THE ELGAR COMPANION TO DEVELOPMENT STUDIES

In memory of my father,
David Michael Clark
28 October 1943–25 October 2003

The Elgar Companion to Development Studies

Edited by

David Alexander Clark

Research Associate, Global Poverty Research Group, Universities of Manchester and Oxford and Institute for Development Policy and Management, University of Manchester, UK

Edward Elgar

Cheltenham, UK • Northampton, MA, USA

Published by
Edward Elgar Publishing Limited
Glensanda House
Montpellier Parade
Cheltenham
Glos GL50 1UA
UK

Edward Elgar Publishing, Inc.
136 West Street
Suite 202
Northampton
Massachusetts 01060
USA

A catalogue record for this book
is available from the British Library

Library of Congress Cataloguing in Publication Data
The Elgar companion to development studies / edited by David Alexander Clark.
    p. cm. – (Elgar original reference)
    Includes bibliographical references and index.
    1. Development economics. 2. Economic development. I. Clark, David, 1972– II. Series.

    HD75 E42 2006
    338.9—dc22

                                            2005058953

ISBN-13: 978 1 84376 475 5 (cased)
ISBN-10: 1 84376 475 X (cased)

Printed and bound in Great Britain by MPG Books Ltd, Bodmin, Cornwall

Contents

Figures

Tables

Contributors

Irma Adelman, Professor in the Graduate School, University of California at Berkeley, Berkeley, CA, USA.

David Alexander, Scientific Director, Region of Lombardy Advanced School of Civil Protection, Milan, Italy.

Sabina Alkire, Research Associate, Global Equity Initiative, Harvard University, Cambridge, MA, USA.

Ron Ayres, Professor of Economics and Head of Department of Economics and International Business, University of Greenwich, London, UK.

Amiya Bagchi, Professor of Economics and Director, Institute of Development Studies Kolkata, India.

Pranab Bardhan, Professor of Economics, University of California at Berkeley, Berkeley, CA, USA.

Tony Barnett, ESRC Professorial Research Fellow, Development Studies Institute, London School of Economics and Political Science, London, UK.

Kaushik Basu, C. Marks Professor of International Studies and Professor of Economics and Director, Programme on Comparative Economic Development, Cornell University, Ithaca, NY, USA.

Robert H. Bates, Eaton Professor of the Science of Government in the Department of Government and Faculty Research Fellow in the Center for International Development, Harvard University, Cambridge, MA, USA.

Anthony Bebbington, Professor, Institute for Development Policy and Management, and Director of Research, School of Environment and Development, University of Manchester, Manchester, UK.

Henry Bernstein, Professor of Development Studies in the University of London, School of Oriental and African Studies, London, UK.

Christopher Bertram, Professor of Social and Political Philosophy, Department of Philosophy, University of Bristol, Bristol, UK.

David Birch, Professor of Communication and Director of the Corporate Citizenship Research Unit, Deakin University, Melbourne, Australia.

Jan Breman, Professor in Comparative Sociology, Amsterdam School of Social Sciences, Amsterdam University, The Netherlands; and Professor, International Institute for Asian Studies, Leiden, The Netherlands.

Daniel W. Bromley, Anderson-Bascom Professor of Applied Economics, University of Wisconsin-Madison, Madison, WI, USA.

Terence J. Byres, Emeritus Professor of Political Economy in the University of London, School of Oriental and African Studies, London, UK.

John Cathie, Assistant Director of Research, Department of Land Economy, University of Cambridge, Cambridge, UK.

Ha-Joon Chang, Reader in the Political Economy of Development, Faculty of Economics, University of Cambridge, Cambridge, UK.

David A. Clark, Research Associate, Global Poverty Research Group and Institute for Development Policy and Management, University of Manchester, Manchester, UK; Research Associate, Southern Africa Labour and Development Research Unit, University of Cape Town, Cape Town, South Africa.

Avi J. Cohen, Associate Professor of Economics, York University, Toronto, Canada.

Paul Cook, Professor of Economics and Development Policy and Director of the Centre on Regulation and Competition, University of Manchester, Manchester, UK.

John Cullis, Reader in Economics and member of the Centre for Public Economics, University of Bath, Bath, UK.

Herman E. Daly, Professor, School of Public Policy, University of Maryland, College Park, MD, USA.

Stefan Dercon, Professor of Development Economics, University of Oxford, Oxford, UK.

Robert Dixon, Reader in Economics, University of Melbourne, Melbourne, Australia.

Edgar J. Dosman, Professor of Political Science and Senior Research Fellow of the Centre for International and Security Studies, York University, Toronto, Canada.

Nigel Dower, Honorary Senior Lecturer in Philosophy, University of Aberdeen, Aberdeen, UK; and Academic Consultant, Cosmopolitan Agendas, Aberdeen, UK.

Andrew S. Downes, Professor of Economics and University Director, Sir Arthur Lewis Institute of Social and Economic Studies, University of the West Indies, St Michael, Barbados.

Jean Drèze, Visiting Professor, G.B. Pant Social Science Institute, Allahabad, India; and Honorary Professor, Delhi School of Economics, University of Delhi, India.

Tim Dyson, Professor of Population Studies, London School of Economics and Political Science, London, UK.

Walter Elkan, Emeritus Professor of Economics, Brunel University, London, UK.

Frank Ellis, Professor of Development Studies and Director of the Overseas Development Group, University of East Anglia, Norwich, UK.

Michael Ellman, Professor of Economic Systems Amsterdam School of Economics, University of Amsterdam, Amsterdam, The Netherlands.

Louis Emmerij, Senior Research Fellow, Graduate Center, and Co-Director of the UN Intellectual History Project, City University of New York, New York, USA.

Arturo Escobar, Professor of Anthropology and Director, University of North Carolina at Chapel Hill, NC, USA; and Research Associate, Colombian Institute of Anthropology and History, Bogota, Colombia.

Mike Faber, former Director and Emeritus Professorial Fellow, Institute of Development Studies, University of Sussex, Brighton, UK.

Osvaldo Feinstein, Consultant and former Manager and Adviser at the World Bank's Operations Evaluation Department, Washington, DC, USA.

Shailaja Fennell, University Lecturer in Development Studies and Fellow of Jesus College, University of Cambridge, Cambridge, UK.

Alexander J. Field, Michel and Mary Orradre Professor of Economics, Santa Clara University, Santa Clara, CA, USA.

Adolfo Figueroa, Professor of Economics, Catholic University of Peru, Lima, Peru.

Ben Fine, Professor of Economics in the University of London, School of Oriental and African Studies, London, UK.

James E. Foster, Professor of Economics, Vanderbilt University, Nashville, TN, USA.

Sakiko Fukuda-Parr, Research Fellow, Belfer Center for Science and International Affairs, Kennedy School of Government, Harvard University, Cambridge, MA, USA; and former Director of the Human Development Report Office, United Nations Development Programme, New York, USA.

Bas de Gaay Fortman, Professor of Political Economy of Human Rights, Utrecht University, Utrecht, The Netherlands.

Des Gasper, Associate Professor of Public Policy and Management, Institute of Social Studies, The Hague, The Netherlands.

Dharam Ghai, former Director, United Nations Research Institute for Social Development, Geneva, Switzerland; and Advisor, International Labour Organisation, Geneva, Switzerland.

Chien Yen Goh, Representative and Senior Researcher, Third World Network, Penang, Malaysia.

Ian Goldin, Director, School of 21st Century Studies, University of Oxford, Oxford, UK.

Jaqui Goldin, Director, The Africa Project, South Africa; and Chairperson, African Water Issues Research Unit, University of Pretoria Water Institute, University of Pretoria, South Africa.

Marshall Goldman, Kathryn Wasserman Davis Professor of Russian Economics (Emeritus), Wellesley College, and Associate Director, Davis Centre, Harvard University, Cambridge, MA, USA.

Denis Goulet, O'Neill Professor Emeritus in Education for Justice, Department of Economics and Policy Studies, and Faculty Fellow of the Kellogg Institute for International Studies and Kroc Institute for International Peace Studies, University of Notre Dame, Notre Dame, IN, USA.

C.A. Gregory, Reader in Anthropology, Australian National University, Canberra, Australia.

Alastair Greig, Reader in Sociology and Head of School of Social Sciences, Australian National University, Canberra, Australia.

G.C. Harcourt, Emeritus Reader in the History of Economic Theory and Emeritus Fellow of Jesus College, University of Cambridge, Cambridge, UK; Professor Emeritus, University of Adelaide, South Australia.

Paul G. Hare, Professor of Economics and Director of Research, School of Management and Languages, Heriot-Watt University, Edinburgh, UK.

John Harriss, Professor of Development Studies, Development Studies Institute, London School of Economics and Political Science, London, UK.

Barbara Harriss-White, Professor of Development Studies and Director of Queen Elizabeth House, Oxford University, Oxford, UK.

John M. Hartwick, Professor of Economics, Queen's University, Kingston, Ontario, Canada.

Sam Hickey, Lecturer in Development Studies, Institute for Development Policy and Management, University of Manchester, Manchester, UK.

Ailsa Holloway, Director of the Disaster Mitigation for Sustainable Livelihoods Programme, University of Cape Town, Cape Town, South Africa.

Stephen Howe, Professor in the History and Cultures of Colonialism, University of Bristol, Bristol, UK.

David Hulme, Professor of Development Studies, Director of the Chronic Poverty Research Centre and Co-Director of the Global Poverty Research Group, University of Manchester, Manchester, UK.

Sriya Iyer, Lecturer in Economics and Fellow of St. Catharine's College, University of Cambridge, Cambridge, UK.

Selim Jahan, Senior Adviser, Employment for Poverty Reduction, Bureau for Development Policy, United Nations Development Programme, New York, USA; former Deputy Director, Human Development Report Office, United Nations Development Programme, New York, USA.

Richard Jolly, Honorary Professorial Fellow and former Director, Institute of Development Studies, University of Sussex, Brighton, UK.

Mushtaq Khan, Professor of Economics in the University of London, School of Oriental and African Studies, London, UK.

Ray Kiely, Reader in Globalisation and Development Studies, School of Oriental and African Studies, London, UK.

Geeta Kingdon, Research Officer, Department of Economics, University of Oxford, Oxford, UK.

Colin Kirkpatrick, Hallsworth Professor of Development Economics and Director of the Impact Assessment Research Centre, University of Manchester, Manchester, UK.

Stephan Klasen, Professor of Economics, University of Göttingen, Göttingen, Germany.

Atul Kohli, David Bruce Professor of International Affairs, Princeton University, Princeton, NJ, USA.

Khalid Koser, Lecturer in Human Geography, Migration Research Unit, University College, London, UK.

Heinz D. Kurz, Professor of Economics, University of Graz, Graz, Austria.

Sanjaya Lall, formerly Professor of Development Economics and Fellow of Green College, University of Oxford, Oxford, UK.

Keith M. Lewin, Professor of Education and Director of the Centre for International Education, University of Sussex, Brighton, UK.

Colin Leys, Emeritus Professor of Politics, Queen's University, Kingston, Canada.

Kristoffel Lieten, Professor of Child Labour Studies, University of Amsterdam and International Institute of Social History, The Netherlands; and Director of the Institute for Research on Working Children, The Netherlands.

Angela W. Little, Professor of Education (with reference to Developing Countries), Institute of Education, University of London, London, UK.

Peter Lloyd-Sherlock, Reader in Social Development, School of Development Studies, University of East Anglia, Norwich, UK.

Julian May, Associate Professor and Head of School of Development Studies, University of KwaZulu-Natal, Durban, South Africa.

J.S.L. McCombie, Fellow in Economics, Downing College, and Reader and Director of the Centre for Economic and Public Policy, Department of Land Economy, University of Cambridge, Cambridge, UK.

Anna McCord, Research Associate, Southern Africa Labour and Development Research Unit; and Visiting Research Fellow, Centre for Social Science Research, School of Economics, University of Cape Town, South Africa.

Santosh Mehrotra, Regional Economic Adviser for Asia, United Nations Development Programme, Bangkok, Thailand and Adviser, Planning Commission, Government of India; and formerly Senior Economic Advisor at the Human Development Report Office, UNDP, New York, USA.

Luiz de Mello, Senior Economist, Economics Department, Organisation for Economic Cooperation and Development, Paris, France.

Rachel Murphy, Senior Lecturer in East Asian Studies, Centre for East Asian Studies, University of Bristol, Bristol, UK.

Peter Nolan, Sinyi Professor of Chinese Management, Chair of the Development Studies Committee and Fellow of Jesus College, University of Cambridge, Cambridge, UK.

S.R. Osmani, Professor of Development Economics, University of Ulster, Belfast, UK.

Arvind Panagariya, Jagdish Bhagwati Professor of Indian Political Economy and Professor of Economics, Columbia University, New York, USA.

Mića Panić, Fellow of Selwyn College, University of Cambridge, Cambridge, UK; and Vice Chairman of the United Nations Committee for Development Policy, United Nations, New York, USA.

David Parker, Research Professor in Privatisation and Regulation and Director of the Cranfield Centre for Competition and Regulation Research, Cranfield University, Bedfordshire, UK; and Co-Director of the Regulation Research Programme in the Centre on Competition and Regulation, University of Manchester, Manchester, UK.

Prabhat Patnaik, Professor, Centre for Economic Studies and Planning, Jawaharlal Nehru University, New Delhi, India.

David Pearce, formerly Emeritus Professor of Environmental Economics, University College London, London, UK.

Ruth Pearson, Professor of International Development and Director of the Centre for Development Studies, University of Leeds, Leeds, UK.

Jonathan R. Pincus, Lecturer in Economics, School of Oriental and African Studies, London, UK; and Senior Country Economist, United Nations Development Programme, Hanoi, Vietnam.

Mozaffar Qizilbash, Professor of Politics, Economics and Philosophy, Department of Economics and Related Studies, University of York, York, UK.

Carole Rakodi, Professor of International Urban Development, University of Birmingham, Birmingham, UK.

Mamphela Ramphele, formerly Managing Director, World Bank, Washington, DC, USA.

Gustav Ranis, Frank Altschul Professor of International Economics, Yale University, New Haven, CT, USA.

Martin Ravallion, Senior Advisor, Development Research Group, World Bank, Washington, DC, USA.

Carl Riskin, Distinguished Professor of Economics, Queens College, City University of New York, USA; and Senior Research Scholar, Weatherhead East Asian Institute, Columbia University, New York, USA.

Ben Rogaly, Senior Lecturer in Human Geography, University of Sussex, Brighton, UK.

Caterina Ruggeri Laderchi, Economist, Poverty Reduction and Economic Management, World Bank, Washington, DC, USA.

David Satterthwaite, Senior Fellow, International Institute for Environment and Development, London, UK.

John S. Saul, Emeritus Professor of Social and Political Science, York University, Toronto, Canada.

Amartya K. Sen, Lamont University Professor and Professor of Economics and of Philosophy, Harvard University, Cambridge, MA, USA (winner of the 1998 Nobel Prize in Economics).

John Sender, Professor of Economics in the University of London, School of Oriental and African Studies, London, UK; and Senior Research Fellow, African Studies Centre, Leiden, The Netherlands.

D. John Shaw, former Economic Adviser and Chief, Policy Affairs Service, UN World Food Programme, Rome, Italy; and consultant to the Commonwealth Secretariat, Food and Agriculture Organisation (FAO) and the World Bank.

Ajit Singh, Professor of Economics and Senior Fellow of Queens' College, University of Cambridge, Cambridge, UK.

Ronald Skeldon, Professorial Fellow in Geography, University of Sussex, Brighton, UK.

Leslie Sklair, Emeritus Professor of Sociology, London School of Economics and Political Science, London, UK.

Robert M. Solow, Institute Professor Emeritus, Massachusetts Institute of Technology, Cambridge, MA, USA (winner of the 1987 Nobel Prize in Economics).

Devi Sridhar, Rhodes Scholar, Institute of Social and Cultural Anthropology, University of Oxford, Oxford, UK.

Guy Standing, Director of the Socio-Economic Security Programme, International Labour Organisation, Geneva, Switzerland.

Howard Stein, Visiting Professor, Center for Afroamerican and African Studies and Department of Epidemiology, University of Michigan, Ann Arbor, MI, USA.

Frances Stewart, Professor of Development Economics and Director of the Centre for Research on Inequality, Human Security and Ethnicity (CRISE), Department of International Development, University of Oxford, Oxford, UK.

Paul Streeten, Emeritus Professor of Economics, Boston University, Boston, MA, USA.

Hugh Stretton, Emeritus Professor of History and Visiting Research Fellow in Economics, University of Adelaide, SA, Australia.

Moshe Syrquin, Professor of Economics, Department of International Studies, University of Miami, Coral Gables, FL, USA.

A.P. Thirlwall, Emeritus Professor of Applied Economics, University of Kent, Canterbury, UK.

C. Peter Timmer, Senior Research Fellow, Center for Global Development, Washington, DC, USA; and Thomas D. Cabot Professor of Development Studies, Emeritus, Harvard University, Cambridge, MA, USA.

Irene Tinker, Professor Emerita, Department of City and Regional Planning and Department of Women's Studies, University of California at Berkeley, Berkeley, CA, USA.

Jan Toporowski, Research Associate, School of Oriental and African Studies, London, UK; Senior Member, Wolfson College, Cambridge, UK; and Research Associate, Research Centre for History and Methodology of Economics, University of Amsterdam, The Netherlands.

Mark Turner, Professor of Development Policy and Management, University of Canberra, Canberra, Australia.

Jan Douwe van der Ploeg, Professor of Rural Sociology, Wageningen University, The Netherlands; and Member of the Council for Rural Areas, The Netherlands.

John Weeks, Professor of Economics in the University of London and Director of the Centre for Development Policy and Research, School of Oriental and African Studies, London, UK.

John Weiss, Professor of Development Economics, University of Bradford, Bradford, UK; and Director of Research, Asian Development Bank Institute, Tokyo, Japan.

Bruce Weisse, former Research Associate, Centre for Business Research, University of Cambridge, UK.

Howard White, Research Fellow, Institute of Development Studies, University of Sussex, Brighton, UK.

Tom Woodhouse, Adam Curle Professor of Conflict Resolution and former Director and founder of the Centre for Conflict Resolution, University of Bradford, Bradford, UK.

Michael Woolcock, Senior Social Scientist, Development Research Group, World Bank, Washington, DC, USA; and Lecturer in Public Policy, Kennedy School of Government, Harvard University, Cambridge, MA, USA.

Reviewers

The editor and contributors would like to thank the following for refereeing papers:

David Alexander
Philip Arestis
Pranab Bardhan
Tony Barnett
Armando Barrientos
Stephanie Barrientos
Robert H. Bates
Anthony Bebbington
Henry Bernstein
Ana Maria Bianchi
Stephanie Blackenburg
Sissela Bok
Mark Bray
Tony Brewer
Daniel W. Bromley
Terry Cannon
Michael Carter
John-Ren Chen
Robin Cohen
Andrea Cornwall
John Cullis
Jocelyn DeJong
Stefan Dercon
Steven Devereux
Robert Dixon
Ronald Dore
Nigel Dower
Andrew S. Downes
Jean Drèze
Jay Drydyk
Tim Dyson
Michael Edwards
Walter Elkan
Frank Ellis
Michael Ellman
Arturo Escobar
Shailaja Fennell
David Fieldhouse

Ben Fine
Tom Fox
Sakiko Fukuda-Parr
Rajat Ganguly
Ugo Gentilini
Clive George
Jaqui Goldin
Marshall Goldman
Edward Graham
Alastair Greig
Steve Haggblade
G.C. Harcourt
David Harrison
Peter Hazell
Jeffrey Henderson
Mandy Heslop
Suet Ying Ho
Geoff Hodgson
David Hulme
Barbara Ingham
Sriya Iyer
Jyotsna Jalan
Jane Jaquette
Rhys Jenkins
Albert Jolink
Richard Jolly
Gareth Jones
Tania Kaiser
Vibha Kapuria-Foreman
Cristobol Kay
Ray Kiely
Geeta Kingdon
Colin Kirkpatrick
Stephan Klasen
Atul Kohli
Khalid Koser
David Laitin
Sanjaya Lall

Todd Landman
Keith M. Lewin
David Lewis
Colin Leys
Marco Manacorda
Julian May
Gay Meeks
Santosh Mehrotra
Lyla Mehta
Luiz de Mello
Diana Mitlin
Karen Moore
Jonathan Morduch
John Mukum Mbaku
Rachel Murphy
Gerd Oberleitner
Wendy Olsen
S.R. Osmani
David Parker
David Pearce
Ruth Pearson
Mark Pelling
J.D. Pitchford
Thomas Pogge
Mozaffar Qizilbash
Rati Ram
Gustav Ranis
Ingrid Rima
Gilbert Rist
Ben Rogaly
Ruhi Saith
Malcolm Sawyer
Susanne Schech
Ken Shadlen
D. John Shaw
Ajit Singh
Ronald Skeldon
Matt Smith

Asun Lera St Clair
Guy Standing
Howard Stein
Frances Stewart
Susan Stout
Marilyn Strathern
Paul Streeten

Moshe Syrquin
Hamid Tabatabai
Finn Tarp
A.P. Thirlwall
Robert Tignor
C. Peter Timmer
Irene Tinker

John Toye
Hulya Ulku
John Weeks
Howard White
Philip Woodhouse

Common abbreviations

AIDS	Acquired Immune Deficiency Syndrome
ECLA	Economic Commission for Latin America
EEC	European Economic Community
EU	European Union
FAO	Food and Agriculture Organisation
FDI	Foreign Direct Investment
GATT	General Agreement on Tariffs and Trade
GDP	Gross Domestic Product
GNP	Gross National Product
HDI	Human Development Index
HIPCs	Heavily Indebted Poor Countries
HIV	Human Immunodeficiency Virus
IBRD	International Bank for Reconstruction and Development
ILO	International Labour Organization
IMF	International Monetary Fund
ISI	Import Substitution Industrialisation
LDCs	Less Developed Countries
MDGs	Millennium Development Goals
MNCs	Multi National Corporations
NGOs	Non Governmental Organisations
NICs	Newly Industrialised Countries
NNP	Net National Product
ODA	Official Development Assistance
OECD	Organisation for Economic Cooperation and Development
OPEC	Organisation of Petroleum Exporting Countries
PPP	Purchasing Power Parity
PRSP	Poverty Reduction Strategy Papers
R&D	Research and Development
TNCs	Transnational Corporations
UN	United Nations
UNCTAD	United Nations Conference on Trade and Development
UNDP	United Nations Development Programme
UNESCO	United Nations Educational, Scientific and Cultural Organization
UNICEF	United Nations Children's Fund
UNIDO	United Nations Industrial Development Organization
WHO	World Health Organization
WTO	World Trade Organization

Preface

This book began life in mid–late 2002 during my time as a Visiting Scholar in Development Studies, University of Cambridge. After leaving Cambridge the book nearly became a casualty of an unfortunate chain of events: a period of employment in an unsatisfactory environment, a family bereavement and a period of illness. In retrospect it is a miracle the book survived. I owe an incalculable debt of gratitude – that words cannot describe – to family, friends and colleagues for their support during this time. I also owe a debt of gratitude to the book itself which, like a true 'companion', travelled with me and provided therapy.

The tide finally turned in mid-2004, when I was fortunate enough to take a job at the University of Manchester. This provided the book with new impetus and momentum. I should begin, however, by apologising to the book's many contributors – especially those who signed up early on – for taking so long to complete the project. I am especially grateful to Tim Dyson, Michael Ellman, Ben Fine, Denis Goulet, Geoff Harcourt, Martin Ravallion, Robert Solow, Paul Streeten, Tony Thirlwall and others, who helped to get the ball rolling. Looking back, the book has succeeded beyond my wildest expectations and I hope the reader will agree that it was worth the wait. The book was originally intended to provide the reader with an overview of key development topics through a series of encyclopaedia style entries. While it can be used for this purpose, it has evolved into something with more depth and breadth than the average reference book. From its inception, the book has strived to embrace different disciplines, methodologies and schools of thought. It has tried to strike different balances between theory and practice, and it has sought to provide detailed commentaries on each of the topics. Above all, it has tried to include different points of view. Several contributors are among the original pioneers of development studies; others are from those currently working on the cutting edge of development research. Some contributions have broken new ground while others advance a particular intellectual position.

I am extremely grateful to Peter Nolan and Geoff Harcourt for advice, encouragement and moral support. Peter has been a constant source of inspiration over the years, whose passion for development is driven by a sense of justice, integrity and fair play second to none. Geoff is a kind, considerate and compassionate person, who has selflessly commented on many of the contributions in this volume. I owe a similar debt of gratitude to Dudley Horner, David Hulme and Mozaffar Qizilbash. Apart from the aforementioned, Shailaja Fennell, Richard Jolly, Geeta Kingdon, Rachel Murphy, Amartya Sen, Leslie Sklair and Paul Streeten have provided extensive advice. I am also grateful to Ron Ayres, Robert Chambers, Ha-Joon Chang, Walter Elkan, Frank Ellis, Faldie Esau, Colin Leys, Gay Meeks, Karen Moore, Siddiqur Osmani, John Toye and countless others for helpful comments and suggestions. Jaqui Goldin deserves a special mention for liaising with contributors and providing research support for one of the entries. Margaret Pugh copy-edited the final manuscript and Karine Pardé helped with translations.

Above all I am grateful to family and friends. My parents and sister have been a constant source of encouragement and support over the years. This book is for my father, who passed away in late 2003. He was a good man who cared about other people and always tried to do the right thing. I miss him dearly. Finally I am grateful to my mother, sister and aunt and uncle (Linda and Dave Morris) for support during difficult times. I am also grateful to Joyce Bentley-Smith (who recently passed away), David Brewer, Dudley Horner, John and Audrey Lippiatt and Mozaffar Qizilbash for their kindness and support.

David A. Clark
14 October 2005

Introduction: Development Studies in the Twenty-First Century

*David A. Clark**

Introduction

Development studies is a vast and rapidly expanding field of inquiry, which brings together contributions from many different disciplines and perspectives. As it has expanded, it has been divided into subdisciplines (such as economic growth, social development, governance and development ethics), which are typically shared with single disciplinary subjects such as economics, sociology/anthropology, politics and philosophy. This book provides an overview of key topics in development from a variety of different perspectives. It also attempts to reflect on the nature, scope and state of development studies at the beginning of the twenty-first century.

History and expansion

The origins of development studies are often traced back to the advent of development economics in the post war era. The late 1940s and early 1950s witnessed a rapid expansion in development economics, as the concepts, methods and tools of mainstream economics were applied to the problems of post-war reconstruction and development in Europe. The same methods and tools were quickly transferred to the study of poor countries in Africa, Asia and Latin America following the first wave of political independence and a vast new industry was born. Early contributions included P.N. Rosenstein-Rodan's wartime essay 'Problems of industrialisation of Eastern and South-Eastern Europe' (1943), Ragnar Nurkse's *Problems of Capital Formation in Underdeveloped Countries* (1953), W. Arthur Lewis's classic paper, 'Economic development with unlimited supplies of labour' (1954), Robert Solow's 'A contribution to the theory of economic growth' (1956) and Walt Rostow's (now) controversial book, *The Stages of Economic Growth: A Non-Communist Manifesto* (1960). Since then, research has flourished and increasing numbers of courses and textbooks have been devoted to development economics (an early classic is Kindleberger, 1958). Some of the most notable contributions from economists focused on economic growth, capital accumulation, structural changes in the economy, the transfer of technology and international trade (topics extensively covered in this book by some of the original pioneers).[1] For many writers at this time, development was basically about economic development.

Economists were not the only ones to make significant contributions to development thinking in the 1950s and 1960s. The rapidly expanding literature on economic growth and development was complemented with social, political and psychological studies of modernisation, exemplified in the work of Talcott Parsons (1960), Daniel Lerner (1958)

* I am extremely grateful to David Hulme and John Toye for helpful comments on this Introduction. I have also benefited from useful conversations with Peter Nolan and James Foster. The usual disclaimers apply.

and David McClelland (1961). In essence these theories argued that development depends on displacing traditional 'values, attitudes and norms' with modern ones (see Webster, 1990). In particular, the weakening of traditional ties and power structures (especially the kinship system), the growth of individual motivation and the rise of an entrepreneurial class were seen as key features of the social and cultural modernisation required for economic growth and structural change. These theories have been largely discredited in recent years for envisaging a single pathway to development and equating modernisation with westernisation. More radical critiques of development from sociology and politics followed in the mid–late 1960s and culminated in the notion of 'dependency' – the mirror image of modernisation.[2] The original (strong) version of dependency emphasised the 'development of underdevelopment' in the periphery (southern countries) due to the process of exploitation driving capitalist development in the centre (northern countries) (for example, Frank, 1967). The notion that development and underdevelopment 'are opposite faces of the same coin' (ibid., p. 33) has been hotly disputed in Marxist circles (Warren, 1973, 1980), prompting a shift within the dependency school from the notion of 'impossibility' to the idea of 'distorted development' in the periphery.[3]

As work on the problems of poor countries gathered momentum during the post-war period and priorities changed (to incorporate broader concerns with poverty and inequality, as well as the traditional emphasis on economic and cultural aspects of modernisation in poor countries), researchers increasingly began to look beyond economics and politics and towards the boundaries of other disciplines for answers. The chief drivers of this transformation towards 'cross-disciplinary' development studies were the early pioneers of what has become the human development movement. Led initially by a small but highly influential group of economists such as Dudley Seers, Richard Jolly, Mahbub ul Haq and Paul Streeten, these individuals initiated a 'counter revolution' in development thinking that increasingly created space (from the early 1970s onwards) for combining economic and social analysis in the field of development. Initially the emphasis shifted from economic growth to employment and 'redistribution with growth' (Seers, 1969; Chenery et al., 1974). This was quickly followed by a shift towards basic needs construed first in terms of inputs (the provision of goods and services) (ILO, 1976) and later reborn with a focus on outcomes (basic opportunities) (Streeten et al., 1981; Stewart, 1985). Today the emphasis has broadened even further to incorporate the full range of human capabilities and freedoms people have reason to value (for example, Sen, 1987, 1992, 1999, and Human Development Index in this volume). Although less clearly structured, the late 1960s and the 1970s also witnessed attempts to focus development studies on issues and analytical frameworks that centred less on economic issues. Writers such as Huntingdon (1968) wrote of 'political development' while sociologists (Apthorpe, 1970) argued for 'social planning' to accompany economic planning.

Since the 1970s, many other valuable contributions have been made to development thinking, which, strictly speaking, transcend development economics and other single disciplinary subjects. Apart from work on poverty, inequality and the quality of life in poor countries, a great deal of cross-disciplinary research has focused on changes in the size and structure of populations, patterns of migration and the process of urbanisation over the course of economic development. The rapid expansion of work in this area has created rich opportunities for collaboration across fields as diverse as economics, statistics, sociology, history and ethics; and has given rise to a 'separable' discipline known as demography, which has developed its own methodologies, tools and techniques for analysing population dynamics. Another rapidly expanding area of cross-disciplinary research has origins in institutional economics. This work typically combines historical studies of institutions (such as property rights, organisations, and economic and political systems) with an analysis of efficiency, economic performance and development. Other areas of research in development studies that combine insights from more than one discipline include agriculture and livelihoods, education and health, globalisation and imperialism, conflict and crisis management, and the analysis of social groups and divisions (among many other topics and issues).

While the roots of development studies are often traced back to the advent of development economics in the 1940s and 1950s, a closer look reveals a much richer pedigree in other areas ranging from ancient philosophy on the one hand to classical political economy and modern social science on the other. For example, Martha Nussbaum (1988, 1990) has drawn out the implications of Aristotle's theory of political distribution and his analysis of human flourishing for contemporary development discourse. Moreover, the conclusions of Adam Smith's (1776) masterpiece *The Wealth of Nations* are almost entirely about the economic development of England. In fact Adam Smith – like Karl Marx – analysed many of the inherent contradictions of capitalist development and was deeply concerned with social issues and the plight of the ordinary man (see the entries on Adam Smith and Karl Marx in this volume).[4] In the late nineteenth and early twentieth centuries, landmark studies with relevance for development continued to emerge. Notable examples include Charles Booth (1892) and Seebohm Rowntree's (1901) pioneering studies of poverty in London and York, which have profoundly influenced development studies (and policy) in the 1990s. In addition, plenty of social anthropologists were actively working in traditional 'untouched societies' prior to the Second World War (see Hulme and Turner, 1990, pp. 9–10). There are also links between contemporary development studies and colonial administration. In fact the first development courses in the UK were for colonial administrators and date back to the early twentieth century.[5]

Nature, dilemmas and challenges

There is now widespread agreement (at least within contemporary development studies) that no single discipline can adequately deal with the breadth or complexity of development. Instead what is required to deepen our understanding of development issues is a blending of analysis and methods from different disciplines (see, for example, Hulme and Turner, 1990, p. 13; Tribe and Sumner, 2004, p. 3). The blending or mixing of disciplines can take different forms. In an effort to clarify 'different types of mixing', Ravi Kanbur (2002, p. 483) has proposed the following distinctions, which have recently been adopted and discussed by David Hulme and John Toye (2005):

- *Cross-disciplinarity* – a generic term referring to any analysis or policy recommendation based substantively on analysis and methods of more than one discipline; there are two main variants:

- *Multidisciplinarity* – refers to work in which individual discipline-based researchers (or teams) do their best, within their disciplinary confines, to examine an issue and subsequently collaborate to develop together an overall analytical synthesis and conclusions; and
- *Interdisciplinarity* – refers to research that attempts a deep integration of two or more disciplinary approaches from the beginning and throughout an entire research exercise.[6]

On the whole, multidisciplinarity is a highly additive form of cross-disciplinary research. In contrast, interdisciplinarity is far more integrative (see also the discussion in Molteberg et al., 2000). There are, of course, many different ways of mixing and combining multi- and interdisciplinary work in development studies, many of which can be found in the pages of this book.

The issue of whether development studies should be viewed as 'a discipline in itself' – as opposed to a rapidly expanding 'subject' area that cuts across disciplines – 'is a matter of considerable dispute' (Tribe and Sumner, 2004, p. 4). However, following John Loxley (2004), it is possible to identify some defining characteristics of development studies:

> There are four essential features of IDS [international development studies] which, taken together, give the field a very distinctive identity. The first is that the central focus is on developing countries per se, which distinguishes it from Global Political Economy (GPE) and International Relations (IR) programs . . . The second, distinctive feature of IDS is that it is interdisciplinary [i.e. cross-disciplinary] in nature. Its basic premise is that any attempt to understand the developing world and how it is inserted into the world economic and political system requires the collective insights of a number of different academic disciplines . . . The third distinctive feature of IDS is that it allows, if not encourages, studies at the international, national and sub-national (regional or local) levels. It can, therefore, accommodate students with a wide, eclectic, range of interests . . . The fourth distinctive feature of IDS is that it is at once theoretical, policy-oriented, and empirical. Some students will incline more to one than the others but all students are more than likely to be exposed to each. (Loxley, 2004, pp. 26–8)

These characteristics are not controversial. Yet development studies continues to lack a commonly agreed definition or mission statement (see Thomas, 2004), although some progress in this direction is being made. In the UK, for example, recognition of development studies as a distinct field of inquiry has recently been made through the creation of a development studies subpanel for the 2008 higher education Research Assessment Exercise (RAE). In addition the (British–Irish) Development Studies Association (DSA) is collaborating with the higher education Quality Assurance Agency (QAA) to generate a 'benchmark statement' for degree courses in development studies.[7] While the DSA/QAA has not yet finalised a benchmark statement, the following description of development studies has been drafted for the RAE:

> [Development studies] covers issue-driven research concerning the analysis of global and local processes of cultural, demographic, economic, environmental, political and social change in low and middle income parts of the world, with particular reference to structures and institutions; the changing relationships between developed and developing countries; and the critical interrogation of theories of these processes and relationships, and of development policy. (RAE, 2005, p. 1)

The document includes the following boundary statement:

> Development studies research is commonly – but not exclusively – inter-disciplinary, multi-disciplinary and heterogeneous in nature. There is a substantial degree of overlap between development studies and several cognate disciplines and disciplinary sub-fields. However, the defining emphasis in development studies is on theories, analyses, interpretations and evaluations of processes of change, their outcomes, their management and their contribution to development policy. (ibid.)

Some researchers have tried to avoid defining development studies – preferring instead to treat it as a cross-disciplinary subject that people can interpret differently. Others are keen to reopen the debate on the nature and role of development studies.[8] One point that should be kept in mind is that the precise nature and character of development studies varies across regions. For example, we might distinguish between English, European (Scandinavian) and Canadian forms of development studies.[9] At least some of the variation reflects different colonial histories and intellectual traditions, as well as cultural and linguistic barriers, which prevent cross-collaboration. There are also differences between Northern and Southern forms of development studies. In terms of the 'essential features of IDS' espoused by Loxley, Southern varieties tend to be more applied than theoretical and much more concerned with local issues. Another issue relates to how far it is meaningful to talk of 'global' development studies. In France, the emphasis is typically on African studies and the analysis of underdevelopment. In the USA, development economics has dominated and those research organisations with broader remits – such as the Earth Institute – have increasingly concerned themselves with poverty studies rather than development studies.[10] Yet despite these variations, it is possible to identify some defining features of a truly international form of development studies which, taken together, separate it from other fields of study.

The study of development matters for several different reasons (see Loxley, 2004). More than 5.3 billion people currently live in low- or middle-income countries (World Bank, 2005a, table 1, p. 293). Together these people constitute five-sixths of the world's population, which Loxley (2004, p. 35) points out 'should be a sufficient, pragmatic, reason for studying the conditions in which they live and the problems they confront in trying to improve their well-being'. About 1.1 billion of these people are estimated to be living below the international poverty line on less than a dollar a day (World Bank, 2005b, pp. 21–2) and between 300 million and 420 million are trapped in poverty that persists for many years (CPRC, 2004, p. 9). Many more people are vulnerable to becoming poor. There are also gross deprivations and disparities in terms of basic human capabilities, such as life expectancy, child mortality and adult literacy (see Table 1). Such statistics provide a strong moral case for an interest in development issues.

Another reason for studying international development might be described as 'enlightened self interest' (Loxley, 2004, p.35). As the process of globalisation has accelerated, the North and South have become increasingly interdependent. Many of these interdependencies are economic – notable examples include trade relations and capital flows. Other forms of mutual interdependence relate to environmental and health concerns such as global warming or the transmission and prevention of infectious diseases. There is also growing concern about political stability, global security and, most recently, international

Table 1   Key indicators of poverty and development

	Population (millions) 2004	Number below dollar a day poverty line (millions)*	Low estimate of chronic poverty (millions)#	High estimate of chronic poverty (millions)#	Life expectancy at birth (years) 2003	Under five mortality rate (per 1000) 2003	Adult literacy rate (% ages 15 and older) 2003
East Asia and Pacific	1870.2	277.0	53.7	84.9	70.5	41	90.4
Europe and Central Asia	472.1					36	
Latin America and the Caribbean	541.3				71.9	33	89.6
Middle East and North Africa	294.0					56	
South Asia	1447.7	524.7	133.9	187.5	63.4	86	58.9
Sub-Saharan Africa	719.0	216.4	91.0	121.3	46.1	171	61.3
All	6345.1	1099.1	298.3	421.7	67.1	84	84

Notes:
*   Where data are available.
#   Estimate of the number of people still below the dollar a day poverty line after five years.

Sources: CPRC (2004, p. 9), World Bank (2005a, pp. 257, 295) and UNDP (2005, p. 222).

terrorism. Loxley has also argued that development studies 'forces us to reflect on how we live in the developed world and to confront some difficult questions about the long-term viability of our lifestyle and the values underlying it' (ibid., p. 36).

One of the most significant challenges facing development studies in the twenty-first century is to find ways of becoming more cross-disciplinary. While development studies has long aspired to cross-disciplinarity, its achievements in systematically establishing robust, cross-disciplinary, analytical frameworks have been modest.[11] In recent years concerns have been raised about the 'fragmentation of science' (Molteberg et al., 2000, p. 318) and the 'splintering of theoretical and applied knowledge', which creates 'blind spots' and threatens to undermine the coherence and relevance of development research (Hulme and Toye, 2005, pp. 3 and 7). Several commentators have emphasised the benefits of greater cooperation between disciplines. A notable example is Ravi Kanbur, who states that '[t]he case for cross disciplinarity in development studies and development policy is very strong indeed' (Kanbur, 2002, p. 483). Yet even among the most open-minded and progressive thinkers, it is possible to detect a note of 'cautious optimism' regarding the prospects for cross-disciplinary development studies. Kanbur (p. 484) ends up making the case for 'small steps' rather than 'the deep integration of methods . . . [and] different disciplines'. He reports that at the 2001 Quant-Qual Cornell conference,

> [Participants] were concerned that creating a true hybrid might lose the strengths of each approach, with the gains lost in disciplinary and methodological confusion . . . Rather 'sequential mixing' was preferred, where each approach would do its best, learn from other approaches, adapt these lessons, and then do its best again. (ibid., p. 484)

Even John Harriss (2002), who argues that disciplines can be 'constraining' and 'repressive' as well as productive, stops short of endorsing true interdisciplinarity by 'respecting the importance of contributions from within individual disciplines' (p. 488). Different disciplines, he says, 'have different contributions to make' and it is 'very far from the case that all development research has to be in some way cross-disciplinary' (p. 494).

While the payoffs from successful forms of cross-disciplinary research are potentially quite high, progress in this direction can be fraught. In the course of making a case for cross-disciplinary work, Hulme and Toye observe:

> [A]s long as many economists still claim that economics can be 'contaminated' by the 'softer' disciplines of other social sciences and many non-economists dismiss as 'reductionist' economists' analyses of human action, it will require considerable energy, intellectual courage and integrity to design and implement a cross-disciplinary research strategy on poverty and well-being. (2005, p. 4)

In practice, a combination of adverse incentives, institutional constraints and human failings hamper the potential for cross-disciplinary research in development studies. The following points are particularly noteworthy:

● *Professional prestige*   Lipton (1970, p. 11) and Lehmann (1979, p. 3) were among the first to point to the lack of professional prestige in cross-disciplinary development research, which compels scholars (especially the best researchers) to work within the confines of established disciplines and publish in specialised 'quality' journals, instead of venturing beyond disciplinary boundaries.[12]

- *Institutions and incentives*   A range of institutions and incentives which include forms of university evaluation (such as single subject peer review), access to funding and other resources, probable impact on career prospects (inside and outside academic research – especially in the USA) and willingness to master a second discipline (given time constraints and intellectual demands) or collaborate with colleagues working in other disciplines (with alien methodologies and different views of the world) inevitably constrains the potential for cross-disciplinary research.
- *Envy, distrust and rivalry*   The incentives and institutions that divide disciplines provide fertile ground for envy, distrust and rivalry between scholars from different disciplines, which in turn generates further divisions.[13] This leads to the 'intellectual stereotyping' of other disciplines (as either objective or subjective, quantitative or qualitative, positivist or post-positivist, generalised or contextualised, etc.) and 'ideologies of disciplinary rivalry [that] provide the currency for a debate in which self-justification is a stronger motive than the search for understanding' (Hulme and Toye, 2005, p. 11).
- *Conflicting ideologies*   Different disciplines have also been divided by politics and ideology. For example, Hulme and Turner (1990, p. 13) note that in the 1980s, sociologists and anthropologists were often excluded from development policy and planning on the grounds 'that they are all left wing ideologues'[14] and are more likely to voice criticism and dissent than those from other disciplines. To take another example, feminists and post-modernists on the one hand and mainstream economists on the other find it difficult, if not impossible, to establish constructive dialogues on development issues (and other matters) for ideological reasons.

There are, however, grounds for optimism. Many of the barriers and institutions that discourage cross-disciplinary research in development studies are being eroded. Since the 1970s, a growing number of researchers have recognised that development problems are multifaceted and require input from more than one discipline. This favourable change in attitudes has gained momentum in recent years as examples of highly successful and innovative research projects that combine work from different disciplines have proliferated.[15] More money has also been made available for cross-disciplinary research. For example, in the UK both the Economic and Social Research Council and the Department for International Development have made multi-million pound investments in multi- and interdisciplinary research centres such as the Global Poverty Research Group (www.gprg. org), the Chronic Poverty Research Centre (www.chronicpoverty.org) and the Centre for Research on Inequality, Human Security and Ethnicity (www.crise.ox.ac.uk). Finally, despite the lack of professional prestige in cross-disciplinary research, there is some anecdotal evidence to suggest that communication across disciplines – at least in terms of citations in the top-ranking economics journals – has increased in recent years (see Hulme and Toye, 2005). There has also been growth in the number of international development journals with a cross-disciplinary focus.[16]

More progress in all of these areas is required, however, if the full potential of cross-disciplinary research is to be realised. In the USA in particular, where development economics reigns supreme, more funding and credos could be assigned to multi- and inter-disciplinary forms of development studies. More weight could also be attached to leading cross-disciplinary development journals, most of which are regarded as 'peripheral'.

Perhaps the most widely recognised requirement for effective collaboration across disciplines is 'mutual professional respect' (White, 2002, p. 519; see also Kanbur, 2002, p. 484; Hulme and Toye, 2005). Researchers must be willing to look beyond the boundaries of their own discipline; they must recognise that different disciplines offer different insights and different ways of thinking about the same problem; and above all they must be willing to accept constructive criticism and build on the insights of other disciplines (see Hulme and Toye, 2005). This involves cultivating the twin virtues of 'critical friendship' and 'co-determining the future' – qualities that Michael Edwards (2002) argues will contribute to a more positive future for development studies. A healthy tension between discipline and 'anti-discipline' is also required (Harriss, 2002). In particular the ability to question conventional ways of viewing the world from within established disciplines and perspectives has provided crucial breakthroughs in development studies (see ibid., 2002) and social science generally (see Kuhn, 1962).

So which pathway should development studies take? Should it aim to be multidisciplinary or should it strive to be more interdisciplinary? To a large extent the answer depends on the research questions and the context in which they are asked. Different disciplines have different contributions to make. They can be mixed in a variety of ways and may be more relevant in one context than another. In general, multidisciplinary research – which relies on teams of people from different disciplines and perspectives – can be expensive and difficult to manage. On large projects especially cases of professional rivalry, envy and resentment between team members, distrust and ignorance of other disciplines, and lack of cooperation are not uncommon.[17] When multidisciplinary research succeeds – and it often does – the results are usually additive (rather than positive sum), as no researcher has a complete overview or integrated understanding of the research.[18]

On the other hand, interdisciplinary forms of research – involving individuals or groups of like-minded people committed to mastering the same disciplines – are easier to manage and less expensive (at least in terms of salaries). While interdisciplinary work is more challenging intellectually and in terms of research time (Hulme and Toye, 2005, p. 26), the results are likely to yield higher returns. Instead of merely adding insights from different disciplines, the results of such research, if successful, should integrate disciplines as far as possible in order to create a new perspective and generate a whole that is greater than the sum of the parts (Molteberg et al., 2000, p. 319; Tribe and Sumner, 2005, pp. 7–8).[19] Many of the 'pioneers of development' and some recent Nobel Prize winners have made their reputations on the strength of pathbreaking interdisciplinary research – notable examples include Albert Hirschman (who boasts of 'trespassing'), Gunnar Myrdal, Douglass North, Dudley Seers, Amartya Sen and Paul Streeten (see their biographies in this book). Of course it is not difficult to find examples of less-successful attempts to become interdisciplinary.[20] One worry is that interdisciplinary research could lack rigour if the conceptual and methodological standards of established disciplines are abandoned (Hulme and Toye, 2005, p. 25). Another worry is that there may not be enough 'renaissance people' with the necessary training and expertise in more than one discipline to move things forward in the next few years (ibid., p. 35).

Some of the difficulties facing cross-disciplinary forms of development studies are symptoms of more general problems in social science. In some academic departments and research institutes charged with the study of development, significant amounts of time and other resources are wasted in unproductive and potentially harmful activities such as micro management, personal rivalries, empire building, public relations and image-building exercises, unnecessary interference with other people's research and excessive fund-raising activities.[21] In the worst-case scenarios, academic research is arrested or becomes driven entirely by the agenda of self-seeking individuals who exploit their position of power. Thus, intellectual freedom and a supportive research environment are vital ingredients of healthy research. As John Stuart Mill passionately argued almost 150 years ago, intellectual freedom is essential for the development of great thinkers:

> Who can compute what the world loses in the multitude of promising intellects combined with timid characters, who dare not follow out any bold, vigorous, independent train of thought, lest it should land them in something which would admit of being considered irreligious or immoral? . . . No one can be a great thinker who does not recognize, that as a thinker it is his first duty to follow his intellect to whatever conclusions it may lead. Truth gains more even by the errors of one who, with due study and preparation, thinks for himself, than by the true opinions of those who only hold them because they do not suffer themselves to think . . . There have been, and may again be, great individual thinkers, in a general atmosphere of mental slavery. But there never has been, nor ever will be, in that atmosphere, an intellectually active people . . . [W]here the discussion of the greatest questions which can occupy humanity is considered to be closed, we cannot hope to find that generally high scale of mental activity which has made some periods of history so remarkable. (Mill, 1859, p. 39)

One final observation follows from these remarks. In so far as resources which ought to be invested in the study of development are pumped into undesirable activities (such as empire building and self-aggrandisement), there is a prima facie case for reforming the way in which research funding is allocated. More small grants for inter-disciplinary researchers in place of larger grants for giant multidisciplinary research projects may stimulate research and generate higher returns. Unfortunately there is a striking contrast here between the trend towards gigantism in publicly funded social science research, where nowadays – following the models of the natural sciences – it is agreed that good social science research needs large teams and vast facilities and the opportunities that less 'strategically managed' trusts and endowments (such as Leverhulme, Nuffield and MacArthur) create for individuals.

Another dilemma for development studies is the longstanding accusation that it is 'Eurocentric'. This has at least two significant dimensions. The first is that the concepts and frameworks it uses are largely derived from a European perspective (meaning Europe and the USA). The rise of governance (initially 'good governance') as a development issue illustrates this well with a focus on using European models of democracy as ideal types to judge what was happening, and prescribe what should be happening, in developing countries. The second dimension relates to the degree to which the thought leaders in development studies are citizens of OECD countries and, especially, Western Europe and North America. Development studies – like all branches of academia – clearly has such a bias, and this bias is reinforced by those in Western institutions underutilising the ideas and writings of colleagues in developing countries. Where Africans, Asians and Latin

Americans make a major contribution they commonly migrate to the universities of the USA and Europe.

Perhaps the single greatest challenge for development studies – especially in the North – lies elsewhere. Scholars must not only be able to talk to each other and relate their work to other social science disciplines. They must also be able to detach from intellectual disciplines in an effort to engage with the views and experiences of ordinary people.[22] Credible development research cannot be conducted in the vacuum of a university or library. Sadly there is no shortage of such research. There is also resistance to fieldwork and/or talking to poor people in some parts of the development studies profession. For example, on arrival in Peru for exploratory fieldwork, the most senior member of the research team employing me – a highly respected professor – booked out of a prearranged guesthouse and into a hotel, where he stayed for the duration of the trip (apart from excursions to the local university and one brief trip to a nearby township he was isolated from any contact with the day-to-day life of Peruvians).[23] Nor has the spectre of paternalism been completely laid to rest. I recall a senior researcher – behind closed doors at least – declaring 'we are not naïve . . . we are the experts'. These examples may be extreme, but they underline two important points. First, development studies must respect the voices of the poor. As social scientists, we have at least as much to learn from the poor as they have to learn from us. Second, research that does not engage with the poor and disadvantaged in a coherent and logical fashion may end up damaging the interests and prospects of the very people it is supposed to help.

Content and philosophy of the book

This book consists of 136 short entries written by an international panel of experts who discuss theoretical, ethical and practical issues relating to economic, social, cultural, institutional, political and human aspects of development in poor countries. It also includes a small selection of intellectual biographies of leading development thinkers. The book is organised along the lines of an encyclopaedia and entries are listed alphabetically. All of the entries, however, provide far more depth and discussion than those found in the average encyclopaedia or handbook. An effort has been made to cover all the major areas and issues in development studies. Some entries are devoted to emerging issues – such as the study of chronic poverty – which are likely to be of interest to the reader. Like all handbooks and encyclopaedias this collection is neither definitive nor fully comprehensive. Perhaps the most crucial casualty from among the commissioned entries is 'Health and Nutrition', which failed to materialise at the last minute.[24] Due to constraints on space it has been necessary to restrict the number of intellectual biographies to a small selection of post-war thinkers plus the seminal contributions of Adam Smith and Karl Marx.[25]

The book is extremely diverse and includes contributions that can be characterised as interdisciplinary, multidisciplinary and single disciplinary. While cross-disciplinary research is a defining feature of development studies and has huge potential, no book on development would be complete without considering the contribution of single disciplinary subjects. In the following pages a special effort is made to cover work in development economics through a series of entries on economic growth, structural transformation, international trade, foreign investment, sustainable consumption, technology, structural adjustment, cost-benefit analysis, labour markets and the debt crisis (among many other topics). A serious effort is also made to address important topics in development sociology such as class, ethnicity and structure and agency. Most entries, however, include elements from two or more disciplines. The contributions in this book are diverse in many other ways. They are pitched at different levels, incorporate different mixtures of theoretical and applied work, embrace different methodologies and represent different views of the world.

Above all, this book does not represent any single person's or organisation's view of development studies.[26] No person or institution should have a monopoly on defining the boundaries of such a momentous subject. Instead, the content and structure of the book evolved gradually over a period of several months stretching from late 2002 to early 2005. A preliminary list of key entries was drawn up by the editor and refined in consultation with experts from economics, politics and sociology. It was then made available for comment to students, academics and practitioners, who provided careful scrutiny. As a result the list was modified and underwent considerable expansion. During this process, all of the contributors to this volume were offered an opportunity to comment on various incarnations of the list and several have written on topics of their own design and choosing (for example, Amiya Bagchi, Herman Daly, G.C. Harcourt, Rachel Murphy and Amartya Sen).

All entries, without exception, have been peer reviewed to ensure rigour and clarity. Contributors, however, have been left with the flexibility and freedom to define the boundaries of their topics, to focus on the questions and issues that matter for them and, crucially, to express their own point of view. Some contributors have taken the opportunity to advance a particular argument (for example, Amartya Sen on the merits of the Human Development Index), while others have broken new ground (for example, James Foster who develops what he describes as a 'new general income standard framework' in his piece on Inequality Measurement). In some cases there have been trade-offs between summarising key issues for the reader and advancing an intellectual position. On balance, such trade-offs have been worthwhile. The philosophy behind the book has preserved rather than stifled intellectual freedom, spurred academic vigour and ingenuity and generated a much more interesting and provocative book. This should give *The Elgar Companion to Development Studies* a unique place among existing encyclopaedias and handbooks.

Notes

1. See, for example, Robert Solow on the Domar Model, G.C. Harcourt on the Harrod Growth Model, Robert Dixon on the Solow–Swan Model, Heinz Kurz on Endogenous Growth, Avi Cohen on Cambridge Controversies in Growth Theory, Moshe Syrquin on Structural Transformation and Arvind Panagariya on International Trade. An early source of dissent was Peter Bauer, who provided a neoliberal critique of government intervention, protectionism, economic planning and foreign aid throughout the 1950s and 1960s (for example, Bauer, 1957; see the biography of Bauer in this volume).
2. These ideas are seen as having their roots in Latin America and particularly in the UN's Economic Commission for Latin America (ECLA) and scholars such as Raul Prebisch.
3. See Ayres and Clark (1998) for a balanced assessment of the empirical evidence. See also the entries on Modernisation Theory, Dependency, Capitalism and Development, and Colonialism in this book.
4. The work of other classical economists such as Thomas Malthus, John Stuart Mill, David Ricardo and William Petty is also relevant. Meier and Baldwin (1962) provide an overview of contributions to development thinking from Classical Political Economy and the writings of Karl Marx and Friedrich Engels.
5. According to archive material drafted by Professor Malcolm Grant and kindly provided by the Development Studies Committee at the University of Cambridge, the Development Studies course at Cambridge 'started life in 1929 as the Course for Colonial Administrative Probationers. Previously this

had been a short course in London, but in 1925 the Colonial Office asked Cambridge and Oxford Universities to provide the courses . . . In 1958 [the Cambridge course] . . . was renamed the Overseas Services Course, and continued until 1963 when the course was further renamed the Course on Development and a more flexible programme [was] adopted'. Ron Clarke (1999) reflects on the connections between development studies and administrative training in the post-war period.

6. Molteberg et al. (2000) and Tribe and Sumner (2004) have drawn a slightly different set of distinctions between 'interdisciplinarity', 'mulitidisciplinarity' and 'transdisciplinarity'. In their scheme 'interdisciplinarity' is roughly akin to cross disciplinarity; multidisciplinarity is defined along the same lines as above; and transdisciplinarity is used to refer to 'a highly integrative form' of development studies that involves the unification of disciplines (Molteberg et al., 2000, pp. 318–19).

7. See the DSA's revised benchmark statement dated February 2005 (DSA, 2005).

8. An example of the former is Jenny Lunn, who is currently working on the Royal Geographical Society's 'Global Perspectives' Research Project. In contrast, Susanne von Itter tells me that the European Development Association is keen to reopen the debate on the nature and role of development studies.

9. The collections edited by De Bandt et al. (1980) and Bowles (2004) provide European and Canadian perspectives on development studies.

10. An internet search using the Lycos and Excite search engines suggests a growing number of degree courses in development studies in the USA. Examples include the interdepartmental degree programme in international development studies at the University of California founded in 1987, and the development studies programme at Brown University's Watson Institute for International Studies.

11. The livelihoods approach (for example, Ellis, 2000) is one of the few detailed elaborations of such frameworks (see also Livelihoods Approach, this volume). Another example is the capability approach (Sen, 1987, 1992, 1999), which integrates contributions from economics, social science and philosophy (see Capability Approach, this volume).

12. This is especially the case in economics, which is the only social science officially recognised as a practising profession (see Hulme and Toye, 2005). It must also be noted that the World Bank, which has the largest concentration of well-resourced researchers working on development, prioritises research concepts and approaches that come out of single-discipline economics.

13. Lipton (1970, p. 11) reports that even highly successful attempts to work in more than one discipline, such as Gunnar Myrdal's, 'are often mistrusted . . . by more narrow minded colleagues'. Sadly there is often envy, distrust and rivalry within as well as between disciplines.

14. Of course this statement is not entirely true, as Hulme and Turner point out.

15. The rapidly expanding literature on well-being and human development is a prime example and combines work from disciplines as diverse as economics and philosophy (see Clark, 2002b). Hulme and Toye (2005, p. 26) cite some additional examples, which include emerging studies of poverty that systematically combine econometric analysis with sociological life histories.

16. The most notable include the *Journal of Development Studies* (first published in 1964) and *World Development* (first published in 1973). Over the years the content and disciplinary focus of these journals has diversified. Harriss (1999, p. 498), for example, remarks that 'it is clear that the three economists who were the first editors of the JDS [*Journal of Development Studies*] had no idea of contributing to the establishment of a new inter-disciplinary field. They referred in their short preface (it was only a paragraph) in JDS 1(1) to the aim of publishing work from among a large amount of new research that was being done by economists on economic development, and – very much as a sub-plot – to encouraging more work on political development'.

17. Myrdal (1962) famously argued that we should declare our value judgements and biases. My views on this topic have inevitably been coloured by an entirely negative experience of one cross-disciplinary research project. For the record, my experiences of such projects at Manchester/Oxford and Cambridge have been positive.

18. Howard White (2002) makes a compelling case for advances in understanding that have occurred in three areas of research through cross-disciplinarity.

19. According to Paul Streeten (1974, p. 26), 'the only forum where interdisciplinary studies in depth can be conducted successfully is under one skull'.

20. Lipton (1970, p. 11) mentions the case of Everett Hagen, when suggesting that '[a]ttempts by first-rate [single discipline] specialists to work in other disciplines . . . often produces results that are not highly regarded by the new discipline and not understood in the old'.

21. These comments are not meant to imply that this is more of a problem for development studies than for other social science subjects. There are numerous examples of research departments and institutes that produce high-quality development research and do not devote significant amounts of time and other resources to genuinely wasteful activities.

22. I have tried to make this point in relation to the rapidly expanding literature on well-being in development studies. In particular, I have called for a new form of 'empirical philosophy' that is firmly rooted in social reality (Clark, 2002a, b). Arguably, most areas of development studies would benefit from greater integration between theoretical and applied work. For example, compare the literature on well-being (highly conceptual, less applied) with parallel work on sustainable livelihoods (conceptually weaker, highly applied). Interestingly there has not been much in the way of meaningful exchanges between these two strands of research.

23. Robert Chambers (1997) has crusaded for development studies researchers to adopt participatory approaches to knowledge creation. One may agree or disagree with his crusade, but self-evidently researchers who seek to avoid any interaction with the people whose lives they are writing about are missing an important source of information and potentially reinforcing processes of social exclusion.

24. Kirkpatrick et al. (2002) includes papers on 'health and nutrition' and 'reproductive health'. Other lost entries in the present volume include 'Apartheid', 'Africa's Agricultural Crisis', 'Rural Non-Farm Economy' and 'Subjective Well-Being'.

25. An effort was made to select some representative examples of prominent thinkers from different disciplines and perspectives. There are, of course, several notable omissions. Originally the goal was to restrict the number to no more than 20 biographies, although in the end the actual number crept up to 23. The fact that a biography appears (or does not appear) in this volume does not necessarily imply a value judgement about the relative merits of a particular contribution to development thinking. One worthy candidate for a biography was reluctant to be included.

26. In a previous job my senior research colleagues did attempt to set conditions on this volume in terms of additional editors, selection of issues and focus. These pressures were not accommodated.

References

Apthorpe, R. (1970), 'Development studies and social planning', in R. Apthorpe (ed.), *People Planning and Development Studies*, London: Frank Cass, pp. 1–28.

Ayres, R.I. and D.A. Clark (1998), 'Capitalism, industrialisation and development in Latin America: the dependency paradigm revisited', *Capital and Class*, **64**, 75–104.

Bauer, P.T. (1957), *Economic Analysis and Policy in Underdeveloped Countries*, Cambridge: Cambridge University Press.

Booth, C. (1892), *Life and Labour of the People in London*, London: Macmillan.

Bowles, P. (ed.) (2004), 'Special Issue: International Development Studies in Canada', *Canadian Journal of Development Studies*, **25** (1).

Chambers, Robert (1997), *Whose Reality Counts? Putting the Last First*, London: Intermediate Technology Publications.

Chenery, H., M. Ahluwalia, C. Bell, J. Duloy and R. Jolly (1974), *Redistribution with Growth: Policies to Improve Income Distribution in Developing Countries in the Context of Economic Growth*, Oxford: Oxford University Press for the World Bank and IDS, Sussex.

Clark, David A. (2002a), *Visions of Development: A Study of Human Values*, Cheltenham, UK and Northampton, MA, USA: Edward Elgar.

Clark, D.A. (2002b), 'Development ethics: a research agenda', *International Journal of Social Economics*, **29** (11), 830–48.

Clarke, R. (1999), 'Institutions for training overseas administrators: the University of Manchester's contribution', *Public Administration and Development*, **19**, 521–33.

CPRC (2004), *Chronic Poverty Report 2004/05*, Chronic Poverty Research Centre, University of Manchester, UK.

De Bandt, J., P. Mándi and D. Seers (eds) (1980), *European Studies in Development*, London: Macmillan.

DSA (2005), 'Revised Submission to the Quality Assurance Agency relating to the Benchmarking of Development Studies for Undergraduate provision in British Universities', Development Studies Association, February, www.devstud.org.uk/consultation/DSA%20Benchmarking-QAA%20Submission%20Feb% 202005.pdf, 5 September 2005.

Edwards, M. (2002), 'Is there a "future positive" for development studies', *Journal of International Development*, **14** (6), 737–41.

Ellis, F. (2000), *Rural Livelihoods and Diversity in Developing Countries*, Oxford: Oxford University Press.

Frank, Andre Gunder (1967), *Capitalism and Underdevelopment in Latin America: Historical Studies of Chile and Brazil*, London: Monthly Review Press.

Harriss, J. (1999), 'The DSA at twenty-one: a critical celebration of development studies', *Journal of International Development*, **11** (4), 497–501.

Harriss, J. (2002), 'The case for cross-disciplinary approaches in international development', *World Development*, **30** (3), 487–96.

Hulme, D. and J. Toye (2005), 'The case for cross-disciplinary social science research on poverty, inequality and well-being', *Journal of Development Studies*, forthcoming.

Hulme, D. and M. Turner (1990), *Sociology and Development*, London: Harvester Wheatsheaf.

Huntingdon, S. (1968), *Political Order in Changing Societies*, New Haven, CT: Yale University Press.

ILO (1976), *Employment, Growth and Basic Needs: A One World Problem*, Geneva: International Labour Organisation.

Kanbur, R. (2002), 'Economics, social science and development', *World Development*, **30** (3), 477–86.

Kindleberger, Charles P. (1958), *Economic Development*, London: McGraw-Hill.

Kirkpatrick, Colin, Ron Clark and Charles Polidano (eds) (2002), *Handbook on Development Policy and Management*, Cheltenham, UK and Northampton, MA, USA: Edward Elgar.

Kuhn, Thomas (1962), *The Structure of Scientific Revolutions*, Chicago: University of Chicago Press.

Lehmann, D. (ed.) (1979), *Development Theory: Four Critical Case Studies*, London: Frank Cass.

Lerner, Daniel (1958), *The Passing of Traditional Society: Modernising the Middle East*, New York: Free Press.

Lewis, W. Arthur (1954), 'Economic development with unlimited supplies of labour', *Manchester School*, **22**, 139–91.

Lipton, M. (1970), 'Interdisciplinary studies in less developed countries', *Journal of Development Studies*, **7** (1), 5–18.

Loxley, J. (2004), 'What is distinctive about international development studies?', *Canadian Journal of Development Studies*, **25** (1), 25–38.

McClelland, David (1961), *The Achieving Society*, Princeton, NJ: Van Nostrand.

Meier, Gerald M. and Robert E. Baldwin (1962), *Economic Development: Theory, History and Policy*, London: John Wiley & Sons.

Mill, John Stuart (1859), *On Liberty*, reprinted in J.S. Mill (1988), *On Liberty and Other Essays*, (Oxford World's Classics, edited by J. Gray), Oxford: Oxford University Press.

Molteberg, E., C. Bergstrøm and R. Haug (2000), 'Interdisciplinarity in development studies: myths and realities', *Forum for Development Studies*, **27** (2), 317–30.

Myrdal, Gunnar (1962), *Value in Social Theory*, London: Routledge & Kegan Paul.

Nurkse, Ragnar (1953), *Problems of Capital Formation in Underdeveloped Countries*, Oxford: Oxford University Press.

Nussbaum, M.C. (1988), 'Nature, function and capability: Aristotle on political distribution', *Oxford Studies in Ancient Philosophy*, supplementary vol., pp. 145–84.

Nussbaum, Martha C. (1990), 'Aristotelian social democracy', in Bruce Douglas, Gerald Mara and Henry Richardson (eds), *Liberalism and the Good*, New York: Routledge, pp. 203–52.

Parsons, Talcott (1960), *Structure and Process in Modern Societies*, Glenco, IL: Free Press.

RAE (2005), 'UOA 43: Development Studies', Draft as at 16 July, www.rae.ac.uk/pubs/2005/04/docs/j43.doc, 31 August 2005.

Rosenstein-Rodan, P.N. (1943), 'Problems of industrialisation of Eastern and South-Eastern Europe', *Economic Journal*, **53** (210/211), 202–11.

Rostow, W.W. (1960), *The Stages of Economic Growth: A Non-Communist Manifesto*, Cambridge: Cambridge University Press.

Rowntree, B.S. (1901), *Poverty: A Study of Town Life*, London: Macmillan.

Seers, D. (1969), 'The meaning of development', *International Development Review*, **11** (2), 2–6.

Sen, Amartya K. (1987), *The Standard of Living: The Tanner Lectures*, Cambridge: Cambridge University Press.

Sen, Amartya K. (1992), *Inequality Re-examined*, Oxford: Clarendon.

Sen, Amartya K. (1999), *Development As Freedom*, Oxford: Oxford University Press.

Smith, Adam (1776), *An Inquiry into the Nature and Causes of the Wealth of Nations*, reprinted in Edward T. Cannon (ed.) (1976), *The Wealth of Nations*, Chicago: University of Chicago Press.

Solow, R. (1956), 'A contribution to the theory of economic growth', *Quarterly Journal of Economics*, **70**, 65–94.

Stewart, Frances (1985), *Planning to Meet Basic Needs*, London: Macmillan.

Streeten, P. (1974), 'Some problems in the use and transfer of an intellectual technology', *The Social Sciences and Development*, Washington, DC: World Bank, pp. 3–54.

Streeten, Paul P., S.J. Burki, Mahbub ul Haq, Norman Hicks and Frances Stewart (1981), *First Things First, Meeting Basic Human Needs in Developing Countries*, Oxford and New York: Oxford University Press.

Thomas, A. (2004), 'The study of development', Notes for presentation at the Development Studies Association Annual Conference, 6 November, Church House, London, www.devstud.org.uk/conference/workshops/3.2-devstud.htm, 31 August 2005.

Tribe, M. and A. Sumner (2004), 'The nature of development studies: an exploration from the standpoint of the British–Irish Development Studies Association', paper prepared for the DSA Annual Conference, 6

November, Church House, London, www.devstud.org.uk/conference/workshops/3.2-devstud.htm, 31 August 2005.

Tribe, M. and A. Sumner (2005), 'The nature of development studies – a United Kingdom perspective', *EADI Newsletter 1–2005*, pp. 7–8.

Warren, B. (1973), 'Capitalism and industrialisation', *New Left Review*, **81**, 3–44.

Warren, B. (1980), *Imperialism: Pioneer of Capitalism* (edited by J. Sender), London: New Left Books.

Webster, Andrew (1990), *Introduction to the Sociology of Development*, 2nd edn, Basingstoke: Macmillan.

White, H. (2002), 'Combining quantitative and qualitative approaches in poverty analysis', *World Development*, **30** (3), 511–22.

World Bank (2005a), *World Development Report 2006: Equity and Development*, Oxford: Oxford University Press for the World Bank.

World Bank (2005b), *Global Economic Prospects: Trade, Regionalism and Development*, Washington, DC: World Bank.

UNDP (United Nations Development Programme) (2005), *Human Development Report 2005: International Cooperation at a Crossroads – Aid, Trade and Security in an Unequal World*, Oxford: Oxford University Press.

Ageing and Development

There is no universally accepted definition of what constitutes old age. There is general dissatisfaction with defining old age in purely chronological terms, but there would appear to be no better alternative. Later life age is perceived and understood in a multitude of different ways, often with important cultural variations (Keith et al., 1994). These may refer to biological processes and physical appearance, key life events (for example, retirement or some other form of disengagement), or social roles (grandparenthood or ceremonial duties).

Population ageing (defined as an increase in the percentage of a population aged 65 years or older) is a global trend. Although the oldest population structures are in richer countries, the majority of the world's older people live in the South. By 2030 there will be nearly three times as many people aged 60 or more in the South than in the North. It is difficult to predict the point where population ageing may tail off in the future. Current projections show that 36 per cent of Japanese will be aged over 65 by 2050, but we should not assume that this figure represents a high-water mark for future trends.

According to some commentators, ageing may be desirable from the point of view of an individual, but is bad for society as a whole. In an influential report, the World Bank observes: 'The world is approaching an old age crisis . . . The proportion of the population that is old is expanding rapidly, swelling the potential economic burden on the young' (World Bank, 1994). This associates later life with dependency, vulnerability and an inherent lack of capability. Yet research from developing countries challenges these negative generalisations, showing that older people are a very heterogeneous group. Key contributions made by older people include the care of grandchildren (including AIDS orphans), sharing pension benefits, continued economic activity (salaried and unsalaried), and the provision of accommodation to other household members. It is important to avoid generalising about later life from either a negative or a positive perspective. Some older people have high levels of vulnerability and dependence, others may be making more social and economic contributions than at any previous time in their lives, and the great majority are both dependent and depended upon.

With reference to economic development, it is claimed that older people use up savings and sell off assets, are unproductive, and have expensive needs, whose cost reduces the resource base of the economy as a whole. Microeconomic research has challenged these claims, observing that many elders continue to save, albeit at a lower rate than previously (Disney, 1996). One reason for this may be that sustaining the size of future bequests increases the likelihood that younger family members will take an interest in their well-being. There is similar uncertainty about the relationship between an ageing workforce and levels of productivity. It is sometimes claimed that older workforces tend to be less entrepreneurial, ambitious and flexible, yet older workers may have accumulated a higher stock of human capital and experience.

1

Another conventional wisdom is that ageing holds back development because investment is lost to the mounting costs of social provision. Yet this process is not inevitable, and is influenced by the ways in which people experience later life. The cost of supporting an elderly population with high levels of protracted chronic disease and general dependence will be greater than that for a healthy, active population.

Developed countries spend large amounts on formal social protection, and a high share of this is devoted to programmes of direct relevance to older people. These programmes are expensive, and are often viewed as beyond the financial and institutional means of many developing and, increasingly, developed countries. This has led to concerns that pressures on public policy caused by population ageing are likely to cause a global 'old-age crisis' (World Bank, 1994). In most low-income countries, social policies focus on the needs of other age groups, such as mothers, children and 'workers'. Instead of sustaining existing programmes, the main challenge for such countries will be to factor older people into social policies for the first time. Across middle-income countries, the scale of social policy interventions for older people is extremely varied, ranging from minimal interventions to schemes which rival those of the North (Lloyd-Sherlock, 2002). Typically, access to services and benefits is restricted to relatively privileged groups, raising concerns about equity and the social exclusion of poor older people. Social protection for all groups has been threatened by structural adjustment, abrupt transitions from socialist welfare models, and the rapid growth of unregulated private sector welfare agencies.

Debates about public policy for older people are strongly derived from the experiences of the North, and have been dominated by controversies about pension reform (Lloyd-Sherlock, 2000). Recent reforms have mainly sought to replace unitary public sector pension funds with more pluralistic arrangements, including a significant private sector component. The arguments in favour of this arrangement are that it promotes competition (and hence efficiency), stimulates capital markets and relieves the public sector of an activity it was not well suited to perform. Some of these contentions have been challenged by studies of reformed systems in countries such as Chile and the UK.

Debates about pension reform overlook several key issues. The first is that the majority of the world's older people do not receive a pension, and are unlikely to do so in the foreseeable future. Second, the debate ignores successful pension programmes which do not fit within the parameters of the new neoliberal model: examples include publicly administered provident funds in Singapore and Malaysia, and non-contributory schemes in a number of countries (Charlton and McKinnon, 2001). These call into doubt the 'one-size-fits-all' approach to pensions of some international agencies.

Older people are usually associated with chronic health conditions that are expensive to treat, and lifetime health expenditure is often heavily concentrated in the period immediately before death. This has given rise to fears of an ageing-related healthcare cost explosion in the North, and the view that comprehensive geriatric care is beyond the financial means of most developing countries. In fact, the impact of ageing on health spending is strongly mediated by a range of other factors, including how the health sector is organised and financed. Despite containing a similar proportion of elderly people as the UK, the USA spends twice as much of its GDP on healthcare. This difference is mainly due to inefficiencies in the US private health insurance market. Health sector reforms being applied in many countries are likely to have a large effect on their capacity to service older people more efficiently, but the growing literature on these reforms makes scant reference to this. In those developing countries relatively unscathed by HIV/AIDS, mortality rates continue to fall, reducing the 'cost of dying' effect on health spending. In poorer countries the social sectors currently fail to meet the basic needs of many people, old and young. In these cases, it is meaningless to project the impact of population ageing on expenditure based on the experiences of the rich North.

The view that healthcare for older people is inherently expensive ignores the potential contributions of appropriate primary healthcare (PHC) programmes to older people. As initially conceived, PHC places a strong emphasis on mother and child health, to the exclusion of groups such as the elderly (Rifkin and Walt, 1986). In developing countries where many elderly people lack access to basic services, the potential benefits of extending PHC to meet their specific needs may be substantial.

In the North, social policy for older people is increasingly influenced by 'grey politics'. With democratisation and demographic ageing, it is to be expected that older people in developing countries will gain political influence. However, it should not be assumed that these people will constitute a single, unified interest group. In several Latin American countries there have been significant mobilisations by older people with formal sector welfare entitlements, but these have not taken up the cause of older people in general.

Divisions between formal social policy interventions and informal means of support for older people are often blurred, and increasing attention is now being paid to the interface between them. This is particularly significant in the area of long-term care for vulnerable older people. As the number of people surviving to a very old age increases, the demand for care services is projected to soar.

In the North, the state usually only finances or provides a small part of care services. Most are being met by either the private sector or informal carers. As such, a burning issue is how to effectively combine the state, family and private sector in order to ensure that care provision is adequate (Walker, 1992). In the private sector there are problems of regulation, equity and supply. There is an urgent need to recognise the contribution of informal carers, and to support and compensate them.

In the South it is widely assumed that care and social services are not a policy priority, since traditional household and community structures are still able to play this role. In most developing countries the great majority of older people continue to live with other family members (Sokolovsky, 2000). However, this does not guarantee satisfactory care. Contexts of poverty and rapid change put families under strain and reduce their capacity to meet these needs. Increased female participation in the salaried labour force is likely to constrain the supply of informal care, regardless of household structure. Rapid rises in the numbers of very old are likely to stimulate demand for residential care, but these services remain very underdeveloped in the South.

The issues of care for and care by the elderly contain strong gender dimensions. Although cultural attitudes to supporting the aged vary, women are almost always the main providers of care, whether the responsibility falls to youngest daughters, daughters-in-law, sisters or some other female relation. Women also predominate as paid carers, either in institutions or working in private households. In poorer, three-generation households, this may add to the multiple responsibilities of employment, domestic chores and childcare. Where older people are themselves the providers of care, women also tend to predominate. Grandparenting often represents an extension of a woman's previous domestic responsibilities. Since women are more likely to survive their male spouses, they are more likely to provide care to their spouses, rather than receive it. Women are also more likely to be widowed, which may reduce their access to informal care in cultures that discriminate against widowhood.

Patterns of care are strongly influenced by intergenerational exchange and reciprocity. Even when they have little current income, many older people still own houses and other valuable assets, such as land. Research has found that both explicit and implicit contracts about inheritance and asset transfer may have an important effect on current care arrangements. However, practices and traditions of inheritance and exchange vary around the world. In India, for example, inheritance is usually patrilineal, increasing the vulnerability of elderly widows (Agnes, 1999).

Discussions about ageing and development must recognise that later life experiences are fluid and diverse, spanning up to four decades of a person's life. Despite this, it is possible to make some generalisations about older people. As a group, they are less likely to be engaged in salaried economic activity. They are more exposed to age-related risks, such as physical decline and some kinds of chronic disease. Older people are also exposed to the general stereotypes and prejudices of society at large: attitudes which may become self-fulfilling prophecies. Taken together, these mean that the capabilities of older people tend to be restricted, and become increasingly so as they progress through later life to death.

These common characteristics do not justify the portrayal of older people as a special-interest group, whose interests are separate from, and possibly in conflict with, those of other generations. Older people do not exist in isolation (despite the best efforts of some societies to promote this), and so their well-being is intimately bound in with that of society as a whole. As with gender, policy needs to recognise both difference and interdependence.

PETER LLOYD-SHERLOCK

References

Agnes, F. (1999), 'Law and women of age. A short note', *Economic and Political Weekly*, **30**, October, 51–4.
Charlton, R. and R. McKinnon (2001), *Pensions in Development*, London: Ashgate.
Disney, R. (1996), *Can We Afford to Grow Old?*, Cambridge, MA and London: MIT Press.
Keith, J., C. Fry, A. Glascock, C. Ikels, J. Dickerson-Putman, H. Harpending and P. Draper (1994), *The Aging Experience. Diversity and Commonality Across Cultures*, London: Sage.
Lloyd-Sherlock, P. (2000), 'Old age and poverty in developing countries: new policy challenges', *World Development*, **18** (12), 2157–68.
Lloyd-Sherlock, P. (2002), 'Formal social protection for older people in developing countries: three different approaches', *Journal of Social Policy*, **31** (4), 695–714.
Rifkin, S. and G. Walt (1986), 'Why health improves: defining the issues concerning "comprehensive primary healthcare" and "selective primary healthcare"', *Social Science and Medicine*, **23** (6), 559–66.
Sokolovsky, J. (2000), 'Living arrangements of older persons and family support in less developed countries', UN Population Division Technical Meeting on Population Ageing and Living Arrangements of Older Persons, New York, February.
Walker, A. (1992), 'The care for elderly people in industrial society: a conflict between the family and the state', in P. Krishnan and K. Mahadevan (eds), *The Elderly Population in the Developed and Developing Worlds*, New Delhi: B.R. Publishing Co, pp. 1–30.
World Bank (1994), *Averting the Old Age Crisis. Policies to Protect the Old and Promote Growth*, Oxford: Oxford University Press.

Agriculture and Economic Growth

Historically, no country has been able to sustain a rapid transition out of poverty without raising productivity in its agricultural sector. The process involves a successful structural transformation where agriculture, through higher productivity, provides food, labour and even savings to the process of urbanisation and industrialisation. A dynamic agriculture raises labour productivity in the rural economy, pulls up wages, and gradually eliminates the worst dimensions of absolute poverty. Somewhat paradoxically, the process also leads to a decline in the *relative* importance of agriculture to the overall economy, as the industrial and service sectors grow even more rapidly, partly through stimulus from a modernising agriculture.

Despite this historical role of agriculture in economic development, both the academic and donor communities lost interest in the sector, starting in the mid-1980s, mostly because of low prices in world markets for basic agricultural commodities. Low prices, while a boon to poor consumers, made it hard to justify policy support for the agricultural sector or for funding agricultural projects.

However, three revolutions are under way that are creating radically new opportunities and challenges in agriculture. The first revolution is in knowledge of basic genetic structures and mechanisms. One result of this knowledge is the development of agricultural biotechnology, but even without genetically modified organisms (GMOs), the genetic revolution will push out the frontier of agricultural productivity dramatically (Mew et al., 2003; Timmer, 2003). Many of these productivity gains can be in developing countries, where they are needed most.

Second, even in poorer developing countries a supermarket revolution is transforming food retail markets, and the supply chains that provision them, at a faster pace than anyone imagined just five years ago (Reardon et al., 2003). There are important new opportunities for farmers in these countries to diversify out of low-value crops into new commodities with greater demand potential, and thus to capture some of the value added being generated by supermarkets. But the strict quality, safety, hygiene and labour standards demanded by supermarkets are also a severe challenge to participation by small farmers and there is concern that rural poverty might worsen as supermarkets expand.

Finally, understanding of the determinants of poverty and the mechanisms for reducing it in a sustainable fashion has also undergone a revolution in the past decade. Part of this understanding is recognition that economic growth is the main vehicle for reducing poverty and that, in many circumstances, the agricultural sector is an important arena for connecting the two (Timmer, 2002). Another part stresses the direct impact on poverty reduction that comes from rising rural wages and incomes. Most of the world's poor live in rural areas, or migrated from them in search of better opportunities. It seems almost obvious that growth in agricultural productivity is the surest way to end poverty. But with low prices for staple cereals in world markets and population growth slowing, the connection is not so clear. Agriculture must be dynamic and profitable if it is to help reduce rural poverty, and growing staple cereals has not been a source of dynamism in rural economies for two decades. A profitable agriculture will depend on diversification into crops and livestock with better demand prospects than for cereals, and into production for the agri-business sector, which can add value through processing and enhanced consumer appeal.

This diversification process has been a policy objective in Asia since the mid-1980s (and in Japan and Korea since well before that). But in low-income Asia, diversification will depend on continued availability of low-cost rice, especially in rural markets. In Africa and Latin America, having cheap corn, wheat and rice available in rural markets will be important if diversification is to be successful. Low-cost staple foods are also important to the poor directly, because they devote such a large share of their budget to them.

What links growth in agricultural productivity to aggregate economic growth?
This seemingly simple question is complicated and controversial. The least-controversial elements are the basic linkages that were first articulated to a general economics audience by Lewis (1954) and Johnston and Mellor (1961). These linkages have long been part of the core of modern development theory and practice (Timmer, 1988, 2002). Because economic growth usually has a direct impact on poverty, any contribution agriculture makes to speeding overall economic growth will, in most circumstances, also directly contribute to reducing poverty (Dollar and Kraay, 2002).

Second, market failures and political biases have led to a systematic undervaluation of output from rural economies and correcting these can have economy-wide benefits. The historic bias against the rural sector in developing countries left them starved for resources and discriminated against by macroeconomic and trade policies (Lipton, 1977; Timmer, 1993). Failures in rural credit and labour markets – some of which can cause 'poverty traps' – have provided the analytical context for much of modern development economics (Dasgupta, 1993). But even commodity markets for many products from developing countries 'fail' in the sense that agricultural surpluses from rich countries are dumped there, depressing world market prices below long-run costs of production.

A final set of linkages makes growth originating in the agricultural sector tend to be more 'pro-poor' than it would be if the source of growth came from the industrial or service sectors (Mellor, 1976; Ravallion and Datt, 1996; Timmer, 2002). New agricultural technologies that improve farm productivity strengthen this connection.

Direct contribution via Lewis and Johnston–Mellor linkages
The 'Lewis linkages' between agriculture and economic growth provide the non-agricultural sector with labour and capital freed up by higher productivity in the agricultural sector. These linkages work primarily through factor markets, but there is no suggestion that these markets work perfectly in the dualistic setting analysed by Lewis (1954). Chenery and Syrquin (1975) argue that a major source of economic growth is the transfer of low-productivity labour from the rural to the urban sector. If labour markets worked perfectly, there would be few productivity gains from this structural transfer.

The 'Johnston–Mellor linkages' allow market-mediated, input–output interactions between the two sectors so that agriculture can contribute to economic development. These linkages are based on the agricultural sector supplying raw materials to industry, food for industrial workers, markets for industrial output, and the foreign exchange needed to import capital goods (Johnston and Mellor, 1961). Again, for the Johnston–Mellor linkages as with the Lewis linkages, it is difficult to see any significance for policy or economic growth unless some of the markets that serve these linkages are operating imperfectly (or, as with many risk markets, are missing altogether). That is, resource allocations must be out of equilibrium and face constraints and bottlenecks not immediately reflected in market prices if increases in agricultural output are to stimulate the rest of the economy at a rate that causes the 'contribution' from agriculture to be greater than the market value of the output, that is, the agricultural income multiplier is greater than one (Timmer, 1995).

Indirect contributions from agriculture

Writing in the mid-1960s, Mosher was able to assume that 'getting agriculture moving' would have a high priority in national plans because of its 'obvious' importance in feeding people and providing a spur to industrialisation (Mosher, 1966). That assumption has held only in parts of East and South East Asia, and has been badly off the mark in much of Africa and Latin America. In the latter regions, a historically prolonged and deep urban bias led to a distorted pattern of investment. Too much public and private capital was invested in urban areas and too little in rural areas. Too much capital was held as liquid and non-productive investments that rural households use to manage risk. Too little capital was invested in raising rural productivity.

Such distortions have resulted in strikingly different marginal productivities of capital in urban and rural areas. New growth strategies – such as those pursued in Indonesia after 1966, China after 1978 and Vietnam after 1989 – altered investment priorities in favour of rural growth and benefited from this disequilibrium in rates of return, at least initially. For example, in Indonesia from the mid-1960s to the mid-1990s, farm GDP per capita increased by nearly half, whereas it had declined from 1900 to the mid-1960s. In China, the increase from 1978 to 1994 was nearly 70 per cent, whereas this measure dropped by 20 per cent between 1935 and 1978 (Prasada Rao et al., 2002). A switch in investment strategy and improved rates of return on capital increases factor productivity (and farm income) because efficiency in resource allocation is improved.

One explanation for more rapid and pro-poor economic growth as urban bias is reduced is provided by Mellor's model of agricultural growth, rural employment and poverty reduction which emphasises the role of the rural non-tradables sector in pulling underemployed workers out of agriculture into the non-agricultural rural economy. The Mellor model explicitly integrates manufactured export performance (the source of much dynamism in East Asia's economies since the 1960s) and the non-tradables sector in the rural economy (which includes a wide array of local agro-processing) to explain subsequent reductions in poverty. This model, drawing on Mellor's earlier work in India (Mellor, 1976) and more recently in Egypt (Mellor, 2000), explains why countries with substantial agricultural sectors that experienced rapid growth from labour-intensive manufactured exports had such good records of overall economic growth *and* poverty reduction.

Getting agriculture moving

There is no great secret to agricultural development in principle. Schultz (1964) and Mosher (1966) had identified the key constraints and strategic elements by the mid-1960s. New agricultural technology and incentive prices in local markets combine to generate profitable farm investments and income streams that simultaneously increase commodity output and lift the rural economy out of poverty (Hayami and Ruttan, 1985). The process can be speeded up by investing in the human capital of rural inhabitants, especially through education, and by assistance in the development of new agricultural technology, especially where modern science is needed to play a key role in providing the genetic foundation for higher yields.

Beyond this level of general understanding, however, the diversity of rural circumstances has sharply impeded agricultural development in practice and made it country specific. The mechanisms for both technology development and provision of rural price incentives are no longer as clear as they were in the 1960s, especially in Africa. The Consultative Group on International Agricultural Research (CGIAR), manager of such centres as the International Rice Research Institute (IRRI) in the Philippines, has produced many breakthroughs for the world's staple grains, but not for the mixed farming systems prevalent in unirrigated areas. Core funding for the system has been falling for nearly two decades as the market prices of these crops have dropped to historic lows, under the weight of productivity gains in developing countries and government-subsidised crop surpluses in rich countries. Few countries have the scientific resources to conduct basic crop research on their own, so the question of where agricultural technology will come from for the additional 3 billion people expected in the next 50 years remains unanswered.

Despite the country specificity of how to implement an agricultural development strategy, the Schultz–Mosher insights suggest that there are several common elements to that strategy. First, obviously, is a supportive macroeconomic policy, one that yields low inflation, a reasonably stable exchange rate, positive real interest rates, and perhaps some monitoring of disruptive short-run capital flows. Second, 'getting prices right' extends good macro policy to the trade arena, where an open economy with low barriers to both internal and external trade should generate a level playing field for producers and consumers alike. The need to keep these barriers low is one of the major arguments against interventionist price policies for staple foods, even when a case can be made on the basis of protecting the poor or stabilising the economy. These two components are the essentials of 'good economic governance' which underpin modern economic growth.

What remains after this? The externalities from rural growth outlined above argue for a significant public role in funding agricultural research and rural infrastructure. Once these are in place as the basis for profitable farming, policy attention and budget priorities should turn to the rural non-tradables sector. Part of the profitability for this sector will come from a labour-intensive export sector that is successfully linked into the global economy, and in many countries this will include the agri-business sector. Rapid growth in this export sector creates demand for labour directly as well as for the goods and services of the rural economy that raise demand for labour indirectly.

An additional challenge, and opportunity, comes from the rapid consolidation of the food retail sector – the rapid rise of supermarkets. The challenge to higher rural incomes from this process is its tendency to have such high standards for quality, safety, hygiene and farm labour practices that many of a country's own farmers are excluded from the supply chains that provision their consumers, even poor consumers (Reardon et al., 2003). Globalisation permits procurement officers to source food supplies from anywhere in the world, so local farmers compete not just against each other for local consumers, but also against the global market. But farmers increasingly also have access to the global market if they are the low-cost producer meeting global standards. The future of agricultural development will depend on putting productive new technologies into the hands of farmers and creating an open market environment to make the resulting production as profitable to farmers as employment opportunities in other sectors. Where that development is not possible, and there will be many environments where it is not, rural poverty will only be solved by migration to alternative opportunities.

Where the strategy does work, diversifying the rural economy will be key to increasing income opportunities. Placing rural diversification at the centre of agricultural development means that there are two quite different tasks that need to be managed simultaneously: (a) raising the productivity of staple food crops for those farmers who continue to grow them; and (b) using the low costs of these staple foods as 'fuel' for the agricultural diversification effort, including as feed for livestock. Making substantial progress on both of these 'rural' tasks will be among the most 'pro-poor' things the development community can hope to accomplish between now and the target date for the Millennium Development Goals in 2015.

C. PETER TIMMER

References

Chenery, Hollis B. and Moshe Syrquin (1975), *Patterns of Development, 1950–1970*, London: Oxford University Press.

Dasgupta, Partha (1993), *An Inquiry into Well-Being and Destitution*, Oxford: Clarendon.

Dollar, David and Aart Kraay (2002), 'Growth is good for the poor', *Journal of Economic Growth*, 7, 195–225.

Hayami, Y. and V. Ruttan (1985), *Agricultural Development: An International Perspective*, revised and expanded edition, Baltimore, MD: Johns Hopkins University Press.

Johnston, B.F. and J.W. Mellor (1961), 'The role of agriculture in economic development', *American Economic Review*, **51** (4), 566–93.

Lewis, W.A. (1954), 'Economic development with unlimited supplies of labour', *The Manchester School*, 22, 3–42.

Lipton, M. (1977), *Why Poor People Stay Poor: Urban Bias in World Development*, Cambridge, MA: Harvard University Press.

Mellor, John W. (1976), *The New Economics of Growth: A Strategy for India and the Developing World*, Ithaca, NY: Cornell University Press.

Mellor, John W. (2000), 'Agricultural growth, rural employment, and poverty reduction: non-tradables, public expenditure, and balanced growth', prepared for the World Bank Rural Week 2000, March.

Mew, T.W., D.S. Brar, S. Peng, D. Dawe and B. Hardy (2003), *Rice Science: Innovations and Impact for Livelihood*, Proceedings of the International Rice Research Conference, 16–19 September 2002, Beijing, China, International Rice Research Institute, Chinese Academy of Engineering, and Chinese Academy of Agricultural Sciences.

Mosher, A.T. (1966), *Getting Agriculture Moving: Essentials for Development and Modernization*, New York: Praeger.

Prasada Rao, D.S., Angus Maddison and Boon Lee (2002), 'International comparison of farm sector performance: methodological options and empirical findings for Asia-Pacific economies, 1900–94', in Angus Maddison, D.S. Prasada Rao and William F. Shepherd (eds), *The Asian Economies in the Twentieth Century*, Cheltenham, UK and Northampton, MA, USA: Edward Elgar, pp. 27–52.

Ravallion, M. and G. Datt (1996), 'How important to India's poor is the sectoral composition of economic growth?', *World Bank Economic Review*, **10** (1), 1–25.

Reardon, T., C.P. Timmer, C.B. Barrett and J.A. Berdegue (2003), 'The rise of supermarkets in Africa, Asia, and Latin America', *American Journal of Agricultural Economics*, **85** (5), 1140–46.

Schultz, T.W. (1964), *Transforming Traditional Agriculture*, New Haven, CT: Yale University Press.

Timmer, C.P. (1988), 'The agricultural transformation', in H. Chenery and T.N. Srinivasan (eds), *Handbook of Development Economics*, Vol. 1, Amsterdam: North-Holland, pp. 275–331.

Timmer, C.P. (1993), 'Rural bias in the East and South East Asian rice economy: Indonesia in comparative perspective', in A. Varshney (ed.), *Beyond Urban Bias*, London: Frank Cass, pp. 149–76.

Timmer, C.P. (1995), 'Getting agriculture moving: do markets provide the right signals?', *Food Policy*, **20** (5), 455–72.

Timmer, C.P. (2002), 'Agriculture and economic growth', in Bruce Gardner and Gordon Rausser (eds), *The Handbook of Agricultural Economics*, Vol. IIA, Amsterdam: North-Holland, pp. 1487–546.
Timmer, C.P. (2003), 'Biotechnology and food systems in developing countries', *Journal of Nutrition*, **133** (11), 3319–22.

Assets, Markets and Entitlement

While the developmental role to be played by governments was under question during the 1990s, the nature and role of the 'markets' assumed to be more efficient in the allocation of resources has received far less critical attention. As a way of addressing this lacuna, the 'livelihoods approach' advanced by Moser (1995), Ellis (2000) and others provides a useful starting-point by linking work to assets and markets. This framework recognises two important activities that are undertaken by the poor based upon their own knowledge and understanding of their environment. First, the poor engage in the active management of a complex asset base while endeavouring to make ends meet, and second, in doing so, the poor engage in iterative processes of response and adaptation to external and internal events that change their day-to-day environment, some of which are determined by the markets they confront when trying to use their assets, others by the risks that they face and the strategies that they adopt to manage these. From the perspective of this framework, the more assets people command in the appropriate mix, the greater their capacity to buffer themselves against external shocks. Likewise, the better markets function to their favour, the more likely are their chances of success when using these assets to generate a livelihood.

Assets and markets can also be said to form the foundation for what Amartya Sen (1981) terms 'entitlement mapping'. This mapping defines the set of commodity bundles that can be claimed on the basis of a given asset, or in Sen's language, an endowment, and reflects the capacity of individuals or other social agents to exchange their endowment resources for commodities that they require or desire. This may be achieved either through the use of endowments in production processes that yield outputs available for consumption or sale, or by their non-market or market direct exchange. The mapping might also imply acquiring complementary resources through factor markets such as finance, productive inputs or information. Although not suggested by Sen, the 'capabilities approach' to well-being could potentially incorporate the use made by an individual of the various commodity bundles that are commanded by the set of endowments available to that individual (Sen, 1985). Put another way, this would refer to the functionings that follow from work, trade and accumulation. It is also noteworthy that participants in the South African Participatory Assessment extended their concerns to include the ability to work *safely*, trade *fairly* and accumulate *securely* (May et al., 1998).

Although Sen's notions of entitlement and capability have been enthusiastically adopted by many analysts of development, others are concerned that the mutation of the original terminology and framework used by Sen can lead to analyses that are confusing and even misleading (for example, Gasper, 1993). However, much of the dynamism and insight of the approach can still be retained by thinking more simply about assets and markets. At one level, markets determine the one-dimensional real income which an asset bundle can command while also shaping the distinctive patterns that characterise the income-claiming mechanisms utilised by agents. For example, a semi-subsistence peasant farmer (endowed with unskilled labour and land) and a semi-skilled artisan (endowed with skills, market information and tools) may on average be able to command the same commodity bundles, that is they may have the same real income on average. However, as Sen demonstrated, they are subject to very distinctive forms of vulnerability and poverty risk. The peasant farmer is exposed to production shocks (what Sen calls 'direct entitlement failures'), while the artisan is subject to the risk of sales constraints and changes in the price of the commodity he or she sells relative to the price of subsistence goods ('trade entitlement failure').

By describing this process as a livelihood strategy, attention is drawn to the combination of productive activities, the operation of markets, the exercise of socially defined rights such as access to charity or publicly provided social security, the coping or adaptive actions undertaken to protect future production and consumption behaviours that are involved. Indeed, Chambers and Conway's (1992, p. 7) well-known definition views a livelihood as comprising 'the capabilities, assets (stores, resources, claims and access) and activities required for a means of living'.

In the pure exchange economy of economic theory, when markets are perfect, that is, price rationed, Sen's entitlement mapping may become no more than the budget set defined by the asset and the given set of relative prices. However, it is important to recognise that the determinants of the rate of return that can be achieved from this asset by different activities have both physical and institutional dimensions. While exchange activities, for example, have agro-climatic and technical determinants, the rate of return that is realised from these activities is also based on the rules that structure the markets in which these exchanges take place. The concept of 'real markets' is useful in this regard as a way of drawing attention to the specific set of power and institutional relationships which constitute real or political markets, as compared to the abstract notion of perfectly functioning markets (Mackintosh, 1990; Harriss-White, 1996). Furthermore, markets may also be missing, such as when financial markets do not extend to those without collateral, or when property markets do not exist under conditions of communal tenure in rural Africa, or when plots are simply occupied without being owned in shanty or informal settlements on the urban fringe. Markets may also be thin when there are few buyers or sellers, barriers to entry, scarce market information or where low volumes are traded. An example is when distress sales of livestock take place in isolated areas leading to low local prices or when small-scale farmers attempt to sell surplus crops that are not consumed locally.

With the rise of new institutional economics, the recognition that economic exchange is not simply about anonymous markets but is a form of social and political interaction has become more common. As such, a variety of types of economic exchange are recognised, which are shaped by, or embedded in, social and cultural variables such as institutions of kinship, social stratification and organisational form. Karl Polanyi distinguished a typology of three types of economic exchange: reciprocal, redistributive and market. While Polanyi argued that only the last was not embedded in social–structural or cultural–structural relationships (Polanyi, 1944, p. 57), Granovetter (1985) and more recently Barber (1995) contend that all forms of economic behaviour are embedded in social structure, although they differ on the exact nature of this structure. At issue is the extent to which the partners in a form of exchange are free to operate as *homo economicus*: 'economising, rationalising individuals, considering only price, not other obligations, buying cheap and selling dear, treating all buyers and sellers impersonally, equally and honestly' (Barber, 1995, p. 398). For Granovetter, social structure appears to be limited to networks of interpersonal exchange, whereas Barber is concerned with wider structures of kinship, stratification, gender and class. Indeed, Barber goes further, and holds out the social embeddedness of economic action as a way of meeting the challenge of what he refers to as the 'absolutisation of the market', referring to the assumption that the notion of the market is beyond question and can be taken for granted (ibid., p. 388). Finally, the embeddedness of economic activities is recognised as carrying costs, which vary as development proceeds, and which may offset, or change the distribution of the benefits of economic exchange.

To some extent, this view reflects Sen's later thinking as his analysis broadened to cover hunger rather than only famine, and incorporated a gender dimension to the analysis. This approach also has close parallels in the work of Rein (1983) who prefers a wider conceptualisation of claims, whereby individuals assemble a package of income through their effective claiming from a range of sources, including from markets. The state, private sector and domestic group are identified as the other institutions against which claims can be made. Rein emphasises that this claiming is an active and strategic process by which individuals demand, extract, request or enforce their bids for resources, operating as individuals, households and in wider groupings such as community associations, trade unions and pressure groups.

In addition, Rein stresses that the process of claim packaging is linked to the dynamic and fluid nature of household composition. This is particularly important in view of debate over the permeability of household boundaries, power relations within the household and the allocation of labour by the household (Guyer and Peters, 1987; Kabeer, 1991). In essence, these writers argue that negotiations and conflict integrally affect individual claims on income over the assets that exist within the household. Clearly, there will be trade-offs between the possible activities that can be engaged in, both in terms of the activities themselves, as well as between the interests of the members of the household itself. Put differently, these activities underpin the livelihood strategy of the household, and are an outcome of decisions and conflict over the use of the household's assets. The strategy that results may well benefit some members of the household at the cost of others. Furthermore, like any strategy, its composition and success will be determined by the constraints and opportunities that are available to the household as a whole and to the individual members.

As a further complication, an individual's position outside the household can affect the division of entitlement within the household due to the increased power that person has in negotiating intra-household distribution. An example would be the greater say that an employed woman might enjoy over the returns from the use of household assets. Feminist analysts have also pointed out that the power of the individuals within the household is affected by state-enforced legal rules which authorise particular patterns of power relationships within the household. An example of this is legislation that asserts that the household head and principal breadwinner is male and that assets such as land are owned or controlled by a male head, or legalisation that requires that the head of the household, usually male, can enter into contracts, such as for the sale of crops or to access credit.

A conclusion that seems to follow from this discussion is that poverty measurement itself would be better thought of in terms of access to assets and (real) markets rather than simply access to income, or better still, in terms of capabilities if problems of measurement could be resolved. This is not a new idea: writing in a rejoinder to Sen, Townsend (1985, p. 661) recommends the use of total resources, meaning an income equivalent of wealth and income in kind, as a measure of deprivation. More recently, Zimmerman and Carter (2003) suggest that a dynamic asset poverty line may be identified which they term the 'Micawber Threshold'. This divides those able to engage in a virtuous Victorian circle of accumulation from those who cannot. Named after Wilkins Micawber of Charles Dickens's *David Copperfield* who encouraged young lads to sacrifice and accumulate, Zimmerman and Carter follow Lipton's (1988) example and use the term the Micawber threshold to evoke the idea that there may be types and depths of poverty from which not even a forward-looking willingness to scrimp and save can enable escape.

JULIAN MAY

References

Barber, B. (1995), 'All economies are "embedded": the career of a concept and beyond', *Social Research*, **62** (2), 387–413.

Chambers, R. and G. Conway (1992), 'Sustainable rural livelihoods: practical concepts for the twenty-first century', IDS Discussion Paper 296, Institute of Development Studies, University of Sussex, Brighton.

Ellis, F. (2000), *Rural Livelihoods and Diversity in Developing Countries*, Oxford: Oxford University Press.

Gasper, D. (1993), 'Entitlements analysis: relating concepts and contexts', *Development and Change*, **24** (4), 679–718.

Granovetter, M. (1985), 'Economic action and social structure: the problem of embeddedness', *American Journal of Sociology*, **91**, 481–510.

Guyer, J. and P. Peters (1987), 'Introduction to conceptualizing the household: issues of theory and policy in Africa', *Development and Change*, **18** (2), 197–214.

Harriss-White, B. (1996), *A Political Economy of Agricultural Markets in South India: Masters of the Countryside*, London: Sage.

Kabeer, N. (1991), 'Gender, production and well-being: rethinking the household economy', IDS Discussion Paper 288, Institute of Development Studies, University of Sussex, Brighton.

Lipton, M. (1988), 'The poor and the poorest: some interim findings', World Bank Discussion Papers 25, World Bank, Washington, DC.

Mackintosh, M. (1990), 'Abstract markets and real needs', in H. Bernstein, G. Crow, M. Mackintosh and C. Martin (eds), *The Food Question: Profits versus People*, London: Earthscan, pp. 43–53.

May, J., P. Ewang, F. Lund and W. Wentzal (1998), *The Experience and Perceptions of Poverty: The South African Participatory Poverty Assessment*, Durban: Praxis.

Moser, C. (1995), 'Urban social policy and poverty reduction', *Environment and Urbanization*, **7** (1), 159–71.

Polanyi, K. (1944), *The Great Transformation*, New York: Farrar.

Rein, M. (1983), *From Policy to Practice*, London: Macmillan.

Sen, A.K. (1981), *Poverty and Famines: An Essay on Entitlement and Deprivation*, Oxford: Clarendon.

Sen, A.K. (1985), *Commodities and Capabilities*, Amsterdam: North-Holland.

Townsend, P. (1985), 'A sociological approach to the measurement of poverty – a rejoinder to Professor Amartya Sen', *Oxford Economic Papers*, **31**, 659–68.

Zimmerman, F.J. and M.R. Carter (2003), 'Asset smoothing, consumption smoothing and the reproduction of inequality under risk and subsistence constraints', *Journal of Development Economics*, **71**, 233–60.

Basic Needs Approach

Introduction
A basic needs approach (BNA) to development is one that gives priority to meeting people's basic needs – to ensuring that there are sufficient, appropriately distributed BN goods and services to sustain all human lives at a minimally decent level.

The BNA to development was initiated in the mid-1970s. It was first taken up by the International Labour Organization (ILO) and subsequently by Robert McNamara, President of the World Bank. For a short time, towards the end of the 1970s, it dominated much donor development policy, although it did not get full support from developing-country governments, who saw it as a diversion from their demands for improved terms in the international system. The debt crisis, and political changes in some major donor governments, led to its rapid and complete abandonment in the early 1980s. Although academic publications about the approach continued, it seems to have been discarded permanently as an overt strategy. Yet the BNA provided one of the important roots of the human development approach – which has much in common with the BNA, especially its practical applications.

This entry will provide a brief survey of the BNA, first considering its place in the evolution of development thought; second, discussing its definition and main characteristics; third, reviewing macro approaches to meeting BNs; finally it will consider some limitations of the approach, and its relationship to capabilities and to human development.

BNA in the evolution of development thought
Thinking about development tends to follow a complex dynamic – in which the problems thrown up by the strategies of previous decades inform new thinking, which in turn gets translated into approaches and policies. The BNA was one of the reactions to the consequences of statist pro-growth policies adopted by many countries in their early development strategies, which, while successful in some respects, left many people in great poverty, with high unemployment and many unfilled basic needs.

On becoming independent in the 1950s and 1960s, developing countries adopted a planned interventionist approach aimed at the promotion of growth and industrialisation. In some respects this was successful, as growth and industrialisation did accelerate, and social indicators, such as infant mortality and literacy rates, also improved. However, a dualistic pattern of development resulted, with a small relatively privileged modern sector leaving the rest of the economy with low incomes and investment. Growth in employment, especially in the industrial sector, lagged behind population growth and unemployment and underemployment emerged as serious problems. The incidence of poverty remained very high as a proportion of the population in most developing countries, and the absolute numbers of people falling below a given poverty line increased. The ILO summarised the position: '[I]t has become increasingly evident, particularly from the experience of the developing countries, that rapid growth at the national level does not automatically reduce poverty or inequality or provide sufficient productive employment' (ILO, 1976, p. 15).

Problems of employment and poverty led to new approaches to development. It was argued that countries had been pursuing the wrong objective: Dudley Seers and the ILO pointed to the need to 'dethrone GNP' (see discussion in Robinson and Johnston, 1971). Initially, the ILO suggested that employment expansion should be the overriding goal. But it was soon accepted that employment is not wanted for itself, but for the recognition, production, and above all incomes that it brings. Consequently, the focus moved to the incomes of the poor, formalised in the publication, *Redistribution with Growth* (Chenery et al., 1979), which advocated giving much higher weight to the incomes of the poor in the development objective. The associated development strategy was to continue to promote growth, but to redistribute the fruits of growth to the poor in the form of productive assets. Yet this attractive but rather complex approach gained little political support.

This is where the BNA comes in. First, it was argued that what the poor need is not money incomes alone, but essential goods and services to give everyone the opportunity to lead full lives – that is, *basic* goods and services. Money incomes might not be sufficient to secure adequate supplies of BN goods and services because important core elements, such as education, health services and good water supplies, depend on public production and distribution, not private incomes. Second, there is a simplicity and urgency about pointing to the need for BN – especially when expressed in concrete terms, as access to health services, to clean water, to enough food, and to schools and shelter – that, it was believed, would gain much more ready acceptance in both the North and South than arguments about the injustice of inequality: 'the basic needs approach appeals to members of the national and international community and is therefore capable of mobilising resources' (Streeten et al., 1981, p. 22).

The ILO proposed the objective of meeting minimum needs throughout the world by the year 2000 at the 1976 World Employment Conference. This received near unanimous support. Shortly after this the World Bank adopted the approach. Both institutions agreed that the overriding aim should be to eradicate poverty, and that in concrete terms this would best be achieved through the BNA.

What is the BNA?
The BNA is often identified with a list of particular goods and services that must be made available to all. It has thus been accused of being materialistic (subject to commodity fetishism, according to Sen, 1993) and paternalistic by dictating the consumption patterns of the poor. In fact the approach is more sophisticated than this, and does not merit either charge if one reads the early documents. A certain reductionism has tended to creep into practical interpretations, however, which explains the prevalence of such criticisms.

The ILO (1976) defines BN as 'the minimum standard of living which a society should set for the poorest groups of its people' (p. 7), which they state includes meeting the minimum requirements for personal consumption of food, shelter and clothing; and access to essential services such as safe drinking water, sanitation, health, education and transport; and 'the satisfaction of needs of a more qualitative nature: a healthy, humane and satisfying environment, and popular participation in the making of decisions that affect the lives and livelihood of the people and individual freedoms'. By making participation part of the approach, the ILO indicates that what is to be provided is not intended to be determined paternalistically, but people themselves should contribute to defining their needs.

Every author writing on BNA insists that non-material, as well as material needs must be included, the non-material to cover such elements as employment, participation, political rights, cultural flourishing and so on (for example, ILO, 1976; Ghai, 1977; Streeten et al., 1981). However, in practical interpretations, the BNA has focused primarily on material goods and services. The major architects and proponents of the BNA agree that the list of BN should not be determined arbitrarily and from outside. Several approaches were proposed for identifying BN. One is participatory – getting people themselves to determine their own BN; another is consultative – requesting governments to identify the core needs. A third approach is to start by defining the quality of life that should be aimed for – both with respect to its main characteristics, for example, being healthy, nourished, educated, and also the minimum acceptable levels of these characteristics – and then derive the goods and services needed (that is, the BN goods and services) empirically as those that would be necessary to produce the opportunity for a such a 'full' life. This relationship has been described as the meta-production function by Fei, Ranis and Stewart (Stewart, 1985, ch. 2):

$$\mathbf{FL} = f(a, b, c, d, \dots),$$

where **FL** is a vector of full-life characteristics that might include health, nutrition, educational achievements, participation, employment, political rights and so on; and *a, b, c, . . .* are the goods and services needed to achieve the minimum acceptable **FL** characteristics. This assumes that the full-life characteristics have been defined, and for this too, a variety of approaches are possible, including participatory ones, through an 'overlapping consensus' or drawing on other normative underpinning.

Thus potentially, the BNA is quite complex, encompassing non-material as well as material needs, and allowing for participation and observation of the meta-production function in order to determine what the actual BN requirements are in terms of goods and services. But in practice, and in popular discussion, the BNA is typically interpreted as involving a quite specific list of requirements – normally including education, health services, food requirements, and sometimes shelter and clothing. The minimum levels are generally also defined roughly – for example, enough food to avoid malnutrition, universal access to primary education, universal functional literacy, clean water for all, universal access to primary healthcare, and reasonable quality of shelter for all. This is not a scientifically derived list, nor one based on participation, though participatory exercises suggest it contains what most people do consider minimum requirements. None the less, it is difficult not to accept that fulfilling these needs would mean huge progress towards eliminating poverty.

Those who advocate a BNA are generally rather pragmatic, determined to speed up poverty eradication, quite prepared to widen the definition of requirements and improve the derivation of specific needs and levels of minimum requirements as knowledge and methods improve, but in the meantime wanting to get on with the job of reorientating development policy by using a reasonably acceptable list of BN.

Macro planning for BN

The BNA suggests a threefold approach to macro planning: supply, demand and organisational. For success, it is necessary to ensure that *supplies* of the BN goods and services are adequate. This is a sharp departure from the income-orientated approach of *Redistribution with Growth*, or many other poverty-reduction strategies, because they focus only on demand (that is, incomes) of the poor, and just assume sufficient supplies would be forthcoming. But since many of the BN goods and services are public goods, like health and education services, sanitation and water supplies, this cannot be assumed, but must be planned; moreover, food is a key element and supply rigidities in food production could lead to inflation and failure, unless adequate supplies are ensured. However, it is also essential to focus on the *demand* side, and see that the poor have sufficient incomes, through employment and self-employment or income transfers to be able to buy adequate food, and to make full use of schools, health clinics and so on. There is also the important issue of ensuring adequate allocation of resources within the household towards BN goods. Finally, there is an *organisational* aspect of planning for BN. Because so many BN goods and services are produced in the public sector, public sector efficiency (central and local) needs to be secured in each of the BN sectors. It is apparent that the BNA does not substitute for economic growth, but requires it since economic growth is essential to generate the incomes the poor need and the public revenue to ensure that the sector supplies are adequate. Relatively equal distribution of income is also needed, as well as appropriate allocation of public revenue to the BN sectors.

Analysis of country experience in meeting BN shows that success requires reasonable performance in each of the three macro approaches, though sometimes one may lead – for example, in Taiwan and South Korea equitably distributed economic growth ensured good performance on BN, but adequate supplies of BN goods and organisational efficiency were also present. In contrast, in Cuba, good BN was achieved primarily by a focus on the supply side. Failures in BN, which are manifold, can occur because any one of the three macro approaches is not fulfilled (that is, lack of growth; maldistributed growth; or a weak public sector with low efficiency).

Weaknesses in the BNA and its relationship to the capability approach

The BNA lost support largely because other concerns came to dominate the donor community – namely stabilisation and adjustment – while it was never taken up with enthusiasm by developing countries partly because it tended to be understood, wrongly, as meaning an end to industrialisation and growth, which as shown above was not the case. One set of problems with the approach, for which there are a variety of answers but no single solution, is the apparent arbitrariness in choice of the core BN goods and services and in the determination of the levels to be aimed at. More fundamentally, the BNA lacked theoretical elegance, and seemed to be an approach that developed countries advocated for developing countries but did not apply to themselves.

When the world recovered sufficiently from the debt crisis, the lost decade of the 1980s and the obsession with stabilisation, to pay attention once more to the need to reduce poverty, the capability approach of Amartya Sen seemed much more attractive than a retreat to BNA. In its reductionist form, the capability approach is very similar to the BNA: the objective of enhancing what people can be or do (a person's capabilities) is virtually identical with the full-life objective of the BNA; and in order to achieve this for the most deprived, a subset of basic capabilities has been identified.

In empirical work, the criteria used to assess success or failure with respect to capabilities are the same as in the BNA (for example, Drèze and Sen, 1989). However, the capability approach has a much more elegant philosophical foundation; moreover, in principle it applies to rich as well as poor people. The capability approach focuses more on individual capacities and needs than the BNA. Consequently, Sen has emphasised the special needs of certain groups (such as the disabled) who may require more material resources to achieve a given set of capabilities than others. In principle, the needs of the old and disabled should and can be an important aspect of BN too, but as practised the approach was a more broad-brush one, directed at the poor in general rather than those with special needs. Despite these differences, when it comes to identifying, measuring and targeting basic capabilities, the capabilities approach encounters the same problems that the BNA does. Moreover, the pragmaticism of the BNA does have advantages in guiding day-to-day policy, as it points directly to the need to ensure adequate supplies of some basic goods and services and to ensure that people have enough incomes to purchase them.

Human development, initiated by the UNDP in its 1990 *Human Development Report*, brought together ideas from the BNA and from capabilities, and people previously involved in each worked on the first report – Amartya Sen representing the capabilities approach; and Mahub ul Haq, Gustav Ranis, Frances Stewart and Paul Streeten the BNA. The human development approach has many of the virtues of both – the immediacy and pragmaticism of the BNA and the elegance of the capabilities approach. It is noteworthy, however, that human development alone did not seem to impart the urgency needed, and so the Social Summit endorsed a set of objectives, which became the Millennium Development Goals, bringing a BN type of approach to the fore again.

FRANCES STEWART

References

Chenery, Hollis, Montek S. Ahluwalia, C.L.G. Bell, John H. Duloy and Richard Jolly (1979), *Redistribution with Growth: Policies to Improve Income Distribution in Developing Countries in the Context of Economic Growth*, Oxford and London: Oxford University Press.
Drèze, Jean and Amartya Kumar Sen (1989), *Hunger and Public Action*, Studies in Development Economics, Oxford: Clarendon.
Ghai, Dharam P. (1977), *The Basic-Needs Approach to Development: Some Issues Regarding Concepts and Methodology*, Geneva: International Labour Office.
Hopkins, Mike and Rolph van der Hoeven (1983), *Basic Needs in Development Planning*, Aldershot: Gower.
ILO (1976), *Employment, Growth and Basic Needs: A One-World Problem*, Geneva: ILO.
Robinson, R. and O. Johnston (eds.) (1971), *Prospects for Employment in the Nineteen Seventies*, London: HMSO.
Sen, A.K. (1993), 'Capability and wellbeing', in M.C. Nussbaum and A.K. Sen (eds), *The Quality of Life*, Oxford: Clarendon, pp. 30–53.
Stewart, Frances (1985), *Planning to Meet Basic Needs*, London: Macmillan.
Streeten, Paul P., Shahid J. Burki, Mahbub ul Haq, Norman Hicks and Frances Stewart (1981), *First Things First, Meeting Basic Human Needs in Developing Countries*, Oxford, UK and New York: Oxford University Press.
UNDP (1990), *Human Development Report, 1990*, Oxford: Oxford University Press.

Bauer, Peter Tamas (1915–2002)

Peter Bauer made an outstanding contribution to development economics by treating the subject as part of mainstream liberal economics at a time when others denied its relevance to Third World countries. He also challenged the widely held view that the development of Third World countries required massive government intervention, protection from competition, detailed economic planning and, above all, major injections of foreign aid. Bauer would have none of that, and instead showed with great cogency how time and again development had been held back by intervention in the operation of free markets and by failing to use the price mechanism. He also differed from most others by the use he made of his extensive knowledge of economic history and by the importance he attached to studying the history of institutions.

Peter Tamas Bauer was born in Budapest on 6 November 1915 to Hungarian–Jewish parents. Educated at a Catholic school he then went on to study law at Budapest University. He first came to England in 1934 and embarked on an economics degree at Gonville and Caius College, Cambridge. After graduating in 1937 he returned to Hungary to complete his law degree, but then came back to England in 1939 to work for a City merchant firm engaged in trade and rubber plantations in the Far East. It was not until he was 28 years old that he embarked on his academic career, first as research fellow and in 1947 as Reader in agricultural economics at the London School of Economics. His later interest in the marketing of primary products from Asia and Africa had its roots in these early years when he had already written several important papers on the history, operation and effects of British agricultural marketing schemes.

He moved back to Cambridge in 1948 and soon found himself teaching economics to new recruits to the Colonial Service who were required to attend a course to prepare them for their career overseas. In 1956 Bauer became Smuts Reader in Commonwealth Studies in Cambridge and in 1960 he was appointed to a professorship at the London School of Economics, having meanwhile published four pathbreaking books on what came to be called development economics. In 1975 he was elected a Fellow of the British Academy and in 1982 he was created a life peer.

Bauer is probably best known for his critique of foreign aid, because it aroused such heated debate. But by then he had long since established his reputation with two major field studies, *The Rubber Industry* (1948) and, above all, *West African Trade* (1954). One fascinating feature of these early studies – and of his teaching on the courses for Colonial Office cadets – is that they were substantially financed by the Colonial Office whose views on economic development were diametrically opposed to Bauer's. While Bauer was steeped in liberal economics, the Colonial Office was imbued with the interventionist ideas that characterised the Fabian Socialism of that time and which found an echo also in Shaftesbury Conservatism. Together they found expression in the colonial development and welfare acts of that period.

West African Trade showed in great detail how government controls which were devised to protect and further the interests of African smallholders had exactly the opposite effect. The marketing boards were a case in point. They were set up as statutory monopsonies to protect small cultivators of cocoa and palm oil who, it was assumed, were exploited by non-indigenous middlemen. The latter were therefore deprived of the right to buy on their own account, forced to become licensed buyers for the marketing boards, and paid a commission to buy at prices determined by the boards. There were several unforeseen results. Middlemen now had an assured income, while growers, by contrast, faced a single buyer, where previously several middlemen had competed for their crops. Further, the boards accumulated large funds that were supposed to be used to remove the fluctuations in incomes which growers had previously experienced as a result of world market price fluctuations. When world market prices started to rise rapidly after the end of the Second World War and continued to remain high for over a decade, the increased proceeds that accumulated in the 'stabilisation' funds were really a form of taxation which deprived cultivators of the benefits of increased incomes. Finally, export taxes further reduced cultivators' incomes.

Bauer went on to show how the huge accumulation of forced savings and tax revenue came to be spent by governments in large measure on ill-conceived large-scale development projects instead of being available to cultivators to invest in improving the productivity of their smallholdings. It was widely assumed by governments and most academics that peasants had limited wants and were guided in their behaviour by tradition rather than by economic rationality. They were thought incapable of taking long views and of saving and investing productively. Any surplus income, it was sometimes said, would be spent on drink and on other frivolous consumption. Bauer pointed out the contrary: the many instances where small cultivators had shown themselves to be astute businessmen. He liked particularly to cite the rise of cocoa growing in the Gold Coast (now Ghana) at the start of the twentieth century when 'peasants' had not only invested heavily in a crop that was totally new to them but had done so in the knowledge that there would be a long waiting period before their investment would bear fruit. The establishment and expansion of rubber smallholdings in Malaya and elsewhere in South East Asia was another example.

Post-war governments were determined to accelerate economic development in their colonies and were convinced that only they knew how to promote it. The rise in primary product prices which should have accrued to the growers was instead siphoned off to pay for such large-scale development projects as the hugely expensive Volta River hydroelectric and aluminium smelting project in West Africa and the Owen Falls Dam, expected to usher in an industrial revolution in Uganda, as also the wholly misconceived and notorious Tanganyikan Groundnut Scheme. All were examples of the widely held belief at that time that industrialisation was the way forward, as the writings of Raul Prebisch and Hans Singer had convinced many people that the terms of trade for primary products were bound to continue to decline. Bauer and B.S. Yamey in their classic textbook, *The Economics of Underdeveloped Countries* (1957), were the first to challenge this questionable finding, and to argue that investment decisions should be determined by their prospective yield, not by whether a project was agricultural or industrial.

Industrialisation was to be financed by taxing small cultivators, and 'encouraged' by offering prospective industrialists heavy protection from competing imports as well as monopoly powers within the country. Bauer again showed how this not only was a tailor-made recipe for inefficiency, but also further reduced the real incomes of small cultivators who formed the majority of the population by raising the prices of precisely those goods they were most likely to buy.

The intimate knowledge which Bauer gained from his two major field studies – one in Asia and one in Africa – alerted him to the serious flaws that came to be the increasingly entrenched orthodoxy of the new development economics as it evolved from the 1940s onwards, and which was characterised by what Bauer liked to describe as 'the disregard of reality'. He thus came to challenge the conventional wisdom that contact with the developed West obstructed or distorted the economic advance of poor countries. He also challenged the view that poor countries were locked in a 'vicious circle of poverty' – too poor to save and therefore unable to invest to reduce their poverty, a view widely canvassed by Gunnar Myrdal and others. By way of refutation Bauer often pointed to poverty-stricken, and densely populated Hong Kong, which pulled itself up almost entirely by its own bootstraps. These refutations of what were widely held views appeared in a long series of journal articles, some of the most powerful written jointly with B.S. Yamey, many of which have been reprinted in some half a dozen books. But Bauer also wrote extensively for newspapers and periodicals and lectured tirelessly in his inimitable Hungarian accent.

If Bauer is best known for his views on foreign aid, *Dissent on Development* (1971) includes the most comprehensive exposition. The view commonly held at that time was that foreign aid was essential to promote development. Third World countries were assumed to have low levels of domestic savings and an inadequate supply of foreign exchange from exports and it was taken for granted that aid was needed to make up these deficiencies. It was essential because, it was widely believed, development in the so-called Third World could not begin until there was a comprehensive infrastructure in place – roads, airports, harbours and power stations, as well as schools, health centres, urban housing and a clean water supply, which could only be provided by foreign aid, without which there could be no development. Bauer challenged this view, arguing that aid was neither a necessary nor a sufficient condition for development. He pointed to the spectacular development of Hong Kong and Singapore – not to mention Britain and Japan in earlier times – as evidence that aid was not necessary for development to take place. He also referred again to his earlier fieldwork, pointing out that a developed infrastructure had not been a precondition for the emergence of the major cash crops of South East Asia and West Africa.

Aid, Bauer argued, is not a sufficient condition either for development to take place, as witness the many countries in receipt of aid over long periods where there has been little or no development. In many of these countries governments have pursued very mistaken policies, including discrimination against minorities like Asians in East Africa and the Chinese in South East Asia who have shown the entrepreneurial talents that are a crucial cornerstone to development. He further argued that since aid is invariably paid to governments, it has often helped to keep in power inefficient, corrupt and elitist governments that often have suppressed the human rights of their own people.

Bauer's writings on foreign aid made him still more unpopular. He was widely regarded as being uncaring and his arguments based on cogent reasoning and meticulous attention to the evidence were often dismissed because they were not part of the temper of the times in academic economic circles. It is, however, also true that Bauer sometimes overplayed his hand, as when he failed to note that, for example, Puerto Rico and Taiwan certainly benefited from injections of foreign capital because other ingredients essential for development were in place. He was, therefore, widely regarded as insufficiently scientific, incompetent and wrong. It was only very gradually that it came to be realised that it was more often mainstream development economics, not Bauer's writings, which was seriously flawed, and that policies based on it, promoted by international agencies and by the consultancy reports of leading academics, were doing a great deal of harm and were frustrating or undermining the aspirations and efforts of the very people they were supposed to help.

Ultimately the recognition that Bauer had been right in many respects was helped by the growing volume of evidence which suggested that foreign aid simply did not work and that interventionist regimes and economic planning were holding back development instead of promoting it. The spectacular growth of the Pacific Rim countries based in vital respects on market principles also helped to alert people to the importance of government policies in encouraging or frustrating business enterprise. Finally, the collapse of socialist regimes in Eastern Europe and eventually the Soviet Union profoundly influenced thinking about the proper role of government in development, encouraging recognition that it had been mistaken to dismiss Bauer's arguments out of hand. One result is that there has been a major change in the policies pursued by the World Bank and other aid agencies.

Bauer had been among the first to recognise that what was holding back development was less a failure of markets than government failure – the inability of governments to take advantage of market forces and to allow prices to determine the allocation of resources, including labour. Countries that maintain overvalued exchange rates, control prices below their equilibrium levels, and fix minimum wages and maximum hours of work may sometimes produce short-term gains for their people but inevitably hold back the development which alone can raise standards of living in the long run. Overvalued exchange rates reduce incomes from exports; controlled prices reduce the incentive to increase production, and labour legislation reduces the volume of employment. All this is now widely accepted, though still not as widely as one might wish. If one examines which countries have developed and which have not, differences in government policies play a prominent part, as Bauer has always maintained, while differences in natural resource endowments or in the volume of foreign aid received, pale into insignificance. What Bauer may have sometimes failed to recognise is that governments in a number of instances have helped the process of development along in a positive way, instead of the more common negative resort to trying to control prices which tends to retard the process of development. This was the case in several of the Pacific Rim countries, though not in Hong Kong.

There is one other factor emphasised by Bauer as significant to development, but generally ignored by other economists: namely, culture. Attitudes towards material advancement differ between societies and between groups within societies. Thus, for example, Bauer found that the Chinese in Malaya played a prominent part in economic life and exhibited a marked economic superiority over the indigenous Malays mainly because they were more industrious, ingenious, thrifty, ambitious and resourceful. Similarly, Asians have played a vital economic role in East Africa, as Huguenots did in seventeenth-century England. While it has often been immigrants who have exhibited these characteristics to a marked degree, there are also essential differences within the indigenous population associated with differences in culture and religion. Thus, Bauer noticed a marked difference between the enterprising Ibo of Nigeria and the less enterprising Hausa. But he also observed how these aptitudes changed in response to changing economic opportunities.

Peter Bauer's writings were wide ranging. For example, he repeatedly challenged the view that a rapidly increasing population retarded economic development, by pointing to England in the nineteenth century and Hong Kong in the twentieth. He also addressed issues not directly related to development but bearing on his overriding concern for liberty for which he was awarded the Milton Friedman Prize for Advancing Liberty by the Washington Cato Institute shortly before his death. One such issue concerned income equality, the deliberate promotion of which Bauer regarded as misdirected and harmful and as unnecessary provided there was equality of opportunity. He poured scorn on the notion that the power exercised by the rich is more objectionable than that often exerted by politicians and civil servants, just because the latter were supposed to be exercised in the public interest – a misleading assertion since the rich, unlike governments, are unable to restrict the choices of their fellow men, except when governments confer that privilege upon them by granting them monopoly powers or exclusive rights.

When the World Bank issued its first commemorative volume in 1984 entitled *Pioneers in Development* (Meier and Seers, 1984), Peter Bauer was included as one of them – the only one who had always worked in the classical liberal tradition inaugurated by Adam Smith. Many then still looked down upon him. Today his analysis and views on policy have come to be much more widely accepted, and many former critics acknowledge that in many respects he had been right all along.

WALTER ELKAN

References and further reading

Bauer, P.T. (1948), *The Rubber Industry*, London: Longmans, Green.
Bauer, P.T. (1954), *West African Trade: A Study of Competition, Oligopoly and Monopoly in a Changing Economy*, Cambridge: Cambridge University Press.
Bauer, P.T. (1957), *Economic Analysis and Policy in Underdeveloped Countries*, Cambridge: Cambridge University Press.
Bauer, P.T. (1961), *Indian Economic Policy and Development*, London: Allen & Unwin.
Bauer, P.T. (1971), *Dissent on Development: Studies and Debates in Development Economics*, London: Weidenfeld & Nicolson, (revised edn, 1976).
Bauer, P.T. (1981), *Equality, the Third World and Economic Delusion*, London: Weidenfeld & Nicolson.
Bauer, P.T. (1984a), 'Remembrance of studies past', in G.M. Meier and D. Seers (eds), *Pioneers in Development*, Oxford: Oxford University Press for the World Bank, pp. 25–43.
Bauer, P.T. (1984b), *Reality and Rhetoric: Studies in the Economics of Development*, London: Weidenfeld & Nicolson.
Bauer, P.T. (1991), *The Development Frontier: Essays in Applied Economics*, London: Harvester Wheatsheaf.
Bauer, P.T. (2000), *From Subsistence to Exchange and Other Essays*, Princeton, NJ: Princeton University Press (with an introduction by Amartya K. Sen).
Bauer, P.T. and B.S. Yamey (1957), *The Economics of Underdeveloped Countries*, London: James Nisbet.
Bauer, P.T. and B.S. Yamey (1968), *Markets, Market Control and Marketing Reform*, London: Weidenfeld & Nicolson.
Blundell, J., J.M. Buchanan, M. Desai, J.A. Dorn, R. Harris, D. Lal, V.C. Price, R. Sally, P.J. Shah, A. Walters and B. Yamey (2002), *A Tribute to Peter Bauer*, Institute of Economic Affairs, London, www.IEA.org.uk.
Dorn, James A. (2002), *Peter Bauer's Legacy of Liberty*, Washington DC: Cato Institute.
Meier, Gerald M. and Dudley Seers (eds) (1984), *Pioneers in Development*, New York: Oxford University Press for the World Bank.
Sen, Amartya (2000), 'Introduction to P. Bauer', in Bauer (2000), pp. ix–xi.
Stern, N.H. (1974), 'Professor Bauer on development: a review article', *Journal of Development Economics*, **1** (3), 191–211.
Yamey, Basil S. (1987), 'Peter Bauer: economist and scholar', *Cato Journal*, **7** (1), 21–7.
Yamey, Basil S. (2002), 'Obituary: Lord Bauer', *The Independent*, 1 June.

Boserup, Ester (b. 1910)

Ester Boserup was a truly original scholar who challenged prevailing theories regarding agricultural change and population growth, and became the guru of the women and international development movement. She wove her examination of population, agriculture and household labour distribution into a unified model that strengthened her analysis of the separate disciplines. More uniquely, she focused on the interplay of economic and non-economic factors in the process of social change, both today and in the past. By viewing human societies as dynamic relationships between natural, economic, cultural and political structures, Boserup argued that global change could not be explained within the framework of a single discipline.

Boserup's model was first articulated in *The Conditions of Agricultural Growth: The Economics of Agrarian Change under Population Pressures*, published in 1965, where she postulates that population density compelled societies to invent new technologies in order to increase food production. She traces the intensification of agriculture from earliest times when hunters and gatherers began to cultivate the forests in order to provide a more reliable source of food. They slashed and burned the jungle, then planted crops among the stumps, utilising the nutrients produced by the burn. As production fell, another plot was burned. Men prepared the plots and provided protection as women farmed using a stick to make a hole. Labour requirements were low, estimated at 15 hours per week for women, 14 hours per week for men. Women were thus an important economic commodity; daughters were exchanged for a bride price paid by the husband's family both for her labour and her fertility.

As population increased and new lands became scarce, the length of time plots were left to fallow decreased and labour requirements increased as fallow periods were reduced from over 15 years to annual planting to multicropping. New technologies had to be invented to clear and till the land; draft animals fertilised the soil as they pulled the plough. Boserup further emphasised that the division of labour within the family was assigned by age and sex, and this distribution varied across regions and cultures. Men began to work longer hours on the farm than women, though women continued to plant, weed and harvest before the advent of modern machinery.

Agricultural change affected land-owning patterns, which evolved from communal or tribal control during slash-and-burn periods to individual ownership. Disparities of income began to appear; poorer families sent women and men to labour on the fields of the more wealthy. As migration patterns increased, racial discrimination grew both in the countryside and in the growing urban centres. Cities became a magnet for employment and education, enticing both rich and poor.

Boserup demonstrated the impact of colonialism on agriculture, noting that colonial enclave economies did not encourage increased agricultural output. Expatriates preferred the tastes of home, and shipping food by boat was also easier than transporting overland on bush roads, depressing local agriculture. Men's labour was sought, sometimes by force, to work on plantations growing export crops, as farms became more dependent on the labour of women who produced food only for the family. At the same time, men's power over women and land resources was privileged, undermining many traditional rights of women.

Boserup expanded her model in 1970 in *Woman's Role in Economic Development*. She looked at the redistribution of labour between women and men that resulted from agricultural change, and how the reallocation of work affected women's status within the family. In slash-and-burn societies, women were the primary farmers; their labour as well as their reproductive value was indicated by the payment of a bride price from the husband to her family. As men became dominant in agriculture, women's worth was primarily based on fertility. The bride price was replaced by a dowry, a payment from the bride's family to that of the husband. With an increase in income differentiation, wealthier families could afford to remove their wives from field labour, a change that enhanced the family status but also restricted women's mobility.

This pattern continues today. In those areas where women farm and men can purchase their labour and where land-use rights can be expanded, primarily in West Africa, polygamy continues. In Muslim areas where a dowry is the rule, the incidence of polygamy is largely confined to the wealthy. In these areas of male farming, upper-caste/status women are in seclusion but women from the lower classes frequently work as casual labourers. Because upper-class women do not work in the fields, casual labourers must replace them; the added cost to the household further depresses women's value and entitlements. This example makes clear that class hierarchies affect age and sex status relationships as well.

Boserup distinguished between female and male towns as she distinguished farming systems. Female towns are centred on markets where women dominate the trade. Male towns are of two types: they may have a surplus of men in the population or they may be towns where women are in seclusion and therefore unseen. A semi-male town is one where women dominate the traditional markets while the modern sector is exclusively the domain of men. Most towns include migrants of ethnicities whose cultures diverge regarding women's occupations.

Market towns trade both agricultural and non-agricultural commodities. Because historically women produced many of the household products they needed, increased opportunities for trade encouraged specialisation. Products may originate in rural areas but trading is done in towns, and women and men offer their tailoring and food at markets. Boserup called this activity the 'bazaar and service sector', which was a more focused concept than the more widely used residual category 'informal sector'. Her category is more accurate. When the International Labour Organization (ILO) studies looked at the informal sector, they searched for small enterprises that hired workers. This classification effectively screens out most women or family-run micro enterprises, such as street-food vending, home-based work, or urban agriculture. Boserup noted that many women preferred such work to factory jobs because it more easily meshed with household responsibilities. This is also true of other economic activities that women can conduct from home.

Boserup's model has had a significant impact on the interpretation of economic history, particularly the causal relationship between population and agricultural change. By insisting that population increase promoted the search for technological innovation that led to agricultural intensification, she contradicts Thomas Malthus who argued that the world has a limited carrying capacity and too many people would outrun food availability. Rather, Boserup argues that low population density inhibits economic and agricultural growth. Although she championed the idea that humans adapt to population pressure, she recognises that the process alters institutions and age–race–sex hierarchies, changes that create new winners and new losers. In terms of environment, growing populations put pressure on resources, particularly land and water, and the new technologies that increase agricultural production often have a negative impact, such as chemical fertilisers and pesticides degrading the environment. Further, rapid technological change creates conflicts with national cultures through its radical influence on traditional ways of life: cultural attitudes and behaviour, which may have made sense in an earlier production system, lose their relevance.

Boserup has had a towering impact on the field of women in international development. Her book, with its reams of data, legitimised the scholarship of women activists around the world who were demanding that women's economic activities should be recognised and rewarded, not ignored and undercut, as most international assistance programmes were doing in the 1960s. The book drew attention to women's contribution to productive work, and critiqued the gender-biased allocation of resources that resulted from the underestimation of women's role as producers.

In addition, Boserup's detailed review of the negative impact of colonialism on women contradicted the presumption that economic development improves women's status. It fuelled postcolonial scholarship, which argues that Western views of women of the South treat them as the 'other', objectifying and trivialising them.

Boserup's holistic approach enhanced her reputation but also resulted in neglect. Disciplinary specialisation and expert opinions tend towards narrow views of the world and of economic development. In each of the areas of agriculture, economic history, population and women's studies, her writings are more often quoted than read because they raise such a panoply of issues. But her work provides insight into current trends, and her penetrating analyses often anticipated contemporary debates. For example, her stance that food subsidies had a negative impact on agriculture has been a recurrent theme and her observations that improvements in women's health and education were perhaps the best ways of achieving family planning were noted at the UN Population Conference in Bucharest in 1974 and anticipated resolutions made at the UN Population Conference in Cairo in 1994.

Ultimately, Ester Boserup has contributed immensely to the understanding of economic development in the South: she helps explain why some areas are reluctant to adopt new agricultural technology, why men resist the loss of their patriarchal control over women, and how the world can adapt to a population over six billion. Her ideas continue to stimulate new scholars and activists.

IRENE TINKER

Further reading

Boserup, E. (1965), *The Conditions of Agricultural Growth: The Economics of Agrarian Change under Population Pressure*, London: George Allen & Unwin.

Boserup, E. (1970), *Woman's Role in Economic Development*, London: George Allen & Unwin.

Boserup, E. (1981), *Population and Technological Change: A Study of Long-term Trends*, Chicago: University of Chicago Press.

Boserup, E. (1990), *Economic and Demographic Relationships in Development: Essays Selected and Introduced by T. Paul Schultz*, Baltimore, MD: Johns Hopkins University Press.

Boserup, E. (1999), *My Professional Life and Publications 1929–1998*, Copenhagen: Museum Tuscularnum Press.

Cambridge Controversies in Growth Theory

The Cambridge controversies, so-called because the protagonists were principally associated directly or indirectly with Cambridge, England or Cambridge, Massachusetts, raged from the mid-1950s to the mid-1970s. If remembered at all, they are usually portrayed today as a storm in a teacup over anomalies involving the measurement of capital in aggregate production function models. When theories of endogenous growth and real business cycles took off in the 1980s using aggregate production functions, contributors usually wrote as if the controversies had never occurred and the Cambridge, England contributors had never existed.

The still-unresolved controversies were over three deep issues. The first is the meaning and measurement of the concept of capital in the analysis of industrial capitalist societies. The second is Joan Robinson's complaint that equilibrium was not the outcome of an economic process and therefore an inadequate tool for analysing processes of capital accumulation and growth. The third issue is the role of ideology and vision in fuelling controversy when the results of simple models are not robust. This summary of implications for modern growth theory (taken largely from Cohen and Harcourt, 2003) focuses on the first and third issues, together with the complementary internal neoclassical critiques of aggregate production functions over problems of empirical testing and aggregation.

Meaning and measurement of capital in the scarcity theory of price

The marginal revolution shifted the explanation of price away from the classical difficulty-of-production focus to the neoclassical focus on utility and relative scarcity. Price was explained as proportional to marginal utility, which depended on scarcity. Neoclassical capital theory was the arena for extending the principle of relative scarcity to explain *all* prices, including factor prices in models with production and time.

The neoclassical perspective on capital (and growth) begins with a one-commodity Samuelson/Solow/Swan aggregate production function model

$$Q = f(K, L),$$

where the one produced good (Q) can be consumed directly or stockpiled for use as a capital good (K). With usual assumptions like exogenously given resources and technology, constant returns to scale, diminishing marginal productivity, and competitive equilibrium, this simple model exhibits what Samuelson (1962) called three key 'parables': (i) The real return on capital (the rate of interest) is determined by the technical properties of the diminishing marginal productivity of capital; (ii) a greater quantity of capital leads to a lower marginal product of additional capital, and thus to a lower rate of interest, and the same inverse, monotonic relation with the rate of interest also holds for the capital/output ratio and sustainable levels of consumption per head; (iii) the distribution of income between labourers and capitalists is explained by relative factor scarcities/supplies and marginal products. The price of capital services (the rate of interest) is determined by the relative scarcity and marginal productivity of aggregate capital, and the price of labour services (the wage rate) is determined by the relative scarcity and marginal productivity of labour (L).

The parables of this one-commodity model depend on a physical conception of capital (and labour) for their one-way causation – changes in factor quantities cause inverse changes in factor prices, allowing powerful, unambiguous predictions like parable 2.

But problems for these parables arise in general models with heterogeneous capital goods. Heterogeneous capital goods cannot be measured and aggregated in physical units; instead, capital valuation must be used (Wicksell, 1911 [1934]). Their value can be measured either as the cost of production, which takes time, or the present value of the future output stream they produce. In either case, since the measure involves time, it presumes a rate of interest – which in the simple model is determined in a one-way manner by the quantity of capital. This additional circularity, or interdependence, causes Wicksell effects. Wicksell effects involve changes in the value of the capital stock associated with different interest rates, arising from either inventory revaluations of the same physical stock due to new capital goods prices (price Wicksell effects) or differences in the physical stock of capital goods (real Wicksell effects).

In the Cambridge controversies, the problems created for neoclassical parables by Wicksell effects were termed 'reswitching' and 'capital-reversing'. Reswitching occurs when the same technique – a particular physical capital/labour ratio – is preferred at two or more rates of interest while other techniques are preferred at intermediate rates. At lower values of the interest rate, the cost-minimising technique 'switches' from a to b and then ('reswitches') back to a. The same physical technique is associated with two different interest rates, violating parables 1 and 2.

With capital-reversing, a lower capital/labour ratio is associated with a lower interest rate. In comparing two steady-state equilibrium positions, it is as though capital services have a *lower* price when capital is 'more scarce'. Capital-reversing implies that the demand curve for capital is *not* always downward sloping, violating parables 2 and 3.

Because of Wicksell effects, in models with heterogeneous capital goods (or heterogeneous output), the rate of interest depends not only on exogenous technical properties of capital, but also on endogenously determined prices like the interest rate. The endogeneity of prices allows multiple equilibria which complicates the one-way parable explanations of income distribution. Differences in quantities no longer yield unambiguously signed price effects. The power and simplicity of one-commodity models emanates from eliminating these endogenous price effects and measurement problems, thereby preserving simple, one-way, parables.

Neoclassicals fight back – aggregate production functions 1956–1966

Solow (1955–56) recognised that problems in measuring aggregate capital due to Wicksell effects could be overcome only 'in very special cases' (p. 108), and presciently commented that 'the real difficulty of [capital] comes not from the physical diversity of capital goods. It comes from the intertwining of past, present and future' (p. 102). He countered with an *empirical* defence of one-commodity models as capturing the essential features of the growth process. Solow's (1956, 1957) one-commodity production function model enabled him to measure the respective contributions of capital deepening and technical progress to growth in output per head over time.

There were also three, less successful, *theoretical* attempts to fend off problems of heterogeneous capital. First, Swan (1956) introduced the metaphor of 'putty capital'. He collapsed the ever-present tension between capital as physically heterogeneous capital goods and as homogeneous funds flowing to equalise rates of return, through his metaphor of meccano sets, which can be timelessly and costlessly reshaped into appropriate quantities of 'capital' in response to the pull of relative factor prices. Subsequent metaphors included butter, lego and putty. But all of these metaphoric feints, which effectively collapse heterogeneous capital goods into a one all-purpose commodity, only avoid, but do not solve, Wicksell's problems.

Solow (1963) provided a second theoretical response, attempting to avoid problems of capital by focusing on the rate of return on investment. In the Irving Fisherian tradition, this was capital theory without any mention of either 'capital' or 'its' marginal product. Solow's model addressed the question, 'what is the expected marginal return to a little more saving/investment in a fully employed economy?' and served as the basis for empirical estimates of rates of return. Pasinetti (1969) argued that neither Fisher's nor Solow's approach provided an intuitively satisfying explanation of the rate of return unless an 'unobtrusive postulate' that disallowed capital-reversing was slipped into the analysis, although Solow disputed this.

The third theoretical neoclassical response attempted to extend one-commodity results to more general heterogeneous commodity models. Samuelson's 'surrogate production function' included what appeared to be a variety of physically distinct capital goods, but also assumed equal factor proportions in all industries, making relative prices independent of changes in distribution between wages and profits. As Samuelson subsequently realised, this effectively collapsed his model back to one commodity.

By the late 1960s, Samuelson's (1966) judicious article, 'A summing up', admitted that outside of one-commodity models, reswitching and capital-reversing may be usual, rather than anomalous, theoretical results and that the three neoclassical parables 'cannot be universally valid'. On a theoretical level, the 'English' Cantabrigians won the round over aggregate production functions. Even neoclassicals like Hahn (1972), showed no mercy for aggregate production functions, which 'cannot be shown to follow from proper [general equilibrium] theory and in general [are] therefore open to severe logical objections' (p. 8). They fell out of favour in the 1970s and early 1980s until their revival with endogenous growth and real business-cycle theories.

Lack of resolution, empirical evidence and aggregation problems
The fight was far from over because *there was no agreement on the significance of these results*. The two sides used different criteria to judge the agreed-upon outcomes of the controversy. The different criteria involve another ongoing and unresolved controversy: has there been continuity in the evolution of economic theory from Adam Smith to the present, or discontinuity, with the marginal revolution setting neoclassical economics on a different path from earlier classical political economy and Karl Marx? The 'English' Cantabrigians believe in discontinuity; most neoclassicals, in continuity.

While neoclassical economics envisages the lifetime utility-maximising consumption decisions of individuals as the driving force of economic activity, with the allocation of given, scarce resources as the fundamental economic problem, the 'English' Cantabrigians argue for a return to a classical political economy vision. There, profit-making decisions of capitalist firms are the driving force, with the fundamental economic problem being the allocation of surplus output to ensure reproduction and growth. Because individuals depend on the market for their livelihoods, social class (their position within the division of labour) becomes the fundamental unit of analysis. The potential rate of profits on capital arises from differing power and social relationships in production, and the realisation of profits is brought about by effective demand associated with saving and spending behaviours of the different classes and the 'animal spirits' of capitalists. The rate of profits is thus an outcome of the accumulation process. Robinson argued – citing Thorstein Veblen and raising the spectre of Marx – that the meaning of capital lay in the property owned by the capitalist class, which confers on capitalists the legal right and economic authority to take a share of the surplus created by the production process.

Imagine the controversies as a crucial thought experiment between two competing visions of economics. From a Cambridge, England perspective, how much more decisive could the results have been? Capital theory was the arena for extending the principle of scarcity to explain the return to capital through marginal productivity. It was precisely on this key point of what determines the rate of return that the 'anomalous' reswitching and capital-reversing results occurred. The three neoclassical capital parables were shown only to hold in a one-commodity model (where classical theory was equally valid). All attempts to extend the parable results to more general models of heterogeneous goods failed, because Wicksell effects made the links between capital and interest bi-directional rather than one way. What else would it take to convince an economist to shift visions?

For neoclassicals, none of this was obvious. The controversies were conducted largely in neoclassical terms about neoclassical models. Reswitching and capital-reversing prompted much useful neoclassical work to try to refine the theory through secondary hypotheses and additional assumptions; Burmeister's (2000) 'regular economies' are a good example. But there was little sense of a viable alternative vision waiting in the wings, and even less sense that the neoclassical vision was at stake.

Furthermore, neoclassical one-commodity models remained intact and fruitful as a basis for empirical work. As explicit simplifications, they could get by with the less rigorous notion that relative scarcities are the *empirically dominant* determinant of relative prices, even if Wicksell effects are theoretically possible. Solow's rationale for empirical work has always been straightforward: assuming that the data may be regarded 'as if' they were generated by the underlying simple model, the estimation procedures serve to provide orders of magnitude of the key parameters of the model. These 'lowbrow' models remain heuristically important for the intuition they provide, as well as the basis for empirical work that has provided good statistical fits and plausible parameter values for aggregate production functions. For these reasons, aggregate production functions have not only survived the Cambridge controversies, but they have also prospered in modern growth theory.

But as Fisher (1971, 1992, 2003), Felipe (2001), Felipe and McCombie (2001, 2003) and Fisher and Felipe (2003) have shown, the 'as if' empirical defence of aggregate production functions is unjustifiable. This internal neoclassical critique goes back to Phelps Brown (1957) and was formalised by Simon (1979), who, in his Nobel lecture, noted that the good statistical fits to aggregate production functions 'cannot be taken as strong evidence for the [neo-] classical theory, for the identical results can readily be produced by mistakenly fitting a Cobb–Douglas function to data that were in fact generated by a linear accounting identity (value of output equals labour costs plus capital cost)' (p. 497).

In a separate internal critique, Fisher has shown that:

> The conditions for successful aggregation are so stringent that one can hardly believe that actual economies satisfy them. If no optimization condition is imposed . . . aggregation over sectors is possible . . . only if micro production functions are additively separable in capital and labor. Even after imposing sensible efficiency conditions . . . the existence of a labor aggregate, for example, requires that all firms employ different labor types in the same proportions. This requires the absence of specialization in employment. Similarly, where there are many outputs, an output aggregate will exist . . . only if all firms produce all outputs in the same proportions. This requires the absence of specialization in production . . . Without such conditions (and equally stringent ones for capital), the aggregates cannot be generated, and the aggregate production function will not exist. (Fisher, 2003, p. 229)

Thus, to this day, the two Cambridges and growth theorists cannot agree about the significance of either the results or the supporting evidence. Such disagreements about significance are an endemic problem in economic analysis. What is the meaning of a simple model whose clear-cut results are not sustained when restrictive assumptions are loosened? Is it none the less a valuable parable, useful heuristically and empirically to isolate crucial tendencies that get obscured in more general models? Or is it a mistake whose insights must be discarded while searching for a better explanation in a completely different direction?

With neither side able to deliver a knockout punch, issues of faith and ideology entered the ring with claims about the significance of the results and competing visions of economics. When one-commodity results are not robust in more general models, the lack of definitive evidence leaves room for ideology to play a role in the decision to hang on to a theory or vision. The intensity and passion of the Cambridge controversies were generated not by abstract technical questions about Wicksell effects, but by strong ideological undercurrents like the ethical justification of the return to capital, and fundamental methodological questions about the extent to which equilibrium is a useful tool of economic analysis and about comparing deeply differing visions of economics.

AVI J. COHEN

References

Burmeister, E. (2000), 'The capital theory controversy', in Heinz D. Kurz (ed.), *Critical Essays on Piero Sraffa's Legacy in Economics*, Cambridge: Cambridge University Press, pp. 305–14.

Cohen, A.J. and G.C. Harcourt (2003), 'Whatever happened to the Cambridge capital theory controversies?', *Journal of Economic Perspectives*, **17**, 199–214.

Felipe, J. (2001), 'Endogenous growth, increasing returns, and externalities: an alternative interpretation of the evidence', *Metroeconomica*, **52**, 391–427.

Felipe, J. and J. McCombie (2001), 'The CES production function, the accounting identity and Occam's Razor', *Applied Economics*, **33**, 1221–32.

Felipe, J. and J. McCombie (2003), 'Comment', *Journal of Economic Perspectives*, **17**, 229–31.

Fisher, F. (1971), 'Aggregate production functions and the explanation of wages: a simulation experiment', *Review of Economics and Statistics*, **53**, 305–25.

Fisher, F. (1992), *Aggregation: Aggregate Production Functions and Related Topics*, Cambridge, MA: MIT Press.

Fisher, F. (2003), 'Comment', *Journal of Economic Perspectives*, **17**, 228–9.

Fisher, F. and J. Felipe (2003), 'Aggregation in production functions: what applied economists should know', *Metroeconomica*, **54**, 208–62.

Hahn, F.H. (1972), *The Share of Wages in the National Income*, London: Weidenfeld & Nicolson.

Pasinetti, Luigi L. (1969), 'Switches of technique and the "rate of return" in capital theory', *Economic Journal*, **79**, 503–31.

Phelps Brown, E.H. (1957), 'The meaning of the fitted Cobb–Douglas function', *Quarterly Journal of Economics*, **71**, 546–60.

Samuelson, Paul A. (1962), 'Parable and realism in capital theory: the surrogate production function', *Review of Economic Studies*, **29**, 193–206.

Samuelson, Paul A. (1966), 'A summing-up', *Quarterly Journal of Economics*, **80**, 568–83.

Simon, H.A. (1979), 'Rational decision making in business organizations', *American Economic Review*, **69**, 493–513.

Solow, Robert M. (1955–56), 'The production function and the theory of capital', *Review of Economic Studies*, **23**, 101–8.

Solow, Robert M. (1956), 'A contribution to the theory of economic growth', *Quarterly Journal of Economics*, **70**, 65–94.

Solow, Robert M. (1957), 'Technical change and the aggregate production function', *Review of Economics and Statistics*, **39**, 312–20.

Solow, Robert M. (1963), *Capital Theory and the Rate of Return*, Amsterdam: North-Holland.

Swan, T.W. (1956), 'Economic growth and capital accumulation', *Economic Record*, **32**, 343–61.

Wicksell, K. (1911 [1934]), *Lectures on Political Economy*, vol. 1, London: George Routledge & Sons.

Capability Approach

Over the last decade Amartya Sen's 'capability approach' (CA) has emerged as the leading alternative to standard economic frameworks for thinking about poverty, inequality and human development generally. In countless articles and several books that tackle a range of economic, social and ethical questions (beginning with the Tanner Lecture 'Equality of what?' delivered at Stanford University in 1979), Professor Sen has developed, refined and defended a framework that is directly concerned with human capability and freedom (for example, Sen, 1980, 1984, 1985a, 1987, 1992, 1999). From the outset, Sen acknowledged strong connections with Adam Smith's (1776) analysis of 'necessities' and living conditions and Karl Marx's (1844) concern with human freedom and emancipation. Later Sen (1993, p. 46) recognised that 'the most powerful conceptual connections' (which he initially failed to appreciate) relate to Aristotle's theory of 'political distribution' and his analysis of *eudaimonia* – 'human flourishing' (see Nussbaum, 1988, 1990).

While the roots of the CA can be traced back to Aristotle, Classical Political Economy and Marx, it is possible to identify more recent links. For example, Sen often notes that Rawls's *Theory of Justice* (1971) and his emphasis on 'self-respect' and access to primary goods has 'deeply influenced' the CA (Sen, 1992, p. 8). Another connection, which is not really discussed, relates to Isaiah Berlin's (1958) classic essay 'Two concepts of liberty', which mounts a fierce attack on the positive concepts of freedom that inspired Sen (but see Sen, 1999, p. 349, n.1 for a tribute to Berlin). Sen also takes the trouble to compare and contrast the CA with some close rivals, which concentrate on entitlements, the priority of liberty, human rights and human capital (Sen, 1984, 1985b, 1997, 1999, 2005). In doing so he generally shows that each approach has something to offer, but only the CA can address *all* relevant concerns.

The CA, however, probably has the most in common with the basic needs approach (BNA) to development pioneered by Paul Streeten et al. (1981) and Frances Stewart (1985), among others (see Basic Needs Approach, this volume). In an early paper entitled 'Goods and people', Sen tries to distinguish between the CA and BNA through a fivefold critique of the latter (Sen, 1984, pp. 513–15). Some of Sen's criticisms, however, appear to misrepresent the BNA (Alkire, 2002, pp. 166–70). In particular the argument that the BNA lapses into a form of 'commodity fetishism' has been challenged. While this is a valid criticism of the original formulation of basic needs (for example, ILO, 1976), the architects of the 'new basic needs' approach have reiterated that '[t]he concept of basic needs as we understood it, was not (as is sometimes thought) centred on the possession of commodities. Instead, it was concerned with providing all human beings, but particularly the poor and deprived, with the opportunities for a full life' (Streeten in Haq, 1995, p. ix; Streeten et al., 1981, p. 21). Nevertheless, it is now widely recognised that the CA manages to bring together many of the concerns of basic needs theorists (originally expressed in a rather ad hoc manner) into a single coherent philosophical framework (Streeten, 1984; Alkire, 2002; Stewart and Deneulin, 2002). Moreover, unlike the BNA, the CA extends beyond the analysis of poverty and deprivation and often concerns itself with well-being generally. Finally, Alkire (2002, p. 170) observes that 'the single most important function of the CA is to make *explicit* some *implicit* assumptions in the BNA about the value of choice and participation (and the disvalue of coercion)' (original emphasis).

Conceptual foundations

The conceptual foundations of the CA can be found in Sen's critiques of traditional welfare economics, which typically conflate well-being with either opulence (income, commodity command) or utility (happiness, desire fulfilment) (see Crocker, 1992 and Clark, 2002a, pp. 29–34 for more extensive discussions of these critiques). Sen distinguishes between commodities, human functioning/capability and utility as follows:

Commodity → Capability (to function) → Function(ing) → Utility (eg. happiness).

He begins by considering income or commodity command. Like Adam Smith, Sen (1983) emphasises that economic growth and the expansion of goods and services are necessary for human development. However, like Aristotle, he reiterates the familiar argument that 'wealth is evidently not the good we are seeking; for it is merely useful and for the sake of something else' (Sen, 1990, p. 44). In judging the quality of life, we should consider what people are able to achieve. Sen then observes that different people and societies typically *differ* in their capacity to convert income and commodities into valuable achievements. For example, a disabled person may require extra resources (wheelchairs, ramps, lifts and so on) to achieve the same things (moving around) as an able-bodied person. Moreover, a child typically has very different nutritional requirements from a manual labourer, pregnant woman or someone with a parasitic disease. Similarly, the commodity requirements for more complex social achievements (such as 'appearing in public without shame' or 'entertaining family and friends') typically depend on 'cultural' factors such as social convention and custom or status and class, *inter alia* (Sen, 1985a, pp. 25–6; 1999, pp. 70–71). In comparing the well-being of different people, not enough information is provided by looking only at the commodities each can successfully command. Instead we must consider how well people are able to function with the goods and services at their disposal.

Sen also challenges the welfare or utility approach, which concentrates on happiness, pleasure and desire-fulfilment. (The choice-based approach is regarded as a 'non-starter' as people do not always choose in accordance with their own personal interests but often wish to consider wider concerns (Sen, 1985a, pp. 18–20).) Following Rawls he recognises that utility does not distinguish between different sources of pleasure and pain or different kinds of desires (Rawls, 1971, pp. 30–31; Sen, 1984, p. 308). In particular, utility fails to discriminate against 'offensive tastes' (such as taking pleasure in another person's misery), although this approach could be modified to deal with this criticism (Cohen, 1993, p. 31). More fundamentally, Sen points out that there is more to life than achieving utility: 'Happiness or desire fulfilment represents only one aspect of human existence' (Sen, 1984, p. 512). While it is important to take note of utility, there are many other things of intrinsic value (notably rights and positive freedoms) that are neglected by the welfare approach (Sen, 1987, p. 8; 1992, p. 54; 1999, p. 62). This might not be a serious problem in cases where utility levels reflect personal circumstances and deprivations. However, Sen (1999, p. 62) indicates that 'utility can be easily swayed by mental conditioning or adaptive expectations'. Among other things he cites evidence from a post famine health survey in India that suggests significant disparities between the externally observed health of widows and their own subjective impressions of their physical state (Sen, 1985a, pp. 82–3).

These considerations lead to the conclusion that neither opulence (income, commodity command) nor utility (happiness, desire fulfilment) constitute or adequately represent human well-being and deprivation. Instead what is required is a more direct approach that focuses on human function(ing)s and the capability to achieve valuable function(ing)s. Sen (1985a, 1993) makes the following distinctions:

- *Functioning* – 'A functioning is an achievement of a person: what she or he manages to do or be. It reflects, as it were, a part of the "state" of that person' (Sen, 1985a, p. 10). Achieving a functioning (for example, being adequately nourished) with a given bundle of commodities (for example, bread or rice) depends on a range of personal and social factors (for example, metabolic rates, body size, age, gender, activity levels, health, access to medical services, nutritional knowledge and education, climatic conditions and so on). A functioning therefore refers to the *use* a person makes of the commodities at his or her command.
- *Capability* – A capability reflects a person's *ability* to achieve a given functioning ('doing' or 'being') (Saith, 2001, p. 8). For example, a person may have the ability to avoid hunger, but may choose to fast or go on hunger strike instead. (Note that Sen typically uses the term 'capability' in a much broader and more general sense to refer to capabilities in plural or the actual ability to function in different ways – see below.)
- *Functioning* n-*tuple* – A functioning *n*-tuple (or vector) describes the combination of 'doings' and 'beings' that constitute the state of a person's life. The functioning *n*-tuple is given by the utilisation (through a personal utilisation function) of the available commodity bundle. Each functioning *n*-tuple represents a possible lifestyle.

- *Capability set* – The capability set describes the set of *attainable* functioning *n*-tuples or vectors a person can achieve. It is likely that a person will be able to choose between different commodity bundles and utilisations. The capability set is obtained by applying all feasible utilisations to all attainable commodity bundles (Sen, 1985a; Saith, 2001). Sen (1985a, 1992, 1999) emphasises that capabilities reflect a person's real opportunities or positive freedom of choice between possible lifestyles.

Sen (1985a) provides a formal treatment of this framework. However, most discussions and applications of the CA dispense with mathematical formalisation, which is not strictly necessary for most purposes. In practice, Sen uses the term 'capability' in a broader sense than above to refer to 'the alternative combination of functionings the person can achieve, from which he or she can choose one collection' (Sen, 1993, p. 31; see also Sen, 1992, p. 40; 2005, p. 153). So instead of describing specific abilities (such as being able to avoid hunger), the notion of 'capability' is effectively used as a synonym for the capability set (see also Qizilbash, 2006 on different uses of the term 'capability' in Sen's work). Sen argues that capability or freedom has intrinsic value and should be regarded as 'the primary informational base' (Sen, 1993, pp. 38–9).

One of the chief strengths of Sen's framework is that it is flexible and exhibits a considerable degree of internal pluralism, which allows researchers to develop and apply it in many different ways (Alkire, 2002, pp. 8–11, 28–30). Three points are noteworthy. First, Sen does not subscribe to a fixed or definitive list of capabilities. Instead he argues that the selection and weighting of capabilities depend on personal value judgements (which are partly influenced by the nature and purpose of the evaluative exercise). While Sen often provides examples of intrinsically valuable capabilities – such as being able to 'live long, escape avoidable morbidity, be well nourished, be able to read, write and communicate, take part in literary and scientific pursuits and so forth' (Sen, 1984, p. 497; see also Clark, 2002a, table 3.1) – he refuses to endorse a unique list of capabilities as 'objectively correct' for practical and strategic reasons (Sen, 1993, p. 47; Clark, 2002a, p. 54; Qizilbash, 2002). Second, Sen indicates that the CA can be used to assess individual advantage in a range of different spaces. For example, the assessment of poverty might involve concentrating on a relatively small subset of basic capabilities. Evaluating well-being or human development on the other hand seems to require a much longer and more diverse list of capabilities (see, for example, Sen, 1993, pp. 31–2, 40–42). The focus of the CA can be broadened further to include 'agency', which recognises that individuals often have values and goals (such as preserving the environment, purchasing free trade products or opposing injustice, tyranny and oppression) that transcend and sometimes even conflict with personal well-being (see Sen, 1985a, 1985b; 1992, ch. 4). The CA has also been adjusted to focus on inequality, social justice, living standards and rights and duties (among other things). Finally, Sen (1999, p. 77) recognises that the CA is not sufficient for all evaluative purposes. By itself the CA does not provide a complete theory of justice or development (see Sen, 1983, 1988; 1992, p. 77; 2005). We need to take note of other principles such as personal liberty, economic growth and efficiency.

Sen's CA has also been praised for broadening the informational base of evaluation, refocusing on people as ends in themselves (rather than treating them merely as means to economic activity), recognising human heterogeneity and diversity (through differences in personal conversion functions), drawing attention to group disparities (such as those based on gender, race, class, caste or age), embracing human agency and participation (by emphasising the role of practical reason, deliberative democracy and public action in forging goals, making choices and influencing policy), and acknowledging that different people, cultures and societies *may* have different values and aspirations.

The CA has been criticised from several different angles. In many cases key strengths are reconstrued as potential weaknesses by critics (notable examples include contrasting viewpoints about the merits of incompleteness). The best-known set of criticisms relate to the issue of 'how far Sen's framework is operational' (Sugden, 1993, p. 1953). The first of these criticisms concerns the identification of valuable capabilities. Several commentators have criticised Sen for failing to supplement his framework with a coherent list of important capabilities (for example, Williams, 1987, p. 96; Nussbaum, 1988, p. 176; Qizilbash, 1998, p. 54). Others have argued that Sen goes too far in terms of insisting that certain capabilities simply are valuable (Sen, 1992, p. 40), 'given the extent of disagreement among reasonable people about the nature of a good life' (Sugden, 1993, pp. 1952–3). This line of attack, however, misrepresents Sen's actual position and conflicts with the available evidence on value formation (see the following section). A second line of criticism casts doubt on the usefulness of the CA for making interpersonal comparisons of well-being in the presence of potential disagreements about the valuation of capabilities including the relative weights to be assigned to these capabilities (for example, Beitz, 1986). Sen, however, is remarkably optimistic about achieving agreement about evaluations: he suggests that the intersections of different people's rankings are 'typically quite large' (Sen, 1985a, pp. 53–6). He has also proposed a range of methods including 'dominance ranking' and the 'intersection approach' for extending incomplete orderings (see Sen, 1985a, 1993; Saith, 2001). Finally, the informational requirements of the CA can be extremely high (see Sen, 1994; Alkire, 2002, pp. 181–93). Evaluating social states typically depends on acquiring data on multiple functionings. In some cases, however, the relevant social indicators are simply not available. Moving from functioning to capability complicates the exercise drastically as additional information is required on counterfactual choices (which cannot be observed) as well as actual choices. Despite these operational difficulties many credible innovative attempts have been made to measure well-being in the functioning *and* capability space (see the final section below).

Completing the capability approach

Attempts to complete the CA often focus on augmenting Sen's framework with a theory of the good to guide moral judgements. Many different ethics of human well-being and need have emerged in development studies, social science and philosophy (see Saith, 2001; Alkire, 2002, ch. 2; Clark, 2002a, ch. 3). Nussbaum (1990, 1995, 2000, 2003), Desai (1995), Alkire and Black (1997), Alkire (2002, ch. 4), Clark (2002a, ch. 4; 2003) and Robeyns (2003) have all generated lists of human capabilities in an effort to apply Sen's framework. The methodologies employed vary in style and sophistication and range from the ad hoc selection of capabilities by 'experts' to more complex rules and procedures for identifying capabilities as well as participatory approaches that listen to the voices of the poor.

The best-known and most influential attempt to complete the CA can be found in the writings of the feminist philosopher, Martha Nussbaum. Nussbaum's version of the CA differs from Sen's in several respects (see Nussbaum, 2000, pp. 11–15; 2003, pp. 43–4; Sen, 1993). The most notable difference is that Nussbaum draws heavily on Aristotle in an effort to develop a definite list of 'central human capabilities' (see Nussbaum, 1990, 1995, 2000). The headings of the latest version of this list (which has basically not changed much over the years) are: (1) life; (2) bodily health; (3) bodily integrity; (4) senses, imagination and thought; (5) emotions; (6) practical reason; (7) affiliation; (8) other species; (9) play; and (10) political and material control over one's environment (Nussbaum, 2000, pp. 72–5; 2003, pp. 41–2; 2005a, pp. 41–2). According to Nussbaum, this list 'isolates those human capabilities that can be convincingly argued to be of central importance in any human life, whatever else the person pursues or chooses' (Nussbaum, 2000, p. 74). It therefore provides basic political principles that should be embodied in constitutional guarantees, human rights legislation and development policy (Nussbaum, 1995, p. 87; 2000, pp. 74–5).

While Nussbaum's general approach has evolved since the appearance of her first list in 1990, it is possible to identify a number of tensions and contradictions in her writings – particularly between her proposed methodology and style of essentialism (see Clark, 2002a, ch. 3). The most serious of these tensions relates to the way in which her list is compiled. Nussbaum has always maintained that her list is subject to ongoing revision and should emerge through some sort of intercultural ethical inquiry. In particular she encourages us to encounter and learn from other cultures and societies in an effort to move towards a shared account of the core human capabilities (Nussbaum, 1995, p. 74). This approach involves 'internal criticism' of local values and practices by appealing to external standards (see Nussbaum and Sen, 1989). In theory this approach is promising, although in practice there are times when one might want to challenge the motives for encouraging 'value rejection' in poor countries. In the end it seems that 'we must accept any *genuinely rational* assessment of [local] values that local people see fit to provide' (Clark, 2002a, p. 78, original emphasis). In other words it is not so much the method itself that is fraught but its potential for abuse.

Nussbaum claims that recent lists represent 'years of cross cultural discussion' (Nussbaum, 2000, p. 76). Comparing the most recent lists with the original shows that the core categories have not changed (Nussbaum, 1990 v. 2003 and 2005a). Some descriptive content has been added and some parts of the list have been reorganised. No categories, however, have been added or deleted. Moreover, revisiting the original list indicates that nearly all Nussbaum's capabilities are actually derived from the writings of Aristotle (Nussbaum, 1990, notes 52–65; Clark, 2002a, p. 78). Some commentators have suggested that it is paternalistic for a middle-class North American philosopher to determine capabilities for other cultures and societies and have advocated the deployment of more participatory approaches (Stewart, 2001, p. 1192; Clark, 2002a). While Nussbaum's book *Women and Human Development* (2000) draws on two brief field trips to India, her case studies 'may be rather thin in both number (two) and depth (perhaps from single meetings reliant on interpreters), for Nussbaum's ambitious project' (Gasper, 2001, p. 4; see also Gargarella, 2001). In the end Nussbaum's list should be viewed 'not as a headcount of present-day opinions, but as a hypothesis about what would over time become an acceptable starting point for discussions in each society, as a rational interpretation, implication and evolution of their values' (Gasper, 2004, p. 187).

Meanwhile Sen (1999, 2004, 2005) has advocated a more direct approach for eliciting relevant information about the formation of human values, which emphasises the constructive role of democracy and the importance of public participation and discussion:

> The problem is not with listing important capabilities, but with insisting on one predetermined canonical list of capabilities, chosen by theorists without any general social discussion or public reasoning. To have such a fixed list, emanating entirely from pure theory, is to deny the possibility of fruitful public participation on what should be included and why . . . public discussion and reasoning can lead to a better understanding of the role, reach and significance of particular capabilities ... (Sen, 2004, pp. 77, 81)

In the event of a conflict between values or traditions, Sen argues: 'it is the people directly involved who must have the opportunity to participate in deciding what should be chosen', not local elites (political or religious) or cultural 'experts' (domestic or foreign) (Sen, 1999, pp. 31–2). Sabina Alkire (2002, esp. ch. 4) has developed a promising methodology for applying Sen's approach at the micro level, which draws on participatory tools and techniques (pioneered by Robert Chambers and associates) in an effort to answer the question: 'How do we identify valuable capabilities?' (p. v). However, Alkire does not systematically identify valuable capabilities through fieldwork herself (except in so far as they arose in her three 'impact assessment' case studies of development projects in Pakistan). Nor does she consider the implications of such an exercise for the many different conceptions of poverty and well-being described in her book.

This brings us to David Clark's plea for 'empirical philosophy' (Clark, 2002a, p. 5; 2002b), and his attempt to confront abstract concepts of human well-being and development with the values and experiences of the poor (see Clark, 2000, 2002a, 2003, 2005; see also Okin, 2003). Clark developed and applied a methodology and survey instrument for investigating perceptions of well-being among the urban and rural poor in South Africa (Clark, 2002a, ch. 4). He found that the most frequently mentioned aspects of a good life in South Africa were jobs, housing, education, income, family and friends, religion, health, food, good clothes, recreation and relaxation, safety and economic security, *inter alia* (a result that is not inconsistent with the findings of most participatory poverty assessments). Respondents were asked to elaborate on the reasons for valuing these items, before being asked to evaluate an expert defined list of capabilities (see Clark, 2002a, pp. 108–36). The most significant finding to emerge from this study is that most people appear to share a common vision of the good, which is not fundamentally at odds with the capabilities advocated by scholars like Nussbaum and Sen. Most theories of well-being and need, however, ought to say more about (i) the practical side of survival and development in poor countries; (ii) the psychology of human well-being, that is, mental functioning; and (iii) some of the 'better things' in life such as recreation (Clark, 2002a, pp. 136–44).

Of course the CA may turn out to be just as susceptible as utility to the problem of adaptive preferences and cultural indoctrination (Nussbaum, 1988, p. 175; Sumner, 1996, pp. 60–68). This is a very real concern. The available evidence from South Africa, however, suggests that adaptation and indoctrination have not generally distorted responses to questions about the selection and value of capabilities (Clark, 2002a, pp. 103, 129–31; Clark and Qizilbash, 2002, 2005; Qizilbash and Clark, 2005). Others have expressed concern that Sen's notion of deliberative democracy is too idealistic, as it neglects political power and may lead to decisions that undermine capabilities or worsen the position of the poor (Stewart and Deneulin, 2002, pp. 63–4). Finally, Qizilbash (2002) has appealed to advocates of the CA and related perspectives to unite against 'common foes' instead of dwelling upon relatively minor disagreements concerning the components of well-being.

Clarification and enlargement
Several attempts have been made to clarify and enlarge on other aspects of Sen's original framework. Four interrelated areas of work are briefly considered.

First, several attempts have been made to clarify the concept of capability – particularly in relation to functioning (see Clark, 2002a, ch. 2, appendix). Sen (1992, p. 41) refines the notion of capability to include *genuine* choice with substantial options. The goodness of the capability set should be judged in terms of the quality as well as the quantity of available opportunities (Sen, 1985a, p. 69; 1993, pp. 34–5; Crocker, 1998). There may also be a case for evaluating capability sets in terms of the *diversity* of options. Sen (1992, ch. 9.9) also emphasises the importance of 'responsible choice'. He accepts that it might be better to concentrate on outcomes (functionings achieved) if intelligent choice is complicated by uncertainty (see also Kanbur, 1987) or social conditioning robs a person of the courage to live in a particular way. Some capabilities (for example, being able to live long), however, do not appear to involve a very meaningful notion of choice (Williams, 1987, pp. 96–8; Crocker, 1995, pp. 163–4), while others (for example, being able to avoid cholera or malaria) depend more on public action and social policy than on individual choice (Sen, 1992, pp. 64–9). Furthermore, choosing to realise some capabilities may involve huge opportunity costs, which implies we should focus on 'sets of co-realisable capabilities' (Williams, 1987, pp. 98–100; Sen, 1987, p. 109). Paul Streeten (2000, p. 159) has suggested that it may be 'better to separate freedom of choice, and to look at poverty and deprivation in terms of observable achievements'. More radical critics have shunned the value of freedom as choice (Gasper, 2002, esp. pp. 456–8).

A second strand of research criticises Sen's CA for underplaying the importance of negative *vis-à-vis* positive freedom (Carter, 1996; Qizilbash, 1996, p. 147). In some respects negative freedom seems to feature more prominently in versions of the CA that distinguish *internal* capabilities from the external conditions required to achieve these capabilities (see, for example, the discussion of Nussbaum's approach in the next paragraph). Sen, however, does acknowledge 'the special significance of negative freedom' for the CA (Sen, 1992, p. 87). He argues that capability failure can stem from the violation of personal rights as well as the absence of positive freedoms (Sen, 1985b, lecture 3). Moreover, in contrast to some capability theorists (who tend to shun personal liberty, for example, Nussbaum, 2005b, pp. 176–7), Sen argues that negative freedom has *intrinsic* as well as instrumental significance (Sen, 1985b, pp. 218–21).

A third line of research is concerned with notions of agency and personhood. Several commentators have argued for a sharper distinction between internal powers and skills and actual opportunities or outcomes (Nussbaum, 1988; Crocker, 1995; Qizilbash, 1996; Gasper, 1997, 2002). The precise distinctions proposed vary slightly and have evolved. A notable example is Nussbaum's (2000, pp. 84–6) distinction between *basic*, *internal* and *combined* capabilities. Basic capabilities reflect 'the innate equipment of individuals that is necessary for developing more advanced capabilities, and a ground for moral concern'. Many of these latent powers and skills are transformed into internal capabilities (with the support of the surrounding environment) over the course of a normal life and become 'developed states of the person' or 'mature states of readiness', which 'are, so far as the person herself is concerned, sufficient conditions for the exercise of requisite functions'. Finally, combined capabilities 'may be defined as internal capabilities *combined with* suitable external conditions for the exercise of the function' (pp. 84–5, original emphasis). Gasper (2002, p. 447) has criticised Sen for failing to modify his terminology in line with these distinctions. He has also argued for a richer conception of human personality, which incorporates the variety of values and motives that influence human action (Gasper, 2002; 2004, p. 180). These motivations extend well beyond Sen's (1977) classic distinction between acts based on 'sympathy' (feelings for other people) and 'commitment' (goals beyond personal well-being).

The fourth and final area of research concerns itself with means and ends. Some commentators have suggested that Sen pays insufficient attention to 'the means of freedom' (Qizilbash, 1996), while others have emphasised the links between human capital and human capability (Streeten, 1994, 2000; Haq, 1995; Sen, 1997, 1999; Bebbington, 1999). While both these approaches 'put humanity at the centre of attention . . . the narrower view of the human capital approach fits into the more inclusive perspective of human capability' which takes note of the direct relevance of human capabilities for well-being and their indirect role through facilitating social change and promoting economic activity (Sen, 1997, pp. 1959–60; 1999, pp. 292–7). The latest version of Sen's CA explicitly recognises five broad categories of *instrumental* freedoms (political freedom, economic facilities, social opportunities, transparency guarantees and protective security), which contribute to the expansion of human capabilities (Sen, 1999, esp. ch. 2). The empirical links and interconnections between different capabilities and freedoms have also been examined (Sen, 1999; Clark, 2002a, 2005). One promising approach, which has not been fully worked out, involves developing a matrix of means and ends to help think through the many complex interconnections between different capabilities together with the policy implications (May, 2000, pp. 8–9).

Public policy and action

As we have seen, the CA suggests that the overriding objective of development is the expansion of human capabilities rather than economic growth. While growth may be necessary for development, it is not always sufficient. In broad terms it is possible to distinguish between 'growth mediated' and 'support led' development (Drèze and Sen, 1989; Sen, 1999, ch. 2). The former operates through rapid and broad-based economic growth, which facilitates the expansion of basic capabilities through higher employment, improved prosperity and better social services. The latter works primarily through proficient welfare programmes that support health, education and social security. Public action also plays an important role in supporting capabilities directly and providing political pressure for state intervention in times of crisis and hardship.

At the micro level, policy action might focus on selecting beneficiaries (according to functioning poverty) for public works programmes, welfare payments or micro-finance projects, *inter alia* (for example, Drèze and Sen, 1989; Alkire, 2002). Such projects should take note of 'adequate income', which considers the amount of money each person needs to achieve minimal functioning (Sen, 1992, ch. 7; 1993, pp. 41–2). The problem with this kind of approach is that it is difficult to identify people with relatively efficient conversion functions in advance. Such people need less money than others to avoid capability failure, but have powerful incentives to conceal their advantage in order to maximise personal income and well-being. This means that development projects based on adequate income will alleviate functioning poverty, but at a higher cost than is necessary and with undesirable distributive consequences (Balestrino, 1994, pp. 400–401). Other small-scale development projects such as community literacy programmes and health initiatives tackle capability failure directly. The CA also provides a strong justification for the promotion of interpersonal equity in the space of basic capabilities.

More work is required to bring out the policy implications of the CA. To this end the Human Development and Capability Association (HDCA) is currently working on a series of policy briefs (www.hd-ca.org). Some commentators have suggested that the CA requires a complementary theory of obligations and duties (Gasper, 2004, p. 178); others have pointed to possible tension between the goal of basic capability *equality* on the one hand and the objective of (overall) capability *expansion* on the other (Alkire, 2002, pp. 177–8). Some thinkers have argued that democratic processes may not be sufficient to bring about the necessary changes or have called for collective action to influence public policy (Stewart and Deneulin, 2002, pp. 69–70; Fukuda-Parr, 2003, p. 309). More controversially, some critics have taken issue with the regularity and selectiveness of the examples Sen uses to justify policy insights or have challenged his reading of the empirical evidence (Nolan and Sender, 1992; Corbridge, 2002).

Applications and guide to further reading
Attempts to apply the CA have mushroomed in recent years. Among other things the CA has been used to investigate poverty, inequality, well-being, social justice, gender, social exclusion, health, disability, child poverty and identity. It has also been related to human needs, human rights and human security as well as development more broadly. Most empirical studies fall into *at least* one of three categories. First, there have been numerous attempts to apply the CA to the measurement of poverty and well-being (for example, Sen, 1992, 1999; Chiappero Martinetti, 1994, 1996, 2000; Balestrino, 1996; Klasen, 1997, 2000; Majumdar and Subramanian, 2001; Clark and Qizilbash, 2002, 2005; Qizilbash and Clark, 2005). The best-known measure is the Human Development Index, which covers income (opportunities), life expectancy, and education (see Human Development Index, this volume). While most applications focus on functioning, some studies have tried to capture capabilities in terms of freedom to choose (for example, Schokkaert and Van Ootegem, 1990) or human talents and skills (for example, Jasek-Rysdahl, 2001). Second, several studies have investigated the links between income (or expenditure) and various capabilities (for example, Sen, 1985a, 1999; Balestrino, 1996; Ruggeri Laderchi, 1997; Klasen, 2000). Many of these studies provide empirical support for the CA by suggesting that income and capabilities do not always go together. Finally, a third strand of work highlights group disparities by pointing to gross inequalities in terms of life expectancy, nutrition and literacy and so on, along the lines of gender, race, class, caste and age (for example, Sen, 1985a, 1999; Majumdar and Subramanian, 2001).

Sen (1990, 1993), Saith (2001) and Alkire (2002) provide excellent introductions to the CA. In addition several edited books consider a range of different issues relating to the CA (Sen, 1987; Nussbaum and Sen, 1993; Nussbaum and Glover, 1995; Comim et al., forthcoming). There have also been several major international conferences on the CA since 2001, which have generated a lot of new research – especially by younger scholars (http:// cfs.unipv.it/sen/index.html). A growing number of special journal issues have also been devoted to the CA. These include *Giornale Degli Economisti e Annali di Economia* (Vol. 53, 1994), *Notizie di Politeia* (Vol. 12, Nos 43–44, 1996), *Journal of International Development* (Vol. 9, No. 2, 1997; and Vol. 12, No. 7, 2000), *Review of Political Economy* (Vol. 14, No. 4, 2002), *Feminist Economics* (Vol. 9, Nos 2–3, 2003), *Social Science and Medicine* (Vol. 60, No. 2, 2005), *Journal of Human Development* (Vol. 6, No. 2, 2005) and *Social Indicators Research* (Vol. 74, No. 1, 2005). The sheer number, quality and diversity of practical applications that have emerged in recent years arguably lays to rest any remaining concerns about the possibility of making the CA operational.

DAVID A. CLARK

References

Alkire, S. (2002), *Valuing Freedoms: Sen's Capability Approach and Poverty Reduction*, Oxford: Oxford University Press.

Alkire, S. and R. Black (1997), 'A practical reasoning theory of development ethics: furthering the capabilities approach', *Journal of International Development*, **9** (2), 263–79.

Balestrino, A. (1994), 'Poverty and functioning: issues in measurement and public action', *Giornale Degli Economisti e Annali di Economia*, **53**, 389–406.

Balestrino, A. (1996), 'A note on functioning poverty in affluent societies', *Notizie di Politeia*, **12**, 97–105.

Bebbington, A. (1999), 'Capitals and capabilities: a framework for analyzing peasant viability, rural livelihoods and poverty', *World Development*, **27** (12), 2021–44.

Beitz, C.R. (1986), 'Amartya Sen's resources, values and development', *Economics and Philosophy*, **2** (2), 282–91.

Berlin, Isaiah (1958), 'Two concepts of liberty', reprinted in Isaiah Berlin (1969), *Four Essays on Liberty*, Oxford: Oxford University Press, pp. 118–72.

Carter, I. (1996), 'The concept of freedom in the work of Amartya Sen: an alternative analysis consistent with freedom's independent value', *Notizie di Politeia*, **12** (43/44), 7–22.

Chiappero Martinetti, E. (1994), 'A new approach to the evaluation of well-being and poverty by fuzzy set theory', *Giornale Degli Economisti e Annali di Economia*, **53**, 367–88.

Chiappero Martinetti, E. (1996), 'Standard of living evaluation based on Sen's approach: some methodological suggestions', *Notizie di Politeia*, **12** (43/44), 37–53.

Chiappero Martinetti, E. (2000), 'A multi-dimensional assessment of well-being based on Sen's functioning approach', *Rivista Internationale di Scienzie Sociali*, **108**, 207–31.

Clark, D.A. (2000), 'Concepts and perceptions of development: some evidence from the Western Cape', Southern Africa Labour and Development Research Unit (SALDRU) Working Paper 88, University of Cape Town.

Clark, D.A. (2002a), *Visions of Development: A Study of Human Values*, Cheltenham, UK and Northampton, MA, USA: Edward Elgar.

Clark, D.A. (2002b), 'Development ethics: a research agenda', *International Journal of Social Economics*, **29** (11), 830–48.

Clark, D.A. (2003), 'Concepts and perceptions of human well-being: some evidence from South Africa', *Oxford Development Studies*, **31** (2), 173–96.

Clark, D.A. (2005), 'Sen's capability approach and the many spaces of human well-being', *Journal of Development Studies*, **41** (8), 1339–68.

Clark, D.A. and M. Qizilbash (2002), 'Core poverty and extreme vulnerability in South Africa', Discussion Paper No. 2002-3, School of Economics, University of East Anglia, UK. Revised version: www.geocities.com/poverty_in_southafrica.

Clark, D.A. and M. Qizilbash (2005), 'Core poverty, basic capabilities and vagueness: an application to the South African context', Global Poverty Research Group (GPRG) Working Paper 26, Universities of Manchester and Oxford, www.gprg.org/pubs/workingpapers/pdfs/gprg-wps-026.pdf.

Cohen, G.A. (1993), 'Equality of what? On welfare, goods and capabilities', in Nussbaum and Sen (eds), pp. 9–29.

Comim, F., M. Qizilbash and S. Alkire (eds) (forthcoming), *The Capability Approach: Concepts, Measures and Applications*, Cambridge: Cambridge University Press.

Corbridge, S. (2002), 'Development as freedom: the spaces of Amartya Sen', *Progress in Development Studies*, **2** (3), 183–217.

Crocker, D.A. (1992), 'Functioning and capabilities: the foundation of Sen's and Nussbaum's development ethic', *Political Theory*, **20** (4), 584–612.

Crocker, David A. (1995), 'Functioning and capability: the foundation of Sen's and Nussbaum's development ethic, part II', in Nussbaum and Glover (eds), pp. 153–98.

Crocker, David A. (1998), 'Consumption, well-being and capability', in David A. Crocker and Toby Linden (eds), *Ethics of Consumption: The Good Life, Justice and Global Stewardship*, New York: Rowman & Littlefield, pp. 366–90.

Desai, Meghnad (1995), 'Poverty and capability: towards an empirically implementable measure', in *Poverty, Famine and Economic Development*, Aldershot, UK and Brookfield, US: Edward Elgar, pp. 185–204.

Drèze, Jean and Amartya K. Sen (1989), *Hunger and Public Action*, Oxford: Clarendon.

Fukuda-Parr, S. (2003), 'The human development paradigm: operationalizing Sen's ideas on capabilities', *Feminist Economics*, **9** (2–3), 301–17.

Gargarella, Roberto (2001), 'Women and human development: review', International Development Ethics Association (IDEA) *Newsletter*, June, www.carleton.ca/idea/newsletter/reports_062001_2.html.

Gasper, D. (1997), 'Sen's capability approach and Nussbaum's capabilities ethic', *Journal of International Development*, **9** (2), 281–302.

Gasper, Des (2001), 'Women and human development: review', International Development Ethics Association (IDEA) *Newsletter*, June, www.carleton.ca/idea/newsletter/reports_062001_7.html.

Gasper, D. (2002), 'Is Sen's capability approach an adequate basis for considering human development?', *Review of Political Economy*, **14** (4), 435–61.

Gasper, Des (2004), *The Ethics of Development*, Edinburgh: Edinburgh University Press.

Haq, Mahbub ul (1995), *Reflections on Human Development*, Oxford: Oxford University Press.

ILO (1976), *Employment, Growth and Basic Needs: A One World Problem*, Geneva: International Labour Organization.

Jasek-Rysdahl, K. (2001), 'Applying Sen's capability approach to neighbourhoods: using local asset maps to deepen our understanding of well-being', *Review of Social Economy*, **59** (3), 313–29.

Kanbur, Ravi (1987), 'The standard of living: uncertainty, inequality and opportunity', in Geoffrey Hawthorn (ed.), *The Standard of Living*, Cambridge: Cambridge University Press, pp. 70–93.

Klasen, S. (1997), 'Poverty, inequality and deprivation in South Africa: an analysis of the 1993 SALDRU survey', *Social Indicators Research*, **41**, 51–94.

Klasen, S. (2000), 'Measuring poverty and deprivation in South Africa', *Review of Income and Wealth*, **46** (1), 33–58.

Majumdar, M. and S. Subramanian (2001), 'Capability failure and group disparities: some evidence from India from the 1980s', *Journal of Development Studies*, **37** (5), 104–40.

Marx, Karl (1844), *Economic and Philosophic Manuscript* (English translation), London: Lawrence & Wishart, 1977.

May, Julian (ed.) (2000), *Poverty and Inequality in South Africa: Meeting the Challege*, London: Zed Books.

Nolan, P. and J. Sender (1992), 'Death rates, life expectancy and China's economic reforms: a critique of A.K. Sen', *World Development*, **20** (9), 1279–303.

Nussbaum, M.C. (1988), 'Nature, function and capability: Aristotle on political distribution', *Oxford Studies in Ancient Philosophy*, supplementary vol., 145–84.

Nussbaum, Martha C. (1990), 'Aristotelian social democracy', in Bruce Douglas, Gerald Mara and Henry Richardson (eds), *Liberalism and the Good*, New York: Routledge, pp. 203–52.

Nussbaum, Martha C. (1995), 'Human capabilities, female human beings', in Nussbaum and Glover (eds), pp. 61–104.

Nussbaum, Martha C. (2000), *Women and Human Development: The Capabilities Approach*, Cambridge: Cambridge University Press.

Nussbaum, M.C. (2003), 'Capabilities as fundamental entitlement: Sen and social justice', *Feminist Economics*, **9** (2–3), 33–59.

Nussbaum, M.C. (2005a), 'Well-being, contracts and capabilities', in Lenore Manderson (ed.), *Rethinking Well-Being*, Perth: API Network, pp. 27–44.

Nussbaum, M.C. (2005b), 'Women's bodies: violence, security, capabilities', *Journal of Human Development*, **6** (2), 167–83.

Nussbaum, Martha C. and Jonathan Glover (eds) (1995), *Women, Culture and Development*, Oxford: Clarendon.

Nussbaum, Martha C. and Amartya K. Sen (1989), 'Internal criticism and Indian rationalist traditions', in Michael Krausz (ed.) *Relativism, Interpretation and Confrontation*, South Bend, IN: University of Notre Dame Press, pp. 299–325.

Nussbaum, Martha C. and Amartya K. Sen (eds) (1993), *The Quality of Life*, Oxford: Clarendon.

Okin, S. M. (2003), 'Poverty, well-being, and gender: what counts, who's heard?', *Philosophy and Public Affairs*, **31** (3), 280–316.

Qizilbash, M. (1996), 'Capabilities, well-being and human development: a survey', *Journal of Development Studies*, **33** (2), 143–62.

Qizilbash, M. (1998), 'The concept of well-being', *Economics and Philosophy*, **14**, 51–73.

Qizilbash, M. (2002), 'Development, common foes and shared values', *Review of Political Economy*, **14** (4), 463–80.

Qizilbash, M. (2006), 'Capabilities, happiness and adaptation in Sen and J.S. Mill', *Utilitas*, **18** (1), 20–32.

Qizilbash, M. and D.A Clark (2005), 'The capability approach and fuzzy measures of poverty: an application to the South African context', *Social Indicators Research*, **74** (1), 103–39.

Rawls, John (1971), *A Theory of Justice*, Oxford: Clarendon.

Robeyns, I. (2003), 'Sen's capability approach and gender inequality: selecting relevant capabilities', *Feminist Economics*, **9** (2–3), 61–92.

Ruggeri Laderchi, C. (1997), 'Poverty and its many dimensions: the role of income as an indicator', *Oxford Development Studies*, **25** (3), 345–60.

Saith, R. (2001), 'Capabilities: the concept and its operationalisation', QEH Working Paper Series 66, Queen Elizabeth House, University of Oxford.

Schokkaert, E. and L. Van Ootegem (1990), 'Sen's concept of the living standard applied to the Belgian unemployed', *Reserches Économiques de Louvain*, **56** (3–4), 429–50.

Sen, A.K. (1977), 'Rational fools: a critique of the behavioural foundations of economic theory', reprinted in *Choice, Welfare and Measurement*, Oxford: Blackwell, 1982, pp. 84–106.

Sen, Amartya K. (1980), 'Equality of what', in Sterling M. McMurrin (ed.), *The Tanner Lectures on Human Value*, Salt Lake City, UT: University of Utah Press, pp. 195–220.

Sen, A.K. (1983), 'Development: which way now?', *Economic Journal*, **93**, 745–62.

Sen, Amartya K. (1984), *Resources, Values and Development*, Oxford: Basil Blackwell.

Sen, Amartya K. (1985a), *Commodities and Capabilities*, Oxford: Elsevier Science.

Sen, A.K. (1985b), 'Well-being, agency and freedom: the Dewey lectures', *Journal of Philosophy*, **82** (4), 169–221.

Sen, Amartya K. (1987), *The Standard of Living: The Tanner Lectures*, Cambridge: Cambridge University Press.

Sen, Amartya K. (1988), 'The concept of development', in Hollis Chenery and Thirukodikaval N. Srinivasan (eds), *Handbook of Development Economics*, Vol. 1, North-Holland: Elsevier Science, pp. 10–26.

Sen, Amartya K. (1990), 'Development as capability expansion', in Keith Griffin and John Knight (eds), *Human Development and the International Development Strategy for the 1990s*, London: Macmillan, pp. 41–58.

Sen, Amartya K. (1992), *Inequality Re-examined*, Oxford: Clarendon.

Sen, Amartya K. (1993), 'Capability and well-being', in Nussbaum and Sen (eds), pp. 30–53.

Sen, A.K. (1994), 'Well-being, capability and public policy', *Giornale Degli Economisti e Annali di Economia*, **53**, 333–47.

Sen, A.K. (1997), 'Editorial: human capital and human capability', *World Development*, **25** (12), 1959–61.

Sen, Amartya K. (1999), *Development As Freedom*, Oxford: Oxford University Press.

Sen, A.K. (2004), 'Capabilities, lists and public reason: continuing the conversation', *Feminist Economics*, **10** (3), 77–80.

Sen, A.K. (2005), 'Human rights and capabilities', *Journal of Human Development*, **6** (2), 151–66.

Smith, Adam (1776), *An Inquiry into the Nature and the Causes of the Wealth of Nations*, reprinted in Edwin Cannon (ed.) (1976), *The Wealth of Nations*, Chicago: University of Chicago Press.

Stewart, Frances (1985), *Planning to Meet Basic Needs*, London: Macmillan.

Stewart, F. (2001), 'Women and human development: the capabilities approach by Martha C. Nussbaum', *Journal of International Development*, **13** (8), 1191–2.

Stewart, F. and S. Deneulin, (2002), 'Amartya Sen's contribution to development thinking', *Studies in Comparative International Development*, **37** (61), 61–70.

Streeten, P. (1984), 'Basic needs: some unsettled questions', *World Development*, **12** (9), 973–8.

Streeten, P. (1994), 'Human development: means and ends', *American Economic Review*, **84** (2), 232–7.

Streeten, P. (2000), 'Freedom and welfare: a review essay on Amartya Sen, *Development as Freedom*', *Population and Development Review*, **26** (1), 153–62.

Streeten, Paul P., Shahid J. Burki, Mahbub ul Haq, Norman Hicks and Frances Stewart (1981), *First Things First, Meeting Basic Human Needs in Developing Countries*, Oxford and New York: Oxford University Press.

Sugden, R. (1993), 'Welfare, resources, and capabilities: a review of *Inequality Re-examined* by Amartya Sen', *Journal of Economic Literature*, **31**, 1947–62.

Sumner, L.W. (1996), *Welfare, Happiness and Ethics*, Oxford: Clarendon.
Williams, Bernard (1987), 'The standard of living: interests and capabilities', in Geoffrey Hawthorn (ed.), *The Standard of Living*, Cambridge: Cambridge University Press, pp. 94–102.

Capitalism and Development

Capitalism is a system of economic and social relations characterised by the dependence of the bulk of the population on the sale of their labour power for subsistence. Although wage labour and private ownership of the means of production have existed sporadically and in various forms over the millennia, capitalism is of relatively recent origin, making its first appearance in the English countryside some four to five hundred years ago (Wood, 2002).

Capitalism and economic development are closely associated in historical time. Maddison, who has produced the most careful estimates of economic growth over the very long run, calculates that the size of the global economy approximately doubled between 1000 and 1500, tripled between 1500 and 1820, but then increased 49-fold over the next 178 years (Maddison, 2001, p. 46). This period, which coincides with the emergence of industrial capitalism in Europe and the areas of European settlement in North America and Oceania, was clearly marked by unprecedented rates of capital accumulation, technological change and consumption growth. Improvements in living standards spread, for the first time, beyond an elite minority to the great bulk of the population. Indicators of welfare including education, health, nutrition and housing recorded truly outstanding gains in comparison with previous historical periods.

Marx's enduring achievement was to recognise from his vantage point in the mid-nineteenth century that the vigorous industrial capitalism of his era was not simply the result of the natural build-up of scientific and technological advances over the centuries, or of the steady accumulation of wealth following on from specialisation, the division of labour and the resulting expansion of markets as imagined by Adam Smith. Marx looked beyond these apparent stimuli to the growth of manufacturing industry to consider the transformation of *social relations* underlying these changes. For Marx, capitalism's unique dynamism stems from a new *social* division of labour that compels capitalists to compete in markets through investment in innovation and forces workers to sell their labour to meet their subsistence needs. For the first time in history, the extraction of economic surplus from the direct producers could no longer be achieved through political, judicial and/or military coercion, but needed economic means to realise the increases in labour productivity required for accumulation. As he wrote with Engels in a famous passage of *The Communist Manifesto*, the 'bourgeois mode of production', as he called it, '[could] not exist without constantly revolutionizing the instruments of production, and thereby the relations of production, and with them the whole relations of society' (Marx and Engels, 1998, p. 38).

Marx did not romanticise the development of capitalism. The process through which the new social division of labour becomes established is brutal and pitiless. Capital comes into the world, in his famous phrase 'dripping from head to foot, from every pore, with blood and dirt' (Marx, 1954, p. 712). But for all its violence and cruelty, capitalism for Marx was historically progressive both economically, in developing the technological forces of production, and politically from the perspective of the creation of the wage-dependent proletariat capable of organising politically to advance the interests of ordinary people. Moreover, Marx believed that capitalism was no less economically and politically progressive in non-European societies, and he would have been appalled by the prospect of twenty-first century 'anti-capitalists' carrying his portrait through the streets of Seattle and Genoa. Marx, in a word, was an arch-globaliser. 'To the great chagrin of reactionaries', he wrote with Engels, '[capitalism] has drawn from under the feet of industry the national ground on which it stood' (Marx and Engels, 1998, p. 39). Old national industries using local raw materials and selling into local markets were increasingly replaced by new industries catering to globalised tastes, using imported inputs and exporting to distant markets. Cheaper commodities 'are the heavy artillery' that breaks down xenophobia, superstition and ignorance. Capitalism could not be resisted: 'it would create a world after its own image' (ibid., pp. 39–40).

Marx did not write much about imperialism, as his main preoccupation was the analysis of the advanced capitalism of his day that he encountered in Britain. But what he did write, contained mostly in his journalism and letters, was consistent with his view of capitalist penetration as historically progressive. British colonisation of India, although 'actuated only by the vilest interests' and 'stupid in her manner of enforcing them', had introduced modern production methods, the railroad and the telegraph, and in doing so had unified the national market and destroyed the social basis of the old regime (Marx, 1968, p. 93). Britain had unwittingly fomented a social revolution in India, the first in Asia, which would lead to the rise of a politically self-conscious nationalist bourgeoisie, and a propertyless working class in opposition to it. He would not have been surprised that, one hundred years after he published these observations, India achieved independence as the seventh-largest economy in the world in terms of industrial output and was the home of the largest indigenous capitalist class in the developing world (Desai, 2002, p. 236).

What would have astonished Marx, however, was the thought that the most systematic and influential attacks on his vision of capitalism as historically progressive would ultimately be launched not by his many detractors but by his most devoted followers. Although Lenin's early work on agrarian capitalism in Russia endorsed the traditional Marxist line, his *Imperialism: The Highest Stage of Capitalism*, written in 1916 (Lenin, 1966), marked a sea change in Marxist thinking on capitalism and development. Lenin argued that imperialism marked the arrival of a decaying monopoly capitalism bereft of the dynamism and impulse to innovation that had so impressed Marx. Monopoly capital, unable to find sufficient investment outlets for the super-profits accumulated at home, channelled its energies into imperialist struggles to control the colonies where abundant resources and cheap labour could still generate profits. Subsequent Soviet policy, picking up the theoretical premises of Lenin's *Imperialism* and welding them to the USSR's immediate security interests, emphasised the dependence of monopoly capitalism on colonial exploitation, and the resulting identity of interests between advanced country proletarians and nationalist movements in the colonies (Warren, 1980, pp. 108–9).

Western Marxists largely retained Lenin's theoretical apparatus after the Second World War, identifying capitalism with monopoly, overaccumulation and imperialism. For these authors, late capitalism was exploitative and parasitic, draining the developing world of capital and labour without contributing to the development of the forces of production. Among the most influential of these authors was the American Marxist Paul Baran, who argued in *The Political Economy of Growth* (1960) that monopoly capitalists in the advanced countries would block development in the rest of the world to prevent the rise of trade competition, while local elites would waste the domestic surplus on luxury consumption and inflated levels of state spending. Andre Gunder Frank's *Capitalism and Underdevelopment in Latin America* added that multinational corporations would boost profits at home by draining capital from the developing world, although it was not entirely clear why monopoly capitalists would be so eager to transfer capital home given that the absence of profitable investment outlets had set the process in motion in the first place.

For Baran, Frank and the *dependistas* and world system theorists that followed them in the 1960s and 1970s, capitalism is an obstacle to development. In a world structured by monopoly capitalism, imperialism and neocolonialism, the benefits of economic growth accrue disproportionately to the advanced countries. Unequal exchange relationships enable the 'core' countries to siphon off the capital from the 'periphery', limiting the scope for productive investment in poor countries. Capitalism in the periphery is thus distorted, relative to an imagined ideal type of capitalism. It is over-reliant on primary product exports, technologically dependent on the core economies and its domestic markets are stunted, dominated by imported luxuries for the wealthy elite. Development could only be achieved outside of the exploitative investment and trade relationships that are part and parcel of world capitalism.

The irony, of course, was that as these various neo-Marxist, anti-capitalist positions gained in popularity in the 1960s and 1970s, the economies of the developing world were growing at historically unprecedented rates. From 1961 to 2001 the combined growth of the developing economies averaged 4.8 per cent per annum, as compared to 3.1 per cent for the Organisation for Economic Cooperation and Development (OECD) over the same period. Moreover, these growth rates were achieved in the same way that the now advanced countries had achieved them: namely, through rapid shifts out of low-productivity activities into manufacturing and other technologically intensive sectors. The developing countries' share of global manufacturing output rose from 5 per cent in 1955 to 19 per cent in 1986, and their share of global manufactured exports from 2 to 35 per cent. Agriculture as a share of developing countries' non-oil exports fell from 77 to 29 per cent, and minerals from 29 to 6 per cent (Schwartz, 2000, p. 39).

These changes did not, of course, occur everywhere or at the same pace. At the turn of the millennium, China produced 37 per cent of manufactured output in the developing countries, and three Latin American countries (Mexico, Brazil and Argentina) added another 23 per cent. But unevenness does not imply that successful developers were somehow exceptions to a general rule of intensifying underdevelopment. Uneven growth has always been as much a characteristic of OECD economies as less developed countries (LDCs). Moreover, and more importantly, successful developers are heavily concentrated among the largest developing countries. Between 1960 and 2001, the ten-largest developing countries by population grew at a combined rate of 5.9 per cent per year; nearly double the rate of growth of the US economy. These countries also recorded a combined 65 per cent reduction in infant mortality, a 60 per cent increase in male life expectancy and 52 per cent drop in adult female illiteracy over the same period. Given that these countries account for 70 per cent of LDC population, these improvements in quality of life are truly historic by any measure (see Table 2).

Dependency theory was wrong about the relationship between capitalism and development. As Marx would have predicted, capitalist development has initiated a revolutionary transformation of social relations and the technological basis of production in the former colonies including those in Sub-Saharan Africa (Sender and Smith, 1986; Sender, 1999). This transformation has occurred at a pace and with an intensity that may have even surprised Marx. Yet what is perhaps most interesting about dependency theory and other forms of pessimism about the prospects for capitalist development is not their predictive failure, but the tenacity with which its proponents cling to the central proposition that capitalism is an obstacle to development in poor countries despite substantial evidence to the contrary.

Bill Warren, in his seminal book *Imperialism: Pioneer of Capitalism*, explained the durability of dependency theory in terms of the ideological support that these views lend to nationalist movements. In a range of developing countries, the need to oppose neo-colonialism has proved to be an effective rallying cry to unite disparate political factions under one nationalist banner. But, as Warren points out, the ideology of dependency is a double-edged sword: while it has helped to forge bourgeois nationalist movements in the developing world, it could only succeed as ideology by denying the fundamental importance of politically independent states to the development of indigenous

Table 2   Selected development indicators for the ten-largest developing countries, 1960–2001

	Population 2001 (millions)	Real average annual GDP growth 1960–2001 (%)	Change in infant mortality rate 1960–2001 (%)	Change in male life expectancy at birth, 1960–2001 (%)	Change in adult female illiteracy 1970–2001 (%)
China	1271.8	8.0	−77	96	−66
India	1032.4	4.4	−54	38	−34
Indonesia	209.0	6.3	−74	58	−69
Brazil	172.4	4.6	−73	22	−64
Pakistan	141.5	5.5	−40	40	−22
Bangladesh	133.3	3.6	−66	49	−21
Nigeria	129.9	3.1	−11	19	−53
Mexico	99.4	4.3	−74	26	−69
Vietnam	79.5	6.9*	−80	57	−63
Philippines	78.3	3.6	−72	31	−75
Population weighted average	–	5.9	−65	60	−52

Note: *For 1984–2001 only.

Source: Authors' calculations from World Bank (2003).

capitalism (Warren, 1980, p. 185). The presumed powerlessness of the state in developing countries shifts the focus of political movements from concrete policy demands to rhetorical pronouncements on the evils of nebulous world systems, and in doing so provides a blanket excuse for development failures. This tendency remains apparent within recent anti-capitalist movements, which blame development disasters on the World Bank, the International Monetary Fund, the World Trade Organization and multinational corporations while curiously exonerating developing-country governments.

In this context, anti-capitalists and their erstwhile neoliberal opponents in the multinational organisations have much more in common than either would wish to admit. Both have, in their own way, failed to address the central role of states in the development of capitalism. While anti-capitalists see the state as a powerless pawn in a globalised system dominated by external actors, neoliberals view the state as an obstacle to what they see as the natural course of market-led growth that will flourish as long as states do not intervene in the functioning of perfect or near-perfect markets. But this is ahistorical in the extreme. Capitalism has spread by creating an increasing number of national economies and nation states. 'When capitalism was born, the world was far from being a world of nation states. Today it is just that' (Wood, 1999, p. 9). Since its initial emergence in the English countryside, capitalism has always required the nation state to create social, political and economic conditions favourable to accumulation (Wood, 2002, p. 177). Concerted state action to establish and protect property rights, create national markets, support capitalists' efforts to penetrate external markets, and to train and discipline labour is as much a feature of contemporary capitalist development as it was in the nineteenth century (Chang, 2002).

JOHN SENDER
JONATHAN R. PINCUS

References

Baran, Paul (1960), *The Political Economy of Growth*, New York: Monthly Review Press.
Chang, Ha-Joon (2002), *Kicking Away the Ladder: Development Strategy in Historical Perspective*, London: Anthem Press.
Desai, Meghnad (2002), *Marx's Revenge: The Resurgence of Capitalism and the Death of Statist Socialism*, London: Verso.
Frank, Andre Gunder (1967), *Capitalism and Underdevelopment in Latin America: Historical Studies of Chile and Brazil*, New York: Monthly Review Press.
Lenin, V.I. (1966), *Imperialism: The Highest Stage of Capitalism*, Moscow: Progress Publishers.
Maddison, Angus (2001), *The World Economy: A Millennial Perspective*, Oxford, Paris: Development Centre of the Organisation for Economic Cooperation and Development.
Marx, Karl (1954), *Capital: A Critique of Political Economy*, Volume I, London: Lawrence & Wishart.
Marx, Karl (1968), 'The British Rule in India' (*New York Daily Tribune*, 25 June 1853), in Shlomo Avineri (ed.), *Karl Marx on Colonialism and Modernization*, Garden City, New York: Doubleday, pp. 83–9.
Marx, Karl and Friedrich Engels (1998), *The Communist Manifesto*, London: Verso.
Schwartz, Herman (2000), *States Versus Markets: The Emergence of a Global Economy*, 2nd edn, London: Macmillan.
Sender, John (1999), 'Africa's economic performance: limitations of the current consensus', *Journal of Economic Perspectives*, **13** (3), August, 89–114.
Sender, John and Sheila Smith (1986), *The Development of Capitalism in Africa*, London: Methuen.
Warren, Bill (1980), *Imperialism: Pioneer of Capitalism*, London: Verso.
Wood, Ellen Meiksins (1999), 'Unhappy families: global capitalism in a world of nation states', *Monthly Review*, **51** (3), July–August, 1–12.
Wood, Ellen Meiksins (2002), *The Origin of Capitalism: A Longer View*, London: Verso.
World Bank (2003), *World Development Indicators, 2003*, World Bank: Washington, DC.

Child Labour

Child labour has been part and parcel of the development of mankind. Children through-out history at an early age have been initiated to perform tasks that helped the clan or community to survive and that prepared them for adult life. Work was an act of self-actualisation in the most explicit sense. Socialisation and the acquisition of skills and knowledge were a natural process which did not need a special institution like education. The work of children was done within the community realm and did not involve exploita-tion by external forces. Such arrangements have continued in ethnic communities in many developing countries until quite recently, but also in these communities child labour has changed its nature and thereby has become a social problem.

European context

With the development of modern society in Western Europe in the eighteenth and much of the nineteenth centuries, the condition of poor children was seen as a social problem, and the focus in the first reform movement then was on destitution and vagrancy. The solution was to make these children employable in factories and workshops. Employers willing to engage children were seen as benefactors, both in the United States and on the European continent. It was not until the formation of an industrialised capitalist society was well under way that work done by children came to be seen as a problem that needed to be rectified.

Liberal reformers, trade union leaders and radical mill owners started a long process of mobilising and sensibilisation, which in the second half of the nineteenth century con-centrated on regulating child labour. The first pieces of national legislation (in England in 1833, in Prussia in 1939, in France in 1841, in the Netherlands in 1872) restricted the working days in factories to 8 hours below the age of 12 and prohibited it below the age of 9. Much later in the century, child labour was further restricted but total prohibition in all countries took many decades of legal wrangling, economic development and polit-ical struggle. The first US federal legislation, restricted to industries engaged in interstate commerce, was enacted in 1916 but was subsequently struck down by the Supreme Court.

The examples in the developed capitalist countries indicate that child labour legislation was tardy, addressed only the youngest cohort of children, usually excluded agriculture and household industries and was enacted and implemented when the incidence of child labour by and large had already disappeared. The gradual introduction of universal edu-cation, in Europe in the last quarter of the nineteenth century and the early twentieth century, brought all children into the schooling system. It did not do away with the phe-nomenon of working children – children work in out of school hours – but it ostensibly reduced the harmful effects. The work done by children in the developed world after the Second World War indeed re-emerged in a new form: regulated work which allowed young adolescents to take part in a consumer society.

Present perspectives

Child labour as a serious social problem in the meantime remained prevalent in many parts of the world, and interest in child labour re-emerged in the last quarter of the twen-tieth century. It was then looked at as a problem, which applied mainly, if not exclusively to developing countries. From at least five different perspectives it was considered as a 'bad'. From the late 1980s onwards, various national and international actors brought child labour into the political limelight.

From the labour market perspective, children are perceived as constituting a reserve army of labour and as exerting a downward pressure on wages. In the human development perspective, child labour reduces access to education and thereby hampers the knowledge base and productive development of the country as well as the individual prospects of the child in adulthood. The social responsibility perspective is of an ethical nature. Child labour is considered to involve exploitation, alienation, oppression and exclusion from the benefits and opportunities available in society and thus imposes social inequality. In the child-centred perspective, child labour is seen as violating the right of the child to unimpaired growth and participation and as hampering its right to welfare. Finally, from the social order perspective it is argued that in modern society there is a generalised interdependency between social groups and as long as there is a sharp cleavage between the haves and the have-nots, the comfortable and orderly life of the wealthy will be under pressure. Education would help to create a national ethos and discipline and thereby facilitate the cohabitation in a polarised society.

The different approaches have brought together diverse actors such as trade unions, NGOs and governments in a worldwide movement against child labour. The national activities have drawn inspiration from and in turn have given inputs to major initiatives at the international level. Both the ILO and the UN have adopted conventions which have been ratified by most countries and thereby have become enforceable documents. The UN in 1989 adopted the Child Rights Convention, which requires governments to provide for a minimum age for admission to employment. Convention 182 of the ILO, which was adopted in 1999, makes a distinction between light forms of child labour and the so-called worst forms of child labour. The latter comprise: (a) all forms of slavery or practices similar to slavery, such as the sale and trafficking of children, debt bondage and serfdom and forced or compulsory labour; (b) the use, procuring or offering of a child for prostitution and the production of pornography; (c) the use, procuring or offering of a child for illicit activities, in particular for the production and trafficking of drugs; and (d) work which, by its nature or the circumstances in which it is carried out, is likely to harm the health, safety or morals of children. This Convention within a short time span has been widely ratified, and in its wake has led to the ratification of Convention 138, which was adopted in 1977 and which sets the general minimum age for work at 15 (14 for developing countries) and at 13 (12 for developing countries) for light work.

Explanations

Yet, despite the multiple civil society initiatives and the official commitment to implement international regulations, child labour remains an intractable problem. Explanations for the continuing involvement of child labour have been manifold.

Some have argued that childhood is culture specific and that it would be wrong to impose a Eurocentric view of a labour-free childhood on communities where childhood is regarded differently. This school of thought claims to have received official support by the current stress on participation, considering children as citizens with rights, which might even include the right to work.

Others have argued that illiterate and poor parents continue to make decisions in favour of short-term gains rather than long-term investment in education. In particular, neoclassical economists have constructed their explanation on the rational choice theory. Parents are supposed to have a choice between the luxury axiom and the substitution axiom, that is, they can decide to substitute adult labour for child labour depending on their appreciation of their income and the opportunities offered by the labour market. The onus for child labour in this model rests with the poor families, not with the employers.

Another explanation stresses the combination of dire poverty as a push force and the search for a cheap and obedient labour force by unscrupulous entrepreneurs. Child labour is not necessarily more prevalent in the poorest region. For child labour to occur, there needs to be a demand for child labour and this usually occurs when there is moderate to high demand for adult labour as well. Under conditions of a high demand for labour and a weak bargaining position of labour, destitute families may find a way out of dire poverty by taking recourse to child labour.

The causation can be looked at through the prism of variables that usually coincide with child labour (like poverty and illiteracy), but over and above these variables, it is important to focus on the wider issues at stake. Child labour relates to poverty and powerlessness and these basically have been conditioned and continue to be conditioned by the international economic system, whatever name it has. Conditions that keep billions in the developing countries on the edge of deprivation have a fundamental impact on the prevalence of child labour.

Definition

The problem with all explanations, particularly if they are based on a statistical multivariate analysis, is that child labour is ill-defined. Work done by children is not necessarily bad or harmful. Various gradations could be considered, from harmful to beneficial. A distinction must be made between child labour, on the one hand, and activities considered part of a natural process of socialisation, on the other. Child labour is such work done by children, either as wage earners or self-employed or as workers in the household or family enterprise, including farming, that is likely 'to be hazardous or to interfere with the child's education, or to be harmful to the child's health or physical, mental, spiritual, moral or social development'. That definition, which is included in Article 32 of the UN Child Rights Convention adopted in 1989, implies that not all work done by children can be regarded as child labour. To treat all work by children as equally unacceptable confuses the issue; on the other hand to treat all work done by children as a free choice worthy of respect negates the exploitative, harmful and inhuman treatment to which many millions of children are exposed.

Magnitude

A rigorous application of the definition will help to approach many controversies surrounding child labour. Unless one is clear about what constitutes child labour, it will be impossible to agree on the tolerability, on the magnitude of the problem and on the solutions.

An agreement on numbers may not be that important. Excessive numbers have been useful as advocacy statistics and have helped to sensitise the world community to the problem of child labour. Yet, the variation in numbers, which one finds in reports on many countries and on many industries, is so wide that arbitrariness seems to prevail.

Much time, energy and finance has been invested in macro studies, and the outcome, because of definitional complexities, may not be very useful for policy purposes. Many countries do not keep statistics on child labour for the simple reason that something which is not supposed to exist, and often exists within the confines of the household, should not be included in official data. The ILO (2002), however, has come up with precise data: 250 million according to the 1995 estimate and 210.8 million according to the 2000 estimate, of which 186 million are said to be exploited in the worst forms of work. These numbers include two types of child labourer: all children up to age 12 doing any type of work, and children between 12 and 14 doing harmful work. In addition, there are supposed to be 59 million children between 15 and 17 years doing hazardous work.

The ILO figures are useful as an icon. They draw attention to a problem and at the same time indicate the common acceptance that the problem exists, which is a big step forward. The figures suggest that most child labourers (60.1 per cent of the world total) are to be found in Asia, followed by Africa (22.7 per cent) and Latin America and the Caribbean (8.3 per cent). The work participation ratio on the other hand is the highest in Sub-Saharan Africa (29 per cent of the children), followed by Asia (19 per cent), Latin America (16 per cent), the Middle East/North Africa (15 per cent), the ex-socialist countries (4 per cent) and the developed economies (2 per cent).

The data, however, have not always been collected either with a solid and precise methodology or with a clear definition of what child labour is. Very often 'some work' done by children has been counted as 'child labour'. Being economically active is not the same as being a child labourer. Most of 'the economically active children' work for a few hours in their own household or on the family farm, and even those working outside the household in many cases work only a few hours per day. Such work done by children who are not attending school, and by children who are attending school, is not necessarily an activity that falls under the definition of child labour as stated in ILO Conventions 138 and 182 and the Convention on the Rights of the Child. It is striking that the survey instruments on child labour have not specifically focused on trying to identify child labourers in accordance with the above conventions or national legislation. Instead, economically active children and occasionally even children not attending school have been taken as a proxy for child labour.

Solutions

The inclusion of excessive numbers of children in the category 'child labour' mixes the concepts and confuses the policy options. Many children who in some of the statistics have been counted as child labourers could rather be considered as deprived children who have not been enrolled in or who have dropped out of school. By getting all these children into school, even if they would continue doing some work in out-of-school time, much of the problem of child labour would be solved. Compulsory and universal education is considered as the best substitute for child labour, and much effort has been put into making this happen.

A hard-core problem, however, would remain, namely those children living in abject economic conditions who have to work for survival and those children who under conditions of semi-bondage are attached to unscrupulous businessmen. Interventions focusing on these hard-core child labour segments have been of a diverse nature. International political pressure, corporate social responsibility initiatives and consumer boycotts have led to a perceptible reduction of child labour in specific industries, for example in carpets, sports goods and textiles. Yet this has tended to affect child labour in export-orientated industries only. A vast number of child labourers in other industries, in agriculture and in the service sector are unaffected by international pressure. However, activities of civil society organisations and national as well as local governments also appear to have brought about a change in consciousness and practice, which is becoming apparent in a gradual decline of the incidence of child labour in many developing countries.

KRISTOFFEL LIETEN

Further reading

Boyden, Jo, Birgitta Ling and William Myers (1998), *What Works for Working Children*, Stockholm: Radda Barnen/UNICEF.
Fyfe, Alec (1989), *Child Labour*, Cambridge: Polity.
Hindman, Hugh (2002), *Child Labour. An American History*, New York: M.E. Sharpe.
ILO (2002), *A Future Without Child Labour*, Geneva: International Labour Office, 90th Session, Report I(B).
Lavalette, Michael (ed.) (1999), *A Thing of the Past? Child Labour in Britain in the Nineteenth and Twentieth Century*, Liverpool: Liverpool University Press.
Lieten, G.K. (ed.) (2004), *Working Children Around the World. Child Rights and Child Reality*, New Delhi: IHD/Amsterdam: Institute for Research on Working Children (IREWOC) Foundation.
Nardinelli, Clark (1990), *Child Labour and the Industrial Revolution*, Bloomington, IN: Indiana University Press.

Child Poverty

Child poverty should be a much more important subject of development studies than it has been hitherto. This is because: (1) children comprise a high share of the population in developing countries (a third to a half) so reducing poverty necessarily means reducing child poverty; (2) reducing poverty for children reduces future poverty, through an intergenerational transfer of poverty; and (3) some features of child poverty have irreversible effects for the current cohort of children, so there is a permanent pay-off from addressing them.

Global attention on children and child poverty gained huge attention after the UN Convention on the Rights of the Child (CRC) in 1989, ratified since by all countries of the world (except the USA and Somalia) – the most ratified of UN conventions. Apart from focusing on child survival, development and protection, it also highlighted children's agency – and that has been a major advance in the study of child poverty. It also rejects cultural relativism in favour of universal human rights to set a minimum standard of protection and respect to which all children are entitled. Unlike the basic needs literature of the 1970s, which focused on areas of health, nutrition, education and shelter above all others, the CRC emphasised these needs, but also the notion of these needs as rights of children, and obligations of others to meet those rights.

Income has been the normal measure of poverty. While it is fairly well established that the income-poor have a higher than average fertility rate, it is difficult to establish from survey data at least in developing countries what proportion of children in a society are income-poor – or at least that task has not been attempted in developing countries on the basis of household surveys. However, non-income measures of poverty are also increasingly used now. This entry discusses the conceptual issues around child poverty, and then examines the empirical evidence, some policy issues, and prospects for the future of child poverty in development policy and practice.

Conceptual issues

Even national poverty lines based on income have not been used to measure child income poverty in developing countries. Hence, discussions of child poverty have always focused on the other aspects of deprivation – survival (especially to age 5), access to education (especially primary and secondary schooling), nutritional status, and access to safe water and improved sanitation. Although survival rates and school enrolment rates tend to go up with the level of household income, there is not always a complete correspondence between money and non-money metric measures of well-being. For example, child malnutrition rates in India are much higher than the incidence of income poverty (based on a national poverty line).

In the developing world, the discussion of poverty generally, and childhood poverty in particular, has been concerned with *absolute* poverty, whether it is of income or along other social dimensions. In rich countries, however, the focus in regard to income poverty has not been on absolute poverty, that is, the inability to purchase or consume a fixed minimum package of goods and services. Rather, it has been defined as a *relative* state. In reality, this is a measure of inequality, not poverty. This definition, adopted by the European Union in 1984, is the most commonly used definition in industrialised countries. Only in the USA is an absolute measure of poverty used: the official poverty line is set in dollars (adjusted periodically to reflect changing prices) (IRC, 2002).

In the absence of income-poverty figures for children in developing countries, non-income dimensions of poverty have dominated the discussion. Hence, the measurement of child poverty has always intersected with other disciplines: public health, education, nutrition and water/sanitation engineering. The standard measure of child health status in a country has been infant (under one year) and child (one to five years) mortality. But health status is not determined independently from the consumption of food, nutritional status, childcaring practices and the mother's education level. Education is to be valued in itself, but also has many instrumental purposes: for instance, it ensures the demand for health services, and the utilisation of those services when available, thus impacting health indirectly.

In rich countries as well as developing ones, the non-income dimensions of child poverty have also been seen as important. However, the concerns with the non-income dimensions of child poverty in rich countries are somewhat different. Concerns have tended to focus on issues like child abuse and child deaths from maltreatment, child deaths by injury, teenage births, or in the educational sphere, inability to solve basic reading tasks or apply basic mathematical knowledge. As long as issues of physical survival and development of children remain crucial, it is unlikely that in developing countries these issues are likely to become dominant in development discourse.

While demographers, economists, educationists and public health specialists have focused their attention on measurement along the dimensions of child mortality, child malnutrition, child schooling and access to water/sanitation, sociologists/social psychologists have drawn attention to the fact that measurement of these discrete aspects does not capture the subjective dimensions of the child's perceptions of 'poverty', which are complex and not quantifiable. Children need to be separated from their adult nexus, and treated on their own terms – only then can the true scale of their poverty be determined (Feeny and Boyden, 2003). It is also argued that the statistical obsession prevents us from understanding childhood poverty as a process, and ignores how children perceive their situation and what their aspirations are for the future. It ignores the fact that while they experience loss (of income, health, or education), they also retain resourcefulness, courage and optimism.

Empirical issues
Since there are no figures available for the income dimension of childhood poverty in developing countries, the focus here will be on the non-income dimensions. For each dimension, the regions/countries with the most serious problems in the world will be identified, rather than attempting a comprehensive treatment of the empirical issues. The statistics in this section are taken from UNDP (2003), unless otherwise stated.

Education
Of the 680 million children of primary school age in developing countries, 115 million do not attend school – three-fifths of them girls. Thus in India, despite a gross enrolment rate (including many over- and under-age children) of over 100 per cent, many children of relevant school age are not in school. In India, 40 million children are not in primary school, while China, Indonesia, Pakistan, Bangladesh, Nigeria, Ethiopia, Brazil and Mexico account for a significant share of the rest. Also, the survival rate to grade 5 of new entrants is three-quarters in Sub-Saharan Africa, and two-thirds in South and West Asia (see UNESCO, 2003). Reflecting these results, one-quarter of adults in developing countries cannot read or write. And of the world's 879 million illiterate adults, two-thirds are women.

Malnutrition
South Asia has both the largest number of malnourished children for any region in the world, but more importantly, a much larger proportion of South Asian children are malnourished (nearly half) than Sub-Saharan African children (a third). South Asia also has among the largest proportion of babies who are born with low birth weight. Low birth weight is a reflection of the nutritional and health status of women in their life cycle, and particularly of their health status during pregnancy (since birth weight is determined *in utero*). In other words, here too the gender dimension is noteworthy: the nutritional and health status of girls, and of those same girls as they become mothers, is a crucial determinant of the life-chances and well-being of children.

Health
The interesting (apparent) paradox is that infant mortality rates (IMRs) and under-five mortality rates (U5MRs) are much higher in Sub-Saharan Africa than they are in South Asia. While India's IMR is 67 (in 2001), Nigeria's is 110 per 1000 live births. In South Asia, the physician network is much larger and more widespread, so the life-saving medical facilities are better, especially in the private sector, than in Africa. By contrast, China's

IMR of 31 was achieved largely during the socialist period, as a result of the widespread public health system of barefoot doctors and primary health centres.

Births attended by skilled health professionals are an important determinant not only of maternal mortality rates, but also of child survival (since a significant share of infant deaths occur in the first four weeks after birth). South Asia and Sub-Saharan Africa have the worst indicators in this respect. Only 43 per cent of births in India and 20 per cent in Pakistan are attended by such skilled health personnel. In countries that have succeeded in bringing maternal and infant mortality down dramatically, such as China, Sri Lanka and Costa Rica, 89, 97 and 98 per cent of births, respectively, are so supervised. Similarly, the overwhelming majority of one-year-olds are fully immunised against preventable diseases, while just over half in India and Pakistan are.

Water and sanitation

Diarrhoeal diseases are among the biggest killers of children. A major cause of such diseases is unsafe water and poor sanitation. South Asia has succeeded in ensuring sustainable access to an improved water source for over 70 per cent of its rural population; the urban population fortunately has almost full coverage. The African urban population too has almost full coverage for safe water, but there is a sharp difference with South Asia in rural water coverage.

No region in the world has such poor sanitation facilities in rural areas as South Asia, far worse than even Sub-Saharan Africa. In fact, what makes environmental health conditions in South Asia much worse is the much higher density of population compared to Sub-Saharan Africa, in fact ten times as dense. The combination of poor sanitation with a much higher density of population makes for perhaps an unhealthier living environment for the poor in urban South Asia than anywhere else in the world. In fact, one explanation of poorer nutritional outcomes for South Asian children may be their poor absorptive capacity for food, given that diarrhoeal disease (due to poor sanitation and overcrowding) affects their absorption of any nutritional intake.

This sectoral analysis does not reveal whether the malnourished children are also those not going to school or whether those suffering from the risk of premature mortality are also suffering from a lack of water and sanitation – primarily since the sources of data for each type of deprivation tend to be different. A recent study for UNICEF (Gordon et al., 2003), based on the Demographic and Health Surveys done for 46 countries (including India and China) in the 1990s, arrived at composite figures for child poverty or absolute deprivation for the *same group of children* along several dimensions. Children were defined as being absolutely poor if they suffered from two or more different types of severe deprivation of basic human need: malnutrition (whose height and weight for their age were more than -3 standard deviations below the median of the international reference population); children who only had access to surface water (for example, rivers) for drinking or who lived in households where the nearest source of water was more than 15 minutes away; children who had no access to private or communal toilets; children who had not been immunised against any diseases or young children who had a recent illness involving diarrhoea and received no medical treatment; children in dwellings with more than five people per room or with no flooring material (for example, a mud floor);

children between 7 and 18 who had never been to school and were not currently attending school; and children between 3 and 18 with no access to radio/TV/telephone/
newspapers at home.

Children who suffered from two or more of these deprivations accounted for a third of
all developing-country children (37 per cent or 674 million). Rates were highest in Sub-
Saharan Africa (65 per cent) and South Asia (59 per cent); and lowest in Latin America
and the Caribbean (17 per cent) and East Asia and the Pacific (7 per cent). Rural children
faced much higher levels of poverty than urban children.

Policy issues

Just as there are multiple non-income dimensions of child poverty, so the interventions
have to be multisectoral. The more important point is that each sectoral intervention
impacts synergistically with other interventions. This is illustrated in the form of a life
cycle of an educated girl. An educated girl is likely to marry later than a girl who remains
without any education – this is especially true if the girl's education extends to at least a
junior secondary level and she engages in economic activity outside the home. Also, an
educated girl will have fewer children, will seek medical attention sooner for herself and
her children, and is likely to provide better care and nutrition for herself and her children
(Carnoy, 1992). This would reduce the probability of morbidity through disease and
hence the survival of her children beyond the age of 5. Over time, the survival of her children will change the behavioural pattern of the family in respect to fertility and contraception – thus, lowering the overall fertility rate. Smaller household size improves the care
of children, and lower fertility reduces the size of the school-age population. These benefits of girls' education accrue from generation to generation. In other words, in order to
maximise the complementarities among basic social services, it is crucial to focus on universal primary education early on, particularly for girls – but it also assumes that
health/family planning/water and sanitation services are available.

These facts about how to address child poverty in their non-income dimensions have
been known for at least a quarter of a century, if not longer. The remarkable successes of
China, Sri Lanka and Kerala; of Costa Rica and Cuba; of South Korea, Malaysia,
Vietnam, Thailand and Indonesia; and of Mauritius and Botswana in the latter half of
the twentieth century in dramatically improving the survival chances of children and their
educational status had shown that a combination of simple, low-cost measures could
transform the lives of children, and in a generation transform the entire nation. Timing
was all-important in these high achievers relative to other countries. As those investments
were made early in the development process, the demographic transition was hastened;
not just death rates, but birth rates declined too. Those simple measures consisted of: universal primary education, and over time at least junior secondary education; primary
healthcare services, ensuring a nutritional floor for the population. In most high achievers, these policies were state supported, ensuring basic services for all, instead of relying
upon the trickle-down of the benefits of economic growth. Where the role of the state in
public health was not large (for example, South Korea), rapid economic growth ensured
that the nutritional floor rose as first total employment and then wages rose. What was
common was that there was also investment in health and education of the population
before economic take-off. Finally, certain cross-sectoral interventions favoured the status

of women, bringing gender parity in schooling, and thus their greater participation in the labour force (Mehrotra and Jolly, 2000).

Earlier in the twentieth century, other late developers had experienced the remarkable effects of these synergies. The Soviet Union had demonstrated the successful functioning of these synergies, and thereafter, the centrally planned economies of Central and Eastern Europe – with the effect of reducing fertility rates, and thereby improving child well-being.

In recent decades, a number of global factors have tended to act as a brake against the synergies generating a virtuous cycle of human development for children (Mehrotra and Delamonica, 2006). First, by and large, the high achievers had resource allocations to the health and education of their populations *usually* above the average for developing countries in their region. However, economic growth rates, which allow increasing resource allocation to social services, have been much lower in the last quarter of the twentieth century than in the third quarter. Second, most developing-country governments with an overextended state faced budget deficits, relative to GDP, that were high and unsustainable, and thus came to rely on the international financial institutions, which systematically sought to cut total public expenditures with a view to reducing budget deficits. Per capita health and education expenditures were often, though not always, affected (as social sectors were seen by governments as soft targets), resulting in a rallying cry by UNICEF for 'adjustment with a human face' (Cornia et al., 1987). These factors will continue to impact the income dimensions of child poverty into the future.

Third, an unexpected new health crisis arose with the emergence of the HIV/AIDS pandemic after 1980, which has ravaged Sub-Saharan Africa in particular, where three-quarters of the world's HIV positive patients are located. It has not only broken the virtuous cycle reducing child poverty in such high achievers as Botswana and Zimbabwe, but has also dramatically reduced life expectancy through a variety of ways: it has increased hunger by affecting the health of adult farmers, both men and women; it has created 10 million new orphans just as the public health system was already overstretched; HIV/AIDS has killed civil servants and school teachers on a continent already severely capacity constrained, thus debilitating health and education systems. When all this happens at the same time as tax revenues of the state have been devastated by falling commodity prices and resulting high external debt, the cumulative effect on human development is catastrophic. All these interlinked factors have severely compromised child well-being.

Prospects for the future

The prospects for child well-being look extremely uncertain in the developing world globally, except in China, parts of South Asia, and South East Asia. China has experienced dramatic declines in poverty since 1980, along with a sharp reduction in child labour. Despite the upsurge in child labour in the immediate aftermath of the Asian economic crisis post-1997, child well-being has resumed its upward trend in much of Asia.

However, everywhere else the fiscal crisis of the state and many other factors leave little ground for optimism. As we saw, the evidence is that where major improvements were made in child well-being in the developing world in the second half of the twentieth century, the state had a major role to play; hence, the state's fiscal capacity is critical. The HIV/AIDS pandemic is only tightening the resource constraints, while devastating whole societies in mainly Sub-Saharan Africa. At least in Africa, there is little prospect of much improvement in child well-being without increasing the current official development assistance level. Nor is there much prospect of rapid growth without much greater market access to poor countries' products in rich countries. Without these prerequisites, the fiscal constraints of states in most low-income countries will not be relaxed. Much faster debt relief on bilateral and multilateral debt is required in low-income countries than has been available under the Highly Indebted Poor Countries II initiative. Without these changes, the call for 'adjustment with a human face' still has validity.

Meanwhile, within the limits of current fiscal constraints some action is indeed possible. Additional tax revenue can be raised. The countries with the worst child poverty indicators in Sub-Saharan Africa and South Asia have seen tax revenue to GDP ratios stagnate through the 1980s and 1990s, the period of adjustment. The educational opportunities of school-age children cannot be widened unless governments are willing to reduce military expenditures and increase both health and education expenditures. In fact, the evidence from the high achievers was precisely that their defence expenditure to GDP ratio was consistently lower than for other countries. Second, primary-level services in health as well as in education need to be prioritised, especially in those regions where unmet need is greatest: South Asia, Sub-Saharan Africa and the Middle East. Third, perhaps the private sector may have to be given an increasing role at tertiary levels of service, provided that the regulatory capacity of the state is simultaneously strengthened, so that poor families, especially children, are not affected adversely. Since the 1950s, South Korea focused public resources on education at the primary level, thus equalising opportunities for all; the private sector absorbed the majority of secondary- and tertiary-level students – a strategy contrary to that adopted in most low-income South Asian and African countries.

Child advocates tend to underplay the obvious fact that poor children live in poor families. Common to anti-poverty policy in most industrialised countries was the establishment of a child allowance or family social security benefit. Given high fertility rates in developing countries, the likelihood of a child allowance having counterproductive effects are great. However, some minimal forms of social security, especially for those families engaged in the informal sector of the economy – the majority – could reduce vulnerability and indigence. Given the fiscal crisis facing most states, there is no immediate prospect that the right to social security as spelt out in Article 26 of the Convention on the Rights of the Child will be realised at public expense. While health and education investments by the state will be a key to reducing child poverty, innovation in financing social security will be essential to reducing vulnerability (Mehrotra and Biggeri, 2006). So to alleviate child poverty there is not only a need for a revitalised public health and public education system, but also a social security system for poor families working in the informal sector or agriculture.

SANTOSH MEHROTRA

References

Carnoy, M. (1992), *The Case for Investing in Basic Education*, New York: UNICEF.
Cornia, G.A., R. Jolly and F. Stewart (1987), *Adjustment with a Human Face*, Oxford: Oxford University Press.
Feeny, T. and J. Boyden (2003), *Children and Poverty: A Review of Contemporary Literature and Thought on Children and Poverty*, Richmond, VA: Christian Children's Fund.
Gordon, D., S. Nandy, C. Pantazis, S. Pemberton and P. Townsend (2003), *Child Poverty in the Developing World*, New York: UNICEF.

IRC (Innocenti Research Centre) (2002), *Child Poverty in Rich Nations*, Florence: UNICEF, www.unicef.org/irc.

Mehrotra, S. and M. Biggeri (2006), *Asian Informal Workers: Global Risks, Local Protection*, London: Routledge.

Mehrotra, S. and E. Delamonica (2006), *Eliminating Human Poverty: Macroeconomic Policies for Equitable Growth*, London: Zed Books.

Mehrotra, S. and R. Jolly (eds) (2000), *Development with a Human Face. Experiences in Social Achievement and Economic Growth*, Oxford: Oxford University Press.

UNDP (2003), *Human Development Report*, Oxford: Oxford University Press.

UNESCO (2003), *Global Monitoring Report 2003*, Paris: UNESCO.

Chronic Poverty

In recent years the idea of chronic poverty has entered the lexicon of international development both as an analytical device and in policy making. The earliest references to the term in the development studies literature emerged in the late 1980s in the work of Ravallion (1988), Gaiha (1989) and in Iliffe's (1987) discussions of 'structural poverty'. While throughout the 1990s its usage occurred with increasing frequency in the literature on poverty and deprivation in OECD countries, and particularly the USA (Corcoran, 1995), it was not until around 2000 that it became a regularly used concept in development studies. This coincided with the establishment of the Chronic Poverty Research Centre (CPRC) and publications by quantitative poverty analysts (for example, Baulch and Hoddinott, 2000; Jalan and Ravallion, 2000). By contrast, it seems likely that poor communities have long recognised poverty that persists. For example, in Zimbabwe people refer to 'poverty that lays eggs' and in Ghana to 'a beggar with two bags' (someone who has to beg during the season of plenty as well as the hungry season) (CPRC, 2004, p. 3).

Chronic poverty is commonly distinguished from transitory (or transient) poverty. This has analytical significance (see below) and is also important for policy. In a country where poverty is largely transitory, short-term social safety nets, microfinance and skills acquisitions should be emphasised. By contrast, in a country where there are significant numbers of chronically poor people, more radical policies will be needed – redistribution of assets, massive infrastuctural investment, reduced social exclusion and long-term social security (Hulme and Shepherd, 2003a, p. 404).

The meaning of chronic poverty

Poverty occurs when a person experiences the deprivation of one or more basic need(s), capabilities or right(s). The distinguishing feature of chronic poverty is its duration – 'the chronic poor [are] those individuals and households who experience poverty for extended periods of time or throughout their lives' (Hulme, 2003, p. 399). Specifying exactly what constitutes 'poverty' and 'an extended period of time', however remain topics of debate for those researching chronic poverty.

What is poverty?

For chronic poverty, the arguments about what constitutes poverty follow well-established debates within poverty studies more generally. At the grandest level are heated debates about whether poverty can be understood as a set of characteristics that can be examined and measured across populations so that generalisations can be made about 'causes' or whether it must be approached as 'an ongoing process involving an interlinked uniquely structured set of varying experiences of suffering, unmet needs and false beliefs which have harmful knock-on effects for the person involved in the process' (Bevan, 2004, p. 10). The former approach (positivist) attempts to make generalisations about the causes of poverty and produce policy recommendations from such analysis. The latter (critical realist) investigates the processes and social relations that create poverty, rather than mere correlates, but finds it hard to generalise.

Second is the issue of how chronic poverty might be conceptualised and measured. While most writers are now in agreement that poverty is best understood in multidimensional terms (for example, inadequate nutrition, lack of access to clean water and primary education, low income) much of the analysis of chronic poverty, and especially quantitative analysis, has focused on income/consumption poverty. Only in relatively rare situations have quantitative studies used non-monetary indicators. When these have been conducted they reveal that the choice of indicator makes a significant difference in 'who' is identified as being chronically poor (Baulch and Masset, 2003).

Third, and assuming that an income/consumption poverty line is used, is the question of whether chronic poverty is purely about 'extreme' poverty, in terms of the depth of poverty that people experience, or moderate poverty. Intuitively, those who experience extreme poverty at a moment in time (whether this is defined in terms of official, national 'lower' poverty lines or the US$1 per day global standard) would appear the most likely to stay poor for a long time. However, work in South Africa reveals that the extreme and moderate income-poor have almost identical probabilities of being trapped in poverty for an extended period (Aliber, 2001). Given this situation much research has adopted 'upper' poverty lines when assessing chronic poverty. While researchers on chronic poverty commonly acknowledge that this is multidimensional, and have collected qualitative evidence that chronically poor people usually experience several forms of deprivation on a long-term basis, theorising on this issue has been limited. The main response has been to utilise the asset pentagon of the livelihoods approach (Ellis, 2000) in fieldwork and to report low levels of capital in several different dimensions (for example, low human capital because of ill health and illiteracy, lack of access to social networks, no physical equipment).

For how long does poverty have to be experienced to be chronic?
The second set of definitional issues relates to the conceptualisation of time within chronic poverty. At the simplest level, the *Oxford English Dictionary* defines 'chronic' as 'persisting for a long time (usu. of an illness or a personal or social problem)'. In the empirical literature many writers have defined 'chronic' as the period of time separating out the waves of the panel data they are analysing. This has ranged from as little as 2 years (Grootaert and Kanbur, 1995), which seems a relatively short period, to as long as 13 years (Sen, 2003). There are at least three main problems with such an empirical approach to duration – it is arbitrary, it is highly variable across studies and there may be important aspects of time that it fails to consider.

In recent attempts (Hulme et al., 2001; Hulme and Shepherd, 2003a; CPRC, 2004) to think through how time might be conceptualised in chronic poverty four main criteria have been identified:

- when an individual experiences poverty (however defined) for his/her entire life course;
- when an individual experiences poverty for more than five years;
- when poverty is transmitted from one generation to the next, that is, when the childhood that parents create for a child produces an asset base for that child that leads to them being poor later in life (especially through the human capital chain); and
- when a person dies a preventable death because of his/her poverty.

The first criterion, poverty that is experienced throughout an entire life course, is one that has not been challenged. When a life is spent entirely in poverty then 'chronic' seems an absolutely logical description! However, once one moves to the second criterion – trying to specify for how long poverty has to be experienced in a life course that includes both spells in poverty and spells out of poverty – setting a criterion becomes much more difficult. Hulme and Shepherd (2003a, p. 405) proposed a 'crude five year criterion' on the grounds that 'in most cultures five years is seen as a significant period of a life course', that survey waves are often five years apart (aiding empirical analysis) and that empirical studies indicated that people who are poor for five years have a high probability of remaining poor in the future. The arguments behind such a criterion have not gone unchallenged (Bevan, 2004).

The third criterion, the intergenerational transmission of poverty, has been widely accepted and is of central importance as this looks beyond the life course into the ways in which deprivation can be 'handed down' to children and even grandchildren. While there are many elements to the intergenerational transmission of poverty, most attention has focused on transfers of human capital, especially low educational achievement and illiteracy, cognitive impairments and health problems. In particular, poor nutrition and healthcare, *in utero* and in early childhood, can lead to long-term health problems, some of which (that is, stunting) are almost irreversible.

Finally, an interest in chronic poverty means that it is essential to incorporate into the analysis those who die preventable deaths, as they experience 'a long period' of being deprived of all their capabilities for the 'lost' years of their lives. If, as is the contemporary norm, those who have died poverty-induced deaths are removed from analysis and measurement then households whose children die may be 'observed' to escape income (and other forms of) poverty while similar households who manage to raise their children (and thus more nearly achieve the lives to which they aspire) will be reported as 'failing' to escape poverty – because their children have survived!

Spells and components approaches to income/consumption chronic poverty
The discussion so far has focused on what is known as the 'spells' approach to assessing chronic poverty. This focuses on transitions into and out of poverty and is widely held to overestimate transitory poverty because of measurement error, especially when the object of analysis is income or consumption. A second methodology, the 'components approach', attempts to isolate the permanent or underlying component of poverty from transitory shifts, and is measured either by average income or consumption over a period of time, or by a prediction of income based on known household characteristics (Jalan and Ravallion, 2000). The spells approach corresponds more to the intuitive idea of

chronic poverty as persistent poverty, while the identification of the chronically poor in the components approach is also influenced by the depth of poverty. Both approaches provide valuable insights (McKay and Lawson, 2003).

Poverty dynamics and poverty trends

Chronic poverty is a facet of *poverty dynamics* rather than *poverty trends*, and as such its quantitative analysis requires household-level panel data. For example, McKay and Lawson (2003), consider the approximate 20 per cent decline in Uganda's aggregate national poverty rate over the 8 years from 1992 to 1999 (poverty trend). This does not imply, as is often assumed, that 20 per cent of individuals or households that were permanently poor have moved out of poverty, or that all households have become 20 per cent richer. In fact, this aggregate poverty trend masks important poverty dynamics: about 19 per cent of households were poor in both years (the chronically poor), and while almost 30 per cent of households moved out of poverty, another 10 per cent moved in (the transitory poor).

Time, poverty and chronic poverty

The discussion so far has described the evolution of the concept of chronic poverty and, in many ways, revealed just how much further theoretical work needs to be done. One of the contributions of recent chronic poverty research, however, has been the way in which it has highlighted the need for more thought about how time is conceptualised in poverty. Arguably, the advances in poverty theory that have been achieved in terms of examining poverty depth and severity, mapping poverty and in understanding the multidimensional nature of poverty (for example, capability poverty and the Human Development Index) have not been matched by a corresponding understanding of how time can be effectively incorporated (see Clark and Hulme, 2005 for a discussion).

Who is chronically poor?

CPRC (2004, p. 9) estimates that between 300 and 420 million people live in chronic poverty, using a five-year criterion and US$1 per day poverty line. However more recent unpublished work by CPRC suggests that these earlier figures were underestimates. These people are not a homogeneous group. People are trapped in poverty for a range of often overlapping reasons (see below). Some live in spatial poverty traps, including remote rural areas, urban slums, and regions experiencing prolonged violent conflict. Others are chronically poor based on their position within households, communities and countries. Those who are chronically poor based on discrimination include marginalised ethnic, religious or caste groups, including indigenous and nomadic peoples; migrant, stigmatised and bonded labourers, refugees and internally displaced people; people with disabilities; people with ill health, especially HIV/AIDS; and, to different extents, women and girls. Those whose chronic poverty is related to household composition and life-cycle position include: children; older people; widows; households headed by older people, disabled people, children and, in certain cases, women.

Why are people chronically poor?

Understanding chronic poverty is difficult as there are generally multiple and overlapping factors involved and these vary greatly from place to place. The available evidence indicates that chronic poverty rarely has a simple single cause. Rather, different forces, from the household to the global level, interact to trap people in poverty. The most comprehensive attempt to identify the causes of chronic poverty is in the *Chronic Poverty Report 2004/05* (CPRC, 2004), which is an initial attempt to catalogue the main factors. It divides the causes into 'maintainers' (which make poverty persistent and trap people in poverty) and 'drivers' (which cause individuals, households and communities to fall or slide into types of poverty – severe, recurrent, multidimensional – that are hard to escape.

The maintainers highlighted in the Report are:

- no or low economic growth and/or growth that is not broad based;
- social exclusion and adverse incorporation;
- adverse geography and agro-ecology;
- cultural aspects of poverty transmission;
- high capability deprivation;
- living in a weak, failing or failed state; and
- weak and failed international cooperation.

The drivers identified in the Report are:

- lack of access to assets;
- shocks that are severe, sudden, unpredictable and sequential and/or affect many people. Health shocks are especially significant; and
- a weak institutional environment that does not support resilience to and recovery from shocks (especially where healthcare and social protection are lacking, when violent conflict is not prevented or resolved and when markets collapse).

These drivers and maintainers operate and interact at every level – individual, household, community, country and global – so that action to tackle chronic poverty must operate at these different levels and seek to create virtuous circles out of such interactions. These policies and processes, which help people to escape from chronic poverty, are identified in the report as 'interrupters'.

What policies are needed to tackle chronic poverty?
The identification of policies to reduce chronic poverty is in its infancy. CPRC (2004) argues that this will require the pursuit of 'good' general policies for poverty reduction – such as peacebuilding and conflict prevention, HIV/AIDS prevention, slowing down global warming, making trade fair and reducing debt – and additional policies or a greater emphasis on certain policies. In its first attempt to identify policies that would tackle chronic poverty CPRC (2004, pp. 50–62) proposed the following framework:

- prioritise livelihood security for chronically poor people through social protection and health policies and policies that tackle childhood poverty;
- promote broad-based growth and redistribute assets to chronically poor people in ways that permit them to pursue economic opportunities;

- tackle the issue of empowerment more seriously and recognise that this is about political change; and
- the international community must accept its obligation to provide real transfers of resources that are predictable, and the need to promote social solidarity across households, communities and nations.

Conclusion

Recently, chronic poverty has been put on the agenda of development research and policy. Whether it will become a significant addition to this agenda or a passing fad remains to be seen. It is clear that to merit continued intellectual and policy attention much more theoretical and empirical work will be required. To be relevant to policy, a substantial body of robust empirical findings will need to demonstrate the 'value added' by focusing on the chronically poor as well as on the poor or the severely poor. Recent work (Hulme and Shepherd, 2003b; BASIS, 2004; CPRC, 2004; Krishna, 2004; *inter alia*) provides insights but does not yet make a convincing case.

To contribute more to the understanding of the processes that underpin poverty and poverty reduction then theoretical development will be essential. This will involve work to (1) more adequately integrate the concept of time into poverty analysis; (2) resolve how to make the study of chronic poverty genuinely multidimensional, perhaps by relating it to the concept of core poverty and systematically exploring how chronic poverty deals with the 'vagueness' of different measures of poverty (Clark and Qizilbash, 2003); and (3) produce cross-disciplinary work that combines the strengths of positivist and realist approaches (that is, representativeness, generalisability, an understanding of structural processes and specificities) without compromising the integrity of either approach.

DAVID HULME

References

Aliber, M. (2001), 'Study of the incidence and nature of chronic poverty and development policy in South Africa: an overview', CPRC Working Paper 3, Chronic Poverty Research Centre, Institute for Development Policy and Management, University of Manchester, UK.

BASIS (2004), Conference on Combating Persistent Poverty in Africa, Washington, DC, 15–16 November, www.basis.wisc.edu/persistentpoverty.html.

Baulch, B. and J. Hoddinott (2000), 'Economic mobility and poverty dynamics in developing countries', *Journal of Development Studies*, **36** (6), 1–24.

Baulch, B. and E. Masset (2003), 'Do monetary and non-monetary indicators tell the same story about chronic poverty?', *World Development*, **31** (3), 441–54.

Bevan, P. (2004), 'Exploring the structured dynamics of chronic poverty', Well-Being in Developing Countries Working Paper, No. 6, University of Bath, UK.

Clark, D.A. and D. Hulme (2005), 'Towards a unified framework for understanding the depth, breadth and duration of poverty', GPRG Working Paper, No. 20, Global Poverty Research Group, Universities of Manchester and Oxford, UK, www.gprg.org/pubs/workingpapers/pdfs/gprg-wps-020.pdf.

Clark, D.A. and M. Qizilbash (2003), 'Core poverty and extreme vulnerability in South Africa', CPRC Conference Paper, Chronic Poverty Research Centre, University of Manchester, UK, www.chronicpoverty.org/conferencepapers.htm.

Corcoran, M. (1995), 'Rags to rags: poverty and mobility in the United States', *Annual Review of Sociology*, **21**, 237–67.

CPRC (2004), *The Chronic Poverty Report 2004/05*, Chronic Poverty Research Centre (CPRC), University of Manchester, UK, www.chronicpoverty.org.

Ellis, F. (2000), *Rural Livelihoods and Diversity in Developing Countries*, Oxford: Oxford University Press.

Gaiha, R. (1989), 'Are the chronically poor also the poorest in rural India?', *Development and Change*, **20** (2), 295–322.

Grootaert, C. and R. Kanbur (1995), 'The lucky few amidst economic decline: distributional change in Côte d'Ivoire as seen through panel datasets, 1985–1988', *Journal of Development Studies*, **31** (4), 603–19.

Hulme, D. (2003), 'Chronic poverty and development policy: introduction', *World Development*, **31** (3), 399–402.

Hulme, D., K. Moore and A. Shepherd (2001), 'Chronic poverty: meanings and analytical frameworks', CPRC Working Paper, No. 2, Chronic Poverty Research Centre, Institute for Development Policy and Management, University of Manchester, UK.

Hulme, D. and A. Shepherd (2003a), 'Conceptualizing chronic poverty', *World Development*, **31** (3), 403–24.

Hulme, D. and A. Shepherd (eds) (2003b), 'Special Issue: Chronic Poverty and Development Policy', *World Development*, **31** (3), 399–665.

Iliffe, J. (1987), *The African Poor: A History*, Cambridge: Cambridge University Press.

Jalan, J. and M. Ravallion (2000), 'Is transient poverty different? Evidence from rural China', *Journal of Development Studies*, **36** (6), 82–99.

Krishna, A. (2004), 'Escaping poverty and becoming poor: who gains, who loses, and why?', *World Development*, **32** (1), 121–36.

McKay, A. and D. Lawson (2003), 'Assessing the extent and nature of chronic poverty in low income countries: issues and evidence', *World Development*, **31** (3), 425–39.

Ravallion, M. (1988), 'Expected poverty under risk-induced welfare variability', *Economic Journal*, **98**, 1171–82.

Sen, B. (2003), 'Drivers of escape and descent: changing household fortunes in rural Bangladesh', *World Development*, **31** (3), 513–34.

Class

Social classes are among the most fundamental divisions of society. While all are agreed that classes are large-scale groupings of people and are generally identified according to economic criteria, there is considerable contestation over the precise meaning and utilisation of the concept. Marxist definitions and usages emphasise ownership or control over the means of production while followers of Max Weber broaden the meaning to include an individual's market position in the system of economic production, distribution and exchange. However, some definitions blend class with status, thus adding to the conceptual confusion.

The concept of class was first employed in sociological and political analysis to comprehend societal transformations of European societies, especially from feudalism to industrial capitalism. In the post-Second World War years it was extensively utilised by social scientists wishing to analyse the developing societies which had been created under very different circumstances from the industrial powers. Modernisation theorists saw economic growth as the engine which would lead to traditional stratification systems being swept away and gradually replaced by those found in the already 'developed' countries. Following Weber, an entrepreneurial middle class was identified as the key promoter of modern values that acted as the catalyst of modern economic development. Orthodox Marxists also believed that economic development would lead to profound changes in the class structure but instead of a prosperous order stabilised by a growing middle class, they predicted that industrialisation would be marked by the decline of the peasantry and the polarisation of the bourgeoisie and proletariat.

However, both perspectives were oversimplifications and failed to capture the complexity and diversity of what was actually happening in developing countries. For example, there were many studies from the 1950s to the 1970s which ordered populations into strata according to variables such as wealth, income and education. They revealed a multiplicity of classes ranging from landless labourers through to different types of peasants to land owners, industrial capitalists, a middle class, unskilled workers in formal urban employment and those engaged in the burgeoning informal economies of major cities. While these studies provided much data and clearly demonstrated the diversity of classes in developing countries, they did little to explain the process of societal change and often avoided discussion of class conflict (Turner, 1978). Arbitrary divisions based on relations of order were used rather than interrelationships between groups of people differentially located in the economy. One contemporary manifestation of this approach in some developing countries can be seen in opinion poll research where populations are divided into 'classes' according to consumption patterns or subjective self-identification and the views of these different classes are compared.

Incorporating questions of class consciousness into analysis gave fresh insights into the turbulent politics and social changes which were taking place across the developing world. The predominantly rural populations of developing countries began to receive particular attention from the 1970s onwards. Revolutions in countries such as China, Cuba and Nicaragua were frequently explained in class terms involving an intelligentsia leading a disgruntled peasantry. But which classes had most revolutionary potential and which possessed the capacity to promote modern development? Paige (1975, pp. 61–2) saw sharecroppers and migrant labourers as having 'a strong incentive for collective action' and transforming into 'a class-conscious proletariat'. Scott (1976), by contrast, saw insurrectionary tendencies rising among the peasantry as the moral economy of the traditional order was overthrown by the penetration of capitalism and the central state. Wolf (1969) noted that external power was often needed to transform class awareness into class consciousness among poor peasants and landless labourers. Some peasant class consciousness, said Scott (1985), does not involve violent revolts but can be seen in everyday forms of resistance such as foot-dragging, sabotage, false compliance and slander.

The concept of class was also recruited to explain events at the national level and in rapidly growing urban settlements. In Latin America various authors tracked the consciousness of the working class (Petras, 1981) while others looked to class alliances involving the middle class with other classes (Cardoso and Faletto, 1979). Others peered more deeply into the rich and powerful and found 'class segments', such as land owners and producers for export markets, which could form the basis for internal class competition and conflict (Zeitlin et al., 1976; Hawes, 1987). Many researchers pondered the problem of class structure where there was no substantial domestic bourgeoisie. One response was to identify a 'bureaucratic bourgeoisie', comprising leading officials of the state, who did not personally own the means of production but effectively controlled them (Shivji, 1976; Alavi, 1982). In another class-related approach to national development, O'Donnell (1973) sought to explain the emergence of 'bureaucratic authoritarianism'. Different stages of development are characterised by different class configurations, authoritarianism being when military leaders and state technocrats ally with foreign capital and clamp down on class pressures from below.

The issue of class alliances in the development process was highlighted by dependency theorists who approached class analysis from the perspective of an international division of labour, rather than focusing exclusively on national class structures. Development was seen as a process of 'combined and uneven development' or 'unequal exchange' where national class formations performed specific functions within the overall process of capital accumulation. Dominant sections of the capitalist class were located within the core regions of the world capitalist system, while dependent classes were mainly found on the periphery. Within this framework, the local bourgeoisie in peripheral countries were unable to perform the historical role the bourgeoisie played in European development. Dependency theorists labelled this peripheral bourgeoisie a comprador class or a 'lumpenbourgeoisie', tied to foreign interests (Frank, 1974). The possibility of overcoming this dependency rested on achieving national liberation under a local class alliance uniting 'popular classes' such as the working class, the peasantry and the middle classes. However, the developmental potential of such hopes has yet to be realised. Furthermore, by the 1990s, the developmental success of some newly industrialising countries (for example, Malaysia, Thailand, South Korea, Indonesia and Mauritius) suggested that global class relations were not so rigidly organised as to preclude peripheral development. This undermined the dependency claim that development could be accomplished only through the rise of subordinate classes.

Yet, despite global economic growth over the past decade, there has been a widening of inequalities between classes both within and between nations. This has resulted in development studies turning towards the more practical problem of 'poverty alleviation' or 'poverty reduction' – especially the eradication of extreme poverty – rather than the issue of class inequality (Nederveen Pieterse, 2004, pp. 64–6). This has had the effect of de-emphasising concepts such as class, where the explanatory value rests on structural relations between economically defined social groups. This contrasts markedly with gender: gender relations and gender inequality have become central analytical issues.

The poverty-reduction literature in development studies rarely mentions class relations and its more fine-grained focus on locality suggests that the concept of class is too blunt an instrument to understand inequality, let alone poverty. As a consequence – especially at the subnational level – analysis has become more multivariate, recognising that certain social groups within a region experience poverty and inequality disproportionately. For instance, more women than men live in absolute poverty and experience lack of empowerment; certain ethnic minorities (and even majorities) have worse life chances than others (Sachs, 2005a). Age and disability are also related to resource and power distribution within societies (CPRC, 2004). At the micro-analytical level, there has been a trend to acknowledge that inequality and poverty impact on different groups in diverse ways and that class is only one conceptual tool among many in understanding the diversity of developmental processes. Much contemporary development analysis focuses on how the interaction of different variables compounds poverty and inequality.

This greater awareness that class intersects with other variables to produce social outcomes has impacted on the politics of development. Over the past two decades more energy has been spent on the role of broader-based social movements that reflect a multiplicity of social groups and interests. This concept of new social movements cuts across the concept of class. Gender, ethnicity, sexuality, nationality, race and ideological persuasion are elements of this broader framework. It embraces a range of social movements including civil rights movements, the women's movement, ethnic rights groups, migrants, students, the homeless, the peace movement and the environment movement (World Social Forum, 2002).

While class analysis has historically tended to search for political parties that represent class interests – for example, a liberal-minded, middle class-based party for modernisation or a proletarian-based workers' party for revolution – the new social movement literature places less weight on class roots and more weight on local culture and social diversity. According to Touraine (1985), these new social movements are not merely interested in the development of material prosperity and the redistribution of resources. They are engaged in issues concerning personal control of our lifeworld, from culture, work, participation, organisation and quality of life. They also sow doubts about the sustainability of mainstream development processes, while suggesting alternative ways to reshape the future (George, 2004). Unlike most class-based political movements, they 'are interested not in development alternatives but in alternatives to development, that is, the rejection of the entire paradigm altogether' (Escobar, 1995, p. 214).

These new social movements, however, continue to reflect concerns associated with class conflict. Many have targeted transnational corporations through exposing unethical practices such as environmental degradation and worker exploitation. These movements also proclaim that the path of capitalist modernity leads not to greater equality through spreading prosperity, but towards planetary chaos as the ecological 'limits of growth' approach. Thus, while the concept of a ruling or hegemonic class reappears in the new social movement literature and practices, the resistance to this class rule is seen as more fragmentary and heterogeneous than earlier class analysis anticipated.

At the more macro-analytical level of international political economy, where class retains a more central role, the focus has shifted onto the strategies of capital expansion associated with new regimes of accumulation, technological control and cultural globalisation (Rapley, 2004). The advanced capitalist countries have witnessed a decline of the industrial working class and the rise of the service economy, subcontracting and self-employment. These transformations in production systems have reconfigured class relations in 'post-industrial', 'postmodern' or 'post-Fordist' society.

These social transformations in class structure have been closely associated with the globalisation of production. An important innovation in class analysis has been the framework of a 'transnational class structure' (Sklair, 2001). As Robinson (2004, p. 36) points out, the traditional focus of class analysis has always been that 'class formation is conditioned by the history, politics, and culture of respective national societies'. The globalisation of production requires analysing class from a more holistic perspective. The underlying dynamic of this shift has been the transformation from 'national circuits of capital' – where the state performed an important role in regulating capital movements, class compromises and wage rates – to 'international circuits of capital', where neoliberalism encourages global capital mobility by making national borders more porous.

The rise of neoliberal globalisation has imposed a set of new rules and competitive conditions which are increasingly generalised across the world (Greig et al., forthcoming). The success of this new regime of capital accumulation rests on removing the wide range of nationally regulated structures which had helped maintain the post-war class compromise between capital and labour in advanced capitalist countries. Capital now has greater freedom and mobility across national boundaries, heightening labour competition and placing downward pressure on wages and other benefits. This applies to all countries regardless of their level of economic development. According to the 'global capitalist' thesis there now exists a global ruling class – a transnational capitalist class – that attempts to regulate the conditions of its own reproduction through transnational institutions such as the WTO and the IMF: 'The locus of class and group relations in the new epoch is not the nation state but the global system' (Robinson, 2004, pp. 39–40).

This neoliberal globalisation might thus appear to support Marx's prediction that one of the historical roles of the capitalist class is to give a 'cosmopolitan character to production and consumption in every country' and promote the 'universal inter-dependence of nations' (Marx, 1969, pp. 46–7). However, many commentators note that neoliberalism has 'marginalised' specific social groups, thus placing them outside the framework of class analysis. As Hoogvelt (1997, p. 89) points out, globalisation means that many people are shifting from 'a structural position of exploitation to a structural position of irrelevance'. The conditions of those outside the market economy can only be partly understood through class analysis and this reinforces the importance of the multivariate local analyses discussed earlier.

For many who constitute the new global working class, the experience of participating in the modern market economy can be both exploitative and liberating (Kabeer, 2002). The low wages and poor conditions found in global sweatshops must be weighed up against the opportunities for workers – especially women workers – to escape the constraining bonds of traditional ties (Sachs, 2005b). Yet, these transformations are not necessarily inconsistent with Marx's dialectical understanding of the process of class struggle.

Class remains a contested concept in the field of development studies. Since the mid-1980s (Booth, 1985), the value of class as a developmental agency has been challenged by approaches that illustrate how class intersects with other variables, such as gender, ethnicity and identity to compound poverty and inequality. This is also reflected in political developments where new social movements represent a diverse range of concerns opposed to neoliberal globalisation. On the other hand, the process of globalisation has forced others to re-examine the national roots of class relations and posit the value of class analysis at a transnational level.

ALASTAIR GREIG
DAVID HULME
MARK TURNER

References

Alavi, H. (1982), 'State and class under peripheral capitalism', in H. Alavi and T. Shanin (eds), *Introduction to the Sociology of 'Developing' Societies*, London: Macmillan, pp. 289–307.

Booth, D. (1985), 'Marxism and development sociology: interpreting the impasse', *World Development*, **13** (7), 761–87.

Cardoso, F.H. and E. Faletto (1979), *Dependency and Development in Latin America*, Berkeley, CA: University of California Press.

CPRC (2004), *The Chronic Poverty Report 2004/05*, Chronic Poverty Research Centre (CPRC), University of Manchester, UK, www.chronicpoverty.org.

Escobar, A. (1995), *Encountering Development*, Princeton, NJ: Princeton University Press.

Frank, A.G. (1974), *Lumpenbourgeoisie Lumpendevelopment*, New York: Monthly Review Press.

George, S. (2004), *Another World Is Possible If . . .*, London: Verso.

Greig, A., D. Hulme and M. Turner (forthcoming), *Challenging Global Inequality: The Theory and Practice of Development in the Twenty-First Century*, London: Palgrave.

Hawes, G. (1987), *The Philippines State and the Marcos Regime: The Politics of Export*, Ithaca, NY: Cornell University Press.

Hoogvelt, A. (1997), *Globalisation and the Postcolonial World*, Basingstoke: Macmillan.
Kabeer, N. (2002), *The Power to Choose*, London: Verso.
Marx, K. (1848 [1969]), *Manifesto of the Communist Party*, Moscow: Progress Publishers.
Nederveen Pieterse, J. (2004), *Globalization or Empire?*, New York: Routledge.
O'Donnell, G.A. (1973), 'Modernization and bureaucratic authoritarianism: studies in South American politics', Institute of International Studies, University of California, Berkeley.
Paige, J. (1975), *Agrarian Revolution: Social Movements and Export Agriculture in the Underdeveloped World*, New York: Free Press.
Petras, J. (1981), *Class, State and Power in the Third World*, London: Zed Books.
Rapley, J. (2004), *Globalization and Inequality*, Boulder, CO: Lynne Rienner.
Robinson, W.I. (2004), *A Theory of Global Capitalism*, Baltimore, MD: Johns Hopkins University Press.
Sachs, J. (2005a), *Investing in People: A Practical Plan to Achieve the Millennium Development Goals* (UN Millennium Project), New York: Earthscan.
Sachs, J. (2005b), *The End of Poverty*, London: Penguin.
Scott, J.C. (1976), *The Moral Economy of the Peasant: Rebellion and Subsistence in South East Asia*, New Haven, CT: Yale University Press.
Scott, J.C. (1985), *Weapons of the Weak: Everyday Forms of Peasant Resistance*, New Haven, CT: Yale University Press.
Shivji, I.G. (1976), *Class Struggles in Tanzania*, London: Heinemann.
Sklair, L. (2001), *The Transnational Capitalist Class*, Oxford: Blackwell.
Touraine, A. (1985), 'An introduction to the study of social movements', *Social Research*, **52** (4), 749–87.
Turner, M. (1978), 'Interpretation of class and status in the Philippines: a critical evaluation', *Cultures et développement*, **10** (2), 265–96.
Wolf, E. (1969), *Peasant Wars of the Twentieth Century*, New York: Harper & Row.
World Social Forum (2002), 'Call of social movements', http://forumsocialmundial.org.br/eng/portoalegrefinal_english.asp.
Zeitlin, M., W.L. Neuman and R.E. Ratcliff (1976), 'Class segments: agrarian property and political leadership in the capitalist class of Chile', *American Sociological Review*, **41**, 1006–29.

Colonialism

'Colonialism' is very much a twentieth-century word, which only began to be used widely in the post-1945 era of decolonisation and the Cold War. The closely related though usually broader concept of 'imperialism', whose uses were often blurred or intertwined with the term colonialism, is only a little older, dating from the mid-nineteenth century. Colonialism was a word initially and mainly used to describe the then declining overseas empires of the European powers, and was employed mostly by those empires' fierce critics. These highly political and polemical origins continue to colour its usage. Large argumentative literatures have grown up over whether 'colonialism' is an apt term or tool of analysis for – among many contentious examples – US policies in Iraq, British ones in Northern Ireland, Chinese in Tibet, or Israeli in occupied Palestinian territories. In every such case, using the word tends to imply hostility to the actions concerned. Many uses of the tag, in addition, appear to be merely metaphorical or loosely allusive. Alongside this, however, the concept of colonialism has been ever more widely used, in seemingly or intentionally less partisan though sometimes still ill-defined fashion, among historians and other scholars. Belief that colonialism is among the most crucial categories for understanding modern world history has become ever more widespread. One consequence is the swelling popularity since the 1980s of the label 'postcolonial' for what might previously have been called 'Third World', 'developing' or 'less-developed' countries and regions. Some analysts of Asian, African and other formerly colonised societies protest that this perspective tends to overstate the importance of the European colonial impact and its legacies, giving indigenous social forces and dynamics, or elements of historical continuity before, across and beyond the colonial era, less than their due.

Beyond the thorny questions of definition and polemical (ab)use, historians and others have engaged in many complex, often heated debates over the character and legacies of colonialism. These include, centrally, its relationship with ideas about development.

On one side stand a range of arguments which see colonial expansion as having been crucial to the economic development and industrialisation of Britain and other European imperial powers, with a particularly crucial role sometimes attributed to profits from the Atlantic slave trade and New World colonial slave labour. For a later period, a strong relationship was posited between colonialism and industrial capitalism. The British radical-liberal J.A. Hobson argued a century ago that European expansion was driven by the search for new fields of investment. The claim still remains both influential and contentious. So, even after the decline of world communism, does V.I. Lenin's view of imperialism as 'the monopoly stage of capitalism'. Following Hobson and/or Lenin, many left-wing writers and anti-colonial nationalists believed that the modern European empires involved a systematic robbing of colonies to enrich the metropoles. Unlike earlier imperial systems, these modern empires were specifically capitalist creations, founded, shaped and driven by the profit motive.

The other side of the coin is that African, Asian and other colonial economies had their prospects or patterns of economic development destroyed, blocked or distorted by their subjection to alien rule. Colonised regions were typically coerced into becoming sources of underpriced raw materials for European industry and of cheap, often forced or enslaved, labour. They were effectively prevented from developing industries of their own, except in the few cases where such development fitted the needs of their European rulers. Profits were largely repatriated to the imperial metropoles rather than invested within the colonies. Taxes and other state revenues were mainly expended not on welfare, infrastructure or other socially and economically productive purposes but on the military and policing, which meant forcing the colonised to pay for their own subjugation. Even where there was not blatant exploitation, there was neglect: very few colonial governments spent significantly on education, healthcare or social welfare; except in the very last years of the colonial era.

The net result was a pattern variously described by radical theorists as 'blocked' or 'dependent' development, the 'development of underdevelopment', or, after the end of formal colonial occupation, 'neocolonialism'. It left most ex-colonial societies trapped in extreme poverty, their economies heavily dependent on structurally unequal external links rather than being self-reliant. And since the end of the colonial period, the pattern has in many cases been perpetuated by multinational companies and financial institutions, as well as by institutions and elite cultural habits which remain abjectly reliant on or imitative of the old imperial models.

A more positive view of colonialism's consequences for development urges that it was through colonial rule that European technologies, cultures and institutions – the means through which Europe itself had been able to develop and industrialise – were spread through the rest of the world. The result was that, far from being systematically or deliberately 'underdeveloped', almost all former colonies developed more rapidly than they would have done if they had remained independent. Colonial regimes on the whole provided more effective and honest government than pre-colonial states had done: and, indeed, they created modern state structures where these had previously not existed. Imperial metropoles' investment in infrastructure, modest though it usually was, enabled colonial products to reach world markets previously inaccessible to them. Postcolonial economic failures should be blamed not mainly on the colonial legacy, but on the incompetence, greed, oppressiveness or misguided ideological leanings of post-independence regimes and elites. Former colonial status is clearly no insuperable barrier to economic success, as the experience of several East Asian countries suggests. Moreover, this positive assessment of colonialism's developmental consequences argues, for much of the less-developed world the era of colonial rule was either too far in the past (as with most of Latin America) or was simply too short-lived (as in much of tropical Africa) for it to be plausible to grant it overriding contemporary significance.

Neither of these starkly opposed views, surely, takes sufficient account of the sheer diversity of colonial situations. In some, the colonial impact entirely transformed economic and other conditions; but in others had a far more limited impact, or simply continued or intensified already established trends. In British India, while early nationalist economic historians argued that indigenous industry was deliberately destroyed by the British, other scholars suggest that the impact of colonial state policies or of British capitalists has been exaggerated: Indian entrepreneurs, industries and trading networks retained considerable wealth and power. Stressing only the damaging effects of colonialism underrates the power of indigenous activity and initiative. In parts of Africa, especially the most remote rural areas, the direct economic effects of colonial rule were limited, at least until near the end of the colonial era, when European rulers began to pursue far more interventionist policies than hitherto. In some African regions, though, it is of course arguable that the greatest, most damaging effects of European intervention came before the establishment of colonial rule, with the ruinous consequences of the slave trade. Some analysts suggest, too, that colonialism as such was more effect than cause of the wider transformations with which it was associated: that it was the growing gulf between relative European wealth, state power and perhaps above all superior technology – an imbalance already evident well before the colonial empires reached their peak – which made modern colonialism possible, far more than vice versa.

The transformative power of colonialism was most obvious, perhaps, in colonies of large-scale European settlement. In some, white migrants and colonists became numerically dominant (as in Australia, New Zealand and almost all of the Americas), displacing or even exterminating indigenous populations. Such settler communities rapidly became the most prosperous, fastest-growing societies in the nineteenth and early twentieth century world. They have sometimes, not inaptly, been called 'neo-Europes'. Elsewhere – places like Algeria, Kenya, Zimbabwe and South Africa – settlers remained minorities, but politically and economically dominant ones. Their activities tended to result in colonialism bringing more rapid and sweeping economic change, but also more pervasive violence (including, in the mid–late twentieth century, bitter wars of decolonisation), than in most non-settlement colonies.

Modern European colonialism was clearly crucial, too, in shaping the networks of long-distance trade, and world financial and monetary integration. For centuries, global trade was in great measure trade within empires – with a consistent pattern of Europe (and later the neo-Europes) importing raw materials, exporting manufactures. Colonial rule monetised previously barter-based economies, spread the use of its own currencies, or tied others to them. British imperial power, especially, depended heavily on sterling's position as a world currency – and vice versa. It is increasingly often pointed out by historians that the origins of what is now called 'globalisation' lay substantially in the colonial systems of the past.

The links between colonialism and globalisation may be traced also in terms of ecological change and of population movements. Colonial expansion and conquest carried European plants and animals as well as people across the oceans, transforming the ecological balances, the economies and the landscapes of the entire world – though most rapidly and sweepingly those of the neo-Europes. They also 'globalised' diseases previously unknown to the Americas and the Pacific: indigenous peoples throughout the New World and on many Pacific islands were reduced to a fraction of their former numbers, or entirely destroyed, as a result. In parts of Africa, too, the collision with Europe was demographically catastrophic: it has been estimated that the population of the Belgian Congo diminished by nine or ten million in the decades following conquest. In the longer run, though, for those who survived this initial impact, the trend was often reversed. Infant mortality rates dropped, life expectancy increased, some previously endemic diseases were controlled or eradicated, and much of the colonised world began to emulate the population explosion which Europe had experienced much earlier.

The colonial empires' networks of trade, conquest and power were crucial also in inducing other kinds of demographic change. They carried tens of millions of Europeans all over the globe. These were mainly voluntary migrations; but millions more people, especially Africans, traversed oceans and continents against their will, transported as slaves across the Atlantic, the Red Sea and Indian Ocean. Chinese, Indian, and many other smaller diasporas also formed parts of the waves of migration that followed and helped form the tides of empire. And after the end of formal colonial empire, flows of mass migration still often followed routes first established in colonial times, but now sometimes reversed the direction of earlier imperial migrancy; going from ex-colonies to former metropoles, from poor regions to rich, from south to north, from country to city.

In recent years much academic and political attention has tended to shift from the economic or political effects of colonialism to its cultural dimensions. This has included much debate over the ideological justifications for colonialism which Europeans constructed: especially their association with theories of race and with multifarious colonial-era beliefs in the supposed physical, moral and/or intellectual inferiority of colonised peoples, but also over colonial ideologies' ideas about gender. The cultural responses of the colonised are also much studied: the varying mixtures of resistance, rejection, collaboration, attempted assimilation or even mimicry with which conquered peoples reacted to colonial rulers and their cultures.

In all these spheres and more, then, the character and continuing consequences of colonialism remain intensely contentious. At the peak of their strength in the first half of the twentieth century, European colonial powers, plus their offshoot the United States, ruled well over 80 per cent of the world's land, and effectively controlled all the oceans too. That direct physical dominance mainly came to an end, with remarkable rapidity, between the end of the Second World War and the 1960s. But its effects remain indubitably important, both for formerly colonised and for ex-imperial, peoples. And a wide range of critics – especially socialists and 'Third World' nationalists, but also such disparate currents as contemporary anti-globalisation protesters and militant Islamists – argue that the twenty-first century world witnesses not just the continuing consequences of old-style European colonialism, but a new kind of global colonial power headed by the USA and its allies.

STEPHEN HOWE

Further reading

Abernethy, David B. (2000), *The Dynamics of Global Dominance*, New Haven, CT and London: Yale University Press.
Doyle, Michael (1986), *Empires*, Ithaca, NY and London: Cornell University Press.
Fieldhouse, David K. (1999), *The West and the Third World*, Oxford: Blackwell.
Inikori, Joseph E. (2002), *Africans and the Industrial Revolution in England*, Cambridge: Cambridge University Press.
Osterhammel, Jurgen (1997), *Colonialism*, Princeton, NJ: Markus Wiener.
Pagden, Anthony (2001), *Peoples and Empires*, London: Weidenfeld & Nicolson.
Said, Edward W. (1993), *Culture and Imperialism*, London: Chatto & Windus.
Young, Robert J.C. (2001), *Postcolonialism*, Oxford: Blackwell.

Conflict and Conflict Resolution

Conflict research is a relatively new field of academic endeavour. The field has generated a set of terms and terminologies which it is useful to clarify at the outset. 'Conflict settlement' or 'conflict management' means the reaching of an agreement between relevant parties that enables them to end an armed conflict. It puts to an end the violent stage of conflict behaviour. This suggests finality, but in practice conflicts that have reached settlements are often reopened later. Conflict attitudes and underlying structural contradictions may not have been addressed. 'Conflict resolution' is a more comprehensive term, which implies that the deep-rooted sources of conflict are addressed and transformed. This implies that behaviour is no longer violent, attitudes are no longer hostile, and the structure of the conflict has been changed. More recently, some analysts have used the term 'conflict transformation' to represent a significant step beyond conflict resolution. This term, however, more accurately reflects conflict resolution at its deepest level, which implies transformation in the institutions and discourses that reproduce violence, as well as in the conflict parties themselves and their relationships. It corresponds to the underlying tasks of structural and cultural peacebuilding.

Although conflict studies drew on a wide range of disciplines, many of the founders of the academic field of peace and conflict studies identified the roots of violent conflict in the failure of the development process. Adam Curle, for example, the founder of the first Department of Peace Studies in the UK in 1973, came from a background that combined anthropology, psychology and development education. Curle moved from the Center for Studies in Education and Development at Harvard to take up the first Chair of Peace Studies at the University of Bradford, which, together with the Richardson Institute for Conflict and Peace Research at the University of Lancaster and the Centre for the Analysis of Conflict at the University of Kent (a relocation of the original 1966 Centre based at University College London) was to become a focal point for conflict resolution

in the UK. His academic interest in conflict resolution was a product of front-line experiences of conflict in Pakistan and in Africa, where he not only witnessed the threats to
development from the eruption of violent conflicts, but was increasingly drawn into the
practice of peacemaking, especially as a mediator. Most importantly, during the intensive
and searing experiences of the Biafran War he felt a compelling need to understand more
about why these conflicts happened. Violence, conflict, processes of social change and the
goals of development began to be seen as linked themes. *Making Peace* (1971) defines
peace and conflict as a set of peaceful and unpeaceful relationships, so that 'the process
of peacemaking consists in making changes to relationships so that they may be brought
to a point where development can occur' (p. 16). Given his academic background, it was
natural that he should see peace broadly in terms of human development, rather than as
a set of 'peace-enforcing' rules and organisations. And the purpose of studying social
structures was to identify those that enhanced rather than restrained or even suppressed
human potential.

The term 'conflict resolution' was coined in the 1950s by Kenneth Boulding, who
founded the first academic centre concerned with conflict analysis and edited the *Journal
of Conflict Resolution*, published from the University of Michigan in the USA. Boulding
defined the term as having two components: the analytic and descriptive study of conflict,
and the normative element of positive conflict management (the theory and practice of
peaceful resolution). There has been, since Boulding first launched his journal in 1957, a
steady growth in the literature and there is now a base of knowledge which, though still
in need of development, is capable of guiding policy at a variety of levels of conflict. The
momentum for the development of this work came from the realisation that deep-rooted
and protracted social conflicts, occurring most frequently in areas undergoing rapid
processes of development, or marked by levels of serious underdevelopment, were resistant to resolution by conventional forms of power-political intervention (whether based
on military or other forms of coercion).

Boulding focused largely on the issue of preventing war because of what he saw as the
failures of the discipline of international relations to explain why wars occurred and to
develop effective preventive structures. If war was the outcome of inherent characteristics
in the sovereign state system, then it might be prevented in Boulding's view by a reform
of international organisation, and by the development of a research and information
capability. From this capability, data collection and processing could enable the advance
of scientific knowledge about the build-up of conflicts, to replace the inadequate insights
available through standard diplomacy. In the first issue of the *Journal of Conflict
Resolution* in March 1957, Quincy Wright had an article proposing a 'project on a world
intelligence centre', anticipating what has more recently come to be called 'early warning
and conflict prevention'. For Boulding, in these formative years of conflict theory, conflict resolution meant the development of a knowledge base in which 'social data stations'
would emerge, forming a system analogous to a network of weather stations which would
gather a range of social, political and economic data to produce indicators that might be
used for conflict prevention.

Many other key thinkers were responsible for the development of the field during the
1970s and 1980s. Prominent among these was Johan Galtung, whose output since the
early 1960s has been prodigious and whose influence on the institutionalisation and ideas

of peace and conflict research is seminal. He saw the range of peace research reaching out far beyond the enterprise of war prevention, to encompass study of the conditions for peaceful relations between the dominant and the exploited, rulers and ruled, men and women, Western and non-Western cultures, humankind and nature. Central here was the search for positive peace in the form of human empathy, solidarity and community, the priority of addressing 'structural violence' in peace research by unveiling and transforming structures of imperialism and oppression, and the importance of searching for alternative values in non-Western value systems or 'cosmologies'.

John W. Burton formulated the defining core of conflict theory in the late 1960s and the 1970s, centred around the theory and practice of problem-solving and the principles of non-zero-sum, or positive-sum conflict outcomes. Burton spent a period in the mid-1980s at the University of Maryland, where he assisted Edward Azar with the formation of the Center for International Development and Conflict Management. Here both Azar and Burton worked on the concept of protracted social conflict, which became an important part of an emerging overall theory of international conflict, combining both domestic–social (developmental) and international dimensions and focused at a hybrid level between interstate war and purely domestic unrest. This model, which saw the potential for the outbreak of violent conflict to be a result of the interplay of four primary factors (communal content; denial of human needs; state failure; and international linkage – where the conflict spilled over state borders), provided a good basic analysis of the conflict dynamics that characterised the primarily civil wars that dominated the international system after 1945.

During the 1990s the academic ideas which marked this field in the early years matured around the concept of conflict prevention, which became central to the policy-making concerns of the international community. Fifty years after the pioneers of the conflict resolution field first examined the idea, conflict prevention has become mainstreamed as the leading edge of international and multilateral conflict management policy. Mechanisms for peaceful change and systems for anticipation of future conflict issues are now being designed into the security architectures of regional and international organisations through the commitment to programmes of conflict prevention.

Active measures to prevent conflict can be divided into two types. The first is aimed at preventing situations with a clear capacity for violence from degenerating into armed conflict. This is called 'light' or 'direct' or 'operational' prevention. Its practitioners do not necessarily concern themselves with the root causes of the conflict, or with remedying the situation that led to the crisis which the measures address. Their aim is to prevent latent or threshold conflicts from becoming severe armed conflicts. Examples of such action are diplomatic interventions, long-term missions and private mediation efforts. 'Deep prevention' or 'structural prevention', in contrast, aims to address the root causes, including underlying conflicts of interest and relationships. At the international level this may mean addressing recurrent issues and problems in the international system, or a particular international relationship which lies at the root of conflict. Within societies, it may mean engaging with issues of development, political culture, and community relations. In the context of post-Cold War conflicts, light 'operational prevention' has generally meant improving the international capacity to intervene in conflicts before they become violent; deep 'structural prevention' has meant economic and political measures to address the sources of conflict by encouraging economic development, meeting the needs for identity, security and access of diverse groups, strengthening shared norms and institutions, addressing the sources of conflict in poverty, marginalisation and injustice, and developing domestic, regional and international capacity to manage conflict. This distinction between 'light' and 'deep' prevention can be related in turn to the immediate and more profound causes of war.

UN concerns in relation to conflict prevention evolved from *An Agenda for Peace* (UN, 1992), through the Brahimi Report (UN, 2000), to the Secretary General's Report on Conflict Prevention to the 55th Session of the General Assembly in June 2001 which made conflict prevention a priority of the organisation, and where Kofi Annan urged his staff to develop a 'culture of prevention'. Similarly UN SCR 1366 of August 2001 identified a key role for the Security Council in the prevention of armed conflict. A Trust Fund for Preventive Action has been established and a system-wide training programme on early warning and preventive measures initiated. The so-called 'Annan Doctrine', which prioritised conflict prevention, has influenced a wide range of actors to follow suit, and the European Union, the Organization for Security and Cooperation in Europe (OSCE), the Association of South East Asian Nations (ASEAN), the African Union and many other international actors have now declared their commitment to conflict prevention as a core component of their foreign and international policy.

Another area in which progress has been made is related to post-conflict peacebuilding. During the past ten years the literature on post-conflict peacebuilding has burgeoned, while within the conflict resolution field a number of scholar-practitioners have led a revision of thinking about the complex dynamics and processes of post-conflict peacebuilding, including the idea that effective and sustainable peacemaking processes must be based not merely on the manipulation of peace agreements made by elites, but more importantly on the empowerment of communities torn apart by war to build peace from below.

John Paul Lederach, working as a scholar-practitioner within a Mennonite tradition which shares many of the values and ideas of the Quakers, and with practical experience in Central America, has also stressed the importance of this approach, which he calls 'indigenous empowerment'. Both Curle and Lederach acknowledge the influence of the radical Brazilian educator, Paolo Freire, whose *Pedagogy of the Oppressed* was published in 1970, in the development of their ideas. Freire, working with the poor in Brazil and Chile from the 1960s, argued against the 'banking' or teacher-directed nature of education as a form of oppression, and in favour of 'education as liberation'. Freire was a visiting professor at Harvard in 1969, during the period when Adam Curle was director of the Harvard Center for Studies in Education and Development and beginning his own journey towards peace education. Curle's *Education for Liberation* was published in 1973, with strong influences from Freire, and his *Making Peace* (1971) represented his attempt to integrate his ideas on education and peacemaking in the broader project of liberating human potential and transcending violence. For Lederach, cognate ideas were explored and advanced in a series of highly influential publications from the mid-1990s (Lederach, 1995, 1997).

Within the conflict resolution field, then, peacebuilding from below became linked with the idea of liberating communities from the oppression and misery of violence in a project whose main goal was the cultivation of cultures and structures of peace (in Galtung's terms, 'positive peace'). The pedagogy appropriate for this was defined as elicitive and transformative, rather than prescriptive and directive. Thus for Lederach:

The principle of indigenous empowerment suggests that conflict transformation must actively envision, include, respect, and promote the human and cultural resources from within a given setting. This involves a new set of lenses through which we do not primarily 'see' the setting and the people in it as the 'problem' and the outsider as the 'answer'. Rather, we understand the long-term goal of transformation as validating and building on people and resources within the setting. (Lederach, 1995, p. 212)

The approach also suggests that it is important to identify the cultural modalities and resources within the setting of the conflict in order to evolve a comprehensive framework that embodies both short- and long-term perspectives for conflict transformation. The importance of cultural relevance and sensitivity within conflict resolution theory has emerged, partly in response to learning from case experience, and partly as an explicit critique of earlier forms of conflict resolution theory where local culture was given marginal significance. What has emerged then is the recognition of a need for what Lederach has called a 'comprehensive approach' to conflict resolution which is attentive to how short-term intervention, which aims to halt violence, is integrated with long-term resolution and development processes.

This long-term strategy will be sustainable if outsiders/experts support and nurture rather than displace resources which can form part of a peace constituency; and if the strategy addresses all levels of the population. Lederach describes the affected population as a triangle. At the apex are key military and political leaders – those who usually monopolise media accounts of conflict. In the middle, at level two, are regional political leaders (in some cases more powerful than central government in their areas), religious and business leaders, and those who have extensive influence in sectors such as health, education and also within the military hierarchies. Finally at the grassroots level, level three, are the vast majority of the affected population: the common people, displaced and refugee populations, together with local leaders, elders, teachers, church groups and locally based NGOs. At this level also, the armed combatants are represented as guerrillas and soldiers in militias. Most peacemaking at the level of international diplomacy operates at level one of this triangle, but for conflict resolution to be successful and sustainable the coordination of peacemaking strategies across all three levels must be undertaken. In this new thinking, peacebuilding from below is of decisive importance for it is the means by which, according to Lederach, a peace constituency can be built within the setting of the conflict itself. Once again this is a departure from conventional practice where peacemaking resources from outside the conflict (diplomats, third party interveners, and so on) are valued more highly than peacemaking assets, which may exist within the community.

In much the same way that both conflict prevention policy and gender-sensitive approaches became 'mainstreamed' in the agendas of international organisations in the 1990s, post-conflict peacebuilding also emerged as an explicit policy objective of a wide variety of key actors concerned to define their role in the resolution of international conflict. The process of post-conflict peacebuilding as far as the UN was concerned was defined in *An Agenda for Peace* in 1992 and included:

comprehensive efforts to identify and support structures which will tend to consolidate peace and advance a sense of confidence and well-being among people. Through agreements ending civil strife, these may include disarming the previously warring parties and the restoration of order, the custody and possible destruction of weapons, repatriating refugees, advisory and training support for security personnel, monitoring elections, advancing efforts to protect human rights, reforming or strengthening governmental institutions and promoting formal and informal processes of political participation. (UN, 1992, p. 2)

During the 1990s most of the large international intergovernmental and non-governmental organisations published their own definitions and guidelines. In 1997 the Development Assistance Committee (DAC) of the OECD produced its guide on *Conflict, Peace and Development Cooperation on the Threshold of the 21st Century* in which it argued that donor agencies working in the area of economic development should use peace and conflict impact assessments in order to link development policy with the task of building sustainable peace in conflict areas.

TOM WOODHOUSE

References and further reading

Burton, J. and F. Dukes (eds) (1990), *Conflict: Readings in Management and Resolution*, Volume 3 of the Conflict Series, London: Macmillan.
Curle, A. (1971), *Making Peace*, London: Tavistock.
Curle, A. (1973), *Education for Liberation*, London: Tavistock.
Freire, P. (1970), *Pedadogy of the Oppressed*, New York: Seabury.
Galtung, J. and C. Jacobsen (2000), *Searching for Peace: The Road to TRANSCEND*, London: Pluto.
Lederach, J.P. (1995), *Preparing for Peace: Conflict Resolution Across Cultures*, New York: Syracuse University Press.
Lederach, J.P. (1997), *Building Peace – Sustainable Reconciliation in Divided Societies*, Washinton, DC: USIP Press.
Ramsbotham, O., T. Woodhouse and H. Miall (2005), *Contemporary Conflict Resolution*, 2nd edn, Oxford: Polity.
UN (1992), *An Agenda for Peace*, Report of the Secretary General (A/47/277–S/24111), 17 June, www.un.org/Docs/SG/agpeace.html, 5 November.
UN (2000), *Comprehensive Review of the Whole Question of Peacekeeping Operations in All Their Aspects*, Report of the Panel on UN Peace Operations (A/55/305–S/2000/809), 21 August (the Brahimi Report).
UN (2001), *Prevention of Armed Conflict*, Report of the Secretary General (A55/985–S2001/574), 7 June.

Corporate Social Responsibility

'Corporate social responsibility' (CSR) is defined by the World Business Council for Sustainable Development (WBCSD) as 'the commitment of business to contribute to sustainable economic development, working with employees, their families, the local community and society at large to improve their quality of life' (WBCSD, 2002, p. 2). While this now tends to be a widely accepted definition by most companies active in this area, worldwide, it is broad enough to encompass many culturally specific variations – both for companies themselves and for national/local cultures and communities. It is increasingly recognised, for example, that a specifically Northern perspective, developed mostly from Europe and America, may not necessarily be the most suitable for developing countries in the South 'as different actors engage with its meaning and application' in different ways and contexts (Birch and Moon, 2004, p. 19).

Tom Fox takes this further by stating: 'The contemporary CSR agenda is failing to fulfil its potential contribution to development [*because*] it is skewed by the dogma that often limits it to voluntary business activities, by its domination by actors in the North, and by its focus on large enterprises' (Fox, 2004, p. 34). While this has certainly been the case for some time, there is growing evidence emerging from a variety of countries, for example Brazil, the Philippines, India and South Africa (see Birch and Moon, 2004) that, as Fox recognises, 'distinctive local agendas are emerging' (Fox, 2004, p. 30). Nevertheless, it is important to increasingly position CSR as an 'essentially contested' concept (see Crane et al., 2003) – not so much in its core principles, but in the varying realisations of, and priorities given to, the implementation of CSR practices.

The WBCSD, for example, has developed a framework of 26 CSR-related questions covering corporate values and issues, the impact of the company, and its outreach and influence in particular communities. While most, if not all, of these questions, are conceptually relevant for any company operating anywhere in the world, the answers given to them might differ markedly according to social, economic and cultural contexts. For example, question 6 asks a company to ask itself 'Are our activities contributing to the development of a sustainable economy?'. Answering that in the context of a company's operations in a wealthy developed economy like Australia for example, is, without a doubt, going to be very different from answering the question in the context of a rural community in the Sudan.

The challenge, of course, is how to ensure that companies, particularly transnational ones, recognise the importance of cultural specificities with respect to CSR, particularly when most CSR policies and protocols are developed in comfortable head offices of large companies in developed countries, and not their operational sites in developing ones. Corporate concerns like reputation, staff retention and becoming an employer of first choice – all central to the Northern business case for CSR – may well need to be replaced with some very specific, and more basic, concerns, like ensuring a supply of clean water, effective sanitation and a good health system for workers in those countries where such issues cannot be taken as an unproblematic business concern.

Overall, the WBCSD argue that '[a] coherent CSR strategy, based on integrity, sound values and a long-term approach, offers clear business benefits to companies and a positive contribution to the well-being of society' (WBCSD, 2002, p. 6). To do this they recognise the need to move towards 'corporate concern for the "triple bottom line" – financial, social and environmental performance' – but that requires radical change throughout the corporations (ibid., p. 7). 'It is not', they say ' "either or". The new paradigm is "and also" ' (ibid.). As such, the fundamental thinking behind CSR is driven by a recognition that there are opportunities for growth and development – but, more often than not, using Northern economic paradigms. The challenge is to inject into the opportunities recognised by the WBCSD, an understanding, awareness and motivation for success in business and its relations with society, which might more usefully come from non-economic paradigms of thinking that might not have been applied to the corporate world before – at least with any particular consistency; in effect, a new, multiple bottom-line, economics. This will have particular challenges (and benefits) for developed nations, but is much more likely to resonate effectively with developing ones.

CSR and new economics thinking
Issues of sustainability, in some form or another, have been on the world agenda, in developed economies at least, for some considerable time, and they come in the wake of

a long history of thinking and writing (though not very deeply embedded in most corporate cultures) in corporate environmental and social responsibility and (more recently) corporate citizenship. Increasingly now, especially within a European context, these issues are being positioned by some people (though not all by any means) within the context of 'the new economy' understood as 'no less than a socio-economic revolution that impacts on all aspects of our relationships with others and ourselves' (Zadek et al., 2000, p. 5).

At the heart of this call for a new economics, is a much deeper understanding of the importance of stakeholder dialogue and influence. CSR, as part of this new economics, therefore, 'implies a strategy that moves from a focus on short-term transaction to longer-term values-based relationships with these stakeholders'. According to Zadek, and others, this 'is exactly what one would expect in the New Economy, where loyalty will be based on a company's ability to build a sense of shared values and mission with key stakeholders' (Zadek et al., 2000, p. 8). The challenge, of course, for developing countries, in particular, is the power differential between companies and community which often makes it very difficult for NGOs and others to position themselves, in the same way as powerful NGOs in developed countries, as potential 'key' stakeholders that companies should not only engage with but also listen to, and act upon, that engagement.

Just as companies now have to engage with multiple bottom lines as a clear and definable expression of CSR – economic, social, environmental, cultural and so on – without always receiving clear guidance as to how these multiple bottom lines function effectively and sustainably in a modern business context, so too they need to increasingly engage with multiple communities, diverse voices, and a very wide range of social and cultural power differentials in those communities. Just as there are increasing calls, from both within and outside of business, to more fully integrate these bottom lines, with serious challenges being made upon leaders and managers to more effectively report, both internally and to the wider public, on the company's CSR performance against these bottom lines, so too there are increasing calls from developing countries for companies to recognise, disaggregate and maintain, cultural and community diversity.

Serious, sustained and significant cultural change needs to take place within the corporate world, and for that change to be understood and recognised by government and community, in both developed and developing economies – but in differing, culturally specific, ways. This change is not simply to satisfy some call from left field either to make business more accountable, or to satisfy some new ageist whim for more environmentally and socially responsible companies. This change is designed to increase the rewards for all, including financial profit, in a world that must seek sustainable success for more and more people if fewer and fewer people are to be disadvantaged and marginalised.

The key to successful CSR, therefore, lies in recognising cultural diversity and difference so that there is not a single paradigm (Western/Northern in its orientation for example) applicable to all societies. As Benjamin Goldsmith makes clear in his analysis of CSR and the importance of a positive reputation in India, 'Western and other non-Indian values do not necessarily translate directly to Indian society. Building the valuable business asset, which a positive reputation is in India, means understanding a lot about Indian culture, history, business, bureaucracy, and politics' (Goldsmith, 1997, p. 327). This is true of any culture, but what we need to do, more and more, in the field of CSR, is to test out the validity of its existent, predominantly 'developed' point of view for its effectiveness in establishing culturally specific and localised realisations of CSR.

For example, while little might have saved Union Carbide's disastrous time in India, after the release of gas at its Bhopal plant killed almost 7000 people (more than double this if unofficial figures are accepted), in retrospect Union Carbide could have better recognised the need to build a more positive reputation for the company in order to better protect it from such crises (see Goldsmith, 1997, p. 336). Similarly had the Enron Corporation, for example, taken more notice of such things, especially stakeholder inclusivity, cultural difference, accountability and transparency, their multi-billion dollar enterprise in the power plant project in Dhabol, India, in 1995 might not have failed as it did (ibid., p. 329). Similarly, KFC, despite recognising cultural difference and including vegetarian food on its menu when it opened its first franchised store in Bangalore in 1995, failed to adequately recognise a serious social issue in the guise of local resistance to its sourcing policies from large-scale farmers (ibid., p. 332). McDonald's has learned from such examples, however, using mutton rather than beef in its burgers and by 'adopting and projecting an attitude of openness and commitment', spending three years pre-launch in preparing local suppliers to meet franchise standards (ibid., p. 334).

It becomes clear, from examples like this, that everyone in a company from the board to casual staff must recognise that their business is a significant social enterprise shaping community values, attitudes and cultures, and as such the role of the directors, in particular, hands-off though they may well be from the daily management of the company, needs to become more about positioning the company as a public culture, and not, as has happened so often in the past, maintaining its privacy (as Enron did) and therefore creating unnecessary distance from the community at large. In this way, business becomes an integral part of the building of society, and in that respect, reorientating business as a public culture has significant synergies with contemporary theories of developmental economics, especially the people-centred and human well-being policies of Mahbub ul Haq (1995, 2000) and the need for an integrated approach to development in the work of Amartya Sen (1999), particularly the importance he attaches to the role of public discussion as a vehicle of social change and economic progress.

Peter Schwartz and Blair Gibb give a good, positive, example of this in their book *When Good Companies Do Bad Things* (1999), when they discuss the Indian division of Unilever, Hindustan Lever, recognising the importance of development projects as 'a business necessity' (ibid., p. 87). They describe the establishment in 1976 by Hindustan Lever of a long-term Integrated Rural Development Programme, involving the lives, health and income levels in 600 rural villages while, as a result of this development project, dramatically increasing their business in milk production. As McIntosh et al. (1998) make clear, what made Hindustan Lever successful in this was 'a deep knowledge of village culture' as each year the company sends 50 of its MBA intake to live in the villages for several weeks, often experiencing rural life for the very first time (ibid., p. 217).

In conclusion, then, as I have tried to demonstrate here, CSR cannot be separated from an understanding of the moral basis of management as a means of business significantly contributing to the development of sustainable society, through a more developed understanding of highly diverse cultures and communities, otherwise developing economies will continue to be trapped in an old, Northern-driven, economics, continuing a situation where long-term social deterioration is sacrificed for short-term economic growth (see Clark and Roy, 1997, p. 29).

DAVID BIRCH

References

Birch, David and Jeremy Moon (eds) (2004), Special issue on 'Corporate Social Responsibility in Asia', *Journal of Corporate Citizenship*, **13**, 18–23.

Clark, Cal and K.C. Roy (1997), *Comparing Development Patterns in Asia*, Boulder, CO and London: Lynne Rienner.

Crane, A., D. Matten and J. Moon (2003), 'Can corporations be citizens?', Working Paper 13, International Centre for Corporate Social Responsibility, University of Nottingham, UK.

Fox, Tom (2004), 'Corporate social responsibility and development: in quest of an agenda', *Development*, **47** (3), 29–36.

Goldsmith, Benjamin E. (1997), 'Corporate citizenship in India: multinational corporate experiences and best practice', in Noel M. Tichy, Andrew R. McGill and Lynda St. Clair (eds), *Corporate Global Citizenship: Doing Business in the Public Eye*, San Francisco: New Lexington Press, pp. 326–47.

Haq, Mahbub ul (1995), *Reflections on Human Development*, Oxford: Oxford University Press.

Haq, Mahbub ul (2000), *Human Development in South Asia 1999*, Oxford; Oxford University Press.

McIntosh, Malcolm, Deborah Leipziger, Keith Jones and Gill Coleman (1998), *Corporate Citizenship: Successful Strategies for Responsible Companies*, London: Financial Times & Pitman Publishing.

Schwartz, Peter and Blair Gibb (1999), *When Good Companies Do Bad Things: Responsibility and Risk in an Age of Globalization*, New York: John Wiley & Sons.

Sen, Amartya (1999), *Development as Freedom*, New York: Knopf.

WBCSD (2002), *Corporate Social Responsibility: The WBCSD's Journey*, Geneva: World Business Council for Sustainable Development Publications.

Zadek, S., N. Hojengard and P. Raynard (2000), *The New Economy of Corporate Citizenship*, Copenhagen: The Copenhagen Centre.

Cost–Benefit Analysis for Development

Introduction

The starting-point for cost–benefit analysis (CBA) in a development context is that a quantitative assessment of project costs and benefits is important and that a financial perspective alone will not capture the gains to society at large (the so-called 'economic effects'). The aim of this entry is to set out briefly the underlying theoretical framework of CBA, which has remained basically unchanged since the development of 'modern cost–benefit methods' (Irvin, 1978) and then to explain how recent developments have modified the practice of CBA. By practice we mean the application of CBA techniques in project (or more generally in policy) analysis by either international or bilateral donor agencies or the use of such techniques by national governments.

Current applications of CBA

The seminal works in the literature on CBA were written in the late 1960s and early 1970s (Little and Mirrlees, 1969, 1974; UNIDO, 1972; and Squire and van der Tak, 1975). These set out how costs and benefits for development projects could be compared systematically and incorporated in a measure of project worth. The close timing of the various contributions was not accidental. Aid flows, which were then largely project based, had become quantitatively significant, but in the era of what were perceived as widespread policy distortions, there were doubts concerning the effectiveness of conventional appraisal techniques in assessing the full economic impact of projects. Expectations were high that a rational system of appraisal based on this literature could be established.

The original literature was concerned primarily with an assessment of the efficiency of projects in tradable sectors, principally industry and agriculture, where aid financing was then important. In the era of import substitution there was strong evidence that many projects were only financially viable because of the shelter granted by trade protection. By using world prices as the measure of value for goods that are tradable on the world market, the distortionary impact of protection can be stripped away and projects assessed in terms of trade efficiency criteria. Also at that time controls in various markets (such as interest rate ceilings or fixed exchange rates) created macro prices that deviated, sometimes very significantly, from opportunity costs. The literature devoted considerable attention to ways of estimating 'true' economic values (usually termed 'shadow prices') for key parameters, such as the discount rate for capital and the shadow price of foreign exchange.

As a result of major policy shifts neither of these concerns are anything like as pressing today. Aid funds now rarely go directly to tradable sectors, which are seen as the preserve of the private sector. This means that project CBA must be applied in the sectors of physical and social infrastructure, which are now the principal recipients of aid funds. For these non-traded activities the simple 'world price valuation' principle no longer applies, and each branch of infrastructure poses its unique challenge for benefit valuation. In addition, structural adjustment and related reforms have meant that while some macro distortions may still remain, their quantitative significance has been much reduced for many countries.

A few years ago two of the principal authors of the original CBA methodology reflected on the neglect of this approach in the World Bank, the institution that had been most active in promoting their work initially (see Little and Mirrlees, 1994). However, their position was a little purist in that while the full procedures of their method were never applied, principally the weighting system for distinguishing between saved and consumed income and between income going to different social groups a simplified form of CBA, involving use of world prices for traded goods, an adjustment to the domestic price of non-tradable inputs and the application of a shadow wage for surplus labour, has been used by most donors and even by some developing-country governments.

Today the primary focus of CBA is in the infrastructure field, broadly defined. This is true both for donors and for national governments, where the latter undertake economic assessments of projects. Key issues are benefit valuation in these sectors, the financial sustainability of such projects, the distribution of project benefits and costs (particularly the poverty impact), and any environmental consequences. The last two concerns have assumed increased importance in recent years with the reassessment of aid priorities that followed the adjustment reforms of the 1980s.

Applied welfare economics
Although the current policy environment differs significantly from that of earlier decades CBA methodology is sufficiently flexible to cope with the demands of the new agenda. CBA is simply applied welfare economics and the work of Little and Mirrlees and others, although set out in a superficially different manner, is in this tradition; see Curry and Weiss (2000) and Londero (2003) for surveys. Put simply, projects can be seen as disturbances to an economy that affect households, enterprises and the government. Project

output that is tangible and marketable can in principle have three possible effects – at the simplest level it may simply affect foreign trade – by raising exports or replacing imports. This is the traded good case noted above. Alternatively if the good is non-traded, in the sense that project output is not exported or imported or a close substitute for goods that are, then it may either add to consumption (the demand margin) or displace from the market goods supplied by another enterprise (the supply margin). Each of these three cases gives a different basis for valuation. In the traded good case the world price of the item defines its value. At the demand margin, value is determined by what consumers are willing to pay for an additional unit of the good. At the supply margin, when other suppliers are displaced by project output, valuation is by costs saved. The common unifying theoretical thread is that in a perfect market with no trade barriers each definition of value would be equal. In real-world conditions there will be wedges, sometimes large ones, between these three bases for value, which practical CBA has to estimate.

In practical project applications in sectors such as transport, power and water, the concepts of demand margin (for incremental consumption of a good) and supply margin (where costs of other producers are saved) are used widely to obtain estimates of tangible economic benefits. Application to social sectors is much more limited. For education projects, rate of return estimates are sometimes derived using measures of willingness to pay for education based on earnings differentials associated with additional years of study. This approach is far from routine, however, partly because education has external benefits to society at large, which will not be picked up in this calculation. Where benefit valuation is controversial a version of cost-effectiveness is being applied increasingly. This takes as given the desirability of an activity and asks how can it be done at the least cost. For example, for health projects it is rare to see benefits valued because of the controversy attached to valuations of life and reductions in illness. These benefits are quantified in non-monetary terms based on healthy years of life saved (often adjusted for illness in the disability-adjusted life years or DALYs). Costs per year of life saved can then be compared across different health projects (see ADB, 2000).

Choosing the numeraire: does it matter?

Initially much theoretical debate focused on the unit or numeraire in which to express project costs and benefits. If we weight incomes equally for all then the choice is simply one of measuring income in a particular currency and in domestic or world prices (these prices for equivalent goods will differ whenever there is some form of protection via tariffs or controls). The Little and Mirrlees solution, followed by much of the subsequent literature, was to use local currency and world prices (units of so-called 'border rupees'). However, provided that identical assumptions are used, choice of world or domestic prices or foreign or local currency for the unit in which all costs and benefits are measured would make no difference to the analysis. While the world price–local currency unit tended to dominate practice in the 1970s and 1980s (for example, the World Bank material used world prices, as did the British government publication ODA, 1988), more recently some disadvantages with its use have become more apparent. This is most obvious once there is a distributional analysis tracing the gainers and losers from a project as it can be confusing to conduct this when economic calculations are in world prices. This is because the procedure for distributional analysis involves combining two sets of income flows – one from the financial arrangements of a project (tracing profits, taxes, subsidies and so on) and the other arising from externalities, policy controls or market imperfections. If these latter economic impacts are measured at world prices they cannot be added directly to the income flows from the financial analysis, since for consistency both types of income flow must be in the same units. Although the flows can be made comparable, the procedure is intuitively clearer and simpler if economic calculations are done initially in domestic prices. Also a problem arises in the treatment of real exchange rate adjustments. This can be handled directly in domestic price units by adjusting the shadow price of the foreign exchange parameter for any deviation of the existing real rate from its long-run (over the life of project) equilibrium level. In a world price system an equivalent adjustment to the standard conversion factor (SCF), which is the parameter used to adjust non-traded to traded prices, would be required and there are ambiguities surrounding the definition of the SCF (for direct equivalence with a domestic price calculation the SCF should be a weighted average of world to domestic prices for traded goods).

Distribution effects and poverty impact

The original literature showed how one could formally weight income changes for different groups (with the poor having weights of above and the rich weights below unity). The aim was to bias project selection towards the poor by boosting the indicators of project worth in this way. For a variety of reasons this approach was never formally applied. Instead, today the same aim is to be achieved by targeting some projects directly at the poor. In so far as this is incorporated in CBA this is done by estimating how a project's economic net present value, that is the net income change for an economy the project creates, is distributed between gaining and losing groups. Those in various groups (like consumers, workers or investors) who are below the poverty line can in turn be identified, so that the income changes to those who are poor can be estimated. In principle it is possible to do this with no more than the data from the original economic rate of return calculation, although in the absence of further information some of the groups involved may be very aggregate. The formal methodology for tracing distribution effects follows UNIDO (1972), but ADB (2001) gives practical guidance on how this might be done. This approach is potentially useful and clearly fits in with current donor priorities. It will only work, however, where all project effects can be expressed in monetary terms. Further, in some important sectors the full distributional impact may be very difficult to establish. The benefits from a road project are a good example. Some will accrue to hauliers if their costs fall; some will accrue to producers if additional output is induced by the road; some will accrue to consumers if prices are reduced through falling transport costs or extra production; and some will accrue to workers if employment expands. Disentangling these effects will be extremely complex and for many projects would require a major research study. Finally, even when an estimate of gains to the poor can be derived, there is the further complication of what is assumed for the without-project counterfactual and how the poor would have been affected if the funds involved had instead been spent on the notional marginal project.

Environmental externalities and intangibles

From the outset the CBA literature was quick to acknowledge the possibility of both external and intangible effects, but it was also eager to diminish expectations that they could be quantified easily. Current thinking emphasises the need to build into appraisal an awareness of environmental impacts and where possible to quantify these as either costs or benefits. Progress has been made, but we are still a considerable way from a routine application of environmental valuation. In principle, the welfare economics approach of willingness to pay to receive environmental benefits (at the demand margin) or to accept compensation for environmental cost or cost savings on alternative forms of environmental treatment displaced by a new project (at the supply margin) provide the conceptual basis for valuation. In the absence of a rigorous assessment, value transfer is one short-cut approach applied in practice, where, for example, damage figures estimated in one context are applied in another. A further issue that has been debated intensely is the question of discount rate for environmental effects. Given that environmental impacts, by their nature, are generally long term, there is acknowledgement that some special adjustment is required to deal with their long-run impacts. Recent theoretical insights provide a rationale for using discount rates that fall over time, so future benefits and costs are valued more highly than they would be with a constant rate (Pearce et al., 2003).

For some projects there may be effects that defy sensible quantification (so-called 'intangibles'); for example, impact on wildlife, on community lifestyles or on culture. CBA should not attempt to measure the intrinsically unmeasurable and should set out both tangible quantifiable effects and a description of other intangible consequences. The ultimate decision takers can then make their own subjective trade-offs between these.

Conclusions

Project CBA is still relevant and useful as a separate line of study, as there remain a number of reasons why financial calculations alone may be misleading as a guide to the impact of a project on the economy. Today these reasons are much less to do with macroeconomic distortions than with the absence or limitations of markets for a range of infrastructure activity. In addition, poverty and environmental issues that are central to the current development agenda remain to be considered at the project level.

JOHN WEISS

References

Asian Development Bank (2000), *Handbook for the Economic Analysis of Health Sector Projects*, Manila: ADB.
Asian Development Bank (2001), *Handbook for Integrating Poverty Impact Assessment in the Economic Analysis of Projects*, Manila: ADB.
Curry, S. and J. Weiss (2000), *Project Analysis in Developing Countries*, London and Basingstoke: Macmillan.
Irvin, G. (1978), *Modern Cost–Benefit Methods*, London and Basingstoke: Macmillan.
Little, I. and J. Mirrlees (1969), *Manual of Industrial Project Analysis in Developing Countries*, vol. 2, Paris: OECD.
Little, I. and J. Mirrlees (1974), *Project Appraisal and Planning for Developing Countries*, London: Heinemann Educational.
Little, I. and J. Mirrlees (1994), 'The costs and benefits of analysis: project appraisal and planning twenty years on', in R. Layard and S. Glaister (eds), *Cost Benefit Analysis*, 2nd edn, Cambridge: Cambridge University Press, pp. 199–231.
Londero, E. (2003), *Shadow Prices for Project Appraisal: Theory and Practice*, Cheltenham, UK and Northampton, MA, USA: Edward Elgar.
Overseas Development Agency (ODA) (1988), *Appraisal of Projects in Developing Countries. A Guide for Economists*, 3rd edn, London: HMSO.
Pearce, D., B. Groom, C. Hepburn and P. Khounduri (2003), 'Valuing the future: recent advances in social discounting', *World Economics*, **4** (2), 121–41.

Squire, L. and H. van der Tak (1975), *Economic Analysis of Projects*, Baltimore, MD: Johns Hopkins University Press.
United Nations Industrial Development Organization (UNIDO) (1972), *Guidelines for Project Evaluation*, New York: United Nations.

Crisis Management

The dictionary definition of the term 'crisis' indicates a decisive moment or turning-point, usually associated with a time of great danger or difficulty. In this entry, 'crisis' is treated as synonymous with 'emergency' and 'disaster'. There are other meanings, associated for example with the economic strictures of global capitalism or the degradation of the world's environment, but the most immediate sense of the term is that of sudden disaster, which of course may nevertheless have economics or environmental depredation among its root causes. This entry will describe both the worldwide impacts of disaster and the current system of aid and relief. It will examine the role of vulnerability and marginalisation in worsening the plight of populations afflicted by catastrophe and will discuss some of the dilemmas and pitfalls of providing aid.

At least 80 per cent of the impacts of natural disaster, and an even higher proportion of casualties, occur in the developing world. The cost of disaster may be low relative to what it is in the Western countries and Japan, but relative to national wealth it tends to be

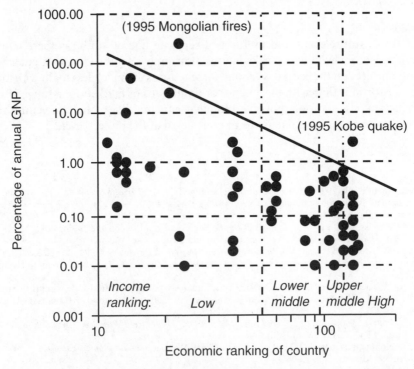

Figure 1   Economic impact of major disasters: 1990s worldwide data on 58 events

much greater. Thus a major hurricane, flood or earthquake may easily cause damage worth more than 2 per cent of a poor country's annual GNP. Very occasionally, as in the case of the Mongolian environmental fires of 1995, it may cost more than the entire year's GNP, whereas in the fully developed countries few disasters cost more than 0.5 per cent of GNP (Figure 1). The poorer countries thus bear a disproportionate burden of catastrophe. They have also acquired a marked dependency on the world relief system (Figure 2), which has grown considerably in recent years. At the same time, the number of disasters and emergencies has increased, spurred by growing inequality and poverty, changing climate and the proliferation of local conflicts. Hence, more than 150 million people are affected by disaster each year, most of them in poor countries.

Besides natural and technological disasters, in the world today about 25 complex emergencies are in progress (Figure 3). These are protracted crisis situations characterised by the breakdown of social and economic order, civil administration and general security. In such situations, emergency relief operations and development initiatives must be carried out under conditions of military instability, and success is unlikely to be durable until peace breaks out, order is restored, civil administration is built up and regular commercial activities take place again.

Meanwhile, in response to growing needs, humanitarian aid organisations have proliferated. In Dhaka, capital of Bangladesh, where it is estimated that a quarter of the 9 million inhabitants have been driven to the city by natural disaster, almost a thousand

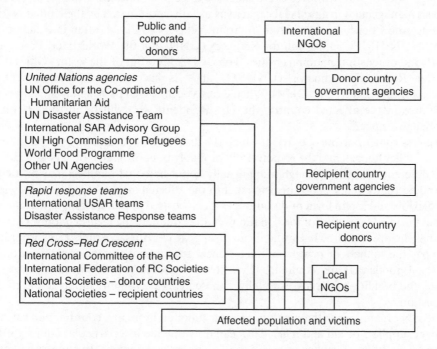

Source: Partly after Borton (1993).

Figure 2 The international disaster relief system

Figure 3   Complex emergencies active in early 2004

international NGOs are at work, representing a wide spectrum of interests and competencies. Whereas the larger and older agencies, such as Oxfam and Save the Children, have built up considerable expertise in managing emergencies, many of the smaller and younger ones are less knowledgeable and capable. All suffer from the training deficit, in that high rates of staff turnover cause expertise to be lost more easily than it is retained.

Crisis management in an official capacity is usually coordinated by the United Nations Office for the Coordination of Humanitarian Aid (UN–OCHA), often in collaboration with the UN High Commission for Refugees (UNHCR), the World Food Programme (WFP) and other supranational entities. The OCHA grew out of the former Office of the Disaster Relief Co-ordinator (UNDRO) and its successor, the Department for Humanitarian Affairs (UN–DHA). When a crisis occurs, OCHA will first consult its representative in the affected country, the UN Resident, who will be in touch with the national government.

The government of the country in which the disaster has occurred may issue an international relief appeal, and the response will probably be coordinated by UN–OCHA. Up to 70 different countries (though more usually about half that number) may participate by sending funds, relief goods or personnel to the affected area. Generally, money is the most flexible and useful form of donation, as it can be used to purchase materials and supplies in the local area, pay for local manpower and stimulate the local economy. However, cash has the obvious drawback that it can disappear in bribes, corruption, expropriation or to pay the soldiers of private militias. Hence, governments often supply a list of specific relief goods that are required, such as items of clothing, bedding, cooking utensils, rations and building materials, especially if these items are in short supply in the country in question.

The UN organisations that work in disaster function more in a coordination role than as direct suppliers of aid and relief. They can only operate in a particular country if they are given the full and explicit permission of the host government. In countries wracked by civil war this may be difficult to obtain, either because the government fears that aid and relief will go to rebel forces, or because there are issues of who *is* the government in certain areas of the country. Hence, in disasters in places like Angola, Sudan and the Democratic Republic of the Congo, at times the major NGOs, such as Oxfam and the International Federation of Red Cross and Red Crescent Societies have more efficiently supplied aid because they have developed strategies for circumventing bureaucracy and government obstructionism.

In any case, all relief organisations suffer the modern dilemmas of international aid. One of the most pressing of these involves the question of how to maintain neutrality. When the Red Cross was founded after the battles of Solferino and Magenta in northern Italy in 1859, it adopted the principle of providing assistance to all who need it, regardless of their political, military, religious or social allegiance. This is the guiding doctrine of humanitarian organisations throughout the world, but it has come under severe stress in recent years, as there have been many instances of the expropriation of humanitarian aid for military or political ends. Bribery, corruption, intimidation and violence have been used variously to achieve this. There have been military attacks on aid convoys, aid agency vehicles have been hijacked, relief goods have been denied import licences, passage or storage facilities, and supplies have been expropriated for use by soldiers and militiamen. The last thing that NGOs want is to be the source of aid to armies that perpetuate conflicts, deny civilian populations assistance and commit atrocities, but it can be hard to avoid such a situation where there is no absolute control over the delivery of relief goods on the ground.

A second dilemma is that relief aid may create dependency among the recipients. It can be very difficult in poor communities to ensure that recovery from and mitigation of disaster are self-sustaining, but as the world's attention shifts from one disaster to the next, the sources of aid can dry up abruptly, leaving the recipients in potentially a worse situation than they would have been if they had had to fend for themselves.

A third dilemma concerns how to shift the focus from simply providing relief after disaster has struck to creating communities that are resistant to catastrophic impacts when they occur. In the Turkish earthquakes of 1999, most of the buildings that collapsed with heavy loss of life were modern, reinforced-concrete apartment blocks that should have been able to resist the tremors. The Province of Kerman, in which the Bam earthquake of December 2003 occurred, has an average of one ruinous seismic event every 8.9 years, and yet buildings collapsed wholesale in Bam. But despite the obvious need for better mitigation, the lion's share of disaster aid still goes on alleviating the consequences rather than tackling the causes, even though there is considerable sensitivity to the issue within the global humanitarian aid community.

Although the incidence of poverty and marginalisation in local populations correlates very substantially with vulnerability to disaster, the two phenomena are not entirely synonymous. An element of resilience, the inverse of vulnerability, is provided by grassroots community organisation that at least in theory can be cheap or free. The knack of it is to give poor communities a political and economic voice and thus combat the marginalisation that leaves them vulnerable to disaster. This strategy has been tried with (albeit limited) success in, for example, Mexico City and Lima, Peru, but it is far from being a panacea and immensely far from universal adoption.

Disaster is a recurrent, often a cyclical, process and hence the areas of the world where it occurs are well known. Thus China, Bangladesh, the Philippines and Indonesia come out top of the list for the principal natural calamities: earthquakes, floods, tropical storms and large landslides. The central, eastern and southern parts of Africa suffer the most from droughts, and frost damage to crops is felt most severely in Brazil. Given the need to respond in a timely manner to disasters, much attention has been given to the definition of early-warning parameters. These can include geophysical variables, but they are also likely to embrace socio-economic factors, such as patterns of migration and economic trends. This approach reflects a growing consensus that disaster is a product of hazard and vulnerability. Indeed, radical interpretations made by academics since the 1970s have suggested that geophysical phenomena are mere triggers of calamity, and vulnerability (comprising poverty, marginalisation and lack of coping strategies) is the real indicator of potential for disaster.

So the impact of disaster can be disproportionately felt in the areas of high vulnerability. When disaster strikes, as it does more than 250 times a year around the world, the global aid community is likely to become involved right from the start. It is a powerful system (see Figure 2), but one that has had its ups and downs over the years, in line with the variations in global politics. Thus, international aid, including disaster relief, reached a peak in 1995, fuelled by the 'peace dividend' that followed the dissolution of the Soviet bloc. It has since declined and most donor countries spend only 0.2–0.35 per cent of their GNP on aid, not the 0.8 per cent pledged at the UN's Rio de Janeiro Conference on Environment and Development in 1992. Moreover, like other forms of international aid, disaster assistance is given strategically. When international relief appeals have been announced, countries have consistently donated more readily and generously to their allies, former client-states or former colonial possessions.

It could be argued that the first truly 'modern' humanitarian disaster was the starvation consequent upon the Nigerian civil war of 1966, which was the first such event to be viewed contemporaneously on world television (actually, the famine in Biafra was artificially engineered for the benefit of one of the belligerent parties). Since then, international disaster relief has grown enormously in size, scope and sophistication. Stockpiles are maintained at key points for immediate delivery to future disaster areas, and the aid agencies have made great progress in perfecting and standardising relief goods from the humble plastic bucket to electrical generators and prefabricated water tanks.

It is important to block the supply of unsolicited donations in kind (and unorganised volunteer forces that are not self-sufficient in the field), as these can drain local resources which must be diverted to cope with them. For example, after the Armenian earthquake of December 1988, 5000 tonnes of drugs and consumable medical supplies, constituting 25–30 per cent by value of the total aid supply, were sent by foreign donors to Yerevan and had to be dealt with in warehouses at that city's airport. Less than one-third of the drugs were immediately usable: of the rest, 11 per cent were inappropriate medicines, 8 per cent were past their expiry date, and much of the remainder were inadequately labelled (with some 238 brand names in 21 different languages). After this and similar cases elsewhere, for instance involving the donation of inappropriate clothing, it is difficult not to regard some of the aid as a form of dumping of surplus production in disaster areas.

The length of time a victim can survive trapped under rubble after a major sudden-impact disaster will vary markedly with the form and severity of injury, if any, the nature of entrapment and the prevailing weather conditions. Although people can survive for up to 15 days, the overwhelming majority of those extracted alive are brought out on the first day, perhaps even within the first 12 hours. Yet foreign urban search-and-rescue (USAR) teams are regularly sent across the world to participate in relief efforts. In Armenia in 1988, 1200 foreigners rescued 60 victims alive. In the Turkish earthquake of August 1999, 2300 rescuers arrived, while in Bam, Iran, in December 2003, USAR teams from 31 different countries had 1600 workers in the field by the third day after the disaster, but they only managed to save 30 victims. At least the Iranian government allowed timely entry of the overseas forces: after the Gujarat earthquake of January 2001, in which a million houses were damaged, the Indian government took 30 hours to waive visa requirements for foreign rescuers. In any case, foreign rescue help simply arrives too late to be efficient at saving lives in the field. Hence, the most promising strategy for the future will probably be the transfer of technology, expertise and training to local teams established in areas of high risk of disaster. In a similar vein, the time taken to transport and set up field hospitals means that they often end up providing back-up and routine care rather than mass-casualty treatment. One can conclude that the international relief system is still a long way from being efficient.

Nevertheless, the demand for medical care is a critical factor in many large international disasters. When an earthquake struck El Salvador in 1986, four hospitals were put out of action by damage and structural collapse. Relief goods were freighted in by C130 aircraft from Toronto. Exactly the same thing happened in the January 2003 earthquake in El Salvador, which strongly suggests that lessons had not been learned and preparations had not been made in the intervening 15 years. The loss of all hospitals in the Bam area during the December 2003 earthquake underlines the seriousness of the problem, given that overwhelming numbers of injured people may require treatment (some accounts give the number of seriously injured in the 1976 Tangshan, China, earthquake, the worst in the twentieth century, as 900 000).

In conclusion, if 'war is the continuation of politics by other means', as Karl von Clausewitz wrote, disaster is economics carried on by other means. Economic causes are at the root of many modern conflicts, the so-called 'resource wars', and economic considerations ally with strategic ones in the distribution of relief aid. Many lessons have been learned in the provision of disaster relief, but the complexity of modern emergency situations means that unprecedented logistical, tactical, moral and ethical demands are being made on the relief agencies.

DAVID ALEXANDER

Further reading

Albala-Bertrand, José-Miguel (1993), *The Political Economy of Large Natural Disasters, with Special Reference to Developing Countries*, Oxford: Oxford University Press.
Blaikie, Piers, Terry Cannon, Ian Davis and Ben Wisner (2003), *At Risk: Natural Hazards, People's Vulnerability, and Disasters*, 2nd edn, London: Routledge.
Borton, John (1993), 'Recent trends in the international relief system', *Disasters*, **17** (3), 187–201.
Cahill, K.M. (ed.) (1999), *A Framework for Survival: Health, Human Rights and Humanitarian Assistance in Conflicts and Disasters*, 2nd edn, London: Routledge.
Cuny, Frederick C. (1983), *Disasters and Development*, Oxford and New York: Oxford University Press.
Curtis, D., J. Macrae and M. Duffield (eds) (2001), 'Special Issue: Politics and Humanitarian Aid: Debates, Dilemmas and Dissension', *Disasters*, **25** (4), 269–357.
Duffield, Michael (1996), 'The symphony of the damned: racial discourse, complex political emergencies and humanitarian aid', *Disasters*, **20** (3), 173–93.

IFRCRCS (annually), *World Disasters Report*, Geneva: International Federation of Red Cross and Red Crescent Societies.

ISDR (2002), *Living With Risk: A Global Review of Disaster Reduction Initiatives*, Geneva: Inter-Agency Secretariat of the International Strategy for Disaster Reduction.

Kreimer, A. and M. Arnold (eds) (2000), *Managing Disaster Risk in Emerging Economies*, Washington, DC: World Bank.

Leader, N. (2000), *The Politics of Principle: the Principles of Humanitarian Action in Practice*, Humanitarian Policy Group Report no. 2, London: Overseas Development Institute.

Lewis, James (1999), *Disasters in Disaster-Prone Places: Studies of Vulnerability*, London: Intermediate Technology Publications.

Macrae, Joanna (2002), *International Humanitarian Action: A Review of Key Trends*, ODI Briefing Paper, London: Overseas Development Institute.

Macrae, J. and N. Leader (eds) (2000), *The Politics of Coherence: Humanitarianism and Foreign Policy in the Post-Cold War Era*, Humanitarian Policy Group Briefing Paper no. 1, London: Overseas Development Institute.

Newkirk, Ross T. (2001), 'The increasing cost of disasters in developed countries: a challenge to local planning and government', *Journal of Contingencies and Crisis Management*, **9** (3), 159–70.

PAHO (1994), *A World Safe from Natural Disasters: The Journey of Latin America and the Caribbean*, Washington, DC: Pan American Health Organization.

Pelling, Mark (ed.) (2003), *Natural Disasters and Development in a Globalizing World*, London: Routledge.

Rieff, D. (2002), *A Bed for the Night: Humanitarianism in Crisis*, New York: Simon & Schuster.

Slim, Hugo (1997), 'Doing the right thing: relief agencies, moral dilemmas and moral responsibility in political emergencies and war', *Disasters*, **21** (3), 244–57.

Twigg, John and Bhat, Mihir (1998), *Understanding Vulnerability: South Asian Perspectives*, London: Intermediate Technology Publications.

Varley, Anne (ed.) (1994), *Disasters, Development and Environment*, Chichester: John Wiley.

Culture and Development

Discourses on culture and development vary according to their conceptions of culture and of development and according to their standpoint. The 'culture and development' problematique has typically: (1) arisen from a conception of 'culture' as a relatively fixed, homogeneous set of mental programmes (categories, frameworks, images, values, norms) shared by members of a population; (2) contained an instrumental concern with how far such 'cultures' impede or promote 'development', largely conceived of as economic growth; and (3) involved outsiders looking at another group or country and seeking relatively simple explanations for perceived development success or failure. All three features are problematic. Alternatives exist, however, in each respect.

This entry refers to conceptions of culture, discourses about the implications of cultures and cultural dynamics for development, and ethical issues that arise when values clash and the value-content of 'development' is seen as dependent on culture. It questions the style of discourse in which developers seek to encapsulate the nature of 'others' yet rarely treat their own culture(s) so simply.

Cultural diversity is quite often ignored in social science, not least in development economics. People are presumed to be everywhere the same in perceptions and values, or those are considered superficial phenomena with expressive but not causal roles. Most conceptions of culture are less shallow than this, but vary in their degree of adequacy. Culture discourses reject the theory that all people behave identically as calculating acquisitive individuals, and treat sceptically claims that there are universally attractive and appropriate methods of governance and management. Van Nieuwenhuijze inverted economists' presumption and proposed that 'everything must be taken as culture-specific until it is proven to be general' (1986, p. 107) rather than the reverse.

Conceptions of culture

We encounter diverse definitions of 'culture'. It may refer to, for example: (1) learned rather than genetically inherited thoughts and behaviour; (2) a distinctive set of practices, a 'way of life'; (3) a system of values and attitudes that sustains a way of life; (4) more dynamically and openly, the shared learned malleable rules, values, ideas and methods through which members of a group deal creatively with their environment. In development agency discourse and even in much development studies and everyday usage, 'culture' often more crudely refers to (5) the 'non-economic': whatever is marginal to or beyond the traditional categories of economics. Overall, 'culture' in 'culture and development' discourse can refer thus to numerous diverse matters, such as arts, religion, language, nationalism, minorities, identity and stereotyping, communities and communalism, 'social capital' and social networks, gender relations, and forms of generating, expressing, pursuing and managing conflicts (Schech and Haggis, 2002).

Culture as a system of practices

In some conceptions, culture includes artefacts, practices and institutions, perhaps as well as ideas and values. This has merits, but raises issues in explaining and assessing change: does every change in practices imply a change in culture? Other conceptions use the hypothesis that practices stem from ideas and values while taking into account various conditions which can change; thus some changes in practices derive only from new external conditions and not from supposedly more fundamental changes of mentality.

Culture as a system of values and attitudes

A widespread approach for trying to understand and cope with cultural differences may be described as 'culture defined for management purposes'. It takes 'culture' as a type of mental programming/information-processing system which is distinct from species-wide programming and from person-specific qualities (learned or inherited). Group-specific qualities and their 'programmes' are the group's culture. People within a 'culture' are presumed to share many major values and mental tools, which mould and even dictate their behaviour in numerous important ways. The programming is deep, for it comes largely during the intense and formative first two decades of a human life, by socialisation in a group or groups. In fact, nearly everyone interacts and is socialised within a number of groups (family, schools, work groups and peer groups, locality, nation and so on) and hence belongs to a number of cultures. Much current discussion focuses on national units and national differences, which reflects not only the power of this level but the management purposes of multinational corporations (Hofstede, 1991; Trompenaars and Hampden-Turner, 1997) and the ongoing concerns of empire. Comparisons are made between the declared values and attitudes of Japanese, Americans, Germans, and nowadays also Chinese, Iraqis and any other national group.

This stress on distinct, diverse, dominant mental packages often leads to notions of 'other cultures' as obstacles (to economic growth or Westernisation) that need drastic reform, but sometimes to viewing them as resources. Such notions are prone to periodic inversion, as seen in the evolution of commonplace views about the instrumental efficacy of Chinese or Japanese cultures. The about-turns in intellectual fashion suggest that the underlying conception of culture is oversimplified. Amartya Sen (2004) warns against 'freeze-frame theorizing': extrapolating from present discrepancies in performance to assert fundamental and enduring cultural differences.

Culture as one source of influence on creative actors
The image of culture as a package of mental programmes is too rigid and crude, argue most anthropologists and practitioners of cultural studies, an interdisciplinary field which has arisen since the 1960s (During, 1993; Schech and Haggis, 2000). Most of our shared mental programming is rather general, not highly determinant. Behaviour is influenced by some shared ideas at various levels, but such ideas are frequently ambiguous, plural and often contested within life spheres, and in competition across overlapping life spheres. And they evolve, especially in an interconnected globalised world; frequently in unexpected, even dramatic, ways.

   Most cultural analysts now use a more complex, flexible and active concept of culture, as an evolving network of meanings, a language for engaging in experience. People make and remake meanings, groups and identities. This takes us back towards the original sense of culture as cultivation (as in 'agriculture'). Culture is constantly being contested and remade, not an exact and immutable set of programmes. While interpretation, reinterpretation and evolution are not excluded in the conception of culture as a system of values and attitudes, the activist conception of culture emphasises them far more. Dictation by culture appears to be more stressed the more remote that authors are from the diverse reality.

Some studies of culture and development
Work continues on possible barriers to economic growth formed by cultures in poor groups and countries, sustaining what in the 1950s and 1960s was a predominantly North American tradition with a social psychology slant. Leading exemplars were David McLelland's (1961) theories of achievement motivation and Oscar Lewis's (1969) idea of a 'culture of poverty', which was reduced sometimes to a notion of a supposedly unitary pattern of 'escapism, impulse gratification, despair and resignation' (UCSB, 2006). Robert Putnam's (Putnam et al., 1993) interpretation of 'social capital' is perhaps the leading current exemplar of barriers-and-keys work, and adds a stress on networks as well as norms. It has been taken up by the World Bank as a possible 'missing link' to explain or excuse why structural adjustment programmes imposed in Africa, Latin America and the former Soviet Union in the past 25 years, based on narrow economic models, were frequently disastrous (Dasgupta and Serageldin, 2000). Critics consider the attempt to reduce culture to another factor of production to be fatuous (Fine, 2000).

   Kabeer (2000) provides an exemplary empirical and theoretical study of Bengali women workers in London and Dhaka, which sifts and synthesises various explanatory strands. Women engaged actively in labour market choices, influenced by remuneration, the requirements of the work, and various evolving concerns, including for autonomy, affiliation, esteem and stimulation; within a field of choice delimited by ideas about what is and is not admissible. These predominant values varied, however, according to people's home region in Bangladesh, and were also differently interpreted and weighted by different women and variously negotiated or contested with their families and peers. Choices were influenced by other contextual factors too; in London, for example, the availability of free schooling and healthcare reduced the pressure to earn, and together with widespread racism in the 'host' English culture group contributed to the prevalence of working from home. In both London and Dhaka, the Bengali women were not culture-less, gender-less 'economic men'; nor were they 'cultural dopes', cast and constrained in a single mould.

Other work starts from observed cultural energies and dynamics, including but not only in the arts, and considers their roles in social change. Among the most important work of this type are studies of communalism and nationalism, notably on the invention of 'trad-itions', national myths and national identities (for example, Hobsbawm and Ranger, 1992). Various authors suggest that nationalism is a modern formation that motivates and sustains the painful introduction of modern impersonal large-scale systems by mobilis-ing the languages and emotions of supposed traditional community (for example, Gellner, 1983; Kaviraj, 1992).

Dominant discourses of culture and development
Why are such varied matters lumped together as 'cultural'? In many languages this sort of concept has not existed. It has arisen, first, in reaction to the modern idea of a univer-sal 'economic man' and 'a world view according to which man as the subject deals with the reality surrounding him in a subject–object relationship: more precisely, in such a way that maximal returns are drawn from systematic effort' (van Nieuwenhuijze, 1986, p. 97). The concept of 'culture' has become used to stress aspects of life that are downgraded or ignored in that conception. Second, whereas in the West the concept of 'social' became the main repository for 'the jumble of non economic concerns that play second fiddle to the economic preoccupation' (ibid., p. 101), for low-income countries 'culture' acquired that role, perhaps because the immediate means are lacking with which to match the scope of 'social policy' and 'social services' in the Western welfare state. More importantly, the power hierarchy and distance in relation to the West have encouraged a stereotyping, gen-eralising discourse from the West about others. It arises especially when the West's other generalising discourse of 'economic man' has not fitted well – 'the label "cultural" serves to indicate matters that are sensed rather than identified, apprehended rather than under-stood' (ibid., p. 103) – or when claiming that extending equal opportunities to others would be pointless or somehow unfair to the West.

Edward Said and others have indicated how European and American 'Orientalist' authors built and sustained, since the eighteenth century or earlier, essentialist, hostile and self-idealising representations of 'the Orient' (Said, 1978, 1994). Ironically, the sim-plified generalisations not only generated resentful reactions but helped to create some of the unities which they posited. Some authors have investigated further the cultures of pur-ported developers and historical underdevelopers. Kiernan's *The Lords of Human Kind* (1972) and Davis's *Late Victorian Holocausts* (2001) are seminal, dismaying accounts of widespread European imperial-era arrogance and inhumanity; for example in British rulers' self-congratulation on civilising late nineteenth-century India while presiding with planned neglect over a series of ameliorable mega famines. Thinkers like Theodore

Roszak (1972) present dominant modern culture in the West as the systematised exploitation of all environments, human and non-human, based on reduction of everything to appetites and resources. They argue that this degrades the exploiters too and jeopardises everyone's flourishing and sustainability. Others suggest that nowadays values of doing and having dominate values of being (Fromm, 1978). Another stream of work investigates ethnographically the cultures of present-day development agencies and professionals (for example, Porter et al., 1991; Hobart, 1993; Crewe and Harrison, 1998; Quarles van Ufford and Giri, 2003). Characteristic findings concern the power of agencies' own convenience and of myths which legitimise their style of operation. More such research is required on cultures not of the weak but of the strong, and on the obstacles those can form for human development.

Value differences

If cultures centrally include values, even if with some internal disagreement; if cultures differ; and if development centres on choices, action and change, then central to discussion of culture and development must be consideration of value differences and disagreements (Gasper, 2004). 'Development', understood as economic growth, was earlier seen as a neutral tool that could promote whatever one's culture's goals were; but gradually the content, purposes and manner of development have been recognised as deeply normative matters, involving cultural and ethical choices. Many disagreements concern the relations between individual rights and group authority and rights; and many involve gender relations, since regulated group practices often concern reproductive life – matters of marriage, inheritance, family property and child custody (Nussbaum and Glover, 1995; Okin et al., 1999). In such discussions, crude conceptions of culture – as fixed, uniform and determinant – can reinforce the power of existing or aspirant elites.

Even positions which are uncomfortable with ethical debate and adopt a normative relativism – that values are purely culture specific, not universal – often espouse a universal value that all cultures should be able to determine their own notion of and path to development rather than let stronger culture groups impose their ideas. Declared universal values, such as that one or in the Universal Declaration of Human Rights, might be grounded in various ways: in a proposed theory, or a demonstrable area of consensus between diverse traditions (as argued in, for example, Küng, 1997), or a mixture of the two methods. The World Commission on Culture and Development (WCCD, 1995) used a mixture, employing both the near-universally endorsed Universal Declaration and the theoretical perspective of 'human development' from Sen and the UNDP.

Development studies and practice sorely need culturally aware approaches in explanation and prescription, but not the misconception of cultures as 'wired-in', fixed, consensual behavioural programming. Sen's normative framework is one attempt to be appropriately culturally sensitive and flexible within a universalist normative perspective (Sen, 1999). The 'cultural theory' of Mary Douglas and her school (for example, Hood, 1998; Rayner and Malone, 1998) shows an attempt at cultural analysis as a methodology for investigating differences and commonalities, rather than as an apparatus for simplistically pigeonholing other people.

DES GASPER

References

Crewe, E. and E. Harrison (1998), *Whose Development? An Ethnography of Aid*, London: Zed Books.

Dasgupta, P. and I. Serageldin (eds) (2000), *Social Capital*, Washington, DC: World Bank.

Davis, Mike (2001), *Late Victorian Holocausts: El Niño Famines and the Making of the Third World*, London: Verso.

During, S. (ed.) (1993), *The Cultural Studies Reader*, London: Routledge.

Fine, B. (2000), *Social Capital versus Social Theory*, London: Routledge.

Fromm, E. (1978), *To Have or To Be?*, London: Jonathan Cape.

Gasper, D. (2004), *The Ethics of Development*, Edinburgh: Edinburgh University Press.

Gellner, E. (1983), *Nations and Nationalism*, Oxford: Blackwell.

Hobart, M. (ed.) (1993), *An Anthropological Critique of Development*, London: Routledge.

Hobsbawm, E. and T. Ranger (eds) (1992), *The Invention of Tradition*, Cambridge: Cambridge University Press.

Hofstede, G. (1991), *Cultures and Organizations: Software of the Mind*, London: McGraw-Hill.

Hood, C. (1998), *The Art of the State*, Oxford: Clarendon.

Kabeer, N. (2000), *The Power to Choose: Bangladeshi Women and Labour Market Decisions in London and Dhaka*, London: Verso.

Kaviraj, S. (1992), 'The imaginary institution of India', in P. Chatterjee and G. Pandey (eds), *Subaltern Studies VII*, Oxford and Delhi: Oxford University Press, pp. 1–39.

Kiernan, V. (1972), *The Lords of Human Kind: European Attitudes to the Outside World in the Imperial Age*, Harmondsworth: Penguin.

Küng, H. (1997), *A Global Ethics for Global Politics and Economics*, London: SCM Press.

Lewis, O. (1969), *On Understanding Poverty: Perspectives from the Social Sciences*, New York: Basic Books.

McLelland, D. (1961), *The Achieving Society*, Princeton, NJ: Van Nostrand.

Nussbaum, M. and J. Glover (eds) (1995), *Women, Culture, and Development: A Study of Human Capabilities*, Oxford: Clarendon.

Okin, S.M., A.Y. At-Hibri, A. An-Na'im, H.K. Bhabha, S.L. Gilman, J.E. Halley, B. Honig, W. Kymlicka, M.C. Nussbaum, B. Parekh, K. Pollitt, R. Post, J. Raz, S. Sassen, C.R. Sunstein and Y. Tamir (1999), *Is Multiculturalism Bad for Women?*, Princeton, NJ: Princeton University Press.

Porter, D., B. Allen and G. Thompson (1991), *Development in Practice*, London: Routledge.

Putnam, R., R. Leonardi and R. Nanetti (1993), *Making Democracy Work: Civic Traditions in Modern Italy*, Princeton, NJ: Princeton University Press.

Quarles van Ufford, P. and A. Giri (eds) (2003), *A Moral Critique of Development*, London: Routledge.

Rayner, S. and E. Malone (eds) (1998), *Human Choice and Climate Change*, 4 vols, Colombus, OH: Battelle Press.

Roszak, T. (1972), *Where the Wasteland Ends: Politics and Transcendence in Post Industrial Society*, London: Faber & Faber.

Said, E. (1978), *Orientalism: Western Conceptions of the Orient*, London: Penguin (2nd edn, 1995)

Said, E. (1994), *Culture and Imperialism*, London: Vintage.

Schech, S. and J. Haggis (2000), *Culture and Development: A Critical Introduction*, Oxford: Blackwell.

Schech, S. and J. Haggis (eds), (2002), *Development: A Cultural Studies Reader*, Oxford: Blackwell.

Sen, A. (1999), *Development as Freedom*, Oxford and New York: Oxford University Press.

Sen, A. (2004), 'How does culture matter?', in M. Walton and V. Rao (eds), *Culture and Public Action*, Stanford, CA: Stanford University Press, pp. 37–58.

Trompenaars, F. and C. Hampden-Turner (1997), *Riding the Waves of Culture: Understanding Cultural Diversity in Business*, London: Nicholas Brealey.

UCSB (2006), 'Culture of poverty', online glossary, Department of Anthropology, University of California Santa Barbara, www.anth.ucsb.edu/glossary/glossary.html.

van Nieuwenhuijze, C. (1986), 'Culture and development', in R. Apthorpe and A. Krahl (eds), *Development Studies: Critique and Renewal*, Leiden: Brill, pp. 95–108.

World Commission on Culture and Development (WCCD) (1995), *Our Creative Diversity*, Paris: UNESCO (2nd edn, 1996).

Debt Crisis

The current level of international debt owed by developing countries to creditor countries (bilateral debt) and institutions (multilateral debt) is a colossal 2.6 trillion dollars, or roughly 500 dollars for every man, woman and child living in developing countries. The annual outflow of debt service payments (interest and amortisation) from developing countries is now over 250 billion dollars which is three times greater than the inflow of ODA. In several highly indebted countries, debt service payments exceed expenditure on health and education, so in this sense alone, debt presents a real crisis for these countries.

Debt arises through the process of international lending and borrowing which has been a feature of international economic life at least since the Medicis of Florence started to make loans to the English and Spanish monarchs in the fourteenth century. Traditionally, the role of foreign borrowing was to supplement domestic saving to allow countries to invest more than they save, and therefore to grow faster, but most debt in recent times has been created by countries financing balance-of-payments deficits on the current account, which also allows investment to exceed domestic saving, but some of the borrowing may be for consumption purposes. It can be shown theoretically that the creation of debt will raise the rate of growth of a country's national income if the productivity of investment financed by borrowing exceeds the rate of interest on loans, and will raise the rate of growth of a country's output if new inflows exceed lost saving arising from the servicing of past debt (see Thirlwall, 2006).

The problems posed by international debt arise because debt has to be serviced and repaid in *foreign* currency (for example, dollars). The world debt problem is therefore a foreign exchange problem. It represents the inability of debtors to earn enough foreign exchange through exports to service foreign debts, and at the same time to sustain the growth of output (which requires foreign exchange to pay for imports). Either debt service payments have to be suspended or growth curtailed, or a combination of both. Unfortunately for the debtor countries, it is the improvement of living standards that has suffered over the last 25 years.

The huge resource transfers to service debt of over 250 billion dollars a year are all part of the 'transfer problem' first analysed by Keynes in the wake of the reparations imposed on Germany after the First World War by the Treaty of Versailles in 1919. Keynes (1919) mocked the folly and futility of the whole exercise on the grounds that it was likely to be self-defeating, and so it turned out to be. Similarly today, the attempt to extract such large transfers, particularly in Africa, is leading nowhere. Their economies continue to suffer, and the poor become progressively poorer.

There are two aspects to the transfer problem. First there is the budgetary task for governments of acquiring domestic resources (for example, tax revenue) for the repayment of debt; and second there is the task of turning the resources into foreign exchange – or the 'pure' transfer problem as Keynes called it. Then there is the 'transfer burden' which is the export surplus that has to be generated to acquire the necessary foreign exchange, plus the possibility of a deterioration of the terms of trade if, in order to sell more exports, prices must be reduced. Even if prices do fall, there is still no guarantee that export *earnings* will increase if the quantity sold does not rise in proportion to the fall in price (that is, demand is inelastic). In these circumstances, the transfer becomes impossible without a contraction of domestic output to compress imports. There is substantial evidence that indebted countries, at least collectively, are caught in this trap, since for a large part of their trade they compete with each other; and competitive price reductions leave earnings unchanged. It is the contraction of living standards that generates the export surplus by reducing the import bill. This damages the developing countries, and the whole world economy.

The other side of the coin is that if total trade is static, increased exports from debtor countries take markets away from domestic producers in other countries, and extracting the surplus from the debtors reduces welfare all round. This was one of Keynes's major objections to the excessive reparations imposed on Germany, that the transfers from Germany would be generated at the expense of the victors. History has lessons to teach. The magnitude of the transfers expected from developing countries in recent years has been greater as a proportion of total output and trade than that imposed on Germany after the war. What we witness today in the world economy is a vast charade of money being recycled from creditors to debtors and back again to creditors, while the total volume of debt grows and the pressure on debtor countries to adjust – a euphemism for deflation – increases.

The 'crisis' aspects of debt can be looked at from different standpoints: from the point of view of individual borrowing countries; of the lenders (private banks and sovereign governments); or of the entire world economy. Debt becomes a crisis for individual countries if they have to cut back on essential government expenditure and imports to service debt, and if debt default causes international lending to dry up in the future. It becomes a crisis for the banking system if particular banks are heavily exposed to a few countries who suspend repayment. In the early 1980s, for example, loans to Brazil and Mexico from the nine largest banks in the United States were equal to 40 per cent of shareholders' capital. If these debts had been written off, a major part of the capital and reserves of the banking system would have been wiped out, and because of the intricate network of interbank lending there would have been the possibility of a chain of bank collapses. Debt becomes a crisis for the world economy if there is a major default which then leads to a massive contraction of bank lending throughout the world, and therefore deflation by countries in order to equilibrate their balance of payments. These are all ingredients of recession, such as the Great Depression of the 1930s.

The origins of the debt crisis of the 1980s, which still lingers today particularly in Africa and Latin America, is no mystery. The massive balance-of-payments surpluses of the oil producers which accrued in the 1970s were on-lent through the banking system to developing countries which were anxious to sustain growth in the face of balance-of-payments deficits. Credit looked cheap, and borrowers looked good risks from the lenders' point of view. Commodity prices were relatively high, and the export earnings of developing countries were buoyant. But then in 1980, circumstances suddenly changed. World interest rates more than doubled, the world economy plunged into recession, commodity prices tumbled, and export earnings languished. The consequence for developing countries was that their debt service payments relative to export earnings rose from under 20 per cent to a peak of nearly 30 per cent in 1986 (and to over 50 per cent in some countries). Mexico was the first country in 1982 to suspend the repayment of loans due to the private banking system and sovereign lenders, and Brazil in 1987 was the first country to suspend interest payments to foreign creditors. Fortunately, however, a repetition of the Great Depression of the 1930s was avoided. Many banks in developed countries did find themselves in difficulties; lending did contract sharply in the early 1980s, but then rose again as difficulties were resolved by various forms of international cooperation and the rescheduling of debt. The growth of the world economy also recovered, improving the foreign exchange earnings of developing countries, and so reducing the overall debt service ratio to below 20 per cent (again). In some regions and countries, however, the ratio has remained high: over 30 per cent in Latin America and the Caribbean, and 25 per cent in the so-called 'severely indebted low-income countries'. In Africa, the ratio is under 20 per cent because most of the debt is now on very soft terms, but still many African countries spend more on debt service than they do on fighting poverty.

This is the reason why in 1996 the World Bank launched the Heavily Indebted Poor Country Initiative (HIPC) to help the world's poorest indebted countries (relaunched in 1999 as the Enhanced HIPC Debt Relief Initiative). The idea is to give debt relief to highly indebted countries if they can demonstrate good governance consistent with sustained growth and a poverty reduction programme outlined in a poverty reduction strategy paper (PRSP). To be eligible for relief, countries must satisfy two further conditions: first the country must be very poor, defined as eligible for concessional assistance from the International Development Association (IDA) of the World Bank and eligible for support under the IMF's Poverty Reduction and Growth Facility; and second, the country must have an unsustainable debt burden defined as a debt to export ratio of more than 150 per cent, or a debt–government expenditure ratio in excess of 250 per cent. To date, no more than fifteen countries have received assistance out of 40 countries that are eligible.

The magnitude of debt is so large in total, however, that there is really no solution to the 'crisis of debt' without a massive programme of debt forgiveness, which leaves a manageable debt that the debtors can service. There has to be debt write-off if there is to be an easing of the transfer burden. Without forgiveness, further borrowing to repay debt increases the size of debt service payments and simply makes matters worse, creating what might be called a 'debt trap'. Since lenders, borrowers and the whole world community have benefited from the debt-creation process, there is a strong economic and moral case for saying that the same three parties should share the burden of relief. It is not fair that the debtor countries should bear the whole of the adjustment burden. Up to now the world community (including the creditor countries and institutions) have done relatively little to ease the plight of the debtors, although there are three good reasons why it should. First, the world community received an external benefit when the debt was created by the on-lending process in the 1970s, preventing output contraction in countries with balance-of-payments deficits, and thereby avoiding a world slump. Second, much of the debt problem arose in the first place through no fault of the developing countries themselves, but as a result of events in the world economy beyond their control – rising oil prices, rising interest rates, world recession and falling commodity prices. Third, the mutual interdependence of the world economy means that if one group of countries is ailing, the health of other countries is impaired, so that debt relief could actually confer a global benefit by easing the deflationary pressures on debtor countries associated with the huge debt overhang.

A.P. THIRLWALL

References

Keynes, J.M. (1919), *The Economic Consequences of the Peace*, London: Macmillan.
Thirlwall, A.P. (2006), *Growth and Development: with Special Reference to Developing Economies*, 8th edn, London: Palgrave-Macmillan.

Democracy and Development

Democracy defined

There are many definitions of democracy (Sartori, 1968). They range from a political system based on government legitimacy stemming from the freely given consent of the governed to a system in which the power of the government is limited and the government is accountable to its citizens. For our purposes we adopt a descriptive, procedural, structural and factual definition of democracy. We define democracy to be a political system that is characterised by the existence of competitive political parties in which the majority respects the rights of minorities and there are institutions which limit the power of government and ensure its accountability.

Procedurally, varying degrees of democracy are distinguished by the following set of political characteristics: the manner in which political leaders are selected; the institutions that specify the breadth of political participation; the degree of freedom of assembly and of the mass media; the extent of political representation and suffrage; the existence of political parties that are based primarily on varying political and social ideologies rather than on purely ascriptive characteristics, such as religion or ethnicity, or on the personality of the party leader; by the manner of functioning of the judicial system and whose interests it represents; and whether there is reasonable expectation of the rotation of power and the means of achieving it (elections versus coups).

The actual forms of government in less-developed countries are quite varied. They range from traditional monarchies to either dictatorships or left- or right-wing constitutional democracies. The form of government and whose interests it represents is critical to economic development because governments have the sole legal monopoly on the exercise of power (Lin and Nugent, 1995) and they create the institutions and promulgate the policies which provide the framework within which economic development takes place. They initiate changes in policy direction as well as institutional reforms.

Some definitions of democracy include concern for the achievement of equality in its various dimensions: political, social and economic. Marxist countries claim that their political systems are democratic because they stress equality, especially in its economic aspects. Political democracy is the least controversial. It is achieved when the state aggregates a wide range of ideologies, exercises limited power, performs a minimal set of functions, acts in the public interest and is accountable for its actions and performance. Social democracy is attained when both the constitution and political institutions guarantee possibilities for equal ethnic, religious and gender participation. Economic democracy refers to the levelling of inequalities in the distribution of wealth.

It is argued that democratic systems equalise disparities. In my view, while there is some association between greater democracy and smaller disparities, this is not necessarily because democracy, as a system, results in greater equality. After all, actual inequality varies substantially over time in a given country without a change in its political system. Rather, it is because democracy cannot persist for any length of time if inequalities among groups of citizens are too vast. The tensions which result from such inequalities will either lead to the dissolution of the polity through civil unrest or civil war leading to the collapse of the polity, or the tensions must be contained by varying degrees of repression and authoritarian rule.

Associations between democracy and development: mechanisms

The channels of association between development and democracy are multiple. They take place through the social and economic conditions that are systematically connected with the process of socio-economic development and are indeed necessary for it. Happily, many of the socio-economic conditions required for development overlap with those that are also necessary for the evolution of democracy. For both, certain minimal levels of social development must be attained. Nevertheless, the association between economic and political development is not strong, especially in the early phases of economic development, because politically many of the socio-economic forces are double-edged.

First, for economic development, the growth of a domestic professional middle class of sufficient size is needed to permit the replacement of expatriate managers with indigenous ones. Politically, the growth of the local middle class has both positive and negative effects. On the positive side, the growth of a domestic, educated middle class permits informed political choices. The expansion of a local middle class also serves to decrease overall national domestic inequality, by bridging the gaps between vast degrees of wealth, on the one hand, and widespread abject poverty, on the other. On the negative side from the point of view of the growth of democracy, the enlargement of an indigenous middle class also generates a segment of the population whose norms are global, rather than purely national. This may be counterproductive in the medium run. For the middle class itself may develop political aspirations that are not consonant with current national form of government. It may become restless and disaffected, and generate political instability and domestic strife of varying degrees of intensity. Rather than bridging the growing gaps between the masses and the elites, it may foment political unrest and civil strife aimed at toppling the current rulers.

Second, both the quantity and quality of education (Almond and Coleman, 1960; Schultz, 1981) must grow to enable transition from an economy that is mainly agrarian to one that is industrial. This transition is integral to the process of economic development. The expansion of literacy is needed for even moderate degrees of industrialisation to generate an indigenous, industrial labour force and is therefore vital to the process of economic development itself. Politically, sufficient levels of literacy permit wide exposure to multiple types of mass communication media (not only TV) reflecting different points of view. This has the potential to generate an informed citizenry. However, for political development, not only the quantity but also the quality of education matters. In the early phases, educational systems promote rote learning rather than independent reasoning and problem solving. Such educational systems can be employed as tools for indoctrination and propaganda, as in Islamic Madrasas. Rote education can spread sectarian values that enhance hatred of different religions, tribes, ethnicities and cultures. It therefore has the potential to generate civil wars and terrorism and can be inimical to both political stability and democracy. The rise of democracy therefore requires an educational system that does not promote sectarian values and hatred of other groups and that encourages critical reasoning rather than rote learning.

Third, urbanisation (Hoselitz, 1960) influences both economic and political development. When, as in the early phases of development, infrastructure in the form of electricity, roads and communication media is scarce, one can economise on infrastructure needs through agglomeration of industry and population in urban centres. Urbanisation thereby reduces the cost of industrialisation. However, urbanisation also enhances economic and social disparities between urban centres and rural areas and exacerbates income and opportunity differentials among regions. Urbanisation also increases economic and social disparities among different tribes and religious groups since different ethnic groups typically tend to predominate in particular geographic areas. Also, rural–urban migration generally exceeds the growth of formal employment opportunities in cities. Overt urban unemployment replaces disguised rural underemployment and the distribution of income within urban areas becomes more skewed. As a result, after a while, the process of urbanisation leads to social and political unrest. Urbanisation thus has both positive and negative effects on democracy during the early and middle phases of development. On the positive side, urbanisation increases political awareness through enhancement of formal and informal communication. On the negative side, urbanisation enhances economic and social dualism, raising social and political tensions and impeding the rise of democracy.

Fourth, at some point, as local demand for domestic manufactures is exhausted, economic development entails a shift towards open development strategies. Politically, this shift generates a higher degree of exposure to developed-country political ideologies, especially through the spread of mass media such as TV. The internalisation of the new political norms by the middle class can lead to the articulation of demands for greater domestic democracy. It may lead to anti-government sentiments that take the form of anti-government demonstrations, clashes with the forces defending central government power and political instability. In the short run, the instability may be met with greater repression and authoritarianism. In the long run, as the need for repression becomes too severe for the police to enforce (as in Russia and, to a lesser extent, China) democracy may evolve.

Finally, development consists of accelerated economic and social change. In and of itself, the process of change induces psychological and social strains which must be managed somehow by the political system. At first, the fact of enrichment of some without concomitant benefits to the many may give rise to hope that a trickle-down of benefits will occur shortly. The enrichment of some may lead to an explosion of expectations and generate insistent demands for a less concentrated, more egalitarian development process. If, as is typically the case during the early and middle phases of development, the benefits from development fail to trickle down to the majority sufficiently rapidly to satisfy rising popular expectations, the ensuing disaffection with the unequal process of development may de-legitimise the existing government. The result may be an escalation of social tensions into outright civil and political strife and even bloody civil wars. This, of course, makes the development of democracy impossible. But there may be a sufficient lapse of time between the rise of expectations and their expression in system breakdown to permit institutions and investment into less unequal economic development. It is noteworthy that, while development had led to increasing inequalities between groups, tribes and regions of the country in Sub-Saharan Africa during the 1960s, it is not until the 1990s that the burgeoning inequalities have led to a predominance of civil wars and intertribal genocide, when bloody civil wars became ubiquitous. To avoid this heartbreaking outcome requires a combination of economic institutions that spread the benefits of development more widely with political institutions that enable the constructive management of social tensions and channelling of expectations so that they can more readily be matched with the capacity of the political and economic systems to deliver. The growth of national consciousness, as distinct from purely ethnic, clan or religious allegiances may help in this regard; so can the spread of institutions for popular participation and of educational systems aimed at inculcating national, as distinct from sectarian values. Government corruption can impede the evolution of egalitarian, participatory development. And the spread of mass communication media can work either way, depending on the content of the message spread by the media. Leadership commitment to more egalitarian and more participatory development is necessary to avoid the breakdown of the political system and give the rise of democracy a chance.

Associations between democracy and development: direction and strength

The statistical association between development and democracy is non-linear and varies with time. When the sample used to study the connections between economic and political development is limited solely to developing countries and is subdivided by broad levels of socio-economic development (Adelman and Morris, 1967, 1973) the basic non-linearity in association stands out. Adelman and Morris found that, during the 1960s, in the least developed countries (mainly Sub-Saharan Africa) the statistical relationship between the rate of growth of per capita GNP and democracy was quite weak (R^2 less than 5 per cent) and negative. On the average, countries with more autocratic, more repressive regimes had more rapid rates of economic growth and higher levels of per capita GNP. However, these countries were characterised by increasingly divisive, dualistic growth. Furthermore, the socio-economic conditions for democracy were almost entirely absent. Illiteracy, poverty and lack of national, as distinct from tribal, identities posed insurmountable obstacles to the formation of a participatory, inclusive democracy. Therefore, political mobilisation for development occurred solely through the exercise of leadership by autocrats whose authority was based on traditional, tribal concepts of legitimacy or on success in leading the country's struggle for independence.

By the 1990s, the mild indication that less democracy was associated with faster economic growth has been replaced by an equally mild indication that greater democracy is associated with more rapid growth (Adelman, 1999). Also, there are now a few least developed countries that are experiencing more widespread, less dualistic, growth promoted by increases in agricultural productivity and rural development. Nevertheless, the 1990s have harvested the political fruits of the concentrated, regionally, ethnically and religiously biased process of economic development of the previous quarter of a century. Armed struggles to depose the political elites and civil wars are taking place in the overwhelming majority of countries in this group. The civil wars are associated with both less rapid economic growth and less democracy, explaining the mild positive relationship between democracy and rates of economic growth during the 1990s.

The sample of countries at an intermediate level of development includes all Moslem countries in North Africa, the Middle East and Asia, other than Turkey, as well as the least developed countries in Latin America. During the 1960s, the correlation between democracy and rates of growth of per capita GNP continued to be weak and negative (Adelman and Morris, 1967, 1973). There was also essentially no systematic relationship among levels of per capita GNP, the nature of the political system and the strength of leadership commitment to economic modernisation in this intermediate group.

This was due to a combination of factors characteristic of development in this group of countries. First, the levels of social modernisation are still below the threshold needed to permit reliable evolution of representative political institutions. Second, there are substantial inconsistencies in paths of social modernisation typical of this sample of countries. Tensions within individuals also grow, as different aspects of their outlook progress to conflicting degrees. Politically, these social tensions were reflected in a persistent lack of national integration, periodic outbursts of violence, and marked political instability. Neither the form of the political system nor the extent of leadership commitment to development had progressed very far. States were generally authoritarian, repressive and routinely violated the human rights of their citizens; bureaucrats and political elites were generally venal and corrupt; and governments were unstable and had a weak grip upon power. Third, there was a failure of leadership to produce substantial tangible improvements in the living levels not only of the poor but also of large segments of the middle class. And fourth, the major focus of the leadership was not economic and social modernisation but rather the creation of a national polity (that is, nation-building). As a result, during the 1960s, these countries experienced a marked rise in social tensions and political instability and a prevalence of military coups, reflecting primarily the discontent of the elites.

By the 1990s, differences in political systems had become strongly associated with inter-country differences in rates of growth of per capita GNP (R^2 of 38.6 per cent) (Adelman, 1999). Higher economic growth rates were related to more democratic systems; party systems that are more competitive and more personalistic rather than purely tribal in nature; lower degrees of centralisation; and greater freedom of opposition and press. Less dualism is also correlated with more democratic political systems. The political contrasts among more and less democratic countries explain a major share of the distinctions in economic performance between the good South Asian performers in this group (India, Sri Lanka, Thailand and Indonesia) on the one hand, and the poor performers in the Middle East (Iraq, Jordan, Lebanon and Syria), on the other. But the overall explanatory power of greater, though modest democracy, its influence on growth rates, and the direction of its association with economic growth persist even when the Middle-Eastern countries are excluded from the sample of transitional countries or when an extra variable, regional war, is included to account for the poor performance of the Middle-Eastern nations.

However, one should not overestimate the degree of democracy typical of the transitional countries in this group. In the average country in this set, while two or more effective political parties operate, there is no reasonable expectation of rotation or sharing of control at the national level. The dominant political party is still not ideological or class based. Rather, it is intensely personalistic and characterised by extensive political opportunism. And some political parties continue to represent regional, religious, cultural, or ethnic groupings of the population. Furthermore, while political parties are free to organise, they are generally limited in their political activities and in their freedom to oppose the dominant party; and the freedom of the press is restricted or intermittent.

The developing countries at the highest level of socio-economic development (mostly Latin American but including also South Korea and Taiwan), which were characterised by bureaucratic authoritarianism during the 1960s, became mostly democratic, to varying degrees, during the 1990s. Nevertheless, the statistical results for both the 1960s and the 1990s for this subset of developing countries are the same: The statistical association between the *speed* of economic growth and the level of development of democratic institutions was still insignificant during both the 1960s and the 1990s, but there was a strong, positive association (R^2 of 65 per cent) between greater levels of democracy and higher *levels* of per capita GNP in both periods. There was also a very close association between the strength of leadership commitment to economic development and the rate of economic growth.

The positive correlation between the emergence of democratic institutions and economic development in this group of countries can be attributed to several factors. The degree of social modernisation had passed the threshold required to permit the development of democratic institutions even during the 1960s. Literacy rates, the size of the middle class, urbanisation, and the degree of national integration and sense of national unity were all high; the extent of dualism had, on the average, diminished and the severity of social tensions and political strife had subsided. Institutions that establish the rule of law, guarantee property rights and enforce contracts had been established.

The Adelman–Morris statistical results are consistent with those of other, more recent, empirical studies. In various samples of developing and developed countries, Alesina (1997) finds negligible associations (R^2 of less than 5 per cent) between growth rates of per capita GNP from 1960 to 1990 and variations in degrees of democracy, coupled with strong correlations (R^2 of 56 per cent) between an index of democracy and levels of per capita GNP in 1960. By contrast, in linear regressions lumping together countries at all levels of socio-economic development, Barro (1991, 1997) finds large correlations between rates of growth of per capita GNP and indicators of democracy. In explaining this association, Barro argues that the direction of causality runs from greater levels of economic modernisation to higher degrees of democracy. As indicated in the earlier section on mechanisms of association between democracy and development, the author believes that it is a case of mutual associations with third factors. Higher levels of social and institutional development are essential to the attainment of both greater democracy and higher levels of economic development.

Irma Adelman

References

Adelman, Irma (1999), 'Society, politics and economic development, thirty years after', in John Adams and Francesco Pigliaru (eds), *Economic Growth and Change*, Chelthenham, UK and Northampton, MA, USA: Edward Elgar, pp. 71–101.

Adelman, Irma and Cynthia Taft Morris (1967), *Society, Politics and Economic Development*, Baltimore, MD: Johns Hopkins University Press.

Adelman, Irma and Cynthia Taft Morris (1973), *Economic Growth and Social Equity in Developing Countries*, Palo Alto, CA: Stanford University Press.

Alesina, Alberto (1997), *The Political Economy of Growth*, World Bank Conference on Economic Development, Washington, DC: World Bank.

Almond, Gabriel A. and John Coleman (1960), *The Politics of Developing Areas*, Princeton, NJ: Princeton University Press.

Barro, Robert (1991), 'Economic growth in a cross-section of countries', *Quarterly Journal of Economics*, **106**, 407–43.

Barro, Robert (1997), *Determinants of Economic Growth: A Cross-Country Empirical Study*, Cambridge, MA: MIT Press.

Hoselitz, Bert E. (1960), *Sociological Aspects of Economic Growth*, Glencoe, IL: Free Press.

Lin, J. Yifu and Jeffrey Nugent (1995), 'Institutions and economic development', in Jerry Berman and T.N. Srinivasan (eds), *Handbook of Development Economics*, vol. IIIA, Amsterdam: Elsevier, pp. 2300–370.

Sartori, Giovanni (1968), 'Democracy', in *International Encyclopaedia of Social Sciences*, vol. 4, London and New York: Macmillan, pp. 112–21.

Schultz, Theodore W. (1981), *Investing in People*, Berkeley, CA: University of California Press.

Dependency

'Dependency' refers to the way in which the 'South' was subordinated to the needs and requirements of the 'North' during the latter's capitalist revolution, especially through colonialism, and to the severe price the South continues to pay for the legacy of this today. Giovanni Arrighi (1991, p. 57) has even asserted the existence of a 'seemingly iron law' according to which a country's location in the global hierarchy of national income and wealth created by imperialism continues to be the best predictor of its economic prospects, pointing out that the ranking has remained remarkably stable from the 1930s to the present day: 'the nations of the world . . . are differentially situated in a rigid hierarchy of wealth in which the occasional ascent of a nation or two leaves the rest more firmly entrenched than ever they were before' (ibid., p. 52).

At the heart of the dependency approach is the view that 'developing' countries are not just 'behind' the economically advanced countries but remain subordinated to them by various mechanisms that must be abolished by radical change from below. Like any other term, 'dependency' can be abused. Third World elites, for example, may sometimes plead 'dependency' to divert attention from their privileged status and hide their responsibility for policies or corruption that help to keep the majority of their fellow countrymen in poverty. None the less, dependency is a real feature of contemporary international relations.

The concept of dependency was first used by Latin American writers seeking to account for the fact that in spite of having won formal independence from Spain or Portugal before the middle of the nineteenth century, a hundred years later their countries had mostly failed to develop into modern, industrialised societies. In the 1950s it became the basis of influential analyses of development by scholars such as Celso Furtado, Theotonio Dos Santos, Osvaldo Sunkel and Fernando Henrique Cardoso, several of whom were linked to the United Nations Economic Commission for Latin America (ECLA), under the leadership of Raul Prebisch (see Blomström and Hettne, 1984; and Kay, 1989). Other writers have used other terms to designate the same general phenomenon. For example Lenin, writing in 1916 with reference to Latin America, called it 'semi-colonialism'; Franz Fanon and Kwame Nkrumah, referring in the 1960s to post-independence Africa, called it 'neo-colonialism'; while Andre Gunder Frank, studying the Latin American experience from the early nineteenth century to the 1960s, called it 'underdevelopment'.

Frank (1969) formulated a general 'law' of dependency, or underdevelopment, which held that the development of the West, the 'metropoles', had been made possible by the subordination and exploitation of the former colonies, the 'periphery', at the expense of the periphery's stagnation and impoverishment, and continued to be so. In Frank's view, real economic development at the periphery had only occurred during the two world wars, or during the depression of the 1930s, when trade and investment links between the metropoles and the periphery were broken, or weakened. The solution to the problem of underdevelopment was therefore to end the condition of dependency through a revolutionary break. Other dependency theorists have advocated less radical alternatives, but all have have called for a reduction in the influence of the imperial states and corporations backed by them – one or another form of 'de-linking', 'autarchy', a 'new international economic order' and so on.

The continuing relevance of the concept of dependency lies above all in the analyses it produced of the impact of imperialism, past and present, on the former colonies. Their economic structures tend to reflect the original reason for making them colonies: the production of primary commodities for export, and the creation of an infrastructure of railways, roads, ports and telecommunications orientated to exports, not the promotion of an integrated national economy offering viable internal markets for more than basic goods. In the most extreme cases the whole economy may be based on the export of just one or two commodities (for example, Fiji's sugar), and be extremely vulnerable to world market fluctuations or bad weather. The well-known decline in the terms of trade for developing countries is closely related to the unbalanced nature of their economies, as a result of which so many of them 'consume what they do not produce, and produce what they do not consume'. Moreover, the decline in the terms of trade contributed significantly to growing indebtedness, which eventually obliged so many countries to accept the 'structural adjustment' programmes imposed as a condition of further aid by the IMF and the World Bank. Not only was this a new form of dependency, but structural adjustment also tended to reinforce many of the features of these countries' economies – especially their reliance on a few primary commodity exports – which were at the root of their economic difficulties.

Economic dependency is reflected in the social structure. Primary commodity production in the colonial era was based on family labour on independent smallholdings, or on very low-wage labour on foreign-owned estates or mines. The typical result is, on the one hand, a large, poor and poorly educated majority, still engaged in relatively low-skill work or, increasingly, crowding into cities with unemployment rates of up to 80 per cent, and still heavily dependent on domestic subsistence production by relatives in the countryside; and on the other, a small local professional and business elite, deriving its income from state revenues or from the intermediary tasks they perform for foreign firms and agencies – acting in effect as '*compradores*', so-called after the intermediaries in the Portuguese coastal enclaves in nineteenth-century China.

This kind of social structure in turn accounts for the well-known political weaknesses of so many countries in the South. Urban elites dominate political life, and the 'civil society' institutions that are taken for granted in industrialised countries (such as trade unions, business associations, craft associations, nationwide churches and national newspapers, not to mention democratic parties), and which in various ways make the elites more accountable to the popular majority, are often weak or even, in some cases, absent. Especially in periods of economic retrogression, such as Africa experienced from the late 1980s onwards, for example, people fall back on local and ethnic attachments, making national politics of any kind, let alone democratic politics, extremely difficult, and sometimes precipitating violence, civil wars and even genocide. As a result, external forces continue to play a crucial role in determining political outcomes, whether by buttressing dictators, like Mobutu in Congo/Zaire and Bokassa in the Central African Republic; or by intervening to overthrow governments, like Chile's in 1973 and Iraq's in 2003 – or by declining to intervene, even to prevent genocide, as in Rwanda in 1993.

During the 1960s and early 1970s the most important debates about development tended to be framed in dependency terms. Three related issues in particular were hotly debated: whether dependency made development impossible, or merely difficult; whether or not underdeveloped countries suffered from 'super-exploitation', as many activists believed; and what alternative might actually exist to capitalist development, since dependency theory suggested that was impossible, or at least very difficult.

Frank (1969) argued that 'underdevelopment' (his term for dependent development) presented an absolute barrier to development. At the other extreme, Bill Warren (1980) argued that capitalism would eventually embrace the whole world, ending dependency and levelling up living standards everywhere. Most dependency thinkers were unconvinced by Warren, but also tended to take a less pessimistic position than Frank, taking comfort from the emergence in the 1980s of the NICs (especially South Korea and Taiwan). Recent research suggests, however, that the circumstances which allowed these NICs to make their historic breakthrough were exceptional, and are not likely to be repeated elsewhere. A reasonable judgement would seem to be that dependency makes development very difficult if not impossible for most underdeveloped countries today.

The question of exploitation is closely connected to this. Many activists, especially, and in the North as well as the South, see the impoverished majority of the South as 'super-exploited', and organisations like Fair Trade seek to counteract this. Geoffrey Kay (1975, p. 55), however, famously declared that 'capitalism has created underdevelopment not simply because it has exploited the underdeveloped countries, but because it has not exploited them enough'. Two different senses of 'exploitation' are clearly involved here. If India had the same level of investment per head of population as Belgium, so that Indian workers were exploited by capitalists to the same degree as Belgian workers are, Indian and Belgian workers would enjoy the same living standards. Today some levelling of workers' living standards has gradually been occurring as companies large and small move their production away from the North in search of lower wage costs. The impact of this in the South, however, remains limited and local, and the extent to which the living standards of consumers in the North are sustained by the low wages and prices paid to producers in the South continues to be one of the many unfairnesses (to say the least) of globalised capitalism.

The most serious problem for dependency theorists and activists was the question of what alternative development path dependent countries should pursue in order to overcome their dependency. Many dependency theorists, like the Russian 'populists' a hundred years earlier, have tended to advocate a return to some form of smallholder agriculture and local craft production. But as Gavin Kitching (1989) forcefully pointed out, they have rarely been able to show – and all too often have not seen the necessity of showing – how productivity could be raised under these conditions. In other words, they have not shown how any development would actually take place on this basis, which has tended to make dependency an unhelpful starting-point for policy makers and activists.

For a time some kind of socialist alternative did seem to be feasible, but harsh experience showed how hard this is to realise in practice. The distribution of power, both economic and political, in the contemporary world is such that a truly autonomous development strategy aimed at promoting the interests of the impoverished majority is extremely difficult for any individual country to realise on its own. Even a programme of redistributive state spending out of massive oil revenues, such as that pursued by the Chavez government in Venezuela, becomes a target of violent reaction by the possessing classes, with imperial backing. Many dependency thinkers now believe that the realisation of egalitarian development is only likely to be achieved if there is coordinated action on the part of a wide range of countries, and most probably only if there is a serious reaction against the logic and power of global capitalism in the imperial centres themselves – something not easy to envisage in the short term, which is what urgently concerns the poor in the South today.

It is easy, therefore, to be driven back to a reformist position, hoping at best to shift the existing arrangements and rules marginally in favour of the countries of the South, to give them some room for manoeuvre within the existing global capitalist system. Yet no convincing case has been made for a genuinely developmental alternative to socialism as a response to dependency. True, there is considerable variation in the way different countries and regions of the world have fared under the burden of dependency, and in their relative positions within the persisting global hierarchy, as documented by Arrighi. But the burden of dependency is felt more or less everywhere.

Africa may provide the most striking case in point – of the starkest structural constraints of dependency, and of the inescapable need to draw on the socialist imagination in order to overcome them. To be sure, Africa was perhaps the most economically backward region of any during the original period of Western imperialism, and some people still maintain that its historical backwardness has simply persisted to the present time. But this is to ignore the costs of the way in which Africa has been subordinated to the needs and requirements of Western colonial powers, from the era of the slave trade to the most recent era of neocolonialism. Although the concept of dependency was first developed in Latin America, it is unavoidable for any honest student of Africa.

For as Manfred Bienefeld (1988, pp. 85–6) has written:

> [B]oth those on the right and the left would do well to remember that the present African crisis was most clearly foreseen by those looking at Africa from a dependency perspective in the 1960s . . . After all it was their contention that a continuation of a 'neo-colonial' pattern of development would lead to disaster because it would produce a highly import- and skill-dependent economic structure that would depend critically on external markets and external investors and decision makers; that dependence would eventually become disastrous in its implications because the long term prospects for Africa's terms of trade were almost certainly poor; moreover, that dependence would be further reinforced because it would also create within African

countries a degree of social and political polarization that would lay the foundations for an increasingly repressive response once those contradictions became critical. Finally, that view was also very clear as to the fact that this entire edifice was essentially constructed on the backs of the peasantry who would have to pay for it eventually.

And, Bienefeld concludes, 'this describes exactly the present circumstances of Africa'.

Generally, it is clear that the price of the grossly unbalanced structure of wealth and power in the world continues to be exacted from those at the bottom end of the global hierarchy, through the mechanisms which dependency theory has unambiguously identified. Wherever else development theory may take us, then, it must begin by focusing on dependency and the forces that sustain it, and how they are to be overcome.

JOHN S. SAUL
COLIN LEYS

References and further reading

Amsden, A. (2003), 'Goodbye dependency theory, hello dependency theory', *Studies in Comparative International Development*, **38** (1), 32–8 (a comment on Arrighi, Silver and Brewer in the same issue, cited below).

Arrighi, Giovanni (1991), 'World income inequalities and the future of socialism', *New Left Review*, **189**, 39–65.

Arrighi, Giovanni, Beverly J. Silver and Benjamin J. Brewer (2003a), 'Industrial convergence, globalization and the North–South divide', *Studies in Comparative International Development*, **38** (1), 3–31.

Arrighi, Giovanni, Beverly J. Silver and Benjamin J. Brewer (2003b), 'Response', *Studies in Comparative International Development*, **38** (1), 39–42 (a reply to Amsden, cited above).

Bienefeld, Manfred (1988), 'Dependency theory and the political economy of Africa's crisis', *Review of African Political Economy*, **43**, 68–87.

Blomström, Magnus and Björn Hettne (1984), *Development Theory in Transition: The Dependency Debate and Beyond: Third World Responses*, London: Zed Books.

Frank, Andre Gunder (1969), *Capitalism and Underdevelopment in Latin America*, revised edn, New York: Monthly Review Press.

Kay, Cristóbal (1989), *Latin American Theories of Development and Underdevelopment*, London: Routledge.

Kay, Geoffrey (1975), *Development and Underdevelopment: A Marxist Analysis*, London: Macmillan.

Kitching, Gavin (1989), *Development and Underdevelopment in Historical Perspective: Populism, Nationalism and Industrialisation*, London: Routledge.

Leys, Colin (1996), *The Rise and Fall of Development Theory*, Oxford: James Currey.

Warren, Bill (1980), *Imperialism, Pioneer of Capitalism*, London: Verso.

Development Ethics

Introduction

Development ethics, now recognised as a distinct field in moral philosophy and as an interdisciplinary normative approach, borrows freely from social scientists and development practitioners. This new field functions as a kind of 'disciplined eclecticism': *eclectic* in its choice of subject matter, *disciplined* in its mode of study. Although development can be fruitfully studied as an economic, political, technological, or social phenomenon, the ultimate goals of development are those of human existence itself: to provide all with the opportunity to live full and meaningful lives, including that opening to transcendence designated in a 1986 Sri Lankan workshop as the 'full life paradigm'. Reflecting on long years as advisor to the UN's Economic Commission for Latin America, economist David Pollock (1980) poses this central development question in philosophical terms: 'What are the transcendental values – cultural, ethical, artistic, religious, moral – that extend beyond the current workings of the purely economic and social system?'. Development is best understood by studying the value conflicts it poses in four respects:

- debates over *goals*: economic growth, meeting basic needs, cultural survival, ecological balance, power transfers;
- competing *political systems* and *institutions*: divergent notions of legitimacy, authority, access to power, governance;
- contending *economic systems*: rival claims on resources and differing rules of access to resources; and
- conflicts between *modernity* and *tradition* which may pit individually chosen behaviour versus prescribed social customs or secular laws against those favouring a religious basis for the conduct of public life.

Development has always been an ambiguous term used *descriptively* or *normatively* to depict a present condition or project some desired alternative. Descriptive usage prevails in reports issued by international financial institutions, governmental planning and aid agencies, NGOs, academic works and testimonial writings. Normative usage appears there too but especially in works of advocacy which criticise development as presently conducted, advocate alternative visions deemed ethically superior, or totally repudiate development. Moreover, the same term 'development' refers both to the *ends* of social change and to the *means* employed to reach these: to the vision of a better life (materially richer, institutionally more 'modern', technologically more efficient), or to projects, programmes, and policies embodying that vision. Development practice is likewise fraught with ambiguities: under its banner parade bewilderingly diverse prescriptions for action. Development is inextricably an economic and political matter, a social and cultural issue, a problem of resource and environmental management, a question of civilisation and values.

Development ethics as now practised has emerged from two streams which increasingly converge in topics treated, if not in methodology and research procedures. The first flows from initial engagement in action by planners and project managers, through to the formal articulation of ethical strategies to guide future actions. The second stream originates in an internal critique of conventional ethical theory conducted by philosophers who then elaborate a distinctive way of doing ethics as normative praxis of development. Development ethics is no mere *application* of principles drawn from particular philosophical systems: Kantianism, Marxism, Rawlsian justice theory, virtue ethics, consequentialism, utilitarianism, positivism, or other 'rival versions of moral enquiry' (MacIntyre, 1990). It is practised in all the diverse ways in which philosophy is conducted. Nor does it draw upon a common set of initial assumptions or exhibit a uniform methodology or corpus of common conclusions. It is perhaps best represented as a cognitive plunge into the concrete realities of struggles by communities of the need to free themselves from the triple curse of underdevelopment – de-humanising misery, hopelessness and powerlessness. These struggles, and the institutional and programmatic responses to them, constitute the raw materials of the distinctive philosophical reflection undertaken by development ethicists as they craft ethical strategies and evaluative criteria. An existential, indeed an *agonistic*, conception of philosophy is clearly at play here, one which endorses the view of the Brazilian educator Paulo Freire that 'in underdevelopment people are mere *objects* of history; in development they become *subjects* of their own social history' (personal comment). The research procedure favoured by many development ethicists is phenomenological analysis, that is, the methodical unearthing and dissection of values and counter-values embedded, often in latent form, in development projects, programmes and policies.

Historical context

Before the 1980s, philosophers, social scientists and religious scholars who studied development's value dimensions did so only tangentially. And most economists, who enjoyed a predominant and entrenched position in development, paid little attention to the value implications of development. One important treatment of ethical values by an economist writing in the English language prior to Sen's *On Ethics and Economics* (1987) came from Gunnar Myrdal, in appendices to *Asian Drama* (1968) and *Objectivity in Social Research* (1969). In the 1970s, numerous Third World writers invoked categories of neo-colonialism, dependency and liberation to issue ethical condemnations of economic exploitation or cultural invasion perpetrated by rich countries on the poor.

In 1987 the International Development Ethics Association (IDEA) was formed by: Central American analytical philosophers, probing questions raised by the diffusion of technology and by social transformations occurring in their distinctive cultural settings; US analytical philosophers looking beyond Western theoretical sources to craft applied ethical norms to guide action in spheres of global change and international public policy; and Yugoslav praxis humanists searching for a non-dogmatic Marxism suited to the study of social and political change in the midst of accelerating technological complexity. The three groups agreed that the proper tasks of ethics are to diagnose vital problems facing human societies undergoing rapid change; to offer rationally grounded normative guidance to development policy makers; and to clarify value dilemmas surrounding these problems and policies, both in disciplined philosophical language and in what Ivan Illich (1981) calls 'vernacular' discourse aimed at informing the wider citizenry. Centuries earlier Niccolò Machiavelli and Adam Smith had stripped moral philosophy of its norm-setting role in society, the former by making a consciously amoral calculus of power and interest the guiding norm of politics, the latter by declaring the independence of economic 'laws' from moral philosophy. Along with later 'economic philosophers' such as Thorstein Veblen, Mahatma Gandhi and Myrdal, IDEA sought to restore value questions to the centre of theoretical, methodological and thematic debates on development, and invited economists, specialists of other disciplines and practitioners to lend critical attention to these questions.

Although it has only recently emerged as a coherent field, the roots of development ethics can be traced to several bodies of thought on how ethics applies to economics. Among these is Gandhi's implicit economic model based on trusteeship, the priority of meeting the needs of all over the satisfaction of desires of the few, favouring cooperation over competition, the pursuit of a right livelihood which brings economic sustenance while spiritually liberating its adepts from excessive attachment to material goods, and the gradual adoption of technology so as not to de-structure society culturally or socially. In the West one recalls Karl Polanyi (1957) urging that institutions of trade, money and market be placed at the service of reciprocity, redistribution and exchange so as to foster humane patterns of economic organisation. Quaker economics with its emphasis on community solidarity, non-violence and simple living, allied to creativity and industriousness – 'doing well by doing good' – has long exercised some modest influence in British and American economic thought.

The most self-conscious precursor of development ethics as a formal discipline, however, is Économie et Humanisme (EH), a French research centre of Christian inspiration. Its Manifesto, issued in 1942 by the mathematician–priest–social planner L.-J. Lebret, together with economists and professionals from the worlds of agriculture, fisheries, industry, handicrafts, labour unions and philosophy, invites others of every persuasion to join them in a common enterprise based 'on the direct observation of facts, which supplies us with a precise method for studying complex social wholes' (Dubois et al., 1942, p. 2, translated by author). EH criticises liberal capitalism and state socialism alike as depersonalising systems which generate mass unemployment, depopulate rural regions, increase urban squalor, shatter cultural vitality and stifle freedom. Differences encountered in the 400 ports and fishing sites studied between 1929 and 1942 – extending from Denmark to Italy, from England to Tunisia – forced Lebret's teams to adopt flexible research and planning approaches which combined quantitative and qualitative elements and could be adapted to varied localities. EH's interdisciplinary methodology was unwieldy, however, and because of the sheer number of analytical measures and the complexity of visual aids it employed to display synthesis, proved difficult to communicate to policy makers. Notwithstanding these deficiencies, EH pioneered in critically examining the theoretical and value bases of competing economic systems, and in creating instruments for linking the analysis of small units to an understanding of national and global units. Linking local to global units of analysis remains a vital task facing students of development and calls for new expanded definitions of development.

Current issues
Over several decades, development debates have been characterised by diverse efforts to craft comprehensive definitions of development. It has been defined as maximum self-sustained economic growth, institutional modernisation, the diffusion of technological progress, mass consumption, and the revolutionary political empowerment of oppressed masses. Sen's (1999) notion of development as freedom has gained wide acceptance in international development agencies, NGO circles, and in academic writings. Freedom is specified as a comprehensive set of capabilities which ought to be available to all, within opportunity structures and a system of effective entitlements which render possible the full array of 'functionings' which lead to human flourishing.

Alternative models, many of which are compatible with Sen's view, centre on participatory decision making, the elimination of unjust economic and social inequalities, sustainability, and optimum life sustenance, esteem and freedom. Development as an object of study is a mountain peak in a common chain of interpenetrating topics: human rights, democracy, cultural diversity and world order. Development ethicists explore norms and criteria of evaluation on a wide range of discrete issues: technology and its transfer; economic transitions; national development strategies; resource use; migration; war and peace; gender equity; urban life; rural poverty; inequality; the transformation of humanitarian aid, especially in zones of conflict, into developmental self-help; participatory decision making, governance and democracy; the 'rights and risks' mode of conducting benefit–cost analysis in large projects; rules for fair (and free?) trade; debt and debt forgiveness; non-reductionist indicators of human development; the rights and wrongs of globalisation, privatisation, aid, foreign investment and so on.

Development ethicists aspire to integrate their normative study of human well-being, individual and societal, with other normative disciplines, including descriptive, classificatory, analytical and policy disciplines. Notwithstanding the importance it assigns to the critique of goals and to the assessment of performance, development ethics may be usefully portrayed as a 'means of the means' which extracts, from within instrumentalities and constraints surrounding technical and political options, value allegiances and procedures to be followed in negotiating, with those who must bear them, tolerable value sacrifices attendant upon alternative courses of action. The econometrician Max Millikan (1962, p. 34) argued that planning ought to be the presentation of certain key alternatives to the community in ways which will help shape the evolution of the community's value system. It is a mistake, he adds, to assume that a society in transition has a clear view of its goals and a firm vision of its value objectives. Therefore, the planner's task cannot consist solely in showing the most efficient way to achieve these aims, since the actual path followed by a society in pursuing goals will be largely determined by the alternative futures portrayed by the planners.

Ethicists can easily forget that development is the art of creating new possibilities and, through this forgetfulness and its implied validation of the status quo may, in many circumstances act as plantation preachers who provide good conscience to economic masters while offering spiritual solace to their slaves. And they are easily tempted to subordinate the demands of morality to the uncritical acceptance of what are presumed to be economic imperatives or political necessities. Consequently, they do not discharge their task properly if they uncritically harness human aspirations to a life of greater justice and freedom to the development model which their technical and political colleagues favour: namely, economic growth, technical efficiency, integration into a competitive global economy, even structural change. Human values are not to be treated as mere means – aids or obstacles – to developmental ends; development is no self-validating absolute goal but a relative good, desirable only with reference to a particular view of the meaning of life. Although under certain aspects development is sought for its own sake, at a deeper level it is subordinated to the good life. As the UNDP's *Human Development Report 1992* observes:

> Human development is thus a broad and comprehensive concept. It covers all human choices in all societies at all stages of development. It broadens the development dialogue from a discussion of mere *means* (GNP growth) to a discussion of the ultimate *ends*. . . . The concept of human development does not start with any predetermined model. It draws its inspiration from the long-term goals of a society. It weaves development around people, not people around development. (UNDP, 1992, p. 2, original emphasis)

Conclusion

The essential task of development ethics is to render development decisions and actions humane. Stated differently, it is to ensure that painful changes launched under the banners of development do not result in anti-development which destroys cultures and exacts undue sacrifices in individual suffering and societal well-being – all in the name of profit, some absolutised ideology or efficiency imperative.

Most fundamentally, the primary mission of development ethics is to demand change and to keep hope alive. By any purely rational calculus of future probabilities, development efforts of many countries seem likely to fail. Poor classes, nations and individuals can never catch up with the rich as long as these continue to consume wastefully and to devise ideological or pragmatic justifications for not practising solidarity with the less developed. In all probability, technological and resource gaps will continue to widen and vast resources will continue to be devoted to destructive armaments. Exacerbated feelings of national sovereignty will, in all likelihood, continue to coexist alongside an ever more urgent need to institute new forms of global governance. By any likely scenario projected over the next 50 years, development in much of the world will remain the privilege of a relative few, while underdevelopment will continue – unnecessarily – to be the lot of vast numbers of human beings. Only some trans-rational calculus of hope, situated beyond closed boundaries of possibility, can elicit the creative energies and vision which authentic development requires. This calculus of hope must be ratified by ethics.

DENIS GOULET

References

Dubois, Alexandre, Jean-Marius Gatheron, Louis-Joseph Lebret, Marie-Réginald Loew, Marie-Fabien Moos, René Moreux, François Perroux and Gustave Thibon (1942), *Manifeste d'Economie et Humanisme* (Economy and Humanism Manifesto), Marseille, www.economie-humanisme.org/ResourcesPDF/Manifeste%201942.pdf.

Illich, Ivan (1981), *Shadow Work*, London: Marion Boyards.

MacIntyre, Alasdair (1990), *Three Rival Versions of Moral Enquiry: Encyclopaedia Genealogy and Tradition*, Notre Dame, IN: University of Notre Dame Press.

Millikan, Max (1962), 'Criteria for decision-making in economic planning: the planning process and planning objectives in developing countries', in *Organization, Planning and Programming for Economic Development*, US Papers Prepared for the UN Conference on the Application of Science and Technology for the Benefit of the Less Developed Areas, Vol. VIII, Washington, DC: US Government Printing Office.

Myrdal, Gunnar (1968), *Asian Drama: An Inquiry into the Poverty of Nations*, 3 vols, New York: Pantheon.

Myrdal, Gunnar (1969), *Objectivity in Social Research*, New York: Pantheon.

Polanyi, Karl (1957), *The Great Transformation: The Political and Economic Origins of Our Time*, Boston, MA: Beacon Press.

Pollock, David H. (1980), 'A Latin American strategy to the year 2000: Can the past serve as a guide to the future?', in *Latin American Prospects for the '80s: What Kind of Development?*, Norman Patterson School of International Affairs, Carleton University, Conference Proceedings vol 1, November, Ottawa.

Sen, Amartya (1987), *On Ethics and Economics*, Oxford: Basil Blackwell.

Sen, Amartya (1999), *Development As Freedom*, New York: Alfred A. Knopf.

UNDP (1992), *Human Development Report 1992*, New York and Oxford: Oxford University Press.

Further reading

Clark, John (2003), *Worlds Apart: Civil Society and the Battle for Ethical Globalization*, Bloomfield, CT: Kumarian.

Crocker, David (1991), 'Toward development ethics', *World Development*, **19** (5), 457–83.

Fox, Jonathan and L. David Brown (2000), *The Struggle for Accountability: The World Bank, NGOs, and Grassroots Movements*, Cambridge, MA: MIT Press.

Goulet, Denis (1971), 'An ethical model for the study of values', *Harvard Educational Review*, **41** (2), 205–27.

Goulet, Denis (1995), *Development Ethics: A Guide to Theory and Practice*, London: Zed Books.

Hausman, Daniel M. and Michael S. McPherson (1996), *Economic Analysis and Moral Philosophy*, Cambridge: Cambridge University Press.

Nussbaum, Martha C. (2000), *Women and Human Development*, Cambridge: Cambridge University Press.

Pelletier, Denis (1996), *Économie et Humanisme: De l'Utopie Communautaire au Combat pour le TiersMonde 1941–1966* (Economy and Humanism: from Communitarian Utopia to Struggle of Behalf or the Third World), Paris: Les Éditions du Cerf.

Diploma Disease

The Diploma Disease is the title of Ronald Dore's controversial book (1976, 1997a) on education, qualification and development. It provides the theme of two documentary films broadcast on Japanese and British television networks, the title of a teaching video, the subject of edited collections (Oxenham, 1984; SLOG, 1987), special issues of development and education journals (see IDS, 1980; AIE, 1997, 2000) and reviews and encyclopaedia entries (Little, 1992, 1997a).

The diploma disease is a ritualised process of qualification-earning whose consequences were thought to be especially deplorable in developing countries. 'It is something that societies, not individuals, get through the aggregation of the (mutually interacting) unintended consequences of ... "processes common to all societies"' (Dore, 1997b, p. 24). Those processes derive from modern bureaucratic organisations that 'rationalise' recruitment of persons for jobs by the use of educational records, especially in general education subjects. This renders schooling a 'positional good' whose value depends on how many other people have it. One consequence of this is qualification escalation, a rise in the qualifications required for a particular job. If the raised qualification enhances productivity then this process is economically efficient. If it leads to improved quality of life and citizenship it is socially rational. Dore questions this assumed efficiency and rationality, for reasons that have to do with the processes of learning and motivation. Distinguishing three motives for learning – learning for its own sake, learning to do a job, and learning to get a job – Dore suggests that in many societies learning to get a job has come to dominate the learning process. In displacing the other two motives for learning it undermines the potential of schools to develop human capital. The 'misallocation of social resources and the degradation of the teaching-learning process were thus the two "deplorable consequences" which prompted [Dore] to speak of the diploma disease' (ibid., p. 27).

The thesis draws strength from two lively theoretical debates contemporary to the 1960s and 1970s – (1) between human capital and screening theorists about variations in earnings; and (2) between the nurture and nature theorists about variations in human abilities. Dore's leanings were towards screening and nature.

While labour economists, sociologists and comparative educators have shown interest in the general thesis, those in development studies derive added value from its elaboration of three general propositions linked to the concept of 'late development'. Dore proposed that the later development starts (that is, the later the point in world history that a country starts on a modernisation drive):

1. the more widely education certificates are used for occupational selection; and
2. the faster the rate of qualification inflation; and
3. the more examination-orientated schooling becomes at the expense of genuine education (Dore, 1997a, p. 72).

Evidence for these 'late development' propositions was drawn from the experiences of England, Japan, Sri Lanka and Kenya, placed on a continuum from early to late development.

Three qualifications to the late development propositions followed. The size and prestige of public sector employment and the presence of a vibrant small-scale private sector would temper the first. The ability of governments to resist popular pressure for educational expansion would temper the second; and the strength of pre-modern educational traditions the third.

Drawing on the experiences of radical reform then current in China, Cuba and Tanzania, Dore also explored the prospects for stemming some of the processes linking jobs, qualifications and education, and develops his own modest proposals.

The original book and thesis met with mixed reactions. The plaudits stressed the elegance, wit, vigour and brilliance of the argument. Some critics questioned some of the basic tenets of the thesis, while others displayed a less than adequate reading and understanding of the (quite complex) argument (see Little, 1992, 1997a for summaries of the critiques and Dore's 1997b response).

Twenty years after its original publication, researchers have commented on the diagnosis and predicted course of the disease in the countries addressed originally by Dore. Aspects of the thesis in relation to England are explored by Wolf (1997, 2002). The England of the 1970s was relatively 'disease free'. Since then qualifications have proliferated; so too the number of young people sitting them. Wolf attributes this to a rational cost–benefit analysis by young people and their parents and the simple faith of politicians in the link between economic prosperity and education rather than to an increasing bureaucratisation of the workplace. While government planned and created a number of new vocational qualifications, uptake by young people was modest. These qualifications were viewed as the 'lemons' of the diploma world. Instead, young people opted for university courses in unprecedented numbers, transforming the higher education sector and the value attached to university diplomas in the labour market and increasing the pressure on young people to stay on in school. Despite these pressures, several associated with the symptoms of the diploma disease, there is little evidence that the quality of school education has been reduced.

Japan's case is explored by Amano (1997). The restructuring of the Japanese economy and society after the Second World War established extremely clear bureaucratic links between levels of jobs, incomes, labour market entrants and educational qualifications. Over time and as numbers expanded, Japanese employers began to pay attention not only to the level of qualification held by recruits but also to the institution or school attended. Japan became a 'which institution' rather than a 'which level' credentialling society. This process was assisted by developments in the educational assessment system itself and the development of the standard score system that ranked individuals, high schools and universities. But there are signs that the diploma disease may have run its course for some segments of the student population. Not all are participating in the examination and increasing numbers are turning against the traditional academic meritocratic values of school.

The Sri Lankan case is explored by Little (1997b). While confirming much of the original diagnosis for the Sri Lanka of the early 1970s, she identifies two processes that changed its subsequent course. The first was economic liberalisation introduced in 1978, the growth of the private sector and the paradoxical institutionalisation of political criteria for recruitment to government jobs. The second was the increasing competition between the country's two major ethnic groups – the majority Sinhalese and minority Tamils – for economic and political resources, the intensification of a civil war and the re-emergence of the Sinhala anti-state militancy that had made such an impression on Dore, some 17 years earlier (Dore, 1997b, p. 24). Since 1978, economic and educational growth increased, the gap between job seekers and jobs available decreased and political criteria for resource allocation increased.

Following Dore's thesis, one might infer that the value attached to educational qualifications would decline. Evidence suggests the contrary. Two reasons are advanced. First, the civil war, the politicisation of recruitment to government jobs and the resurgence of Sinhala militancy served to enhance, rather than diminish, the legitimacy of qualifications as a 'just' allocator of scarce resources, including jobs. Despite earlier problems associated with examinations and university entry, most ordinary Sinhala and Tamil war-tired citizens regard examinations as the only legitimate and fair way of allocating scarce resources in a conflict-ridden society. Second, economic liberalisation served to increase the supply of courses and qualifications by foreign suppliers and open up many more opportunities for the youth to travel abroad for further education and for jobs (Hettige, 2000; Little and Evans, 2005). Foreign suppliers of qualifications work alongside domestic suppliers in an ever-expanding market of qualifications and provide opportunities to labour markets worldwide. Where Dore's original analysis had focused on the emergence of national education systems and the use of credentials within national economies, more recent analyses suggest that the landscape of youth aspirations for education and jobs extends beyond the shores of Sri Lanka to a greater degree than in the periods about which Dore wrote. Not all youth can so aspire and there is a growing tendency for aspirations beyond national boundaries and participation in 'international' examinations to be the preserve of the better off (Lowe, 2000).

The case of Kenya – the most recent 'developer' in Dore's continuum of 'late development' – is addressed by Toyoda (1997) and Somerset (1997). Charting the massive expansion in primary and secondary enrolments in the 1975–92 period and the raising of the first major selection hurdle from Primary 7 to 8, Toyoda confirms that the demand for education and qualifications is as high as ever. Somerset describes the attempts made in Kenya to reform the quality of the Primary 7 and 8 selection exams in order to mitigate the worst effects of the examination on the process of learning, in particular the rote and ritualistic learning so abhorred by Dore. Arguing that many poor-quality national examination systems test 'passive, inert knowledge', Somerset (1997, p. 91) suggests that good examinations test active ideas and require learners 'to think about what they know, and to restructure it in some way', thus supporting, not subverting pedagogy.

Reflections

In a set of 'reflections' Dore (1997c) reassesses the original diagnosis in the light of (1) the experiences of England, Japan, Sri Lanka and Kenya; (2) the experiences of countries which held out some promise of reform, in particular China, Cuba and Tanzania; and (3) other research that has addressed aspects of the thesis over the past 25 years. 'How rudely history erupts in sociologists' attempts to arrive at generalisations about long-term trends!' he bewails (ibid., p. 189). While the original diagnosis had acknowledged the role of specific class structures, educational traditions and small-scale private sectors in modifying the three propositions about trends, the thesis did not provide for the impact on trends of traumatic historical events. Such events include the enormous changes in Japan as a result of the Second World War (Amano, 1997), the impact of the collapse of the Soviet Union on the economic and educational system of Cuba (Eckstein, 1997), the effects of civil war in Sri Lanka (Little, 1997b) and the switch from Maoist socialism to market socialism in China (Lewin, 1997).

Reflecting on the process of qualification inflation, Dore notes how some governments have called a halt to qualification spirals, even in the absence of traumatic historical events, and how employers inflate criteria within the same level of certificate via the grade of the level and the institution attended by the student. The propensity to do this, Dore suggests, may 'reflect a society's predisposition to believe in the human capital theory or screening theory explanation of how education systems work' (Dore, 1997c, p. 191).

Fundamental to the diploma disease thesis is the notion that the bureaucratisation of working life was a long-term and irreversible trend. Writing in the early 1970s, Dore did not foresee 'Thatcherism, Reagonomics and the neo-liberal marketist individualist revolution in the Anglo-Saxon world' (ibid., p. 194), all of which advocated that the public sector introduce performance-related pay systems and short-term contracts, in marked contrast to the security of a job for life offered by public and many large private corporation bureaucracies (especially in Japan). And if bureaucratisation is so important for the diploma does its reversal mean the end of the disease? Dore's reflection on Cooksey and Riedmiller's (1997) account of recent developments in Tanzania, especially the decline in primary level enrolments, suggests this might be so. 'The IMF and the World Bank's imposition of Thatcherite anti-public sector policies as a condition for survival loans, has so cut back on the bureaucratically organised jobs in government and the parastatals that the drive has gone out of the search for qualifications' (Dore, 1997c, p. 194).

Implicit in the original thesis were twin assumptions about the impact of qualification seeking qualifications on learning and working. The first was that the effects of a qualification-earning educational experience – ritualistic, tedious and suffused with anxiety and boredom, destructive of curiosity and imagination – would be the same for all ability groups. The second was that those 'who have been subjected to a ritualistic examination-oriented learning as children and adolescents are likely to turn into ritualistic, performance-evaluation workers, incapable of the sort of entrepreneurial initiative-taking which developing countries need' (Dore, 1997a, p. xxvii). Dore now suggests that it is not the brightest who are likely to suffer most from qualification-orientated schooling, but 'those who are bright without being the brightest, those who are within sight of whatever are socially defined as the desirable prizes in the competition, but by no means certain of reaching them without a very great deal of anxious effort' (Dore, 1997c, p. 200). And the complexity of relationships between learning motivations developed in school and in the workplace has been amply demonstrated by subsequent studies (SLOG, 1987; Little and Singh, 1992; Little, 2003).

Notwithstanding the caveats and qualifications to the original thesis it is interesting that several of Dore's concerns and issues, raised in the context of developing countries in the 1960s and 1970s, are now surfacing at a policy level in some developed countries. Wolf's

(2002) account of young people's views of vocational qualifications in England and the fate of vocational qualifications resonates with Foster's (1963) vocational school fallacy, identified in the Ghana of the 1950s and influential in Dore's thinking. Her questioning of the social rationality underpinning the expansion of higher education in the UK and elsewhere, resonates with Dore's descriptions of qualification escalation in developing counties. And some of the basic questions raised by Dore on the impact of external examinations on student motivations for learning are now attracting high-level policy interest in the United States and England and systematic reviews of research (for example, see Kellaghan et al., 1996; Harlen and Deakin Crick, 2003). The reviews underline the importance of understanding the motivation of learners and teachers in the process of education and the development of human capital. Harlen and Deakin Crick identify negative and positive impacts of summative evaluation on learners. Their recommendations for policy makers include one with clear links to the notion of human capital and lifelong learning. 'Not only is there growing recognition of the value of learning to learn and of the drive and energy to continue learning, but there is empirical evidence that these are positively related to attainment' (ibid., p. 203).

The debate about qualifications, examinations, motivation and learning will run for many more years to come.

ANGELA W. LITTLE

References

Amano, I. (1997), ' Education in a more affluent Japan', *Assessment in Education*, **4** (1), 51–66.

AIE (1997), special issue 'The Diploma Disease Twenty Years On', *Assessment in Education*, **4** (1).

AIE (2000), special issue 'Globalisation, Qualifications and Livelihoods', *Assessment in Education*, **7** (3).

Cooksey, B. and S. Riedmiller (1997), 'Tanzanian education in the nineties: beyond the diploma disease', *Assessment in Education*, **4** (1), 121–36.

Dore, R.P. (1976), *The Diploma Disease: Education, Qualification and Development*, London: George Allen & Unwin.

Dore, R.P. (1997a), *The Diploma Disease: Education, Qualification and Development*, 2nd edn, London: Institute of Education, University of London.

Dore, R.P. (1997b), 'The argument of the diploma disease: a summary', *Assessment in Education*, **4** (1), 23–32.

Dore, R.P. (1997c), 'Reflections on the diploma disease twenty years later', *Assessment in Education*, **4** (1), 189–206.

Eckstein, S. (1997), 'The coming crisis in Cuban education', *Assessment in Education*, **4** (1), 107–20.

Foster, P.J. (1963), 'The vocational school fallacy in development planning', in M.J. Bowman and C.A. Anderson (eds), *Education and Economic Development*, Chicago: Aldine, pp. 142–66.

Harlen, W. and R. Deakin Crick (2003), 'Testing and motivation for learning', *Assessment in Education*, **10** (2), 169–207.

Hettige, S.T. (2000), 'Economic liberalisation, qualifications and livelihoods in Sri Lanka', *Assessment in Education*, **7** (3), 325–34.

IDS (1980), special issue 'Selection for Employment Versus Education?', *Institute of Development Studies Bulletin*, **11** (2).

Kellaghan, T., G.F. Madaus, and A. Raczek (1996), *The Use of External Examinations to Improve Student Motivation*, Public Service Monograph, Washington, DC: American Educational Research Association.

Lewin, K.M. (1997), 'The sea of items returns to China: backwash, selection and the diploma disease re-visited', *Assessment in Education*, **4** (1), 137–60.

Little, A.W. (1992), 'The diploma disease and related literature', *Encyclopaedia of Higher Education*, Oxford: Pergamon.

Little, A.W. (1997a), 'The diploma disease twenty years on: an introduction', *Assessment in Education*, **4** (1), 5–22.

Little, A.W. (1997b), 'The value of examination success in Sri Lanka 1971–1996: the effects of ethnicity, political patronage and youth insurgency', *Assessment in Education*, **4** (1), 67–86.

Little, A.W. (2003), 'Motivating learning and the development of human capital', *Compare*, **33** (4), 437–52.

Little, A.W. and J. Evans (2005), 'The growth of foreign qualification suppliers in Sri Lanka: de facto decentralisation?', *Compare*, **35** (2), 181–91.

Little, A.W. and J.S. Singh, (1992), 'Learning and working: elements of the diploma disease thesis in England and Malaysia', *Comparative Education*, **28** (2), 181–200.

Lowe, J. (2000), 'International examinations; the new credentialism and reproduction of advantage in a globalising world', *Assessment in Education*, **7** (3), 363–78.

Oxenham, J.C.P. (ed.) (1984), *Education versus Qualifications: A Study of Relationships between Education, Selection for Employment and the Productivity of Labour*, George Allen & Unwin: London.

SLOG (1987), 'Why do students learn? A six country study of student motivation for learning', Institute of Development Studies Research Report Rr 17, University of Sussex, Brighton.

Somerset, A. (1997), 'Treating the diploma disease in Kenya: a modest counter proposal', *Assessment in Education*, **4** (1), 91–106.

Toyoda, T. (1997), 'Kenya 1975–1995: an introductory note on educational expansion', *Assessment in Education*, **4** (1), 87–90.

Wolf, A. (1997), 'Growth stocks and lemons: diplomas in the English market-place 1976–1996', *Assessment in Education*, **4** (1), 33–50.

Wolf, A. (2002), *Does Education Matter? Myths about Education and Economic Growth*, London: Penguin.

Disability and Development

Disability is any long-term impairment, which leads to social and economic disadvantages and to the denial of rights. Impairment is defined as any loss or 'abnormality' of psychological, physiological or anatomical structure or function. The development of the concept of the 'handicap' has emphasised environmental shortcomings, which prevent disabled people from participating in social life and working in the economy on a par with others (Yeo, 2001).

Disability is a serious development problem worldwide, and one for which data are unusually defective. Global estimates are built from scant and irregular surveys with inconsistent classifications, and from case material. Over 600 million people, or approximately 10 per cent of the world's population, are thought to live with a disability – at least two-thirds of them in developing countries (DFID, 2000). The proportion of the population deprived by disabilities increases with levels of economic development. With development, disability undergoes its own epidemiological transition, involving a decline in disabilities attributable to malnutrition/infectious disease and increases in both life expectation and survival rates from disabling accidents and degenerative disease (Harriss-White, 1996). The prevalence of moderate to severe disability worldwide increases from 2 per cent in infancy to 55 per cent in people over 80 (Yeo and Moore, 2003).

Although disability cuts across class, region, the rural–urban divide, the income distribution, and social segmentation by gender, ethnicity and religion, disability and poverty are strongly associated. As many as 50 per cent of disabilities are preventable and linked to poverty. Disabled people are estimated to account for 20 per cent of the world's poorest people – and for this reason alone disability reduction ought to be an essential element of development – whether conceived of as poverty reduction or capability expansion (ibid.). Yet disability is strikingly absent from utilitarian, welfare and Rawlsian theories of justice and well-being, and, as Sen pointed out in late 2004, both capability expansion and poverty reduction require attention to the earnings gaps of disabled people and the large and hidden 'conversion gap' made up by the costs of achieving parity with non-disabled people (Sen, 2004).

   Disability causes private poverty through exclusion from education and labour markets, inadequate social transfers, wear and tear and extra costs for treatment and palliative equipment (and its maintenance), other income forgone by those upon whom a disabled person is dependent, the costs of adaptation to hostile working and home environments, and the costs of accessing public goods and services. In underdeveloped market economies, people's bodies tend to be valued for their ability to function like machines. Work becomes a major defining element of social worth (Erb and Harriss-White, 2002). Wherever the reservation wage coexists with unemployment there are social norms barring entry to the labour market and barring self-employment. The socially acceptable body is key to such rules. Disabled people are unable to participate at an equal level with non-disabled people, which results in extraordinarily high rates of disabled unemployment. (There is little data for developing countries but in the USA the unemployment rate for disabled people is 71 per cent (Russell and Malhotra, 2002).) Economic exclusion creates a subclass of 'deserving poor', dependent on intra-household entitlements, charitable philanthropy and exiguous state transfers.

   Poverty causes disability along several direct pathways involving malnutrition, inadequate access to preventive and curative medical care, the prevalent risk of accidents and occupation-related injury. Chronic poverty results in limited access to education, employment, land and shelter, poor sanitation, healthcare, and to insufficient and/or unhealthy food. These factors force poor people to accept adverse incorporation in the workforce – with poor payment, insecure terms and conditions and unhealthy and hazardous workplaces. All these conditions are known to increase the risk of impairment. Social attitudes to impairment commonly involve a combination of ridicule, fear and discrimination which together lead to disability. Those who are discriminated against or disabled have been found to face raised probabilities of exclusion from formal/informal education and employment; they have poor access to (private) healthcare and quackery. They may also be disenfranchised from, or have lowest priority for, limited resources (food, water, inheritance rights to land and other economic assets). As a result, they suffer limited social contacts, low social expectations and self worth; they tend to be excluded from formal politics and severely deprived in the capability space of rights assertion. The set of interconnected social relations of disability thus reinforce poverty in all its dimensions: private income poverty, lack of access to public goods and services, capability deprivations, social exclusion and poor social and political participation (Yeo, 2001).

   Ironically, despite individual discrimination, disability is a social condition affecting the person, his or her household and its wider social relations; despite the shock of sudden accident or disabling illness, disability is a process over time often reinforcing clientelist and pauperising relations of debt and dependency. Up to 25 per cent of the population may be adversely affected as a result of disabilities – either through the direct cost of treatment, the indirect cost to those not directly affected (such as 'carers'/family members), and the opportunity costs of income forgone from incapacity (Harriss-White, 1999, p. 138). The 'indirect cost' of caring for a disabled child falls disproportionately on mothers or female relatives who must take time away from other reproductive work, income earning or school attendance in order to stay home and care for the child. In South India, economic losses to a rural region from the three costs of what is locally understood as 'incapacity' were estimated at up to 8 per cent of production in agriculture and the local non-farm economy (Erb and Harriss-White, 2002). In a Tanzanian survey, households with a disabled member were found to have a mean consumption less than 60 per cent of the average for the population, which led to the claim that 'disability is a hidden face of African poverty' (reported in Yeo and Moore, 2003).

Disability is socially regulated. In village studies, gender, ethnicity and social class have been found to affect the extent to which a given level of 'incapacity' is socially recognised and compensated for. Old age is defined not by age but instead by the onset of disabling incapacity from work. Gender determines the differential power and control men and women have over the socio-economic determinants of their mental health and lives, their social position, their status and treatment in society, their work and their susceptibility and exposure to specific physical and mental health risks. There coexists a tendency to think of people with disabilities as desexualised and genderless while also feminising the issue. Disabled women certainly face a risk of the simultaneous double discrimination of social exclusion and inclusion on abusive terms. They have been found to be socially recognised as disabled at a significantly more advanced stage of disability than men. Disabled women may be vulnerable on several counts: for example through the lack of permanent marriage partners, or the inability to defend themselves if attacked or raped, or the inability to make decisions on matters of sexuality due to powerlessness resulting from various forms of patriarchal discrimination and the lack of easily accessible and intelligible communication materials on health (Harriss-White, 1996).

The experience of disabled children in developing countries has been characterised by dependency, social isolation, vulnerability, powerlessness and last but not least (mortal) neglect and rejection. Disabled children may be unable to defend themselves, left alone at home, and undervalued by those around them. Disadvantages of these kinds make them particularly vulnerable to physical, sexual and emotional abuse. Such children are also less likely than their siblings to attend school, to go on outings, or to experience conditions where they have to solve problems or to contribute to household chores. Even when special needs schools exist, funding is limited, teachers often lack training and proper equipment, and the stigma surrounding disability can make parents feel ashamed to send their children to school. Only 1–2 per cent of disabled children in developing countries receive an education. As a consequence many disabled children lack self-esteem and confidence, which, in later adulthood reinforces unemployment and poverty (Yeo and Moore, 2003).

Disability is bottom of the list of priorities for development policy and activism. At its most conventional, disability is an 'add-on' and not argued to be intrinsic to effective poverty reduction. Lack of funding is often cited as a reason for its low priority, but it is a strange paradox for poverty reduction agencies to lack the resources to work with some of the poorest of the poor. Donor agencies rarely demand that disability be mainstreamed, as for instance 'gender' and 'environment' have attempted to be. Donor organisations facing intense pressures to make visible change find it risky, unfamiliar and challenging to work with people who are marginalised and spatially dispersed; they have been shown to be less aware of disabled people's needs than of those of other kinds of poor people and more inarticulate in representing them (ibid.).

Three different models have wide currency in addressing disability as a development challenge: the medical model, the charity model and the social model. In the medical model, disabled people are defined by their impairment; and medical/technical solutions are offered to alleviate their impairment. This is an individualistic approach focused on the medical and occupational rehabilitation of disabled people rather than on the social barriers disabled people face. The charity model focuses on helping disabled people through shelter and elementary welfare. It does not recognise the rights of disabled people or the role that discrimination plays in their livelihoods. The social model (whose development has been championed by disabled activists) focuses on the idea that an impaired person only becomes disabled when social and physical barriers limit his or her opportunities. At its most extreme, the body is denied to be impaired (and indeed there are cultures where deviant social practice, such as refusal to accept the parental choice of a marriage partner, is a sufficient condition for a woman to be considered disabled). More generally, three major types of social discrimination are emphasised in the social model: institutional (such as lack of schooling), environmental (such as being unable to participate socially and politically or to work for use or income, due to physical barriers), and attitudinal (such as facing low expectations, fear or embarrassment by others) (Lang, 2000; Yeo, 2001).

The costs of developmental responses to disability have featured prominently in literature on policy. Vocational training and job placement are strong points of cost-effective entry for social and economic integration, providing a mechanism for breaking the 'disability cycle' of isolation, dependence and chronic poverty. In addition, the social model puts emphasis on collective improvements in living conditions, such as dependable water supplies, sanitation, better nutrition, conflict prevention and safer transport, all of which can prevent the transition from chronic poverty to impairment, but which require more substantial resources. Community-based rehabilitation (CBR) is an attempt to provide medical care, by building on and validating existing local knowledge and information systems while also facilitating access to relevant information and ideas outside the community. It combines the elements of physical rehabilitation, medical care and social inclusion with the long-term goals of both individual and collective empowerment. Justified as cost effective, CBR has been criticised as being limited in its impact, necessarily small in scale and vulnerable to outsiders' imposed notions of 'community' (Harriss-White, 1996). However, specialist NGOs such as 'Basic Needs' is institutionalising innovative adaptations to CBR for the specially stigmatising conditions of mental ill health and mental disability.

But for disability to be mainstreamed in development, there needs to be a concerted effort to create a reliable data bank, to research the long-term social costs of exclusion as well as the short-term costs of inclusion, to dynamise participatory research to empower disabled people, and to reduce poverty in consultation with disabled people, their organisations and supportive professionals. While disabled people know best their own needs, some disability professionals have in the past had self-interested political agendas. There have been well-publicised instances of humiliation or abuse of disabled people from the very professionals who ought to be empowering them to claim human rights, civil and legal rights, and economic and social rights (ibid.). People with disabilities have themselves urged on development agencies a fourth model, one based on rights (DFID, 2000). Trends in best practice are towards full 'equality of opportunity' for persons with disabilities, entailing structural change, preparing people for greater participation, tackling discrimination in a number of areas and changing social attitudes among people who are not disabled. Equal treatment is necessary but not sufficient; an added allowance (or, as the UN terms it, a 'reasonable accommodation' to cover what Sen calls the 'conversion gap') is necessary to make rights 'real' for people with disabilities. The United Nations has passed 22 Standard Rules on Equalisation of Opportunities for Persons with Disabilities. These fall into three categories. The first is 'preconditions for equal participation' such as awareness-raising, medical care, rehabilitation and support services. The second is 'target areas for equal participation' such as accessibility, education, employment, income maintenance and social security, family life and personal integrity, culture, religion and recreation/sports. The third consists of 'implementation measures' such as information and research, policy making and planning (Yeo and Moore, 2003). Where disabled people have been consulted, they put highest priority on equal treatment, restorative equipment, sexual fulfilment, access to rights and entitlements, mobility, credit, employment and livelihoods (Erb and Harriss-White, 2002). If development is self-realisation through social agency as well as improvements in material conditions then the quality of the lives of people with disabilities must be one of its most sensitive indicators.

BARBARA HARRISS-WHITE
DEVI SRIDHAR

References

DFID (2000), *Disability, Poverty and Development*, London: Department for International Development, UK Government.

Erb, S. and B. Harriss-White (2002), *Outcast from Social Welfare*: *Adult Disability in Rural South India*, Bangalore: Books for Change.

Harriss-White, B. (1996), *The Political Economy of Disability and Development with Special Reference to India*, Geneva: United Nations Research Institute for Social Development.

Harriss-White, B. (1999), 'Onto a loser: disability in India', in B. Harriss-White and S. Subramanian (eds), *Illfare in India*, New Delhi; Sage, pp. 135–62.

Lang, R. (2000), 'Perceiving Disability and Practising Community-based Rehabilitation: A Critical Examination with Case Studies from South India', PhD Thesis, University of East Anglia, Norwich.

Russell, M. and R. Malhotra (2002), 'Capitalism and disability', in L. Panitch and C. Leys (eds), *A World of Contradictions: Socialist Register*, London: Merlin, pp. 211–28.

Sen, A.K. (2004), 'Disability and justice', Keynote Speech at the Disability and Inclusive Development Conference, World Bank, 30 November to 1 December, http://siteresources.worldbank.org/DISABILITY/214576-1092421729901/20291152/Amartya_Sen_Speech.doc, 16 January 2005.

Yeo, R. (2001), 'Chronic poverty and disability', Chronic Poverty Research Centre Working Paper no. 4, Institute for Development Policy and Management, University of Manchester, Manchester.

Yeo, R. and K. Moore (2003), 'Including disabled people in poverty reduction work: "nothing about us without us"', *World Development*, **31** (3), 571–90.

Disaster Mitigation

What is disaster mitigation?

Disaster mitigation as a development concept largely has its origins in the context of disasters and disaster risk management. It specifically describes measures, strategies and activities that minimise the adverse impact of natural, technological or other threats through what are known as 'structural' and 'non-structural' mitigation measures. Disaster mitigation efforts primarily focus on managing the 'risk factors' that drive the potential for disaster loss by targeting the hazard or threat itself (for instance an upstream dam designed to avert downstream flooding). This is often referred to as 'structural mitigation', as it requires infrastructure or engineering measures to 'keep the hazard (that is, the flood) away from those at risk'.

However, disaster mitigation efforts also target those that are at risk, by reducing their vulnerability to a specific threat (for instance, through the enforcement of land-use regulations and public education in a flood plain). This is often called 'non-structural mitigation', as it promotes risk-reduction behaviours and attitudes to 'keep people away from hazards and threats' (in this instance, a potential flood). Non-structural mitigation efforts also include education, empowerment and social mobilisation initiatives that reduce the vulnerability of specific at-risk groups, such as women- and child-headed households in areas that are exposed to natural and other threats.

Why is disaster mitigation relevant to development?
Although mitigation as an organising concept has been extensively applied in disaster-related fields, it has been less explicitly applied in developmental contexts. This is in part due to past and continuing disjunction between developmental action and what is popularly viewed as disaster management – a perception which defines actions that are disaster related as somehow separate from development concerns. Yet, there is increasing evidence that sustainable development and poverty reduction objectives are not achievable if disaster risk is not more effectively managed, and losses avoided or minimised wherever possible. This applies at all scales, from regional and national levels to the experience of individual households and families.

Repeated disaster losses undermine development
For instance, extreme weather events such as cyclones, hurricanes and powerful winter storm systems can trigger widespread flooding and disruption to services, as well as damage and destruction to physical infrastructure that result in sizeable losses and development setbacks even in developed nations. Similarly, poor families affected by repeated drought shocks in areas isolated from essential public services are also witness to the erosion of their already precarious asset base, levels of health and potential for sustaining their livelihoods. In urban areas, poor residents of densely congested informal settlements may find their homes destroyed by recurrent fires, landslides or floods that might never be declared 'national disasters'.

It is clear that this repeated destruction of household assets as well as erosion of household livelihoods sets back development potentials at household, community, national and even regional levels where powerful transboundary threats – including extreme weather systems – have the potential to trigger severe losses across many countries.

What is also clear is that poor households, communities and countries bear disproportionately high losses compared with their wealthier neighbours. Evidence suggests, for instance, that poor countries repeatedly shocked by tropical storm systems, other extreme weather events, earthquakes, droughts and epidemics, sustain significantly larger losses proportionate to GNP than wealthier nations, who have the capacity to absorb the impact and recover more quickly.

These examples illustrate reasons why ongoing strategies to 'mitigate' the effect of expected shocks and stresses such as extreme weather events should be viewed as integral elements of development planning. This is because they help avoid the unnecessary losses and hardships that compromise and undermine potentials for development – particularly in poor households, communities and countries.

However, it is not only people who sustain losses when exposed to external shocks and stresses. Our natural environment, especially with respect to its more fragile ecological zones, is particularly vulnerable to external forces. Intense and rapidly spreading wild-fires can destroy natural vegetation, which in mountain areas have the potential to desta-bilise steep slopes. Intense and protracted drought processes can accelerate rates of soil erosion.

In these instances, robust development planning and action in fire or drought exposed areas should ideally incorporate appropriate *disaster mitigation* strategies to minimise the chance of such destructive losses. In the former example, this might include restoring the natural fire regime in a wooded area. This would allow ecologically robust natural burn processes to occur within controlled parameters and avoid the accumulation of an ageing and highly dangerous fuel load. In the second, the use of careful ploughing techniques that minimally damage the topsoil of drought-prone agricultural land can assist in miti-gating the impact of rainfall scarcity. In this context, many effective mitigation measures are drawn from generations of indigenous knowledge, which reflect a deep understanding of naturally occurring hazard processes. Examples of this include the use of contour ridges or terraced agricultural practices in Asia to reduce the risk of land instabilities on steep hillsides. They also include the long-established practice of flood-plain recession cul-tivation in riverine areas of Asia, Africa and the Middle East that face recurrent drought risks. In this instance, residents protect their livelihood security in the dry season by cul-tivating the nutrient-rich flood-plain as the floods recede.

'Development' has potential to increase disaster losses

In the same way we recognise that repeated losses from disasters undermine development opportunities, it is now understood that poor development practices also increase the probability of disaster loss and hardship. As 'development' forces expansion into areas that are more ecologically vulnerable, our exposure to potential losses increases. This includes urban, recreational and commercial development in coastal zones as well as estu-arine areas that increase the likelihood of losses triggered by storm surges and coastal flooding. It also includes development of wooded mountain regions and risks associated with land instabilities, fires, flash floods and avalanches. Moreover, the expansion of agri-cultural activities into areas that are already under pressure increases the likelihood of losses from drought. Today, we are especially conscious of the links between disasters and the rapid growth of cities, particularly those in developing countries, characterised by the rapid in-migration of poor households seeking to escape rural poverty or – in many instances – armed conflict. In addition to pressing needs for social and other essential ser-vices, affordable housing is an urgent priority. However, this rapid largely unplanned urban growth is reflected in non-engineered formal and non-formal housing, seldom built in compliance with building codes and regulations. These homes, and the families who live within them, are highly vulnerable to natural and other threats, which may include land-slides, earthquakes, extreme weather, communicable disease outbreaks and informal set-tlement fires. Such 'development' within cities places the lives and livelihoods of tens of thousands of people at risk annually.

Sound and sustainable development minimises disaster loss

Disaster mitigation has a direct role to play in minimising the processes of risk accumulation that drive the possibility of disaster events. For instance, the protection of wetlands has long been valued for ensuring the continuity of rich and diverse ecosystems. It is increasingly recognised that wetlands also offer 'free environmental services' that include the properties of flood attenuation and flood mitigation. It makes environmental sense to nurture not only these protective services, but also good mitigation practice, to minimise the potential for destructive floods.

Similarly, effective poverty reduction and social assistance programmes that support the most economically at-risk members of a community are important disaster mitigation mechanisms. In wealthier countries where grants and pensions are accessible as government-supported social safety nets, those most at risk are economically cushioned from external shocks. In other contexts, community-based saving schemes, money clubs and farming cooperatives also provide a buffer against modest shocks for their individual members – even if these are not sufficiently robust to withstand extreme loss.

In countries where HIV/AIDS and other communicable diseases compromise individual and household capabilities to manage everyday stresses, let alone more extreme shocks such as drought and flood events, accessible equipped and affordable health services are crucial disaster mitigation mechanisms. In fact, health and education services have been identified as central to the developmental reduction of disaster-related losses. It is recognised that measures should be taken to reduce the risk of disaster-related losses to such services and facilities wherever possible. This, in the case of health services, ensures service continuity in times of stress when life-saving medical services are most needed, and similarly for schools, avoids costly disruptions to learning. Schools and other buildings are also often depended on as community evacuation centres when an area is affected by an endangering weather system, flood, fire or earthquake – and, unknowingly may place large numbers of children at risk if they are not appropriately risk proofed for expected threats.

As our knowledge of effective risk-reduction measures increases, it is possible to apply and adapt mitigation solutions in different contexts. For instance, Latin America and the Caribbean's extensive experience in hurricane- and earthquake-proofing schools and health facilities is equally relevant to other developing contexts that face similar threats.

Disaster mitigation and risk reduction

In the past, disaster mitigation was largely viewed as an element of disaster management. Today it is regarded as a critical component of developmental risk reduction, in which vulnerabilities and disaster risks are reduced and sustainable development opportunities strengthened. This approach shifts from a focus on 'managing disaster events' to the developmental and ongoing 'reduction of disaster risks'. In this context, disaster risk is viewed as the likelihood of loss due to the interplay between an *external* threat (such as a drought or extreme weather event) and *internal* conditions of vulnerability.

An example of this would be the impact of a significant – but not necessarily severe – wind and rainstorm. Residents of well-built houses with solid foundations, walls and roofs would withstand this without difficulty. This might be in contrast to the experience of informal settlement residents whose homes are made of wood and corrugated iron sheeting and who live in areas without municipal storm water drainage, and who might be flooded out, lose their possessions, be temporarily displaced or become ill.

In this example, it is not the external threat (the storm) that was responsible for the disproportionate impact on the informal settlement residents. It was their underlying conditions of economic, social and environmental vulnerability that contributed to the storm's adverse impact and hardship. In many developing countries, the risk profile of informal settlements is significantly driven by this interplay of economic, social and political marginalisation processes. Located far from a city's main business and commercial nodes, and with limited access to dependable transport, informal settlement residents are economically and spatially marginalised. Moreover, as many have their origins in outlying areas characterised by minority political, ethnic or religious affiliations, their political leverage is limited in achieving appropriate support developmental intervention from the local authorities.

In this instance, among the disaster mitigation strategies that may be considered are those that focus on structural measures, including effective low-cost techniques to better weather-proof flimsy non-engineered structures. They might also involve the rehabilitation of neighbouring wetlands if applicable and strengthened systems for disseminating weather-warning information to the residents of settlements at risk. Appropriate non-structural mitigation measures may also include the establishment of representative consultative processes between the local authorities and settlement residents to collaboratively upgrade the areas most at risk.

Effective disaster mitigation today calls for greater attention to these developmental drivers of disaster risk, and gives greater emphasis to measures that reduce the vulnerability or, its reciprocal, to, enhance the resilience of those most at risk. In flood-, fire-, storm- and drought-prone areas, effective mitigation practice requires the same transparent and participatory decision-making processes that are applied to other forms of development.

In the same way, our investments in development are less likely to be undermined if they incorporate disaster mitigation measures for known and expected risks – irrespective of whether they are capital-intensive housing projects or community-based rainwater harvesting initiatives. However, the relative effectiveness of selected mitigation interventions is itself determined by the degree to which chosen measures are sustainable and/or can adapt to a rapidly changing physical and social environment. For instance, structural coastal defences to prevent erosion and storm surges can eventually be pounded away by the ceaseless motion of waves. Moreover, rapid unplanned urban growth can overwhelm municipal capabilities to provide essential protective services and also lead to unplanned occupation of high-risk areas.

We live in a world characterised by increasing climate variability and population densification in hazard-exposed areas – both accompanied by the likelihood of increased disaster loss. If indeed we are to achieve our aspirations for sustainability in this increasingly risk-prone environment, then disaster mitigation is a non-negotiable component of development planning and implementation.

AILSA HOLLOWAY

Further reading

Abramovitz, J. (2001), 'Averting unnatural disasters', in Lester R. Brown, Christopher Flavin, Hilary French and others (eds), *The State of the World 2001*, Worldwatch Institute, New York, London: W.W. Norton, pp. 123–42.

International Federation of Red Cross and Red Crescent Societies (2002), *World Disasters Report: Focus on Reducing Risk*, Bloomfield, CT and London: distributed by Kumarian Press and Eurospan.

Pelling, M. (2003), *The Vulnerability of Cities: Natural Disasters and Social Resilience*, London: Earthscan.

Twigg, T. (2004), *Good Practice Review 9: Disaster Risk Reduction, Mitigation and Preparedness in Development and Emergency Planning*, London: Humanitarian Practice Network, Overseas Development Institute.

United Nations (2002), *Living with Risk: A Global Review of Disaster Reduction Initiatives*, United Nations Inter-Agency Secretariat, International Strategy for Disaster Reduction, United Nations, Geneva.

United Nations Development Programme (2004), *Reducing Disaster Risk: A Challenge for Development*, Bureau for Crisis Prevention and Recovery, United Nations, Geneva, www.undp.org/bcpr/disred/rdr.htm.

Wisner, B., P. Blaikie, T. Cannon and I. Davis (2003), *At Risk: Natural Hazards, People's Vulnerability and Disasters*, London: Routledge.

The Domar Model

The uniform custom is to speak of the Harrod–Domar model, rather like the Arrow–Debreu model or the Modigliani–Miller theorem. In fact, the Harrod (1939, 1948) and Domar (1946, 1947) models have a lot in common: dependence on a simple fixed-proportions model of production; arrival at the same famous necessary condition for equilibrium growth. But there was no reciprocal influence; Domar (1957, p. 92) tells us that he stumbled upon Harrod's 1939 article just after he had sent his own 1947 paper to the printer. And in the end there are many differences in focus and in the commentary accompanying the skeletal elementary algebra of both authors. Just because the formal models were so simple, much of the economics had to be supplied by interpretative remarks and reflections.

The Domar (like the Harrod) model can usefully be discussed on its own. My recollected impression is that Harrod attracted more attention in the 1950s, perhaps because his discussion of investment decisions was both richer and more obscure than Domar's; but some varieties of growth theory in the 1980s and 1990s sound more like Domar than like Harrod.

Domar gets to the Harrod–Domar condition – which really does have to be attributed to them both – in a direct supply-and-demand way. A constant level of (net) investment I will generate a constant level of income Y from the demand side: $Y = I/\alpha$, where α is the marginal and, by assumption, average propensity to save, and the price level is assumed not to be varying. This is just the instantaneous multiplier. But a constant level of net investment will lead to capital accumulation and a perpetually increasing productive capacity or potential output (P), so $dP/dt = sI$, where s is an incremental output–capital ratio, also assumed to be technologically given and constant.

Domar then points out that if a dollar of investment creates s dollars of capacity 'locally,' it will likely add less than s dollars to economy-wide capacity. That is because some existing capital and capacity may be rendered obsolete or uncompetitive, or because new capacity may draw labour, natural resource inputs or other factors away from older capacity, or because there is an induced shift in the mix of goods sorted by capital intensity. Besides, some of the new investment may turn out to have been misdirected and unviable. In Domar's phrase, some capacity, somewhere, may have to be 'junked'. On the economy-wide scale, the incremental and average output–capital ratio is then $\sigma < s$, also constant, and the appropriate supply-side equation is $dP/dt = \sigma I$.

Domar says that his agenda could be carried out in principle if s and σ are variable; he must mean variable in time, but still exogenous. He knew perfectly well that investment decisions are far from mechanical. But it will not do to say that s and σ are today whatever economic conditions and expectations cause them to be. He is talking about long-run growth. The parameters do not have to be literally constant; but they have to change slowly, smoothly and predictably for the model to make sense in its own context.

Suppose the economy starts in equilibrium with $P_0 = Y_0$. Then a necessary condition for equilibrium growth is obviously that $dP/dt = dY/dt$, or $\alpha^{-1}dI/dt = \sigma I$, or $r = \alpha\sigma$ where r is the growth rate of investment (and, under fixed coefficients, of income) that is *required* if the economy is to remain in balance with $P_t = Y_t$. Domar is very insistent that this is not a statement about how fast the economy will grow, but a statement about how fast the economy can grow and must grow if it is to remain at 'full employment'. I put those last two words in quotation marks because they are the words actually used, although neither paper, despite their titles, contains any explicit analysis of employment and unemployment. Domar was quite aware of this gap, but left any serious consideration of the labour market to occasional remarks in passing. At one point he writes that his procedure amounts in practice to treating capital as the only factor of production.

In one passage Domar assumes explicitly but casually that employment is a function of Y/P; but this makes no sense because employment itself has a scale, while Y/P is dimensionless. I think Domar understood this full well, and meant to make the employment or unemployment *rate* a function of Y/P. Then 'full employment' would mean the employment rate consistent with $Y/P = 1$. That would be reminiscent of – indeed an anticipation of – Okun's Law, a perfectly good short-run device. But this is about growth and the long run, and a more fundamental treatment of the labour market is called for.

If investment and output actually grow at a rate $g < r$, then eventually Y/P tends to $g/\alpha\sigma = g/r$. In other words there will be persistent 'unused capacity and unemployment'. Domar was acutely aware of the possibility that an assumed growth rate g will lead to a utilisation rate $g/\alpha\sigma$ so small that further growth of investment even at rate g cannot be sustained. He left it at that. This was precisely the sort of potential instability that Harrod discussed at length, but obscurely and – in my personal judgement – unsuccessfully.

Towards the end of the 1947 article, Domar brings up a very interesting question: '[I]t was shown that a state of full employment [sic] can be maintained if investment and income grow at an annual rate of $\alpha\sigma$. The question now arises as to what extent the argument can be reversed: suppose income is guaranteed to grow at the $\alpha\sigma$ rate; will that call forth sufficient investment to generate the needed income?'. Each year's income Y is 'guaranteed' (or firmly expected) to grow by the amount $Y\alpha\sigma$. For simplicity assume there is no autonomous investment. Presumably the expected growth of output would induce enough investment to create a matching increment in capital, thus an amount satisfying $sI = Y\alpha\sigma$, or $I = Y\alpha\sigma/s$.

Domar now considers two cases. If $s \approx \sigma$, that is, if investment is well directed and 'creative destruction' is limited, the induced investment will be about $Y\alpha$ and will just match the amount of saving. Macroeconomic equilibrium will be maintained. This is a case in which a credible public guarantee of growth at rate $\alpha\sigma$ will induce the private actions that validate the guarantee. If, on the other hand, $\sigma < s$, then induced investment is less than saving, and a (contractionary) disequilibrium is likely; the mere guarantee will fail because it can not force the discard of old equipment in the amount $(s - \sigma)I$; less than the required amount of new investment will be undertaken: '[A] substantial difference between s and σ simply indicates that with the available labour force and the current progress of technology, the maintenance of full employment under a given α requires the accumulation of capital at a faster rate than it can be used' (1957, p. 81). 'Animal spirits' in the form of new products, aggressive competition and all that can create the required investment (or even more), but then it is not the guarantee of growth that is doing the work.

Clearly Domar, like Harrod, believed that the more worrisome threat to macroeconomic equilibrium was the danger of a contractionary failure, the likelihood that investment and income would grow more slowly than the required rate, with excess capacity and unemployment as the outcome. It is interesting that although he discussed policy in passing, he did not devote much space to the provision of incentives to invest. (There is, however, a paper that finds some use for accelerated depreciation allowances (1957, ch. VIII).) Perhaps a one-asset economy is not suitable for that line of thought.

Domar merely mentioned two lines of policy: one was to reduce α, to discourage saving; the other was the promotion of more rapid technological progress, not so much to increase productivity but to stimulate autonomous investment, leaving less for the acceleration principle to do. Naturally he preferred the second.

Domar himself noted that his model treated capital as the only explicit factor of production. This made it easy, perhaps even natural, to leave aside any tendency to diminishing or, for that matter, increasing returns. To do otherwise would have complicated the model itself and the corresponding theory of investment. As it happens, recent work in the theory of growth, especially that connected with the so-called AK models along with many mild generalisations, has moved back in that somewhat Domaresque direction, paying attention to only one factor of production. In that incarnation, the one-factor models tend to be very optimistic, more so than Domar would have found plausible. He would not have approved of the recipe for economic development sometimes distilled from the Domar model: just save more.

Robert M. Solow

References

Domar, E.D. (1946), 'Capital expansion, rate of growth, and employment', *Econometrica*, **14** (April), 137–47. Reprinted as Chapter III in E.D. Domar, *Essays in the Theory of Economic Growth*, Oxford and New York: Oxford University Press, 1957.

Domar, E.D. (1947), 'Expansion and employment', *American Economic Review*, **37** (March), 34–55. Reprinted as Chapter IV in E.D. Domar, *Essays in the Theory of Economic Growth*, Oxford and New York: Oxford University Press, 1957.

Harrod, R.F. (1939), 'An essay in dynamic theory', *Economic Journal*, **49** (March), 14–33.

Harrod, R.F. (1948), *Towards a Dynamic Economics*, London: Macmillan.

East Asian Crisis

From May 1997 to late 1998 several East Asian countries were hit by a major economic crisis, which initially took the form of collapsing values of their currencies and soon spread to declining national incomes and ballooning unemployment. Unlike Latin America, where the *absence* of periodic debt or currency crises leaves economists edgy and pondering about what is happening to the world, in East Asia it was the occurrence of a crisis that threw economists into a deep quandary.

For nearly four decades the bulk of East Asia was a model of economic propriety. These countries were conservative in their fiscal policy, played safe on the international market and experienced booms in their exports and national income like no other region in the world. On 1 March 1997, *The Economist* magazine, while pointing to some cracks in the East Asian economies, nevertheless, noted that 'on most structural issues, these economies have got a large number of big things absolutely right: high savings, prudent monetary and fiscal policies, openness to trade'. And then, noting that the baht had risen a little – by 15 per cent – over two years, it asserted that 'in general, though, the Asian currencies are not over valued'. Little did the magazine know then that this was being written on the eve of the biggest currency collapse and general economic dislocation that this region had known.

When in May 1997, the Thai baht came under some speculative attack, the initial reaction everywhere was that this was a minor market correction that would be weathered easily by the economy. But the problem persisted and then, on 2 July, the baht, which was traditionally kept pegged to the US dollar, was permitted to float and soon it was depreciating rapidly. There was dismay when the crisis, far from being quickly doused, was found to be spreading to other East Asian countries. Within months the contagion of currency crisis spread to the Philippines, Indonesia and Malaysia, and, then with a bit of a lag it hit Korea. In the month of July itself, the Thai baht lost 25 per cent of its value, the Philippine peso lost 13 per cent, the Indonesian rupiah lost 5.7 per cent and the Malaysian ringgit lost 4.4 per cent (Rakshit, 2002). The worst was yet to come.

The crisis would continue for nearly two years, leaving scars that would last for much longer on some countries, such as Indonesia. In the case of Indonesia it is arguable that the crisis lasted longer because it fed into political instability. That the crisis would come to a close in two years is also testimony to the overall strength of these economies and smart policy response, especially in the case of Korea and Malaysia.

During the first 6 months of the crisis – from June to December 1997 – all these five countries saw their share prices plunging and their currencies losing value. The falls in average share prices were 24 per cent for Thailand, 36 per cent for the Philippines, 44 per cent for Indonesia, 46 per cent for South Korea and 49 per cent for Malaysia. These problems carried over to the real economy, with national incomes falling in all five countries over 1998. The GDP of the Philippines fell by 0.5 per cent, for Korea the fall was

5.8 per cent, for Malaysia it was 7.5 per cent, Thailand's GDP fell by 9.4 per cent and Indonesia's declined by an astonishing 13.2 per cent (ibid.). While these countries were the worst hit, the contagion also affected Japan and even Brazil. As a result of the crisis numerous firms went bankrupt, and there were runs on banks, some of which actually collapsed, including Japan's Hokkaido Takushoku.

The above are the broad contours of the East Asian crisis. Because it was so unexpected, it has led to greater soul searching than any other crisis. Clearly, this was a very different crisis from the ones that Latin American countries have periodically faced. The grounds for the latter were laid through budgetary overspending and general fiscal profligacy. The East Asian crisis drew home the point that in today's globalised economy, with international capital flowing all over the globe, virtually any country is fair game for the spark of currency crisis, especially because it is now clear that a crisis is only partly caused by fundamentals and much depends on the beliefs of agents and these could be founded on nothing to start with but quickly become self-fulfilling (Wan, 2004). The best bet for a country is to build up strengths so that the spark of crisis does not escalate to a general economic downturn.

With hindsight we know the changes in the global economic structure which prepared the ground for the East Asian crisis. Inter-country capital flows began growing rapidly when, a few years after the breakdown of the Bretton Woods system in 1973, many countries began to ease capital controls. Initially, the predominant capital flows were between the industrialised countries. But thanks to the sharp oil price rise of the 1970s, many of the East Asian countries felt an acute need for dollars and began a process of relaxing capital controls and, by 1990, capital was surging into East Asia, and would maintain an inflow rate of 148 billion dollars per annum for the next six years. Moreover, what we now know, in retrospect, is that the proportion of short-term debt was exceedingly high in these countries; and it was the sudden outflow of this money that caused the crisis (Furman and Stiglitz, 1998). Finally, behind most of these crises was a facilitating political factor. A large number of banks in this region had a disproportionately large share of non-performing assets. This was, in large measure, a reflection of the countries' political structure and pervasive influence of crony capitalism.

The East Asian crisis has caused a major rethinking of policies for countries caught in a currency crisis. Initially, the belief was to administer to these countries the standard prescription that the IMF offered to countries in crisis, to wit, to cut back on government spending, open the economy more and push up interest rates to attract money. In November 1997 when Hong Kong was expecting a speculative attack, it raised the overnight interest rate to 300 per cent. But it has been argued that these prescriptions, borrowed largely from the previous Latin American experience, were misplaced in the Asian context and actually exacerbated the economic problems of the region (see Furman and Stiglitz, 1998; and Wan, 2004).

One of the excesses indulged in by East Asian firms in the late 1990s was to borrow foreign exchange for domestic use. So when the price of the dollar rose sharply in terms of their own currency, these firms found their debt burden rising and balance sheets worsening suddenly. And with the domestic interest rates rising at the same time, they were caught in a dreadful bankruptcy trap. This is the only way to understand why exports did not pick up sufficiently from, for instance, Indonesia, when the value of the rupiah collapsed (as textbook economics would predict). The reason is that firms went bankrupt and did not have even the little working capital needed to be in business. The recognition of the role of the balance-sheet problem of firms has also given rise to some new theoretical writings on the problem of currency and debt crises (Krugman, 2000).

There was another important lesson in the East Asian crisis. Just as we have for some time become aware of contagion between *countries*, by which a currency problem of one nation can spark off problems in a seemingly unrelated country, with globalisation there has occurred a linking of *markets* that was not there earlier. This 'market contamination' phenomenon helps us understand why the housing market, the stock market and the foreign exchange market were so hopelessly intertwined in this crisis (Basu, 2003).

Note that as companies began to do badly and banks went bankrupt (in some cases because of overlending to companies that invested heavily in the housing market and the housing market was not doing well) the stock prices in these countries – let us here consider Thailand for illustration – naturally fell. In earlier times, when currencies did not flow freely across borders, this crisis would have remained contained. But nowadays with so much cross-country lending, consider people in New York who may have invested money in the Bangkok stock exchange. When the stock prices begin to fall they will try to take their money out of stocks, like all investors; but unlike domestic investors, most of them will then proceed to convert their money back to dollars (since they had converted to bahts, in the first place, only in order to buy Thai stocks). But when they do this, the demand for bahts will fall and that of dollars will rise, causing the baht to lose value. Hence, a domestic market problem tends to convert to an exchange rate crisis in today's globalised environment. And of course once the exchange rate collapses the contamination of the problem spreads to all goods and services that are exported or imported.

It is easy to reach wrong policy conclusions from this analysis. It is true that capital mobility was a channel though which crisis spread. But to curtail capital mobility would be the wrong conclusion to reach. The boom of the late twentieth century owes much to the mobility of capital and no serious economist would argue that this mobility should be stopped. This would be the classic case of throwing away the baby with the bathwater. We have to keep the door open for savings and capital to flow from where there is excess to where the returns are high and this responsibility has to lie, essentially, with the private sector.

The lesson that many economists have taken away from the Asian crisis, however, is that capital flows must not be equated with the flow of goods and services. While we may want to remove all hindrances from the flow of goods and services, some friction in the flow of capital may be worthwhile and some disincentives on building up too large a fraction of short-term capital to total capital may be worth instituting. The key issue is not the free flow of capital but what form the capital takes and how it is used. Adding some friction to the flow of capital or discouraging the excessive use of short-term capital could then be viewed as *instruments* for diverting the capital to more efficient use.

But these are just the broad contours of policy for countering crises of the kind that East Asia faced. The crisis is still too recent for us to have worked out the full details of what the right response should be. In the next few years, the theory of currency collapse and the policy ideas on how to stave it off will no doubt evolve as we debate and ponder one of the biggest crises of the twentieth century. And once these ideas have matured we will be able to sit back for a while until a new mutant crisis hits the world and sends us back to the drafting board.

KAUSHIK BASU

References

Basu, Kaushik (2003), 'Globalization and the politics of international finance: the Stiglitz verdict', *Journal of Economic Literature*, **41**, 885–99.

Furman, Jason and Joseph E. Stiglitz (1998), 'Economic crises: evidence and insights from East Asia', *Brookings Papers on Economic Activity*, no. 2, pp. 1–135.

Krugman, Paul (2000), 'Balance sheets, the transfer problem, and financial crises', in P. Isaard, A. Razin and A. Rose (eds), *International Finance and Financial Crisis*, Norwell, MA: Kluwer Academic Publishers, pp. 31–44.

Rakshit, Mihir (2002), *The East Asian Currency Crisis*, Oxford and New Delhi: Oxford University Press.

Wan, Henry (2004), *Economic Development in a Globalized Environment: East Asian Evidences*, Norwell, MA: Kluwer Academic Publishers.

Economic Aid

Definition

Capital flows to developing counties may be either official or private. With the exception of charitable contributions through NGOs, which are of limited quantitative significance (4 per cent of the value of official aid), aid is a part, indeed the largest part, of official flows. Official aid flows go either directly from the aid agency to support activities in the recipient country (bilateral aid) or to an international organisation such as the UN or the World Bank (multilateral aid).

The donors' club, the Development Assistance Committee (DAC), defines 'aid' as flows from official agencies to developing countries and multilateral institutions which satisfy two criteria: (1) primarily intended for development purposes (which rules out both military aid and export credits), and (2) highly concessional, defined as having a grant element of at least 25 per cent. The grant element is the grant equivalent divided by the face value, where the grant equivalent is the face value of the loan less the present value of repayments discounted at 10 per cent. A grant has a grant element of 100 per cent and a loan with an interest rate of 10 per cent a grant element of 0 per cent. DAC maintains a two-part list of 'eligible recipients'. Flows meeting the above criteria to countries on DAC's Part I list (mostly low- and middle-income countries) are called official development assistance (ODA), and those to countries on Part II (high-income countries, including those in Eastern and Central Europe) are called official aid (OA).

Origins of aid

The origins of aid can be traced to three factors: (1) the aftermath of the Second World War; (2) the Cold War; and (3) the demise of colonialism. Immediately after the Second World War, Europe received substantial aid flows from the United States under the Marshall Aid plan. The perceived success of this plan led to the view that similar efforts could be directed towards achieving development. The political will to do so increased with the emergence of the Soviet Union as a superpower: the USA and the USSR used aid to build political support among the newly independent countries. Until the 1960s other developed countries made contributions to the United Nations but did not have their own bilateral programmes. Countries such as Great Britain initially planned to phase out financial support to colonies as these countries became independent. However, the wave of African independence in the 1960s changed this view as many of these countries seemed to require substantial subventions. At the same time other donors with no colonial past, such as Sweden, were beginning bilateral programmes motivated by their social democratic orientation.

Aid volume
The value of aid increased in nearly every year since the 1960s until the early 1990s, when it peaked at US$62.7 billion in 1992. In the next four years the total then fell, down to US$47.9 billion in 1997, but has since recovered, most markedly in the years since 2001, reaching US$105 billion in 2005 (DAC, various years). These trends are more muted, but still present, when real aid is considered. Aid's share of donor income also declined in the 1990s. This share has, on average, fallen from a high of close to 1 per cent in the early 1960s to fluctuate between 0.30 and 0.35 per cent for two decades, but then fell to its present level of around 0.20 per cent once aid declined. There is a UN target that aid should be 0.7 per cent of GNP. But that target is further away than ever from being met.

While the fall in aggregate aid has been partly driven by the collapse of US aid to less than 0.1 per cent of GNP, falling aid is a general phenomenon. Comparing each donor's aid peak in the late 1980s or early 1990s, out of 21 donor countries in DAC, 11 recorded a substantial decline in aid performance compared to (a fall of more than 0.1 per cent of GNP), and five others a small fall. Only one country, the UK has experienced no change, in fact being a story of a decline from the mid-1990s, reversed in the most recent years. Four countries have had increasing aid ratios, which in the case of Denmark brings it up to the position of 'top-ranking donor' based on share of GNP.

Underlying these country-level trends have been shifts in the relative importance of different donors. The US share fell from over half in the 1960s to well under a fifth by the end of the 1990s. Japan's increasing aid made it the largest single donor in the early 1990s, accounting for just over a fifth of all DAC bilateral aid. The USA remains the second-largest donor in absolute terms, with a programme just over double that of the next rank of donors (France, Germany and the United Kingdom, with shares of DAC aid of around 10 per cent).

DAC donors dominate the aid scene, more so today than in the past since aid from what were the two main groups of non-DAC donors (the Soviet bloc and OPEC) has been declining over time, becoming relatively insignificant by the end of 1990s. In 2000, non-DAC donors provided US$1120 million of ODA (net) – that is just over 2 per cent of the value of DAC aid – of which US$780 million was bilateral.

One reason why aid has fallen in the 1990s has been the diversion of aid towards former-communist countries, which are mostly Part II countries. But this is not the whole picture: in 2000, OA was US$7.8 billion compared to total ODA of US$49.5 billion, meaning that OA 'accounted for' about 60 per cent of the 'shortfall' in ODA compared to its nominal peak in 1992. Other likely reasons for the fall are also related to negative repercussions from the end of the Cold War, which (1) resulted in the decline of aid from the Soviet bloc and one DAC donor (Finland), and (2) the demise of US aid, which has always been the most politically motivated and so consequently declined once the Cold

War was won. In addition, the United States has traditionally given 20–25 per cent of its aid to Israel. The graduation of Israel off Part I of the DAC list thus badly hit the volume of US ODA since the money has continued to flow to Israel, rather than be reallocated to countries eligible for ODA.

Multilateralism

Multilateral aid has risen from one-fifth of aid in the 1960s to a third of the total by 2000. The impetus for this increase in the 1970s and 1980s was the role of the Bretton Woods institutions in financing the response of developing countries to first the oil-price shocks and then the debt crisis, reinforced in the 1970s by the expansion of the World Bank under the presidency of Robert McNamara. For European countries, an additional factor has been the increase in the size of the aid programme of the European Union, which has gone from just over 3 per cent of total aid in the 1970s to nearly 9 per cent in the most recent years; for EU members this share rose from 11 to 20 per cent from 1989–90 to 2000. But a further factor underlying the rising multilateral share in the 1990s has been the shrinking aid programme, since multilateral contributions are to some extent a 'fixed cost' in a donor's aid programme.

The geographical allocation of aid

The share of aid going to low-income countries rose during the 1980s, but fell back somewhat during the 1990s to around two-thirds of the total. At the same time, aid to high-income countries has declined, the rise being among low–middle-income countries. Mirroring these changes was a rise and fall in aid to Sub-Saharan Africa. The share of both Europe and Far East Asia has gone up. These increases reflect new aid programmes to former communist countries in both former Soviet Union and Eastern Europe, and also China and Vietnam. Since aid has been falling, so have per capita aid receipts in many of the poorest countries: Sub-Saharan Africa has been triply hit by a falling share of a shrinking aid budget compounded by a growing population, resulting in a drop of real aid per capita of over 40 per cent between 1990 and 2000.

Higher aid to lower–middle-income countries is in part explained by aid recipients graduating from the low-income to the low–middle-income country category. Such improvements in income present donors with a dilemma. Withdrawing aid from good performers, as they no longer need it, can send the wrong signal and so create adverse incentives. In practice, donors have been slow and reluctant to phase out aid, only doing so when a country's fortunes are very well established (for example, Botswana). But failing to graduate good performers off aid at a time of falling real aid budgets means that the neediest countries are receiving a smaller slice of a shrinking cake.

At the country level there is considerable disparity in aid per capita, which is explained both by differences in income and also by country size. There is a small-country bias by which small countries get more aid per capita than large ones, so a region with lots of small countries (Sub-Saharan Africa, the Caribbean and the Pacific) will get more aid per capita than a region with a few large countries (South America), or a region with even one very large country (China in East Asia and India in South Asia).

The main approach towards the explanatory analysis of the allocation of development aid distinguishes between recipient need (RN) measured by variables such as income per capita, infant mortality and balance-of-payments difficulties and donor interest (DI) captured by colonial and strategic dummies, foreign investment arms sales and donor–recipient trade links. This literature thus casts some light on the motivations for aid. Where aid is altruistically motivated, then RN should play the major role in explaining the allocation of aid. But if donors use aid as a means of promoting their own strategic interests, then DI variables will dominate. The main finding has been that DI has been dominant in the allocation of bilateral aid – especially for the United States, and less so for Scandinavian countries – whereas the RN model better explains multilateral allocations (Maizels and Nissanke, 1984; McGillivray, 2003).

Hence, while there is a moral case for aid, it is clear that the actual motivation for aid is a combination of altruism and self-interest. Self-interest may be enlightened self-interest in the sense that development is a global public good. Poverty in the developing world will have adverse consequences in terms of environment, pestilence (for example, AIDS), war and refugees, whereas Third World prosperity will provide growing markets for our goods. This view has been forcibly argued on several occasions, such as in the Pearson (Commission on International Development, 1969) and Brandt (Independent Commission on International Development Issues, 1980) reports. But a narrower self-interest has been behind much aid. The United States has been the most explicit in using its aid for both political and commercial advantage, and has experienced the sharpest decline in volume post-Cold War. But it is not the only country to make the case for self-interest – Margaret Thatcher publicly stated that British aid should serve British interests. Use of aid to promote the donor's commercial and political interests will usually undermine its effectiveness in poverty reduction, distorting allocation by country, sector and project design. Dependency theorists argue that self-interest is the sole reason for aid, which is used to reinforce the subordinate positions of poorer countries by, for example, financing projects to promote exports of raw materials and imposing conditions for the receipt of aid to open their markets, a view forcibly expressed by Teresa Hayter in *Aid as Imperialism* (1971), and several subsequent publications.

Aid effectiveness
Aid effectiveness – how well it achieves its objectives, which are usually stated in terms of poverty reduction – can be measured at micro (project) level and macro level, how aid effects a country's development performance usually measured by economic growth. Project evaluations carried out by donor agencies find the majority of projects, usually between 70 and 80 per cent, to be satisfactory. Certain sectors (agriculture) and regions (Sub-Saharan Africa) have a lower percentage of satisfactory projects. However, these assessments are not usually based on rigorous evaluations. Very little is known about the impact of aid on poverty – though we do know that a very small percentage (around 10–15 per cent) is used to directly benefit the poor (White, 1996).

During the 1980s the view emerged that projects could not be successful if the policy environment were not 'right', being one rationale for the move towards supporting structural adjustment programmes. The link between policy and aid effectiveness became more firmly established by the World Bank's *Assessing Aid* report (World Bank, 1998). In response, several donors have tried to reallocate their aid towards countries with 'good policies', with moves for this approach (called 'selectivity') to displace the former practice of conditionality (which have aid in return for promises of reform), which is widely perceived to have failed. Where governments are good, there is moreover less need for projects, the money can simply be given to the government to spend as it sees fit (budget support) or donors can be part of a general framework for a specific sector (the sector-wide approach). However, there are strong academic criticisms of the research underpinning the move to selectivity. Hansen and Tarp (2001) and others have found that the econometric finding that aid only works with 'good policy' is not robust to different specifications, samples and definitions. Lensink and White (2000) have raised questions as to what constitutes good policy, how it should be measured, and practical problems in applying selectivity. An alternative approach that avoids these problems is to select on the basis of outcomes rather than policies. Moreover, the question is still open as to how aid should most effectively be used to reduce poverty, which is meant to be the common cause of donors today.

HOWARD WHITE

References and further reading

Commission on International Development (1969), *Partners in Development* (The Pearson Report), New York: Praeger.
DAC (various years), *Development Cooperation Report*, Paris: OECD.
Hansen, H. and F. Tarp (2001), 'Aid and growth regressions', *Journal of Development Economics*, **64**, 547–70.
Hayter, T. (1971), *Aid as Imperialism*, Harmondsworth: Penguin.
Independent Commission on International Development Issues (1980), *North–South: A Programme for Survival: The Report of the Independent Commission on International Development Issues* (The Brandt Report), London: Pan Books.
Lensink, Robert and Howard White (2000), 'Assessing aid: a manifesto for aid in the twenty-first century?', *Oxford Development Studies*, **28** (1), 5–17.
Maizels, A. and M.K. Nissanke (1984), 'Motivations for aid to developing countries', *World Development*, **12** (9), 879–900.
McGillivray, Mark (2003), 'Modelling aid allocation: issues, approaches and results', WIDER Discussion Paper no. 2003/49, United Nations University, Helsinki, Finland, www.unu.edu/hq/library/collection/PDF_files/WIDER/WIDERdp 2003.49.pdf.
Tarp, Finn and Peter Hjertholm (eds) (2000), *Foreign Aid and Development*, London: Routledge.
White, H. (1996), 'How much aid is used for poverty reduction?', *IDS Bulletin*, **27** (1), 83–99.
World Bank (1998), *Assessing Aid*, Washington, DC: World Bank.

Education for All and the Millennium Development Goals

Introduction
The World Education Forum in Dakar in April 2000 identified six targets for educational development (see Table 3) within a framework for action to support education for all (EFA) (UNESCO, 2000). These Dakar Goals (DGs) encompassed the expansion of early childhood education, the achievement of universal primary education by 2015, meeting the learning needs of young adults, achieving a 50 per cent improvement in literacy levels by 2015, eliminating gender disparities in primary and secondary schooling by 2005, and improving quality in terms of measurable learning outcomes related to literacy, numeracy and essential life skills. Development partners promised that no country with a feasible plan to achieve the goals would fail as a result of lack of resources.

The Millennium Development Goals (MDGs) were declared in September 2000 (UN, 2000). These goals included two of the DGs: universalising primary education by 2015

Table 3   The six Dakar Goals

Goals
1. Expanding and improving comprehensive early childhood care and education, especially for the most vulnerable and disadvantaged children
2. Ensuring that by 2015 all children, particularly girls, children in difficult circumstances, and those belonging to ethnic minorities, have access to and complete free and compulsory primary education of good quality
3. Ensuring that the learning needs of all young people and adults are met through equitable access to appropriate learning and life skills programmes
4. Achieving a 50% improvement in levels of adult literacy by 2015, especially for women, and equitable access to basic and continuing education for all adults
5. Eliminating gender disparities in primary and secondary education by 2005, and achieving gender equality in education by 2015, with a focus on ensuring that girls' full and equal access to and achievement in basic education is of good quality
6. Improving all aspects of the quality of education and ensuring excellence for all so that recognised and measurable learning outcomes are achieved by all, especially in literacy, numeracy and essential life skills

Source: UNESCO (2000).

and eliminating gender disparities by 2005; and six other goals: eradicating poverty, reducing child mortality, improving maternal health, combating HIV/AIDS, ensuring environmental sustainability, and developing a global partnership for development (see Millennium Development Goals, this volume).

Subsequently two global monitoring reports (UNESCO, 2002, 2003) have been published on education, which chart progress towards the goals. These identify the status and progress of countries towards those goals which can be quantitatively assessed, and comment on qualitative developments. In brief, total enrolments in primary schools increased from about 600 million to 650 million between 1990 and 2000. Despite registering the largest relative gains, Sub-Saharan Africa (SSA) remained the region furthest from universalising participation. About 44 million children failed to attend school in SSA, with a further 32 million out of school in South and West Asia (SWA). Girls' enrolments have been increasing faster than boys'. In SWA and the Arab states girls comprise between 60 and 66 per cent of those out of school, and about 53 per cent in SSA. Sixteen countries were judged far from the goal of universalisation in 2015, 13 of which were in SSA. About 21 countries seemed unlikely to achieve gender parity in primary education by 2015, and 45 countries are likely to miss gender parity at secondary school by 2015 (UNESCO, 2003).

Several issues are noteworthy:

● First, the MDGs that relate to education are often cited as just those that apply to universalising primary schooling and gender equity in schools. Much educational target setting by governments and their development partners has focused on these and most performance indicators linked to disbursement of external assistance relate to aspects of these. This is unfortunate and misleading. The eradication of poverty and hunger is unlikely without educational investment broadly distributed, not least because educational achievement is correlated everywhere with income and employment (Blaug, 1972; Psacharopoulos, 1987; Woodhall, 1987; Knight and Sabot, 1990; Appleton, 2001; Hanushek, 2003) and because there are few if any cases of industrialisation which were not accompanied by increased access and participation in education (World Bank, 1993; Landes, 1998). Reductions in child mortality and improvements in maternal health are also widely correlated with the educational status of mothers (Cochrane, 1979; Cochrane et al., 1980). Combating HIV/AIDS, malaria and other diseases is in part a problem of public health education and awareness, environmental sustainability depends in part on understanding the interdependence of eco-systems and the consequences of environmental degradation which is best acquired systematically, global partnerships for development are unlikely to be equitable if vast differences remain in educational endowments.

- Second, it is generally recognised that quantitative targets have acquired more significance (UNESCO, 2002) in much of the dialogue surrounding EFA, and that qualitative improvement may have been underemphasised as a result. This may not be surprising. Establishing the proportion of a population with access to primary schooling may not be easy but has a relatively low level of ambiguity. Determining whether educational quality is improving is fraught with problems of definition, values, and differentiated outcomes that are difficult to resolve and may be very problematic to generalise about across countries and cultures.

- Third, the MDGs and DGs can be interpreted in different ways. Most obviously some or all can be linked to human rights (UNESCO, 2003) where their achievement takes precedence over other goals that are merely desirable. Alternatively all the goals can be seen as ambitions to be achieved while recognising the trade-offs that may be necessary between goals and in terms of the timescales over which each might be achieved. A question is therefore whether universal enrolment at primary level should take precedence over improved enrolment levels at secondary or tertiary level.

- Fourth, the specification of MDGs and DGs does not recognise interaction between goals. Two examples make the point. If primary schooling is to be universalised in low-enrolment countries, many new teachers will have to be trained. Assuming that such teachers need to have completed secondary schooling at a minimum then, where secondary systems are very small, they must be expanded in advance of meeting demand for new primary teachers (Lewin and Caillods, 2001; Lewin and Stuart, 2003). The sustainability of universal primary schooling depends on adequate growth in the national economy to support its costs. This growth depends on far more than investment in primary schooling, especially where increasing proportions of national wealth are associated with knowledge and skill acquired at higher levels (Becker, 1993; Wood and Ridao-Cano, 1996; Mayer and Wood, 1999; Hanushek, 2003). Where as much as 70 per cent of investment in formal education is at primary level, as is the case in some of the poorest countries, other levels may be starved of support, creating shortages of higher-level human resources.

- Fifth, some MDGs and DGs appear unattainable for technical reasons. Thus achieving gender equity at primary and secondary school levels by 2005 was clearly impossible for countries with the greatest differences in gender balance when it was announced in 2000. It could only have been achieved by implausible actions – attracting back into the higher grades of primary and secondary schools girls who had left school, discouraging boys from continuing in higher grades and so on. The goals themselves are largely uncontentious; their technical specification is sometimes flawed.

The MDGs and DGs are important in shaping national planning and external assistance to poor countries. It has become almost mandatory to frame development plans which are subject to scrutiny and support externally, in terms of the goals and derived targets. Poverty reduction strategy programmes required for budgetary support invariably take them as one reference point. Benchmarks have been established to guide target setting for key system variables (Bruns et al., 2003). A critical perspective on the MDGs and DGs and the processes that surround their application needs to explore problems of origin, ownership and definition; questions concerned with monitoring progress involving standards and performance criteria; mechanisms of accountability; and omissions and possible conflicts of interest.

Origin, ownership and definitions

The MDGs and DGs have the legitimacy provided by the conferences that generated them and by their repeated affirmation in subsequent meetings of international development partners at the global, regional and national levels. There are several issues that arise:

First, as global targets they are largely blind to the differences between countries and education systems, and are mostly silent on distributional issues at the intra-country level. This may not matter too much at the highest level of generality (for example, enrolling all children in primary school by 2015) since it is easy to get consensus that this is desirable. It is problematic as overall goals are translated into more specific targets. Thus, identifying desirable levels for the pupil–teacher ratio, class size and teachers' salaries as a percentage of GDP percentage of private sector provision and so on, based on regional norms, best-practice judgements or simply casual empiricism, acquires very different meanings in different systems. Starting-points are very different, and prospects for the achievement of goals very varied.

Second, the goals are the product of a process at the international level, which is not embedded in any national political system. The significance of commitments made by representatives of states in international meetings are mediated by the realities of power, resource availability, national politics, and the transience of those who make the commitments. If the commitments are not embedded nationally, with a fair degree of consensus, they are unlikely to shape policy or its implementation. If they are, they will be differentiated quite strongly between country cases, and be in conflict with globally homogeneous targets.

Third, targets may be defined in different ways. Some of the possibilities include absolute definitions, for example, primary education as a human right (all girls and boys should complete primary); median benchmarking (the average pupil–teacher ratio in primary and secondary schools is x and y, therefore x and y are targets for each school);

successful practice comparison (countries which have universalised primary have pupil–teacher ratios of x, therefore x is the target); best-case approaches (achievement levels at grade 6 in literacy and mathematics are a and b in the highest-performing reference country, therefore a and b are targets); arithmetic or other statistical types of equity (achievement of group n is less than that of group m; group n should have the same level as group m); compensatory approaches (marginalised group e has spending per child of f compared to an average of g, spending per child for group e should be increased by h per cent more than the average to compensate for marginalisation). Which types of targets are identified, on which basis, clearly have implications for the extent to which they may be understood, accepted, and acted on. It may also shape which group's interests may be threatened, and which supported, when decisions are made over resource allocation which involves trade-offs.

Goals, standards and performance criteria

The second set of problems surrounds the use of targets in planning and implementing policy. The reality is that external assistance to the poorest countries is linked to conditionalities which seek to tie progress to disbursement. The indicators chosen then shape priorities, sometimes perversely. Some dilemmas include the following:

- First, the level at which targets are set carries implications for organisational and individual responses. Where criterion referencing is used, the criteria selected can be problematic. If they are set too high their achievement will be beyond the capability of a majority; if they are set too low their achievement will be trivial to most. Many of the MDGs and DGs have largely been achieved in middle-income countries. For some of the poorest their achievement by 2015 is widely regarded as improbable. In those policy systems, unachievable outcomes may simply come to be ignored in practice. Targets and criteria need to be defined differentially if they are to be feasible; they need to be seen to be achievable.
- Second, to be useful, targets must define criteria and measure standards of achievement. Often there are alternative ways of measuring performance (100 per cent completion of primary schooling within the primary school age range; or completion defined to include obtaining a primary school leaving certificate which is criterion referenced; or 100 per cent completion for children of any age born after 2010; or completion defined to include post-primary accreditation of those who drop out). Which standards are applied clearly has implications for apparent success.

Accountablity

If targets are to be useful it should be clear who is accountable for their achievement and what consequences flow. There are two problems here.

One problem relates to the locus of responsibility. If target setters are far removed from target getters (those with the responsibility for their achievement), disjunctions may occur which lead to low levels of credibility, commitment and accountability. If chains of accountability are diffuse and spread across many organisations and organisational levels, they are unlikely to invite effective ownership. If target setters have not had experience of target getting, they may set unrealistic targets that lack credibility.

Also, target achievement may paradoxically penalise the successful and reward the lag-gards. If the price of success is the withdrawal of subsidy and additional support to achieve the target, it may be more attractive to fall short. If the price of success is another more demanding target, the same is true. Falling short of the target, especially if the causes are lost in a fog of confused accountability, may be more attractive than succeed-ing. There may be an element of moral hazard if reaching targets has high stakes.

Possible contradictions

Whatever targets are set, they may have different significance for different actors. Two examples make the point.

First, targets adopted by developing-country governments may or may not coincide with public service agreements and other organisational goals which development part-ners work within, whether they be development agencies answerable to national govern-ments, or national or international NGOs with boards of directors. The scope for confusion is substantial, with many different stakeholders responsible in different ways for the achievement of goals and targets.

Second, target getting is generally seen as the responsibility of governments. At the post-primary level, development strategies increasingly assume contributions to educa-tional provision from non-government providers. Where these are wholly private (and especially where they are for-profit organisations), there is no obvious incentive to recog-nise national targets; where private provision is subsidised it is unclear what, if any, responsibility is shared.

Concluding remarks

Issues related to goals and targets draw attention to many of the problems which can be encountered in practice. They do not constitute a case to abandon targets as a useful tool in the planning and implementation process. Rather they are a reminder that targets have a variety of characteristics that need to be understood by users.

The analysis suggests that such targets should be:

- generated and owned though a process which embeds them in national policy debate and seeks to generate a consensus among key stakeholders and ownership by implementers;
- feasible to achieve over defined time periods taking into account stated priorities across the education sector;
- set and defined by those with some experience of implementation;
- differentiated across countries to reflect different starting-points, priorities, historic realities, political possibilities and resource constraints;
- designed to recognise that redistributive targets (reducing the variance in class size, pupil–teacher ratios and so on) may be as important as achieving a desired average value;
- linked to other targets and tested for consistency, constructive interaction and destructive interference;
- presented in forms that can be understood by key stakeholders at different levels of the education system; and

- integrated with medium-term budget allocations and coherent implementation strategies that can be sustained.

A final observation is that it may be useful to consider the value of goals and targets focused on rates of increase rather than on desired end points. Most existing targets specify outcomes at points in the future. Current overviews of progress on EFA suggest that many of the poorer countries are at risk of failing to meet these. Past experience indicates that targets that are not thought feasible are dropped in advance of their achievement dates – the goals and targets set in 1990 at the World Conference on Education for All, which included universalising primary education by 2000, receded into the background before the Dakar conference; the gender equity target for 2005 is widely regarded as not feasible and will be changed. It is almost inevitable that some targets for some countries will have to be rescheduled or revised if they are to be believable by those closest to the responsibility of achieving them. There is a case not only to differentiate timeframes between countries, but also to reconceptualise some goals and targets in terms of rates of change and improvement. These new goals could prove more durable, would not have to be continually revised as they became implausible, and might just be a more useful tool in planning at the national, regional and local levels that could be more widely understood and used to guide action.

KEITH M. LEWIN

References

Appleton, S. (2001), 'What can we expect of universal primary education', in R. Reinikka and P. Collier, *Uganda's Recovery: The Role of Firms, Farms and Government*, Washington, DC: World Bank, pp. 371–406.
Becker, G.S. (1993), *Human Capital*, 3rd edn, Chicago: University of Chicago Press.
Blaug, M. (1972), *Introduction to the Economics of Education*, London: Penguin.
Bruns, B., A. Mingat and R. Raktomalala (2003), *A Chance for Every Child: Achieving Universal Primary Education by 2015*, Washington, DC: World Bank.
Cochrane, S. (1979), 'Fertility and education: what do we really know', World Bank Staff Working Paper no. 26, Washington, DC: World Bank.
Cochrane, S., J. Leslie and D. O'Hara (1980), 'The effects of education on health', World Bank Staff Working Paper no. 405, Washington, DC: World Bank.
Hanushek, E. (2003), *The Economics of Schooling and School Quality*, Cheltenham, UK and Northampton, MA, USA: Edward Elgar.
Knight, J. and R. Sabot (1990), *Education, Productivity and Inequality: The East African Natural Experiment*, Oxford: Oxford University Press.
Landes, D. (1998), *The Wealth and Poverty of Nations: Why Some are Rich and Some are Poor*, New York: W. W. Norton.
Lewin, K.M. and F. Caillods (2001), *Financing Secondary Education in Developing Countries: Strategies for Sustainable Growth*, Paris: International Institute for Educational Planning.
Lewin, K.M. and J.S. Stuart (2003), *Researching Teacher Education: New Perspectives on Practice, Performance and Policy*, UK Department for International Development, Research Series Monograph 49a.
Mayer, J. and A. Wood (1999), 'South Asia's export structure in a comparative perspective', *IDS Working Paper No. 91*, Institute for Development Studies, Brighton.
Psacharopoulos, G. (1987), *Economics of Education: Research and Studies*, Oxford: Pergamon.
UN (2000), *United Nations Millennium Declaration*, New York: United Nations, www.un.org/millennium/.
UNESCO (2000), *A Framework for Action*, World Education Forum, Dakar, UNESCO, Paris, www.unesco.org /education/efa/ed_for_all/dakfram_eng.shtml.
UNESCO (2002), *Education for All: Is the World on Track?*, Global Monitoring Report 2002, Paris: UNESCO, www.unesco.org/education/efa/monitoring/monitoring_2002.shtml.
UNESCO (2003), *Gender and Education for All: The Leap to Equality*, Global Monitoring Report

2003, Paris: UNESCO, http://portal.unesco.org/education/en/ev.phpURL_ID=23023&URL_DO=DO_TOPIC&URL_SECTION=201.html.

Wood, A. and C. Ridao-Cano (1996), *Skill, Trade and International Inequality*, Institute of Development Studies, Working Paper 47, University of Sussex, Brighton.

Woodhall, M. (1987), 'Earnings and education', in Psacharopoulos (ed.), pp. 21–24.

World Bank (1993), *The East Asian Miracle: Economic Growth and Public Policy*, Washington, DC: World Bank.

Education, Returns to

What are returns to education?

The returns to education are the benefits of education, net of its costs. Returns to education may be both economic (for example, increased earnings) and non-economic (for example, lower infant mortality, the joy of learning, better participation in a democracy). Similarly, returns to education may be private – that is, accruing to the educated individual only – or they may be social. Estimates of returns to different levels of education (primary, secondary, higher), different types of education (general versus vocational) and to different subjects (medicine, law, agriculture, humanities and so on) are used for various policy and evaluation purposes. For instance, intra-sectoral budgetary allocations are sometimes justified on the basis of the estimated returns to different levels and types of education. Similarly, some governments look at the economic returns to different degree subjects in setting fees for different university courses.

How are returns to education estimated?

Much of the focus in the economics of education literature has been on the estimation of the *economic* returns to education. A very large body of research has examined the association between education and individuals' productivity. Productivity is measured either by a farmer's physical output or, in urban settings, by the individual's wages/earnings; the latter assumes that labour markets are competitive and that workers are paid their marginal product. The rates of return to education are computed either by the cost–benefit method or by the Mincerian regression method.

The cost–benefit method

The rate of return to education is the ratio of schooling benefits to schooling costs. These benefits and costs can be depicted as in Figure 4, which shows age–earnings profiles for people with university education and for people with secondary education. The area marked with positive signs measures the *gains* from university education and the area marked with negative signs measures the *costs* of university education for a secondary school completer (both direct costs of university such as fees and books as well as indirect opportunity costs of forgone earnings).

The internal rate of return to education is defined as that interest rate which just equates the net present value of the costs and benefits of education.

Mincerian earnings function method

This method also requires cross-section data on a sample of workers of varying ages and education levels. It is far more commonly used than the cost–benefit approach as it allows

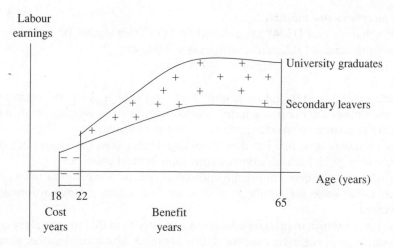

Figure 4   Age–earnings profiles, by education level

for flexible ways of controlling for other worker characteristics. It involves least squares regression of log of earnings on workers' years of schooling, years of experience and square of experience, as in equation (1):

$$\ln Y = \alpha + rS + \beta E + \gamma E^2 + \varepsilon, \tag{1}$$

where $\ln Y$ is the natural logarithm of earnings, α is the intercept, S is years of schooling with its coefficient r being the marginal return to an extra year of schooling, E is years of experience, E^2 is experience squared, β and γ are coefficients on experience and its square and ε is an error term. Age–earnings profiles typically show that earnings increase with experience but at a decreasing rate and this provides the basis for the inclusion of both experience and its square. Jacob Mincer (1974) showed that the coefficient on 'years of education' in such an earnings function gives the extra lifetime earnings an individual will earn as a result of one extra year of schooling.

United States 1973: $\ln Y = 6.20 + 0.107S + 0.081E - 0.0012E^2$ ($R^2 = 0.285$)
South Africa 1993: $\ln Y = 4.66 + 0.159S + 0.057E - 0.0008E^2$ ($R^2 = 0.316$)
India 1995: $\ln Y = 4.70 + 0.106S + 0.068E - 0.0011E^2$ ($R^2 = 0.520$).

The three Mincerian earnings functions show that the marginal returns to education in the years shown were 10.7 per cent in the USA, 15.9 per cent in South Africa and 10.6 per cent in India. The US equation is taken from Mincer (1974) and the ones for South Africa and India are computed by the author with data used in Kingdon and Knight (2004) and Kingdon (1998), respectively.

Strictly speaking the coefficient on S is simply the marginal benefit and not the marginal return to schooling since it does not take into account the direct costs of education. Private returns to education are always higher than the social returns if education is publicly subsidised.

Evidence on returns to education

George Psacharopoulos (1994) has collated findings from studies of rates of return to education from scores of different countries (see Table 4).

From these patterns, Psacharopoulos infers that:

- The social rate of return to education is at least as high as any reasonable measure of the opportunity cost of capital, that is, investment in people is as or more conducive to economic growth than investment in machines.
- The private returns to education are always higher than the social rates of return because of public subsidisation of education in most countries.
- The discrepancy between private and social returns is greatest at university level. This raises issues of equity as well as of how education expansion should be financed.
- The rate of return to primary education is greater than that to secondary education which, in turn, is greater than the return to higher education. In other words, there are diminishing returns to extra years of education.
- The same diminishing returns apply across countries: the more developed the country, the lower the returns to education at all levels. The high returns to education in low-income countries must be attributed to their relative scarcity of human capital.

While Psacharopoulos's worldwide patterns of returns to education have become widely quoted, Bennell (1996) finds unsafe inferences: he argues that many of the original studies on which Psacharopoulos's synthesis draws rely on poor-quality data and utilise

Table 4   Evidence on returns to education, by estimation method

Country	Mean p.c. income US$	Social			Private		
		Primary	Secondary	Higher	Primary	Secondary	Higher
Low income	299	23.4	15.2	10.6	35.2	19.3	23.5
L middle income	1402	18.2	13.4	11.4	29.9	18.7	18.9
U middle income	4184	14.3	10.6	9.5	21.3	12.7	14.8
High income	13 100	n.a.	10.3	8.2	n.a.	12.8	7.7
World	2020	20.0	13.5	10.7	30.7	17.7	19.0

Country		Mean years of schooling	Coefficient on years of schooling
Low income	301	6.4	11.2
L middle income	1383	8.4	11.7
U middle income	4522	9.9	7.8
High income	13 699	10.9	6.6
World	3665	8.7	10.1

Source: Psacharopoulos (1994).

methods that are flawed. Moreover, it does not appear that the rate of return to primary education is always greater than that to higher education. A number of studies find that the return to primary education is now lower than that to post-primary education (Appleton et al., 1999, for three African countries; Kingdon, 1998, and Kingdon and Unni, 2001, for India; Moll, 1996, for South Africa; Söderbom et al., 2006, for Kenya and Tanzania; and Aslam, 2005 for Pakistan). The likely explanations for the decline of primary returns (compared to the 1960s and 1970s) are shifts in labour supply and a fall in quality of schooling. Nevertheless, a further update of global patterns of returns to education in Psacharopoulos and Patrinos (2004) – based on a larger number of more recent and more comparable studies – appears to confirm the patterns noted in Psacharopoulos (1994).

The ability bias challenge to measuring the returns to education

Innate ability and years of education are likely to be highly correlated since more able people find it easier to learn cognitive skills and pass school grades. In this context, does the return to education represent a return to human capital (skills acquired through education) or does it merely represent a return to ability?

The idea that education enhances workers' productivity has come to be known as the human capital interpretation of education. However, the screening or credentialist hypothesis challenges this interpretation, arguing that employers may be using education as a way of identifying the most able workers. In other words, the apparent large economic returns to education may really accrue not so much to education as to ability, with which education is usually highly correlated.

If true, the screening hypothesis potentially has far-reaching implications, the chief one being that the efficiency rationale for public investments in education would be much weakened: society would derive less benefit from the education of individuals although the individuals themselves would still enjoy private returns to education. This challenge has inspired a number of studies which aim to isolate the effect, on productivity (earnings), of education and ability. Many imaginative ways of separating out the effects of education and ability have been tried in the applied literature, the main ones being the following:

- Controlling for ability by using IQ type tests. The results of these studies, both in developed and developing countries, did not reject the human capital interpretation. With a measure of IQ included in the earnings function, the returns to education typically fell only a little. However, the criticism of these studies has been that no IQ test can adequately capture all aspects of innate ability and, in any case, there is scepticism about whether any IQ test can be truly orthogonal to education.
- Controlling for ability using a sample of identical twins, that is, regressing the difference in earnings on the difference in education between pairs of identical twins. The results show substantial returns to education even after the strong controls for both genetic and environmental ability, and they vindicate the human capital interpretation of education (Ashenfelter and Krueger, 1994; Rouse, 1999).
- Controlling for ability using an instrumental variables (IV) approach. An IV approach requires a variable that is well correlated to years of schooling but otherwise uncorrelated with earnings. The idea is to find some exogenous event or

circumstance that leads to an extra bit of education being assigned to certain people in a way that was not related to their ability level, and then to examine whether and how much this extra bit of education (acquired irrespective of ability) raises earnings. Various instruments have been used in the literature, such as birth quarter and number of schools constructed in an area in a given time period (for the latter, see Duflo, 2001). In each case, the authors establish the validity of their instrument – that is, show that it is correlated with years of schooling but not with earnings, except via its correlation with years of schooling. The findings of such studies are reviewed in Card (2001) and are seen as a fairly decisive rejection of the screening hypothesis.

There have been other attempts in the literature to test whether measured returns to education represent a return to human capital or merely a return to ability. These include comparing returns to schooling among groups that are likely to face screening – such as waged workers, migrants, new recruits and so on – and those that are unlikely to be paid according to their educational credentials, such as non-migrant (or local) workers and existing workers (as opposed to new recruits) and so on. Although there is some evidence of 'weak' screening in some developing countries – that is, workers being paid according to their education signal at recruitment and in the early years of employment – the results of most such studies support the notion that education does increase worker productivity. In particular, employers pay educated workers more than uneducated workers even after long tenure, that is, even after they have had an opportunity to observe the workers' true ability and productivity.

Finally, several other observations appear to militate against the screening/credentialist view that returns to education are really a measure of the returns to ability. For example, educated farmers produce greater output than uneducated ones (Jamison and Lau, 1982) and there are no employers involved and thus no question of credentialism. This also shows that the idea that education enhances productivity does not depend on the use of wages as a measure of productivity. Second, telling evidence in favour of the human capital explanation of education is that there are substantial returns to education in the informal and self-employed sectors in many countries, a sector where there is little credentialism.

Taken together, the evidence points strongly in the direction of a human capital interpretation of education. Education raises human capital which raises productivity, and this is the efficiency rationale for the promotion of education.

Further challenges in measuring the returns to education
There are two important benefits of education that are not usually included in the estimates of returns to education: external economic benefits and non-economic benefits.

Economic externalities of education
If the education of an individual has beneficial effects on the learning of others near him/her, then education has a positive 'externality' which ought to be included in the calculation of the return to education. Some progress has been made in estimating and including the size of such external benefits in the calculation of the returns to education.

For instance, it has been shown that having an educated neighbour can increase a farmer's output significantly (Appleton and Balihuta, 1996; Weir and Knight, 2004).

Non-economic returns to education

Education has well-documented large non-economic benefits as well. Many studies show that education – particularly of women – reduces infant mortality and fertility rates (Subbarao and Raney, 1995; Ainsworth et al., 1996; Drèze and Murthi, 2001). Moreover, there is persuasive evidence that education has beneficial social externalities: others' education in the neighbourhood has a negative association with household-level child mortality and fertility, and causality has been attributed to education. However, it is not straightforward to assign monetary values to these non-economic benefits or to integrate them into a single monetary or non-monetary measure of the overall return to education. One such attempt to estimate the total return to education is by Walter McMahon (2001).

GEETA KINGDON

References

Ainsworth, M., K. Beegle and A. Nyamete (1996), 'The impact of women's schooling on fertility and contraceptive use: a study of fourteen Sub-Saharan African countries', *World Bank Economic Review*, **10** (1), 85–122.

Appleton, S. and A. Balihuta (1996), 'Education and agricultural productivity in Uganda', *Journal of International Development*, **8** (3), 415–44.

Appleton, S., J. Hoddinott and P. Krishnan (1999), 'The gender wage gap in three African countries', *Economic Development and Cultural Change*, **47** (2), 289–312.

Ashenfelter, O. and A.B. Krueger (1994), 'Estimates of the economic returns to schooling from a new sample of twins', *American Economic Review*, **84** (5), 1157–73.

Aslam, M. (2005), 'Returns to education by gender in Pakistan', mimeo, University of Oxford.

Bennell, Paul (1996), 'Rates of return to education: does the conventional pattern prevail in Sub-Saharan Africa?', *World Development*, January, **24** (1), 183–99 (and Psacharopoulos's reply, p. 201).

Card, David (2001), 'Estimating the return to schooling: progress on some persistent econometric problems', *Econometrica*, **69** (5), 1127–60.

Drèze, Jean and M. Murthi (2001), 'Fertility, education, and development: evidence from India', *Population and Development Review*, **27** (1), 33–63.

Duflo, Esther (2001), 'Schooling and labor market consequences of school construction in Indonesia: evidence from an unusual policy experiment', *American Economic Review*, **91** (4), 795–813.

Jamison, D. and L. Lau (1982), *Farmer Education and Farm Efficiency*, Baltimore, MD: Johns Hopkins University Press.

Kingdon, G. (1998), 'Does the labour market explain lower female schooling in India?', *Journal of Development Studies*, **35** (1), 39–65.

Kingdon, G. and J. Knight (2004), 'Unemployment in South Africa: the nature of the beast', *World Development*, **32** (3), 391–408.

Kingdon, G. and J. Unni (2001), 'Education and women's labour market outcomes in India', *Education Economics*, **9** (2), 173–95.

McMahon, Walter (2001), *Education and Development: Measuring the Social Benefits*, Oxford and New York: Oxford University Press.

Mincer, J. (1974), *Schooling, Experience and Earnings*, New York: National Bureau of Economic Research.

Moll, Peter (1996), 'The collapse of primary schooling returns in South Africa, 1960–90', *Oxford Bulletin of Economics and Statistics*, **58** (1), 185–210.

Psacharopoulos, G. (1994) 'Returns to investment in education: a global update', *World Development*, **22** (9), 1325–43.

Psacharopoulos, G. and H. Patrinos (2004), 'Returns to investment in education: a further update', *Education Economics*, **12** (2), 111–34.

Rouse, Cecilia (1999), 'Further estimates of the economic return to schooling from a new sample of twins', *Economics of Education Review*, **18** (2), 149–57.

Söderbom, M., F. Teal, A. Wambugu and G. Kahyarara (2006), 'The dynamics of returns to education in Kenyan and Tanzanian manufacturing', *Oxford Bulletin of Economics and Statistics*, forthcoming.

Subbarao, K. and L. Raney (1995), 'Social gains from female education: a cross-national study', *Economic Development and Cultural Change*, **44** (1), 105–28.
Weir, S. and J. Knight (2004), 'Externality effects of education: dynamics of the adoption and diffusion of an innovation in rural Ethiopia', *Economic Development and Cultural Change*, **53** (1), 93–114.

Endogenous Growth

Ever since the inception of systematic economic analysis at the time of the classical econo-mists from William Petty to Adam Smith and David Ricardo the problem of economic growth – its sources, forms and effects – was high on the agenda of economists. In the early authors, economic growth, or rather economic development, was considered as gen-erated from within the socio-economic system as a consequence of the purposeful activ-ities of humans. These activities generated a number of effects, some intended, others not. History was therefore seen as the 'result of human action, but not [of] human design' (Ferguson, 1793, p. 205). Adam Smith placed special emphasis on the role of an ever-deeper division of labour on labour productivity. Capital accumulation, by increasing the extent of markets, was seen to be a prime mover of economic development and product-ivity growth. An aspect of the division of labour was that research and development became the 'sole trade and occupation of a particular class of citizens', engaging 'philoso-phers or men of speculation, whose trade it is, not to do any thing, but to observe every thing: and who, upon that account, are often capable of combining together the powers of the most distant and dissimilar objects' (Smith, 1776 [1976], p. 21). The writings of the classical economists foreshadow the concepts of induced and embodied technical progress, learning by doing, and learning by using. Labour did not constrain growth because it was considered to be created endogenously and attuned to the needs of capital accumulation.

Karl Marx, too, considered the development of the productive powers of society and of economic growth as the outcome of the forces at work in a capitalist economy. Capital accumulation and innovation are seen as the necessary result of competitive conditions in which the single capitalist can survive only if his business expands and is continually modernised: 'Accumulate, accumulate! This is Moses and the prophets'. Labour-saving technical progress feeds an industrial reserve army of the unemployed which constrains the aspirations of the working class.

The idea of an economic system growing exclusively because some exogenous factors make it grow is of a much later date. We encounter it, for example, in Alfred Marshall and in Gustav Cassel. It was, however, only with the neoclassical models of Robert Solow and Trevor Swan that it gained prominence. In Solow's (1956) model, the steady-state growth rate is given from outside: it equals the (exogenous) rate of growth of the working popu-lation plus the (exogenous) rate of labour-saving technical progress.

The idea of endogenous growth figured prominently in post-Keynesian growth theory championed by Nicholas Kaldor and Joan Robinson, with the emphasis on the role of effective demand in the long run. However, it became particularly prominent from the 1980s onward even in mainstream economics due to a growing disenchantment with and critical assessment of the theoretical features and empirical implications of the Solovian model. Key properties of the 'new' or 'endogenous' growth models are:

- the steady-state rate of growth is determined by the behaviour of agents;
- innovation occurs in response to profitability;
- the emphasis is on explaining *intensive* growth, that is, growth of per capita income;
- capital accumulation and innovation generate externalities; and
- the endogenous mechanisms at work prevent the returns to capital from falling.

A few remarks on the most prominent new growth models are apposite (see Romer et al., 1994; Barro and Sala-i-Martin, 1995; Jones, 1998; and Kurz and Salvadori, 2003).

One class of models sets aside all non-accumulable factors of production (labour and land) and assumes that all inputs are 'capital' of some kind. The simplest version of this class is the so-called 'AK model', or 'linear model', which assumes that there is a linear relationship between total output, Y, and a single factor capital, K, both consisting of the *same* commodity:

$$Y = AK, \tag{1}$$

where $1/A$ is the amount of that commodity required to produce one unit of itself. The rate of return on capital r is given by:

$$r + \delta = \frac{Y}{K} = A, \tag{2}$$

where δ is the exogenously given rate of depreciation. This model is essentially a variant of Ricardo's 'corn model' in which corn is produced by means of corn, land is a free good and $\delta = 1$. There are a large variety of models of this type in the literature. In the two-sector version in Rebelo (1991) it is assumed that the capital good sector produces the capital good by means of itself and nothing else. It is also assumed that there is only one method of production to produce the capital good. Therefore, *the rate of profit is determined by technology alone*.

Then the saving–investment mechanism jointly with the assumption of a uniform rate of growth determines a relationship between the growth rate, g, and the rate of profit, r. Rebelo obtains either:

$$g = \frac{A - \delta - \rho}{\sigma} = \frac{r - \rho}{\sigma}, \tag{3}$$

or:

$$g = (A - \delta)s = sr. \tag{4}$$

Equation (3) is obtained when savings are determined on the assumption that there is an immortal representative agent maximising the following intertemporal utility function:

$$\int_0^\infty e^{-\rho t} \frac{1}{1 - \sigma} [c(t)^{1-\sigma} - 1] dt,$$

subject to constraint (1), where ρ is the given discount rate or rate of time preference, $1/\sigma$ is the elasticity of substitution between present and future consumption ($1 \neq \sigma > 0$), and $Y = c(t) + \dot{K}$ (where $c(t)$ is consumption at time t and $\dot{K} = dK/dt$ is net investment). Equation (4) is obtained when the average propensity to save s is given. Hence, in this model the rate of profit is determined by technology alone and the saving–investment mechanism determines the growth rate. Obviously, the lower ρ and σ (the higher s), the higher is the steady-state rate of growth. With a constant population, g gives of course the rate of growth of per capita income.

King and Rebelo (1990) assumed that there are two kinds of capital: real capital and human capital. There are two lines of production, one which produces a consumption good that serves also as a physical capital good, whereas the other produces human capital. The production functions relating to the two kinds of capital are assumed to be homogeneous of degree one and strictly concave. There are no diminishing returns to (composite) capital for the reason that there is no non-accumulable factor such as simple or unskilled labour. The rate of profit is uniquely determined by the technology and the maximisation of profits. The growth rate of the system is then endogenously determined by the saving–investment equation. The greater the propensities to accumulate human and physical capital, the greater the growth rate.

The linear models do not really contain any new insights into the growth process. They were anticipated in a two-sectoral framework by Robert Torrens and by Karl Marx in his schemes of extended reproduction. The most sophisticated linear model of endogenous growth, taking into consideration fixed capital and joint production and allowing for a choice of technique, was elaborated by John von Neumann (1937 [1945]). A macro version of the model was first put forward by E.D. Domar.

Another class of models preserves the dualism of accumulable and non-accumulable factors but restricts the impact of an accumulation of the former on their returns by a modification of the aggregate production function. Jones and Manuelli (1990), for example, allow for both labour and capital and even assume a convex technology. However, a convex technology requires only that the marginal product of capital is a decreasing function of its stock, not that it vanishes as the amount of capital per worker tends towards infinity. Jones and Manuelli assume that:

$$m(k) \geq bk, \text{ each } k \geq 0,$$

where $m(k)$ is the per capita production function and b is a positive constant. The special case contemplated is:

$$m(k) = f(k) + bk, \tag{5}$$

where $f(k)$ is the conventional Solovian per capita production function. As capital accumulates and the capital–labour ratio rises, the marginal product of capital will fall, approaching asymptotically b, its lower boundary. With a given propensity to save, s, and assuming capital to be everlasting, the steady-state growth rate g is endogenously determined: $g = sb$. Assuming, on the contrary, intertemporal utility maximisation, the rate of growth is positive provided that the technical parameter b is larger than the rate of time preference ρ. In the case in which it is larger, the steady-state rate of growth is given by equation (3) with $r = b$.

The models dealt with up until now can hardly be said to contain any original novelties or to provide new insights into the process of economic development and growth. More interesting in this respect are a large and growing class of models contemplating various factors counteracting any diminishing tendency of returns to capital and generating a growth in per capita income. Here the focus will be on the following two subclasses: human capital formation and knowledge accumulation. In both kinds of models *positive external effects* play an important part; they offset any fall in the marginal product of capital and are the source of a growing income per person.

Models of the first subclass attempt to formalise the role of human capital formation in the process of growth. Elaborating on some ideas of Uzawa (1965), Lucas (1988) assumed that agents have a choice between two ways of spending their (non-leisure) time: to contribute to current production or to accumulate human capital. Lucas's conceptualisation of the process by means of which human capital is built up is the following:

$$h = \upsilon h(1 - u), \tag{6}$$

where υ is a positive constant.

With the accumulation of human capital there is said to be associated an externality: the more human capital society as a whole has accumulated, the more productive each single member will be. This is reflected in the following production function:

$$Y = AK^{\beta}(uhN)^{1-\beta}h^{*\gamma}, \tag{7}$$

where the labour input consists of the number of workers, N, times the fraction of time spent working, u, times h which gives the labour input in efficiency units. Finally, there is the term h^* designed to represent the externality. The single agent takes h^* as a parameter in his/her optimising by choice of c and u. However, for society as a whole the accumulation of human capital increases output both directly and through the externality. Here we are confronted with a variant of a *public good* problem. The individual optimising agent faces constant returns to scale in production: the sum of the partial elasticities of production of the factors he/she can control, that is, the individual's physical and human capital, is unity. Yet for society as a whole the partial elasticity of production of human capital is not $1 - \beta$, but $1 - \beta + \gamma$. As is well known, whenever there is a public good problem there is room for economic policy designed to correct an insufficient private supply of the good.

It can be shown (see Kurz and Salvadori, 1998) that if the above-mentioned externality is *not* present (γ in equation (7) equals zero) and therefore returns to scale are constant, endogenous growth in Lucas's model is obtained in essentially the same way as in the linear models: the rate of profit is determined by technology and profit maximisation alone; and for the predetermined level of r the saving–investment mechanism determines g. Yet, as Lucas himself pointed out, the endogenous growth is positive *independently* of the fact that there is the above-mentioned externality. Therefore, while complicating the picture, increasing returns do not add substantially to it: growth is endogenous even if returns to scale are constant. If returns to scale are not constant then neither the competitive technique nor the associated rate of profit is determined by technical alternatives and profit maximisation alone. Nevertheless, these two factors still determine, in steady states, a relationship between the rate of profit and the rate of growth. This relationship, together with the relationship between the same rates obtained from the saving–investment mechanism, determines both variables.

Models of the second subclass attempt to portray technological change as generated endogenously. The proximate starting-point of this kind of models was Arrow's (1962) paper on 'learning by doing'. Romer (1986) focuses on the role of a single variable called 'knowledge' or 'information' and assumes that the information contained in inventions has the property of being available to anybody to make use of it at the same time. In other words, information is considered essentially a non-rival good. Yet, it need not be totally non-excludable, that is, through some institutional arrangements (for example, patent rights) it can be monopolised at least temporarily. It is around the two different aspects of publicness – non-rivalry and non-excludability – that the argument revolves. Discoveries are made in research and development (R&D) departments of firms. This requires that resources be withheld from producing current output. The basic idea of Romer's model is that there is a trade-off between consumption today and knowledge that can be used to produce more consumption tomorrow. He formalises this idea in terms of a 'research technology' that produces 'knowledge' from forgone consumption. It is boldly assumed that knowledge is cardinally measurable.

Romer stipulates a research technology that is concave and homogeneous of degree one,

$$\dot{k}_i = G(I_i, k_i),\qquad(8)$$

where $\dot{k}_i = dk_i/dt$, I_i is an amount of forgone consumption in research by firm i and k_i is the firm's current stock of knowledge. The production function of the consumption good relative to firm i is:

$$Y_i = F(k_i, K, \mathbf{x}_i),\qquad(9)$$

where K is the accumulated stock of knowledge in the economy as a whole and $\mathbf{x}_i$ is the vector of all inputs different from knowledge. The function is taken to be homogeneous of degree one in k_i and $\mathbf{x}_i$ and homogeneous of a degree greater than one in k_i and K. Romer assumes that factors other than knowledge are in fixed supply. Spillovers from private R&D activities increase the public stock of knowledge K. Again, a positive externality is taken to be responsible for per capita income growth. And again there is room for economic policy in order to overcome a socially suboptimal generation of new knowledge.

Assuming, contrary to Romer, that the above production function (9) is homogeneous of degree one in k_i and K involves a constant marginal product of capital: the diminishing returns to k_i are exactly offset by the external improvements in technology associated with capital accumulation. In this case it can be shown that, similar to the models previously dealt with, the rate of profit is determined by technology and profit maximisation alone, provided, as is assumed by Romer, that the ratio K/k_i equals the given (!) number of firms. Once again, endogenous growth does not depend on an assumption about increasing returns with regard to accumulable factors, whereas a growing per capita income does. Such an assumption would only render the analysis a good deal more complicated. In particular, a steady-state equilibrium does not exist, and in order for an equilibrium to exist the marginal product of capital must be bounded from above. This is effected by Romer in terms of an ad hoc assumption regarding equation (8).

Finally, there are so-called 'neo-Schumpeterian' models of growth which take into account the fact that self-seeking behaviour which leads to technical and organisational innovation and economic growth typically generates both positive and negative externalities; see in particular Aghion and Howitt (1998). These models revolve around Joseph Schumpeter's concept of 'creative destruction'. A firm that innovates successfully manages to obtain a temporary monopoly position and can reap extra profits. Wages growing in line with labour productivity at the same time render capital stocks embodying older vintages of technical knowledge obsolete. This poses, among other things, once again the question of what is the socially optimal rate of technical innovation.

In conventional theory, whenever increasing returns that are (dominantly) internal to the firm, externalities, public goods (or bads), incomplete and asymmetric information and so on are involved, there is a problem of market failure. Since the literature on 'new' or 'endogenous' growth revolves around precisely these phenomena, the question of public policy, institutional arrangements and mechanism design are close at hand. While capital accumulation is still at the centre of the analysis, these wider issues, which figured prominently in the classical authors, have been brought back into the picture.

HEINZ D. KURZ

References

Aghion, P. and P. Howitt (1998), *Endogenous Growth Theory*, Cambridge, MA and London: MIT Press.

Arrow, K.J. (1962), 'The economic implications of learning by doing', *Review of Economic Studies*, **29**, 155–73.

Barro, R.J. and X. Sala-i-Martin (1995), *Economic Growth*, New York: McGraw-Hill.

Ferguson, A. (1793 [1966]), *An Essay on the History of Civil Society*, 6th edn, Edinburgh: Edinburgh University Press.

Jones, C.I. (1998), *Introduction to Economic Growth*, New York: W.W. Norton.

Jones, L.E. and R. Manuelli (1990), 'A convex model of equilibrium growth: theory and policy implications', *Journal of Political Economy*, **98**, 1008–38.

King, R.G. and S. Rebelo (1990), 'Public policy and economic growth: developing neoclassical implications', *Journal of Political Economy*, **98**, 126–50.

Kurz, H.D. and N. Salvadori (1998), 'The "new" growth theory: old wine in new goatskins', in F. Coricelli, M. Di Matteo and F.H. Hahn (eds), *New Theories in Growth and Development*, London: Macmillan, pp. 63–92.

Kurz, H.D. and N. Salvadori (2003), 'Theories of "endogenous" growth in historical perspective', Chapter 6 in H.D. Kurz and N. Salvadori, *Classical Economics and Modern Theory*, London: Routledge.

Lucas, R.E. (1988), 'On the mechanics of economic development', *Journal of Monetary Economics*, **22**, 3–42.

Neumann, J. von (1945), 'A model of general economic equilibrium', *Review of Economic Studies*, **13**, 1–9. English translation of 'Über ein ökonomisches Gleichungssystem und eine Verallgemeinerung des Brouwerschen Fixpunktsatzes', in *Ergebnisse eines mathematischen Kolloquiums*, **8** (1937), 73–83.

Rebelo, S. (1991), 'Long run policy analysis and long run growth', *Journal of Political Economy*, **99**, 500–521.

Romer, P.M. (1986), 'Increasing returns and long-run growth', *Journal of Political Economy*, **94**, 1002–37.

Romer, P., G. Grossman, E. Helpman, R. Solow and H. Pack (1994), 'Symposium on new growth theory', *Journal of Economics Perspectives*, **8** (1), 3–72.

Smith, A. (1776), *An Inquiry into the Nature and Causes of the Wealth of Nations*, reprinted in *The Glasgow Edition of the Works and Correspondence of Adam Smith* (1976), Oxford: Oxford University Press.

Solow, R.M. (1956), 'A contribution to the theory of economic growth', *Quarterly Journal of Economics*, **70**, 65–94.

Uzawa, H. (1965), 'Optimum technical change in an aggregate model of economic growth', *International Economic Review*, **6**, 18–31.

Environment and Development

In his book *Human Well-being and the Natural Environment*, Partha Dasgupta remarks that he has long drawn attention to the neglect by development economists of environmental economics and he also alleges that environmental economics has made 'no contact with poverty in poor countries'. 'The two fields of specialisations had passed each other by and had weakened in consequence' (Dasgupta, 2001, p. viii). The former judgement has certainly been correct as far as the academic literature on development economics is concerned. Major undergraduate textbooks in development economics typically devote a token chapter to the environment, and some have no chapter at all. But Dasgupta's second judgement about the neglect of poverty by environmental economists is too harsh. Some major texts in environmental economics certainly do not address issues such as the environment–poverty nexus while others make a constructive effort to do so. Moreover, the picture is changing fast: development economics is being 'greened'. The intellectual origins of this greening go back to the 1970s when economic growth theorists turned their attention to problems of tracing out theoretically optimal economic growth paths in the presence of an exhaustible natural resource (for example, Dasgupta and Heal, 1979). The practical policy origins lie in changes in the World Bank in the 1980s. Against formidable resistance, a few individuals fought to have environmental issues formally recognised in the economic appraisals of Bank lending and policy. In turn, Bank lending increasingly focused on poverty alleviation. Today, the Bank is a leading institution both in conceptualising and applying environmental economics to development issues. In this respect, the practical world of development economics has recognised environmental economics. Additionally, environmental economists have been at the forefront of practical approaches that link environment and poverty. This 'coming together' of development and environmental issues has spawned a small number of books (for example, Bojö et al., 1990) and surveys (for example, Blackman et al., 2001) seeking to condense what we know about these linkages. There is also a leading journal, *Environment and Development*, which specialises in the discipline. So, a past failure to cross-fertilise environmental and development economics there has certainly been, but the picture is changing rapidly.

At the risk of some caricature, there are two broad views of the link between economic development and the natural environment. The first view, frequently articulated by developing-country politicians, and supported by the more conventional development economists Dasgupta complains about, says that the prime goal of developing-country policy and of international aid institutions is to raise the per capita income levels of the poor, and that improving the environment has little or nothing to do with this goal. Environmental improvement involves diverting resources away from high-income-increasing activities towards low-productivity activities. Hence positive environmental policies will decrease per capita incomes compared to the counterfactual baseline of what would have happened without environmental policy. This is the 'trade-off' view and it can be found in many guises, for example in the widespread view that environmental policy has been one of the factors explaining 'productivity slowdowns' in some advanced economies. On the trade-off view, then, the environment is something of a luxury, an issue which can be attended to only when per capita incomes have risen to some target level. Perhaps unwittingly, development-cum-environmental economists may have encouraged this view by finding inverted 'U'-shaped relationships between development and environmental degradation. As incomes grow, things get worse on the environmental front, but the situation is reversed after some turning-point in income per capita is achieved. This alleged relationship has come to be known as the 'environmental Kuznets curve' since it parallels a similar relationship between income growth and equality postulated by Nobel Prize winner Simon Kuznets.

One of the misleading conclusions that some people have derived from this literature is that developing countries can afford to wait before they address environmental issues – the problem will correct itself as economic growth occurs. No such conclusion can be derived, however. First, the empirical foundations of environmental Kuznets curves are not as strong as is usually made out. Second, the cost of high levels of air pollution and water pollution in terms of forgone well-being and economic growth is now known to be formidable. There is more than a suspicion that development policies giving more emphasis to environmental quality would enhance, not inhibit, real income growth. While sufficient evidence exists to show that investing in environmental assets can yield significant positive net benefits, many of the benefits in question show up in 'non-market' form, that is, gains in human well-being that are not registered in conventional measures of economic progress such as gross national product. This raises the other major problem with any 'defence' of environmental investments in poor countries. Gains that show up in the marketplace, as traded goods and services, or as assets such as roads and machinery, appear far more 'real' than gains in human health or increased supplies of fuelwood or wildlife. Economics teaches that those gains in well-being are just as 'real' as the gains secured from roads and machinery. The fact that they often have no identifiable market, and the fact that they may be more difficult to measure, is not really relevant to making policy or investment decisions. None the less, the perception is there that non-market gains are not as important as marketed gains, that what the environmental economist deals with is, in some sense, unreal gains and losses. In part, this perception reflects the first problem raised above – a prior belief that the rate of return to environmental investment is not as high as the rate of return to 'real' investment. In large part, however, it reflects the fairly understandable, but unjustified, bias that comes about because some things have markets and some do not.

The alternative view of the development–environment linkage is that development itself depends upon environmental quality in certain critical ways. Hence, while there may be a short-term trade-off between environmental improvement and income per capita, in reality the two are complements, at least as far as certain environmental improvements are concerned. Development requires the environment to be improved. Observations about inverted 'U'-shaped curves may not be relevant. For what the curves may be measuring is a past development path, whereas a sounder development path might be one in which the environment is not so readily sacrificed. What has happened in the past carries no particular implication for what could or should happen. Those arguing for this positive view of the environment–development link would point to various interdependencies of the following kinds.

The poor depend on natural resources far more directly than do the rich. This does not mean that the poor consume more natural resources than the rich. It simply means that reducing the availability of those natural resources they do consume, places their livelihoods at risk. Examples would be the direct dependence on water from wells or rivers and dependence on fuelwood from natural sources. Reactions to changes in the availability or quality of these resources may also impair human health – for example, by having to walk further to collect wood and water, or by cutting down on cooked food to save fuel. Environmental degradation can severely impair the health of the poor (a) because it is more likely that the poor are most exposed to environmental risks, and (b) because their health states are such that they will be more vulnerable to changes in environmental quality.

Demonstrating these linkages is none the less immensely complex. Figure 5 attempts to capture the role that environment plays in the development process (Pearce, 2005). The arrows show the interactive mechanisms with '+' denoting a compounding effect, and '–' an amelioration effect. Thus population growth would have a compounding effect (+) on poverty if we believe that population growth simply dissipates capital stocks, but an ameliorating effect (–) if, with Boserup (1965) it is argued that population growth stimulates technological change. Population will also tend to degrade environments because of increased pressure on land, and more pollution and congestion. If environments degrade, poverty is worsened because poor sanitation, water contamination, air pollution, soil

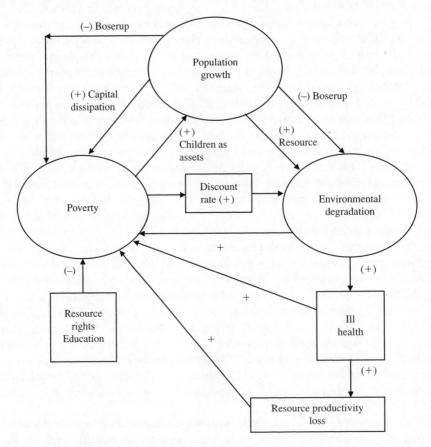

Figure 5   Environment and development: the linkages

depletion and so on all affect human health. This in turn lowers resource and labour productivity, worsening poverty. While not a necessary relationship, poverty worsens the environment because low incomes are correlated with high personal discount rates. In keeping with the theory of natural resource depletion, high discount rates accelerate rates of depletion of natural resources.

Inspection of Figure 5 shows just how easy it is to generate 'vicious cycles' of poverty and environmental degradation. The figure illustrates a number of policy interventions via the clearer definition of resource property rights and via education, both of which can alleviate poverty directly. Resource rights can also conserve natural assets by converting 'open access' situations – in which no-one owns the environment and everyone has a private incentive to deplete it beyond an optimal point – to communal or even private ownership, thus giving the resource more chance of protection.

While simplistic in many respects, the figure captures the essence of the linkages that environmental development economists seek to investigate.

DAVID PEARCE

References

Blackman, Allen, Mitchell Mathis and Peter Nelson (2001), *The Greening of Development Economics: A Survey*, Washington, DC: Resources for the Future.
Bojö, Jan, Karl-Göran Mäler and Lena Unemo (1990), *Environment and Development: An Economic Approach*, Dordrecht: Kluwer.
Boserup, Ester (1965), *The Conditions of Agricultural Growth*, Chicago: Aldine.
Dasgupta, Partha (2001), *Human Well-being and the Natural Environment*, Oxford: Oxford University Press.
Dasgupta, Partha and Geoffrey Heal (1979), *Economic Theory and Exhaustible Resources*, Cambridge: Cambridge University Press.
Pearce, David (2005), 'Environment and economic development: the economics of sustainable development', Manuscript.

Ethnicity

While lacking precise definition, the term 'ethnicity' commonly refers to collectivities that share a myth of origin. Most who apply the term emphasise the importance of ancestry; others, the importance of history, most often migration (*volkerwanderun*) and settlement, but also of political passage, be it escape from oppression or the colonisation of new territory (Weber, 1968). Common to many definitions is the sharing of a 'culture', the most notable aspect of which is language. Indeed, many ethnic groups are known by the same name as that of the language they speak.

The boundary between nationalism and ethnicity remains ill-defined and the logic mobilised by the students of the one often parallels that invoked by students of the other. So often do they overlap that the distinction will not be tightly drawn in this entry. To be noted is that limitations of space prevent even a selective review of the rich literature on ethnicity in the advanced industrial nations, especially that originating from the United States.

Sparking much of the research on ethnicity in developing areas is the tension between state building and ethnic self-assertion. Also important is the tension between theoretic expectations and observable behaviour.

The power of ethnicity

While many factors account for the attention given to ethnicity, among the most important is the tension between ethnic groups and the state. Limiting attention to the last century, while attempting to lay the foundations for peace following the First World War, diplomats sought to base political order on sovereign states, a task made difficult by the claims for sovereignty articulated by ethnic groups (MacMillan, 2001). The tension between ethnicity and state building emerged again mid-century, when the collapse of colonial empires bequeathed a multitude of newly independent nations (see, for example, Emerson, 1960 and Apter, 1963). The leaders of these nations faced political challenges from subnational groupings: some religious, some linguistic, some regional – and many ethnic. After the Second World War, the Soviet Union and the United States defended the integrity of states within their respective spheres of influence. But the subsequent collapse of the Soviet Union limited the ability of the first and the incentives of the second to continue to do so. The subsequent recrudescence of ethnic conflict in the Balkans and the collapse of states in Africa re-emphasised the magnitude of the tensions between ethnicity and state building.

The limitations of theory

In analysing the behaviour of ethnic groups, scholars initially drew on the works of those who sought to describe and explain the rise of modern Europe. One cluster drew on Karl Marx and Friedrich Engels; a second on Durkheim (1933), Weber (1968) and others (such as Tonnies, 1963). The first focused on the rise of capitalism, emphasising industrial development and class struggle. The second focused on modernisation, emphasising its impact on organisation and culture. For both, the power of ethnicity appeared anomalous and therefore a problem demanding exploration. Attempts to address this anomaly inspired much of the subsequent research.

For Marxists, the power of ethnicity in capitalist societies was problematic because social organisation and political institutions are structured by the means of production: social classes, not ethnic groups, should dominate politics in the modern era. For the second group of theorists, the contemporary power of ethnicity remained problematic because the forces of modernisation should erode its organisational and cultural foundations. Urbanisation should fragment primary ties, replacing them with interest-based relationships. Literacy should enable people to transcend parochial affiliations. And mass participation should strengthen the power of nationalism, leading to the break-up of colonial empires, perhaps, but also to the rise of nation states.

The continued power of ethnic groups provoked theoretical innovations in both schools of scholarship. Among Marxists, many responded by focusing on the transition to capitalism rather than upon its consolidation. In doing so, they joined their Leninist colleagues in viewing the rise of capitalism as a global rather than national phenomenon. Major portions of the economies of the newly independent states contain 'pre-capitalist' modes of production in which labour retains control over the means of production; to a greater extent than in the centre, economies in the periphery remain rural and agrarian. The forces of capitalism – the market for commodities on the one hand and for factors of production (including capital) on the other – spread from the advanced industrial societies to the agrarian periphery. The table was thereby set for the rise of ethnic groups in the developing nations.

In one variant of this tableau, the forces of ethnicity represent sectoral interests, usually those of agriculture as it declines relative to the industrial core. Thus Gellner's (1983) justly famous discussion of Ruritania, and Hechter's (1986) study of clashes between the centre and periphery in the process of state formation. In another variant, ethnicity represents a class interest (for example, Breton, 1964; Sklar, 1967). As development proceeds, a rising bourgeoisie seeks to consolidate its position. In markets for goods, it seeks to restrict competition from 'foreigners'; appealing to communal sentiments, it promotes trade protection. In markets for labour, it champions ethnic quotas. In markets for land, it champions the property rights of the 'sons of the soil' against the claims of 'strangers'. The bourgeoisie thus appeals to communal sentiments in order to consolidate its position in the new economic order. This last variant has also been applied, of course, to ethnic relations in advanced industrial nations, particularly South Africa and the United States, where ethnic groups occupy different positions in the class system (Wright, 1977; Greenberg, 1980).

Varieties of explanation

Among those who adhere to modernisation theory, some respond to its failure of prediction by reaffirming the power of 'primordial' identities (Geertz, 1963). As the forces of modernisation spread, less-educated, more rural and more 'traditional' segments of society enter politics (Deutsch, 1961). When the rate of social mobilisation exceeds the capacity of elites to control or to shape them, then primordial sentiments displace national identities in defining the collective interest in politics – thus reconciling the co-variation of modernisation and ethnicity.

Others emphasise the role of elites rather than masses in accounting for the power of ethnicity. When competing for office, politicians mobilise political supporters. Ethnic groups provide low-cost means for rallying constituents; and by targeting distributive benefits to their members, politicians can build a loyal political base, thus assuring themselves of office (Bates, 1973; Brass, 1985). This approach shares with Marxian interpretations an instrumentalist view of ethnicity: communal appeals are made to advance private interests. It differs in that the goals are political rather than economic.

Combining elements of both approaches is a third, often referred to as 'constructivism' (for example, see Hobsbaum and Ranger, 1983 and Anderson, 1991). In keeping with the primordialists, constructivists view ethnic identities as a cultural endowment; but in keeping with instrumentalists, they view ethnic identities as malleable. Distinguishing their position is the belief that while identities can be reshaped, they can be altered only at significant cost.

Primordialism seeks to explain the persistence of tradition: as in the writings of Kaplan (1994), primordialists often interpret contemporary conflicts as the renewal of age-old antagonisms – ones that antedate the formation of a nation state. Interpretivists and constructivists seek to explain change. Because some ethnic groups are virtually the creations of those who compete for positions of advantage in the modern state, most scholars feel that the last two advance the stronger argument (see Anderson et al., 1967).

Theoretical convergence

Mid-century scholars such as Mitchell (1956), Epstein (1958) and Gluckman (1960) noted that in some situations, such as in labour relations, appeals to class solidarity dominate appeals to ethnic identity; in other settings, such as during elections, appeals to ethnic interests dominate those to class solidarity. These findings received subsequent confirmation in later studies by Melson and Wolpe (1970) and Melson (1971) (see also Anderson et al., 1967) and gave rise to the notion of 'situational selection'. They also provided a point of entry for rational choice theory to approach the study of cultural politics.

The notion of 'situational selection' suggests that people organise their perceptions and choices depending on how an issue is framed. Ethnic identities are not eroded (as the Marxists and modernisation theorists once thought), but rather retained; supplemented with new identities, such as that of a worker; and, in some settings, activated. When class solidarity is valuable, ethnic differences are set aside; when competing for the spoils of office, they are reaffirmed. Viewed from this perspective, ethnicity can be seen as a choice or a strategy, the value of which varies with the situation.

An important feature of the 'situation' is, of course, the behaviour of leaders who seek to mobilise collective action, be it in the form of a labour or ethnic movement. As Posner (2004a) demonstrates, leaders appear to choose purposefully, assessing the relative advantages of ethnic mobilisation against other means of recruiting political support.

To invoke an ethnic identity may be a choice, but, as emphasised by Dickson and Scheve (2004), the expected value of the choice depends upon the anticipated behaviour of others. Departing from Posner's decision-theoretic reasoning, Dickson and Scheve build a game-theoretic model in which political entrepreneurs choose the strength of ethnic appeals while anticipating the response of political rivals. A notable implication of their model is that the relationship between policy preferences and electoral support would be discontinuous in democratic settings – something that seems to be validated by Ferree's (2002) research into electoral behaviour in multiethnic South Africa. Notable too is Dickson and Scheve's use of Akerlof and Kranton's (2000) model of social preferences – a model that provides a flexible but tractable way of incorporating social identities into the decisions of individuals who are rational.

While the early literature on situational selection invoked dominance, the more recent literature thus invokes contingency. The value of a strategy depends on the expected response of others. In some circumstances, the assertion of a political identity may be dangerous, unless others also affirm it: dissent abides by this logic (Kuran, 1989). In other situations, affirming an identity may become more profitable the fewer the numbers who affirm it: thus the logic of collaboration. In such situations, no strategy is unambiguously best and multiple outcomes become possible.

One implication is that small changes in behaviour can generate large consequences; choices can cascade, as persons, reacting to the decisions of others, recalculate the costs and benefits of affirming their identity. Thus does Laitin (1998) explore variation in the identities chosen by Russians left stranded in non-Russian republics after the break-up of the Soviet Union. Another implication is that there is a role for leadership, symbolism and communication; each plays a role in shaping the expectations that drive the selection of an equilibrium (Hardin, 1995). Thus do Prunier (1998) and others (Human Rights Watch, 1999) emphasise the power of *radio milles collines* in provoking ethnic fears in Rwanda.

A third approach explores intertemporal decision making and, in particular, the problem of commitment. Commitment problems arise when preferences can alter over time; to form binding agreements, people must look for ways to demonstrate that their pledges are credible. Such problems arise in economic settings, as when people seek to invest; given the gains to be made from the opportunistic appropriation of investments, pledges to repay may be doubted, and economic opportunities therefore lost. Problems of credibility also arise in political settings; antagonistic groups may be unwilling to disarm for fear of being oppressed, resulting in the continuation of costly but unproductive military expenditures.

Because ethnic groups provide opportunities for repeated interaction, they enable the use of punishment strategies to render opportunistic defection costly (Platteau, 1994). Development economists stress that because ethnic groups are endowed with this form of social capital, they can mobilise financial capital for private investment. Thus Greif's (1993) study of the Maghrebi traders and Fafchamps's (2001) research into ethnic networks in Africa (see also Bates and Yakovlev, 2002). By contrast, those who focus on the politics of ethnic groups tend to stress the paucity, rather than the availability, of mechanisms for imparting credibility to pledges of political restraint (Azam, 1994). Because of the absence of such mechanisms, some argue, multiethnic societies fail to produce negotiated cost-sharing agreements; given the variation in preferences (Alesina et al., 1999) and the externalities to which public goods give rise (Miguel and Gugerty, 2002), they therefore undersupply public goods. Interactions between ethnic groups, still others emphasise, can also generate 'security dilemmas' in which each group's search for security (as by arming) renders others less secure (Posen, 1993; Fearon, 1996). In such settings, fear becomes rational (Bates et al., 1998; Weingast and de Figueiredo, 1999) and insecurity the norm. Some, such as Posen (1993), therefore relate ethnic diversity to conflict. Laitin and Fearon (1996) demonstrate that peace rather than conflict most often prevails in ethnically variegated settings, however. Bates and Yakovlev (2002) find that ethnic diversity becomes politically dangerous when the size of the largest ethnic group approaches 50 per cent of the population. Collier and Hoeffler (1999b) confirm Bates and Yakovlev's finding, but only for non-democratic states.

Recent research into the role of ethnic groups thus places the subject at the interface between rational choice theory and the study of culture. It treats ethnicity as a strategy, but one that taps the power of symbolism, of history, and of interpretation and rhetoric. By focusing on ethnicity, those committed to rational choice theory are thus challenged to probe not only the economic and political wellsprings of human behaviour but also forces that, for want of a better term, we designate as cultural. The viability of this programme rests on the degree to which rational behaviour is possible in ethnic settings; and this possibility in turn rests on the capacity of persons to discern and perceive ethnic identities and on their assessment of the capacity of others to do so as well.

Empirical work

Research into ethnicity has given rise to several lines of empirical research. As in the work of Ferree (2002) and Posner (2004a), one mobilises survey research and electoral data and studies to investigate the impact of ethnic diversity on political accountability and democratic behaviour. As exemplified by Scarritt and Mozaffar (1999) or Fearon (2003), a second employs aggregate cross-national data and explores the impact of ethnic diversity on political conflict. By collecting time-varying, cross-national data, Posner (2004b) makes possible the measurement of the impact of political conflict on ethnic identity as well, thus allowing for the impact for endogeneity. Still other scholars seek to perform experiments. Thus Habyarimana et al.'s (2004) research in Uganda, which explores the capacity of persons to infer and attribute ethnic membership. By probing the common knowledge condition for rational behaviour, they seek to determine whether ethnicity can indeed provide a rational basis for trust, cooperation, and collective action, as scholars have claimed.

Ethnicity has proven capable of challenging the boundaries of nations. So too does its study reshape the boundaries of scholarship.

ROBERT H. BATES

References and further reading

Akerlof, G. and R. Kranton (2000), 'The economics of identity', *Quarterly Journal of Economics*, **115**, 715–53.

Alesina, A., R. Baqir and W. Easterly (1999), 'Public goods and ethnic divisions', *Quarterly Journal of Economics*, **114**, 1243–84.

Anderson, B. (1991), *Imagined Communities*, London: Verso.

Anderson, C.W., F.R. von der Mehden and F. Young (1967), *Issues of Political Development*, Englewood Cliffs, NJ: Prentice-Hall.

Apter, D. (ed.) (1963), *Old Societies and New States*, New York: Free Press of Glencoe.

Azam, J.P. (1994), 'How to pay for peace? A theoretical framework with reference to African countries', *Public Choice*, **83**, 173–84.

Bates, R.H. (1973), *Ethnicity in Contemporary Africa*, Program of Eastern African Studies, Syracuse University, Syracuse, NY.

Bates, R.H., B. Weingast and R. de Figueiredo (1998), 'The politics of interpretation, rationality and culture', *Politics and Society*, **26** (4), 603–42.

Bates, R.H. and I. Yakovlev (2002), 'Ethnicity, capital formation and conflict', in C. Groodtaert and T. Van Bastelaer (eds), *The Role of Capital in Social Development*, Cambridge and New York: Cambridge University Press, pp. 310–40.

Brass, P. (ed.) (1985), *Ethnic Groups and the State*, London: Croom Helm.

Breton, A. (1964), 'The economics of nationalism', *Journal of Political Economy*, **72** (4), 376–80.

Collier, P. and A. Hoeffler (1999a), 'Ethnicity, politics, and economic performance', Washington, DC: World Bank, Typescript.

Collier, P. and A. Hoeffler (1999b), 'The political economy of ethnicity', in B. Pleskovic and J. Stiglitz (eds), *Proceedings of the Annual Bank Conference on Development Economics*, Washington, DC: World Bank, pp. 387–99.

Deutsch, K.W. (1961), 'Social mobilization and political development', *American Political Science Review*, **55** (3), 493–510.

Dickson, M. and M. Scheve (2004), 'Social identity, political speech, and electoral competititon', New York: New York University, Department of Politics, Typescript.

Durkheim, É. (1933), *The Division of Labor in Society*, New York: Free Press of Glencoe.

Emerson, R. (1960), *From Empire to Nation*, Boston, MA: Beacon Press.

Epstein, A.L. (1958), *Politics in an Urban African Community*, Manchester: Manchester University Press, Published on behalf of the Rhodes-Livingstone Institute.

Fafchamps, M. (2001), 'Networks, communities and markets in Sub-Saharan Africa', *Journal of African Economies*, **10** (2), 109–41.

Fearon, J.D. (1996), 'Commitment problems and the spread of ethnic conflict', University of Chicago, Typescript.

Fearon, J. (2003), 'Ethnic structure and cultural diversity by country', *Journal of Economic Growth*, **8**, 195–222.

Ferree, Karen (2002), 'Voters and Parties in the Rainbow Nation: Race and Elections in the New South Africa', PhD Dissertation, Department of Government, Harvard University.

Geertz, C. (1963), 'The integrative revolution: primordial sentiments and civil politics in the new states', in D. Apter (ed.), *Old Societies and New States*, New York: Free Press of Glencoe, pp. 105–57.

Gellner, E. (1983), *Nations and Nationalism*, Ithaca, NY: Cornell University Press.

Gluckman, M. (1960), 'Tribalism in modern British Central Africa', *Cahiers d'Études Africaines*, **1** (1), 55–70.

Greenberg, S. (1980), *Race and State in Capitalist Development*, New Haven, CT: Yale University Press.

Greif, A. (1993), 'Contract enforceability and economic institutions in early trade: the Maghribi traders' coalition', *American Economic Review*, **3** (83), 525–48.

Habyarimana, J., M. Humphreys, D. Posner and J. Weinstein (2004), 'Ethnic identifiability: an experimental approach', Paper presented at the Annual Meeting of the American Political Science Association, Chicago, 2 September, www.polisci.ucla.edu/faculty/posner/pdfs/ethnic_identifiability.pdf.

Hardin, R. (1995), *One For All: The Logic of Group Conflict*, Princeton, NJ: Princeton University Press.

Hechter, M. (1986), *Internal Colonialism*, Berkeley and Los Angeles, CA: University of California Press.

Hobsbaum, E. and T. Ranger (eds) (1983), *The Invention of Tradition*, Cambridge: Cambridge University Press.

Human Rights Watch (1999), *Leave None to Tell*, London: Human Rights Watch.

Huntington, S.P. (1968), *Political Order in Changing Societies*, New Haven, CT and London: Yale University Press.

Kaplan, R.D. (1994), 'The coming anarchy', *The Atlantic Monthly*, **273** (2), 44–76.

Kuran, T. (1989), 'Sparks and prairie fires: a theory of unanticipated political revolution', *Public Choice*, **61**, 41–74.

Laitin, D. (1998), *Identity in Formation*, Ithaca, NY: Cornell University Press.

Laitin, D. and J. Fearon (1996), 'Explaining interethnic cooperation', *American Political Science Review*, **90** (4), 715–35.

Laitin, D. and D. Posner (2001), 'The implications of constructivism for constructing ethnic fractionalization indices', *APSA–CP (Newsletter of the Organized Section in Comparative Politics of the American Political Science Association)*, 12, 1–14.

MacMillan, M. (2001), *Paris 1919*, New York: Random House.

Marx, A. (1998), *Making Race and Nation*, Cambridge and New York: Cambridge University Press.

Melson, R. (1971), 'Ideology and inconsistency: the case of the "cross pressured" Nigerian voter', *American Political Science Review*, **65** (1), 161–71.

Melson, R. and H. Wolpe (1970), 'Modernization and the politics of communalism', *American Political Science Review*, **44** (4), 1112–30.

Miguel, T. and M.K. Gugerty (2002), 'Ethnic diversity, social sanctions, and public goods in Kenya', Berkeley, CA: Typescript.

Mitchell, J.C. (1956), *The Kalela Dance*, Manchester: Manchester University Press on behalf of the Rhodes-Livingstone Institute: Rhodes Livingstone Papers no. 27.

Platteau, J.-P. (1994), 'Behind the market stage where real societies exist', *Journal of Development Studies*, **30** (3–4), 533–77 and 753–817.

Posen, B. (1993), 'The security dilemma and ethnic conflict,' *Survival*, **35** (1), 27–47.

Posner, Daniel (2004a), 'The political significance of cultural difference: why Chewas and Tumbukas are allies in Zambia and adversaries in Malawi', Los Angeles: Department of Political Science, University of California.

Posner, Daniel (2004b), 'Measuring ethnic fractionalization in Africa', *American Journal of Political Science*, **48** (4), 849–63.

Prunier, G. (1998), *The Rwanda Crisis: History of a Genocide*, London: Hurst.

Scarritt, J. and S. Mozaffar (1999), 'The specification of ethnic cleavages and ethnopolitical groups for the analysis of democratic participation in Africa,' *Nationalism and Ethnic Politics*, **5**, 82–117.

Sklar, R.L. (1967), 'Political science and national integration – a radical approach', *Journal of Modern African Studies*, **5**, 1–11.

Tonnies, F. (1963), *Community and Society*, New York: Harper & Row.

Weber, M. (1968), *Economy and Society*, New York: Free Press of Glencoe.

Weingast, B. and R. de Figueiredo (1999), 'Rationality of fear: political opportunism and ethnic conflict', in B. Walter and J. Snyder, (eds), *Civil Wars, Insecurity and Intervention*, New York: Columbia University Press, pp. 261–302.

Wright, H. (1977), *The Burden of the Present: Liberal-Radical Controversy over Southern African History*, Cape Town: D. Philip.

Famine as a Social Phenomenon

Throughout history, famine has been seen primarily as a consequence of niggardliness of nature, occasionally aggravated by the malfeasance of man. As most people lived at the edge of subsistence as a normal course of affairs, an occasional crisis such as a severe drought or a devastating flood would be enough to cause an acute food shortage leading to mass starvation and excess mortality. It was understood that a large part of famine mortality was caused not directly by starvation as such, but by diseases stemming from malnutrition and mass migrations related to widespread hunger. None the less, the root cause of famine was seen to lie in the shortage of overall food availability caused by some natural disaster.

This view of famine, which puts the blame squarely at the feet of nature, has undergone fundamental changes in modern times. It's not that nature has been completely absolved of its responsibility, but increasing recognition is being given to the culpability of men – through the institutions they create and the policies they pursue in economic, social and political spheres. In this new perspective, the occurrence of famine has much less to do with geography and climate and much more with the nature of social organisation.

To see the role of man and society in the causation of famine, it is useful to distinguish between two stages or aspects of any famine, namely: (a) the emergence of a potential famine situation, and (b) the translation of potential into actual famine. Human culpability is easier to understand in the latter context, especially in the contemporary world where technology has made it possible to vastly improve the productivity of land and to transport food from one place to another a lot faster than was imaginable even a century ago. If a potential famine situation is transformed into actual famine in this day and age, there is every reason to suppose that there has been a colossal human failure – to get the food to those who need it. The exact nature of this failure may vary from case to case; it may even be deliberate in some cases. Much modern research on famine has been concerned with understanding the social and political causes of this failure, especially for the famines that continue to ravage much of Africa.

More fundamentally, even the emergence of a potential famine situation usually involves failure of social organisation, and this is true even when nature has a role to play. This is the message of two centuries of social analysis of famine, starting from the seminal work of Thomas Malthus. It is common knowledge that Malthus attributed famine to an unequal race between growth of food production and population growth, the latter outstripping the former. His insight is enshrined in the famous formulation that food production grows at an arithmetical rate while population grows at a geometric rate. When formulated this way, Malthus's theory seems to have offered a wholly deterministic view of famine, as if caused by the inexorable laws of nature pertaining to the biology of food production on the one hand and human reproduction on the other. In reality, though, Malthus's analysis was much more subtle and nuanced than that. Nature did have a big role to play in his theory, but man was not a mere helpless victim of a remorseless nature – human agency had a role to play too.

Although Malthus believed that population growth had an inherent tendency to outstrip food production, he also believed that there were mechanisms that helped maintain a rough balance between population and food supply over long periods. He identified two types of mechanism: preventive and positive checks. The mechanism of preventive checks operates through economic incentives and involves human agency. As population growth outstrips food supply, the price of food goes up, making it difficult for people to raise a family. In response, they may decide to postpone marriage, or not marry at all, or to have fewer children if they are married. This will slow down the pace of population growth until it comes back in line with food supply.

When for some reason preventive checks do not work, the positive checks will come into play. Malthus reckoned famine to be the last and the most dreadful of them all. First would come epidemics, wars and so on: 'Should success still be incomplete, gigantic inevitable famine stalks in the rear, and with one mighty blow, levels the population with the food of the world' (Malthus, 1798, pp. 139–40).

Famine is thus seen as a consequence of the failure of human agency to apply the preventive checks. Malthus also speculated on the reasons as to why preventive checks seemed to work better in some societies than in others. This is where social organisation really came to the fore in his analysis. Preventive checks are meant to maintain a satisfactory standard of living in the future by controlling reproductive behaviour at present. But incentives for such control would exist only if people expected to retain their rights on the fruits of labour in future. Security of property rights was thus a critical factor in providing incentives for preventive checks. Malthus argued that despotic political institutions weakened this incentive while liberal institutions strengthened it. On this reasoning, he maintained that England, with its liberal institutions, would be better able to avoid famines than the 'backward' societies in Asia and Africa, where despotism was rampant. Leaving aside the question of whether Malthus was right in his characterisation of Asia and Africa, the important analytical point to note here is the emphasis he placed on the nature of social organisation as a major influence on preventive checks, and hence on the likelihood of the occurrence of famine.

In an important way, though, the role of social organisation was rather limited in Malthus's analysis. Its only function was to determine the extent to which control of reproductive behaviour would keep famine at bay by maintaining population size in line with aggregate food availability. There was no place for the idea that social organisation can determine the likelihood of famine also by operating on the food side of the equation – by affecting the manner in which the available food is distributed among the members of the population. This idea was brought to the forefront of famine analysis by the seminal work of Amartya Sen (1981).

Sen pioneered the 'entitlement approach' to famine, which went beyond the traditional concern with aggregate food availability and focused on the forces that determined different individuals' ability to access the available food. Based on his empirical investigation of the Great Bengal famine of 1943 and several other twentieth-century famines of Asia and Africa, he made the startling claim that contrary to popular belief famine is not always caused by a decline in overall food availability. For the famines he studied, he found that food availability did not decline much compared to the preceding years, and yet millions of people went hungrier than before and many more people died from starvation-related causes than in normal times. Famine, he concluded, is a case of people not having enough food to eat, but not necessarily of there not being enough food to go around. Famine analysis should, therefore, be concerned with the reasons why a large number of people lose their ability to stave off starvation at the same time. Any enquiry into these reasons would put the focus squarely on the nature of social organisation that shaped people's differential access to food. The entitlement approach to famine was meant to provide that focus.

The analysis is built upon three basic conceptual categories, namely, the endowment set, the entitlement mapping and the entitlement set. The endowment set is defined as the combination of all resources legally owned by a person. The entitlement set is defined as the set of all possible combinations of goods and services that a person can legally obtain by using the resources of his/her endowment set. The entitlement mapping is simply the relationship between the endowment set on the one hand and the entitlement set on the other. Roughly speaking, it shows the rates at which the resources of the endowment set can be converted into goods and services included in the entitlement set. This conversion can take place in different ways. For example, endowments can be converted into food through production (as when a farmer uses his land to produce food), or through exchange (as when a labourer works for a wage and then uses that wage income to buy food), or through transfer (as when poor people receive free or subsidised food from government agencies).

Whether a person has enough food to eat obviously depends on the size and richness of his/her entitlement set. When the entitlement set does not contain enough food to enable that person to avoid starvation, he/she is said to suffer from the failure of food entitlement. A famine occurs when a large number of people within a community suffer from such entitlement failures at the same time.

This way of looking at famine offers a powerful organising framework for analysing its causes (Osmani, 1995). Since the entitlement set is determined solely by the endowment set and the entitlement mapping, any instance of entitlement failure must be caused by a shrinkage of the endowment set or by an adverse change in entitlement mapping or by a combination of the two. Thus the entitlement approach requires that the search for the causes of famine be directed along two channels – namely, what happened to the endowment sets and what happened to the entitlement mappings of different groups of population. For example, a farmer might lose his endowment of land or livestock, leading to his entitlement failure. Or, a labourer may find that the entitlement mapping that converts his labour power into food has moved adversely – say, because employment opportunities have shrunk or real wages have slumped. That too will cause an entitlement failure.

The nature of social organisation plays a critical role in this type of analysis. Each of the two proximate causes of entitlement failure – namely, loss of endowment and adverse movement in entitlement mapping – can be influenced by a variety of social processes defined broadly to include economic and political processes. For example, people may lose their land or livestock because of a debt trap created by an exploitative credit market or by the dislocations caused by war. Landless labourers may find that their entitlement mapping has become unfavourable as their wages fail to keep pace with inflation created by government policies, as happened during the Bengal famine of 1943. A whole ethnic or religious community may find its entitlement mapping suffer in a civil war as its adversaries use legal or illegal power to block its access to food, as happened in the famines that ravaged the Biafra region of Nigeria in the 1960s and the Darfur region of Sudan in 2004.

This kind of social analysis is obviously essential when famine is not accompanied by any decline in aggregate food availability. But even when food availability does decline and plays a causal role in precipitating famine, social analysis of the kind envisaged by the entitlement approach is still essential. It is not enough to know that food availability has declined, it is necessary to explore precisely how the decline has translated itself into entitlement failure – operating either via endowment loss or via adverse movement in entitlement mapping. This further analysis is called for by the common observation that the incidence of famine is typically asymmetric in nature, that is, famines cause distress to some groups of people more than others, and some not at all. We shall never know why this is so by looking simply at aggregate availability of food. By contrast, the social analysis demanded by the entitlement approach should be able to explain such asymmetries by looking separately at what has happened to the entitlement sets of different socio-economic classes and why.

The entitlement approach gives primacy to social processes not only in explaining how a potential famine situation emerges, but also in determining whether a potential famine will translate into an actual one. Sen has famously observed that famines do not happen in independent democratic societies these days. As the signs of an impending famine become apparent, democratic governments feel obliged to take steps to protect the entitlements of the most vulnerable people. This is because the social processes that characterise democracy – involving free media, civil society and political opposition – make it impossible for governments to ignore signs of widespread entitlement failure. The absence of famine in India since independence despite some close calls is a testimony to the power of democracy. By contrast, closed undemocratic societies that are unencumbered either by a free media or an active opposition, can easily let a manageable crisis get out of hand, as happened in the case of the devastating famine that occurred in China in the wake of the Great Leap Forward during 1958–61.

It can be argued that the advance of democracy and the rule of law has played at least as big a role as advances in the technology of food production as well as the demographic transition in practically eliminating famines from Asia by the end of the twentieth century. Famines are now largely confined to some of the countries of Sub-Saharan Africa. According to one estimate, of the 25 famines that the world has seen in the second half of the twentieth century, all but three occurred in Africa (von Braun et al., 1998, p. 3). Sadly, famines continue to ravage Africa in the early years of the twenty-first century.

A complex combination of fragile ecology and even more fragile political system – giving rise to civil wars and poor governance – has allowed famine to continue to stalk that part of the world. There are a number of ways in which wars and conflicts create a predisposition towards famine, especially when the balance between food supply and population is already quite precarious (von Braun et al., 1998). First, military expenditure reduces the food entitlement of vulnerable groups by diverting resources away from productive activities and social expenditure. This may sometimes take the form of diverting human resources – as happened, for example, when forced conscription of young men into the army disrupted the productive activities of rural households in Ethiopia in 1990/91. Second, the destruction and dislocations caused by war lead to both loss of endowments and adverse changes in entitlement mapping. In fact, mass migration and 'ethnic cleansing' associated with civil wars has been the most proximate cause of recent famines in Africa. Third, warring factions, including the state, often use food as a weapon of war by blocking the enemies' access to food and healthcare – the most recent instance being the famine in the Darfur region of Sudan in 2004. Fourth, a state that has been rendered dysfunctional by civil war and/or poor governance cannot undertake necessary measures to protect the entitlements of vulnerable groups when an already precarious food situation gets worse because of some exogenous shocks such as drought, soil erosion, pest attack, cattle epidemic and so on.

Political conflicts have assumed such a high degree of salience in modern-day African famines that they almost seem to set these famines apart from most others known in history. This realisation has prompted some analysts to argue that the existing tools of famine analysis – including the entitlement approach – are inadequate for the purpose of understanding and, by extension, preventing the African famines. The search for new methodology, and new tools of analysis, is thus at the forefront of current research on famines (for example, de Waal, 1990; Devereux, 2002). It is arguable, however, that, suitably applied, the entitlement approach is perfectly adequate for the job at hand. The processes underlying the modern-day African famines may be different from the ones that have characterised past famines, but that is not a problem for the entitlement approach because it does not postulate any specific process behind famines (Osmani, 1995). What this approach essentially does is to ask the analyst to search for the social processes that lead to widespread entitlement failures, either by causing loss of endowments or by worsening the entitlement mapping. The challenge of identifying the nature of these processes as they operate in modern-day Africa has yet to be fully met.

S.R. OSMANI

References

de Waal, A. (1990), 'A re-assessment of entitlement theory in the light of recent famines in Africa', *Development and Change*, **21**, 469–90.
Devereux, S. (ed.) (2002), Special issue: 'The New Famines', *IDS Bulletin*, **33** (4), 1–126.
Malthus, T.R. (1798), *An Essay on the Principle of Population as It Affects the Future Improvement of Society*, London: J. Johnson.
Osmani, S.R. (1995), 'The entitlement approach to famine: an assessment', in K. Basu, P. Pattanaik and K. Suzumura (eds), *Choice, Welfare, and Development: A Festschrift in Honour of Amartya K. Sen*, Oxford: Clarendon, pp. 253–94.
Sen, A.K. (1981), *Poverty and Famines: An Essay on Entitlement and Deprivation*, Oxford: Clarendon.
von Braun, J., T. Teklu and P. Webb (1998), *Famine in Africa: Causes, Responses and Prevention*, Baltimore, MD: Johns Hopkins University Press.

Food Security

Food security, or its converse food insecurity, is a very general idea, which embodies a wide range of concepts and concerns as to the underlying causes of the food problem in developing countries. In many countries the problem manifests itself in the form of endemic hunger and malnutrition and this 'hidden hunger' affects millions of people in the world economy (Drèze and Sen, 1993). Food insecurity is in part a problem of the lack of effective demand among the poor, which in its extreme form results in a famine situation where access to the means of subsistence is denied to a population.

The ideas and policies that underlie food security discussions can be considered separately from those questions applying to famine situations (see Famine as a Social Phenomenon, this volume). Although famine can be regarded as an extreme form of food insecurity, more often this situation signifies the complete breakdown of the social, political and economic system in a country or region. The question of famine relief and the methods best suited to the alleviation of starvation itself are often best considered in the light of logistics, transportation improvements and methods of bring expeditious relief to affected areas such as refugee camps, as well as supplies of food, medicines clean water and shelter for those affected.

The origins of the concept of food security

The concern with food insecurity issues arises from the agricultural policy changes in the world economy in the 1970s and the focus on the causes of the so-called, 'world food crisis' of that decade. Increasingly it was recognised that the problem of world hunger and the associated causes of that hunger constituted a number of different problems with interconnecting causes. In the context of Sub-Saharan Africa the agricultural and food supply problem was considered as the major development priority for the continent as a whole (see, for example, World Bank, 1981). In the last two decades the food security issue on the continent has intensified rather than abated. The complexity of the causes have indeed increased and countries such as Zimbabwe have in the course of two decades gone from not having had a serious food insecurity problem, to the brink of famine and endemic countrywide food shortage with the economy on the verge of collapse. Food insecurity can be caused by government policy failure or market failure, or indeed natural causes including HIV/AIDS. In Sub-Saharan Africa some 35 million people are affected by HIV/AIDS which has serious consequences for food security.

The food crisis has a number of aspects other than the supply of foodstuffs and the availability of food, including the ability of the poor to acquire access to available supplies. The food problem is as much a problem of poverty itself and increasingly a problem of chronic ill health, unemployment, lack of purchasing power and entitlement to medicines as well as food and above all to acquire the means of subsistence. At the most general level, food security has been defined as 'access by all people at all times to enough food for an active, healthy life' (Reutlinger, 1985, p. 7).

Chronic food insecurity

The idea of food security can be refined to consider both its long- and short-term aspects. Long-term food insecurity, or chronic insecurity is defined in terms of the persistent existence of malnutrition and the associated lack of development and growth in low-income developing countries or in regions of those economies. The policy recommendations for chronic food insecurity include minimum daily food intake, nutritional policy measures and often more general, non-economic measures to offset or improve malnutrition and under nutrition in whichever form it takes. The problems of long-term endemic malnutrition in the first instance requires policy actions that are concerned with the alleviation of this dire form of under nutrition. The permanent alleviation of chronic food insecurity is most likely to be achieved by the process of economic growth and development itself. In Sub-Saharan Africa, chronic food insecurity and HIV/AIDS reinforce each other in a continental pandemic where mortality rates have the potential to undermine economic progress (Human Science Research Council, 2004).

Transitory food insecurity
The inability to attain food security in the short run, or transitory food insecurity, is defined as a temporary decline in a household's or region's or nation's access to food. Therefore the concept of food insecurity applies at several levels. Food insecurity is considered to arise from the instabilities of food production and price or in household incomes. Transitory food insecurity can be considered as a decline in domestic production or a rise in world agricultural commodity prices. Drought and seasonal supply fluctuations form part of this aspect of the food security question. Food insecurity can be seen as arising from local, regional or international food markets through excessive supply and price fluctuations. The rapid commodity price rises in the 1970s resulted in many countries having insufficient currency reserves to meet food import requirements. The world food crisis of the 1970s saw a reassessment of the issues surrounding the causes of the intransigent nature of world hunger. The optimism with regard to ridding the world of food shortage and hunger in the immediate aftermath of the Second World War was giving way to a recognition that these problems were far more complex than Malthusian supply-side solutions might at first suggest.

Transitory food insecurity may result from inappropriate government policy such as the destabilisation of the trend consumption of food by government policies themselves. The recent failures of land reform policy in Zimbabwe and the destabilisation of the food supply and the overall economy would be a twenty-first century example of government policy failure in providing food security to a country. The wars of the twentieth century together with agricultural policy and general economic policy failures as well as genocide have resulted in the death of hundreds of millions of people. These wars, both local and international, have brought famine in their wake. The catastrophic famine caused by the Soviet agricultural policy in the 1930s, the equally disastrous 1960s policy failures in China and the many other government policy-induced failures in numerous developing countries bear testament to the disregard of food security in government policy making (Bradford De Long, 2004).

Economy-wide definitions of transitory food insecurity seek to stabilise trend consumption of food by focusing upon the short-term nature of the food problem in many developing countries. The food security policy objective takes the form of the stabilisation of consumption without adversely affecting the rate of economic growth in the economy, or the balance of payments (Cathie and Dick, 1986). Food security objectives are determined by the trade-offs between nutritional goals and the economic objectives of growth and development.

A policy of food consumption stability for the nation as an aggregate is not necessarily the same thing as consumption stability for large sections of the population. A policy of subsidised prices for consumers, for food security purposes, may very well result in adverse effects upon the supply of agricultural products through price disincentives. The problem of food insecurity has been considered by some analysts to consist of both the supply and the financing of the supply of food to meet minimally adequate consumption requirements without domestic price increases, regardless of world market conditions (Valdes, 1981). The causes of food security are considered to be shortfalls in domestic production and instability of world food prices (cereals). Food insecurity arises from inappropriate agricultural policies as well as inadequate employment or income growth in a developing economy.

Food security policies

To some considerable degree the definition of the concept of food security can pre-empt the policy conclusions and predetermine the policy recommendation of the analysis. Chronic food insecurity is often best considered within the context of emergency and direct feeding programmes and projects, where alleviation of human misery is the objective. Transitory food insecurity, however, involves consideration of a country food policy in the context of a broader macroeconomic framework where the objectives of such a policy are considered in respect of other objectives of economic policy. Since food security policies are not without their costs, the relative efficiency of economic policies concerned with transitory food insecurity can then be assessed against other objectives of economic policy. The implicit assumption that the cost of meeting transitory food insecurity should be borne by the international community alone often obscures the adverse effects that such policies can have upon the economies of recipients of international largesse. Food aid policy as a secondary outcome of agricultural policy in rich countries has among its many objectives a transitory food security element, however this source of assistance has proved to be unreliable in a number of ways. The notion that the international community will always provide for developing-country food shortfalls is not borne out of the evidence of the experience of policies, such as those conducted by the major donors over the last 50 years (Wallerstein, 1980; Cathie, 1982).

Transitory food insecurity is measured as deviations from trend consumption levels or of food consumption targets. This approach, where it adopts a high level of aggregation and when a large number of countries are examined, is not particularly helpful in identifying the source and causes of the food insecurity. At this high level of aggregation the analysis more often as not pre-empts the policy conclusion that food insecurity can only be solved by international assistance, whether it be financial (in the form of an IMF food facility loan), or the Export Earnings Stabilisation Scheme STABEX of the EU, or indeed of buffer stock policy advocated by the Food and Agriculture Organization of the United Nations. The highly aggregated estimation of food insecurity actually ignores how transitory food insecurity affects individual households in the economies concerned in so far as increases in food production in one part of a country may offset decreases in another. A similar circumstance may also apply to household incomes.

The advocacy of international assistance for food insecurity may under particular country situations be quite inappropriate for the correction and the alleviation of the causes of that insecurity. International assistance in the form of continuous food aid handouts may very well prevent the governments concerned from undertaking policy change that would ultimately relieve the causes of the basic insecurity. The food-first approach recognised that dependence may cause government to put off policy decisions, or to even consider having a food policy at all. Dependence on international charity of food hand-outs may in the longer run perpetuate the food insecurity problem (Lappe and Collins, 1980). Relying on foreign governments or international bureaucracies may not prove less risky than relying on the international marketplace, or for that matter the weather.

The major concern of the literature on food insecurity has been to justify international policies to alleviate transitory and chronic food insecurity. Policies, which are advocated, include *inter alia* IMF financial facilities for covering the import bill, buffer stocks to offset price and supply instabilities, and regularised, institutionalised food aid quantities. Twenty years ago the Brandt Commission (1983) endorsed these policies, which arguably have not improved the overall situation towards reducing food insecurity.

An examination of food insecurity not only requires a distinction between the long run and medium run as well as the short run but also a country-specific analysis of the food situation in each developing country (Maxwell, 2001). This requires an analysis of consumption, production, imports and indeed the analysis of the economic policy of the country concerned as a whole. A partial examination of the food insecurity of a large number of countries (or regions) and at a high level of aggregation may obscure the causes of the problem. The policy recommendations resulting from highly aggregated data may be both inadequate and inappropriate. In low-income countries, where typically food forms some 70–80 per cent of the disposable income of the population, that is to say where formal sector employment exists, a food policy is central to overall macroeconomic policy (Cathie and Dick, 1986).

Transitory food security policy aims to stabilise food consumption without affecting the rate of growth of the economy by allowing an adverse balance-of-payments problem either to slow the rate of consumption for food products, or to cause imports of non-food items to be restricted in favour of food. The problem of food insecurity arises because either the market mechanisms to overcome short-run falls in consumption do not exist, as in the subsistence sector, or as in the informal sector of the economy they may not be fully functioning. In addition to market failure contributing to food insecurity, government-induced distortions to the operation of market mechanisms may also prevent individuals from providing for their own family needs. The introduction of land rights, or the establishment of appropriate exchange rate policies as well as savings institutions such as micro-credit and other schemes may very well provide a lasting means to overcome food insecurity.

The food security problem manifests itself in different forms in different countries and generalised international policies may overlook the very nature of the problem and the source of its causes as it is in a particular country or region of the world. Food security is as much a national responsibility as it is an international concern. International policies, including humanitarian responses, by their very nature can only have a short-term responsibility and international agencies permanently established to alleviate hunger and malnutrition imply its unending continuation.

JOHN CATHIE

References

Bradford DeLong, J. (2004), 'Slouching towards Utopia? The economic history of the twentieth century IV: genocide', www.j-bradford-delong.net/TCEH/Slouch_power 4.html.

Brandt Commission (1983), *Common Crisis North–South: Cooperation for World Recovery*, London: Pan World Affairs.

Cathie, John (1982), *The Political Economy of Food Aid*, Aldershot: Gower.

Cathie, John and Hermann Dick (1986), *Food Security and Macroeconomic Stabilisation: A Case Study of Botswana 1965–1984*, Tübingen: Mohr.

Drèze, Jean and Amartya K. Sen (1993), *The Political Economy of Hunger*, Oxford: Clarendon.

Human Sciences Research Council (2004), 'Food security in South Africa: key issues for the medium term', Position Paper, Pretoria.

Lappe, Francis and Joseph Collins (1980), *Food First*, London: Abacus.

Maxwell, Simon (2001), 'The evolution of thinking about food security', in S. Devereux and S. Maxwell (eds), *Food Security in Sub-Sahara Africa*, London: ITDG Publishing, pp. 13–27.

Reutlinger, Shlomo (1985), 'Food security and poverty in LDCs', *Finance and Development*, **22** (4), 7–11.

Valdes, Alberto (ed.) (1981), *Food Security for Developing Countries*, Boulder, CO: Westwood Press.

Wallerstein, Michael (1980), *Food for War – Food for Peace: United States Food Aid in Global Context*, Cambridge MA and London: MIT Press.

World Bank (1981), *Accelerated Development in Sub-Sahara Africa: An Agenda for Action*, Washington, DC: World Bank.

Foreign Direct Investment

The literature on foreign direct investment (FDI) is vast and multifaceted. A considerable part of it focuses on the reasons why a given country is selected by multinational corporations (MNCs) to relocate production overseas. Of particular importance from the viewpoint of economic development is how FDI may contribute to enhance growth in the host country, primarily through capital accumulation and productivity gains.

It is hard to define FDI. Conventionally, it can be thought of as a form of international inter-firm financial transaction that involves significant equity stake and effective management decision power in, or ownership control of, foreign enterprises. But FDI can also encompass more generally non-equity forms of cross-border ventures involving the supply of tangible and intangible assets by a foreign enterprise to a domestic firm without foreign control. These ventures include a host of investment modalities, such as licensing, leasing, franchising, start-up and international production sharing agreements, as well as broad research and development cooperation. In any case, MNCs are the main vehicles for FDI.

FDI has risen rapidly over time, outpacing the growth in international trade (see Table 5; see OECD, 2003, and UNCTAD, 2003, for more information on FDI trends). OECD countries account for the lion's share in outward FDI but are also important recipients of inward FDI, with most FDI activity consisting of mergers and acquisitions in the services sector, particularly in the 1990s, rather than 'greenfield' investments. Among developing countries, some have been more successful than others in attracting FDI, which remains concentrated in a few emerging market economies in South East Asia, China and Latin America. These trends – which have fluctuated over time – have been motivated by new investment opportunities brought about by reform-driven privatisation programmes, as well as globalisation and internationalisation trends in production, operations and investment, among others. The substantial increase in FDI flows in the 1990s was little affected by the downturn in cross-border mergers and acquisitions that occurred after 2000. The sectoral composition of FDI has also shifted over time: inflows were concentrated in manufacturing in the 1970s and 1980s and continued to be important in the 1990s, despite the take-off in services-orientated FDI. Microeconomic data are not readily available for

Table 5   Foreign direct investment flows, 1970–2001

	1970	1980	1990	2001
	Outflows (in billions of US dollars)			
OECD	14.2	61.3	270.4	651.0
of which: G7	11.3	49.6	213.4	417.8
Latin America	0.0	0.4	1.1	3.0
Middle East and North Africa	0.0	0.5	0.4	0.7
South East Asia (excl. China)	0.0	0.2	8.5	27.6
Sub-Saharan Africa	0.1	0.8	0.1	3.7
China (incl. Hong Kong)	0.0	0.0	0.8	15.9
	Inflows (in billions of US dollars)			
OECD	9.4	53.8	177.0	572.1
of which: G7	6.0	37.3	114.5	330.3
Latin America	1.1	7.3	8.4	68.5
Middle East and North Africa	0.3	−3.3	2.9	4.0
South East Asia (excl. China)	0.5	2.9	15.4	42.6
Sub-Saharan Africa	0.7	0.0	1.0	10.9
China (incl. Hong Kong)	0.0	0.2	3.5	67.1
	Inflows (in per cent of GDP)			
OECD	0.4	0.7	1.0	2.3
of which: G7	0.3	0.6	0.8	1.6
Latin America	0.6	0.8	0.7	3.4
Middle East and North Africa	0.5	−0.6	0.5	0.5
South East Asia (excl. China)	0.3	0.5	1.2	1.7
Sub-Saharan Africa	1.1	0.0	0.3	3.3
China (incl. Hong Kong)	0.0	0.1	0.8	5.1
	Inflow (in per cent of exports of goods, f.o.b.)			
OECD	4.2	4.2	6.9	13.7
of which: G7	3.7	4.1	6.5	12.0
Latin America	6.6	6.4	5.7	19.4
Middle East and North Africa	2.1	−1.3	1.8	2.3
South East Asia (excl. China)	3.0	2.0	4.0	4.8
Sub-Saharan Africa	6.4	0.1	1.4	13.8
China (incl. Hong Kong)	0.0	0.5	2.6	14.7

Source: CEPII (2004).

most developing countries, but the distribution of FDI across sectors of economic activity seems to vary considerably in different countries. Inward FDI is large as a percentage of exports in Latin America, reflecting the region's relatively low share in world trade.

The FDI determinants

Several factors affect a firm's decision to invest abroad. Important FDI determinants are found at the level of the firm (see, for example, the literature pioneered by Buckley and

Casson, 1976, and Dunning, 1977). International trade patterns are a powerful FDI determinant, but differentials across countries in rates of return on investment (reflecting the relative abundance, or scarcity, of factor endowments among countries), the absorptive capacity of the host country, institutions and policies also matter (see, for example, Aggarwal, 1980; Batra and Ramachandran, 1980; Helpman, 1984; Dunning, 1993; and Markusen and Maskus, 2001).

FDI and trade are closely related. Empirical evidence suggests that most FDI occurs among countries bound by foreign trade agreements or within close geographical proximity (see the early studies surveyed by de Mello, 1997). FDI can be complementary to trade because there must be a significant volume of commercial exchange between the foreign investor and the host country to justify production relocation. Optimal relocation theory predicts the timing at which firms replace trade with foreign-located operations (see, for example, Buckley and Casson, 1981). Also, FDI can, and often does, take place as a means of bypassing trade restrictions in the recipient economy. Alternatively, FDI and trade can be thought of as substitutes to the extent that production relocation may reduce the scope for trade between the home and host countries. Once production relocates abroad, imports from the home country may fall at an initial stage of import substitution, but exports from the host country to the home country may subsequently rise. The composition of imports is also likely to change. It is therefore common that bilateral trade and FDI complement or substitute for each other in different phases of the FDI cycle.

But, regardless of whether trade and FDI are substitutes or complements, which is an empirical question, the trade–FDI nexus depends on the absorptive capacity of the recipient economy. Local production takes place only when the basic skills needed for production relocation are present and further training is possible, where needed. This allows foreign investors to use domestic non-reproducible inputs and labour of the quality level needed to set up operations in the host country and sustain productive activities thereafter. The labour force has to be sufficiently well educated and trained and domestic non-reproducible inputs have to satisfy minimal quality standards to justify investment and technology transfers into the host country. This has led to the idea of a 'development threshold' for FDI. Empirical evidence suggests that, if FDI takes place before this threshold is attained, it may result in the creation of a dual economy, with foreign firms engaging primarily in assembly-type activities with a higher ratio of exports to domestic sales and higher imported input content than domestic firms, and limited spillovers to the domestic market (see, for example, Borensztein et al., 1998).

Linked to absorptive capacity and attractiveness to FDI is the idea that institutions matter. These include the degree of political stability and government intervention in the economy; the existence of property rights legislation and ensuing law enforcement institutions; the property and profit tax system, and the extent and severity of bureaucratic impediments and foreign ownership limitations, among others. Property rights legislation, particularly on intellectual property, offers foreign investors guarantees against expropriation and is a powerful determinant of not only the volume of FDI but also the scope for FDI-induced technological transfers.

Policy also matters. Many countries, particularly in the developing world, encourage inward FDI through incentives, which can be fiscal (for example, tax rebates and exemptions), financial (for example, subsidised loans and grants), and non-financial (for example, basic infrastructure provision). These incentives are not cost free, but these costs are believed to be outweighed by the benefits that inward FDI brings to the host country. To a large extent, country-specific FDI incentives tend to reflect competition for foreign capital, but the decisions to invest in a given country do not appear to be overly sensitive to the incentives offered by the host country, the costs of which are often underestimated. Related to policies in general is the macroeconomic framework within which foreign investors operate in the host country, with macroeconomic volatility having a considerable deleterious impact on MNCs' employment and investment decisions. For industries with costly capacity, MNCs tend to invest in more stable markets.

Scale factors, affecting the absorptive capacity of the host country, affect the volume and type of FDI inflows. The size of the domestic market, in conjunction with the growth prospects of the host country, also plays a role when foreign investors decide to relocate production overseas, or to engage in export-bound production in the host country. Typically, a large domestic market may encourage FDI in downstream industries geared for domestic demand, whereas in smaller economies FDI may take place in industries or sectors producing primarily exportable goods and services. By affecting relative prices, the foreign exchange regime of the host country also plays a part in determining the outward orientation of FDI-related activities.

FDI and growth
The impact of FDI on growth is expected to be manifold (see the surveys by Lall, 1978, and de Mello, 1997). This is because FDI is a composite bundle of capital stocks, know-how and technology. Consequently, its impact is expected to be greater, the greater the value-added content of FDI-related production, and productivity spillovers to domestic firms, by which FDI leads to increasing returns in domestic production.

Through capital accumulation, FDI can enhance growth as a result of the use of a wider range of intermediate goods, as well as new technologies, in production. Technological change can take the form of product innovations, by which new products are created, but also process innovations, by which (not necessarily new) goods are produced using newer technologies transferred via FDI. FDI is also expected to be growth enhancing through the introduction of alternative management practices and organisational arrangements, and through human capital accumulation, since it provides specific productivity-increasing labour training and skill acquisition in the recipient economy.

Growth is also affected by the degree of complementarity, or substitution, between FDI and domestic investment. Under complementarity, innovations embodied in foreign investment may create, rather than steal, rents accruing to the older technologies used in domestic production. It may be argued that there needs to be some degree of complementarity between FDI and domestic investment because the existing factor endowments in the host country are an important FDI determinant. But technologies that are complementary to the FDI-related innovations may subsequently substitute for older technologies. As a result, a faster rate of technological change embodied in FDI-produced goods may lead to a higher rate of capital obsolescence and scrapping in the host country, which is expected to affect output growth via total factor productivity gains. Again, different degrees of complementarity and substitution are likely to be present in different periods of the investment cycle.

The scope for FDI to enhance growth varies in different schools of thought. In conventional neoclassical growth models, long-run growth can only result from technological change and/or population/labour force growth, which are both considered to be exogenous. FDI would affect output growth only in the short run and, in the long run, under diminishing returns, the recipient economy would converge to its steady state, as if FDI had never taken place, leaving no permanent impact on output growth. The only vehicle for growth-enhancing FDI would be through permanent technological shocks.

But more recent models show that FDI may raise long-run growth. Even if diminishing returns prevail in individual firms, and hence the marginal product of capital tends to decline as capital is accumulated, the presence of externalities places a wedge between social and private rates of return to investment. In the aggregate, externality-generating factor accumulation prevents the unbounded decline of the marginal productivity of capital. In other words, FDI-related externalities account for the non-diminishing returns needed to promote growth in the long run. As a result, foreign investors may increase productivity in the recipient economy and FDI can be deemed to be a catalyst for domestic investment and technological progress. Due to their externality effects, knowledge and technology transfers are expected to be the most important mechanisms through which FDI promotes growth in the host country. The ultimate test of these hypotheses is nevertheless empirical and the evidence available so far is far from unequivocal. Whereas a strong FDI–growth nexus is reported by several researchers (see, for example, Balasubramanyam et al., 1996, and those surveyed by de Mello, 1997), more recent empirical work has cast some doubt on these early findings (see, for example, Carkovic and Levine, 2002).

Conclusion

Foreign direct investment has risen over time as a percentage of both GDP and trade flows. Developed countries are not only the main investors overseas but also the main recipients of FDI. Greater international integration and pro-market reform in many parts of the world – with the liberalisation of trade and investment regimes, privatisation, and deregulation of product and labour markets in general – have contributed to the rise in FDI in the developing world. Differentials in rates of return on investment, reflecting differentials in factor endowments, as well as firm-level factors, play an important role, but so do foreign trade patterns, institutions and policies. In addition, the concentration of FDI in a few leading emerging markets and in the developed world suggests that the effect of FDI on growth and development is not uniform across countries.

LUIZ DE MELLO

References

Aggarwal, J.P. (1980), 'Determinants of foreign direct investment', *Weltwirtschaftliches Archiv*, **116**, 739–73.
Balasubramanyam, V.N., M. Salisu and D. Sapsford (1996), 'Foreign direct investment and growth: new hypotheses and evidence', Discussion Paper EC7/96, Department of Economics, Lancaster University.
Batra, R.N. and R. Ramachandran (1980), 'Multinational firms and the theory of international trade and investment', *American Economic Review*, **70**, 278–90.
Borensztein, E., J. de Gregório and J.W. Lee (1998), 'How does foreign direct investment affect growth?', *Journal of International Economics*, **45** (1), 115–35.
Buckley, P.J. and M. Casson (1976), *The Future of Multinational Enterprises*, London: Macmillan.
Buckley, P.J. and M. Casson (1981), 'The optimum timing of foreign investment', *Economic Journal*, **91**, 75–87.

Carkovic, M. and R. Levine (2002), 'Does foreign direct investment accelerate economic growth?', University of Minnesota, unpublished manuscript.

CEPII (2004), CHELEM (Comptes Harmonisés sur les Échanges et l'Économie Mondiale) database, Paris: CEPII.

de Mello, L. (1997), 'Foreign direct investment and growth: a survey', *Journal of Development Studies*, **34**, 1–34;

Dunning, J.H. (1977), 'Trade location of economic activity and multinationals: a search for an eclectic approach', in B. Ohlin, P.O. Hesselborn and P.M. Wijkman (eds) *The International Allocation of Economic Activity*, London: Macmillan, pp. 395–418.

Dunning, J.H. (1993), *Multinational Enterprises and the Global Economy*, Reading, MA: Addison-Wesley.

Helpman, E. (1984), 'A simple theory of trade with multinational corporations', *Journal of Political Economy*, **92**, 451–71.

Lall, S. (1978), 'Transnationals, domestic enterprises and the industrial structure in host LDCs: a survey', *Oxford Economic Papers*, **30**, 217–48.

Markusen, J.R. and K.E. Maskus (2001), 'General-equilibrium approaches to the multinational firm: a review of theory and evidence', NBER Working Paper no. 8334, National Bureau of Economic Research, New York.

OECD (2003), *Economic Outlook no. 73*, Paris: OECD.

UNCTAD (2003), *World Development Report*, Geneva: United Nations/UNCTAD.

Gender and Development

Since the 1970s women, and then gender, have moved progressively into central focus of development studies. From being a critical and political irritant, the concern for 'gender' has now become *de rigeur* for development analysts, practitioners and even critics.

This entry sets out to establish the varied paths which the focus on gender and development have followed. As in other areas of development studies, the theory, analysis and practice of gender and development have been subject to evolution and change over the last four decades and it is important both to chart these changes and to distinguish it from other elements of political and social change. Gender and development is best conceptualised as an approach to development analysis, which uses a gender lens to inform and shape policy and practice in a manner which takes into account both the centrality of gender relations as an organising dimension within households, communities and public policies, and the implications of the near universal dynamic that places women in a subordinate position in relation to men.

Gender and development: what it is not

Gender and development is not an alternative development paradigm, or a substitute for an international women's liberation movement, or a humanising addition to main (male) stream development studies, although it is common practice to assume that these are all the same. But clearly if gender and development refers to the deployment of a gender lens on development activity it cannot be separated into an alternative development paradigm. Gender must inform all development activity which is concerned with global and local inequalities; it is central to development activity not an alternative construction. Sen and Grown (1987) called their articulation of Third World women's perspectives *Development, Crises and Alternative Visions*; development from a gender perspective may well mean rethinking both what desirable development might look like and the strategies to achieve it; but this redirection has to be centred on gendering development itself, rather than creating an alternative paradigm called 'gender and development'.

Nor can we see gender and development as a substitute for the international women's movement, although as many of us have recorded, the impetus for inserting a gender perspective into international development analysis and policy indubitably came from a commitment to international feminism (Pearson et al., 1984; Pearson and Jackson, 1998; Pearson, 2005). Increasingly in a globalised world of instantaneous electronic communication and information sharing via the worldwide web, international networks have grown up offering access to a wide range of information, solidarity and activities which can be seen as part of an international women's movement. And feminist groups committed to reversing the subordination of women have used the opportunities offered by the international conferences convened by the UN system throughout the 1990s as a platform to press for women's rights in the context of the environment, human rights, population and development, social development and the series of world conferences on women which culminated in the Beijing conference in 1995. (Note that Beijing was the last of these international conferences for a variety of reasons, not least because the feminist movement considered that the reactionary change in global politics since would make it difficult to uphold the commitments embodied in the Beijing Platform for Action. Beijing +5 and +10 held in New York had little resonance beyond the immediate UN system and achieved only limited participation from international women's organisations.)

But nor is gender and development to be thought of just as a humanising addition to main (male) stream development studies, though the perusal of most development studies courses and texts continue to give that impression. If gender is seen as a universal organising principle of all human activity in the social, economic and cultural sphere, it is logical that gender analysis should be central to all scholarship, policy and practice that is aimed at engaging with and eliminating international inequality and poverty. But as evidenced in the recent articulation of the Millennium Development Goals, in public discourse gender is present only in terms of targeting primary education and by implication eliminating maternal mortality; there is no specific mention of gender equality in the seven out of the eight goals, and no explicit references to the aspects of development directly concerned with the challenging of women's subordination such as violence, reproductive and sexual rights, and social and political marginalisation (Sweetman, 2005). It would indeed appear that in spite of all the efforts to ensure that gender analysis is at the heart of all development endeavours it has remained a marginal and optional add-on.

Over the past 15 years or so, the reaction by committed feminists to the marginalisation of gender analysis in development policy has led to the demand to mainstream gender in all development activity. However, this too has proved problematic. While many international development organisations have adopted a policy of mainstreaming, as required in the Beijing Platform for Action agreed in 1995, this has not proved universally successful (Watkins, 2004). There has been a discernible coyness about senior management taking institutional responsibility for ensuring adequate and comprehensive incorporation of gender analysis throughout the organisation and its activities. Instead, there has often been a tendency to use a policy of gender mainstreaming to eliminate specifically targeted provision for women, even though gender inequality persists and needs to be addressed directly. This use of the notion of gender mainstreaming to reduce resources to support gender and development activities has led many activists to conclude that it is the technicisation of 'gender' that has allowed the development sector to retreat from a commitment to ending women's subordination under the umbrella of mainstreaming development.

There are clearly different paths towards implementing a gendered approach to development and a high level of contestation about the efficacy of different experiences and strategies. With this in mind the remaining part of this entry attempts to make clear the different elements which are included in the concept of gender and development and their relevance to contemporary development studies and practice.

Gender and development: what it is

Gender and development encompasses a wide range of contributions and inputs which I have divided into three main themes: (1) the ways in which development policy and intervention of both international donors and national governments and NGOs have evolved and changed over the past decades; (2) gender analysis of development issues policies and practices; and (3) gender and global change which encompasses planned and unplanned changes in the global economy and social order which both impact on and are influenced by the changing nature of gender identities and roles. These three themes are discussed in turn below but it should be emphasised that their order does not represent the periodisation of their evolution nor does it reflect any implicit hierarchy among the different themes.

The gendering of international development policy
There are three terms ('women in development', 'women and development' and 'gender and development': WID, WAD and GAD) which refer to the way in which donor and policy-related approaches have *included* women within the realm of development activity and benefits have evolved since the 1970s. Since the pathbreaking volume by Danish economist (demographer) Ester Boserup, *Women's Role in Economic Development*, was published in 1970, development agencies all over the world, encouraged by their feminist staff, have striven to 'integrate women into the development process'.

The development of a WID approach reflected this desire to include women both as participators and beneficiaries of development programmes. The 1970s was not just the era of civil rights, new wave feminism, anti-colonial struggles and the Cold War; it was also an age of optimism about the efficacy of development planning to deliver economic growth and improvements in the living standards of the world's poor through a managed market-led process. If development was to succeed, then women should share in that success.

However, the optimism about uninterrupted economic development was short-lived and by the end of the 1970s the emphasis was on anti-poverty strategies. Rather than focus on women achieving equality with men in a context of continuous improvement, policy towards women shifted to initiatives which were designed to meet women's basic needs, often in the form of income-generating projects for women's groups. Aware of the fact that projects targeted at women often 'misbehaved' (Buvinic, 1986), policy makers were challenged to mainstream development initiatives aimed at women, and to ensure that women participated in all projects and programme implementation rather than reserving small budgets and ring-fenced projects for women alone. This approach was reinforced by the so-called 'efficiency' approach to gender and development which stressed women's potential as productive labour in an increasingly commodified economy; the adjustment required by new economic policies required women as well as men to respond to market pressures, so that women's productive role in the development process was emphasised rather than their non-(or un)productive activities in non-traded or reproductive work.

These approaches have zigzagged between an emphasis on what Young (1988, p. 1) called, 'women's condition' (that is, women's material circumstances) and women's position (relative to men's). Although the concern remained with poor women and men as the objects of development policy and activity, the focus on gender quality was lost during the 1980s and 1990s in the face of anti-poverty and economic growth considerations. Only in more recent times have development agencies returned to a more holistic consideration of women's empowerment – a catch-all term which encompasses the improvement of women's individual, intra-household, economic, political and social status, and autonomy.

WAD

While all the above approaches can be said to be about 'women in development' the literature makes a parallel distinction between WID, WAD and GAD. In the mid-1980s following the UN's Decade for Women (1976–85), an influential think-tank comprising women professionals from Third World countries issued what amounted to a manifesto for the advancement of women's position in development (Sen and Grown, 1987). The proposed 'women and development' framework questioned the uncritical modernist approach of WID and argued that the problem was not women marginalised from development but the development model itself and the terms on which women were integrated. Development needed to be reformulated in a way which would valorise women's unpaid work, challenge differentials between male and female workers and prioritise the collective responsibility of nation states for resourcing and organising reproductive services such as health and education which would support struggles for women's equality.

GAD

However, the neoliberal political and economic trajectory of the 1980s made such a position institutionally untenable (despite advances made through the series of UN world conferences on women in 1975, 1985 and 1995 (Beijing)); the reality was the structural adjustment policies of the Washington Consensus. Instead of the vision of women's participation in a transformatory development *strategy*, the market-orientated economic adjustment policies of the 1990s were primarily concerned with the potential for women to contribute to the labour-intensive export sectors in which developing countries were to compete in the expanding international market. However, feminist development studies had evolved a new paradigm – 'gender and development' – which foregrounds not the identities of women as opposed to men in developing countries, but the gender ideologies, structures and norms which construct the different positioning of both men and women. GAD had its antecedents in early efforts to analyse development issues from a development perspective (see Wellesley Editorial Committee, 1977; Young et al., 1981) and has more recently been applied to a range of issues and policy arenas within developing countries.

Looking at development through a gender lens

Using a gender lens to interrogate different development arenas has resulted in insights which have been both useful to development policy makers and have contributed to our intellectual understanding of the fluidity of gender differences over time and place. For instance, a gender analysis of structural adjustment moved the focus from UNICEF's admirable concern with 'women and children' as vulnerable groups to an understanding of the male bias in economic policies. The World Bank has long since recognised the importance of understanding gender roles and differences in the context of changing the productive behaviour of rural households (Blackden and Morris-Hughes, 1993). However, gender analysis of structural adjustment called on feminist deconstruction of the household, analysis of domestic labour and unpaid work on family farms and businesses, to demonstrate the inherently male bias of economic policies which assumes that all labour is interchangeable, equally market responsive and not embedded in non-market obligations and priorities (Elson, 1995).

Gender analysis of other cross-cutting issues has been revealing. Ecofeminist attempts to link women with nature reflect romantic assumptions about women and nature in both a conceptual and spiritual sense. Preserving harmony between people and nature would seem to rest on women's unpaid and beneficent activities and women's timeless knowledge of all things natural is drawn upon to either resist change or to give women prime responsibility for environmental management. However, a GAD approach rejects this essentialist link and instead explores the ways in which women's and men's relationships with the environment are seen to emerge from the dynamics of both gender relations and livelihood systems. Depending on their context, some women may be locked into environmental resource dependence (such as gathering wood for cooking fuel – for sale as well as for own domestic use) and, deprived of access to more lucrative activities, have little incentive for environmental sustainability or improvement (Green et al., 1998).

Similarly a gendered analysis of population growth and change is also revealing. The role of feminist NGOs and researchers in moving the population and development community from population or family planning policy to the notion of reproductive rights which stresses women's rights to bodily integrity and autonomy is well known, and includes successful campaigns against invasive and non-reversible contraceptive techniques and invasive 'cultural' procedures such as female genital mutilation. However, researchers often pay much less attention to the gender bias in particular populations. Yet in spite of the careless truism that women comprise one-half of the world's population, the reality is that in some regions and including the most populous countries of India and China, women's share of the population is continuing to fall. In India's 2001 census, the sex ratio of children up to the age of 6 years has declined from 945 females per 1000 males in 1991 to just 927 females ten years later. In some provinces in China there are only 870 girls per thousand boys, and in some provinces the ratio is as low as 770 (Rahmeen, 2004).

Masculine juvenile sex ratios are increasingly easy to achieve as technology of pre-birth sex selection and abortion make other measures such as infanticide and neglect of girl children less necessary. But a gender analysis is necessary to investigate the interaction of population limitation policies, strong cultural and economic son preference and the status of women which can account for the fact that the elimination of women from the population has accelerated rather than declined as economic growth and income have risen.

Similar gender analyses could be provided for a range of other issues including the HIV/AIDS pandemic and disaster, conflict and reconstruction. Severe food shortages (famines) for example often present at moments in time when there has been sustained male out migration in the face of ongoing declines in harvests, leaving a predominantly female population in the areas of production failures or in relief or refugee camps. Women who are seeking survival for themselves and their children outside the accepted gender order where they are offered protection within the household or the community are vulnerable to a range of aggression including sexual harassment by border officials, host governments or aid agency personnel, as well as local populations and particularly from militia groups representing opposing ethnic groups. Even access to emergency relief is often perilous for unprotected and displaced women in disaster and conflict situations (El Bushra, 2004).

Gender analysis of global change

The ways in which global processes have changed the nature of international production, trade and labour forces can also be illuminated by gender analysis of global change. Over the last three decades it has been clear that when poor (cheap labour) economies produce for international markets, women's lower wages can offer a distinct competitive advantage. However, not only are women paid less; they are often excluded from (even rudimentary) social protection and non-wage benefit provisions, but offer higher productivity particularly in occupations which require manual dexterity, application to repetitive tasks and adherence to strict industrial discipline (Pearson, 1998; Razavi, 1999).

Recent changes in the global economy – towards longer commodity chains constructed through serial subcontracting relationships – have removed many women workers in developing economies further from the realm of the protected and organised formal sector workforce; in fact most women workers involved in exports of manufactures in textiles, garments, sportswear and footwear work in unregulated factories and workshops or as home-based producers. Even electronics labour processes are utilising more and more outsourced suppliers and very little of the workforce is unionised or covered by labour protection legislation. New global markets – in cut flowers, tropical fruits and vegetables – have offered new employment opportunities to women who are the preferred labour force for planting, weeding, pruning, picking and packing but again this work is insecure, seasonal and unprotected. In the lively debates about corporate social responsibility and regulation of labour, it is often women's voices who have most loudly welcomed initiatives such as the Ethical Trade Initiative (ETI) and corporate codes of conduct, whereas trade unions which have traditionally represented male formal sector workers have looked on voluntary initiatives as undermining collective bargaining and unions' monopoly on the representation of labour (Pearson and Seyfang, 2002).

Gender analysis of global change also throws light on a range of migratory processes, both legal and illegal which facilitate a range of reproductive activities and services to be carried out by (cheap) labour often originating in low-wage developing countries. In the case of childcare and domestic workers (nannies and maids) it is the irregularity of the immigration process as well as the undocumented nature of the work that renders women particularly vulnerable in these occupations (Ehrenrich and Hochschild, 2003). Other global processes are illegal as well as being unregulated – including sex work, human trafficking and opiates markets, part of the 'underbelly of globalisation' which offers poor women a (highly risky) survival strategy (Sassen, 2002). A gender analysis reveals that women are heavily represented in all these activities, as sex workers, drugs mules, and (often but not always) unwilling victims of trafficking between countries and regions in their attempt to escape poverty or to improve the opportunities of parents, children and other household members.

The politicisation of religion is another area where political changes at a global scale merit subjection to gender analysis. Recent attention to fundamentalist movements has focused on the security challenges they pose to Western so-called 'democratic' states whether they are secular or not. However, it has long been recognised that imposition of fundamentalist interpretations of every world religion places restrictions on the domestic and public roles of women, including restrictions on mobility, dress, education, employment, and marriage and sexuality decisions. Moreover, the security measures taken by

Western states in the face of real and perceived threats from fundamentalist groups also have a gendered effect; curfews may prevent the circulation of armed men – but they also prevent women in labour accessing medical assistance in childbirth; they prevent women and children escaping domestic violence and abuse. And the issue of women's rights is used as a political pawn by all sides in the argument: from the mobilisation of American opinion which justified the invasion of Afghanistan in order to free Afghani women from the gendered oppression of the Taliban to the similar rhetoric concerning the liberation of Iraqi women from the oppression of the Saddam regime. Fundamentalist movements on the other hand seek to justify the oppression of women in the name of timeless tradition or culture – challenging the construction of universal rights to equality which are seen to be an imposed Western construct. Women are often the instruments and objects of policies in the international and political realm – too often just as instruments rather than as subjects in their own rights. In Afghanistan, for example, in spite of all the rhetoric the Ministry for Women has a miniscule budget and a very marginal position in the current administration agreed with international backing (see WLUML, 2005). In Iraq the justification for the invasion by the US–British-led coalition used the rhetoric of human rights and democracy; however at this moment (of going to print) it would appear that the new Iraqi constitution will relegate women to an official inferiority governed by Sharia Law and institutional inequalities (UN, 2005; WHR, 2005).

These three aspects of gender and development – the gendering or international development policy, the interrogation of development policy through a gender lens, and the analysis of global change – are of course interconnected. However, it is important in the field of gender and development as in other aspects of development policy and practice to disentangle actors, perspectives, objectives and processes. This is essential not only in order to improve the implementation of development policy and to facilitate grounded and informed analysis and critique of development policy but also in order to facilitate the political mobilisation necessary to move forward towards the goals of gender equity.

RUTH PEARSON

References

Blackden, M. and E. Morris-Hughes (1993), *Paradigm Postponed: Gender and Economic Adjustment in Sub-Saharan Africa*, Technical Department, Africa Region, Washington, DC: World Bank.

Boserup, E. (1970), *Women's Role in Economic Development*, New York: St Martin's Press.

Buvinic, M. (1986), 'Projects for women in the Third World: explaining their misbehaviour', *World Development*, **14** (5), 653–64.

Ehrenrich, B. and A. Hochschild (2003), *Global Women: Nannies, Maids and Sex Workers in the New Economy*, London: Granta Books.

El Bushra, Judy (2004), 'Fused in combat: gender relations and armed conflict', in H. Afshar and D. Eade (eds), *Development, Women and War: Feminist Perspectives*, Oxford: Oxfam, pp. 152–71.

Elson, D. (ed.) (1995), *Male Bias in the Development Process*, 2nd edn, Manchester: Manchester University Press.

Green, C., S. Joekes and M. Leach (1998), 'Questionable links: approaches to gender in environmental research and policy', in Jackson and Pearson (eds), pp. 259–83.

Jackson, C. and R. Pearson (eds) (1998), *Feminist Visions of Development: Gender Analysis and Policy*, London: Routledge.

Pearson, R. (1998), 'Nimble fingers revisited: reflections on women and Third World industrialisation in the late twentieth century', in Jackson and Pearson (eds), pp. 177–88.

Pearson, R. (2005), 'The rise and rise of gender and development', in U. Kothari (ed.), *A Radical History of Development Studies*, London: Zed Books, pp. 157–79.

Pearson, R. and C. Jackson (1998), 'Interrogating development: feminism, gender and policy', in Jackson and Pearson (eds), pp. 1–16.

Pearson, R. and G. Seyfang (2002), ' "I'll tell you what I want": women workers and codes of conduct', in R. Jenkins, R. Pearson and G. Seyfang (eds), *Corporate Responsibility and Labour Rights: Codes of Conduct in the Global Economy*, London: Earthscan, pp. 43–60.

Pearson, R., A. Whitehead and O. Harris (1984), 'Introduction: the continuing subordination of women in the development process', in K. Young , C. Wolkowitz and R. McCullagh (eds), *Of Marriage and the Market*, London: Routledge & Kegan Paul (2nd edn, 1984).

Rahmeen, Manesh (2004), 'Population of India to overtake China's within 30 years', *The Guardian*, 12 July, www.guardian.co.uk/china/story/0,,1259205.00.html#article_continue.

Razavi, D. (1999), 'Export oriented employment, poverty and gender: contested accounts', *Development and Change*, **30** (3), 653–83.

Sassen, S. (2002), 'Counter-geographies of globalization: the feminization of survival', paper presented at the conference on Gender Budgets, Financial Markets, Financing for Development, Heinrich-Boell Foundation, Berlin, 19–20 February, www.transformaties.org/bibliotheek/sassgender.htm.

Sen, G. and K. Grown (1987), *Development, Crisis and Alternative Visions*, New York: Monthly Review Press.

Sweetman, C. (2005), 'Editorial: Special Issue on the Millennium Development Goals', *Gender and Development*, **13** (1).

UN (2005), *UN News Service*, www.un.org/news, 3 August 2005.

Watkins, F. (2004), *Evaluation of DfID Development Assistance: Gender Equality and Women's Empowerment: DfID's Experience of Gender Mainstreaming 1995–2004*, London: Department for International Development.

Wellesley Editorial Committee (ed.) (1997), *Women and National Development: The Complexities of Change*, Chicago: University of Chicago Press.

WHR (2005), *Challenging Fundamentalism: A Web Resource for Women's Human Rights*, www.whrnet.org/fundamentalisms/, 7 August 2005.

WLUML (2005), *Women Living Under Muslim Law*, www.wluml.org, 3 August 2005.

Young, K. (1988), 'Reflections on meeting women's needs', in K. Young (ed.), *Women and Economic Development: Local, Regional and National Planning Strategies*, Oxford: Berg, pp. 1–30.

Young, K., C. Wolkowitz and R. McCullagh (eds) (1981), *Of Marriage and the Market*, London: CSE Books.

Global Inequalities

Like income distribution, concern with global inequalities in income and living standards has fluctuated over the years. Adam Smith referred to the injustices of colonisation, and David Ricardo, John Stuart Mill and Karl Marx made national and international inequalities a central part of their analysis. But in the twentieth century, attention largely faded until the post-Second World War period, when Arthur Lewis, Gunnar Myrdal, Jan Tinbergen and some UN economists argued the need for economic development in poorer countries in part to help to narrow global gaps. Attention surged in the 1970s with calls for a new international economic order but these were then sidelined until the late 1990s, when there was a revival of interest as development in China and India accelerated but Sub-Saharan Africa and other least developed countries lagged far behind.

With the new millennium, development thinking has once again focused on worldwide trends in income inequalities between countries and between individuals. Though clearly interrelated, the first has important implications for global and national stability and inequalities of economic, political and military power. The second has implications for justice and human rights. In a world where human rights – economic, social and cultural as well as political and civil – are increasingly emphasised to be universal, and tourism and the media make the realities of inequality only too visible, it is difficult to defend the fact that an individual's life chances are so largely determined by birth place, skin colour and nationality.

Income inequalities, 1820–2000

World income inequality has worsened dramatically over the past two centuries. In 1820, the gap between average income in Western Europe, North America, Australasia and Japan was about twice that of the rest of the world, and approximately three times that of Africa. By 1998, the gap was 7:1. Between the United States, the world's leader today and Africa, the poorest region, the gap is now 20:1 (Maddison, 2001). The gap between the world's richest country and the world's poorest increased from about 3:1 in 1820 to about 70:1 in 2000.

Over this period, the ratio of the estimated incomes of the richest 5 per cent of people in the world to the poorest 20 per cent increased from 6:8 in 1820 to 10:3 in 1890 to 12:2 in 1910, to 14:8 in 1950 and to 16:4 in 1992. Even if the poorest 20 per cent all had equal incomes, this would imply a gap between the richest five and the poorest 5 per cent rising from at least 23 to at least 65 times.

Branko Milanovic (2005) has analysed global inequalities in terms of three concepts: concept one is inequality between states, which he terms 'unweighted international inequality'; concept two is inequality between countries, weighted by population, termed 'weighted international inequality'; and concept three is income distribution between individuals within the world, termed 'true world inequality' by Milanovic. For each of these, Milanovic estimates long-run trends in the Gini coefficient – a measure of overall income inequality, in which 0 represents perfect equality and one perfect inequality. All three concepts show very large increases in inequality over the last two centuries. The Gini coefficient for concept one inequality rises from 0.20 in 1820 to 0.29 in 1870, 0.37 in 1913, 0.46 in 1960, 0.47 in 1978 and 0.54 in 2000. Over the same period, the Gini coefficient for concept two inequality rises from 0.12 in 1820 to 0.26 in 1870, to 0.37 in 1913, to 0.55 in 1960, thereafter falling slightly to 0.54 in 1978 and then to 0.50 by 2000. Concept three – 'true world inequality' – rises from 0.50 in 1820 to 0.56 in 1870, 0.61 in 1913, to 0.64 in 1960, 0.66 in 1978, before dropping slightly to 0.62 in 1988 and rising slightly again to 0.64 in 2000 (ibid.).

Different assumptions, different indicators and different time periods lead to different results. Some researchers have used data on consumption rather than incomes, some have focused on the years from 1950 or 1970 to 2000, for which more data are available, especially on national levels of income distribution. In general, gaps are smaller and trends lower if one uses purchasing power parity measures rather than per capita GNP converted at current exchange rates. Some researchers using income data claim that global inequality remained more or less constant during the 1970s and then declined substantially during the 1980s and 1990s (Sala-i-Martin, 2002). Much of the difference in results depends on how people in China and India are being counted. Given the rapid growth of these two countries over the 1980s and 1990s, groupings which include people from China and India – such as the shares of the bottom 20 or 40 per cent of the world's population and Gini coefficients – show improvement. Measures which exclude them – such as the shares of the poorest 10 per cent of the world's population – show deterioration.

For similar reasons, most analysts agree that the proportion of the world's population in extreme absolute poverty – with incomes below some very basic level of poverty – has fallen sharply. One long-run estimate – using the $1 a day measure of poverty – shows a decrease from an estimated 84 per cent in 1820 to 66 per cent in 1910 to 55 per cent in 1950 and to 24 per cent in 1992 (Bourguignon and Morrison, 2002). But while the *proportion* of poor people has declined steadily, their *number* has continued to rise, as a result of rapidly rising population. The total numbers in poverty rose from about 1 billion in 1820 to 2.8 billion in 1992. The estimated numbers in *extreme* poverty over the same period rose from 890 million to some 1290 million. (For these calculations, an international definition of poverty is used, defined as having consumption of less than $2 a day in 1985 prices and extreme poverty as less than $1 a day, also in 1985 prices.)

All of these estimates depend greatly on the definition of inequality adopted, the methodology used for the calculations and the accuracy and the availability of data. The most important source of data over the long term is that of Angus Maddison, who has made estimates of income, population and productivity – for 22 countries in 1820 increasing to 152 countries for 1998. Most authors use the Maddison series until 1950 or 1970, but often other sources thereafter. Many make other estimates, depending on the focus of their interest and research. More difficult is the availability of evidence on income inequality within countries, which for all countries is notoriously unreliable and for many countries is simply not available. For concept 3 inequality, Milanovic uses data from household surveys.

Estimates have also been made of trends in global inequality, using earnings data collected by the International Labour Office. These suggest even greater increases in global inequality, in part because of rising region-specific inequality, notably within China and Russia (Galbraith and Kum, 2002).

Over the long run, the increase of inequality *between* countries has been a major factor accounting for the global increase of inequality between people. Growing inequality *within* countries is a secondary factor. Over the nineteenth century and the first half of the twentieth, relatively slow growth in the Asian region combined with accelerating growth in Western Europe and the United States to produce rising global inequality. Declining inequality within Europe also contributed somewhat to the drop in global inequality between individuals.

After 1950 and especially after 1980, new factors emerge. Very rapid economic growth in China after 1980 and increasing rates of growth in India in the 1990s have helped narrow relative global gaps among people. Given that China and India together comprise nearly half the population of developing countries, it is hardly surprising that their economic performance has a great influence on the global situation. At the same time, because of stagnant and often declining economic situation in Sub-Saharan Africa, which now comprises most of the poorest countries of the world and some 10 per cent of the world's population, the income and consumption gaps between the richest and the poorest 10 per cent of the world people have widened (Maddison, 1995).

Human development, life expectancy and other human indicators
Although many gaps in income inequality have risen over the last two centuries, many inequalities in human indicators have narrowed, especially since 1950. Life expectancy rates have risen in both developed and developing countries, infant and child mortality rates have fallen, and the proportion of children enrolled in schools has increased, along with literacy rates. Judged by such measures, there was more human progress in the twentieth century than in any previous period of history. Moreover, the time lag between

industrial countries achieving progress measured by these human indicators and developing countries achieving the same progress has often shortened considerably. For instance, it took the developed countries about 100 years, from the mid-nineteenth century to the 1940s, to reduce infant mortality from about 200 to about 70 per 1000 live births. The same transition took the developing countries only about 35 years (Patel et al., 1995). As another example, in 1900, only one country – Norway – had achieved an infant mortality rate below 100 per 1000 live births. By 2000, all but about 25 countries had infant mortality rates below 100 and the average infant mortality rate in developing countries was about 60. That said, such quantitative indicators often underemphasise the qualitative dimensions, which may still represent important and sometimes widening differences with the situation in developed countries.

Issues and controversies

One major controversy concerns 'convergence'. Under neoclassical economic theory, market forces are expected to encourage investment to flow to countries where wage rates are lower, thus in time encouraging increases in production, growth and the incomes of poorer countries. This, it is argued, should lead to convergence, to a narrowing of the gaps between developed and developing countries. The rapid progress of Korea, China and more recently of India could be cited as examples. In contrast, analysts working within a structuralist paradigm, like Myrdal (1956) and Seers (1983) have argued that richer countries build up advantages of income and power that create backwash effects, leading poorer countries to fall ever further behind. Structuralists also point to the way that richer countries dominate global institutions, often leading to a bias against poorer countries in the way they operate. Such analysts might cite the many developing countries where economic growth has been insufficient to show any real signs of narrowing even relative economic gaps as evidence.

A related issue is how much global inequality matters. Some argue that global inequality simply reflects the outcomes of differences in productivity and governance between countries and people, and as such should be of no international concern providing that the international processes creating them have been legal. A growing number of people and policy makers in both developed and developing countries reject this view. They argue that global inequality matters for several types of reason: global inequalities inhibit the fulfilment of the human rights of millions of poor people in the poorest countries; extremes of inequalities create problems which affect all countries, for instance when diseases flourish in poor countries and get exported to richer ones or when the environment suffers in countries too poor to take action; and extremes of inequality often create resentments and hostilities which lead to instability. Pressures to migrate are also stimulated, even though such migration is increasingly subject to strict controls.

Future prospects

If poorer countries maintain higher growth rates of per capita income over a number of years, as in most of Asia since 1980, the size of the relative gap in per capita income between these and richer countries will narrow. Moreover, if the growth rates in these countries are sustained at very much higher levels than in industrial countries – as recently in China and a small number of other developing countries – the absolute gaps may also start to narrow within a decade or two. In contrast, if the starting-point is one of large differences in per capita income and lower economic growth, as for most of the poorest countries in the world today, it will take many years, and often many decades or even centuries, before the absolute gaps begin to narrow. Worse still, if levels of per capita income are declining or growing at rates below those of the developed countries, as in many countries of Sub-Saharan Africa since 1980, relative gaps as well as absolute ones will widen.

One can conclude therefore that without major changes in approach, policy and action, large absolute gaps in income are likely to remain a feature of the global economy for decades and even centuries to come. And as long as such gaps continue, they will provide pressure for migration, be a source of international tension and serve as the economic base for large and continuing inequalities in economic, military and political power.

RICHARD JOLLY

References and further reading

Bourguignon, François and Christian Morrison (2002), 'Inequality among world citizens: 1820–1992', *American Economic Review*, **92** (4),727–44.
Galbraith, James K. and Hyunsub Kum (2002), 'Inequality and economic growth: data comparisons and econometric tests', Working Paper 21, University of Texas Inequality Project.
Maddison, Angus (1995), *Monitoring the World Economy 1820–1992*, Development Centre Studies, Paris: OECD.
Maddison, Angus (2001), *The World Economy: A Millennium Perspective*, Development Centre Studies, Paris: OECD.
Milanovic, Branko (2005), *Worlds Apart: Measuring International and Global Inequality*, Princeton, NJ: Princeton University Press.
Myrdal, Gunnar (1956), *An International Economy: Problems and Prospects*, New York: Harper.
Patel, Surendra J., Krishna Ahooja-Patel and Mahesh S. Patel (1995), *Development Distance Between Nations*, International Development Studies Series no. 1, New Delhi: Ashish.
Sala-i Martin, Xavier (2002), 'The disturbing "rise" of global income inequality', NBER Working Paper 8904, National Bureau of Economic Research, Cambridge, MA.
Seers, Dudley (1983), *The Political Economy of Nationalism*, Oxford: Oxford University Press.
World Bank (2005), *World Development Report 2006: Equity and Development*, Oxford: Oxford University Press.

Globalisation and Development

Over the last decade or so globalisation has become an umbrella term to describe and theorise the driving forces in the contemporary world. In some cases, it is replacing development as the central motif in theorising the relations between different parts of the world and explaining the dynamics (more often the lack of dynamics) of what can still be usefully described as the Third World.

The central feature of all approaches to globalisation current in the social sciences is that many important contemporary problems cannot be adequately studied at the level of nation states, that is, in terms of national societies or international relations. However, what to put in the place of this conventional state-centrist social science methodology is an extremely controversial question. Globalisation researchers have focused on three new phenomena that have become significant in the last few decades (though some scholars trace the origins of these back for centuries): (i) the electronic revolution, notably transformations in the technological base and global scope of the electronic mass media, and most of the material infrastructure of the world today; (ii) the subsequent creation of transnational social spaces in the economic, political and culture-ideology spheres; and (iii) qualitatively new forms of cosmopolitanism in transnational social relations.

These three new phenomena may be considered to be the defining characteristics of globalisation in a generic sense. In the absence of global catastrophe they are irreversible in the long run because the vast majority of the people in the world appear to accept, at varying levels of discourse, that generic globalisation could serve their own best interests, even if it is not necessarily doing so at present. The forces of globalisation affect the lives of most people all over the world, big landlords as well as subsistence farmers in villages, corporate executives as well as labourers in sweatshops in major cities, well-paid professionals as well as informal workers in tourist sites, comfortable manual workers as well as desperate migrants in transit in the hope of better lives. These oppositions have thrown up a substantial literature on resistances to globalisation, much of it emanating from groups under pressure in the Third World and those who support them, notably non-governmental organisations.

There is no single agreed definition of globalisation and there are many ways to summarise the vast literature on the subject. The method chosen here categorises approaches to globalisation on the basis of who or what is said to be driving it. This gives four research clusters: world-systems; global culture; global polity and society; and global capitalism. It is not incidental that these bear certain resemblances to the most influential theories of development.

The world-systems approach is based on the distinction between core, semi-peripheral and peripheral countries in terms of their changing roles in the international division of labour dominated by the capitalist world-system. World-systems as a model in social science research, inspired by the work of Immanuel Wallerstein (1974, 1980, 1988), has been developed in a large and continually expanding body of literature since the 1970s. Although the work of world-systems theorists cannot be said to be fully a part of the globalisation literature as such, its institutionalisation undoubtedly prepared the ground for globalisation in the social sciences.

The second approach derives specifically from research on the globalisation of culture. Global culture theorists argues that globalisation is driven by a homogenising mass-media-based culture, and that this threatens national and/or local cultures and identities. Although these researchers cannot be identified as a school in the same way as world-systems researchers can be, there are some common themes running through their works. First, they are all interested in the question of how specific identities can survive in the face of an emerging global culture. Second, they tend to prioritise the cultural over the political and/or the economic. A distinctive feature of this approach is that it problematises the existence of global culture, as a reality, a possibility or a fantasy. The inspiration for this debate is the emergence of what Marshall McLuhan (1987) famously called 'the global village', the very rapid growth that has taken place over the last few decades in the scope and scale of the mass media. The basic idea is that the spread of the mass media, especially television and now the internet, means that everyone in the world can be exposed to the same images, almost instantaneously. This, the argument goes, turns the whole world into a sort of global village. The debate has been enlivened by studies of the cultures of globalisation in the plural, and attempts to connect globalisation, modernity and post-colonialism.

A subset of the global culture approach, characterised as globo-localism, derives from those whose main concern is to try to make sense of the multifaceted and enormously complex web of local–global relations, with an emphasis on the territorial dimension. The main research question for cultural globalisation is the autonomy of local cultures in the face of an advancing global culture. Competing claims of local cultures against the forces of globalisation have forced themselves onto the sociological, cultural and political agendas all over the world. For some this is simply a rerun of older cultural and media imperialism debates, for others it introduces new dimensions, for example issues of hybridity and cultural heterogeneity.

The conception of global polity and society provides the inspiration for the third approach to globalisation. The concept of global polity and/or society, it is argued, has become a believable idea only in the modern age and, in particular, advances in science, technology, industry and universal values are increasingly creating a world that is different from any past age. The globalisation literature is full of discussions of the decreasing power and significance of the nation state and the increasing significance (if not actually power) of supranational, transnational and global institutions and systems of belief, for example what the *New York Times* called the 'second superpower', namely the rise of global public opinion facilitated by globalising social movements and international non-governmental organisations. This had led to the conclusion that, while globalisation itself can have many causes, the most desirable driver for the future will be the organisation of global governance through global civil society and/or polity. Within this general approach we may locate the significant literature connecting globalisation with modernity, around the theme that modernity has become a progressively global phenomenon. Ideas of space–time distanciation and time–space compression were generated to illustrate how processes of globalisation compress, stretch and deepen space–time for people all over the world thus creating some of the conditions for a global polity and society. There is a powerful psychological need for progressive writers to believe in the possibilities of global social values and institutions to protect them (which I share). The reason for this is simple: now that humankind is vulnerable to destruction through nuclear and toxic catastrophes, a democratic and just human society on the global level, however utopian, seems to be the best long-term guarantee of the continued survival of humanity. Those who are prosecuting the war on terrorism have used such arguments, often cynically, to great effect.

A fourth approach locates the main driver of globalisation in the structures of an ever-more globalising capitalism. McMichael (2000), for example, focuses on the issue of capitalism and Third World development and provides both theoretical and empirical support for the thesis that globalisation is a qualitatively new phenomenon and not simply a quantitative expansion of older trends. He contrasts the Development Project of the late 1940s up to the early 1970s, modelled on the parallel development of national economies under an international development regime, with the Globalisation Project from the 1980s onwards, modelled on development through integration into a globalised world market and directed by a public–private coalition of global managers. Sklair (2002) has proposed an explicit model of capitalist globalisation, global systems theory, based on the concept of transnational practices, practices that originate with non-state actors and cross state borders. These are analytically distinguished in three spheres: economy, polity and culture-ideology. The research agenda of this theory is concerned with how transnational corporations, the transnational capitalist class and the culture-ideology of consumerism operate to transform the world in terms of the global capitalist project. The contrast between generic and capitalist globalisation in global system theory opens up the space for theoretical discussion of alternative forms of globalisation.

Each of the four approaches to globalisation has its own distinctive strengths and weaknesses. The world-system model tends to be economistic (minimising the importance of political and cultural factors), but as globalisation is often interpreted in terms of economic actors and economic institutions, this does seem to be a realistic approach. The globalisation of culture model, on the other hand, tends to be culturalist (minimising economic factors), but as much of the criticism of globalisation comes from those who focus on the negative effects of homogenising mass media and marketing on local and indigenous cultures, the culturalist approach has many adherents. The global polity and society approach tends to be both optimistic and all-inclusive, an excellent combination for the production of world-views, but less satisfactory for social science research programmes. Finally, the global capitalism model, by prioritising the capitalist global system and paying less attention to other global forces, runs the risk of appearing one-sided. However, three questions remain: (1) How important is that one side (global capitalism)? (2) Can capitalist globalisation develop the Third World? And (3) what, exactly, is wrong with capitalist globalisation? Attitudes to capitalist globalisation range from happy fatalism (things are getting better all the time) through optimistic fatalism (things will surely get better for those who are hurting today) to depressed fatalism (things will get worse for those who are hurting and may never get much better but there is nothing anyone can do about it). However, Marx-inspired crisis theory suggests that the problems with capitalism are a consequence of contradictions within the capitalist mode of production itself. Global system theory complements this argument by globalising it. As capitalism globalises its crises intensify, notably class polarisation and ecological unsustainability. The generally acknowledged failure of the development project gives the search for alternatives to capitalist globalisation added urgency.

This account of globalisation and development is largely based on the European and North American literature and it does not preclude the possibility of other and quite different conceptions of globalisation being developed elsewhere, for example through the prism of debates on Orientalism and post-colonial discourses. It is very likely that an introduction to globalisation studies to be written ten years from now will reflect non-Western perspectives much more strongly. Perhaps the application of globalisation to development studies will be considered to be yet another discourse of Orientalism.

LESLIE SKLAIR

References and further reading

Jameson, F. and M. Miyoshi (1998), *Cultures of Globalisation*, Durham, NC: Duke University Press.

Lechner, F. and J. Boli (2003), *The Globalisation Reader*, 2nd edn, Oxford: Blackwell.

McLuhan, M. (1987), *Understanding Media: The Extensions of Man*, London: ARK.

McMichael, P. (2000), *Development and Social Change: A Global Perspective*, 2nd edn, London: Sage.

Mittelman, J. (2000), *The Globalisation Syndrome: Transformation and Resistance*, Princeton, NJ: Princeton University Press.

Sklair, L. (2002), *Globalization: Capitalism and its Alternatives*, Oxford: Oxford University Press.

Wallerstein, I. (1974, 1980, 1988), *The Modern World System*, 3 vols, New York: Academic Press.

Globalisation and Development Policy

Globalisation is an often discussed and seldom understood phenomenon. Broadly defined, globalisation is an increase in human activities that cross national boundaries. These may be economic, social, political cultural, technological or even biological, as is the case with disease.

Globalisation is not new. Indeed, the ever-increasing integration of people and societies around the world has been both a cause and effect of human evolution. Yet while globalisation has generally proceeded apace throughout human history, the process has occurred more in fits and starts than through any simple linear progression. Technological innovations, such as the invention of the marine chronometer or fibre optics, have propelled surges in globalisation, while changes in policy, institutions or cultural preferences have restrained and sometimes even reversed integration. In the fifteenth century, for instance, the Chinese emperor Hung-hsi banned maritime expeditions, effectively slowing Asian globalisation. Similarly, the proliferation of nation states and imposition of border controls throughout the early twentieth century generated new obstacles to the movement of persons, goods, ideas and capital across spans of ocean and earth. In recent decades, global integration has accelerated once more.

The factors which drive the current wave of globalisation are not dissimilar to those accounting for previous waves. Rapid technological progress, particularly in transportation, communication and information technology, have dramatically lowered the cost of moving people, goods, capital and ideas across the globe. In addition, there has been a concerted effort among many states to reverse the isolationist impact of policies enacted during the first half of the twentieth century, leading to a relaxation of trade barriers and rules governing capital flows and foreign investment, not least in Eastern Europe and in China. Whether or not the current wave of accelerated globalisation will continue in the coming decades depends on continued progress in these dimensions. Growing conflicts and terrorism fears, leading to increased barriers and costs to trade and movement, rising protectionism and mercantilism, and stricter controls on migration could all contribute to a slowing of globalisation. Policy makers have a key role to play in influencing these factors and ensuring that globalisation is a force for development.

The relationship between globalisation and development has multiple dimensions; both are broad concepts with wide-ranging interpretations. Just as globalisation goes well beyond mere economic facets, so too has the term 'development' increasingly been defined along multiple dimensions. Along with fundamental changes in our thinking about how increases in income are best achieved, our understanding of the very notion of development has itself evolved. Indeed, over the past 50 years, practitioners and institutions within the development community have generally moved away from a myopic focus on rudimentary economic variables to a more holistic approach that incorporates aspects of health, education and human development. We now see the objectives of development as ensuring that all people have the ability to shape their own lives – 'development as freedom' in the words of the Nobel Laureate Amartya Sen (1999). Overcoming poverty is a means to the end of empowering poor people with greater opportunity and security.

While prior asymmetrical trade patterns and differences in political power remain persistent, global integration can under certain circumstances be a powerful force for the reduction of poverty and the empowerment of poor people. Poor people are less likely to remain poor in a country that is exchanging its goods, services and ideas with the rest of the world. Yet while integration and participation in the global economy has generally been a powerful force for poverty reduction, the reach and impact of globalisation remains uneven. In addition, the accelerated pace of globalisation has been associated with a rapid rise in global risks which have outpaced the capacity of global and national institutions to respond. The increasing global impact of national policies, ranging from nuclear armaments to contributions to climate change and biodiversity, points to the need for more effective global governance and the need for global externalities to be taken into account when drafting national policies. If the globalisation train is to pull all citizens behind it, policies are required to ensure that the poor benefit and that the engine of growth does not lead to global and national environmental destruction.

The first area for action in support of a beneficial globalisation is to ensure that global trade negotiations yield a more balanced outcome; rich countries must not seek to impede the ability of poor countries to produce and trade in a wide range of goods and services. Unfortunately, this is presently not the case. Goods produced by poor people face on average double the tariff barriers of those produced in the most advanced countries. The practice of generously subsidising agricultural production, widespread in many high-income countries, has also had a devastating impact on many poor producers, denying them not just export markets but also hindering their capacity to sell their produce in their own country. With around $300 billion per year devoted to agricultural protection alone, the rich countries' policies have created a fundamentally imbalanced playing field. Current policies compound the downward trend in commodity prices, increase instability, and undermine the potential for diversification into value-adding manufactured products. Reforming the world trade system and ensuring more equitable access for the products of poor countries is an essential step to allowing more of the world's people to enjoy the benefits of globalisation.

The second area for action to support development is the increased provision of aid, assistance and debt relief to countries who demonstrate their commitment to the effective and equitable use of the additional resources. As Figure 6 shows, aid volumes have declined in real terms over the past four decades, falling from around 0.48 per cent of rich countries' GNP to 0.23 in 2001, despite the fact that donor countries are richer now than ever and that aid has never been more effectively used. With the ending of the Cold War in the 1990s, geopolitical objectives became less important in determining aid allocations, and aid increasingly was allocated to countries able to use it most effectively. Not surprisingly, the impact of aid on growth and poverty reduction has more than doubled over recent years, in terms of its impact on growth and poverty reduction.

Compared to private investment, and even to remittances, the value of aid flows is small. Domestic investment in developing countries in recent years has reached around $1.5 trillion, compared to aid levels hovering around $55 billion per year, and foreign investment of around $200 billion (World Bank, 2004b). In all countries, what matters most is the ideas and policies which drive sustainable growth and poverty reduction. In the poorest countries, the resource transfers are, however, particularly important, and much higher levels of aid are urgently required for investments in health, education, infrastructure and in combating HIV/AIDS and other diseases. These investments cannot be

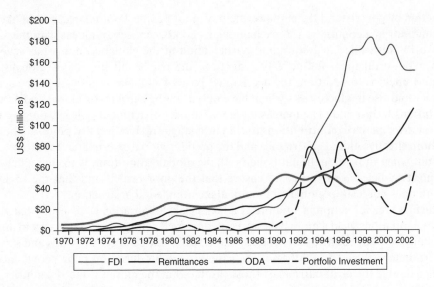

Sources: World Bank (2004a, b).

Figure 6   Nominal flows of aid, capital and remittances to developing countries

financed by domestic savings alone, particularly for countries which are currently crushed under burdens of debt and escaping the ravages of past corruption and mismanagement. The provision of increased foreign assistance, and the implementation of more rigorous schemes of monitoring and evaluating the effective use of that aid, are thus critical to ensuring that the gains provided by globalisation are not erased by the spectre of bad governance and ineffective use of aid.

The third area for action is migration. Historically, migration has been a vital means for escaping poverty, and until the eighteenth century was associated with mass seasonal and permanent movements across Europe, Asia and Africa. This historical pattern has been greatly reduced by the development of nation states and, more recently, around the beginning of the twentieth century of passports and a growing range of mechanisms to identify and control individual movement. Migration remains for many poor people the most effective means to escape poverty. Recorded remittances of well over $100 billion are double the amount of annual foreign assistance (World Bank, 2004a). Whereas barely 20 per cent (around $10 billion) of aid is transferred to developing countries in the form of capital flows, the totality of remittance flows represent real transfers. These flows could be increased if the transactions costs were reduced from their current average of around 15 per cent of the flows to around 1 per cent, which is closer to the cost of transfers between rich countries. While remittances tend to flow directly to individuals and communities, aid goes to governments and foreign investment flows to a small number of firms. The loss of skills associated with migration is a severe problem, not least for poor regions such as Africa or the Caribbean, where it is estimated that up to two-thirds of educated doctors and teachers have left. Positive flows include the ideas and investment which come from this diaspora, such as is evident in the pivotal role of Indian emigrants in the Bangalore information technology boom.

The fourth area of action in support of globalisation is in those areas commonly referred to as international public goods. Foremost among these is the need for global peace and stability. Wars, big and small, destroy the foundation of growth and development. While many have local origins, they feed off global flows, from the sale of commodities such as diamonds and oil, to the trade in arms and ammunition. Managing the wide range of environmental externalities associated with domestic policies is also vital. Chief among our environmental concerns are the looming water and energy crises, both of which will have increasing international dimensions, and climate change. How these are managed are among the biggest development challenges facing our planet and vividly illustrate that the development agenda for nation states is a global concern. The management of science and technology in favour of development is another vital area for global action.

The combating of diseases, not least HIV/AIDS and malaria, as well as the development of higher-yield and stress-resistant crops can only be addressed at the global level, and requires a pooling of resources and the management of intellectual property and technology, including the internet, to overcome the widening scientific and digital divide. Finally, among the global and national challenges is the crucial question of cultural and political independence and stability. All countries and societies feel strongly about the need to protect their identity which at times they perceive to be threatened by foreign trends and influences.

Globalisation need not spell homogeneity, particularly if governments and societies are aware of this threat and take the necessary actions, through their policies and educational and other practices. Managing globalisation so its benefits are widely shared and the negative impacts identified and mitigated is a global, national, local and community responsibility.

IAN GOLDIN*

References and further reading

Goldin, I. and K. Reinert (2006), *Globalization for Development: Trade, Finance, Aid, Migration, and Policy*, Basingstoke: Palgrave Macmillan and World Bank.
Sen, A.K. (1999), *Development as Freedom*, New York: Knopf.
Stiglitz, J. (2002), *Globalization and its Discontents*, New York: Norton.
World Bank (2004a), *Global Development Finance*, Washington, DC: World Bank.
World Bank (2004b), *World Development Indicators*, Washington, DC: World Bank.

Green Revolution and Biotechnology

The term 'green revolution', originally coined in 1968 by William Gaud, then the head of the US Agency for International Development (USAID), describes the sharp rise in grain yields brought on by the dissemination of new water-seed-fertiliser technologies introduced in the 1950s and 1960s. Although productivity improvements were recorded in rich and poor countries alike, the economic and political impact of these changes was greatest in the developing world.

According to the UN Food and Agriculture Organization, over the period from 1961 to 2001, wheat yields increased by 3.5 times and rice yields doubled in the developing world. As a result of higher productivity and expanded area under cultivation, total cereal production tripled in Asia and Latin America over the same period. In Africa, a region that is widely assumed to have missed out on the benefits of the green revolution, total cereal production expanded 2.5-fold. Higher production levels worked to stabilise and in some cases lower domestic food prices and to increase farm incomes. Greater local availability of food grains also helped countries to conserve scarce foreign exchange, which is vital to achieving macroeconomic balance. Both China and India moved from deficit to surplus in the balance of trade in cereals despite a doubling of the population, and the share of food grains in total imports declined dramatically in a wide range of developing countries.

In the popular imagination, the green revolution is most closely identified with the development of modern varieties (MVs) of wheat and rice. These varieties were 'semi-dwarf' in stature and therefore could absorb more nutrients from the soil without lodging or falling over. Pioneering work in the development of modern wheat varieties was carried out in the 1950s by Norman Borlaug of the Office of Special Studies, a cooperative venture between the Mexican ministry of agriculture and the Rockefeller Foundation. This agency served as a model for international agricultural research centres such as the International Maize and Wheat Improvement Centre (CIMMYT) established in Mexico in 1967 and the International Rice Research Institute (IRRI) in the Philippines in 1960. Borlaug, who was awarded the Nobel Peace prize in the 1970s for his work with high-yielding wheat, is the scientist most commonly associated with the advent of MVs and hence the green revolution itself.

But the popular conception of the green revolution as the product of new developments in plant breeding is unduly limiting. To begin with, the success of rice and wheat MVs was founded on prior and equally significant innovations in ammonia production, which succeeded in dramatically reducing the cost of synthesising fixed nitrogen. Semi-dwarf MVs enabled farmers to make better use of cheaper and more readily accessible sources of synthetic nitrogen, and as such the green revolution was as much a product of chemical engineering as plant breeding.

More fundamental still to increased production was the supply of water in a timely manner and in appropriate amounts. Water control, in the influential formulation of Shigeru Ishikawa, was the 'leading input in Asian agriculture' (Ishikawa, 1974, p. 90). Improved irrigation and drainage worked to stabilise yields, increase cropping intensities (crops per year) and, finally, to create the agro-ecological conditions required for the adoption of improved fertiliser-sensitive varieties. From this perspective, post-1960 productivity gains were more a replication of previous experience, for example in Meiji Japan, than a revolutionary technological change. Intensification of production would not have been possible in the newly independent countries of Asia without prior, large-scale investment in the expansion and improvement of irrigation systems. The inferior performance of Sub-Saharan Africa relative to Asia must be understood in these terms: in 2000, irrigated cropland as a share of arable was less than 5 per cent in the former as compared to 40 per cent in the latter.

Much of the required investment in irrigation systems, and ancillary investments in transportation, storage and fertiliser production, was undertaken by the public sector.

The state was directly involved in other ways, some of which were more or less explicitly modelled on farm programmes in the United States. Price supports were often used to stabilise output prices and thus ensure farmers a minimum return on their investments in the new technologies. National agricultural research centres were established, and these institutions were largely responsible for the development of second-generation seed varieties that adapted earlier MVs to local conditions. Elaborate agricultural extension systems were put in place to promote the use of the new seeds and fertilisers. Rural banks, cooperatives and other lending institutions were set up to provide credit for the purchase of new inputs. Large bureaucracies sprang up to administer and coordinate these various systems, and to liaise with donor agencies anxious to support them. There was waste and inefficiency, and at times unnecessary coercion of farmers and farm labourers. But, on the whole, the green revolution was the product of an era of public sector optimism and an example of effective state intervention in the development process.

State action was not, of course, equally effective in all locations. Constraints to the adoption of green revolution technologies were as often social and political as they were ecological. James Boyce, for example, showed how agrarian structure in West Bengal and Bangladesh thwarted the development of water control systems and thus slowed the pace of technical change (Boyce, 1987). Boyce showed that landlords whose access to economic surplus depended on political power, debt bondage or other forms of extra-economic coercion were unlikely to cooperate among themselves to invest in and maintain irrigation and drainage systems, or to recognise the advantages of productivity-enhancing technologies. The Bengal case serves as an important reminder that the new water-seed-fertiliser technologies did not arrive as a *deus ex machina*, complete with appropriate social relations of production, and that deeply entrenched pre-capitalist social relations could prove highly resistant to the economic incentives associated with technical innovation. Intensification in Latin America has been most successful on newly colonised land made available through public investment in irrigation. The forcible removal of traditional rural elites in Japan, Korea, China and Vietnam by occupying armies or communist regimes created, by design or fortuitously, the social basis of the green revolution in these countries.

The green revolution did not meet with universal approbation. Critics initially attacked the new technologies on equity grounds, but in recent years the environmental challenge has gathered pace. The view that the green revolution would penalise the poor was widely held during the early years of state-led intensification programmes, when some observers argued that the water-seed-fertiliser technologies favoured farmers better endowed with land and capital, and that higher productivity on larger, more-intensive farms would lower output prices and perhaps raise input prices. These effects would penalise small farmers who had not made, or could not make, the transition to the new seeds. Moreover, the introduction of mechanisation, which, it was assumed, would accompany the new seeds, would decrease demand for hired labour, thus imposing an additional burden on the poor (Griffin, 1974). By the second decade of implementation these fears had diminished as it became increasingly apparent that the adoption of water-seed-fertiliser technology was unrelated to farm size. By 1990, for example, 74 per cent of Asia's rice area was planted to MVs, including nearly all of the irrigated area and a large proportion of rain-fed rice land (Pingali et al., 1997, p. 4). Use of MVs was also associated with increased demand for hired labour and positive indirect employment effects. Access to irrigation, and therefore public investment, has proved to be the most important determinant in the adoption of new rice and wheat varieties (Hazell and Ramasamy, 1991; David and Otsuka, 1994).

The environmental critique of the green revolution has proved more formidable. Ecologists claim that agricultural intensification contributes to soil erosion, salinisation, water logging, desertification, loss of biodiversity and water pollution from overuse of nitrogen fertilisers. Reliance on genetically homogeneous monocultures selected for yield has increased the susceptibility of plants to diseases and insect pests. The use of chemical pesticides to protect crops has compounded the problem by destroying the 'natural enemies' or pest predators that would otherwise have kept insect pest populations in check. Excessive use of both fertilisers and pesticides was due in large part to explicit and implicit input subsidies designed to maximise yields without due consideration of the economic, environmental and human health costs.

Moreover, some observers attribute slowing yield growth in wheat and rice, and in some cases actual yield declines, to the long-term effects of intensification (Conway, 1997; Pingali et al., 1997). Although solutions to some problems, such as soil nutrient deficiency and toxicity, are readily to hand, others, like soil salinity and water logging, are not so easily resolved. Declining yield growth is particularly worrying in view of increased competition for land and water resources from industry and household use in a range of developing countries. Cities and industrial zones are cutting into well-irrigated lowlands in China, Thailand and Indonesia. Further expansion of cultivated areas will come at the expense of primary forests or fragile upland ecosystems, most of which are unsuited to intensive agriculture owing to poor soils or limited scope for irrigation.

It is in this context that enthusiasm for the potential of biotechnology must be understood. Molecular marker technology can accelerate and reduce the costs of conventional plant breeding. More controversially, breeders can now transfer genes within or across species to create novel plants with economically desirable characteristics. Transgenic crops have been created to resist pests or withstand herbicide applications, to thrive under dry or saline conditions or to achieve higher yields. Proponents of biotechnology argue that transgenic crops represent the next phase of the green revolution, delivering both higher productivity and lower environmental costs: they see herbicide-resistant crops as a means to eliminate tillage and therefore reduce fertiliser use and runoff; pest-resistant cotton and rice as an alternative to chemical insecticides; and drought-resistant and salt-tolerant crops as the key to raising productivity on millions of hectares of marginal crop land.

Critics of biotechnology question the desirability of moving transgenic varieties from the lab to large-scale production before the risks to the environment and human health are well understood. They argue that while there may be a role for transgenic varieties in the distant future, the risk of environmental disruption in the present is too great to justify immediate adoption of these technologies. Moreover, the potential of existing, alternative technologies more suited to the needs of farmers in the developing world has not yet been exhausted. In view of the widening gaps between yields on experiment stations and farmers' fields, many suspect that raising the theoretical yield ceiling is less urgent than providing farmers with the knowledge and tools that they need to adjust agronomic practices to the specific agro-ecological conditions found in their own fields (Pretty, 1995; Conway, 1997).

A crucial difference between the development of green revolution MVs and recent transgenic innovations is that the latter are for the most part privately controlled (Conway, 1997). The dominance of large multinational chemical and seed companies in the research, development and marketing of agricultural biotechnologies has been accompanied by the privatisation of agricultural science. Intellectual property rights cover an expanding array of biological materials and enabling technologies, and even public institutions such as agricultural research centres and universities increasingly license their discoveries to private companies. Gone are the days when a public sector scientist like Norman Borlaug could, on short notice, ship samples of 600 unreleased Mexican wheat varieties to his Indian counterparts as occurred in 1963 (Perkins, 1997, p. 236).

The US government, which has forced protection of intellectual property to the top of the international trade agenda, sees well-defined property rights as a necessary incentive to research and innovation. Experience to date suggests that private control over agricultural technology has directed efforts towards potentially profitable products and applications, but not necessarily those that are the most socially useful. Herbicide-tolerant soybeans may help rich country farmers cut costs and provide a fillip to chemical sales, but they are generally not suited to conditions in developing countries. There is less money to be made developing varieties suited to Africa's highly varied agro-ecosystems. The problem is compounded by the decline in public funding for agricultural research. Research centres grouped under the Consultative Group on International Agricultural Research (CGIAR), which expanded rapidly in the 1970s, faced shrinking budgets by the 1990s (Pardey and Beintema, 2001, p. 4). Cash-strapped national agricultural research centres, particularly in Africa, are forced to operate at increasing distance from the technological frontier.

In retrospect, the green revolution was brought about by a confluence of contributing factors, including a backlog of biological and chemical innovations, massive public investment in infrastructure and institutional development, enthusiastic donor support for public sector investment, research and extension programmes, changes in agrarian social structure and an open access intellectual property rights regime. It is unlikely that these conditions can be replicated in the current international environment. Those who hope for a new green revolution for Sub-Saharan Africa, or a second-generation green revolution building on advances in biotechnology, are likely to be disappointed. This does not mean an end to agricultural productivity growth, but rather that further progress is likely to be evolutionary and local rather than revolutionary and global.

JONATHAN R. PINCUS

References

Boyce, James K. (1987), *Agrarian Impasse in Bengal: Institutional Constraints to Technological Change*, Oxford: Oxford University Press.

Conway, Gordon (1997), *The Doubly Green Revolution: Food for All in the Twenty-First Century*, London: Penguin.

David, Cristina C. and Keijiro Otsuka (eds) (1994), *Modern Rice Technology and Income Distribution in Asia*, London: Lynne Rienner and the International Rice Research Institute.

Griffin, Keith (1974), *The Political Economy of Agrarian Change*, London: Macmillan.

Hazell, Peter B.R. and C. Ramasamy (1991), *The Green Revolution Reconsidered: The Impact of High-Yielding Rice Varieties in South India*, Baltimore, MD and London: Johns Hopkins University Press.

Ishikawa, Shigeru (1974), *Economic Development in Asian Perspective*, Tokyo: Kinokuniya Bookstore.
Pardey, Philip G. and Nienke M. Beintema (2001), 'Slow magic: agricultural R&D a century after Mendel', International Food Policy Research Institute, Washington, DC, 26 October.
Perkins, John H. (1997), *Geopolitics and the Green Revolution: Wheat, Genes and the Cold War*, Oxford: Oxford University Press.
Pingali, P.L., M. Hossain and R.V. Gerpacio (1997), *Asian Rice Bowl: The Returning Crisis?*, Wallingford: CAB International and the International Rice Research Institute.
Pretty, Jules (1995), *Regenerating Agriculture*, London: Earthscan.

Haq, Mahbub ul (1934–1998)

Mahbub ul Haq was one of the most influential economists of his time. He contributed to putting human priorities – equity, poverty, education, health, peace, employment, equal rights of women, political freedom and social justice – on the agenda of development strategies. He was a visionary who led his life as a mission, challenging entrenched power structures. He deployed the tools of economics – concepts, data and analysis – with immense creativity, coupled with personal powers of persuasion to influence policies in his own country and elsewhere. He is best known for having created the concept of human development and the Human Development Index.

Evolution of life and work

Mahbub ul Haq was born on 22 February 1934 in Jammu. His father was a school teacher who valued learning and independent thinking. Mahbub received his first BA in economics from Government College, Lahore, Pakistan, after which he took a second BA at Cambridge University. There, fellow students first thought Mahbub shy. But they soon realised that they were utterly mistaken. In his soft voice, he began to take on Harry Johnson on trade cycle theories, Nicholas Kaldor on the relevance of expenditure tax to finance a welfare state for Pakistan, and Joan Robinson on the Maoist model. After Cambridge, Mahbub went on to Yale University to study for his doctorate (Sen, 1998).

Mahbub returned to Pakistan in 1957 at the age of 23, to join the Planning Commission of Pakistan. This experience deepened his appreciation that the real obstacles to progress lay in widespread poverty, illiteracy and ill health, concentration of wealth, the counter-productive regulations to which the political elites were wedded. Yet in those days, he was an unreconstructed growth man (Streeten, 2004). He wrote: 'The underdeveloped countries must consciously accept a philosophy of growth and shelve for the distant future all ideas of equitable distribution and welfare state. It should be recognised that these are luxuries which only developed countries can afford' (Haq, 1966, p. 30). This was written under Ayub Khan's military regime which was in power between 1958 and 1969. Later he wrote:

> I expressed my views with a certain exuberance which is the privilege of youth, arguing that GNP growth must supersede all other goals. Though I have written much else since then, my detractors have seldom allowed me to forget my original writings, perhaps believing that evolution of ideas is an unforgivable sin. (Haq, 1976 p. 8)

His experience with practical planning led to his first book, *The Strategy of Economic Planning*, published in 1963. This was a major contribution to development studies, which contained one of the first systematic accounts of the widening economic gulf between East and West Pakistan – an issue that would receive much attention soon afterwards (Haq, 1963).

In 1970, still in his 30s, Mahbub joined the World Bank, where he soon became a close friend and influential adviser to Robert McNamara. He crafted McNamara's famous 'Nairobi speech' – the 1973 Presidential address that brought poverty to the forefront of the agenda of the World Bank and consequently of international development more generally. Mahbub's attention focused on poverty and inequality both across and within countries as a central moral issue of the time. His second book, *The Poverty Curtain: Choices for the Third World*, published in 1976, provides a graphic, disturbing, picture of two worlds – 'one embarrassingly rich and the other desperately poor' – separated by what he termed 'the poverty curtain' (Haq, 1976). The book argued that growth strategies adopted in most developing countries enriched the elite and failed to benefit the masses. He then set out to define new development strategies for a direct attack on mass poverty, with fundamental reforms in national and international economic systems. The following book, *First Things First*, which he co-authored with Paul Streeten and others, put forward meeting the basic needs of all people as a central objective of development (Streeten et al., 1981). The basic needs approach became an influential concept in shaping policy agendas of national governments and donor programmes of the 1970s.

In 1982 Mahbub returned to public life in Pakistan, first as Deputy Chairman of the Planning Commission, then becoming Minister for Planning and Development in 1983 and Minister for Finance, Planning and Economic Affairs in 1985. During this time, he was quite frustrated; the feudal landed gentry, the elite class, the bureaucracy and military rule were major barriers to his reform agenda.

But these frustrations did not stop Mahbub from extending the frontiers of his creative thinking and influence as he turned to international debates. The 1980s was a time when developing countries faced economic crises of growing debt and sharp declines in world commodity prices. Leading economists, the World Bank and the IMF argued for macroeconomic balances and structural adjustments as key priorities for developing countries. Mahbub played a pioneering role in the North–South Roundtable that sought an alternative to these policies. The Roundtable brought together leading progressive economists of the North and South starting with Barbara Ward, his mentor since Cambridge days, as well as Richard Jolly, Paul Streeten and Lal Jayawardena, who met annually for open debate on global policy challenges and policy choices. It was through this process that many of the ideas that came to be defined as of human development were articulated. Central to these debates was the idea that development was about people, and that improvements in human living conditions and life chances can be improved quite dramatically and rapidly even in poor countries through properly targeted social intervention, and did not depend entirely on growth of GDP.

In 1989, Mahbub persuaded William Draper III, the UNDP administrator, to sponsor the *Human Development Report*, as an alternative to the World Bank's *World Development Report* which monitored development trends and identified key global challenges. Mahbub asked Draper for one condition – freedom. Mahbub brought together a group of powerful economists and friends, notably: Amartya Sen, Frances Stewart, Gus Ranis, Keith Griffin, Sudhir Anand and Meghnad Desai. The report was a daring venture. Not only did it argue that the ultimate end of development was to improve human well-being and economic growth was only a means, but it also made the argument on the basis of frank and objective analysis of development failures and successes (Haq, 1995a). This was unprecedented in UN reports, which scrupulously avoid criticising governments. The report dared to rank countries by the Human Development Index (HDI) that estimated the progress of a country in expanding the capabilities that individuals have to lead lives to their full potential (Anand and Sen, 1994; Haq, 1995b; Jahan, 2002). Governments were alarmed, yet the vast majority of delegates applauded the initiative, welcoming an analytical report that was objective rather than ideologically or politically mandated, and that provided valuable information, analysis and policy options. The report survived the controversy and a UN General Assembly resolution in 1994 endorsed its editorial independence. By the time Mahbub returned to Pakistan in 1996 to establish the new Human Development Centre in Islamabad, he had the satisfaction of seeing that the Human Development Reports were already well-established and well-respected across the world.

Mahbub ul Haq passed away on 16 July 1998, at the age of 64, leaving behind his wife, Khadija Haq, an accomplished economist, and two children – Toneema and Farhan.

Human development: concept, measurement, and development strategies
Mahbub's goal in creating the *Human Development Report* and the HDI was to advocate a new development paradigm that recognised that the ultimate purpose of development was to improve people's lives, and that economic growth is only a means to this end. The concept of human development is simply defined as a process of enlarging choices. It builds on Mahbub's earlier work on basic needs. But human development is also a more elaborate and complete framework that is an attempt to apply the ideas about capabilities and functioning that the economist and philosopher Amartya Sen had been developing at the time. Human beings have and can expand their capabilities – and freedoms – to be and do what they value in life. Development is about expanding these capabilities to allow people to have more choices and freedoms to live full lives (Sen, 1989; UNDP, 1990). The Human Development Reports developed a body of concepts, measurement tools and policy strategies that operationalised Sen's ideas about development as expansion of capabilities and freedoms that formed a 'human development approach' to development (see Fukuda-Parr, 2003; Fukuda-Parr and Kumar, 2003).

Mahbub was a masterful communicator, able to explain complex concepts in simple terms. He explained human development as development *of*, *for* and *by* the people. It is about the development of people's capabilities through investing in their health and education. It is development for people where the benefits of growth are translated into the lives of people, of all people, rich and poor, men and women. And development is about action by people themselves to influence the processes that shape their lives whether it is economic entrepreneurship or political pressure for gender equity and social justice.

Mahbub used the power of numbers to persuade as well as to analyse the importance of economic trends that required priority attention. Quantitative information was a cornerstone of the Human Development Reports, which presented indicators of the many dimensions of human lives, in innovative ways, such as gender gaps in education, urban–rural divides in access to healthcare, North–South gaps in income, or contrasts between expenditures for education versus arms. He was also convinced that there was a need for a summary measure to monitor progress in 'human development' in contrast to GDP per capita. Amartya Sen recounts how he argued against this idea but was in the end persuaded by it, and agreed to help Mahbub develop the HDI, a composite measure that includes adjusted income, literacy, education and life expectancy and that ranks countries. This would be the only way to 'break the dominance of the GNP'. Otherwise, people will look at the multitude of human development indicators but would go back to GNP to assess progress (Sen, 1998).

The HDI had considerable impact on drawing the attention of presidents, ministers of finance, journalists and others to their countries' literary levels, educational attainment, child mortality and such social indicators that have been around but ignored over years. It led countries to do more – like Egypt which made its own analysis and gave greater priority to girls' education; or Brazil which developed an HDI for each of the municipalities of the country and major anti-poverty programmes to redress the vast disparities that exist within the country.

Mahbub was concerned with the importance of measuring inequality and political freedom in assessing the progress of human development. He made several attempts to track these trends by supplementing the basic HDI with other measures, namely, the income-adjusted HDI, the gender-adjusted HDI, the human poverty index (HPI), the gender empowerment measure (GEM), the political freedom index and the human freedom index. While the gender and human poverty measures were successful, the distribution-adjusted HDI and the freedom indices contained technical weaknesses that could not be overcome (UNDP, 1993, 1994, 1995, 1997).

In addition to the HDI and associated measurement tools, the Human Development Reports 1990–96 created by Mahbub contained a wealth of innovative ideas on a wide range of policy issues. They include concepts such as *jobless growth* (1993) – economy grows through productivity gains, but without resultant job increases or benefits of growth being translated into the lives of poor people; *human security* (1994) – security is about people's lives and so should focus on defending people, not national borders and should extend to securing jobs, health, environment, personal safety and so on. Mahbub also used the Human Development Reports quite effectively during the early 1990s to put forward some of his innovative policy proposals. The 20:20 proposal, asked for 20 per cent of domestic resources and 20 per cent of official development assistance to be devoted to basic social services. He revived the idea of the Tobin tax as a means for generating resources for human development in the developing world. He also talked of using the *peace dividend* for human development and proposed the creation of a global fund. He suggested major reforms in global institutions such as the creation of a global central bank or the Economic Security Council so that economic and social crises – such as the HIV/AIDS pandemic – would receive the same attention as political security issues. He did not hesitate to call for change in the policies of governments, including those of the most powerful – such as in the closed markets of Europe and the United States to developing-country goods, the arms sales of the P-5 countries that fuel violent conflicts, and the gender inequalities in Japan.

Mahbub believed that the ideas presented in the global Human Development Reports had to be translated into national contexts. He piloted the National Human Development Reports in four countries in 1991. Today nearly 300 National Human Development Reports have been produced in more than 120 countries. All these national reports have become important documents for national policies and strategies, for serving as a depository of innovative data and also crucial advocacy tools.

Before his premature death, Mahbub published two Human Development Reports for South Asia and started work on a third under the Human Development Centre in Islamabad. These reports, especially the third one on governance that was completed and published posthumously, boldly raised issues such as corruption and flaws in the functioning of democratic institutions. In the year he died, Pakistan and India undertook nuclear tests and the conflict over Kashmir flared up, while efforts to resolve sectarian violence in Sri Lanka and elsewhere were stymied. Mahbub ardently worked towards persuading politicians to join together to fight poverty rather than engage in self-destructing conflicts.

Mahbub the visionary

Mahbub's vision was a world where, as he often used to say: security would be reflected in the lives of the people, not in the weapons of the countries; poverty would be tackled not as a mere flu, but as a body cancer; gender equality would not receive a band-aid approach, but would be mainstreamed; people would be empowered to guide both the state and the market, both of which, in the last analysis, must serve the interests of the people; poor nations would get an equitable access to global market opportunities, not charity; and peace and development would coexist (Haq, 1993).

'In decades ahead', Mahbub wrote, 'it is battle on freedom from want that will continue to challenge our most creative energies' (ibid., p. 3). For Mahbub the primary means to achieve change were ideas – 'Ideas were the prime movers of history; revolutions came thereafter' (Haq, 1976, p. 11). He believed that the evolution of a new idea had three stages: the first stage is characterised by organised resistance; the second could be described as widespread and uncritical acceptance of new ideas; and the third is where there is a critical evaluation of ideas and their practical implementation.

Courage was another crucial element in changing the world. In his final book, *Reflections on Human Development*, a collection of essays published in 1995, Mahbub wrote,

> Throughout the time I have been associated with the production of the Human Development Reports, I have realized that what endeared them to the world was their raw courage, their ability to state facts professionally, but honestly, their refusal to make any intellectual compromises with institutional constraints. (Haq, 1995a, p. 11)

Mahbub was open minded, always ready to take on new ideas, and was excited to launch new ideas which would develop into 'an intellectual journey' as they would generate debate, and through that process, be strengthened or dropped. He kept a plaque, which said, 'It is too late to agree with me, because I have already changed my mind'.

He had trust in hope and the vision of common people, because human progress towards social justice was ultimately won by the efforts and struggles of people. From the fall of the Berlin wall to the end of apartheid in South Africa, the unthinkable was happening as a result of people taking action in their own hands. He saw nothing good in pessimism and he used to say that pessimists should not be in the development business. Most people see things as they are and ask 'Why?'; but Mahbub was one of those few people who dreamed things that never were and ask 'Why not?'.

Mahbub the human being

In his personal life, Mahbub was dedicated to his family. Khadija, his wife, was a constant intellectual companion and an integral part of what he accomplished in his life. He was very proud of his children – Toneema and Farhan. To his many friends, he was a pillar of strength, grace and consideration.

Mahbub valued knowledge, wisdom and honesty. He once said: 'Honesty is a gift that only friends can give to friends'. In the dedication of his last book, *Reflections on Human Development*, he wrote 'To Toneema and Farhan, Let knowledge be your sword and wisdom be your shield'. Mahbub was a fighter who loved challenges.

Mahbub was very fond of poetry. His book *An Elusive Dawn* (1985) is a translation of the works of Faiz Ahmed Faiz, the famous Pakistani poet, and won critical acclaim, including from the poet himself. His two favourite poems were 'Do we dare?' by T.S. Elliot and 'The Road Not Taken' by Robert Frost. Mahbub's life was about daring to disturb the world and take the road less travelled to change the world for humanity, and correct injustices.

Paul Streeten says that human beings are either a mollusc or a mammal. Molluscs are hard on the outside, unyielding and tough, but soft and mushy underneath. Mammals are soft, warm and yielding outside, but firm inside held together with a strong backbone. Paul describes Mahbub as a quintessential mammal, whose gentle appearance concealed a tenacity and strength of character that was the core of the life he led as a mission.

Mahbub often said to his friends, 'in the ultimate analysis, human destiny is a choice, not a chance' – whether in his personal life or in his life as a public official this belief defined the way Mahbub ul Haq approached all challenges. It was by choice that he stood against sectarianism and bigotry, and fought for public intervention to promote peace, security and human well-being. In every aspect of life, Mahbub never let chance dictate his choices.

SAKIKO FUKUDA-PARR
SELIM JAHAN

References

Anand, Sudhir and Amartya Sen (1994), 'Human development index: methodology and measurement', reprinted in Fukuda-Parr and Kumar (eds) (2003), pp. 114–27.

Fukuda-Parr, S. (2003), 'Operationalizing Sen's capability approach', *Feminist Economics*, **9** (2–3), 301–17.

Fukuda-Parr, Sakiko and A.K. Shiva Kumar (eds) (2003), *Readings in Human Development*, Oxford and New Delhi: Oxford University Press.

Haq, Mahbub ul (1963), *The Strategy of Economic Planning: A Case Study of Pakistan*, Oxford and Karachi: Oxford University Press.

Haq, Mahbub ul (1976), *The Poverty Curtain: Choices for the Third World*, New York: Columbia University Press.

Haq, Mahbub ul (1985), *An Elusive Dawn: Selections from the Poetry of Faiz Ahmed Faiz*, Centre for Social Sciences and Humanities, Islamabad: University Grants Commission.

Haq, Mahbub ul (1993), 'Towards an Agenda for Development', mimeo, Human Development Report Office, UNDP, New York, September.

Haq, Mahbub ul (1995a), *Reflections on Human Development*, Oxford and New York: Oxford University Press.

Haq, Mahbub ul (1995b), 'The birth of the human development index', reprinted in Fukuda-Parr and Kumar (eds) (2003), pp. 103–13.

Jahan, Selim (2002), 'Evolution of the human development index', reprinted in Fukuda-Parr and Kumar (eds) (2003), pp. 128–39.

Sen, Amartya K. (1989), 'Development as capability expansion', reprinted in Fukuda-Parr and Kumar (eds) (2003), pp. 3–16.

Sen, Amartya K. (1998), 'Mahbub ul Haq: the courage and creativity of his ideas', Speech at the Memorial Meeting for Mahbub ul Haq at the United Nations, New York, 15 October (published in the *Journal of Human Development*, **1** (1), 2000).

Streeten, Paul (2004), Personal correspondence.

Streeten, Paul, Shahid, J. Burki, Mahbub ul Haq, Norman Hicks and Frances Stewart (1981), *First Things First: Meeting Basic Human Needs in the Developing Countries*, Oxford: Oxford University Press.

UNDP (1990), *Human Development Report 1990: Concept and Measurement of Human Development*, Oxford and New York: Oxford University Press.

UNDP (1993), *Human Development Report 1993: People's Participation*, Oxford and New York: Oxford University Press.

UNDP (1994), *Human Development Report 1994: New Dimensions of Human Security*, Oxford and New York: Oxford University Press.

UNDP (1995), *Human Development Report 1995: Gender and Human Development*, Oxford and New York: Oxford University Press.

UNDP (1997), *Human Development Report 1997: Human Development to Eradicate Poverty*, Oxford and New York: Oxford University Press.

The Harrod Model of Growth and Some Early Reactions to It

Roy Harrod himself saw his 1939 article, 'An essay in dynamic theory', and his 1948 book, *Towards a Dynamic Economics*, as putting forward a new, exciting way of seeing and doing economics. It would, he wrote, make 'the old static formulation of problems [seem] stale, flat and unprofitable' (Harrod, 1939, p. 15). His primary purpose was to set out some fundamental relationships between rates of change of levels of key variables at a moment of time (instead of, as in static analysis, relationships between levels). He abstracted from lags between variables in key relationships – they could come in later – and from all but the necessary attention to the impact of certain expectations on economic behaviour and decision making. This led him to distinguish between four concepts of the rate of growth of economies: expected (g_e), actual (g), warranted (g_w) and natural (g_n). The first two are self-explanatory; the last two are very much his innovations. g_w is rather inelegantly defined by Harrod (ibid., p. 16) as 'that rate of growth which, if it occurs, will leave all parties satisfied that they have produced neither more nor less than the right amount'. This would lead decision makers to repeat the rates of growth they had first planned and then subsequently achieved. The natural rate of growth (g_n) reflected the supply-side characteristics of the economy; it was determined by the rate of growth of the labour force and the rate at which through technical advances the labour force improved its productivity over time. Harrod supposed g_n to be independent of g_e, g and g_w; on reflection, an unacceptable simplification once the embodiment of technical advances in the stock of capital goods by investment and the accompanying impact on productivity of the labour force are recognised.

Two questions then arose. First, if the economy does not immediately grow at g_w as an aggregate outcome of the activities of individual business people, could the signals given out by the economy, in particular, the implications of the revealed discrepancies between what was initially expected and what was actually achieved, be such as to induce the decision makers to take such actions as to move g_e and g towards g_w? That is to say, is g_w a stable or an unstable rate of growth? Second, even if g_w were to be achieved, would it also necessarily coincide with g_n, so that both full employment of labour and normal capacity working of the stock of capital goods would be achieved?

In outline, this is how Harrod and his interpreters posed the questions. With hindsight we may see that his contributions fit into two major strands of the preceding literature. The first relates to Karl Marx's schemes of reproduction, Marx (1885 [1978]), a link of which Harrod candidly admitted (to Joan Robinson who pointed it out to him) he was not aware when he wrote his two classics. Marx asked in effect what conditions must be fulfilled as between the three departments of the economy – wage, capital and luxury goods – in his two schema, simple and expanded reproduction, respectively, in order that, as we would say now, both aggregate demand and aggregate supply, and their respective compositions, would match? That is to say, each department could in effect take in its own washing and the appropriate portions of the other departments' washing as well (see Sardoni, 1981). Having established the very special conditions implied, Marx conjectured that it would be a fluke if individual business people operating in a competitive environment and pursuing their own goals brought these conditions into being. He argued that if they did not, then instability and even crises would result. Harrod's contribution was to provide a precise set of answers to such fundamental questions concerning the laws of motion of capitalism.

The second strand to which he contributed is, of course, the Keynesian revolution. Keynes (1936) had analysed the employment-creating effects of accumulation and argued that it was unlikely that, left to itself, a capitalist economy would even on average bring about a level of accumulation that would offset leakages into full employment saving. He had little systematically to say about the capacity-creating effects of current investment expenditure, especially if it were to be acted upon so as to produce full employment in the short run. Harrod did not explicitly (as did Evsey Domar) pose questions about the latter – what were the conditions that would make aggregate demand be such as to ensure that the economy advanced along g_n, that is to say, would ensure the equality of g_e, g, g_w and g_n? If these equalities were not attained, what factors in the economy would provide signals that would lead decision makers to act in such a manner as to establish them?

So we have two basic questions: first, what determines g_w and is g_w stable? Second, if $g_w \neq g_n$ initially, what forces are present, at least in a long-term sense, to bring them to equality?

First, we derive an expression for g_w. Harrod built on the analysis in his 1936 book on the trade cycle of the relationship between the accelerator which determined planned investment expenditure and the multiplier which determined the equilibrium level of income associated with planned investment expenditure. He concentrated on a point in time, deriving the conditions by which the aggregate level and rate of growth of expected sales in the economy would be achieved by creating through investment the capacity for production to match them and the aggregate demand to match the forthcoming aggregate supply. As Amartya Sen (1970) has shown, the desired expressions may be derived as follows: we write the saving function as $S_t = sY_t$ where S is overall saving, s is the marginal (equals the average) propensity to save, Y is income (also realised sales and output) and t is the current period of time; the investment function is $I_t = q(X_t - Y_{t-1})$, where I is planned investment expenditure, q is the desired incremental capital–output ratio (the accelerator) and X is the expected level of sales of time t. Harrod assumed that national income is always the short-period equilibrium level of income, so abstracting from the groping process whereby the stabilising signals given out by any initial gap between planned investment and planned saving tend to take the economy toward the equilibrium point, Keynes's level of effective demand, so that planned and actual investment equal planned and actual saving ($sY_t = I_t$). It follows that:

$$Y_t = \tfrac{1}{s}I_t = \tfrac{1}{s}q(X_t - Y_{t-1}).$$

What is the condition for $X_t = Y_t$? Write:

$$\frac{Y_t}{X_t} = \frac{q}{s}\left(\frac{X_t - Y_{t-1}}{X_t}\right) = \frac{q}{s}g_e.$$

$Y_t/X_t = 1$ if and only if $g_e = s/q$. This is the expression for Harrod's g_w. Moreover, the actual growth exceeds, equals, or falls short of g_e if g_e itself exceeds, equals or falls short of g_w.

Harrod noted that *unless* the economy is on g_w, then, even though accumulation plans are always realised, they would not have been made in the first place, had the actual outcomes been correctly expected. This leads to the analysis of g_w's stability.

We may put it this way: having ruled out by assumption the stabilising signals of a gap between planned investment and planned saving in the short period, Harrod sensed the destabilising signals of such a gap in the long period. Suppose that $g > g_e > g_w$. Then business people would be encouraged to undertake an even greater rate of accumulation in the future, so driving the economy even further away from g_w. This occurs because, if we look at levels, the saving relationship, the slope of which, q, is the accelerator, is both greater than unity and s, the slope of the saving function (constrained to be much less than unity), so that the saving relationship is intersected from below. There is excess demand to the right of the intersection (and excess supply to the left), providing exactly the opposite signals to the short-period signals. Moreover, even if the economy is on g_w there is no guarantee that g_w will correspond to g_n because they are determined by independent factors.

There were two principal early reactions to Harrod's instability problem and the non-equality of g_w and g_n. The best-known is, first, the neoclassical model of economic growth associated with Robert Solow (1956) of Cambridge, Massachusetts and Trevor Swan (1956) (who was then Professor of Economics at the Research School of Social Sciences of the Australian National University); two eminent Keynesian economists, it should be noted. They asked the following question: suppose an all-wise, Keynesian-inspired, government were to keep the economy at full employment in all short periods. Would then the operation of neoclassical forces, Marshall's 'dynamical principle of "Substitution" . . . seen ever at work', Marshall (1890 [1961], p. xv), responding to appropriate signals through the price mechanism, lead to a change in q so as to give it a value that makes $g_w = g_n$? As is well known, at least in a simple one-commodity model, the price mechanism does the trick by so changing the relative prices of the services of labour and capital as to lead business people, faced with different techniques of production, to choose the value of q that, given the value of s, brings about the desired equality. Solow argued that Harrod's assumption of a constant value of q was too strong, too ad hoc, and likely to be the cause of the instability result, that a capitalist economy is immensely unstable, either pushing upwards to an inflationary Heaven or downwards to a deflationary Hell. This is not really fair to Harrod, for he was considering a point in time so that q could be both momentarily a constant and the outcome of sensible economic choice in a given situation.

The other main response came, surprise surprise, from the other Cambridge in the persons of Nicholas Kaldor, Richard Kahn, Joan Robinson and Luigi Pasinetti. In Kaldor's classic 1955/56 article, 'Alternative theories of distribution', he accepts a constant q (indeed, goes further, making it independent of economic signals through profits) and supposes that the decision makers in aggregate are providing a rate of planned accumulation that would put the economy on g_n. He adopts the Keynesian view that investment leads and saving responds. He then assumes on the basis of empirical findings that saving out of profits is greater than saving out of wages at the margin ($s_\pi > s_w$) and that, *as a long-term tendency*, prices are more flexible than money wages. This means that if at full employment (Y_f), planned S/Y_f were to be, say, less than $\bar{I}/Y_f$, the resulting excess demand situation would tend to make prices rise faster than money wages so redistributing Y_f from wages to profits and raising the value of S/Y_f until g_w, initially not equal to g_n because of an inappropriate value of s, is brought to equality with g_n when $S/Y_f = \bar{I}/Y_f$.

Joan Robinson also independently suggested this outcome and, furthermore, provided a version of the possible attainment of g_w in her famous banana diagram (Robinson, 1962, p. 48). From Kalecki's theory of distribution she derived a relationship between actual accumulation and achieved profitability; from Keynes's theory she derived the 'animal spirits' function which related desired accumulation to expected profitability, itself a function of actual profitability in a situation where financial conditions and long-term expectations are givens. She tells a story of how, if the economy is not immediately at the point where, *in a given situation*, the two relationships intersect, the resulting gap between expected and actual rates of profit (the latter created by the accumulation induced by the expected rate of profit, an earlier Kaleckian as well as Kaldorian insight) will take the economy through the Keynesian mechanism whereby the actual rate of profit determines the value of the expected rate of profit, towards the stable intersection point. Here, what was expected and what occurs coincide, the economy is growing at g_w. However, the very passage of time may destroy the underlying given conditions, changing the positions of the relationships, so that like Marx, she predicts that the accumulation process leads to cyclical growth, often unstable and sometimes crisis prone. And, of course, even if g_w *is* attained in Harrod's and her stories, though this would be optimum for the business people in the given situation because *their* plans have been achieved and they are the principal decision makers who drive the economy along, it certainly need not to be so for the wage-earners. Not only may they find that some of their number are unemployed, they are also unable to signal that it would be profitable to employ them, which indeed it would not be if 'animal sprits' are sluggish and weak.

Stephanie Blankenburg (a lecturer at SOAS, London) has reminded me (a euphemism for making me aware of it), that Harrod's model, along with Lewis's model, provided the basis for a range of central debates on development policy in the 1950s and 1960s (personal correspondence). Specifically, if g_n exceeds g_w, so that the effective labour force grew faster than accumulation and planned investment outstripped planned saving, high unemployment and inflation would be found to go together in many developing economies. The Harrod model provided the necessary policy framework by suggesting policies of population control (to reduce g_n) and fiscal and other policies to impact on the saving ratio and the capital–output and capital–labour ratios, in order to raise s, reduce q, and so increase g_w (and g_n). Together, the object was to bring about equality between g_n and g_w (and, so, g and g_e). The Harrod model is now out of fashion, due to the resurgence of neoliberal thinking and because it was perceived to be too simplistic a framework for understanding capital accumulation in pre-industrial and pre-capitalist conditions.

G.C. HARCOURT

References

Harrod, R.F. (1936), *The Trade Cycle. An Essay*, Oxford: Clarendon.
Harrod, R.F. (1939), 'An essay in dynamic theory', *Economic Journal*, **49**, 14–33.
Harrod, R.F. (1948), *Towards a Dynamic Economics*, London: Macmillan.
Kaldor, N. (1955/56), 'Alternative theories of distribution', *Review of Economic Studies*, **23**, 83–100.
Keynes, J.M. (1936), *The General Theory of Employment, Interest and Money*, London: Macmillan.
Marshall, A. (1890 [1961]), *Principles of Economics*, 9th (Variorum) edn, London: Macmillan.
Marx, K. (1885 [1978]), *Capital*, Vol. II, Harmondsworth: Penguin.
Robinson, Joan (1962), *Essays in the Theory of Economic Growth*, London: Macmillan.
Sardoni, C. (1981), 'Multi-sectoral models of balanced growth and the Marxian schemes of expanded reproduction', *Australian Economic Papers*, **20**, 383–97.
Sen, A.K. (1970), *Growth Economics. Selected Readings*, Harmondsworth: Penguin.
Solow, R.M. (1956), 'A contribution to the theory of economic growth', *Quarterly Journal of Economics*, **70**, 65–94.
Swan, T.W. (1956), 'Economic growth and capital accumulation', *Economic Record*, **32**, 334–61.

Hill, Polly (1914–2005)

Polly Hill was born on 10 June 1914 into one of Cambridge's most distinguished academic families: her father was A.V. Hill, a Nobel Prize winning physiologist, and her mother's brother was J.M. Keynes. Polly Hill graduated from Cambridge in 1936 with a degree in economics, but her academic career did not begin until 1954 when she took up a post as a research fellow in the University of Ghana. This was the beginning of her distinguished career as a 'field economist', as she liked to describe herself. Over the next 30 years she published nine books and over 50 articles including the classic study that established her reputation *The Migrant Cocoa-Farmers of Southern Ghana* (1963). Polly Hill's economics has little in common with that of her celebrated uncle: she was more of a 'specific empiricist' than a 'general theorist'; and more concerned with inequality and poverty in the developing countries than unemployment in the developed countries. What she did have in common with her uncle was a concern to question conventional wisdom. Her questioning was grounded in the countryside of west Africa and southern India; her views were based on some 13 years' fieldwork and she had little time for those development economists who based their analyses and policy conclusions on, in her considered opinion, worthless official statistics and false assumptions about the economic motivations of farmers. A favourite saying of hers best sums up her approach to development: 'We are so ignorant of the conditions of poverty in the developing world that we do not know how ignorant we are' (personal communication). This belief informed her field

research and her critiques of those whose theories were, in her opinion, founded on ignorance.

Her first job on leaving university was as an editorial assistant with the *Economic
Journal*. She held this position for two years (1936–38) and then took a position with the
Fabian Society where she wrote her first book, *The Unemployment Services* (1940), which
was concerned to expose the inefficiency and inhumanity of the system of unemployment
relief and to advance policy conclusions to overcome these deficiencies. This book is
informed by a commitment to social and economic justice, a moral philosophy that per-
meates all her books.

With the outbreak of the war she was obliged to become a civil servant. She worked
successively in the Treasury, the Board of Trade and the Colonial Office and resigned in
1951 when, after a period of unemployment, she became a journalist for the weekly *West
Africa*. In 1953 she married and went to live in Ghana with her husband.

From 1954 to 1965 she was employed as a research fellow at the University of Ghana
when, as she puts its, she became a pupil of the migrant cocoa farmers of Ghana. This was
the beginning of her career as 'field economist', a term that best describes the unique fieldwork methods she pioneered. She began her research using the standard questionnaire
method and wrote up the result of this research in her second book, *The Gold Coast Cocoa
Farmer: A Preliminary Study* (1956). When she subsequently realised that this method had
led her to accept uncritically some false conventional assumptions about the backgrounds
of these farmers, she abandoned the method in favour of one that would enable her to make
empirical discoveries. Her new method was based on one that combined the methods of an
economic historian, a human geographer and an economic anthropologist. She made intensive studies of villages, conducted extensive archival work, and situated her findings in the
relevant comparative and historical context. All her subsequent works were based on original data that she collected using her meticulous and rigorous scholarly methods.

Her next book, *The Migrant Cocoa-Farmers of Southern Ghana* (1963), the product of
many years of painstaking research, demonstrated the fruitfulness of her approach and
established her reputation as a scholar of renown. Her carefully documented findings on
the behavioural patterns of the cocoa farmers turned conventional orthodoxy on its head.
She charted the economic aspects of the migratory process over the years 1894–1930 and
mapped the geographical dimensions of it. She also demonstrated that the matrilineal
farmers adopted an entirely different mode of migration from patrilineal farmers. The
book caught the attention of geographers, historians and anthropologists and its informal status as a 'classic' was officially recognised in 1997 when the International African
Institute reissued the book in its Anthropological Classics series.

Her subsequent fieldwork in Ghana covered almost every domain of economic activity:
she studied trade, traders and marketing, farmers, fisher-people and pastoralists. In 1966
she began fieldwork in rural Hausaland, northern Nigeria, financed by the Institute of
Social and Economic Research at Lagos. The following year she returned to Hausaland and
spent six months at Batagarawa, near Katsina City. This was financed by the Centre for
Research on Economic Development at the University of Michigan. In 1970–71 she did a
further 15 months fieldwork in a very densely populated rural area near Kano city. She also
consulted the Nigerian national archives and did some original work on the history of rural
farm slavery. Numerous articles and books followed (Hill, 1970, 1972, 1977).

In 1972, after five years of self-funded research, she eventually got the academic recognition too long denied her when she was appointed Smuts Reader in Commonwealth Studies at Cambridge University, a position with a fixed term of six years. She was also appointed as a permanent fellow of Clare Hall Cambridge. In 1975 she returned to rural Fanteland in southern Ghana for three months more fieldwork. An indefatigable fieldworker she decided, at age 63, to undertake fieldwork in rural Karnataka in southern India when immigration restrictions prevented her from returning to Nigeria. She found, to her surprise, that the fieldwork techniques she developed for understanding economic inequality in west Africa were applicable there. *Dry Grain Farming Families: Hausaland (Nigeria) and Karnataka (India) Compared* (1982) followed.

She was 67 years old when she went on her last overseas fieldwork trip and she would have continued doing fieldwork in the tropics had her health allowed it. Her 'field economist' days over, she began working on *Development Economics on Trial: The Anthropological Case for the Prosecution* (1986). Her long experience of working in the tropics made her acutely aware of the 'old-fashioned, stereotyped, Western-biased, overgeneralised crudity and conceptual falsity of so many conventional economic premises' (1986, p. xi). The polemical intent of this book was to expose these assumptions; its constructive purpose was a practical demonstration that many of the findings of economic anthropology are relevant to development economics. She saw these two subdisciplines not as opponents but as complements in an intellectual division of labour: fieldworkers are needed to provide the empirical data that is to serve as the basis for generalisation.

This was her swansong as an economist but not as a scholar. In 1990 she privately published *The History of the Isleham Fen in the 1930s*. She also edited, with R. Keynes, *Lydia and Maynard: Letters between Lydia Lopokova and John Maynard Keynes* (1989). In her eighties she worked on the history of early Cambridge Women Students but, to her great disappointment, was unable to find a publisher. Another passion she developed late in life was poetry and she compiled collections of her work which she distributed privately to friends. Polly Hill died on 21 August 2005 aged 91.

What was Polly Hill's contribution to development economics? She was a student of rural poverty rather than urban and of tropical, dry-grain farming practices rather than wet-rice cultivation. Like Francesca Bray (1986) who exposes the wheat-centric bias of development theory in her *The Rice Economies: Technology and Development in Asian Societies*, Hill argues that the specificities of climate and crops create limits on generalisation in agricultural development economics. Her life work has provided a model for those interested in a 'field economist' approach to development; it has also provided data of the kind that those interested in secondary-level, synthetic generalisations need. Grand theorists concerned with universal generalisations, be they neoclassical economists or neo-Marxist, will find that her work calls the fundamental usefulness of their project into question.

C.A. GREGORY

References

Bray, F. (1986), *The Rice Economies: Technology and Development in Asian Societies*, Oxford: Basil Blackwell.
Hill, P. (1940), *The Unemployment Services*, London: Routledge.
Hill, P. (1956), *The Gold Coast Cocoa Farmer: A Preliminary Study*, Oxford: Oxford University Press.
Hill, P. (1963), *The Migrant Cocoa-Farmers of Southern Ghana*, Cambridge: Cambridge University Press.

Hill, P. (1970), *Studies in Rural Capitalism in West Africa*, Cambridge: Cambridge University Press.

Hill, P. (1972), *Rural Hausa: A Village and a Setting*, Cambridge: Cambridge University Press.

Hill, P. (1977), *Population, Prosperity and Poverty: Rural Kano 1900 and 1970*, Cambridge: Cambridge University Press.

Hill, P. (1982), *Dry Grain Farming Families: Hausaland (Nigeria) and Karnataka (India) Compared*, Cambridge: Cambridge University Press.

Hill, P. (1986), *Development Economics on Trial: The Anthropological Case for a Prosecution*, Cambridge: Cambridge University Press.

Hill, P. (1990), *The History of Isleham Fen in the 1930s*, Cambridge: (privately published).

Hill, P. and R. Keynes (eds) (1989), *Lydia and Maynard: Letters between Lydia Lopokova and John Maynard Keynes*, London: A. Deutsch.

Hirschman, Albert Otto (b. 1915)

One of the 'pioneers in development' (Meier and Seers, 1984), Albert Hirschman is an economist whose approach to development issues combined economics with other social sciences, introducing new concepts and perspectives to understand development issues, providing new and valuable insights for the design and evaluation of development strategies, policies, programmes and projects. His work has been widely used by economists as well as by political scientists, historians, sociologists, policy makers and development practitioners.

Albert Otto Hirschman was born in 1915 in Berlin, and left Germany in 1933. He studied economics at the Sorbonne in Paris, continuing at the London School of Economics in the mid-1930s. In the summer of 1936 he enlisted with the Spanish Republican Army, and then he went to Italy, receiving his doctorate in 1938 from the University of Trieste. That year Mussolini's racial laws were introduced and Hirschman, who was an active anti-Fascist militant, returned to Paris. He served in the French Army in 1939–40 and emigrated to the United States in 1941 with a Rockefeller Foundation Fellowship. After two years at the University of California (Berkeley) and three years in the US Army, he joined the Federal Reserve Board in Washington DC in 1946 (invited by A. Gerschenkron, the eminent economic historian), where he worked on problems of post-war reconstruction in Western Europe. From 1952 to 1956 he lived in Bogotá (Colombia), until 1954 as an economic adviser to the government and since then as a private consultant. In 1956 he became a visiting professor at Yale University, continuing as professor of international economic relations at Columbia from 1958 to 1964, and as professor of political economy at Harvard from 1964 to 1974. Hirschman then moved to the Institute for Advanced Study, at Princeton University, New Jersey, as a professor of social science, and Emeritus since 1985.

His multidisciplinary and creative approach is evident in his early work: for example, in *National Power and the Structure of Foreign Trade*, written in 1942 (and published in 1945), he discussed the relations between the economic and the political dimension of foreign trade, taking into consideration both theoretical and historical aspects, drawing on multiple sources in economics, politics, history, literature and statistics published in several languages. In this work he developed a new statistical index of concentration (which has been applied by other economists also to industrial concentration issues), and discussed perhaps for the first time the theme of dependence in the context of foreign trade.

Hirschman introduced several concepts that expanded the tool-kit of social scientists (economists and also political scientists, sociologists and historians). Some of these concepts are inducement mechanisms; inverted sequences; exit, voice and loyalty; perversity, futility and jeopardy; backward and forward linkages; latitude; trait-making and trait-taking characteristics; trespassing; self-subversion; tunnel effect; possibilism; hiding hand; hidden rationalities; *fracasomania*; the principle of conservation and mutation of social energy; and the unintended consequences of human action.

'Linkages' is one of the most celebrated Hirschmanian concepts; it led to a vast literature and to a myriad of applications in different disciplines, particularly in development studies, and in policy and project applications. A linkage is a more or less compelling sequence of investment decisions occurring in the course of economic development. Among the dynamic linkage effects, Hirschman distinguishes between *backward* and *forward* linkages. The former are those in which the direction of the stimulus towards further investment flows from the finished article back to the semi-processed or raw materials from which it is made, or the machines which help make it. Whereas forward linkages are those when the stimulus towards additional investment flows forward in the product chain towards the use (either as input or final demand goods) of the products.

Although this concept is closely connected to the input–output model, which was a factor contributing to its success, an important aspect to take into account, and which was missed in several applications, is that linkage effects need time to unfold whereas the input–output matrix used in applications generally is static. Nevertheless, the concept was widely used to understand the development process and to guide the design of development strategies and policies. Another type of linkage considered by Hirschman, the *consumption* linkage, is defined as the stimulus towards domestic production of consumer goods that will be undertaken as newly earned incomes are spent on such goods. Although this type of linkage can be seen as the initial step in the process of import substitution industrialisation, when consumption linkages are given their due, the expansion of agricultural incomes can be just as stimulating for overall growth as an industrial spurt, and the linkage concept can thus underpin a development strategy that tilts investment priorities towards agricultural improvements (see Hirschman, 1986). All these linkages, including also others such as fiscal linkages, called attention to the ways in which 'one thing leads (or fails to lead) to another'.

Whereas the linkages concept has been mostly used by economists, the 'exit, voice and loyalty' triad, presented by Hirschman in 1970, became one of the key concepts used by political scientists and development practitioners. As indicated in the subtitle of his classic book, exit, voice and loyalty are 'responses to decline in firms, organisations and states'. *Exit* means withdrawal from a relationship, and assumes the possibility of choice. Hirschman contrasts exit with *voice*, which is an option exercised by those who do not exit but protest, complain or demand improvements, remaining (being loyal) in the organisation, state or firm. Voice provides key information for improving the way organisations work. The combination of exit and voice facilitates the integration of the economist's approach, which tends to privilege exit (competition) and the political scientist's focus on voice (although the latter can also be seen as playing a key role in the articulation of demand for greater quality of public services).

The role of 'disappointment' is considered in *Shifting Involvements* (1982) as resulting from the confrontations of expectations and experience. Although Hirschman focuses his analysis of disappointment in the context of private–public cycles (swings from the private-orientated to the public life and back again), without particular reference to development issues, the concept can be fruitfully applied to development matters, as shown by R. Picciotto (see Rodwin and Schon, 1994).

In the analysis of *The Rhetoric of Reaction* (1991), Hirschman identified another triad which is useful in the discussion of development policies: the 'perversity thesis', or thesis of the perverse effect, according to which any purposive action to improve some aspect of the political, social or economic order only serves to exacerbate the condition one wishes to remedy; the 'futility thesis', which holds that attempts at social transformation will not be feasible; and the 'jeopardy thesis', which argues that the cost of the proposed change or reform is too high as it endangers some previous, valuable accomplishment. In addition to these theses of the reactionary rhetoric, Hirschman also considers the symmetric theses in the progressive rhetoric; particularly relevant is the consideration of the 'imminent danger thesis', the opposite of the jeopardy thesis. Whereas the former concentrates only on the dangers of action, the latter wholly focuses on the risks of inaction. The 'mature' position, Hirschman emphasised, should canvass and assess the risks of both action and inaction, thus overcoming 'the rhetoric of intransigence' with their unilateral emphasis on either action or inaction.

It is worthwhile in this context to refer to Hirschman's 'possibilism', which consists in the discovery of paths, however narrow, leading to an outcome that appears to be foreclosed on the basis of probabilistic reasoning alone. Possibilism can be contrasted with approaches that posit the existence of no alternatives.

His observations in Latin America led him to introduce the notion of '*fracasomania*', a term coined by Hirschman to call attention to a failure complex, the tendency of Latin Americans to a self-deprecatory attitude, and an unjustified feeling of ineptness and inferiority. Hirschman pointed out that *fracasomania* could become a self-fulfilling prophecy, leading to real failures. As an antithesis of *fracasomania* he elaborated the idea of a 'bias for hope'.

Related to this positive bias is the 'principle of the hiding hand', presented by Hirschman in *Development Projects Observed* (1967). After reviewing a set of projects financed by the World Bank, he observed that had project designers anticipated all the risks and difficulties that could affect the projects, they would have considered most of those projects as infeasible. However, the creativity to find solutions for problems faced during project implementation would also have been underestimated. Thus, it was as if a 'hiding hand' led development practitioners to tackle what may have appeared *ex ante* as infeasible projects. Furthermore, Hirschman also dealt with concrete aspects of design, construction and operation of development projects, providing a useful taxonomy of uncertainties and a set of valuable suggestions. For example, he showed that projects whose *latitude* is limited by being 'site-bound' or whose construction is 'time-bound' have a number of advantages over those that do not present these characteristics.

Hirschman's influence is not limited to development economists, but also reached other social scientists and development practitioners, including policy makers at the highest level and the staff of international financial institutions. In fact, it is remarkable that his influence has not decreased with the passage of time: new applications are found for concepts that he introduced (for example, the triad 'exit, voice and loyalty' is a key concept underpinning the World Bank's 2004 *World Development Report*, which focuses on making services work for poor people). Furthermore, Hirschman's influence is not limited to Latin America, the area in which he focused his work, but also extends to other regions of the world. Thus, a very practical and influential application of exit, voice and loyalty was introduced some years ago in India, and this successful innovation (the Bangalore 'Citizen Report Card') is being replicated in other regions (his books have been translated into French, Spanish, Italian, Portuguese, German, Japanese, Hungarian and Swedish). However, it should be noted that the strong preference of mainstream economists for the use of formal models restricted Hirschman's influence on them, although several leading economists (such as Kenneth Arrow and Amartya Sen) praised his work.

Hirschman has been a constructive dissenter, rejecting traditional views and developing alternative ways of looking at issues. For example, when economists were writing about 'balanced growth' in the 1950s, he made the case for 'unbalanced growth'; whereas the majority of economists were focusing on resource allocation and on equilibrium, Hirschman stressed the importance of resource mobilisation and disequilibrium. The basic proposition of *The Strategy of Economic Development* (1958, p. 5) was that 'development depends not so much on finding optimal combinations for given resources and factors of production as on calling forth and enlisting for development purposes resources and abilities that are hidden, scattered or badly utilised'. He also played the dissenter role with respect to his own writings, 'self-subversion' as he called it. Combining direct observations of development processes with creative (lateral) thinking, and through an imaginative use of social science findings and literary works, Hirschman provided new interpretations of a myriad of development issues, with a 'bias for hope'. He also designed a set of concepts that enriched the tool-kit of social scientists (economists and non-economists) and of development practitioners, using story-telling in a heuristic way. At the same time, Hirschman portrayed the 'grandeur of the development enterprise', stimulating social scientists to apply their talents, and the concepts that he introduced, to development studies and practice (in the design and evaluation of policies, programmes and projects), showing fruitful ways in which disciplinary boundaries can and should be trespassed.

OSVALDO FEINSTEIN

References and further reading

Foxley, Alejandro, Malcom McPherson and Guillermo O'Donnell (eds) (1986), *Development, Democracy and the Art of Trespassing. Essays in Honor of Albert Hirschman*, Notre Dame, IN: University of Notre Dame Press.

Hirschman, Albert O. (1945), *National Power and the Structure of Foreign Trade*, Berkeley, CA: University of California Press.

Hirschman, Albert O. (1958), *The Strategy of Economic Development*, New Haven, CT: Yale University Press.

Hirschman, Albert O. (1963), *Journeys Toward Progress: Studies of Economic Policy-Making in Latin America*, New York: Twentieth Century Fund.

Hirschman, Albert O. (1967), *Development Projects Observed*, Washington, DC: Brookings Institution.

Hirschman, Albert O. (1970), *Exit, Voice and Loyalty*, Cambridge, MA: Harvard University Press.

Hirschman, Albert O. (1971), *A Bias for Hope: Essays on Development in Latin America*, New Haven, CT: Yale University Press.

Hirschman, Albert O. (1977), *The Passions and the Interests*, Princeton, NJ: Princeton University Press.

Hirschman, Albert O. (1981), *Essays in Trespassing: Economics to Politics and Beyond*, Cambridge: Cambridge University Press.

Hirschman, Albert O. (1982), *Shifting Involvements*, Princeton, NJ: Princeton University Press.

Hirschman, Albert O. (1984), *Getting Ahead Collectively*, New York: Pergamon.

Hirschman, Albert O. (1986), *Rival Views of Market Society and Other Recent Essays*, New York: Viking.

Hirschman, Albert O. (1991), *The Rhetoric of Reaction: Perversity, Futility, Jeopardy*, Cambridge, MA: Harvard University Press.

Hirschman, Albert O. (1995), *A Propensity to Self-Subversion*, Cambridge, MA: Harvard University Press.

Hirschman, Albert O. (1998), *Crossing Boundaries: Selected Writings*, New York: Zone Books.

Meier, Gerald M. and Dudley Seers (1984), *Pioneers in Development*, Oxford and New York: Oxford University Press.

Meldolesi, Luca (1995), *Discovering the Possible: the Surprising World of Albert O. Hirschman*, Notre Dame, IN: University of Notre Dame Press.

Rodwin, Lloyd and Donald A. Schon (eds) (1994), *Rethinking the Development Experience. Essays Provoked by the Work of Albert O. Hirschman*, Washington, DC: Brookings Institution.

Santiso, Javier (2000), 'La Mirada de Hirschman sobre el Desarrollo o El Arte de los Traspasos y las Autosubversiones (Hirschman's view of development or the art of trespassing and self-subversion)', *Revista de la CEPAL*, no. 76, pp. 91–106.

Teitel, Simon (ed.) (1992), *Towards a New Development Strategy for Latin America: Pathways from Hirschman's Thought*, Washington, DC: Inter-American Development Bank.

World Bank (2004), *World Development Report*, Oxford: Oxford University Press.

History and Development Studies

History can be regarded as a sequence of frozen presents. It is frozen in the sense that the facts of history cannot change, although our knowledge of those facts is continually evolving as we discover new facts and find new ways of arranging both new facts and the newly discovered aspects of the past. Thus we can use history for generating and motivating our hypotheses about how societies and economies develop. Adam Smith, the father of political economy in the Anglo-Saxon world, had used his construct of the mercantile system to motivate his discussion of how economic life should be ordered. Karl Marx had erected his edifice of critical political economy on a mountain of Blue Books giving the history of development of the British economy along with its contemporary contours. His critique of the received doctrines of political economy was based on perhaps the most learned history of classical political economy that was ever penned. In our own times, Douglass North and his followers have arrived at their construct of the institutional basis of the advanced capitalist economies on what they think are the main movements in the history of Western capitalist nations (North and Thomas, 1973). With all this evidence, it is surprising that the teaching of the history of economic development and of economic thought has been banished from most major departments of economics in the USA and the UK, and that the same practice has been imitated in most other departments of economics around the world.

Why does history matter? In analysing movements in the era of capitalism, it matters for three reasons, working together, or in many cases, against one another, either pushing economic and human development on its way or hindering it at every step. These three are (a) the forces of static and dynamic increasing returns, which interact with other processes such as network effects and intergenerational biological effects to create sequences of path dependence, (b) institutional or more broadly, structural inertia and structural breaks, or, in some cases, (c) accidents or serendipity.

Josiah Tucker (1774) and Adam Smith (1776) were the first two political economists to focus on increasing returns as a major motive force in economic development (Bagchi,

1998). Tucker pointed out the advantages that a rich nation (or region) enjoys as against its poorer rivals. These follow not only from the greater stock of productive and investible capital that the rich nation possesses but also from the greater technical knowledge that the rich nation has because of its specialisation in manufactures requiring such knowledge. Furthermore, the rich nation can learn more because of its better knowledge base to start with. It can embody that knowledge in more equipment because of its command over a larger investible capital. Thus the race between the rich nation and the poorer one becomes almost like a race between a hare and a tortoise where the former has a head start. Adam Smith considered the division of labour to be the principal engine of economic progress. The increasing division of labour is pushed forward by an expanding market and the latter in turn is extended by the greater productivity yielded by the increasing division of labour. Smith (1776, Book I, chapter 1) also considered the process of a continually finer division of labour to be a motive force behind the invention of machines. Tucker stressed the spread effects and backwash effects later embodied in theories of cumulative causation elaborated by Myrdal (1957) and Kaldor (1972). Karl Marx (1867) advanced this analysis by pointing out that under capitalism, machines reproduce machines and that the invention of new knowledge itself becomes part of the production process.

Dynamic economies of scale generated by static economies of scale, learning, capital accumulation, adaptation of complementary and competitive production and organisational structures, and innovations to overcome imbalances created by new vintages of equipment and organisational changes can be reinforced by network effects. The more a particular type of equipment or a particular way of doing business is adopted by a number of firms or users, the cheaper it becomes for the producer of that kind of equipment or the practitioner of that style of business to produce that equipment or intensify that particular style of doing business. The combination of dynamic economies of scale and network effects can then generate a path dependence in production structures, consumption patterns and business organisation and business behaviour (David, 1985; Arthur, 1989).

There is another kind of path dependence with effects that can persist for generations that economists have tended to neglect. This is best brought out by eminent practitioners of 'auxology' or human (biological) growth such as John Tanner (Tanner, 1981; Eveleth and Tanner, 1990; Bogin, 1999). A girl's physical and cognitive development is greatly influenced by the condition of her mother during the period she is in her womb, by the nutrition she receives after birth and by the stimulation and care she receives as a child. If she is conceived by a healthy mother, is born at the proper time and receives adequate nutrition and care and stimulation when she is growing up, she is likely to develop into a healthy, intelligent individual capable of functioning as an equal of others in a democratic society. (I am assuming that she receives the education appropriate to her abilities and aptitude.) But if the girl is conceived by, say, an anaemic mother who is underweight in relation to her stature, she is likely to be born with a low birth weight. Her chances of surviving her infancy will be low. If she survives but does not receive adequate nutrition for the first five years, not only her physical capacity but also her cognitive abilities will suffer in comparison with children who have received proper nurture, and were born of healthy mothers. When she grows up, she is likely to obtain only low-paid jobs because of her physical and cognitive disabilities, even if there is no overt discrimination against women (which is a rather strong assumption). If she gives birth to a child while still in her teens, it is likely that her baby will also be underweight and without corrective nutrition, she will also grow stunted and liable to go through the same trauma as her mother. Unfortunately, the latter kind of fate awaits girls in many poor families in poor countries and even in rich countries. Thus class differences become transmitted from generation to generation, unless strong public action corrects deficiencies in nutrition, care and social norms of marriage or cohabitation and the education of all children, and especially, girls.

The rise of Britain as the first 'industrial nation' can be largely explained by the fact that it was the first country that provided the social and institutional conditions that allowed the process of cumulative causation in the economic sphere to become a strong force. If, however, cumulative causation operated forever or was confined to only one country or region, then no region or nation could ever have caught up with Britain. Other industrialising countries could catch up because the growth of the pioneers had spread effects, and because labour migrated from more backward regions to the growing regions. The outward movement of labour from the backward regions raised their per capita resource endowments and more importantly, the bargaining power of labour. Moreover, the congested sites of accumulation suffered diseconomies of agglomeration. The jinx of backwardness can also be exorcised by deliberate policies to bring about social transformation. On the other hand, the influence of favourable resource endowments can be wholly negated by policies obstructing social transformation and structural breaks.

I will illustrate these general propositions by invoking the history of major Latin American countries as against that of the USA, and by examining the reasons for differences in the regional growth within India. Several countries in Latin America such as Brazil, Argentina and Mexico were rich in their endowments of land and other natural resources as was the United States of America. But while the USA was free of feudal institutions to start with and an entrenched planter oligarchy, thriving on slave labour, was severely enfeebled by the American Civil War, the Latin American countries inherited semi-feudal institutions from the time of their independence. In practically all these countries, landlord rule was further consolidated by the *criollo* ruling class after independence. The social structure impeded the growth of a free market in various ways, kept the peasants and workers impoverished, allowed a very large part of the social surplus to be wasted in conspicuous consumption and badly dented investment incentives of domestic capital. These structural differences would go a long way to explain both their increasing backwardness compared with the USA and the dependence of the ruling class of these countries on the favour of imperialist powers, starting with Britain and ending with the USA (Furtado, 1963; Bagchi, 1982; Morris, 1992; Long and Roberts, 1994a; Hoff and Stiglitz, 2001). (Long and Roberts, 1994b, contains a detailed bibliography of the agrarian structures and their evolution in Latin America since the nineteenth century.) In most Latin American countries, only feeble efforts were made to alter inherited agrarian structures and give land to the actual producers. Export orientation of landlord-dominated agriculture exacerbated inequality, rural–urban differences and waste of investible resources. These effects were exacerbated by the debt crisis and the structural adjustment policies that were largely brought about by the capital flight in which the rich of these countries played the leading role.

In many cases, the socio-political differences between landlord- or enclave-dominated rural areas, and social systems characterised by a greater degree of equality, would go a long way to explain the relatively low levels of human development in the former compared with their potential. It is not an accident that Cuba under communist rule, with a much lower level of per capita income than Brazil or Colombia, shows higher levels of human development in such areas as education and health. The Cuban case also illustrates the importance of a structural break for altering the pattern of economic and human development – a break that was attained through a revolutionary movement.

In India, the British introduced basically three types of land tenure systems for the field crops cultivated by peasants. Under the first system (*zamindari* or *taluqdari*), the peasants paid taxes to revenue farmers who paid more or less fixed amounts to the government but who were free to increase their imposts on the peasants. Under the second system (*raiyatwari*), the peasants or the presumed cultivators of the land paid their taxes directly to the government, which could, and did raise their taxes when it judged that the yield of the land had increased. The third system conferred true private property on the owners since they got the land permanently, or on a very long lease, on payment of a one-off fee, and did not have to pay an annual tax as a condition of ownership. Planters, who were predominantly European, enjoyed this privilege, and we will ignore it.

The colonial government had thus an incentive to invest in public infrastructure, mainly large-scale irrigation and roads, in the *raiyatwari* areas, and thereby improve land productivity, and it did so. By contrast, revenue farmers had neither the means nor the incentive to invest in such infrastructure. As a consequence, in British India, land productivity either declined or remained stagnant in the *zamindari* areas (regions containing the major part of the population) but improved in the *raiyatwari* regions. Ironically, these differences persisted in post-independence India (Bagchi, 1976; Banerjee and Iyer, 2002). Except for a few states such as Kerala and West Bengal, where pro-peasant land reforms have been carried out, the states that had been under the *zamindari* system also perform worse in respect of health and education than the other states. The local governments in the former states are dominated by landlords and spend too little on public infrastructure and deny the poor access to the infrastructure that is built with public money (Bagchi, 2002; Banerjee and Iyer, 2002). The differences between these two groups of states also extend to credit networks, especially in rural areas. Peasants in *raiyatwari* areas were much freer than in *zamindari* areas to offer their land and other assets to banks or micro-credit institutions or *nidhis* (Ray, 2003). We generally find a much denser network of credit institutions catering to farmers in the former than in the *zamindari* areas. Again, these differences persist in contemporary India: there is a much greater penetration of bank branches into the towns and villages of southern India, and the credit/deposit ratios are also higher in the southern region than in the rest of India. But those ratios have tended to decline in most parts of India under the impact of economic liberalisation.

We will exemplify our point about the influence of serendipity, initial conditions and structural breaks with some illustrations from East and South East Asia. After the Second World War and especially in the wake of the Korean War, the US government wanted to build up Japan, South Korea, Taiwan, the Philippines and Thailand as bastions against the threat of the spread of communism. The exports of these countries were given favourable access to the US market. They also received substantial volumes of US aid, military assistance and military contracts, especially after the outbreak of the US–Vietnamese war. This serendipitous advantage caused by the geo-political situation took care of the balance-of-payments deficits that often accompanied ambitious industrialisation programmes. Yet South Korea and Taiwan pushed ahead along the industrialisation path whereas Thailand and the Philippines lagged far behind. We can adduce two basic reasons for this difference. The first is that in South Korea and Taiwan, thoroughgoing, pro-peasant land reforms were carried out. But this did not happen in Thailand and the Philippines. A second, connected reason is that Taiwan and South Korea promoted literacy and education much earlier and more consistently than the other two countries.

Fernand Braudel (1958) had advocated the writing of history with different time spans to take care of the speed with which different factors influencing the human condition change. The longest time spans, the '*longue durée*' in Braudel's phrase, in this classification can be assigned to mental states or ideologies ruling in particular societies, including their ruling groups, the constraints imposed by geography and by basic socio-political structures. Patrick O'Brien (1996) has invoked the Braudelian paradigm to explain the differences between Britain and France in respect of the timing of the onset of industrialisation between the two countries and the much slower rate of release of labour from agriculture in France.

Taking the contrast between typical Latin American realms and the industrially advanced East Asian countries, again, it is noticeable how strong nationalism is among the ruling classes in East Asia as compared with its weakness among those of countries of Latin America. One index of this is that on the few occasions on which the East Asian countries have had to go to the IMF for assistance in the case of a balance-of-payments crisis, the governments have taken strong steps to see that this does not happen again, or at least not because of their own policies. In Latin America, by contrast, balance-of-payments crises have been endemic. Apart from the difficulties generated by the typical structural adjustment programmes (SAPs), a major contributory factor has been the systematic export of capital by the ruling classes in Latin America. They have often taken advantage of the temporary stability of exchange rates induced by the SAPs to export more capital, thus ensuring that there would soon be another balance-of-payments crisis. Another illustration of the *longue durée* in the ideological sphere is the continued female foeticide and infanticide in a whole swath of countries stretching from China and South Korea in the East through South Asia (barring Sri Lanka) to West Asia and North Africa in the West (Sen, 1999). In China, under Maoist communism, this tendency had gone down; but with the embrace of 'market socialism', it has assumed ferocious proportions again. In all these countries, including India, new technologies of pre-natal sex selection have made it easier to carry out this inhuman practice and the rich seem to be indulging in it more extensively than the poor.

Development studies often degenerate into a search for instant solutions that come unstuck almost as soon as they are proposed. One reason is that there is no attempt to understand the constraints that social and political structures and mental habits pose in the way of promoting human development for everybody and to work towards bringing about changes in those constraints that are the most constricting. A deep knowledge of history of those constraints, and the opportunities that may be opened up with their removal is essential for success in studies of economic and human development and their implementation.

AMIYA BAGCHI

References

Arthur, B. (1989), 'Competing technologies, increasing returns, and lock-in by historical events', *Economic Journal*, **99**, 116–31.

Bagchi, Amiya K. (1976), 'Reflections on patterns of regional growth in India under British rule', *Bengal Past and Present*, **95** (1), 247–89.

Bagchi, Amiya K. (1982), *The Political Economy of Underdevelopment*, Cambridge: Cambridge University Press.

Bagchi, Amiya K. (1998), 'Development', in H.D. Kurz and N. Salvadori (eds), *The Elgar Companion to Classical Economics*, Cheltenham, UK and Northampton, MA, USA: Edward Elgar, pp. 213–17.

Bagchi, Amiya K. (2002), 'Agrarian transformation and human development: instrumental and constitutive links', in V.K. Ramachandran and M. Swaminathan (eds), *Agrarian Studies: Essays on Agrarian Relations in Less-Developed Countries*, New Delhi: Tulika, pp. 153–65.

Banerjee, Avijit V. and Lakshmi Iyer (2002), 'History, institutions and economic performance: the legacy of colonial land tenure systems in India', unpublished, Department of Economics, Massachusetts Institute of Technology, Cambridge, MA, USA.

Bogin, B. (1999), *Patterns of Human Growth*, 2nd edn, Cambridge: Cambridge University Press.

Braudel, F. (1958), 'History and the social sciences: the *longue durée*', *Annales E.S.C.*, no. 4; translated from the French and reprinted in Fernand Braudel (1980), *On History*, London: Weidenfeld & Nicolson, pp. 25–54.

David, P.A. (1985), 'Clio and the economics of QWERTY', *American Economic Review*, **75**, 332–37.

Eveleth, P.B. and J.M. Tanner (1990), *Worldwide Variation in Human Growth*, 2nd edn, Cambridge: Cambridge University Press.

Furtado, C. (1963), *The Economic Growth of Brazil: A Survey from Colonial to Modern Times*, Berkeley, CA: University of California Press.

Hoff, Karla and Joseph E. Stiglitz (2001), 'Modern economic theory and development', in G.M. Meier and J.E. Stiglitz (eds), *Frontiers of Development Economics*, New York and Oxford: Oxford University Press for the World Bank, pp. 389–459.

Kaldor, Nicholas (1972), 'The irrelevance of equilibrium economics', *Economic Journal*, **82**, 1237–55.

Long, N. and B. Roberts (1994a), 'The agrarian structures of Latin America, 1930–1990', in L. Bethell (ed.), *The Cambridge History of Latin America, vol. VI: Latin America since 1930, Economy, Society and Politics*, Cambridge: Cambridge University Press, pp. 325–90.

Long, N. and B. Roberts (1994b), 'Bibliographical essays', in L. Bethell (ed.), *The Cambridge History of Latin America, vol. VI: Latin America since 1930, Economy, Society and Politics*, Cambridge: Cambridge University Press, pp. 537–608.

Marx, K. (1867), *Capital: A Critique of Political Economy*, vol. 1, translated from the German by E. Aveling and S. Moore, London: Swan Sonnenschein 1887; reprinted Moscow: Foreign Languages Publishing House, 1960.

Morris, Cynthia Taft (1992), 'Politics, development, and equity in five land-rich countries in the latter nineteenth century', *Research in Economic History*, **14**, 1–68.

Myrdal, Gunnar (1957), *Economic Theory and Underdeveloped Regions*, London: Gerald Duckworth.

North, Douglass C. and Robert P. Thomas (1973), *The Rise of the Western World: A New Economic History*, Cambridge: Cambridge University Press.

O'Brien, Patrick K. (1996), 'Path dependency, or why Britain became an industrialized and urbanized economy long before France', *Economic History Review*, **49** (2), 213–49.

Ray, Mamata (2003), 'Regional financial institutions: lending behaviour and path-dependence, Madras 1921–1969', PhD thesis, University of Calcutta.

Sen, Amartya K. (1999), *Development as Freedom*, New York: A.A. Knopf.

Smith, A. (1776 [1976]), *An Inquiry into the Nature and Causes of the Wealth of Nations*, vol. II of *The Glasgow Edition of the Works and Correspondence of Adam Smith*, edited by R.H. Campbell, A.S. Skinner and W.B. Todd, Oxford: Oxford University Press.

Tanner, J.M. (1981), *A History of the Study of Human Growth*, Cambridge: Cambridge University Press.

Tucker, Josiah (1774), *Four Tracts on Political and Commercial Subjects*, 2nd edn, printed by R. Raikes and sold by J. Rivington, Gloucester and London.

HIV/AIDS and Development

HIV and AIDS

HIV (human immunodeficiency virus) is a general term for what may be thought of as a group of closely related viruses known as HIV-1. Another virus, HIV-2 is responsible for a small epidemic in parts of West Africa but this appears to be a less vigorous organism and is increasingly displaced by HIV-1. There are many subtypes of the HIV-1 group and some of these may themselves be further subdivided.

These viruses cause a breakdown of the human body's ability to defend itself against infections and other diseases. Infection is through exchange of body fluids. This occurs in most cases through sexual intercourse but mother to child transmission during birth, contaminated medical equipment such as re-used syringes, infected blood and blood products and injection drug equipment are all important pathways for infection to take place. Globally, most infections occur via heterosexual intercourse. In parts of Russia, the Baltic, Central Asia, China, India and South East Asia, such heterosexual epidemics are rooted in a preceding epidemic associated with intravenous drug use and shared injecting equipment.

When the immune system no longer functions effectively, a person's health fails with a characteristic range of opportunistic infections finally overwhelming the system. This is called AIDS: acquired immunodeficiency syndrome. Where people's health is poor to begin with, the chances of infection increase. This is often the case with poor people who do not have access to medical care and who are likely to live in unhealthy conditions and/or do dangerous or unhealthy work. Where people's health status includes untreated or partially treated sexually transmitted infections like genital warts, genital herpes or any of a range of common sexually transmitted infections, the chances of contracting HIV from an infected partner increase dramatically. Poor diet is probably a factor contributing to the rate of transition from infection to illness and to the rate at which the illness develops.

Without expensive anti-retroviral therapy (ART) which is available to many people with HIV infection and AIDS in richer communities (but not to all people in rich countries, it depends on the local system of health provision), the end result of HIV infection is death from AIDS. The mean period from infection to death is around 8.5 years although some people are 'early progressors' and become sick and die within a year or so, while others are 'later progressors' and survive for as long as 20 years. Initial infection results in a mild 'flu-like illness and the person soon recovers. During the intervening period until they become sick, they may lead a normal life and be completely unaware of their status. They are infectious during this period and so each person may infect each of his/her sexual partners.

Because this disease is mainly sexually transmitted, it has very important social and economic implications for development. It affects the structure of populations and therefore the supply and quality of labour.

Estimates and terminology

In talking about HIV/AIDS it is most important be clear as to the difference between HIV (the virus) and AIDS (the illness).

In the absence of surveys of whole populations (which would be logistically impossible and very expensive) rates of *HIV infection* can only be estimated on the basis of sample surveys of particular populations, for example women attending ante-natal clinics. In contrast, reported rates of AIDS illness may be fairly inaccurate, depending on the ability of clinicians to diagnose and on the efficiency with which reporting systems enable diagnosis counts to reach national authorities and then international databases. Poor countries are more likely to have poorer statistics.

HIV rates are described in terms of the level of *seroprevalence* – the percentage of the whole population or the adult population estimated to be HIV+ at the time of reporting. AIDS cases are reported in terms of the number of cases per 100 000 of the population. Another measure which appears in discussions of HIV and AIDS is the notion of *incidence* which describes the number of new infections or cases which occur in a particular period, usually a year.

In some of the worst-affected countries, notably Botswana and Swaziland, national adult seroprevalence has reached 40 per cent. Readers may like to ask themselves whether rates of 'only' 5 per cent (Ghana in 2003) or 'only' 1 per cent (Russia in 2003) can really be considered 'low'. Readers may also like to reflect on the question of 'data accuracy'. Data often have an inevitable element of estimation. When this turns out to be an over-estimate, much may be made of the 'political' or even 'self-interested' attitudes of those who produce such estimates. In fact these are hard calls to make and – as with the 2004 Demographic and Health Survey study of Kenya showing that national HIV prevalence was closer to 6.7 per cent than the previously estimated 9.4 per cent of adults – the response may well be 'so what!'. That 6.7 per cent may be 40 per cent lower than 9.4 per cent, but it is still pretty worrying. It means that in a few years' time 6.7 per cent of the adult population will be suffering from severe illness. And it does not stop there, as there will be more in the future. That must be a development impact.

HIV/AIDS – the global situation
Tables 6 and 7 summarise the global HIV/AIDS situation as at the end of 2005 as estimated by UNAIDS, the United Nations Joint Programme on HIV/AIDS.

HIV/AIDS and population
The most seriously affected areas of the world are in Africa. But it is probable that some countries and regions in South Asia (India has the world's largest number of HIV infections – reflecting its huge population size), South East Asia and China, will follow this pattern in the next decade.

In some of the hardest-hit countries, AIDS has begun to alter population structures in ways which have not been seen before. Because it is mainly sexually transmitted, HIV/AIDS picks off society's young adults and mature workers and carers.

It is important to recognise that AIDS deaths are *premature deaths*. In countries where HIV spreads mainly through sex between men and women, the majority of infected people acquire HIV by the time they are in their twenties and thirties. Without anti-retroviral treatment, they can be expected to die of AIDS within ten years of initial infection.

Particularly in Sub-Saharan African countries, where such large proportions of the population have HIV or have already died of AIDS, these premature deaths are altering

Table 6   Global HIV/AIDS estimates, end of 2005

People living with HIV/AIDS	40.3 million (range 36.7–45.3 million)
New HIV infections in 2005	4.9 million (range 4.3–6.6 million)

Source: UNAIDS (2005, p. 3).

Table 7   The global HIV/AIDS epidemic by major world regions, 2005

Region	Adults and children living with HIV/AIDS	Adults and children newly infected with HIV	Adult prevalence (%)*	Adult and child deaths due to AIDS
Sub-Saharan Africa	23.8–28.9 million	2.8–3.9 million	6.6–8.0	2.1–2.7 million
North Africa & Middle East	230 000–1.4 million	35 000–200 000	0.1–0.7	25 000–145 000
South & South East Asia	4.5–11.0 million	480 000–2.4 million	0.4–1.0	290 000–740 000
East Asia	440 000–1.4 million	42 000–390 000	0.05–0.2	20 000–68 000
Oceania	45 000–120 000	2400–25 000	0.2–0.7	1700–8200
Latin America	1.4–2.4 million	130 000–360 000	0.5–0.8	52 000–86 000
Caribbean	200 000–510 000	17 000–71 000	1.1–2.7	16 000–40 000
Eastern Europe & Central Asia	990 000–2.3 million	140 000–610 000	0.6–1.3	39 000–91 000
Western and Central Europe	570 000–890 000	15 000–39 000	0.2–0.4	<15 000
North America	650 000–1.8 million	15 000–120 000	0.4–1.1	9000–30 000
Total	40.3 million (36.7–45.3 million)	4.9 million (4.3–6.6 million)	1.1 (1.0–1.3)	3.1 million (2.8–3.6 million)

Notes: *The proportion of adults (15 to 49 years of age) living with HIV/AIDS in 2005, using 2005 population numbers. The ranges around the estimates in this table define the boundaries within which the actual numbers lie, based on the best available information.

Source: UNAIDS (2005, p. 3).

the structure of the population with resultant effects on households, communities and ultimately whole countries. Households experience many costs – both quantifiable and hard to quantify – associated with coping and caring as well as with livelihoods. Many of these costs have a gender dimension. Cumulative household and individual costs weaken communities' ability to cope with the exigencies of already impoverished livelihood strategies. Ultimately, whole nations experience the effects. Economists have calculated that in Africa the AIDS epidemic costs national economies between 1 and 2 per cent of GDP growth per year. But there are of course many other less easily estimable costs of which we know nothing.

HIV will kill at least a third of the young men and women of countries where it has its firmest hold, and in some places up to two-thirds. In 2002, UNAIDS commented: 'Despite millennia of epidemics, war and famine, never before in history have death rates of this magnitude been seen among young adults of both sexes and from all walks of life' (UNAIDS, 2002, p. i).

AIDS and development

Anti-retroviral treatments are used to treat AIDS in rich countries. They are costly and complex but for many people they extend active and participative life for many decades – as long as treatment continues. However, these medications are available to only a very small proportion of the world's poorest people who need them. The World Health Organization has set an ambitious target of providing treatment to 3 million people who need it by 2005. This is a drop in the ocean of real demand.

In the absence of effective and available vaccines – which are not currently on the medium-term horizon – or economically feasible and effective treatments, AIDS will wipe out half a century of development gains as measured by life expectancy at birth. From 44 years in the early 1950s, life expectancy rose to 59 in the early 1990s. Now, a child born between 2005 and 2010 can once again expect to die before his or her 45th birthday. In some parts of Africa, life expectancy at birth has decreased to levels not seen for millennia.

Life expectancy and child mortality rates have been widely used as markers for development. In Botswana, life expectancy at birth is now estimated to be 39 years instead of 71 without AIDS. In Zimbabwe, life expectancy is 38 instead of 70. In fact, children born today in Botswana, Malawi, Mozambique, Rwanda, Zambia and Zimbabwe have life expectancies below 40 years of age. They would have been 50 years or more without AIDS.

Due to these substantial increases in child mortality, only five out of 51 countries in Sub-Saharan Africa will reach the International Conference on Population and Development goals for decreased child mortality. The Millennium Development Goals are threatened by the HIV/AIDS epidemic – and not only in Africa.

Wider development impacts

The premature death of half of the adult population, typically at ages when they have already started to form their own families and have become economically productive, can be expected to have a radical effect on virtually every aspect of social and economic life.

Conclusion

The conclusion is very simple. HIV/AIDS presents a wide range of development challenges. There is no area of development policy which can omit to take HIV/AIDS into account. It will affect industrial production, agriculture, mining and above all the households in poor countries. In as much as households are essential to social and cultural reproduction but their contributions are not measured in official statistics, it is inevitable that the full social and economic impact of HIV/AIDS will go unnoticed until the effects are very large. While HIV/AIDS is currently seen at its worst in Africa, India, China and Russia, all confront substantial epidemics in the decade ahead. The epidemic has economic, social, cultural and political implications for development.

Guide to further reading

The following sources are useful for people wanting to follow up these issues in more detail. Goudsmit's (1997) book is first because it is vital when dealing with disease to have a good understanding of the mechanics of that disease. So, with HIV/AIDS, it is essential to have knowledge of the virology, clinical features and epidemiology. Goudsmit is a good starting-point. Barnett and Blaikie's (1992) *AIDS in Africa* was the first field-based study of the social and economic effects of the epidemic – and many of its lessons have still to be taken on board! Barnett and Whiteside's (2006) *AIDS in the Twenty-First Century* is a comprehensive account of the social and economic impact of the epidemic and also gives some basic epidemiology. Moatti et al. (2003) provide an excellent review of the issues to do with anti-retroviral treatments. This can be found in electronic form at www.iaen.org – the website of the International AIDS and Economics Network. The annual *Report on the Global HIV/AIDS Epidemic* should also be a key source and is available together with much else of use at www.unaids.org. Another important source for epidemiological data is the US Bureau of the Census www.census.gov.

Tony Barnett

References and further reading

Barnett, T. and P. Blaikie (1992), *AIDS in Africa: Its Present and Future Impact*, London: Wiley, and New York: Guilford Press.
Barnett, T. and A. Whiteside (2006), *AIDS in the Twenty-First Century: Disease and Globalisation*, 2nd revised edn, London and New York: Palgrave-Macmillan.
Goudsmit, J. (1997), *Viral Sex: The Nature of AIDS*, Oxford: Oxford University Press.
Moatti, J.-P., T. Barnett, B. Coriat, Y. Souteyrand, J. Dumoulin and Y.A. Flori (eds) (2003), *Economics of AIDS and Access to HIV/AIDS Care in Developing Countries: Issues and Challenges*, Paris: ANRS (Agence Nationale de Recherches sur le Sida: National Agency for AIDS Research).
UNAIDS (2002), *Report on the Global HIV/AIDS Epidemic 2002*, Geneva: UNAIDS.
UNAIDS (2005), AIDS Epidemic Update: December 2005, Geneva: UNAIDS, www.unaids.org/epi/2005/doc/report_pdf.asp.

Human Capital

A central concern in development economics is why some countries are rich and others poor. Some would explain these differences in terms of historical endowments, others in terms of contemporary institutions. Many would attribute these differences to *human capital* – the capacity of human beings as productive agents to promote increases in income through the acquisition of skills and the accumulation of knowledge. Basic health and education, which are central to human capital acquisition, are also central to the process of development. Valuable in their own right, such investments are highly complementary with other dimensions of progress such as generating income and poverty alleviation.

Human capital comprises the collective accumulation of investments in education, training and health that raises the productive capacity of people (Becker, 1975). The notion of investment in human beings that increases the economic efficiency of individual decision making has roots in the writings of Adam Smith and Alfred Marshall. Smith was the first to link human capital investments and labour market skills with wages and income distribution. Central to the notion of human capital is that individuals and governments may invest in education and health to improve production. In so far as this yields returns both to individuals and to society, the economic effects of human capital investment, and the patterns of the returns to that investment, matter for economic development (Becker, 1975). Consequently, human capital investment is of consequence at both the microeconomic and macroeconomic levels. This entry reviews the microeconomic and macroeconomic models of human capital, and empirical studies of human capital and development.

Microeconomics of human capital

At the micro level, two aspects of human capital are worthy of attention – first, it encapsulates both skills and knowledge: skills that enhance productivity and knowledge that generates innovation. Investing in human capital raises the market value of future labour supply and it is deliberately accumulated by investment in training and education by individuals. Second, earnings from investments in human capital are equal to a rate of return on those investments, with an important role being played both by earnings over the lifetime and human capital wealth (Rosen, 1998). If viewed in this way, then investments in human capital are determined by a complex set of factors such as school quality, earnings and the background characteristics of families.

An august lineage of economists have devoted themselves to the elaboration of the concept of human capital, and to its elucidation in microeconomic models, such as, for example, Schultz (1961), Mincer (1974), Becker (1975) and others. Economists such as Theodore Schultz linked the skills element with the health and well-being of populations more widely as measured by their better health, lower mortality, or greater life expectancy. An initial conception of human capital was thereby broadened to focus both on skill and knowledge acquisition, and on investments in health capital. Contemporary studies of human capital therefore focus on how different kinds of human capital investments interact. One example is studies of the relationship between workers' earnings and their health and nutritional status, after controlling for workers' experience post-schooling (Strauss and Thomas, 1995). Another example is whether health investments are related to gender bias, altering the level of education that girls and boys attain (Miguel and Kremer, 2001). All this suggests that human capital valuation today includes a range of factors – education in the form of primary schooling for basic literacy and numeracy, basic health such as access to maternal and child healthcare, but equally better opportunities to obtain both education and healthcare. Consequently, empirically quantifying the returns to schooling and health have been pre-eminent concerns. Randomised trials in order to test the impact on human capital investments of the supply of education provision have been undertaken (Duflo, 2001).

Human capital theory at the individual level is also concerned with earnings and consequently, with experience. Empirically, both schooling and experience on the job matter. Mincer's work on this issue, in which he argued that schooling explained less than 7 per cent of earnings differentials and that experience was important for any cohort of individuals with similar schooling levels, has largely driven the empirical research on this issue in developing and developed countries alike (Mincer, 1974). More recent work has shown a positive impact of schooling on subsequent earnings (Krueger and Lindahl, 2000). But in primarily agricultural societies, human capital investments will also be related to access to land and credit markets, which are characterised by asymmetric information and market failures. For example, in the face of exogenous shocks such as adverse weather, families with land will be more able to borrow in order to finance human capital investments compared to the landless (Jacoby and Skoufias, 1997). Similarly, credit market imperfections will affect schooling decisions if children are kept home from school for their labour or for old-age security. But identifying the direction and degree of causality between these variables is fraught with difficulty. Empirical studies of human capital at the micro level, especially using data from poor countries, have therefore faced specific problems with respect to the presence of omitted variables, and problems of measurement when aggregating multiple sources of human capital (Schultz, 2003).

Macroeconomics of human capital
At the macro level, human capital investment is important for development, and models of endogenous growth have formalised this relationship. In these models, an endogenous accumulation of human capital is considered in the context of the Solow growth model (Solow, 1956; Lucas, 1988; Romer, 1990). Lucas (1993) argued that human capital is the 'engine of growth'. Endogenous growth models postulate that many countries are poor because they are less well-endowed with human capital. In these models, the inputs of production are usually distinguished as physical and human capital. Human capital is deliberately accumulated. Income, physical capital and human capital are assumed to grow at a common rate, which is determined both by the savings rate and by the propensity to invest in human capital. The larger is the ratio of saving in human capital relative to that of physical capital, the larger is the long-run ratio of both variables. The long-run rate of growth is then a product of the fraction of income saved to accumulate physical capital and the fraction used to augment the quality of human capital through education. In these models, the positive externalities associated with human capital formation outweigh the effects of the rising capital–output ratio.

These models have sparked debate about 'convergence' among nations, and whether or not they imply that rich countries, or regions, may grow faster than poor ones. This is because the assumption of diminishing rates of return on physical capital is counteracted by an ever-expanding stock of human capital. If rich countries, or some regions within countries, are better endowed with human capital, then perpetual – and higher – growth therein is possible. But many models also assume that the effect of human capital investments, for example in education, would affect the productivity of labour equally across different jobs in the economy. This assumption is relaxed in models of endogenous growth that link education with technological diffusion. For example, education may affect growth because education increases the capacity of individuals to undertake technological innovations, increasing the speed of technological diffusion (Nelson and Phelps, 1966). The key implication for developing countries is that investments in human capital will increase as the economy becomes more developed technologically. As economies develop, there is greater emphasis on research and development activities, and correspondingly greater investments in the higher education sector compared to primary and secondary schooling. Human capital investments are also self-sustaining – greater investments in education and health lead to higher growth which in turn generates further resources for investment in human capital. Such symbiotic reciprocity is evident in many regions of the world, for example, in South East Asia, China and in states such as Kerala and Himachal Pradesh in India. The historical experience of countries in East Asia, such as Japan, Taiwan, Hong Kong and South Korea, all provide testimony to rapid economic growth, attributable to an educated and well-trained labour force.

The importance of human capital is also illustrated by its central role in poverty alleviation. Coordination failures sustain poverty traps in developing countries. A direct way out of the vicious circle of poverty traps is the acquisition of human capital. Human capital also ameliorates other factors, which sustain poverty traps such as high fertility and high mortality, by allowing parents to conduct the appropriate trade-off between increased 'quantity' of children, in favour of better 'quality', as measured by human capital investments in them. This trade-off explains the relationship between high incomes, high levels of human capital and low birth rates (Becker, 1975).

Finally, the importance of human capital for development arises from it being worthy in itself – an educated and healthy population is intrinsic for progress. But it has even greater value than this: human capital enables individuals to achieve a larger set of opportunities to increase their welfare. In poor countries, this is most particularly true for the empowerment of girls, who are often discriminated against by the unequal allocation of resources in the home. Human capital also engenders social externalities more widely: in many poor societies, human capital functions both as a signalling and as a sorting mechanism, ordering for example the marriage market. A more literate labour force may encourage democratic institutions or greater discussion of social welfare issues. In hierarchical and racially disparate societies, human capital acquisition will be important for the upward mobility of groups.

Empirical studies of human capital

Empirical studies of human capital have shown that there is a very close relationship between increases in living standards and increases in education and health. Human capital may therefore explain why the standard of living varies enormously between countries and why the pattern of growth rates differs too. In empirical research, human capital is measured by a number of indicators: literacy rates, primary and secondary school enrolments, life expectancy, institutions of higher education, and so forth. Before the nineteenth century, there is little empirical evidence that investment in human capital was important. But in the twentieth century, macro-level studies that looked at increases in total factor productivity have found that human capital investments, as measured by schooling, nutrition and health, are significant for economic growth (Barro and Sala-i-Martin, 1995). In this study, for a large sample of countries, for the 1965–85 period, years in schooling is significantly correlated with subsequent growth and public spending on education in particular, has a positive effect on growth. Mankiw et al. (1992), take three samples of countries over the 1960–85 period: 98 oil-producing countries, 76 developing countries, and 22 OECD countries. This study finds that differences in savings rates and population growth account for over 50 per cent of income differences between countries. When the Solow model is augmented for differences in human capital formation (proxied by secondary school enrolment rates), it 'explains' 80 per cent of the differences in per capita income, and human capital formation is significant for all three samples. More recent studies test the model over a longer time period and for different continents, such as East Asia, Latin America and Sub-Saharan Africa. These results are less conclusive, but are still broadly consistent with the predictions of the augmented Solow model.

The state of human capital in poor countries today presents a mixed picture. Although there are individual examples of countries in which education and health are poorly provided, overall health and education provision is approaching that in richer nations (Schultz, 2003). A study of the rates of return to education in developing countries shows that the highest rate of return comes from investment in primary education (Psacharopoulos, 1994). The rate of return declines with the level of schooling, and with the level of development. In most countries, social rates of return are less than private rates of return, as the costs of education are borne by the state, occasioned by the innate public goods characteristics of health and education. But some poor economies suffer from significant underprovision of education. In the short run, educational investments may not raise economic growth if not matched by corresponding increases in the rate of growth of physical capital, as has been witnessed in parts of Africa, but in the long run, educational investments are usually very productive.

This suggests that investment in education needs to focus both on the quantity and on the quality of education. Focusing on school quantity affects both earnings and the returns to schooling. An Indonesian policy experiment conducted on 61 000 primary schools, using a 'difference in difference' estimator, which controls for variation across cohorts and across regions, isolates the effect of a programme to increase school quantity (Duflo, 2001). Each school built per 1000 children in the sample increases the education of children aged 2–6 by 0.12 years, and increases subsequent wages up to 3.8 per cent. Increases in the exogenous returns to education using the exogenous variation in schooling, is of the order of up to 9.1 per cent. Recent evidence also shows that there are strong positive effects of school quality measures on earnings and on educational returns (Bedi and Edwards, 2002). This study of Honduran males aged 14–35 shows that an increase by one standard deviation in school quality measures (such as teacher quality, student–teacher ratio, the table–student ratio, and the provision of electricity) increases educational returns by 1.2 per cent. Other studies of education, for example in India, also reflect the importance of school quality (Drèze and Kingdon, 2001). In a survey of 96 studies, the evidence provides little support to reduce class sizes; instead, it is found that the teacher's experience and education, and school facilities, are critical (Psacharopoulos, 1994). The moral of the story provided by the empirical research on human capital then is to provide schools with greater incentives to increase both quantity and quality, in order that the returns to education will be high in developing countries.

Marshall's prophecy
Differences in economic development are associated with differences in human capital. Microeconomic and macroeconomic models of human capital, historical experience and empirical studies support this claim. Consequently, the Dakar framework pledges to provide universal primary education in poor countries by 2015 even though a quarter of children in these countries today still receive no primary education. An education is worth

investing in, especially for girls. But it is equally important to target both the quantity and the quality of education.

The simple lesson to be learned from the theory of human capital is that it is possible to explain why some countries are rich and others poor by differences in their endowment and acquisition of human capital. In 1890, in the *Principles of Economics*, Alfred Marshall argued that 'The most valuable of all capital is that invested in human beings' (1961 edition, p. 564). Alfred Marshall's prophecy was prescient – if the most valuable of all capital is indeed that invested in human beings, then for developing economies especially, there can be no better investment than that in human capital.

SRIYA IYER

References

Barro, Robert and Xavier Sala-i-Martin (1995), *Economic Growth*, New York: McGraw-Hill.
Becker, Gary (1975), *Human Capital*, New York: Columbia University Press.
Bedi, A.S. and J.H.Y. Edwards (2002), 'The impact of school quality on earnings and educational returns – evidence from a low-income country', *Journal of Development Economics*, **68**, 157–85.
Drèze J. and G.G. Kingdon (2001), 'School participation in rural India', *Review of Development Economics*, **5**, 1–24.
Duflo, E. (2001), 'Schooling and labour market consequences of school construction in Indonesia', *American Economic Review*, **91**, 795–813.
Jacoby, G.H. and E. Skoufias (1997), 'Risk, financial markets, and human capital in a developing country', *Review of Economic Studies*, **64** (3), 311–35.
Krueger, A. and M. Lindahl (2000), 'Education for growth: why and for whom?', *Journal of Economic Literature*, **39** (4), 1101–36.
Lucas, R.E. (1988), 'On the mechanics of economic development', *Journal of Monetary Economics*, **22** (1), 3–42.
Lucas, R.E. (1993), 'Making a miracle', *Econometrica*, **61** (2), 251–72.
Mankiw, N., P. Romer and D. Weil (1992), 'A contribution to the empirics of economic growth', *Quarterly Journal of Economics*, **107**, 407–38.
Marshall, Alfred (1890), *Principles of Economics*, Volume 1 Text, 9th (Varorium) edn 1961, with annotations by C.W. Guillebaud, London: Macmillan & Co Ltd for the Royal Economic Society.
Miguel, E. and M. Kremer (2001), 'Worms: education and health externalities in Kenya', National Bureau of Economic Research Working Paper 8481, Cambridge, MA, September, pp. 1–64.
Mincer, Jacob (1974), *Schooling, Experience and Earnings*, New York: Columbia University Press.
Nelson, R. and E. Phelps (1966), 'Investment in humans, technological diffusion, and economic growth', *American Economic Review: Papers and Proceedings*, **61**, 69–75.
Psacharopoulos, G. (1994), 'Returns to investment in education: a global update', *World Development*, **22** (9), September, 1325–43.
Romer, P. (1990), 'Endogenous technological change', *Journal of Political Economy*, **98**, 71–101.
Rosen, S. (1998), 'Human capital', in the *The New Palgrave: A Dictionary of Economics*, Vol. 2, E–J, 681–90, London: Palgrave.
Schultz, T.P. (2003), 'Human capital, schooling and health', *Economics and Human Biology*, **1**, 207–21.
Schultz, T.W. (1961), 'Investments in human capital', *American Economic Review*, **51**, 1–17.
Solow, R. (1956), 'A contribution to the theory of economic growth', *Quarterly Journal of Economics*, **70**, 65–94.
Strauss, J. and D. Thomas (1995), 'Health and labour productivity: sorting out the relationships', in G.H. Peters and D.D. Hedley (eds), *Agricultural Competitiveness: Market Forces and Policy Choice: Proceedings of the Twenty Second International Conference of Agricultural Economists*, Aldershot, UK: Dartmouth. pp. 570–90.

Human Development

The emergence of the human development approach

Modern economics has always been concerned with human welfare. One area of the subject – welfare economics – is dedicated to its study. Yet over time some development economists became convinced that a concern with per capita income growth had led some economists to 'forget' that human beings were both the *ends* as well as the means of development. This central insight was shared by a number of influential economists – including Mahbub ul Haq, Amartya Sen, Paul Streeten and Frances Stewart – and became the central tenet of the human development approach.

Within development economics, the idea of human development emerged from a number of interrelated debates in the 1970s. One key concern in these debates was that the benefits of per capita income growth often do not 'trickle down' to the poorer sections of society. A natural reaction to this worry was to pursue 'redistribution with growth' (Chenery et al., 1974). A different response, which argued for a focus on basic needs, came from the International Labour Organization (1976) and Paul Streeten and others (including Frances Stewart and Mahbub ul Haq). Many of the central ideas of the human development approach were very forcefully expressed by Streeten and his co-authors in *First Things First: Meeting Basic Human Needs in the Developing Countries* (1981), which articulated the 'basic needs approach' to development. They wrote that 'the basic needs concept is a reminder that the objective of development effort is to provide all human beings with the *opportunity* of a full life' (Streeten et al., 1981, p. 21, original emphasis). However, the basic needs approach did not attempt to redefine development itself. Streeten and his co-authors did, none the less, express the worry that in focusing on the *means* rather than the ends of development, some economists may be guilty of what Karl Marx called 'commodity fetishism' – where commodities can acquire a value that is independent of the needs or ends they help to fulfil (ibid.).

Many of these themes can also to be found in early formulations of Amartya Sen's capability approach, which suggested that commodities are not of value in themselves, but only valuable to the extent that they give people the *ability* or *opportunity* to live valuable or flourishing lives. This approach insists that 'capability' – understood in terms of the range of lives (constituted by 'beings' and 'doings' or 'functionings') from which a person can choose – is an important 'space' (if not the only relevant 'space') for the evaluation of the quality of life, egalitarian justice and development. While the capability approach initially emerged in a paper – entitled 'Equality of what?' (Sen, 1980) – about the question of what it is that egalitarians ought to equalise, Sen began to articulate the approach in the context of development in numerous subsequent essays (for example, Sen, 1990). The capability approach also formed part of Sen's broad critique of mainstream welfare economics. In the context of development, Sen went beyond the basic needs school in arguing that we should *redefine* development. He suggested that we needed to move away from the 'traditional' view of development which focused on per capita income growth and to see development as the expansion of human capabilities. His approach allowed the concerns of the basic needs school to be expressed in a broader intellectual framework, with a strong philosophical pedigree established through repeated references to Karl Marx's writings from the 1840s (for example, Marx 1844) and Aristotle's *Nicomachean Ethics*. The philosophical aspect of Sen's work led to an engagement with the writings of the eminent philosopher Martha Nussbaum, who developed her own variation on the capability approach in the late 1980s, based on an interpretation of Aristotle's work (Nussbaum, 1988). However, apart from the Aristotelian connection, the idea of treating human beings as ends – which is central to the human development approach – is also famously expressed by Immanuel Kant who suggested that we should act so as to treat 'humanity . . . in every case as an end withal, never as means only' (Kant, 1987, p. 58).

Many of these ideas were distilled and brought to a large policy-orientated audience by Mahbub ul Haq. Haq's first exposition of his notion of human development appeared in a speech entitled 'People in development' which was given at the United Nations in 1988 (and later published in modified form in his *Reflections on Human Development*, 1995). In this speech, Haq was most concerned with the dominance of national income and its components in development plans. A people-centred view of development would, in his view, replace this focus on national income accounts with a 'human balance sheet'. Haq's view was forcefully developed (in collaboration with others) over time in a series of Human Development Reports published annually by the United Nations Development Programme (UNDP) since 1990. These reports broadly endorsed the notion of development as an expansion of human capabilities. Yet the term 'choice' often replaces Sen's notion of capability – so that development is thought of as a 'process of enlarging choices' (UNDP, 1990, p. 1). This echoes Sen's approach in as much as Sen sees development as an expansion in the range of lives from which people can choose – and to that degree sees it as an expansion of choice or freedom. However, the Human Development Reports treat income as one of the 'choices' people might have, while in the capability approach income and capability are distinct evaluative spaces. None the less, while the precise formulation of the idea of 'human development' in the Human Development Reports differs from Sen's notion of development as capability expansion, the language of the UNDP's reports reflects the influence of a broad range of intellectual frameworks – including the capability approach and the basic needs approach. The UNDP's notion of human development is best conceived of as reflecting a number of key concerns shared by certain development thinkers who worried that human beings were in danger of being forgotten in the obsession with per capita income growth and national income accounts.

Since the UNDP's work on human development highlighted worries about focusing exclusively on economic growth and national income accounting it was natural for the UNDP to look for an alternative to gross domestic product (GDP) per capita which might influence economic policy. The now well-known Human Development Index (HDI) emerged from this desire to produce an index which would show up the limitations of per capita GDP, while at the same time being relatively easy to calculate. The HDI included three dimensions – income, health (measured by life expectancy) and knowledge (measured by a weighted average of the adult literacy rate and either mean years of schooling or the combined enrolment ratio). However, it was clearly stated in the very first *Human Development Report* that the HDI did not capture all the dimensions of human development (UNDP, 1990, p. 16).

The evolution and growing influence of the approach

Over time the Human Development Reports have addressed a wide range of themes such as security, participation, political freedom, human rights and democracy, gender, poverty, environmental concerns, consumption, global inequalities and culture *inter alia*. Because the human development approach has brought a distinct perspective to the analysis of development issues it can articulate an alternative viewpoint on a range of contemporary concerns. The distinctive flavour of the human development approach emerges in the various Human Development Reports and in research which has been inspired by the approach. For example, regarding those among the elderly or disabled who may not be especially productive, a concern with human beings as ends rather than merely means implies a quite different approach to one which would follow from an exclusive focus on GDP per capita. Furthermore, by emphasising the multidimensionality of well-being, the human development approach has highlighted the importance of articulating the dimensions or components of well-being (Qizilbash, 1996; Nussbaum, 2000; Alkire, 2002; and Clark, 2002).

In addressing various issues the paradigm of development has also changed imperceptibly over time. Recognising the importance of the environmental dimension, for example, the conception of development shifted from 'human development' to 'sustainable human development'. The UNDP unsurprisingly developed this broader paradigm under the influence of the well-known report of the World Commission on Environment and Development (1987) or 'Brundtland Commission' which defined 'sustainable development' as development which meets the needs of the present, without compromising the ability of future generations to meet their needs. In the *Human Development Report 1994* this notion was wedded to the idea of human development through an emphasis on inter-generational equity. Similarly gender equality was a central theme of the *Human Development Report 1995*. The original formulation of the notion of 'human development' in the early Human Development Reports has, none the less, survived with limited modifications over the years.

In successive Human Development Reports further measures, particularly measures of gender inequality (such as the gender empowerment measure (GEM) and the gender-related development index) and poverty (the human poverty index) have also emerged. Issues about the precise manner in which the HDI is constructed have, in the meantime, also led to a large literature about weaknesses and refinements of the HDI. The UNDP has adjusted the index in the light of this literature. While some of this literature merely proposes minor modifications of the HDI, other contributions propose more radical adjustments. For example, some of the literature suggests ways in which the HDI and related poverty measures based on the capability approach can be adjusted for inequality. There are also significant criticisms of the methodology used in some of the UNDP measures. Worries are regularly expressed about the weights attached to the components of these measures. Among advocates of the capability approach, worries were naturally also expressed about the inclusion of per capita income (even if the logarithm of per capita income is used) and implicit trade-offs between the various components of these measures.

In response to these critiques and worries, various defences of the HDI have emerged. In particular, Amartya Sen has sometimes argued that while the simplicity or 'vulgarity' of the HDI opens it up to a whole series of criticisms, it is the very same simplicity that is the key to its success. Furthermore, it can be argued that even if the HDI is 'vulgar' or unattractive because it embodies a number of evaluative decisions about weights and trade-offs, at least these decisions are transparently presented in the Human Development Reports. These decisions are thus open to public debate. In contrast, while the construction of GDP also involves evaluative decisions – making it 'vulgar' in the same way as the HDI is vulgar – these decisions are not so transparently presented. Regarding the income component of the HDI, Sudhir Anand and Amartya Sen (2000) justify the inclusion of the income component on the grounds that it captures those capabilities which are closely related to income. Finally, in responding to criticisms of the HDI, defenders of the human development approach sometimes claim that the HDI has been 'too successful', in as much as discussion of the HDI has distracted attention from all the detailed information which is presented in the Human Development Reports. The many tables in these reports attempt to capture – on an international scale – something like the 'human balance sheet' that Mahbub ul Haq had in mind. In his reflections on the first decade of human development, Sen (2000) suggested that the plurality of concerns – which the many tables in the Human Development Reports attempt to capture – is fundamental to the human development approach and is obscured by any aggregative index such as the HDI.

Regarding the evolution of the human development approach, Sakiko Fukuda-Parr has argued that one of the important shifts in emphasis in the Human Development Reports since the mid-1990s has been the increasing focus on *agency* – that is, people's capacity to shape their own destinies. Fukuda-Parr suggests that this change can be seen in the *Human Development Report 1995*. In her view, the GEM (which appeared in that report) is a measure of agency because it measures 'the extent to which women have influence in decision making, in politics, professional life, and in organizations' (Fukuda-Parr, 2003, p. 309). This new emphasis on agency is also apparent in Amartya Sen's most recent discussions of development, particularly in his *Development as Freedom* (1999). Sen has increasingly argued that people ought not to be viewed as *patients* or mere recipients of development policies, but as agents who can themselves bring about change. Sen (2004) also sees agency as important in advocacy relating to environmental issues. For this reason, he has argued that we should be concerned with sustaining freedoms, not just 'sustainable development' when this is understood in terms of sustaining living standards.

Apart from the work of the UNDP and the important contributions of the leading figures who developed the human development approach, many other scholars and policy makers now engage with the concerns of human development. The literature on human development has grown and crossed disciplinary boundaries. This interdisciplinarity is unsurprising since the human development approach has always claimed a strong philosophical pedigree, and presented an overarching view which can inform debates in different disciplines. The literature covers a very wide range of topics, including the definition of development, gender, the environment, the relation of income growth to human development, corruption and the multidimensionality of well-being and poverty. Furthermore, while the human development approach is sometimes contrasted with mainstream economics (which tends to focus on income), researchers in the mainstream of the economics profession have begun to engage with issues relating to human development. While some of this engagement has unsurprisingly been critical (for example, Srinivasan, 1994), important constructive work has also emerged, particularly on the multidimensionality of well-being and poverty. Apart from this broadening of the intellectual 'reach' of the human development approach, Human Development Reports are now produced in most countries and regions of the world. In these national reports, policy issues that are particularly pertinent to specific countries are addressed at some length in a way that they cannot be in the annual international Human Development Reports prepared by the UNDP. The human development approach has thus continued to grow in influence. It is a vibrant part of the landscape of development thought and policy work.

MOZAFFAR QIZILBASH

References

Alkire, S. (2002), 'Dimensions of human development', *World Development*, **30** (2), 181–205.
Anand, S. and A.K. Sen (2000), 'The income component of the Human Development Index', *Journal of Human Development*, **1** (1), 83–106.
Aristotle (1980), *The Nicomachean Ethics*, translated by D. Ross, Oxford: Oxford University Press.
Chenery, Hollis, Montele S. Ahluwahlia, C.L.G. Bell, John H. Dulow and Richard Jolly (1974), *Redistribution with Growth*, Oxford: Oxford University Press.
Clark, David A. (2002), *Visions of Development: A Study of Human Values*, Cheltenham, UK and Northampton, MA, USA: Edward Elgar.
Fukuda-Parr, S. (2003), 'The human development paradigm: operationalising Sen's ideas on capabilities', *Feminist Economics*, **9** (2–3), 301–18.
Haq, Mahbub ul (1995), *Reflections on Human Development*, Oxford and New York: Oxford University Press.
International Labour Organization (1976), *Employment, Growth and Basic Needs: A One World Problem*, Geneva: ILO.
Kant, Immanuel (1987), *Fundamental Principles of the Metaphysic of Morals*, translated by T.K. Abbot, New York: Prometheus Books.
Marx, Karl (1844), 'The economic and philosophical manuscripts', in David McLennan (ed.), *Karl Marx. Selected Writings*, Oxford: Oxford University Press, pp. 75–112.
Nussbaum, M.C. (1988), 'Nature, function and capability: Aristotle on political distribution', *Oxford Studies in Ancient Philosophy*, **6** (supplementary volume), 113–37.
Nussbaum, Martha C. (2000), *Women and Human Development: The Capabilities Approach*, Cambridge: Cambridge University Press.
Qizilbash, M. (1996), 'Capabilities, well-being and human development: a survey', *Journal of Development Studies*, **33** (2), 143–62.
Sen, Amartya K. (1980), 'Equality of what?', in S.M. McMurrin (ed.), *Tanner Lectures on Human Values*, Cambridge: Cambridge University Press and reprinted in A.K. Sen (1982), *Choice, Welfare and Measurement*, Oxford: Blackwell, pp. 353–69.
Sen, Amartya K. (1990), 'Development as capability expansion', in Keith Griffin and John Knight (eds), *Human Development and the International Development Strategy for the 1990s*, London: Macmillan, pp. 41–58.
Sen, Amartya K. (1999), *Development as Freedom*, Oxford: Oxford University Press.
Sen, A.K. (2000), 'A decade of human development', *Journal of Human Development*, **1** (1), 17–23.
Sen, A.K. (2004), 'Why we should save the spotted owl', *London Review of Books*, **26** (3), 10–11.
Srinivasan, T.N. (1994), 'Human development: a new paradigm or reinvention of the wheel?', *American Economic Review*, **84** (2), 238–43.
Streeten, Paul, Shahid J. Burki, Mahbub ul Haq, Norman Hicks and Frances Stewart (1981), *First Things First: Meeting Basic Human Needs in the Developing Countries*, Oxford: Oxford University Press.
United Nations Development Programme (various years), *Human Development Report*, Oxford: Oxford University Press.
World Commission on Environment and Development (1987), *Our Common Future*, Oxford: Oxford University Press.

Human Development and Economic Growth

Recent literature has contrasted human development, described as the ultimate goal of the development process, with economic growth, described as an imperfect proxy for more general welfare, or as a means towards enhanced human development. This debate has broadened the definitions and goals of development, but still needs to define the important interrelations between human development (HD) and economic growth (EG). To the extent that greater freedom and capabilities improve economic performance, human development will have an important effect on growth. Similarly, to the extent that increased incomes will increase the range of choices and capabilities enjoyed by households and governments, economic growth will enhance human development. This entry analyses these relationships and the two-way linkages involved, focusing on the relatively narrow education and health dimensions of human development. It will first review some of the theoretical debates on EG/HD linkages, then review the conclusions suggested by empirical analysis. Finally it will examine the policy implications of these linkages.

Growth and its impact on human development
Human development finds its theoretical underpinnings in Sen's capabilities approach which holds 'a person's capability to have various functioning vectors and to enjoy the corresponding well-being achievements' to be the best indicator of welfare (Sen, 1985, p. 203). This perspective shifts the analysis of development to the vector of not only attributes (as is the more traditional utilitarian or even the original basic needs view of human welfare, see Streeten, 1979), for example, income, education, health, but also the vector of possible opportunities available to individuals. Naturally, there is a link between the two – these opportunities are affected by certain attributes of the individual: a starving, uneducated person would have fewer choices than a healthy, educated person. Yet the capabilities approach goes far beyond individual attributes, to analyse the role of the social environment on human choice and agency, that is, does an individual in an open, free society enjoy a larger set of potential functionings than one in a closed, oppressive society? However, while capabilities make an appealing goal for development, the number of possible human functionings is large, and many are almost by definition unobservable.

The first major attempt to translate the capabilities approach into a tractable ranking of nations came in the 1990 UNDP *Human Development Report*. Its objective was to 'capture better the complexity of human life' by providing a quantitative approach to combining various socio-economic indicators into a measure of human development (UNDP, 1990, p. 11). This was in contrast to the perceived prevailing wisdom in development economics, as embodied in the World Development Reports, whose 'excessive preoccupation with GNP growth and national income accounts has . . . supplanted a focus on ends by an obsession with merely the means' (UNDP, 1990, p. 9). Yet the transformation from a normative theory of capabilities into a quantitative variable was by no means an obvious task. The use of life expectancy, literacy and GDP as components of a Human Development Index admittedly constitutes a rough proxy and simplification of the original capabilities theory (for example, Kelley, 1991; Srinivasan, 1994). Notably missing were measures of political freedom and income inequality. Furthermore, any quantitative ranking raises difficult measurement questions, such as accounting for the decreasing marginal utility of income, and the necessarily arbitrary weighting of each component of HD. Nevertheless, the Human Development Reports have had a strong influence on development thinking, causing developing countries to publish their own national-level human development reports and indices and modify their policies.

Income growth clearly strikes one as the main contributor to *directly* increasing the capabilities of individuals and consequently the human development of a nation since it encapsulates the economy's command over resources (Sen, 2000). For example, while the citizens of the Indian state of Kerala have life expectancies and literacy rates comparable to those of many developed countries, the fact that they cannot enjoy many of the benefits of citizens of such countries (such as better housing, transportation or entertainment) demonstrates the importance of GDP as an instrument for achieving a wide range of capabilities. However, GDP also has a strong effect on literacy and health outcomes, both through private expenditures and government programmes. Thus, in so far as higher incomes facilitate the achievement of crucial human development objectives, it also has an *indirect* effect on human development.

The impact of economic growth on a nation's human development level, of course, also depends on other conditions of the society. One important component is the role of the distribution of income. At the micro level there is great potential for a positive causality – individual and household consumption can be an important element in increasing human development and may respond more closely to the real needs of the population than do government programmes. However, individual consumption may not always go towards goods which contribute maximally to human development. In societies where women contribute more to family income and have more influence on household decision making, expenditures on human development-orientated goods are likely to be relatively higher. For example, among Gambian households, the larger the proportion of food under women's control, the larger household calorie consumption (von Braun, 1988). Similarly, in the Philippines it has been shown that consumption of calories and proteins increases with the share of income accruing directly to women (Garcia, 1990). Also see Hoddinot and Haddad (1991) who look at the impact of intra-household income distribution on child welfare.

At a macro level, the distribution of the increased income from economic growth will also have a strong impact on human development. Since poorer households spend a higher proportion of their income on goods which promote health and education, economic growth whose benefits are directed more towards the poor will have a greater impact on human development. For example, Birdsall et al. (1995) show that if the distribution of income in Brazil were as equal as that in Malaysia, school enrolments among poor children would be 40 per cent higher.

The effects of economic growth on government human development expenditures are bound to complement private expenditure channels. In fact, Anand and Ravallion (1993) find that most of the effects of economic growth on HD are likely to flow through government budgetary expenditures, central or local. However, the strength of this effect depends entirely on the effectiveness of expenditure targeting and delivery. The government must identify priority sectors such as primary education and health that have the highest potential for HD improvement. Government expenditures for HD should be distributed predominantly to low-income groups since it is here that the highest marginal impact will be had. Government must also have the institutional capacity to efficiently allocate these expenditures. Studies by Rajkumar and Swaroop (2002) have demonstrated that the effectiveness of public expenditure is conditional on the quality of governance, with government accountability likely to play an important role. While empirical evidence here is spottier, theory suggests that a decentralised, locally accountable government system may have advantages in resource allocation and service delivery.

Human development and its impact on growth

Human development, in turn, has important effects on economic growth. If a central element of economic growth is allowing agents to discover and develop their comparative advantage, an increase in the capabilities and functionings available to individuals should allow more of them to pursue occupations in which they are most productive. In this sense human development can be seen as the relaxing of constraints, which may have interfered with profit maximisation. Furthermore, although human development represents a broader concept, many of its elements overlap significantly with the more traditional notion of human capital. Thus, to the extent that human capital affects economic growth, human development is bound to have an impact on economic growth.

More specifically, each of the various components of human development is likely to have a distinct impact on economic growth. Education, for instance, has a strong effect on labour productivity. In agriculture, Birdsall and James (1993) use data from Malaysia, Ghana and Peru to show that each extra year of a farmer's schooling is associated with an annual increase in output of 2–5 per cent. In Indonesia, Duflo (2001) estimates an increase in wages of 1.5 to 2.7 per cent for each additional school built per 1000 children. In addition to its direct effect on productivity, education also affects the rate of innovation and technological improvements. Foster and Rosenzweig (1995) demonstrate that increased education is associated with faster technology adoption in Green Revolution India. Similarly, higher education levels have been shown to increase innovation in businesses in Sri Lanka. In this sense human development may also enter into an Uzawa–Lucas type endogenous growth model as a factor affecting growth rates through its effect on technological change. Statistical analysis of the clothing and engineering industries in Sri Lanka (Deraniyagala, 1995), to cite just one example, showed that the skill and education levels of workers and entrepreneurs were positively related to the rate of technical change of the firm. Education alone, of course, cannot transform an economy. The quantity and quality of investment, domestic and foreign, together with the choice of technology and the overall policy environment, constitute other important determinants of economic performance. The quality of private entrepreneurs, of public policy makers and of investment decisions generally, is bound to be influenced by the education of both officials and managers; moreover, the volume of both domestic and foreign investment and the rates of total factor productivity will undoubtedly be higher when a system's human capital level is higher.

Health has also demonstrated positive effects on economic growth beyond its inherent desirability as an end in itself. Strauss and Thomas (1998) review a large literature documenting how improvements in health and nutrition improve productivity and incomes. Schultz (2000) finds correlations between height and income in his analysis of data from Ghana, Côte d'Ivoire, Brazil and Vietnam. A range of labour productivity gains have been observed, associated with calorie intake increases in poor countries (Cornia and Stewart, 1995), including studies of farmers in Sierra Leone (Strauss, 1986), sugar cane workers in Guatemala (Immink and Viteri, 1981), and road construction workers in Kenya (Wolgemuth et al., 1982). In these cases, productivity enhancement appears to follow fairly immediately as current intakes of calories or micro nutrients are increased.

Education and health may also have strong indirect impacts on economic growth through their effect on the distribution of income, and education even more so through its impact on health (for example, Behrman and Wolfe, 1987b provide evidence of the impact of women's education on family health and nutrition). As education and health improve and become more broadly based, low-income people are better able to seek out economic opportunities. For example, a study of the relation between schooling, income inequality and poverty in 18 countries of Latin America in the 1980s found that one-quarter of the variation in workers' incomes was accounted for by variations in schooling attainment; it concludes that 'clearly, education is the variable with the strongest impact on income equality' (Psacharopoulos, 1992, p. 48). And a more equal distribution of income is known to favour growth for both economic and political economy reasons.

Education may also affect per capita income growth via its impact on the denominator, that is, population growth. For example, a study of 14 African countries in the mid-1980s showed a negative correlation between female schooling and fertility in almost all countries, with primary education having a negative impact in about half the countries and no significant effects in the other half, while secondary education invariably reduced fertility (Behrman and Wolfe, 1987a; Thomas et al., 1991; Birdsall et al., 1995; Jayaraman, 1995; Thomas and Maluccio, 1995).

The joint HD/EG linkages
The two-way relationship between economic growth and human development suggests that nations may enter into either a virtuous cycle of high growth and large gains in human development, or a vicious cycle of low growth and low rates of HD improvement. Levels of EG and HD are mutually reinforcing, leading towards either an upward spiral of development, or a poverty trap. The existence and persistence of these cycles depends on the strengths of the linkages previously cited between EG and HD. Countries may also find themselves in a lop-sided state, at least temporarily, with relatively good growth and relatively poor HD, or vice versa.

There may be various reasons for 'economic growth lopsided' nations, that is, those which have high rates of GDP growth relative to the improvement in human development indicators, including government corruption, low social expenditures, or inequitably distributed incomes. A recent analysis of such cases raises concerns about the sustainability of such states, for example, Ranis et al. (2000) found that of the eight EG-lopsided nations in 1960–70, all eight moved to the vicious cycle of low EG/low HD. These results suggest that good economic growth not accompanied by increases in human development may prove to be ultimately unsustainable.

'Human development lopsided' nations, on the other hand, fared better over the last 40 years, with four nations moving into virtuous cycles and four others moving into vicious cycles. In the 50 per cent of favourable cases, early progress in human development meant that they were able to take advantage of policy reforms to generate growth. Thus, a high level of human development early in a nation's history can, with the right policy decisions, translate into a virtuous cycle of good growth and human development supporting each other. The policies involved, such as encouraging higher levels of investment, technology change and an improved distribution of income, can leverage the successes in human development into sustainable economic gains.

This contrast clearly points to an important conclusion for development sequencing, that is, human development seems to be a necessary prerequisite for long-term sustainable growth. Human development may, moreover, exhibit threshold effects, in the sense that nations must attain a certain HD level before future economic growth becomes sustainable. This emphasis on levels differentiates human development from human capital in endogenous growth theory. While *changes* in human capital and labour quality matter most for endogenous growth, it is the *level* of human development that determines a nation's sustainable growth path.

The above findings also have strong implications for government policy. If HD improvements are indeed a precondition for sustainable EG, government policy and public funding may be necessary to move a nation above the HD threshold level. Nations stuck in vicious cycles, or low-HD poverty traps may need targeted government investments to meet the fixed costs of HD improvements that will lead to later economic growth. These fixed-cost investments may include schools, hospitals, and the necessary governance improvements to implement investment projects effectively.

The crucial lesson that emerges is that the old-fashioned view of 'grow first and worry about human development later' is not supported by the evidence. Improving levels of education and health should have priority or at least move together with efforts to directly enhance growth.

GUSTAV RANIS

References

Anand, Sudhir and Martin Ravallion (1993), 'Human development in poor countries: on the role of private incomes and public services', *Journal of Economic Perspectives*, **7** (1), 133–50.

Behrman, J.R. and Barbara L. Wolfe (1987a), 'Investments in schooling in two generations in pre-revolutionary Nicaragua: the roles of family background and school supply', *Journal of Development Economics*, **27**, 395–419.

Behrman, Jere and Barbara L. Wolfe (1987b), 'How does mother's schooling affect the family's health, nutrition, medical care usage and household sanitation?', *Journal of Econometrics*, **36** (1–2), 185–204.

Birdsall, N. and E. James (1993), 'Efficiency and equity in social spending: how and why governments misbehave', in Michael Lipton and Jacques van der Gaag (eds), *Including the Poor*, New York: Oxford University Press for the World Bank, pp. 335–58.

Birdsall, N., D. Ross and R. Sabot (1995), 'Inequality and growth reconsidered: lessons from East Asia', *World Bank Economic Review*, **9**, 477–508.

Cornia, G.A. and F. Stewart (1995), 'Two errors of targeting', in F. Stewart (ed.), *Adjustment and Poverty: Options and Choices*, London: Routledge, pp. 82–107.

Deraniyagala, S. (1995), 'Technical change and efficiency in Sri Lanka's manufacturing industry', PhD dissertation, University of Oxford, UK.

Duflo, Esther (2001), 'The medium run effects of educational expansion: evidence from a large school construction program in Indonesia', Massachusetts Institute of Technology, Department of Economics Working Paper: 01/46.

Foster, A. and M. Rosenzweig (1995), 'Learning by doing and learning from others: human capital and technical change in agriculture', *Journal of Political Economy*, **103** (6), 1176–209.

Garcia, M. (1990), 'Resource allocation and household welfare: a study of personal sources of income on food consumption, nutrition and health in the Philippines', PhD dissertation, Institute of Social Studies, The Hague.

Hoddinott, John and Lawrence Haddad (1991), 'Household expenditures, child anthropometric status and the intrahousehold division of income: evidence from the Côte d'Ivoire,' Research Program in Development Studies, Discussion Paper 155, Woodrow Wilson School, Princeton University, NJ.

Immink, M. and F. Viteri (1981), 'Energy intake and productivity of Guatemalan sugarcane cutters: an empirical test of the efficiency wage hypothesis', *Journal of Development Economics*, **9**, 251–71.

Jayaraman, R. (1995), 'On the meta-production front: an evidence-gathering exercise', Processed for UNDP, New York.

Kelley, Allen C. (1991), 'The Human Development Index: "handle with care"', *Population and Development Review*, **17** (2), 315–24.

Psacharopoulos, G. (1992), 'Poverty and income distribution in Latin America: the story of the 1980s', *Technical Paper No. 351*, Washington, DC: World Bank.

Rajkumar, Andrew S. and Vinaya Swaroop (2002), 'Public spending and outcomes: does governance matter?', World Bank Working Paper no. 2840, World Bank, Washington, DC.

Ranis, Gustav, Frances Stewart and Alejandro Ramirez (2000), 'Economic growth and human development', *World Development*, **28** (2), 197–219.

Schultz, T. Paul (2000), 'Productive benefits of improving health: evidence from low-income countries', Yale University, mimeo.

Sen, Amartya (1985), 'Well-being, agency and freedom: the Dewey Lectures 1984', *Journal of Philosophy*, **82** (4), 169–221.

Sen, Amartya (2000), 'A decade of human development', *Journal of Human Development*, **1** (1), 17–23.

Srinivasan, T.N. (1994), 'Human development: a new paradigm or reinvention of the wheel?', *American Economic Review*, **84** (2), 238–43.

Strauss, John (1986), 'Does better nutrition raise farm productivity?', *Journal of Political Economy*, **94** (2), 297–320.

Strauss, John and Duncan Thomas (1998), 'Nutrition, and economic development', *Journal of Economic Literature*, **36** (2), 766–817.

Streeten, Paul (1979), 'Basic needs: premises and promises', *Journal of Policy Modelling*, **1**, 136–46.

Thomas, D. and J. Maluccio (1995), 'Contraceptive choice, fertility, and public policy in Zimbabwe', Living Standard Measurement Survey Working Paper 109, World Bank, Washington, DC.

Thomas, D., J. Strauss and M.H. Henriques (1991), 'How does mother's education affect child height', *Journal of Human Resources*, **26**, 183–212.

United Nations Development Programme (UNDP) (1990), *Human Development Report*, Oxford: Oxford University Press.

von Braun, J. (1988), 'The impact of new crop technology on the agricultural division of labor in a West Africa setting', *Economic Development and Cultural Change*, **37**, 513–35.

Wolgemuth, J.C., M.C. Latham, A. Hall and D. Crompton (1982), 'Worker productivity and nutritional status of Kenyan road construction labourers', *American Journal of Clinical Nutrition*, **36**, 68–78.

Human Development Index

The concept of human development draws on the greatness of human potentiality despite our narrowly circumscribed lives. Lack of schooling, meagre healthcare, inadequate economic opportunities, violation of political liberties, denial of civil rights, and other hostile influences can powerfully limit and frustrate human lives. The perspective of human development is based on the recognition that the hindrances that people face can be removed through social efforts as well as individual initiatives.

The human development approach

The Human Development Reports were published by the United Nations Development Programme (UNDP), from 1990. The movement was led by the visionary Pakistani economist, Mahbub ul Haq, who died in 1998. A firm belief in the basic importance of enriching the lives and freedoms of ordinary human beings has been a central concern in the social sciences for a very long time. This applies not only to Adam Smith, but also to earlier writings, even to Aristotle, who argued in *Nicomachean Ethics* that 'wealth is evidently not the good we are seeking; for it is merely useful and for the sake of something else'. We have to judge the success of a society, including its economy, not just in terms of national wealth or the gross national product (the ubiquitous GNP), but in terms of the freedoms and capabilities that people enjoy, to live as they would value living.

The broadness of that perspective has often been undermined through seeing development in the narrow perspective of expansion of the supply of objects of convenience (represented, for example, by the GNP, or the gross domestic product, the GDP). That expansion is important, but not for its own sake, and we have to take into account the variability of the relation between economic growth and the expansion of basic human freedoms and capabilities. It is this relatively neglected heritage that the human development approach tries to reclaim. That basic ambition informs the tables and analyses presented in the Human Development Reports.

By the time Mahbub ul Haq became the pioneering leader of the human development approach, there were several movements of discontent which were seeking an approach broader than what standard economic measurement provided. There were development theorists arguing for the recognition of 'basic needs'. There were advocates of various indicators of 'physical quality of life'. There were writers focusing on disparities in 'living conditions'. There were international organisations (even within the UN family, for example UNICEF) which emphasised the importance of ascertaining 'the state of the world's children'. There were relief organisations, from Oxfam to CARE (Christian Action for Research and Education), concerned with hunger, morbidity and mortality, rather than only with income poverty. There were humanists voicing the need for social justice in the distribution of opportunities that people have. And there were also some obdurate theory-spinners wondering whether the foundations of economic and social evaluation could not be radically shifted from commodities to capabilities, thereby moving the focus of attention from what people own (or have) to what they can actually do (or be). The human development approach, under Mahbub ul Haq's stewardship, tried to make room for all these concerns.

Use of an index of human development
The difficulty, however, of trying to replace a simple and coarse number like the GNP by an avalanche of tables (and a whole set of related analyses) is that the latter does not have the handy usability that the crude GNP has. People could make respectful references to the breadth and reach of the human development approach, and then slip back into relying only on the GNP when it comes to summary statements. The Human Development Index (HDI) was devised explicitly as a rival to GNP – indeed as a similarly coarse measure as the GNP but not oblivious of everything other than products and incomes. Not surprisingly, it has a boorishness that is somewhat similar to that of the GNP (for this unflattering description, I hope I would not be accused of being too disrespectful of the HDI, which I had a hand in constructing, for Mahbub ul Haq, in late 1989). By focusing on some of the aspects of human lives – such as longevity and education – the HDI takes us well beyond the narrow limits of concentrating only on objects of convenience. It is a quick and imperfect glance at human lives, which – despite the crudeness it shares with the GNP – is sensitive, to a significant extent, to the way people live and can choose to live.

However, the breadth of the human development approach must not be confused with the slender specificity of the Human Development Index. The latter – the HDI – can compete with the GNP in terms of ready usability, in a way that the very broad and sophisticated human development analysis – with many tables and complex concerns – cannot. This explains why the HDI, despite its rough and unrefined nature, has been used as something of a flagship of the 'human development approach' since its appearance in the *Human Development Report 1990* – the first report of what has been a continuing series since then.

The components of the HDI

The HDI is based on three components, namely, indicators of basic education, of longevity and of income per head. It is, thus, not exclusively focused on economic opulence, as is the GNP. In particular, it takes note of the fact that even with the same level of economic opulence, differences in life expectancy and basic education tend to reflect significant variations in the quality and reach of human lives. The HDI, thus, serves the purpose of broadening the limited vision of the GNP and other narrowly income-based indicators.

The weighting of the three components of the HDI is somewhat arbitrary. There certainly is more room for public discussion on the weights to be used, and indeed within the general format of the HDI, the weights attached to the distinct components have been parametrically varied over the years. The weighting exercise is done implicitly, while sticking formally to putting the same weight on the normalised value of each component. The maximum and minimum values of each component used in 'normalising' the figures (for example, between a minimal life expectancy and a maximum value) determines what weight is in effect attached to a given increase in that component. For example, the value of a one-year increase in life expectancy would be twice as large if the normalisation is done between 50 and 80 years, compared with taking the limits to be 30 and 90 years.

Education and life expectancy

Within its educational component, the HDI takes note of literacy as well as ongoing schooling. It is not hard to appreciate that education enhances the ability of people to do what they value doing. The use of life expectancy has, however, received more critical attention.

The fact that longevity is very often taken to be a primary accomplishment of a good society perhaps does relate in some ways to the presumption that people are, in some sense, 'happier' (or 'more well') if they live on rather than dying off (at least so long as they are not too overwhelmed by the debility of old age). But aside from the complexity of that judgement (an issue of some intellectual antiquity), there are also critically important issues of freedom that are also linked to longevity. These concerns include not only the fact that people tend, by and large, to value living longer, but also the central recognition that being alive is typically a necessary requirement for carrying out the plans and projects that we have reason to value and pursue.

The point was put well by the seventeenth-century English poet, Andrew Marvell, in a poem dedicated to his 'coy mistress':

> The grave's a fine and private place,
> But none, I think, do there embrace.

I do not know precisely how coy Marvell's 'coy mistress' was, or whether she liked being embraced by Andrew Marvell or not. But clearly Marvell sought it, and he was, in general, right in pointing to the fact that we value life at least partly because of the things we can *do*, *if alive*. The value of living must reflect the importance of our valued capabilities – our ability to do what we would like to do – since living is typically a necessary condition for having those capabilities. This is one of the reasons why the focus on longevity in the HDI reflects an implicit valuation of human freedom – our capability to do what we value doing.

Income *vis-à-vis* the income component of the HDI

However, human capabilities depend not only on longevity and education, but also on many other factors. By including an income component to the informational basis of the HDI, note is taken of the relevance of 'the command over resources to enjoy a decent standard of living'. This is a concession to the reasons that give relevance to the GNP, without excluding everything else. Indeed, unlike in the GNP, the income component of the HDI has a specific and constrained role:

1. it is not the only influence on the HDI, and
2. by incorporating diminishing returns to income in the income component of the HDI, there is an attempt here to take note of the greater importance of incremental income near poverty levels (rather than counting the poor person's precious dollar to be no more significant than the millionaire's marginal dollar).

Indeed, there have been attempts, in various Human Development Reports, to reflect distributive concerns *within* the measure of the income component of the HDI.

Some limitations of the HDI

Let me end by briefly mentioning some limitations of the HDI. First, the well-being and freedom that we enjoy have much internal diversity, and they are influenced by a great variety of factors – political, economic, social, legal, epidemiological and others. These factors are distinct, but they also interrelate with each other. The HDI is based on a heroic selection and puts the focus on some of these features, while totally neglecting others. The problem cannot be rectified by including more factors into this one numerical index, since the inclusion of more variables reduces the importance of each of the other – already included – variables. The loss of informational sensitivity involved in moving from a complex reality to just one number (formally, from an *n*-tuple or a vector to a scalar) cannot but be great. Depending on the purpose at hand, the particular informational focus of any index, like the HDI, may well be contingently justified, but it cannot do justice to the variety of purposes that can be served by the human development approach in general.

Second, when the ingredients of a judgement are diverse, any aggregate index with *given* weights over its diverse constituent elements would tend to oversimplify the evaluative exercise. As is well known from indexing theory, much would depend on the questions that the index is meant to address.

Third, another concern involves the time dimension. We have reason to be interested in the current situation as well as future prospects. Indeed, sometimes we are particularly interested in *changes* over time. For example, if a further spread of AIDS and the unfolding of that pandemic would reduce life expectancy sharply, it would be particularly relevant to examine that and also to see how this would tend to restrain or reduce the future values of HDI, of which life expectancy is a component.

Of course, this is not, in itself, an argument against the HDI as an indicator, since we can distinguish between different questions, in particular, 'what is the present situation?' and 'what are the prospects of the future?'. But since some commentators seem to be keen on getting all the different information – concerning the future as well as the present – through just one real number (through some all-inclusive index), it is worth noting that any expectation that today's HDI may adequately reflect *both* the present situation and the future prospects would be hard to satisfy.

The usefulness of the HDI is dependent on understanding its purpose and limits. It is aimed at broadening the informational narrowness of the GNP or GDP. This it does, but it cannot capture the breadth of the human development approach in general. No one number can, no matter how much we try to pack into that number.

AMARTYA K. SEN

Further reading

Anand, Sudhir and Amartya Sen (1994), 'Human development index: methodology and measurement', Occasional Paper 12, HDRO, UNDP, New York; reprinted in Fukuda-Parr and Kumar (eds) (2003), pp. 114–27.

Aristotle (4th Century BC [1980]), *The Nicomachean Ethics*, translated by David Ross, The World's Classics, Oxford: Oxford University Press.

Desai, Meghnad (1994), *Poverty, Famine and Economic Development*, Aldershot, UK and Brookfield, US: Edward Elgar.

Fukuda-Parr, Sakiko and A.K. Shiva Kumar (eds) (2003), *Readings in Human Development* Oxford and New Delhi: Oxford University Press.

Grant, James P. (1978), *Disparity Reduction Rates in Social Indicators*, Washington, DC: Overseas Development Council.

Griffin, Keith and John Knight (1990), *Human Development and the International Development Strategies for the 1990s*, London: Macmillan.

Haq, Mahbub ul (1995), *Reflections on Human Development*, Oxford and New York: Oxford University Press.

Morris, Morris D. (1979), *Measuring the Conditions of the World's Poor: The Physical Quality of Life Index*, Oxford: Pergamon.

Nussbaum, Martha (1998), 'Nature, function and capability: Aristotle on political distribution', *Oxford Studies in Ancient Greek Philosophy*, supplementary vol., 145–84.

Nussbaum, Martha and Amartya Sen (eds) (1993), *The Quality of Life*, Oxford: Clarendon.

Sen, Amartya (1980), 'Equality of what?', in S. McMurren (ed.), *Tanner Lectures on Human Values*, vol. I, Cambridge: Cambridge University Press, pp. 195–220.

Sen, Amartya (1985), *Commodities and Capabilities*, Amsterdam: North-Holland.

Sen, Amartya (1989), 'Development as capability expansion', *Journal of Development Planning*, **19**, 41–58.

Stewart, Frances (1985), *Planning to Meet Basic Needs*, London: Macmillan.

Streeten, Paul, Shahid J. Burki, Mahbub ul Haq, Norman Hicks and Frances Stewart (1981), *First Things First: Meeting Basic Needs in Developing Countries*, Oxford and New York: Oxford University Press.

UNDP (1990), *Human Development Report*, Oxford: Oxford University Press (published annually since 1990).

Human Rights

Human rights reflect a determined effort to protect the dignity of each and every human being against abuse of power. This endeavour is as old as human history. What is relatively new is the international venture for the protection of human dignity through internationally accepted legal standards and generally accessible mechanisms for implementation. That mission got a major impetus with the founding of the United Nations in 1945.

While the primary focus of the international project for the realisation of human rights used to be on ways and means of limiting and governing political power, other institutions than the state are coming within its range of attention, too, including those of the corporate world. Recently, a 'human rights approach' to poverty has gained a prominent place on the development agenda. It is precisely in this connection that, beside their original protective function, human rights have acquired a transformational (emancipatory) role, too.

From idea to international mission
The spiritual source of human rights lies in the fundamental belief that the protection of human dignity and equality is a responsibility of society at all its different layers and levels. This should generally limit and govern any use of power over human beings. The starting-point is the acknowledgement of every person's right to exist. People count and in principle no individual counts more, or less, than any other. No one, in other words, is to be excluded from the typical human rights term 'everyone'.

This idea has a great and diverse cultural backing. However, human dignity as a fundamental standard of judgement easily gets twisted into a norm applying 'to us but not to all those others'. Thus, the Romans already based their legal system upon the rule that freedom is of inestimable value; yet they institutionalised slavery. Indeed, human history manifests a continuous tendency to justify abuse of power by constructing certain individuals and groups regarded as obstacles to the fulfilment of certain ambitions, into categories to which the fundamental ideas of human dignity and equality would not apply. Thus, crucial qualifications of human rights such as 'inalienable' and 'universal' tend to meet with a great deal of practical resistance.

Even more problematic than the support for protection of everyone's human dignity as such is the way in which that is to be done. With the formation of nation states the system became to protect people's basic dignity by law. Rights have been defined that pertain to all individual human beings as well as to communities. Incorporation in national bills of rights was followed by a major international endeavour. The principal documents on which the international project for the realisation of human rights is based – the Universal Declaration of Human Rights of 1948 and the two principal International Covenants (for Civil Political Rights, and for Economic, Social and Cultural Rights, respectively, both in force since 1976) – are known together as 'the International Bill of Human Rights'. More specific conventions followed, against torture and racial discrimination, for example, and on child rights and women's rights. While all states fall under the international mechanism based upon human rights as an essential element in the Charter of the United Nations – with the Geneva-based Human Rights Council as major supervisory body – the treaties require specific procedures of access and ratification. Separate committees are charged with supervision of the implementation of the various distinct human rights covenants and conventions.

Indivisibility and interdependence
The interests that are accordingly protected by international human rights law are of a *fundamental* character in the sense of being directly linked to basic human dignity. Human rights, then, function as abstract acknowledgements of fundamental freedoms

and titles that support people's claims to live in freedom while sustaining their daily livelihoods. The category of rights that protect fundamental freedoms – originally called the 'first generation of human rights' – has been termed 'civil and political rights' while the cluster that protects basic entitlements has become known as 'economic, social and cultural rights' (the so-called 'second generation'). Obviously, the two are intertwined. It makes not much sense, for example, to tell a starving person that he/she has fundamental freedoms, including free speech. Nor would a 'right to food' be meaningful when people are not free to say that they are hungry. (The latter has actually happened in practice, for instance in cases of famine in Ethiopia and the Sudan.) Notably, implementation of civil and political rights would be meaningless without a simultaneous realisation of 'survival rights' while for a realisation of economic, social and cultural rights, civil and political rights function as 'empowerment rights', enabling collective action addressing the structures behind non-implementation. This indivisibility and interdependence of distinct categories of human rights received formal recognition in the final declaration of the United Nations Human Rights Summit in Vienna 1993. It includes the incorporation of a 'third generation' in the system: the 'rights of collectivities'. Generally, the ordering in first, second and third reflects diminishing degrees of international attention to the rights in question. Thus, the protection of minorities appears to be one of the most problematic elements in the international endeavour for the realisation of human rights.

With regard to economic, social and cultural rights two misconceptions ought to be mentioned. The first is that civil and political rights (CPR) would relate merely to negative freedom in the sense of a liberty from interference by others in the enjoyment of one's freedoms while economic, social and cultural rights (ESCR) would be based purely on positive freedom in the sense of opportunity. At first sight this might seem to be a logical qualification: *no* torture, *no* detention without trial, *no* censorship and so on versus a *positive* responsibility to secure enough food for everyone, good education, public health and so on. Yet, CPR actually require a positive investment, too: well functioning judicial systems, including good prisons and solidly established democratic institutions. Furthermore, the fulfilment and protection of ESCR not only places a large burden on the fiscal capacity of states; these rights can also be violated through public policies that intervene negatively in people's own entitlements to ensure satisfaction of their basic needs.

The second fallacy is that contrary to CPR, ESCR would be rights without remedies, and mere 'aspirations'. In real life, implementation of rights is never automatic. Litigation always requires action on the part of the rights-holders first, and the possibility to clearly identify duty-bearers, next. Furthermore, in legal disputes the interests of one person or collectivity always have to be weighed against those of others in the light of distinctive rights and principles. This applies to both categories of rights. Thus, there are certain contexts in which the 'justiciability' of CPR becomes highly problematic – civil war, for example – while in particular cases of concrete and identifiable violations the implementation of ESCR can be legally enforced (see our reference to the South African *Grootboom* case below). Crucially, moreover, the impact of human rights is not confined to their instrumental role of legal resources. These rights also play their part as political tools of a transformational nature. This vital point too, will be further explained below.

The human rights deficit

In terms of the role and rule of law, society is expected to function in such a way that rights are respected, and claims based on entitlements connected to those rights get honoured. Dispute settlement is confined to cases in which there are conflicting claims protected by different rights (between landlord and tenant, for example). Yet, in the case of human rights adequate embodiment in positive law is all too often missing, while they get violated in and from centres of political power, too. There are notable differences in context here. Whereas in some countries freedom of speech, for example, is protected by a historically *acquired* right, in other countries it is merely based on an internationally *declared* right that is still structurally violated from the national political centre. In the case of economic, social and cultural rights, general recognition at the centres of power in the global economy is even lacking.

Thus, the global endeavour for the realisation of human rights suffers from a huge *deficit* that is all too often submerged in the general euphoria of human rights declarations, conferences, committee meetings and workshops. This deficit manifests itself in four distinct realms: (1) the precarious struggle against impunity of state-related perpetrators of violations of civil and political rights; (2) the apparent lack of protection of minorities; (3) the persistent inability of state law to protect people behind the walls of privacy, and its paralysing effects on the struggle against domestic violence; and (4) the non-fulfilment of ESCR in a world in which so many people's basic needs apparently remain denied.

Indeed, for people living in daily hardship, human rights mean protection of entitlements that they simply do not have. Thus, everyone has an internationally acknowledged right to health but hundreds of millions of people lack access to sanitary services and clean water. Accordingly, for the poor, human rights tend to constitute an abstract recognition of their basic needs without the actual entitlements that would enable them to satisfy these. Entitlement, in an economic context, means actual protected access to resources and actual protected command over goods and services. Clearly, then, for poor people it is actual entitlement that matters more, rather than universally declared rights.

Human rights strategies

In fact, while the whole idea of rights is based upon the expectation that evident violations would lead to contentious action resulting in redress, *human* rights often remain without effective implementation. This is due to two crucial obstacles: first, the often prevailing inadequacy of law as a check on power, and second, the lack of reception of these rights in many cultural and politico-economic contexts.

Yet, the implication of such critical constraints in the operational impact of universal human rights is not that these rights lose all meaning in processes of development and the attack on poverty. While in Western history individual human rights got a place in the statute books at the end of processes of societal transformation, in most of the developing world these internationally accepted standards stand at the beginning of emancipation and social change. Their function, in other words, is not so much *protection* (what ought to be protected would still have to be acquired), but rather *transformation*. Moreover, these internationally recognised rights play their part not merely as legal resources (implying a reliance on functioning legal systems) but also as political

Table 8   Human rights in a functional as well as an instrumental setting

Functional Instrumental	Protective	Transformational
Legal resources	Judicial action (case by case)	Legal literacy programmes aiming at awareness building
Political instruments	Dissent and protest against policies and actions violating human dignity	Collective action addressing power relations embodying structural injustice

instruments in the sense of internationally enacted standards of legitimacy that are meant to govern any use of power.

Actually, a judicial case-by-case approach to concrete violations of human rights is just one possible option in efforts to realise human rights. Legal literacy programmes are a way of raising awareness on people's rights in general. A political case-by-case approach uses protest and other forms of dissent as ways of protecting fundamental interests against policies and action that violate people's human dignity. Even in the lives of those already facing daily hardships, such resistance often appears to be necessary. But the most pressing challenges lie in persistent *non-implementation* of human rights. It is the economic, political and social structures behind such situations that would have to be addressed. Here collective action would be called for, aiming at structural reforms.

These four distinct types of human rights strategies may be illustrated by a simple matrix showing the focus of human rights with regard to two major functions, protection and transformation, as well as two categories of means towards implementation: legal resources and political instruments (see Table 8).

Human rights and development

The character of human rights as 'declaratory' rather than 'conclusive' concerns economic, social and cultural rights in particular and manifests itself especially in countries in the South. This has to do with a *socio-economic* context: no jobs, no access to land and hence extreme pressure on scarce productive resources. Such conditions appear to breed frustration and aggression rather than recognition of other people's freedoms and needs. But there is also a *political* setting that finds its background in the history of colonialism and its effects on the distribution and control of power, both internationally and in local contexts. As a result the struggle for *social justice* in the developing world faces serious constraints. Internationally that endeavour has not yet yielded impressive fruits. As a result of decisions taken in the name of economic progress, the poor often have to face increasing hardships from day to day. In that dim light the idea emerged to connect the struggle for human development to human rights.

The *Human Development Report 2000* (UNDP, 2000) with its special focus on human rights, may be seen as a first response to UN Secretary General Kofi Annan's appeal for a 'mainstreaming'. Indeed, the persistent efforts towards integrating development, security and governance through a compelling focus on the human being – *human* development, *human* security and *human* rights – may be seen as central to the Human Development Reports of the UNDP. It is basic human dignity that links the three together.

Notable in the discourse that is usually employed in this connection is, first of all, the use of the term 'approach'. Apparently, the idea is no longer to plan, steer or direct but just to *approach* poverty and the need for development. This terminology is in line with the earlier shift in emphasis from development as programming structural improvement of the economy to *human development* as 'a process of expanding the real freedoms that people enjoy'. The language used here is Amartya Sen's (see, for example, his *Development as Freedom* published in 1999). It is, indeed, particularly his thinking that appears to have influenced the Human Development Reports in general and the 2000 Report on the human rights approach in particular. In an earlier publication to which the *Human Development Report 2000* refers, Sen (1999b) had already summarised the case for human rights from a developmental perspective in three aspects: '(1) their *intrinsic* importance, (2) their *consequential* role in providing political incentives for economic security, and (3) their *constructive* role in the genesis of values and priorities' (p. 99, original emphasis). Fundamental freedoms, in other words, have *intrinsic* as well as *instrumental* value: without freedom there *is* no development, and with freedom, development as a process of uplifting personal well-being is enhanced.

Implications of a human rights approach to poverty and destitution

In its *Guidelines on Poverty Reduction* (2001) the Development Assistance Committee (DAC) of the Organisation for Economic Cooperation and Development (OECD) already noted an 'increasing focus on the "rights approach"', which links empowerment to international agreements on human and political as well as economic, social and cultural rights'. Possibly stimulated by the appointment of a Special Rapporteur on the Right to Development by the United Nations Commission on Human Rights, the World Bank has proclaimed this right as a new guideline to its policies. In line with the United Nations General Assembly Declaration on the Right to Development of 1986, this is held to imply, among other things, a persistent focus on participation from the grassroots and distributional equity (article 2 [3]).

Notably, rights-based approaches to poverty go beyond development approaches tuned to increasing productivity as the way towards progress (usually interpreted as pure 'positive-sum games'). In rights approaches, poverty is seen as 'a pronounced deprivation in well-being', as the World Bank has put it in its *World Development Report 2000/2001*, or, in current UNDP terminology, as 'a brutal denial of human rights'. Hence, the primary focus in such strategies is not on some abstract and general phenomenon – the number of people who have to survive on less than so much per day – but on *human beings* and their daily hardships, here and now.

Behind the non-implementation of poor people's rights lie complicated social, political and economic structures. In rights approaches the primary responsibility to address these is with the rights-holders themselves. Yet, when people get faced with insurmountable constraints to the realisation of their rights, other actors are to be called to their duties. In cases of concrete violations, such responsibilities of other actors tend to be quite evident. When a government orders poor people's shacks to be bulldosed down, for example, the duty bearer in respect of their right to shelter becomes easily identifiable: the state. Such situations may even lead to court cases, as has happened in the South African *Grootboom* case (Constitutional Court of South Africa, 4 October 2000). More common, however, are general patterns of structural non-implementation of the rights of the poor. In such a setting, human rights imply a duty for actors to engage in *policies* that respect fundamental freedoms and basic entitlements following from internationally declared standards. This applies not just to the state but also to institutions of the corporate world.

Finally, rights approaches imply a strong *normative* component guiding the execution of power by all actors. This element, too, distinguishes rights-based strategies clearly from needs-based approaches to poverty and destitution. When human rights are seen as not just *legal resources* but also *political instruments*, this means that power is to be regarded as legitimate only if international human rights standards are followed. *Legitimacy*, in other words, becomes the core concept, referring to the right institutions and principles, the right procedures and also normatively acceptable outcomes. Hence, rights-based approaches to overcome poverty imply efforts to address economic injustices as well, in the first place at the level of the global economy as such.

BAS DE GAAY FORTMAN

References and further reading

Gaay Fortman, Bas de (1999), 'Beyond income distribution: an entitlement systems approach to the acquirement problem', in J. van der Linden and A. Manders (eds), *The Economics of Income Distribution: Heterodox Approaches*, Cheltenham, UK and Northampton, MA, USA: Edward Elgar, pp. 29–75.

Gaay Fortman, Bas de (2003), 'Persistent poverty and inequality in an era of globalisation: implications of a rights approach', in Paul van Seters, Bas de Gaay Fortman and Arie de Ruijter (eds), *Globalisation and Its New Divides: Malcontents, Recipes, and Reform*, Amsterdam: Dutch University Press and West Lafayette, IN: Purdue University Press, pp. 149–67.

Klein Goldewijk Berma and Bas de Gaay Fortman (1999), *Where Needs Meet Rights. Economic, Social and Cultural Rights in a New Perspective*, Geneva: WCC Publications.

OECD (2001), *DAC Guidelines on Poverty Reduction*, Paris: OECD, June 2000, Vol. I, 1.4.2, no. 59.

Sen, Amartya (1999a), *Development as Freedom*, Oxford: Oxford University Press.

Sen, Amartya (1999b), 'Human rights and economic achievements', in J.R. Bauer and D. Bell (eds), *The East Asian Challenge for Human Rights*, Cambridge: Cambridge University Press, pp. 88–100.

UNDP (1998), *Integrating Human Rights with Sustainable Development*, New York: United Nations Development Programme.

UNDP (2000), *Human Development Report 2000*, Oxford: Oxford University Press.

Human Security

Even though the term 'security' has a literal meaning, it has different connotations to different people. It also depends on the context in which it is being used. So far, both in the literature as well as in practice, the term 'security' has been largely treated as synonymous with 'territorial security' or 'national security'. But recent events in the world clearly demonstrate that it is not territorial security, but 'human security' – security of jobs and income, food security, health security, personal security and so on – which are more important and relevant. The conflicts in today's world are not so much between states as they are between people. The idea of human security, though simple, is likely to revolutionise society in the twenty-first century.

Human security: concept and definition

The concept of security has for too long been interpreted narrowly: as security of territory from external aggression, or as protection of national interests in foreign policy, or as global security from the threat of a nuclear holocaust. It has been related more to nation states than to people. Forgotten was the legitimate concern of common people who sought security in their daily lives. For many of them, security symbolised protection from the threat of disease, hunger, unemployment, crime, social conflict, political repression and environmental hazards. For most people, a feeling of insecurity arises more from worries about daily life than from the dread of a cataclysmic world event.

Human security may be termed as the 'freedom from certain deprivations' as well as 'freedom from specific perceived fears'. For example, freedom from income poverty and hunger refers to security in terms of actual deprivation, where as the desire to be secure from violence or personal assault may imply security against perceived threats. But both are aspects of human security. The relative importance of these two phenomena is a subjective issue. In fact, they are interlinked. The actual food shortage may result in a perception of fear for food security. On the other hand, the perception of food shortage may lead to a large-scale hoarding and result in an actual famine.

In both actual deprivation and perceived fear, the *degree of hurtfulness* and the *rate of suddenness* may be of importance. People feel insecure and threatened when something hurts severely and suddenly. Otherwise, people try to adapt to changed situations. But at the same time, it should not mean that a prolonged suffering in the form of, for example, slow famine, is not a problem of human security. Often the degree of hurtfulness and the suddenness of phenomena like war may quickly draw the attention of the national and the international community to it as a *crisis*. But it must be recognised that even before the spillover, the seeds of human security were there. Thus the issue of human insecurity should be seen from the perspectives of both *loud emergencies* as well as *silent ones*.

A consideration of the basic concept of human security must focus on five essential characteristics:

- Human security is *people centred*. It is concerned with how people live in a society, how they exercise their choices and whether they live in peace or conflicts.
- Human security is a *universal concern*. It is relevant to people everywhere, in rich nations and poor. There are many threats that are common to all people – such as unemployment, drugs, crime, pollution and human rights violation. Their intensity may differ from one part of the world to another, but all these threats to human security are real and growing.
- Human security can be *national* or *local* and some security concerns are *global*. Economic security in terms of jobs and income may encompass more national and local contexts. But there are also global challenges to human security – challenges that arise because threats within countries rapidly spill beyond national frontiers. Environmental threats are one of the clearest examples: land degradation, deforestation and emissions of greenhouse gases affect climatic conditions around the world.
- The components of human security are *interdependent*. When the security of people is endangered anywhere in the world, all nations are likely to get involved and this

has become increasingly true in a more interdependent globalised world. Disease, pollution, drug and human trafficking, ethnic conflicts, and terrorism are no longer isolated events, confined within national borders. Their consequences travel across the globe. In today's world, human deprivation anywhere is a threat to human security everywhere.

- Human security is easier to *ensure through early prevention* than through later intervention. It is less costly, in every aspect, to meet these threats upstream than downstream. This is true of economic security, political security, communal security and so on. Often things explode down stream, as earlier and timely preventive measures were not taken upstream. In most cases, preventive development is the best guarantee for human security.

In defining human security, it is important that the notion of human security is not equated with human development. Human development is a broader concept – defined as the process of widening the range of people's choices. Human security means that people can exercise these choices safely and freely. There is of course, a link between human security and human development: they are mutually reinforcing. Progress in one area enhances the chances of progress in the other, but failure in one area also heightens the risk of failure in the other.

Human security: as people see it

It is quite difficult to provide a rigorous and precise definition of human security. This is because like other fundamental concepts such as human freedom, human security is more easily identified through its absence, rather than its presence. And most people instinctively understand, as the *Human Development Report 1994* (UNDP, 1994) indicates, what insecurity means:

'When we have enough for the children to eat, we are happy and we feel secure' – Shoemender in Thailand;

'I feel secure when I am living with my family and friends' – Primary school pupil in Kuwait;

'What makes you feel insecure above all is violence and delinquency' – Man in Ecuador;

'I shall feel secure when I know that I can walk the streets at night without being raped' – Fourth-grade school girl in Ghana;

'My security is in the name of the Lord who has made the heaven and the earth. I feel secure because I am at liberty to worship whom I like and how I like' – Woman in Nigeria;

'Before education was free, but from this year every student has to pay. Now I do not feel very secure about finishing my education' – Secondary school student in Mongolia;

'Security for me means that my job and position are safe and I can continue to provide for my family and also for something for investment and friends' – Public Administrator in Cameroon;

'Robberies make me insecure. I sometimes feel as though even my life will be stolen' – Man in Namibia;

'I believe that a girl cannot feel secure until she is married and has someone to depend on' – Woman in Iran;

'Human security indicates faith in tomorrow, not so much to do with food and clothing, as with stability of the political and economic situation' – Woman in Kyrgyzstan;

'I feel secure because I feel fulfilled and have confidence in myself. I also feel secure because God is great and watches over me' – Woman in Paraguay.

Components of human security

There have always been two major components of human security: *freedom from fear* and *freedom from want*. And the idea was to give equal weight to territories and to people. But for long, in a Cold War era, the concept was tilted in favour of the first component rather than the second. With the changed realities in the 1990s, the concept of security changed in two basic ways: from an exclusive stress on territorial security to a much greater stress on people's security and second, from security through armaments to security through sustainable human development. The world made a transition from the narrow concept of national security to an all-encompassing concept of human security.

The components of human security may be examined at different levels. At one level, it may be categorised in terms of individual and collective security; at another level, it can be arranged as local, national or global security; at yet another level, it can be looked at as economic, political or social security. At any level, there can be conformities or conflicts – whether between individual or collective security or between national or global security.

Since human security is conceptually anchored in the human development paradigm, its components should be looked at in relation to human well-being – in terms of individual and collective security in the national as well as global context. In the national contexts, people's security can be considered under seven main categories: economic security, food security, health security, environmental security, personal security, community security and political security. At the global level, challenges to human security come from various sources: disparities in economic opportunities, international migration, conflicts and refugees, global environmental phenomena, the drugs trade, human trafficking, international terrorism and so on.

Indicators of human security

What best indicates the presence or absence of human security? It may be an easy question, but there is no easy answer to it, particularly if quantitative indicators with too scientific a rationale are sought. Indicators for human security should be rather common-sense indicators, which would not necessarily be a measure of human security, but rather be indicative of it. Five observations may be pertinent in this regard:

- Indicators of human security should be theoretically anchored into the paradigm of human development. Therefore, in many cases, human development indicators – whether input or outcome indicators – can serve as a good proxy for human security. For example, in terms of input indicators, the human development indicator of access to health services can be a good proxy for health security, Or in terms of outcome indicators, the human development indicator of the unemployment rate can be a good surrogate for economic security.

- Simple comparison of individual indicators can be more powerful than composite indices. For example, if the food production per capita of a country and the food import dependency ratio of a country are contrasted with the daily calorie supply as a percentage of requirements for the people, it can give a strong signal for food security in that society. On a consistency basis, if the per capita food production goes down while the food import goes up consistently, but the daily calorie supply as percentage of requirements declines, this can be a serious indication for food insecurity in that country. It can be a simple, but quite useful approach.

- Human security indicators should be simple, minimum, meaningful and easy to understand. At the same time, they should encompass, as much as possible, the various aspects of human security. In identifying the indicators of human security, the contextual differences between the developing and the developed world should be taken into account and a balance between the two should be made.

- The choice of human security indicators should be largely data driven, as choice of indicators based on theoretical considerations may not be practical. Yet in terms of human security data, there may be two major problems. First, in many cases, there are no consistent time-series data on some indicators, making any meaningful monitoring of human security quite difficult. Second, data may not be available for all countries, as a result of which intercountry comparisons are not possible.

- Even though human security indicators, individually and collectively identify human security threats, they should not be mistaken as a complete scientific early warning system.

For selected components of human security in the *national* context, the following indicators, which do not represent a comprehensive list, may be proposed: *economic security* – unemployment rate and real earnings or wages; *health security* – access to health services, safe water and basic sanitation, incidence of HIV/AIDS; *environmental security* – deforestation rate, emission of greenhouse gases; *personal security* – number of deaths from traffic accidents, number of robberies and incidence of domestic violence; *political security* – number of refugees and internally displaced people. For the *global* level, income disparities between nations, the amount of revenue generated by the drug trade, and the number of people trafficked across borders can be good indicators for human security.

Policy implications

In today's world, human insecurity demands new policy responses, both nationally and internationally. Over the past five decades, humankind has gradually built up an edifice of global security – an edifice of nuclear deterrents, power balances, strategic alliances, regional security pacts and international policing through the superpowers and the United Nations. Much of this global security framework needs change to ensure the security of all people the world over. Some global concerns require national action – others, a coordinated international response.

Within the national context, economic, food and health security required a pro-poor macroeconomic framework ensuring the access of poor people to basic social services and productive resources, generating pro-poor economic growth, the benefits of which would be translated into the lives of poor people. In order to ensure environmental security, pro-poor policies must be environmentally sensitive so that economic growth also becomes environmentally sustainable. Issues like personal security or community security would require respecting human rights of individuals and groups. Changes in the legal framework, ensuring democratic governance, freedom of the press and the judiciary, are essential elements for all this.

In the national contexts, policies for social integration are necessary for human security. Disparities among groups, inequalities in opportunities among racial and ethnic groups need to be addressed for broad-based social inclusion. Specific measures have to be taken with regard to sex disparities and gender issues.

Experience shows that where there are multiple problems of personal, economic, political or environmental security, there is a risk of national breakdown. Timely preventive action in political as well as economic terms can help avoid such crisis and disaster. A stitch in time saves nine is most appropriate with regard to human security.

SELIM JAHAN

Reference and further reading

Jahan, Selim (1993), 'Human security: an affordable goal?', mimeo, Human Development Report Office, UNDP, New York, October.

Jahan, Selim (1996), 'Human security indicators: a suggested list', paper presented at the International Conference on Human Security, Dalhousie University, Halifax, Canada, 15–16 August.

UNDP (1994), *Human Development Report: New Dimensions of Human Security*, Oxford: Oxford University Press.

Income Distribution

Income distribution as a central topic in development has waxed and waned over the last half-century. In the immediate post-Second World War period, income distribution was seen as central, linked to such issues as the need for land distribution and the generation of a surplus by transferring underused labour from rural to urban areas, as outlined in the theory of Arthur Lewis. Income distribution then faded as an issue until the 1970s, when priorities for generating employment and meeting basic needs were often seen as requiring macro strategies of redistribution with growth. In the 1980s and 1990s, income distribution faded once more as attention shifted to policies of economic stabilisation and structural adjustment. By the early twenty-first century, income distribution became once again an important point of focus, both for policy and analysis. This was stimulated in part by concerns that globalisation was creating forces in many countries that were exacerbating greater inequalities of income distribution, which required positive corrective action.

Concerns with income distribution in development reflect values and objectives, theory and analysis. The links with values and objectives are readily apparent – although it is important to stress that attention to income distribution goes well beyond concern with poverty, both conceptually and analytically. A focus on income distribution encompasses issues of equity, justice and power. Theory and analysis exercise their own important influence on perceptions and policy. Neoclassical economic theory tends to treat income distribution as an outcome and to direct attention to policy issues of price and the efficient allocation of resources. In contrast, structural analysis, neo-Marxian analysis and, more recently, human development analysis give much greater place to income distribution as a causal factor, both in understanding and modelling the process of development and in identifying crucial variables influencing outcomes. Accordingly, within these three paradigms, income distribution takes on an importance in setting the national objectives of development and in developing strategy within the political–economic parameters of the situation.

Empirical research has uncovered other relationships. There is evidence, for example, that inequality within countries can inhibit economic growth and slow poverty reduction. It can have repercussions on civic, social and political life and institutions, undermining social solidarity. And there is evidence that social stress in more unequal societies is associated with lower levels of health for all social classes, not merely the poorest. Research has also shown that inequality between geographic, ethnic or social groups – 'horizontal inequality' – is correlated with higher risks of civil conflict within countries.

Patterns and trends in income distribution

Though data are not comprehensive, far from reliable and not fully comparable, information on income distribution is available for nearly 80 developing countries and for some 25 countries in transition (UNDP, 2004). These show that most developing countries have higher levels of inequality than both industrial countries and countries in transition, judged by two common measures: (1) the ratios of the shares of income or consumption of the richest 10 or 20 per cent of the population to the shares of the poorest 10 or 20 per cent; and (2) the Gini coefficient, which provides a measure of the overall distribution of income (with a scale in which 0 indicates perfect equality and 1 perfect inequality).

Using the latest data available, mostly for the years 1998–2000, the median ratio between the average income or consumption of the richest and the poorest 20 per cent in developing countries is about ten, but with a very wide range. The ratios rise to 32 in Brazil and about 34 or more in South Africa and five other countries in Sub-Saharan Africa. In contrast, the ratio is well under ten in most countries of South and South East Asia. In China the ratio of the richest 20 per cent to the poorest 20 per cent is estimated to be 11 and in India about five, though in both countries it may be rising quite rapidly.

In recent years, the median ratio of income or consumption of the richest to the poorest 20 per cent in the high-income OECD countries has been about 5.5, ranging between 3.5 and 4.5 in Scandinavia and Japan and 6 to 8 elsewhere, with the United States the highest at 8.5. In the transition countries, the median ratio of the consumption or earnings of the richest 20 per cent to the poorest 20 per cent is about five. The ratio was the highest in the Russian Federation (about 10.5) while in Uzbekistan, the Czech Republic and Slovakia the ratio was four or less.

In contrast, in developing countries, using data for 2000 or the most recent data available (UNDP, 2004), the median Gini coefficient is about 0.45 compared with 0.33 in the industrial countries and 0.30 in countries in transition. Among developing countries, the highest and the lowest Gini coefficients are 0.71 in Namibia and 0.29 in Rwanda. Within the transition countries the Gini coefficients range from 0.46 in the Russian Federation to 0.24 in Hungary. These may be compared with the Gini coeffiicients in the high-income OECD countries, which range between about 0.25 in Sweden and Norway to 0.41 in the United States.

Theories and causes
Until the 1970s, the Kuznets curve, developed by the Nobel Laureate economist Simon Kuznets (1955), exercised a dominant influence on thinking about income distribution and development. On the basis of data from 18 developing countries – about all for which there was at that time data – Kuznets suggested that overall income inequality tended to rise in the initial stages of development, then to level out and later to decline as countries became more developed. This explained what seemed at that time to be the pattern of income distribution, in which income distribution in the middle-income countries was more unequal than in the poorer and the more-developed countries.

With more recent data, these patterns no longer seemed to hold (Chenery et al., 1974; Atkinson, 1997; Champernowne and Cowell, 1998; Ferreira, 1999; Birdsall, 2000). In the immediate post-war period, a dominant view had been that inequality served as a positive influence on economic growth, on the grounds that rich people saved more than poorer people and that this inequality led to higher rates of saving and thus to higher rates of investment and growth. However, by the 1970s, this view began to be questioned. Often poorer groups saved a higher percentage of their low incomes, especially when savings in kind were counted; and the savings of richer groups were often transferred abroad, rather than being invested within the country; and by the 1970s, evidence was emerging that physical capital was much less important for growth than education and health, savings and investment which added to or protected human resources.

Over the 1980s, income distribution faded from concern, at least from the mainstream development agenda, as promoted by the World Bank and the IMF. Orthodoxy focused on policies of stabilisation and structural adjustment, privatisation and liberalisation, backed up by neoclassical forms of analysis. However, evidence accumulated that income distribution was often worsening as a result of these policies and by the late 1990s, attention was once more being given to income distribution, though mostly as the counterpart of achieving poverty reduction rather than as an objective in its own right or as a necessary component of a more complex process of development. In addition, empirical studies of the late 1990s were suggesting that the relationship between income distribution and economic growth was positive or, at worst, neutral. Thus the pursuit of policies of redistribution could in principle have a positive effect on economic growth and development, and at least not a negative one.

The World Bank attributes the renewed interest in inequality to three reasons. First, recent empirical work on the link between inequality and growth has tended to find a negative relationship, especially between inequality of asset distribution and growth. The Bank finds that the more equal the distribution of assets such as land, the higher growth rates tend to be. Second, with poverty reduction in many countries being slow at best, there is a need to re-examine public policies of redistribution in order to explore new ways to accelerate poverty reduction – from safety nets to social expenditures. Third, several recent empirical studies have identified impacts of inequality – independent of the poverty level – on health outcomes, such as morbidity or mortality rates or as a cause for violence.

Country experience and policies

Some of the most successful countries in terms of economic growth, poverty reduction and human development are also those that have followed objectives and strategies of equitable development. These include South Korea, Malaysia, Mauritius, Sri Lanka and Tunisia as well as the smaller countries of Botswana, Barbados, Costa Rica and the Indian states of Kerala and Tamil Nadu. This experience combined with analytical models of pro-poor growth and distribution suggests a range of policies and strategies, which can help achieve more equitable income distribution, poverty reduction and growth. These include:

- *Macro strategies of redistribution with growth*, in which over time, the additions to income from economic growth are allocated to forms of investment disproportionately benefiting the poorest groups in a country.
- *Pro-poor policies in rural and urban areas*, especially in agriculture and informal urban and peri-urban production and related sectors serving the poorest or generating income for them (McCulloch and Baulch, 1999).
- *Pro-poor policies in health, education and other social sectors*, especially benefiting the poorest sectors of the population.
- *Attention to the gender impact* of public expenditure and legislation relating to inheritance and rights of women.

- *Measures to improve the position of children and minority groups*, especially by targeting social expenditures in health and education and other welfare services.
- *Transfers of income and assets*, in ways that increase productivity and production with a minimum of disruption. These encompass taxation, reform or withdrawal of inequitable subsidies, reallocation of government budgets and expenditure, as well as land redistribution and reform of inheritance law and arrangements.
- *Human rights legislation and institutions*. These are often ignored in economic strategy – but in fact have a major role to play in favour of poor and marginalised groups, especially if backed up by participatory approaches and clear government commitments.

The list of potential policies is long. The priorities and relevance for each country must be judged in relation to the national context, economic and social priorities and political feasibility. The main influence is likely to be perceptions of the links between income distribution and achievement of more mainstream economic, social and political goals. Recent analysis and evidence suggests that more equitable income distribution is often positively associated with other economic and social objectives.

RICHARD JOLLY

References

Atkinson, A.B. (1997), 'Bringing income distribution in from the cold', *Economic Journal*, **107** (441), 297–321.
Birdsall, Nancy (2000), 'Why inequality matters: the developing and transitional economies', Paper prepared for Conference on the World Economy in the Twenty-First Century: Challenges and Opportunities, Mt Holyoke College, South Hadley, MA, 18–19 February.
Champernowne, D.G. and F.A. Cowell (1998), *Economic Inequality and Income Distribution*, Cambridge: Cambridge University Press.
Chenery, Hollis B., Montek S. Ahluwalia, C.L.G. Bell, John H. Duloy and Richard Jolly (1974), *Redistribution with Growth: Policies to Improve Income Distribution in Developing Countries in the Context of Economic Growth*, London: Oxford University Press.
Ferreira, Francisco H.G. (1999), 'Inequality and economic performance: a brief overview to theories of growth and distribution', www.worldbank.org/poverty/inequal/index.htm.
Kuznets, Simon (1955), 'Economic growth and income inequality', *American Economic Review*, **45**, 1–28.
McCulloch, Neil and Bob Baulch (1999), 'Tracking pro-poor growth: new ways to spot the biases and benefits', *id21 Insights*, September.
UNDP (2004), *Human Development Report 2004*, Oxford and New York: Oxford University Press.

Inequality Measurement

Development is fundamentally concerned with differences in achievements – over time and space, across individuals, groups and countries – and several key themes from development involve inequality measurement in one form or another. Lucas (1988), for example, has stressed the importance of accounting for cross-country variations in per capita income. Kuznets (1955) hypothesised an inverted 'U'-shaped relationship between a developing country's per capita income and its level of income inequality. Many recent development models have explored the instrumental impact of inequality on development, or vice versa (Ray, 1998). Sen (1997, 1999) has emphasised its inherent ethical dimensions while broadening its evaluative basis to other categories of achievements besides income.

Advances in inequality measurement occurred sporadically until 1970 when Atkinson published a remarkable paper that presented a welfare-based measure, revived the axiomatic contributions of Dalton (1920), and used contemporary results from risk analysis to provide a welfare basis for the Lorenz curve and its ranking. Along with Kolm's (1969) deep, but difficult, treatise, and Sen's (1973) exceptionally clear and thought-provoking monograph, it set the agenda for a literature at the crossroads of welfare economics, philosophy, applied economics, and mathematics and statistics. Subsequent work has extended the normative approach to inequality measurement, offered sophisticated characterisations of measures in term of the axioms they satisfy, constructed inequality rankings beyond the Lorenz criterion, and explored the implications of multidimensionality. This entry provides a brief introduction to the contemporary literature on inequality measurement. See Foster and Sen (1997), Cowell (2000), and Lambert (2002) for more thorough presentations and Ray (1998) and Fields (2001) for development perspectives.

Elements
Inequality measurement begins with a specification of the individual unit of analysis, such as the person, household, ethnic group or country. Next, the quantitative variable of interest is identified, which is often a measure of resources such as income, earnings, expenditures, or wealth. For simplicity, the unidimensional variable in question will be called 'income' here (multidimensional aspects are discussed below); it is assumed to take on positive values. Group variables are often an average of individual levels, and when the unit is a household, an 'equivalence scale' is typically employed to account for differing needs across units. The process yields a 'distribution', which is a list of units and their respective income levels.

Inequality comparisons are made using inequality rankings and inequality measures. An 'inequality ranking' is a rule for comparing distributions in terms of inequality. A 'complete' ranking compares all distributions; a 'partial' ranking may leave some comparisons indeterminate. 'Lorenz dominance' compares distributions using a figure called the 'Lorenz curve', which, for every population share *p* between zero and one, plots the share of the total income received by the lowest *p* of the population. A completely equal distribution has a Lorenz curve on the diagonal where the income share *is* the population share. Inequality is reflected in departures below the diagonal. One distribution is more equal than another according to Lorenz dominance if it has a higher Lorenz curve for some *p* and no lower for all *p*. When Lorenz curves cross, this partial ranking does not apply.

An 'inequality measure' is a function or mathematical formula assigning each distribution a number to indicate its level of inequality. A key characteristic of an inequality measure, as opposed to a 'poverty measure' (Sen, 1976) or 'welfare function', is its *relative* nature: it is concerned only with the relative positions of incomes and not with their absolute levels. This is usually captured in the requirement that a *proportional* increment to all incomes does not affect overall inequality (the scale invariance axiom given below). An alternative approach specifies that an *equal* increment across all incomes must leave inequality unaffected (Kolm, 1969).

Basic axioms
There are a number of basic properties for relative inequality measures to satisfy. The axiom of 'Lorenz consistency' ensures that the inequality measure agrees with the judgement of Lorenz dominance when it applies. The 'symmetry' axiom states that the order

of the income receiving units does not matter. 'Replication invariance' requires that if all units were cloned or replicated a certain number of times, the inequality level would be unchanged. 'Scale invariance' requires that if all incomes were multiplied by a positive constant, the inequality level would be unchanged. Finally, the 'transfer principle' states that if a regressive transfer (from poor to rich that preserves total income) were made, then inequality should rise. A basic result is that Lorenz consistency is equivalent to the other four axioms (Foster, 1985): Whenever all measures satisfying the four axioms agree that one distribution has more inequality than another, the distributions must be ranked by Lorenz dominance (and vice versa). Inequality measures that have greater sensitivity to transfers at the lower end of the distribution are called 'transfer sensitive'. Shorrocks and Foster (1987) characterised the unambiguous partial ranking implied by all Lorenz-consistent and transfer-sensitive inequality measures and showed how additional comparisons are possible when Lorenz curves cross. For distributions with a fixed mean, Atkinson's (1970) theorem provides a normative dimension to the Lorenz criterion: it shows that Lorenz dominance also signals higher welfare according to a class of equity-preferring social welfare functions.

Income standards
Different inequality measures have very distinct motivations, interpretations and properties. Even so, a unifying framework encompassing virtually all inequality measures can be constructed using the concept of an 'income standard', which defines for any given distribution a *representative* income level for that distribution. The most common examples of income standards are the mean or median, but there are many other examples focusing on different aspects of the distribution, for example, the income at the 75th percentile or the income share of the lowest 10 per cent. Income standards satisfy certain properties: *symmetry* and *replication invariance* (as noted above); *normalisation* (if all units receive the same income, then the standard is that level); *monotonicity* (the standard will not decrease when a single income is increased); and *linear homogeneity* (a positive constant times all incomes leads to the same constant times the standard). Income standards are the basic building blocks of inequality measures.

Assembling inequality measures
Measuring inequality is simple in the two-income case, where it is natural to use the difference between the larger (say b) and the smaller (say a) income, normalised by either b or a to obtain $1 - a/b$ or $b/a - 1$. Other formulae are possible, but all relative measures rank two-person distributions in the same way and can be expressed in terms of a ratio involving a and b.

In the many-income case, aggregation becomes important and different inequality measures often disagree. None the less, virtually all relative measures have the same general form. They first summarise the distribution using a pair of income standards, A and B, with one always higher than the other, say $A \leq B$. Then they evaluate the inequality between the two standards using an expression involving their ratio such as the two given above. Such a measure inherits symmetry, replication invariance and scale invariance from its constituent standards; the transfer principle relies on the relative curvatures of the two.

Ratios

The '90/10 ratio', defined as B/A where B is the 90th percentile income and A is the 10th percentile income, is used in labour economics to assess the spread in the distribution of earned income. (An alternative version measures the difference in the log incomes at these percentiles, which reduces to the logarithm of B/A.) This form of inequality measure conveys precise information about one aspect of the distribution in a particularly intuitive way and, depending on the focus of the investigation, other pairs of percentile incomes can be used (for example, 90/50 or 75/25). The 'range' is the limiting example where A is the minimum and B the maximum income (also measured as $1 - A/B$). Note that the income standard employed in these ratios is quite crude, as it collapses the entire distribution to one particular percentile income. This can be useful in the presence of severe data constraints. However, the resulting measure violates the transfer principle and even ranks some pairs of distributions *opposite* to Lorenz dominance.

The 'decile dispersion ratio' is defined as B/A where A is the mean income among the lowest 10 per cent of the population and B is the mean of the top 10 per cent. More generally, if A is the mean of the top q per cent of the population and B is the mean of the lowest p per cent, the resulting measure might be called the (q/p) 'dispersion ratio'. This reduces to twice the 'Kuznets ratio' (the share of income received by the richest fifth over the share of the poorest two-fifths) when q is 20 and p is 40. A dispersion ratio conveys meaningful information about the distribution, has graphical links to the Lorenz curve, and can be used when data are limited. However, it also ignores part of the distribution and just violates the transfer principle.

Gini coefficient

The 'Gini coefficient' is obtained from the formula $1 - A/B$ where B is the mean and A is the 'Sen income standard' defined as the expected value of the minimum of two incomes drawn randomly (with replacement) from the distribution. The Sen standard places greater weight on lower incomes (the weights on the highest, middle and lowest income are one-ninth, three-ninths and five ninths, respectively, in the three-income case), and hence its value cannot exceed the mean. The increasing weights also ensure that it satisfies a transfer principle for income standards, and hence is an equity-preferring 'welfare function'. Indeed, the Sen standard is twice the area under the 'generalised Lorenz curve', which is obtained from the Lorenz curve by multiplication by the mean and underlies the unambiguous welfare ranking known as 'generalised Lorenz dominance' or 'second-order stochastic dominance' (Shorrocks, 1983). The Gini coefficient is very commonly used and has helpful interpretations as: the expected difference between two incomes divided by twice the mean; twice the covariance between income and income ranks divided by the mean; twice the area between the Lorenz curve and the diagonal (so it is obviously Lorenz consistent); and the percentage welfare loss due to inequality (using the Sen welfare function). Weymark (1981) has extended the definition to obtain the class of 'generalised Ginis'.

Atkinson and generalised entropy measures

Several inequality measures rely on an important standard that generalises the mean and was introduced into the inequality literature by Kolm (1969) and Atkinson (1970). For a given non-zero parameter q, the *general mean* is found by raising each income to the qth power, averaging across the transformed incomes, and raising the result to the $1/q$th power; for zero, it is the *geometric mean*. This transformation emphasises low (high) incomes when q is below (above) 1. For a completely equal distribution, the general mean equals the mean; for an unequal distribution, the general mean is increasing in q and tends to the min (or max) income as q tends to negative (or positive) infinity. With q below 1 the general mean satisfies a transfer principle and becomes the equity-preferring welfare function Atkinson called the 'equally distributed equivalent income'.

The Atkinson family of inequality measures is expressed as $1 - A/B$ where B is the arithmetic mean and A is a general mean with q less than 1, and thus it measures the percentage loss in welfare due to inequality. The parameter $1 - q$ indicates the measure's degree of inequality aversion, with greater $1 - q$ indicating greater sensitivity to transfers at the lower end of the distribution. This general method for constructing *normative* inequality measures from welfare functions and vice versa has been further explored by Blackorby and Donaldson (1978). A second family of measures known as the 'generalised entropy measures' is also based on the general means: for q below 1 it is a function of the ratio A/B from the Atkinson measures; for q above 1, where the general mean exceeds the mean, it uses B/A where B is the general mean and A is the mean; and for q equals unity, it is Theil's measure discussed below. These measures include multiples of the 'mean log deviation' (or 'Theil's second measure'), which is the logarithm of the ratio of the arithmetic mean to the geometric mean, and the 'squared coefficient of variation', which is the variance over the squared mean. From the curvature properties of general means, all the Atkinson and generalised entropy measures satisfy the transfer principle, and thus are Lorenz consistent; transfer sensitivity holds for q below 2.

Limiting measures

Two frequently used measures of inequality cannot be written in terms of a ratio of two income standards: 'Theil's measure', whose formula has its origins in information theory, and the 'variance of logarithms', which is the *variance* applied to the distribution of the logarithm of incomes. Both are limits of measures that are functions of ratios of general means (Foster and Shneyerov, 1999). While the Theil measure satisfies the transfer principle, the variance of logarithms does not and the extent of its Lorenz inconsistencies can be most remarkable (Foster and Ok, 1999).

Subgroups

The univariate approach is often extended to include additional dimensions of relevance to well-being and inequality. Some variables are purely descriptive (for example, ethnicity, region, or gender), with no direct effect on well-being, but lead to a salient partitioning of the population into subgroups. They can help create a *multilevel* understanding of inequality, where subgroups are viewed as income-receiving units for evaluating *between-group inequality* (the inequality across subgroup income standards) as well as subpopulations for evaluating *within-group inequality* (a weighted sum of subgroup inequality levels). 'Decomposability' axioms require overall inequality to be the sum of these two components. Following Theil's (1967) introduction of this concept, several measures (including the generalised entropy, Atkinson's and the variance of logarithms) have been axiomatically characterised using decomposability axioms (Bourguignon, 1979; Shorrocks, 1980; Foster and Shneyerov, 1999). 'Subgroup consistency' is a less-restrictive axiom that requires overall inequality to rise whenever one subgroup inequality level rises and the others are unchanged (holding population sizes and income standards of all subgroups fixed). Shorrocks (1988) characterised the generalised entropy and Atkinson families using subgroup consistency. The Gini coefficient satisfies neither axiom, unless subgroup distributions do not overlap; an extra term measuring the degree of overlap can make the Gini decomposition exact.

Differing needs
A classification variable may also convey welfare-relevant information (for example, differential needs across a heterogeneous population). If the quantitative impact can be modelled and income levels can be adjusted (as with equivalence scales) then the analysis can proceed as before. However, if the link is not precisely known or if the difference in needs across units is purely ordinal, an alternative measurement strategy must be found (see, for example, Shorrocks, 2004).

Many dimensions
A more complete assessment of well-being and inequality may require examining several dimensions at once, as suggested by the basic needs approach or Sen's (1997) capabilities model. Kolm (1977) and Atkinson and Bourguignon (1982) construct rankings applicable in the multidimensional case and the resulting literature has produced several new inequality measures in this context. One unavoidable problem is the fundamental absence of comparability *across* the dimensions. The Human Development Index deals with this through an ad hoc normalisation process, but there are clearly deep issues here both methodologically and conceptually. Another research question is how to gauge the contributions of the individual variables to overall inequality. Shorrocks (1982) has explored this in the case where the various dimensions are different sources of income, and derived a useful 'source decomposition' formula. Research continues on this and other questions in the multidimensional environment.

JAMES E. FOSTER

References
Atkinson, A.B. (1970), 'On the measurement of inequality', *Journal of Economic Theory*, **2**, 244–63.
Atkinson, A.B. and F. Bourguignon (1982), 'The comparison of multi-dimensioned distributions of economic status', *Review of Economic Studies*, **49** (2), 183–201.
Blackorby, C. and D. Donaldson (1978), 'Measures of relative equality and their meaning in terms of social welfare', *Journal of Economic Theory*, **18** (1), 59–80.
Bourguignon, F. (1979), 'Decomposable income inequality measures', *Econometrica*, **47**, 901–20.
Cowell, F.A. (2000), 'Measurement of inequality', in Anthony B. Atkinson and François Bourguignon, *Handbook of Income Distribution*, Vol. 1, Amsterdam: North-Holland, pp. 87–116.
Dalton, H. (1920), 'The measurement of inequality of incomes', *Economic Journal*, **30** (119), 348–61.
Fields, Gary S. (2001), *Distribution and Development: A New Look at the Developing World*, Cambridge, MA and London: MIT Press.
Foster, J.E. (1985), 'Inequality measurement', in H. Peyton Young (ed.), *Fair Allocation*, Providence, RI: American Mathematical Society, pp. 31–68.
Foster, J.E. and E.A. Ok (1999), 'Lorenz dominance and the variance of logarithms', *Econometrica*, **67**, 901–8.
Foster, J.E. and A. Sen (1997), 'On economic inequality: after a quarter century', in Sen, pp. 107–219.

Foster, J.E. and A.A. Shneyerov (1999), 'A general class of additively decomposable inequality measures', *Economic Theory*, **14**, 89–111.

Kolm, Serge-Christophe (1969), 'The optimal production of social justice', in Julius Margolis and Henri Guitton (eds), *Public Economics*, London: Macmillan, pp. 145–200.

Kolm, Serge-Christophe (1977), 'Multidimensional egalitarianisms', *Quarterly Journal of Economics*, **91**, 416–42.

Kuznets, S. (1955), 'Economic growth and income inequality', *American Economic Review*, **45** (1), 1–28.

Lambert, Peter (2002), *The Distribution and Redistribution of Income*, 3rd edn, Manchester: Manchester University Press.

Lucas, R. (1988), 'On the mechanics of development', *Journal of Monetary Economics*, **22**, 3–42.

Ray, Debraj (1998), *Development Economics*, Princeton, NJ: Princeton University Press.

Sen, Amartya K. (1973), *On Economic Inequality*, Oxford: Clarendon.

Sen, A.K. (1976), 'Poverty: an ordinal approach to measurement', *Econometrica*, **44**, 219–31.

Sen, Amartya K. (1997), *On Economic Inequality* (enlarged edn with a substantial new annexe co-written with James E. Foster), Oxford: Clarendon.

Sen, Amartya (1999), *Development as Freedom*, New York: Alfred Knopf.

Shorrocks, A.F. (1980), 'The class of additively decomposable inequality measures', *Econometrica*, **48** (3), 613–25.

Shorrocks, A.F. (1982), 'Inequality decomposition by factor components', *Econometrica*, **50** (1), 193–211.

Shorrocks, A.F. (1983), 'Ranking income distributions', *Economica*, **50** (197), 3–17.

Shorrocks, A.F. (1988), 'Aggregation issues in inequality measurement', in W. Eichorn (ed.), *Measurement in Economics*, New York: Physica-Verlag, pp. 429–51.

Shorrocks, A.F. (2004), 'Inequality and welfare evaluations of heterogeneous income distributions', Research Paper no. 2004/1, World Institute for Development Economics Research, Helsinki.

Shorrocks, A.F. and J.E. Foster (1987), 'Transfer sensitive inequality measures', *Review of Economic Studies*, **54**, 485–97.

Theil, Henri (1967), *Economics and Information Theory*, Amsterdam: North-Holland.

Weymark, J.A. (1981), 'Generalised Gini inequality indices', *Mathematical Social Sciences*, **1**, 409–30.

Informal Sector Employment

The argument that poverty is mainly a question of insufficient or inadequate economic activity – whether voluntary or imposed – has become less convincing since the 1970s, when case studies on what became known as the informal sector in various parts of the world began to reveal the highly active existence of men, women and children crowding at the bottom of the urban economy in Third World countries. A stream of empirical micro studies, initially undertaken by anthropologists in urban locations within the Third World, has expanded our knowledge of how workers succeed in living on the fruits of their labours outside the formal sector of the economy. The formal–informal dichotomy can be regarded as a new variation on the dualism theories of the past. In the colonial era a contrast was constructed between an invasive Western capitalist sector and an opposing Eastern non-capitalist people's economy. In post-colonial development theory the concept of dualism was applied to the dichotomy of traditional and modern. According to this view, the rural agricultural order was still predominantly pre-capitalist while the urban-based industrial economy was described as capitalist. In the most recent phase of the dualism doctrine capitalism is the label of only the advanced segment of the urban milieu: the formal sector. The modes of production in the lower economic terrain, with their non-capitalist stamp, are characterised as the informal sector.

In operationalising these variations on dualism, the contrasts are more significant than the specific characteristics of each moiety. For instance, it is entirely normal to describe the informal sector by summing up the absence of elements found in the formal sector.

In the absence of a more analytical definition, the landscape of the informal sector becomes synonymous with the kaleidoscope of unregulated, poorly skilled and low-paid workers. Highlighting this chaotic assortment, Keith Hart coined the term 'informal economy' in his famous paper of 1973, based on fieldwork in the Ghanaian city of Accra.

Sometimes the term refers to the modality of employment, and sometimes it refers to the organisation of economic activity as a whole. The first definition refers to the income from work, performed either on one's own account and at one's own risk or as waged labour, for which no explicit written or oral contract stipulating the rights and obligations of the parties has been agreed; where there is no legal protection for the conditions of employment, and the activities are only summarily recorded in the government's accounts, if at all. Focusing on the organisation of activity emphasises characteristics like the small scale of enterprises, the predominance of familial employment and property, low capital intensity and simple technology, fluctuating production, easy entry to and exit from the lower echelons of the economy, the preponderance of local markets and the lack of government recognition and support. In the former case the dualism is attributed to the nature of employment and labour relations, while in the latter the economy is split into two circuits, each with its own method of production. The assumption that these are parallel dichotomies is incorrect. The criteria do not produce a clear and consistent classification. The resulting confusion stems from the tendency to incorporate elements of both definitions in the analysis. The hybrid often chosen seems to arise from the fact that informality is frequently associated with self-employment. This was also how Hart initially described it (Hart, 1973, p. 66).

Despite the ambiguous and overlapping criteria, the duality of the urban order is explained in both definitions with reference to the nature of government intervention. The rules applying in the formal sector refer to both the proper use of labour and set quality standards that the goods and services offered must meet. The informal sector is less burdened by public regulation, partly because of the authorities' inability to get a grip on the wide range of activities through conditions and licensing, and partly as a result of the way in which economic actors resist registration, inspection and taxation by the government.

Since the introduction of the informal sector concept, opinion has been divided as to its socio-economic impact. Some authors, inclined to a more positive assessment, have pointed to the accelerated shift in livelihood patterns away from agriculture and villages to cities and towns in the Third World since the mid-twentieth century. Even if the masses of migrants flooding into urban areas were fortunate enough to establish a foothold, the vast majority of them could gain no access to the formal sector. It was still too small to cope with the continuous influx of newcomers. Under the circumstances the informal sector acted as a catchment reservoir for jobseekers who had been forced out of their rural agricultural existence. In this explanation, the emphasis is on the stamina, the flexibility, the will to adapt, the ingenuity and the attempts made for upward mobility of the footloose workforce flooding into Third World cities. The more integrated they became in their new milieu of work and life and the more skills they acquired, the better qualified they would be for the formal sector of the economy. In making this leap forward they would form trade unions to strengthen their bargaining power *vis-à-vis* both employers and government.

The more critical analysis of researchers who have observed that the formal sector remained inaccessible for reasons other than the inferior quality of the new urbanites' labour, and their other defects, rejects such an optimistic view. The failure of the new-comers' efforts to find stable and reasonably paid work is in this alternative perception due mainly to a development strategy that, in the face of excess supply, seeks to keep the price of labour as low as possible, allows no room for collective action to reduce these people's vulnerability and refuses to provide this footloose workforce with official support. In short, the lack of registration, organisation and protection does not have its origin in the free play of social forces, but is the product of economic interests that benefit from the state of informality in which a wide range of activities in all branches of the economy are kept, systematically and on a large scale, through evasion of labour laws and taxation.

Indeed, the informal sector is not a separate and closed circuit of work and labour. To fully understand the mechanisms at work we must focus on the interaction between the formal and informal sectors, and particularly on the dependence of the latter on the former, and its subordination to it. My own analysis refutes in the first place the long-held idea that the informal sector is a characteristic feature of urban economic activity. To the extent that there is a duality, the tendency to split into two sectors manifests itself in a way that transcends the nature of the urban economy. By drawing the same distinction in the rural economy, it is possible to identify the ties between formal and informal segments in town and hinterland – manifested in the circulation of both labour and capital – and include them in an understanding of the economic order as a whole.

In the second place, I reject the view that informality refers largely or exclusively to self-employment. What often appears to be own-account work is in fact a disguised form of wage labour, for orders sourced out through intermediaries such as (sub)contractors or jobbers. Both in small-scale enterprises and in the chain of dependency made up of brokers and ending with home workers, wages are paid not time-rated, but calculated on the basis of piecework. To record this as self-employment is to overlook the fact that such labouring modalities actually bear the hallmark of an employer–employee relationship expressed in the form of wage payment.

The different views on the informal sector did not stop most studies focusing, until recently, on its time-bound nature. Whatever the school of thought authors adhered to, they almost always felt they could assume that informality was a temporary phenomenon born of the slow expansion of the formal sector economy. The acceleration that would inevitably happen would lead to a simultaneous shrinking of the informal sector. Underlying this prognosis was the assumption of parallel development whereby the process of transformation seen in the Third World from the second half of the twentieth century onwards would essentially follow the same path already travelled by developed societies. The formalisation of industrial activity was bound to lead to technological mod-ernisation and scale expansion, while labour productivity would also increase as capital was added. This transformation was meant to be accompanied by growing state involve-ment designed to increase public control over the use of capital, labour and other resources. The informal sector workers would gain a voice in society by taking collective action to represent their own interests. These analyses, made in the 1970s, seem to have lost more and more of their currency over the years.

The fact that the informal sector has continued to grow rather than decline in magni-tude and significance is undoubtedly the most obvious indication of this reverse trend. The earlier estimates that less than half the working population lived on the proceeds of the informal sector have since been revised to include at least three-quarters or even nine-tenths of all those who are gainfully employed. A complex of economic and social mechanisms has led to a rapid fall in the volume of labour in agriculture. Transfer to other areas of economic activity in both urban and rural areas has occurred under conditions characteristic of work in the informal sector, can be summarised as sustained spatial mobility, no stable but casual employment and piecework rather than time-rate work. The growing pressure in the bottom layers of the economy outside agriculture has not been relieved by the expansion of formal sector employment. There are in fact signs that this segment has shrunk over the past few decades. The recognition of this unexpected dynamic has led to a reconsideration of the view that the process of economic growth in the Third World is essentially a delayed repetition of the industrialisation and urbanisation scenario that laid the foundations for the Western welfare state in the early twentieth century.

This critical review of the initial notion of an evolutionary trajectory based on the Western model has major policy implications. The new political correctness is to state that efforts should no longer focus on formalising the labour system. In a major deviation from the previous route to development, the suggestion now is that the privileges enjoyed by an exceedingly small proportion of the working population must end. The protection enjoyed by the elite within the workforce – who in Third World countries represent no more than a tenth of the total population living on the fruits of its labour power – is detrimental, according to this argument, to the efforts of the vast majority to improve the conditions in which they live. This 'unfair' competition could be avoided by abolishing security of employment, minimum wages and maximum working hours, and secondary labour rights which used to apply in the formal sector. But should we not then worry that things will get even worse for the quality of the labouring existence? No, those who call for flexibility to give employers a free hand to hire and fire as they please suggest that this approach would actually lead to more, and better work, and a rise in wages in real terms. The idea that efforts should no longer be focused on increasing formalisation of the labour system seems to have become the received wisdom in the milieu of policy makers. In *The Informal Sector in the 1980s and 1990s* (1991), for instance, H. Lubell insists on the benign effects of this dynamic. Analyses focusing on the positive side of the regime of economic informality are designed to refute the idea that anyone leaving the formal sector and joining the informal sector will automatically experience a deterioration in their standard of living. Such a view often tends to culminate in an ode to the virtues of micro enterprise. The World Bank has been a leading proponent of the policy of informalisation, which goes together with the erosion of the rights of formal sector workers. This was the basic message of the *World Development Report 1995*, which discusses the position of labour in the globalised economy.

The erosion of the welfare state in Western societies, as well as its halting development where it had only just come into sight, can be seen as confirmation of a trend in which the slowly advancing emancipation of labour in recent decades appears as if it is being reversed into its opposite – subordination and growing insecurity. The progressive polarisation of social classes accompanying these dynamics has given rise to a debate that concentrates on the inclusion–exclusion contrast. It seems to mark the return of the old dualism concept in yet another form.

JAN BREMAN

References and further reading

Breman, J. (1976), 'Dualistic labour system? A critique of the "informal sector" concept', reprinted in J. Breman (1994), *Wage Hunters and Gatherers: Search for Work in the Urban and Rural Economy of South Gujarat*, Oxford: Oxford University Press, pp. 3–45.

Breman, J. (1995), 'Labour get lost: a late-capitalist manifesto', reprinted in J. Breman (2003), *The Labouring Poor in India: Patterns of Exploitation, Subordination and Exclusion*, New Delhi: Oxford University Press, pp. 167–93.

Breman, J. (1996), *Footloose Labour, Working in India's Informal Economy*, Cambridge: Cambridge University Press.

Breman, J. (2003), *The Making and Unmaking of an Industrial Working Class in India*, Oxford and New Delhi: Oxford University Press and Amsterdam: Amsterdam University Press.

Hart, K. (1973), 'Informal income opportunities and urban employment in Ghana', *Journal of Modern Africa Studies*, **11** (3), 61–89.

Lubell, H. (1991), *The Informal Sector in the 1980s and 1990s*, Development Centre of the Organisation for Economic Cooperation and Development, Paris: OECD.

World Bank (1995), *World Development Report: Workers in an Integrating World*, Oxford: Oxford University Press.

Institutions and Development

Unbundling of institutions

It is now common in the institutional economics literature to define institutions in the very general sense of rules of structured social interaction. In any society there is, of course, a plethora of such rules (including those that undergird even a so-called 'free market' economy). In the context of economic development, the focus is on those rules that act as a substitute for missing markets in an environment of pervasive risks and severe transaction and information costs that individuals and groups face in their economic transactions with others. In the literature on rural development at the micro level there have been many attempts to understand institutions like land tenure, informal arrangements for credit and risk-sharing, and interlocking of credit contracts with those for future delivery of labour services or output, in the context of missing credit, insurance and futures markets and imperfect enforceability of various formal contracts. (For an overview of some of the major theoretical issues in this literature and empirical references, see Bardhan and Udry, 1999.) Radical economists have often cited some of these production relations in a poor agrarian economy as institutional obstacles to development; but if we carry out a programme of abolishing them without paying attention to their microeconomic functional rationale, we may not always help the intended beneficiaries of such programmes. Merely abolishing land tenancy by legislation, for example, often drives tenancy underground or leads to pre-emptive eviction. On the other hand, understanding an institution in terms of its functional role under a given set of constraints, is neither to condone the constraints nor to claim an adequate explanation of the mechanism of the historical emergence of the institution – something that some institutional economists have not always been careful about.

In the recent literature (see Acemoglu et al., 2002; Rodrik et al., 2002) there have been some interesting attempts to quantify the effects of institutional quality on economic performance at the macro level, using cross-country statistical analysis, and to determine the relative importance of geographical as opposed to institutional factors in explaining differential economic performance in different parts of the world. Those who emphasise geography as destiny, more than institutions, point to the disease environment of the tropics, types of crops and soil, transportation costs and so on which afflict many of today's poor countries. But others point out that many such geographically handicapped countries were relatively rich in 1500 (the Moghal, Aztec and Inca empires occupied some of the richer territories of the world in 1500; Haiti, Cuba and Barbados were richer than the United States in early colonial times). This 'reversal of fortune' obviously has more to do with colonial history and the legacy of extractive institutions put in place.

In much of this literature the institution that is emphasised most in explaining differential economic performance is that of ensuring security of private property rights against the predatory state or other marauding individuals and groups. The empirical literature has tried to quantify the effect of the property rights institutions – or what is called in this literature the 'rule of law' variable – on economic performance from cross-country aggregative data. Since these institutions may be endogenous (that is, economically better-off countries may have more of those institutions, rather than the other way round), the literature tries to resolve the identification problem by finding exogenous sources of variations in those institutions.

What is often ignored in this literature is that the rule of law involves actually a whole bundle of rights, and we need to 'unbundle' it. For example, one part of rule of law may involve various democratic rights of political participation, association, mobilisation and expression of 'voice'. An analysis of cross-country variations in human development indicators (which includes education or health variables like mass literacy or life expectation) shows that an institutional variable measuring voice or participation rights may be just as important as that measuring security of property rights as an explanatory variable (see Bardhan, 2004, ch. 1). In other words, the part of 'rule of law' that refers to democratic participation rights may explain a significant amount of variations in human development indices across countries. Those who emphasise property rights often ignore the effects of participatory rights, and there is some obvious tension between these two types of rights included in the standard package of rule of law.

Comparative historical analysis
In contrast to the quantitative empirical literature a comparative historical analysis of institutions in the development process for Western Europe and North America has been tried by North (1981, 1990) and Greif (1992, 1997). North has pointed to the inevitable trade-off in the historical growth process between economies of scale and specialisation on the one hand, and transaction costs on the other. In a small, closed, face-to-face peasant community, for example, transaction costs are low, but the production costs are high, because specialisation and division of labour are severely limited by the extent of market defined by the personalised exchange process of the small community. In a large-scale complex economy, as the network of interdependence widens the impersonal exchange process gives considerable scope for all kinds of opportunistic behaviour and the costs of transacting can be high. Greif examined the self-enforcing institutions of collective punishment for malfeasance in long-distance trade in the late medieval period and explored the institutional foundations of commercial development, which involved intertemporal and interspatial transactions among people largely unknown to one another. These often required multilateral reputation mechanisms supported by frameworks of credible commitment, enforcement and coordination.

Many developing countries in the world have a long history of indigenous mercantile institutions of trust and commitment (based on multilateral reputation mechanisms and informal codes of conduct and enforcement) – examples of such institutions of long-distance trade and credit abound among mercantile families and groups in pre-colonial and colonial India, Chinese traders in South East Asia, Arab 'trading diasporas' in West Africa, and so on. But these relation-based traditional institutions of exchange in developing countries often did not evolve into more complex (impersonal, open, legal–rational) rules or institutions of enforcement as in early modern Europe. As the scale of economic activity expands, as the need for external finance and managerial talent becomes imperative, and as large sunk investments increase the temptation of one party to renege, relational implicit contracts in traditional clan-based organisations and reputational incentives become weaker. As Li (2003) has pointed out, relation-based systems of governance may have low fixed costs (given the pre-existing social relationships among the parties and the avoidance of the elaborate legal–juridical and public information and verification costs of more rule-based systems), but high and rising marginal costs (particularly of private monitoring) as business expansion involves successively weaker relational links.

A major institutional deficiency that blocked the progress of the mercantile into the industrial economy in many poor countries relates to the financial markets. Even when caste- or clan-based mercantile firms thrived in their network of multilateral reputation and enforcement mechanisms, the latter were often not adequate for supporting the much larger risks of longer-gestation large sunk-cost industrial investment. These firms, by and large, had limited capacity (in terms of either finance or specialised skills) to pool risks and mobilise the capital of the society at large in high-risk high-return industrial ventures (their own reinvested profits and trade credit from suppliers were not enough).

The usual imperfections of the credit and equity markets emphasised in the literature on imperfect information are severe in the early stages of industrial development. First of all, the investment in learning by doing is not easily collateralisable and is therefore particularly subject to the high costs of information imperfections. At an early stage when firms are not yet ready for the securities market (with its demands for codifiable and court-verifiable information), there is often a need for some support and underwriting of risks by some centralised authority (with, of course, its attendant dangers of political abuse). There is also the problem of interdependence of investment decisions with externalities of information and the need for a network of proximate suppliers of components, services and infrastructural facilities with large economies of scale. Private financiers willing and able to internalise the externalities of complementary projects and raise large enough capital from the market for a critical mass of firms are often absent in the early stage of industrialisation. Historically, the state has played an important role in resolving this kind of coordination failure by facilitating and complementing private sector coordination – as the examples of state-supported development banks in nineteenth-century France, Belgium and Germany, and more recently in Japan, Korea, Taiwan and China suggest. There are, of course, many examples of state failures in this respect and politicisation of financial markets in other developing countries.

In general, economies at early stages of development are beset with coordination failures of various kinds, and alternative coordination mechanisms – the state, the market, the community organisations – all play different roles, sometimes conflicting and sometimes complementary, in overcoming these coordination failures, and these roles change in various stages of development in highly context-specific and path-dependent ways. To proclaim the universal superiority of one coordination mechanism over another is naive, futile and a-historical.

Persistence of dysfunctional institutions

Finally, a crucial question in institutional economics is: why doesn't a society discard its inefficient institutions and adapt its legal and institutional set-up to facilitate productivity-enhancing innovations? Such innovations have gainers and losers, but in most cases the gainers could potentially compensate the losers. The problem is that it is politically difficult for the gainers from a change to credibly commit to compensate the losers *ex post*. There may not exist an easy way whereby politicians and powerful social groups could make a deal with the rest of society, giving up some of their control on existing rules and institutions that are inefficient, allow others to choose policies and institutions that bring about improvements in productivity, and then redistribute part of the gains to those politicians and groups. Such deals have severe commitment problems; those in power cannot credibly commit to not using this power in the process, and others cannot credibly commit to redistribute once the formerly powerful really give up their power for the sake of bringing about new rules and institutions.

A central issue of development economics is thus the persistence of dysfunctional institutions over long periods of time, as we discuss in Bardhan (2004, ch. 2). In particular, the history of underdevelopment is littered with cases of formidable institutional impediments appearing as strategic outcomes of distributive conflicts. Acemoglu and Robinson (2002) develop a theory where incumbent elites may want to block the introduction of new and efficient technologies because this will reduce their future political power; they give the examples from nineteenth-century history when in Russia and Austro-Hungary the monarchy and aristocracy controlled the political system but feared replacement and so blocked the establishment of rules and institutions that would have facilitated industrialisation. These replacement threats are, of course, often driven by extreme inequality in society.

In explaining the divergent development paths in North and South America since the early colonial times, Engerman and Sokoloff (2002) have provided a great deal of evidence of how in societies with high inequality at the outset of colonisation rules and institutions evolved in ways that restricted to a narrow elite access to political power and opportunities for economic advancement. Initial unequal conditions had long lingering effects, and through their influence on public policies (in distribution of public land and other natural resources, the right to vote and in secret, primary education, patent law, corporate and banking law and so on) tended to perpetuate those institutions and policies that atrophied development. The classic example of inefficient rules and institutions persisting as the lopsided outcome of distributive struggles relates, of course, to the historical evolution of land rights in developing countries. In most of these countries the empirical evidence suggests that economies of scale in farm production are insignificant (except in some plantation crops) and the small family farm is often the most efficient unit of production. Yet the violent and tortuous history of land reform in many countries suggests that there are numerous roadblocks on the way to a more efficient reallocation of land rights put up by vested interests for generations.

Pranab Bardhan

References

Acemoglu, D., S. Johnson and J.A. Robinson (2002), 'Reversal of fortune: geography and institutions in the making of the modern world income distribution', *Quarterly Journal of Economics*, **117** (4), 1231–94.

Acemoglu, D. and J.A. Robinson (2002), 'Economic backwardness in political perspective', NBER Working Paper no. 8831, National Bureau of Economic Research, Cambridge, MA.

Bardhan, P. (2004), *Scarcity, Conflicts and Cooperation: Essays in Political and Institutional Economics of Development*, Cambridge, MA: MIT Press.

Bardhan, P. and C. Udry (1999), *Development Microeconomics*, Oxford: Oxford University Press.

Engerman, S.L. and K.L. Sokoloff (2002), 'Factor endowments, inequality, and paths of development among new world economies', NBER Working Paper no. 9259, National Bureau of Economic Research, Cambridge, MA.

Greif, A. (1992), 'Institutions and international trade: lessons from the commercial revolution', *American Economic Review*, **82** (2), 128–33.

Greif, A. (1997), 'Microtheory and recent developments in the study of economic institutions through economic history', in D.M. Kreps and K.F. Wallis (eds), *Advances in Economic Theory*, Vol. II, Cambridge: Cambridge University Press, pp. 79–113.

Li, J.S. (2003), 'Relation-based versus rule-based governance: an explanation of the East Asian miracle and Asian Crisis', *Review of International Economics*, **11** (4), 651–73.

North, D.C. (1981), *Structure and Change in Economic History*, New York: Norton.

North, D.C. (1990), *Institutions, Institutional Change and Economic Performance*, Cambridge: Cambridge University Press.

Rodrik, D., A. Subramanian and F. Trebbi (2002), 'Institutions rule: the primacy of institutions over geography and integration in economic development', Harvard University, unpublished.

Internal Migration and Rural Livelihood Diversification

The vast majority of migrants in the global system move within their nation's boundaries. In 2000 in China alone, there were an estimated 180 million rural migrants working in the cities. The same year, the total figure for international migrants living in various parts of the developing and developed world was 175 million (United Nations Population Fund, 2004). Even though the total volume of internal mobility worldwide far outweighs that of international migrants, internal migration has attracted only a fraction of the attention of international migration in the media and scholarly literature. The neglect of this more prevalent form of mobility is serious because the majority of critical links between migration and development are likely to occur domestically rather than through international migration. While rural to urban migration is not the only form of internal migration to occur in developing countries, it is arguably the most dramatic, contributing to the acceleration of urbanisation and the formation of mega-cities, and subjecting the movers to cultural and economic changes that are as least as challenging as those experienced by international migrants.

Rural labourers in developing countries who migrate to the cities commonly find that they are 'economically accepted and socially rejected'. They are accepted, albeit grudgingly, because they carry out 'the three ds' – the dirty, dangerous and difficult jobs that enable cheap and rapid urban construction, competitive export manufacturing and the provisioning of menial services to urban residents. They are rejected because they are seen by the urban mainstream as threatening. Highly visible at railway stations, street markets and the outskirts of cities, urban planners speak of them as 'flooding' the cities and blame them for straining urban resources such as water supplies and transport and for committing crime. The social rejection of migrants is manifest by abuses such as bulldosing their accommodation, confiscating their stalls, and condoning their intimidation by the police (Nelson, 1976; Skeldon, 1990).

Given that migrants are generally viewed with disdain by city dwellers, why do they leave their homes in the first place? In answering this question, many scholars find it convenient to focus on the 'push factors' in the origin areas and 'pull factors' in the destination areas. Factors in origin areas that propel migration include increases in farm input costs, inefficient credit markets, inadequate infrastructure, adverse environmental conditions, high population-to-land ratios, underemployment arising from technical innovation, inequitable patterns of land distribution resulting from local class relations or inheritance customs, restrictive traditional values and oppressive family relationships. Attractions of the cities include demands for labour with certain attributes, higher urban wages, the presence of fellow villagers and relatives who help with finding accommodation and employment, the lure of 'bright city lights', opportunities for increased freedom, and better facilities (Nelson, 1976; Skeldon, 1990; Murphy, 2002).

National planners commonly debate whether the outcomes of rural to urban migration are good or bad for development and whether it is better to encourage people to stay on the farm or to become fully integrated and civilised urban residents. This entry reviews analyses of the positive and negative outcomes from migration. It then goes on to show that migration, so often regarded as a social pathology, is simply one of the ways in which the rural poor try to improve their well-being. This can be seen from the role of migration in contributing to household livelihood diversification strategies and from the ways in which migrants and villagers use 'an ideology of return' (King, 1985) to sustain spatially extended networks to multiply their sources of material and emotional support.

The consequences of migration
The positive and negative consequences of migration can be delineated with reference to modernisation and political economy theories. Although these theories have passed from favour in the mainstream development studies literature, they are nevertheless worthy of attention because their assumptions continue to influence greatly the content of the migration reports and policies devised by international development institutions and national governments.

Planners and scholars sympathetic to a modernisation perspective argue that migration enables rational individuals to respond to different economic conditions in origin and destination areas by redistributing their labour from low-productivity rural peripheries to high-productivity urban cores. Adapting Lewis (1958), these scholars maintain that the cheap rural labour allows industry to accumulate capital, which is directed towards industrial expansion, further propelling the demand for migrant labour (Fei and Ranis, 1964). In this explanation, only 'surplus' or 'zero value' labour migrates, and once the supply of surplus labour is depleted from the countryside and urban labour markets become saturated with workers, rural wages rise and urban wages fall in accordance with supply and demand. While this is happening, capital is said to flow from the high- to low-wage sectors, further mitigating differences in wage rates. In this model, labour mobility finally adjusts itself in response to the equalisation of rural and urban wage rates with a general move towards equilibrium.

Although many modernisation scholars recognise that equilibrium fails to occur in reality, they none the less contend that at an aggregate level, migration improves the distribution of labour and other resources both within and among regions. To illustrate redistribution within regions, out-migrants are said to assist not only themselves, but also those who remain behind because they alleviate pressure on the land, leading to higher productivity per head and facilitating technical innovation in farming. With regard to redistribution between regions, migration is credited with accelerating the diffusion of modern cultural and economic resources from urban cores to rural peripheries (Galbraith, 1980; Unwin, 1989).

Political economy theorists focus on the negative consequences of migration, arguing that exchanges between the urban core and rural periphery can never be balancing because they are inherently unequal. They argue that these inequalities result from histories of uneven capitalist expansion and colonial exploitation, adverse terms of trade in agricultural and industrial goods, and government policies affecting regional patterns of investment. Migration is denounced as both the child and parent of inequality because it helps to sustain the spatial and sectoral inequalities that propel movement from origin areas (Connell et al., 1976; Lipton, 1980; Bernstein, 1992). Origin areas are also said to lose more than they gain from migration because it is not only 'zero value' labour that migrates. Even if at the aggregate level only surplus labour leaves, at the village and household level often vital young and skilled labour is lost, leaving the elderly and the very young to fend for themselves (Murphy, 2002). In some localities where male out-migration dominates, married women are left alone to take over labour-intensive farm work, and in parts of Sub-Saharan Africa, the onset of mass male out-migration has been shown to coincide with women shifting to less arduous but also less nutritious food crops, such as from millet to yam. In other origin areas where either women or both sexes leave, it is often the older men who take over the farming, and they too generally face increased workloads.

While policy makers and scholars have devoted attention to identifying the positive and negative outcomes of labour migration, in reality a variety of outcomes result with the balance depending on local conditions and local migration patterns (de Haan, 1999; Murphy, 2002). Migration therefore defies neat classification as either 'good' or 'bad' and there is no one-size-fits-all policy response.

Rural livelihood diversification

Scholars have increasingly come to see migration not as a one-off adjustment by the individual to changing conditions in the origin and destination areas but as part of rural livelihood diversification. Rural livelihood diversification refers to the actions of households in deploying their labour and other resources across a range of farm and non-farm activities. When migration forms part of livelihood diversification, it involves a continuous movement of labour and other resources between origin and destination, in a pattern that is referred to as 'circulation' (Hugo,1982; Skeldon, 1990). In circulation, the rural family farm provides social security for the migrant in the event of injury, sickness, pregnancy, unemployment or old age. And the money remitted by the migrant compensates for previous family investment in education, and provides cash for farm inputs and livelihood expenses. But as political economy scholars note, in this arrangement, the migrants' labour generates wealth for the cities while the countryside shoulders the burden of reproducing this labour.

Rural households try to maintain a hold on the loyalty of their migrant members despite their physical separation by invoking familial cultural values. In environments as diverse as China and Sub-Saharan Africa, children are raised with the belief that they owe their parents a debt for the gift of life. This means that parents have a continuous claim on their children's earnings. In some cultures, such as the Philippines and Thailand, this sense of debt may be cultivated more strongly in females than in males with the result that households are more likely to entrust their daughters with the task of migrating to earn wages (Lauby and Stark, 1988; Mills, 1997). When new opportunities for earning wages afford subordinate individuals increased leverage, patriarchs often intensify the ideological measures aimed at preserving the family's authority over its primary resource – labour. But asserting ideological pressure is not always successful. This is because some household members gain increased leverage for arranging their own lives. As an example, sojourning enables some sons to accumulate the economic resources necessary for earlier marriage and separation from parents (Murphy, 2002).

Many development debates have centred on the position of diversified rural households in a changing world: are they a transitional category or a permanent but changing part of a world in transition? For national governments influenced by modernisation theories, farmers will ultimately be transformed into permanent wage labourers and disappear. Similarly, for some political economy theorists, circulation is a transitional process, albeit an unstable one, with uncertain outcomes arising from the resistance and reluctant behavioural adaptation of rural people to the pressures of proletarianisation (Standing, 1985). For other political economy theorists, economically diversified or 'rural–proletarian' households are a fixed feature of the economy that result from endemic structural inequalities and rural underdevelopment. These scholars point out that circulation is 'deeply rooted in a variety of cultures and found at all stages of socio-economic change' (Chapman and Prothero, 1985, p. 25).

More recently, some development scholars have argued that poverty alleviation through rural livelihood diversification is not a transitional economic arrangement preceding the realisation of modernisation teleology, but is a satisfactory end in itself (Ellis, 1998; Hussain and Nelson, 1998; de Haan, 1999). This perspective shifts the policy debate away from whether it is better to try to keep rural dwellers 'on the farm' or to encourage them to become a permanent part of the urban working class. Instead, the implication is that governments should adopt policies which increase the freedom and range of options for rural households to diversify their livelihoods, while enacting measures to protect the vulnerable from abuse and destitution in both the city and the countryside. This is not to deny, as comparative studies of China and Mexico reveal, that migration networks are in transition, evolving and maturing with 'daughter migrant communities' and native place associations eventually becoming established in the destination areas (Roberts, 1997). None the less, in many developing countries, diversified households that flexibly pursue creative migration strategies are a seemingly 'permanent' part of a changing countryside.

An irony is that although diversification through circulation is often pursued to strengthen a family economically it entails the prolonged physical separation of family members. This can have a detrimental impact on well-being. It can lead to heavier work burdens, worries, emotional estrangement and loneliness. It also involves the wide spatial mobility of poor and educationally deprived young people, factors commonly associated with high levels of transmission of sexual diseases. Migrants often avail themselves of the relative freedom and anonymity of destination areas to seek comfort for their isolation and hardship with temporary sexual partners. At the same time, some poor migrant women find it necessary to provide sexual services to obtain material and emotional support (Chant and Radcliffe, 1992; Nelson, 1992). Mining and long-distance trucking are examples of sectors particularly associated with prostitution and sexually transmitted infections. When the migrants return home they often infect their rural partners, with wives and girlfriends being particularly vulnerable because power inequalities make it difficult for them to insist on safe sex (Lurie et al., 1997).

The 'ideology of return'

Over time, migration may become less circulatory and more 'permanent'. Even migrants who seldom visit their villages commonly live long term in the cities with an 'ideology of return' – a belief that they will one day return, and this belief helps them to evade moral censure for forgetting their families, and to avoid confronting their ambivalence towards social relationships in the native place. Many migrants initially delay permanent resettlement because they lack the funds for achieving goals in the village such as building a new house, earning enough for a marriage ceremony or accumulating sufficient savings for a nest egg. They nevertheless maintain a homeward orientation, committing increasing portions of their wages to the needs of both family in the village and the requirements of an urban lifestyle, so less money remains for the attainment of their goals. Over time, some migrants form even higher life goals that require more resources, or else they become accustomed to urban life, so indefinitely postpone resettlement while maintaining links with the native place. For migrants in some countries and in some economic sectors, a stable life in the city becomes possible because high levels of industrialisation create the economic demand for a permanent and skilled workforce rather than the itinerant and unskilled workforce that characterises labour-intensive production. This causes employers to improve wages and living conditions, thereby enabling the migrants to bring their spouses and dependants with them to the cities (Skeldon, 1990).

As migrants gain increasing permanence in the cities and lose the intention to return, their remittances decline in amount and frequency. Even so, the ideology of return is so deeply inculcated that they maintain social ties with the native place. This link to home is expressed through life-cycle ceremonies and through investment in the social networks associated with home. In China, Papua New Guinea and much of Africa, both 'permanent' urban residents and sojourners participate in native place funeral associations which send the bodies of the dead back 'home' for burial (ibid.). And in Latin America, urban residents financially sponsor Saints' festivals and construction projects in their native villages. Even after three or four generations have resided continuously in the city, their settlement may turn out to be not so permanent after all. For instance, following the fallout from structural adjustment in Sub-Saharan Africa, the cities failed to provide sufficient resources to sustain the livelihoods of their residents. But the continued actions of individuals and families in sustaining reciprocal ties across generations enabled them to return to their rural ancestral homes to claim access to land, food and social support (Potts, 1995). So, even permanently absent migrants continue to influence their home communities.

Conclusion

Rather than deliberate on whether it is better to keep migrants on the farm or help them integrate into the cities, a more helpful approach is to view migration as a strategy for improving livelihoods. This perspective recognises that migration is not a social aberration or marker of chaos but simply a way for the poor to try to improve their lot. The appropriate response of national development planners is therefore to encourage policies which protect the rights, wages, health and general well-being of poor people in the cities and the countryside; and provide welfare security for those who may be adversely affected by labour migration, for instance, migrants who lose their city jobs, migrants and family members vulnerable to illness and the elderly who hold the fort on the farm.

RACHEL MURPHY

References

Bernstein, Henry (1992), 'Agrarian structures and change: Latin America', in H. Bernstein, B. Crow and H. Johnson (eds), *Rural Livelihoods: Crises and Responses*, Oxford: Oxford University Press, pp. 27–50.

Chapman, Murray and R. Mansell Prothero (1985), 'Themes on circulation in the Third World', in M. Chapman and R.M. Prothero (eds), *Circulation in Third World Countries*, Routledge: London, pp. 1–27.

Chant, Sylvia and Sarah Radcliffe (1992), 'Migration and development: the importance of gender', in S. Chant (ed.), *Gender and Migration in Developing Countries*, London; Belhaven, pp. 1–29.

Connell, John, Biplab Dasgupta, Roy Laishley and Michael Lipton (1976), *Migration from Rural Areas: The Evidence from Village Studies*, Oxford: Oxford University Press.

de Haan, Arjan (1999), 'Livelihoods and poverty: the role of migration – a critical review of the migration literature', *Journal of Development Studies*, **36**, 1–47.

Ellis, Frank (1998), 'Household strategies and rural livelihood diversification', *Journal of Development Studies*, **35**, 1–38.

Fei, J. and Gustav Ranis (1964), *Development of the Surplus Labour Economy*, Homewood, IL: Richard D. Irwin.

Galbraith, John Kenneth (1980), *The Nature of Mass Poverty*, Harmondsworth: Penguin.

Hugo, Graeme J. (1982), 'Circular migration in Indonesia', *Population and Development Review*, **8**, 59–83.

Hussain, Karim and John Nelson (1998), 'Sustainable livelihoods and livelihood diversification', IDS Working Paper no. 69, (May), Institute of Development Studies, University of Sussex, Brighton, UK.

King, Russell (1985), *Return Migration and Regional Economic Problems*, London: Croom Helm.

Lauby Jennifer and Oded Stark (1988), 'Individual migration as a family strategy: young women in the Philippines', *Population Studies*, **42** (3), (November), 473–86.

Lewis, W. Arthur (1958), 'Economic development with unlimited supplies of labour', in A.N. Agarwala and S.P. Singh (eds), *The Economics of Underdevelopment*, Oxford: Oxford University Press, pp. 400–449.

Lipton, Michael (1980), 'Migration from rural areas of poor countries: the impact on rural productivity and income distribution', *World Development*, **8**, 1–24.

Lurie, Mark, Abigail Harrison, David Wilkinson and Salim Abdool Karim (1997), 'Circular migration and sexual networking in rural KwaZulu/Natal: implications for the spread of HIV and other sexually transmitted diseases', *Health Transition Review*, **7** (3), 17–27.

Mills, Mary Beth (1997), 'Contesting the margins of modernity: women, migration and consumption in Thailand', *American Ethnologist*, **24**, 37–61.

Murphy, Rachel (2002), *How Migrant Labor is Changing Rural China*, New York and Cambridge: Cambridge University Press.

Nelson, Joan (1976), 'Sojourners versus new urbanites: causes and consequences of cityward migration in developing countries', *Economic Development and Cultural Change*, **24**, 721–59.

Nelson, Nici (1992), 'The women who have left and those who have stayed behind: rural–urban migration in Central and Western Kenya', in S. Chant (ed.), *Gender and Migration in Developing Countries*, Belhaven: London, pp. 109–38.

Potts, Deborah (1995), 'Shall we go home? Increasing urban poverty in African cities and migration processes', *Geographical Journal*, **161** (3), 245–64.

Roberts, Kenneth D. (1997), 'China's tidal wave of migrant labor: what can we learn from Mexican undocumented migration to the United States?', *International Migration Review*, **31** (2), 249–93.

Skeldon, Ronald (1990), *Population Mobility in Developing Countries: A Reinterpretation*, London: Belhaven.

Standing, Guy (1985), 'Circulation and the labour process', in Guy Standing (ed.), *Labour Circulation and the Labour Process*, London: Croom Helm, pp. 1–46.

United Nations Population Fund (2004), *Meeting the Challenges of Migration: Progress Since the International Conference on Population and Development*, New York: UNFPA, www.unfpa.org/publications/detail.cfm, 21 November 2004.

Unwin, Tim (1989), 'Urban–rural interactions in developing countries: a theoretical perspective', in Robert B. Potter and Tim Unwin (eds), *The Geography of Rural–Urban Interactions in Developing Countries*, London: Routledge, pp. 11–32.

International Trade

The core theories of international trade can be divided into those based on (1) cost differences among countries and (2) economies of scale. But the ultimate test of the benefits of trade must be empirical: is openness crucial to faster growth?

The theories based on cost differences have their origin in the famous Ricardian theory of comparative advantage that is also seen as the foundation of international trade as a separate field of study. While the cross-country differences in technology account for the differences in the costs in this theory, differences in factor endowments form the basis of the related Heckscher–Ohlin (H–O) theory.

The strength of the Ricardian theory lies in its ability to simultaneously refute the assertions – commonplace even today among policy analysts and politicians – that a country with high wages cannot compete against a country with low wages or that a country with low productivity cannot withstand competition from a country with high productivity. The theory also dispels any fears that trade is a zero-sum game so that if one country benefits from it, another must lose.

The basic message of the Ricardian theory can be understood with the help of a simple example based on two countries, two goods and one factor of production, labour. Suppose it takes 1 unit of labour to produce a bushel of wheat and 2 units of labour to produce a shirt in England (Table 9). Suppose also that it takes 2 units of labour to produce a bushel of wheat and 6 units to produce a shirt in Spain. Thus, England is absolutely more productive than Spain in the production of both goods. Yet, it has as much to benefit from trade as Spain.

Table 9   Labour costs per unit (in person days)

	Wheat	Shirt
England	1	2
Spain	2	6

To explain, note that while the labour cost in England is a half of that in Spain in wheat it is only a third for shirts. England has a cost advantage in both goods but its advantage is more in shirts. Conversely, labour cost in Spain is twice as much as England in wheat but 3 times as much in shirts. Its cost disadvantage is relatively less in wheat. According to Ricardian theory, both England and Spain will benefit if they specialised in the good in which their cost advantage is the most (shirts for England) or the cost disadvantage is the least (wheat for Spain) and then exported the good in which they specialise in return for the other.

To see how this works, suppose that initially each country produces what it consumes so that they do not trade. Next, suppose we transfer 2 units of labour out of wheat and into shirts in England thereby reducing the output of wheat by 2 bushels and increasing that of shirts by 1. Simultaneously, transfer 6 units of labour out of shirts and into wheat in Spain, thus, increasing the output of wheat by 3 bushels and reducing that of shirts by 1 unit there. The net outcome of these reallocations is an increase in the total output of the two countries taken together by 1 bushel of wheat. If England now exports 1 shirt to Spain for 2.5 bushels of wheat, each nation can consume an extra half bushel of wheat. The more each country specialises in the good of its comparative advantage, the more extra output can be generated and, thus, the larger the benefit from specialisation and trade.

In Ricardian theory, there is only one factor of production, labour, so that trade benefits all – trade raises the real incomes or wages of all workers. This strong result is modified once we allow for more than one factor of production as in the H–O theory, which assumes that countries have identical technologies for all products at their disposal but differ in terms of factor endowments. Thus, assume that there are two factors of production, land and labour, and modify the above example so that shirts use more labour per unit of land than wheat (that is, a shirt is more labour intensive in production than wheat). Also assume that England has more workers per unit of land than Spain (that is, England is labour abundant relative to Spain). Assuming that spending patterns are similar across individuals, the H–O theory then predicts that England will export shirts, which use its abundant factor, labour, more intensively and Spain will export wheat, which uses its abundant factor, land, more intensively.

While the H–O theory also yields the conclusion that trade benefits both countries overall, it additionally brings into play the income distribution conflict. Thus, continuing with our example, in England, the imports of the land-intensive product effectively reduce the demand for land and lead to a decline in the real income of land owners while the exports of the labour-intensive product increase the demand for labour and raise the real income of workers. Even though in principle, gainers gain sufficiently to be able to compensate the losers and still be better off, since such compensation does not take place in practice, the opening to trade turns into a battle between the gainers and losers.

This distributional conflict has almost always been at the heart of the debate on trade liberalisation. For example, recently, in the United States and other rich countries, trade liberalisation has received much resistance on the ground that it benefits skilled labour and hurts unskilled labour because these countries export skilled labour-intensive goods and import unskilled labour-intensive goods. Among other things, organised labour has begun to demand higher labour standards in the poor countries, which predominantly export unskilled labour-intensive goods, as a cost of further opening of markets. Raising labour standards including minimum wages in the poor countries will, of course, undermine their competitiveness and have the same effect as protection in so far as the interests of unskilled labour in the rich countries are concerned. Linking environmental standards to the market-opening measures, which is also advocated by organised labour, has a similar effect.

Most recently, some have come to question the benefits of trade that takes the form of outsourcing, especially in the United States. Outsourcing refers to the imports of services through electronic means as, for example, the back office services and customised software provided by workers in Bangalore to customers in New York. Like the traditional trade in goods, this phenomenon can also lead to adverse effects on the incomes of the specific factors whose services are imported through outsourcing but the claims by many that it leads to an overall decline in income of the importing nation are misplaced. What outsourcing has done is to turn some previously non-tradable services into tradable services. This is not unlike the decline in the cost of transportation that turned many non-tradable goods into tradable goods.

Differences in costs are not necessary to give rise to beneficial trade provided that production is subject to economies of scale. For example, suppose the United States and Japan face identical cost conditions in the production of large as well as small cars in the sense that for a given number of large cars, the average cost of production is the same in both countries and the same applies to the small cars. Suppose further that the average cost of production of each type of car declines with the expansion of output. In the absence of trade, each country produces what it consumes. But if trade is allowed, one country, say, the United States can specialise in the large cars and the other, Japan, in the small cars (or the opposite). This specialisation allows both types of cars to be produced on a larger scale and hence at a lower average cost. One way to see the benefits is to note that the pre-trade worldwide output of each type of car can now be produced with fewer resources. Alternatively, the same resources allow a larger output of the two types of car. This enables both countries to achieve a higher consumption level than before trade.

The presence of the economies of scale also accommodates the phenomenon of intra-industry trade in a natural way. If goods are differentiated and consumers like variety and each variety is subject to economies of scale, a trade-off arises between the number of varieties and the exploitation of economies of scale. In equilibrium, finite varieties are produced. Trade allows each country to consume the varieties produced by the other countries so that the gains from trade arise from increased variety as well.

Although economists generally accept the merits of free trade, in the policy domain, the issue has always been controversial. During the past century or more, many reasons have been offered for why protection may be good. The theoretically cleanest case arises when a country is large in the world markets such that it has monopoly power as a seller and monopsony power as a buyer. In this situation, restrictions on imports that reduce the demand lead to a decline in the price paid to exporters and, thus impose the burden of the tariff partially on the latter. While this constitutes a logically correct case for protection, economists uniformly reject it since two can play this game. Tariffs by one country to exploit this monopoly power can lead other countries doing the same so that the net change may be simply a reduction in the gains from trade without any improvement in the terms of trade.

The other arguments for protection are 'second-best' arguments in the sense that they are based on settings in which superior policies are available. For example, if the wages are higher than their competitive level in an import-competing sector, it shrinks beyond its Pareto-efficient level. Some protection can then move the sector closer to the efficient level. The first-best policy to correct the wage distortion, however, is to subsidise the use of labour in the sector with a higher wage such that the level of employment in the sector is restored to where it would be in the absence of the wage distortion. Once this is done, free trade is still the optimal policy. The same analysis applies to other distortions arising out of environmental or other externalities.

While the principle of comparative advantage has a wide acceptance, from the development perspective, many question whether trade actually helps accelerate economic growth. Although under plausible circumstances, theory suggests that trade leads to an acceleration of growth, it is possible to construct models in which it does not lead to higher growth, or even causes a decline. Indeed, in the standard neoclassical model, the growth rate is constrained by the growth rate of the labour force so that trade has no impact on the growth rate. Therefore, the issue is ultimately empirical.

Unfortunately, the econometric evidence based on cross-country regressions has been subject to much controversy. Critics argue that the evidence presented by free trade advocates to date is insufficient to establish a causation running from low or lower trade barriers to faster growth. They question the indices of protection used in the studies as well as the methodology. In my view, even if the evidence is not fully compelling, its overall weight favours the view that openness promotes growth.

But even if we reject this evidence altogether, I have recently argued that this does not give the critics their contrary case (Panagariya, 2004). An examination of country experience shows that the countries that have grown rapidly on a sustained basis have almost always done so while experiencing very high growth in exports and imports. I analyse the developing countries that have grown at rates of 3 per cent or more in per capita terms during 1961–99. I consistently find that these growth miracles are accompanied by rapid growth in trade. Even in terms of trade *policies*, either low or declining trade barriers accompany the miracle growth rates. It is rare to find examples of countries that were highly protected and managed to grow rapidly on a sustained basis without also lowering the barriers.

In parallel, I look at growth débâcles – cases of prolonged stagnation or declining incomes in per capita terms. Contrary to the claims of the critics, I find little evidence to support the claim that rapid growth in imports is a principal cause of such débâcles – generally, they are accompanied by very low or negative growth in imports.

The message from my research is loud and clear: we may not know precisely what it is that triggers growth but we do know that countries that are open (as were Singapore and Hong during 1960–2000) or react to growth opportunities by opening up (as Korea did beginning in the early 1960s) are successful in sustaining growth and those that choose autarkic policies (as India did during 1960–80) are condemned to low growth even if they manage to raise their savings and investment rates and achieve macroeconomic stability.

ARVIND PANAGARIYA

Reference and further reading

Bhagwati, J., A. Panagariya and T.N. Srinivasan (1998), *Lectures on International Trade*, 2nd edn, Cambridge, MA: MIT Press.
Panagariya, A. (2004), 'Miracles and Débâcles: in defense of trade openness', *World Economy*, **27** (8), 1149–71.

Kaldor, Nicholas (1908–1986)

Nicholas Kaldor was without doubt one of the leading and most original economists of his generation. His early work, undertaken while he was at the London School of Economics, made notable contributions to the theory of the firm and welfare economics. This was very much in the neoclassical tradition, although he became a Keynesian soon after the *General Theory* appeared in 1936. He spent most of his academic life at the University of Cambridge, where he was made Reader in Economics in 1949 and Professor in 1966. He became a trenchant critic of neoclassical economics, especially of its assumption of constant returns to scale (this was before the development of endogenous growth theory), its neglect of the role of demand factors in economic growth and the marginal productivity theory of distribution (see Thirlwall, 1987; Targetti and Thirlwall, 1989; and Targetti, 1992).

Kaldor had a long-held interest in the application of economic theory to development problems and the resulting policy implications. This largely stemmed from his role as taxation advisor to a number of less-developed countries that began in 1956 and which brought him into close contact with development issues.

Taxation and economic development

Kaldor's interest in taxation may be traced from his appointment by the British Chancellor of the Exchequer, Hugh Gaitskell, to the Royal Commission on Taxation and Profits in 1951. He disagreed with many of the conclusions of the Commission and drafted a famous 'Memorandum of Dissent', but it was his book *An Expenditure Tax* (1955) that made his name in this area. He became a tax advisor to many developing countries ranging from India (in 1956) to Venezuela (in 1976). His report on Indian tax reform (Kaldor, 1956) was a classic in exposing the widespread deficiencies of the tax system of a less-developed country. It became the template that, with suitable modifications, he used in advising other developing countries. Kaldor (1964a, Part III) contains a useful collection of some of his papers on taxation.

He considered that one of the major problems was that whereas the tax potential (taxes as a proportion of GDP) of developing countries was not greatly different from that of the advanced countries, the actual proportion raised was about half as much, namely 15 per cent as opposed to about 30 per cent. Kaldor saw this as the result of massive tax avoidance and evasion and the effect of the wealthy elite in blocking tax reform. Many less-developed countries, moreover, had an inequitable tax system, where taxes on property and profits were less than on wages and salaries. It is little wonder that his proposals for substantial tax reform for many of the less-developed countries were met with such hostility from the wealthy that the implementations of his recommendations were greatly watered down by the various governments. This was especially true of his proposal for an Indian expenditure tax, which was first diluted and then eventually rejected as a consequence of intense political pressure.

Kaldor's two-sector model of development

For Kaldor, the key to understanding the growth of a country in the early stages of development is the role of demand for industrial output emanating from the agricultural sector. Like Arthur Lewis (1954), Kaldor assumed that there is disguised unemployment in the agricultural sector and rigid wages in the industrial sector, which exceed the agricultural wage. Consequently, there is a perfectly elastic supply of labour to the industrial sector. Moreover, capital accumulation is as much a consequence of development as a cause. For these reasons, Kaldor considered that growth is not determined by the supply side. For Lewis, growth occurs as the capitalist industrial sector expands, and both the level and share of profits rise, which are reinvested in the industrial sector. However, a shortcoming of this explanation is the assumption that all the industrial output would automatically be sold.

Kaldor posed the question where, with a relatively closed economy, is this demand for the industrial output going to come from? An important source must be the rural sector and Kaldor developed a model of development that took this into account. Like much of his work, his insights are found scattered in a number of his papers and he nowhere presented a fully articulated model. The nearest he came was in his posthumously published 1984 Mattioli lectures (Kaldor, 1996). Nevertheless, his insights have been formalised by others, one of the closest in spirit to Kaldor being the approach of Thirlwall (1986), which is followed here.

Kaldor starts by assuming a closed economy that consists of two sectors, namely, agriculture and industry. Agriculture produces food and industry produces an investment good. The growth of agriculture is determined by its share of investment in its output and the productivity of its investment. Part of the agricultural output is consumed in the rural sector and the remainder is sold to industry in exchange for the investment good. A key insight of Kaldor is that the overall rate of growth of the economy is determined by the complementary nature of the growth of agriculture and industry, acting through the demand side. On the one hand, agriculture provides food for the industrial workers and the cheaper food is, *ceteris paribus*, the more industrial output can be retained and invested in the industrial sector and the faster will be industry's growth rate. On the other hand, the growth of demand for investment goods from the agricultural sector will also be lower because of the lower growth of purchasing power in the agricultural sector. This will, *ceteris paribus*, reduce the growth of the industrial sector. Consequently, there is a potential conflict between the demand and supply sides. Kaldor devised a model where the terms of trade between the two sectors could serve to equilibrate and maximise the growth of demand and supply.

The analysis may be best illustrated in terms of a diagram (see Figure 7). The volume of the investment good that agriculture obtains for a given quantity of agricultural goods depends on the terms of trade $P = P_I/P_A$, where P_I and P_A are the prices of the investment and agricultural good, respectively. Consequently, the lower are the terms of trade, the higher is the rate of agricultural investment, and the faster is agriculture's growth rate. This is shown in Figure 7 by the curve g_A which traces out the maximum level of agricultural growth for a given terms of trade. (The income elasticities of demand for agricultural and industrial goods are assumed to be unity, so that their growth rates may be both drawn on the horizontal axis of the figure. This does not affect the argument.) Likewise,

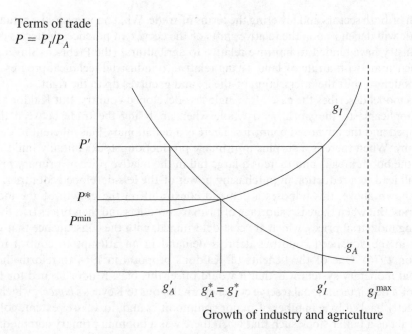

Figure 7   Kaldor's two-sector growth model

as the terms of trade move in industry's favour, so less industrial output has to be exchanged for a given volume of food and so there are greater industry profits that can be reinvested. Hence the growth of industry is given by the upward-sloping curve g_I. There is a limit to the terms of trade given by P^{min} where industrial growth is zero. At this point, because of the assumed downward wage rigidity in the industrial sector, the whole of industrial output is going to pay the industrial workers and there is no investment in industry. The maximum growth rate of industry is given by g_I^{max} and this occurs when the whole output of industry is invested in industry.

The equilibrium growth rate of the two sectors is given by the intersection of the two growth curves and occurs at g_I^* and g_A^* where the terms of trade are given by P^*. The role of demand in constraining growth may be simply illustrated using this model. Suppose, for some reason, the terms of trade are initially above P^* and are given by P'. At these relative prices industry could accumulate capital such that, *if demand conditions warranted*, it could grow at the rate g_I'. But at this relative price, the fastest agriculture can grow is g_A' and, consequently, industry is limited by the growth of demand for its output from the agricultural sector to this rate.

As agriculture is subject to diminishing returns owing to the fixity of land, in the absence of technical change, this will lead to a progressive leftward shift of the g_A curve and declining agricultural and industrial output. If the g_I curve is relatively stable, it may be seen that growth will ultimately depend upon the extent to which the rate of land-saving technical change will offset this shift. An increase in the growth of productivity of industry will shift the g_I curve downwards to the right, thereby also increasing the rate of growth of both sectors and lowering the terms of trade. What happens to the actual terms of trade will depend upon the relative shifts of the curves. In practice, the terms of trade of industry have tended to improve relative to agricultural (the Prebisch–Singer effect), commensurate with a rate of land-saving relative to industrial technical progress that is fast enough to shift the intersection of the g_A and g_I curves up to the right.

This model describes the case of a single less-developed country. But Kaldor also saw it as applicable to the world as a whole when analysing the trade between the less-developed and the advanced countries. There is a deflationary bias inherent in the world economy. When there is a surplus in primary production, stocks initially build up. But when the boom breaks and there is a large fall in the relative price of primary products, this will lead to a reduction in purchasing power of the less-developed countries. As has been shown above, this imposes a demand constraint on the growth of the industrial countries. But when there is a shortage of primary products and their prices rise, this leads to rising industrial prices, which are cost determined, with the consequence that governments in the advanced countries depress demand in an attempt to control inflation (Kaldor, 1976). One of the benefits of Kaldor's proposal in 1964 to reform the international monetary system was that it would offset this bias. Kaldor argued for the creation of a new international reserve currency, analogous to Keynes's *bancor*, which would be directly backed by a number of major commodities and, to a lesser extent, gold. This would act as a buffer stock such that when there was a boom in primary commodity production, intervention would ensure that their prices, and hence the purchasing power of the less-developed countries, would not fall (Hart et al., 1964. Kaldor was the principal architect of this scheme, which never got off the drawing board).

Economic growth in an open economy
When growth occurs and the economy becomes more open, Kaldor did not see a reduction in the importance of demand conditions. Instead, the key source of demand shifts from agricultural to that emanating from outside the country, namely exports. In addition, Kaldor laid great emphasis on the importance of increasing returns to scale (long before it became fashionable in the endogenous growth models) and it is useful to consider this first. In fact, he saw the origins of the industrial revolution in the development of the factory system, which allowed huge improvements in the level of productivity through specialisation and the division of labour. Moreover, the scope for technological improvement increases with the degree of mechanisation and the degree of roundaboutness of production (Kaldor, 1977). A corollary is that the capital–labour ratio is not solely determined by the ratio of factor prices, as in the neoclassical schema, but also by the extent of the division of labour, itself both a cause and consequence of increasing returns to scale. The prevalence of increasing returns and the importance of demand gives rise to virtuous and vicious circles of economic growth. A rapid growth of demand and output leads to increasing productivity growth due to increasing returns to scale (of both the static and dynamic variety), induced technical change and an increased rate of capital accumulation. The increased productivity growth leads to an increased competitive advantage, faster growth of exports and hence a positive feedback leading to a faster growth of output in a process of cumulative causation. The converse is also true; countries could be locked in a vicious circle of low output and productivity growth (Myrdal, 1957;

Kaldor, 1981). It is mainly for this reason that growth occurred, and still occurs, unevenly across countries.

Kaldor (1966) cited the famous Verdoorn law as evidence of the existence of returns to scale. This is a deceptively simple relationship between the growth of labour productivity (p_I) and output (g_I) for industry of the form $p_I = \alpha + \beta g_I$, where α is exogenous productivity growth and β is the Verdoorn coefficient, which in a wide range of studies takes a value of about a 0.5. This implies that every increase in industrial output growth of one percentage point gives rise to an increase in employment and productivity growth each of one-half of a percentage point. The Verdoorn law has been subject to a number of criticisms ranging from simultaneous equation bias to omitted variable bias (the growth of the capital stock). Nevertheless, it appears to be robust (see the papers in McCombie et al., 2002). If there is no binding supply constraint, what then limits the rate of growth of output?

As was noted above, the answer is the growth of exports acting through the dynamic Harrod foreign trade multiplier (or, more generally, the Hicks super-multiplier) and the existence of a balance-of-payments constraint. Developing countries require exports to provide the finance for the import of necessary capital goods as well as sophisticated consumer goods. The income elasticity of demand for imports is generally greater than unity, which requires that exports grow faster than the domestic economy for current account equilibrium. If changes in relative prices are unimportant in altering trade flows, then the growth of imports and exports will be determined by the relative income elasticities of demand, as Kaldor came to believe. Changes in relative prices will be largely ineffective if the Marshall–Lerner condition is only just satisfied. Also, the fear of importing inflation may lead to attempts by the government to prevent the exchange rate falling. A country cannot permanently run a balance-of-payments deficit (except to the extent it is financed by pure aid and/or long-term foreign direct investment). In these circumstances, the growth of exports must equal the growth of imports and it is these growth rates that determine the growth of the output. The rate of growth of output that is consistent with current account equilibrium (that is, the balance-of-payments constrained growth rate, g_{BP}) is given by $g_{BP} = g_X / \pi = \varepsilon g_W / \pi$, where g_X, g_W, ε and π are the growth of exports, the growth of world income, the world income elasticity of demand for exports and the domestic income elasticity of demand for imports. (This relationship is known as Thirlwall's law. See Thirlwall, 1979.) Thus, if world demand for a less-developed country's exports was, say, only growing at 4 per cent and the demand for imports was high, with an income elasticity of demand for imports of 2.5, then the maximum growth rate of the less-developed country is 1.6 per cent per annum. This may be well below the maximum rate of growth of productive potential (see McCombie and Thirlwall, 2004).

This led Kaldor somewhat controversially to advocate the use of quotas and tariffs, in certain circumstances, not to generate a trade surplus, but to allow trade to be balanced at a faster domestic growth rate. However, Kaldor (1964c), at a time when he was more sanguine about the efficacy of exchange rate adjustments, also argued that a dual exchange rate would be better than tariffs and quotas. Under this arrangement there would be a fixed official exchange rate for the staple exports and essential imports. Foreign exchange for non-essential imports could only be purchased at a free rate given by a floating exchange rate which, given the shortage of foreign exchange, would give a domestic price of foreign currency that was at a premium over the fixed exchange rate. The exporters of manufactured goods would be free to exchange their foreign exchange earnings at this higher rate. Consequently, as Kaldor pointed out, the premium would represent the equivalent of an *ad valorem* import duty combined with an *ad valorem* export subsidy, which manufacturing required in the earlier stages of development because of increasing returns to scale and the infant industry argument. The dual exchange rate would 'combine the advantages of free trade from the point of view of fostering international specialisation and the division of labour with the advantages of protection for the promotion of local industrialisation' (Kaldor, 1964b, p. 189).

J.S.L. McCombie

References

Hart, R.A., N. Kaldor and J. Tinbergen (1964), 'The case for an international commodity reserve currency', memorandum submitted to UNCTAD, Geneva, reprinted in Kaldor (1964b).
Kaldor, N. (1955), *An Expenditure Tax*, London: George Allen & Unwin.
Kaldor, N. (1956), *Report of a Survey on Indian Tax Reform*, Ministry of Finance, Government of India, Delhi.
Kaldor, N. (1964a), *Essays on Economic Policy*, Vol. I, London: Duckworth.
Kaldor, N. (1964b), *Essays on Economic Policy*, Vol. II, London: Duckworth.
Kaldor, N. (1964c), 'Dual exchange rates and economic development', *Economic Bulletin for Latin America*, **9** (2), 214–23, reprinted in Kaldor (1964b).
Kaldor, N. (1966), *The Causes of the Slow Rate of Economic Growth of the United Kingdom: An Inaugural Lecture*, Cambridge: Cambridge University Press.
Kaldor, N. (1976), 'Inflation and recession in the world economy', *Economic Journal*, **86** (344), 703–14.
Kaldor, N. (1977), 'Capitalism and industrial development: some lessons from Britain's experience', *Cambridge Journal of Economics*, **1** (2), 193–204.
Kaldor, N. (1981), 'The role of increasing returns, technical progress and cumulative causation in the theory of international trade and economic growth', *Économie Appliquée*, **34** (4), 593–617, reprinted in Targetti and Thirlwall (eds) (1989).
Kaldor, N. (1996), *Causes of Growth and Stagnation in the World Economy* (Raffaele Mattioli Lectures, Milan, 1984), Cambridge: Cambridge University Press.
Lewis, W.A. (1954), 'Economic development with unlimited supplies of labour', *The Manchester School of Economic and Social Studies*, **22** (2), 139–91.
McCombie, J.S.L., M. Pugno and S. Bruno (2002), *Productivity Growth and Economic Performance: Essays on Verdoorn's Law*, Basingstoke: Palgrave.
McCombie, J.S.L. and A.P. Thirlwall (eds) (2004), *Essays on Balance of Payments Constrained Growth: Theory and Evidence*, London: Routledge.
Myrdal, G. (1957), *Economic Theory and Underdeveloped Regions*, London: Duckworth.
Targetti F. (1992), *Nicholas Kaldor: The Economics and Politics of Capitalism as a Dynamic System*, Oxford: Clarendon.
Targetti F. and Thirlwall, A.P. (eds) (1989), *The Essential Kaldor*, London: Duckworth.
Thirlwall, A.P. (1979), 'The balance of payments constraint as an explanation of international growth rate differences', *Banca Nazionale del Lavoro Quarterly Review*, **128**, 45–53.
Thirlwall, A.P. (1986), 'A general model of growth and development along Kaldorian lines', *Oxford Economic Papers*, **38** (2), 199–219.
Thirlwall, A.P. (1987), *Nicholas Kaldor*, Brighton: Wheatsheaf.

Kalecki, Michał (1899–1970)

The Polish economist Michał Kalecki is best known for having worked out essential features of Keynes's *General Theory* prior to the publication of that work. Although the significance of that book, and Kalecki's own anticipation of it, remain matters of some debate, there is little in the *General Theory*, or in Keynes's writings, apart from general issues of financial and commodity price stabilisation, that would be applicable to developing countries. Kalecki, however, did devote a significant part of his work to elucidating the problems of developing countries, and he continues to have a small but important following among development economists.

Kalecki was made aware of the political economy of development during his formative years as an economist, in the 1920s. His earliest writings in economics were analyses of commodity markets and industrial development in Poland. These were rooted in the political debates in Poland at that time around the works of Rudolf Hilferding, Rosa Luxemburg and Henryk Grossman, all of whom accorded an important role to developing countries in their analyses of capitalism. Rosa Luxemburg, in particular in her book *The Accumulation of Capital* (1913 [1951]) which Kalecki knew well, examined in detail the impact of capitalism on traditional economies. In his decade of work at the United Nations, from 1945 to 1955, Kalecki studied the economic problems of developing countries and started his consultancy work for some of their governments, notably Israel and Mexico. Following his return to Poland in 1955, he was active in seminars and research projects on developing countries, and advised the governments of India and Cuba. This work was brought to an abrupt halt in 1968, when his Polish collaborators in these projects came under political attack, and were purged from university positions. His influence was marginalised even if the institutions in which he worked continued in a more politically subservient fashion.

Kalecki's first published intervention in development economics was a review of Mihail Manoilescu's *Die Nationalen Produktivkrafte und der Aussenhandel* (published in English as *The Theory of Protection and International Trade*, 1931). Manoilescu had put forward an early version of the import-substitution argument in favour of developing-country protectionism. Because developing-country productivity in industry is higher than in agriculture, even if that industrial productivity may be lower than in industrialised countries, improvements in efficiency can be obtained by expanding industry behind protective tariff barriers. The resulting overall improvement in productivity may result in a higher output available to an economy, than might have been obtained from relying on low-productivity agricultural exports to pay for industrial imports. Kalecki criticised one possible neoclassical objection to this theory, namely that developing countries experience capital scarcity, and that market forces would tend 'naturally' to equalise the marginal productivity of capital or labour in industry or agriculture. According to Kalecki, such capital scarcity was not binding in agricultural countries, since rural unemployment or underemployment allowed investment to be undertaken unconstrained by 'the supply of new saving' up to the point of full employment. At the same time, he criticised the notion that protection for new industries was a sufficient condition for economic development: 'To represent free trade as the *only* obstacle to the economic progress of backward countries is to divert attention from such urgent social problems as land reform and others' (Kalecki, 1938, p. 711, original emphasis).

The critical issue for developing countries was how such investment could be organised. When Kalecki returned to this question, as a government adviser to Israel in 1950, he considered two possible alternatives for countries such as Israel with minimal indigenous investment goods capacity. In this situation, countries could rely on foreign direct investment, or on government-organised investments. The first possibility he considered to be of dubious benefit, because it was unlikely to be on a sufficient scale or attracted to industries that could supply the domestic market, and hence limit inflationary pressures in them. State-organised investments should therefore be undertaken with a view to maximising the exports needed to finance the import of industrial machinery, developing domestic investment capacity, and minimising domestic inflation. Private sector investment was to be regulated to ensure that it did not absorb scarce foreign exchange in ventures that were not high on the government's development priorities (Kalecki, 1951).

Kalecki went on to expand on these themes in his subsequent work on economic development. In the first place, he examined the political and social formation in which economic development could take place. He had no illusions about the existence in developing countries of some 'naturally' entrepreneurial capitalist class. Instead he highlighted those features of economic and social backwardness that served as obstacles to industrial development, in a way that was later taken up by the 'structuralist' school of development economists. The crucial issues opening up the possibilities for such development were political leadership and land reform. Land reform was critical because upon it depended the ability of the agricultural sector to supply food to a growing industrial sector whose workers still had a large income elasticity of demand for foodstuffs. Otherwise, real wages fell, or food imports rose, alleviated perhaps by food grants from the agricultural surpluses of the industrialised countries. Without land reform, the financial accumulation from higher agricultural production or prices would be absorbed by rural debt service or rents, which would then finance luxury consumption rather than being invested in the expansion of agricultural production.

The analytical foundation of Kalecki's 'structuralist' view was in his reflux theory of saving, investment and profits. In an industrialised capitalist economy, a government financial deficit expands the sales revenue of firms without increasing their costs, so that their profits and savings rise. Similarly, if firms undertake additional investment, using their own savings or bank credit, then this new expenditure ends up as additional profits for firms. Hence the 'reflux' of firms' spending into their profits, so that for firms as a whole there is no immediate problem of financing any investment credits. In a developing economy, government expenditure and investment 'leaks' out of the system into incomes of non-productive social groups (landowners, merchants and moneylenders). But the key leakage occurs through foreign trade, as a result of the large increase in imports of capital equipment, raw materials and finished goods that is attendant upon an investment boom in a developing country. This in turn drains the scarce foreign exchange reserves of such a country.

Kalecki had little faith in the ability of foreign companies to overcome the foreign exchange constraint by means of foreign direct investment. He considered that such investment was very expensive in terms of the amount of profit that foreign companies repatriated, openly or covertly, through transfer pricing. He gave one of the earliest expositions of the effects of such pricing practices (Kalecki, 1954). He considered that official loans usually came with political strings and requirements for favourable terms for companies from countries granting such loans. However, he favoured long-term trade agreements between countries. These he felt allowed governments to plan more securely with assured markets abroad.

A key political requirement for economic development, according to Kalecki, was the installation in power of an 'intermediate regime'. This was a government based on the 'lower-middle class', the urban professional classes and small businessmen who have an interest in economic development and are willing to push through crucial land reforms. But they may not necessarily be in favour of socialism and may be bought off by big business and foreign companies (Kalecki, 1964). This is perhaps the most troublesome of Kalecki's political concepts. He had in mind the Nasser government in Egypt. But that, like many of the intermediate regimes of Latin America was, initially at least, based on an alliance of military leaders and trade unions. In India, Jawaharlal Nehru was remarkably cautious in challenging the power of the big landowners who delivered the Congress votes in the rural areas.

With an intermediate regime in place, the key to economic development was planning industrialisation. Kalecki considered this to be a financial problem, even though he did not consider developing countries to be subject to a saving constraint. Formal finance for domestic investment could always be obtained through domestic loans. But if it became necessary to finance investment out of taxes, then Kalecki favoured taxes on profits and higher incomes, because this would have least impact on lower-income groups, and may even reduce inflationary pressure by reducing luxury consumption. Capital imports (foreign credits) can ease the foreign exchange constraint, and indeed may support general government spending programmes by allowing the import of specialist health equipment, as well as investment goods (Kalecki, 1963). However, foreign credits came in different forms and were frequently politically motivated. The best form of loan was one repayable in finished goods rather than in foreign currency (Kalecki and Sachs, 1966).

There was not, in Kalecki's view, any financial constraint on the amount of investment that could be undertaken by governments. Financial problems arose because of the financial liabilities to which investment may give rise, and because of the way financial resources, expended on investment, subsequently circulate in the economy at large. This circulation determines whether an investment drive is sustainable, or dissipates into inflation and luxury consumption. Kalecki's account of inflationary pressures in developing countries was 'structural' rather than the demand-led inflation that, in his view, characterised industrialised economies. Given low wages in developing countries, any substantial investment effort would result in higher demand for 'necessities'. If the supply of such necessities did not increase, then the resulting inflation would reduce real wages, so that the workers themselves would be largely financing the investment drive. At the same time, without land reform, the additional incomes of the food producers would be absorbed by higher rents and debt repayments, increasing demand for luxury goods among merchants, moneylenders and landowners.

These foreign exchange and domestic considerations made Kalecki sceptical of the benefits of installing the most capital-intensive (labour-productive) variants of particular investment projects. These had been advocated by Maurice Dobb and Amartya Sen, subject to a constraint of maintaining the level of real wages. In Kalecki's view, the choice of different variants in particular industries was not wide, while inflating capital requirements increased demand for wage good necessities or imports at a time when such demand was already likely to be high (Kalecki, 1972, ch. 10).

Kalecki's work on development economics won sufficient following in what were then called 'Third World countries' to arouse the anxiety of the US foreign policy establishment, which recognised hostility towards American capitalism behind Kalecki's suspicion of multinational enterprises, foreign direct investment, the Washington institutions of the International Monetary Fund and the World Bank, and commercial international loans. Following his death, Kalecki's work was continued by a small but significant group of economists who had worked or studied with him. Notable among them were Joan Robinson, Thomas Balogh and Eprime Eshag, and the still active Julio Lopez-Gallardo, Ignacy Sachs and Bruce McFarlane. However, circumstances and the prevalent ortho-doxy on economic development have shifted considerably from issues that Kalecki exam-ined. The kind of technocratic economic planning and étatist investment that Kalecki advocated is now widely viewed as a sink of corruption and venality, to be remedied by 'financial liberalisation' and 'appropriate' fiscal and monetary policies. In fact the worst corruption has occurred at the point of interaction between 'free' enterprise and govern-ments, where effective government is reduced to providing opportunities for business. The rotting infrastructure in many developing countries today reflects less the futility of eco-nomic planning *per se* than the inability to pursue it consistently and the incapacity of the private sector to provide such infrastructure.

Behind this shift of circumstances and issues have been two important changes in inter-national politics and finance. The first was the collapse of the Soviet Union and not only the system that Kalecki advocated of long-term international trade contracts used by the Communist bloc's Council for Mutual Economic Assistance, but also the bipolar inter-national political system that fostered Kalecki's 'intermediate regimes': 'The intermediate regimes are the proverbial clever calves that suck two cows: each bloc gives them financial aid, competing with the other. Thus has been made possible the "miracle" of getting out of the USA some credits with no strings attached as to internal economic policy' (Kalecki, 1964, p. 10). Foreign credits for developing countries are now much more influenced by the commercial interests of US corporations. This has removed crucial international political support for 'intermediate regimes'. The second major international change has been the rise of international finance, which has greatly expanded the possibilities for securing commercial foreign credits. The resulting international debt and 'emerging market' crises have placed the economic and financial policies of developing countries, including successful industrialisers like the East Asian economies, under the direct super-vision of the International Monetary Fund. In addition to the obvious political difficulties of pursuing sustainable development policies that effectively benefit the many living in poverty, the challenge facing any government seeking to pursue a Kaleckian development strategy, is how to take advantage of the opportunities offered by inter-national finance, while insulating the economy from the instability emanating from the international financial system.

JAN TOPOROWSKI

References

Kalecki, M. (1938), 'Foreign trade and the national forces of production', *Economic Journal*, **48** (192), 708–11.
Kalecki, M. (1951), 'Report on the main current economic problems of Israel', reprinted in Jerzy Osiatyński (ed.), *Collected Works of Michał Kalecki, Volume V: Developing Economies*, Oxford: Clarendon, 1993.
Kalecki, M. (1954), 'The Problem of financing economic development', reprinted in Jerzy Osiatyński (ed.), *Collected Works of Michał Kalecki, Volume V: Developing Economies*, Oxford: Clarendon, 1993.
Kalecki, M. (1963), 'Problems of financing economic development in a mixed economy', reprinted in Jerzy Osiatyński (ed.), *Collected Works of Michał Kalecki, Volume V: Developing Economies*, Oxford: Clarendon, 1993.

Kalecki, M. (1964), 'Observations on social and economic aspects of "intermediate regimes"', reprinted in Jerzy Osiatyński (ed.), *Collected Works of Michał Kalecki, Volume V: Developing Economies*, Oxford: Clarendon, 1993.

Kalecki, M. (1972), *Selected Essays on the Economic Growth of the Socialist and the Mixed Economy*, Cambridge, UK: Cambridge University Press.

Kalecki, M. and I. Sachs (1966), 'Forms of foreign aid: an economic analysis', reprinted in Jerzy Osiatyński (ed.), *Collected Works of Michał Kalecki, Volume V: Developing Economies*, Oxford: Clarendon, 1993.

Luxemburg, R. (1951), *The Accumulation of Capital* (translated by Agnes Schwartzschild), London: Routledge and Kegan Paul.

Manoilescu, M. (1931), *The Theory of Protection and International Trade*, London: P.S. King & Son.

Kindleberger, Charles Poor (1910–2003)

Few economists have made a more important contribution over the past century to our understanding of the processes that are responsible for economic progress and stagnation than Kindleberger. He did so by adopting an approach to the study of economic development shunned by most of his contemporaries as being 'unscientific'. At a time when formal modelling became all the rage he made no attempt to extract an elegant theoretical model of economic growth from his encyclopaedic knowledge of international economic history. Nor was he interested in using this knowledge to formulate 'laws' of economic development. Yet his contributions in the field are likely to be read long after most of the currently fashionable theories of economic growth have been forgotten.

Life and work

Charles Poor Kindleberger was born in New York in 1910 (see Kindleberger, 1991). After completing primary and secondary education he enrolled in 1928 at the University of Pennsylvania with the intention of studying Greek and Latin. However, he soon switched to economics as the Wall Street collapse and the start of the Great Depression in 1929 changed his interests. Like many of his contemporaries he wanted to understand the reasons behind such a disastrous breakdown of the economic system. He graduated in 1932. For his postgraduate studies, Kindleberger went to Columbia University where he obtained his MA in 1934 and PhD in 1937.

In 1936 he started more than a decade of work in government and international service. He was able, therefore, to observe as an insider the making of history in one of the most important periods of the twentieth century, including the beginning of a remarkable worldwide economic transformation. The forces for change that brought about this transformation, especially in the international sphere, remained at the centre of his professional interest and work for the rest of his life.

He started briefly as a research economist at the US Treasury (summer 1936) before moving first to the Federal Reserve Bank of New York (1936–39), which was concerned with international aspects of the New Deal, and then to the Bank for International Settlements in Basle, Switzerland (1939–40). After the outbreak of the Second World War he worked for the US Federal Reserve Board in Washington (1940–42), the US Office of Strategic Services (1942–44) and the State Department, where he stayed until 1948. In the last of these, he was employed first as Chief of the Division for German and Austrian Economic Affairs and then as Adviser on the European Recovery Programme (the Marshall Plan).

In 1948 Kindleberger joined the Economics Department at the Massachusetts Institute of Technology (MIT) where he was Professor of Economics and Ford International Professor of Economics from 1951 until his retirement in 1976. Eminent academics rarely 'retire', especially those with the curiosity, enthusiasm and energy that Kindleberger possessed in abundance. Not surprisingly, he continued to teach at the MIT and elsewhere for another decade and to write and lecture for the rest of his long life.

He was (predominantly in international economics and economic history) a prolific writer. His first paper was published when he was 24 (on competitive exchange rate depreciation between Denmark and New Zealand), his first book three years later (*International Short-Term Capital Movements*, 1937) and his last major work when he was 86 (*World Economic Primacy: 1500–1990*, 1996). In all, Kindleberger wrote and edited over thirty books and countless articles. He received many honours at home and abroad and in 1985 became President of the American Economic Association.

He died in the summer of 2003.

Diversity of the development problems and effective policies

Having been involved in policy making during one of the most difficult periods in history, Kindleberger was aware to a greater extent than most economists that neither economics nor any other social science is capable of explaining within its own analytical framework something as complex as economic growth and stagnation. At best, each can provide a partial explanation of the processes involved and account for some of the reasons for the diversity of national approaches to economic growth.

Theoretical models of economic growth invariably have three important limitations. First, all those factors that can be ignored in short-run, partial equilibrium analysis now occupy centre-stage. Physical environment, historical experience, culture, ideology and socio-political relations are of critical importance in determining how available productive resources are employed in the process of economic development and the efficiency with which they are used. Second, as many of these factors often differ significantly from country to country it is impossible, contrary to policy implications that emerge from the models, to employ effectively the same development strategy in all cases. Finally, the same growth strategy may not be appropriate at all stages of development even in the case of a single country. As the volume and quality of productive resources, and the efficiency with which they are used, change different policies and institutions will be needed to deal with new challenges.

It is for these reasons that Kindleberger's approach to economic development relies to such an extent, in addition to theoretical growth models and statistical analysis, on comparative international history. Economic history provides an important account not only of long-run economic successes and failures but also of the reasons, economic and other, behind them. Consequently, those who specialise in the theory of economic growth or trade unaware of 'the [wide] range of possibilities exemplified by history may generalise from a single case or a few cases, and fail to appreciate the need for care in the choice of assumptions and models, along with the frequent need to change them' (Kindleberger, 1990a, p. 351). Kindleberger warns, therefore, that '[o]nly fools would rely on purely deductive reasoning' (Herrick and Kindleberger, 1983, p. 497).

Theoretical models and their practical limitations

To isolate the role of some important aspect of economic development, theoretical growth models invariably focus on the contribution of a particular factor to eradicating poverty and improving economic welfare. As everything else is assumed away, the remedy recommended by the models is confidently expected to enable any country that adopts it to achieve sustainable economic development.

In contrast, Kindleberger's study of comparative economic history reveals that, at best, this *may* happen. Even then, it is not a single policy that will be responsible for the outcome but a country's capacity to transform its economy: that mix of economic and non-economic changes and policies that has so far eluded most nations. How people react to major structural shifts in the world economy 'will depend in many cases on the political power of given sectors, regions, factors, classes . . . and their readiness to use it. Ideology and culture will [also] play a role' (Kindleberger, 1978a, p. 239).

The study of economic development requires, therefore, a broader approach. Kindleberger demonstrates this in his analysis of some of the models that have been debated and disputed over the last two hundred years (see also Kindleberger, 1964a).

Arthur Lewis's model of *growth with unlimited supplies of labour* published in the early 1950s has, of course, a long history going back to David Ricardo and Karl Marx. Rates of growth in capitalist economies depend on the supply of cheap labour. Surplus labour keeps real wages fixed at a low level. This ensures that profits are high, stimulating investment and growth. In contrast, labour shortage leads to rising wages, falling profits, lower investment and declining rates of growth.

Kindleberger's analysis of the experience of Western Europe in the 1950s and the 1960s as well as over a much longer period exposes the model's limitations (Kindleberger, 1967, 1989). To begin with, surplus labour is 'a permissible rather than an initiating or even determining factor' (Kindleberger, 1967, p. 8). Many economies in the world with an abundance of surplus labour have made little or no economic progress. Moreover, as labour becomes scarce, in the long run technical progress makes it possible to raise efficiency levels and, consequently, both wages and profits – stimulating further growth. Higher wages enable wage earners also to save. The result is an increase in aggregate savings, making it possible to finance further investment. Finally, if there are no obstacles to international factor mobility, inadequate domestic saving can be supplemented by external borrowing and growth-inhibiting labour shortages by allowing immigration.

The important conclusion that emerges from this analysis of comparative international economic history is that the most advanced economies have achieved the same end – a high standard of living – by employing different growth strategies.

The same conclusion also follows from Kindleberger's analysis of the Prebisch–Singer theory of unequal international exchange between the periphery (developing countries) and the centre (industrial countries) caused by the long-term decline in the *terms of trade* of primary commodities relative to manufactures (Kindleberger, 1958, 1964b).

He does not dispute the fact that there has been a long-term decline in primary commodity prices compared to those of manufactures (Kindleberger, 1956). But, having analysed these trends, Kindleberger concludes that it would be difficult to offer a systematic explanation that would support any theory attempting to link changes in a country's terms of trade to its level of development (Kindleberger, 1958). Raul Prebisch's statistical analysis was 'unacceptable' because it ignored the fact that industrial countries were often important exporters of primary products and developing countries of manufactures (Kindleberger, 1964b, p. 342).

Structural changes can improve terms of trade through diversification into primary products as well as into manufactures. There are important differences in the impact of individual non-oil commodities on income distribution, and on development of the infrastructure and other sectors (Kindleberger, 1962, ch. 12). What really matters, therefore, is the ability of a country to diversify its exports in response to changes in international market conditions. 'Continuous attention to terms of trade is . . . in fact, a symptom of incapacity to adapt' (Kindleberger, 1958, p. 85).

Kindleberger is particularly sceptical of the accepted wisdom in his numerous writings on *foreign trade*, a field in which his knowledge of comparative international history was unrivalled. This is hardly surprising, as there are few areas of economics in which the mainstream theory is so much at odds with empirical evidence.

Economists may disagree about many things, but most tend to agree that: (i) external trade plays an important, even key, role in economic development; (ii) countries that adopt an export-led development strategy are far more likely to be successful than those that opt for import substitution; and (iii) countries which liberalise their trade grow faster than those that persist with protection. In fact, although there is a general consensus about these propositions in their normative sense, they have always been among the most contentious policy issues in economics. The reason for this is that they are based on assumptions that ignore non-economic factors and take the underlying conditions and capacity to change to be 'equal' everywhere.

Kindleberger uses historical experience of industrial countries to question the general validity of each of the three propositions. The experience shows that 'the relationships between foreign trade and growth are varied and complex . . . [and] . . . occasionally remote' (Kindleberger, 1961, p. 305). The critical factor is domestic capacity for economic transformation. A country cannot benefit from 'large potential gains from trade' if it lacks productive 'capacity to make use of them' (Kindleberger, 1962, p. 204). Hence, 'foreign trade is neither a necessary nor a sufficient condition' to explain either economic growth or the lack of it (ibid., ch. 12).

As for the relative merits of *export-led* and *import-substitution* strategies, both can stimulate *or* retard economic progress. The outcome will be determined by the capacity for major economic and social change – which varies between countries (Kindleberger, 1961, 1962, 1990b; Herrick and Kindleberger, 1983). Consequently, which of these strategies is adopted 'must be considered in a realistic context' *before* a particular policy package is implemented.

The same applies to overall *trade policy* (the choice between freer trade and protection) where decisions tend to be made frequently for political reasons. Which of the two policy options is chosen, including the extent and speed of its implementation, often depends on whether it happens to be in the interest of powerful economic and political groups rather than whether it will benefit the country as a whole (Kindleberger, 1951, 1975b). This is also true internationally. The world's dominant economies will put pressure on other countries to liberalise their trade partly to enable powerful domestic producers to gain access to global markets and partly to prevent potential competitors in other countries from developing fully their productive capacity, as it might threaten their own dominance (Kindleberger, 1975a).

National and international economic order

One of the most important and controversial issues in economic development concerns the control and use of productive resources. Which form of organisation, the state or 'the market', is most likely to achieve and sustain improvements in social welfare? Is the optimum solution at the international level to leave macroeconomic management to individual nation states, to rely on the benevolence of the world's dominant economy or to entrust it to supranational organisations? Despite claims to the contrary, few economists manage to consider them objectively and pragmatically. Kindleberger belonged to the few.

His personal preference, as his various writings make clear, is to rely on 'the markets'. But, this is not allowed to cloud the judgement of Kindleberger the scholar. Historical experience shows that neither political centralisation nor decentralisation is equally effective at all stages of development. In peacetime, with economies 'moving on trend', federal, pluralistic forms of organisation will normally be more effective. In times of crises centralisation, leadership and coordination of economic activity become essential (Kindleberger, 1996, p. 220).

In both cases, social factors are 'in many ways the strategic element' in economic development (Kindleberger, 1965, p. 385). This means that special attention must be paid to public goods; and the very nature of these 'goods' is such that the state has to play a major role in providing them (Kindleberger, 1975b, 2000, chs 8 and 19). Moreover, history shows that 'markets, people, ideas' have a 'pronounced tendency . . . to go to excess' (Kindleberger, 1990b, p. 7). Government intervention is needed to prevent such crises, especially in financial markets, and to deal with their consequences (Kindleberger, 1978b, 1984).

A highly integrated international economic system requires a unified approach to macroeconomic management. That means in practice that it is managed either informally by the world's dominant economy or formally by specially created supranational institutions. Kindleberger favoured the former. He gives the reasons for this in his analysis of the collapse of the international economic order in the interwar period and its contribution to the Great Depression in the 1930s (Kindleberger, 1973). The problem, as his last major work makes clear, is that such systems are unstable. Sooner or later all dominant economies lose their supremacy, mainly for socio-political reasons (Kindleberger, 1996).

Hence, international organisations ought to be encouraged and 'built on' (ibid., 2000, ch. 20). He is not confident, however, that this will work, as 'their record makes it hard to feel confident that the world economy can be effectively handled in crisis by supranational entities' (Kindleberger, 1996, p. 226).

Conclusion

Kindleberger was involved early in his career in solving exceptionally difficult economic problems during the Great Depression, the Second World War and the post-war reconstruction. The experience enabled him to ask in his research the right questions and to assemble an extraordinary wealth of historical evidence 'to test the validity and generality [of a number] of economic laws and models' (Kindleberger, 1989, p. ix). Such a formidable combination of practical experience and scholarly erudition should have left a permanent mark on both economic theory (so that it reflects more accurately real problems and policy preoccupations) and economic history (making it more robust analytically).

Yet, although respected and read widely, the professional influence that he ought to have enjoyed eluded him. The reason, as he recognised towards the end of his life, was that his work lacked the analytical depth to leave a permanent influence on the study and application of economics. He reflected that he 'could be regarded intellectually as a grasshopper who moves from problem to problem, gets a limited amount of mileage out of each one by the use of intuition, with limited statistics, no econometrics, and minimal formal analysis' (ibid., p. 138). He seemed satisfied with the narrative approach to economics even though he realised years earlier, after completing an important study, that 'in the course of attacking the partial equilibrium explanations, I may have uncovered the materials needed for a general theory of growth' (Kindleberger, 1964a, p. 4).

That is a major contribution in itself: to indicate a much more promising approach to one of the most important economic problems and to collect a wealth of historical evidence that should enable other economists to complete the task.

MIĆA PANIĆ

References

Herrick, Bruce and Charles P. Kindleberger (1983), *Economic Development*, 4th edn, New York: McGraw-Hill.

Kindleberger, Charles P. (1937), *International Short-Term Capital Movements*, New York: Columbia University Press.

Kindleberger, Charles P. (1951), 'Group behaviour and international trade', *Journal of Political Economy*, **59**, 30–46.

Kindleberger, Charles P. (1956), *The Terms of Trade: A European Case Study*, Cambridge, MA: MIT Press.

Kindleberger, Charles P. (1958), 'The terms of trade in economic development', *Review of Economics and Statistics*, Supplement, **40**, 72–90.

Kindleberger, Charles P. (1961), 'Foreign trade and economic growth: lessons from Britain and France, 1850 to 1913', *Economic History Review*, Second series, **14**, 289–305.

Kindleberger, Charles P. (1962), *Foreign Trade and the National Economy*, New Haven, CT and London: Yale University Press.

Kindleberger, Charles P. (1964a), *Economic Growth in France and Britain, 1851–1950*, Cambridge, MA: Harvard University Press.

Kindleberger, Charles P. (1964b), 'Terms of trade for primary products', in M. Clawson (ed.), *Natural Resources and International Development*, Baltimore, MD: Johns Hopkins University Press, pp. 339–65.

Kindleberger, Charles P. (1965), *Economic Development*, 2nd edn, New York: McGraw-Hill.

Kindleberger, Charles P. (1967), *Europe's Postwar Growth: The Role of the Labour Supply*, Cambridge, MA: Harvard University Press.

Kindleberger, Charles P. (1973), *The World in Depression, 1929–1939*, Berkeley, CA: University of California Press (revised and enlarged, 1986).

Kindleberger, Charles P. (1975a), 'The rise of free trade in Western Europe, 1820–1875', *Journal of Economic History*, **35**, 20–55.

Kindleberger, Charles P. (1975b), 'Germany's overtaking of England, 1806–1914', *Weltwirtschaftliches Archiv*, **III**, 253–81 and 477–504.

Kindleberger, Charles P. (1978a), *Economic Response: Comparative Studies in Trade, Finance and Growth*, Cambridge, MA: Harvard University Press.

Kindleberger, Charles P. (1978b), *Manias, Panics and Crashes: A History of Financial Crises*, New York: Basic Books (revised and enlarged, 1989).

Kindleberger, Charles P. (1984), *A Financial History of Western Europe*, London: George Allen & Unwin.

Kindleberger, Charles P. (1989), *Economic Laws and Economic History*, Cambridge: Cambridge University Press.

Kindleberger, Charles P. (1990a), *Historical Economics: Art or Science?*, New York and London: Harvester Wheatsheaf.

Kindleberger, Charles P. (1990b), 'Historical economics: a bridge between liberal arts and business studies?', in Kindleberger (1990a), pp. 3–11.
Kindleberger, Charles P. (1991), *The Life of an Economist: An Autobiography*, Oxford and Cambridge, MA: Basil Blackwell.
Kindleberger, Charles P. (1996), *World Economic Primacy, 1500–1990*, Oxford and New York: Oxford University Press.
Kindleberger, Charles P. (2000), *Comparative Political Economy: A Retrospective*, Cambridge, MA: MIT Press.

Kuznets, Simon (1901–1985)

In this entry I present some highlights of the contributions of Simon Kuznets, focusing on issues of continuous relevance for development and globalisation. I have relied on several excellent papers on Kuznets written after he was awarded the Nobel Prize in 1971 or as memorials after his death in 1985. These should be consulted for further details, in particular Lundberg (1971), Easterlin (1979), Abramovitz (1986), Kapuria-Foreman and Perlman (1995) and Fogel (2001).

A puzzle

Simon Kuznets was awarded the 1971 Nobel Prize in economics 'for his empirically founded interpretation of economic growth which has led to new and deepened insight into the economic and social structure and process of development'. Yet, two decades after his death it is only in the guise of the 'Kuznets curve' that he may be found in the literature of growth or of economic development. This is puzzling. Over a 60-year period Kuznets produced 31 books and over 200 papers, many of which were deservedly considered pathbreaking. Growth and distribution appear prominently in his studies but he was mostly known as the principal actor in the conceptual development of national income accounting and careful measurement of income and capital formation. Many assumed that the Nobel Prize had been awarded for this work, whereas in fact this contribution was strangely omitted from the Nobel citation.

Biography

Kuznets was born in Russia in 1901, emigrated to the United States in 1922, and completed his economic studies at Columbia University obtaining a PhD in economics in 1926. His dissertation, written under Wesley Clair Mitchell, was published in 1930 as *Secular Movements in Production and Prices* (1930). It complements the two other books from this period, *Cyclical Fluctuations* (1926) and *Seasonal Variations* (1933) in presenting and analysing the cyclical, seasonal, and secular movements in production and prices in a comparative framework. Mitchell brought Kuznets into the newly founded National Bureau of Economic Research (NBER) where he remained as a staff member from 1927 to the early 1960s. He served as Professor of Economics and Statistics at the University of Pennsylvania (1931–54), Professor of Political Economy at Johns Hopkins University (1954–60), and Professor of Economics at Harvard University (1960–71). His initial appointment at the University of Pennsylvania was in statistics 'because the economics department did not want immigrant Russian Jews' (Kapuria-Foreman and Perlman, 1995, p. 1530). Kuznets served as President of the American Economic Association in

1954 and before that in 1949 of the American Statistical Association, the last person to have held both positions.

After his retirement from Harvard in 1971 he continued a most active academic career publishing no less than 50 papers and two volumes of essays. The main theme at this stage was demographic change and its relation to economic growth and income distribution.

Institution building

Kuznets was also instrumental in the institutionalising of the continuous development and publication of comparable national income systems. The present wealth of statistics in every country and in international organisations owes much to these efforts. In the United States the first official estimates of national income published by the Department of Commerce were the work of Kuznets, on loan from the NBER in the early 1930s. While these may not be the first ever estimates of national income they were the first to lead to an institutionalised effort then imitated around the world.

Most of his massive statistical enterprises were carried out with little or no assistance. Yet from early on he was aware that the development of national income accounts was a continuing project that would require discussion and collaboration of many scholars for long periods of time. He thus helped to establish in 1935 the Conference on Research in National Income and Wealth and for years was one of the major contributors to its publications. He was also among the founders of the International Association for Research in Income and Wealth (IARIW) in 1947, an association that brings together academics and official statisticians. At about the same time the Social Science Research Council (SSRC) followed his suggestion and established in 1948, with him as chairman, the Committee on Economic Growth. The committee recruited leading economists in 11 countries to study long-term growth. He advised various countries on the development of their national income accounts. He helped found the Falk Institute for Economic Research in Israel, which carried out the first basic studies of Israel's economy.

From business cycles to growth

Kuznets started his comprehensive project on the economic growth of nations not much before 1950. However, already in his earlier studies in the late 1920s he showed interest in growth and its impact, positive and negative, on various groups of the population.

The 1930 book on secular trends looks at long-term movements in production and prices in many products in six countries. Continuous growth is the first feature noted: 'Our modern economic system is characterized by ceaseless change' (p. 1), 'a process of uninterrupted and seemingly unslackened growth' (p. 3). Yet, at the national or sectoral level the picture is less uniform; we observe shifts in leadership among nations and, within a nation, the lead shifts from one branch to another as retardation inevitably reaches former leaders. Kuznets contrasts the secular retardation at the sectoral level 'with our belief in the fairly continuous march of economic progress' (p. 5) and asks why not balanced growth? The answer combines demand effects and technological change: progress of technique makes new goods available (tea, cotton, radios and so on) but eventually demand reaches saturation, the pace of technical change slackens, new goods emerge, and possibly also competition from younger nations.

Measuring national income

At the NBER, Kuznets worked on the conceptual development and the measurement of national income and capital formation for more than two decades. It is difficult to visualise today what the situation was like with regard to information for the aggregate economy. Kuznets's effort at estimating national income, while not the first, was so distinctive that it became the benchmark in the field.

For Kuznets the design of national income accounts had to start with a clear view of what the basic purposes of economic activity are. For him national income estimates are primarily indicators of economic welfare and less so measures of short-run productive capacity. This led him to dwell during the next half-century on some conceptual problems which recur in his work, and in some memorable disputes: the problems of scope, netness/grossness and valuation.

In measuring national product we have to distinguish between economic activity and social life at large (scope), and between the costs and net returns of economic activity (net and gross). We also have to decide on the common base at which the various activities will be valued. The answers to these questions depend on the purpose of economic activity which in turn refers to the social values of the place and time. The solutions can therefore never be absolute. The practice to include only market transactions leaves out important categories such as household activities and increased leisure.

The most contentious issue during the early stages of conceptualisation was the treatment of government services. Originally, Kuznets argued for treating most of government expenditures as intermediate products; he viewed them as consisting of intermediate services to business or as necessary outlays for the maintenance of the fabric of society at large; a 'necessary regrettable' (Nordhaus and Tobin, 1972), but not a source of final utility to ultimate consumers. Neither the US Department of Commerce nor the UN System of National Accounts adopted Kuznets's approach (see also the section on costs and benefits of growth).

When relative prices differ across space or over time, computing growth at base year prices or at end of period prices will yield different results. These reflect different vantage points from which economic growth is seen. Kuznets argues that 'economic growth should always be examined from the vantage point of the present, if only because this is a more complete view than that from the past looking forward . . . in every generation the indices must be revised and history partially rewritten' (1956, p. 7). Similarly, since measurement depends on theory, as theory advances past measures would have to be revised. Theoretical and empirical knowledge are therefore always tentative and provisional.

Kuznets presented estimates of national income in its three principal forms. The first two were income received by individuals or factors, essential for distribution studies, and value added by industrial origin, essential for industrial shifts of economic activity and for growth accounting. The third approach, national product as the sum of expenditures for final use provided the empirical scaffolding for the Keynesian framework. In the postwar period, the short-run perspective of the Keynesian approach and the related requirements of the political system for a more active macroeconomic policy to maintain full employment with price stability lead to the development of systems of national income adequate for measuring short-term changes in current economic performance, but not as gauges of economic growth and welfare (1972). The short-run approach, focusing more on production than on consumption, prevailed in part because of the spread of Keynesian theory but also, paradoxically, because of the application of the Kuznets system of national income accounts to the war effort.

In 1942, Kuznets and his former student and now Chairman of the Planning Committee of the War Production Board (WPB), Robert Nathan, applied the national income accounts in a rudimentary input–output framework to estimate the economy's productive capacity and identify binding constraints of materials, labour and other resources. Their work played a crucial role in mobilising the economy's war capacity and maintaining a high level of civilian consumption during the war. In four years the share of material procurement in GNP rose from 4 per cent to 48 per cent (Nathan, 1994; Kapuria-Foreman and Perlman, 1995). This little-known chapter in Kuznets's professional life led John Kenneth Galbraith to argue that 'Simon Kuznets and his talented people had been the equivalent of several infantry divisions in their contribution to the American war effort' (1980, p. 80).

Economic growth of nations

Before Pearl Harbor Kuznets already had a clear outline for a research project on the economic growth of nations which he presented to Mitchell and referred to in a 1943 letter towards the end of his service at the WPB. A more detailed outline was circulated and discussed at the NBER in 1945–46. Mitchell and Arthur Burns, who was soon to succeed Mitchell as director, were not supportive of Kuznets's ambitious project. The missed opportunity on the part of the NBER was taken up by the SSRC under whose aegis most of the growth study was done.

'Modern economic growth' (MEG) is the term applied by Simon Kuznets (1966) to describe the economic epoch of the last 250 years, distinguished by the pervasive application of science-based technology to production. An economic epoch is a relatively long period (over a century) with distinctive characteristics that give it unity and differentiate it from other epochs (1966, p. 2). The principal quantitative characteristics commonly observed in the growth of the presently developed countries are: high rates of growth of per capita product, of population and of factor productivity, and a high rate of structural transformation. Major aspects of structural change include the shift away from agriculture, increase in the scale of productive units, shifts in organisation and in the status of labour, and shifts in the structure of consumption (see Structural Transformation, this volume).

'Advancing technology is the permissive source of economic growth, but it is only a potential, a necessary condition, in itself not sufficient' (1973a, p. 247). Its realisation requires institutional and ideological adjustments. Kuznets illustrates this with some examples from MEG: the modern large-scale plants needed to exploit inanimate power are not compatible with illiteracy or slavery, or with the rural mode of life or the veneration of undisturbed nature. In *Modern Economic Growth* (1966) he suggests the special attitudes that are as important as the technological and social epochal innovations to initiate and sustain growth. He summarises those attitudes in a triad: secularism – material attainment in this world; egalitarianism – denial of inborn differences among human beings; and nationalism – capacity of the state to provide stability and a historically community of feeling with an elite dedicated to modernisation.

Structural shifts

The high rate of growth of labour productivity is inevitably associated with a high rate of structural shifts. These comprise changes in the shares of output and inputs in economic activity with implicit changes in the status of employment, the conditions of work and life, the forms of enterprise, and the structure of foreign trade and other interactions with the rest of the world. Changes in the proportion of workers actively engaged by sector are due to differential productivity growth, demand responses to the fall in costs because of improved technology and in response to the continuous emergence of new goods, and the evolution of comparative advantage.

The consequences are a disjunction between the sectoral attachment of labour of successive generations. Associated with the higher mobility and migration were higher skill and educational requirements, largely the result of the new technology but also a response to the need for objective criteria for evaluation, given the increase in the number of migrants in the additions to the labour force. The outcome was a shift from social status to overt criteria of the capacity to perform. The trend away from status was magnified by the demographic transition; a decline in mortality followed, with a lag, by a reduction in birth rates reflecting the increased needs for human capital investment in the younger generation. The young thus became the carriers of the new knowledge and this contributed to the de-authorisation of tradition. Structural shifts thus emerge as an important strand in the process of modernisation.

The shifts in positions of various socio-economic groups often led to breakdowns and conflict. The resolution mechanism needed to preserve the consensus for growth and structural change came in the form of the national sovereign state, which relies on a sense of community, of common interest, among its members to serve as arbiter of intra-national conflicts; and as referee among new institutional devices to channel the improved technologies into efficient use and mitigate the negative effects and reduce the resistance to growth (Kuznets, 1980).

Costs and benefits of growth

From his earliest work on the measurement of national income, Kuznets stressed the importance of delimiting what enters into the economic calculation and the dividing line between final and intermediate. This has a close relation to the question of what are the benefits and the costs of economic growth, a theme that often reappears in his writings.

In the private sector, the dividing line between intermediate and final goods had shifted with the increased complexity of society during the process of economic growth.

In the 1970s, after the publication of ten long articles in *Economic Development and Cultural Change* (1956–1967) and the 1966 monograph, Kuznets returned frequently to the discussion of the measurement of costs and benefits of growth, an issue that rose to prominence at the time (1971, 1972, 1973a, 1973b, 1978). Why then? 'The sudden rise in interest' in 'old questions' would seem to be the result of the renewed interest in the study of economic growth in the previous 25 years and the rising concern at the time with negative byproducts of the growth of output and population that led some to advocate zero population and output growth (1972, 1973b; see also Nordhaus and Tobin, 1972).

In his 1971 *Economic Growth of Nations*, Kuznets refers to non-conventional costs and argues that a significant part of these are due to deficiencies in the 'conventional national economic accounting that treats some outputs that are really costs of production as *final* rather than as *intermediate* products' (1971, p. 75, original emphasis). We have reached this point, in part, by relying on national income measures well suited as indices of short-term changes but not adequate as gauges of economic growth (1972). 'In theory there can be no "costs" in *net* product properly defined as a gauge of economic growth' (1980, p. 428, original emphasis).

In addition to reclassification of measured quantities, Kuznets considers various 'hidden' costs such as the time spent in commuting to work, air and water pollution, and more subtle effects of urban life 'represented by the difficulties of maintaining privacy and of escaping from the vulgarities of mass media and from irrational domestic violence' (1971, pp. 95–6).

Kuznets warns of a bias in emphasising the negative or problem aspects and neglecting the positive aspects of technological innovations and growth. It may well be that 'emphasis on neglected negative byproducts is a useful goad to reform and change . . . [but] it is a balanced view . . . that we must seek' (1978, pp. 77–8).

Two points not usually acknowledged are:

1. 'The negative effects of growth have never been viewed as so far outweighing its positive contribution as to lead to its renunciation' (1973a, p. 254); and
2. If depletion of natural resources are to be counted then so should additions to resources resulting from new discovery and knowledge. Similarly with pollution: 'it is illogical and biased to enter a minus sign for pollution or deterioration' and not to include the original contribution of resources and of improvements in their use when represented by new technology (1973b, p. 583).

Theory and measurement

Kuznets was a student of Mitchell and became probably the leading practitioner of the latter's inductive approach to research. He had great respect for facts and theory but a strong scepticism towards formal statistics. Kuznets and others at the NBER were not engaged in measurement for the sake of measurement; instead, they were motivated by a desire to quantify macro variables of significance (Patinkin, 1976, p. 1107).

There is no formal theory in Kuznets but there is much theoretical speculation to comprehend empirical regularities, systematic differences, and underlying causes. In 'Toward a theory of economic growth' (1955) he maintains the impossibility of a purely economic theory of growth. A more general theory is a worthwhile goal but a very remote one for the present. The central problem is how to endogenise what economics mostly regards as givens: technology, population, tastes and institutions.

Kuznets was keenly aware of the limitations of the statistical information, always warning the reader of all its possible deficiencies. He worried about imposing too much structure on deficient data, preferring simpler forms of data analysis such as frequency distributions with various levels of classification to regression analysis (Fogel, 2001). 'There is little question that, unless critically analyzed, much of the apparently quantitative record for the early periods of developed economies and even the current statistics for underdeveloped countries is almost worthless' (Kuznets, 1957, p. 548).

Assessment

Kuznets did more than anyone else to convert economics from a speculative discipline into an empirical science. Leaders in his fields recognised his contributions during his lifetime and continue to do so today. A brief sample of accolades: 'Kuznets is a wise man; to my mind the wisest among now living economists' (Lundberg, 1971, p. 461), 'a giant in 20th century economics' (Paul Samuelson, in the *Boston Globe*, 1985, p. 43), 'the pioneer of quantitative economic history . . . revolutionized the analytical scope of economic history by giving it a quantitative underpinning' (Maddison, 2005, pp. 1–9).

And yet, in the economics profession there seems to be a 'profound ignorance of what Kuznets managed to accomplish in his approximate 60 years of professional work' (Kapuria-Foreman and Perlman, 1995, p. 1525) and, as argued above, in the current literature of growth and development Kuznets and his work (except for the 'Kuznets curve') have all but disappeared. A systematic exposition and appraisal which, as Moses Abramovitz (1986) pointed out in his obituary article, Kuznets would welcome as a step in the scientific process of verification, criticism, and reformulation of ideas, is long overdue.

MOSHE SYRQUIN

References

Abramovitz, M. (1986), 'Simon Kuznets: 1901–1985', *Journal of Economic History*, **46**, 241–6.
Boston Globe (1985), 'Simon Kuznets, Economics Pioneer, Nobel Winner, Harvard Professor', 11 July, p. 43.
Easterlin, Richard A. (1979), 'Simon Kuznets', in *The International Encyclopedia of the Social Sciences*, New York: Free Press, pp. 393–7.
Fogel, R.W. (2001), *Simon Kuznets, 1901–1985: A Biographical Memoir*, Washington, DC: National Academy of Sciences.
Galbraith, John K. (1980), 'The National Accounts: arrival and impact', in Norman Cousins (ed.), *Reflections of America: Commemorating the Statistical Abstract Centennial*, Washington, DC: US Department of Commerce, Bureau of the Census, pp. 75–80.
Kapuria-Foreman, Vibha and Mark Perlman (1995), 'An economic historian's economist: remembering Simon Kuznets', *Economic Journal*, **105**, 1524–47.
Kuznets, Simon (1926), *Cyclical Fluctuations: Retail and Wholesale Trade, United States, 1919–1925*, New York: Adelphi.
Kuznets, Simon (1930), *Secular Movements in Production and Prices: Their Nature and their Bearing upon Cyclical Fluctuations*, Boston, MA and New York: Houghton Mifflin.
Kuznets, Simon (1933), *Seasonal Variations in Industry and Trade*, New York: NBER.
Kuznets, Simon (1955), 'Toward a theory of economic growth', in R. Lekachman (ed.), *National Policy for Economic Welfare at Home and Abroad*, Garden City, NY: Doubleday, pp. 12–85.
Kuznets, Simon (1956), 'Quantitative aspects of the economic growth of nations. I. Levels and variability of rates of growth', *Economic Development and Cultural Change*, **5**, 1–94.
Kuznets, Simon (1957), 'Summary of discussion and postscript to W.W. Rostow, John R. Meyer, and Alfred H. Conrad – the integration of economic theory and economic history', *Journal of Economic History*, **17**, 545–53.
Kuznets, Simon (1966), *Modern Economic Growth*, New Haven, CT: Yale University Press.
Kuznets, Simon (1971), *Economic Growth of Nations: Total Output and Production Structure*, Cambridge, MA: Harvard University Press.
Kuznets, Simon (1972), *Quantitative Economic Research: Trends and Problems*, Fiftieth Anniversary Colloquium, vol. 7, New York: NBER.
Kuznets, Simon (1973a), 'Modern economic growth: findings and reflections' (Nobel address), *American Economic Review*, **63**, 247–58.
Kuznets, Simon (1973b), 'Concluding remarks', in Milton Moss (ed.), *The Measurement of Economic and Social Performance*, Studies in Income and Wealth 38, New York: Columbia University Press, pp. 579–92.
Kuznets, Simon (1978), 'Technological innovations and economic growth', in Patrick Kelly and Melvin Krantzberg (eds), *Technological Innovation: A Critical Review of Current Knowledge*, San Francisco: San Francisco Press, pp. 335–56.

Kuznets, Simon (1980), 'Driving forces of economic growth: what can we learn from history?', *Weltwirtschaftliches Archiv*, **116**, 409–31.

Lundberg Erik (1971), 'Simon Kuznets' contribution to economics', *Swedish Journal of Economics*, **73** (4), 444–61.

Maddison, Angus (2005), 'Measuring and interpreting world economic performance 1500–2001', *Review of Income and Wealth*, **51** (1), 1–36.

Nathan, Robert R. (1994), 'GNP and military mobilization', *Journal of Evolutionary Economics*, **4** (1), 1–16.

Nordhaus, William and James Tobin (1972), 'Is growth obsolete?', *Economic Growth*, Fiftieth Anniversary Colloquium, Vol. 5, New York: NBER.

Patinkin, Don (1976), 'Keynes and econometrics: on the interaction between the macroeconomic revolutions of the interwar period', *Econometrica*, **44** (6), 1091–123.

Labour Markets

Labour markets are peculiar, in that unlike other markets the service that is bought or sold at the time of initial exchange is rarely known. In developing countries, traditionally labour markets accounted for only a minor part of the arrangement of work. Either non-wage forms of production or some quasi-feudal arrangement prevailed, in which peasants supplied a proportion of their work time or produce in return for access to land or other means of production. Estates, plantations and mines typically brought in indentured migrant workers, sometimes paid money wages, sometimes given just board, lodging and a rented plot on which to produce basic foodstuffs.

Gradually, those practices have given way to the two main forms of arrangement, usually characterised as 'wage labour' and 'own-account' work (including unpaid family work). But labour markets are much more complex than this might imply. Essentially, individuals offer to supply time, effort and the application of 'skills' (an unclear idea in itself) in return for some remuneration, which might or might not be a monetary payment.

The best way of understanding the evolution of labour markets is to unpack the elements of the package involved. At the back of one's mind, one must think that labour *per se* is a commodity – it is bought and sold – but the worker is not a commodity, in principle. He or she retains some ownership rights, except in the limiting cases of slavery and bonded labour.

On the supply side, the worker may agree to enter a bargain to work so many hours for so many days. Some analysts would use the term 'contract' rather than 'bargain'. But for the overwhelming majority who labour in developing countries, there is no contractual arrangement. The agreement between worker and employer, or between worker and middleman, is likely to be informal, easily abrogated with impunity on the employer's side, usually less easily on the worker's side. The term 'contract' is a misnomer. Only when there are labour laws and written contracts should that term be used.

It is important to distinguish between 'labour', 'employment' and 'work'. Labour is work performed for remuneration. Not all work is labour. Some productive forms of work are not counted as part of economic activity, which is a statistical artefact that has had severe ramifications for the perceived nature of economic development and the treatment of women. Thus, the work of care, for children, the elderly, the sick and others, has been excluded, as has all forms of *voluntary* and *community work*.

Not all labour is employment in that for many performing labour the relationship is casual, precarious and indirect. Thus, a woman working as a 'homeworker' or 'outworker' may be paid on a piecerate basis, supplied with raw materials or petty means of production by a merchant, moneylender, landlord or middleman. This is scarcely the same situation as someone who is expected to turn up at a specific worksite at a specified time to work under direct supervision for a certain amount of time; that is employment, which has been a minority experience in developing economies.

This leads to a feature of labour markets – control. Employers in developing countries have used a wide variety of controls, many indirect, such as rental arrangements, share-cropping and debt bondage, obliging workers to labour to pay off a debt or using the existence of a debt to force the worker to remain at their disposal. And the means of production may be owned by the employer or by a merchant or middleman contracting to 'out-workers'.

Labour market analysts too rarely take account of these 'informal' arrangements, which are the reality for many millions of people around the world. The form that the wage relationship takes is also a neglected topic, and is shaped by historical and cultural practices, the character of production and the needs of employers. In effect, labour is controlled by a mix of forms of remuneration, usually including a money wage but also various non-wage benefits and a range of sanctions or potential deductions. The resultant mix may be messy, and usually means that workers are uncertain about what they will receive, living a working life of uncertainty and vulnerability.

These historical features of labour markets – in particular, employment and income insecurity – induced twentieth-century reformers to try to make labour markets less like other types of market, to reduce the extent of oppression, exploitation and insecurity. In short, a process of *decommodification* was launched. Protective regulations were passed limiting hours of work, requiring respect for workplace safety and health measures, requiring employers to pay the wages they had agreed to pay, requiring them to follow decent procedures of dismissal and requiring them to allow workers sick leave, vacation and so on.

Legislation proliferated. One result was a vast number of international conventions and recommendations developed within the ambit of the International Labour Organization (ILO), set up in 1919 to offset politicised unrest among the growing working classes in industrialising economies. Although progress was slow in developing countries, and distorted in state socialist economies, labour market *regulation* made global advance in the post-1945 era. It was more than symbolic that the ILO received the Nobel Peace Prize in 1969, since that was about the time of the high-water mark in the development of protective labour market regulation. Thereafter, there was certainly not 'de-regulation' – there being no such thing – but systematic re-regulation, towards less protection for workers and more for capital.

Looking back, the era of protective regulation may not have eradicated many of the insecurities associated with labour markets, but it did set a moderating framework in many parts of the world. A statutory instrument given prominence was the *minimum wage*. The idea was to set a floor below which no employer was supposed to go. In developing countries, it was never very effective in doing so. In some countries, it was always restricted to certain sectors or type of enterprise. And it rarely reached outworkers, casual workers and all those classified as in the informal economy. Nevertheless, in the 1970s and 1980s the minimum wage was derided as a labour market rigidity, in an intense attack orchestrated by the World Bank and neoclassical economists who saw it as preventing labour markets from 'clearing' and hindering the growth of employment.

Accordingly, governments allowed the real value of the minimum wage to fall, cut back labour inspection, introduced reforms to make more exceptions, made the minimum lower for young workers, and so on. The minimum wage has shrunk as a weapon against income insecurity. There never was strong evidence that it had much effect as a 'rigidity' or that it reached the growing number of workers in informal labour relations. But its current weak status reflects the evolution of regulatory systems in the past three decades.

Historically, the vulnerability of workers confronted by powerful employers led to attempts to form *trade unions*. These have varied in form, mostly being groups with similar types of work, defined in terms of sectors of production or occupational groups. In developing countries, others have been set up with explicit political objectives.

As far as the labour market is concerned, unions have tried to obtain more security for their members and raise their income, trying to make labour less like other commodities. They have used three main tactics – lobbying governments to change laws and regulations, indulging in collective bargaining with employers or groups of employers, and in some cases with government, and trying to regulate labour supply, in part to hold up the wage rate.

For many years, unions were regarded as the main instrument for limiting the unequal power of capital and labour at all levels of society. But even in countries where the unionisation rate (the percentage of the workforce in unions) was quite high, unions have been on the retreat (an exception being South Africa, due to political factors). Unions have always been attacked for interest and ideological reasons. But since the 1970s, that attack has been more systematic, the claim being that unions have been a source of rigidity, preventing labour markets from 'clearing' by holding up wages, imposing high non-wage labour costs and forcing governments and employers to operate employment protection rules, supposedly lowering employment growth.

Again, the international financial agencies were at the forefront of this incessant critique, as were the supply-side economists predominating in the United States. The Pinochet regime in Chile became a demonstration project, advised by US economists, leading the way in measures to break the perceived power of unions and to decentralise labour bargaining to individual production units. Since then, albeit less drastically or visibly, in numerous other countries restrictions have been placed on unions while there has been a trend towards individual employment contracts, beginning with managerial and professional employees and filtering down to types of skilled worker. The rollback has been fostered by the spread of multinationals into developing countries, bringing with them US, European or Japanese labour practices.

The outcome of these changes is that labour markets have again become more like a market for lemons, with workers in a weaker bargaining position. What is happening is a restructuring of what might be called the 'social income', with a declining proportion of workers having access to community support networks, to enterprise-level benefits, or the hope of acquiring them, and the promise of state benefits, such as healthcare and pensions. Fewer have been able to rely on protective labour regulations. Although the vast majority of workers in developing countries never had much in terms of state benefits, the trend had long been assumed to be towards more being protected in that way. Now the reverse is the case. In recent years, the components of social income consisting of non-wage forms of remuneration and protection have been shrinking, making trends in money incomes a misleading guide to changes in welfare, poverty and inequality (Standing, 2002).

Although life in low-income countries has always been insecure, the insecurities in labour markets have been associated with demographic trends in patterns of labour.

The position of *women* has been crucial. For a long time, their role was almost ignored; then discussion focused on their 'invisibility' and on women as a 'labour reserve'. Ester Boserup (1970) did much to change this perspective, and since then more has been written about women workers than on any other labour market issue.

Although women have always been involved in labour market activity, their recorded participation in the labour force has increased substantially in the past 50 years. Although partly due to improved interest in measuring their work activity, that has much to do with the changing character of labour relations, since women have always been relegated largely to precarious jobs, which have been spreading relative to regular, protected full-time jobs. Their greater involvement has also been due to the spread of export-orientated labour-intensive industries, in which women have predominated as low-cost labour, mostly recruited for short periods from rural areas as teenagers, soon to be discarded and expected to return to their villages. No country has industrialised without mobilising large numbers of women workers.

Women have comprised a larger share of *migrants*, internal and international, than is often appreciated. Extensive internal migration has usually accompanied the emergence of labour markets in developing countries, much of it being short-term labour circulation, with migrant workers returning to participate in agriculture and depending on remittances from rural areas. Indeed, migrants have contributed to the growth of flexible labour markets that are characteristic of the early twenty-first century global economy.

Migrants are absorbed in labour markets more easily than was once believed. A popular model of labour market dynamics in the 1970s, the so-called Harriss–Todaro model, postulated that migrants entered urban areas by joining a queue, such that as urban unemployment rose migration would slow and even halt. Labour markets rarely operate so simply. Migrants often enter urban areas by taking jobs that pay less than urban residents expect or can afford to accept. In some cases, employers prefer to employ migrants because they are more exploitable, or can be discarded with fewer costs, or because they wish to possess a diversified workforce.

Labour markets are often depicted in *dualistic* terms, the most popular dualism being a division between 'formal' and 'informal' sectors. This is a crude and arbitrary approach; too much is compressed into each 'sector', whereas in reality there is a continuum of labour relations in terms of precariousness and income level (ILO, 2004). A trend in many developing countries is that so-called 'formal' enterprises (modern, large) have been informalising their labour, by outsourcing, and by using more casual labour and contract labour. Ironically, this has meant that some workers in so-called 'informal' firms (small, more traditional) have more security and protection by regulations than many labouring for formal firms.

Another clumsy dualism used to describe and analyse labour markets is the distinction between 'skilled' and 'unskilled' labour. The terms are rarely defined. It is remarkable that very little is known about levels and distributions of competencies, and claims such as the assertion that country *x* is underdeveloped because of a shortage of skilled labour cannot be supported by available data. Most governments that collect labour statistics present data on the distribution of jobs, or at best the proportion reporting their main 'occupation' (a misnomer). To give just one example, if a person who has qualified as a medical doctor is working as a taxi driver, his/her medical skill is unlikely to be recorded in labour market statistics. In short, the conventional distinction between skilled and unskilled says more about the division of labour than about the distribution or level of skills.

Generally, labour market statistics are still deficient and distorting. The main means by which social scientists assess patterns and trends is the *labour force approach*, developed in the 1930s and 1940s in response to the Depression and concern over mass unemployment in industrialised countries such as Germany, the UK and the USA. Since then, labour force surveys, with concepts attuned to industrialised labour markets, have been replicated in most parts of the world. These analyse labour by means of a trichotomy of employed, unemployed and economically inactive. Observers have pointed to the inadequacy of that approach in developing countries. But mainstream thinking still concentrates on data from it.

Thus, unemployment and labour force participation rates are often presented for comparative analysis when these reflect institutional differences, underlying economic and social structures and differences in reference periods and definitions of job seeking. Observers have tried to respond by developing concepts of *underemployment*, visible and invisible. But these have been presented on an ad hoc basis, rather than as an alternative way of assessing labour market performance.

A related phenomenon that has attracted a disproportionate amount of attention is so-called 'voluntary unemployment', the claim being that young labour force entrants, particularly those in urban areas with secondary schooling, prefer to remain unemployed than take available low-income, informal jobs. This is used to suggest that unemployment is less serious than the measured rate might suggest. Whether or not the social suffering is overestimated, the notion of voluntary idleness can be misleading. Often, the fact that on average the unemployed have more schooling than the average merely reflects the fact that younger cohorts are most prone to unemployment and have more schooling than their predecessors, and the fact that urban populations have more schooling while urban unemployment is often higher than rural.

The worst consequence of the labour force approach is that it has encouraged the neglect of most work that is not labour, that taking place outside labour markets. Although vital, and occupying the time and energy of millions of women, in particular, the tasks summarised by the term 'care work' have been ignored, as has community work. These are extraordinarily important for everybody in developing countries. Until that neglect is redressed, we will continue to undervalue forms of work that are intrinsically more productive (having greater use value) than many jobs regarded as desirable by those who measure development by the number of jobs generated, and policy makers will continue to penalise those doing such work by the tendency to link social security entitlements to the performance of labour.

What are likely to be the main labour market trends? Almost certainly, they will become even less like they were expected to become in the mid-twentieth century. Even in the public sector, long perceived as the standard setter, employment relations have become less secure (influenced by structural adjustment strategies). We should anticipate that flexible, informal and unstable labour relations will remain pervasive, so that the old labourist dream of strong *employment security* will not be the norm. However, new agencies and institutions will emerge to pool and allocate workers to productive enterprises, thus implying more outsourcing of the employment relationship. This would be potentially beneficial for workers and for enterprises, if regulated with mutual benefit in mind.

Without such agencies, a future of chronic labour market insecurity beckons, and would be a defeat for human development.

Among the promising trends is the emergence of organisations that are not old-style unions but are representing workers in several complementary ways, in the labour market, as consumers and as citizens more generally. These include the Self-Employed Women's Assocation (SEWA) of India, which has a membership of hundreds of thousands of women, organised in part to bargain for better working conditions, mainly for street vendors and outworkers, such as bidi rollers and garment makers. In other parts of the world, similar organisations are gaining strength, and may become the great bodies moderating the insecurities and commodifying tendencies endemic to labour markets. Voice regulation is essential, and in some places is gaining strength. Reformers who fear commodification should welcome that and promote it. Atomised, individualised labour markets are not compatible with human development or real freedom.

GUY STANDING

References

Boserup, E. (1970), *Women's Role in Economic Development*, New York: St. Martin's Press.
International Labour Organization (2004), *Economic Security for a Better World*, Geneva: ILO.
Standing, G. (2002), *Beyond the New Paternalism: Basic Security as Equality*, London: Verso.

Land Reform

Land reform is understood here as the redistribution of property rights in agricultural land. Its dynamics and outcomes are bound up with issues of class and popular politics; forms of agricultural production and their effects for the productivity of land and labour; and the ways in which agricultural growth contributes to processes of economic growth more generally, not least as a stimulus to industrialisation. The notion of land reform has been applied variously to the dispossession of large landholdings in favour of small 'family' farmers or 'peasants' (which remains its 'classic' reference point); the nationalisation or socialisation of large commercial farms; and the decollectivisation of state farms and other corporate entities in the former Soviet bloc, China and Vietnam.

Land reform in any expansive sense is a central motif in the making of the modern world. From the French Revolution onwards, land reforms – of different kinds and by very different means – have a long, diverse and complex history in both North and South. That history predates development discourse, hence development studies, in the contemporary (post-Second World War) sense, and discloses questions and problems that today's development policy agendas might absorb or avoid in various ways. Land reforms have commonly combined a number of goals: social justice in the face of oppression, enhanced livelihoods and security for those employed in farming, and aspirations to a more productive agriculture. These goals, and their tensions, are evident in both major land reforms that emerged from social revolution in (mostly) agrarian societies and the (intermittent) advocacy by development agencies of land reform – properly designed, packaged and managed as policy intervention – over the last 60 years or so, including currently by the World Bank.

A starting-point: 'land to the tiller'
The slogan of 'land to the tiller' is emblematic of many of the major land reforms of modern history. It denotes the ambition to transform an agrarian structure that, in stylised terms, consists of large landholdings owned by a class of landed property and worked by a class of small agricultural producers or 'peasants', subjected in various ways to exactions of rent and tribute. Landlords have a predatory character: their income is used for luxury consumption and reproducing their social power, including military means and religious status, rather than for productive investment in enhancing the yields of land or of the labour that works it. Such a pre-capitalist, for example 'feudal', agrarian structure lacks the drive to invest in productivity – on the part of both landowners and their subject tenants – intrinsic to capitalism.

Any economic dynamic thus requires, as a necessary if not sufficient condition, a redistribution of 'land to the tiller(s)': those farmers whose energies are consequently freed of the burdens of rent and tribute, and of the social oppression that typically underwrites them. A key point in this model is that while property rights in land undergo a radical change, the form of agricultural production – 'peasant' or 'family' farming – remains, albeit now constituted on a basis that is, in principle, socially equitable and economically more productive.

Rural social movements to achieve 'land to the tiller' were part of major social upheavals in many agrarian societies in modern history, culminating with particular intensity from about 1900 to the 1970s: the period *par excellence* of what Eric Wolf (1969) termed 'peasant wars of the twentieth century'. Examples include Mexico and Russia in the 1910s, Eastern and Southern Europe and China in the interwar period (continuing in China into the 1940s and 1950s), and in the post-war period Bolivia in the 1950s, Vietnam and Algeria in the 1950s and 1960s, Peru in the 1960s, and Mozambique and Nicaragua in the 1970s and 1980s. In all these instances peasant political action contributed to redistributive land reform, in some cases combining struggles against large landed property and its social power with anti-colonial or anti-imperialist struggles.

Land reform as development policy I: state-led development
The resonances of land reform effected by 'peasant wars'/social revolution remained potent in the post-war period of state-led development: in continuing (or renewed) impulses of social revolution, as in China and Vietnam; in strategies to pre-empt its possibility (or 'threat'), as in Italy, Japan and Korea in the 1940s and 1950s under US military occupation, and in the US-led Alliance for Progress in Latin America in the 1960s following the Cuban revolution; between the 1950s and 1970s in other state-led development strategies pursued by modernising regimes of varying nationalist complexions, from Nehru's India and Nasser's Egypt to the Iran of the last Shah.

This wide range of examples suggests that in this period more and less comprehensive land reforms were pursued for different purposes, by different social and political forces, through more and less radical means, and with various outcomes. It is widely accepted that some 'modernising' land reforms accelerated the pace of capitalist development in agriculture, while – the other side of the same coin – in many cases the poorest categories of the rural population obtained less than richer 'peasants' and embryonic capitalist farmers – in India, Egypt, Iran, and much of Latin America, for example – and especially women farmers and agricultural workers who generally continue to have the weakest land rights (Razavi, 2003).

Land reform as development policy II: market-based development

Land reforms of the various kinds indicated culminated in the 1970s, including in Portugal whose belated democratic revolution was triggered by the costs of colonial wars in Africa. Several commentators accurately remarked on, and also lamented, the disappearance of land reform from the agenda of development policy during the initial moment of the neoliberal ascendancy in development doctrine in the 1980s, concentrated at it was on urgent measures of structural adjustment. It is striking, then, that land reform has been reinserted in the development policy agenda from around 1990. Less surprising is that it has been reinvented in the terms of current orthodoxy: 'Previous land reforms have been unduly confiscatory, statist or top-down. "New wave" land reform, which is decentralised, market-friendly and involves civil society action or consensus, is sometimes feasible and consistent with just and durable property rights' (IFAD, 2001, p. 75). 'Market-friendly' land reform deploys a 'willing seller–willing buyer' mechanism, typically with special credit provision to potential buyers among the rural poor and land-hungry who qualify by dint of need and serious intent to farm. Such 'new wave' land reform – like other manifestos of 'pro-poor' growth – claims a 'win–win' scenario: it will help overcome rural poverty by distributing property rights more widely, fostering small-scale farming with its beneficial employment and efficiency effects (see below) while simultaneously stimulating more effective land markets.

Three approaches to land reform

While there is substantial agreement, across the ideological spectrum of ideas about modernisation, of the desirability of dispossessing predatory landed property, this conceals sharply divergent viewpoints about the type of farming most conducive to economic development following redistribution of land to the tiller. First, in the Marxist tradition there is a strong, if not exclusive, impulse towards economies of scale in agriculture as in industry. Reform that dispossesses predatory landed property in favour of 'peasants' assists the development of capitalism by establishing conditions for a fuller differentiation of rich, moderately endowed and poor peasants, the final destination of which is the formation from their ranks of classes of agrarian capital, established on large farms, and proletarian labour.

By the same logic, following the Bolshevik, Chinese and Vietnamese revolutions with their initial redistributions of land to the tiller, policies of socialist development favoured, and imposed, the formation of larger agricultural units across a spectrum of organisational forms from state farms to producer cooperatives and communes. In other instances, where large-scale capitalist farms already existed – rather than simply predatory landed property – there was a tendency to nationalise such modern enterprises, and benefit from their economies of scale, rather than divide them into 'family' farms, for example, in the case of Cuba's sugar plantations after 1959 and in Algeria, Ethiopia, Mozambique and Nicaragua following their 'national liberation' struggles.

Second, mainstream development discourse tends to be more agnostic about any intrinsic virtues of large- and small-scale farming, but not about how optimal farm size should be determined, namely by the particular combinations of factor productivities in different branches of agriculture and the relative prices of commodities in markets for farming inputs and outputs. For neoliberal theory, the optimal size and type of farm enterprise for different kinds of agricultural goods in different countries will be decided by the operation of those markets, both domestic and international, once the 'distortions' induced by subsidies, administrative pricing, state marketing of inputs and outputs, and other interventionist measures, are removed.

A third viewpoint is that of agrarian populism which champions an agrarian structure of small 'family' farmers as most conducive to efficiency and growth, in terms of the factor endowments of poorer countries (plentiful labour, scarce capital) and in terms of equity: employment and income distribution effects. The populist case for land reform has a long lineage that includes the great Russian agricultural economist and opponent of the Soviet collectivisation of agriculture A.V. Chayanov (1888–1937). Today it incorporates two central controversies in development debate: the so-called 'inverse relationship' and notions of 'urban bias' in development policy. The former maintains that smaller farms manifest higher productivities of land – output per area – than larger farms, as well as generating higher net employment (albeit at necessarily lower levels of labour productivity). While much contested analytically and empirically, the inverse relationship is a central plank in continuing populist economic arguments for redistributive land reform, including subdividing large(r) commercial farms to accommodate the landless and land-hungry rural poor. The other controversy concerns 'urban bias': the notion that development policies in the South favoured cheap food policies in the interests of strong urban constituencies and a (mistaken) emphasis on industrial development, at the expense of smaller and poorer farmers.

Both the inverse relationship and 'urban bias' have long been central to the work on agricultural development, including their advocacy of land reform, by two influential development economists: Michael Lipton, from his seminal book on *Why Poor People Stay Poor* (1977) through the 2001 IFAD report which he directed, and Keith Griffin also since the 1970s (see most recently Griffin et al., 2002). 'Urban bias' is also a notable component of the World Bank's encompassing critique, from the 1980s, of state-led development strategies and their outcomes (Karshenas, 1996), with the added argument that poorer countries would do best to remove policy 'distortions' that impede the contributions of agriculture to their export performance, on the principle of comparative advantage, as well as that of domestic markets.

The state of play today
Fierce controversy surrounds the theoretical rationale, motives, likely extent, and outcomes for agricultural growth and rural poverty reduction – *and* for social and political stability – of 'new style', 'market-friendly' land reform, and will continue to do so (Ghimire, 2001; Byres, 2004). Just as striking as the reappearance of land reform on the agenda of (neoliberal) development policy are those countries where its applications, promoted by the World Bank, have a high profile: Brazil, with its powerful radical landless people's movement, the MST (*Movimento Sem Terra*); Colombia with its long and

continuing history of *La Violencia*; Central America as part of the 'post-conflict' settlement of major civil wars; and South Africa in its fraught moment of transition from apartheid (1990–94) and since.

The MST – given Brazil's high levels of urbanisation and industrialisation, and extreme social inequality – is especially emblematic for more radical interpretations that identify a series of intensified land struggles from below across the South. These struggles may contain elements of historically familiar 'peasant' movements but, in this view, are principally generated by the pressures of the 'semi-proletarian' condition: that is, the ways in which so many of the labouring poor have to secure their reproduction (livelihoods, 'survival') by combining a range of activities across different sites of the social division of labour, including farming, in the absence of adequately paid and secure wage employment (Moyo and Yeros, 2005). This impulse from below is seen as one element in the volatile and highly contradictory course of events since 2000 in Zimbabwe – a unique case of sweeping, regime sanctioned, confiscatory land redistribution at the present time. Of course, the embracing of land struggles from below, in Brazil and elsewhere, draws inspiration from the revolutionary forces and moments of the past and scorns any good intentions of World Bank-style 'market-friendly' but state-managed land reform.

What both stances do indicate, irrespective of their other virtues and vices, are aspects of the changed conditions of development wrought by 'globalisation' and the era of structural adjustment. 'Market-friendly' land reform seeks to fill the gaps between now conventionalised formulae of 'pro-poor growth' and evidence of growing poverty and inequality in many regions of the South, despite the promised benefits of openness to world markets and the tough love of aid conditionality. The view of a pervasive 'semi-proletarian' condition as a major force in land struggles from below recognises the intensifying, if hardly novel, crisis of secure wage employment as a livelihood base of the great majority of the working poor in an increasingly 'globalised' South. In so doing, it also highlights one of the problematic elements in the Marxist tradition of 'the agrarian question' as applied to today's South, namely its emphasis on raising the productivity of farm labour and thereby reducing the economically active population in agriculture (as in the course of capitalist development in the North).

Some core issues pervade all the different experiences of land reform listed here: which land should be appropriated? How are its owners to be compensated, if at all? Who should benefit? How effectively are the twin moments of appropriation and redistribution implemented? What kinds of farming does land reform promote? What other measures may be necessary to secure a more productive agriculture from land reform? And, crucially, which social and political forces are driving land reform – and seeking to manage it? At the same time, there is a great variety of responses to these questions, in different circumstances and with different outcomes, not least in today's changing social conditions when the pursuit of livelihoods by 'footloose labour', in Jan Breman's (1996) term, straddles countryside and town, farming and other occupations, more than ever before, and when investment in agriculture and its commodity chains attracts an ever-greater range of urban and international capital. The pace and effects of contemporary agrarian change highlight both the continuing intrinsic interest and relevance of issues of land reform and their links with the dynamics and contradictions of processes of capitalist development more broadly.

HENRY BERNSTEIN

References

Breman, Jan (1996), *Footloose Labour: Working in India's Informal Economy*, Cambridge: Cambridge University Press.

Byres, T.J. (ed.) (2004), 'Redistributive Land Reform Today', special issue of *Journal of Agrarian Change*, **4** (1–2).

Ghimire, Krishna B. (ed.) (2001), *Land Reform and Peasant Livelihoods. The Social Dynamics of Rural Poverty and Agrarian Reform in Developing Countries*, London: Intermediate Technology for UNRISD (United Nations Research Institute for Social Development).

Griffin, Keith, Azizur Rahman Khan and Amy Ickowitz (2002), 'Poverty and the distribution of land', *Journal of Agrarian Change*, **2** (3), 279–330.

IFAD (2001), *Rural Poverty Report 2001, The Challenge of Ending Rural Poverty*, Rome: International Fund for Agricultural Development.

Karshenas, Massoud (1996), 'Dynamic economies and the critique of urban bias', in Henry Bernstein and Tom Brass (eds), *Agrarian Questions. Essays in Appreciation of T.J. Byres*, London: Frank Cass, pp. 60–102.

Lipton, Michael (1977), *Why Poor People Stay Poor. A Study of Urban Bias in World Development*, London: Temple Smith.

Moyo, Sam and Paris Yeros (eds) (2005), *Reclaiming the Land. The Resurgence of Rural Movements in Africa, Asia and Latin America*, London: Zed.

Razavi, Shahra (ed.) (2003), 'Agrarian Change, Gender and Land Rights', special issue of *Journal of Agrarian Change*, **3** (1–2).

Wolf, Eric (1969), *Peasant Wars of the Twentieth Century*, New York: Harper and Row.

Least Developed Countries

The term least developed countries (LDCs) refers to a subset of developing countries characterised by exceptionally low indicators of economic and social development. It was invented by the United Nations to designate a group of countries that tended to lag behind other developing countries in economic growth and social progress. In the late 1960s, the UN established a few criteria for the identification of LDCs. These included per capita GDP of $100 or less (1968$), share of manufacturing in GDP of 10 per cent or less, and adult literacy of 20 per cent or less. In subsequent years, the criteria were updated and others added.

On the basis of the initial criteria and the work done by UNCTAD, the General Assembly approved a list of 24 LDCs in 1971. The number rose to 50 by 2003, accounting for over 10 per cent of the world population. Only one country – Botswana – has graduated out of the status of LDC. The initial list of countries included, Afghanistan, Botswana, Burundi, Ethiopia, Nepal, Somalia, Sudan, Uganda and Tanzania. In subsequent years, apart from small island states in Africa and the Pacific, new entrants included Angola, Bangladesh, Cambodia, Congo/Zaire, Eritrea, Liberia, Madagascar, Mozambique, Myanmar, Senegal, Sierra Leone and Zaire, *inter alia*. Of the 50 LDCs in 2003, 34 were from Sub-Saharan Africa, ten from Asia, and six from the Pacific Ocean or the Caribbean.

Characteristics and development experience of LDCs

In general, the economies of LDCs are characterised by low per capita income, the predominance of primary production, low savings and tax revenue, poor physical infrastructure, low stock of human skills, high population growth, poor communications networks, high concentration of exports and vulnerability to natural disasters and external economic shocks. The LDCs display relatively high infant and maternal mortality and malnutrition, low life expectancy and low levels of adult literacy and school enrolment rates. They have also been exceptionally prone to internal conflicts and political instability. But as might be expected of such a large group of countries, they show considerable diversity in economic, social and political characteristics.

While some countries such as Angola, Burundi, Cambodia, Liberia, Nepal, Rwanda, Somalia, Sudan, Uganda and the former Zaire have become bywords for violent conflicts and political instability, others such as Lesotho, Malawi, the Maldives, Samoa, Senegal, Tanzania and Zambia have benefited from peaceful and orderly political regimes. In terms of economic development, at the lower end, countries like Burundi, Democratic Republic of the Congo, Eritrea, Ethiopia, Malawi, Mozambique, Sierra Leone and Tanzania, had GDP per capita below $200 in 1998 (1995$). At the other end, even excluding the island states that tend to have higher per capita incomes, are countries like Angola, Bhutan, Djibouti, Laos, Lesotho, Mauritania and Zambia with GDP per capita in excess of $400. Again ignoring island states and those with very small populations, despite overall poor performance, a number of countries were able to achieve growth in per capita GDP over 1990–98 of 2 per cent or more. These include Bangladesh, Cambodia, Laos, Lesotho, Eritrea, Ethiopia, Malawi, Nepal, Sudan and Uganda (all these statistics are from UNCTAD publications cited below).

Social indicators also show considerable diversity. For instance, countries like Afghanistan, Angola, Liberia, Malawi, Mali, Niger and Sierra Leone have infant mortality rates in excess of 130 per 1000 live births. The corresponding figures in countries like Bangladesh, Eritrea, Myanmar and Sudan are 80 or below. Adult literacy rates in excess of 70 per cent are found in Cape Verde, Democratic Republic of the Congo, Lesotho, Malawi, the Maldives, Myanmar, Tanzania and Zambia. At the lower end, countries with less than 35 per cent adult literacy comprise Afghanistan, Burkina Faso, Ethiopia, Mali, Niger, Sierra Leone and Somalia. With regard to schooling, Angola, Cambodia, Laos, Lesotho, Malawi, Myanmar, Nepal and Zambia have more than 80 per cent primary school enrolments. In contrast, the corresponding figures for Bhutan, Ethiopia, Liberia, Mali, Niger and Somalia are less than 40 per cent.

Overall, the LDCs' economic performance and social indicators have lagged well behind those of other developing countries over the past two decades. While the per capita GDP fell by 0.1 per cent per annum in LDCs over 1980–90, it rose by 1.9 per cent in other developing countries (ODCs). In 1990–98, the respective figures were increases of 0.9 and 3.6 per cent, respectively. Excluding Bangladesh, which accounts for about a quarter of total LDC output, the per capita output growth in LDCs falls further to −0.9 per cent and 0.4 per cent per annum over the two periods. Thus while the per capita GDP in LDCs in 1980 was over 30 per cent of that in all developing countries, it had fallen to just under 23 per cent by 1998.

The rate of population growth in ODCs slowed down from 2.3 per cent per annum over 1960–70 to 1.7 per cent during 1990–97. In LDCs, it rose from 2.4 to 2.6 per cent over the same period. Similarly, the gap between the LDCs and ODCs remains wide in social indicators such as under five mortality rate (108 and 65 per 1000 births), life expectancy (49 and 62 years), adult literacy (49 and 82 per cent) and school enrolments: for secondary and tertiary education, the rates are 16 and 65 per cent and 1.6 and 17.7 per cent, respectively.

The contrast in economic structure and communications is equally striking. In 1990, 75 per cent of the labour force in LDCs was found in agriculture, as compared with 32 per cent in ODCs. In 1997, while the share of primary products in total exports was 69 per cent in the former, it was 32 per cent in the latter. It is also of interest to note that both the export concentration ratio and the export instability index were much higher in LDCs relative to ODCs. While there were five telephone lines per 1000 people in LDCs in 1999, in all developing countries, the figure was 69 per 1000 people.

The experience of LDCs with regard to trade, development assistance and foreign investment has been quite disappointing since the 1980s. Their share of world exports, already very low at 0.4 per cent, has declined further. LDCs, in contrast to ODCs, have relied heavily upon concessional resource flows. In 1985, concessional loans and grants accounted for over 96 per cent of all financial flows to LDCs. This share had declined to over 84 per cent by 1998 but rose again to over 94 per cent in 2000. For all developing countries, the corresponding figures were 71, 21 and 27 per cent, respectively. The concessional funds per capita in constant dollars declined in LDCs from $28.1 to $18.4 between 1985 and 1998, while for all developing countries, the fall was more moderate from $10.8 to $10.0.

The situation in the LDCs has also deteriorated on the debt front. The total external debt more than doubled between 1985 and 1998, rising from $71.3 billion to $138.7 billion. As a proportion of the GDP of LDCs, external debt rose from 61 to 85 per cent. On the other hand, thanks in part to debt–service rescheduling and accumulated arrears, the burden of debt service fell somewhat over the period from $4.5 billion in 1985 to $4.2 billion in 1998. As a proportion of exports of goods and services, the debt–service ratio halved from 30 to 15 per cent. This appears to have been the only bright spot in an otherwise extremely dismal picture on the external economic relations of the LDCs.

There are diverse and complex reasons for the poor performance of the LDCs as a group. First, a high proportion of them – nearly 21 out of 50 – have experienced grave episodes of violence and instability over the past two and a half decades. These episodes have resulted in death and disabilities for millions of persons, while also seriously disrupting the processes of economic and social development. Second, because of their heavy reliance upon primary product exports, they have suffered from fluctuating prices and declining terms of trade for most of this period. Third, the sheer underdevelopment of their human resources and physical infrastructure condemns them to lower social and economic progress than countries with superior endowments. Fourth, the LDCs have had their share of governance failures in terms of poor institutions, management problems and inefficient use and misappropriation of resources. Finally, as seen below, they have been served poorly by the international community in terms of both advice on development strategies and policies, and keeping to the commitments made to them regarding development assistance and trade and technology concessions.

The response of the international community

The development policies pursued in the LDCs have been influenced even more than in ODCs by the advice and pressure from the Bretton Woods institutions and bilateral donors. The policy prescriptions have far too often consisted of standard packages of economic liberalisation, privatisation and deregulation that the financial institutions have crafted for all developing and transition economies. On the whole, the LDCs in the 1990s had a better record of carrying out economic reforms, especially with regard to liberalisation of prices, markets, trade and payments, than ODCs. But as pointed out by UNCTAD in its 2000 Report on the LDCs, these reforms did not address the deep structural problems experienced by most LDCs. These include inadequate social and economic infrastructure, weakness of market development, the thinness of the entrepreneurial class, and low production capabilities in the private sector. These difficulties were compounded by the inadequacy and uncertainty of aid flows, the poor quality and coordination of delivery of aid, the scale of debt relief and the erosion of government capacity.

The growing gap in economic and social performance and infrastructure between the LDCs and the ODCs has prompted the multilateral agencies to adopt a number of measures to accelerate their development. The UN specialised agencies are devoting an increasing share of their resources to assist them. An UNCTAD Inter-Governmental Group on the LDCs has been meeting regularly since 1975 to discuss their problems, review progress made and identify emerging critical issues. The WTO has created a special technical assistance programme to help them in their work relating to multilateral trade agreements and for negotiations relating to the adhesion to WTO of non-members among them. The Bretton Woods institutions have developed special debt relief mechanisms for heavily indebted poor countries (HIPCs).

The UN has convened or co-sponsored three world conferences in 1981, 1991 and 2001 to deal specifically with the problems faced by the LDCs and the measures that can be taken at national and global levels to accelerate their progress and integration into the global economy. These conferences brought together UN member states, international and regional agencies, the business community and voluntary development and humanitarian organisations. They set detailed targets for economic and social development for the LDCs. They specified overall macroeconomic and sectoral measures that the LDCs need to take to achieve these targets. The last two conferences also laid considerable stress on respect for human rights, equality for women, observance of the rule of law and promotion of transparency and accountability.

The conferences also laid down policy measures for the rich countries in the areas of development assistance, commodity agreements, liberalisation of market access for LDC exports, debt relief and transfer of technology on easier terms. For the most part, the industrialised countries failed to live up to their commitments: the aid targets were not met, the tariff escalation on processed goods and quantitative restrictions on competing agricultural products were largely maintained and HIPC debt relief schemes worked too slowly, for too few countries and on too small a scale to make a major impact on the resource flows to the LDCs. In the 2001 Conference, the industrial countries, especially the European Union, made specific commitments to enhance aid flows, reduce debt burden, ensure quota-free access to all exports except arms, facilitate adhesion to the WTO on more flexible terms, augment technical assistance and promote investment, develop enterprises and strengthen technological capabilities. It remains to be seen the extent to which these commitments will be implemented in the coming years. In the meanwhile, the continuing deprivation and marginalisation of the LDCs, especially in Sub-Saharan Africa, remains one of the most important, if not the most important issue, on the international agenda for development.

DHARAM GHAI

Note

The statistics cited in this entry are mostly from the UNCTAD *Least Developed Countries Report* (2000). An UNCTAD official kindly provided the latest data relating to 50 LDCs in 2003.

Further reading

UN (1982), *Report of the United Nations Conference on the Least Developed Countries, 1981*, New York: UN.
UN (1992), *Report of the United Nations Conference on the Least Developed Countries, 1991*, New York: UN.
UN (2001), *Report of the United Nations Conference on the Least Developed Countries, 2001*, New York: UN.
UNCTAD, *The Least Developed Countries*, Geneva: UN (published annually since 1984).
UNCTAD (2000), *The Least Developed Countries: 2000 Report*, Geneva: UN.

The Lewis Model

W. Arthur Lewis's 1954 paper was a *tour de force* which virtually laid the foundations of development economics as a *sui generis* subject. Underdeveloped economies, especially the Asian economies which were the focus of his attention, were characterised, he argued, neither by neoclassical full employment, nor by Keynesian unemployment: they had substantial labour reserves, with the marginal product of labour close to zero in the traditional subsistence sector, but not unemployed non-labour resources. Consequently neither the neoclassical nor the Keynesian paradigms were of much help in analysing their problems; we had to go back to the classical world with its assumption of a virtually unlimited labour supply for the capitalist sector at a subsistence wage rate (this had to exceed by a certain given amount the average product per person in the overcrowded subsistence economy).

Once the capitalist sector got established, it would continue to grow through the reinvestment of surplus, whose size relative to its own, and of the economy's output, would increase through technological progress which raised labour productivity. As long as the surplus of the capitalist sector, in excess of what it contributed to consumption, was invested (thus ruling out Keynesian aggregate demand problems), and there was no shortage of natural resources raising rents at the expense of profits (the problem that worried David Ricardo), through for instance technological progress in agriculture, the rate of profit in the capitalist sector could not fall; it could only rise, and with it the growth rate of the sector, until labour reserves began to get used up, putting pressure on wages.

How was this classical picture of capitalist dynamics to get started? Lewis clearly saw the state as playing a leading role (he saw the USSR and India as growing a class of 'state capitalists' who were 'determined to create capital rapidly on public account'). He also visualised private capitalists coming up, as new opportunities arose and the market widened (in which case 'state capitalism' in 'mixed economies' like India could also be seen as a progenitor of private capitalism). 'State capitalist' investment, he argued, could also be financed through credit creation, in addition to taxation and savings. The inflationary impact of such credit creation, which could be protracted if the inflation-hit classes defended their real incomes through increases in their money claims, would none the less eventually peter out since such investment would give rise to increased real incomes. The transitional pains caused by such inflationary financing would be more bearable the more such investment was directed towards short-gestation projects for raising consumer goods output (such as irrigation works), and the smaller the value of the Keynesian multiplier in the economy (the 'turnover tax' system in the Soviet Union being a classic example of a mechanism for truncating the multiplier). In addition to inflationary financing, the state, Lewis argued, had to introduce protection for the industrial sector (we shall discuss this argument below). 'But once a capitalist sector has emerged', through all these measures, 'it is only a matter of time before it becomes sizeable'.

This process of rising capitalist surplus, and investment, in national income would of course stop when surplus labour disappears. But it may stop even before that for several possible reasons: first, through the increase in wages in the capitalist sector which comes about because the absorption of surplus labour from the subsistence sector raises the average income per remaining person in the latter; second, if the capitalist sector, dependent upon imports from the subsistence sector, finds its terms of trade becoming adverse, precisely because its own rapid growth creates excess demand pressures for such imports, and thereby lowers its rate of profit (through, for instance, a rise in the product wage if its workers depend upon the subsistence sector for their food requirements); third, if the subsistence sector itself becomes more productive, and hence raises the wage rate for the capitalist sector (this argument has nothing to do with trade between the two sectors, and its strength would be reduced if the greater productivity of the subsistence sector also turns the terms of trade *in favour of* the capitalist sector); and finally, if the workers in the capitalist sector succeed in obtaining higher wages through trade union action. But if, despite these possible hurdles, conditions remain favourable for the capitalist surplus to grow more rapidly than population, then 'there must come a day when capital accumulation has caught up with labour supply'.

Several criticisms have been levelled against the Lewis model, most of them anticipated by Lewis himself. A zero marginal product of labour, it has been argued, is neither necessary nor sufficient for the existence of surplus labour in the subsistence sector as suggested by Lewis (Sen, 1966); but Lewis himself says of 'disguised unemployment' in the subsistence sector that if some family members are removed from the scene then the others would have to work harder ('the argument includes the proposition that they would be willing to work harder under these circumstances'), which makes zero marginal product, strictly speaking, irrelevant. It has also been suggested that since the average income per remaining person in the subsistence economy starts increasing *immediately* as labour gets drawn from it, the capitalist sector has to face an increasing supply price of labour from the very outset, and not a horizontal one as suggested by Lewis. But since there are several sources of labour reserves, of which the disguised unemployment on the family farms is only one (we must not forget the substantial open unemployment which also exists in such economies), the proposition of a horizontal supply curve still retains validity; besides, one can argue quite plausibly with Lewis that it is only a *noticeable* increase, not *any* increase, in the average income in the subsistence sector which can push up wages for the capitalist sector. The shifting of the terms of trade against the capitalist sector, not necessarily because of excess demand for subsistence sector goods (which Lewis mentions and which had been recognised by Dobb (1967, p. 78) in 1951) but because of the exercise of monopoly power by the landlords in traditional agriculture, has also been held as a constraint on Lewisian capitalist dynamics (Chakravarty, 1974; Mitra, 1977). Such exercise of monopoly power, however, presupposes that landlords have significant control over the state, that is, that the basic premise of the Lewisian argument, namely the coming into being of a state committed to capitalist (or 'state capitalist') industrialisation, has not been fulfilled. In other words, it does not constitute a critique of Lewis, no matter how significant a phenomenon it may be. (Even in the case of India where this argument was advanced with much force for the decade following the mid-1960s, it is now clear that the balance of class forces underlying state power *shifts* through time, so that the power of the landlords does not always remain equally significant.)

The real problem with the Lewis model, however, lies in his assumption that the process of capitalist investment can be completely dissociated from the consumption demand of workers and peasants, or, more generally, in his belief that capitalist investment is always savings constrained. As the surplus of the capitalist sector rises as a proportion of the capitalist sector's income, if the capitalists decide not to consume more than a fixed fraction of this surplus, then their savings as a proportion of *this sector's income* (and of course of the *national* income), must increase over time, and with it *ex hypothesi* their investment. In other words, if the capitalist sector is not to slip into demand deficiency, investment as a proportion of this sector's output must go on increasing, the ever-increasing investment providing the growing market for itself and hence constituting its own sole rationale and justification. This vision, however, of investment occurring solely and blindly for investment's sake (a vision that had been advanced vigorously by the Russian economist Mikhail Tugan-Baranovsky (see Kalecki, 1971)), is scarcely a plausible one even for a planned ('state capitalist') economy, let alone for a capitalist economy where the anticipated growth of the market crucially determines investment behaviour (a fact sought to be captured by hypotheses like the 'accelerator').

If, on the other hand, capitalist investment as a proportion of the capitalist sector's output remains more or less constant, thereby avoiding the Tugan-Baranovsky scenario, and capitalists' consumption absorbs the remainder of the surplus (hence satisfying the 'no glut' assumption of Lewis), then we are faced with a different problem, namely that the surplus labour in the economy may never get absorbed. If the investment ratio within the capitalist sector is given by s and the incremental capital–output ratio by v, then the growth rate of this sector is given by s/v, and if the rate of growth of labour productivity through technological progress in this sector is m and the rate of population growth is n, then the labour reserves would never get used up if $(s/v - m) \leq n$. In such a case, productivity growth in the subsistence sector, and the consequent increase in the capitalist sector's wage rate, which Lewis sees as a hindrance to capitalist dynamics, could actually promote a more vigorous capitalist dynamics by enlarging consumer demand and thereby stimulating capitalist investment. Capitalist dynamics in short is better sustained through a relatively more balanced expansion of consumption and investment than under a Tugan-Baranovsky scenario.

Lewis's assumption of investment being forever savings constrained also precludes any consideration of the foreign exchange constraint. To explore this let us move to his 'open economy' discussion. Since food is produced both by the high-productivity-per-person advanced country agriculture and the low-productivity-per-person underdeveloped country agriculture, the wage rate in the latter (in terms of food) is a fraction of what it is in the former. Since labour mobility across these two worlds is restricted by fiat, and since capital mobility, which too could in principle offset this wage differential, is also restricted, though because of a range of complex factors that govern capital movements, this wage differential persists.

It follows that the commodities which the latter exports would fetch a correspondingly lower price than what the former exports, and that any benefit of technological progress in the latter's export sector would lower its world price without raising export sector wages while any such progress in the former's export sector can be appropriated as higher wages (if world food prices are equalised and the differential within the advanced country between the wage rate and the income per person in food production is not to widen, then some income subsidy would have to be given to advanced country food growers). In short as long as surplus labour exists in the underdeveloped economies they are doomed to be victims of adverse factoral terms of trade. But precisely because their marginal product of labour in agriculture is way below the average product while the two hardly differ in manufacturing, the theory of comparative cost dictates that underdeveloped countries should specialise in manufacturing and import their food in exchange for manufactured goods exports. To get to this pattern of trade they need to protect their manufacturing sector from imports from the advanced countries. As Lewis was to argue even more forcefully later (Lewis, 1978), what the developing world needs is not the growth that comes its way under the existing pattern of international specialisation (the conventional 'export-led growth'), but a deliberate promotion of its own agricultural and industrial revolutions, through protectionism and state intervention, which eliminates its surplus labour. The 'Lewis model' demonstrates how this can be done.

Three comments are in order on this remarkable argument. First, the cause for the higher productivity per person in agriculture in advanced countries, which Lewis (1978) locates in the 'agricultural revolution', lies rather in the forcible acquisition by European migrants of enormous tracts of temperate land through the eviction of the original inhabitants (this was compounded by the destruction of traditional industries in Asia by unrestricted imports from advanced countries): the so-called 'agricultural revolution' in Britain and elsewhere is a much exaggerated phenomenon (see Patnaik, 1997 for details) which distracts attention from this fact.

Second, since tropical agriculture is characterised by the overcrowding of persons on scarce land, but since access to a whole range of *exclusively* tropical produce, from fresh fruits to tea, coffee, sugar and cotton, is essential for the maintenance of the living standards in the advanced countries, the Lewisian argument suggests a conflict of interest between the advanced and the backward countries, both because the latter's breaking away from the current specialisation would raise the prices of all these commodities to the former, and because it would also entail a loss of export markets for the manufactured goods of the former. Thus, despite his claim of adhering to the classical tradition, Lewis is in fact breaking away from the Ricardian notion that free trade benefits all countries. A faithful pursuit of the Ricardian logic of comparative advantage would itself show, according to Lewis's argument, that the actual pattern of international trade reflects the conflicting interests of different countries. The pursuit of a Lewisian agenda by the underdeveloped countries, it follows, would invite opposition from the developed countries.

Third, Lewis underestimates the possibility that in the face of this opposition the resolve of the capitalist class in the underdeveloped countries (including the 'state capitalists') may crumble. The fact that capitalist industrialisation in the underdeveloped countries behind protectionist barriers faces a foreign exchange constraint is not because domestic manufacturing production is 'inefficient' (which is both debatable and *per se* irrelevant to the argument), or because these countries cannot physically do without a range of imports for which their newly erected manufacturing sectors behind protection-ist barriers are incapable of earning the requisite foreign exchange (large underdeveloped countries like India and China, which are precisely the repositories of massive labour reserves are certainly capable of producing virtually all their requirements); to a very sig-nificant extent the foreign exchange constraint reflects the desire of the upper classes, including the bourgeoisie, for advanced country goods in preference to the goods which they themselves produce. Such preference, a legacy of the colonial past, would certainly subvert a Lewisian growth trajectory, even if there were no other factors (for example, the current globalisation of finance) militating against the *dirigiste* growth strategy that Lewis approved of. He talked of the workers in the capitalist sector imitating the capitalist way of life, and thereby causing a reduction in the rate of capital accumulation, but he did not reckon with the possibility that the capitalists in the underdeveloped countries may imitate the way of life of the capitalists in the developed countries and cause a similar choking off of accumulation.

PRABHAT PATNAIK

References

Chakravarty, S. (1974), 'Reflections on the growth process of the Indian economy', *Indian Left Review*, reprinted in his *Selected Economic Writings*, Oxford and Delhi: Oxford University Press, 1993.

Dobb, M.H. (1967), *Papers on Capitalism, Development, and Planning*, Part 2, London: Routledge & Kegan Paul.

Kalecki, M. (1971), 'The problem of effective demand with Rosa Luxemburg and Tugan-Baranovski', in M. Kalecki *Selected Essays on the Dynamics of the Capitalist Economy*, Cambridge: Cambridge University Press, pp. 146–55.

Lewis, W.A. (1954), 'Economic development with unlimited supplies of labour', *The Manchester School*, **22**, May, 139–91.

Lewis, W.A. (1978), *The Evolution of the International Economic Order*, Princeton, NJ: Princeton University Press.

Mitra, A. (1977), *Terms of Trade and Class Relations*, London: Frank Cass.

Patnaik, P. (1997), *Accumulation and Stability Under Capitalism*, Oxford: Clarendon.

Sen, A.K. (1966), 'Peasants and dualism with or without surplus labour', *Journal of Political Economy*, **74**, October, 425–50.

Lewis, (William) Arthur (1915–1991)

William Arthur Lewis was born on 23 January 1915 in the small Caribbean country of St Lucia. After receiving his primary and secondary education in St Lucia, he entered the London School of Economics and Political Science in 1933 where he read for the Bachelor of Commerce degree. His excellent performance landed him a scholarship to pursue a doctorate in industrial economics at his alma mater. He completed his PhD degree in 1940 with a thesis, which was subsequently published as a book entitled *Overhead Costs* (1949a).

Lewis joined the London School of Economics and Political Science in 1938 as an assistant lecturer. He rose to the rank of Reader in Colonial Economics in 1947 before joining the Department of Economics at the University of Manchester in 1948 as the Stanley Jevons Professor of Political Economy. He left the University of Manchester in 1958 to become the Principal of the University College of the West Indies (UCWI) and later the Vice Chancellor of the independent University of the West Indies (UWI). Lewis was the economic adviser to the prime ministers of Ghana (1957–58) and the West Indies Federation (1961–62) and deputy managing director of the United Nations Fund for Development for a brief period. He was offered the post of Professor of Economic and Political Affairs at Princeton University in 1963 and later the post of James Madison Professor of Political Economy. He remained at Princeton University until his retirement in 1983. During his attachment at Princeton University, he took leave to be the President of the Caribbean Development Bank (CDB) and visiting Professor of Economics at the University of the West Indies, Cave Hill Campus. In addition to receiving a knighthood from the Queen of England in 1963, he was awarded the Nobel Prize in economics jointly with Professor Theodore W. Schultz, for his 'pioneering research into economic development research with particular consideration of the problems of developing countries' (see Wilkinson, 1999; Downes, 2004). He died in 1991.

Lewis's work covered three broad areas, namely industrial economics, the history of the world economy from the mid-nineteenth century and development economics. His work in industrial economics was undertaken during the period from 1938 to 1948 and covered such topics as the nature of overhead costs, the two-part tariff, market structure (monopoly and competition in the retail sector) and the pricing policies of public corporations. Much of his work is still relevant today especially as it relates to the pricing of electricity and telephone services and the design of competition policy.

Between 1944 and the late 1980s, Lewis was concerned with issues of economic development and the history of the world economy. It is in these two areas that he made seminal contributions to the field of development studies, an interdisciplinary subject which involves three basic elements: theoretical or philosophical, empirical or historical and practical or technical (Toye, 1980; see also Lipton, 1970).

Although Lewis is well known for his work as a development economist, his methodological approach to the study of developing countries involves the elements of the development studies framework. He was concerned with historical processes, the philosophy of the international economic order and domestic and regional economic policy. He was an applied economist who approached a problem from its institutional background. Because of his emphasis on policy matters, he argued that one must have a good idea of the sociological background of an economic issue and also its political linkages (Lewis, 1986). Indeed, he published papers and a monograph on the political problems confronting the Caribbean and West Africa based on his advisory experience in these regions (see Lewis, 1965; Emmanuel, 1994).

In the area of development studies, Lewis's work covered several areas: development theory, economic growth, development planning, education and human resource development, economic integration and politics of developing states. His analysis of world economic history sets the background against which these development areas were analysed. As he explained, a good part of his academic life was spent on two important questions: what determines the terms of trade between industrial and primary products and whether the 'Great Depression' was a unique event that had never happened before or whether it was one of a series of such events (Lewis, 1986). A collection of Lewis's papers and a bibliography of his books are contained in Emmanuel (1994).

As a development economist, Lewis is probably best known for three important works: his dual-economy model of economic development with unlimited supplies of labour, the theory of economic growth and development planning – the essentials of economic policy.

His celebrated 1954 article and its later extensions published in 1958, 1972 and 1979 examined the process of economic development in the context of a two-sector economy using classical methodological principles. His model illustrates the process of economic transformation of a country whereby excess labour in the subsistence sector would be gradually absorbed by the capitalist sector. Implicit in this process is the industrialisation of the economy coupled with the gradual modernisation of the agriculture sector. In effect, Lewis advocated a 'balanced development strategy'. His basic framework has been employed to examine rural to urban migration, urban unemployment and the determination of shadow wage rate in project evaluation (see The Lewis Model, this volume).

Probably Lewis's main contribution to development studies as an interdisciplinary subject is provided in his encyclopaedic text, *The Theory of Economic Growth* (1955). Without using a single mathematical formula, which is characteristic of 'modern' growth theory, Lewis was able to explain the factors which underlie the growth and development process of a country drawing on economics, sociology, psychology, management, demography, politics and anthropology. With a simplicity of language and exposition and a historical backdrop, Lewis was able to highlight and analyse many of the factors which are now associated with the popular 'endogenous growth theory' (see Gylfason, 1999). Lewis argued that the 'proximate causes of economic growth are the effort to economize, the accumulation of knowledge and the accumulation of capital' (Lewis, 1955, p. 164).

One of his famous statements is that the 'central problem in the theory of economic development is to understand the process by which a community which was previously saving and investing 4 or 5 percent of its national income or less converts itself into an economy where voluntary saving is running at about 12 to 15 percent of national income or more' (Lewis, 1954 in Emmanuel, 1994, p. 920). His explanation of the effort to economise focuses on the value system of the population and the nature of the economic institutions which encourage people to postpone current consumption for future consumption. He analysed such factors as the attitude to work, wealth and social status, the spirit of risk and entrepreneurship, the management of resources, trade relations, economic freedom and markets, the family and other social institutions.

In the context of the accumulation of knowledge, Lewis argued that economic growth depends on both technological and social knowledge (popularly called 'social capital'). He traced the growth of knowledge in different societal contexts and showed how such knowledge has been applied to the production of new and better goods and services which have enhanced economic and social welfare. Lewis placed great emphasis on training and the need to develop the human resources of a country. This issue is further developed in Lewis's work on education and development where he distinguished between education as a 'consumption good' and an 'investment good' (see Lewis, 1961). In his administrative roles as head of the University of the West Indies and president of the Caribbean Development Bank, he was able to put into practice the idea that the accumulation of knowledge is a key element in the growth and development process. Rapid capital accumulation is vital to the economic development process. Lewis links this vital element to the savings of a country along with its ability to borrow externally to finance development projects. It is important that the institutional framework be developed to promote both savings and investment – stock market, banking system and other financial institutions.

The role of the state in the development process was a major preoccupation for Lewis both in his academic writings and his advisory role to governments in Africa, Asia and the Caribbean. In his two books on planning, *The Principles of Economic Planning* (1949b) and *Development Planning: The Essentials of Economic Policy* (1966), he discussed the operational role of the government in the development process. As a social democrat, he believed that government action was needed to secure economic outcomes that were not easily obtainable through the market. He defined democratic socialism as 'political democracy plus economic equality' and was concerned with issues of inequality and unemployment. Governments in developing countries need to engage in some form of development planning to overcome obstacles and hasten the process of economic and social development. He advocated 'planning through the market' and was critical of 'planning by direction' or centralised planning. Although formal development planning is not in vogue today, with countries engaged in structural adjustment programmes in response to the process of globalisation, many of the issues raised by Lewis are still relevant – the need for a 'strong, competent and incorrupt administration', the promotion of foreign trade, the appropriate allocation of public resources (finance), the role of the private sector, and the need for balanced growth and development. Lewis was also concerned about the need to promote political stability in developing countries (especially in Africa) not only to attract foreign investment, but also to enhance social capital formation and economic growth.

He was also conscious that economic growth has its costs and wrote an insightful appendix to his book, *The Theory of Economic Growth* where he examined the costs and benefits of the growth and development process and the need to manage the transition process very carefully. He noted the increase in human wealth and choice, the greater control over the environment, gender dimension ('women benefit from these changes even more than men' (1955, p. 422)) and international power and dominance. But he lamented the change in social relationships, ethnic and racial discrimination, the inequality in the distribution of income and wealth, the growth of individualism, the environmental damage and geographical polarisation which can accompany the economic growth process. These topics are still high on the development studies agenda.

As indicated earlier, Lewis made seminal contributions to the study of the economic history of the international economy. This area of study preoccupied his attention up to the late 1980s. Indeed, his empirical studies of world trade and investment form the precursor to the discussion today on globalisation (see, for example, Lewis, 1978). He worked on the issue of international transmission of growth and viewed the deterioration in the factorial terms of trade experienced by primary producing countries as a result of their low productivity in the production of food. He argued for several years that there was a need to raise productivity in the agricultural sector of developing countries through the education of farmers, control of social erosion, providing irrigation systems and improving rural institutions. For small developing economies, he argued that regional integration was a viable development strategy since they need to form coalitions in order to face the vagaries of a dynamic global economic and political environment. His strategy of regional industrial development in the Caribbean is a classic illustration of his suggestion (Lewis, 1950).

As an interdisciplinary, policy-orientated subject, development studies is not an easy field of enquiry for one person. Although his focus was on economics, Lewis was able to draw on the richness of his intellect and his exposure to the problems of development to make valuable contributions to the study of economic, social and political issues. His keen understanding of history and institutions formed the backdrop for his analysis of important economic issues facing the developing world. Although he did not employ modern econometric techniques in his work, he was a great exponent of the use of empirical data as the foundation for applied economic analysis and policy making, He has made lasting contributions in the areas of development theory, development planning, economic growth, human resources development and economic policy formulation. His exposition of the issues makes his writing easily accessible to a wide range of persons working in the area of development studies.

ANDREW S. DOWNES

References

Downes, A.S. (2004), 'William Arthur Lewis: 1915–1991. A Biography', in D. Rutherford (ed.), *Bibliographical Dictionary of British Economists*, Bristol: Thoemmes Press.
Emmanuel, P.A.M. (1994), *Sir William Arthur Lewis Collected Papers 1941–1988*, Vols I, II and III, Barbados: Institute of Social and Economic Research (Eastern Caribbean), University of the West Indies.
Gylfason, T. (1999), *Principles of Economic Growth*, Oxford: Oxford University Press.
Lewis, W.A. (1949a), *Overhead Costs: Some Essays in Economic Analysis*, London, George Allen & Unwin.
Lewis, W.A. (1949b), *The Principles of Economic Planning*, London: George Allen & Unwin.
Lewis, W.A. (1950), 'Industrialisation of the British West Indies', *Caribbean Economic Review*, **2** (1), 1–61.
Lewis, W.A. (1954), 'Economic development with unlimited supplies of labour', *The Manchester School*, **22** (2) 139–91.
Lewis, W.A. (1955), *The Theory of Economic Growth*, London: George Allen & Unwin.
Lewis, W.A. (1958), 'Unlimited labour: further notes', *The Manchester School*, **26**, (1), 1–32.
Lewis, W.A. (1961), 'Education and economic development', *Social and Economic Studies*, **10** (2), June, 113–27.
Lewis, W.A. (1965), *Politics in West Africa*, London: Allen & Unwin.
Lewis, W.A. (1966), *Development Planning: The Essentials of Economic Policy*, London: George Allen & Unwin.
Lewis, W.A. (1972), 'Reflections on unlimited labour', in L.E. DiMarco (ed.), *International Economics and Development: Essays in the Honour of Raul Prebisch*, New York: Academic Press, pp. 75–96.
Lewis, W.A. (1978), *Evolution of the International Economic Order*, Princeton, NJ: Princeton University Press.
Lewis, W.A. (1979), 'The dual economy revisited', *The Manchester School*, **47** (3), 211–29.
Lewis, W.A. (1986), 'Autobiography: W Arthur Lewis', in W. Breit and R.W. Spencer (eds), *Lives of the Laureates: Seven Nobel Economists*, Cambridge, MA: MIT Press, pp. 1–19.
Lipton, M. (1970), 'Interdisciplinary studies in less developed countries', *Journal of Development Studies*, **7** (1), October, 5–18.
Toye, J. (1980), 'Does development studies have a core?', *IDS Bulletin*, Institute of Development Studies, University of Sussex, Brighton, **11** (3), 14–20.
Wilkinson, A. (1999), *Sir Arthur Lewis: A Bibliographical Portrait*, Barbados: Institute of Social and Economic Research, University of the West Indies.

Livelihoods Approach

The purpose of this entry is to set out the framework for undertaking policy work on poverty reduction that has become known as the 'sustainable livelihood approach', or just the 'livelihoods approach'. This framework was developed in the late 1990s in order to capture for a variety of policy purposes the multiple strands that comprise people's efforts to attain and sustain an adequate living. The framework (see Figure 8) attempts to capture not just what people do in order to make a living, but the resources that provide them with the capability to build a satisfactory living, the risk factors that they must consider in managing their resources, and the institutional and policy contexts that either help or hinder them in their pursuit of a viable or improving living.

In the livelihoods approach, resources are referred to as 'assets' or 'capitals' and are often categorised between five or more different asset types owned or accessed by family members (Carney, 1998; Scoones, 1998): human capital (skills, education, health), physical capital (produced investment goods), financial capital (money, savings, loan access), natural capital (land, water, trees and so on) and social capital (networks and associations). These asset categories are admittedly a little contrived, and not all resources that people draw upon in constructing livelihoods fit neatly within them. Nevertheless, they can serve a useful purpose in distinguishing asset types that tend to have differing connections to the policy environment. For example, human capital connects to social policies (education and health), while natural capital connects to land use, agricultural and environmental policies.

It is worth mentioning in passing that the social capital category remains somewhat elusive as a livelihood asset category despite a decade or so of academic musings about it (Harriss, 1997). While it can readily be accepted that the quality of certain types of social connectedness can make a big difference to people's livelihood prospects, this quality factor is difficult to pin down. For example, kinship ties can play roles both as valuable support networks and as demands on resources to meet familial obligations. Likewise, some types of social linkage seem more designed to keep the poor in their place than to assist them to overcome their poverty (for example, bonded labour, caste systems, some types of traditional authority).

This caveat aside, the livelihoods framework regards the asset status of poor individuals or households as fundamental to an understanding of the options open to them. One

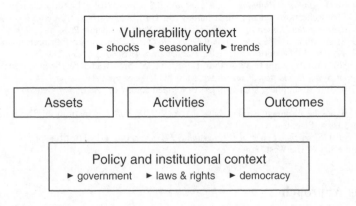

Sources: Ellis (2003a, 2003b).

Figure 8   The basic livelihoods framework

of its basic tenets, therefore, is that poverty policy should be concerned with raising the asset status of the poor, or enabling existing assets that are idle or underemployed to be used productively. The approach looks positively at what is possible rather than negatively at how desperate things are. As articulated concisely by Moser (1998, p. 1) it seeks 'to identify what the poor have rather than what they do not have' and '[to] strengthen people's own inventive solutions, rather than substitute for, block or undermine them'.

As illustrated in Figure 8, the things people do in pursuit of a living are referred to in the livelihood framework as livelihood 'activities'. These activities may be remote as well as nearby. They include, for example, activities that are made possible by migration as well as those that are on the doorstep of the resident household. The risk factors that surround making a living are summarised as the 'vulnerability context', and the structures associated with government (national and local), authority, laws and rights, democracy and participation are summarised as the 'policy and institutional context'. People's livelihood efforts, conducted within these contexts, result in outcomes: higher or lower material welfare, reduced or raised vulnerability to food insecurity, improving or degrading environmental resources, and so on.

It can be noted that Figure 8 contains no lines or arrows denoting causalities between its elements. The reason for this is that the construction of a livelihood is a process unfolding over time, in which there are complex interdependencies between the factors represented by the different categories of the framework. Of course, there are subsets of this process for which causalities can be defined, for example, between assets, activities and outcomes; but the spirit of the sustainable livelihoods approach is that the key factors inhibiting the achievement of improving livelihoods are likely to vary from one setting to another, and are therefore unlikely to be accurately identified if too many prior relationships of cause and effect are imposed *ex ante* on particular groups of the rural or urban poor (Ellis, 2005).

The livelihoods approach originates in a literature on food security and famines (Sen, 1981; Swift, 1989) from which it derives particular strengths for understanding vulnerability and coping (see Vulnerability and Coping, this volume). The concept sets out to be people-centred and holistic, and to provide an integrated view of how people make a living within evolving social, institutional, political, economic and environmental contexts (Carney, 1998; Bebbington, 1999). It has proved to have considerable strengths, especially in recognising or discovering:

- the multiple and diverse character of livelihoods;
- the prevalence of institutionalised blockages to improving livelihoods;
- the social as well as economic character of livelihood strategies;
- the principal factors implicated in rising or diminishing vulnerability; and
- the micro–macro (or macro–micro) links that connect livelihoods to policies.

The multiple and diverse character of livelihoods (Ellis, 1998, 2000) means that people seldom obey the assignment to economic sectors and subsectors that remains the principal entry point to development policies. On the contrary, people's livelihoods are cross-sectoral in character, and mobility, flexibility and adaptability are crucial attributes for staying out of poverty or improving living standards. Indeed, for rural households, those who have a proportion of income sources that are unconnected to agriculture tend to do better than those who remain dependent on agriculture and closely adjacent activities (for example, working on other farms). Diverse livelihoods permit the occurrence of virtuous spirals of accumulation, in which cash earned in one branch of activity can be used to build assets in another branch of activity. For example, in livelihoods research conducted in eastern and southern Africa (Ellis and Freeman, 2004) it was found that the top income quartile of rural households had the greatest proportion of their incomes originating in non-farm activities and, at the same time, their farm productivity measured as agricultural net income per hectare was four times that of the lowest income quartile of households.

Successful diverse livelihood strategies require a facilitating, or at least not actively hampering, institutional context within which to evolve. Unfortunately, public sector policy contexts often tend to be blocking rather than enabling. Poorly remunerated public officers regard local-level enterprise as a target for income supplementation, and district councils under decentralised government are continuously seeking new ways of raising revenue. For this reason, livelihoods tend to be hemmed in by dense thickets of fees and fines and permits and licences and taxes that mean that all but the most energetic and well-connected of citizens are defeated by the burden these impose on initiative. In effect, the transaction costs of building sustainable livelihoods are raised, and 'entry barriers' close off options, especially for the poor who are least able to navigate and negotiate ways round such barriers.

The foregoing considerations mean that macro–micro links are not just about markets and prices, which is the conventional economic way of looking at them. They are also about policy and institutional contexts that are enacted or take shape at the central level, and are interpreted and implemented in local settings. The transmission from central to local does not always work well, and central initiatives to do with improving the conditions for poverty reduction can fizzle out long before they reach the village; moreover, district-level public service may continue to operate in ways that disable livelihood options even when central policy is to remove such blockages. In the opposite direction, knowledge about the true institutional constraints confronting people in local settings may not be transmitted upwards, thus failing to get addressed in the formulation of new policies.

The first-round poverty reduction strategy papers (PRSPs) that emerged as the overarching policy framework governing donor–government relations in the early years of the twenty-first century displayed little if any awareness of the cross-sectoral and mobile nature of people's livelihoods. Instead, when stripped of the fashionable development rhetoric within which they tend to be couched, most early PRSPs ended up looking rather like old-fashioned sectoral expenditure plans from the mid-twentieth century. The livelihoods approach emphasises making the effort to connect micro-level understandings of people's livelihoods to the macro-level policies that are supposedly designed to help them construct their own pathways out of poverty. Therefore a livelihoods approach to PRSPs would place much greater emphasis on reducing and eliminating institutional blockages to efforts made by people themselves to improve their livelihoods.

The livelihoods approach does not claim to provide a definitive solution to poverty eradication in low-income countries. Livelihoods work often takes place in unpromising economic and political environments – economic stagnation and failing states – the problems of which go far beyond the scope of the livelihoods framework to tackle. What the livelihoods approach can do is to contribute in a serious way to the policy discussion that is provoked by the intense donor–government interaction that accompanies international poverty reduction efforts. This contribution may sometimes be about anticipating food security crises, an area where livelihoods approaches and their antecedents have actually done rather well, or it may be about rebuilding livelihoods in conflict zones, or curbing the tax-raising powers of district authorities, or reducing barriers to internal and international labour mobility, or seeking equal land rights between women and men. Such a list could be extended indefinitely, the main point being that livelihoods approaches encourage particular questions to be asked about blockages to building or rebuilding viable livelihoods, therefore directing attention to the policy initiatives required to modify or remove such blockages in order to give individuals and families greater scope to construct their own routes out of poverty.

FRANK ELLIS

References

Bebbington, A. (1999), 'Capitals and capabilities: a framework for analyzing peasant viability, rural livelihoods and poverty', *World Development*, **27** (12), 2021–44.

Carney, D. (ed.) (1998), *Sustainable Rural Livelihoods: What Contribution Can We Make?*, London: Department for International Development (DFID).

Ellis, F. (1998), 'Survey article: household strategies and rural livelihood diversification', *Journal of Development Studies*, **35** (1), 1–38.

Ellis, F. (2000), 'Rural livelihoods and diversity in developing countries', Oxford: Oxford University Press.

Ellis, F. (2003a), 'Human vulnerability and food insecurity: policy implications', *Forum for Food Security in Southern Africa*, Theme Paper No. 3, London: Overseas Development Institute, August, www.odi.org.uk/food-security-forum/publications.html.

Ellis, F. (2003b), *A Livelihoods Approach to Migration and Poverty Reduction*, Paper Commissioned by the Department for International Development (DFID), October, www.livelihoods.org/hot_topics/migration/policy.html.

Ellis, F. (2005), 'Sustainable livelihoods', in T. Forsyth (ed.), *The Routledge Encyclopedia of International Development*, London: Routledge, pp. 668–9.

Ellis, F. and H.A. Freeman (2004), 'Rural livelihoods and poverty reduction strategies in four African countries', *Journal of Development Studies*, **40** (4), 1–30.

Harriss, J. (ed.) (1997), 'Policy arena: "missing link" or analytically missing? The concept of social capital', *Journal of International Development*, **9** (7), 919–71.

Moser, C.O.N. (1998), 'The asset vulnerability framework: reassessing urban poverty reduction strategies', *World Development*, **26** (1), 1–19.

Sen, A.K. (1981), *Poverty and Famines: An Essay on Entitlements and Deprivation*, Oxford: Clarendon.

Scoones, I. (1998), 'Sustainable rural livelihoods: a framework for analysis', IDS Working Paper, No. 72, Institute of Development Studies, University of Sussex, Brighton.

Swift, J. (1989), 'Why are rural people vulnerable to famine?', *IDS Bulletin*, **20** (2), 8–15.

Marx, Karl (1818–1883)

Marx's contribution to development theory and practice is greater than that of any other individual. This entry will examine some key areas that he has influenced.

Communist planning

The planning system in the communist countries stemmed directly from Marx's writings about capitalism and its overthrow, and from the interpretation of these writings by the leaders of those countries, notably Lenin, Stalin and Mao Tsetung. Marx's writings were translated and printed in huge numbers in all the communist countries. This constitutes the most direct and obvious impact of Marx on 'development' in the twentieth century.

The central proposition in the *Communist Manifesto* and *Capital* was the irrationality and injustice of the capitalist mode of production. Marx and Engels believed that rational economic management serving the interests of all members of society, would be achieved by establishing the obverse of the capitalist mode of production, through nationalisation and centralisation of the means of production, and elimination of the market-based price system and the profit motive:

> The proletariat will use its political supremacy to wrest, by degrees, all capital from the bourgeoisie, to centralise all instruments of production in the hands of the State, i.e., of the proletariat organised as the ruling class; and to increase the total of productive forces as rapidly as possible . . . [I]n the course of development, [when] class distinctions have disappeared . . . all production [will be] concentrated in the hands of a vast association of the whole nation . . . (Marx and Engels, 1848, p. 53)

The basic principle of communist economics was the construction of the 'whole economy as a single factory'. The communist planning system attempted to overcome the anarchy of the market through directive-based material balance planning, state-administered prices and by cutting economic agents off from direct contact with the international economy. The central paradox of the communist-administered economy is that it was at least as anarchic as the system it replaced. Far from abolishing waste, it produced waste on a grand scale. It abolished production for profit but was unable to orientate production towards production for use. It abolished the short-termism of competitive capitalism but substituted for this an even more profound short-termism of current plan fulfilment. It steered economic activity in directions that were widely acknowledged as being socially undesirable, but was unable to shift away from this pattern.

The development results of communist planning were mixed. Through common ownership of the means of production, the communist economies were able to establish comprehensive systems of universal free education and free healthcare, heavily subsidised public housing, public transport, domestic electricity and water supply, free or heavily subsidised sports, literature, music, art and cinema, heavily subsidised basic food supply, guaranteed employment for all, and extensive systems of old-age provision. They achieved high levels of 'human development' relative to their level of GNP per capita.

Both the USSR and Communist China achieved high rates of savings, investment and output growth, but the inefficiencies in the way in which growth was achieved limited the degree of progress in living standards. In the USSR, by the 1960s, levels of food intake, housing space and consumption of a narrow range of consumer durables approached the levels in contemporary Western Europe. However, thereafter, growth of living standards slowed down, and ground to a halt in the 1980s. In China, after considerable improvement in living standards during the mixed economy period of the 1950s, there was little improvement in the ensuing two decades. Indeed, by the mid-1970s the World Bank estimated that China still had 270 million people living in poverty as defined by international norms.

Throughout his writings, Marx cautioned that a successful proletarian revolution could only happen once the necessary social conditions had developed. He believed that unless the socio-economic conditions were fully mature, having been brought to that position by capitalist development, a purely political revolution was likely to descend into terror:

> The first direct attempts of the proletariat to attain its own ends, made in times of universal excitement, when feudal society was being overthrown, necessarily failed, owing to the then underdeveloped state of the proletariat, as well as to the absence of the economic conditions for its emancipation, conditions that have yet to be produced, and could be produced by the impending bourgeois epoch alone. The revolutionary literature that accompanied these first movements of the proletariat had necessarily a reactionary character. It inculcated universal asceticism and social levelling in its crudest form. (Marx and Engels, 1848, p. 61; quoted in Avineri, 1968, pp. 191–2)

Marx consistently opposed what he considered to be pointless and premature political putsches. He was deeply critical of Jacobinism in the French Revolution, of the impossibility of a successful proletarian revolution in France either in 1848 or, even, in 1870 in the Paris Commune. In fact, it was precisely in the underdeveloped countries, which had not gone through the process of capitalist industrialisation, that the communist revolutions of the twentieth century took place. Almost all of them descended into different degrees of political terrorism against a large body of the population. In the extreme cases of Kampuchea and the USSR, a large number of people were executed, and in the case of China and the USSR, decisions taken by a highly centralised party apparatus helped to precipitate the worst famines of the twentieth century, in which tens of millions of people died.

Class analysis
Marx's writings are permeated with the analysis of social classes. In part this stemmed from his burning sense of the injustice of historical and contemporary class relations. Marx reserved some of his most powerful writing to ridicule and condemn the arguments used to justify class inequality:

> In the tender annals of Political Economy, the idyllic reigns from time immemorial. Right and 'labour' were from all time the sole means of enrichment, the present year always excepted. As

a matter of fact, the methods of primitive accumulation are anything but idyllic. (Marx, 1867, p. 714)

Marx's class analysis was also intimately bound up with his analysis of the economic growth process. He placed the generation and distribution of 'economic surplus' between different classes at the heart of his analysis of growth both historically and in contemporary capitalism. The emergence of the industrial proletariat in modern capitalism was central to the possibility of the mass of the population taking control of the world they had created through their own labour. The proletariat was the instrument that would achieve the 'negation of the negation', in other words would overturn human beings' alienated condition of life, which Marx believed would reach its fullest point of development under capitalism.

There is a vast literature analysing class relations in developing countries, which ultimately was inspired by Marx (see also Class, this volume). The literature includes classic works by the leaders of the communist countries, such as Lenin's *Development of Capitalism in Russia* (Lenin, 1956) and Mao Tsetung's numerous writings on China's class structure (Mao, 1971). It includes also a huge academic development literature on class analysis and economic growth, and on the sociology and history of class stratification. Most of the academic Marxist analysis focuses on the injustice and exploitative nature of capitalist class relations, rather than upon the role of the capitalist class in leading the process of economic advance. Indeed, much of the academic literature in this field is hostile to the possibility of a progressive function for capitalism.

Non-communist planning

The inter-war collapse of primary commodity prices and the rise of protectionism deeply damaged poor countries and demonstrated the anarchic nature of capitalism. There was a widespread disbelief that capitalism could offer a path for rapid economic development. The Soviet Union's industrialisation experience in the 1920s and 1930s, and its highly successful recovery after the Second World War, made the Soviet model of development highly appealing for developing countries (Baran, 1957; Dobb, 1963, 1967). It was widely felt that the international economy could not be relied upon to stimulate economic development, and that foreign trade and investment were mechanisms for exploiting poor countries and maintaining them in a state of underdevelopment (Frank, 1967). The arguments for socialist planning were supported by the application of Marx's analysis of the role of the capital goods sector in the evolution of the capitalist economic system. By expanding the production of 'capital goods to produce more capital goods', it was thought that developing countries could liberate themselves from dependence on the international economy (Dobb, 1963; Raj, 1967). Large swathes of the economics profession involved in policy formation in developing countries were influenced by Marxist views of development, with more or less explicit admiration for the Marxist model of development in the USSR.

Under these combined influences, across a wide spectrum of developing countries, different forms of 'socialist' planning became the dominant form of development policy. These were widely built around inward-looking protectionist policies, which aimed to construct relatively self-sufficient economies, with a central role for state-led expansion of the capital goods industries.

Marxist history

A large part of Marx's writing was focused on the historical context within which he analysed modern capitalism. Viewed from the perspective of Britain in the middle of the nineteenth century, the non-European world appeared to Marx to be stagnant. He considered that 'Indian society has no history at all' (Marx, 1960a, p. 76) and that China was 'vegetating in the teeth of time' (ibid., p. 188). He identified several features that he considered were common to these societies, such as absence of private property in land, isolated and self-sufficient village communities, and a large role for public hydraulic works (Anderson, 1974, p. 472). One stream of Marxist historiography, following Marx's view of non-European societies emphasised the apparent long-term socio-economic stagnation in large parts of the developing world. Marxist writers in this vein saw common elements of an 'Asiatic mode of production' across many different countries and, even, across continents (Wittfogel, 1957; Anderson, 1974; Melotti, 1977).

Within the communist countries, such a view of their history was unpopular, as it denigrated their history. Marx's writings on the Asiatic mode of production were not widely available, and were notable for their absence from university courses on Marxist economics and history. Instead, the view was widely held that Marx saw all countries as following the same path from slavery to feudalism to capitalism, and finally, to socialism and communism. Mao Tsetung (1939) wrote: 'As China's feudal society had developed a commodity economy and so carried within itself the seeds of capitalism, China would of herself have developed slowly into a capitalist society even without the impact of foreign capitalism'. In this view, colonialism and imperialism were held responsible for underdevelopment by interrupting the process of indigenous capitalist development: 'Regardless of their national peculiarities, the pre-capitalist orders [sic] in Western Europe and in Japan, in Russia and in Asia, were reaching at different times and in different ways their common historical destiny' (Baran, 1957, p. 162). Their failure to follow this path was attributed instead to the 'violent, destructive, and predatory opening up of the weaker countries by Western capitalism' (ibid.). In the view of Marxist writers in this tradition, incorporation into the global capitalist system meant that it was 'fruitless to expect the underdeveloped countries of today to repeat the stages of economic growth passed through by the modern developed societies, whose classical capitalist development arose out of pre-capitalist and feudal society' (Frank, 1967, p. xvi).

Capitalist dynamism and universalism

Marx's own view of the function of capitalism in economic development was different from that of most Marxists (a notable exception is Warren, 1980). He considered that capitalism was the only force capable of propelling the forces of production forward so as to create the conditions for the proletariat to take control of the world they had themselves created. For Marx, the bourgeoisie's drive to accumulate and push forward technical progress was the key to economic advance in all parts of the world:

> The bourgeoisie, during its rule of scarce one hundred years, has created more massive and more colossal productive forces than have all the preceding generations together. Subjection of Nature's forces to man, machinery, application of chemistry to industry and agriculture, steam-navigation, railways, electric telegraphs, clearing whole continents for cultivation, canalization of rivers, whole populations conjured out of the ground – what earlier century had even a

presentiment that such productive forces slumbered in the lap of social labour? (Marx and Engels, 1848, pp. 39–40)

Far from considering that colonialism hindered the process of capitalist development Marx considered that the forcible intrusion of capitalism was critical to stimulating economic progress in developing countries. As we have seen, he considered that these were mired in long-run stagnation. Only the forcible intrusion of the advanced capitalist powers could shake the underdeveloped countries out of their torpor:

> The bourgeoisie, by the rapid improvement of all instruments of production, by the immensely facilitated means of communication, draws all, even the most barbarian, nations into civilization. The cheap prices of commodities are the heavy artillery with which it forces the barbarians' intensely obstinate hatred of foreigners to capitulate. It compels all nations, on pain of extinction, to adopt the bourgeois mode of production; it compels them to introduce what it calls civilization into their midst, that is, to become bourgeois themselves. In one word it creates a world after its own image. (Ibid., p. 39)

Marx considered that free trade was the path to the most rapid growth of the global economy, and to the consequent dissolution of the capitalist system through the forces it generated itself:

> Free Trade dissolves the hitherto existing nationalities and pushes to its climax the tension between proletariat and bourgeoisie. In one word, the system of free trade precipitates the social revolution . . . [The bourgeoisie] has resolved personal worth into exchange value, and in place of the numberless indefeasible chartered freedoms, has set up that single, unconscious freedom – Free Trade. (Marx and Engels, 1968, pp. 64–5 and 36–7, quoted in Avineri, 1968, p. 252)

Marx considered that the character of capitalist development was inherently international and universal: 'The need of a constantly expanding market for its products chases the bourgeoisie over the whole surface of the globe. It must nestle everywhere, settle everywhere, establish connections everywhere' (Marx and Engels, 1848, p. 38). He regarded it as axiomatic that communism would emerge as a global movement, to match capitalism's basic impulse to establish a global system of production and a global culture:

> The bourgeoisie has through its exploitation of the world market, given a cosmopolitan character to production and consumption in every country. To the great chagrin of Reactionists, it has drawn from under the feet of industry the national ground on which it stood. All old-established national industries have been destroyed or are daily being destroyed . . . In place of the old local and national seclusion and self-sufficiency, we have intercourse in every direction, universal interdependence of nations. And as in material, so also in intellectual production. The intellectual creations of individual nations become common property. National one-sidedness and narrow-mindedness become more and more impossible, and from the numerous national and local literatures, there arises a world literature. (Ibid., pp. 38–9)

Although Marx was writing in an epoch of predominantly small-scale, family-owned firms, he considered that the basic law of capitalist development was towards an ever-larger scale of operations, which could take advantage of scale economies and achieve accelerated technical progress:

The battle of competition is fought by cheapening commodities. The cheapness of commodities depends, *ceteris paribus*, on the productiveness of labour, and this again on the scale of production. Therefore the larger capital beats the smaller . . . Everywhere the increased scale of industrial establishments is the starting-point for a more comprehensive organization of the collective work of many, for a wider development of their material motive force – in other words, for the progressive transformation of isolated processes of production, carried on by customary methods, into processes of production socially combined and scientifically arranged. (Marx, 1867, pp. 626–7)

Marx firmly believed in the impulse provided to economic progress by the incentive of capitalist competition, especially among large firms:

Big industry universalised competition . . . established means of communication and the modern world market . . . By universal competition it forced all individuals to strain their energy to the utmost . . . It produced world history for the first time, insofar as it made all civilized nations and every individual member of them dependent for the satisfaction of their wants on the whole world, thus destroying the former natural exclusiveness of separate nations. (Marx, 1960b, p. 56)

Conclusion

Marx's view of development can be criticised from many perspectives, including the simplicity of his conception of human nature (Fromm, 1956), his view that large parts of the developing world had been locked for centuries into long-run stagnation (Anderson, 1974), and for his confidence that human beings could and should 'dominate nature'. However, writing from the perspective of the early twenty-first century, Marx's views (as opposed to those of most Marxists) seem extraordinarily prescient to understanding the challenges of development today. Much of the period since the late nineteenth century, including the attempt to establish communism in poor countries and to construct 'socialist planning' in the non-communist Third World, can be seen as an intermission in the process of global capitalist development which was the focus of Marx's analysis. Since the 1970s, these forces have been released with renewed force, in the epoch of modern globalisation and the global business revolution.

Capitalism has stimulated human creativity in ways that have produced immense benefits. In the recent epoch of globalisation, capitalism has broadened its scope at explosive speed, 'nestling everywhere', 'settling everywhere'. Global oligopolies have emerged in almost every sector, competing fiercely with each other to achieve technical progress and reduce costs of production across the value chain. In this revolutionary epoch, the benefits from the exercise of capitalist freedoms have become even greater. Human beings have been liberated to an even greater degree than hitherto from the tyranny of nature, from control by others over their lives, from poverty, and from war. The advances achieved by the globalisation of capitalism have appeared all the more striking, when set against the failure of non-capitalist systems of economic organisation in the twentieth century.

However, capitalist freedom is a two-edged sword. In the epoch of today's capitalist globalisation, its contradictions have intensified. The freedoms of capitalist globalisation have intensified selfish, competitive and greedy behaviour. They comprehensively threaten the natural environment. They have intensified inequality in both rich and poor countries. They have stimulated a high degree of instability in global finance. The world's dominant capitalist power refuses to dismantle its vast stock of nuclear arms, which are sufficient to obliterate the entire global civilisation. The present stage of development of global capitalism has produced contradictions latent within the system exactly as was envisaged by Marx. As human beings have taken to new heights their ability to free themselves from fundamental constraints, so they also have reached new depths in terms of the uncontrollability of the structures they have created, which have resulted in intense threats to the very existence of the human species.

Marx was confident that the capitalism itself would produce the conditions for its own replacement by communism (the 'negation of the negation'). It remains an open question whether human beings can, indeed, regain control over the global mechanism that they have created. Marx hoped that this would happen sooner rather than later. However, ultimately, he believed it would be a long process before communism was finally realised by means of the evolution of forces within capitalism. Marx could not foresee the threat to the very existence of the species posed by nuclear weapons or the ecological disaster unfolding around us. The dramatic nature of the challenge they pose to human existence may accelerate the process of human beings taking control over their destinies, since the contradictions of the current phase of capitalist development can only be resolved globally.

Far from opposing today's capitalist globalisation, Marx would undoubtedly have welcomed it as the force that could lead mankind to establish communism on a global scale: 'Communism is only possible as the act of dominant peoples "all at once" and simultaneously, which presupposes the universal development of the productive forces and the world intercourse bound up with them' (Marx, 1960b, p. 25).

PETER NOLAN

References

Anderson, P. (1974), *Lineages of the Absolutist State*, London: Verso Books.
Avineri, S. (1968), *The Social and Political Thought of Karl Marx*, Cambridge: Cambridge University Press.
Baran, P. (1957), *The Political Economy of Growth*, New York: Monthly Review Press.
Dobb, M. (1963), *Economic Growth and Underdeveloped Countries*, London: Lawrence & Wishart.
Dobb, M. (1967), *Capitalism, Development and Planning*, New York: International Publishers.
Frank, A.G. (1967), *Capitalism and Underdevelopment in Latin America*, New York: Monthly Review Press.
Fromm, E. (1956), *The Sane Society*, London: Routledge.
Lenin, V.I. (1956), *The Development of Capitalism in Russia*, Moscow: Progress Publishers.
Mao Tsetung (1939), 'The Chinese Revolution and the Chinese Communist Party', www.etext.org/Politics/MIM/classics/mao/sw2/mswv2.23.html, 29 September 2005.
Mao Tsetung (1971), *Selected Readings from the Works of Mao Tsetung*, Peking: Foreign Languages Press.
Marx, K. (1867 [1967]), *Capital*, vol. 1, New York: International Publishers.
Marx, K. (1960a), *On Colonialism*, Moscow: Progress Publishers.
Marx, K. (1960b), *The German Ideology*, New York: International Publishers.
Marx, K. and F. Engels (1848), *Manifesto of the Communist Party*, reprinted in Marx and Engels (1968), Vol. 1.
Marx, K. and F. Engels (1968), *Selected Works*, Moscow: Progress Publishers.
Melotti, U. (1977), *Marx and the Third World*, London: Macmillan.
Raj, K.N. (1967), 'Role of the "machine tools sector" in economic growth', in C. Feinstein (ed.), *Socialism, Capitalism and Economic Growth*, Cambridge: Cambridge University Press, pp. 217–26.
Warren, B. (1980), *Imperialism, Pioneer of Capitalism*, London: Verso Books (edited by John Sender).
Wittfogel, K.A. (1957), *Oriental Despotism*, New Haven, CT: Yale University Press.

Media Communications and Development

Media technologies such as printing, radio, television and the internet have the unique capacity to simultaneously reach many people in dispersed locations. This entry explores two main domains in which media impacts on development. First, the media is used by national governments, NGOs and international development agencies to direct planned change in fields such as reproduction, health, agricultural extension, natural resource management and local governance, a practice referred to as 'development communication'. Second, media is an integral component of the global political economy. It involves flows of symbols, values, information and capital within and across national borders and is also the means by which new transnational forms of community are configured.

In both development communication and global communication, media may exert a hegemonic effect by producing and distributing knowledge that favours the values and interests of the powerful and by representing marginal groups in ways that highlight their inherent inadequacies rather than the structural causes of their deprivation. Yet media can also be a tool of resistance. People rework received information and messages to suit their own purposes and use media for distributing alternative representations of themselves and the world.

Development communication

'Development communication' refers to the planned and systematic use of communication to help individuals and communities introduce and accept change (Fraser and Restrepo-Estrada, 1998, p. 5). Development communication may be generally informative or else tailored towards particular objectives and audiences.

Development communication involves ensuring that citizens are well informed about national policies and events and are able to participate productively in the social and economic life of the community. In the case of television the objectives of development communication are often facilitated in inadvertent ways in the course of fulfilling the more primary purpose of entertaining. As David A. Clark reports for South Africa, the poor value television because it enables them to see other places, follow national and international events and find out about prices, consumer products and fashions (2002, pp. 44–5, 52). In many countries, there are, however, more strategic efforts to use the media for development objectives which involve radio and television producers adding purposeful messages to existing media products. As examples, soap operas in Sub-Saharan Africa demonstrate condom usage; television dramas in Brazil examine domestic violence; radio stories in India discuss new crop and animal varieties. Other programmes are more explicitly pedagogic. For example, television reportage documentaries in China are followed by panel discussions to educate viewers about points of law including obligations within the family, consumer rights and civic duty (Chu, 2005).

Some development communication fuses targeted information with folk media such as theatre, dance, puppetry and song. These media use cultural symbols that resonate with audiences and are also easily integrated into mass media, reaching even more people. But in the absence of community participation in the production process, a folk medium may be unsuited to the development message, causing the intervention to fail. For instance, in Karnataka, India, planners tried to promote birth planning through a song honouring the goddess Yellamma, whose devotees were mainly poor and had large families, and this stirred up indignation within the community (Melkote and Steeves, 2001, p. 255).

Many media items are produced specifically for a coordinated campaign. For example, UNICEF produced a series of cartoon films about a small Asian girl called Meena.

Her appearance was generically Asian so she resembled a local child in several countries. The episodes depicted her everyday experiences of discrimination on account of being a girl. The producers hoped that the emotional scenes would help to change parental and societal attitudes towards girl children (Fraser and Restrepo-Estrada, 1998, pp. 29–31). Other forms of development communication facilitate the implementation of particular projects within communities. For instance, in parts of Jiangxi province, China, the local government used county television programmes to instruct farmers in the cultivation technique for a new variety of rice which was less labour intensive. This technique required that farmers broadcast seeds rather than plant them close together and later transplant them in rows (Murphy, 2005).

While development communication may empower people by providing them with information and alternative ways of seeing their situation, the process is often top down. Different kinds of people are ranked by their distance from modernity (Pigg, 1992), and those who are poor, rural, women or ethnic minorities are persuaded to work towards a prescribed vision of a desirable life through attitudinal and behavioural change. The educator Paulo Friere argues that the persuasive thrust of development communication entails a unidirectional flow of knowledge, which is always used for neutralising potentially hostile forces in the consciousness of the oppressed (Friere, 1973, pp. 96–7). He suggests that development interventions are not dialogic because its architects do not understand that knowledge is created through the mutual learning of the teacher and the pupil engaged in a common process of problem-solving (ibid., pp. 114–23). For Friere, the inequality embedded in persuasion forms part of wider structural inequalities which are internalised by the oppressed, making them conservative and unsure of both themselves and outsiders (ibid., pp. 132–5).

Participation has become a 'buzz' word in development practice, yet studies show that even a participatory project can be manipulated through the consultation process to serve the interests of dominant stakeholders (Cooke and Kothari, 2001). Good development communication is nevertheless participatory in the sense that target communities are involved as much in the production as in the reception of media products. Case studies of local radio stations in Brazilian slums (Schelling, 1999) and in Filipino villages describe community dynamism in analysing and debating livelihood problems and mobilising everyone to contribute to solutions, for example donating labour to build a bridge. In the Filipino countryside, public debate and dramatised life stories on the radio have also addressed social problems, and in one instance, the men in a region voluntarily quit gambling (Fraser and Restrepo-Estrada, 1998, pp. 190–218). Development communication carried out *by* rather than *for* the people has the further advantage of community members actively representing themselves rather than being represented by development agencies and governments, enabling them to escape such debilitating labels as 'passive', 'backward' and 'victim' (Hewitt and Smyth, 1999; Lidchi, 1999) which obscure the root causes of deprivation.

While the state and development agencies use the media to construct better citizens, citizens for their part are able to use the media to disseminate knowledge in ways that exercise their rights as citizens. The media plays a role in facilitating 'rightful resistance'. Rightful resistance is when oppressed people identify and exploit divisions among the powerful (O'Brien, 1996). It usually involves the marginalised applying pressure to those in power who have failed to live up to a professed ideal or government policy. As examples, in China, farmers learn of national tax laws through news programmes then use this knowledge to resist unfair exactions, even contacting journalists to expose local cases of corruption (O'Brien, 1996). And Iranian women use a women's magazine, *Zanam*, to argue that in order to support Islam and fulfil their role as dutiful Muslim women, they need certain rights and resources. So, the women shape public consensus on the position of women in Islam in ways that are favourable to them (Gheytanchi, 2001).

Globalisation, communication and development
Since the early days of print, radio and film, the circulation of information and symbols has shaped and reflected power relations in the global political economy. The transnational flow has been primarily from the developed to developing world, with media products prioritising Western values, interests and perspectives. Before the Second World War missionaries, colonial administrators and pedagogues produced films aimed at fostering loyalty among colonial subjects to Western civilisation. These films portrayed colonial subjects as developmentally immature, childlike and in need of instruction. Such paternalistic pedagogy fed into a later developmental discourse, which became a potent instrument through which the West constructed and managed the Third World (Escobar, 1995; Goldfarb, 2002).

During the 1970s and 1980s, some observers in developing countries and international agencies became increasingly concerned at how new media technologies were serving Western cultural and economic dominance. A 1980 UNESCO commission under the leadership of Sean MacBride reported: '[I]n the communication industry there are a relatively small number of predominant corporations which integrate all aspects of production and distribution, which are based in the leading developed countries and which have become trans-national in their operations', and this corporate dominance privileges commercial profit over human development (MacBride, 1980 cited in Hoover, 1993).

The United Nations and UNESCO responded by trying to establish a 'New World Information and Communication Order'. In 1983, UNESCO convened an international summit to discuss ways for developing countries to escape their financial and cultural dependence on the economic powers and to create a more equitable system of access to media and communication technologies. The main suggestion to arise was that developing countries should be supported in their efforts to establish local television stations, news agencies and media production because these would better serve the needs of viewers and help to preserve their cultures and identities. While Third World leaders saw the UNESCO proposal as a chance for justice and for creating media products that would promote social cohesion and development, many Western leaders vilified it as a threat to freedom and criticised developing countries for their press censorship and lack of democracy.

Concerns about global inequities in media production and representation continue to the present day. In recent years much of this debate has centred on the ways in which media and development institutions in the North portray 'development' to others in the North such as child sponsors, NGO donors, international volunteers, ethical investors, fair trade consumers and news watchers (Smith and Yanacopulos, 2004). A key dimension of this debate centres on how, in their efforts to enhance their public profile and attract revenue, NGOs and news agencies use images of the poor which some people see as dramatic, patronising and voyeuristic and dismissive of the subjects' agency (DFID, 2001; Smith and Yanacopulos, 2004). Even when indigenous photographers produce images about development, the stylistic and content demands of US/Western purchasers dominate the 'global political economy of images' to the extent that inequalities in the North–South relationship are still reproduced through representation (Clark, 2004). Clark illustrates this argument by relating the case of a Bangladeshi photographer who responded to the post-9/11 appetite of Western newspapers for negative and threatening images of Muslims by honing in on a peaceful crowd of protesters to capture one close-up of an angry Muslim face (ibid.).

One of the most famous thinkers to address global inequalities in media flows and access is Manuel Castells (1996, 1997). He argues that the information revolution has involved a shift from an industrial to 'informational' system or 'network society'. In the industrial system, wealth and power resided in control over the production of material goods, with information serving this end. Now, information is both the raw material and the final product. According to this explanation, the whole world is connected in its economic functions through communication flows, and exclusion from these flows is tantamount to exclusion from the global economy. Significant segments of society in developing countries, which are marginalised from the network's organising principles and institutions, construct alternative identities grounded in religious fundamentalism or ethnic separatism. They do this by tapping into the segmentation of the network, the ways in which VCRs and emails can be disconnected from flows to create individualised communication and mental images that can be mobilised for struggle and even illegal activities. While Castells's explanation is useful in highlighting inequalities in access to new media technologies, it is flawed in assuming that the majority of people conform unproblematically to the cultural norms of a network society dominated by modern capitalist centres of power. The framework is also limited in relegating struggle to outside the network, thereby overlooking how contestation may transform the network society itself.

In recent years scholars have responded to implicit assumptions that media is either a source of cultural imperialism or a force for inculcating modern ideas by pointing out that people in developing countries are not passive cultural dupes. Case studies reveal that individuals actively bring their own resources, expectations and beliefs to the interpretation process. For instance, a study of audience reception of the television series 'Dallas', revealed that different ethnic groups made sense of the story line in different ways. Israeli Arabs and Moroccan Jews stressed kinship and the motivations of family members in relation to family hierarchy and the survival of the dynasty; Russian immigrants were cynical and accused the scriptwriters of manipulating the viewers; and Americans and groups of kibbutz members focused on the psychological dramas of interpersonal relationships (Leibes and Katz cited in Thompson, 1995, p. 174). The creative reworking of cultural symbols and messages extends also to media production: studies of musicians in Indonesia (Sen and Hill, 2000) and Africa show that artists appropriate elements of Western pop and integrate them with indigenous forms to create hybrid styles.

Increasingly, scholars argue that media flows are not unidirectional, as in the cultural imperialism and modernisation approaches, but multidirectional (Giddens 1999; Straubhaar 2002). Media products from developing countries are becoming ever more popular with Western audiences, Bollywood and Kung Fu films being obvious examples. Regional media networks such as Al-Jazeera and Channel NewsAsia, which are independent from the ownership of Western global media networks, provide important alternative voices not only for their regional audiences but also for the world. More generally, the communications revolution enables people to participate in virtual communities creating forms of citizenship based on culture and identity rather than on rights and obligations to a nation state. These communities are formed through flows of information and symbols that transcend space and borders: examples include the circulation of home videos, emails and ethnic music tapes within diaspora communities, and the use of videos, images, electronic newsletters and chat rooms by global environmental activists.

Multidirectionality and plurality in media production and distribution are also facilitated by access to new technologies that are relatively cheap and give individuals direct access to information and a mass audience. NGOs, lobby groups and individuals use the internet to link up with support groups in other countries and to publicise their cause: examples include the indigenous Zapista movement in Mexico and Chinese intellectuals and mothers who use the website to ask about people who disappeared during the Tiananmen crackdown. Some observers of these trends talk about the emergence of a 'global civil society', transnational alliances which are based on solidarity rather than on a benefactor/beneficiary relationship (Smith and Yanacopulos, 2004). They argue that global communication offers a way for increased North–South equality because different institutions and individuals within the global civil society represent themselves and their own views. Notwithstanding the importance of new technology in facilitating organisation and advocacy, cautionary notes raised by some commentators include that large numbers of the poor are illiterate; that many more have never used a telephone let alone the internet; and that face-to-face interactions and land phones have often proved to be the most effective means of social and political organisation for many marginalised people (Kole, 2004).

While optimism about the empowering potential of new technologies needs to be tempered with recognition of the 'digital divide', media communication nevertheless plays an important role in development. World Bank President, James Wolfensohn, has argued that access to communications in developing countries is as important as securing housing and clean water (cited in Mutume, 2000). But like housing and clean water, provisioning depends on political will. If there is political will, internet points and mobile phones are relatively easy and inexpensive to distribute. One success story is the initiative coordinated by the Pan Asian Network and Grameen Bank to make mobile phones and internet connections available to poor rural women in Bangladesh. These women earn money by charging others to use their phones and they are able to obtain market information about agricultural prices in other regions and even other countries.

Conclusion

Media is used to inculcate values and aspirations among people in developing countries through pedagogic projects which urge attitudinal and behavioural change and through transnational media flows which often promote Western values and lifestyles. Such media products commonly represent people from developing countries in ways that suggest they are inherently inferior or in need of instruction and civilisation. Within developing countries, there is also a process of 'internal orientalism', a complex and contested term which describes a process whereby national elites accept the Western image of their country as backward, and then project backwardness on to subgroups such as peasants or ethnic minorities who are portrayed as distant from modernity and development. These groups become the particular focus of pedagogic interventions to help move the nation forward.

Recognising the role of the media in prescribing certain worldviews does not deny that development communication and global media flows are important in increasing people's access to symbols and information. Although modernisation and cultural imperialism approaches to the media imply that values are inculcated in audiences, ethnographic studies reveal that people are active and creative in interpreting media messages and using them in their own media production. The recent expansion in media communications offers new opportunities for marginal people to obtain access to information and to represent themselves and their worldview. Development interventions should focus on increasing people's access to and control over media, enabling them to obtain useful knowledge and to articulate and solve their own problems.

RACHEL MURPHY

References

Castells, Manuel (1996), *The Rise of the Network Society: The Information Age: Economy, Society and Culture*, Oxford: Blackwell.

Castells, Manuel (1997), *The Power of Identity – The Information Age: Economy, Society and Culture*, Vol. 2, Oxford: Blackwell.

Chu, Yingchi (2005), 'Legal report: citizenship education through a television documentary', in Vanessa L. Fong and Rachel Murphy (eds), *Chinese Citizenship: Views from the Margins*, London: Routledge, pp. 68–95.

Clark, David A. (2002), *Visions of Development: A Study of Human Values*, Cheltenham, UK and Northampton, MA, USA: Edward Elgar.

Clark, David J. (2004), 'The production of a contemporary famine image: the image economy, indigenous photographers and the case of Mekanic Philipos', *Journal of International Development*, **16**, 693–704.

Cooke, Bill and Uma Kothari (2001), 'The case for participation as tyranny', in Cooke and Kothari (eds), *Participation: The New Tyranny* London: Zed Books, pp. 1–15.

DFID (2001), *Viewing the World Report*, London: Department for International Development (DFID) www.dfid.gov.uk/pubs/files/viewworldfull.pdf.

Escobar, Arturo (1995), *Encountering Development: The Making and Unmaking of the Third World*, Princeton, NJ: Princeton University Press.

Fraser, Colin and Sonia Restrepo-Estrada (1998), *Communicating for Development: Human Change for Survival*, London: I.B. Tauris.

Friere, Paulo (1973), *Education for Critical Consciousness*, New York: Continuum (first published in 1969).

Gheytanchi, Elham (2001), 'Civil society in Iran: politics of motherhood and the public sphere', *International Sociology*, **16** (4), 557–76.

Giddens, Anthony (1999), *Runaway World: How Globalisation is Reshaping Our Lives*, London: Profile.

Goldfarb, Brian (2002), *Visual Pedagogy*, Durham, NC: Duke University Press.

Hewitt, Tom and Ines Smyth (1999), 'Street lives and family lives in Brazil', in Tracey Skelton and Tim Allen (eds), *Culture and Global Change*, London: Routledge, pp. 212–20.

Hoover, Stewart M. (1993), 'All power to the conglomerate', *Media and Values*, issue 61, winter, www.medialit.org/reading_room/article 91.html.

Kole, Ellen S. (2004), 'Connecting women from developing countries to the internet: searching for an appropriate paradigm', www.xs 4all.nl/-ekole/public/isaconnect.html, April 2004.

Lidchi, Henrietta (1999), 'Finding the right image: British development NGOs and the regulation of imagery', in Tracey Skelton and Tim Allen (eds), *Culture and Global Change*, London: Routledge, pp. 87–101.

MacBride, Sean (1980), *Many Voices, One World*, International Commission for the Study of Communication Problems, Paris: UNESCO.

Melkote, Srinivas R. and H. Leslie Steeves (2001), *Communication for Development in the Third World*, New Delhi: Sage.

Murphy, Rachel (2005), 'Citizenship education in rural China: the dispositional and technical training of cadres and farmers' in Vanessa L. Fong and Rachel Murphy (eds), *Chinese Citizenship: Views from the Margins*, London: Routledge, pp. 9–26.

Mutume, Gumisai (2000), 'Media/information technology', *Asian Times*, 23 February.

O'Brien, Kevin (1996), 'Rightful resistance', *World Politics*, **49** (1), 31–55.

Pigg, Stacy Leigh (1992), 'Inventing social categories through place: social representations and development in Nepal', *Comparative Studies in Society and History*, **34** (3), 491–513.

Schelling, Vivian (1999), 'The people's radio of Vila Noassa Senhora Aparecida: alternative communication and cultures of resistance in Brazil', in Tracey Skelton and Tim Allen (eds), *Culture and Global Change*, London: Routledge, pp. 167–79.

Sen, Krishna and David Hill (2000), *Media, Culture and Politics in Indonesia*, Oxford: Oxford University Press.

Smith, Matt and Helen Yanacopulos (2004), 'The public faces of development: an introduction', *Journal of International Development*, **16**, 657–64.

Straubhaar, Joseph (2002), '(Re)asserting national media and national identity against the global, regional and local levels of world television', in Joseph M. Chan and Bryce T. McIntyre (eds), *In Search of Boundaries: Communication, Nation-states and Cultural Identities*, London: Ablex, pp. 181–286.

Thompson, John (1995), *The Media and Modernity: A Social Theory of the Media*, Cambridge: Polity.

Microfinance

As the economic base of a society becomes more complex and diverse, a range of new institutions is needed for managing risk and coordinating exchange. New financial institutions were needed, for example, when the relatively simple credit and accounting systems that had underpinned subsistence agriculture in early nineteenth-century Europe proved inadequate for servicing the increasing scale and scope of livelihoods based on manufacturing and services. Even without fundamental changes in a particular economy, however, technological and organisational innovations can help lower the costs of providing more extensive financial services, thereby helping that economy (and its constituent social groups) to more efficiently respond to its particular challenges and opportunities. In the late twentieth century, Bangladesh and Indonesia became well known for their innovative rural credit systems serving millions of poor farmers (and especially women), as did several countries in Latin America (such as Bolivia). Implementing effective financial institutions for managing economic life is a major development challenge, one that, done well, can be especially beneficial to the poor.

Over the last two decades, an increased awareness of the actual and potential importance of providing financial services to the poor – in developing and developed countries alike – has sparked great interest among scholars and practitioners in a range of organisational responses broadly referred to as 'microfinance'. Anthropologists have long been fascinated with indigenous mechanisms for extending credit, and indeed there is a remarkable similarity to the ways traditional communities from Africa to Asia have devised informal solutions to this problem. For a variety of reasons, however, even the best-designed financial institutions struggle to meet the needs of the poorest, and yet it is the poor who are in the weakest position – by virtue of having, by definition, few material assets – to confront the range and severity of risks (for example, disease, crop failure, property expropriation, physical security) to which they are routinely exposed. Being unable to offer adequate collateral, moreover, means that the poor are usually unable to secure loans from commercial banks. Together, these factors also mean that the poor are least well positioned to take advantage of new entrepreneurial opportunities as and when they present themselves.

At best, microfinance organisations help the poor respond to these risks and opportunities in much the same way that wealthier members of society do: namely, by enabling greater smoothing of consumption over time, by diversifying income streams and asset portfolios, and by securing access to a broader range of 'competitive' credit markets (which thereby lessens the dependence on local moneylenders, whose interest rates are often usurious). Some microfinance organisations go further, arguing that their programmes also enhance members' capacity to set and achieve financial goals by offering ongoing training and group support that builds business confidence (for example, by diversifying access to ideas and markets), social skills (for example, learning to negotiate, to speak in public forums), and financial competence (for example, gaining skills in basic accounting).

There are a host of good and bad reasons why orthodox financial institutions struggle to meet the needs of the poor, and thus a basis for why policy makers may need to make some specific interventions. The 'bad' reasons are that poor borrowers are often politically marginalised and expedient, with little recourse when discriminated against, exploited, or overlooked by state, market or informal financial service providers. The 'good' reasons are that lending to the poor is generally a costly enterprise: banks solely concerned with making a profit will inevitably find it more attractive to make and manage a single loan to one rich person than the same amount spread over ten small loans to ten poor people. The larger costs associated with lending to the ten poor people are not merely driven by the additional paperwork: the more intractable issue is one of information asymmetry, in which the rich person's assets provide the banker with an immediate signal of creditworthiness, irrespective of that person's diligence or trustworthiness. Such assets can, of course, be leveraged as security for the extension of credit; even the viable prospect of future assets, as signalled by admission into an elite college, means that penniless but college-bound 18 year olds in rich countries will be offered credit cards and car loans. Poor borrowers in rich and poor countries alike, by contrast, have few material assets, current or future, to offer as collateral or a signal of creditworthiness. All of these factors can combine to generate a large market failure in the extension of financial services to the poor, with millions of diligent potential borrowers left to get by using informal services that too often are unreliable and usurious, thereby compounding their already difficult lives.

The most innovative and effective solutions to these problems, as pioneered and propounded by the microfinance movement in the 1980s, have focused on getting around the information asymmetry issue. (Earlier initiatives in the 1960s and 1970s sought merely to address the cost problem by subsidising rural banks, but this approach was widely deemed a financial and developmental failure.) This has taken several forms. One approach to discerning honesty and diligence has focused on tapping into the social knowledge of poor borrowers, who often live in close proximity to one another and are thus well placed to observe one another's behaviour; by giving joint liability loans to groups, the fortunes of members are bound to one another and thereby give them an immediate incentive to choose as fellow group members those known to be hard working and reliable. Group lending also means that larger loans can be extended with only a single 'contract' being drawn up: members then on-lend to another one, assuming responsibility for monitoring the use and repayment of the loan, in the process absorbing an otherwise costly element of it.

Microfinance programmes often, but do not necessarily, use group-based savings and credit mechanisms. In Indonesia, for example, rural banks have devised lending protocols that enable them to lend to individuals. Even among the better-known group-based approaches, there are interesting variations: while some offer an independent financial organisation for the poor, others (for example, selected NGOs in India) seek to act as a temporary intermediary or 'bridge' between poor communities and the commercial banking sector, simultaneously helping the poor to establish a verifiable financial history that will be recognised by the commercial banks *and* negotiating with the banks to encourage them to adopt more 'poor-friendly' policies and procedures (such as allowing groups to hold accounts, using simple forms, recognising thumb-prints instead of signatures for illiterate borrowers and so on).

As social movements around the world have sought to rapidly expand and scale up the reach of microfinance programmes, they have also become the subject of considerable debate. Proponents, for example, argue that microfinance programmes can be cost effective, even profitable, in the medium to long term, and do not need permanent external subsidies to be commercially viable; academic critics point out that even the highest-profile programmes (such as Grameen Bank in Bangladesh) absorb an enormous amount of external funding via their training institutes, and in any event took many years to establish their credibility and to discern a context-specific set of lending instruments; they also suggest that 'costs' are less of a burden on the poor than the absence of access, security, and savings services, and that as such microfinance programmes should worry less about charging high interest rates on loans (as do programmes in Bolivia) and more on ensuring their financial viability, accessibility and longevity. In any event, like other popular development practices, few microfinance programmes have been subject to rigorous evaluation protocols, making it hard for supporters and critics alike to substantiate their claims.

Nevertheless, given the centrality of monetary exchange to contemporary economic life, it seems eminently desirable to seek effective and inclusive ways of making financial services available to as many people as possible. The perennial challenge is to keep finding innovative, cost-effective and accessible ways of doing so for the benefit of the millions of people throughout the world who continue to be denied, by design or default, such services.

MICHAEL WOOLCOCK

Further reading

Bornstein, David (1997), *The Price of a Dream: The Story of the Grameen Bank*, Chicago, IL: University of Chicago Press.
Consultative Group to Assist the Poor (CGAP) (2005), *CGAP: Building Financial Institutions for the Poor*, www.cgap.org/, 16 August 2005.
Drake, Deborah and Elisabeth Rhyne (eds) (2002), *The Commercialization of Microfinance: Balancing Business and Development*, Bloomfield, CT: Kumarian Press.
Morduch, Jonathan (1999), 'The microfinance promise', *Journal of Economic Literature*, **37** (4), 1569–614.
Pitt, Mark and Shahidur Khandker (1998), 'The impact of group-based credit on poor households in Bangladesh: does the gender of participants matter?', *Journal of Political Economy*, **106** (5), 958–96.

Migration for Rural Work

Migration between rural areas for employment, whether within or across national boundaries, has confounded measurement by most large-scale surveys, and has consequently received little attention either in public policies or in academic research. Yet in-depth studies have shown just how critical this kind of spatial movement is, both for the workers and for the businesses that employ them (for example, Breman, 1985, 1990). One study found that the half a million agricultural wage workers resident in a single Indian district was at least matched in numbers by seasonal migrant workers, entering the region to harvest rice twice a year (Rogaly et al., 2001). In the United States, an exceptional large-scale survey which attempted an estimate found that 56 per cent of the 1.6 million farm workers in crop-based agriculture were migrants (Oxfam America, 2004, p. 7).

Much rural–rural migration is seasonal, which is, at least in part, a response to the seasonality of demand for workers in rural areas. This in turn relates to (though is not always determined by) the seasonality of production: agriculture is a key case in point, but other rural industries are also seasonal, including brick-making and road construction. Moreover, people who migrate from rural areas may have seasonal labour requirements on land they cultivate, in other enterprises, or wage labour commitments to others in their usual place of residence.

Although agricultural mechanisation continued its spread in the second half of the twentieth century, there are certain production processes that have remained labour intensive. The extent of this varies. For example, rice production in eastern India relies on transplanting and harvesting by hand, while threshing is partly mechanised. Lettuces grown in the UK are harvested by mechanical rigs, in which the lettuces are packed and boxed, ready to be transported to supermarkets. However, teams of workers are required both to cut lettuces and to place them on the conveyor belt, and, once the belt enters the rig, to label and box them (Taylor and Rogaly, 2004).

The political economy of demand for rural migrant workers
The demand for migrant workers by rural-based enterprises is only partly shaped by the technological requirements of the particular production process, and the local availability of labour. There are social and political determinants too, and all of these factors operate in relation to the action (or inaction) of states, and the political economy of the wider markets faced by rural producers. Demand is therefore historically and geographically contingent and rarely explainable by a particular parameter. Actual rural–rural migrations are not only shaped by that demand, of course, but also by the decisions made and pressures faced by those who migrate for rural work. That part of the story will briefly be explored in the next section.

Rural agricultural enterprises, like urban ones, are located in value chains (see Kritzinger et al., 2004). The demand for labour at any point in the value chain, and the wage paid, is influenced by the conditions elsewhere in the chain. Currently in UK agriculture, for example, growers of fresh fruit and vegetables rely increasingly on contracts with very large retailers (Lawrence, 2004). The price of fresh produce is set by the retailer, who is able to find alternative sources of the same fruit and vegetables globally. Because growers are under pressure to reduce their margins, they often seek to reduce the cost of labour. If it is found that hiring migrant workers reduces costs, then growers will seek such workers, reflecting the huge imbalance of power between themselves and the retailers.

Migrant workers are seen as useful by rural enterprises for other reasons too. Importantly, they enable companies to increase their power over the terms and conditions of local workers. Employers I have interviewed in both India and England talked about their problems with local workers in terms of motivation and application to the task. The availability of migrant workers brings downward wage pressures to bear, and may make for a more 'pliable' workforce. In general, migrant workers have fewer commitments in their workplace than in their place of usual residence. They are thus more likely than local workers to be prepared to work nights, work at very short notice, and to vary their shift patterns.

The case of Californian fruit is instructive as it has long been a subsector with high levels of demand for seasonal migrant workers. Indeed one analysis of data from the early part of the twentieth century calculated that the profitability of Californian fruit relied on not bearing the year-round costs of reproducing the labour force (Mitchell, 1996). In another Californian study, the degree to which agricultural growers could control wage workers, preventing them from absconding or from shirking, was found to be related to the legality of their migration and their citizenship status (Wells, 1996, pp. 68–9).

Being an undocumented migrant worker makes it riskier to protest or to join a union, as the ultimate sanction is not only loss of job but deportation. Rural migrants, regardless of citizenship status, are often provided with accommodation. This can also be a means of control, as workers are likely to depend on it, with no home of their own within commuting distance. In providing accommodation, employers gain an extra lever over their workforce, and may be able to decrease the net wage paid by more than the equivalent of reasonable rent. Cases were recently reported in rural areas of eastern England where migrant workers were subject to high portions of their wages being deducted for 'rent' – above the limit for such charges set by the Agricultural Wages Board (House of Commons, 2003). In the UK, for those crops where the time of harvest is unpredictable, because it is related to fluctuations in consumer demand (such as spring onions), growers need to be able to call on migrant workers when they need them and to despatch them when the work is done. When workers live on site, it becomes far easier for employers to demand extreme flexibility in terms of hours of work, as has been shown in research on migrant domestic workers (Anderson, 2000).

Many rural migrant workers in the UK, as is increasingly the case in the US (Oxfam America, 2004), are housed by labour contractors or gangmasters, who are their direct employers. These workers are then moved from site to site according to very short-term demand fluctuations. Intermediaries may be necessary to match workers to seasonal jobs in rural areas. However, the use of intermediaries is not universal. In late twentieth-century Gujarat in India, sugar-cane farmers clubbed together to form cooperative factories for sugar processing. In this 'cooperative capitalism', intermediaries were used to recruit and manage migrant workers. Local wage workers were deliberately excluded from employment in the sugar fields, in what has been interpreted as a means of social control (Breman, 1990). This structuring of labour demand and the workings of sugar owners' class power was closely intertwined with the local caste structure, because most of the land was owned by Kanbi Patels, the dominant peasant caste. In a study of rice production in West Bengal, demand worked differently with employers doing their own recruitment without intermediaries, and competing with each other at labour marketplaces in times of extreme labour shortage. Caste power in West Bengal was more diffuse, and the shortage of labour more keenly felt at the time of harvest and planting (Rogaly et al., 2002).

As in the contemporary UK fresh produce sector, in West Bengal demand for rural migrant workers has been shaped by the wider market conditions, as well as by the way in which state policies and party politics have played out in relation to worker protection. Producers of rice in West Bengal have been in crisis since the turn of the millennium, when, after two decades of relative prosperity, a combination of factors led to a fall in the price of rice (Harriss-White and Ghosh, 2002). There followed downward pressure on wages for agricultural workers, including migrants, although this was modified by the actions of the ruling political party in attempting to continue the negotiated cross-class compromise over wages, which had kept relative peace in rural areas of the state since it came to power in 1977.

Lifeworlds of rural migrant workers

A continuing collapse of rice prices in West Bengal would have severe consequences for the livelihoods of the hundreds of thousands of people involved in migrating into or across the state for short periods to transplant or harvest rice. This rural–rural migration, as elsewhere, is motivated in large part by the need to access cash, and the higher earnings available through a combination of higher wages and consecutive days of employment. In some circumstances a cycle of debt may operate in which migrant workers are effectively bonded. Loans or advances in the lean season are repaid by work in the peak season but more loans are required during that period, leaving few net earnings to take home. (Mosse et al. (2002) analyse the debt relations of migrant workers seeking seasonal urban work in construction.) In the West Bengal study, there was a greater degree of debt-induced compulsion for migrant brick workers than for the rice workers. The brick workers' season was also much longer, lasting six to nine months.

The power of rural migrant workers in relation to employers is not fixed. It varies across place and time in a number of ways. Importantly, in tight labour market conditions, when there are relatively few people and a large number of unfilled vacancies, migrant workers may be able to press for better deals, including rates of pay. They are also likely to be more confident about refusing work with a particular employer after discussing the details of accommodation, work expected, distance to be travelled each day (Rogaly et al., 2004). In the early twentieth-century Californian case analysed by Mitchell, mobility itself was used subversively, with workers setting up their own camps, which became spaces for organisation and contestation of working conditions (ibid., ch. 3).

Those who migrate to rural areas for temporary work are necessarily combining this with other forms of livelihood. Migration has to be fitted around commitments to family, employers and other patrons at home, one's own productive enterprises, including agriculture, and any studying or other employment that one is engaged in. Such commitments change over a lifetime, as does the capacity to do manual work. Individuals are likely, therefore, to move in and out of rural–rural migration, although it often becomes a way of life for a period. Rural–rural migration is also likely to be related to the life cycle of a household – both because of households' varying income, and because of changes in the ratio of workers to dependents.

While the lives of rural migrant workers travelling without families may be of much use to employers seeking a truly flexible source of labour for a limited period, the absences induced by this kind of migration are often disruptive, both materially and emotionally. The temporary nature of employment of rural migrant workers means that homes are not usually made at the place of work. Home is a place to return to regularly or a place that will be created in the future after a period of itinerant migration for rural work. This involves much planning and negotiation with immediate family, other relatives and/or neighbours. However, rural–rural migration, like other migration, can also be an act of rebellion, of asserting independence from parents. The most arduous work can be tolerated in order to change places, get away from the claustrophobia of home, explore the world, and form intimate, and even amorous relations with others (Shah, 2003).

Summary

As we have seen, demand for migrant workers in rural areas is high both in northern and in southern countries, and includes both internal and international migrants, depending on the context. It is important to understand the political economy of rural–rural migration, how migrant workers are exploited through their lack of citizenship or local belonging, and how in some circumstances capital uses migrant workers to divide the labour force. There is usually great inequality involved in terms of the alternatives open to employers and would-be workers if the migration does not take place. The UK fresh produce sector is an extreme case in point, where the retailers hold the rest of the fresh produce value chain in thrall, especially those at the bottom of the chain: migrant harvest workers and packers (Lawrence, 2004). However, as we have seen, this inequality can vary seasonally, annually and across space. Rural–rural migration is an ongoing process or way of life for part of migrant workers' lives. It involves continued investment in relations at home, but may also be an expression of rebellion against them. The diversity of circumstances in which rural–rural migration takes place, and the contingency of power relations between workers, intermediaries and owners of land and other capital, belie generalisation about the degree to which this movement is forced or voluntary.

BEN ROGALY

References

Anderson, B. (2000), *Doing the Dirty Work: The Global Politics of Domestic Labour*, London: Zed Books.
Breman, J. (1985), *Of Peasants, Migrants and Paupers: Rural Labour Circulation and Capitalist Production in West India*, Oxford and New Delhi: Oxford University Press.
Breman, J. (1990), ' "Even dogs are better off": the ongoing battle between capital and labour in the cane-fields of Gujarat', *Journal of Peasant Studies*, **17** (4), 546–608.
Harriss-White, B. and P.K. Ghosh (2002), 'A crisis in the rice economy', *Frontline*, **19** (9), 14–27 September, www.frontlineonnet.com/fl1919/19190440.htm.
House of Commons (2003), *Environment, Food and Rural Affairs Committee Fourteenth Report of Session 2002–03, Gangmasters*, HC 691, London: HMSO.
Kritzinger, A., S. Barrientos and H. Rossouw (2004), 'Global production and flexible employment in South African horticulture: experiences of contract workers in fruit exports', *Sociologia Ruralis*, **44** (1), 17–39.
Lawrence, F. (2004), *Not on the Label: What Really Goes Into the Food on Your Plate*, London: Penguin.
Mitchell, D. (1996), *The Lie of the Land: Migrant Workers and the California Landscape*, Minneapolis, MN: University of Minnesota Press.
Mosse, D., M. Mehta, V. Shah, J. Rees and the KRISP Project Team (2002), 'Brokered livelihoods: debt, labour migration and development in tribal Western India', *Journal of Development Studies*, **38** (5), 59–88.
Oxfam America (2004), *Like Machines in the Fields: Workers without Rights in American Agriculture*, Boston, MA: Oxfam.
Rogaly, B., J. Biswas, D. Coppard, A. Rafique, K. Rana and A. Sengupta (2001), 'Seasonal migration, social change and migrants' rights: lessons from West Bengal', *Economic and Political Weekly*, **36** (49), 4547–59.

Rogaly, B., D. Coppard, A. Rafique, K. Rana, A. Sengupta and J. Biswas (2002), 'Seasonal migration and welfare/illfare in Eastern India: a social analysis', *Journal of Development Studies*, **38** (5), 89–114.
Rogaly, B., D. Coppard, K. Rana, A. Rafique, A. Sengupta and J. Biswas (2004), 'Seasonal migration, employer–worker interactions, and shifting ethnic identities in contemporary West Bengal', in F. Osella and K. Gardner (eds), *Migration, Modernity and Social Transformation in South Asia*, New Delhi, Thousand Oaks, CA and London: Sage, pp. 281–310.
Shah, A. (2003), 'Understandings of the state: an anthropological study of Rural Jharkhand, India', unpublished PhD thesis, London School of Economics and Political Science.
Taylor, B. and B. Rogaly (2004), *Migrant Working in West Norfolk*, Norwich: Norfolk County Council.
Wells, M. (1996), *Strawberry Fields: Politics, Class and Work in Californian Agriculture*, Ithaca, NY and London: Cornell University Press.

Migration, International

International migration is the movement of people across international borders. Within this simple definition lies a multiplicity of complexity covering different types of migrants, different duration of movement, different reasons for migrating and different entry categories. These differences in international migration resonate in a range of development outcomes. For example, the movement of unskilled workers on short-term labour contracts has very different development implications for both origin and destination countries from the movement of highly skilled or professional workers. The entry of large numbers of illegal migrants, termed 'irregular migrants' in much of the literature, poses quite distinct policy issues compared with migrants who enter a country legally.

Global dimensions

The United Nations (2002) estimated that in the year 2000, some 175 million people were living outside their country of birth, representing about 3 per cent of the world's population at that time. The majority, some 104 million, were to be found in the developed countries of the world where they accounted for about 8.7 per cent of the population compared with just 1.5 per cent of the population of the developing world. The global stock figure of 175 million had increased from 75 million in 1965 and from 154 million in 1990. Impressive though these gross numbers appear, the growth rate of migrant stock in the 1990s at 1.3 per cent per annum was virtually the same as that for the growth of the population of the world as a whole, at 1.4 per cent per annum. The bald numbers should temper any impression that international migration is somehow out of control and that we are in an era of unprecedented global population movement. However, the UN estimates have to be used with a great deal of care. They are useful to the extent that they provide a common methodology applied across space and through time but they are likely to exclude the effects of the many forms of short-term and temporary movements that are coming to characterise the modern global system of international population movement.

International migrants include those who are moving to settle, those going to work under some type of contract, both for skilled and professional occupations and for unskilled jobs, and those going overseas to study. The majority of those in the last two categories are moving temporarily. To these must be added the numbers who are entering countries illegally or staying on after the terms of their legal entry have expired. There are also those who flee to other countries for reasons of persecution in their home country and who enter as refugees or claiming asylum. Estimates exist of the number of refugees, some 15.9 million in 2000, but it is much more difficult to generate estimates for the other major types of international migrants and particularly of the numbers of irregular migrants. However, even including all these categories of movers, it is still a tiny minority of the world's population that cross international borders. The vast majority of those who move do so within their country of birth as internal migrants, and often as rural to rural or rural to urban migrants. Nevertheless, small numbers of international migrants can have profound developmental implications for both countries of origin and countries of destination.

Causes
The reasons why people migrate across international borders are many but are conditioned by three underlying sets of factors, economic, political and demographic. As the UN estimates suggest, most migrants move either within or towards the more developed countries, or from poorer to richer economies. However, this generalisation masks significant trends in the international migration system. It is difficult to explain current patterns of migration to the United States, for example, without taking into consideration prior American foreign policy. Migration from the Philippines, the Republic of Korea, Taiwan Province of China and Vietnam is more pronounced than from countries in which there has been little American involvement. The migration to the United Kingdom from South Asian nations or to France from North Africa cannot be explained without reference to previous colonial links. Yet, factors other than political ties must also be incorporated into any explanation of global migration in the twenty-first century. The two principal sources of migration to Canada are China and India and, together, they account for over one-quarter of all current settler arrivals. In an increasingly globalising economy, competition for brains has emerged as a major development issue. Developed countries in North America, Australasia and Europe are specifically targeting the educated and skilled from developing countries and particularly from those countries in Asia that are rapidly expanding their educated and skilled populations. Such targeting can be implemented through the regular immigration channels of developed countries or through specialised programmes specifically designed to allow fast entry of the skilled such as H1-B visa entry in the United States and the Highly Skilled Migration Programme in the United Kingdom. Some 53 per cent of those admitted to the United States under the H1-B programme in 2001 came from India and China.

Underlying these trends are shifts in the demography of destination societies. Where once Europe dominated migration to the Americas, today the major sources lie in Latin America and Asia. Western and southern Europe have shifted from areas of mass emigration to mass immigration as a sustained fertility decline to well below replacement levels has led to a slowing and eventually to a decline in national labour force growth. 'Replacement migration' is seen as being necessary to replenish at least partially the diminished age cohorts in both skilled and professional categories as well as in those jobs that native populations no longer wish to undertake, the so-called '3-D' jobs, or those that are dangerous, demanding or dirty and are, in reality, insecure, poorly paid and boring. It is not just in Europe that a general transition from emigration to immigration can be observed but also in those societies in East and South East Asia where there has been rapid economic development over the last forty years accompanied by sustained declines in fertility. The Republic of Korea, Taiwan Province of China, as well as Hong Kong SAR, Singapore, Malaysia and Thailand, have emerged as significant destinations for international migrants, having passed through turning-points in a 'migration transition' from net emigration to net immigration.

Increasingly, international migration appears to be characterised by movement at both ends of the skill spectrum: educated and skilled at one end and the less educated who are prepared to undertake unskilled jobs, particularly in construction and in the agricultural sector, at the other. In reality, the picture is more complex, with a broader range of people migrating and better-educated people undertaking unskilled jobs. The 'de-skilling' of migrant labour can be seen: those educated as teachers in the Philippines, for example, can earn more as domestic workers in Hong Kong. Women may be particularly likely to be subject to such de-skilling. Even the less skilled among the international migrants, however, do not appear to be the poorest from developing countries and absolute poverty is rarely the main driving force behind these movements. The migrants require some capital, both physical and human, in order to support their migration in the first place. International migration, rather than being a failure of development, echoes the process of development itself. Both the migration out of Europe during the second half of the nineteenth century and the migration out of much of the developing world today are closely linked to accelerated rates of economic growth in the areas of origin. Thus, programmes to foster development are unlikely to stem migration but are more likely, initially at least, to encourage migration.

The international migrations are seen to provide the labour to maintain competitiveness in technical fields in the most developed countries on the one hand and to provide the foot soldiers for the basic services to support the more highly skilled on the other. Many of these migrations are directed towards the largest cities of the developed world such as London, New York, San Francisco, Toronto, Sydney, Singapore and Hong Kong, the 'global cities'.

Consequences

The impact on the countries of origin can be profound and essentially revolve around two groups of issues, brain drain and remittances. The loss of skilled personnel, even temporarily, might be thought to have a negative impact on the development prospects of the economies of origin. Yet, there are no simple generalisations. The 'tiger economies' of East Asia experienced marked outmigration of students and professionals from the 1960s yet have hardly demonstrated a 'brain-drain' effect. Quite the reverse: with increased rates of return from the 1970s, particularly of students, there has been a 'brain gain' as those either trained in or with experience of the developed world went back to participate in and promote development in their home economies. However, in those countries of Sub-Saharan Africa from which small numbers of students and professionals have left and where there is little in the economy to draw them back, a brain drain may indeed exist. It is estimated that about one-third of educated Ghanaians and Sierra Leoneans live abroad, for example. The exodus of ethnic Russians from Central Asian countries may be a contributory factor in poor economic growth and a rise in poverty in these areas. Thus, almost paradoxically, there may be little brain-drain effect from those areas where the absolute loss of the educated is greatest as in Asia but a small loss may have a marked impact on small, fragile economies as in parts of Africa. The loss of the educated must always be gauged against whether they could be productively employed at home: where they cannot, emigration provides a social and political as well as an economic safety valve.

Perhaps the most significant developmental issue related to migration is the volume of money and goods sent home in the form of remittances. World Bank estimates placed the global flows to developing countries alone through official channels at US$72.3 billion in 2001 (Ratha, 2003, p. 157). This amount is much greater than official development assistance and was equivalent to 42 per cent of total FDI flows to developing countries in that year. If the amounts sent back home by migrants through unofficial channels could be added accurately, the total value of remittances would be increased substantially. For example, a survey in Bangladesh suggested that only about 46 per cent of remittances flowed through official channels (cited in Siddiqui, 2003, p. 5). There is no question that the flows are significant. There is much more debate about their developmental impact. Given that the international migrants are not among the poorest and usually come from very specific small areas in countries of origin, remittances can increase intra-village and interregional inequalities. There are, nevertheless, important externalities: remittance income used for construction creates demand for local materials and local labour that may eventually draw in workers from surrounding and poorer areas. Thus, links can be important between international and local internal migrations. Also, no clear distinction between investment and consumption purposes can be drawn for remittances. Spending money on an event of apparent conspicuous consumption such as a wedding feast in the village can be interpreted as an investment in the demographic and social future of that village, for example.

Diasporas
Migration can be conceptualised as developing through networks of human interaction in which individuals and families seek to gain access to resources in different places that allow them to minimise risk. Failure at one point of the network can be balanced against return at another point and human circulation or short-term migration within the networks is common. The networks established across international borders make up the transnational community or diaspora. The significance of the diaspora for development is that it provides the source for return migrants, for those with human and physical capital to contribute to the development of the home economies. The Chinese Overseas and the Viet Kieu (overseas Vietnamese) are playing an important role in promoting businesses and trade in and from their home countries and the overseas destinations with which they are familiar. Conversely, diaspora communities can have security implications either in the support of separatist or dissident groups in origin areas or in the undermining of societies and economies in destination areas.

Trafficking and smuggling
International migration operates through the filter of the migration policies of states that control or manage the entry or exit of migrants. Where these policies are restrictive and

demands for labour exist, a fertile ground for irregular migration is created. The broker who facilitates the illegal migration is the smuggler or trafficker. A distinction is drawn between the two. The trafficker engages in deception, possibly uses force and exploits and abuses the prospective migrant. Smugglers, on the other hand, merely facilitate an illegal movement across a border, prospective migrants voluntarily contact smugglers to arrange their passage. In practice, a clear distinction is often difficult to draw as it is known that migrants who willingly enter smuggling networks can be subject to harassment along the way and to exploitation at the destination while the smuggler awaits full payment of the cost of the illegal transfer. Particular attention has been directed towards the trafficking of women into the sex sector and of children into the worst forms of child labour. Much of the former at least is more closely associated with smuggling, and men as well as women are often the victims of traffickers and smugglers.

Conclusion

International migration is perhaps the most obvious human dimension of globalisation. The migrations are not the result of a failure of development but are an integral part of the whole process of development itself. The resultant global inequalities, in effect, underlie so much of international population movement. There are unquestionably negative consequences associated with migration, but the movement of peoples has brought benefits to countries of origin, to countries of destination, as well as to most of the migrants themselves. A geographically static population would be a society and economy without development. While the impact of international migration on destination societies can be seen to undermine traditional values and raise issues of national security, its transformative role can be positive for both economic development, through the supply of key skills, and for social welfare, through the provision of enhanced livelihood choices. The effective management of international migration remains one of the principal challenges for the twenty-first century.

RONALD SKELDON

References and further reading

Abella, Manolo I. (ed.) (1994), 'Turning points in labor migration', *Asian and Pacific Migration Journal*, **3** (1), special issue.
Castles, Stephen and Mark Miller (2003), *The Age of Migration: International Population Movements in the Modern World*, 3rd edn, Basingstoke: Palgrave.
Nyberg-Sørensen, Ninna, Nicholas Van Hear and Poul Engberg-Pedersen (eds) (2002), 'The migration–development nexus', *International Migration*, **40** (5), special issue.
Ratha, Dilip (2003), 'Workers' remittances: an important and stable source of external development finance', *Global Development Finance*, Washington, DC: World Bank, pp. 157–75.
Salt, John (ed.) (2000), 'Perspectives on trafficking of migrants', *International Migration*, **38** (3), special issue.
Siddiqui, Tasneem (2003), 'Migration as a livelihood strategy of the poor: the Bangladesh case', paper presented at the international conference on Migration, Development and Pro-Poor Policy Choices in Asia, United Kingdom Department for International Development, Dhaka, 22–24 June, www.livelihoods.org.
Skeldon, Ronald (1997), *Migration and Development: A Global Perspective*, London: Longman.
Skeldon, Ronald (2002), 'Migration and poverty', *Asia-Pacific Population Journal*, **17** (4), 67–82.
Stark, Oded (1991), *The Migration of Labor*, Oxford: Blackwell.
United Nations (2001), *Replacement Migration: Is it a Solution to Declining Populations?*, Population Division, Department of Economic and Social Affairs, New York.
United Nations (2002), *International Migration Report 2002*, Population Division, Department of Economic and Social Affairs, New York.

Militarism and Development

Looking back at development trends in the second half of the twentieth century, two contrasting tendencies stand out. The first is a steady improvement in living standards in many countries, evident for instance in rising per capita incomes, declining mortality rates, better nutrition, higher education levels and expanding civil liberties. The second tendency consists of periodic wrecking of these achievements in specific countries as a consequence of armed conflict. Afghanistan, Angola, Cambodia, Congo/Zaire, Ethiopia, Iraq, Lebanon, Pakistan, Sierra Leone, Somalia, Sri Lanka, Sudan, Vietnam and former Yugoslavia are some examples – among many – of countries where armed conflicts have played havoc with social progress and left behind them a long trail of destruction and misery.

Development economics, however, has focused almost exclusively on the first tendency. The standard textbooks have virtually nothing to say on the relation between armed conflicts and development. Even in the broader field of 'development studies', armed conflicts have received little attention until quite recently. Tawney's (1933) view of war as 'the most neglected factor in social development' (p. 15) remains largely applicable today.

Defining militarism is not an easy task. Seen as a characteristic of states, it is commonly understood in at least four different senses: military rule, high levels of military spending, a propensity for aggression, and a preponderant influence of military institutions or culture in civilian affairs. These features are related, but only loosely so. For instance, military rule need not imply any of the other characteristics (Berg and Berg, 1991). A further difficulty is that states need not be seen as having the monopoly of militarism.

Militarism will be broadly understood here as a propensity to use military power, or the threat of it, for political settlements. Including the *threatened* use of military power in the definition is important, especially in view of the role of nuclear threats in contemporary military strategy. Note also that this does not require military or even authoritarian rule. The US government, for instance, clearly satisfies the proposed criterion of militarism. The reference to 'military power' encompasses guerrilla armies and private militias, but not pub brawls or individual murders. The proposed definition has its limitations, but it will do for our purposes. Militarism in this sense may be contrasted with various alternatives – collective security arrangements, the rule of international law, peaceful negotiations, total disarmament, among others.

There are at least three important classes of social costs associated with militarism. These relate to security, development and democracy, respectively.

To start with, militarism is a major source of insecurity and violence in people's lives. This may sound paradoxical, since the ostensible purpose of building military power is often to ensure 'national security'. The problem is that unilateral investment in military power for defence purposes tends to be collectively self-defeating: each state attempts to enhance its own security through military strength, but as other states do the same, collective security often decreases instead of increasing. This is a typical example of the 'prisoner's dilemma' well known to game theorists, or more generally of a 'social trap' (Rapoport, 1992). Arms races can be seen as the culmination of this self-defeating process: as each side tries to enhance its own security by outdoing the other side, a dangerous process of escalation sets in. Indeed arms races have often ended in devastating wars.

Second, militarism often interferes with development. In development economics, this issue has been examined primarily in terms of the impact of high military expenditure on economic growth (see Military Expenditure and Economic Growth, this volume). There is a large literature on this, with mixed findings, though the balance of evidence suggests that military expenditure tends to slow down economic growth (Sandler and Hartley, 1995). However, this is only one particular link between militarism and development. For instance, aside from slowing down economic growth, high military expenditure is often associated with relatively poor social indicators, possibly because of the trade-off between military expenditure and social expenditure, or because of a similar trade-off in the domain of policy priorities (Dixon and Moon, 1986). Similarly, to the extent that militarism enhances the probability of armed conflict, it is also a major threat to development, given the devastating economic and social consequences of war (Stewart and Fitzgerald, 2000). Once we acknowledge that development is not just about economic growth, but also about social progress in a larger sense, we also get a fuller view of the adverse consequences of militarism on development.

The third and least studied casualty of militarism is democracy. In situations of armed conflict (or preparation for it), there is a tendency to suppress human rights, political opposition and democratic freedoms. This can be seen even in countries with a relatively strong democratic tradition. During the First World War, for instance, the governments of Britain and the United States pioneered the art of modern propaganda, later applied to marketing. Even outside situations of active conflict, the military establishment tends to have a strong anti-democratic influence.

The anti-democratic influences of the military establishment have many aspects, including hostility to human rights, extensive propaganda activities, promotion of a culture of secrecy, intensive lobbying for military projects, and the spread of corruption. At an obvious level, military activities involve a high concentration of power, and in this respect they are fundamentally at odds with democratic ideals. Another anti-democratic influence of the military establishment is the spread of a culture of secrecy. A certain amount of secrecy is perhaps inevitable in military matters, but the culture of secrecy has a tendency to spread well beyond the bounds of necessity. Closely related to secrecy is the role of the military establishment in spreading corruption. Defence contracts are particularly attractive channels for illegal inducements: the deals are sheltered from the public gaze, the number of 'partners' tends to be small, and the amounts are huge. It is no wonder that in many countries some of the biggest scams that have been exposed relate to military expenditure.

This brief account of the relation between militarism and development may appear to be 'one-sided'. Indeed, there are also positive connections between militarism and each of the social objectives examined here – security, development and democracy. For instance, it has been argued that war tends to be a period of rapid social change, including positive social change (Marwick, 1988). The swift change in gender relations in Britain during the First World War is an interesting if controversial example, as is the role of the world wars in the origin of the 'welfare state'. Similarly, military expenditure can have some positive 'externalities', such as civilian uses of military infrastructure (for example, roads and satellites), commercial applications of defence research, and the involvement of the army in disaster relief. However, the positive links between militarism and development tend to be much more speculative than the adverse connections reviewed in this entry.

To illustrate the point, consider the consequences of militarism in India and Pakistan during the last 50 years or so. This is a situation where there has been a persistent tendency to settle disputes through military means ('militarism' in the sense used here), at the expense of other means such as peaceful negotiation and regional détente. The adverse consequences are fairly clear: five wars have been fought; the region came perilously close to nuclear war on several occasions; human rights and civil liberties have been comprehensively suppressed, especially in conflict zones such as Kashmir; crippling defence budgets have displaced social expenditure; defence-related scams have flourished; and so on. The consequences of militarism have been particularly stark in Pakistan, but even India has paid a heavy price for it (Drèze and Sen, 2002). This is not to deny that military power may have had its positive uses from time to time. In India, for instance, the army has often played a positive role in disaster relief, and sometimes also in bringing communal violence under control. But it would be hard to argue that these 'positive externalities', as they are called in economics, outweigh the devastating toll of militarism in the subcontinent. The same applies to most of the armed conflicts mentioned at the beginning of this entry.

JEAN DRÈZE

References

Berg, A. and E. Berg (1991), 'The political economy of the military', in G. Psacharopoulos (ed.), *Essays on Poverty, Equity and Growth*, Oxford: Pergamon, pp. 203–39.
Dixon, W. and B. Moon (1986), 'The military burden and basic human needs', *Journal of Conflict Resolution*, **30** (4), 660–84.
Drèze, J.P. and A.K. Sen (2002), 'Security and democracy in a nuclear India', in Drèze and Sen (eds), *India: Development and Participation*, Oxford and New Delhi: Oxford University Press, pp. 275–305.
Marwick, Arthur (ed.) (1988), *Total War and Social Change*, Basingstoke: Macmillan.
Rapoport, Anatol (1992), *Peace: An Idea Whose Time Has Come*, Ann Arbor; MI: University of Michigan Press.
Sandler, T. and K. Hartley (1995), *The Economics of Defense*, Cambridge: Cambridge University Press.
Stewart, F. and V. Fitzgerald (eds) (2000), *War and Underdevelopment: The Economic and Social Consequences of Conflict*, Oxford: Oxford University Press.
Tawney, R.H..(1933), 'The study of economic history', *Economica*, **13** (39), 1–21.

Military Expenditure and Economic Growth

Most economists take the view that unproductive public expenditure generally slows down economic growth. When it comes to military spending, however, they have often argued the opposite – that public expenditure boosts economic growth. The objectivity of the economics profession in this matter is not entirely clear, if only because economists are among the major recipients of defence-related research funds (especially in the United States). Be that as it may, the relation between military expenditure and economic growth has received considerable empirical scrutiny, and while the debate is far from settled, the basic issues at least are somewhat clearer than they used to be. The following is a brief introduction to this literature, with special focus on developing countries.

Emile Benoit (1973, 1978) set the ball rolling with some surprising statistical findings, allegedly showing that military expenditure enhances economic growth in developing countries. The statistical techniques, however, left much to be desired, and prompted a number of devastating rejoinders (for example, Lim, 1983; Deger, 1986; Grobar and

Porter, 1989). To illustrate, Benoit's interpretation of his 'chief regression results' involved some startling statistical reasoning, including the notion that the portion of R^2 ('the square of the statistical magnitude R') not accounted for by the regression variables can be discounted when assessing the statistical significance of a particular variable – a convenient way of magnifying t-statistics.

On a more positive note, Benoit's work stimulated a great deal of further thinking and empirical work on the subject. A superficial view of this body of work suggests that it is largely inconclusive: some studies find no significant relation between military expenditure and economic growth, others a negative relation, and others still a positive one. On closer examination, however, the balance of evidence seems to support the hypothesis that military expenditure reduces economic growth.

The basic question addressed in most studies is whether a high 'military burden' (usually defined as the share of military expenditure in GDP) tends to lower economic growth in developing countries. How could this fail to be the case? One common but misleading answer is associated with what might be called 'military Keynesianism': the notion that military expenditure promotes growth by stimulating aggregate demand and reducing excess capacity. This thesis need not retain us here, since lack of demand is not a major constraint on medium-term growth in most developing countries. Even where demand needs to be stimulated, there is no reason to do it by building missiles rather than roads or schools. A fair evaluation of the opportunity cost of the military burden has to consider the *next best use* of public resources (taking into account all the relevant constraints), not an arbitrary alternative (such as a corresponding reduction of total public expenditure) which makes little sense in the given context.

A more plausible argument is that military expenditure stimulates economic growth through various kinds of 'spillover effects' on civilian production, as argued in some detail in Benoit's original study. For instance, research and development (R&D) for military purposes often has civilian applications – even the internet is a revamped offspring of the Pentagon. The R&D argument has some relevance in industrialised countries, where sophisticated technology has extensive civilian applications. In developing countries, where advanced military technology has much less to contribute to basic civilian needs, military R&D is unlikely to give a major boost to technological innovation in the civilian sector. However, military expenditure in developing countries may have other types of spillover effects, such as civilian uses of military infrastructure (for example, roads and satellites) and the role of the army in disaster relief.

Another possible spillover effect is the military influence on civilian attitudes and human capital. One version of this idea is that the military establishment contributes to the process of modernisation by fostering values such as efficiency, discipline and national unity (Benoit, 1978, pp. 277–8). The argument used to be popular among political scientists in the 1960s, but little empirical evidence has materialised in support of it. A more persuasive version is that military service contributes to the diffusion of skills. Weede (1992), in particular, has argued that military participation can be seen as 'a kind of school and an agency for human-capital formation' (p. 227).

While some of these arguments are plausible, it should be noted that in order for spillover effects to boost economic growth they have to be strong enough to compensate for the expenditure involved. For instance, it is not enough to argue that military facilities such as roads and satellites provide some services to the civilian population. It also has to be shown that the 'indirect' provision of these services through military expenditure is *more efficient* than the direct provision of civilian facilities. Otherwise, civilian needs are better served through direct provision. This point is quite crucial in interpreting empirical findings on spillover effects.

On the other hand, the most obvious reason why military expenditure might slow down economic growth is the 'crowding-out effect': military expenditure entails a diversion of productive resources (including human capital), potentially usable for civilian investments. In addition, there may be a 'distortion effect': apart from displacing other investments, military expenditure may reduce the efficiency of resource allocation in the economy, for example, by distorting relative prices and fostering rent-seeking activities. Finally, the possibility of *negative spillover* effects (much neglected in the literature) is worth noting. Examples include the use of civilian facilities for military purposes and the environmental damage caused by military training. Even in the formation of human capital, there may be negative spillovers: it is by no means obvious that military training and socialisation enhance a person's preparedness to contribute to civilian life. In some countries, demobilised soldiers are notoriously problematic citizens.

The net effect of military expenditure on economic growth is a matter of empirical investigation. Much of the empirical evidence (aptly reviewed in Ram, 1995) consists of statistical analyses of international cross-section data, focusing on the association between military burdens and economic growth. The standard regression equation is of the form:

$$g_{i,t} = \mathbf{X}_{i,t} \cdot \beta + m_{i,t} \cdot \gamma + \varepsilon_{i,t} \tag{1}$$

where $g_{i,t}$ is the growth rate of per capita GDP in country i and period t, $\mathbf{X}_{i,t}$ gives the corresponding values of a vector of conditioning variables, $m_{i,t}$ is the military burden (or, in some models, the *growth* of the military burden) in country i and period t, and $\varepsilon_{i,t}$ is the error term. The choice of conditioning variables may be based either on a structural model of the relation between military expenditure and economic growth, or on ad hoc statistical tests. Typical components of $\mathbf{X}$ include human capital, regional dummies and the savings or investment rate. In many studies, there is a single reference period, in which case (1) boils down to a simple cross-section equation. In other cases, there are two or three periods (for example, successive five-year intervals); a few studies use annual time-series data. The parameter of primary interest is γ, interpreted as the effect of military expenditure on economic growth.

Note that this exercise resembles the proverbial search for a needle in a haystack. Indeed, in most countries military expenditure is small relative to total investment. Thus, variations in military expenditure are unlikely to account for much of the variation in growth rates, even if (say) there is one-to-one crowding-out between military expenditure and investment and if the latter drives economic growth. The bulk of the variation in growth rates reflects other factors, only some of which can be expected to figure in the regression. If key variables are omitted (or misspecified), the coefficient of military expenditure is likely to be biased, or to have a high standard error, or both. The notoriously unreliable nature of military expenditure data (at least until recently) makes the exercise all the more heroic. Considering these limitations, it is interesting that econometric analysis has yielded reasonably consistent evidence of the negative effects of military expenditure on economic growth.

The main exception pertains to a class of models known as 'Feder-type models' (Ram, 1995). Econometric estimates based on these models typically suggest that the impact of military expenditure is either insignificant or positive. However, these models are fundamentally flawed, because the regression equation derived from Feder-type models (i) ignores crowding-out effects by construction (by including investment among the conditioning variables) and (ii) involves a major simultaneity bias (because economic growth is regressed on the *growth* of military expenditure). It is worth noting that Gershon Feder is not responsible for these flaws. The original model (Feder, 1983) made sense in the context for which it was built, that is, the issue of how *export performance* affects economic growth. It is the transplantation of this model in a different context, without the required modifications, that seems to have failed.

If we exclude Feder-type models, and Benoit's unconvincing analysis, most of the studies surveyed by Ram (1995) find that that the impact of military expenditure on economic growth is either negative or insignificant. The fact that several studies find no significant relation between the military burden and economic growth, even outside the Feder-type models, should not be read as strong evidence *against* the hypothesis of a negative effect of the former on the latter. Rather, it reflects the demanding nature of 'significance tests' based on a low tolerance for type-I errors.

The picture is aptly summarised by Sandler and Hartley (1995, p. 220), where Feder-type models are called 'supply-side models':

> Models that include demand-side influences, where defense can crowd out investment, found that defense had a negative impact on growth. In contrast, almost every supply-side model either found a small positive defense impact or no impact at all. The findings are amazingly consistent despite differences in the sample of countries, the time periods, and econometric estimating procedures. Since we suspect that these supply-side models exclude some negative influences of defense on growth, we must conclude that the net impact of defense on growth is negative, but small.

One limitation of many of the studies surveyed by Ram (1995) concerns the possibility of 'feedback' effects: if economic growth influences the military burden, then regressing the latter on the former would lead to biased estimates of the impact of military expenditure on economic growth. In particular, if this feedback effect is positive, then the estimated coefficient of the military burden is likely to be biased *upwards*. In some studies, economic growth is regressed on *lagged* values of the military burden, but even then a bias may persist, in so far as lagged economic growth is likely to be correlated with economic growth in the reference period. A more credible answer is to estimate a simultaneous-equations model, where military expenditure is one of the dependent variables. This is the spirit of the 'Deger-type models', initially developed by Saadet Deger (see Deger, 1986; and Deger and Sen, 1995). These models consistently find that the military burden has a negative impact on growth.

Subsequent to the publication of Ram's (1995) survey, evidence of the negative effects of military expenditure on growth has been consolidated in a major way by Knight et al.

(1996). This study involves a considerable refinement of earlier estimation techniques, which makes full use of the panel aspects of the data (the latter are available for three successive five-year periods and 79 countries). The model has two equations, one for the growth rate and one for the investment rate. The conditioning variables are derived from a modified neoclassical growth model *à la* Solow–Swan. The results clearly indicate that military expenditure reduces growth, through both a 'crowding-out effect' and a 'distortion effect'.

Even though the literature on this subject is already bloated in some respects, much potential remains for further research, especially in the light of recent improvements in data quality and econometric techniques. In particular, there is a case for investigating composition effects, that is, how different *types* of military expenditure affect economic growth. It has been suggested, for instance, that the opportunity cost of military expenditure is low for 'military investments' (Brauer, 1991), and high for military imports (Looney, 1994). Another crucial compositional issue relates to the employment intensity of military expenditure. Some studies suggest that a high level of 'military participation' is good for economic growth (Weede, 1983, 1992). This points to the need for joint estimation of the effects of military expenditure and military participation on economic growth.

To conclude, there is consistent evidence that high levels of military expenditure are detrimental to economic growth. However, one caveat is in order: it does not follow from these findings that a *reduction* in military expenditure can be expected to generate swift and tangible economic benefits. There is a possibility of 'ratchet effects' of various kinds in the process of expenditure reduction. The literature on disarmament, for instance, highlights the difficulties involved in the 'conversion' of military industries to civilian production. Similar issues arise with respect to the demobilisation of soldiers. In some countries, there is also a possibility that the haphazard reduction of military expenditure under pressure in the 1990s has contributed to a surge in internal violence, as underpaid or demobilised soldiers turned to looting, crime and other forms of 'economic violence' (Keen, 1998). Reaping 'peace dividends' seems to require broader measures than an indiscriminate reduction in military expenditure.

JEAN DRÈZE

References

Benoit, Emile (1973), *Defense and Economic Growth in Developing Countries*, Lexington, MA: Lexington Books.
Benoit, Emile (1978), 'Growth and defense in developing countries', *Economic Development and Cultural Change*, **26** (2), 271–80.
Brauer, Jurgen (1991), 'Military investments and economic growth in developing nations', *Economic Development and Cultural Change*, **39** (4), 873–84.
Chan, S. and A. Mintz (eds) (1992), *Defense, Welfare and Growth*, London: Routledge.
Deger, Saadet (1986), *Military Expenditure in Third World Countries: The Economic Effects*, London: Routledge & Kegan Paul.
Deger, S. and S. Sen (1995), 'Military expenditure and developing countries', in Hartley and Sandler (eds), pp. 275–308.
Feder, Gershon (1983), 'On exports and economic growth', *Journal of Development Economics*, **12** (1–2), 59–73.
Grobar, Lisa, and Richard Porter (1989), 'Benoit revisited: defense spending and economic growth in LDCs', *Journal of Conflict Resolution*, **33** (2), 318–45.
Hartley, K. and T. Sandler (eds) (1995), *Handbook of Defense Economics*, Amsterdam: North-Holland, Elsevier Science.
Keen, David (1998), *The Economic Functions of Violence in Civil Wars*, Adelphi Papers 320, Oxford: Oxford University Press for the International Institute for Strategic Studies.

Knight, M., N. Loayza, and D. Villanueva (1996), 'The peace dividend: military spending cuts and economic growth', *IMF Staff Papers*, 43.

Lim, D. (1983), 'Another look at growth and defense in less developed countries', *Economic Development and Cultural Change*, **31** (2), 377–84.

Looney, Robert E. (1994), *The Economics of Third World Defense Expenditures*, London: JAI Press.

Ram, Rati (1995), 'Defense expenditure and economic growth', in Hartley and Sandler (eds), pp. 251–74.

Sandler, T. and K. Hartley (1995), *The Economics of Defense*, Cambridge: Cambridge University Press.

Weede, Erich (1983), 'Military participation ratios, human capital formation, and economic growth: a cross-national analysis', *Journal of Political and Military Sociology*, **11** (1), 11–19.

Weede, Erich (1992), 'Military participation, economic growth, and income inequality: a cross-national study', in Chan and Mintz (eds), pp. 211–30.

Millennium Development Goals

The Millennium Development Goals (MDGs) are a set of goals for a range of development indicators, including income poverty and child mortality, setting targets most of which are supposed to be met by 2015. The goals have been endorsed by many governments and international agencies and are argued by some to have refocused development efforts on the poor.

History

The MDGs were preceded by the International Development Targets (IDTs), which were formally adopted at the Thirty-Fourth High Level Meeting of the Development Assistance Committee (DAC) in Paris during May 1996. From the outset there was some disquiet that these 'international goals' were set by an expert group in Paris. There were two defences against this criticism. First, developing-country governments do not have to sign up to precisely these poverty reduction goals but may adopt their own with a similar spirit. Second, the IDTs were based on resolutions passed at international conferences, and in this sense had already been endorsed by most developing countries.

Discontent about the origins of the IDTs manifested itself at the Millennium Summit in New York, 6–8 September 2000, which adopted the *Millennium Declaration* (UN, 2000) containing a list of goals, which overlapped with the IDTs but was not the same. A year later the UN document, *Road Map Towards the Implementation of the United Nations Millennium Declaration* (UN, 2001), laid out a finally agreed list of MDGs shown in Table 10, which incorporates some later minor modifications.

The goals

The MDGs comprise eight goals with 18 separate targets, together with a list of 48 indicators to monitor the targets. An important difference between the IDTs and MDGs is that the eighth goal adds targets relating to the direct contribution of the developed countries to meeting the goals, with mention of aid, debt relief and tariff barriers. It is significant that such actions (for example, debt reduction, higher aid) have been added. However, the wording of most of these is vague ('address . . .', 'deal comprehensively with . . .', 'more generous . . .' and so on), compared to the precise numerical goals for developing-country performance, with neither quantified targets nor deadlines, thus reflecting the unequal nature of the global partnership.

Table 10   The Millennium Development Goals

Goals and targets	Indicators
Goal 1: Eradicate extreme poverty and hunger Target 1: Halve, between 1990 and 2015, the proportion of people whose income is less than one dollar a day	1. Proportion of population below US$1 per day 2. Poverty gap ratio (incidence multiplied by depth of poverty) 3. Share of poorest quintile in national consumption
Target 2: Halve, between 1990 and 2015, the proportion of people who suffer from hunger	4. Prevalence of underweight children under five years of age 5. Proportion of population below minimum level of dietary energy consumption
Goal 2: Achieve universal primary education Target 3: Ensure that, by 2015, children everywhere, boys and girls alike, will be able to complete a full course of primary schooling	6. Net enrolment ratio in primary education 7. Proportion of pupils starting grade 1 who reach grade 5 8. Literacy rate of 15–24 year olds
Goal 3: Promote gender equality and empower women Target 4: Eliminate gender disparity in primary and secondary education, preferably by 2005, and to all levels of education no later than 2015	9. Ratio of girls to boys in primary, secondary and tertiary education 10. Ratio of literate women to men 15–24 years old 11. Share of women in wage employment in the non-agricultural sector 12. Proportion of seats held by women in national parliament
Goal 4: Reduce child mortality Target 5: Reduce by two-thirds, between 1990 and 2015, the under-five mortality rate	13. Under-five mortality rate 14. Infant mortality rate 15. Proportion of one-year-old children immunised against measles
Goal 5: Improve maternal health Target 6: Reduce by three-quarters, between 1990 and 2015, the maternal mortality ratio	16. Maternal mortality ratio 17. Proportion of births attended by skilled health personnel
Goal 6: Combat HIV/AIDS, malaria and other diseases Target 7: Have halted by 2015 and begun to reverse the spread of HIV/AIDS	18. HIV prevalence among 15–24 year-old pregnant women 19. Condom use rate of the contraceptive prevalence rate A. Condom use at last high-risk sex

Table 10   (continued)

Goals and targets	Indicators
	B. Percentage of population aged 15–24 years with comprehensive correct knowledge of HIV/AIDS
	C. Contraceptive prevalence rate
	20. Ratio of school attendance of orphans to school attendance of non-orphans aged 10–14 years
Target 8: Have halted by 2015 and begun to reverse the incidence of malaria and other major diseases	21. Prevalence and death rates associated with malaria
	22. Proportion of population in malaria risk areas using effective malaria prevention and treatment measures
	23. Prevalence and death rates associated with with tuberculosis
	24. Proportion of tuberculosis cases detected and cured under DOTS (directly observed treatment short course)
Goal 7: Ensure environmental sustainability	
Target 9: Integrate the principles of sustainable development into country policies and programmes and reverse the loss of environmental resources	25. Proportion of land area covered by forest
	26. Ratio of area protected to maintain biological diversity to surface area
	27. Energy use (kg oil equivalent) per $1 GDP (PPP)
	28. Carbon dioxide emissions per capita and consumption of ozone-depleting CFCs (Ozone depleting potential tons)
	29. Proportion of population using solid fuels
Target 10: Halve, by 2015, the proportion of people without sustainable access to safe drinking water	30. Proportion of population with sustainable access to an improved water source, urban and rural
	31. Proportion of people with access to improved sanitation
Target 11: By 2020, to have achieved a significant improvement in the lives of at least 100 million slum dwellers	32. Proportion of people with access to secure tenure
Goal 8: Develop a Global Partnership for Development	
Target 12: Develop further an open, rule-based, predictable, non-discriminatory trading and financial system. Includes a commitment to good governance, development, and poverty reduction – both nationally and internationally.	Some of the indicators listed below will be monitored separately for the least developed countries, Africa, landlocked countries and small island developing states

Table 10   (continued)

Goals and targets	Indicators
Target 13: Address the special needs of the least developed countries. Includes: tariff and quota free access for least developed country exports; enhanced programme of debt relief for relief for heavily indebted poor countries (HIPCs) and cancellation of official bilateral debt; and more generous official development assistance (ODA) for countries committed to poverty reduction.	*Official Development Assistance* 33. Net ODA as percentage of DAC donors' gross national income (GNI) (targets of 0.7 per cent in total and 0.15 per cent for least developed countries) 34. Proportion of ODA to basic social services (basic education, primary healthcare, nutrition, safe water and sanitation) 35. Proportion of ODA that is untied
Target 14: Address the special needs of landlocked countries and small island developing states (through Barbados Programme and Twenty-Second General Assembly provisions)	36. ODA received in landlocked countries as a proportion of their GNI 37. ODA received in small island developing states as a proportion of their GNI
	Market Access 38. Proportion of total developed-country imports (by value and excluding arms) from developing countries admitted free of duty 39. Average tariffs imposed by developed countries on agricultural products and textiles and clothing from developing countries 40. Agricultural support estimate for OECD countries as a percentage of their GDP 41. Proportion of ODA provided to help build trade capacity
Target 15: Deal comprehensively with the debt problems of developing countries through national and international measures in order to make debt sustainable in the long term	*Debt Sustainability* 42. Total number of countries that have reached their HIPC decision points and number that have reached their completion points (cumulative) 43. Debt relief committed under HIPC initiative 44. Debt service as a percentage of exports of goods and services
Target 16: In cooperation with developing countries, develop and implement strategies for decent and productive work for youth	45. Unemployment rate of 15–24 year olds, each sex and total
Target 17: In cooperation with pharmaceutical companies, provide access to affordable, essential drugs in developing countries	46. Proportion of population with access to affordable essential drugs on a sustainable basis

Table 10 (continued)

Goals and targets	Indicators
Target 18: In cooperation with the private sector, make available the benefits of new communications	47. Telephone lines and cellular subscribers per 100 people 48. A. Personal computers per 100 people 48. B. Internet users per 100 population

Source: World Bank (2004).

Why the MDGs are important and some problems

Targets can be seen as important for a number of reasons:

1. *Helping to define an organisation's purpose.* Targets can have a positive motivational role both within and across organisations. As a prominent supporter of the MDGs, the Department for International Development has posters that set out each target prominently displayed in its offices worldwide. The entrance foyer of the World Bank has a permanent display of the goals suspended from the ceiling. Where several development organisations are working in the same area, then targets can create a sense of common purpose across these agencies. Setting targets can be argued to have played the role of increasing the cohesiveness of the international development community, helping to focus the renewed attention to poverty in the 1990s, influencing both the country allocation of development aid towards lower-income countries and the sectoral allocation of development programmes towards areas of priority need for the poor (although there is debate as to what this means, some arguing that it is incorrectly equated with social service provision).
2. *Focus on outcomes*, offsetting the past tendency of performance systems to focus on inputs, helping orientate country programme and project design to priority areas. In the past donor agencies judged their performance based on how much money they disbursed, whereas the MDGs imply judgement on results, the wording indicating the link which exists between adoption of the MDGs and the current dominance of results-based management.
3. *Creating a basis for the accountability* of development agencies whose performance is to be judged on outcomes. DFID has a Public Service Agreement (a supposed 'contract with the public') containing MDG-like goals over a shorter time frame. The World Bank is moving towards monitoring MDG-related indicators as a basis for performance measurement.
4. *The goals create a basis for a rights-based approach*, by which the governments of developing countries can solicit international support for poverty-orientated initiatives, and the citizens of those countries have a basis for claiming rights to basic health and education.

However, focus on a single indicator can risk distorting programmes or sacrificing quality. For example, achieving the goal of universal primary education may mean getting more children into already overcrowded classrooms, with few materials and poorly motivated teachers, thus meeting the target for quantity at the expense of the quality of education. Meanwhile, achieving the target of having a national strategy for sustainable development does not mean that this strategy is implemented. Indeed, the resources put into developing a formal strategy may well divert resources from existing activities that are actually promoting sustainability.

Moreover, performance targets may simplify problems, focusing on what is identifiable and measurable while ignoring what really matters but is more complex. The complexity and multidimensionality of poverty is well understood. Even if a target is well identified it may have adverse organisational effects by discouraging innovation. Managers are likely to rely on tried and tested methods where there is a clear target to be achieved, rather than risk missing that targets by trying out a new approach. Targets may also undermine other forms of accountability. In the bid to satisfy performance criteria, particular problems or interests may be missed. Moreover, the focus on outcomes may deflect attention from the costs borne in achieving those outcomes, so that the efficiency focus of traditional management systems is lost.

Use of performance targets requires good data, which is unfortunately not always available for many MDG indicators, especially in low-income countries where monitoring is most important.

Finally, critics point out that development goals are not new. There have been many in the past which have long passed their target dates with scant if any progress towards the goal being met. What, they ask, is different about the MDGs? Defenders can answer that the MDGs appear to command broader international support than has been the case for previous targets and that, driven by the results agenda, agencies are genuinely using the goals to make a difference to how they do their work.

Progress toward goals
Progress toward the MDGs is mixed. Some countries, particularly those in East Asia , are well on track to meet the targets – and in some cases have already done so. But many others, notably in Sub-Saharan Africa, have made insufficient progress and are very unlikely to reach the targets. The former centrally planned economies of Eastern Europe experienced sharp declines in GDP, deterioration of social service provision and declining real transfers in the 1990s with a consequent increase in poverty and higher mortality. These countries may well not meet the goals, although in East Asia, the formerly centrally-planned economies of China and Vietnam are among the strongest performers.

Experience is also mixed by goal (see Table 11). Most countries are expected to achieve gender equality in schools and nearly two-thirds may attain the targets for access to water, and primary school completion. But close to half will not attain the target for maternal mortality and almost as many will fail to attain those for under-five mortality.

What will it take to reach the goals?
Issues underlying achieving the MDGs include (i) to what extent will the goals be met by relying on economic growth alone, or is government-backed social spending also

Table 11   Progress towards the MDGs

	Likely	Possible	Unlikely	Very unlikely	No data	Total
Number of countries						
Child malnutrition	23	11	5	21	92	153
Primary school completion	45	28	19	16	44	153
Gender equality in school	75	14	10	9	45	153
Child mortality	31	43	30	21	29	153
Maternal mortality	31	27	20	31	44	153
HIV/AIDS prevalence	38	11	13	22	69	153
Access to water	22	15	19	0	97	153
As percentage of countries with data						
Child malnutrition	38	19	9	35		100
Primary school completion	42	26	18	15		100
Gender equality in school	69	13	9	8		100
Child mortality	25	35	24	17		100
Maternal mortality	28	25	19	28		100
HIV/AIDS prevalence	45	14	15	26		100
Access to water	39	27	34	0		100

Source: Carvalho (2003, pp. 63–4).

required? (ii) how to build political will, and (iii) ensuring adequate government systems are in place.

Realistic projections of likely growth rates for most developing countries, or even optimistic ones, imply a shortfall in meeting many of the targets, with few met in the poorest countries where the need is greatest. The conclusion from this point may be either to further accelerate growth or to strengthen channels for better social outcomes independent of growth. Some would argue that the growth approach has been pursued for the last two decades, or longer, and proved to provide an inadequate social return. But others would respond that where growth performance is poor, the right policies (whatever they may be, but most holding this position claim them to be a market-based open economy with a democratic political system) have yet to be properly implemented.

The call for greater social spending assumes that governments will be willing to do this, usually diverting resources from activities that benefit the better-off to ones benefiting the less well-off. Such policies may prove difficult to implement for political reasons, even where there is the will to do so. When politics are not a constraint then the capacity to implement may be, especially if the required policies require an expansion in service delivery at local level. In the short run, funds may have to be devoted to capacity development, rather than actual service delivery.

Conclusion

The MDGs are the latest in a long line of development targets, which have a sorry history as failed promises. There is, however, reason for optimism that the new goals are being taken more seriously and having an impact on how some development agencies do their business – DFID is probably the leader in this respect, but others are coming into line. But, the statement of a goal is not the same as a strategy as to how to reach it. The adoption of the MDGs has not resolved debates at the centre of development policy, leaving considerable room for disagreement as to how the goals might best be met.

HOWARD WHITE

References and further reading

Black, Richard and Howard White (2004), *Targeting Development: Critical Perspectives on the Millennium Development Goals*, London and New York: Routledge.

Carvalho, Soniya (2003), *2002 Annual Review of Development Effectiveness: Achieving Development Outcomes: The Millennium Challenge*, Washington, DC: World Bank, http://lnweb18.worldbank.org/oed/oeddoclib. nsf/DocUNIDViewForJavaSearch/57BCB3B42521CBAE85256CDE006DEC0D/$file/ARDE_2002.pdf, 22 February 2005.

UN (2000), *United Nations Millennium Declaration,* Document A/RES/55/2, New York: United Nations, www. un.org/millennium/declaration/ares 552e.pdf.

UN (2001), *Road Map Towards the Implementation of the United Nations Millennium Declaration: Report of the Secretary-General*, Document A/56/326, New York: United Nations.

World Bank (2004), 'About the Goals', www.developmentgoals.org/About_the_goals.htm, 17 December 2004.

Missing Women

In contrast to most industrialised countries, where females outnumber males by a considerable margin, there are a number of developing countries, including most countries of South Asia, the Middle East and North Africa as well as China and Taiwan, where the number of males exceeds the number of females. While this imbalance had been known for some time and was blamed on differential neglect of females in these regions (for example, Visaria, 1961; D'Souza and Chen, 1980), the issue rose to much greater prominence in development policy discussions when Amartya Sen claimed in the late 1980s that up to 100 million women were 'missing' in the developing world due to gender discrimination in survival opportunities (for example, Sen, 1989, 1990a). To him, 'missing women' referred to additional females that would be alive today in the affected regions had there been equal treatment of the sexes in the distribution of survival-related goods. It is thus a way to assess the cumulative survival disadvantage women have suffered, leading to increasing decimation of their cohorts and thus representing the most serious form of gender discrimination. Sen's work gave rise to three strands of literature that will be briefly reviewed here. One considers measurement issues across space and time, another examines the causes of this female disadvantage, and a third examines policy issues.

Measurement issues

Central to the measurement of missing women is a comparison between the actual sex ratio (the number of males divided by the number of females) in a country with an expected sex ratio that would obtain if the sexes had been treated equally in the distribution of survival-related goods. If the actual exceeds the expected sex ratio, the difference between the two is the percentage of females missing in a country (see columns 7 and 9 in Table 12). And holding the number of males constant, the additional females that would have to be alive in order to equate the actual with the expected sex ratio is then the absolute number of missing women (see columns 6 and 8 in Table 12).

Table 12 Missing women, latest estimates and trends

	Latest estimates (mid-1990s to early 2000s)						Previous estimates (1980s to early 1990s)	
	(2) Actual number of women	(3) Actual sex ratio	(4) Expected sex ratio	(5) Expected number of women	(6) Missing women	(7) Percentage missing	(8) Missing women	(9) Percentage missing
China	612.3	1.067	1.001	653.2	40.9	6.7	34.6	6.3
Taiwan	10.8	1.049	1.002	11.3	0.5	4.7	0.7	7.3
South Korea	22.2	1.008	1.000	22.4	0.2	0.7	−0.0	−0.1
India	495.7	1.072	0.993	534.8	39.1	7.9	38.4	9.4
Pakistan	62.7	1.081	1.003	67.6	4.9	7.8	4.3	10.8
Bangladesh	63.4	1.038	0.996	66.1	2.7	4.2	3.8	8.9
Nepal	11.6	0.997	0.992	11.7	0.1	0.5	0.6	7.7
Sri Lanka	8.6	1.005	1.006	8.6	0.0	0.0	0.3	3.4
West Asia	92.0	1.043	1.002	95.8	3.8	4.2	3.9	7.1
of which: Turkey	27.9	1.027	1.003	28.5	0.7	2.4	0.8	3.2
Syria	6.7	1.047	1.016	6.9	0.2	3.1	0.4	5.0
Afghanistan	11.1	1.054	0.964	12.1	1.0	9.3	0.6	9.7
Iran	29.5	1.033	0.996	30.6	1.1	3.7	1.1	4.5
Egypt	29.0	1.048	1.003	30.3	1.3	4.5	1.2	5.1
Algeria	14.5	1.018	1.005	14.7	0.2	1.2	0.3	2.7
Tunisia	4.3	1.021	1.000	4.4	0.1	2.1	0.2	4.5
Sub-Saharan Africa	307.0	0.987	0.970	312.5	5.5	1.8	4.9	1.9
Total (World)	1774.8				101.3	5.7	94.7	6.5

Note: Actual and expected sex ratios refer to the number of males per females in the entire population. Turkey and Syria are subsumed in West Asia and are therefore not added separately. The negative numbers of missing women in South Korea (columns 8 and 9) suggest that there was excess male mortality in that country at the time. The years for the latest (previous) estimates are: China 2000 (1990), Taiwan 1999 (1990), South Korea 1995 (1985), India 2001 (1991), Pakistan 1998 (1981), Bangladesh 2001 (1981), Nepal 2001 (1981), Sri Lanka 1991 (1981), West Asia 2000 (1985), Afghanistan 2000 (1979), Iran 1996 (1986), Egypt 1996 (1986), Algeria 1998 (1987), Tunisia 1994 (1984), and Sub-Saharan Africa 2000 (1990).

Source: Klasen and Wink (2003).

While the actual sex ratio is based on the most recent census count or demographic population estimate, the central issue in this calculation is how to estimate the expected sex ratio. As in no society of the world are males and females treated the same or behave the same in ways that are relevant for health and mortality (for example, there are significant differences between males and females in most countries in rates of alcohol and nicotine abuse, in traffic behaviour and in violence against self and others; see for example, Waldron, 1993), there is no obvious standard against which to assess the current sex-specific mortality conditions in a country. This problem is compounded by the fact that there is a slight imbalance of the sexes at birth (there are between 3 and 7 per cent more males at birth) and that females have a distinct biological survival advantage in infancy and old age (and possibly in between as well, although here the literature is less conclusive due to the problems stated above, see ibid.).

In order to get a rough idea of the magnitude of the problem, Sen (1988, 1989, 1990a) used the sex ratio prevailing in Sub-Saharan Africa as the expected sex ratio for his calculation of missing women and arrived at a figure of close to 100 million in South Asia, China, Egypt and West Asia alone in the late 1980s.

Ansley Coale (1991) picked up this issue but used a more detailed methodology for estimating the expected sex ratio. Instead of assuming a constant expected sex ratio as Sen had done, Coale considered in his calculations that the expected sex ratio depends on the sex ratio at birth, the sex-specific mortality across the age groups, the age structure of the population (as in younger populations one would expect more males due to the higher sex ratio at birth, while in older populations the survival advantage of females leads to a more female population as they predominate in older cohorts), and sex-specific international migration. He assumed a constant sex ratio at birth (that prevailing in industrialised countries of about 1.06) and assumed that the 'biological' pattern of sex-specific mortality (that is, in the absence of discrimination) would approximate the mortality patterns of the so-called West Model Life Tables, which summarise the mortality experience of some populations in Western Europe and of European descent in the late nineteenth to the early twentieth centuries. With these assumptions, he arrived at a figure of about 60 million missing women in the early 1990s in South Asia, China, West Asia and Egypt.

Klasen (1994) argued that the assumptions of a constant sex ratio at birth and the West Model Life Tables were underestimating the number of missing women. Using a (empirically derived and more plausible) variable sex ratio at birth (depending on the overall mortality conditions in a country) and a different set of Model Life Tables (the East Tables) which arguably contained less gender bias in mortality, he arrived at a figure of 90 million for the same countries and time period considered by Sen and Coale. All three authors agreed that the problem of 'missing women' was one of the most serious human catastrophes of the twentieth century that had received too little attention and that urgent policy attention was needed to address this massive gender inequity in survival.

Klasen and Wink (2002, 2003) reviewed the debates surrounding measurement and used new census information and population estimates from the late 1990s and the early 2000s to update the number of missing women using their methodology (as well as Sen's and Coale's). Their estimate (based on their preferred method) is reproduced in Table 12, and shows that between the 1980s and early 1990s and the late 1990s and early 2000s, the absolute number of missing women increased worldwide from about 95 million to

102 million. In relative terms, however, the percentage of missing women declined some-what from 6.5 to 5.7 per cent. Particularly noteworthy are significant reductions in the per-centage of missing women in Taiwan, Pakistan, Bangladesh, Nepal, Sri Lanka, and all countries of the Middle-East and North Africa. There has also been a slight reduction in the share of missing women in India, while the share of missing women increased in China. Thus there appear to have been some welcome improvements in some regions, but gender bias in mortality continued to exert a massive human toll.

Causes of female disadvantage

Many detailed studies have assessed particular aspects of this female survival disadvan-tage. It appears clear that most of the survival disadvantage arises in infancy and child-hood, is particularly severe in rural areas of the affected regions, and appears to particularly affect later-born girls in families with several daughters (for example, Chen et al., 1981; Banister, 1987; Das Gupta, 1987; Muhuri and Preston, 1991; Basu, 1992; Banister and Coale, 1994). There also appears to be significant regional differences within the affected countries, most notably in India where gender bias in mortality is particularly severe in North India, and, on average, hardly present at all in some southern states (for example, Drèze and Sen, 1995; Klasen and Wink, 2002, 2003).

Most analysts agree that the most important mechanism that leads to higher female mortality is related to unequal access to healthcare, while there is much less evidence for unequal access to food (for example, Chen et al, 1981; Basu, 1992; Hill and Upchurch, 1995; Alderman and Gertler, 1997; Timaeus et al., 1998; Croll, 2000; Hazarika, 2000). In recent years, the increasing recourse to sex-selective abortions appears to have addition-ally contributed significantly to generating 'missing women' in China, Taiwan and South Korea, and most recently also in India (Banister and Coale, 1994; Park and Cho, 1995; Croll, 2000; Junhong, 2001; Registrar General, 2001). This is also held to be the main reason for the worsening of the problem in China and the relatively small improvements in India (Klasen and Wink, 2002, 2003).

As far as underlying socio-economic determinants of the phenomenon are concerned, it appears that 'investment' considerations appear to play an important role (for example, Rosenzweig and Schultz, 1982; Dyson and Moore, 1983; Klasen, 1999; Croll, 2000). Parents selectively invest in sons in order to secure their own old-age support in systems where sons are mainly responsible for the old-age support of the parents or where sons are important to continue the family name and carry out important symbolic functions (such as ancestor worship). This is aggravated by marriage systems involving substantial dowry payments, thereby increasing the costs of raising girls significantly. In addition, the female disadvantage is also affected by a poor bargaining position of women which in turn is related to their limited access to education, employment and earning in most of the affected countries (for example, Sen, 1990b; Klasen, 1998, 1999). These factors are also able to explain most of the regional variation between countries in excess female mortality as well as the differentials within countries such as India (for example, Murthi et al., 1995; Klasen and Wink, 2002, 2003). The recently observed reduction in excess female mortality in most regions is related to some improvements in women's education, employment and earnings opportunities (which raised female bargaining power and increased the 'investment' value of daughters) as well as rising prosperity in some regions which has lessened the need to ration access to health and nutrition (Klasen and Wink, 2002, 2003).

Policy issues

The massive inequity in survival opportunities poses a serious challenge to development policy makers and this issue has consequently been the focus of considerable policy research (for example, Drèze and Sen, 1989, 1995; World Bank, 2001). From the discussion above, it appears clear that strengthening women's education, employment and earning opportunities is one way to reduce the incidence of excess female mortality.

In addition, however, there are other ways in which state policy has served to affect the discrimination of women in access to survival-related goods. In countries and regions where the state has committed itself to providing free education, healthcare and nutrition to all (or at least the poor), as in Sri Lanka, the Indian state of Kerala, or pre-reform China (prior to 1979), the need for households to differentially ration these resources was greatly diminished, which helped to reduce gender bias in mortality. In Kerala, there is no evidence of gender bias in mortality, and in Sri Lanka is has entirely disappeared from a very high level in previous decades (for example, Drèze and Sen, 1989, 1995; Klasen, 1999; Klasen and Wink, 2002, 2003), and also in China gender bias in mortality was declining between the 1950s and the 1970s (for example, Klasen, 1993).

In contrast, the market reforms in China introduced in the late 1970s (which, from an efficiency point of view, have been a great success) have sharply reduced the public provision of health and nutrition and thereby allowed old discriminatory practices within households to resurface again (Banister, 1987; Drèze and Sen, 1989, 1995; Klasen, 1993, 1999).

More seriously, the strictly enforced one-child policy in China, introduced in the late 1970s and still in force (although recently in a somewhat less strict fashion), has, as an unintended consequence, sharply increased parental efforts to ensure that the one child allowed will be a son. As a result, parents have adopted a range of strategies to ensure this, ranging from hiding daughters, giving them up for (illegal) adoption, and increasingly relying on sex-selective abortions to prevent daughters from being born in the first place (for example, Johansson and Nygren, 1991; Banister and Coale, 1994; Croll, 2000; Junhong, 2001; Klasen, 2003). The sex ratio at birth in China has risen from a normal level of about 1.08 in 1982 to 1.17 in 2000, showing the dramatic effect of sex-selective abortions (Klasen, 2003; Klasen and Wink, 2003). Prohibiting the use of sex-selective abortions (or even pre-birth sex determination) as has been done in China and India has done little to curb the problem as long as the incentive to have sons has not been tackled.

These debates have shown that there are ways to tackle the problem of gender bias in mortality. In the short term, provision of free healthcare, education and food can have a significant impact, and abandoning coercive family planning policies would also make a significant contribution. In the medium term, improvements in women's education, employment and earnings are likely to reduce these problems. But a sustainable long-term solution must also address the underlying social, economic and cultural factors that lead parents to differentially invest in children of the two sexes.

STEPHAN KLASEN

References

Alderman, H. and P. Gertler (1997), 'Family resources and gender differences in human capital investments: the demand for children's medical care in Pakistan', in L. Haddad, J. Hoddinott and H. Alderman (eds), *Intrahousehold Resource Allocation in Developing Countries: Models, Methods, and Policy*, Baltimore, MD: Johns Hopkins University Press, pp. 231–48.

Banister, J. (1987), *China's Changing Population*, Oxford and New York: Oxford University Press.

Banister, J. and A.J. Coale (1994), 'Five decades of missing females in China', *Demography*, **31**, 459–79.

Basu, A. (1992), *Culture, the Status of Women, and Demographic Behaviour*, Oxford: Oxford University Press.

Chen, L.C., E. Huq and S. D'Souza (1981), 'Sex bias in the family allocation of food and healthcare in rural Bangladesh', *Population and Development Review*, **7**, 55–70.

Coale, A. (1991), 'Excess female mortality and the balance of the sexes', *Population and Development Review*, **17**, 517–23.

Croll, E. (2000), *Endangered Daughters*, London: Routledge.

D'Souza, S. and L. Chen (1980), 'Sex differences in mortality in rural Bangladesh', *Population and Development Review*, **6**, 257–70.

Das Gupta, M. (1987), 'Selective discrimination against females in rural Punjab, India', *Population and Development Review*, **13**, 77–100.

Drèze, J. and A. Sen (1989), *Hunger and Public Action*, Oxford: Clarendon.

Drèze, J. and A. Sen (1995), *India Economic Development and Social Opportunity*, Oxford: Clarendon.

Dyson, T. and M. Moore (1983), 'On kinship structure, female autonomy, and demographic behaviour in India', *Population and Development Review*, **9**, 35–57.

Hazarika, G. (2000), 'Gender differences in children's nutrition and access to healthcare in Pakistan', *Journal of Development Studies*, **37**, 73–92.

Hill, K and D.M. Upchurch (1995), 'Gender differences in child health: evidence from the demographic and health surveys', *Population and Development Review*, **21** (1), 127–51.

Johansson, S. and O. Nygren (1991), 'The missing girls of China – a new demographic account', *Population and Development Review*, **17**, 35–51.

Junhong, C. (2001), 'Prenatal sex determination and sex-selective abortion in rural central China', *Population and Development Review*, **27**, 259–82.

Klasen, S. (1993), 'Human development and women's lives in a restructured eastern bloc', in A. Schipke and A. Taylor (eds), *The Economics of Transformation: Theory and Practise in the New Market Economics*, New York: Springer, pp. 253–93.

Klasen, S. (1994), 'Missing women reconsidered', *World Development*, **22**, 1061–71.

Klasen, S. (1998), 'Marriage, bargaining, and intrahousehold resource allocation', *Journal of Economic History*, **58**, 432–67.

Klasen, S. (1999), 'Gender inequality in mortality in comparative perspective', mimeo, University of Munich.

Klasen, S. (2003), 'Sex selection', in P.G. Demeny and G. McNicoll (eds), *Encyclopedia of Population*, volume 2, Basingstoke and New York: Macmillan, pp. 878–81.

Klasen, S, and C. Wink (2002), 'Is there a turning-point in gender bias in mortality? An update on the number of "missing women"', *Population and Development Review*, **28** (2), 285–312.

Klasen, S. and C. Wink (2003), 'Missing women: revisiting the debate', *Feminist Economics*, **9**, 263–99.

Muhuri, P.K. and S.H. Preston (1991), 'Effects of family composition on mortality differentials by sex among children in Matlab, Bangladesh', *Population and Development Review*, **17**, 415–34.

Murthi, M., A. Guio and J. Drèze (1995), 'Mortality, fertility, and gender bias in India: a district-level analysis', *Population and Development Review*, **21**, 745–82.

Park, C.B. and N.H. Cho (1995). 'Consequences of son preference in a low fertility society: imbalance in the sex ratio at birth', *Population and Development Review*, **21**, 59–84.

Registrar General (2001), Provisional Population Totals, Census of India Series 1, Paper 1 of 2001, New Delhi: Ministry of Home Affairs.

Rosenzweig, M. and T.P. Schultz (1982), 'Market opportunities, genetic endowments, and intra-family resource distribution', *American Economic Review*, **72**, 803–15.

Sen, A. (1988), 'Africa and India: what do we have to learn from each other?', in K. Arrow (ed.), *The Balance Between Industry and Agriculture: Proceedings of the Eighth World Congress of the International Economics Association*, New York: St Martin's Press, pp. 105–37.

Sen, A. (1989), 'Women's survival as a development problem', *Bulletin of the American Academy of Arts and Sciences*, **43**, 14–29.

Sen, A. (1990a), 'Gender and cooperative conflict', in I. Tinker (ed.), *Persistent Inequalities – Women and World Development*, Oxford and New York: Oxford University Press, pp. 123–49.

Sen, A. (1990b), 'More than 100 million women are missing', *The New York Review of Books*, 20 December, pp. 61–66.

Timaeus, I., K. Harris and F. Fairbairn (1998), 'Can use of healthcare explain sex differentials in mortality in the developing world?', in United Nations (ed.), *Too Young to Die: Genes or Gender*, New York: United Nations, pp. 154–78.

Visaria, P. (1961), *The Sex Ratio of the Population of India*, Monograph 10, Census of India 1961, New Delhi: Office of the Registrar General.

Waldron, I. (1993), 'Recent trends in sex mortality ratios for adults in developed countries', *Social Science & Medicine*, **36**, 451–62.

World Bank (2001), *Engendering Development*, Washington, DC: World Bank.

Modernisation Theory

Modernisation theory was the dominant sociological theory of development for much of the 1950s and 1960s. Its principal claim was that development was a process in which 'societies' – defined as nation states – pass through similar stages of development on the road to an end state. This end state to which 'development' aspired was a mass consumer society, not unlike the United States in the 1950s. The claims of modernisation theory can be traced back to both the eighteenth-century Enlightenment and the classical sociology of the nineteenth and early twentieth centuries, although modernisation theory essentially downplayed the critical accounts of capitalism and rationalisation that could be found in the works of Karl Marx and Max Weber. In the post-war period, influenced by the functionalist sociology of Talcott Parsons (1962), modern societies were contrasted with traditional societies in such a way that the former were said to represent progress when compared to the latter. It was argued that modern societies were meritocracies in which the best achievers rose to the top, and raised standards for the whole society through investment and wealth creation. This was in contrast to traditional societies, where elites were socially reproduced through birth and inheritance rather than talent, and they tended to consume rather than reinvest their wealth.

Modernisation theorists argued that development represented a transition from tradition to modernity. This was to be achieved through copying at least some of the (perceived) characteristics of Western societies, such as the development of entrepreneurship and the borrowing of advanced technology. Enhanced contact with the West was considered desirable as it hastened the transition to modernity. There were variations in terms of the explanation for the movement from one state to another, such as McClelland's (1961) social psychological explanation based on the development of the *n* factor. This factor was regarded as the development of values based on the need to achieve, which essentially meant an increase in levels of entrepreneurship and innovation. Rostow (1960) put forward a five-stage theory of development, in which nation states rigidly pass through a similar developmental sequence: traditional society; preconditions for take-off; take-off; the drive to maturity; and the age of high mass consumption. The preconditions for take-off and the take-off stages were considered to be the two most important, with the former removing obstacles to growth through the development of entrepreneurial ambition and reinvestment, and the latter consolidating these key features of the development process.

The relationship between this theory and concrete development strategies in the 1950s and 1960s is ambiguous. On the one hand, newly independent states developed pro-industrialisation strategies of import substitution on the grounds that specialisation in primary products led to trading disadvantages in the world economy based on unequal terms of trade. Modernisation theory had little to say on this subject but tended to assume that as with relations with the West more generally, trade was a benign process that promoted development in what had become known as the Third World. At the same time, import substitution industrialisation did involve some protection for selected producers in the Third World, and recognition that specialisation in trading in primary products may have had some gains but these were unequally distributed. These points laid the basis for more radical theories of dependency and underdevelopment in the 1960s and 1970s, which more firmly rejected the claims of modernisation theory. On the other hand, the pro-industrialisation strategies were aimed at *catching up* with the West through the development of advanced technology through independent nation states. In this way, economic growth and development became essentially interchangeable terms for both modernisation theory and development strategy. In these respects the arguments of pro-industrialisers were not so far removed from modernisation theory.

From the late 1960s, modernisation theory increasingly went out of fashion. Perhaps above all, modernisation theory lacked a convincing account of the *causes* of modernisation. Entrepreneurship and innovation may well be important factors in modernising processes, but the question remains as to whether such individual behaviour *reflects* (or at least is only part of) a process of wider social transformation. Of great relevance in this respect is Marx's account of the 'primitive accumulation' of capital through the displacement of peasants from direct access to land, and the resultant generalisation of both wage labour and commodity production – and with these the development of market imperatives which forced 'entrepreneurs' to accumulate or go out of business. The clear implication of this approach is that the kind of entrepreneurial behaviour associated with reinvestment and innovation only takes place in a particular social context, rather than simply being a product of the adoption of certain values.

More broadly, the West as an ideal construct was increasingly challenged in the context of heightened conflict within these societies, as well as the belated recognition that it made little sense to talk about the West in the singular – a point that also applied in many respects to developing countries. Related to these points, the rigid dichotomy of modernity and tradition was increasingly challenged, as such concepts were too vague and overgeneralised, and ignored the continued existence and reinvention of 'tradition' in supposedly modern societies (Webster, 1990). For instance, in Britain the political system continues to give some weight to 'traditional' institutions such as the monarchy and the House of Lords. Conversely, processes of 'modernisation' have not only eliminated but at times actually reinforced 'tradition', in response to the massive social upheavals, inequalities and unevenness associated with 'development'. It therefore makes little sense to discuss Islam, for example, as a traditional religion in the modern world. There are a great variety of Islams, and these are linked in diverse ways to processes of modernisation. Some versions of Islam may attempt to revive tradition, but this is through a process of ideological reinvention, which is in part a response to the wider social and political processes associated with modernisation. For example, the 'Islamic revolution' in Iran in 1979 cannot be understood without some analysis of Western political intervention in that country in the 1950s, and the attempted modernisation process that followed under the authoritarian rule of the Pahlavi regime. Clearly then, modernisation is a far more contradictory and ambiguous process than the linear model which assumes that 'tradition' will simply be abandoned with the onset of development.

Moreover, it was also increasingly argued from the late 1960s that modernisation theory failed to see any conflict between 'advanced' and 'Third World' societies. Indeed, underdevelopment theory went further, and argued that the reason why some countries became advanced was precisely because they had exploited Third World nations. Modernisation theory was therefore guilty of a dualist analysis in which modernity (development) was rigidly separated from tradition (undevelopment), when in fact the former actually occurred for some countries through the exploitation of the latter (Frank, 1969). In this respect the whole world was modern, or capitalist, and some areas developed through the underdevelopment of others. This point applied not only to the colonial era, but also the post-colonial era through the mechanisms of unequal trade and multinational company exploitation.

This theory of underdevelopment was not without its own set of problems, not least that the poorest or most underdeveloped societies were usually those that received low amounts of foreign investment and traded relatively small amounts with Western countries. On the other hand, the fact that Western countries were increasingly investing and trading among themselves undermined the developmental optimism of modernisation theory (Kiely, 1995). It was clear that the West (or more accurately, capitalist companies) was less interested in development (or indeed underdevelopment), than in finding the most profitable investment opportunities across the globe. This meant a failure to modernise much of the Third World, and a relative marginalisation for many countries from the world economy – something that versions of dependency theory at least attempted to grasp (Kay, 1989). Of course such marginalisation was never absolute, and there was investment in certain sectors for market access, cheap labour and raw materials, but this was rarely on a sufficient level to achieve development in the sense of catching up with the West. In cases where investment levels were high, development was often hindered by national elites that were not so much criticised for their 'traditionalism', and more often championed for their anti-communism and their openness to partnerships with Western allies. There are therefore strong grounds for suggesting that modernisation theory was actually little more than ideology, a crude justification for Western economic, political and strategic interests in the Cold War era. This suspicion is also seemingly confirmed by the 'naivety' of the theory's analysis of Western societies as meritocracies which, applied to the United States in the segregationist 1950s, smacks of nothing else but crude apology.

On the other hand, and in a less crudely stagist form, modernisation theory made something of a comeback from the 1980s onwards, both in academic circles (Fukuyama, 1992) and in the wider political context. The context for this revival was the wave of democratisation of many Third World countries in the 1980s and 1990s, the neoliberal turn in development, the end of the Cold War and perceived victory of the West, and the rise of globalisation rhetoric. Together these factors led to the argument that there was no viable alternative to Western-style liberal democracies, which together with the promotion of market-friendly economic policies would lead to some form of 'catch-up' with Western economies (ibid.). This argument was less explicitly tied to earlier modernisation approaches, and did not put forward a rigid model whereby societies went through various stages of development on the road to modernity. Rather, catch-up would occur through the promotion of an appropriate model of limited government or 'good governance', which would draw on the opportunities granted by the world economy (World Bank, 1992). Countries would therefore develop not so much through state-directed policies of import substitution industrialisation, but through neoliberal policies of open trading relationships in which countries exercised their comparative advantage through free and open competition in the level playing field of the world economy. More broadly, some of these arguments were accompanied by a discourse that divided the world into the civilised world (based on liberal democracies and market economies) and rogue states (based on dictatorships and support for terrorism). This account of the world was influential in the 1990s, and increased enormously in the early twenty-first century, in the context of the terrorist attacks against the United States on 11 September 2001, and the wars against Afghanistan and Iraq that followed.

There are enormous problems with this new version of modernisation theory however. Neoliberalism underestimates the extent to which some states exercise double standards, pressurising developing countries to liberalise while they maintain protectionist policies at home. Moreover, even in a situation of open market competition, such competition is likely to be very unequal as established producers enjoy competitive advantages over 'late developers' – in other words, free trade does not constitute a level playing field (Chang, 2002). The theoretical case for import substitution therefore stands, even if the particular forms that it has taken have often been problematic. It is also unclear whether liberal democracy does actually provide the institutional conditions for sustained economic growth, and anyway the commitment of Western countries to promoting democracy in developing countries is highly selective and based more on power politics and less on principle. Moreover, it is highly unlikely that the outcome of 'humanitarian wars' will be the promotion of liberal democracy and longer-term development. In this respect the discourse of humanitarian intervention is close to the classical modernisation theory of the 1950s and early 1960s, as both can be regarded as ideological justifications for the expansion of certain forms of Western power in the world system.

One final criticism of modernisation theory highlights its ideological approach, but at the same time reminds us that a complete rejection of all of its claims has its own set of problems. Post-development theory argues that the development project is inherently Western and based on the exercise of power over subject peoples in the South (Escobar, 1995). The critique here is not so much about whether developing countries *can* develop (either through state- or market-directed policies), and more a case of whether they *should* develop. Post-development theories suggest that an alternative is support for social movements that are said to reject the inherent Westernisation of the development project, and which support a variety of alternatives to the homogenising discourse of development. However, it is unclear that social movements *completely* reject the development project, though of course they often question many of its ethnocentric assumptions. It is one thing to reject the expansion of commodity production, consumer culture and the fetishism of the individual, but quite another to reject the expansion of basic needs, human rights and political participation (Sutcliffe, 1999). Classical modernisation and new modernisation theories may downplay the power relations intrinsic to processes of 'actually existing development', and the downsides of Western-led modernity, but they at least show a commitment to political and social progress that is often lacking in other critical accounts. The problem however, is that too often both the means (Westernise through technology, aspirational values or market forces) and the ends (the West as ideal) are problematic. Therefore, a commitment to development needs to be separated from a commitment to modernisation theories, and the debate continues to take place *within* rather than outside the discourse of development.

RAY KIELY

References

Chang, Ha-Joon (2002), *Kicking Away the Ladder*, London: Anthem.
Escobar, Arturo (1995), *Encountering Development*, Princeton, NJ: Princeton University Press.
Frank, Andre Gunder (1969), *Capitalism and Underdevelopment in Latin America*, New York: Monthly Review Press.
Fukuyama, Francis (1992), *The End of History and the Last Man*, London: Penguin.
Kay, C. (1989), *Latin American Theories of Development and Underdevelopment*, London: Routledge.
Kiely, Ray (1995), *Sociology and Development: The Impasse and Beyond*, London: University College London Press.
McClelland, David (1961), *The Achieving Society*, New York: Free Press.
Parsons, Talcott (1962), *Working Papers in the Theory of Action*, London: Collier-Macmillan.
Rostow, Walt (1960), *The Stages of Economic Growth*, Cambridge: Cambridge University Press.
Sutcliffe, Bob (1999), 'The place of development in theories of imperialism and globalization', in Ronaldo Munck and Denis O'Hearn (eds), *Critical Development Theory*, London: Zed Books, pp. 135–54.
Webster, Andrew (1990), *Introduction to the Sociology of Development*, London: Macmillan, chapter 3.
World Bank (1992), *Governance and Development*, Washington, DC: World Bank.

Myrdal, Gunnar (1898–1987)

If a man has been successively university professor, government adviser, member of parliament, director of a study of American blacks, cabinet minister, bank director, chairman of a planning commission, international civil servant, head of an institute of conflict research, author of a massive study of Asian development and a Nobel Prize winner; if, as a citizen of a small country, he has occupied these positions in different countries and has travelled widely, we should not be surprised if he comes to ask himself some fundamental questions. Gunnar Myrdal was born in 1898 in the province of Darlana in Sweden. He attributed his faith in the Puritan ethics and his egalitarianism to his sturdy farming background.

Through Myrdal's work run five lines of criticism of orthodox or mainstream economic and social theory (his last collection of essays is appositely called *Against the Stream*, 1973). First, his appeal for greater realism, or, as he calls it, 'adequacy to reality', is not a critique of abstraction or selection or simplification. As a most sophisticated social scientist, he is, of course, not only aware but also insists that all theorising must abstract and select. His criticism is that the abstractions follow the wrong lines, that irrelevant features are selected and relevant ones ignored. He called the former 'opportunistic selection' or 'illegitimate isolation', and the latter 'opportunistic ignorance', for the ignored features suit the ideological bias of the theory. Misplaced aggregation and illegitimate isolation contribute to the unrealistic character of the models, which serves certain interests. Underlying his analysis there was a sociology of knowledge, belief and opinion.

A second line of criticism is the narrow definitions of concepts such as development, economic growth and welfare. The actual needs and valuations (much more than narrow self-interest) of people, he argued, not the abstractions of statisticians or the empty constructs of economists and philosophers, should be the basis for formulating policy objectives. Both the American creed in his book on the American blacks *An American Dilemma* (1994) and the modernisation ideals in *Asian Drama* (1968) are formulated as springing from actual valuations of the people. The United Nations accepted this approach in 1969 as the integrated or unified strategy of development, and the United Nations Research Institute for Social Development, on the Governing Council of which Myrdal sat, was entrusted with research on it. The social indicator movement, and later the basic needs and the human development approaches, have also derived strength from it.

His third criticism is directed at the narrow definitions and the self-imposed limits of academic disciplines. The essence of the institutional approach advocated by Myrdal is to bring to bear all relevant knowledge and techniques on the analysis of a problem. According to this institutional approach 'history and politics, theories and ideologies, economic structures and levels, social stratification, agriculture and industry, population developments, health and education and so on must be studied not in isolation but in their mutual relationships' (1968, vol. 1, p. x.) In an interdependent social system, he used to say, there are no economic problems, no psychological problems, no anthropological problems, no political problems, no social problems, there are just *problems*; and all these problems are complex.

His fourth line of criticism is directed at spurious objectivity that, under the pretence of scientific analysis, conceals political valuations and interests. He criticised the way in which economists deduce political conclusions and recommendations from pure, theoretical, positive analysis, normative content from 'the nature of things'. Myrdal argued that this pseudo-science should be replaced by explicit valuations, in the light of which analysis can be conducted and policies advocated. He was not so naive as to believe that simple specification of these value premises is easy or even possible at all, and has shown how complicated and complex the nexus between valuations and facts can be. But ever since his youthful and iconoclastic *The Political Element in the Development of Economic Theory* (1930) he has persistently fought the legacy of natural law and utilitarianism, according to which we can derive recommendations from facts. 'The greatest good for the greatest number' or 'the maximization of social welfare' were targets for his critique.

A fifth line of criticism throughout his writings is directed against biases and twisted terminology. He lays bare the opportunistic interests and the 'diplomacy by terminology' underlying the use of such concepts as 'United Nations' (which should be about governments, not, as the Charter says, 'we the peoples . . .'), 'international' (which should often read 'intergovernmental'), 'values', 'welfare', 'bilateral aid', 'unemployment', 'the free world', 'international cooperation' and 'developing countries'. Consider the history of the terminology of underdevelopment: from backward regions (not yet countries!) to underdeveloped countries to less developed countries to developing countries to emerging countries. We nowadays read newspaper headlines such as 'stagnation in developing countries' or even 'decline in developing countries' without blinking an eyelid. Amartya Sen writes: 'Take the term "developing economy," which refers to countries that are lacking in development, whether or not they are actually "developing" in any under-standable sense. The usage clearly does confound the *need* for development with its *occur-rence* – it is like defining a hungry person as "eating" ' (Sen, 1994, pp. 315–16, original emphasis).

The features against which these lines of criticism are advanced are combined in the technocrat. He isolates economic (or other technical) relations from their social context; he neglects social and political variables and thereby ministers to the vested interests that might otherwise be hurt; he pretends to scientific objectivity and is socially and culturally insensitive. Since the majority of experts, academics and managers are of this type, Myrdal had ruffled many feathers.

An important idea in Myrdal's arsenal is that of circular or cumulative causation (or the vicious – or virtuous – circle) first fully developed in *An American Dilemma*. Traditional theory explains inequality between individuals, regions and countries as the result of differential resource 'endowments'. But resources are also the result, not only the cause, of income and wealth. Unimproved land, which is an endowment, is important for resource-based industries, but not for processing and manufacturing. It is the resource-poor countries, such as Israel, Hong Kong, Singapore, Taiwan, South Korea and Japan which present the success stories of development. Capital, an important factor of pro-duction, is also much more the result than the cause of economic growth. The principle of cumulative causation postulates increasing returns through specialisation and economies of scale and shows how small initial advantages are magnified.

The notion of cumulative causation was applied by Myrdal, following Wicksell (1898), most illuminatingly to price expectations (*Monetary Equilibrium*, 1931, English transla-tion 1939) to the relations between regions within a country (*Economic Theory and Underdeveloped Regions*, 1957a; American title: *Rich Lands and Poor: The Road to World Prosperity*, 1957b). He showed how the advantages of growth poles (François Perroux's term) can become cumulative, while the backward region may be relatively or even absolutely impoverished. This is particularly serious for low-income countries, where 'spread effects' are weak, what he called 'backwash effects' strong, and government action to correct inequalities often absent.

Myrdal also applied the notion to sociological variables, such as the prejudices and dis-crimination against Blacks in the United States, their incomes, and their level of perform-ance (low skills, poverty, high crime rates, disease and so on); to economic variables in the development process; and, above all, to the interaction between so-called 'economic' and 'non-economic' variables. In this way, the relation between better nutrition, better health and better education, higher productivity, higher incomes, and hence ability to further improve health, education and nutrition shows that the inclusion of non-economic vari-ables in the analysis opens up the possibility of numerous cumulative processes to which conventional economic analysis is blind. It also guards against unicausal explanations and panaceas.

Like the Marxists, Myrdal emphasised the unequal distribution of power, property and income as an obstacle not only to equity but also to growth. In his contribution to the World Bank's *Pioneers in Development* (Myrdal, 1984, p. 152), he said that he arrived at his interest in the problems of development, from the Swedish welfare state as a problem of international inequality which should be solved by the creation of an international welfare world, an extension of the Swedish welfare state. But his policy conclusion was not Marxian. He regarded a direct attack on institutions and a shaping of attitudes (what Marx regarded as part of the superstructure) as necessary, though very difficult, partly because the policies which aim at reforming attitudes and institutions are themselves part of the social system, part of the unequal power and property structure. Although a planner, Myrdal dismissed the conventional planning models. A plan, in his view, is a political programme that has to comprise policies on institutions, attitudes and physical quantities, and should not be confined to public government expenditure.

Myrdal was advocating broad, strategic planning of macroeconomic policies, and in particular the avoidance of inflation, with a 'maximum role for the working of the forces in the market' (ibid., p. 37). But while highly critical of the shortcomings of the cumulative muddle of government interventions, he ended by saying that talk about planning and interventions being the 'Road to Serfdom' (Friedrich Hayek) and leading inevitably to the end of democracy and to the police state is bunk (ibid., p. 40).

The approach favoured by Myrdal is one of neither Soviet authority, force and central planning, nor capitalist *laissez-faire*, but of a third way: that of using prices for purposes of national economic management, and of attacking attitudes and institutions directly to make them instruments of reform. The difficulty is that any instrument, even if used with the intention to reform, within a given power structure may come to serve the powerful and re-establish the old equilibrium. Even well-intentioned allocations, rationing, and controls may reinforce monopoly and big business. What looks like social policies in the first round feeds monopolies in the second and third. How does one break out of this lock? Myrdal did not draw revolutionary conclusions but relied on the admittedly difficult possibility of self-reform that arises, in both the American creed and the modernisation ideals, from the tensions between the proclaimed beliefs of politicians and their actions.

Myrdal is not easy to typecast. On many issues, he fired at both sides of the conventional barricades and liked to emphasise the false shared premises of the combatants. Thus in the discussion of the role of the purely *economic* factors in development, to the exclusion of historical, cultural, social, political and psychological, he criticised liberal and conservative economics for assuming the non-economic factors to be fully *adapted* to economic progress and therefore bundled away under *ceteris paribus* clauses, and the Marxists for believing that these factors are responsive and automatically *adaptable*, as a result of what Marxists call the economic substructure, and therefore also beyond analysis and policy. From diametrically opposed premises, liberals (in the English, Manchester School sense, that is, conservatives) and Marxist revolutionaries therefore arrive at the same conclusion: there is no need for direct action on non-economic variables (administration, educational systems, labour markets, caste systems, contempt for certain types of work), for in the one case they are fully suited for the required change and in the other they will inevitably and automatically be shaped by the underlying economic change. Liberals (in the English sense) and radicals share common ground, which prevents them from seeing the need for the conscious planning of institutions.

The options before us, in Myrdal's view, are not confined to the models of capitalist or Soviet development. Social objectives can be pursued by a system of decentralised decision making in which planning is combined with freedom, democracy and a flourishing civil society. But here again, the added option is not one of the apolitical dreams of the futurologists or science fiction writers, but is anchored in political feasibility. He stood nearest to the so-called 'utopian' socialists Charles Fourier (1772–1837), Pierre Joseph Proudhon (1800–1865), the Comte de Saint-Simon (1760–1825), Robert Owen (1771–1858), and others, like the Irish landlord and capitalist William Thompson (1775–1833), and the Ricardian socialist Thomas Hodgskin (1787–1869) whom Marx and Engels contemptuously dismissed as 'unscientific' but who paid careful attention to shaping social institutions and even human attitudes for a better society. According to the Marxists, such planning was impossible or unnecessary: impossible before the revolution, because they formed part of the superstructure determined by economic conditions; unnecessary after the revolution, when human attitudes and social institutions would be automatically adapted to the socialist society.

Independence saw the rapid growth of the 'development industry'. A massive body of research and communications grew up in the 1950s and 1960s, and the mood changed to one of optimism. The new independence, the desire of the ruling elites to emulate the West and the rivalries of the Cold War fed this optimism. The false analogy of European reconstruction under the Marshall Plan was used as the paradigm for development. Since the communists had blamed the colonial powers for lack of development, the response was to drop the colonial doctrine. The existing body of economic analysis came in very handy. It neglected climate, it ignored attitudes and institutions as strategic variables, it regarded consumption as not productive, and it treated the state as exogenous. The conclusion: pour capital into the sausage machine, turn the growth handle, and out comes evergrowing output. There was no anticipation of the very high growth rates of population to come, and the growth of output meant output per head. The optimism is reflected in the changing terminology mentioned above. There is assumed to be a trade-off between equality and growth, and therefore equality, which hinders growth, has to be sacrificed or postponed. There is no deep analysis of land reform, education, corruption, social discipline, and the interests and efficiency of the government.

With this optimism in some respects went excessive pessimism in others. The 'golden age' of the 1950s and 1960s was overpessimistic about exports, the ability of the poor to save, incremental capital–output ratios, and hence economic growth prospects. Economic growth rates turned out to be spectacularly, unprecedently and unexpectedly high. But the golden age was overoptimistic on population growth, and on the productivity of physical investment that produces almost automatically extra output, and it largely ignored human rights, governance, the physical environment and even the role of women, in spite of the influence of Alva, Myrdal's wife.

An important element in Myrdal's thinking was dissent from this optimism. His views contributed to a change in opinion. Reduced emphasis in subsequent writings on physical capital in favour of political institutions and cultural attitudes owed much to Myrdal. In the late 1960s and 1970s the development profession returned to a pessimistic mood (Myrdal would have called it more realistic), rationalised by pointing to the ineffectiveness of development aid, to 'wrong' domestic economic policies in the developing countries, and to the reduced need for aid. At the same time the underdeveloped countries (as Myrdal insisted on calling them against the prevailing euphemism 'developing countries') called for a 'New International Economic Order'. Myrdal had stressed throughout his work the need for reform inside the underdeveloped countries themselves, though the developed countries and the international agencies, through international reform and aid, can make contributions to overcoming internal difficulties. Towards the end of his life he changed his mind and turned against development aid. In his prescient *An International Economy* (1956) he had developed the idea that national integration led to international disintegration. In the nineteenth century, when only minimal duties had been assumed by the state, and fixed exchange rates and balanced budgets had been widely accepted, the international economy had been more integrated. As each nation state attempted to assume more and more responsibilities towards its citizens, including price stability, full employment, income distribution, regional balance, environmental protection, and the paraphernalia of the welfare state, it made the achievement of these objectives by other countries more difficult. The old, apparently irrational constraints produced a more rational world than the new rational national selfishness.

Both *An American Dilemma* and *Asian Drama* are books about the interaction and the conflicts between ideals and reality; and about how, when the two conflict, one must give way. Much of conventional economic theory is a rationalisation whose purpose it is to conceal this conflict. But it is bound to reassert itself sooner or later. When this happens, either the ideals will be scaled down to conform to the reality, or the reality will be transformed by the ideals. Even if the chances of the latter happening are one in a hundred, Myrdal, who called himself a cheerful pessimist (forgetting that he had condemned optimism and pessimism as unworthy of scientists), never afraid to express unconventional and unpopular views in plain language, would be a leader, in thought and action, towards a reality shaped by the enlightened ideals.

PAUL STREETEN

References and further reading

Myrdal, Gunnar (1930), *The Political Element in the Development of Economic Theory* (originally published in Swedish), English translation by Paul Streeten, London: Routledge & Kegan Paul, 1953.

Myrdal, Gunnar (1931), *Monetary Equilibrium* (originally published in Swedish), English expanded translation, London: W. Hodge & Company, 1939.

Myrdal, Gunnar (1944), *An American Dilemma: The Negro Problem and Modern Democracy*, New York: Harper & Brothers.

Myrdal, Gunnar (1951), 'The trend towards economic planning', *Manchester School*, **19**, January, 1–42.

Myrdal, Gunnar (1956), *An International Economy: Problems and Prospects*, London: Routledge and Kegan Paul.

Myrdal, Gunnar (1957a), *Economic Theory and Underdeveloped Regions*, London: G. Duckworth.

Myrdal, Gunnar (1957b), *Rich Lands and Poor*, New York: Harper.

Myrdal, Gunnar (1958), *Value in Social Theory*, edited by Paul Streeten, London: Routledge & Kegan Paul.

Myrdal, Gunnar (1968), *Asian Drama*, 3 vols, New York: Pantheon.

Myrdal, Gunnar (1973), *Against the Stream: Critical Essays on Economics*, New York: Pantheon.

Myrdal, Gunnar (1984), 'International inequality and foreign aid in retrospect', *Pioneers in Development*, in Gerald Meier and Dudley Seers (eds), New York and Oxford: Oxford University Press, pp. 151–65.

Sen, Amartya (1994), 'Economic regress; concepts and features', *Proceedings of the World Bank Annual Conference on Development Economics 1993*, Washington, DC: International Bank for Reconstruction and Development.

Wicksell, Knut (1898), *Geldzins und Güterpreise* (Interest and Prices), Jena: G. Fischer.

National Accounting

The student of national accounting can easily lose sight of the fact that the end towards which economic activity is directed is consumption 'development' and maintenance. In an ideal world, the national accounts of a country would tell us about this state of affairs. Tricky of course is the fact that labour-time is part of the consumption bundle, albeit a negative one. The national accounts do not treat the experience of consumption over time via life expectancy, nor do they treat the distribution of consumption over persons; the national accounts deal only with aggregate consumption in a particular year. The accounts handle the issue of the sustainability of per capita consumption rather crudely, namely by highlighting the stock of produced capital that is maintained over time. Also, the national accounts tell us virtually nothing about whether consumption was 'earned' by hard labour in adverse conditions or by relatively easy button-pressing using ingenious machines in benign settings. A large element of economic progress is the freeing of millions of workers from hard labour by the substitution of machine-power.

When we say that person A comes from a nation with a high average 'income', we may or may not be relaying that person A has a comfortable life. It would be interesting if there were examples of nations with high average incomes but short average life expectancies, or having a large fraction of the population working in dangerous and physically demanding settings and so on. But this is not generally the case. Higher 'income' per capita and better lives on average often go together and this has led to the use of summary statistics associated with the national accounts being used as proxies for the quality of life.

The set-up of the national accounts

The 'rules of the road' for national accounting are vetted by a committee of experts under the auspices of the United Nations. If one consults the current summary statement for nations (United Nations, 2002), one finds two sets of flow accounts in local currency, say dollars: the expenditure account and the value-added account.

The expenditure account measures the dollar value of current final demand or final expenditure, which equals the value of aggregate consumer goods produced per year, C; plus the value of investment goods for produced capital, I; plus the value of government goods, G; and the value of goods for export, X, minus the (local) value of goods imported, M. Goods that are produced only to be used in the production of other goods in the same year are not included. Hence the familiar equation that aggregate current product flow equals $C + I + G + (X - M)$ in current dollars. Gross investment flow, I, includes replacement capital goods ('capital consumption allowance') as well as additional new capital goods which flow through firms. In brief, the net investment goods flows should be viewed as part of consumption goods flows beyond the current period.

In contrast to the flows of goods moving through households and firms, national wealth measures the size of the economy's 'factory' or capacity to generate these flows.

There is of course much interest in measuring national wealth, but this task of stock measurement is distinct from traditional flow accounting. Of interest is how 'factory size' varies with the natural resource base of a nation. Also of recent interest is the environmental cost of current production. Current economies tend to be net garbage producers and a more complete accounting would presumably have the stock of accumulated garbage show up as a negative entry in the consumption vector. The other flow account in the UN document lists so-called value added by sector. Value added should factor back into the dollar value of primary inputs, as it is the services of land, labour and produced capital that are embodied in goods and services during the year. The flour miller buys wheat for x dollars and sells flour to the bread merchant for y dollars. Value added in milling is thus $y - x$ dollars, representing the miller's labour costs, capital and land rentals, plus 'profits' for the accounting period. Hence the sum of value addeds is a measure of the value of primary input flows per year. So-called intermediate inputs such as the wheat to the miller are netted out of the value added in milling.

In the long tradition of double-entry bookkeeping, the expenditure and the value-added accounts are arranged to sum to the same total (apart from statistical discrepancies). A third account, not present, is the listing of the annual value of the services of land, labour and produced capital employed over the year (the income flow to the input flows). It sums to the same total as the other two accounts. Hence input flows can be valued directly as national income flowing to primary inputs, or indirectly as the sum of value addeds by sector. Production requires payment for inputs (wages, capital and land rentals), and these payments get expended 'back' over the period as the expenditures for product. Hence the term 'circular flow of income and expenditure'. The measurement of expenditure and income is not unambiguous. Is job-related expenditure such as the purchase of uniforms to be treated as consumption in the way that restaurant meals are, or should it be netted out of one's wage? Much of government output is not paid for directly by households and firms and hence must be valued with proxies such as the cost of inputs flowing into the government sector. The value of the services of homemakers in partnership with a spouse goes unrecorded because accountants are reluctant to guess at the value of such labour. Imputation in the national accounts is done only as a last resort. Imputations or guesses must be made for the value of farm produce consumed in farm households, which in less developed countries could be a large fraction of agricultural product. In those countries, much final expenditure will go unrecorded since transactions are carried out by barter or in a payments system that cannot be monitored by government accountants. Of course illegal activity such as drug-selling goes unrecorded in every country, rich or poor.

The newer approach to national accounting considers gross *domestic* product (GDP), roughly speaking what is produced within the geographical boundaries of a nation, and abandons gross national product (GNP), what is produced by nationals locally and abroad. GDP includes the labour services of migrants. The UN has thus opted to emphasise how 'productive' local primary inputs are rather than how well a representative citizen is doing. This raises three large questions: what vector of final goods prices should be selected to value the final flow product, how tight is the link between flow inputs and the value of final product, and why do we consider that land, labour, and produced capital are the relevant primary inputs? Should not mineral flows as in say oil be considered separately from land? What about the services of watersheds in providing water for consumption, production and waste removal?

With regard to the first question there may be, to a first approximation, a 'world price vector' for final goods that are traded, but there will be a set of prices for non-traded goods that is different for each country. Consequently it is difficult to infer how 'productive' a nation's input flow vector is by comparing its GDP to that of another nation's. Even in the absence of the non-traded goods problem, the link between final goods prices and input valuations will be affected by distortions caused by local taxes, imperfect competition and information asymmetries, leading to an undervaluation of 'the productiveness' of primary input flows. One would be very hard-pressed for example to distinguish a rise in the efficiency of a nation due to technical change from one due to mitigating a distortion by, say, improving the structure of its tax system.

Cross-country comparisons

There are also wedges between the final goods price vectors of different nations created by tariffs and quotas. Such price distortions have been estimated to cost a nation as much as 10 per cent of its potential value of final demand, that is, input flows are being undervalued by as much as 10 per cent. Summers and Heston (1991) have come up with a time series of final expenditure for 53 countries over 40 years using a common world price vector, but they leave open the question of how efficient each nation is in transforming its inputs into final 'product'. In cross-country comparisons, no one has a satisfactory benchmark for 'the' standard of living. Usher (1963, 1968) took up the question of how an Ethiopian household living reasonably satisfactorily could be living on an annual income of US $40, far below US subsistence levels. We suggest that the reason so much more money is needed to survive in the United States than in Ethiopia lies in the relatively expensive bundle of secondary inputs 'embodied' in 'necessities' in developed economies. A breakfast of Kellogg's Corn Flakes in Madison, Wisconsin is overlaid with many extra costs compared with an Ethiopian breakfast of cornmeal; namely costs of transportation, distribution, advertising, packaging, insurance, banking services, legal services police services and even national defence services. Most financial services, including real estate services, show up in the market price of goods and services sold to households. Inasmuch as government services are paid for by sales taxes, value-added taxes and corporate income taxes, government services are embodied in final goods prices as well.

This is not to say that the extra services 'hidden' in prices have no value. A widget with legal services 'hidden' in its price comes with reasonable assurance that the manufacturer is in a good position to protect itself against product liability. One definition of economic 'development' would be that 'basic consumption goods' become expensive because they acquire a 'shell' of extra inputs associated with the tertiary sector. For 1999, our calculations put value added in the tertiary sector at 0.75 of GDP in the United States, 0.62 of GDP in South Africa, 0.54 in Poland and 0.472 in Bangladesh (United Nations, 2002). While the representative household in a rich country consumes more of the primary dimension of housing, food, clothing, personal transportation, commercial entertainment and leisure goods, there is evidence that the representative household in a nation that appears hopelessly poor in comparison can, in the absence of war, live a life free of the worst depredations of poverty.

Comparisons over years

The question of how well a household is doing is often addressed by comparing the cost of a standard bundle of consumer goods over time, net of inflation. If the cost is declining, one infers that a household is becoming better off. Hence a consumer price index or cost-of-living index. A central difficulty is that the standard bundle requires re-specification every few years because the relative prices of the goods in the bundle change and because new products become part of a household's typical expenditure. These issues get summed up in the term 'index number problem'. It is extremely difficult to measure welfare changes for a representative household over medium and longer time horizons. National accounts produce a 'GDP deflator', a chain index which measures inflation and detours around the matter of 'the standard bundle' of commodities for a household.

In the 1980s, Ward (1982) and others asked how sustainable currently measured GDP was for nations depending on natural resource export flows. If Kuwait is producing and exporting only oil flows, will not its consumption flows decline in future decades as its endowment of oil is depleted? Net national product (NNP), rather than GDP, was seen to measure sustainable income, because provision is made in NNP to replace produced capital worn out over the accounting period; an additional netting out of current resource stock depletion could be performed as well. Some oil-producing countries acknowledged the problem of possible future consumption reduction and began to set aside some of the current export earnings in so-called 'heritage funds'. The intent was to have a large interest income flow available from the fund in the future. For such a nation a net capital loss figure is needed, not a gross measure of current stock depletion. The corresponding net investment or disinvestment figure has become known as 'genuine savings', 'genuine investment', or a more general 'net investment'. Generalised net investment was central in the Solow (1974) model of constant aggregate consumption in an economy relying on a dwindling oil stock. There, sustainability was linked to replacing current capital lost in value terms with new produced capital, that is, zero net investment (Hartwick, 1977). In the formative years of modern national accounting, attention had been directed to a flow measure of national product that could be sustained over more than one accounting period, linked to 'maintaining capital intact'. Arthur Pigou, Friedrich von Hayek and John Hicks were the principals in exchanges in the journals. But John Maynard Keynes's work (his *General Theory*) shifted attention to the definitions of the components of aggregate products, namely C, I, G and $X - M$.

The systematic gap between the annual growth in the value of primary inputs and the value of final expenditure in developed countries has come to be identified with 'exogenous technical progress' or 'productivity' improvement. The most basic notion is that of the inflation-adjusted, dollar value of output per hour of labour increasing over time. In such a circumstance a worker can consume more each year and be unambiguously better off because he/she is more productive. Hence long-run welfare improvement is seen to depend on 'technical progress', the freeing up of some inputs each year to produce 'extra' goods and services. The measurement of this gain is a quite separate activity from traditional national accounting and involves complicated input-measurement issues (Jorgenson et al., 1987): index number problems, again. At any point in time one might say that a nation is rich because workers combine their labour with relatively abundant capital inputs and hence produce much output per hour worked, but over decades, the key to accumulation of much capital is the cumulative impact of positive, labour-saving technical progress. Population growth runs counter to technical progress since, to a first approximation, it lowers the capital–labour ratio.

JOHN M. HARTWICK

References

Hartwick, J.M. (1977), 'Investing rents from exhaustible resources and intergenerational equity', *American Economic Review*, **67** (5), 972–4.
Jorgenson, Dale W., Frank M. Gallop and Barbara M. Fraumeni (1987), *Productivity and US Economic Growth*, Cambridge, MA: Harvard University Press.
Solow, R.M. (1974), 'Intergenerational equity and exhaustible resources', *Review of Economic Studies*, Symposium, 29–46.
Summers, Robert and Alan Heston (1991), 'The Penn World Table (Mark 5): an expanded set of international comparisons, 1950–1988', *Quarterly Journal of Economics*, **106** (2), 327–68.
United Nations (2002), *National Accounts Statistics: Main Aggregates and Detailed Tables, 2000*, New York: United Nations.
Usher, Dan (1963), 'The transport bias in comparisons of national income', *Economica*, **30** (118), 140–58.
Usher, Dan (1968), *The Price Mechanism and the Meaning of National Income Statistics*, Oxford: Clarendon.
Ward, Michael (1982), *Accounting for the Depletion of Natural Resources in the National Accounts of Developing Economies*, Paris: Organisation for Economic Cooperation and Development.

National Economic Planning

Economists are trained to think of markets and prices as the standard tools of resource allocation. To function well, particular markets need an underpinning of institutional structure that is often overlooked or taken for granted. For instance, all markets need property rights, laws relating to contracts and so on; consumer markets often need additional provisions to do with product safety, consumer protection and the like. Resource allocation through markets is well known – under ideal conditions of perfect competition – to have attractive efficiency properties (productive efficiency, Pareto efficiency). Even with good institutions in place, however, markets do at times fail to work well. This can be due to environmental problems (so-called 'externalities' due to pollution, for instance), many types of informational problem (for example, in the credit market, where it is not easy for a bank to determine how good a borrower's investment project is, giving rise to equilibria with *credit rationing* and *collateral* requirements), and poor macroeconomic policy that results in equilibria with substantial *unemployment*.

In the development context, markets often function poorly due to the lack of, or undeveloped state of, the institutions referred to above. In addition, the financial markets that are supposed to mobilise the population's savings and direct it towards profitable investment opportunities frequently suffer from a limited and badly regulated banking network, few or no securities markets, and an absence of public confidence. In these circumstances, governments seeking to foster economic growth and development are faced with an extremely challenging situation.

In the early post-war decades, when general confidence in markets was in any case at a fairly low ebb due to the terrible experience in the 1930s of the Great Depression – allied with the parallel observation that the Soviet Union under central planning appeared to be growing very rapidly – many developing countries started to formulate national development plans. Often these ran for periods of 5–10 years, and their degree of detail was highly variable; most included lists of major investment projects and sectoral priorities, some also included in-depth analysis of key sectors like agriculture, or of important policy areas such as the structure of the tax system. For a while, the preparation of a development plan – a national economic plan – even came to be treated by the major aid agencies as a condition for receiving certain forms of aid, especially project-based aid. Presumably agencies like the World Bank wanted to understand how a particular project fitted into a country's development strategy, in order to help judge whether it would be desirable or not. This was at a time when the emphasis in development economics was very much on promoting faster growth of GDP. Nowadays, most aid agencies place far greater emphasis on the poverty-reducing aspects of a country's development strategy, with the result that the key country document relevant for aid disbursement is most often the so-called poverty reduction strategy paper (PRSP).

What all these national economic development plans generally lacked, though, was an effective implementation mechanism. To a perhaps surprising extent they were merely paper plans. To construct them, a great deal of information was collected and then put together into the plan document. Formally, this would in turn be approved by the relevant government, and be endorsed by the main aid agencies. But then what? Rarely were these plans accompanied by the issuing of detailed instructions to individual firms as in the traditional Soviet-type planning model. Rarely, indeed, were specific resources – public or private – allocated to fund the investment projects identified and highlighted in the plan. At most a few of the public infrastructure projects in the plan would be undertaken, often with the help of foreign assistance or FDI. In addition, in line with the specified sector priorities, import duties, trade controls and other policy measures would be introduced to support favoured sectors. Sometimes the plan objectives included the goals of expanding the exports of some products. More often, the emphasis was on cutting back imports in order to protect domestic producers and to eliminate trade deficits. The resulting policy mix came to be known as 'import-substituting industrialisation' (and empirical studies subsequently confirmed the inefficiency of this approach to development).

Interestingly, therefore, what started out as an exercise at least in part based on observations of apparent market failure often turned out to distort and undermine even those markets that could work well. Countries that engaged in national economic planning frequently operated a plethora of controls on international trade, from complex tariff structures through import quotas and other forms of non-tariff barrier. They also had tax systems with differentiated rates that favoured certain 'key' sectors, diverse forms of licensing and regulation (opening up numerous opportunities for corruption), and credit policies that ensured relatively easy finance for some activities, and much tougher conditions for others.

In most instances where developing countries adopted the approach of national economic planning, economic performance did not turn out especially well. Growth remained slow, living standards mostly failed to improve at all rapidly. However, a few developing countries had started to develop at increasingly rapid rates by the mid-1970s, notably the so-called 'Asian Tigers' but also, later, a few other countries. Some of these countries, such as Japan, appeared to use some form of planning, while others did not. However, subsequent research has shown that even where planning was a possible factor in economic success, this occurred due to the limited powers of the relevant planning authority, and the possibilities for private sector competition. Moreover, economic policy in the Asian Tigers was characterised by a very strong export orientation, and in some cases this was accompanied by land reforms that helped to improve the productivity of agriculture.

Although it is quite hard to generalise about the factors giving rise to economic success, a few characteristics are shared by virtually all the success stories of the past two to three decades. These include:

- strong export orientation (and an increasingly liberal trading environment in general);
- competition between domestic firms both in supplying the domestic market and in export markets;
- tax systems that provide effective business incentives to encourage existing firms to expand and new firms to establish themselves;
- land reform, both to improve agricultural productivity *per se*, and to release labour for absorption into other sectors that are growing rapidly;
- high rates of savings and investment, with efficient investment allocation especially important; public investment to improve infrastructure, such as the development of port facilities, is critical in support of a strong export orientation; and
- improving labour force skills (mostly through improvements in education).

It will be noted that none of these points has much to do with national economic planning *per se*.

It is nevertheless worth considering why national economic planning mostly failed to deliver what was expected from it. First, even in a situation where there are severe market failures, it does not follow that government intervention, such as through the establishment of a planning framework, will improve matters; government failure is at least as widespread as market failure, and can be more damaging if the government insists on monopoly control over a given market (for example, by suppressing potential competition). Second, governments that have tried to assess which sectors are going to succeed in some country, with resources being directed accordingly, have nearly always been wrong. Governments often think that they have better economic information than private agents, but the evidence from their attempts to 'pick winners' is that this is rarely so. Third, constructing a plan for an entire economy is an exceptionally complicated task, requiring both difficult judgements about many uncertain factors not subject to government control (such as the weather, and its impact on the harvest; the state of world markets for major export products; the volume of investment; and so on), as well as a delicate balance between disparate political interests battling to secure resources for their respective constituencies. In much of the literature on national economic planning, these risk factors and political factors are commonly overlooked, the latter often through the simple expedient of assuming that the 'planners' (whoever they may be) are working with a given and agreed national objective. While this is an appealing starting-point for much of the highly technical, theoretical literature on economic planning, it cannot be taken terribly seriously in practice.

Even in the countries where national economic planning was most firmly established, namely the former Soviet Union and the former communist countries of Central and Eastern Europe, rapid growth in the early post-war years soon gave way to slowdown, then economic stagnation, and in the worst cases actual decline. Explaining the region's deteriorating economic performance proved a significant challenge, but the principal elements of the 'story' are now pretty much agreed. They include:

- The need to shift from extensive to intensive growth as it became less easy to find more workers to transfer out of low-productivity agriculture into more-efficient industry. Once enough people had moved out of agriculture, growth could only be sustained through improvements in productivity within industry.
- In an economic system where firms were told what to produce and to whom to supply it (ensuring that firms had guaranteed markets for their output), there was virtually no incentive to innovate, either by improving production processes or by introducing new products. The planners tried to deal with this by setting targets for innovation, and by establishing massive networks of research institutes and the like. Although some of these institutes performed world-class research, the transfer of new ideas into production was slow and in any event bore little relation with what 'customers' would have wanted had they ever been consulted. Central planning and innovation do not sit well together, and this basic shortcoming becomes even more serious in an era when technological change is very rapid.
- Especially for the smaller socialist countries, efficient international trade was fundamental for successful growth and improvements in living standards. Yet the socialist bloc's share of world markets fell dramatically after the 1950s and it became increasingly apparent that attempts by central planners to determine efficient patterns of specialisation across the various socialist countries, associated with extensive restrictions on both trade and inward flows of foreign investment, were actually very damaging.
- Ironically, it turned out that central planners responded badly to major post-war economic shocks such as the two oil-price shocks of the 1970s (resulting from conflicts in the Middle East). The entire socialist bloc sought to keep down the domestic prices of energy, with the result that the smaller countries lacking their own energy resources (such as Hungary) both accumulated external debt, which remains a heavy burden even today, and also effectively encouraged profligate energy use by domestic households and firms. Many of the former socialist countries still consume over twice as much energy per unit of GDP as most OECD countries.

Against this rather negative appraisal of national economic planning, it is interesting to consider where and when it has actually worked. Examples that come to mind concern situations where *national objectives are clear, simple and well defined*, such as the situation in some countries during the Second World War when resources were being mobilised for the war effort. The planning of aircraft production in the UK is a notable example of this. While certainly accompanied by all the well-known inefficiencies of centralised planning, the authorities judged – probably correctly – that if they pulled resources into the war effort using market methods they would generate severe inflation and would also adversely affect many relatively poor people. In other words, the underlying case for the use of planning was not based on any claim for its efficiency, but was much more an argument about real income distribution. A suitable mix of planning plus rationing at controlled prices was considered more acceptable, politically, than reliance solely upon the market mechanism.

After the war, there was of course the well-known Marshall Plan through which a great deal of American assistance was provided to support reconstruction and recovery in Europe. This worked surprisingly quickly and effectively, but not because the plan itself was wonderfully coordinated and controlled. Rather, it was a success because Europe possessed the institutional framework needed to operate a market economy, and also possessed in abundance the skilled manpower required to make it work. Human capital, in this context, turned out to be immensely more important for recovery than physical capital.

Another interesting example is that of China. Since the late 1970s China has been the world's fastest-growing economy, yet it remains a communist country and still operates economy-wide central planning. However, the country has performed so well partly because the central planners never sought to control more than a small fraction of the economy, namely the state-owned enterprises managed directly from Beijing (amounting to well under 20 per cent of the economy, and declining in relative importance). Other state-owned firms were managed at provincial or even lower levels and this decentralisation permitted the beginnings of competition even within the state-owned sector. Until recently, state-owned enterprises have performed relatively poorly in China, but these new competitive pressures, supplemented by increasing competition from the non-state sector, are starting to improve the situation.

Aside from this decentralisation of planning, China did three things that contributed massively to its economic success. First, it reformed agriculture by abandoning the commune system and moving to family farming based on market incentives; second, it opened up to foreign trade, starting in key coastal provinces and gradually extending the more liberal conditions to other parts of the country; and third, it not only permitted hundreds of thousands of very small businesses to start up at the local level, but it also allowed the creation of the so-called TVEs (township and village enterprises). While not strictly private, and often set up jointly by businessmen and local authorities working in partnership, the TVEs had sufficient security to take risks and invest on a massive scale, accounting by the late 1990s for about half China's manufactured exports. This was a truly stunning performance, all the more so when one observes that it was wholly unexpected. Neither the Chinese themselves nor outside observers expected the TVEs to take off in quite the spectacular way that they did. So if the Chinese performance is to be counted as a success for planning, it must be a success for *cautious, limited and extremely decentralised planning*.

To conclude, then, where does all this leave national economic planning? Essentially, I believe, it is an idea that has had its day, especially if one thinks in terms of the very detailed, directive and comprehensive approach adopted in the former socialist countries. Some countries still seek to plan particular sectors, notably the energy sectors, and one can find many examples of long-term energy strategies resulting from such exercises (for example, both Russia and Kazakhstan recently published energy strategies extending to 2020). In practice, I remain quite sceptical about the merits of these efforts, since they are necessarily based on projections for other sectors of the economy which are themselves subject to massive uncertainties. A looser, more aggregated approach – though still possibly distinguishing a few key regions or sectors – can work better in principle, giving rise to indicative planning of the sort popularised in France (especially in the 1960s and 1970s) and often advocated for other countries. Anything else is likely to fall victim to the normal political struggles over resources that occur in all countries, whether democratic or not.

Fundamentally, such struggles are almost always about the distribution of resources across sectors or regions. In other words, politics is nearly always concerned with dividing up the existing cake and not with baking a bigger one, whereas planning at its best ought to be striving to increase the cake itself. One can therefore readily see how planners – who try to stand back and take an 'objective' view of alternative development strategies for a given country – might be overwhelmed by ambitious politicians demanding more resources for 'their' pet project or pet sector 'now'. Such lobbying, though, is a normal part of the democratic process, and it goes on everywhere. The difficulty is always how to design the political system to put some constraints on the process and to limit the opportunities for corruption and unfairness to which it gives rise. It was perhaps a little naïve of those favouring national economic planning to imagine that it could ever operate in isolation from these interest-group pressures.

PAUL G. HARE

Further reading

Blitzer, Charles R., Peter B. Clark and Lance Taylor (1975), *Economy-Wide Models and Development Planning*, World Bank Research Publication, Oxford: Oxford University Press.
Estrin, Saul and Peter Holmes (1983), *French Planning in Theory and Practice*, London: George Allen & Unwin.
Hare, Paul G. (1991), *Central Planning*, Chur, Switzerland: Harwood Academic Publishers.
Hogan, Michael J. (1987), *The Marshall Plan: America, Britain and the Reconstruction of Western Europe, 1947–1952*, Cambridge: Cambridge University Press.
Kornai, János (1992), *The Socialist System: The Political Economy of Communism*, Oxford: Oxford University Press.
Lal, Deepak (1980), *Prices for Planning: Towards the Reform of Indian Planning*, London: Heinemann.
Todaro, Michael P. and Stephen C. Smith (2003), *Economic Development*, 8th edn, Boston, MA: Addison-Wesley.

Nationalism and Development

In his classic essay, 'Economic backwardness in historical perspective', in which he discusses the industrialisation of France, Germany and Russia – following 'the road which England began to tread at an earlier time' – Alexander Gerschenkron (1952) has this to say about 'Ideologies of Delayed Industrialisations':

> To break through the barriers of stagnation in a backward country, to ignite the imaginations of men, and to place their energies in the service of industrial development, a stronger medicine is needed than the promise of better allocation of resources or even of the lower price of bread. (Gerschenkron, 1952 [1992], p. 125)

He went on to argue that what is needed to bring about change in an economically backward country is 'a New Deal in emotions', and faith 'that the golden age lies not behind but ahead of man'. He thought that these might be supplied by socialism, and as he says 'Capitalist industrialisation under the auspices of socialist ideologies may be less surprising a phenomenon than would appear at first sight' (ibid., p. 126). This is an insight that appears to have been vindicated in the development experience of China towards the end of the twentieth century. Yet Gerschenkron's analysis shows that another kind of ideology was more significant in the later nineteenth-century industrialisations. Of Germany he says that 'the lack of both a preceding political revolution and an early national unification rendered nationalist sentiment a much more suitable ideology of industrialisation', and of Russia under the Tsars that 'the state, moved by its military interest, assumed the role of the primary agent propelling the economic progress in the country' (ibid., p. 126). Now, in the light of another half-century of experience of economic development, it is clear that nationalism has been much the greater ideological force than socialism. According to the work of Chalmers Johnson, first on peasant nationalism in China (1962) and later on the role of the Ministry of International Trade and Industry (MITI) in the rapid development of Japan (1982), nationalism – 'the exigencies and requirements of national survival and mobilization in a twentieth century dominated by bigger powers in Europe and America' (Woo-Cumings, 1999, p. 2) – has been the driver of the successful East Asian economies.

'Nationalism' refers to an idea of the existence of community, shared among large groups of people – people who cannot possibly know each other individually. Nationalism refers, then, as Benedict Anderson put it most influentially, to the idea of an 'imagined community', represented as having deep historical roots (Anderson, 1983). Anderson and others argue that nationalism is a distinctively modern phenomenon. It is pointed out that the word itself, in European languages, is of nineteenth-century coinage, and suggested that the imagined community of the nation came to replace face-to-face community relations as societies experienced industrialisation and modernisation, or as an outcome of the experience and practices of colonial rule. In these accounts, nationalism is conditioned upon, and is in part an outcome of economic development, and of the creation of integrated markets across a territory. Other scholars hold, rather, that contemporary nationalisms are built upon long-established sentiments of patriotism that are both reflected in and expressed through particular symbols and narratives, often associated with language (see, for example, Smith, 1986). Yet others believe that nationalisms are deliberate constructions that serve particular interests such as those of an emerging bourgeoisie.

The objective of national economic development has both served and been served by the development of nationalism. In India, for example, the rise of the nationalist movement was greatly influenced by nineteenth-century Indian thinkers who argued that as a result of colonial rule by Britain their country was being impoverished or – in the words of a later generation of dependency theorists who drew upon their arguments – systematically underdeveloped. Writers such as, most notably, Dadabhai Naoroji (whose work, *Poverty and Un-British Rule*, was published in 1901) and R.C. Dutt maintained that India's potential investible surplus was being lost to Britain, and that instead of benefiting Indians, was actually being used to fund their subjugation. The struggle for freedom from British rule was therefore linked with the idea that independence was a necessary condition for the transformation of the economy; and above all else the government of independent India was expected to overcome the 'backwardness' and poverty that were seen as having been brought about by colonialism. As Jawaharlal Nehru memorably put it when, in January 1947, he closed the initial debate in the Constituent Assembly that was entrusted with the task of drawing up the constitution for the new nation state: 'The first task of this Assembly is to free India through a new constitution, to feed the starving people, and to clothe the naked masses, and to give to every Indian the fullest opportunity to develop himself according to his capacity'. A developmental ideology became, therefore, a constituent part of the self-definition of the post-colonial state, that was in turn identified with and sought to consolidate the 'nation'. Economic development was necessary in order to build the nation – even in the literal sense that the new nation was represented symbolically in great new factories, power stations and big dams; while the idea of the nation provided the essential emotional and ideological driver that the effort required.

Influenced in part by the earlier Soviet experience, the instrument of national development in India – as in most other post-colonial states – was economic planning, buttressed by the newly formulated discipline of development economics. These paradigms were, as Satish Deshpande argues, 'particularly amenable to translation into a specifically *nationalist* idiom' (Deshpande, 2003, p. 66, original emphasis). It is a matter of history that in India and many other of the now 'developing countries' in the 1960s and 1970s, planning generally produced disappointing results. But it was not so everywhere. It has come to be recognised that the most successful developing economies, those of East Asia, and Malaysia and Thailand in South East Asia, have interventionist, 'developmental' states, as Chalmers Johnson suggested. Their governments have pursued industrial policies, that have involved, however, the disciplining of private capital and the subjection of their developing industries to competition in international markets. In concluding his influential book on industrial policy in Taiwan, Robert Wade muses on why it has been that so many other countries have not succeeded in industrial development in the way that Taiwan has done. The answer that he comes up with is that Taiwan has had a political elite that has been dedicated to national development: 'a shared sense of the external vulnerability of the nation has helped to concentrate the rulers' minds on performance-enhancing measures as a means of their own survival' (Wade, 1990, p. 377). The context for this is supplied in Johnson's analysis. In East Asia there was a revolutionary nationalism

> that grew from war and imperialism and manifested itself variously: communism in China . . . and the capitalist developmental state in Japan, South Korea and Taiwan. This is also why the East Asian developmental states [with 'hard-bitten' elites that 'chose economic development as the means to ensure national survival'] have more in common with late developing European nations of the past and less with contemporary developing societies in Latin America and elsewhere. (Woo-Cumings, 1999, p. 7)

In Africa, by contrast, nationalism has been but weakly developed. Mahmood Mamdani has shown that the effects of indirect rule during the colonial period in most of Africa, were to 'tribalise' African rural societies and to create what were effectively 'bifurcated states'. The towns came to have to have citizens who spoke the language of civil society. Rural people were rather the subjects – people 'civilised as communities not as individuals' – of the tribal chiefs who were to a significant extent the creations of colonial governments (see Mamdani, 1996). These were not circumstances in which it was possible that nationalist elites like those of the economically successful East Asian states would emerge. Africa shared, after the end of colonial rule, in the mainly economic rhetoric of Third World nationalism. But even less than in India were there political conditions conducive to the formation of developmental nationalist elites like those of East Asia.

JOHN HARRISS

References

Anderson, Benedict (1983), *Imagined Communities*, London: Verso (2nd edn, 1991).
Deshpande, Satish (2003), *Contemporary India: A Sociological View*, Delhi: Penguin Books.
Gerschenkron, Alexander (1952 [1992]), 'Economic backwardness in historical perspective', in B. Hoselitz (ed.), *The Progress of Underdeveloped Countries*, Chicago: University of Chicago Press. Reprinted in M. Granovetter and R. Swedberg (1992) (eds), *The Sociology of Economic Life*, Boulder, CO: Westview Press, pp. 111–30 (page references are to the latter).
Johnson, C. (1962), *Peasant Nationalism and Communist Power: the Emergence of Revolutionary China, 1937–1945*, Stanford, CA: Stanford University Press.
Johnson, C. (1982), *MITI and the Japanese Miracle: The Growth of Industrial Policy, 1925–1975*, Stanford, CA: Stanford University Press.
Mamdani, Mahmood (1996), *Citizen and Subject: Contemporary Africa and the Legacy of Late Colonialism*, Princeton, NJ: Princeton University Press.
Smith, Anthony D. (1986), *The Ethnic Origins of Nations*, Oxford: Blackwell.
Wade, Robert (1990), *Governing the Market: Economic Theory and the Role of Government in East Asian Industrialization*, Princeton, NJ: Princeton University Press.
Woo-Cumings, Meredith (1999), 'Chalmers Johnson and the politics of nationalism and development', in M. Woo-Cumings (ed.), *The Developmental State in Historical Perspective*, Ithaca, NY: Cornell University Press, pp. 1–31.

NGOs and Civil Society

Civil society has been termed 'a notoriously slippery concept' by more than one commentator (Bebbington and Riddell, 1995, p. 880; Edwards, 2004, p. vi), while the struggle to define the notion of non-governmental organisations (NGOs) remains unfinished. Despite this, donor agencies across the spectrum have tended to hinge their 'civil society strengthening' programmes around capacity-building support to NGOs. An important implication is that – if the meanings of both NGO and civil society are multiple and unclear – civil society strengthening programmes implemented via NGOs are not all a cut of the same cloth. While some may aim to foster a broader and more inclusive public sphere for the exercise of democratic politics, others may be promoting a very particular form of liberal democracy coupled with particular forms of market liberalisation. Civil society and NGO are not then merely slippery concepts – they are deeply contested.

Approaches to civil society

The emergence of civil society within social science and social policy debates over the past two decades was catalysed by the popularity and relative success of anti-authoritarian and pro-democracy movements in Eastern Europe, Latin America and Sub-Saharan Africa during the 1980s and early 1990s. In terms of development studies, this coincided with a moment known as the 'impasse' (Booth, 1994), which included a strong disenchantment concerning how the previously dominant state and market paradigms were responding to the continued challenges of uneven development. Two of the ideological positions to emerge from this impasse have provided particularly fertile ground upon which civil society debates have flourished, namely the neoliberal approach, which emphasises a reduced role for the state, and more radical post-Marxist and post-structural approaches, which view the civil arena as a potential locus for alternative forms of development and politics. These 'mainstream' and 'alternative' positions on civil society in international development (Howell and Pearce, 2001), can to some extent be aligned with the two quite distinct analytical approaches to civil society. The first of these understands civil society primarily in terms of associations, while the second understands it as 'the arena . . . in which ideological hegemony is contested' (Lewis, 2002, p. 572; Gramsci, 1971). Both are relevant to development theory, and each has been acted upon in development practice.

The associationalist approach is the more familiar in development studies, and begins with Georg Hegel's delineation of civil society as the arena of association between the household and the state – a 'third sector' distinct from both the state and the market. This sector may be a source of services that neither state nor market is able to deliver, or deliver as effectively and efficiently (for example, Salamon and Anheier, 1997). In a more de Tocquevillian sense, such associations may act as a counterweight to the state and market, exercising some degree of control over them, and promoting processes of democratisation (for example, Putnam, 1993: see also Social Capital, this volume).

Approaches that understand civil society in terms of organisations none the less offer distinct interpretations of the forms such organisations take. Organisations can be understood primarily in terms of their forms and functions (what they are and what they do), or in terms of the state–society and political–economic relationships within which they emerged. The former approach tends to confer more agency to these organisations, while the latter understands organisations in terms of their relationships to particular class, ethnic or other groups within society, and structures of power and resources.

The second approach traces its roots to the work of Antonio Gramsci, although it has also taken form in the works of Jürgen Habermas. Gramsci understood civil society as the arena in which ideas and discourses become hegemonic, serving to stabilise and naturalise capitalist systems of production and exchange. However, he also understood this arena as contested – hegemonic ideas could always be resisted, questioned and potentially destabilised.

These ideas were critical to many post-Marxist and post-structuralist theorists who viewed the (new) social movements of the 1980s and 1990s as potential vehicles through which counter-hegemonic ideas (around, for instance, democracy and patriarchy) could be constructed and promoted (Alvarez et al., 1998; Peet and Watts, 2004). Slightly different approaches emphasise the importance of building a healthy and inclusive public sphere that would allow for democratic deliberation over different socio-political projects (Habermas, 1984).

Within both of these approaches there tends to run a normative thread, suggesting that civil society is in some way a 'good thing' – that a 'civil society' is a good society (Edwards, 2004). However, this tendency has become increasingly problematic in the light of evidence that many organisations operate as sources of exclusion as much as cooperation, while the public sphere can be understood as inherently riven by conflict and inequality. Non-governmental associations pursue a range of often conflicting goals, many of which will not be in tune with general notions of 'the good society' (see Tarrow, 1996), rendering normative positions further problematic. Importantly, the promotion of civil society as 'a good thing' may be viewed as an ethnocentric imposition on other contexts and peoples, particularly given the critique that civil society is a particularly Western concept born of a specific period in European history. For some, the tendency to conceptualise civil society in contradistinction to the state reinforces state–society dualisms, which may not be helpful for understanding social order and change (Mamdani, 1996; Ferguson, 2004). Here, the challenge is to examine how the political trajectories of particular political communities lead to the emergence of social movements, and then to examine these before coming to conclusions about what forms of civil society these movements might comprise.

Non-governmental organisations

The definition of NGOs is equally contested. If one simply took practice as a guide, and considered the range of organisations funded by donor NGO support programmes, the category would include the Red Cross, national and international Oxfams, place-based citizen groups working with place-based groups elsewhere, trades unions, cooperatives, conservative and leftist think-tanks, and many more. These organisations share little except that they are not government, and they have diverse social, political and historical origins, and differing goals, internal structures and geographical reach. Efforts to develop taxonomies of NGOs have sought some pattern (for example, Clark, 1991; Vakil, 1997), and seek to classify NGOs according to what they do, what they are, what they stand for, how they relate to poor populations, whether they are northern or southern – and often some mix of these criteria. However, development studies has increasingly focused on formal, and at least partly professionalised organisations that are concerned in some way with development and relief activities (Vakil, 1997) – organisations at times referred to as non-governmental *development* organisations. As with civil society, NGOs have been considered as the key agents for both neoliberal rollbacks of the state and alternative development, with its focus on people-centred and empowering solutions (Drabeck 1987; Tandon, 2001).

In all these tussles to define NGOs, the focus has remained largely at the organisational level. Yet in more recent years the transnational nature of relationships among NGOs has become clearer. NGOs become one of several means through which 'activists without borders' work together on issues they believe in (Keck and Sikkink, 1998) – and transnational networks might create NGOs as legally recognised organisations through which such networks can act. Such transnationalism is not necessarily heralded as desirable. Ferguson (2004) notes that while the rise of NGOs in Africa is often viewed as a step towards democracy, what may often be happening is that greater control over services and other dimensions of socio-economic life is being transferred to organisations over which local populations have little control, which are themselves more responsive to the demands and dynamics of these transnational relationships and which show little or no inclination to challenge real structures of state and economic power. Reflections on such transnational networks hook up with a related discussion on the concept of a global civil society (Hyden, 1997) – a discussion in which once again one can find both understandings of global civil society that emphasise the existence of global associations as well as views that emphasise the idea of a sort of global public sphere in which hegemonic global ideas are naturalised and contested, and in which the voices of international organisations (including international NGOs) crowd out local voices. The transnationalisation of NGOs and of civil society is not, then, necessarily democratising, and, for some observers, the increasingly transnational community of NGOs might operate more as an essentially neo-imperialist transmission belt for Western ideologies and management practices aimed more at control than empowerment (Townsend et al., 2002).

Such concerns have not stood in the way of efforts to create NGOs, and the number of organisations registered as NGOs has grown remarkably in recent decades. Estimates suggest that NGOs reach around 450–600 million people – roughly 15–20 per cent of the world's poor (Fowler, 2000a, p. 16). This reflects structural changes – most notably democratisation and neoliberalisation – which have opened up greater political and economic space for NGOs. Although precise figures on NGO funding are very difficult to come by, it is currently estimated that development-orientated NGOs disburse between 10 and 15 billion dollars annually (World Bank, 2001), which could be as much as 20 per cent of official aid.

As funding for NGOs has grown, the composition of this funding has changed. The proportion of funds deriving directly or indirectly from donor-country governmental sources has increased, as has that from multilateral sources. Funding from southern governments has also increased, as governments increasingly subcontract the implementation of public programmes. This has steadily brought NGOs closer to governments – in both the North and the South – and arguably 'too close for comfort' (Edwards and Hulme, 1995; Hulme and Edwards, 1997). Observers worry that NGOs have become increasingly subject to the restrictions and upwardly orientated accountability mechanisms that come with public funding, and particularly that such resource dependence can reduce the extent to which NGOs will voice certain criticisms and positions in public debates, or work in fields not fashionable among donors (Wallace et al., 1997). In the terms of the above debates on civil society, the concern is that the apparent strengthening of civil society in an associational sense (more and better-funded NGOs) might weaken it in the public sphere sense, as organisations self-censor in order to ensure funding access, and as they pay less attention to facilitating the participation of social movements and other grassroots actors in public debate, and more attention to ensuring their own visibility and fundability.

NGOs in civil society

NGOs are, then, neither synonymous nor entirely congruent with civil society – whether understood as a realm of associations or a public sphere. Indeed, the relationships both among different NGOs and between them and other types of association have not always been easy. Some social movements and popular organisations have criticised NGOs: for imposing agendas; for not allowing people's organisations sufficient say in the management of the financial resources that NGOs raise; for pursuing their own organisational imperatives at the expense of those of social movements; and for claiming to represent poor people in public debates and in the process marginalising people's own organisations. Other observers refuse to locate NGOs within the civic sphere, arguing that their ideologies, activities and lines of accountability are more characteristic of the private, market sector (for example, Uphoff, 1995; Stewart, 1997), and that they tend to treat bene-ficiaries as clients rather than citizens (for example, Miraftab, 1997). Attempts to resolve this dilemma include the suggestion that NGOs should adopt a 'fourth position' – embedded within the 'values' of civil society but institutionally located at a critical distance from state, market and civil society (Fowler, 2000b) – although this runs counter to suggestions that, if NGOs are to realise a comparative advantage, they may need to focus their attentions more clearly on working with one of these institutional arenas (Bebbington, 1997).

Notwithstanding the non-congruent relationship between NGOs and civil society, donor programmes have often assumed the two to be largely the same, and even where they have not, they have still tended to privilege NGOs within civil society strengthening programmes (Howell and Pearce, 2001). The reasons for this are understandable – it is practically and at times legally more difficult to transfer financial resources to movements and people's organisations that may not be legally constituted or registered, that may lack the internal capacities funding agencies require to ensure adequate use of public resources, and that themselves may not be representative of their ostensible membership. None the less, the focus on development NGOs has tended to obscure the importance of more political actors within civil society.

Three main types of such civil society strengthening programmes might be identified: those which seek to strengthen the capacity of civil society to deliver services, those which strengthen civil society as part of a good governance agenda, and those which seek to strengthen and democratise the public sphere. Much work on NGOs has emphasised their significance as sources of service provision. Efforts to chart the sheer scale of the third sector (Salamon and Anheier, 1997), suggest that NGOs are a vital source of social and economic services. Arguably such a message falls on particularly fertile ground among more neoliberal-orientated agencies concerned to reduce the scope of government in social life (Arellana-López and Petras, 1994), and there remain concerns that NGOs have so far struggled to ensure that such services reach the poorest groups (Riddell and Robinson, 1995).

A second type of programme draws inspiration from the argument that civil society organisations play important roles in holding state institutions to account, and thus in securing the foundations of democracy. Such programmes seek to strengthen organisations' roles in a range of activities – voter registration, citizen education, election monitoring, monitoring public expenditure and policies, human rights work, the liberalisation of the press and so on. Some argue that such programmes are also broadly neoliberal because they tend not to question the relationship among democratic procedure, asset distribution and the exercise of power in society. The success of NGOs in this more political role has been questionable (Mercer, 2002).

The third approach aims to build stable and socially inclusive public spheres – on the grounds that struggles over development are really struggles about hegemony and that therefore ideas about development must be continually contested and reworked in society. Such programmes support advocacy NGOs, unions, social movements, membership groups, interest groups, think-tanks and research institutes. Radical, social justice agencies and conservative donors alike have sought to strengthen the role of like-minded actors in public debate (Hearn, 2001). Indeed, the temptation of some donors to reduce support to research and divert funds towards direct poverty reduction can reasonably be seen as ceding ground to more conservative forces in the struggle to define hegemonic ideas.

Summary

Civil society has borne multiple meanings in development research and practice, and certain of these meanings have assumed most power, reflecting both dominant world-views and underlying material interests. Those meanings have underlain particular types of action with important material effects. NGOs have been both *actors in* and *vehicles of* these struggles over the meaning of civil society. As *actors* they aim to foster particular meanings of civil society. In some respects, their own diversity itself reflects different ideas about the type of civil society that should be worked towards or struggled for, and about the ways in which civil society, state and market should be linked and embedded in each other. As *vehicles* they have sometimes become the means – again, wittingly or unwittingly – through which other actors have aimed to promote particular meanings of civil society and visions of development. Whatever the definition of civil society one might choose, struggles over its meaning have material effects. NGOs are one of many actors engaged in these struggles. NGOs are not the same as civil society – but they play an important role in determining the forms that it takes.

ANTHONY BEBBINGTON
SAM HICKEY

References

Alvarez, S., E. Dagnino and A. Escobar (eds) (1998), *Cultures of Politics/Politics of Cultures. Re-visioning Latin American Social Movements*, Boulder, CO: Westview.
Arellana-López, S. and J. Petras (1994), 'Nongovernmental organizations and poverty alleviation in Bolivia', *Development and Change*, **25** (3), 555–68.
Bebbington, A. (1997), 'New states, new NGOs? Crisis and transition among Andean rural development NGOs', *World Development*, **25** (11), 1755–65.
Bebbington, A. and R. Riddell (1995), 'The direct funding of southern NGOs by northern donors: new agendas and old problems', *Journal for International Development*, **7** (6), 879–93.
Booth, D. (ed.) (1994), *Rethinking Social Development: Theory, Research and Practice*, Harlow: Longman.
Clark, J. (1991), *Democratizing Development: The Role of Voluntary Organizations*, London: Earthscan.
Drabek, A. (1987), 'Development alternatives: the challenge of NGOs', *World Development*, **15** (supplement), Autumn.
Edwards, M. (2004), *Civil Society*, Oxford: Polity.
Edwards, M. and D. Hulme (eds) (1995), *Nongovernmental Organisations Performance and Accountability: Beyond the Magic Bullet*, London: Earthscan.
Ferguson, J. (2004), 'Power topographies', in D. Nugent and J. Vincent (eds), *A Companion to the Anthropology of Politics*, Oxford: Blackwell, pp. 383–99.
Fowler, A. (2000a), 'Civil society, NGDOs and social development: changing the rules of the game', UNRISD Occasional Paper no. 1, Geneva: UN Research Institute for Social Development.
Fowler, A. (2000b), 'NGO futures: beyond aid: NGDO values and the fourth position', *Third World Quarterly*, **21** (4), 589–603.
Gramsci, A. (1971), *Selections from the Prison Notebooks*, London: Lawrence & Wishart.
Habermas, J. (1984), *The Theory of Communicative Action*, Cambridge: Polity.
Hearn, J. (2001), 'The uses and abuses of civil society in Africa', *Review of African Political Economy*, **87**, 43–53.
Howell, J. and J. Pearce (2001), *Civil Society and Development: A Critical Exploration*, Boulder, CO: Lynne Rienner.
Hulme, D. and M. Edwards (1997), *Too Close for Comfort? NGOs, States and Governments*, London: Macmillan.
Hyden, G. (1997), 'Civil society, social capital, and development: dissection of a complex discourse', *Studies in Comparative International Development*, **31** (1), 3–30.
Keck, M. and K. Sikkink (1998), *Activists beyond Borders: Advocacy Networks in International Politics*, Ithaca, NY: Cornell University Press.
Lewis, D. (2002), 'Civil society in African contexts: reflections on the usefulness of a concept', *Development and Change*, **33** (4), 569–86.
Mamdani, M. (1996), *Citizen and Subject: Contemporary Africa and the Legacy of Late Colonialism*, Oxford: James Currey.

Mercer, C. (2002), 'NGOs, civil society and democratization: a critical review of the literature', *Progress in Development Studies*, **2** (1), 5–22.

Miraftab, F. (1997), 'Flirting with the enemy', *Habitat International*, **21** (4), 361–75.

Peet, R. and M. Watts (eds) (2004), *Liberation Ecologies: Environment, Development, Social Movements*, 2nd edn, London: Routledge.

Putnam, R. (1993), *Making Democracy Work: Civic Traditions in Modern Italy*, Princeton, NJ: Princeton University Press.

Riddell, R. and M. Robinson (eds) (1995), *Non-Governmental Organisations and Rural Poverty Alleviation*, Oxford: Oxford University Press.

Salamon, L. and H. Anheier (eds) (1997), *Defining the Non-Profit Sector: A Cross-National Analysis*, Manchester: Manchester University Press.

Stewart, S. (1997), 'Happy ever after in the marketplace: non-government organisations and uncivil society', *Review of African Political Economy*, **71**, 11–34.

Tandon, R. (2001), 'Riding high or nosediving: development NGOs in the new millennium', in D. Eade and E. Ligteringen (eds), *Debating Development*, Oxford: Oxfam, pp. 44–59.

Tarrow, S. (1996), 'Making social science work across space and time: a critical reflection upon Robert Putnam's *Making Democracy Work*', *American Political Science Review*, **90** (2), 389–97.

Townsend, J., G. Porter and E. Mawdsley (2002), 'The role of the transnational community of development non-governmental organizations: governance or poverty reduction?', *Journal of International Development*, **14** (6), 829–39.

Uphoff, N. (1995), 'Why NGOs are not a third sector: a sectoral analysis with some thoughts on accountability, sustainability and evaluation', in Edwards and Hulme (eds), pp. 17–30.

Vakil, A. (1997), 'Confronting the classification problem: toward a taxonomy of NGOs', *World Development*, **25** (12), 2057–70.

Wallace, T., S. Crowther and A. Shepherd (1997), *Standardising Development: Influences on UK NGOs' Policies and Procedures*, Oxford: World View.

World Bank (2001), *World Development Report 2000–2001: Attacking Poverty*, Oxford and New York: Oxford University Press.

North, Douglass (b. 1920)

Douglass C. North received his undergraduate and graduate training in economics (BA 1942; PhD 1952) from the University of California at Berkeley. His early research in economic history focused on the balance of payments, and led to his notable elaboration of an export-led model of US antebellum growth (North, 1961; see also Sutch, 1982). His 1966 textbook helped popularise a new approach to economic history: quantitatively orientated and explicitly informed by theory. This work is remarkable for its brevity (under 200 pages), and lack of attention to details of institutional or legal change that had been a feature of earlier (and bulkier) surveys. Paradoxically, while North stressed the dependence of economic growth on free market institutions, readers received little exposure to the details of the changing legal and regulatory environment that delineated such an evolving economy. His approach to institutions here can be usefully contrasted with the opening chapters of Hughes (1990), which recalled earlier traditions in its treatment of the American legal heritage from Europe, and its consequences.

North's growing interest in institutions ultimately consumed the bulk of his scholarly attentions over the next 35 years. His 1968 article on productivity growth in ocean shipping concluded that declines in piracy and improvements in organisation (rather than technological change narrowly construed) had been the main engine of growth in that sector, sharpening his interest in transaction costs as a potential brake on the growth of output, and on the role of political and economic organisation in potentially overcoming them. A growing explanatory ambition, however, now moved his work beyond sectorally focused empirical studies. Beginning in 1971, a series of articles and books explored at national and international levels the causes and consequences of institutional variation.

Davis and North (1971) drew inspiration from the public choice literature to try to account for when and why interest groups organised to change rules which otherwise constrained them, in the process altering the incidence of transaction costs and prospects for growth. North and Thomas (1973) were even more ambitious, claiming in 158 pages to account for eight centuries of European development. Particularly with respect to the pre-1500 period, North and Thomas attempted to use what they viewed as purely 'economic' variables (that is, technology and demographic changes) to explain the decline of feudalism and the rise of institutions of market economy. Their attempt was notable for its apparent avoidance of 'ad hoc' appeals to institutions, culture or legal persistence as forces in their own right.

North and Thomas's work was criticised by Fenoaltea (1975) for its superficial treatment of the historical record, and by Field (1981) for its inability to deliver on a methodological promise that was probably unattainable. Why, for example, if population growth led to the breakdown of feudalism in the eleventh to the thirteenth centuries, did not population decline after the Black Death reversed the process? North and Thomas's answer was that the rise in the land–labour ratio increased the bargaining power of those cultivators who survived. But this argument ran contrary to that put forward by Evsey Domar (1970) to explain the emergence of serfdom in Eastern Europe, as well as the American slave system. High (or rising) land–labour ratios could not simultaneously be the explanation of freedom in Western Europe and of serfdom/slavery in Eastern Europe and the American South.

North took note of these criticisms, and his thinking eventually evolved to a more nuanced position. Acknowledging loose ends in his earlier writings, he now argued that in order to make sense of these histories one had, either explicitly or implicitly, to recognise an independent role for institutional regimes themselves, and the cultural forces that might reinforce and sustain them. To understand why such regimes sometimes did and sometimes did not change, one needed, moreover, a historical, case-specific methodology. In contrast, North and Thomas had been driven by a powerful imperative to view rules as ultimately derivative of more 'fundamental' givens, such as technologies and endowments. From such a perspective, institutional details were developed primarily to illustrate the power of the model, rather than because such details might be causal in their own right (Field, 1991). Ultimately, institutional variation became epiphenomenal, and could not itself help explain why regions with access to similar endowments and technology experienced different growth paths.

North's subsequent publications reflected a not always successful struggle to reconcile two imperatives: first, to account for institutional variation as the outcome of maximising behaviour constrained only by technology and endowments, and second, to use institutional variation to account for differences in economic performance. His third book on institutions (North, 1981) included responses to criticisms of earlier work. In Chapter 5, North explicitly acknowledged ideology as an independent influence binding individuals together and overcoming free-rider problems. In other words, ideology could have bound together Eastern lords, or American slaveholders, making it possible for them to impose their coercive labour regimes in regions with high land–labour ratios, in spite of the otherwise favourable bargaining conditions for cultivators.

But much of the rest of the book carried forward the language and objectives of earlier work. The implications of criticisms responded to in one part of the book were not systematically acknowledged in its remainder. His 1990 book was similar in this respect. As its title (*Institutions, Institutional Change, and Economic Performance*) suggested, sections of the book, particularly Part III, placed even more explicit emphasis on the consequences of institutional variation. But elsewhere the public choice analysis of why and when institutions change persisted, albeit with more qualifications.

Subsequently, North has pushed forward in trying to understand those features of human cognitive machinery that allow or encourage ideology to influence behaviour. In 1993 he shared the Nobel Prize in economics with Robert Fogel for 'having renewed research in economic history by applying economic theory and quantitative methods in order to explain economic and institutional change'. North's Nobel lecture (North, 1993) reinforced his new emphasis on the political underpinnings of institutional structures, and the likelihood that they would not in fact be optimal. Institutions, he now maintained, were 'not necessarily or even usually created to be socially efficient; rather they, or at least the formal rules, are created to serve the interests of those with the bargaining power to create new rules'. In contrast with the position he and Thomas had articulated in 1973, efficient institutional structures had become the exception rather than the rule.

His Nobel lecture also delineated some of the themes that have occupied him in recent years: an interest in how to integrate research in cognitive science, game theory and evolutionary history to help us understand how individuals learn, how they form 'mental models' of the world, and how these processes impinge on the formation and change of institutional structures. These structures, he has emphasised again and again, even more than technologies, resource endowments, or preferences narrowly understood, govern the course of economic development and explain the different success of human populations in different regions of the world.

North's achievement and recognition has been based on the indefatigable manner in which he has insisted that the economics profession acknowledge at some level the 'importance' of institutions. While he has never entirely abandoned the attempt to develop an endogenous theory of institutional change, his writings have evolved and now include more statements and sections with which a critic of his earlier work could agree. As a result, it is possible, by searching, for almost everyone to find something appealing here.

But the converse also remains true. As North has responded to critics, he has built a large tent and invited in people of different persuasions to celebrate. But it is important that critical sensibilities not be dulled. North's work has not, by its example, encouraged economists and economic historians to emulate the attention to detail common in legal scholarship and work in comparative law. His writing on institutions has been broad-brush, based largely on secondary sources. His attention to institutional detail has been further limited by the space devoted to expositing (or, at times, criticising) the theoretical literature from which he has drawn inspiration.

Second, his tolerance for ambiguity, and his willingness to bring to bear ideas from differing theoretical traditions, generates frustration for those trying systematically to take the measure of his work. One way to try to resolve this is to distinguish between research concerned with the origins of institutional variation and that addressing its consequences. North, for example, has had great interest and considerable involvement in the study of the impact of new institutional regimes in transition economies. This is a clear instance of a focus on the consequences of rule variation, since in this case North has presumed that these policies are intended to foster economic growth and the well-being of the target population, and has not suggested a 'political economic' or public choice model of regime change, as was true in his earlier studies of US and European economic history. In other words, Western policy advisers have been viewed by North as genuinely interested in implementing efficient rule structures, perhaps an historical exception to the tendency described in his Nobel lecture for those with the power to design formal rules to do so with their own economic interest in mind. Or perhaps there is simply no conflict between these imperatives in this instance.

Another and related way to gain insight into what North is attempting is to explore more systematically how our long evolutionary history has conditioned our cognitive and behavioural predispositions (see, for example, Field, 2001). As early as 1978, North described his ultimate goal as a 'generalised theory of social science' (1978, p. 974), and he continues to pursue that objective. As he acknowledges, work that he and others have done in this area is in its infancy, and there is much that remains to be done in developing a unified approach to human behaviour rooted in the behavioural, social and natural sciences, and integrating both experimental and observational evidence. Such work will be critical in resolving the difficult but important questions posed by North during his long and productive academic life.

ALEXANDER J. FIELD

References

Davis, Lance and Douglass C. North (1971), *Institutional Change and American Economic Growth*, Cambridge: Cambridge University Press.

Domar, Evsey (1970), 'The causes of slavery and serfdom: a hypothesis', *Journal of Economic History*, **30**, 18–32.

Fenoaltea, Stefano (1975), 'The rise and fall of a theoretical model: the manorial system', *Journal of Economic History*, **35**, 386–409.

Field, Alexander J. (1981), 'The problem with neoclassical institutional economics: a critique with special reference to the North/Thomas model of pre-1500 Europe', *Explorations in Economic History*, **18**, 174–98.

Field, Alexander J. (1991), 'Do legal systems matter?', *Explorations in Economic History*, **28**, 1–35.

Field, Alexander J. (2001), *Altruistically Inclined? The Behavioral Sciences, Evolutionary Theory, and the Origins of Reciprocity*, Ann Arbor, MI: University of Michigan Press.

Hughes, Jonathan (1990), *American Economic History*, 3rd edn, New York: Scott Foresman.

North, Douglass C. (1961), *The Economic Growth of the United States, 1790–1860*, Englewood Cliffs, NJ: Prentice-Hall.

North, Douglass C. (1966), *Growth and Welfare in the America Past: A New Economic History*, Englewood Cliffs, NJ: Prentice-Hall.

North, Douglass C. (1968), 'Sources of productivity change in ocean shipping, 1600–1850', *Journal of Political Economy*, **76**, 953–67.

North, Douglass C. (1978), 'Structure and performance: the task of economic history', *Journal of Economic Literature*, **16**, 963–78.

North, Douglass C. (1981), *Structure and Change in Economic History*, New York: Norton.

North, Douglass C. (1990), *Institutions, Institutional Change, and Economic Performance*, Cambridge: Cambridge University Press.

North, Douglass C. (1993), Nobel Lecture: 'Economic performance through time', www.nobel.se/economics/laureates/1993/north–lecture.html.

North, Douglass C. and Robert Paul Thomas (1973), *The Rise of the Western World: A New Economic History*, Cambridge: Cambridge University Press.

Sutch, Richard (1982), 'Douglass North and the new economic history', in Roger L. Ransom, Richard Sutch and Gary M. Walton (eds), *Explorations in the New Economic History*, New York: Academic Press, pp. 13–38.

Participatory Research

From a purely methodological point of view, participatory research can be defined as methods for analysing local individuals' and communities' concerns, tapping into their capacity to identify for themselves the characteristics of the phenomenon under study, as well as to appraise its causes, consequences and dynamics. Underpinning these methods is the belief that local people have the ability and the right to analyse their circumstances and to take action. Participatory research aims, therefore, to set in motion new dynamics which challenge existing power relations – a well-structured analytical process is therefore not only limited to 'understanding' but calls for 'consensus and action' as next steps (Gujit and Braden, 1999). Distinctive elements of this type of analysis are the limited role of the external researcher, who acts only as a facilitator in the process, the emphasis on mutual learning between researchers and participants and among participants themselves in the process of constructing knowledge, and the use of visual rather than verbal or written outputs, generally obtained through group activities. The adoption of this type of technique has been claimed to lead to very similar quantitative results to those of standard surveys, and to do so in a more cost-effective, rapid and enjoyable way.

The popularity of these methods is intertwined with the evolution of thinking on the role of participatory processes in development. Such evolution has not been a linear one, and it has been the result of different forces. As a result, the concept has been and remains a contested and evolving one. Cornwall (2000) identifies three big shifts in the thinking on participation in development. At first, in the 1970s, 'popular participation' was called for within the context of rural development and basic needs strategies. The emphasis was on increasing the efficiency and the effectiveness of the projects, of which people were seen as 'beneficiaries'. The retreat of the state in the 1980s saw local participation become associated with the growth of grassroots self-reliance and self-help, either for its political value as a way of promoting local ownership or for its cost-sharing element. In the 1990s, participation moved beyond the boundaries of project or grassroots interventions to other spheres of social, economic and political life.

The evolving meaning of participation in development translated into new methods for participatory research and analysis, and by the early 1990s, 'participatory rural appraisal' (PRA) emerged. PRA built on a variety of other methodological and conceptual developments, including 'activist participatory research', which adopted dialogue and participatory research to enhance respondents' awareness and confidence, agro-ecosystem analysis with its various visual tools, and anthropological methods (for more detail, see Chambers, 1994). The key influence on the development of PRA was, however, 'rapid rural appraisal' (RRA), a technique which seeks to elicit local knowledge to overcome the inherent biases of outsiders. Essential RRA elements which continue to characterise PRA are the so-called principle of 'optimum ignorance' (find out as much as you need to know now) and 'appropriate imprecision' (there is no need to know everything exactly)' (Cornwall, 2000).

What PRA brought to the fore, however, was the ultimate purpose of the research – not extracting information, but 'to enable local people to conduct their own analysis, and often to plan and take action' (Chambers, 1994, p. 958). For many of its proponents, therefore, participatory research is but one tool to enact participation: 'participation is a way of viewing the world and acting in it' (Blackburn and Holland, 1998, p. 3). The tension between seeing participation as a means (say, to lower programme costs) or seeing it as an end remains, however, and is mirrored in the tension between an efficiency and a rights-based argument for the adoption of participatory methods. The former focuses on using participatory methods to collect information, either to substitute or to integrate information from standard surveys. The latter emphasises the epistemological and political aspects of empowering individuals to analyse their realities and identify their own priorities for action.

The tension over this duality of scopes and aims of participatory methods surrounds many of the applications of participatory methods – this will be illustrated by taking the example of poverty analysis (see Poverty, Characteristics of, this volume, and Ruggeri Laderchi, 2005 for a fuller discussion). Poverty analysis is only one of the many areas to which participatory methods have been applied, ranging for example from natural resource management (for example, Veit, 1998; Coriolo et al., 2001), to violence (for example, Moser and McIlwaine, 1999), to participatory monitoring and evaluations (Estrella and Gaventa, 1998) and risk assessments (Smith et al., 2000). A focus on poverty analysis, however, offers an immediate example of the variety of analytical tools available, the different ways participatory research can challenge and integrate results obtained by quantitative methods, and the pressures faced in scaling up and institutionalising participatory analysis. In particular, in the field of poverty analysis it is evident that there is a risk of a divorce between methodological tools and conceptual underpinnings, as local communities might be at pains to act on the structural and systemic causes of poverty, while their input might be sought to inform policy and understanding more than for immediate action.

Participatory poverty research

The core of poverty analysis is constituted by the identification of deprived households on the basis of some indicator of well-being, the description of their characteristics associated with deprivation and possibly the identification of causal relations. Dynamic analysis of how deprivation has evolved in the population, to what extent the well-being of those in poverty has changed, whether new groups have become poor and to what extent, and the distribution of the risk of becoming poor for different groups are also potentially very informative for policy making, but not always possible. A variety of other issues can be explored to understand the constraints and resources the poor face – these relate to the livelihoods of the poor, their coping strategies when faced with shocks, their access to natural resources and to services, their use of formal and informal institutions.

The set of tools applied to these issues include:

- *social maps*, that is, representation of the communities where different types of household and the resources they can access are identified;
- *well-being rankings*, that is, orderings of the households in the communities on the basis of the criteria identified by the group;

- *Venn diagrams*, or other diagrammatic representations of interactions between households and institutions in the community or between institutions; and
- *timelines*, illustrating the seasonality in uses and needs for resources, or depicting the chronological development of different events and so on.

Many of these tools are used in focus group discussions, or in interviews with key informants. Open-ended questionnaires can also be used. It is worth stressing, however, that the variety of these methods and their flexibility distinguishes them from other methods, which elicit self-perception data through structured questionnaires.

All these various activities are likely to take place with different groups, representing different categories of respondents with some a priori assumption on the relevance of the various categories for poverty analysis. Typical examples of such groupings would be by gender, or race, or caste, or by some other salient characteristic. This variety of points of view and techniques aimed at triangulating the perceptions of different types of respondents is an essential element of these research methods, as is the emphasis on the visual and the non-structured. Space is also left for the unexpected to emerge, and for the analysis to adapt to the local context. These characteristics imply that the sequence of activities might differ from locality to locality and in particular across urban and rural contexts. They also imply that researchers need to synthesise the variety of outputs and insights obtained to distil their messages.

The defining features of participatory poverty analysis are made more obvious by contrasting them with the characteristics of standard economic analysis of poverty:

- In terms of well-being indicators, participatory research emphasises community identification of criteria of well-being and ill-being, while economic analysis uses monetary indicators (income or consumption) obtained through closed-ended questionnaires. Participatory analysis can therefore result in localised and often group specific assessments, which might be hard to generalise, especially if it is unclear how statistically representative the assessment was.
- In terms of identification of those who are poor, participatory research provides categories that are likely to be context specific and to refer to a wider spectrum of dimensions than the monetary one captured by economic assessments of poverty. Furthermore, interpersonal comparisons of well-being are hindered by the lack of a common metric of deprivation when comparing assessments from different locations.
- In terms of assessments of the dynamics of change, in participatory exercises it can refer to often undefined (for the researcher) time horizons, rather than to the fixed-term (the time between different waves of a panel survey) basis of economic poverty assessments. At the same time, however, participatory techniques can engage with the analysis of the process of change and the mechanism that generate it in a way which is not possible for standard economic assessments (Shaffer, 2002).

These differences have led to much scepticism on the 'scientific' value of this type of poverty assessments on the part of those trained into economic methods of poverty analysis. In contrast, practitioners of participatory methods have argued that 'a key contribution . . . lies in revealing and bringing together a greater diversity of perspectives' (Abbott and Gujit, 1997, p. 28).

Nevertheless, practitioners have to grapple with some of the issues at the heart of the concept of participation and the empowering role of creating knowledge: how participatory the practice of participatory methods can truly be, especially when time is limited and the mandate of the researcher is delimited by external actors' constraints (say, donors' mandate in a given field); what can be done to bring into the open and mute the role of the researcher in constructing knowledge; what is meant by 'community' and whose voices are being heard, given power dynamics within groups, and their interactions with personal identities and socially constructed categories such as gender (for example, Gujit and Shah, 1998); is it ethical to engage communities in processes which might both require broader action than the one afforded by local action plans, and raise expectations on interventions by outsiders?

Advocates of participatory research point to the need for intellectual honesty and self-reflective criticism on the part of the researcher as means to address most of these difficult issues. They also suggest that all processes of knowledge formation, including those based on 'scientific' and objective sources, should be subject to the same type of scrutiny, though this call has gone largely unheeded by those who use 'scientific' approaches.

The differences in scope and methods listed above can be read as pointing to the high degree of complementarity between different types of poverty analyses. Analyses based on monetary indicators do not capture perceptions and feelings, while those in themselves influence well-being. At the same time, the highly contextual assessments provided by participatory research might provide insights of limited use for arriving at a broader understanding of a phenomenon. It is in this vein that the potential of quantitative and participatory techniques to feed off each other has been advocated to address some of the obvious shortfalls of either method (Booth et al., 1998), though remaining aware of the existence of trade-offs (see Kanbur, 2004 and Shaffer, 2004 in particular). Poverty analysis can be enriched by thinking creatively about these complementarities thanks to the suitability of participatory methods to the analysis of causes and consequences, the dynamics and potential for change and the identification of heterogeneity of behaviours and effects. For example, quantitative surveys have been used to quantify the importance of key livelihood strategies identified by participatory methods (for example, Carter and May, 1999). Alternatively, one can imagine using participatory methods to explore specific findings raised by quantitative research, and the dynamics that brought them about.

It has been suggested, however, that methodological innovation through combined methods and statistical soundness can lead to 'compromises of complementarity' (Abbott and Gujit, 1997), distorting the participatory element of the original method. These compromises seem to have emerged strongly in the context of participatory poverty research, which has been scaled up to arrive at nationwide 'participatory poverty assessments' (PPAs) (as they have come to be known within the World Bank where they originated). The effort to bring the techniques which were used at the local and project level to bear on broad policy debates has faced practitioners with a variety of new challenges, such as how to extend techniques which had been developed in rural contexts of rather stable communities to urban ones, how to ensure that flexible and ultimately uncodifiable practices lead to results which can be generalised and trusted to represent broader realities, and how to maintain the participatory nature of the assessment. These challenges are all the more pressing now that participatory methods are scaled up both in terms of coverage (for example with multicountry studies such as the World Bank's *Voices of the Poor*, Narayan et al., 2000) and in terms of breadth of issues tackled (such as in the case of the institutionalised participation in the elaboration of poverty reduction strategy papers – PRSPs).

At the same time, scaling-up of participatory research has had an enriching effect on the poverty discourse of development's mainstream – consider for example the adoption of multidimensional concepts of poverty (though these are not the exclusive retinue of participatory research) and the emphasis on the insecurity and powerlessness experienced by the poor.

However, it is in terms of engagement with political processes that a larger challenge to participatory research is faced. In the views of some of its detractors, participatory poverty research risks reducing these techniques to their empty shell of data extraction. Even worse, their application contributes to the legitimisation of the powerlessness of the poor, by giving them a voice without fostering further change and by peddling a naïve vision of empowerment (Cooke and Kothari, 2001).

Those within the participation camp see in contrast the possibility of engaging and shaping political processes. McGee and Norton (1999), for example, consider that PPAs offered the opportunity to broaden the conceptual agenda of standard poverty assessments and establish the right of the poor to participate. And over time, PPAs have also become tools for opening up spaces in which poor people's perspectives can influence policy makers' views. This is seen to occur through various channels including generating information and stimulating local level action, as recognised by the PRA tradition, but also having an impact on relationships between actors involved in poverty reduction issues, and providing an opportunity for experimental learning by policy makers (McGee, 2002).

In the mid-1990s Robert Chambers asked 'how much potential these approaches and methods have for making participation more practical and the rhetoric more real?' (Chambers, 1994, p. 953). That question remains relevant. It is posed today when we think of participation as a means to engage with the higher spheres of policy making – in an arena quite removed from the local and programme-based reality in which these methods were born. Over the years, participatory research has gone from the periphery to the mainstream of development studies. In so doing it has raised high hopes and generated some controversies. People from other research traditions claim that it fails to meet the criteria of reliable research. From a different perspective, others maintain that the adoption of this methodology into the mainstream has not been accompanied by a shift towards embracing the political agenda of participation. The experience of the last decade suggests, however, that the versatility of these research methods, and the enthusiasm and dedication of those who see it as a means for bringing change about are likely to keep it right where it is – a useful though debatable tool for listening to the voices of the poor.

CATERINA RUGGERI LADERCHI

References

Abbott, Jo and Irene Gujit (1997), 'Methodological complementarity. Creativity and compromise', PLA Notes 28, International Institute for Environment and Development (IIED), London, pp. 27–32.

Blackburn, James and Jeremy Holland (eds) (1998), *Who Changes? Institutionalising Participation in Development*, London: Intermediate Technology.

Booth, David, Jeremy Holland, Jesko Hentschel, Peter Lanjouw and Alicia Herbert (1998), *Participation and Combined Methods in African Poverty Assessment: Renewing the Agenda*, DFID Social Development Division, Department for International Development, London.

Brock, Karen and Rosemary McGee (eds) (2002), *Knowing Poverty: Critical Reflections on Participatory Research and Policy*, London: Earthscan.

Carter, Michael R. and Julian May (1999), 'Poverty, livelihood and class in rural South Africa', *World Development*, **27** (1), 1–20.

Chambers, Robert (1994), 'The origins and practice of participatory rural appraisal', *World Development*, **22** (7), 953–69.

Cooke, Bill and Uma Kothari (eds) (2001), *Participation: The New Tyranny?*, London: Zed Books.

Coriolo, L., K. McLean, M. Mokoli, A. Ryan, P. Shah and M. Williams (2001), 'Community based rural development: reducing rural poverty from the ground up', *World Bank Rural Strategy Discussion Paper 6*, Washington, DC: World Bank.

Cornwall, Andrea (2000), 'Beneficiary, consumer, citizen: perspectives on participation for poverty reduction', mimeo, Institute of Development Studies, University of Sussex, Brighton.

Estrella, Marisol and John Gaventa (1998), 'Who counts reality? Participatory monitoring and evaluation: a literature review', IDS Working Paper 70, Institute of Development Studies, University of Sussex, Brighton.

Gujit, Irene and Su Braden (1999), 'Learning from analysis. Ensuring reflection in participatory processes', PLA Notes 34, IIED, London, pp. 18–24.

Guijt, Irene and Meera K. Shah (eds) (1998), *The Myth of Community: Gender Issues in Participatory Development*, London: Intermediate Technology.

Kanbur, Ravi (ed.) (2004), *Q-squared. Qualitative and Quantitative Methods of Poverty Appraisal*, Delhi: Permanent Black.

McGee, Rosemary (2002), 'The self in participatory poverty research', in Brock and McGee (eds), pp. 14–43.

McGee, Rosemary and Andy Norton (1999), 'Participation in poverty reduction strategies: a synthesis of experience with participatory approaches to policy design, implementation and monitoring', IDS Working Paper 109, Institute of Development Studies, University of Sussex, Brighton.

Moser, Caroline and Cathy McIlwaine (1999), 'Participatory urban appraisal and its application for research on violence', *Environment and Urbanization*, **11** (2), 203–26.

Narayan, Deepa, Robert Chambers, Meera Kaul Shah and Patti Petesch (2000), *Voices of the Poor: Crying Out for Change*, Oxford: Oxford University Press for the World Bank.

Ruggeri Laderchi, Caterina (2005), 'Participatory methods in the analysis of poverty: a critical review', in CIP-UPWARD, *Participatory Research and Development for Sustainable Agriculture and Natural Resource Management: A Sourcebook*, Los Banos, Laguna, Philippines: CIP-UPWARD, 3 vols, pp. 135–44.

Shaffer, Paul (2002), 'Participatory analysis of poverty dynamics: reflections on the Myanmar PPA', in Brock and McGee (eds), pp. 44–68.

Shaffer, Paul (2004), 'Difficulties in combining income/consumption and participatory approaches to poverty: issues and examples', in Kanbur (ed.), pp. 126–40.

Smith, Kevin, Christopher Barrett and Paul Box (2000), 'Participatory risk mapping for targeting research and assistance: an example using East-African pastoralists', *World Development*, **28** (11), 1945–59.

Veit, Peter (ed.) (1998), *Africa's Valuable Assets: A Reader in Natural Resource Management*, Washington, DC: World Resources Institute.

Planning

The origins of planning

Like so much in economics, it began as a simple notion but as it evolved, planning became a very sophisticated process with all manner of bells and whistles. Its purpose was logical; determine what must be produced today so that goals set for next year can be achieved. It started with the individual and small businessman. As the business unit grew, the processes and interconnections became more complicated and required more regularised procedures. In the corporate world, it came to be called budgeting, but in essence it was planning. In order to ensure that the corporation will have enough production capacity to meet demand, the corporate executive must predict sales and allocate investment resources and working capital to have ready the machinery as well as the inventory and workforce needed to produce the anticipated sales.

The Soviet variant
After seizing control of Russia and realising that the rest of Europe would not follow Russia's example and embrace communism, Vladimir Lenin – and then Joseph Stalin – set themselves the goal of industrialising Russia as quickly as possible. Convinced that a market system with competing firms trying to do each other in was wasteful, Stalin in particular concluded that he could achieve a faster rate of growth if instead business entrepreneurs cooperated with each other and coordinated their activities. If budgeting and coordination made sense at the micro-firm level in Germany and the United States with their large corporations, it should also make sense at a macro level. National coordination or planning, however, was unattainable as long as enterprises were privately owned and business managers could do as they pleased. Such communal efforts would only be possible when enterprises were owned by the state and factory directors knew that they would have to follow state mandates. Of course, state ownership also fits in nicely with Marxist ideology.

Because no country had ever attempted anything so bold and ambitious, the early attempts at planning in the USSR were inevitably crude. The first challenge in the mid-1920s was simply to determine what resources in terms of capital, factories, inventory, labour and raw materials the state had at its disposal. Given how backward Russia was economically, that was no easy task. But once that was done, in 1925–26 some draft control figures were drawn up by Gosplan (the state planning agency). Another set was prepared for 1927–28 and this time the control figures became mandatory. By 1928, Gosplan extended the planning period to five years with the publication of the USSR's 2000-page first five-year plan which was to run from 1928 to 1933.

The plan set production output targets five years in the future for the priority sectors of the economy. This in turn required the setting of production targets for the inputs needed to attain the priority output. To coordinate all these activities, Gosplan created what it called 'material balances'. These balances were nothing more than two columns: one detailing the supplies of a good expected to be available during the course of the planning period and the other a list of uses to which that product was to be put. Thus the supplies of steel included expected production for the year as well as steel imports and a draw-down of inventory. The demand for steel included the steel needed to produce such items as bridges, automobiles, tanks and refrigerators, as well as steel intended to be set aside for export and inventory build-up.

It was then the planners' task to ensure that there were enough inputs to make possible the outputs called for in the plan. This might require an increase in output or a curbing of demand for inputs. This also meant ascertaining the composition of a product – that is, to produce water, the planners needed to provide two units of hydrogen for one unit of oxygen.

Economists like Wassily Leontief understood that these crude material balance relationships lent themselves nicely to a more sophisticated mathematical treatment and he and others came up with the concept of an input–output matrix that would calculate these interrelationships. The problem was that this was before the age of the sophisticated computer and the more detailed the matrix became and the more the economy grew in size and complexity, the more complicated it became to calculate.

This was not the only shortcoming. It quickly became apparent that predicting the future, even a year in advance, was not easy. While drawing up a plan forced the planners and Soviet leaders to think through their priorities and alert them to the measures needed to realise major objectives, it became increasingly clear that the plan and actual economic results had less and less to do with each other. Weather and technological change were particularly problematic. In the case of technology, as long as there were relatively few technological advances, as in the 1930s, there was no serious problem. But by the 1960s and 1970s, whole new industries had come into being. The Soviet Union tried to keep abreast or ahead of such advances by creating an impressive network of research institutions and laboratories. It also relied heavily on espionage. But even with experiments in the laboratories and stolen blueprints, it found itself losing out on more of the new developments in such fields as chemistry, electronics, computers and biotechnology. And when some of its laboratories did come up with pathfinding innovations, the innovations often as not failed to find their way into the commercial production process. Unlike the capitalist world, the Soviet Union had no venture capital phenomena. For the most part, capital was still controlled centrally by the state. This meant that those state bureaucrats in charge of capital allocations were much less willing to expose themselves to risks and thus less likely to benefit from putting technological breakthroughs into production.

Soviet central planning had its proponents in the West, particularly prior to the Second World War. While most of the Western world in the 1930s found itself deep in an economic depression with massive unemployment, the Soviet Union began to boast record rates in economic growth. Not surprisingly, many engineers with no prospects of employment in the United States eagerly accepted jobs building factories, refineries and dams in the Soviet Union.

By the 1960s, however, it became clear that the planning system – at least the Soviet variation – was beginning to outlive its usefulness. Not only was Soviet technology falling further behind, but Soviet consumers were perennially faced with shortages, including food. Whereas in the Tsarist era, Russia was often the world's largest grain exporter, under Soviet planning it became the world's largest importer. But while there were embarrassing shortages, there was also embarrassing duplication and waste. Even when plans were prepared in time and assigned before the beginning of the planning period, the plan targets seemed to diverge more and more from actual output. In addition, no matter how hard they tried, Soviet planners found themselves unable to anticipate consumer demands. It was hard enough to do this when the product mix of goods available to Soviet consumers was simple. As the product mix became more varied, it seemed to be all but impossible.

There were periodic attempts to reform the planning system, but none seemed to solve the challenges of eliminating shortages, duplication and facilitating innovation. By 1985, when Mikhail Gorbachev became the General Secretary of the Communist Party and the head of the Politburo, it had become clear that central planning was not working and that the market system of the West might bring about not only higher but more meaningful economic growth that would ultimately provide a better life for most Russians.

Planning in the non-communist world

While planning is normally thought of as a Soviet or communist phenomenon, there have been many adaptations in the capitalist world as well. The French, for example, adopted a form of macro planning called 'indicative planning'. This stood in contrast to the 'imperative planning' that reflected Soviet practices. What the French did was to project certain levels of GDP growth and then suggest what this might mean for various industries. The Japanese had something similar. For a time this seemed to work reasonably well in large part because Japanese executives concluded that in order to gain market share, if growth for their industry was projected at 6 per cent, they would have to grow at a rate of 8 or even 10 per cent. This was fine as long as Japanese costs were competitive, but after new and cheaper competitors began to operate in Korea, Taiwan and China, the Japanese found themselves at a serious disadvantage.

With time, Japanese planners came under attack for their efforts at micro management. As a subcomponent of macroeconomic planning, the Japanese officials, particularly in the Ministry of International Trade and Industry (MITI) tried to anticipate what they thought would be the future growth sectors of the economy. They would then pressure what they considered the non-growth industries to curtail their activity and redirect their capital and resources to the growth areas. This was not always successful. Critics pointed out, for example, that some of Japan's most successful companies such as Honda and Sony had on occasion been pressured by MITI to shrink rather than expand. In other words, MITI was as often wrong as right.

Limited planning, however, has its advocates. In Taiwan for example, economic officials sought to stimulate the high-tech sector by setting up a high-tech industrial park in Hsinchu, Taiwan. Located amidst some of Taiwan's best universities and technical institutes, Hsinchu was designed to generate start-ups and foreign investors seeking a pool of highly trained specialists. Tax incentives and cheap financing were also made available. Some regions in the United States, such as the 'Research Triangle' in North Carolina, have attempted similar programmes. The Tennessee Valley Authority is an earlier version of regional planning which emphasised the building of hydro-electric power.

It is also worth mentioning a limited but revealing American experiment in planning that was carried out in the early days of the Second World War. As the United States began to ramp up its military production, Professor Leontief, then at Harvard University, was asked to analyse what the country would have to do to produce the military aircraft it would need to fight the war. Using his input–output system, Leontief found that the United States would need not only massive quantities of aluminium, which was easy to anticipate, but also enormous quantities of electrical power which was essential for producing the aluminium – something not many had foreseen.

Prospects

While planning has had some limited success, what is regarded as its dismal failure in the Soviet Union has made most economists wary of its use in the future. Changes in consumer tastes and demands, and rapid technological obsolescence and an ever-more varied and changed product mix, make anticipating demand next year (not to mention five years hence) seem all but impossible. Yet in some ways, what Soviet planners were unable to do, planners at large corporate retail giants like Walmart in the United States and Tesco in the United Kingdom are actually doing. Walmart, for example, now supplies as much as 25 per cent of all the toys and 8 per cent of all retail products other than automobiles sold to American consumers. In the United Kingdom, Tesco accounts for 1 out of every 8 pounds spent in Britain's shops. That means that both companies must anticipate consumer demand and respond quickly to it. Unlike Soviet planning, however, Walmart and Tesco planners have at their disposal sophisticated computers that track sales of specific products in specific regions which enable them to anticipate sales and inventory needs on a seasonal as well as a day-to-day basis. Of course, the fact that 92 per cent or so of retail sales in the United States are made by Walmart's competitors forces Walmart to remain competitive and alert to new styles and trends that Gosplan never had to worry about and never had the technology to track. Yet there is irony in the fact that the market system's Walmart is able to process what is a considerably larger and more varied quantity of consumer goods than the Soviet Union's Gosplan, even in its heyday. Conceivably planning, recognised as such, one day may yet be something more than a historical artefact.

MARSHALL GOLDMAN

References and further reading

'A country within a country', *Financial Times*, 9 July 2004, p. 8.
Gregory, Paul and Robert Stuart (1981), *Soviet Economic Structure and Performance*, 2nd edn, New York: Harper & Row.
Smolinski, Leon (1970), *Technocratic Elements in Soviet Socialism*, 23 October, Hamilton, Ontario: Department of Economics, McMaster University.
'Tesco's tough act', *Financial Times*, 20 April 2004, p. 19.
'The price of huge sales and tiny margins', *Financial Times*, 7 July 2004, p. 8.
US Census Bureau, *Statistical Abstract of the United States*, 2002, 122nd edn, Washington, DC, p. 418.
Walmart Annual Financial Report, 2004.
Zaleski, Eugene (1980), *Stalinist Planning for Economic Growth, 1933–1967*, Chapel Hill, NC: University of North Carolina Press.

Population and Development

As the expression suggests, 'population and development' refers to the field which addresses relationships between population variables on the one hand, and development variables on the other. *Inter alia* populations can vary in their size, density, growth rate, and their age and sex structures, as well as in the levels and patterns of fertility, mortality and migration which together determine features such as population size, growth and structure. The development side of the expression envelops the main areas of socio-economic enquiry – notably the economic, the cultural and the political – including the many variables that are associated with them (for example, relating to levels of income and education). Because population variables are influenced by development variables and vice versa, the field is often concerned with *reciprocal* implications. And it embraces analysis of urban growth and urbanisation too – since these phenomena are influenced both by demographic and by socio-economic processes. Because population and development processes evolve through time, much work in the field has a strong historical dimension. The principal journal is *Population and Development Review* – published quarterly by the Population Council in New York.

The overarching framework for research in the population and development field is provided by the facts of the demographic transition (for example, see Davis, 1945; Kirk, 1996). This transition involves a change from a situation in which populations are subject to high and roughly equal birth and death rates, to one in which low and roughly equal birth and death rates prevail. In virtually all cases, much of the decline in the death rate occurs *before* the birth rate has begun to fall. Therefore the transition itself is a period of population *growth* – during which the birth rate exceeds the death rate to an unusual degree. In Western Europe the demographic transition began in the early nineteenth century, and was completed during the second half of the twentieth. In developing regions the transition started at various times in the twentieth century and is still at various stages of completion early in the twenty-first.

A basic contrast between more- and less-developed regions in their experience of the demographic transition is that in the former death rates declined fairly gradually as a result of changes which were largely *endogenous* to the societies concerned (for example, improvements in sanitation and general living standards). Their birth-rate declines were fairly gradual too. As a result, the resulting average annual rates of population growth were fairly modest (rarely exceeding 1.5 per cent). However, much of the mortality decline which has occurred in the developing regions, especially from around the middle of the twentieth century, resulted from the rapid introduction, from more-developed countries, of effective and relatively inexpensive methods of, and knowledge regarding, death control (for example, insecticides, antibiotics, vaccinations and so on). Consequently even very poor countries have experienced very significant improvements in their death rates – although their birth rates have tended to remain high. The result has been considerable – often extremely rapid – population growth. For example, India's population of about 360 million in 1950 nearly tripled in the period to the year 2000. In Sub-Saharan Africa, demographic growth rates exceeding 3 per cent per year have been common – meaning that populations have often doubled in size, and then almost doubled again, during 1950–2000.

A central concern of researchers in the field has been to assess the socio-economic consequences of the unprecedented demographic increase of recent decades (for example, see McNicoll, 1984; World Bank, 1985). Much research has been economic in focus, although recently there has been growing interest with environmental implications. Clearly, the economic effects of population growth depend partly upon the particular context in which it occurs (for example, in terms of institutional arrangements and energy supplies). It is clear, too, that many countries have been able to raise their average living standards despite experiencing very considerable demographic growth. Accordingly, research has focused on the *net* effects of population increase on economic growth – the debate swaying in different directions at different times. Especially prominent during the 1980s were the arguments of Julian Simon (for example, see 1989, 1995) who – echoing the views of classic mercantile writers like William Petty and Friderich Lütken – maintained that population growth has a net positive impact on economic performance. Also influential in this vein have been the arguments of Ester Boserup (1965), linking rises in population density to advances in agricultural techniques.

Mainstream opinion, however, has generally favoured a negative relationship – a position influenced by the early simulations for India and Mexico conducted by Ansley Coale and Edgar Hoover, and published in their book *Population Growth and Economic Development in Low-Income Countries* (1958). At the start of the twenty-first century, support for a negative relationship has tended to strengthen in econometric analysis (for example, see Kelley and Schmidt, 2001). Furthermore, some development economists now attribute a significant proportion of the economic success of certain countries in East and South East Asia to the so-called 'demographic bonus' resulting from their relatively rapid birth-rate declines of the 1970s and 1980s. Fertility decline reduces the proportion of children in the population, and so raises the proportion of the population in the labour force. Thus, it is argued, there is a 'window of opportunity', lasting several decades, which, if grasped, permits increased savings and investment, including investment in human capital via the education system (for example, see Bloom and Williamson, 1998). Because poorer countries (and poorer people within them) tend to experience higher levels of fertility, and therefore higher rates of natural increase, there is little doubt that in recent decades demographic growth has worked against a reduction in the total number of people in the world living in poverty. Equally, it is generally accepted that rapidly expanding populations pose serious challenges for the provision of basic services and facilities – like education, employment, healthcare, housing and fresh water.

With such considerations in mind, another central concern of scholars working in the field has been with the issue of high fertility. Economists, anthropologists, demographers and others have advanced various theoretical explanations for high fertility – an objective sometimes being to help design more appropriate policies to reduce birth rates and so slow rates of population growth. At the individual and household levels, many of the benefits arising from reduced levels of fertility have been well established. For example, other things equal, in poor settings: high parity births (for example, a mother's fifth or sixth birth) experience sharply increased risks of dying (compared to lower parity births); again, frequent childbearing is far from gender neutral, and it carries considerable health and mortality risks for women; also, much research shows that children in large families tend to get a worse deal (for example, in terms of feeding and education) compared to those in smaller families (Lloyd, 1994).

Most of the theoretical explanations forwarded to account for high fertility have been framed in economic terms – the argument essentially being that parents derive considerable economic benefits from having many children – for example, in terms of the provision of direct family labour, insurance against risk, and support in old age. However the *costs* incurred in bearing and rearing children did not always receive the same amount of consideration. Analysis of the increasing body of fertility and health survey data, which started to become available for many developing countries from the 1970s, underscored the importance of increased levels of *education* – particularly of women – in contributing to later ages at marriage, greater uptake of contraception, and consequently lower levels of fertility (and child mortality). However, particularly from around the 1980s, it became increasingly clear that birth rates were falling in many countries, including many that were poor and where educational levels were low. Mari Bhat (2002), for example, concluded that in the 1990s about two-thirds of all fertility decline in India was attributable to illiterate women. Thus, while levels of fertility (and child mortality) tend to be inversely associated with levels of income and education and other development variables, the strength of these relationships has often waned with time – as mortality and fertility declines have become increasingly pervasive phenomena of the modern world. In turn, this has brought about a new understanding of the demographic transition – one in which conventional development variables are regarded more as *facilitators* than as *determinants* of fertility decline. From this perspective, fertility decline is seen as being primarily a lagged response to the preceding – although largely unrecognised – fact of sustained and massive death-rate decline (for example, see Kirk, 1996).

So the demographic transition is increasingly seen as a *global* process – one which eventually will be completed everywhere. Arguably there has been no more significant dimension of 'development' than the huge improvement in mortality which has been the principal component of the demographic transition, and the ultimate engine behind the process of fertility decline. Moreover, the demographic transition is a key factor underlying many other aspects of societal development. For example, it is mortality decline which enables the process of urbanisation with its manifold consequences – for example, for the division of labour in society and the wider distribution of political power. There are powerful arguments, too, that fertility decline is the critical 'remote' causal process underpinning the transformation of gender relations in the modern world (Dyson, 2001).

Turning to the future, research in the field of population and development will continue to be determined by demographic trends. Several areas of interest can be identified briefly here.

First, the fertility decline of the demographic transition leads inexorably to the process of *population ageing*. Developed countries are already confronting many of the issues which arise from such ageing – for example, relating to pension provision, meeting the healthcare needs of the elderly, and adjusting retirement ages so as to help maintain the labour force. However, while fairly advanced, population ageing in most developed countries has been a comparatively slow process – because their past fertility declines were also relatively slow. In contrast, an increasing number of poorer countries (for example, in East and South East Asia) will soon confront the problems raised by population ageing as, due to their much faster fertility declines, their populations begin to age at rates that will be quite unprecedentedly fast.

Second, and relatedly, there is the increasingly important issue of *very* low fertility. Nearly half of the world's population now live in countries where the average level of fertility is around two live births per woman or less (Wilson, 2001). The extent of future population ageing will depend to a large degree upon just how low levels of fertility go. And there is also the distinct possibility of population *decline* – which over the longer run has the potential to become rapid. While the lowest levels of fertility – not much above one birth per woman – are found in southern Europe, the average level of fertility in China, for example, is also less than two births (United Nations, 2003). Nowadays the issue of very low fertility interests scholars working in the field as much as, if not more than, that of accounting for high fertility.

Third, there remain many questions relating to the socio-economic, environmental and other consequences of demographic growth. For, despite falling levels of fertility, the world's population is still projected to rise from about six to nine billion during 2000–50. Virtually all of the increase will occur in poorer regions (ibid.). Coupled with increasing levels of energy use, a world population of nine billion may pose a serious challenge to global sustainability over the longer run. And, at lower levels of aggregation, falling levels of fertility per woman do not translate quickly into falling rates of population growth – because the age structures of most poor populations remain fairly young. Therefore many countries will experience substantial demographic growth because of inevitable increases in the number of women of reproductive age – a phenomenon termed 'population momentum'. Indeed, the next few decades will witness little reduction in the population *growth* differential between the world's demographically most- and least-advanced regions. Thus Paul Demeny (2003) highlights how the central (medium variant) population projections of the United Nations suggest that the population of Yemen (with a young age structure and high fertility) may well surpass that of Russia (with an old-age structure and very low fertility) some time in the middle of the present century. The details of such projections are almost certainly wrong, but the broad implications are almost certainly right. Such future demographic developments are likely to have major consequences for patterns of international *migration*, and they may well have significant geo-political ramifications too. Issues also arise as to how countries will accommodate much bigger future populations – for example, for Yemen a projected population in 2050 of 102 million (ibid.).

Finally, the field will doubtless remain involved with both the factors fuelling the HIV/AIDS epidemic and its many consequences – particularly *vis-à-vis* the evolving tragedy in Sub-Saharan Africa. Hitherto demographic research has focused chiefly on the mortality effects of HIV/AIDS, although there has also been work on the fertility effects and the growth in orphanhood. Research on the implications for development has focused, *inter alia*, on the likely consequences for families, the health and education sectors, and the wider economy. However, future research *vis-à-vis* the situation in Sub-Saharan Africa seems likely to incorporate some new indications regarding the epidemic's ramifications – indications which pertain to central *loci* in the population and development field. For example, there are signs that in the most adversely affected countries, HIV/AIDS is slowing the pace of urbanisation; indeed, in some countries de-urbanisation could eventually occur. Since urbanisation is a central characteristic and engine of overall development, this may well be a matter of increasing concern. Even more importantly, it is clear that negative rates of population growth will soon apply in some African countries, and that there will be truly extraordinary accompanying population age–structural effects. These happenings are likely to have singular implications for socio-economic and more general societal development.

TIM DYSON

References

Bhat, M. (2002), 'Returning a favour: reciprocity between female education and fertility in India', *World Development*, **30** (10), 1791–803.

Bloom, D. and J.G. Williamson (1998), 'Demographic transitions and economic miracles in emerging Asia', *World Bank Economic Review*, **12** (3), 419–45.

Boserup, E. (1965), *The Conditions of Agricultural Growth*, London: George Allen & Unwin.

Coale, A.J. and E.M. Hoover (1958), *Population Growth and Economic Development in Low-Income Countries*, Princeton, NJ: Princeton University Press.

Davis, K. (1945), 'The world demographic transition', *Annals of the American Academy of Political and Social Science*, **237**, 1–11.

Demeny, P. (2003), 'Population policy dilemmas in Europe at the dawn of the twenty-first century', *Population and Development Review*, **29** (1), 1–28.

Dyson, T. (2001), 'A partial theory of world development: the neglected role of the demographic transition in the shaping of modern society', *International Journal of Population Geography*, **7** (2), 67–90.

Kelley, A. and R. Schmidt (2001), 'Economic and demographic change: a synthesis of models, findings, and perspectives', in Nancy Birdsall, Allen Kelley and Steven Sinding (eds), *Population Matters: Demographic Change, Economic Growth, and Poverty in the Developing World*, Oxford: Oxford University Press, pp. 67–105.

Kirk, D. (1996), 'Demographic transition theory', *Population Studies*, **50** (3), 361–87.

Lloyd, C. (1994), 'Investing in the next generation: the implications of high fertility at the level of the family', in Robert Cassen (ed.), *Population and Development: Old Debates, New Conclusions*, Washington, DC: Overseas Development Council, pp. 181–202.

McNicoll, G. (1984), 'Consequences of rapid population growth: overview and assessment', *Population and Development Review*, **10** (2), 177–240.

Population and Development Review (1975–), New York: Population Council, quarterly.

Simon, J. (1989), 'On aggregate empirical studies relating population variables to economic development', *Population and Development Review*, **15** (2), 323–32.

Simon, J. (ed.) (1995), *The State of Humanity*, Oxford: Blackwell.

United Nations (2003), *World Population Prospects: The 2002 Revision*, New York: United Nations.

Wilson, C. (2001), 'On the scale of global demographic convergence', *Population and Development Review*, **27** (1), 155–71.

World Bank (1985), *Population Change and Economic Development*, Oxford and New York: Oxford University Press.

Population: Policy and Ethics

Population policy has been a contentious subject in Western economic writing since the completion of the tract *An Essay on the Principle of Population* (1798) by Thomas Robert Malthus and its subsequent discussion among the members of the intellectual classes in England at the end of the eighteenth century. This Malthusian inheritance has coloured the thinking of social scientists, and more particularly demographers as they came into contact, and became acquainted with the economies and societies outside Europe in the twentieth century. Concern with the imminence of the Malthusian spectre in developing countries provided a sharp contrast with the statistical evidence of falling rates of population growth in Europe over the nineteenth century confronting demographers in the early decades of the twentieth century. Leading intellectuals in Europe and the United States in the field of demography during the 1920s encountered debates where Malthusian and statistical perspectives encountered eugenic and racial concerns and these cross-cutting themes were evident at the First World Population Conference convened in Geneva in 1927, which led to the setting up of the organisation which became the International Union for the Scientific Study of Population (IUSPP). The IUSSP had a primary aim of bringing together nations to discuss population concerns and to further the study of demography in individual countries as well as a collective endeavour. In the United States the newly formed Population Association of America (PAA) in 1931, similarly reflected the views of a variety of academicians and policy makers, who were equally influenced by the thinking of eugenicists as those of neo-Malthusians, and consequently the meetings of the PAA advocated both population control and selection (Hodgson, 1991). The emphasis on control and selection indicated that both Malthusian and Darwinian principles were dominant influences in the sphere of population policy, and was strongly reflected in the debates on immigration and 'family planning' policies in the United States in the 1930s, where it was considerations regarding the diminishing number of 'superior' races relative to the 'weak' races that were the focus of deliberations.

The imperative to construct population policy spread beyond the control and fashioning of domestic populations with the de-colonisation and nationalisation movements of the 1940s and the onset of the Second World War that resulted in the creation of a new international order (Greenhalgh, 1996). The theory of demographic transition that had been constructed to explain the population trends of industrialised and industrialising countries was extended to the new nations of the world in an attempt to document and understand the trajectories of their populations. The Office of Population Research at Princeton was established in 1936, representing the largest and most directed study on trends in population in the 1940s, and the Kingsley Davis study, *World Population in Transition* (1945) concluded that there would be a rapidly growing population in Asia and parts of Africa that would result in a Malthusian crisis in these regions, in the absence of intervention from governmental and international agencies (Szreter, 1993). Populations projections were the main methodology adopted by demographers in the 1920s and 1930s, and in 1946, the United Nations contributed its own population projections, through the Population Division of its newly established Economic and Social Council. The implication was that there was a need for a population policy, through some form of external imposition, whether moral, economic or political, or a combination therein, to control the world's population and this was translated into a policy mandate by international organisations. The Ford Foundation entered the population field in 1952 with a grant to the Population Reference Bureau and subsequent support for the Population Council in 1954. Ford became an important player in the dissemination of knowledge on family planning through the 1960s with initial forays into India and Pakistan through educational programmes for universities in these countries in the area of demography (Caldwell and Caldwell, 1986). During the 1960s, the Ford Foundation was the most influential international development agency in the field of population, establishing offices across the developing world, to provide a combination of information on reproductive control and provision of devices for such control to slow down the rate of population growth.

The ethical dimension of the international project of constructing population policy was overshadowed, if not obscured, by the modernising zeal of these international institutions. In its stead was the overwhelming presence of a decided moral tone on the superiority of fewer children, tinged with a paternalistic note regarding the need to inform and educate populations in developing countries, particularly those among the poor in the rural sector. The directed and increasing pressure on developing countries was transmitted through cultural and ideational means to national elites, who emerged as the vanguard in the early initiatives to control population (Luke and Watkins, 2002). The top-down and often bureaucratic apparatus of national population policies reflected an equal lack of concern with ethics as was manifest in the national population policies taken up by countries across Asia, Africa and Latin America during the 1970s and 1980s in response to domestic concerns regarding the rapidly growing young population resulting in high 'dependency ratios' (Chamie, 1994). Population policies were regarded as a combination of 'carrots' and 'sticks' that would ensure a convergence of private costs to the household and public costs to the economy of children as advocated in the mainstream economic literature (Cassen, 1994). The population policy of the Indian government hit the international headlines in 1975–76, during the prime ministership of Indira Gandhi, where a combination of anti-poverty strategies and population control policies went badly wrong, with top-down coercive population policies implemented by an army of bureaucrats and local governmental actors. Despite the large numbers achieved with 8.5 million sterilisations in 1976, the policy was widely regarded as largely unsuccessful as a viable population policy on account of the strong-arm tactics employed by the government (Gwatkin, 1979). In the same decade, the Chinese government embarked on a population policy in the early years of the 1970s as a direct consequence of a national campaign to reduce the total population through imposing limits on the number of children in a household, and rapidly transforming into the more restrictive one-child policy in 1979. The Chinese population policy, while becoming more flexible in the late 1980s and permitting families with only a girl child a second child, made considerable headway in lowering the growth rate of its population using a combination of national directives and local initiatives (White, 1994). The evolving Chinese population policy was framed with direct regard to the economic reform process underway in the 1980s and was regarded as a part of the modernisation of the Chinese economy (ibid., 1994).

The increasing engagement of national governments with population policies was couched in terms of economic advancement and drew on the language and symbols of modernity and scientific knowledge in the pursuit of lower fertility levels (Ong Tsui, 2001). The ethical dimension of these national policies for population control began to emerge through the international responses to these policies where there was a telling absence of the unified approval that was given to the international agenda of the 1960s. The criticisms were primarily directed at the element of 'coercion' that was evident in these national policies, and advocated strengthening the role of individual choice in reproductive decision making and the underpinning of population policy with a choice-based approach. Coercion was in fact regarded as a part of national population policies from the 1950s to the 1980s in developing countries as different as Albania and Singapore (Thomas and Grindle, 1994) and the emerging international opposition to these top-down imperatives in the field of population control was the consequence of international women's movements in the preceding decade.

The family-planning approach to population policy was called increasingly into question during the course of the 1980s, by a wide-ranging array of organisations, from feminist to religious in developing countries. The international and national approaches to family planning were criticised for the scant regard paid to the cultural aspects of reproduction in particular societies. The position of women within the household and community was not accorded adequate importance, if any, and recognition and reproductive choices were deemed to be those of the household. Population policies appeared to work against the interests of women in these societies as they were operating on the presumption that reproductive choice was a matter for the household and not the woman. There was an academic response to these criticisms from advocacy groups with models of informed choice by households regarding the optimal number of children beginning to give way to considerations regarding the reproductive rights of women (Kabeer, 1994). There was also a shift in demographic studies, with a move away from tracing the 'demographic transition' towards searching for a better understanding of the relationship between women's education, fertility and economic development (see Population and Development, this volume). Studies using time-series data on populations showed that there was evidence of 'missing women' in national populations and that population policy was not gender neutral in implementation (see Missing Women, this volume). The construction and implementation of population policies also became a matter of interest to development economists with the growing evidence of interrelations between the productive and reproductive spheres at the microeconomic level, which gave rise to a growing literature on the relationship between the position of women and economic development (Basu, 1992).

In 1994 the International Convention on Population and Development (ICPD) in Cairo called for a shift in the focus of population studies and proposed an approach that directly addressed the relationship between sexual and reproductive health and rights (SRHR) and development, thereby making a significant shift from the agenda of the preceding four decades of population policies that had aimed at reducing fertility through family-planning programmes. The Cairo programme was universally adopted and has been celebrated by international agencies for placing the rights of women as the foundation stone for all population programmes. The decade that has followed has shown that the Cairo agenda is a rocky terrain as there has been considerable opposition to the new international perspective on population policy from pro-choice lobbies in the developed world. The anti-abortion campaign has presented the SRHR framework as an ethical travesty and has called for a withdrawal of donor funds to developing countries that might be used to further women's rights at the expense of the unborn child. While the ICPD agenda has become the cause of an ongoing battle between religion-based aid agencies and international agencies, there are also national concerns regarding the impact of new reproductive technologies on social phenomena, such as son preference and female infanticide.

The difficult relation between national directives on population policy and the reproductive rights of women is evident in growing concerns regarding antenatal tests, particularly with regard to access to facilities for amniocentesis tests for determining the sex of the foetus. There is also the conundrum of the negative implications of seemingly successful population policies for the reproductive rights of citizens due to a limited understanding of gender equity and rights within the implementing authorities in the country. An inadequate conceptual framework can result in 'oversight' through an inability to comprehend the full extent of the framework of SRHR or can be the result of the totalitarian nature of the authority, where the 'override' feature (Sen, 1994) results in a disregard for protecting individual rights, or where deviant reproductive behaviour has resulted in sanctions and the denial of certain attributes of the full range of citizenship rights (Greenhalgh, 2003). The dilemmas raised by ideational aspects of national population policy have been the subject of particular study in the case of China's one-child policy, where the intertwining of population and economic policies has been represented by themes such as 'the two strands of production' (White, 1994). The social and cultural transmission of the objectives of population policy through ideological and cultural metaphor in societies has been the subject of much recent research (McNicoll, 2001). The ethical dimension of these conundrums is the current subject of emerging research in the area of population and development where the mechanisms and consequences of social and cultural transmission are identifying important linkages between government policy making, nation building and individual behaviour (Murphy, 2004). The impact of national population policy identified by these recent studies indicate that the interactions between ideational and economic imperatives significantly impact individual decisions regarding work and residence and set in motion new patterns of rural–rural migration as well as the more traditional Lewisian rural–urban migration flows.

Another area where the impact of population policy is becoming visible is with regard to the child population. The growing literature on the rights of the child has focused on absence of a discourse on the relationship between economic development and the experience of childhood, a version of which was enunciated in the Convention on the Rights of the Child (UN, 1989). The CRC directive to ensure that children have access to health, education and other economic, social and cultural provision places a premium on the children who are currently on the earth yet simultaneously has the potential to discriminate against the as yet unborn child. The discrimination against the unborn or unwanted child also forms the central plank of a discussion of discriminatory practices generated by official practice, such as deeming as inferior children resulting from 'unplanned births' in a manner that is reminiscent of the socio-Darwinism of the 1930s (Greenhalgh, 2003). Such recent work by anthropologists of development has played a central role in bringing the study of power to population policy, as well as to the academic discipline of demography. Population policy is increasingly evaluated in terms of the conceptualisation of the rights of various individuals in the household, particularly the reproductive rights of women and the impact on gender equity between men and women (Luke and Watkins, 2002).

It must be recognised that the current movement of regarding population policy as a matter pertaining to the rights of the individual, is at odds with the preference expressed by some governments to consider population growth in terms of the dominant ethnic and racial groups in a society (McNicoll, 2001). Population policy that directly addresses the relative growth rates of ethnic population takes on a confrontational and aggressive political overtone and is often plagued by the dark shadow of eugenics, as was the case in the early decades of the construction of population policy. The competing or conflicting claims of groups in multi-ethnic and multi-religious societies are often articulated in terms of the differential between own and other group rates of growth in population, as in the case of Indian population policy of the 1970s (Gwatkin, 1979). Where the ethnic populations are explicitly identified and incorporated in a nation's population policy with preferences being granted as with the proposed state subsidy for graduate mothers in Singapore in the 1990s, there is a group bias that militates against the mandate of the 1994 Cairo Convention. It is therefore not surprising that state control of reproduction, particularly of reducing fertility, has been a thorny subject that has generated much debate, if not severe criticism, regarding the lack of involvement and participation of the local community. Policy makers appear to suffer from a seeming inability, if not a direct refusal to work with local norms (Watkins, 2000). Where there has been relative success in the construction and implementation of population policy it has been on account of non-governmental organisations (NGOs) and civil society organisations that have contributed to population policies in the dissemination of literature and the public awareness programmes. The ethical dilemma is evident in this sphere where the control of population is a matter of restricting the individual through national control but without adequate involvement of the local sphere. On the other hand, there is increasing concern about the lack of independence of NGOs and civil society organisations as they are increasingly under the sway of northern donor organisations rather than immediately responsive to the local community demands, and that the agenda for fertility control is still being led by the international agenda rather than local considerations.

The top-down policy directives appear to be in contradiction to recent evidence on effective interventions, which points to consistent reduction in fertility being consequent on successful changes in social norms, often in conjunction with economic development (Ong Tsui, 2001). The central role of engagement with local social norms in fertility reductions indicates that shifts in demographic behaviour arise from an intricate intertwining between reproductive and productive patterns. Consequently the parameters of examining population policy are currently much broader than that of the now discredited theory of demographic transition, which emphasises only the changing economic and social context of urbanisation and industrialisation. The control of population through changing and reworking social norms requires a mechanism for cultural transformation that has been absent in many of the coercive policies. The importance of local culture, in particular female predisposition to fertility regulation and its relationship to education, has gained considerable currency in the 1990s (Mason, 2001). The variation in the success of population policy in the local sphere has been attributed to differences in education, fertility awareness and the nature of centre–state relations. Consequently, responsible and sustainable population policy is currently evaluated in terms of its local effectiveness as much as the national imperative and the international commitments in the realm of population policy.

SHAILAJA FENNELL

References

Basu, Alaka (1992), *Culture, the Status of Women and Demographic Behaviour: Illustrated with the Case of India*, Oxford: Oxford University Press.

Caldwell, John and Pat Caldwell (1986), *Limiting Population Growth and the Ford Foundation Contribution*, London: Pinter.

Cassen, Robert (1994), *Population and Development: Old Debates, New Conclusions*, New Brunswick, NJ: Transaction.

Chamie, Joseph (1994), 'Trends, variations and contradictions in national policies to influence fertility', *Population and Development Review*, **20** (Supplement), 37–50.

Davis, Kingsley (ed.) (1945), *World Population in Transition*, Philadelphia, PA: The American Academy of Political and Social Science.

Greenhalgh, Susan (1996), 'The social construction of population science: an intellectual, institutional, and political history of twentieth century demography', *Comparative Studies in Society and History*, **38** (1), 26–65.

Greenhalgh, S. (2003), 'Planned births, unplanned persons: "population" in the making of Chinese modernity', *American Ethnologist*, **30** (2), 196–215.

Gwatkin, Davidson R. (1979), 'Political will and family planning: the implications of India's emergency experience', *Population and Development Review*, **5** (1), 29–59.

Hodgson, D. (1991), 'The ideological origins of the Population Association of America', *Population and Development Review*, **17** (1), 1–34.

Kabeer, Naila (1994), *Reversed Realities: Gender Hierarchies in Development Theory*, London: Verso.

Luke, N. and S.C. Watkins (2002), 'Reactions of developing-country elites to international population policy', *Population and Development Review*, **28** (4), 707–33.

Malthus, Thomas (1798), *An Essay on the Principle of Population*, London: J. Johnson.

Mason, K.O. (2001), 'Gender and family systems in the fertility transition', *Population and Development Review*, **27** (Supplement), 160–76.

McNicoll, G. (2001), 'Government and fertility in transitional and post-transitional societies', *Population and Development Review*, **27** (Supplement), 129–59.

Murphy, Rachel (2004), 'Turning peasants into modern Chinese citizens: "population quality" discourse, demographic transition and primary education', *China Quarterly*, **177**, 1–20.

Ong Tsui, A. (2001), 'Population policies, family planning programs, and fertility: the record', *Population and Development Review*, **27** (Supplement), 181–204.

Sen, Amartya (1994), 'Population: delusion and reality', *New York Review of Books*, **41** (15), 62–71.

Szreter, S. (1993), 'The idea of demographic transition and the study of fertility change: a critical intellectual history', *Population and Development Review*, **19** (4), 659–701.

Thomas, John W. and Merilee S. Grindle (1994), 'Political leadership and policy characteristics in population policy reform', *Population and Development Review*, **20** (Supplement), 51–70.

UN (1989), *Convention on the Rights of the Child*, United Nations General Assembly Document A/RES/44/25, 12 December.

Watkins, S.C. (2000), 'Local and foreign models of reproduction in Nyanza Province, Kenya', *Population and Development Review*, **26** (4), 725–59.

White, Tyrene (1994), 'Two kinds of production: the evolution of China's family planning policy in the 1980s', *Population and Development Review*, **20** (Supplement), 137–58.

Post-Development

In 1992, a collective volume edited by Wolfgang Sachs, *The Development Dictionary*, started by making the radical and controversial claim, 'The last forty years can be called the age of development. This epoch is coming to an end. The time is ripe to write its obituary' (Sachs, 1992, p. 1). If development was dead, what would come after? Some started to talk about a 'post-development era' (Escobar, 1992) in response to this question, and a second collective work, *The Post-Development Reader*, launched the project of giving content to the notion of 'post-development' (Rahnema and Bawtree, 1997). According to the editors of this work, the word 'post-development' was first used at an international colloquium in Geneva in 1991. Six years later it had caught the imagination of critical scholars and practitioners in the development field. Reactions on all sides of the scholarly political spectrum have continued since, resulting in a vibrant, albeit at times somewhat scattered, debate. This debate has brought together practitioners and academics from many social science disciplines and fields.

To fully understand the emergence of the notion of post-development and how it has functioned in the international development debate, it is important to locate it briefly within the development studies field. Over the past 50 years, the conceptualisation of development in the social sciences has seen three main moments, corresponding to three contrasting theoretical orientations: modernisation theory in the 1950s and 1960s, with its allied theories of growth and development; dependency theory and related perspectives in the 1960s and 1970s; and critical approaches to development as a cultural discourse in the second half of the 1980s and the 1990s. Modernisation theory inaugurated a period of certainty in the minds of many theorists and world elites, premised on the beneficial effects of capital, science and technology; this certainty suffered a first blow with dependency theory, which argued that the roots of underdevelopment were to be found in the connection between external dependence and internal exploitation, not in any alleged lack of capital, technology or modern values. For dependency theorists, the problem was not so much with development as with capitalism. In the 1980s, a growing number of cultural critics in many parts of the world questioned the very idea of development. They analysed development as a discourse of Western origin that operated as a powerful mechanism for the cultural, social and economic production of the Third World (for example, Apffel-Marglin and Marglin, 1990; Ferguson, 1990; Escobar, 1995;

Rist, 1997). These three moments may be classified according to the root paradigms from which they emerged: liberal, Marxist and post-structuralist theories, respectively. Despite overlaps and more eclectic combinations than in the recent past, a main paradigm continues to inform most positions at present, making the dialogue difficult at times.

The deconstruction of development led post-structuralists in particular to postulate the possibility of a 'post-development era'. For some, this generally meant an era in which development would no longer be the central organising principle of social life (Escobar, 1995) – one in which, to paraphrase a well-known paper of the period, development would not take place solely 'under Western eyes' (Mohanty, 1991). Others added to this characterisation a re-valorisation of vernacular cultures, the need to rely less on expert knowledge and more on ordinary people's attempts at constructing more humane and culturally and ecologically sustainable worlds, and the important point of taking seriously social movements and grassroots mobilisations as the basis for moving towards the new era (Shiva, 1993; Rahnema and Bawtree, 1997; Rist, 1997; Esteva and Prakash, 1999). In the second half of the 1990s, these analyses and forms of advocacy became themselves the object of poignant critiques and rebuttals. This may be seen as a fourth moment in the historical sociology of development knowledge. In fact, a partial result of this debate was the identification (mostly by liberal and Marxist critics) of a 'post-development school' of post-structuralist orientation. While the critiques of post-development have not constituted a unified body of work, it is possible to identify three main objections to the original post-development proposal: (1) with their focus on discourse, the post-development proponents overlooked poverty and capitalism, which are the real problems of development; (2) they presented an overgeneralised and essentialised view of development, while in reality there are vast differences among development strategies and institutions; they also failed to notice the ongoing contestation of development on the ground; and (3) they romanticised local traditions and social movements, ignoring that the local is also embedded in power relations (see, among the most cogent and spirited critiques of post-development, Berger, 1995; Lehmann, 1997; Crew and Harrison, 1998; Pieterse, 1998; Kiely, 1999; Storey, 2000; for a response, see Escobar, 2000).

Besides evincing contrasting paradigmatic orientations, the debate over post-development spurred by these critiques should also be understood by considering the changed context of knowledge production in the 1990. This context saw the consolidation of new tendencies and fields, in ascendancy since the 1980s, such as post-structuralism, cultural studies, feminist theory, and ethnic and environmental studies, which enabled a different understanding of how development operates. Adopting a sociology of knowledge perspective again, we may say that in the same way that the discursive approaches of the 1980s and early 1990s were made possible by earlier critiques (for example, dependency theory and the cultural critiques of thinkers such as Ivan Illich, Paulo Freire, Julius Nyrere, Orlando Fals Borda, Denis Goulet and Johan Galtung) and by the importation of new tools of analysis (post-structuralism), it is impossible to understand the critiques of the post-development school without the post-development moment itself. Predictably, proponents of post-development have responded to their critics, in turn, by suggesting that the critiques are, themselves, problematic. To the first set of critiques, post-development proponents responded by saying that this argument amounts to a naïve defence of the real. In other words, critics of post-development argue that because of their focus on discourse and culture, the post-structuralists fail to see the reality of poverty, capitalism and the like. For the post-structuralists, however, this argument is not valid, because it rests on the (Marxist or liberal) assumption that discourse is not material, failing to see that modernity and capitalism are simultaneously systems of discourse and practice.

If the first critique of post-development could be seen as operating in the name of the real, so to speak, the second was seen as proposed in the name of (better) theory. This was also problematic to post-development authors on epistemological grounds. Paraphrasing, the critics of post-development said something like: 'You (post-development advocates) represented development as homogeneous while it is really diverse. Development is heterogeneous, contested, impure, hybrid. Your theories are thus flawed'. In response, the post-development theorists acknowledged the importance and validity of this criticism; however, they pointed out that the post-structuralist project was a different one – that of analysing the overall discursive fact, not how it might have been contested and hybridised on the ground. In a similar way that political economy endowed capitalism with a high degree of systematicity and unicity, it made sense at this moment in the conceptualisation of the post-structuralist critique to ascribe a certain relational coherence to development, even in terms of showing development's connection to capitalism and modernity (see, for example, Kamat, 2002). Besides, the post-structuralists argued, the issue was not to provide a more accurate representation of 'the real'; this was everybody else's project, and part of the problem from this perspective. In highlighting the nature and effects of the overall development discourse, the post-structuralist analysts saw themselves less as 'trying to get it right', under the mandate of an epistemological realism that post-structuralism in any case complicates, than as political intellectuals constructing an object of critique for both scholarly and political action and debate.

Finally, to the charge of romanticising the local and the grassroots, advocates of post-development have responded by saying that the (liberal and Marxist) strategy of talking 'in the name of the people' from the distance of the academy or development NGOs will not do. To elaborate, the critics of the concept of post-development chastised their proponents by saying that they do not understand power (power lies in the material and with the people, not in discourse); that what is at stake are people's needs, not theoretical analyses; and that because of their romantic, neo-Luddite and relativist stance they patronise the people and overlook their interests. For the post-structuralists and cultural critics, this commentary is a reflection of the chronic realism of many scholars who invariably label as romantic any radical critique of the West or any defence of 'the local'. In addition, post-structuralist authors pointed out that the realist notion of social change that underlies the commentary fails to unpack its own views of 'the material', 'livelihood', 'needs' and the like (Escobar, 2000).

This debate has contributed to the creation of a lively climate for more eclectic and pragmatic approaches. If anything has come out clearly from the debates around post-development in the 1990s, it is a greater willingness on the part of many authors to constructively adopt elements from various trends and paradigms (for example, Gardner and Lewis, 1996; Peet and Hartwick, 1999; Arce and Long, 2000; Schech and Haggis, 2000). This is particularly the case regarding a series of questions, including the contestation of development on the ground; the re-conceptualisation of social movements from the perspective of networks and local/global articulations; a new rapprochement between political economy and cultural analysis on questions of development; and the examination of the relation between development and modernity as a way to deepen, and make more nuanced, the cultural critiques of the post-structuralists without overlooking the contributions of the liberal and Marxist critiques. These trends are producing a new understanding of how development works and is transformed.

Arce and Long (2000), for instance, have outlined a project of pluralising modernity by focusing on the counter-work performed on development by local groups; these authors focus on the ways in which the ideas and practices of modernity are appropriated and re-embedded in local life-worlds, resulting in multiple, local or mutant modernities. Bebbington (2000) has called for a notion of development that is at once alternative and developmentalist, critical and practicable, focused on the concept of livelihood. Grillo and Stirrat (1997) take their critique of post-development as a point of departure for a constructive redefinition of development theory and practice. Fagan (1999) has suggested that the cultural politics of post-development has to start with the everyday lives and struggles of concrete groups of people, particularly women, thus weaving together Marxist and post-structuralist proposals; Diawara (2000) implicitly makes a similar point by advocating for a consideration of the varieties of local knowledge that are present in the development encounter. The relation between post-development, feminism and post-colonial theory has been another focus of fruitful discussion. Sylvester (1999) warns about the effect on our accounts of the world of our distance from those we write about; she advocates for building connections between post-colonial theory and post-development as a corrective to this problem and as beneficial to both. Other authors find in gender and poverty a privileged domain for weaving together elements of post-development, post-colonial theory, political economy and feminism into a new understanding of development, while maintaining a critical eye on the ethnocentrism and exclusions that often characterised earlier developmentalist representations of women (for example, Marchand and Parpart, 1995; Gardner and Lewis 1996; Schech and Haggis, 2000). Basic issues of paradigmatic differences have also been usefully brought to the fore (Pieterse, 1998).

As we entered the present decade, the panorama of development theory is thus marked by a wide array of positions and growing inter-paradigmatic dialogue. This could be seen as a positive result of the sometimes acrimonious debates on post-development during the 1990s. As the first decade of the new century unfolds, the problems of development continue to be as challenging, if not as intractable, as ever. On the one hand, economic globalisation has taken on such a tremendous force that it has seemingly relegated the debates over the nature of development to the back burner. On the other, global movements and the deepening of poverty continue to keep issues of justice and development on the agenda. For most of these movements, it is clear that conventional development of the kind offered by neoliberalism is not an option. There are, indeed, many alternatives being proposed by movement activists and intellectuals. At the very least, it is becoming clear that if 'another world is possible', to appeal to the slogan of the World Social Forum, then another development should, indeed, also be possible. The knowledge produced by these movements has become an essential ingredient for rethinking globalisation and development. In this way, post-development has also come to mean the end of the dominance of expert knowledge over the terms of the debate. It remains for us, development scholars, to engage with these intellectual and political trends among the movements with the always important aim of rethinking our own perspectives.

ARTURO ESCOBAR

References

Apffel-Marglin, Frédérique and Stephen Marglin (eds) (1990), *Dominating Knowledge*, Oxford: Clarendon.

Arce, Alberto and Norman Long (eds) (2000), *Anthropology, Development, and Modernities*, London: Routledge.

Bebbington, Anthony (2000), 'Re-encountering development: livelihood transitions and place transformations in the Andes', *Annals of the Association of American Geographers*, **90** (3), 495–520.

Berger, Mark (1995), 'Post-Cold War capitalism: modernization and modes of resistance after the fall', *Third World Quarterly*, **16** (1), 717–28.

Crew, Emma and Elizabeth Harrison (1998), *Whose Development? An Ethnography of Aid*, London: Zed Books.

Diawara, M. (2000), 'Globalization, development politics and local knowledge', *International Sociology*, **15** (2), 361–71.

Escobar, Arturo (1992), 'Imagining a post-development era? Critical thought, development, and social movements', *Social Text*, **31/32**, 20–56.

Escobar, Arturo (1995), *Encountering Development*, Princeton, NJ: Princeton University Press.

Escobar, Arturo (2000), 'Beyond the search for a paradigm? Post-development and beyond', *Development*, **43** (4), 11–14.

Esteva, Gustavo and Madhu Suri Prakash (1999), *Grassroots Postmodernism*, London: Zed Books.

Fagan, G.H. (1999), 'Cultural politics and (post) development paradigms', in Ronald Munck and Denis O'Hearn (eds), *Critical Development Theory: Contributions to a New Paradigm*, London and New York: Zed Books, pp. 179–95.

Ferguson, James (1990), *The Anti-Politics Machine*, Cambridge: Cambridge University Press.

Gardner, Katy and David Lewis (1996), *Anthropology, Development, and the Post-Modern Challenge*, London: Pluto.

Grillo, R.D. and R.L. Stirrat (eds) (1997), *Discourses of Development: Anthropological Perspectives*, Oxford: Berg.

Kamat, Sangeeta (2002), *Development Hegemony: NGOs and the State in India*, Oxford and Delhi: Oxford University Press.

Kiely, Ray (1999), 'The last refuge of the noble savage? A critical assessment of post-development theory', *European Journal of Development Research*, **11** (1), 30–55.

Lehmann, David (1997), 'An opportunity lost: Escobar's deconstruction of development', *Journal of Development Studies*, **33** (4), 568–78.

Marchand, M.H. and J.L. Parpart (eds) (1995), *Feminism/Post-Modernism/Development*, London: Routledge.

Mohanty, Chandra (1991), 'Under Western eyes. Feminist scholarship and colonial discourses', in Chadra Mohanty, Ann Russo and Lourdes Torres (eds), *Third World Women and the Politics of Feminism*, Bloomington, IN: Indiana University Press, pp. 51–80.

Peet, Richard and Elaine Hartwick (1999), *Theories of Development*, New York: Guilford.

Pieterse, Jan Nederveen (1998), 'My paradigm or yours? Alternative development, post-development, and reflexive development', *Development and Change*, **29**, 343–73.

Rahnema, Majid and Victoria Bawtree (eds) (1997), *The Post-Development Reader*, London: Zed Books.

Rist, Gilbert (1997), *The History of Development*, London: Zed Books.

Sachs, Wolfgang (ed.) (1992), *The Development Dictionary: A Guide to Knowledge as Power*, London: Zed Books.

Schech, Susanne and Jane Haggis (2000), *Culture and Development: A Critical Introduction*, Oxford: Blackwell.

Shiva, Vandana (1993), *Monocultures of the Mind*, London: Zed Books.

Storey, Andy (2000), 'Post-development theory: romanticism and Pontius Pilate Politics', *Development*, **43** (4), 40–46.

Sylvester, Christine (1999), 'Development studies and postcolonial studies: disparate tales of the "Third World"', *Third World Quarterly*, **20** (4), 703–21.

Poverty and Growth

The link between aggregate economic growth and poverty has been of long-standing interest in development studies. This entry revisits the issue in the light of recent arguments and evidence. After a discussion of the relevant concepts and measures, the entry examines what we currently know about how much poor people benefit from economic growth and what might explain why some growth processes are more pro-poor than others. It ends with a discussion of the possibility of a reverse causation, whereby current poverty limits future growth, which means in turn that poverty is perpetuated.

Concepts and measures

As normally defined, 'poverty' means that one cannot afford certain predetermined consumption needs. This is commonly assessed using a comprehensive measure of real consumption or income (including imputed values for consumption or income in-kind, including from own production) for randomly sampled households in a socio-economic survey. There is a large literature on the conceptual and practical issues that arise in the measurement of welfare using such data; for an overview, see Slesnick (1998).

The most common measure of poverty is the headcount index, given by the proportion of the population living in households with consumption or income below a predetermined poverty line. The headcount index tells us nothing about what has happened to the distribution *below* the poverty line; for example, if the poorest person becomes poorer then the headcount index will not change. Better measures of poverty have been proposed that reflect distribution below the line; for example, see Watts (1968), Sen (1976) and Foster et al. (1984). The discussion in this entry will focus on the headcount index, though noting when results might differ for these 'higher-order' measures. The entry will also confine attention to 'absolute poverty' whereby the poverty line is intended to have a fixed real value. (For further discussion of methods of setting poverty lines, see Ravallion, 1998.)

For making international comparisons of absolute poverty, the World Bank has chosen to measure global poverty by the standards of what poverty means in poor countries, which gave the '$1/day' line (Ravallion et al., 1991). This is converted to local currency using the latest PPP exchange rates for consumption and local consumer price indices are then used to convert the international poverty line to local currency at the time of the household survey. By this measure, there were about 1.1 billion poor in the world around 2000 – about one-fifth of the world's population (Chen and Ravallion, 2001). This is a conservative definition; while one could hardly argue that the people in the world who are poor by the standards typical of the poorest countries are not in fact poor, there are many more people in the world who are poor by the standards of middle-income countries. If instead one uses a poverty line of $2/day, the poverty count rises to 2.7 billion (about one in two people).

In describing the impact of economic growth on poverty it can be useful to exploit the fact that a measure of poverty can be written as a function of the mean of the distribution on which that measure is based and all other parameters of the distribution, which can be loosely interpreted as 'inequality'. This fact can be used to decompose changes in poverty over time into a component attributed to growth in the mean and a component due to changes in distribution (Datt and Ravallion, 1992). A growth process is said to be 'distribution neutral' if all incomes grow at the same rate leaving inequality unchanged. The distributional change is said to be pro-poor if the redistribution component is poverty reducing.

In studying the impact of growth on poverty, the growth rates can come from either the same surveys used to measure poverty or from the national accounts. Using surveys has the advantage that one is measuring growth in *household* income or consumption. Using surveys also means that time periods and definitions match perfectly with the poverty measures. However, using surveys for the growth rates can lead to overestimation of the correlation between poverty reduction and growth due to the inevitable measurement errors in surveys, which are naturally passed on to both the mean and the poverty measures. Ravallion (2001) tries to correct for this by using the growth rate from the national accounts as an instrumental variable for the growth rate in the survey mean. This assumes that the growth rates from the two sources are correlated, but that their errors are not.

While growth rates from these two data sources tend to be highly correlated, there are some worryingly large differences for some countries (including India in the 1990s) and regions (such as Eastern Europe and Central Asia in the 1990s). Discrepancies in levels and growth rates from these two data sources can stem from various factors; for further discussion, see Ravallion (2003a) and Deaton (2005). However, such discrepancies do not imply that poverty measures should instead be based on the mean incomes from the national accounts; indeed, this could well yield an even less accurate measure of poverty, given that there can be no presumption that the national accounts are right and the surveys are wrong, or that the surveys would get the mean wrong but the distribution right (Ravallion, 2003b).

Has growth reduced poverty?
A common empirical finding in the literature is that changes in inequality at country level have virtually zero correlation with rates of economic growth; see, for example, Ravallion and Chen (1997), Fields (2001), Ravallion (2001) and Dollar and Kraay (2002). This also holds for growing poor countries. The Kuznets hypothesis – that with growth in a low-income country, inequality first increases then starts to fall after a certain point – has generally not been borne out by experience in growing developing countries (Bruno et al., 1998; Fields, 2001).

Among growing developing economies, inequality tends to fall about as often as it rises, that is, growth tends to be distribution neutral on average. For example, across 117 spells between successive household surveys for 47 developing countries, the correlation coefficient between annualised changes in the Gini index of inequality and annualised rates of growth in mean household income or consumption from surveys is only 0.06 (Ravallion, 2003b).

The fact that growth tends to be distribution neutral on average makes it unsurprising that the literature has also found that poverty measures tend to fall with growth; see, for example, Ravallion (1995), Ravallion and Chen (1997) and Fields (2001). The elasticity of the $1/day poverty rate to growth in survey means is around –2, though somewhat lower (in absolute value) if one measures growth rates from national accounts (Ravallion, 2001).

However, there is a wide variation in the impact of a given rate of growth on poverty; the 95 per cent confidence interval implies that a 2 per cent rate of growth in average household income will bring anything from a modest drop in the poverty rate of 1 per cent per year to a more dramatic 7 per cent annual decline. (So for a country with a headcount index of 40 per cent, we have 95 per cent confidence that the index will fall by somewhere between 0.4 percentage points and 2.8 points in the first year.) The elasticity tends to be higher (in absolute value) for higher-order poverty measures, which reflect distribution below the poverty line. The gains to the poor from growth are typically not confined to people near the poverty line, but reach deeper.

With positive growth in the developing world as a whole, there has been a declining trend in the incidence of absolute poverty and the total number of poor over the bulk of the 1980s and 1990s. For example, the number of poor by the $1/day standard fell by about 100 million in the 1990s, representing a decline of about 0.7 points per year. In the aggregate, if the rate of absolute poverty reduction experienced in the 1990s is maintained it will be sufficient to achieve the UN's Millennium Development Goal of halving the 1990 $1/day poverty rate by 2015. However, progress is highly uneven and Sub-Saharan Africa, in particular, is not on track for meeting this goal. Growth in the most populous countries (China and India) has clearly been important to bringing down the global headcount of poverty. By the same token, lack of growth in some of the poorest countries has dampened overall progress.

What makes growth more pro-poor?

The available evidence suggests that the same rate of growth can bring markedly different rates of poverty reduction. By probing more deeply into the causes of diverse impacts of growth on poverty, the literature has pointed to some important implications regarding the policies that are needed for rapid poverty reduction, in addition to promoting higher growth.

Two sets of factors can be identified as the main proximate causes of the differing rates of poverty reduction at given rates of growth. A key factor is the *initial level of inequality* (Ravallion, 1997, 2001). While the evidence suggests that one cannot expect absolute poverty to fall without positive growth, the higher the initial inequality in a country (even if it does not change), the less the gains from growth tend to be shared by the poor. In other words, a smaller initial share tends to mean a smaller subsequent share of the gains from expansion. Consider the rate of poverty reduction in a country with a headcount index of 40 per cent and with a 2 per cent rate of growth in per capita income, without any change in distribution. In a low-inequality country – with a Gini index of 0.30, say – the headcount index will be halved in 10 years; by contrast, in a high inequality country, with a Gini index of 0.60, growing at the same rate and with the same initial headcount index, it will take over 50 years (Ravallion, 2004). Poverty can be quite unresponsive to growth in high-inequality countries.

By the same argument, high inequality will help protect the poor from the adverse impact of aggregate economic contraction. Low inequality can thus be a mixed blessing for poor people living in an unstable macroeconomic environment; it helps them share in the benefits of growth, but it also exposes them to the costs of contraction.

While 'initial inequality' is clearly an important proximate determinant of differing rates of poverty reduction at a given rate of growth, to inform policy we need to probe more deeply into the relevant sources of inequality. There are inequalities in a number of dimensions that are likely to matter, including access to both private (human and physical) assets and public goods. Inequalities in access to infrastructure and social services (healthcare and education) naturally make it harder for poor people to take up the opportunities afforded by aggregate economic growth. This has been borne out by empirical investigations of why some Indian states have seen more rapid poverty reduction than others (Ravallion and Datt, 2002).

A second factor is changing income distribution. What happens to inequality in growing economies can make a big difference to the rate of poverty reduction. Among growing economies, the median rate of decline in the $1/day headcount index is 10 per cent per year among countries that combined growth with falling inequality, while it is only 1 per cent per year for those countries for which growth came with rising inequality (Ravallion, 2001). Either way poverty tends to fall, but at very different rates. (And similarly among contracting economies; poverty rises on average, but much more rapidly when inequality is rising than falling.)

What underlies the changes in distribution? There are clearly a great many country-specific idiosyncratic factors. Generalisations across country experience are never easy, but one factor that is likely to matter in many developing countries is the *geographic and sectoral pattern of growth*. Higher growth in a number of developing countries has come with widening regional disparities and often little or no growth in lagging poor areas. For example, the more rapid economic growth seen in India during the 1990s has not occurred in the states where it would have the most impact on poverty nationally (Datt and Ravallion, 2002). Agricultural growth has also lagged in growing economies relative to the (primarily urban) non-farm economy. As a result, the overall growth process in India has tended to become less pro-poor over time. The same thing appears to have been happening in China.

Making growth more pro-poor requires a combination of more growth, a more pro-poor pattern of growth and success in reducing the antecedent inequalities that limit the prospects for poor people to share in the opportunities unleashed in a growth economy. The ideal combination will naturally vary with country circumstances. In some countries attention can safely focus on the overall rate of growth to ensure rapid poverty reduction; elsewhere, a broader approach will be called for. This begs the question as to whether there might be a trade-off between the rate of growth and interventions to make growth more pro-poor. The final section turns to that issue.

Is poverty an impediment to future growth?

While poverty is more often seen as a consequence of low average income, there are reasons for thinking that there is a feedback effect. (Good reviews of the theoretical arguments can be found in Aghion et al., 1999 and Bardhan et al., 1999.) A plausible argument is that the existence of credit market failures means that some people are unable to exploit growth-promoting opportunities for investment in (physical and human) capital. And it will tend to be the poor for whom these constraints are most likely to be binding. With declining marginal products of capital, the output loss from the market failure will be greater for the poor. So the higher the proportion of poor people there are in the economy the lower the rate of growth. Then high current poverty is perpetuated.

There is supportive evidence for this view from cross-country comparisons of growth rates, suggesting that countries with higher initial inequality in incomes have tended to experience lower rates of growth controlling for other factors such as initial average income, openness to trade and the rate of inflation (Alesina and Rodrik, 1994; Persson and Tabellini, 1994; Birdsall et al., 1995; Perotti, 1996; Deininger and Squire, 1998;

Easterly, 2002). At the same time, there are also a number of concerns about the data and methods underlying these findings based on cross-country comparative analysis (Ravallion, 2001). Future research will hopefully throw a clearer light on the magnitude of the efficiency costs of poverty and inequality.

Accepting that there is no aggregate trade-off between mean income and inequality does not, however, mean that there are no trade-offs at the level of specific policies. Reducing inequality by adding further distortions to an economy will have ambiguous effects on growth and (hence) poverty reduction. The challenge for policy is to combine growth-promoting economic reforms with the right policies to help ensure that the poor can participate fully in the opportunities unleashed, and so contribute to that growth. Get the combination of policies right, and both growth and poverty reduction can be rapid. Get it wrong and poverty reduction will be slow or even stalled, and possibly growth too.

MARTIN RAVALLION

References

Aghion, Philippe, Eva Caroli and Cecilia Garcia-Penalosa (1999), 'Inequality and economic growth: the perspectives of the new growth theories', *Journal of Economic Literature*, **37** (4), 1615–60.

Alesina, Alberto and Dani Rodrik (1994), 'Distributive politics and economic growth', *Quarterly Journal of Economics*, **108**, 465–90.

Bardhan, Pranab, Samuel Bowles and Herbert Gintis (1999), 'Wealth inequality, wealth constraints and economic performance', in A.B. Atkinson and F. Bourguignon (eds), *Handbook of Income Distribution*, Vol. I, Amsterdam: North-Holland, pp. 541–603.

Birdsall, Nancy, D. Ross and R. Sabot (1995), 'Inequality and growth reconsidered: lessons from East Asia', *World Bank Economic Review*, **9** (3), 477–508.

Bruno, Michael, Martin Ravallion and Lyn Squire (1998), 'Equity and growth in developing countries: old and new perspectives on the policy issues', in V. Tanzi and K. Chu (eds), *Income Distribution and High-Quality Growth*, Cambridge, MA: MIT Press, pp. 117–46.

Chen, Shaohua and Martin Ravallion (2001), 'How did the world's poorest fare in the 1990s?', *Review of Income and Wealth*, **47**, 283–300.

Datt, Gaurav and Martin Ravallion (1992), 'Growth and redistribution components of changes in poverty measures: a decomposition with applications to Brazil and India in the 1980s', *Journal of Development Economics*, **38**, 275–95.

Datt, Gaurav and Martin Ravallion (2002), 'Has India's post-reform economic growth left the poor behind?', *Journal of Economic Perspectives*, **16** (3), 89–108.

Deaton, Angus (2005), 'Measuring poverty in a growing world (or measuring growth in a poor world)', *Review of Economics and Statistics*, **87** (1), 1–19.

Deininger, Klaus and Lyn Squire (1998), 'New ways of looking at old issues: inequality and growth', *Journal of Development Economics*, **57** (2), 259–87.

Dollar, David and Aart Kraay (2002), 'Growth *is* good for the poor', *Journal of Economic Growth*, **7** (3), 195–225.

Easterly, William (2002), 'Inequality does cause underdevelopment: new evidence', Working Paper 1, Center for Global Development, Washington, DC.

Fields, Gary S. (2001), *Distribution and Development*, New York: Russell Sage Foundation.

Foster, James, J. Greer and Erik Thorbecke (1984), 'A class of decomposable poverty measures', *Econometrica*, **52**, 761–5.

Perotti, Roberto (1996), 'Growth, income distribution and democracy: what the data say', *Journal of Economic Growth*, **1** (2), 149–87.

Persson, Torsten and Guido Tabellini (1994), 'Is inequality harmful for growth?', *American Economic Review*, **84**, 600–621.

Ravallion, Martin (1995), 'Growth and poverty: evidence for developing countries in the 1980s', *Economics Letters*, **48**, 411–17.

Ravallion, Martin (1997), 'Can high inequality developing countries escape absolute poverty?', *Economics Letters*, **56**, 51–7.

Ravallion, Martin (1998), 'Poverty lines in theory and practice', Living Standards Measurement Study Paper 133, Washington, DC, World Bank.

Ravallion, Martin (2001), 'Growth, inequality and poverty: looking beyond averages', *World Development*, **29** (11), 1803–15.

Ravallion, Martin (2003a), 'Measuring aggregate welfare in developing countries: how well do national accounts and surveys agree?', *Review of Economics and Statistics*, **85**, 645–52.

Ravallion, Martin (2003b), 'The debate on globalization, poverty and inequality: why measurement matters', *International Affairs*, **79** (4), 739–54.

Ravallion, Martin (2004), 'Pro-poor growth: a primer', Policy Research Working Paper, Development Research Group, World Bank, Washington, DC.

Ravallion, Martin and Shaohua Chen (1997), 'What can new survey data tell us about recent changes in distribution and poverty?', *World Bank Economic Review*, **11** (2), 357–82.

Ravallion, Martin and Gaurav Datt (2002), 'Why has economic growth been more pro-poor in some states of India than others?', *Journal of Development Economics*, **68**, 381–400.

Ravallion, Martin, Gaurav Datt and Dominique Van de Walle (1991), 'Quantifying absolute poverty in the developing world', *Review of Income and Wealth*, **37**, 345–61.

Sen, Amartya (1976), 'Poverty: an ordinal approach to measurement', *Econometrica*, **46**, 437–46.

Slesnick, Daniel T. (1998), 'Empirical approaches to the measurement of welfare,' *Journal of Economic Literature*, **36** (4), 2108–65.

Watts, Harold W. (1968), 'An economic definition of poverty', in Daniel P. Moynihan (ed.), *On Understanding Poverty*, New York: Basic Books, pp. 316–29.

Poverty Measurement

Poverty measurement is the quantitative assessment of the level and depth of poverty of individuals or in aggregate, for a group or in a region, country or across the world. Why should we be concerned with measuring poverty? Any quantitative measurement involves reductionism, and this will come at a cost, affecting the implications that can be drawn from this exercise. A first point in this respect is that there is clearly a demand for this research activity. Policy makers like headline figures. It focuses the mind and provides crisp sound bites. More positively, it provides explicit and plausibly agreed means to evaluate policies and change. Still, while generating headline figures on the level of poverty appears to be a key activity of any poverty research, it is only one aspect of poverty measurement and analysis, to the frustration of any practitioner in this field.

Quantitative poverty measurement has a long history, with a seminal contribution by Seebohm Rowntree in 1902 but really came to the fore in the 1960s in the United States and subsequently, when more data sources became available, in the 1980s in the developing world. Key methodological contributions on poverty measurement that have defined the current state of the art, have been made by eminent economists such as Amartya Sen, Tony Atkinson, James Foster and Martin Ravallion. They have all written accessible papers and books on the subject, and are definitely worth reading by any student of development studies. This contribution liberally draws on their insights.

Poverty measurement involves three steps. First, it involves the choice and the quantitative measurement of a welfare indicator. Second, it requires the choice of a means of discriminating between poor and non-poor, typically via the poverty line. Finally, it involves aggregating this information in a poverty measure for a particular population. An example would be to count the poor and provide the percentage of the population that is poor, but this is just one method for aggregation. It is by far the most commonly preferred method by policy makers, but it has serious shortcomings. This entry first discusses each of these three steps in turn. Then, it briefly discusses two more crucial issues: first, multidimensionality and its implications for measurement and aggregation, and finally, the risk and the temporal dimensions of poverty measurement.

The choice of the welfare indicator is by far the most critical and most controversial part of poverty measurement. Indeed, while critics of poverty measurement often focus on issues such as the choice of the poverty line, much of the ill-feeling towards poverty analysis is typically caused by the reductionism implied by the welfare indicator used. What one requires is a means of assessing the welfare of a population but in a comparable and quantifiable way. Indeed, poverty measurement is not interested in the measurement of poverty of an individual *per se*, but in making comparisons between groups or countries, or between time periods. Poverty comparisons require welfare indicators that are constructed to be comparable. Perfect comparability can surely not be achieved either conceptually or empirically, so the best practice requires one to be explicit about the choices made.

Most economists would tend to prefer the value of consumption or income, as a means of approximating the budget constraint faced. Often, this approach is referred to as 'money-metric utility' following a simple correspondence (under particular assumptions) in basic textbook economics between the 'utility' that can be obtained by households and the budget constraint faced. Of course, such arguments do not sway those with roots in other disciplines. The presence of multiple dimensions of poverty, some not easily quantifiable, presents a challenge for poverty measurement. However, provided one is dealing with plausibly quantifiable dimensions of well-being, such as education, access to water or nutrition, virtually all issues discussed in this entry can be applied to each of these dimensions, as will be discussed further below.

In general, income is considered harder to measure in poorer societies than consumption, not least in rural settings, and due to inherent fluctuations related to risk and seasonality, income may not give a good indicator of achieved welfare outcomes when measured over a relatively short recall period. Consumption, measured for a particular relatively short period, is then typically preferred by analysts given the tendency of households to try to keep consumption smooth over time. It tends to be constructed in a way that has meaning for many households. It is an aggregate including several crucial basic needs, most notably food and clothing (often constituting well over half the spending in cash or in kind for households in poorer areas), based on its measurement over well-defined recall periods and valued in monetary terms. It is often suggested that subsistence consumption tends to be excluded from household consumption aggregates, but this is generally not true: the focus is on quantities consumed and those coming from own stocks or gathering in the field tend to be included, usually assigning a value based on local market prices. Still, there are important further problems, and essential items for achieved consumption outcomes such as housing or education and health services are typically not well measured in poverty measurement, with notable exceptions in some studies.

Beyond the measurement of household consumption, at least two critical issues remain for a welfare indicator for poverty measurement. The unit of analysis is by necessity usually the household, since income and consumption can typically only be observed at the level of the household. Even so, it involves in practice choices on the meaning of the household, and most large-scale household surveys use a functional definition, referring to those residing in the same dwelling and/or sharing 'from the same pot', but again, in some contexts the biases involved can be substantial. In order to compare poverty outcomes across households with different size and composition, poverty analysis tends to use either per capita consumption (dividing consumption by the number of household members) or a transformation in 'per adult' terms, typically using a weight assigned to each household member based on needs contingent on age (a young child needs fewer calories than an adult), as well as for possible economies of scale of large households (to put it simply, an extra child does not necessarily mean that a larger furnace is to be acquired). The implication is an assumption that each member of a household has the same welfare. Since looking within the household is crucial for understanding poverty, other individual-specific dimensions of welfare would need to be measured beyond simple household consumption and income, such as individual nutrition or health outcomes, or supplementary analysis should be conducted on how individual members benefit from household-level outcomes. A further issue is that the consumption or income values need to be expressed in a comparable way across households. Since monetary values are used, this requires a correction for the purchasing power implied across households. A price deflator, expressing the weighted cost of a particular 'average' bundle of commodities consumed across a population tends to be used in practice.

These procedures result in a standardised indicator of welfare, assumed to be perfectly comparable for a given population. It allows one to describe the distribution of this indicator across this population. Up to this point, all the procedures described and their underlying assumptions are essentially the same for inequality measurement (see Inequality Measurement, this volume). This commonality means that many of the criticisms on the practice of poverty measurement also apply to inequality measurement, including the issues of choosing an appropriate welfare indicator and the multidimensionality of welfare. At this juncture, poverty measurement starts deviating: inequality aims to provide summary statistics for the entire distribution, while poverty refers to the characteristics of some lower part of this distribution, essentially ignoring the rest. Poverty measurement then requires a norm, the poverty line, to assess who is poor and who is not poor. Again, this is highly controversial and crucial choices have to be made; and these choices always involve something arbitrary. A useful guiding principle is that it should reflect a socially accepted norm for what constitutes a reasonable level of welfare. Poverty measurement for policy purposes makes sense only if there is some acceptance that the measure is helpful to illuminate outcomes in a society. But many options exist for how to proceed. One approach is an absolute 'needs-based' approach, from the perception that there is some absolute level of welfare that translates readily into minimal requirements. When consumption is used, it typically contains the value of some agreed bundle of basic food commodities, plus some allowance for essential non-food consumption. The level of food consumption chosen may be linked explicitly to being able to obtain the minimum calorie intake required for basic health living (often suggested to be approximately 2300 Kcal for an adult). This 'basic needs'-based method of absolute poverty calculation is commonly used in World Bank-supported data collection and poverty analysis within some of the poorer developing countries. Others tend to favour a relative poverty line, meaning a line defined relative to mean or other characteristics of the distribution of welfare across the population. The argument is closely linked to the idea of a socially acceptable norm, whereby it is judged that one's position relative to other people is essential for a poverty concept. For example, in the European Union, the poverty line is defined as 60 per cent of median income in a particular country.

Superficially, the origin of the poverty line may not appear to be a problematic issue, as long as it seems reasonable and acceptable, since it is just a means of allowing one to focus on a particular part of the welfare distribution. However, the implications of choosing a particular method can be far-reaching, since poverty measurement is concerned mainly with making comparisons of poverty between geographical areas, groups in society and over time. Using a relative poverty line or a different absolute poverty line per context may mean that one considers a different norm for different countries or groups. For example, an acceptable norm in a rich society may imply having the means to pay for rather fancy, branded clothes, while in a poor society simple clothing may be sufficient. Arguments can be made for such a method and when looking within the group or society in question, this does not have to be a problem. But when making comparisons between societies, for example to prioritise spending between countries, allowing for these different 'needs' will have a different implication from using basic clothing for all societies. Similarly, should one compensate one social group for its culturally determined but more expensive tastes when constructing a poverty line? Or, when evaluating the change in poverty over time, an 'absolute' fixed basket of commodities will have different implications from using an updated relative poverty line, linked to the mean or median welfare outcome in each period, as used in the European Union. For example, adjusting the poverty line to the mean may seem attractive for a broadly growing economy – resulting in lower poverty declines than may be implied by using a fixed line. But when a big crisis hits an economy, halving its GDP, without any change in income inequality then the poverty line is likely to halve as well and no increase in poverty will be observed as if this has no implications for poverty. The alternative, such as using a fixed poverty line reflecting the purchasing power implied by one US dollar in a particular year, as used in the Millennium Development Goals (MDGs), provides then a relatively transparent tool for comparison between countries, and possibly allocating funding between countries, even though as a means for conducting a substantive investigation of poverty within a particular country it may seem wanting (see Millennium Development Goals, this volume). These examples suggest that poverty lines should be chosen to serve best the nature of the poverty comparison one wants to conduct over time, between groups or between countries and regions. Each choice will partly predetermine the findings, and any poverty analysis should be explicit about the reasons for its choice.

The choice of a welfare indicator and poverty line allow us to identify the poor in a particular setting. Poverty measurement aims to go further: to provide a summary statistic of poverty for a particular country or group. Many aggregate poverty measures have been proposed, from the simple headcount (the percentage of a group that is poor) to more complicated and possibly less intuitive aggregations. Different aggregations tend to have different policy implications in terms of which groups are poorer or how to alleviate poverty, so a highly mathematical but important literature has developed since the 1970s on finding criteria to judge whether a particular aggregation corresponds to broadly acceptable value judgements regarding what would constitute an increase or decrease in poverty. For example, one crucial axiom in most applied poverty analysis is that one chooses to focus exclusively on those below the poverty line – whether those above are just marginally so or are indeed very rich, is irrelevant. As a consequence, increasing the welfare level of at least one poor person via a transfer is judged an identical reduction in poverty, irrespective of whether this transfer came from a very rich person, an only marginally non-poor person or from outside the population. Another axiom typically considered necessary for a poverty measure is that a transfer from a not-so-poor to a poorer person should not imply an increase, or more strongly, it should imply a reduction in aggregate poverty (provided that their relative positions are not reversed). A sufficient condition for this to hold is a preference for more equality rather than inequality in a population – something typically agreed by those concerned with poverty, but a value judgement nevertheless.

While reasonable assumptions, some of the most commonly used poverty measures are not consistent with them. For example, the headcount measure of poverty could be reduced by transferring resources from very poor people to not-so-poor people. Of course, few governments would explicitly set out to do this. However, some combinations of policy measures, for example inducing substantial relative price changes, may have exactly this effect, lifting some groups above the poverty line but worsening the position of some of the poorer groups. The reduction of the headcount index may then seem proof of success, but the underlying distributional effect among the poor is not reflected in this particular aggregate measure. If countries are currently hard pressed to meet the MDG to reduce those living below $1 a day, the logic of the measure used is that they could reach this goal at least cost by focusing their policy packages on those just below this poverty line – surely not an intended policy response!

In fact, the headcount index is a limiting case of a general family of poverty measures that are most commonly used in applied poverty analysis. This family, the FGT family of poverty measures, is named after the authors of a classic article on the matter, Foster et al. (1984). It is calculated using data on a population of N, whose welfare levels, c, are ordered from poor to rich. If there are q poor people in this population, and z is the poverty line, then all the poverty measures in this family are defined by

$$P_\alpha = \frac{1}{N} \sum_{i=1}^{q} \left(\frac{z-c}{z} \right)^\alpha,$$

in which α can take a non-negative number starting from zero. If α equals zero, this poverty measure is just the headcount – and its undesirable characteristics were discussed before. When α equals one, then the measure reduces to the poverty gap index, and can be interpreted as the shortfall of the poor's welfare as a percentage of the poverty line and averaged across the population. By implication, it provides a direct measure of the cost (expressed as a percentage of the poverty line) of lifting all the poor out of poverty. In policy terms, it is neutral about transfers taken from the poorest and given to the not so poor: the total gap is what matters, not who is contributing to this gap. Arguably, this is not a desirable characteristic. However, once α is larger than one, we are left with an index that tends to have most of the crucial desirable characteristics of an aggregate poverty measure. For example, the squared poverty gap index, with α equal to two, is a measure often reported in quantitative poverty analysis, sensitive to the inequality among the poor. However, this comes at a cost, in terms of ease of interpretation. It should then not come as a surprise that few policy makers use this index to provide them with headline figures, but rather stick to those with effectively undesirable characteristics.

Much policy-orientated poverty analysis tends to include some basic further analysis, once the headline figures have been obtained. One tool often used is a poverty profile, essentially a discussion of the correlates of poverty outcomes in a country or region. At it simplest, it tends to provide descriptive statistics of the characteristics of the poor versus the non-poor, for example in terms of sex, age, education, asset holdings, access to infrastructure, or geographic location. It also provides a simple means of checking how the poor as identified in one particular way fare in other welfare dimensions, such as health and nutrition. Often, this work is expanded to provide a multivariate analysis of the links between poverty outcomes and these characteristics (in particular, a statistical regression of the poverty measures on a set of characteristics). While suggestive and interesting, a crucial risk in this type of work is the interpretation of the findings: these simple correlates are hardly providing a careful analysis of the causal processes of impoverishment. In practice, caution is often thrown to the wind in much policy research, although increasingly, these micro-level data are also used to study poverty and its causes and consequences more carefully, using new methods and techniques.

In recent years, poverty measurement and analysis has also been enriched by including more explicitly the multidimensionality of poverty in the analysis. A key reason why multiple dimensions should be measured is that the correlation between different dimensions is not strong. Some have argued that this is not the case: different dimensions are positively correlated. But since empirically, the correlation is not perfect, there are definitely good reasons to consider multidimensionality explicitly not only in conceptual work but also in empirical measurement work. For example, intra-household inequality, linked to power relations within the household, would mean that household-based income and consumption measures would not correlate perfectly with individual nutrition or education dimensions. Similarly, the public good nature of crucial aspects of health provision, for example related to health information and immunisation, and therefore the relevance of publicly provided services, means that income and health indicators need not be highly correlated.

As argued before, the steps used to construct a poverty measure are just as relevant to other dimensions of welfare and are not exclusive to work using income or consumption, even if this impression may exist in much of the literature. For example, standard measures of malnutrition, such as wasting or stunting, use exactly the same steps and make similar crucial but implicit assumptions. First, a welfare outcome measure is chosen in such a way that it is comparable across a population. Z-scores for wasting and stunting (usually based on respectively the weight divided by the height, and the height divided by age) provide an outcome measure, assumed to be fully comparable across a population of children of a particular age group. A line is chosen, usually at -2 for malnutrition, or -3 for serious malnutrition, based on some semi-objective reason, the statistical properties of a particular population of healthy children but not necessarily relevant for the population studied. It is a choice made to be able to proceed with statements about malnutrition. Finally, aggregation takes place, by simply counting the children below the norm and this aggregation is typically a headcount index, the percentage of children failing to reach the norm, with all the problems it entails in terms of the most cost effective policy for a marginal reduction in this measure. Similarly, we could define measures of water access 'poverty', for example based on how far one is from safe water. Indeed, much work on other dimensions of poverty could be helpfully enriched by explicitly considering some of the lessons from the problems of measuring income and consumption poverty. Asset poverty work is an example in this respect: while clearly providing a means of linking the poverty debate to some of its underlying determinants, using assets as a quantifiable welfare measure means that it is assumed that a comparable asset index or value can be constructed that, in welfare terms, is directly comparable across a population studied, which may not be able to be true, for example when comparing pastoralists, crop farmers and urban dwellers in a particular setting. This provides a particular challenge to research in this area.

Beyond simply recognising the need to measure different dimensions of poverty, quantitative poverty research has also started to consider key issues on how to use these indicators together. One route would be to consider each of the dimensions worth considering independently of the others. Implicitly, this would suggest that there is limited substitution: for example, the incidence of having limited access to safe water can never be compensated for by having better outcomes in terms of nutrition, relative to a norm. While it is unlikely that those designing the MDGs would have thought in these terms, they provide a long list of headcount 'poverty' measures in different dimensions, that each have to be met (see Millennium Development Goals, this volume). Another route would be to allow for some substitution, and proceed to some form of aggregation of different dimensions. The human poverty index designed for UNDP is one example of such aggregation (see UNDP, 1997). Work to make the properties of such aggregation and the judgements they imply explicit is under way. Note a close parallel of this work with those involved in trying to engage welfare measurement by taking the 'capabilities' approach as the central entry point, since this work also faces the problems of trying to measure in acceptable ways different dimensions of low well-being, and whether choices within the capability set (the options available to people) involve trade-offs or not, and how to account for them in empirical assessments.

One other recent extension to poverty analysis deserves to be mentioned. For many, the need for a poverty line, and the difficult choices involved, is an undesirable characteristic of poverty measurement. It imposes a discrete threshold below which one is poor and above one is not, but its level is not easily justified, not least in dimensions such as income or expenditure, but also in other dimensions, such as education, for example. However, much work has been done on poverty analysis without a poverty line, usually referred to as 'poverty dominance analysis'. Essentially, this work shows that many relevant statements about poverty, such as whether poverty is higher in one group relative to another, could be done by identifying the range of poverty lines for which a statement is valid. For example, it could be that the percentage of rural households that is poor is always higher than the percentage of poor among the urban households for any poverty line considered in a large reasonable range, implying that a strong statement about poverty can be made without poverty. Of course, fewer clear statements about which group is poorer can be made by requiring intervals rather than just one poverty of lines, but its use in policy is highly underrated. Note that others have tried to avoid strict threshold-based poverty analysis, by using 'fuzzy' poverty measures that acknowledge that near the poverty line, identification of the poor may be difficult.

Poverty measurement is still far from exhausting the need to research appropriate methods. For example, most poverty analysis is static, and considers poverty outcomes in one period, and its measurement is devoid of dynamic issues – for example, how to judge the ability of people who may choose to be below the poverty line now to be relatively well-off in the future? Or how to compare two households that are poor today, but one is just poor today while the other is poor in perpetuity? Similarly, it ignores risk, by only considering outcomes after risk affecting this outcome has been resolved – for example, nutrition is considered after locusts have eaten the harvest of one household but not its neighbour's. It may imply poverty of the former but no poverty for the latter. But before the locusts came, they may both have been similarly at risk of poverty, a relevant fact for policy makers, but not at all considered in standard poverty measurement. Both risk and time are active areas of research on poverty and deserve further attention.

In addition, poverty measurement alone does not provide much insight into the processes behind observed poverty outcomes. A description of the characteristics of the poor relative to the non-poor, often referred to as a 'poverty profile', may provide suggestive evidence, but it is typically a static snapshot and agnostic about the dynamic causal processes involved. Understanding the dynamics of poverty and its links with other processes of change in society and the economy is a central research area, supplementing the poverty measurement issues discussed in this entry (see Chronic Poverty, this volume). In particular, lively research areas are further investigations into the dynamic processes that may allow people to escape poverty or that lead to persistence in poverty outcomes and even poverty traps (states of poverty that entrap individuals when they drift into them, and from which they cannot escape, despite the existence of feasible higher welfare outcomes for otherwise similar individuals).

To conclude, quantitative poverty research has provided the world with a striking statistic, that there are 1.2 billion poor people. It is typically presented without any reference to the crucial choices made by the researchers involved in the quantitative treatment of data, in terms of welfare measurement, poverty lines and aggregation. It is a powerful statement and definitely not a statement without meaning. But it has a specific meaning, linked to explicit assumptions. Used as such it can illuminate policies and processes; without it, it risks manipulation and misinterpretation.

STEFAN DERCON

References and further reading

Atkinson, A.B. (1987), 'On the measurement of poverty', *Econometrica*, **55**, 749–64.
Bourguignon, F. and S.R. Chakravarty (2004), 'The measurement of multidimensional poverty', *Journal of Economic Inequality*, **1** (1), 25–49.
Foster, J., J. Greer and E. Thorbecke (1984), 'A class of decomposable poverty measures', *Econometrica*, **52** (3), 761–6.
Ravallion, M. (1994), *Poverty Comparisons: Fundamentals of Pure and Applied Economics*, Chur: Harwood Academic Publishers.
Rowntree, B.S. (1902), *Poverty: A Study of Town Life*, London: Macmillan.
Sen, A.K. (1979), 'Issues in the measurement of poverty', *Scandinavian Journal of Economics*, **81**, 285–307.
Sen, A.K. (1983), 'Poor relatively speaking', *Oxford Economic Papers*, **35** (1), 153–69.
Sen, A.K. (1999), *Development As Freedom*, Oxford: Oxford University Press.
Sen, A.K. and J. Foster (1997), *On Economic Inequality*, Oxford: Clarendon, 2nd edn with a substantial new appendix.
UNDP (1997), *Human Development Report 1997: Human Development to Eradicate Poverty*, Oxford: Oxford University Press.

Poverty, Characteristics of

The global community entered the twenty-first century at a time of unprecedented prosperity. Over the past 20 years the incidence of poverty declined sharply based on national poverty lines. The spurts of economic growth experienced by China and India accounted for much of the poverty reduction. Yet for Sub-Saharan Africa, poverty levels have increased in both absolute numbers and severity. Many African countries have witnessed reversals in development gains over the last few decades. In many ways, Africa is a metaphor of 'poverty in the midst of plenty'.

The share of wealth going to the top 5 per cent of the population globally has increased and in 1960 the 14 richest countries earned 57 per cent of the world's total income and in 2000 the 13 richest countries earned 80 per cent of the world's total income. Eighty per cent of the world's wealth is enjoyed by the top 20 per cent of the 6 billion global population, leaving 80 per cent to survive on the remaining 20 per cent (Wolfensohn, 2003).

The world today has much of the know-how, the resources and the technological and logistical capacity to end poverty. Yet the political will to do so is lacking at the local, national, regional and global levels. Consider the issue of agricultural subsidies by the richest countries, which cost no less than $330 billion per year between 1999 and 2001 (Aksoy and Beghin, 2004, p. 44). These subsidies deprive poor farmers in Burkina Faso and other poor countries of markets for their products and much-needed income to fight poverty.

Private affluence and public deprivation live side by side in most countries of the world, ranging from the United States to Mali. Levels of wealth have reached unprecedented levels among those who are rich, while destitution – often akin to pre-industrial levels – continues to plague those who are poor. Cape Town exemplifies this gap with its spectacular beauty alongside the squalor of the squatter camps on the Cape Flats. Tolerance of inequalities by those in leadership across many lands continues to perpetuate poverty in the twenty-first century. It is this tolerance that lies at the root of the 'know-do' gap with respect to poverty eradication, that is, knowing about poverty but not doing anything about it.

The causes of poverty also shape its characteristics. Apartheid's legacy superimposed on British colonial heritage, has left South Africa with poverty that is marked by race, gender and geography. Poor people are more likely to be black, rural or peri-urban, women and/or children, those without secure land tenure or other fixed property, and those with minimal education. The same applies to much of Africa and South Asia although in many places poverty is widespread in urban areas, where the legacy of the past continues to haunt the present and to cast shadows on the future. Structural adjustment programmes to address macroeconomic and other imbalances have, in many cases, worsened the plight of the poorest people, who end up with little or no safety net. The contrast between the reluctance of the EU and the USA to undertake the requisite structural adjustment to eliminate agricultural subsidies and their insistence, as major shareholders of multilateral financial institutions, on accelerated adjustments in poor countries, is striking.

Poor people interviewed across many countries speak eloquently about 'who poor people are' and 'what characterises poverty'. Deepa Narayan and Patti Petesch (2002) have captured many of the voices of poor people in their study of 14 countries across Africa, South and East Asia, Latin America and the former Soviet Union (see also Wilson and Ramphele, 1989; Moore et al., 1998; Narayan et al., 2000a, 2000b; Clark, 2002). The profile of those living in poverty is portrayed by interviewees to include those who are unemployed, sick, widowed, orphaned, disabled, people lacking assets, those caught up in conflicts and wars such as Bosnia/Herzegovina and those whose 'voices do not carry weight'.

Poverty is characterised by poor people themselves as 'ill-being'. Ill-being is said to come from constant deprivation of the basic necessities of life such as food, medical care and shelter. Many use poignant phrases to describe markers of poverty: 'empty pockets'; 'no money'; 'not having enough to eat'; 'wearing tattered clothes'; unemployed or irregular and/or inadequate income; lack of access to livelihood resources such as agricultural and fishing equipment and dilapidated housing (see, for example, Narayan and Petesch, 2002, pp. 30–80). The 'most poor' are described as: 'those with stunted growth . . . they do not have enough to food . . . they fall sick quickly . . . they are thin [and] their hair is not strong . . . their bodies do not shine even after taking a bath' (ibid., p. 55).

Traditional measures of poverty seem inadequate for the task of capturing the sense of ill-being depicted by those experiencing deprivation. Economists speak of poor people as those living on less than two US dollars per day. They constituted four billion of the world's total population of six billion people in 2003. As if that is not bad enough, of these four billion poor people, around 1.2 billion live on less than one US dollar per day (World Bank, 2000, p. 3). The $1 a day poverty line is seen in the academic literature as highly problematic, both methodologically and conceptually, although it has proved a useful measure for the World Bank and other international institutions.

In investigating deprivation in Philipstown, South Africa, Mary-Jane Morifi (1984, p. 3) observed that 'poverty is expensive'. This fitting insight is confirmed by many of the other studies of deprivation conducted for The Second Carnegie Inquiry into Poverty and Development in Southern Africa (see Wilson and Ramphele, 1989, esp. pp. 43–50). Poor people generally pay more for less, than those who are well off. Inadequate basic services impose burdens for poor people not captured by purchasing power parity measures. They pay more for water and often get poor quality water. They pay more for healthcare, and often get the worst quality care. They pay more for basic food because of lack of access to cheaper supermarkets and other vendors. They even have to pay public servants for public services that better-off people get for free such as policing, social welfare grants, primary schools and other entitlements. Corruption is another burden that falls disproportionately on poor people.

Poor people also receive lower returns for their efforts at earning a livelihood. Take poor fishermen in Ampenan Utara in Indonesia. They lack their own boat, engine and fishing nets. They are compelled to rent these from rich fishermen who charge them half their catch, leaving them with little income at the end of a hard day's work (Narayan and Petesch, 2002, p. 188). Poor people in Andhra Pradesh in India, point to their lack of assets as making them dependent on wage labour which is irregular, low paying and unsafe as is the case in the bauxite mines or lime stone quarries in their province (ibid., p. 155).

Self-employment is also thwarted by lack of access to credit. Poor people pay more for credit – 30 per cent and higher interest rates are charged even by public entities in countries committed to supporting small and medium-sized enterprises. Poor people also face other barriers to entry into the business world because of their poor education, burdens of ill health and lack of infrastructure, clothing and other goods needed to compete in the business sector. Once again, it is the blight of corruption that hits poor people most as they struggle to establish small and medium-sized enterprises.

Poverty is also expensive in other respects. Poor people often speak of having to sacrifice the future because of the insecurity of the present. Contrary to conventional wisdom, poor people have the same aspirations as the rest of the population. They are aggrieved by having to take children out of school or by failing to send them to a secondary school to get better skills because they know that education is essential for better opportunities. Many also speak of the direct correlation between lack of education, larger families and increasing ill-being and pressure on the land and environment. As some young people say: 'I am afraid of having hope' (Ramphele, 2002). This is not fatalism. It is realism that stems from far too many betrayals of youthful optimism. Without hope life becomes a desperate struggle for many poor young people.

Vulnerability is also a key characteristic of poverty. A young Roma man in Bulgaria likened poverty or ill-being to not knowing what will happen tomorrow (Narayan et al., 2000a, p. 36). Vulnerability is inextricably tied to insecure livelihoods. The poor are burdened with job insecurity, lack of secure land tenure, insufficient health security and no insurances against injury or losses from natural disasters that many well-off people are able to insure themselves against. Higher levels of crime and violence within households and in the communities where poor people live add to insecurity.

But it is ill health that seems to catapult many poor people from just getting by, to destitution. The tragedy of the HIV/AIDS pandemic as well as endemic malaria and tuberculosis in the poorest regions of the world, brings out this vulnerability most starkly. Africa carries the largest burden of the ill health spawned by these three major diseases. Of the world's 38 million people living with HIV/AIDS, 25 million live in Africa. Of the world's 14 million AIDS orphans, 12 million are in Africa. Of the 300 million cases of malaria a year, 90 per cent occur in Africa and 25 per cent of childhood deaths in Africa are due to malaria (Sachs, 2005, p. 150). The opportunity costs of disease are enormous and Africa loses 12 billion per year due to malaria, money that could be well spent on improving the living conditions of those who are destitute.

Networks of support are often cited as key means of escaping poverty. Getting a job, a loan, some food, healthcare when sick or even shelter often hinges on access to networks of support. Those poor people finding themselves in households with generations of unemployed who have 'lost the respect of others in the community' typically fall into poverty and despair.

Conclusion

The markers of poverty are those of vulnerability and insecurity in terms of the basic necessities of life as well as safety of the person, powerlessness and 'not having a voice which carries weight'. Poor people are as rational as everybody else, but they lack the means to make rational choices. The responsibility of leadership is to listen to all voices and to respond appropriately. Ending poverty, hunger and insecurity is within our means as a global community. What is lacking is the political will to do so.

MAMPHELA RAMPHELE

References

Aksoy, Atmon and John C. Beghin (eds) (2004), *Global Agricultural Trade and Developing Countries*, Washington, DC: World Bank.
Clark, David A. (2002), *Visions of Development: A Study of Human Values*, Cheltenham, UK and Northampton, MA, USA: Edward Elgar.
Moore, M., M. Choudhary and N. Singh (1998), 'How can we know what they want? Understanding local perceptions of poverty and ill-being in Asia', IDS Working Paper 80, Institute of Development Studies, University of Sussex, Brighton.
Morifi, M.-J. (1984), 'Life among the poor in Philipstown', Carnegie Conference Paper 33, Southern Africa Labour and Development Research Unit, University of Cape Town.
Narayan, Deepa, Robert Chambers, Meera Kaul Shah and Patti Petesch (2000a), *Voices of the Poor: Crying Out for Change*, Oxford: Oxford University Press for the World Bank.
Narayan, Deepa with Raj Patel, Kai Schafft, Anne Rademacher and Sarah Koch-Schulte (2000b), *Voices of the Poor: Can Anyone Hear Us?*, Oxford: Oxford University Press for the World Bank.
Narayan, Deepa and Patti Petesch (2002), *Voices of the Poor: From Many Lands*, Oxford: Oxford University Press for the World Bank.
Ramphele, Mamphela (2002), *Steering by the Stars*, Cape Town: Tafelberg.
Sachs, Jeffrey D. (2005), *Investing in People: A Practical Plan to Achieve the Millennium Development Goals* (UN Millennium Project), New York: Earthscan.
Wilson, Francis and Mamphela Ramphele (1989), *Uprooting Poverty: The South African Challenge*, New York: W.W. Norton.
Wolfensohn, James D. (2003), 'A new global balance: the challenge of leadership', President's Address to the Board of Governors, Dubai, United Arab Emirates, September, http://siteresources.worldbank.org/ NEWS/ Resources/jdwsp-092303.pdf.
World Bank (2000), *World Development Report 2000/01: Attacking Poverty*, Oxford: Oxford University Press for the World Bank.

Prebisch, Raul (1901–1986)

Raul Prebisch was a driving force of development thought and diplomacy in the twentieth century, a leading theoretician and powerful leader who left an indelible imprint on Argentina, his home country, as well as on North–South relations. He was that rare thinker who was also a born administrator and policy maker with a huge capacity for work. Revered by supporters and reviled by critics, Prebisch always aroused controversy and strong passions, but his innovation and achievements are not in doubt. Best known for his work with the United Nations after 1949, particularly with the Economic Commission for Latin America (ECLA) and as founding Secretary General of the United Nations Conference on Trade and Development (UNCTAD), he changed the discourse on international trade and development and the struggle for global equity.

Argentine roots

The key to understanding Prebisch's career lies in his Argentine years. Born in 1901 in the northern city of Tucuman to a middle-class family, Prebisch was repelled by the feudal conditions endured by the Indians working the large sugar estates of his province while wealthy Argentina enjoyed a per capita income second only to the United States. He chose economics to pursue his goal of social reform, and this early ethical commitment to equity remained a life-long animating imperative.

A second formative impulse in Prebisch's career derived form the timing of his arrival in Buenos Aires in 1918 to begin his studies in the Faculty of Economic Sciences. The First World War was in its last stages; the October 1917 Soviet Revolution had just occurred; there were riots in Buenos Aires; the post-war years of turmoil to 1921 were about to begin. Positions had to be taken. Prebisch rejected the Soviet model on both economic and political grounds, and instead chose engagement in the Argentine public service as his primary career to reform the existing order. But he also retained a Faculty link after graduation in 1922, and he was awarded a tenured professorship in the Faculty in 1925. In fact Prebisch was largely self-taught; his professors cowered in the reflected shadows of the British classics, uninterested in the surrounding turmoil shaping Argentina's future. Nevertheless he shared in a broad liberal consensus in mainstream Buenos Aires as the economic revival of the 1920s took hold.

Prebisch rose rapidly to become Under Secretary of Finance in 1930 as Argentina lay in the grip of the Great Depression. Confronted by the economic crisis, he abandoned his liberal free trade orthodoxy and led the shift to an activist state in trade, currency and income tax policy. At the Geneva Preparatory Commission and the World Economic Conference in London in 1933, where he encountered John Maynard Keynes's 'means to prosperity', he gained an additional lesson in the vulnerability of agricultural countries; Argentina was completely ignored by the industrial powers in international trade, and was forced to accept a humiliatingly subordinate position to Britain in commercial relations.

The Argentine Central Bank, which he created in 1935 with himself as general manager, was Prebisch's solution to the instability in the national economy after the onset of the Great Depression in 1929. Its public–private charter provided sufficient autonomy for the bank to play a core regulatory and steering role despite protracted political turbulence in Buenos Aires, while externally it managed a countercyclical policy to tame the international business cycle and oversee a careful but deliberate policy of import-substitution industrialisation. By 1939, the Argentine Central Bank was recognised as one of the leading banking institutions in the world, maintaining close relations with the US Federal Reserve and the Bank of England. Prebisch's record in managing the economy was exemplary; Argentina, alone in South America, did not default on its debt. With war in Europe after September 1939 and the closing of that market to South American goods, Prebisch began negotiations for a regional free trade area and endorsed accelerated industrialisation. Prebisch always saw the Central Bank as his greatest triumph.

Regional leader
The Argentine military government dismissed Prebisch in October 1943 for his pro-Allied views and defence of the autonomy of the Central Bank. Banished from the public sector, he returned to his professorship at the Faculty of Economic Sciences, but his tenure became increasingly precarious, and for five years Prebisch supplemented his income from teaching with extensive work in Mexico and Venezuela as well as numerous advisory missions to central banks throughout Latin America with Robert Triffin of the US Federal Reserve. This period of travel helped to prepare Prebisch for his subsequent international career. First, he discovered Latin America, and developed a regional as opposed to national optic. Second, he met the leaders of a gifted new generation of young economists eager to understand Latin America's position in the world after the Second World War and to promote modernisation.

Building from his work in Argentina, Prebisch began elaborating a 'centre–periphery' concept of the international economy. In 1947 he wrote a book interpreting Keynes for

Latin American readers; while endorsing Keynes's general approach to economic welfare and the state, he criticised his failure to address the faultline in the global system between developed and developing countries. Even before 1943 he had advocated industrialisation in Argentina, led by what he termed 'an intelligent state', and he linked this priority to factors such as 'the persistent decline in the terms of trade' for primary commodity exports. But he had not completed his theoretical work when the Perón regime forced his resignation from the university in November 1948. Rejected by the IMF for a senior appointment, Prebisch's opportunity for fleshing out his ideas came with the invitation from ECLA (opened in Santiago Chile earlier that year), to write an introduction for its first Economic Survey of Latin America to be presented in Havana in May 1949.

The document which Prebisch wrote and presented in Havana, *The Economic Development of Latin America and its Principal Problems* (1950), would be his most enduring contribution at the theoretical level with his concept of a structural rift in the international economy in which the Latin American 'periphery' was linked to the industrial powers as a function of its natural resources, but in a subordinate position which primarily served the interests of the 'centre'. Combining business-cycle theory and what became known as the 'Prebisch–Singer' thesis on terms of trade (see Singer, Hans this volume), he challenged the traditional comparative advantage approach to international trade, maintaining that the existing division of labour between nations exporting primary products and those exporting manufactures concentrated the fruits of technical progress in the industrial countries. The corollary of this structuralist critique was evident: if international market forces left to themselves reproduced inequity, peripheral countries required an activist state to promote industrialisation. The conventional wisdom that agricultural countries could thrive in the future by remaining commodity producers was undermined; infuriated US economists such as Jacob Viner of Princeton University dismissed the Prebisch Manifesto as a dangerous amalgam of unsubstantiated historical conjecture and simplistic hypothesis (see Viner, 1952, pp. 61–4). They entirely missed the point. The cognitive leap offered by Prebisch was dethroning the absolutism of classical theory with an alternative approach that addressed power relations in the international system, and demanded that the industrial as well as raw material producers share responsibilities in international development.

The Prebisch Manifesto was an instant classic in Latin America and became the starting-point for a new theory of underdevelopment. Following the Havana Conference, Prebisch became Executive Secretary of ECLA and transformed it into the most dynamic centre of economic research in the Americas and exciting destination for scholars from Latin America and around the world. While the United States was paralysed intellectually by McCarthyism and Cold War hysteria, ECLA offered intellectual freedom and innovation in distant Santiago. Under Prebisch's direction, his team shaped an indigenous economic paradigm and vocabulary for viewing the region within a single conceptual and policy framework. He also advocated a new approach to hemisphere relations based on mutual economic interests, long-term planning, regional integration, new institutions (such as the Inter-American Development Bank), and commodity price stabilisation. Caricatured by critics as dangerously leftist and irresponsibly protectionist, ECLA under Prebisch's leadership was practical, concerned about inflation and the limits of industrialisation, and the search for a path to modernisation different from US,

Soviet and West European models. When President John Kennedy announced his Alliance for Progress in 1961, he paid Prebisch the compliment of incorporating the ECLA doctrine wholesale.

Global statesman
In 1963, United Nations Secretary General U Thant invited Prebisch to head the UNCTAD Preparatory Committee for a world conference on Trade and Development held in Geneva in early 1964. International trade had become the dominant issue at the United Nations; UNCTAD offered the opportunity to take the ECLA doctrine to the global level in a North–South dialogue to link trade and development in a new negotiating forum challenging the GATT. It was a huge ambition: the industrial countries strongly supported the GATT, while the G-77 of developing counties which comprised Prebisch's constituency was divided and lacked a coherent vision. He succeeded in establishing UNCTAD as a permanent body in 1964, and attracting leading economists to staff the new secretariat in Geneva, but the obstacles to substantive new initiatives were impressive. After failing to achieve his expectations in UNCTAD II, its second world conference in New Delhi in 1968, Prebisch announced his retirement. In fact his achievements were important (such as the Generalised System of Preferences: GSP), but great power diplomacy ruled out a negotiating role for UNCTAD. Apart from specific measures achieved, his four years at UNCTAD laid out the principles and content of the New International Economic Order (NIEO) – the North–South *cause célèbre* of the 1970s.

Prebisch did not retire to stop work. Dean of Latin American economists, he turned his attention to the Latin American Institute for Economic and Social Planning (ILPES) which he had created in 1961, and undertook a major review of the region for the Inter-American Development Bank titled *Change and Development: Latin America's Great Task* (1970). He also accepted special assignments from the UN and Organization of American States (OAS) Secretaries General before founding a major journal, the ECLA *Review* which he edited until he died. Prebisch maintained a formidable regime of travel, conferences, interviews and writing as his role shifted to prophet and elder statesman, moving to a more radical dependency critique of Latin America's 'imitative capitalism' as he observed the growth of corruption, patronage and unproductive private sectors. Saddened by the advent of Ronald Reagan and Margaret Thatcher and the end of the North–South dialogue, he was invited by President Raul Alfonsin to return to Argentina in 1983 when democracy was restored, to assist him in the reconstruction of the economy.

The essential Prebisch
Although various scholars have suggested discontinuities between Prebisch's Argentine and UN careers, a thorough examination of his life, work and voluminous writings reveals a surprising coherence in his approach to innovation. Throughout his life, Prebisch was driven by a search for 'historical moments' in which the timing of a new concept could transform an organisation into a movement. Theory, machinery and policy: this powerful trinity linking an idea to an institutional mechanism in order to nurture rational dialogue and generate new policy comprised the core of the Prebisch vision – in the Argentine Central Bank, ECLA and UNCTAD. In each case his magnetic personality attracted gifted economists from around the world, united behind a shared ethic of

development – Gunnar Myrdal, Hans Singer, Sidney Dell, Wladek Malinowski, Jan Tinbergen, Celso Furtado, Dudley Seers, Enrique Iglesias and many others.

Prebisch's lifelong concern with independent research and education also formed part of the 'essential Prebisch'. He insisted that Latin America and developing countries maintain intellectual autonomy to design development models appropriate to their own needs. He never forgot the Argentine fascination with all things British from his student days, mirrored after 1945 by the slavish adoption of US graduate school fashions throughout Latin America. In each phase of his life, Prebisch formed centres of independent research and training to challenge the monopoly of ideas from the North and test their relevance against local realities to the benefit of thousands of students and young professionals.

Finally, Prebisch believed in balance, in avoiding extremes even if this made him an easy target for critics. He opposed both Marxism and liberal orthodoxy in favour of 'progressive capitalism' guided by an 'intelligent state'. He was the first to criticise Latin American governments for distorting Import Substitution Industrialisation (ISI) with excessive protectionism and flabby states. Globalisation for Prebisch was neither good nor bad but a process to be managed – a process of symmetrical obligations by both developed and developing countries which shared responsibilities in global development; he supported conditionality if applied responsibly and equitably as proposed in Kennedy's Alliance for Progress. The G-77 was an imperfect bargaining tool for developing countries, but it was an essential forum in international negotiations nevertheless. He supported the IMF as an institution but detested its often sterile conditionality. In general his long life demonstrates an unfailing support for rational debate and deliberate policy over ideological thinking of left and right.

Legacy

Prebisch is best understood as Latin America's Keynes, a crossroads thinker whose charisma, warmth and generosity changed the lives of those who knew him. His impact has been huge, globally as well as in Latin America. At the level of ideas, structuralism offered fertile soil for subsequent theorists, and mainstream economists have finally decided that the Prebisch–Singer thesis on terms of trade was valid after all. Many of his ideas which were controversial in his time (for example, regional integration; the need to diversify away from primary production; development as a multifaceted process, including social change) are now taken for granted. Within the United Nations only Dag Hammarskjöld equalled Prebisch in his ability to project a compelling and coherent vision to the global community. His insistence on mutual responsibilities within a multilateral world order to generalise welfare underpins the contemporary clichés of 'global governance' or 'civilising globalisation'. If ISI as practised in Latin America did not diminish the region's vulnerability and was loudly proclaimed a failure, the problem lay less in doctrine than in implementation: Prebisch's developmentalism proved successful in Asia and Europe with stronger states and more-equitable societies.

The end of the North–South dialogue marginalised Prebisch, but his legacy revived as the neoliberal Washington Consensus fashion faded, and has gradually grown since his death in 1986. The four-volume collection of Prebisch's writings from 1919–1948, published by the Prebisch Foundation based in Buenos Aires, has demonstrated the range and creativity of his early work, and has stimulated a Prebisch revival evident in the distinguished lecture series, books and conferences dedicated to the memory of a remarkable scholar, reformer, central banker and teacher. But it is equally clear that the definitive work on so multifaceted and complex a personality as Raul Prebisch remains to be written.

EDGAR J. DOSMAN

References and further reading

Dosman, Edgar J. (2001), 'Markets and the state in the evolution of the "Prebisch Manifesto" ', *CEPAL Review*, **75**, 87–101.

Furtado, Celso (1988), *La Fantasia Organizada*, Buenos Aires: Editorial Universitaria.

Iglesias, Enrique V. (1994), *The Legacy of Raul Prebisch*, Washington, DC: Inter-American Development Bank.

Keynes, John M. (1933), 'Means to prosperity', *Collected Writings*, edited by Donald Moggridge (1972), London: Macmillan and St Martin's Press, Vol. IX, pp. 357–64.

Love, Joseph L. (1980), 'Raul Prebisch and the origins of the doctrine of unequal exchange', *Latin American Research Review*, **15** (3), 45–72.

Love, Joseph L. (1994), 'Economic ideas and ideologies in Latin America since 1930', *Cambridge History of Latin America*, edited by Leslie Bethel, **6** (1), pp. 595–601.

Prebisch, Raul (1947), *Introduccion a Keynes* (Introduction to Keynes), Mexico: Fondo de Cultura Economica.

Prebisch, Raul (1950), *The Economic Development of Latin America and its Principal Problems*, New York: United Nations (E/C.12/R.1).

Prebisch, Raul (1964), *Towards a New Trade Policy for Development: Report by the Secretary-General of the United Nation's Conference on Trade and Development*, New York: United Nations.

Prebisch, Raul (1970), *Change and Development: Latin America's Great Task*, New York: Praeger.

Prebisch, Raul (1984), 'Five stages in my thinking on development', in Gerald M. Meier and Dudley Seers (eds), *Pioneers of Development*, Oxford and New York: Oxford University Press, pp. 175–91.

Prebisch, Raul (1991), *Obras 1919–1948*, Buenos Aires: Fundacion Raul Prebisch.

Shaw, John D. (2002), *Sir Hans Singer: The Life and Work of a Development Economist*, Basingstoke, UK and New York: Palgrave-Macmillan.

Sprout, Ronald (1992), 'The ideas of Prebisch', *CEPAL Review*, **46**, 177–92.

Toye, J. and R. Toye (2003), 'The origins and interpretation of the Prebisch–Singer thesis', *History of Political Economy*, **35**, 437–67.

Viner, J. (1952), *International Trade and Economic Development*, Glencoe, IL: Free Press.

Privatisation

Introduction

Views on the appropriate role of government in the economy have changed dramatically over recent decades. Until the end of the 1970s, most developing countries favoured state ownership as a remedy for the problems of market failure, which were seen as significant constraints to the process of capital accumulation and economic development. It was also argued that state ownership of enterprises was a necessary instrument for development planning to achieve accelerated economic growth and transformation. By the end of the 1980s, however, sentiment had changed in donor agencies and in a growing number of developing countries in the face of mounting evidence of the large financial deficits and economic inefficiencies of the state-owned enterprise sector. As a result, privatisation became a significant component of the economic reform programmes adopted by developing countries, often as part of donor conditionality under structural adjustment lending (World Bank, 1995).

The term 'privatisation' has been used to cover an array of different policies aimed at increasing the involvement of the private sector in the provision of goods and services previously provided exclusively by the state sector. In this entry, the term is used to refer to the transfer of ownership of productive assets from the public sector to the private sector. Privatisation may be through initial public offering of shares or by direct sale to domestic or international companies or individuals. In some cases, privatisation has involved the complete transfer of control and ownership to the private sector, and in others government has retained some degree of control and ownership in the enterprise.

Privatisation activity has grown significantly in developing countries and accounted for about a third of global privatisation sales value between 1990 and 1999. Foreign direct investment and portfolio investment contributed over 40 per cent of total privatisation transactions, by value, in developing countries in the 1980s and continued to be a significant source of funding for privatisation in the 1990s, especially in infrastructure projects (World Bank, 2003; Kirkpatrick et al., 2006b). The regional distribution of privatisation has been uneven, with Latin America accounting for most of the privatisation activity. In contrast, privatisation sales in Sub-Saharan Africa contributed only 3 per cent of total developing-country privatisation proceeds between 1990 and 1999.

Despite the popularity of privatisation as a policy instrument in many developing countries, its adoption has been controversial and politically sensitive. First, the claim that privatisation will produce significant improvements in financial and economic performance has been contested. Second, there is a concern that privatisation will lead to unemployment, worsening income distribution and poverty. Third, the lack of transparency with many privatisation transactions has reinforced the belief that privatisation benefits the privileged few at the expense of the many, and encourages corruption and poor standards of governance. These criticisms of privatisation underline the need for systematic study of its effects, as a means of informing future policy making.

The objectives of privatisation

Any assessment of the results of privatisation needs to begin by identifying the objectives that are set for privatisation. In practice, policy makers have often had a variety of objectives in mind when deciding to adopt privatisation as a policy instrument. First, given the widespread evidence of economic inefficiency, low productivity and lack of competitiveness, it was hoped that by switching from public to private ownership, economic performance would improve. Second, many individual public enterprises, and the state-owned enterprise sector as a whole, had been operating with sizeable financial deficits, requiring subsidisation. Privatisation was seen as a means of reducing the fiscal burden on government. Third, privatisation has been used as a means of raising revenue to meet public expenditure needs. Fourth, privatisation has been adopted to meet broader macroeconomic objectives, for example, to raise the inflow of direct foreign investment or to increase the rate of economic growth. Finally, privatisation may be pursued for political reasons, reflecting a desire to reduce the government's involvement in the economy and increase the share of the private sector.

The theoretical argument for privatisation rests on the assumption that in a competitive market environment, enterprise performance will be superior under private ownership, as compared to public ownership; in other words, property rights are assumed to be the primary determinant of enterprise performance. Property rights provide optimal incentives for principals to monitor the behaviour of their agents in the face of incomplete information, contracts and markets (Boycko et al., 1996). But where there are significant market failures, such as market power or externalities, the public enterprise may produce a socially optimal outcome which maximises social welfare, in contrast to the private enterprise that will maximise private profits and welfare. The idea that public ownership is the solution to the problem of market failure, however, has been challenged by public choice theory which concentrates on the behaviour of agents within government and their tendency to pursue their own interests or the interests of special-interest groups, over the public interest.

The extent to which competition affects performance has important implications for the theoretical case for privatisation. Since competition is generally regarded as a key determinant of performance, policy to increase competition in the market is likely to have a more significant effect on enterprise performance than a change of ownership through privatisation. Conversely, if privatisation is adopted where monopoly or significant barriers to competition exist, the result will be to replace the public monopoly with a private one, while performance remains unaffected. Thus, in the absence of market competition, regulation of the privatised monopoly will be needed if post-privatisation performance is to improve.

To summarise, the theoretical literature offers a number of reasons why, even in the case of market failure, state ownership has important weaknesses (Megginson and Netter, 2001). But the debate over ownership and performance is far from settled, and the alternative to state ownership is not necessarily purely private, unregulated firms (Laffont and Tirole, 1993). As Megginson and Netter (2003, p. 30) put it: 'Many of the theoretical arguments for privatisation are based on the premise that the harmful effects of state intervention have a greater impact under state ownership than under state regulation, not that the harmful effects can be eliminated through privatisation'.

The results of privatisation in developing countries
A review of the evidence on the impact of privatisation can inform policy makers on the conditions and complementary policies that are needed if privatisation is to improve economic performance and promote long-term pro-poor growth in developing countries. Assessing the impact of privatisation is faced with the problem, however, of establishing the counterfactual, that is, knowing what would have happened in the absence of privatisation. A second difficulty arises in the selection of the variables to measure performance, which should reflect the objectives of the privatisation policy. There may be multiple objectives, and the relative weight given to each objective may not be clear, or may shift over time. Privatisation can contribute to one objective while at the same time making it more difficult to achieve another, for example, there will be a trade-off between maximising the sales revenue by offering the private purchaser the opportunity to operate in a monopoly market, and improving economic efficiency by introducing competition into the market.

There is a substantial body of empirical evidence on the impact of privatisation on enterprise performance, derived mainly from comparing performance 'before' and 'after' privatisation (Boubakri and Cosset, 1998; Megginson and Netter, 2001; Nellis, 2003a, b). Shirley and Walsh (2001) provide one review of the empirical work. They examined a total of 52 studies on private–public enterprise performance, spanning the period from 1971 to 1999, covering developing and developed countries in a variety of competitive environments. Of the 52 studies, 32 conclude that the performance of private and privatised firms is superior to that of public enterprises, 15 studies find either that there is no significant relationship between ownership and performance or that the relationship is ambiguous, and five studies conclude that publicly owned enterprises perform better than private firms. In competitive markets, the majority of studies find that private firms perform better, whereas the superiority of private enterprises is less pronounced in monopolistic markets. Parker and Kirkpatrick (2005) have also reviewed the literature and conclude that there has been considerable variation in results across countries and sectors.

Studies of the relationship between privatisation and economic growth in developing countries have produced conflicting results. Plane (1997) and Barnett (2000) find that privatisation has a significant and positive impact on economic growth, whereas Cook and Uchida (2003) find a negative partial correlation between privatisation and economic growth in a sample of 63 developing countries for the period from 1988 to 1997.

The fiscal impact of privatisation has been equally difficult to assess. While revenues from asset sales have been large, in many cases the net revenue gain has been significantly reduced by debt write-offs, costs of reconstruction, recapitalisation and transaction costs. The fiscal impact of privatisation depends on the amount and the use made of the proceeds, and the subsequent changes in financial flows – taxes, transfers and dividends – to and from the budget. Using a sample of Latin American economies, Pinheiro and Schneider (1995) found that the proceeds from privatisation were too small and received too late to have a significant impact on the fiscal balance, and therefore, the objective of improving the fiscal balance through privatisation had not been achieved. In contrast, Davis et al. (2000) found that, on average, privatisation proceeds transferred to the budget were saved and used to substitute for other sources of domestic financing, suggesting that over time the fiscal balance tended to benefit from privatisation.

Most sectoral studies involving developing countries have focused on privatisation in utilities, particularly telecommunications. Wallsten (2001) uses a sample of 30 developing African and Latin American countries between 1984 and 1997, and finds performance gains in the telecommunications sector occurred due to competition and when privatisation was coupled with effective and independent regulation. These findings are confirmed by Fink et al. (2002) using a larger sample of developing countries, which suggest that both privatisation and competition lead to significant improvements in telecommunications performance, but that policy reforms that include independent regulation produced the largest efficiency gains.

The evidence of the electricity sector suggests that privatisation resulted in performance improvements and benefits to consumers (Jamasb et al., 2004). The studies by Zhang et al. (2002, 2005) model the impact of privatising electricity generation in developing countries between 1985 and 2000. The authors confirm that privatisation alone is statistically insignificant in explaining post-privatisation performance, with independent regulation, competition and the sequencing of the reforms being the significant determinants for performance. These findings are complemented by Jamasb et al. (2004) who find that country institutions and sector governance play an important role in the success or failure of privatisation reform.

Divestitures or sales of state-owned water utilities have been rare, with private involvement in the water sector mainly in the form of service and management contracts or concessions. Econometric studies for Asia (Estache and Rossi, 2002) and Africa (Estache and Kouassi, 2002; Kirkpatrick et al., 2006a) fail to find evidence of significant difference in the performance of public and private water enterprises. This may reflect the particular problems of privatising water utilities in developing countries, where organising competition within water services is precluded by the technology of water provision, and by the institutional weaknesses which prevent effective regulation of the monopoly water utilities (Kirkpatrick and Parker, 2005).

Social impact of privatisation
While much of the interest in the impact of privatisation has focused on the economic and financial dimensions of performance, there is a widespread concern with the possible negative social effects, particularly on employment levels (Van der Hoeven and Sziraczki, 1997; Birdsall and Nellis, 2002). State-owned enterprises that are protected by soft budget constraints and a non-competitive market environment are often overstaffed with excessive wage and salary levels. Part of the gains from privatisation may result, therefore, from a reduction in the privatised enterprise's workforce. These long-term efficiency gains will also represent the short-term social costs of adjustment as labour is entrenched. It is more difficult to assess the overall social impact. However, some of the dismissed labour may be successful in finding alternative employment, and there is the potential to redistribute the fiscal gains from privatisation in pro-poor expenditure programmes.

Utility privatisation has often led to an expansion in the network and increased access to the service, including by the urban poor, particularly in urban areas. The quality of the service provided has also tended to improve with privatisation. Often, however, these improvements in access and quality have been accompanied by increases in prices. The overall distributional impact is difficult to assess, and depends on a balance between the benefits of improved access and quality and the negative impact of increased payments by the poor. More generally, while privatisation can contribute to pro-poor and distributional objectives, this outcome requires government commitment and capacity to manage the privatisation process. This may involve short-term safety-net policies to mitigate any immediate adverse impacts on vulnerable groups, and a longer-term policy for regulating privatised utilities in a way that balances the interests of the poor with the concern to maximise the economic efficiency gains of privatisation (Estache et al., 2001).

Conclusion
This entry has considered the impact of privatisation in developing countries. The result has been to reveal a complex and sometimes contradictory picture, with theoretical disagreements on the predicted outcomes, and significant differences in the empirical evidence across sectors and countries. The relationship between privatisation and performance improvement is clearly complex and superior post-privatisation performance is not axiomatic. The evidence points to the roles of competition and regulation in performance and reveals that introducing more market competition and effective state regulation may be crucial in ensuring that economic performance improves (Cook et al., 2004). Government involvement in the post-privatisation process is also needed to ensure

that the outcomes of privatisation are consistent with social redistribution and poverty-reduction objectives.

Privatisation can be an effective instrument for bringing about significant financial, economic and social gains in developing countries. Introducing more competition and effective regulation will play an important part in ensuring this outcome. In addition, a wider range of institutional issues, including legal, management, financial and political capacity within countries, will affect the impact of privatisation on performance. Where institutional capacity is limited, the scale, coverage and sequencing of privatisation need to be consistent with the available resources to manage the post-privatisation process and outcomes. Otherwise, the results of privatisation are likely to disappoint.

PAUL COOK
COLIN KIRKPATRICK
DAVID PARKER

References

Barnett, S. (2000), 'Evidence on the fiscal and macroeconomic impact of privatisation', IMF Working Paper 97/118, Washington, DC: International Monetary Fund.

Birdsall, N. and J. Nellis (2002), 'Winners and losers: assessing the distributional impact of privatization', Centre for Global Development Working Paper no. 6, Washington, DC: Centre for Global Development.

Boubakri, B. and J.-C. Cosset (1998), 'The financial and operating performance of newly privatized firms: evidence from developing countries', *Journal of Finance*, **53** (3), 1081–1110.

Boycko, M., A. Shleifer and R.W. Vishny (1996), 'A theory of privatisation', *Economic Journal*, **106**, March, 309–19.

Cook, P., C. Kirkpatrick, M. Minogue and D. Parker (eds) (2004), *Competition and Regulation in Developing Countries*, Cheltenham, UK and Northampton, MA, USA: Edward Elgar.

Cook, P. and Y. Uchida (2003), 'Privatisation and economic growth in developing countries', *Journal of Development Studies*, **39** (6), 121–54.

Davis, J., R. Ossowski, T. Richardson and S. Barnett (2000), 'Fiscal and macroeconomic impact of privatisation', IMF Occasional Paper no. 194, Washington, DC: IMF.

Estache, A., A. Gomez-Lobo and D. Leipziger (2001), 'Utilities privatization and the poor: lessons and evidence from Latin America', *World Development*, **29** (7), 1179–98.

Estache, A. and E. Kouassi (2002), 'Sector organisation, governance and the inefficiency of African water utilities', World Bank Research Working Paper 2890, Washington, DC: World Bank.

Estache, A. and M.A. Rossi (2002), 'How different is the efficiency of public and private water companies in Asia', *World Bank Economic Review*, **16** (1), 139–48.

Fink, C., A. Mattoo and R. Rathindran (2002), 'An assessment of telecommunications reform in developing countries', World Bank Policy Research Working Paper 2909, Washington, DC: World Bank.

Jamasb, T., R. Mota, D. Newbery and M. Pollitt (2004), 'Electricity sector reform in developing countries: a survey of empirical evidence on determinants and performance', Cambridge Working Papers in Economics 0439, Cambridge, MA: Massachusetts Institute of Technology.

Kirkpatrick, C. and D. Parker (2005), 'Domestic regulation and the WTO: The case of water services in developing countries', *The World Economy*, **28** (10), 1491–1508.

Kirkpatrick, C., D. Parker and Y.-F. Zhang (2006a), 'An empirical analysis of state and private sector provision of water and services in Africa', *World Bank Economic Review*, **20** (1), 143–63.

Kirkpatrick, C., D. Parker and Y.-F. Zhang (2006b), 'Foreign direct investment in infrastructure in developing countries: does regulation make a difference?', *Transnational Corporations*, **15** (1), 143–71.

Laffont, J. and J. Tirole (1993), *A Theory of Incentives in Procurement and Regulation*, Cambridge, MA: MIT Press.

Megginson, W.L. and J.M. Netter (2001), 'From state to market: a survey of empirical studies on privatization', *Journal of Economic Literature*, **39**, 321–89.

Megginson, W.L. and J.M. Netter (2003), 'History and methods in privatization', in D. Parker and D. Saul (eds), *International Handbook on Privatization*, Cheltenham, UK and Northampton, MA, USA: Edward Elgar, pp. 25–40.

Nellis, J. (2003a), 'Privatization in Africa: what has happened? What is to be done?', mimeo, Washington, DC: Center for Global Development.

Nellis, J. (2003b), 'Privatization in Latin America', Center for Global Governance Working Paper no. 31, Washington, DC: Center for Global Development.

Parker, D. and C. Kirkpatrick (2005), 'Privatisation in developing countries: a review of the evidence and the policy lessons', *Journal of Development Studies*, **41** (4), 513–41.

Pinheiro, A. and B. Schneider (1995), 'The fiscal impact of privatisation in Latin America', *Journal of Development Studies*, **31** (5), 751–85.

Plane, P. (1997), 'Privatisation and economic growth: an empirical investigation from a sample of developing market economies', *Applied Economics*, **29** (2), 161–78.

Shirley, M. and P. Walsh (2001), 'Public versus private ownership: the current state of the debate', mimeo, Washington, DC: World Bank.

Van der Hoeven, R. and G. Sziraczki (eds) (1997), *Employment and Privatisation*, Geneva: International Labour Office.

Wallsten, S.J. (2001), 'An econometric analysis of telecom competition, privatization and regulation in Africa and Latin America', *Journal of Industrial Economics*, **49** (1), 1–19.

World Bank (1995), *Bureaucrats in Business: The Economics and Politics of Government Ownership*, London and New York: Oxford University Press for the World Bank.

World Bank (2003), *Private Participation in Infrastructure: Trends in Developing Countries, 1990–2001*, World Bank and Public Private Infrastructure Advisory Facility, Washington, DC: World Bank.

Zhang, Y.-F., D. Parker and C. Kirkpatrick (2002), 'Electricity sector reform in developing countries: an econometric assessment of the effects of privatisation, competition and regulation', Working Paper no. 31, Centre on Regulation and Competition, IDPM, University of Manchester.

Zhang, Y.-F., C. Kirkpatrick and D. Parker (2005), 'Competition, regulation and privatisation of electricity generation in developing countries: does the sequencing of reforms matter?', *Quarterly Review of Business and Economics*, **45** (2–3), 358–79.

Property Rights and Development

Rights

To talk of 'property rights' in development requires that we must first be clear about the distinct concepts of a 'right' and of 'property'.

For an individual to have a right requires that others must have an enforced duty. In the absence of a *duty* for others, rights cannot exist. A duty can be either a moral duty or a legal duty. Moral duties – those that address matters defined by 'ought', 'ought not', 'should' and 'should not' – tend to be adequate when the stakes are low, but the reality of much daily life is that *effective* duties require compulsion from an authority system that agrees to protect the interests of those to whom it (that authority system) has granted rights (Becker, 1977; Bromley, 1989a, 1991; Christman, 1994). Legal compulsion captures the ideas of 'must', 'must not', 'may' and 'may not'. Many duties that are today legally enforced were at one time simply moral duties. The codified realm (the 'law') is often an official version of long-standing customs and norms of behaviour. Custom evolves into law when the future value of a particular durable practice (a custom) is found to be worth reinforcing by official sanction rather than leaving compliance to traditional processes such as pleading and the threat of shame or shunning.

A duty compels those who might interfere with the interests of others (those who have rights) to refrain from doing so on pain of authorised sanction. The individual(s) with rights can compel the coercive authority – whether a 'formal' state or a village council/headman – to come to the assistance of those to whom rights have been granted. Note that rights come *from* the authority system and are enforced by that same system. Individuals do not have meaningful rights until the authority system declares that it is ready to enforce the imposition of duties on others so that those with rights might thereby be protected. Rights *expand the capacities* of the individual by indicating what one can do with the aid of the collective power.

Property and property rights

The second idea requiring clarity is that of property. It is common to see property object-ified by equating it with some tangible object – often a piece of land. However, property is not an object but is, instead, a stream of benefits (values) into the future (Macpherson, 1973, 1978; Bromley, 1991). When one buys a piece of land one acquires not just some physical object but rather *control* over a benefit stream arising from that setting and circumstance. The buyer offers a price that reflects his/her subjective valuation of the discounted present value of all future net income that is expected to flow from the anticipated ownership of the thing (or of the circumstances). If this value exceeds a similar valuation undertaken by the current owner then ownership changes hands. Ownership concerns futurity – value running into the future that the owner controls (for the most part) and may now receive.

The idea of 'property rights' brings together these two ideas. We see that the idea of property rights defines the limits of the law pertaining to the income appropriable from control of income-producing settings and circumstances. Trademarks, copyrights and patents are forms of property rights. All are forms of *rights* in property (the future value), and correlated *duties* for non-owners. When one talks of intellectual property rights in new seeds, or in particular biotechnology products, one is discussing the legal arrange-ments that control the future value of income streams arising from the control of the ideas and benefit streams embedded in those seeds or technologies. Property rights are the social recognition of a *process* that determines which conflicting 'rights claims' shall be upheld (sanctified) by an authority system and its agents. As above, this need not imply a 'state' or 'government' as we might understand that idea in the industrialised economies. A trad-itional leader in some societies reflects and represents the authority system and thus it is here that one finds the enforcement of rights and duties. When those rights and duties pertain to settings and circumstances that entail tangible benefit streams into the future then we can say that we are getting close to the paradigmatic idea of property rights.

Property rights and development

Two common assertions connect property rights and development. The first is that eco-nomic development is impeded by the *lack* of property rights. This is then transformed into an assertion that only private (individualised) property rights will do the necessary work. Note that this prescription is embedded in (follows from) neoclassical economic models that envisage (and justify) the autonomous utility-maximising individual as the correct unit of analytical interest. The thought that an individual embedded in a particu-lar economy and society in Africa or India might not plausibly be modelled as an autonomous individual never enters the mind (or the models) of those seeking to impose 'economic rationality' on a different culture. The normative and value-laden nature of these prescriptive 'truths' can render them useless – indeed harmful – when they are adopted by policy makers who lack the conceptual sophistication to grasp the reasons for their impertinence. In particular, if policy makers seek to impose new property regimes on traditional societies we (and they) should not be surprised to find that little good will come from it and there is a plausible chance that great harm will result.

The second assertion is that natural resource degradation in the developing world persists because of insecure ('private') property rights. The literature on deforestation in the tropics seems unanimous that if only private property rights were more secure then deforestation would be rectified. Interestingly, empirical studies are unable to offer support for this claim (Deacon, 1994, 1995). As above, solid empirical work cannot support assertions that the solution to resource degradation – and stifled development – lies in the imposition of one particular property regime into a culture and an economy where social and economic relations render alien institutions problematic (Bromley, 1999). The problem here is the assumption that private (individualised) property rights are necessary and sufficient for individuals to take good care of assets such as forests, soils, arable and pasture land, and so on. The familiar story is, 'if you own something you will take care of it'. The standard argument is that the future value of this stream of benefits is significant enough that a private owner will act so as to maximise the discounted present value of this stream of benefits and by doing so will act in the best interests of the resource (the asset) into the future. Reality is more complex.

If the owner's time preference for liquidity exceeds the rate at which the natural resource (trees, range forage, agricultural soils) can grow, regenerate, or otherwise produce income, then it is 'optimal' (efficient) for the private owner to exploit the asset in its entirety – to liquidate it – and to use the financial gain for other needs. This process is the result of the 'iron law of the discount rate' (Page, 1977). The theoretical basis for this outcome is well known (Smith, 1968; Clark, 1973).

We see this same doctrine advanced to advocate issuance of title to slum dwellers and other urban poor so that they will take better care of their meagre surroundings and invest to improve them (DeSoto, 2000). While plausible on the face of it, recall that a title as allegedly *secure collateral* is pertinent to credit markets only if there is also a secure income stream against which funds will be advanced. If there is no secure job (and income) associated with such titles then credit markets will fail to bring forth the funds necessary to accomplish that which titles are alleged to insure. If employment is sporadic, uncertain and badly paid then titles are largely irrelevant. This reminds us that 'property rights' cannot be considered in isolation from the larger legal and economic circumstances in which the poor are embedded. That is, the presumption in such policy prescriptions is that the dominant impediment to credit markets fully clearing is the absence of collateral on the part of borrowers. There are many reasons for failure in credit markets.

Nested institutional arrangements
The essential problem is that property rights are but one small part of the institutional architecture of a nation state. When our focus turns to actions that might enhance economic development, it is common to fix attention on some specific problematic situation and to prescribe institutional solutions for that problem. Doing so causes well-meaning advisors to prescribe policies that are isolated from the broader institutional structure within which the problem is situated. Development initiatives that seek to impose particular property relations in a sector – forestry, small-scale agriculture, urban housing, fisheries, irrigation – often overlook the fact that these sectoral problems are themselves embedded in a particular constellation of institutional arrangements and governance structures that may be deeply flawed, conflicted and incoherent.

Development interventions cannot solve problems of deforestation, soil erosion, depleted fisheries, dysfunctional irrigation projects, or inadequate agricultural investment if the full constellation of institutions produces fouled incentives throughout the larger economy. That is, property relations must be understood as part of the larger institutional structure of a society (Bromley, 1989a).

It is important to understand that property regimes can and do show as much variability across cultures as do other social arrangements. But the institutional arrangements of a society – of which property relations are of current interest – must be understood as a reflection of prior values and expectations regarding future opportunities. Just as there is no 'right' culture, there is no 'right' property regime. Rather, there are property regimes responding to, indeed reflecting, manifold interests and priorities (Bromley, 1989b). Property relations – property regimes – are reflections of this *pre-allocative* function of any economic system. And, by being pre-allocative, property relations must be understood as social constructs whose nature and existence are antecedent to all 'economic' behaviour. Property regimes are particularistic structures that gain their rationale because they address fundamental questions about which members of society deserve the protection from the state that property relations entail. Property relations are manifestations of whose interests count in a particular social setting.

Customary (that is, traditional) property regimes have fallen prey to the general dysfunction of most poor countries. Communities of resource users are usually unable to resist the economic and political power from national capitals. Pressure on local property regimes is often subtle. In particular, perhaps crop agriculture is given preference over pastoral activities. It is thereby inevitable that the property regimes central to pastoralism will be undermined. It is not enough that pastoralists have traditional grazing 'rights' in a particular area. If the property regime central to pastoralism is to survive incursion by outsiders, pastoralists cannot be expected to mobilise their own defence of the assets central to their survival. Holders of private property are not expected to defend their own claims to ownership; the authority system does that for them. *Any* structure of property relations requires a commitment from the recognised system of authority that enforcement will be collectively assured – not privately required (Bromley, 1991). When individuals must enforce their own property rights, the concept of a property 'right' becomes a contradiction in terms.

The instrumental nature of institutional arrangements, including property regimes, is best demonstrated when we think about the intersection of the realms of ecological variability and the holding of social and economic capital. In temperate climates, fixed assets such as land hold great economic potential and social status. It is thus to be expected that institutional and technological structures will exist to define and control access to, and control over, land. Most residents of temperate climates regard it as quite normal to view a fixed land base as both an economic asset and as a source of social status. It is less often understood that in a pastoral economy individuals gain social status from holding not land but cattle. That cattle are privately owned and land is not, says less about stages of 'development' than it does about the ecological reality within which pastoralists must make a living. This institutional structure reflects an adaptive response to the reality of provisioning where soils are poor, rainfall is fickle, and irrigation is not in the feasible set. It is not surprising that this structure of flexibility will, at times, confront an alternative property rights structure – private property – constructed for rigidity. But institutional flexibility is a necessary attribute of certain economic systems (Behnke, 1994).

Conflicts between pastoralists and sedentary agriculture in the arid climes must be understood as a conflict over property regimes. Unfortunately, property rights essential for extensive livestock production have been eroded by a long history of conflicts. More recently, a number of state interventions that expropriated pastoralist property rights crucial to their economic systems have clearly favoured farmers over pastoralists in the realignment of property rights. These changes have often created general uncertainty over property rights, thereby inducing a de facto open access situation. The resulting degradation associated with open access resources has substantially increased the (transaction) costs of running the pastoralist economy and adversely affected pastoralists' ability to overcome periods of drought (Bromley, 1991; van den Brink et al., 1995).

Ecological settings that exhibit great variability require property regimes that allow quick and low-cost adaptations to these stochastic circumstances. Livestock as an asset, because of their mobility, provide this flexibility in a way that the immobility of land cannot possibly equal. Small wonder that the institutions over livestock and land differ so profoundly between the temperate climates of the middle latitudes, and the arid and semi-arid reaches of Africa and Asia.

Finally, there is the common assertion that a *secure title* to land is a necessary condition for investment in, or the wise management of, land and related natural resources. Here we see private (and secure) title advanced as the *sine qua non* of agricultural investments and much development assistance since the mid-1980s has been predicated on this idea. Interestingly, this 'truth' is less true than many might like to imagine (Place and Hazell, 1993). In fact, there is plausible evidence that the contrary proposition – prior investment in land is a necessary condition to secure 'title' in that land – is equally probable. That is, rather than investment requiring security, security requires investment (Sjaastad and Bromley, 1997, 2000).

The confusion in this domain has to do with the precise meaning of 'security' and 'title'. In some parts of the world the titling and registration of land has been the immediate precursor to the dispossession of those who imagined that this step would ensure their longevity on the land. Instead, such title became a means whereby money lenders and others with some measure of political influence were able to acquire what the poor once thought was 'their' land. Rather than title enhancing security, it has had quite the opposite effect in some locations. So the pertinent issue in the realm of property rights and development is not one of mere 'title and security' but of *security for whom?*

Implications

Property rights are indeed important for the development process. However, we must be careful to see and to understand the rights structures that already exist in many settings. We must be careful, as well, to avoid the imposition of particular property rights regimes that happen to fit received economic theory, but that do not at all fit local cultures and circumstances. The *ideology of property* is deeply rooted in Western-led development interventions. This often means that we make matters worse not better for those whose lives we like to believe we are improving.

DANIEL W. BROMLEY

References

Becker, Lawrence C. (1977), *Property Rights*, London: Routledge & Kegan Paul.

Behnke, R.H. (1994), 'Natural resource management in pastoral Africa', *Development Policy Review*, **12** (1), 5–27.

Bromley, Daniel W. (1989a), *Economic Interests and Institutions: The Conceptual Foundations of Public Policy*, Oxford: Blackwell.

Bromley, Daniel W. (1989b), 'Property relations and economic development: the other land reform', *World Development*, **17** (6), 867–77.

Bromley, Daniel W. (1991), *Environment and Economy: Property Rights and Public Policy*, Oxford: Blackwell.

Bromley, Daniel W. (1999), 'Deforestation: institutional causes and solutions', in Matti Palo and Jussi Uusivuori (eds), *World Forests, Society and Environment*, Kluwer: Dordrecht, pp. 95–105.

Christman, John (1994), *The Myth of Property*, Oxford: Oxford University Press.

Clark, Colin W. (1973), 'Profit maximization and the extinction of animal species', *Journal of Political Economy*, **81**, 950–61.

Deacon, Robert T. (1994), 'Deforestation and the rule of law in a cross-section of countries', *Land Economics*, **70** (4), 414–30.

Deacon, Robert T. (1995), 'Assessing the relationship between government policy and deforestation', *Journal of Environmental Economics and Management*, **28** (1), 1–18.

DeSoto, Hernando (2000), *The Mystery of Capital*, New York: Basic Books.

Macpherson, C.B. (1973), *Democratic Theory: Essays in Retrieval*, Oxford: Clarendon.

Macpherson, C.B. (1978), *Property: Mainstream and Critical Positions*, Toronto: University of Toronto Press.

Page, Talbott (1977), *Conservation and Economic Efficiency*, Baltimore, MD: Johns Hopkins University Press.

Place, Frank and Peter Hazell (1993), 'Productivity effects of indigenous land tenure systems in Sub-Saharan Africa', *American Journal of Agricultural Economics*, **75** (2), 10–19.

Sjaastad, Espen and Daniel W. Bromley (1997), 'Indigenous land rights in Sub-Saharan Africa: appropriation, security, and investment demand', *World Development*, **25** (4), 549–62.

Sjaastad, Espen and Daniel W. Bromley (2000), 'The prejudices of property rights: on individualism, specificity, and security in property regimes', *Development Policy Review*, **18** (4), 365–89.

Smith, Vernon, L. (1968), 'Economics of production from natural resources', *American Economic Review*, **58** (3), 409–31.

van den Brink, Rogier, Daniel W. Bromley and Jean-Paul Chavas (1995), 'The economics of Cain and Abel: agro-pastoral property rights in the Sahel', *Journal of Development Studies*, **31** (3), 373–99.

Public Works

Public works are a form of social protection in which a wage in cash or in kind is provided in return for labour, in order to provide a safety net at a time when regular wage employment or participation in normal livelihood activities are not possible, due to some economic, political or environmental shock. Public works wages may be paid in the form of cash (cash for work), food (food for work), or inputs such as seeds or fertiliser (inputs for work). Public works generally have as their primary objective the provision of a safety net for the poor who are not able to find work or pursue their normal livelihood activities due to some form of disruption to the labour market. They are intended to provide a basic income and prevent the distress selling of assets in order to meet subsistence needs. Public works frequently involve the creation or maintenance of productive infrastructure, such as roads, irrigation systems or vegetable gardens, which are intended to contribute to an improvement in the livelihood of participants. Depending on the nature of the crisis driving the implementation of public works, other objectives may include skills development through work experience and on-the-job training, the stimulation of economic growth by promoting demand among public works employees, or the maintenance of social and political order in the context of unacceptably high levels of unemployment and poverty.

Programmes are usually self-targeted on the basis of the principal of 'less eligibility', according to which the value of the wage is kept low in order to ensure that participation in the programme is only attractive to the poor. This is often achieved by setting the wage at or below the market wage, on the assumption that only the poor will self-select for public works employment at this wage rate. When employment is offered to all those seeking work, the programme is known as 'universal'. However, where the number of those seeking public works employment exceeds the number of jobs available, access is rationed using a variety of mechanisms including targeting on the basis of group or geographical characteristics, the allocation of employment through lottery systems, and/or community targeting, where employment is allocated by communities among themselves.

The public works wage may be in cash or in kind, and is made in return for a set amount of work, often defined in terms of the completion of a particular task. Whether cash, food or other inputs are the most appropriate mode of payment varies according to the nature of the crisis. Generally cash is more desirable due to the choice it offers to workers in terms of their own consumption priorities, but where food is not readily available at stable prices, or the situation is insecure, food may be the preferred option.

The variety of interventions falling under the umbrella of public works is diverse, ranging from large-scale Keynesian-style direct employment creation schemes, to more limited geographically specific interventions responding to transient labour market problems. Programmes may broadly be divided into three categories; large-scale public sector employment, employment guarantee schemes, and temporary public works employment at times of acute labour market crisis arising from natural disaster or short-term shifts in the business cycle. The US response to the Great Depression exemplifies a classic public sector employment programme. Under the programme, massive state expenditure on public works employment was initiated, absorbing up to 30 per cent of the unemployed in an attempt to stimulate consumer demand and prevent the deepening of the economic recession. Employment guarantee schemes are operational in several states in India, for example the Maharashtra Employment Guarantee Scheme (MEGS) (see Dev, 1995). Under this scheme, employment is defined as a constitutional right, and the state offers a guaranteed number of days of employment each year to any unemployed work seeker, who will be employed on the creation of community assets and paid at the minimum wage. Public works programmes responding to temporary disturbances to the employment cycle arising from disasters such as drought or typhoon damage are frequently implemented in Bangladesh and other southern Asian states, offering temporary employment at these times of acute labour demand shortage. Programmes have also been implemented on a large scale in East Africa as relief interventions in response to the disruption of livelihoods that have occurred as the result of conflict and drought. The Ethiopian food for work programme, for example, which has been in operation since 1980, offered temporary work to up to 1.4 million people in drought-affected communities each year between 1999 and 2003 (see Subbarao and Smith, 2003).

Public works have been implemented throughout the world, with major programmes implemented in Britain and Prussia during periods of industrialisation and conflict, in the United States during the Great Depression, and in Africa, Latin America and Asia during the second half of the twentieth century. In developing countries public works have been used as both development and emergency instruments, while in recent decades they have frequently formed a component of social funds, often with developmental objectives relating to livelihoods and poverty reduction. In Africa, programmes have tended to be short term and contingent on donor funding, while in Asia although multilateral food aid supported large-scale food-for-work programmes during the immediate post-war decades, more recently many programmes have been based on cash transfers, implemented for prolonged periods and primarily domestically funded. While public works generally are not used as instruments to reduce long-term poverty, they can be used to perform this function, as illustrated by MEGS, initiated during the 1970s and still in operation, and the national public works programme in South Korea which was implemented from the 1960s to the 1980s. Both programmes addressed poverty by ensuring sustained access to employment by the poor, thereby guaranteeing a minimum regular income, and in this way promoting income insecurity, and reducing vulnerability.

The design of a public works programme is contingent on the nature of the unemployment problem and the desired outcomes of the programme. When unemployment is an acute transitional problem – for example, during periods of economic restructuring – public works programmes tend to offer short-term employment, but when unemployment is a chronic problem arising from structural changes in the economy, longer-term employment is required if significant and sustained impacts on poverty and livelihoods are to be achieved. The objective of public works is frequently *poverty relief* in the form of a social safety net. However, when the programme objective is *poverty reduction*, higher wage rates and/or prolonged employment duration are required, since the poor use income to satisfy basic consumption needs first, then invest in human capital (education and health) and social capital, and only then invest in activities to promote livelihoods. Hence a public works wage is only likely to impact on productive investment and an improvement in livelihoods if it is greater than the income required to ensure that basic consumption needs are satisfied (Devereux, 2000). Even when wage income is limited in comparison with household needs, public works can have a significant impact by providing a form of income insurance, although a programme can only serve this function if public works employment is available on a sustained basis (Dev, 1995). Evidence from India and southern Africa indicates that this insurance function may be of greater significance than the value of the transfer in terms of sustained poverty reduction, since it reduces income fluctuation and thereby prevents acute distress to the poor. If a public works programme is to contribute to secondary employment and facilitate growth, the scale of the employment created must be large and the infrastructure created economically productive.

The key question in public works is whether to target and how best this should be done. Whether the programme is targeted or universal (available to all those seeking to participate) is often contingent on the amount of funds available, as this dictates the scale of the programme in relation to the number of workers in search of employment/relief. Wage targeting (keeping public works wages at or below the prevailing wage rate), is frequently used to ensure that the poor are the primary beneficiaries of public works programmes. This form of targeting is administratively cheap and results in limited leakage to the non-poor, providing the wage is set sufficiently low. However, in countries with high levels of poverty, low prevailing wages and high unemployment, the use of low wages to promote self-selection of the poor into public works programmes may entail setting the wage so low that it fails to meet the basic subsistence needs of participants, thereby undermining the relief and/or development objectives of the programme. Finding the balance between setting a wage low enough to limit leakage to the non-poor, while also contributing to the livelihoods of participants remains a key challenge in many public works contexts. If the programme aims to target more accurately, the criteria employed need to reflect the priority objectives of the programme and recognise the heterogeneous nature of the unemployed who are seeking assistance. For example, if household poverty reduction is the primary goal, public works employment might be targeted at female household heads, since research has indicated that this group tends to be more vulnerable, and that transfers to female household heads have a greater impact on household welfare than transfers to males. If, however, promoting skills development and future employment prospects is the priority, youths with the ability to travel in search of employment, and many years of potential labour market participation, would be a more appropriate target.

Public works programmes vary considerably in terms of their implementation modalities, which are determined by a range of budgetary, administrative and political considerations, and while some programmes are implemented directly by the state, others are implemented by NGOs, bilateral donors such as the World Food Programme, or private contractors. These different modalities may have a significant impact on targeting and livelihood outcomes, with less of a concern among private sector implementers for the social protection aspects of the programme, such as targeting the poorest, or ensuring timely wage payment, for example.

A key problem associated with public works is the exclusion of households with limited labour, for example child-headed households, or households with limited able-bodied adult members, who by definition are not able to participate in programmes with labour-based entry criteria. Other problems frequently associated with public works programmes are delays in payment (which undermine the safety-net function), implementation at the incorrect time of the year (when employment opportunities are not at their most scarce), and the quality and limited productive value of infrastructure created.

The major areas of contemporary research into public works have been related to the cost effectiveness of public works programmes as safety-net instruments, the impact of public works on poverty and livelihoods, the role of public works in emergency situations, and how to integrate relief-orientated public works into the development process. Subbarao and Ravallion have carried out seminal work examining the cost effectiveness of public works as a transfer instrument (see, for example, Subbarao et al., 1997; and Ravallion, 1998). Their work examines the efficiency of public works as a mechanism to deliver social protection from a primarily economic perspective. The relationship between public works, poverty reduction and livelihoods has been widely explored in the literature, with the main conclusions being the importance of programme duration, wage level and timing in determining the developmental impact of public works. These issues have been discussed in relation to public works programmes in India (for example, Datt and Ravallion, 1994a, b) and southern Africa (for example, Devereux, 2000). The relief and food security potential of public works and options for the integration of emergency-orientated public works responses into the development process has been widely explored in the literature (for an overview of the current debate, see Barrett et al., 2004).

ANNA McCORD

References

Barrett, C., S. Holden and D. Clay (2004), 'Can food-for-work programs reduce vulnerability?', in S. Dercon (ed.), *Insurance Against Poverty*, WIDER Studies in Development Economics, Oxford: Oxford University Press, pp. 361–86.

Datt, G. and M. Ravallion (1994a), 'Income gains for the poor from public works employment', Living Standards Measurement Study Working Paper no. 100, Policy Research Department, Washington, DC: World Bank.

Datt, G. and M. Ravallion (1994b), 'Transfer benefits from public works employment – evidence from rural India', *Economic Journal*, **104**, 1346–69.

Dev, S.M. (1995), 'India's (Maharashtra) Employment Guarantee Scheme: lessons from long experience', in J. von Braun (ed.), *Employment for Poverty Reduction and Food Security*, Washington, DC: International Food Policy Research Institute, pp. 108–43.

Devereux, S. (2000), *Social Safety Nets for Poverty Alleviation in Southern Africa*, Brighton: Institute of Development Studies, University of Sussex.

Ravallion, M. (1998), 'Appraising workfare programs', Policy Research Working Paper, WPS 1955, Development Research Group Poverty and Human Resources, Washington, DC: World Bank.

Subbarao, K., A. Bonnerjee and J. Braithwaite (1997), 'Income generation programs', in K. Subbarao, A. Bonnerjee, K. Ezemerari, J. Braithwaite, C. Graham, S. Carvalho and A. Thompson, *Safety Net Programs and Poverty Reduction: Lessons from Cross Country Experience*, Washington, DC: World Bank, pp. 69–92.

Subbarao, K. and W.J. Smith (2003), 'Safety nets versus relief nets: towards a medium-term safety net strategy for Ethiopia', November, www1.worldbank.org/sp/risk_management/Training/ Ethiopia%20Safety%20Nets. pdf, 5 November 2004.

Purchasing Power Parity

A competitive domestic economy generates equilibrium prices such that identical goods or inputs will have identical prices. This is the Law of One Price (LOOP). A question arises as to whether this principle carries over to the 206 economies whose statistics are recorded by the World Bank in the World Development Reports. If there are two units of a homogeneous good such as identical cars in different countries, say, the UK and Germany, then their price should be the same because if they were different it would be predicted that arbitrage would take place. That is to say, rational individuals would buy the car where it is cheaper, increasing the demand and placing upward pressure on price, and sell it where it is more expensive, thereby making a profit, and at the same time increasing supply, which puts downward pressure on the price of the car. This process will continue until identical cars once again have the identical price in both countries. Here LOOP operates through the mechanism of trade. But this formulation ignores the exchange rate between the two countries. As the UK uses pounds sterling and Germany euros, the exchange rate between the two countries must be involved. The LOOP is now reformulated to state that the price of the two cars will be the same once they have been related through the exchange rate. That is, $PukCar = Es\ PgCar$ where Es is the spot nominal exchange rate quoted in the direct fashion as the number of pounds it takes to buy a euro. Numerically if Es is 0.5 pounds per euro and the German car is €20 000, then for the LOOP to obtain the UK car price is £10 000. If such a process is applied to all (internationally traded) goods then absolute purchasing power parity (PPP) would naturally arise as $Puk = Es\ Pg$ where Puk and Pg are now price indices. Such indices measure the price of all goods in a given economy by calculating how much it costs to buy a representative sample of goods called a 'basket'. Here it is assumed that the same basket is bought in the UK and in Germany and each good given the same weighting in the index. However, given that the inflation rate (movement in the general price level) of a country is measured by its price index, the focus has shifted from a 'real-side' story about trade adjustments for an individual good to a more monetary argument about the exchange rate being the ratio of two price indices as by rearrangement $Es = Puk/Pg$. Other things equal, if the general price level increases in the UK absolute PPP says the exchange rate must involve more pounds per euro for price equality. That is, the pound must depreciate against the euro.

Invoking the injunction that theory should rely on the minimum assumptions required to yield sustained potentially falsifiable predictions, absolute PPP is actually cast in less strong terms and does not require that the LOOP apply strictly for each good but only on average. That is, some goods will be overpriced by reference to the LOOP and other goods will be underpriced, but on average the condition is met. A failure of LOOP does not invalidate absolute PPP. In this way PPP becomes a monetary account of exchange rate determination, as inflation can be viewed as monetarily generated and measured by the (expected) movement in the general price level so that the (expected) exchange rate between two countries will be predicted to reflect their different (expected) inflation experiences. A country's exchange rate will depreciate if its (expected) inflation rate is greater than that of other countries. How do these considerations carry over to developing economies?

In the short run there are a number of 'frictions' that reduce the power of PPP forces, especially where developing economies are concerned. First there is the existence of transport costs, which means that prices can differ by the cost of transporting goods from the low- to the high-price economy. Similarly, but less naturally, the existence of quotas and tariffs on international trade restrict the opportunities for goods arbitrage. Lack of complete information, goods not being truly homogeneous and consumer inertia in making consumption decisions mean that even instrumentally rational individuals may be slow to respond to profit opportunities. Second, the theory developed into a monetary-inflation rate driven account of exchange rate determination but both relative and the general price levels change in a dynamic economy. If a new technology is introduced for producing a good, its price relative to other goods will fall and for the LOOP to apply the exchange rate must be accommodating independent of any overall general price level considerations. More generally all economic shocks, especially those relating to developing economies, such as wars, new investment opportunities and oil crises, could be expected to affect the exchange rate independently of their impact on the inflation rate. Finally, the biggest change in recent decades in the international economy has been the presence of massive financial capital flows triggered by small interest rate differences, and/or the fear of holding assets denominated in a currency that is expected to depreciate. Any modern account of exchange rate movements would necessarily include this consideration.

Long-run considerations raise the issue of the Belassa–Samuelson effect. If PPP is applied in a rigorous way, the one thing that people could not say on return from their foreign holiday is: 'It wasn't half cheap there' as the parity condition is precisely about rates of currency conversion that will equalise the purchasing power of different currencies. It was Belassa (1964) among others who provided a rationale for the: 'It wasn't half cheap there' assertion. The internal price ratio (IPR) for a country is the ratio of the price of its non-internationally traded goods (Pnt) to its internationally traded goods (Pt), that is, $IPR = Pnt/Pt$. The internationally traded goods tend to be manufactures with a common price that are open to technology change and a lowered cost of production. The non-internationally traded goods tend to be services (for example, haircuts) that are much less open to technology change and therefore the possibility of a lowered cost of production. Given this, it is predicted that average factor productivity (AP) in traded goods exceeds that for non-internationally traded goods. That is, $APt > APnt$. A common wage (W) can be assumed in both sectors of an economy (otherwise workers will move from the low- to the high-wage sector to establish equality – a law of one wage) and prices set by $P = W/AP$, yields $Pt = W/APt$ and $Pnt = W/APnt$. Now $APnt$ is unlikely to vary much from country to country. However W, the common wage, is much higher for the so-called 'developed economies' and as such they must have higher internal price ratios as Pnt is higher, other things equal. With the exchange rate reflecting the prices of internationally traded goods the, say, pound–Thai baht rate will appear to be appreciated by reference to PPP and on arrival your holiday service sector type products will look cheap despite PPP!

Given these qualifying arguments it is not surprising that there is a third weaker, less-demanding, PPP concept. This is relative PPP. It is less demanding in that it says *changes* (relative movements) in nominal exchange rates will reflect differences in different countries' inflation rates on equivalent baskets of goods (the weights on the different elements in the basket can be different for different countries but must be constant). For simplicity, convert this principle to a LOOP example. Suppose, as above, the pound/euro rate is £0.5 to €1 but initially the German car was €18 000 and the UK car £10 000 and then the price of the German car fell by €1800 to €16 200. A relative version of the LOOP would predict the exchange rate move in the same proportion, namely 10 per cent to 0.55 pounds per euro. Here the pound is depreciating by 10 per cent to offset the 10 per cent fall in the price of the German car. Note that at no point does the LOOP apply, in that the German car was initially £9000 compared to £10 000 for the UK car whereas after the 10 per cent price movement and 10 per cent exchange rate movement it was £8910. A failure of absolute PPP does not invalidate relative PPP. This reflects the weaker condition that relative PPP requires.

PPP is relevant to development economics in several key ways. First, development economists are often required to make comparisons across countries which inevitably, as with the car example above, raises the question of exchange rates with the worry being that 'analyses based on unreliable or biased data, could result in seriously distorted, if not altogether wrong, analytical and policy conclusions' (Srinivasan, 1994, pp. 4–5). For concreteness, assume that it was thought desirable to direct aid to the 35 poorest countries in the world. How easy would it be to identify them? A natural starting-point would be to compare GDP per capita and select the 35 lowest. However, what exchange rate should be used? One method used by the World Bank involves a synthetic exchange rate commonly called the 'Atlas conversion factor'. This factor is basically the average of a country's exchange rate for that year and the two previous years (to minimise the impact of short-run fluctuations/frictions noted above). This figure corrected for the difference between its inflation rate and those of the G-5 economies (France, Germany, Japan, the UK and the USA) provides the dollar Atlas conversion factor for a country. Looking at the *World Development Report 2000/2001*, Kenya, with a 1999 GNP per capita of $360 by the Atlas method of conversion (World Bank, 2001, p. 274), would be ineligible for aid as it ranked 170 of 206 and outside the poorest 35. However, given the discussion above, using a (sophisticated) method based on official exchange rates would be inaccurate, as such exchange rates do not reflect PPP. Economists have not been unaware of this and two Pennsylvania University economists used the United Nations International Comparison Project (ICP) to create the Penn World Tables (PWT) of national accounts at international prices (see Summers and Heston, 1991). The basics are as follows. The ICP collects data on between 400 and 700 items in each of a set of benchmark countries. The price of each item is then divided by its corresponding US price to yield a relative price. The items are allocated to one of 150 expenditure categories and by an averaging procedure a relative price for each category is obtained. National expenditure on category i which is by definition price (p_i) multiplied by quantity (q_i) is divided by the relative price to provide an estimate of the quantity in that category valued at US prices $(p_i q_i)/(p_i/p\text{US})$. But US prices are not international prices. The relative price ratios for items in the 150 categories are further averaged in a specialised weighted way to give an international relative price across the benchmark countries. Dividing national expenditures on each category by their international relative price gives national output at international prices. The PPP for a country is its ratio of domestic currency expenditures to the international price valuation of its output. Generally the lower a country's GDP when converted to dollars by published exchange rates, the greater is the deviation from the PPP method. Returning to Kenya, GNP measured at PPP for 1999 was higher at $975 and its rank was now 185, thereby qualifying for aid as one of the poorest 35 countries. Numbers matter.

The correction to the PPP method illustrates how using the method based on official exchange rates significantly inflates the gap between poor and rich nations and in doing so generally alters their GNP per capita rankings. Similarly, poverty measured as the proportion of the population below $1 a day and $2 a day as reported in the *World Development Report 2000/2001* (World Bank, 2001, pp. 280–81) are the percentages of the population living below those levels of consumption or income at 1993 prices, adjusted for PPP.

For some development economists the way out of poverty is trade not aid, and again PPP is relevant. Whether an economy is competitive or not is typically captured in a measure of the real exchange rate (θ) that connects to PPP. Define $\theta = EsPf/Pd$ where Es is the spot nominal exchange rate and Pf and Pd are price indices for the foreign and domestic country, respectively. In words, the real exchange rate is the nominal bilateral exchange rate weighed by the relevant price levels measured as indices. If Pf approximates import prices and Pd export prices then it is easy to connect to international competitiveness in that: $\theta = EsPf/Pd \cong$ import price index/export price index ($= 1/$terms of trade). If export prices (Pd) falls, θ will rise so that on this definition of the real exchange rate an increasing θ means increased international competitiveness. Consider the simple example in Table 13.

Despite a doubling of the US price level, country D's traded goods are no more competitive in the USA in Period 2 than they were in Period 1, as D's exchange rate has appreciated from 0.5 to $1 to 0.25 to $1 leaving the real exchange rate unchanged at 1. It is the real exchange rate that indicates international competitiveness not the nominal one. Looking at the nominal exchange rate, D would look less competitive in Period 2 than in Period 1, because the appreciation of the peso would make its export prices high. At this point it is tempting to make a large error. Using the $Pd = EsPf$ formulation implies for

Table 13   The real exchange rate and international competitiveness

Country	USA	D	Nominal exchange rate (Es pesos per $)	Rate real exchange rate (θ)
Period 1 price index	200	100	0.5 to $1	$\dfrac{200}{100} \times 0.5 = 1$
Period 2 price index	400	100	0.25 to $1	$\dfrac{400}{100} \times 0.25 = 1$

Period 1, $100 = 0.5 \times 200$ and for Period 2, $100 = 0.25 \times 400$, and PPP appears to work perfectly when the real exchange rate $= 1$. Unfortunately this appealing reasoning is lost once it is remembered that Pd and Pf are price indices and as such can legitimately be rebased so the real exchange rate will no longer appear as 1. In short, it is a constant real exchange rate that indicates international competitiveness is unchanged and the real exchange rate $= 1$ is not the test for PPP. But what is?

A direct way to test a model is to try to establish the validity of its' assumptions. A somewhat 'tongue in cheek' test of the LOOP is the so-called 'Big Mac' or 'Hamburger' standard. *The Economist* periodically repeats an investigative exercise first undertaken in 1986 in which they priced a MacDonald's Big Mac hamburger in many countries. The idea is that the Big Mac forms a mini-consumer basket that could form a test of the LOOP and predict which way exchange rates should move on PPP reasoning. PPP is not established for this test as the price of Big Macs expressed in dollars varies from country to country. How surprising is this? In a (frictionless) perfect capital market, Big Macs could be transported 'free' and not get colder than they are already. In reality, transport costs and their non-durability mean that they are not internationally traded. Markets are separated so there is no goods arbitrage, although some arbitrage of the inputs might be expected. Further, demand and supply considerations impinge on this 'test'. On the demand side this is a product market where there is product differentiation, variable availability of substitute 'fast food', income and taste differences, making the market ripe for the practice of third-degree price discrimination where the same good is sold at different prices in different markets. On the supply side, cost structures are different as many inputs are local and not usually internationally traded, for example, electricity, making for different marginal costs of production and therefore prices even in the absence of demand-side considerations. Clearly this market would not be described as frictionless and barriers to international trade may not be a big contributor to the Big Mac PPP failure as price differences intra-nationally among the US states exceed those observed internationally, suggesting an industrial structure explanation of price difference.

However, there is a plethora of more serious econometric evidence. Sarno and Taylor (2002) divide this sophisticated literature into six phases, but despite the interest in falsifiable predictions as an indirect test of a model, in the PPP case of a constant real exchange rate, the empirical evidence remains open to interpretation. It is very difficult to completely falsify a prediction econometrically as all types of sub-debate arise. Questions abound. Have the 'right' data been used? Should the data be cross-section, time series, or a combination of both? For what countries and types of exchange rate regime are the data available? Have the 'correct' functional forms been estimated by 'appropriate' techniques? Have the 'correct' tests of significance been applied to the estimated equations? And so on. Sarno and Taylor (2002, p. 87) summarise the current state of the debate as 'PPP might be viewed as a valid long-run international parity condition when applied to bilateral exchange rates obtaining among major industrialised countries'. This of course is comforting for an intellectual discipline whose key concept is market adjustment to equilibrium. With respect to the latter process, the authors note 'the role of non-linearities in real exchange rate adjustment to long-run equilibrium'. It seems that PPP adjustments take place slowly and not in a straight-line fashion and it is therefore not surprising that the World Bank systematically assesses the appropriateness of official exchange rates for conversion purposes.

JOHN CULLIS

References

Belassa, B. (1964), 'The purchasing power parity doctrine: a reappraisal', *Journal of Political Economy*, **72**, 584–96.

Sarno, L. and J.A. Taylor (2002), *The Economics of Exchange Rates*, Cambridge: Cambridge University Press.

Srinivasan, T.N. (1994), 'Data base for development analysis: an overview', *Journal of Development Economics*, **44**, 3–27.

Summers, R. and A. Heston (1991), 'The Penn World Table (Mark 5): an expanded set of international comparisons, 1950–1988', *Quarterly Journal of Economics*, **106**, 327–68.

World Bank (2001), *World Development Report 2000/2001 Attacking Poverty*, Oxford and New York: Oxford University Press.

Rawls, John (1921–2002)

An entry on the relevance of John Rawls to development studies faces a paradox from the start. Rawls himself, both in his seminal work *A Theory of Justice* (1971) and in his later writings, does not have much to say directly about development, either as a process of socio-economic change occurring in any society or as something specifically applying to the poorer so-called 'developing' countries in the 'South' whose general condition and specific high incidence of extreme poverty have been a matter of international concern and action in the last 60 years or so. Development was not really his concern. On the other hand, Rawls's ideas, particularly about social justice in general, about the 'difference principle' as an egalitarian principle of distribution, and, in his later writings, about overlapping consensus as a basis of pluralist societies, have provided much material for other writers, both as something to use in the construction of theories of development and as something to criticise in the underlying rationale of conventional liberal models of development. But they have also provided the basis for the extension to the international/global level in the development of theories of global justice (in ways which Rawls himself did not necessarily approve!).

That Rawls's ideas, whatever his own preoccupations, should have such a central bearing on development thinking is not in the least surprising if we bear two facts in mind. Rawls's main project was the construction of a socially just society and this construction involved (as we shall see in greater detail below) distinctive views both about the 'goods' with which social justice is concerned and about what the principles of social justice are themselves. On the face of it development is rather different, since it is a process of socio-economic change. But reflection quickly shows interesting links with social justice, since this change does not just happen nor is it merely *post eventum* something deemed desirable or undesirable, it is something that is *pursued*. As such it assumes norms and values of some kind that *justify* the pursuit of it. Even the conventional model of development as economic growth, as an object of public policy, assumes a set of values (to do with maximising utility or choice). These values have often remained implicit, even unacknowledged, until challenged by other thinkers who want to propose more complex values which development is about. Thus the explicit discourse of development ethics – as the field of enquiry has come to be called in the last 20 years or so (see Development Ethics, this volume) – is about the normative framework for assessing the state of a society at any given point and for prescribing its development into the future. Since any theory of development then must include some view (whether implicit or explicit) about what principles ought to govern a society and what goods are to be pursued in it, Rawls's views on the last two issues have central relevance to our understanding of development (whether we accept them or reject them). Given the dominance of Rawls's ideas in the late twentieth century and the continued influence of these ideas even now, his views can hardly be avoided when discussing development.

In what follows, I first sketch out the main elements of Rawls's theory as it has a bearing on development, and also indicate some limited respects in which he himself saw what he had to say as having a bearing on development. I then show how these ideas impact on development thinking, and finally indicate how his ideas can be extended into the global sphere, which has interesting implications for the international framework of aid and trade relations within which development is either facilitated or impeded.

Rawls's approach

In his most famous work, *A Theory of Justice* (1971), Rawls develops a distinctive theory of social justice which he takes to be about the principles governing the distribution of the benefits and burdens of social cooperation. He proposes a method for determining these principles that involves people entering an 'original position' in which behind a veil of ignorance they are stripped of any particular knowledge about themselves such as whether they are rich or poor, clever or stupid, or what their particular conceptions of the good or well-being are. This veil of ignorance is meant to guarantee impartiality (hence justice as *fairness*). Behind it people choose the fundamental principles. Rawls assumes that what is to be distributed are the primary goods of liberty, opportunity, income, wealth and the bases of self-respect. The two main principles that would be chosen are: first (having priority), the equal liberty principle and second, the difference principle which has two elements. The first is essentially an egalitarian principle because the presumption is that distribution is to be equal except in so far as an unequal distribution allows for everyone to be better off than under other social arrangements. In effect, Rawls is saying that some inequalities of wealth are just because the pursuit of wealth through enterprise generates wealth, part of which can then benefit the poor either through deliberate redistribution through taxation to fund social welfare and to protect the poor from being even poorer, or through 'trickle-down' processes more generally. The second aspect of the difference principle, is what Rawls calls the 'fair equality of opportunity' principle, which requires that measures like universal access to education and medical provision enable people to develop their talents properly, thus also reducing the impact of differences in people's natural endowments and social circumstances, and contributing to greater equality.

Interestingly enough, Rawls sees these two principles as being the principles that would be accepted in a society which is at a reasonably high level of material development. Where a society is still economically backward, the single general principle would be appropriate:

> All social values – liberty and opportunity, income and wealth, and the bases of self-respect – are to be distributed equally unless unequal distribution of any, or all, of these values is to everyone's advantage. (Rawls, 1971, p. 62)

The thought here is that in a state of economic backwardness it is rational to be more concerned with securing the material conditions of life than with the enjoyment of liberties (in the sense of civil and political rights). While Rawls's reaction here does reflect a quite common view that in economically backward countries civil and political liberties are more of a luxury than a priority (and may have to be sacrificed in the drive to increase economic well-being), this is by no means generally accepted. Sen, for instance, has argued that these freedoms are indeed central to development, not merely as ends in themselves but as means of advancing the social and economic rights (or capabilities) of poor people (Sen, 1999).

In his later writings, such as *Political Liberalism* (1993), Rawls develops a further feature of liberal society and that is the importance of overlapping consensus for political justice between different groups who may have differing and conflicting 'comprehensive doctrines' based on different religious or philosophical foundations. The emphasis here is not merely that of the accommodation of different conceptions of the good but also different moral visions (often shared by groups) of how to live. While Rawls at this stage was not proposing this as a universal theory of justice for all societies (unlike the more ambitious project of *A Theory of Justice*) but one for *liberal* societies, the ideas are of course of relevance to any definition of development (anywhere) that involves social values of some kind and also to the possibility of shared values at a global level (see, for example, Nussbaum, 2000).

Rawls's own view of international relations also underwent some modification over time. In *A Theory of Justice*, the issue is touched on cursorily and conventionally, in that Rawls supposed that a similar original position with representatives of states should be conceived, and he supposed that they would choose the familiar principles of the 'internationalist' tradition of respecting sovereignty, non-intervention, just war and *pacta sunt servanda* ('treaties are to be honoured') (Rawls, 1971, p. 378). What is interesting about this regarding development is that Rawls does not see here any fundamental duty of justice to redistribute wealth across borders, either by aid or by regulating international trade – except in so far as 'pacts' (that is, treaties and international laws) may be agreed, specifying such obligations (though this point is not explicitly discussed).

By the time he wrote *The Law of Peoples*, first as an article and later as a short book (Rawls, 1999), a rather different conception emerges of a more complex set of principles hypothetically agreed between states or 'peoples'. This agreement is not now between all states but between liberal states and hierarchical well-ordered states (that is, authoritarian states which observe the rule of law and have regard for civil rights). The principles now agreed include the protection of civil rights and to some extent the protection of socio-economic rights. Although other kinds of states or peoples called outlaw states and burdened peoples (often nowadays referred to as 'rogue' states and 'failed' states) are not formally part of the 'contract', nevertheless Rawls did by now recognise some international obligations of assistance towards 'burdened states' to enable them to become well-ordered and thus, he assumes, to tackle adequately the problems of poverty. His eighth principle reads thus: 'Peoples have a duty to assist other peoples living under unfavourable conditions that prevent their having a just or decent political and social regime' (Rawls, 1999, p. 37). As we will note later on, many thinkers who want to use the Rawlsian framework to develop a theory of global justice, do not think Rawls himself went far enough.

The relevance of Rawls's ideas to development discourse
In the early decades of international development programmes (1950s to 1970s), one of the key issues debated was the adequacy of the 'development as economic growth' paradigm. It was often initially assumed that what poorer countries needed was rapid

economic growth, caused by modernisation, industrialisation, mechanisation, gearing local agricultural production to international markets and so on. It was generally assumed that such growth would lead – and lead more effectively than alternative strategies – to the reduction of poverty at least in the long run through a gradual 'trickle-down' process ('a rising sea lifts all ships'). This came to be challenged on the grounds that the goal of poverty reduction required active intervention by the state, the development of welfare services, food subsidies for the poor and so on. Development came to be seen as 'growth with equity' or more specifically as incorporating 'basic needs' strategies in which programmes were targeted on helping very poor people to meet their needs. The centrality of widening access to education and medical care was of course generally recognised too.

Although these debates predated Rawls's writing and influence, one can see in Rawls a powerful articulation of a theoretical basis for strategies of the second kind. Rawls's 'difference principle' expresses, albeit in rather a strong form, an ethical intuition that policies should reflect the underlying structure of a socially just society so that they are to be to the advantage of the least well-off groups or at least to protect them from falling below certain minimum conditions necessary for well-being – though Rawls himself did not try to specify a 'minimum' standard, partly because his argument led to standards higher than this. In the late 1970s and the 1980s the debate focused more on a normative issue rather than the earlier more empirical issue of whether economic growth on its own would lead to poverty reduction by trickle-down processes. Now one of the issues was whether distribution of wealth was itself a legitimate concern of public policy and hence of development. Although Rawls developed his position as much as anything in opposition to what he saw as the errors of utilitarianism and to some extent in opposition to Marxist ideas of justice, somewhat surprisingly the most active opposition came from the political right as exemplified by Nozick in *Anarchy, State and Utopia* (1974), where the idea that justice was about active interventionist distribution of goods was rejected as a violation of individual liberty, especially economic liberty. Such economic libertarianism provided an alternative model of justice in society and hence a model of development. If a person became poorer through the repetition of just transactions, that may be regretted, but it was not unjust. For those who want to reject the latter approaches, Rawls provides a powerful account of why in addition to liberties themselves, the distribution of goods (as reflected in the difference principle) was of great importance to the kind of development that one pursues. Furthermore Rawls's later writings provide a rich rationale for why a modern pluralistic society should see itself as maintaining and even increasing such plurality and also respect for cultural difference. If one thinks that development should include the freedom of groups to pursue their different visions of the good life, this again can be seen as part of the model of appropriate development to be pursued.

So we can see that Rawls's ideas can be used to inform a plausible model of development. Certainly compared with the rather ethically thin model of development as economic growth, his ideas can inform an ethically rich account. On the other hand, for many others thinking ethically about development, in some ways Rawls's ideas have been part of the problem. It is not that there is anything wrong with seeing the distribution of wealth as part of the basic structure of a socially just society which in consequence requires *redis*tribution in almost all actual societies, as least to the extent that serious poverty is addressed. It is rather that the theory gives too thin or formalistic an account of what development is actually *about*. Ironically Rawls's approach shared much in common with what he saw as his main opposition, namely Utilitarianism. Both took a fairly general or formal view about what the goods were – either pleasure/utility, preference satisfaction or the primary goods – and both had a commitment to distributive principles, Rawls quite explicitly, Utilitarianism on empirical grounds (such as diminishing marginal utility arguments). There are real differences, but compared with more radical approaches to development they shared features which were problematic (see, for example, Crocker, 1992).

Opposition comes from many sources, including richer accounts of what the *good* is that development quite generally is meant to promote, and accounts which put more emphasis upon the importance of culture and community in determining the character and content of the conception of the good and the relevant moral frameworks. An example of the former is the development of the 'capability' approach in the writings of Sen, Nussbaum and many others who see themselves interpreting or extending the ideas of these two thinkers (see, for example, Crocker, 1995; Clark, 2002; Gasper, 2004). What is significant here is the idea that human well-being cannot be reduced to formal account such as pleasure, utility or the exercise of choice, but needs to be understood in terms of a wide range of powers and potentialities which need developing and expressing. The liberal Kantian/Enlightenment assumptions of the autonomous timeless self have also been more severely criticised by those who see human well-being as being more socially constructed in the matrix of relationship and cultural traditions in which people live. Such criticisms may come from feminists, postmodernists, communitarians of general persuasion or from those concerned with the specific cultural conditions in which most people in the South live who are sceptical of the relevance of these Rawlsian norms for societies in other parts of the world (for overview, see Gasper, 2004).

Global extension

As indicated above, one of the most powerful determinants of how well or badly development is pursued in countries is the nature of the international framework within which it occurs. Does Rawls's theory of justice provide us with a suitable normative framework for assessing international relations? Rawls's own applications of his basic approach, as we have seen, yield an approach which reflects the internationalist tradition in international relations theory. The three main approaches to international relations are realism (which denies or marginalises the relevance of moral norms), internationalism (which postulates a limited 'morality of states' in which the key actors are states themselves and the moral rules are those that have evolved through custom and agreement) and cosmopolitanism (which postulates the world as one moral domain and critically assesses the state system and what states do within it according to how well they promote or exhibit cosmopolitan values).

Rawls's point of view was part of the internationalist tradition, in that states themselves are parties to the original position at the global level – even in his later *The Law of Peoples* (1999), this state-centred position was still assumed (though it reflects, in parallel to the way internationalist thinking itself has developed, a greater interest in the status of individuals and their rights within the international system).

On the other hand, various authors have taken Rawls's approach and put it to a more robust *cosmopolitan* use. Beitz (1979), for instance, postulated the world as one *society* so Rawls's principles should be applied globally. If we regard all human beings as being parties to a global original position (not state representatives), we would endorse a *global difference principle* – and while the real world is so far removed from one conforming to this principle and so the theory belongs to 'ideal theory', it provides a powerful normative basis for arguing for radical changes in global institutions and practices. Unlike Rawls, who tended to see states as independent of each other and largely self-sufficient, Beitz also saw the major differences of natural resources as morally arbitrary and requiring redistribution – an argument clearly relevant to the development prospects of many countries. Other writers, like Thomas Pogge, have also sought to extend the Rawls's theory of justice in a global cosmopolitan way (Pogge, 1989). Even though Rawls himself does not go down this cosmopolitan route, part of his legacy then is to be found in this kind of cosmopolitan application.

NIGEL DOWER

References

Beitz, C.R. (1979), *Political Theory and International Relations*, Princeton, NJ: Princeton University Press.
Clark, D.A. (2002), *Visions of Development: A Study of Human Values*, Cheltenham, UK and Northampton, MA, USA: Edward Elgar.
Crocker, D. (1992), 'Functioning and capability – the foundations of Sen's and Nussbaum's development ethic', *Political Theory*, **20** (4), 584–612.
Crocker, D. (1995), 'Functioning and capability – the foundations of Sen's and Nussbaum's development ethic, Part 2', in M. Nussbaum and J. Glover (eds), *Women, Culture and Development*, Oxford and New York: Oxford University Press, pp. 153–98.
Gasper, D. (2004), *The Ethics of Development*, Edinburgh Studies in World Ethics, Edinburgh: Edinburgh University Press.
Nozick, R. (1974), *Anarchy, State and Utopia*, Oxford: Blackwell.
Nussbaum, M. (2000), *Women and Development: The Capabilities Approach*, Cambridge: Cambridge University Press.
Pogge, T. (1989), *Realizing Rawls*, Ithaca, NY: Cornell University Press.
Rawls, J. (1971), *A Theory of Justice*, Oxford: Oxford University Press.
Rawls, J. (1993), *Political Liberalism*, New York: Columbia University Press.
Rawls, J. (1999), *The Law of Peoples*, Harvard, MA: Harvard University Press.
Sen, A. (1999), *Development as Freedom*, Oxford: Oxford University Press.

Refugees

According to the United Nations Convention relating to the Status of Refugees (1951), a refugee is someone who is: 'outside his own country, owing to a well-founded fear of persecution, for reasons of race, religion, nationality, membership of a particular social group, or political opinion'. There are regional variations on this basic formula, and it has been criticised as being out of date; yet it remains the most commonly accepted definition. The majority of the world's 10 million or so refugees are currently located in the less-developed world: including some 3 million in Africa and another 3 million in Asia (UNHCR, 2003).

The literature on links between 'refugees' and 'development' has tended to focus on three specific interactions. The first is the link between development – or lack of development – and displacement. The second is the developmental impacts of refugees in host countries. And the third is the implications for development in their home country of the return of refugees.

There is considerable debate about the extent to which there is a link between refugee displacement and poverty or underdevelopment in their home country. In 1995 the Office of the United Nations High Commissioner for Refugees (UNHCR) conducted a basic analysis comparing refugee numbers and development indicators (UNHCR, 1995). It was found that the countries with the highest ranking on the Human Development Index (HDI) were least likely to experience population displacements, whereas those with the lowest ranking had the highest propensity to generate large movements of refugees. The same broad correlation remains true today.

What is difficult, however, is to establish a causal relationship. Many poor countries have not generated refugees – Tanzania is a good example. Conversely, some wealthier countries have, and the best recent example is in the former Yugoslavia. Furthermore, many recent refugee movements have been provoked by events such as conflicts, which are not necessarily directly linked with economic development – the Soviet intervention in Afghanistan is an example. Furthermore, the 1951 Convention definition of a refugee clearly excludes people who have fled their home country primarily for economic reasons.

An alternative approach to the link between development and displacement focuses on 'development-induced displacement', particularly in the context of dam construction. In such development schemes, planned reservoir areas can necessitate the relocation of entire settlements. The scale of these displacements is hard to assess, but it was estimated that in the decade up to 1995 over 100 million people were affected (Cernea, 1995). Recent examples include: the construction of the Almatti dam on the Upper Krishna river in India, which has displaced about 240 000 people; the Shuikou and Yantan dams in China which have respectively displaced about 70 000 and 45 000 people; and the Kedung Ombo dam in Indonesia which displaced about 25 000 people (Picciotto et al., 2001). Particular controversy surrounds the ongoing construction of the Three Gorges dam on the Yangtze River in China. It is estimated that this project will lead to the inundation of two cities, 140 towns and 1350 villages, and necessitate the resettlement of over one million people.

Two main debates surround these displacements. First, the vast majority are internal and not international – and so they do not strictly fit the definition of a refugee as being 'outside his own country'. A second, associated debate concerns to what extent such displacements fit the 'persecution' criteria of the 1951 Convention. The distinction is important, because there are significant implications for the assistance of these displacees. In principle, where displacement is internal, the state should assist resettlement – in reality, the World Bank often contributes. If they are really refugees, then they fall under the institutional responsibility of the Office of the UNHCR. It is worth noting, nevertheless, that development-induced displacement presents challenges that are very similar to those presented by conventional refugee displacement, including income restoration, rebuilding social infrastructures and managing relations between the displacees and host communities.

The second main focus of literature considering interactions between refugees and development focuses on the developmental implications of refugees in host countries. It is often assumed that refugees have a negative impact, and there is a particular focus in the literature on the environmental impacts of refugees (Black, 1998). Refugees often need wood for cooking and construction, and significant deforestation can occur around their settlements, resulting in the longer term in deteriorating soil quality. The water table may also be lowered and groundwater polluted. The potentially negative impact on the environment has been cited recently by several countries (for example, Honduras, Pakistan and Turkey) as one reason to turn away refugees. In this light, it is important to place the environmental impact of refugees in proper context. It varies according to the number of refugees and the length of time they stay. It is likely to be more severe where they settle on marginal land, where they live in camps rather than within local settlements, and where their movement is restricted. And recent evidence suggests that even where environments are damaged, they can recover quickly once refugees have gone home.

A more limited literature considers various other impacts that refugees can have. Their receipt of aid means that they can sometimes undercut the wage rates of local people, thus introducing an element of competition, which benefits some and disadvantages others within the local community. Social tensions can arise between refugees and the local community. Sometimes refugee camps can also become the focus for political activities. Once again it is important to place such impacts in their proper context, and to note that they vary according to a whole range of factors associated both with the refugees and with the local community.

Perhaps the clearest examples of a positive impact of refugee settlement were the 'integrated zonal developments' that emerged in several East African countries during the 1960s and 1970s. Rural refugee settlements were planned and deliberately integrated into the local economy, and in some cases they formed the focus for the growth of new villages and even towns. The reasons these developments succeeded were first that there were relatively few refugees involved, and second that host governments had a largely positive attitude towards them.

The final interaction to consider is the implications for development at home of the return of refugees. The first thing to bear in mind, however, is that refugees often return to countries that have been affected for long periods of time by conflict (for example, Afghanistan or Mozambique), and in this context it may be premature to talk of development at least in the short term. It also needs to be noted that there is a significant shortage of research on what happens to refugees after they return – at least in part because they are no longer considered 'problematic' and no longer fall under the institutional responsibility of any international organisation.

The limited literature, nevertheless, indicates that return can pose significant obstacles for refugees (Black and Koser, 1999). Recurrent physical problems include the presence of land mines and the destruction of housing. Economic activity largely depends on access to key resources such as land, labour, working capital and skills. And social confrontation can often arise in the context of the reintegration of returnees with the internally displaced, with those who never fled, and also with demobilised soldiers.

One of the most important variables that can influence the reintegration process is conditions in refugee settlements in exile, and specifically the extent to which refugees have been allowed to gain a degree of self-reliance. Other variables include the type and management of settlements for returnees and the extent and type of assistance made available to them.

A recent extension of the literature considering the links between refugee return and development at home focuses on situations where refugees do not return, but instead remain in host countries permanently and form a 'refugee diaspora' (Al-Ali et al., 2001). It needs to be acknowledged straight away that this probably only applies to that very small percentage of refugees who move long distances and settle in richer countries. Despite their small numbers, they can nevertheless have significant impacts on development at home. Research among Bosnian and Eritrean refugees in several European countries demonstrated that they could participate in a range of activities which benefit their home country. They can send home remittances and invest in land or property. They can participate in elections from abroad. And they can contribute to intellectual debate via the internet. Clearly, however, the desire and ability of refugees to contribute in these sorts of ways vary over time, and cannot always be taken for granted.

KHALID KOSER

References

Al-Ali, N., R. Black and K. Koser (2001), 'Refugees and transnationalism: the experience of Bosnians and Eritreans in Europe', *Journal of Ethnic and Migration Studies*, **27** (4), 615–34.

Black, R. (1998), *Refugees, Environment and Development*, London: Longman.

Black, R. and K. Koser (eds) (1999), *The End of the Refugee Cycle? Refugee Repatriation and Reconstruction*, Oxford: Berghahn.

Cernea, M. (1995), 'Understanding and preventing impoverishment from displacement: reflections on the state of knowledge', *Journal of Refugee Studies*, **8** (3), 245–64.

Picciotto, R., W. van Wicklin and E. Rice (2001), *Involuntary Resettlement: Comparative Perspectives*, New Brunswick, NJ: Transaction.

UNHCR (1995), *The State of the World's Refugees: In Search of Solutions*, Oxford: Oxford University Press.

UNHCR (2003), *Global Refugee Trends*, Geneva: UNHCR.

Religion and Development

Religion is no panacea, but aspects of it can complement as well as motivate development. It can also obstruct or undermine. The avenues by which religion influences development activities in different faiths and regions are haunting in their complexity. The literature is likewise rich and varied. Religious people and institutions may be agents of advocacy, funding, innovation, empowerment, social movements and service delivery. Equally, religious people and institutions can incite violence, model hierarchy, oppose empowerment (women should stay at home); deflect advocacy (we care about the next life); absorb funding (build a new hall of worship); and cast aspersions on service delivery (they are trying to convert you). A further complication: the gusto of development experts who resonate with religion is enthusiastically matched by the repugnance of those who revile it.

To scan busy contemporary intersections between religion and development is to neglect the long and varied historical associations and literatures. As Amartya Sen points out, Ashoka, a convert to Buddhism in the third century BC, explicitly championed religious tolerance – as indeed did Moghul Emperor Akbar in a Muslim state nearly two millennia later (while the Christian Inquisition was in full swing) (Sen, 1999, p. 236). Bartolomé de las Casas, a fifteenth/sixteenth century Dominican friar and Spanish missionary to Latin America, wrote in defence of indigenous persons' rights to self-determination. Abdullahi An-Naim reminds us that Mahatma Gandhi's 'secular' India intended to draw upon and incorporate spiritual insights rather than sideline them (Terchek, 1998; Anheier et al., 2003, pp. 59–61). Many less-salutary writings and incidents could also be mentioned. The point is that religion and development have often been intimately interwoven (for good or ill).

Contemporary intersections between religion and development can be examined and mapped from a variety of perspectives, which inevitably overlap to some degree.

Intrinsic value

Religious faith may open an independent route to serenity and meaning whether one is in prison or in penury, or suffering illness or exclusion or bereavement or other troubles. Thus religion may contribute directly to a person's flourishing or contentedness, and comprise an intrinsically valued dimension of human well-being (Clark, 2002, p. 124 and table I.1; Clark and Qizilbash, 2002, table 4). Attention has been indirectly drawn to this facet of religion (among other forces) by Amartya Sen, who notes that instead of grumbling, many of the extreme poor have reconciled themselves with their lot and seem 'grateful for small mercies'. While Sen regards such unnatural happiness to be a momentous achievement, he points out that their happiness is a poor indicator of their quality of life in other respects. Still, as Aquinas and the Aristotelian tradition among others show, religious practices stand alongside and complement other aspects of human flourishing that are intrinsically valued – such as safety, health, knowledge, meaningful work and play, self-direction, culture and the like (Finnis, 1998; Alkire, 2002a, b).

The contribution of religion to happiness is empirically studied within psychology (for example, Argyle, 1999) but in 'participatory' and 'multidimensional' development initiatives the religious factor also arises. For example, the *Voices of the Poor* study by the World Bank, which synthesised conceptions of well-being articulated by approximately 60 000 people in 60 countries, who consider themselves to be poor and are so considered by their community, found that 'harmony' with transcendent matters (which might include a spiritual life and religious observance) was regularly considered to be part of well-being (Narayan et al., 2000a, b; Alkire, 2002b). If development aims to expand the freedoms people value and have reason to value, and if religion is so valued, then religious freedoms should be part of development (alongside tolerance and democratic practices), as the 2004 *Human Development Report* argued (UNDP, 2004).

Vision of development

Visions of development from faith perspectives may differ significantly from economic development. As Goulet wrote, to religious groups, development experts may seem like 'one-eyed giants' who 'analyse, prescribe and act *as if* man could live by bread alone, *as if* human destiny could be stripped to its material dimensions alone' (Goulet, 1980, p. 481, original emphasis; Ryan, 1995). For example, Seyyed Hussein Nasr's writings critically evaluate modernisation and development with respect to the extent to which it distracts Muslims from their true nature, or enables them to live out their true purposes better (Nasr, 1975, 1997; Akhtar, 1991). The Roman Catholic social teachings, in particular those since *Populorum Progressio*, articulate a faith-based view of development in which the contributions of spiritual disciplines and of ethical action to a person's 'vocation to human fulfilment' are addressed alongside contributions made by markets, public policy and poverty reduction (*Populorum Progressio*, 1967; see also Lebret, 1965; Beckmann, 1981; *Solicitudo Rei Socialis*, 1987; *Centesimus Annus*, 1991; *Veritatis Splendor*, 1993; Reed, 2001).

Further visions of development arise in the liberation theologies, which criticise structural injustice and call for greater religious engagement in political and economic institutions to ensure equitable development processes. While these began with the publication of Gustavo Gutiérrez's *Theology of Liberation*, distinct liberation theologies have emerged on other major faiths (Gutiérrez, 1973; Phongphit, 1988; Akhtar, 1991; Queen and King, 1996; Rowland, 1999). Popular books also explicate development to the faithful – such as Bernardo Kliksberg's *Social Justice: A Jewish Perspective* (2003) or Buddhist Sulak Sivaraksa and Tom Ginsburg's *Seeds of Peace* (1992). From the interfaith perspective, fora such as the World Faiths Development Dialogue (WFDD) have mapped areas of convergence among the faiths' development agendas – relating to relationships of service and solidarity, harmony with the earth, and the vital but limited contribution of material progress (WFDD, 1999; Harper, 2000; Kumar, 2003). Obviously religious and secular ethical approaches to development also have strong commonalities – some of which have also been explored (Daly, 1996; Iguiñez, 2003).

Born-again and Pentecostal forms of Christianity and fundamentalist forms of Islam and Hinduism, which are also on the ascendant, hold yet other visions of development, which tend to emphasise the protection and promotion of the virtuous individual and family through behaviours of sobriety, industry and self-discipline. Pentecostal Christian leaders tend to be dismissive about the state's ability to introduce meaningful change and often advocate liberation through micro enterprise or penny capitalism. They contrast religious visions with 'the world' (with its wasteful demands or spiritually suspect traditions). They would also stress individual responsibility and decision making based on religious principles, even if these upset traditional obligations to family and community (Meyer, 2004; Robbins, 2004).

Resurgent religion
Many had argued that religion would decline with the advent of secular development (Berger, 1999). Instead, religion has arguably surged in numbers as well as visibility, with conservative branches of all religions and religious political parties (such as, temporarily, the Hindutva in India) being particularly ascendant. For example, over the last 100 years, 'the share of the world's population that is Muslim has risen from 12.5 per cent to 20 per cent' (Anheier et al., 2003, pp. 154–5). Jenkins predicts that in 2050, the ratio of Christians to Muslims will be three to two (with 34 per cent of the world being Christian), but by then most Christians would live in Africa and Latin America (2002). Even in countries with low religious attendance and high levels of economic development such as the United States and Switzerland, studies indicate that people still have strong religious beliefs – they just spend less time on them (Iannaccone, 1998; Barro and McCleary, 2003). Such findings have given rise to a vigorous set of studies on the changes of religious values as economies develop – many of which have been able to make use of substantial new data sets on religious affiliation and beliefs (Inglehart et al., 1998; Jenkins, 2002; Esposito and Bourgat, 2003). Pragmatically, it has also underlined the need for the engagement between religion and development to be enduring.

Faith-based organisations
Moving to more practical matters, local, national and international faith-based organisations (FBOs – organisations whose motivation or funding sources derive partly from their faith) are, in some areas, significant purveyors of education, service delivery and

other non-market goods. They may also introduce cultural values. Islamic Relief, Catholic Relief Services, the Aga Khan Development Network and others deliver significant resources. The Christian evangelical development agency World Vision, with a 2003 cash budget of $819 million, plus $431 million in-kind contributions, is among the largest and more studied of such international NGOs (Myers, 1999; Tripp, 1999; Whaites, 1999; and Bornstein, 2002). The economic views of these organisations are quite varied. For some the provision of social services by such private organisations is consistent with neoliberal agendas that would prefer to see the state shrink; other FBOs pose structural challenges and demand greater political responsiveness to social ills.

By far the greatest number of FBOs are local or national. One famous example is the Sarvodaya Shramadana Movement in Sri Lanka, founded by A.T. Ariyaratne in the 1950s, which awakened members to their inner person, and urged them then to change outer structures by common activities such as volunteer work camps – with the famous slogan 'We build the road and the road builds us' (Zadek and Szabo, 1994; Lean, 1995; Tyndale, 2003). In some cases religious institutions also deliver services directly; for example, religious schools may be subsidised and run directly by churches or monasteries and convents. Some government programmes are also faith based – for the separation of religion and state that is apparent in most industrialised countries is less stark in many developing countries (Barro and McCleary, 2004).

The prevalence of FBOs has led to their scrutiny by development institutions but the literature is widely dispersed. Most are case studies with respect to a particular sector or region or organisation (*World Development*, 1980, **8** (7–8); Lean, 1995; Belshaw et al., 2001; *Development*, 2003, **46** (4); Marshall and Keough, 2004). Some are country-wide – such as World Bank findings that for the poor 'in Benin, church-affiliated organizations represent the most prominent and effective protection network' (Kliksberg, 2003, p. 58; Narayan et al., 2000b, pp. 104–5) or that in Malawi 'in the mid-1970s, it is claimed that the annual budget of a prominent ecumenical organisation, the *Christian Service Committee of the Churches of Malawi*, was 1.5 times the size of the entire government allocation for development' (WFDD, 2003, p. 2). The World Bank's *World Development Report 2004: Making Services Work for Poor People* refers frequently to religious schools and organisations as existing delivery mechanisms for essential services.

Religious professionals

The possible impact of religious beliefs on economic behaviour has been the subject of empirical study since Max Weber (1930) at least and has seen resurgence in the 1990s. Staff in secular organisations and governments may be motivated in part by religion, and see their engagement with development as an outgrowth of their values. In some cases, their beliefs may impact their professional behaviour. A study of religious healthcare NGOs in Uganda found that despite being paid lower wages, staff of religious not-for-profit organisations were more likely to charge less, and to use additional funding to decrease fees and increase services, rather than to raise their own salaries. Thus the paper concludes that staff seem partly driven by altruistic concerns, and that such behaviours quantitatively improve their performance (Reinikka and Svensson, 2003). In any institution (religious or secular), religious professionals may also stress the need for respect and dignity among staff and partners and thus an alternative *process* of collaboration (Myers, 1999). Thus faith may have an instrumental impact because people remain motivated although they witness imperfect progress. Indeed, one of Gandhi's reasons for cultivating theism was pragmatic: that it sustains persons in times of failure (Shri Ramaswamy's conversation as recorded by Shri Pyarelal).

The recognition of human imperfection may be the most distinctive and understudied feature of religions. While many approaches to development implicitly attribute human misbehaviour to misunderstanding, or to a lack of education, or to perverse incentives, religious professionals and the groups they animate calmly acknowledge human evil, error and weakness of will, and have structured avenues for expressing regret – and forgiveness – among a community as well as before a deity.

Global encounters

Intersections between poverty-focused development agencies and religious individuals and institutions are also increasingly active. For example, in 1998 James Wolfensohn, president of the World Bank and then-Archbishop of Canterbury George Carey founded a 'World Faiths Development Dialogue' to promote dialogue between religious groups, and between the World Bank and IMF and religious groups. It has supported case studies, and organised publications and workshops with faith and development leaders, on themes of the World Development Reports, on poverty reduction strategy papers (PRSPs) and, in 2002, on the Millennium Development Goals (MDGs) (Marshall and Marsh, 2003; www.wfdd.org.uk). Other fora include the Inter-American Development Bank's initiative on Social Capital, Ethics and Development (www.iadb.org/etica), the World Council of Churches Dialogues with the ILO, the UN, the IMF and the World Bank, and UNFPA's (the United Nations Population Fund) ongoing dialogue with faith leaders.

Religion versus development

Religion may become a practical problem when religious leaders or institutions obstruct development or view it as a threat because it promotes Western liberal secular culture and human rights, or when religious rhetoric is a veneer for other motives. Classic issues of value conflict surround family-planning methods such as contraception and abortion, HIV/AIDS prevention and implicit messages related to sexual morality and women's empowerment; other issues might relate to secularism, sacred sites, dress, or tolerance of outside groups. In development such values and practices may be addressed under the label of 'culture' (Verhelst, 1990; Haverkort et al., 2003; Walton and Rao, 2004). Organisations such as the United Nations Population Fund have actively cultivated respectful modes of cooperation with faith leaders and international religious institutions (UNFPA, 2004; UNDP, 2004). Cooperation with donor countries must also navigate religious values. For example, by 2004 the popularity of the ABC (Abstinence, Being Faithful, Condoms) approach to HIV/AIDS prevention threatened US funding for condoms.

Given that patriarchy is engrained in the cultural forms of many world religions, a separate literature has developed on women and religion. Many topics may relate not to development itself but rather to sexuality, prayer, family life or violence. However, an active interface occurs between religious groups and 'gender and development' agendas such as women's empowerment, reproductive health, education or personal security.

This interface is expressed in meetings as well as literature that draws attention to oppressive or theologically disputable practices towards women, and also to devout women in positions of leadership (Howland, 2001; Ahmed, 2002; Balchin, 2003).

Religious forces in civil society

Another literature addresses religion as a critical factor in civil society support for development priorities. The *Global Civil Society Yearbook* 2004/5 argues:

> There is no way we can understand the logic, strategies and dynamics of civil society anywhere in the Third World unless we bring the transcendental dimension back into our analysis. Religious devotion is a fundamental motive for many social movements in the South, from Latin America to Africa and South Asia. (Anheier et al., 2004/5, p. 45; see also Casanova, 1994; Smith, 1996; Mandaville, 2001; Romero, 2001)

Political and social movements and advocacy campaigns have often drawn upon religious motivations and the support of religious leaders. The churches' mobilisation in support of the anti-apartheid campaign and the Jubilee campaign for debt forgiveness was arguably central to their political visibility. And in Latin America, churches mobilised in support of literacy (Archer and Costello, 1990). In so far as political parties set development agendas that can be exclusive or equity enhancing, the religious influence on political movements is also important. In India, the rise of Hindu nationalism has been linked to the televised Hindu epic series *Ramayana* (Rajagopal, 2001). Religious regimes and parties influence development priorities to some extent. The international MDG campaigns are actively collaborating with faith groups to mobilise the faithful for advocacy and non-violent symbolic actions.

Religious extremism

However benevolent and indeed inspiring some religious expressions may be, development is regularly stymied by conflict and violence – some of which is caused by religious groups (or groups with a religious veneer). An enormous literature has emerged, and gained further momentum after 11 September, on religious contributions to conflict and violence (for example, Armstrong, 2000; Juergensmeyer, 2000). Whether in Sri Lanka or Central Asia and Chechnya, the Middle East or Gujarat, or Bosnia or Southern Africa, armed groups have claimed religious support for their endeavours. Given that conflict both causes and exacerbates poverty, and interrupts development, careful attention needs to be paid to the possible negative consequences of cooperation with religious groups.

Conclusion

Much literature on religion (or faith, or spirituality) and development remains diverse and unconsolidated. Some development publications or collections address religious topics with the air of discovery, and do not refer to previous literature, or to the much more consistent attention that religious groups have paid to development processes. Thus far religious influence on development has not been a primary topic of any international report on world development, health, trade, children, food insecurity, water, refugees, least developed countries, or population, although it has received occasional mention. Religious themes did achieve prominence in the 2004 Human Development Report on Cultural

Liberty, and special issues in *World Development* (1980, vol. 8, no. 4), *Gender and Development* (1999, vol. 7, no. 1), *Daedalus* (2001, vol. 130, no. 4), *Journal of Urban History* (2002, vol. 28, no. 4) and *Development* (2003, vol. 46, no. 4) address religion and development-related issues.

Part of the difficulty arises from fuzzy boundaries: religion cannot be tidily isolated from other factors at work within and among people and groups (Maxwell, 1999). Perhaps the very best writings on religion and development are deeply local historical, anthropological, economic, missiological or sociological studies in which religion takes its place alongside other variables, and in which a much more nuanced account of inter-actions is allowed to emerge than has been possible in this brief sketch.

SABINA ALKIRE

References

Ahmed, Durre S. (ed.) (2002), *Gendering the Spirit: Women and Religion and the Post Colonial Response*, London: Zed Books.

Akhtar, Shabbir (1991), *The Final Imperative: An Islamic Theology of Liberation*, London: Bellew.

Alkire, Sabina (2002a), *Valuing Freedoms: Sen's Capability Approach and Poverty Reduction*, Oxford: Oxford University Press.

Alkire, Sabina (2002b), 'Dimensions of human development', *World Development*, **30** (2), 181–205.

Anheier, Helmut, Marlies Glasius and Mary Kaldor (eds) (2003), *Global Civil Society Yearbook*, London: Oxford University Press.

Anheier, Helmut, Marlies Glasius and Mary Kaldor (eds) (2004/5), *Global Civil Society Yearbook*, London: Sage.

Archer, David and Patrick Costello (1990), *Literacy and Power: The Latin American Battleground*, London: Earthscan.

Argyle, M. (1999), 'Causes and correlates of happiness', in D. Kahneman, E. Diener and N. Schwarz (eds), *Well-Being: The Foundations of Hedonic Psychology*, New York: Russell Sage Foundation, pp. 353–73.

Armstrong, Karen (2000), *The Battle for God*, New York: Knopf.

Balchin, Cassandra (2003), 'With her feet on the ground: women, religion and development in Muslim com-munities', *Development*, **46** (4), 39–49.

Barro, Robert and Rachel McCleary (2003), 'Religion and economic growth across countries', *American Sociological Review*, **68** (5), 760–81.

Barro, Robert and Rachel McCleary (2004), 'Which countries have state religions?', mimeo, Harvard University, Cambridge, MA.

Beckmann, David M. (1981), *Where Faith and Economics Meet: A Christian Critique*, Minneapolis, MN: Augsburg.

Belshaw, Deryke, Robert Calderisi and Chris Sugden (eds) (2001), *Faith in Development: Partnership between the World Bank and the Churches of Africa*, Oxford: Regnum Books/World Bank.

Berger, Peter L. (ed.) (1999), *The Desecularization of the World: Resurgent Religion and World Politics*, Grand Rapids, MI: William B. Eerdmans.

Bornstein, Erica (2002), 'Developing faith: theologies of economic development in Zimbabwe', *Journal of Religion in Africa*, **32** (1), 4–32.

Casanova, José (1994), *Public Religions in the Modern World*, Chicago: University of Chicago Press.

Clark, David A. (2002), *Visions of Development: A Study of Human Values*, Cheltenham, UK and Northampton, MA, USA: Edward Elgar.

Clark, David A. and Mozaffar Qizilbash (2002), 'Core poverty and extreme vulnerability in South Africa', Discussion Paper no. 2002-3, School of Economic and Social Studies, University of East Anglia, Norwich.

Daly, Herman (1996), *Beyond Growth: The Economics of Sustainable Development*, Boston, MA: Beacon Press.

Esposito, John and François Bourgat (eds) (2003), *Modernizing Islam: Religion in the Public Sphere in Europe and the Middle East*, New Brunswick, NJ: Rutgers University Press.

Finnis, John (1998), *Aquinas: Moral, Political, and Legal Theory*, Oxford: Oxford University Press.

Goulet, Dennis (1980), 'Development experts: the one-eyed giants', *World Development*, **8** (7–8), 481–9.

Gutiérrez, Gustavo (1973), *A Theology of Liberation*, Maryknoll, NY: Orbis Books.

Harper, Sharon M.P. (ed.) (2000), *The Lab, the Temple and the Market: Reflections at the Intersection of Science, Religion and Development*, Bloomfield, CT: Kumarian Press/IDRC/CRDI.

Haverkort, Bertus, Katrien van't Hooft and Wim Hiemstra (eds) (2003), *Ancient Roots, New Shoots: Endogenous Development in Practice*, London: Zed Books/COMPAS.

Howland, Courtney (2001), *Religious Fundamentalisms and the Human Rights of Women*, New York: Palgrave-Macmillan.

Iannaccone, L.R. (1998), 'Introduction to the economics of religion', *Journal of Economic Literature*, **36** (3), 1465–95.

Iguiñez Echeverría, Javier (2003), *Desarrollo, Libertad y Liberación en Amartya Sen y Gustavo Gutiérrez* (Development, liberty and liberation in Amartya Sen and Gustavo Gutiérrez), Lima: Centro de Estudios y Publicaciones, IBC.

Inglehart, R., M. Basáñez and A. Menéndez Moreno (1998), *Human Values and Beliefs: A Cross-cultural Sourcebook*, Ann Arbor, MI: University of Michigan Press.

Jenkins, Philip (2002), *The Next Christendom: The Coming of Global Christianity*, Oxford and New York: Oxford University Press.

Juergensmeyer, M. (2000), *Terror in the Mind of God: The Global Rise of Religious Violence*, Berkeley, CA: University of California Press.

Kliksberg, Bernardo (2003), *Social Justice: A Jewish Perspective*, Jerusalem: Gefen.

Kumar, Satish (2003), 'Development and religion: cultivating a sense of the sacred', *Development*, **46** (4), 15–21.

Lean, Mary (1995), *Bread, Bricks, Belief: Communities in Charge of their Future*, Bloomfield, CT: Kumarian Press.

Lebret, L.J. (1965), *The Last Revolution: The Destiny of Over- and Underdeveloped Nations*, translated by J. Horgan, Dublin and Melbourne: Gill & Son.

Mandaville, P. (2001), *Transnational Muslim Politics: Reimagining the Umma*, London: Routledge.

Marshall, Katherine and Lucy Keough (2004), *Mind, Heart, and Soul in the Fight Against Poverty*, Washington, DC: World Bank.

Marshall, Katherine and Richard Marsh (eds) (2003), *Millennium Challenges for Development and Faith Institutions*, Washington, DC: World Bank.

Maxwell, David (1999), *Christians and Chiefs in Zimbabwe: A Social History of the Hwesa People c. 1870s–1990s*, Edinburgh: Edinburgh University Press.

Meyer, Birgit (2004), 'Christianity in Africa: from African Independent to Pentecostal–Charismatic churches', *Annual Review of Anthropology*, **33**, 447–74.

Myers, Bryant L. (1999), *Walking with the Poor: Principles and Practices of Transformational Development*, Maryknoll, NY: Orbis/World Vision.

Narayan, Deepa, Robert Chambers, Meera Kaul Shah and Patti Petesch (2000a), *Voices of the Poor: Crying Out for Change*, Oxford and New York: Oxford University Press for the World Bank.

Narayan, Deepa, Raj Patel, Kai Schafft, Ann Rademacher and Sarah Koch-Schulte (2000b), *Voices of the Poor: Can Anyone Hear Us?*, Oxford and New York: Oxford University Press for the World Bank.

Nasr, Seyyed Hossein (1975), *Islam and the Plight of Modern Man*, London: Longman.

Nasr, Seyyed Hossein (1997), *Man and Nature: The Spiritual Crisis of Modern Man*, Chicago: Kazi Publications.

Phongphit, Seri (1988), *Religion in a Changing Society: Buddhism, Reform and the Role of Monks in Community Development in Thailand*, Hong Kong: Arena Press.

Queen, Christopher S. and Sally King (eds) (1996), *Engaged Buddhism: Buddhist Liberation Movements in Asia*, Albany, NY: State University of New York Press.

Rajagopal, Arvind (2001), *Politics after Television: Hindu Nationalism and the Reshaping of the Public in India*, Cambridge: Cambridge University Press.

Reed, Charles (ed.) (2001), *Development Matters: Christian Perspectives on Globalization*, London: Church House.

Reinikka, Ritva and Jakob Svensson (2003), 'Working for God? Evaluating service delivery of religious not-for-profit health care providers in Uganda', Center for Economic Policy and Research Discussion Paper 4214, Washington, DC.

Robbins, Joel (2004), 'The globalization of Pentecostal and Charismatic Christianity', *Annual Review of Anthropology*, **33**, 117–43.

Romero, Catalina (2001), 'Globalization, civil society, and religion from a Latin American standpoint', *Sociology of Religion*, **62** (4), 475–90.

Rowland, C. (ed.) (1999), *The Cambridge Companion to Liberation Theology*, Cambridge: Cambridge University Press.

Ryan, William (1995), *Culture, Spirituality, and Economic Development: Opening a Dialogue*, Ottawa: International Development Research Centre.

Sen, Amartya K. (1999), *Development As Freedom*, New York: Knopf.

Sivaraksa, Sulak and Tom Ginsburg (eds) (1992), *Seeds of Peace: A Buddhist Vision for Renewing Society*, Berkeley, CA: Parallax.

Smith, Christian (1996), *Disruptive Religion: The Force of Faith in Social-Movement Activism*, London: Routledge.

Terchek, R.J. (1998), *Gandhi*, Oxford: Rowman & Littlefield.

Tripp, Linda (1999), 'Gender and development from a Christian perspective: experience from World Vision', *Gender & Development*, **7** (1), 62–8.

Tyndale, Wendy (2003), 'Idealism and practicality: the role of religion in development', *Development*, **46** (4), 22–8.

UNDP (2004), *The Human Development Report*, New York: United Nations Development Programme.

UNFPA (2004), *Culture Matters: Working with Communities and Faith Based Organisations*, New York: UNFPA.

Verhelst, Thierry G. (1990), *No Life Without Roots: Culture and Development*, London: Zed Books.

Walton, Michael and Vijayendra Rao (eds) (2004), *Culture and Public Action: A Cross-Disciplinary Dialogue on Development Policy*, Palo Alto, CA: Stanford University Press.

Weber, Max (1930), *The Protestant Ethic and the Spirit of Capitalism*, translated by T. Parsons, New York: Charles Scribner's Sons.

WFDD (1999), *Poverty and Development: An Inter-Faith Perspective*, Oxford: World Faith Development Dialogue, www.wfdd.org.uk/documents/publications/poverty_development_english.pdf, 3 May 2005.

WFDD (2003), 'The provision of services for poor people: a contribution to the WDR 2004', World Faith Development Dialogue, Oxford, www.wfdd.org.uk/programmes/wdr/WFDDWDR2004.pdf.

Whaites, Alan (1999), 'Pursuing partnership: World Vision and the ideology of development – a case study', *Development in Practice*, **9** (4), 410–24.

World Bank (2003), *The World Development Report 2004: Making Services Work for Poor People*, Oxford: Oxford University Press for the World Bank, Washington, DC.

World Faiths Development Dialogue (WFDD) (2003), 'The provision of services for poor people: a contribution to WDR 2004', mimeo, www.wfdd.org.uk.

Zadek, Simon and Sue Szabo (1994), *Valuing Organisations: The Case of Sarvodaya*, London: New Economics Foundation.

Catholic documents
Centesimus Annus (1991), London: Catholic Truth Society.
Populorum Progressio (1967), New Delhi: St. Paul Publications.
Solicitudo Rei Socialis (1987), Washington, DC: United States Catholic Conference.
Veritatis Splendor (1993), London: Catholic Truth Society.

Rent Seeking and Corruption

Rent seeking and corruption are overlapping phenomena but each includes activities that are not part of the other. Rent seeking is the activity to create, capture or reallocate rents. Rents, in turn, are incomes that are higher than the next best income that an individual or group could earn given their assets. Rents are always based on the protection, change or reallocation of rights, and therefore, access to rents or attempts to change their allocation typically require the support of the state in protecting, changing or reallocating the underlying rights. Rent seeking is the expenditure that individuals undertake to persuade the state to create rents in their favour or to withdraw rents that harm them. Corruption describes all types of illegal activities by public officials in pursuit of their private interests, which could be economic or political. Clearly, some types of corruption are illegal rent seeking where rent seekers bribe officials to get privileged access to resources that are clearly rents. In these cases, corruption *is* illegal rent seeking. But rent seeking can also include perfectly legal expenditures in lobbying, political contributions and other forms of persuading that would not count as corruption in the strict sense. (In the everyday usage of the word, legal influence buying is often also regarded as corruption, but legal rent seeking is strictly not corruption given the definitions of these concepts.) Corruption can also include the theft of assets or incomes by public officials. At first sight, theft by public officials may appear to be different from rent seeking, but these activities are simply more complex cases of rent seeking where public officials themselves spend resources to acquire positions of power that enable them to directly capture rents. Thus, corruption is always a form of illegal rent seeking, but not all rent seeking is necessarily illegal and therefore corrupt.

Analysing 'unproductive' activities has long been an important area of interest for classical political economists and political scientists (see, for instance, Heidenheimer, 1970; Boss, 1990; Heidenheimer and Johnston, 2002). But more recently, these concerns have become the subject of mainstream neoclassical economic analysis, which has argued that *all* rent seeking is unproductive (Krueger, 1974; Bhagwati, 1983). The attack on corruption and other forms of rent seeking has thus become a central plank in programmes of market-enhancing reforms in developing countries. Policies of liberalisation, privatisation and reducing the scope of state intervention are increasingly justified in terms of the difficulty or impossibility of controlling corruption and rent seeking when states intervene, and for most interventions, these activities make the costs associated with the intervention higher than the expected benefit. But this analysis fails to address the policy issue when the underlying rents created by the intervention are socially beneficial, and it also fails to identify some of the most important determinants of corruption and rent seeking in developing countries. In this way, contemporary policy approaches can result in time and resources being wasted in programmes that are unlikely to achieve reductions in corruption or rent seeking. Even worse, by promoting reforms that reduce the ability of the state to create and manage *any* rents, these reforms may paradoxically *reduce* the prospects of development and therefore of achieving lasting reductions in corruption in developing countries.

Rent seeking and corruption
Rents in the modern literature are defined as incomes that are higher than the next best income that an individual or group can earn. The persistence of these incomes signals that property rights have been constrained in some way. This could be because either the right to enter into or exit from some activities are constrained, creating artificial monopolies, or states may directly tax and transfer incomes to some individuals. They may also protect other rights, like property rights over natural resources, and this may allow owners to control usage and maximise their income, which then includes an element of rent. The protection of intellectual property rights that give innovators access to extra profits (Schumpeterian rents) is another example of state activity that protects a specific rent (Khan, 2000a). Clearly, some types of rent can be socially damaging. These include, in particular, some types of monopolies and transfers that result in the net output of society declining. For instance, granting import licences to selected importers for scarce goods can create artificial monopolies that transfer incomes to the monopolists but also lower the net output of society. But other rents can be socially beneficial. Rents that accelerate the acquisition or development of new technologies, or those that induce disproportionately greater effort by their recipients are examples of such rents.

Some recent extensions of neoclassical theory have recognised the necessary and beneficial role of some rents (see in particular Stiglitz, 1994). These advances have pointed out that the *normal* operation of a market economy requires many types of rent. For instance, the discovery of a trade opportunity requires time and effort, and unless the entrepreneur doing the research was rewarded with a rent at the end, the arbitrage would not be worth it. Thus, even at the simplest level, an *efficient* market requires *rents.* The only question is how long they should last in order to have the positive effect, without the negative effect of high prices outweighing the benefit. When we look at examples of more complex but still beneficial rents, like Schumpeterian rents that reward innovators, or 'learning' rents that states can provide to emerging industries in developing countries, very similar issues apply. A reward for an innovator that lasts forever would be wasteful and would prevent imitation and extension of the innovation. On the other hand, if the rent were competed away instantly, there would be no incentive for future innovators. Advanced countries spend a lot of regulatory effort in getting the balance right. There is no neat theoretical answer because the required incentive would depend on the difficulty of innovation in particular sectors and the risk aversion of innovators, but trial and error can gradually make improvements in the management of these rents.

Similar considerations apply in the case of rents or incentives for emerging industries in developing countries. Support from the state that is too generous or unconditional can result in infants that refuse to grow up. On the other hand, no support at all means that developing countries can only produce things they already have a comparative advantage in, and no technological leapfrogging is possible. It is worth remembering that all successful catching-up experiences of the last 50 years have involved different types of rent management by states to induce rapid learning and technology acquisition. The difference between the success stories and the others that did not succeed lay in the details of their rent management and on whether rents could be removed from non-performers (Khan, 2000b). However, while there is a growing body of literature pointing out the importance of beneficial rents and of rent management, the analysis of *rent seeking* almost always assumes that rents are always damaging and take the form of monopoly rents or transfers to special-interest groups. This is a serious shortcoming in the academic and policy literature on rent seeking because it suggests that the appropriate policy response is always to remove the rent. In fact, in many cases, the appropriate response should be to strengthen the capacity of the state to create and manage certain rents. If this could be done properly, society would benefit even in the presence of some amount of rent seeking.

Rent seeking is defined as the use of resources (by rent seekers) to influence or persuade public officials to create, allocate or transfer rents in ways that benefit the rent seekers. Rent seeking takes place because once rents exist, rational individuals will be willing to spend resources, both legally and illegally, to capture, protect or reallocate rents. Legal forms of rent seeking include all legal processes of buying influence, such as lobbying, contributions to political parties, and expenditures on think-tanks and advertising. Illegal forms of rent seeking include corruption where bribes or illegal political contributions are used to buy favours. It can also include violent forms of 'persuasion' by mafias or warlords trying to capture resources from what remains of the state (Krueger, 1974; Buchanan et al., 1980; Bhagwati, 1983; Khan, 2000b provides a critical overview). The analysis of illegal rent seeking thus significantly overlaps with the analysis of corruption. Rent seeking is always a social cost in the sense that these activities do not directly produce any value. If the underlying rent that rent seekers are trying to capture is damaging, there is a double cost, so that the overall cost of rent seeking is significantly negative. On the other hand, if the underlying rent is socially beneficial, the rent seeking may be associated with a process that has an overall social benefit. For instance, if property rights over a natural resource rent are created through a rent-seeking process, the benefit of the eventual natural resource rent *may* outweigh the cost of the rent seeking. Similarly, if the state can manage learning subsidies for technology acquisition in a developing country, the overall effect of the associated rent seeking may be positive. The beneficiaries may still engage in rent seeking to ensure that they continue to get subsidies but if the state can discipline beneficiaries and ensure that technology acquisition is rapid (as in many East Asian developers), the overall effect of the rent-seeking process can be positive for society.

These possibilities do not counter the observation that in many cases, rent seekers seek rents that have no social benefit, and in these cases, rent seeking is unequivocally damaging. In other cases, where the underlying rent is potentially beneficial, the rent seeking process *may* be socially beneficial if the state has the capacity to manage the rent allocation to ensure that its creation and allocation is beneficial, and if the associated rent-seeking cost is low. In reality, the rent-seeking cost and the management and allocation of the rent are interconnected. The organisation of different rent-seeking processes affects not just the resource cost of the rent seeking but also whether the type of rent created and its allocation and management are likely to be socially beneficial. For socially beneficial rent seeking, the rent-seeking process has to be such that socially beneficial rents are created and managed at relatively low rent-seeking cost. While these cases are less common, it does not follow that trying to remove the rent-creation capacities of states across the board will leave societies better off.

Corruption is defined in much of the social science literature as the abuse of public office by officials for their personal benefit (Nye, 1967; Khan, 1996b; World Bank, 1997). Thus, corruption can include illegal rent seeking where a public official accepts a bribe (the rent-seeking expenditure of the bribe giver) to grant a special privilege (the rent). But it can also include theft and extortion by public officials where no benefit is conferred to a private individual as in the more usual cases of rent seeking (Khan, 2004a). However, from an analytical perspective, even extortion or theft is a variant of rent seeking. The incomes or assets seized by the public official are like rents that are captured by the official. To be able to capture these rents, these officials have to spend resources on maintaining their positions, buying supporters or militias, and these are the equivalent of rent-seeking expenditures. The distinguishing feature of corruption is that the rent created, or the rent-seeking expenditure or both are illegal.

It is tempting to conclude that illegal rent seeking is more damaging than legal rent seeking, but this is not always the case. Legal arrangements do not necessarily reflect social costs and benefits. The creation of some beneficial rents may be illegal. For instance, the creation of property rights over natural resources may not be legally possible in some contexts, and in these cases, corruption may allow the creation of *de facto* if not *de jure* rights (and the associated rents) so that economic efficiency can be achieved. This is a different point from the one made by Leff (1964) who had argued that corruption could be efficient in developing countries. In that argument, the assumption is that the state has the prior ability to create artificial restrictions and damaging rents, so that some corruption may be a second-best way of getting around these restrictions. For instance, if the state has the power to insist on a staggering amount of red tape and form filling that performs no function, corruption can speed up business and allow investments to take place. But in this case, society would be even better off without the damaging rent or restriction in the first place, so that the corruption is not necessary to work around these restrictions. On the other hand, some legal rents and forms of rent seeking may also be very damaging. So it is by no means clear that legal rent seeking does not have damaging consequences, or that illegal rent seeking always is damaging. It is therefore necessary to analyse the types of rent and the extent of rent-seeking costs in the case of both legal and illegal rent seeking before judging their economic impact. However, in one respect corruption does have effects that are quite different from legal rent seeking. Corruption can corrode confidence in the legitimacy of the state and its officials, and extensive corruption that is unchecked for too long can have serious political costs for society.

Note that the social science definition of corruption is considerably narrower than the everyday understanding of the term. First, corruption is defined in such a way that its analysis does not involve moral judgements about the act. This is an advantage, since if corruption is defined as acts that are 'morally wrong', this would result in different acts being identified as corrupt according to different moral standards. For instance, a public official who gives a job to a nephew to maintain his status in his clan would not be considered corrupt if it was thought to be a moral duty to support one's extended family. But it would be corrupt according to the definition here as long as formal rules of conduct for public officials in that country ruled out such acts. There is, of course, the possibility that there may be differences in legal or formal rules of public conduct across countries but, in general, in virtually every country, rules of public conduct do not allow the acceptance of bribes, nepotistic allocations of resources or diversions of public resources for economic or political benefit. This makes it easier to identify corruption without entering into debates about the appropriate moral standards to use. Nevertheless, in everyday usage, people do make moral judgements when discussing corruption, and the difference between the everyday sense of corruption and the definition that is widely used in economic and social analysis needs to be kept in mind. However, there are significant differences between countries in the types of rents that states can legally create, and the rent-seeking expenditures that are legally allowed. This is particularly true between developed and developing countries. In the former, a much greater range of rent seeking has been legalised and is regulated, and this is one important factor explaining the lower incidence of corruption in advanced countries.

Second, corruption is deliberately defined as a *process* rather than identified based on its *outcome*. If corruption were to be defined to include only acts that have damaging *outcomes* for the public, then this would rule out cases where a process was corrupt but its overall effects were neutral or even positive. But, once again, in common usage, corruption is often used to describe actions by public officials that are against the 'public interest', whether or not any rules of conduct are violated; while actions where rules *are* violated but the 'public' does not suffer (or even benefits) are often not described as corrupt. Once again, the difference between everyday conceptions of corruption and its definition in economics and social analysis needs to be kept in mind.

Finally, this definition of corruption places public officials at the centre of the analysis. According to this definition, corruption does not take place if public officials are not involved and, in this sense, corruption is simply a lens through which to examine illegal rent seeking. But in common usage, corruption can refer to reprehensible behaviour by anyone, including interactions exclusively between private individuals or agents. But according to the social science definition, if a private person steals from another, that is *theft*, not *corruption*. Only in the case of theft by public officials is corruption involved. Note that using the social science definition does not imply that illegal acts by public officials are more serious than the illegal acts of private individuals, only that the focus of corruption analysis is on the functioning of the state.

None the less, there are important grey areas that we need to keep in mind. If a small shopkeeper gives a job to a relative without following proper procedures, or charges a fee for providing the job, these acts would very likely be described as nepotism or extortion rather than corruption even in common usage, and here common usage conforms to the economist's definition. But, if the chief executive of a large quoted company did the same thing, this would be commonly described as corruption, and would very likely be treated in the literature on corruption as a corrupt act. This is because many authors treat private sector executives in important economic positions as having semi-public roles. But a more consistent position would be to argue that their activities are regulated by the state so that theft, extortion or fraud by executives in important private sector positions often involves either a failure of public governance, or direct corruption and collusion by public officials.

Limitations of the conventional analysis of rent seeking and corruption

The analysis of rent seeking that emerged with the work of Tullock (1967) and Krueger (1974), soon became an important part of the neoclassical 'counterrevolution' (Toye, 1987) which from the 1970s onwards began to make a concerted case for liberalisation and a radical reduction in the role of the state. The rent-seeking analysis hoped to establish that the cost of state intervention was potentially much greater than the costs identified by conventional neoclassical economics. The previous neoclassical analysis had focused on the deadweight welfare losses that followed from state interventions that created monopolies, restricted market access or transferred incomes to special-interest groups. But the problem for a thoroughgoing critique of the state was that these deadweight losses were arithmetically very small and could not justify a significant rolling back of the state (Posner, 1975).

Rent-seeking theory came to the rescue of the neoliberal reform agenda by pointing out an additional cost of state intervention. It pointed out that any state that creates rents would induce rent-seeking expenditures by individuals hoping to capture these rents. The contribution of the early rent-seeking theorists was to show that under plausible assumptions, this rent-seeking expenditure could be as big as or bigger than the rent that the state intervention inevitably created. If this were true, and if all of this expenditure was a social waste, say because it amounted to a withdrawal of resources from productive investment, then the cost of state intervention would indeed be prohibitive. It would certainly be many times greater than the deadweight losses identified by earlier theory. The policy conclusion was that a competitive market with a minimal state was not just efficient in its own terms; it was also necessary to minimise the state failure associated with high rent-seeking costs.

A very similar analysis developed with respect to corruption, the illegal variant of rent seeking. As in the rest of the emerging rent-seeking theory, it was assumed that corruption would always result in the creation, protection and allocation of *damaging* rents (such as monopolies, contracts to inefficient contractors, or the protection of inefficient industries), *and* it would result in the waste of resources that would be used up in organising and giving bribes. The dual effect of corruption would thus add up to a significant decline in investment and the inefficient allocation of investible resources (Shleifer and Vishny, 1993; Mauro, 1995, 1997; Tullock, 1996). Cross-country evidence seemed to support these claims because countries with a higher corruption index (as measured by the perception of people in that country) tended to have lower growth and investment rates (Mauro, 1995; Knack and Keefer, 1997; Hall and Jones, 1999).

While the new analysis of rent seeking and corruption did add valuable insights, it suffered from serious shortcomings. The rent-seeking approach assumed that there was a 'normal' structure of property rights that did not, or should not, cost anything to maintain. Only 'artificial' rights newly created or transferred by states (such as monopoly rents or subsidies) were subject to rent-seeking expenditures. But it was soon pointed out that this distinction is itself artificial (Samuels and Mercuro, 1984). Societies spend vast amounts to protect, legitimise and restructure rights over assets and incomes, whether already existing or newly created. These expenditures can be justified if the underlying rights are essential for economic growth and political stability. Exactly the same analysis could be applied to the interventions that create, protect or restructure the rights sustaining rents. While some rents destroy value and reduce social stability, others can add to social output or change distribution in ways that enhance a society's stability and viability (Khan, 2000a). The rent-seeking expenditure, too, can be large or small depending on the institutional and political structure in which the rent seeking is taking place (Congleton, 1980; Shleifer and Vishny, 1993; Khan, 2000b). The rent-seeking expenditure is likely to be large only when the political competition over rents is completely unconstrained. In reality, the political competition for rents is always constrained to some extent, and the more regulated it is, the less likely that the rent-seeking cost will be great enough to wipe out the potential benefit of many types of rents. The assessment of the social implications of any structure of rents therefore depends on the types of rents that the rent-seeking process is creating and protecting, and the cost of 'seeking' and protecting these rents. The net effect of any process of rent seeking can be positive or negative, and is not necessarily always negative as conventional rent-seeking theory assumes (Khan, 2000b).

The same observations hold true for the analysis of corruption. Corruption is always a cost if one only looks at the resource cost of organising and giving bribes (the rent-seeking cost). But this is only one side of the exchange that is entailed in any corrupt transaction. The net economic or political effect of corruption also depends on the types of rent and interventions that are taking place. If the rents are themselves socially damaging, the overall effect of corruption will obviously be very damaging. If the rents are socially beneficial, the net economic effect can be positive or negative, depending on the relative magnitude of the social benefit of maintaining the rent and the rent-seeking cost (Khan, 1996a). This is true even if we agree that corruption is always undesirable in a civic or moral sense. The policy solution is to make the rent and the rent seeking associated with it legal and regulated, not to address the corruption by removing the interventionist capacity of the state.

How does this analysis sit with the evidence that countries that are more corrupt perform worse than ones that are less corrupt? In fact, the evidence is more complex than the cross-country regression evidence seems to suggest. The regression results reflect the fact that most poor countries have high levels of corruption and most developed countries have lower levels. Poor countries also tend to have lower growth rates as most of them are falling behind, not catching up. However, the problem for the general conclusion is that there has been a group of high-growth catching-up countries in the last 50 years (such as South Korea or China), and these countries had on average just as high levels of corruption as other developing countries. But unlike most other developing countries, they achieved high growth and investment rates (Khan, 2002, 2004b). Clearly, in these countries, corruption was associated with the creation and protection of rents that were strongly growth promoting.

The conventional analysis also has a problem in explaining why corruption is so widespread in virtually every developing country. The explanation most often put forward in the conventional literature looks at a combination of opportunity and incentives. The opportunity comes from the interventionist capacities of the state that allow states to create restrictions that inhibit economic activity or to create damaging rents that are nevertheless privately beneficial. The incentive comes from the low opportunity cost of being engaged in corruption. The factors explaining the low opportunity cost of corruption include low civil servant salaries, inefficient court systems that fail to punish corrupt public servants, low levels of transparency and accountability, and a high degree of intervention creating more points at which bribes can be collected. The conventional response to corruption is therefore a two-pronged one: liberalise the economy to reduce the possibility of damaging state interventions and at the same time carry out reforms that raise the opportunity cost of corruption.

However, cross-country evidence suggests that these variables have a relatively weak effect in explaining differences in the levels of corruption across countries (Treisman, 2000). Countries that liberalise are often observed to suffer higher corruption (Harriss-White and White, 1996) and raising bureaucratic salaries typically has little effect (Rauch and Evans, 2000). Democratisation and attempts to improve accountability across a very wide range of developing countries has not resulted in reductions of corruption and concerted attempts at improving the 'rule of law' in developing countries seem to have had little effect. The problem for these approaches to corruption is that if there is something common to all developing countries that results in high levels of corruption, then corruption cannot easily be a policy variable that can be addressed to improve economic performance. Second, as we have noted, the developing countries that did begin to catch up with advanced countries did not in general have low levels of corruption.

Alternative approaches to rent seeking and corruption
The conventional literature on rent seeking and corruption was initially primarily interested in deriving policy conclusions about the benefits of liberalisation and rolling back the state. Many of its results were based on a number of special and potentially misleading assumptions. Nevertheless, the analysis opened up the possibility of a deeper investigation of the costs and benefits of state intervention. The analysis of rent seeking and corruption has been very usefully extended to distinguish between the determinants of

differences in the *types* of rent created in different countries. A closer look at the cross-country evidence shows why this is very important. High- and low-growth developing countries cannot be easily differentiated by significant differences in their *levels* of rent seeking or corruption. Rather, it seems that rent seeking in high-growth countries resulted in the creation of value-enhancing rents, while in low-growth countries the outcome was value-reducing rents. To explain why, we have to go well beyond an abstract model of rent seeking and look at other institutional and political factors determining the types of rent that states can create and manage (Khan and Jomo, 2000).

Countries where value-enhancing rents dominated often had strong centralised states, political rent seekers (typically from the non-capitalist 'intermediate' classes who are the most politically organised in developing countries) were usually weakly organised and did not have the power to demand excessive transfers or protect inefficient rent recipients in emerging capitalist sectors for a share of their rent. In these countries, transfers achieved political stability, subsidies for technology acquisition produced dramatic results and new property rights could be created to maximise growth. In contrast, in low-growth economies, states were often weak and unable to determine the types of rent created, large and fragmented political factions could create many inefficient redistributive rents and political entrepreneurs could protect inefficient industries, preventing rapid technology acquisition. In these countries significant transfers failed to achieve political stability, subsidies to emerging sectors and for technology acquisition resulted in waste and inefficiency, and property rights could not be created to maximise social benefit (Khan, 2000b). But in both groups of countries, there was significant rent seeking and corruption as many different types of rent were created during rapid social transformations.

It is also possible to explain why corruption is systematically more extensive in developing countries compared to advanced ones. While rent seeking is likely to be high in every society given that the task of the state is to create and protect rights over assets and incomes (Samuels and Mercuro, 1984), developing countries on average suffer from illegal forms of rent seeking to a far greater extent than advanced countries. Why should this be the case? A number of factors are at play here, and these are relevant for understanding the limits of anti-corruption policies derived from the mainstream analysis that focuses only on the incentives and opportunities of public officials. First, developing countries are by definition going through far-reaching social transformations through which new asset-owning classes are emerging and older ones are declining. The new classes typically do not have the legitimacy to engage in legitimate rent seeking. Consequently, much of their expenditure in influencing and rewarding public officials cannot be made transparent to the extent possible in more advanced countries where capitalist classes have existed for some time and their assets have become legitimate.

Second, when the capitalist sector of the economy is very small, the privileges of the capitalist sector usually mean that rents exist for one or two capitalists in that sector. This is very difficult to present in socially acceptable terms even if the rents in question are socially desirable. In many cases, therefore, both the rents that capitalists can acquire and the payments and expenditures they make to acquire them are not legally defined and transparent. Finally, there is a systematic structural factor driving political corruption in developing countries. The limited fiscal revenues of most developing-country states means that little is available in the budget to transfer in transparent and accountable ways to broad groups of the population in order to achieve political stabilisation. Much of the political stabilisation in developing countries therefore involves off-budget resource transfers through patron–client networks, and by definition, these cannot be regulated by law or legalised.

These factors mean that even if the state leadership is committed to removing or reducing corruption by increasing bureaucratic salaries and carrying out improvements in transparency, sustained reductions in corruption are unlikely until these major structural drivers of corruption are reversed (Khan, 2004a). This in turn requires the emergence of a legitimate and viable capitalist class that can protect its assets and rents through legal rent seeking, and the collection of enough fiscal revenue to maintain social cohesion and political stability through transparent and legal transfers to broad classes of citizens, rather than through illicit transfers to targeted clients. There is little evidence of a developing country achieving sustained reductions in corruption without first achieving these preconditions. These observations should lead us to doubt the efficacy of following anti-corruption strategies as a *precondition* for achieving rapid economic growth in developing countries.

On the contrary, accelerating growth may require states acquiring capacities for creating and managing growth-enhancing rents in the way that rapid developers did in the late twentieth century. These include transfers to maintain political stability, to accelerate the emergence of new entrepreneurs and to accelerate their acquisition of new technologies. As long as the associated rent seeking and corruption can be controlled to remain within limits and does not affect the allocation and management of these and other critical developmental rents, the developmental outcomes may be satisfactory even in the presence of considerable corruption. Economic development in turn creates some of the necessary preconditions for sustained anti-corruption strategies to be effective, though legal rent seeking is likely to continue as long as there are privileged individuals in society enjoying privileged incomes. The real danger in the mainstream approaches is that if developing-country states find it structurally difficult to achieve significant reductions in corruption, anti-corruption strategies that consistently result in failure may lead to social disaffection, and to attacks on state capacities that make it even less likely that the state can assist in viable social and developmental transformations.

Mushtaq Khan

References

Bhagwati, J.N. (1983), 'DUP activities and rent seeking', *Kyklos*, **36** (4), 634–7.
Boss, H.H. (1990), *Theories of Surplus and Transfer: Parasites and Producers in Economic Thought*, Boston, MA: Unwin Hyman.
Buchanan, J.M., R.D. Tollison and G. Tullock (eds) (1980), *Towards a Theory of the Rent-Seeking Society*, College Station, TX: A&M University Press.
Congleton, R.D. (1980), 'Competitive process, competitive waste, and institutions', in Buchanan et al. (eds), pp. 153–79.
Hall, R. and C. Jones (1999), 'Why do some countries produce so much more output per worker than others?', *Quarterly Journal of Economics*, **114** (1), 83–116.
Harriss-White, B. and G. White (1996), 'Special Issue: Liberalization and the new corruption: resolving the paradox (a discussion based on South Indian material)', *IDS Bulletin*, **27** (2), 1–87.
Heidenheimer, A.J. (ed.) (1970), *Political Corruption: Readings in Comparative Analysis*, New York: Holt, Rinehart & Winston.
Heidenheimer, A.J. and M. Johnston (eds) (2002), *Political Corruption: Concepts and Contexts*, 3rd edn, New Brunswick, NJ: Transaction.
Khan, M.H. (1996a), 'The efficiency implications of corruption', *Journal of International Development*, **8** (5), 683–96.

Khan, M.H. (1996b), 'A typology of corrupt transactions in developing countries', *IDS Bulletin*, **27** (2), 12–21.

Khan, M.H. (2000a), 'Rents, efficiency and growth', in Khan and Jomo (eds), pp. 21–69.

Khan, M.H. (2000b), 'Rent-seeking as process', in Khan and Jomo (eds), pp. 70–144.

Khan, M.H. (2002), 'Corruption and governance in early capitalism: World Bank strategies and their limitations', in J. Pincus and J. Winters (eds), *Reinventing the World Bank*, Ithaca, NY: Cornell University Press, pp. 164–84.

Khan, M.H. (2004a), 'Corruption and governance', in K.S. Jomo and B. Fine (eds), *The New Development Economics*, London/New Delhi: Zed Books/Tulika, pp. 200–21.

Khan, M.H. (2004b), 'State failure in developing countries and strategies of institutional reform', in B. Tungodden, N. Stern and I. Kolstad (eds), *Toward Pro-Poor Policies: Aid Institutions and Globalization*, Proceedings of the Annual World Bank Conference on Development Economics, Oxford: Oxford University Press and World Bank, pp. 165–98.

Khan, M.H. and K.S. Jomo (eds) (2000), *Rents, Rent-Seeking and Economic Development: Theory and Evidence in Asia*, Cambridge: Cambridge University Press.

Knack, S. and P. Keefer (1997), 'Why don't poor countries catch up? A cross-national test of an institutional explanation', *Economic Inquiry*, **35** (3), 590–602.

Krueger, A.O. (1974), 'The political economy of the rent-seeking society', *American Economic Review*, **64** (3), 291–303.

Leff, N. (1964), 'Economic development through bureaucratic corruption', *American Behavioral Scientist*, **8**, 8–14.

Mauro, P. (1995), 'Corruption and growth', *Quarterly Journal of Economics*, **110** (3), 681–712.

Mauro, P. (1997), 'Why worry about corruption?', *IMF Economic Issues*, **97** (6), 1–12.

Nye, J.S. (1967), 'Corruption and political development: a cost–benefit analysis', *American Political Science Review*, **61** (2), 417–27.

Posner, R.A. (1975), 'The social costs of monopoly and regulation', *Journal of Political Economy*, **83** (4), 807–27.

Rauch, J.E. and P.B. Evans (2000), 'Bureaucratic structure and bureaucratic performance in less developed countries', *Journal of Public Economics*, **75** (1), 49–71.

Samuels, W.J. and N. Mercuro (1984), 'A critique of rent-seeking theory', in D.C. Colander (ed.), *Neoclassical Political Economy: The Analysis of Rent-Seeking and DUP Activities*, Cambridge, MA: Ballinger, pp. 55–70.

Shleifer, A. and R.W. Vishny (1993), 'Corruption', *Quarterly Journal of Economics*, **108** (3), 599–617.

Stiglitz, J.E. (1994), *Wither Socialism?*, Cambridge, MA: MIT Press.

Toye, J. (1987), *Dilemmas of Development: Reflections on the Counter-Revolution in Development Theory and Policy*, Oxford: Basil Blackwell.

Treisman, D. (2000), 'The causes of corruption: a cross national study', *Journal of Public Economics*, **76**, 399–457.

Tullock, G. (1967), 'The welfare costs of tariffs, monopolies, and theft', *Western Economic Journal*, **5** (3), 224–32.

Tullock, G. (1996), 'Corruption theory and practice', *Contemporary Economic Policy*, **14** (3), 6–13.

World Bank (1997), *The State in a Changing World*, World Development Report 1997, Washington, DC: World Bank.

Robinson, (Edward) Austin (Gossage) (1897–1993)

Austin Robinson was born on 20 August 1897, the eldest son of Albert Robinson, 'an impecunious clergyman', who had married Edith Sidebotham, the daughter of a clergyman. Through scholarships he went to Marlborough where he read Classics and then to Christ's College, Cambridge in 1916. Before going up to Christ's, however, he served in the Royal Naval Air Service, training as a pilot of seaplanes which he loved. The war with its appalling loss of life and gross injustices had a traumatic effect on Austin's generation at Cambridge, though he was never a pacifist 'in the technical sense'. Austin obtained a First in Classics after 15 months and then went with relief to read economics. (Hearing Maynard Keynes lecture on what became *The Economic Consequences of the Peace* (1919) was a major influence on his decision.) Supervisions by C.R. Fay produced ferocious debates that forced Austin to make explicit and coherent arguments. When Fay went to

Canada, Dennis Robertson and Gerald Shove supervised Austin. He graduated with a First in 1922.

Austin became a Fellow of Corpus Christi College in 1923 and by 1925 was lecturing on his favourite subject, Industry. He married Joan Maurice, who had been his pupil, in 1926 and the Robinsons went to India for two years where Austin tutored the young Maharajah of Gwalior. The experience not only kindled his life-long love for India and its people, it also introduced him to the problems of development in a most practical way. He contributed a first-class piece of applied political economy to *The British Crown and the Indian States* (1928).

Austin and Joan returned to Cambridge, Austin starting afresh his long academic career there. It was only seriously interrupted by his distinguished service in Whitehall during the Second World War. He became a university lecturer in 1929 and a Fellow of Sidney Sussex College in 1931. He had known Keynes as an undergraduate and in 1934 Keynes asked him to become assistant editor of the *Economic Journal*, the start of his long association, 60 years service in all, with the Royal Economic Society – editor for 36 years, and secretary for 25 years (he retired in 1970). He was appointed to a Chair in 1950, he retired in 1965 but continued an extremely varied and intense career until his death in 1993.

In the late 1920s, Dennis Robertson asked Austin to write the volume on monopoly for the 'Cambridge Economic Handbook' series. As a result he wrote two classics, *The Structure of Competitive Industry* (1931) which cleared the ground for *Monopoly*, published in 1941. Both were reviewed most favourably in the *Economic Journal* by Philip Sargent Florence (1932, 1941) who praised his originality, common-sense analysis and empirical examples and lively clear style, a legacy of his thorough training in Classics.

Austin was a devout Christian for whom faith without works was inconceivable. His Christianity and interest in development issues came together in his two major studies of African problems in the 1930s, the first of which was under the auspices of the International Missionary Council and took Austin for six months to what is now Zambia. He used the analysis of Keynes's *A Treatise on Money* (1930) to make the rudiments of a national accounting framework in which to think about structural imbalances between rural and industrial sectors, overseas trade and development and the impact of government expenditures and taxation on economic systems. Austin was always interested in individuals and their groupings so in his thoughts about rural underdevelopment and poverty he was keen to use the potential skills and aspirations of people *where they were* rather than advocate large migration and huge urban concentration. He also wrote two big chapters in Lord Hailey's *African Survey* (1938), the quality of which won them 'a place among the classics of economic literature' (see Cairncross, 1993, p. 73).

Austin increasingly assimilated the new lessons Keynes was developing as he wrote *The General Theory* (1936). Austin's review in *The Economist* (1936) is perceptive and accurate; it could still be read with profit by today's students (and their teachers) to enable them to get the essence both of the theory itself and of how the advanced world works. He understood well the significance of the equality of saving and investment and his keen sense of industrial organisation illuminated his explanation of why output levels away from the unemployment rest state were not sustainable, even in the short term. Most of all, he absorbed the need to apply a different theoretical structure to situations of unemployment and underutilisation of capital goods, on the one hand, and situations of full employment and normal utilisation of capital goods, on the other.

Austin spent the war years in two different sections of Whitehall: first, in the offices of the war cabinet, its economics section and what became the Central Statistical Office when they were set up. Inspired by Keynes's *How to Pay for the War* (1940), he instituted through James Meade and Richard Stone reliable estimates of national income and expenditure, 'his chief contribution to the war' (Cairncross, 1993, p. 79). Second, in 1942 Austin became the Economic Advisor and Head of the Programmes Division in the Ministry of Production. His experiences reaffirmed his belief that macroeconomic analysis that is not combined with the microeconomic details of firms and industries will be seriously flawed. Here he was joined by Richard Kahn and Brian Reddaway in the postwar period, whereas James Meade, another of the original Keynesians with wartime experience, was content to put more emphasis on macroeconomic issues. John Toye judges that the path followed by Austin was of greater relevance and so of more use for developing economies (personal communication). Moreover, Austin's profound understanding of Alfred Marshall led him always to connect together the long-term development implications of short-term changes and vice versa. He drew on his wartime experiences in his 1965 Alfred Marshall Lectures, *Economic Planning in the United Kingdom: Some Lessons* (1967). There, he set out a blueprint for policy making in a free society which nevertheless is determined to employ all its citizens and direct its overall development in the long term as well as in the short term.

Austin returned to university life after the war for 40 years and more as an academic. His reputation though was such that the Civil Service and government would not let him go completely. He spent a year in London helping to draft the Economic Surveys for 1948 and for 1948–52 and six months in Paris at the office of the European Community ensuring that the Marshall Plan would go through. He kept his links with government and government service for many decades afterwards – selection boards of the civil service and, through the National Institute of Economic and Social Research and development agencies, he influenced advice given and personnel chosen.

Increasingly in the post-war period Austin was drawn towards the problems of developing countries. He was a founder of and indefatigable worker for the International Economic Association (IEA; its treasurer 1950–59, its president 1959–62, general editor of its volumes 1950–80), one of many institutions of which he was 'a willing slave', combined with, it must be said, an imperious manner. The bulk of the 12 volumes he edited or co-edited for the IEA were concerned with development issues. A selection of the titles alone indicates the breadth of Austin's interest and knowledge: *The Economic Consequences of the Size of Nations* (1960); 'Foreign trade in a developing economy', a chapter by Austin in Kenneth Berrill (ed.), *Economic Development with Special Reference to East Asia* (1964); *Problems in Economic Development* (1965); *The Economics of Education* (edited with John Vaizey, 1966); 'The desirable level of agriculture in industrial economies', a chapter in Ugo Papi and Charles Nunn (eds), *Economic Problems of Agriculture in Industrial Societies* (1969a); *Backward Areas in Advanced Countries* (1969b); *Economic Growth in South Asia* (edited with Michael Kidron, 1970); *The Economic Development of Bangladesh* (edited with Keith Griffin, 1974); *Appropriate Technologies for Third World Development* (1979).

His commentaries, always clearly expressed, combined optimism tempered with caution and a clear delineation concerning what academic economists could speak on with some authority but outside of which they were trespassing without good reason.

His biographer, Alec Cairncross, singled out for special praise a report Austin wrote in the mid-1970s (at the request of his former pupil, the distinguished Indian economist, I.G. Patel) for the United Nations Development Programme. Austin asked why under-employment and unemployment were so persistent in many developing countries? He set out six constraints on a policy of increasing demand to draw these workers into employment and allow incomes to rise. He put orders of magnitude on imports needed to match expanding incomes and on exports needed to pay for them. As a result he felt top priority must be given to increasing the necessary agricultural surplus (as Adam Smith told us). This meant reducing the weakness of the exchange mechanism between town and country – and the import of luxury commodities. A further limitation was inadequate accumulation due to low saving ratios, inefficient methods of finance and the high import content of investment. The fifth and sixth limitations were associated with the paucity of skills available, administrative as well as productive. Austin advocated the creation of 'small-scale, low-capital-intensive occupations' with 'very large numbers of small craftsman, traders, entrepreneurs starting successful small businesses' to bypass the problem (Cairncross, 1993, p. 151). He discussed the dual-economy aspects of development, the contrasts between the modern and traditional sectors, and the choice these raised of whether to go for rapid development through greater growth and low capital inputs per job, or a gradual transition with the consequent need to revitalise and reinvigorate the traditional economy (his own preference in the 1930s). Finally, he recognised the problem associated with the growth of population which could mean the absorption of as much as three-quarters of investment just to stand still. His 1974 Kingsley Martin Memorial Lecture, 'The economic development of Malthusia', a case study of Bangladesh, illustrates well his approach – his well-developed sense of relevant orders of magnitude in the simple (but profound) development model he carried in his head. As John Toye reminds me, 'Austin was very influential in the early days of the UN . . . his criticisms led to a restructuring of the UN Department for Economic Affairs and the redesign of the UN's *World Economic Report*'. He was also 'the driving force behind the setting up of the Overseas Development Institute in London. His purpose was to raise public and political interest in development issues. He served on its council [for] over thirty years . . . and [his] peremptory guidance . . . was invaluable in keeping it on the straight and narrow' (personal communication).

Austin played a major role in the Faculty of Economics and Politics at Cambridge, not only as a teacher and supervisor of graduate students but also as a farsighted administrator. The building that bears his name (it was so christened at the party in its coffee room in honour of his 90th birthday) was very much the outcome of his enthusiasm and persistence. He had long spells as secretary and chairman, doing his best to bring peace and return cohesion to that most faction-ridden of Faculties.

He retired in 1965 (Joan was elected to his chair) but he had nearly 30 years more of remarkably active life. Although he was physically frail towards the end, he was mentally alert and wrote some of his best papers in the 1980s and early 1990s. These included his superb autobiographical essay, 'My apprenticeship as an economist' (1992). It, together with his obituary article of John Maynard Keynes in the March 1947 *Economic Journal*, most typically reflect Austin's great strength as an economist, perceptive human being and elegant stylist.

Sidney Sussex was a central focus of Austin's life; his substantial contributions there over many years fitted perfectly with the ideal of college life as a city state of Plato in which like minds administer and further the affairs of the establishment.

Austin was the role model *par excellence* for the aspiring applied political economist. For him economics was a 'hands on' subject, the sole object of theory being to apply it to explanation and policy. For Austin 'no economist was more dangerous than the pure theorist without practical experience and intuitive understanding of the real world' (Robinson, 1992, p. 721). His Christian practice with works emphasised more than faith and his experiences in the First World War led him to a life of service to his profession, his country, the many institutions with which he was associated and to humanity, especially to those parts of it least able to help themselves, the victims of both oppression and the malfunctionings of social systems.

Austin had a bad fall in May 1993 and was taken to Addenbrookes Hospital in Cambridge. He died peacefully on 1 June 1993, having heard some of his favourite Bible readings and prayers the night before.

G.C. HARCOURT

References

Berrill, K. (ed.) (1964), *Economic Development with Special Reference to East Asia*, London: Macmillan.
Cairncross, A. (1993), *Austin Robinson: The Life of an Economic Advisor*, London: Macmillan.
Hailey, Lord (ed.) (1938), *African Survey*, Oxford: Oxford University Press.
Keynes, J.M. (1919), *The Economic Consequence of the Peace*, London: Macmillan, reprinted in *The Collected Writings of John Maynard Keynes*, vol. 2, 1971.
Keynes, J.M. (1930), *A Treatise on Money* (2 vols), London: Macmillan (reprinted in *CW*, vols 5 & 6, 1971).
Keynes, J.M. (1936), *The General Theory of Employment, Interest and Money*, London: Macmillan (reprinted in *CW*, vol. 7, 1973).
Keynes, J.M. (1940), *How to Pay for the War: A Radical Plan for the Chancellor of the Exchequer*, London: Macmillan (reprinted in *CW*, vol. 22, 1978, pp. 40–155).
Robinson, E.A.G. and others (none explicitly named) (1928), *The British Crown and the Indian States*, London: P.S. King.
Robinson, E.A.G. (1931), *The Structure of Competitive Industry*, Cambridge: Cambridge University Press (revised edn, 1953).
Robinson, E.A.G. (1936), 'Mr Keynes on money', *The Economist*, 24 February, pp. 471–2.
Robinson, E.A.G. (1941), *Monopoly*, Cambridge: Cambridge University Press (reprinted, 1956).
Robinson, E.A.G. (1947), 'John Maynard Keynes 1883–1946', *Economic Journal*, **57**, 1–68.
Robinson, E.A.G. (1960), 'The size of the nation and the cost of administration', in E.A.G. Robinson (ed.), *The Economic Consequences of the Size of Nations*, London: Macmillan, pp. xiii–xxii.
Robinson, E.A.G. (1964), 'Foreign trade: foreign trade in a developing country', in Berrill (ed.), pp. 212–32.
Robinson, E.A.G. (ed.) (1965), *Problems in Economic Development*, London: Macmillan.
Robinson, E.A.G. (1967), *Economic Planning in the United Kingdom: Some Lessons*, Cambridge: Cambridge University Press.
Robinson, E.A.G. (1969a), 'The desirable level of agriculture in advanced industrial economies', in U. Papi and C. Nunn (eds), *Economic Problems of Agriculture in Industrial Societies*, London: Macmillan, pp. 26–50.
Robinson, E.A.G. (1969b), *Backward Areas in Advanced Countries*, London: Macmillan.
Robinson, E.A.G. (mid-1970s), *Future Tasks for UNDP: Report to the Administrator of the United Nations Development Programme*, New York: UNDP.
Robinson, E.A.G. (1974), 'The economic development of Malthusia', *Modern Asian Studies*, **8**, 521–34.
Robinson, E.A.G. (ed.) (1979), *Appropriate Technologies for Third World Development*, London: Macmillan.
Robinson, Austin (1992), 'My apprenticeship as an economist', in Szenberg (ed.), pp. 203–21.

Robinson, E.A.G. and K. Griffin (eds) (1974), *The Economic Development of Bangladesh within a Socialist Framework: Proceedings of a Conference held by the International Economic Association at Dacca*, London: Macmillan.

Robinson, E.A.G. and M. Kidron (eds) (1970), *Economic Development in South Asia*, London: Macmillan.

Robinson, E.A.G. and J.E. Vaizey (eds) (1966), *The Economics of Education*, London: Macmillan.

Sargent Florence, P. (1932), 'Review of *The Structure of Competitive Industry* (1931)', *Economic Journal*, **42**, 66–70.

Sargent Florence, P. (1941), 'Review of *Monopoly*', *Economic Journal*, **51**, 481–3.

Szenberg, M. (ed.) (1992), *Eminent Economists: Their Life Philosophies*, Cambridge: Cambridge University Press.

Robinson, Joan (1903–1983)

Joan Robinson was born in 1903 into an upper middle-class family with a tradition of dissent. She herself was the rebel with a cause *par excellence*. As Joan Maurice she read history at St Paul's Girls' School and came up to Girton College, Cambridge in 1922 to read economics because she wanted to know why unemployment and poverty abounded. She did not think the economics or the economists of that time provided satisfactory answers. She graduated in 1925, married Austin Robinson, one of her teachers, in 1926 and they went to India for two years. This started her life-long affair with the sub-continent and her interest in the problems of developing countries. Although Cambridge was always to be her base, her love of travelling meant that she visited China several times in the post-war years and in her later years she spent part of each year in Kerala State in India. Her first visit to the United States is still remembered with awe and, sometimes, with affection. Joan Robinson became a university assistant lecturer at Cambridge in 1934, a university lecturer in 1937, a reader in 1949 and a professor in 1965. She 'retired' in 1971, remaining active into the last year of her life, despite poor health in her last few years. She died in August 1983.

Joan Robinson said of Alfred Marshall, 'The more I learn about economics the more I admire Marshall's intellect and the less I like his character' (Joan Robinson, 1953; *CEP*, Vol. 4, 1973, p. 125). Marshall had a profound influence on the development of her thought through his *Principles* and the teaching and writings of A.C. Pigou, John Maynard Keynes, Gerald Shove, Dennis Robertson and Austin Robinson. Even as an undergraduate she showed she understood him only too well, see her delightful 'spoof', 'Beauty and the Beast' (Joan Robinson and Dorothea Morison, *CEP*, Vol. 1, 1951).

In her first major publication, *Economics is a Serious Subject* (1932) Pigou's tool-making imagery is dominant. She is wary of applying theory directly to explanation and policy, discerning a conflict between reality and tractability and warning that there must be a trade-off between them.

Yet it was a real problem that led her to develop what became *The Economics of Imperfect Competition* in 1933 – why had not more firms closed down in the depressed conditions of the 1920s and 1930s in the United Kingdom, an inescapable inference of Marshallian–Pigovian theory? Piero Sraffa's 'pregnant suggestion' in 1926 that demand rather than rising marginal costs determined levels of production of firms provided the springboard for her analysis of mini-monopolies operating in competitive environments. The core tool of her book was the marginal revenue curve and the most important influence on her as she wrote it was Richard Kahn. That the unfit were not necessarily eliminated by the slump was a damning indictment of the workings of competitive capitalism, second in importance only to the Keynes–Kalecki theory of effective demand, especially of its unsatisfactory level, in such economies. Joan Robinson subsequently repudiated her 1933 book, especially the 'shameless fudge' (she had something of a 'who's for hockey' vocabulary) whereby demand curves stayed still while business people groped for equilibrium prices by trial and error. In later years this critique was summed up as 'History versus equilibrium' (Joan Robinson, 1974; *CEP*, Vol. 5, 1979, pp. 48–58). She did retain, though, her scepticism about the orthodox theory of distribution which began in her 1933 book.

Keynes's *A Treatise on Money* was published in 1930. Joan Robinson saw Keynes as trying, guiltily, to break out of the Marshallian dichotomy between the real and the money in order to analyse the causes and cures of prolonged unemployment as well as deflation and inflation of the general price level. The discussion of *A Treatise on Money* by the 'Circus' in the early 1930s and Keynes's lectures as the embryonic *General Theory* emerged as an obvious outlet for Joan Robinson's passionate search for truth. She wrote two perceptive interim reports in the early 1930s (Joan Robinson, 1933b, 1933c), arguing that Keynes was trying to make a theory of output and employment but, still under Marshall's influence, it was a long-period theory. By the time *The General Theory* was published in 1936 it had become short-period analysis in its own right with Joan Robinson providing in 1937 a long-period exercise to try to show that the new, short-period, results held in principle in the long period too. The same volume of essays contained a discussion of disguised unemployment (it brought together understanding from her time in India and the new theory) and an explanation of what is now known in the literature as the Harris–Todaro model of migration (Harris and Todaro, 1970) (see Tahir, 1999).

Joan Robinson first met Michał Kalecki in 1936 and the beginning of their long, close intellectual friendship and vigorous debates was probably the single most important stimulus for the sea-change in her views that started about then. (She was the greatest champion of the clear-cut case that Kalecki independently discovered the principal propositions of *The General Theory*.) She came to feel that the Marxian framework through which Kalecki solved the realisation problem was more appropriate than Keynes's Marshallian-based approach for an understanding of the capitalist process. Her mastery of this former approach and framework is exemplified in her superb account of Kalecki on the economics of capitalism (Joan Robinson, 1977; *CEP*, Vol. 5, 1979, pp. 184–96). She shows how the price policies of firms, the different saving behaviour of wage-earners and profit-receivers and the dominant importance of profit-making and accumulation, may be combined in a short-period model of employment and the distribution of income to illustrate the possibility of an underemployment rest state. The same structure underlies the analysis of her *magnum opus* of 1956, *The Accumulation of Capital*, and its sequel of 1962, *Essays in the Theory of Economic Growth*. Moreover, Kalecki's (1936, 1990; Targetti and Kinda-Hass, 1982) critique of the structure of Keynes's theory of investment is mirrored in her own, that it is an unholy mass of *ex ante* and *ex post* factors which need to be separated by taking into account the two-sided relationship between profitability and accumulation: on the one hand, actual accumulation creates actual profitability; on the other, expected profitability creates planned accumulation. These are the ingredients of her famous banana diagram (see Joan Robinson, 1962, p. 48). All this had been preceded by her 1942 *An Essay on Marxian Economics*, criticised by Shove (1944) for its lack of understanding of Marshall rather than Marx and praised by Keynes (in a letter to Mrs Austin [sic] Robinson of 20 August, 1942) for how well written it was 'despite [how] . . . boring [is] an attempt to make sense of what is in fact not sense'. This says more about Keynes than Marx. Joan Robinson's book more than deserves its second edition of 1966.

Joan Robinson developed Keynes's ideas in at least two directions in the post-war years. First, she had a deep understanding of money and its roles in economic systems. Her main concern was with the determination of the rate of interest (Joan Robinson, 1952). She responded to Keynes's injunction to be on guard against the fallacy of composition and explained how the equilibrium rate of interest serves to bring about an uneasy truce between bullishness and bearishness in financial markets at each point in time.

The other development was 'generalising *The General Theory* to the long period', the distinctively Cambridge, England, contributions by Kahn, Kaldor, Joan Robinson, Sraffa and, later, Luigi Pasinetti to the post-war theories of growth. Real post-war problems and Harrod's (1939, 1948) theoretical contributions were the stimuli. In *The Accumulation of Capital*, she developed a model of an unregulated free enterprise economy in which firms, ultimately constrained by finance, determine accumulation while the public, constrained by their command of purchasing power, are free to make the rate of expenditure what they please, '[a] model not unrealistic in essential respects'.

Four questions were considered:

1. comparisons of situations which differ in some respects;
2. tracking the path of one economy when technical conditions, including their rate of change, and other characteristics are given;
3. tracing the consequences of a change in one of the characteristics; and
4. examining short-period reactions to unexpected events.

All of these issues and the analyses of them constituted a return to classical and Marxian preoccupations renewed in the light of the Keynesian–Kaleckian revolution.

Parallel with these developments were the fights over the theory of distribution and the meaning of capital (side-tracked into questions of measurement) in the neoclassical supply and demand approach as compared to the Marxian–Kaleckian–Keynesian view of the world. The Wicksellian analysis in her 1953–54 article, 'The production function and the theory of capital' and in her 1956 book concerned the choice of techniques aspect of her theory of growth, the most difficult but not the most essential part of her analysis. But the Cambridge controversies in the theory of capital, which her writings and the publication in 1960 of Sraffa's *Production of Commodities by Means of Commodities* brought about, overshadowed her positive contributions, especially when the controversies 'hotted up' in the mid-1960s with the 1966 *Quarterly Journal of Economics* symposium on capital-reversal and reswitching. Although she contributed both early and late to the debates, she increasingly came to feel that they were all beside the point, see her 'The unimportance of reswitching' (Joan Robinson, 1975). She pursued relentlessly her methodological critique, the illegitimacy of using comparisons (differences) to analyse processes (changes), the need to be clear about the limitations and applicability of models set in logical time *vis-à-vis* those set in historical time. The former are concerned with what would be different if . . .?; the latter with what would follow, that is to say, happen next, if . . .? (This naturally leads to considerations of path dependence, though neither Kaldor (1934!) nor Joan Robinson received credit for their early awareness of this when path dependence became all the rage in the 1980s and 1990s.)

There was, however, a practical aspect to her work on the choice of techniques as well. In the 1950s, on a visit to China, she gave three lectures, the second of which was devoted to this question (see Tahir et al., 2002). It was set within the context of the analysis associated with Dobb (1954), Galenson and Leibenstein (1955) and Sen (1960) of the appropriate techniques to embody in accumulation in developing economies. (Sen's 1960 book was based on his 1950s PhD dissertation at Cambridge supervised for part of the time by Joan Robinson.) Joan Robinson argued for a middle way, giving weight to employment as well as increasing the annual surplus to be reinvested. The first lecture was concerned with the nature of interdepartmental flows which planners need to have at the back of their heads and the forefront of their minds. The third lecture was in outline her difficult but profound essay, 'The philosophy of prices' (Joan Robinson, *CEP*, Vol. 2, 1960, pp. 27–48), in which she discusses the role of the price mechanism in development, especially its role in the creation of incomes and expenditures. In outline and content the lectures, together with her views on population control, are close to the pragmatic, gradualist, trial-and-error, use of the market, openness and central control that now characterises the Chinese economy.

In 1978 she published *Aspects of Development and Underdevelopment* in which she spelt out in detail the approach she had taken in the 1950s lectures in China and later. Its pages were filled with a mixture of acute analysis, usually well-chosen empirical examples, and a feel for what ought to be done, coupled often with realistic analysis combined with *Realpolitik* but also influenced by her growing pessimism about what was likely to happen.

Joan Robinson was ill for much of the last decade of her life and deeply depressed about the arms race (see Joan Robinson, 1981). She became more and more pessimistic, even nihilistic, concerning economic theory. Two late papers, Bhaduri and Joan Robinson (1980) and Joan Robinson (1980; 1985), reflect this mood. The first is the more optimistic; it contains her final assessment of where the writings of possibly her greatest influence and certainly her most feared critic, Piero Sraffa, might be combined with those of Marx and Kalecki to form a schema through which to understand the laws of motion of capitalism. The latter article was much more radical. Initially titled 'Spring cleaning', it is a plea to clear out the whole house, not just the attic, and start again.

Joan Robinson taught us always to look at the conceptual basis of our theories. The latter should start from actual situations, actual societies with explicit 'rules of the game', institutions, past histories and defined sociological characteristics. When analysing these societies we should ask what levels of abstraction are appropriate to the questions we are trying to answer. We should aim to construct theories that contain the essential elements of reality, expressed in a sufficiently simple form to allow us to see clearly the relationships at work and how they intertwine. Most of all, perhaps, we should remember her injunction that: 'the purpose of studying economics is not to acquire a set of ready-made answers to economic questions, but to learn how to avoid being deceived by economists' (Joan Robinson, 1955; *CEP*, Vol. 2, 1960, p. 17).

G.C. Harcourt

References

Bhaduri, Amit and Joan Robinson (1980), 'Accumulation and exploitation: an analysis in the tradition of Marx, Sraffa and Kalecki', *Cambridge Journal of Economics*, **4**, 103–15.

Dobb, M.H. (1954), *On Economic Theory and Socialism: Collected Papers*, London: Routledge & Kegan Paul.

Feiwel, George R. (ed.) (1985), *Issues in Contemporary Macroeconomics and Distribution*, London: Macmillan.

Galenson, W. and H. Leibenstein (1955), 'Investment criteria, productivity and economic development', *Quarterly Journal of Economics*, **69**, 343–70.

Harris, J.R. and M.P. Todaro (1970), 'Migration, employment and development: a two-sector model', *American Economic Review*, **60**, 126–42.

Harrod, R.F. (1939), 'An essay in dynamic theory', *Economic Journal*, **49**, 14–33.

Harrod, R.F. (1948), *Towards a Dynamic Economics: Some Recent Developments of Economic Theory and their Application to Policy*, London: Macmillan.

Kaldor, N. (1934), 'A classificatory note on the determinateness of static equilibrium', *Review of Economic Studies*, **1**, 122–36.

Kalecki, Michał (1936), 'Some remarks on Keynes' theory', in F. Targetti and B. Kinda-Hass (1982), pp. 245–53.

Kalecki, Michał (1990), *Collected Works*, Vol. 1 (edited by Jersy Osiatynski), Oxford: Clarendon.

Keynes, J.M. (1930), *A Treatise on Money*, 2 vols, London: Macmillan.

Keynes, J.M. (1936), *The General Theory of Employment, Interest and Money*, London: Macmillan.

Pasinetti, L.L., D. Levhari, P.A. Samuelson, M. Morishima, M. Bruno, E. Burmeister, E. Sheshinki and P. Garegnani (1966), 'Paradoxes in capital theory: a symposium', *Quarterly Journal of Economics*, **80**, 503–83.

Robinson, Joan (1932), *Economics is a Serious Subject: The Apologia of the Economist to the Mathematician, the Scientist and the Plain Man*, Cambridge: Heffers.

Robinson, Joan (1933a), *The Economics of Imperfect Competition*, London: Macmillan (2nd edn, 1969).

Robinson, Joan (1933b), 'A parable of saving and investment', *Economica* (N.S.), **13**, 75–84.

Robinson, Joan (1933c), 'The theory of money and the analysis of output', *Review of Economic Studies*, **1**, 22–6 (reprinted in *CEP*, Vol. 1, 1951, pp. 52–8).

Robinson, Joan (1937), *Essays in the Theory of Employment*, Oxford: Basil Blackwell (2nd edn, 1947).

Robinson, Joan (1942), *An Essay on Marxian Economics*, London: Macmillan (2nd edn, 1966).

Robinson, Joan (1951–1980), *Collected Economic Papers* (*CEP*), 6 vols, Oxford: Basil Blackwell.

Robinson, Joan (1952), *The Rate of Interest and Other Essays*, London: Macmillan.

Robinson, Joan (1953), *On Re-Reading Marx*, Cambridge: Students Bookshop (reprinted in *CEP*, Vol. 4, 1973, pp. 247–68).

Robinson, Joan (1953–54), 'The production function and the theory of capital', *Review of Economic Studies*, **21**, 81–106 (reprinted in *CEP*, Vol. 2, 1960, pp. 114–31).

Robinson, Joan (1955), 'Marx, Marshall and Keynes', *Occasional Paper No. 9*, Delhi School of Economics.

Robinson, Joan (1956), *The Accumulation of Capital*, London: Macmillan (2nd edn, 1965; 3rd edn, 1969).

Robinson, Joan (1962), *Essays in the Theory of Economic Growth*, London: Macmillan.

Robinson, Joan (1974), 'History versus equilibrium', London: Thames Polytechnic (reprinted in *CEP*, Vol. 5, 1979, pp. 48–58).

Robinson, Joan (1975), 'The unimportance of reswitching', *Quarterly Journal of Economics*, **89**, 32–9 (reprinted in *CEP*, Vol. 5, 1979, pp. 76–89).

Robinson, Joan (1977), 'Michał Kalecki on the economics of capitalism', *Oxford Bulletin of Economics and Statistics*, **39**, 7–17.

Robinson, Joan (1978), *Aspects of Development and Underdevelopment*, Cambridge: Cambridge University Press.

Robinson, Joan (1980; 1985), 'Spring cleaning', Cambridge, mimeo. Published as 'The theory of normal prices and the reconstruction of economic theory', in Feiwel (1985), pp. 157–65.

Robinson, Joan (1981), *The Arms Race* (The Tanner Lectures on Human Values), Logan, UT: University of Utah Press.

Robinson, Joan and Dorothea Morison (1951), 'Beauty and the beast', in *CEP*, Vol. 1, 1951, pp. 225–33.

Sen, A.K. (1960), *Choice of Techniques: An Aspect of the Theory of Planned Economic Development*, Oxford: Basil Blackwell.

Shove, G.F. (1944), 'Mrs Robinson on Marxian economics', *Economic Journal*, **54**, 47–61.

Sraffa, P. (1926), 'The laws of returns under competitive conditions', *Economic Journal*, **36**, 535–50.

Sraffa, P. (1960), *Production of Commodities by Means of Commodities*, Cambridge: Cambridge University Press.

Tahir, Pervez (1999), 'Joan Robinson: a neglected precursor of internal migration models', in C. Sardoni and P. Kriesler (eds), *Keynes, Post-Keynesianism and Political Economy: Essays in Honour of Geoff Harcourt*, Vol. 3, London: Routledge, pp. 312–33.

Tahir, P., G.C. Harcourt and P. Kerr (2002), 'On Joan Robinson and China', in *Joan Robinsion: Critical Assessments of Leading Economists*, edited by Prue Kerr in collaboration with G.C. Harcourt, London: Routledge, pp. 267–80.
Targetti, F. and B. Kinda-Hass (1982), 'Kalecki's review of Keynes's *General Theory*', *Australian Economic Papers*, **21**, 244–60.

Rural Poverty Reduction

While urbanisation has been proceeding apace in low-income countries, it is nevertheless still true that most people living in poverty do so in rural areas. Overall World Bank poverty data suggests that of the 1.2 billion people living below the poverty line in 1999, roughly 70 per cent lived in rural areas and 30 per cent in urban areas (IFAD, 2001; World Bank, 2003). These are, of course, only broad orders of magnitude. Countries have diverse definitions concerning how their populations are classified between rural and urban categories. In some instances, settlements with populations as low as 5000 people are categorised as urban; in others this cut-off figure may be 50 000 or 100 000. For this reason, certainly some share of the poverty attributed to rural areas will refer to people attempting to gain a living in towns and not engaged in agriculture.

For at least 30 years, if not more, it has been thought that poverty in rural areas would best be tackled by raising productivity in agriculture. Intellectually, the origins of this emphasis can be traced to influential agricultural development economists such as John Mellor, whose writings from the early 1960s focused on small-farm agriculture as a source of economic growth (Johnston and Mellor, 1961; Mellor, 1966; 1976). Mellor went on to be Director of the International Food Policy Research Institute (IFPRI) during the 1980s, and IFPRI remains to this day an organisation that consistently advocates rural poverty reduction through rising agricultural productivity (for example, Delgado et al., 1999; IFPRI, 2002).

Since this entry ends up differing from the mainstream consensus it is just as well to set out the interlocking components that comprise the agriculture-centred argument. Small-farm agriculture possesses attributes that are attractive from the viewpoints of growth and equity. It is labour intensive in character, thus providing income-earning opportunities in labour-abundant and capital-scarce economies (Hayami and Ruttan, 1971). For this same reason, it can be regarded as 'efficient' in the broad economic sense of the word. At the same time, yield-increasing technical change in agriculture, comprising the use of more productive seeds together with complementary inputs like water and fertiliser, is regarded as 'scale neutral', that is, it does just as well in the context of a small-farm structure of agriculture as it would do for a large-farm structure (Lipton and Longhurst, 1989). An additional argument in favour of a small-farm emphasis is that large farms tend to use land less intensively than small ones (Berry and Cline, 1979).

The so-called 'Green Revolution' in rice and wheat that occurred from the early 1970s onwards in Asia and Latin America appeared to provide substantive support for these propositions about the 'growth with equity' attributes of small-farm agriculture. Indeed rising yields and rapid agricultural growth in those regions spawned an elaboration of the basic model that suggested that small-farm agriculture was the driver not just of agricultural growth itself, but indeed of much larger, economy-wide, processes of economic transformation (for example, Johnston and Kilby, 1975; Tomich et al., 1995). This analysis is referred to as the 'regional growth linkage' or 'rural growth linkage' model (for example, Hazell and Haggblade, 1993) and, as these descriptive phrases suggest, it places emphasis on economic change that is linked to agricultural growth, through backward linkages (supply of inputs to farmers), forward linkages (marketing and processing of farm outputs) and consumption linkages (expenditure by farmers on non-farm consumption goods). In this scenario, economy-wide growth and poverty reduction is achieved through the initial and fundamental focus on raising yields on small farms.

While the core ideas that comprise the small-farm agriculture-centred route to poverty reduction originated from a group of mainly American agricultural development economists, a vast body of development theory and practice has provided support over the years. To pick out just a few examples, 'urban bias' as proposed by Michael Lipton in the 1970s (Lipton, 1977) played to a similar view of the virtues of small-farm growth, as indeed did farming systems research (Byerlee and Collinson, 1980) and farmer participatory research (Chambers et al., 1989), both precursors of participatory rural appraisal (Chambers, 1994). More recently, two reports on rural poverty prepared a decade apart for IFAD (Jazairy et al., 1992; IFAD, 2001) subscribe to the agriculture-centred model, in the latter case going so far as to advocate the rapid adoption of genetically modified crops in low-income countries as a route to rural poverty reduction. An econometric analysis of the poverty-reducing effects of agricultural research expenditure concludes that farm productivity growth has a substantial impact on poverty reduction (Thirtle et al., 2003).

There have, of course, all along been minority views sceptical of the universalistic claims of the agriculture-centred approach. These have ranged from some writers dubious of the benefits to the landless of yield growth on farms (Griffin, 1974), to some who emphasised circumstances under which agricultural growth linkages would be weak (Harriss, 1987; Hart, 1993), and others convinced that the motor of growth and poverty reduction lies in industry and services rather than agriculture. Interest in the majority view has also waned with changing fashions in development practice; on the economics side liberalisation has meant that most types of farm-support policy are regarded with disapproval by the donor community; while micro-level work in rural areas has tended to move away from economic to social agendas: community-based natural resource management, gender, participation, rights and so on.

Work dating from the mid-1990s onwards on patterns of rural livelihoods in Sub-Saharan Africa and South Asia seem to pose especially serious difficulties for an agriculture-centred approach to rural poverty reduction (Bernstein et al., 1992; Ellis, 2000). In the first place, the multiple and diverse character of rural livelihoods is emphasised (Bryceson, 1996; Ellis, 1998); most so-called farm households turn out to depend on nearby or remote non-farm sources of income for around half their total livelihoods, on average, including migratory behaviour of varying durations, with associated remittances and other income transfers (Reardon, 1997). However, second, the relationship of poverty and vulnerability to these livelihood patterns turns out to be less obvious than is sometimes supposed. The rural poor and most vulnerable are those most dependent on agriculture, and even more so when they are dependent on food crop production within agriculture. The rural best-off are least dependent on agriculture, but they also attain by far the highest levels of farm output per hectare since they are able to utilise cash generated from non-farm activities in order to hire labour and purchase cash inputs to farming (Ellis and Freeman, 2004). In other words, the agriculture-centred thesis is stood on its head: rising farm yields follow rather than initiate non-farm employment and earnings.

In Sub-Saharan Africa (SSA) it is possible that agriculture could at best make only a modest contribution to poverty reduction in the long run. There are numerous intersecting reasons for this, some external to Africa itself, others associated with domestic factors in SSA countries. Externally, the real prices of both food and export crops have tended to decline inexorably over time, and for food commodities this is not unrelated to industrial-country farm-support policies and export subsidies. Internally, domestic markets for food in fact turn out to be rather limited; it only takes a reasonably good harvest for a food staple like maize for prices to decline to levels that make farming relatively unattractive among competing activities. While international food security experts are preoccupied with the instances when food output fails to meet national requirements, the more common occurrence of quite sufficient domestic food production even without 'Green Revolution' yield gains passes relatively unremarked. Little point, then, in pushing for high-yielding technologies when the domestic market has limited growth potential, and oversupply can quickly occur.

The true balance of pressures and options for rural populations in SSA is shown more by what people do than by economic hypotheses about what ought to pertain. People, as they say, 'vote with their feet' and in SSA, agriculture tends to take a secondary role as the occupation of choice whenever plausible alternatives present themselves. The process thus put in motion has been referred to as 'deagrarianization' (Bryceson and Jamal, 1997; Bryceson and Bank, 2001). It has multiple features: many rural areas are rapidly reaching the point where there is no further scope to subdivide land at inheritance, meaning that a new generation will be unable to attain more than a partial livelihood from farming; returns to farming have tended to be lower and a lot more unstable post-liberalisation than in the days of farm-support policies; members of rural resident families are increasingly mobile and involved in rural–urban interactions. In SSA, there is a powerful gender dimension to this since it tends to be women who remain locked into agriculture while men adopt more mobile livelihood styles.

A reading of first-round poverty reduction strategy papers (PRSPs) reveals that the agriculture-centred approach to rural poverty reduction continues to inform a lot of strategic policy thinking, and a rather narrow sectoral approach to poverty reduction tends to predominate. Livelihoods research suggests, by contrast, that rural poverty reduction depends on intersectoral mobility and adaptability. It can therefore be concluded that blockages and barriers to mobility need to be addressed by poverty policy including fees and fines and permits and roadblocks associated with such mobility, as well as institutional factors that hamper the exit from agriculture such as land tenure systems that make land rental difficult without compromising ownership security, and social restrictions on the mobility of women.

In contrast to the agriculture-centred approach, rural poverty reduction may well be best served by encouraging rapid urban and non-farm growth in low-income agrarian economies. And in this regard, there is undue pessimism about the ability of human agency to create livelihood options in urban areas, as recent experience in cities like

Kampala or Dar es Salaam demonstrates. The latter argument does not, of course, mean that raising farm productivity is entirely without merit as a partial approach to poverty reduction; rather it provides a note of caution, and a counterbalance, to the exaggerated claims of the new agriculture enthusiasts (or rather the early twenty-first-century resurgence of the old agriculture enthusiasts).

FRANK ELLIS

References

Bernstein, H., B. Crow and H. Johnson (1992), *Rural Livelihoods: Crises and Responses*, Oxford: Oxford University Press.

Berry R.A. and W.R. Cline (1979), *Agrarian Structure and Productivity in Developing Countries*, Baltimore, MD: Johns Hopkins University Press.

Bryceson, D.F. (1996), 'Deagrarianization and rural employment in Sub-Saharan Africa: a sectoral perspective', *World Development*, **24** (1), 97–111.

Bryceson, D.F. and L. Bank (2001), 'End of an era: Africa's development policy parallax', *Journal of Contemporary African Studies*, **19** (1), 5–23.

Bryceson, D.F. and V. Jamal (eds) (1997), *Farewell to Farms: Deagrarianisation and Employment in Africa*, Research Series no. 1997/10, Leiden, Netherlands: African Studies Centre.

Byerlee, D. and M. Collinson (1980), *Planning Technologies Appropriate to Farmers – Concepts and Procedures*, Mexico: CIMMYT.

Chambers, R. (1994), 'The origins and practice of participatory rural appraisal', *World Development*, **22** (7), 953–69.

Chambers, R. and R. Conway (1992), 'Sustainable rural livelihoods: practical concepts for the 21st century', IDS Discussion Paper, no. 296, Institute of Development Studies, University of Sussex, Brighton.

Chambers, R., A. Pacey and L.A. Thrupp (eds) (1989), *Farmer First – Farmer Innovation and Agricultural Research*, London: Intermediate Technology Publications.

Delgado, C.L., J. Hopkins and V.A. Kelly with P. Hazell, A.A. McKenna, P. Gruhn, B. Hojjati, J. Sil and C. Courbois (1999), *Agricultural Growth Linkages in Sub-Saharan Africa*, IFPRI Research Report no. 107, Washington, DC: International Food Policy Research Institute.

Ellis, F. (1998), 'Survey article: household strategies and rural livelihood diversification', *Journal of Development Studies*, **35** (1), 1–38.

Ellis, F. (2000), *Rural Livelihoods and Diversity in Developing Countries*, Oxford: Oxford University Press.

Ellis, F. and H.A. Freeman (2004), 'Rural livelihoods and poverty reduction strategies in four African countries', *Journal of Development Studies*, **40** (4), 1–30.

Griffin, K. (1974), *The Political Economy of Agrarian Change: An Essay on the Green Revolution*, London: Macmillan.

Harriss, B. (1987), 'Regional growth linkages from agriculture', *Journal of Development Studies*, **23** (2), 275–89.

Hart, G. (1993), 'Regional growth linkages in the era of liberalization: a critique of the new agrarian optimism', World Employment Programme Research Working Paper no. 37, Geneva: International Labour Office.

Hayami, Y. and V.W. Ruttan (1971), *Agricultural Development: An International Perspective*, Baltimore, MD: Johns Hopkins University Press.

Hazell, P. and S. Haggblade (1993), 'Farm–nonfarm growth linkages and the welfare of the poor', Chapter 8 in M. Lipton and J. van der Gaag (eds), *Including the Poor*, Proceedings of a Symposium Organised by the World Bank and the International Food Policy Research Institute, Washington, DC: World Bank, pp. 190–204.

IFPRI (2002), 'Fighting famine in Southern Africa: steps out of the crisis', IFPRI Briefing Paper, Washington, DC: International Food Policy Research Institute.

International Fund for Agricultural Development (IFAD) (2001), *Rural Poverty Report 2001: The Challenge of Ending Rural Poverty*, Oxford: Oxford University Press for IFAD.

Jazairy, I., M. Alamgir and T. Panuccio (1992), *The State of World Rural Poverty: An Inquiry into its Causes and Consequences*, London: IT Publications for the International Fund for Agricultural Development (IFAD).

Johnston, B.F. and P. Kilby (1975), *Agriculture and Structural Transformation*, Oxford and New York: Oxford University Press.

Johnston, B.F. and J. Mellor (1961), 'The role of agriculture in economic development', *American Economic Review*, **51** (4), 566–93.

Lipton, M. (1977), *Why Poor People Stay Poor: Urban Bias in World Development*, London: Temple Smith.

Lipton, M. and R. Longhurst (1989), *New Seeds and Poor People*, London: Unwin Hyman.

Mellor, J.W. (1966), *The Economics of Agricultural Development*, Ithaca, NY: Cornell University Press.

Mellor, J.W. (1976), *The New Economics of Growth*, Ithaca, NY: Cornell University Press.

Reardon, T. (1997), 'Using evidence of household income diversification to inform study of the rural nonfarm labor market in Africa', *World Development*, **25** (5), 735–47.

Singh, I. (1990), *The Great Ascent: The Rural Poor in South Asia*, Baltimore, MD: Johns Hopkins University Press.

Thirtle, C., L. Lin and J. Piesse (2003), 'The impact of research-led agricultural productivity growth on poverty reduction in Africa, Asia and Latin America', *World Development*, **31** (12), 1959–75.

Tomich, T.P., P. Kilby and B.F. Johnston (1995), *Transforming Agrarian Economies: Opportunities Seized, Opportunities Missed*, Ithaca, NY: Cornell University Press.

World Bank (2003), *Global Economic Prospects 2003*, Washington, DC: World Bank.

Seers, Dudley (1920–1983)

From the founding of the Institute of Development Studies (IDS) in 1966 until his death, Dudley Seers was widely recognised as the pre-eminent European in his chosen field. The manner of his death says much about the character of his working life. He died in March 1983 in Washington, DC part of the way through a journey that was scheduled to last 11 weeks, to span four continents, to involve about 40,000 miles of travel and to embrace five distinct assignments. Five weeks in Fiji working on an 'Employment and Development Mission' were to be followed by two and a half weeks working with the World Bank in Washington helping edit their 'Pioneers in Development' volume, then a trip to Trinidad and Tobago to give a lecture commemorating the life of Eric Williams, followed by a conference in Shanghai on 'The International Economic Order'. On his way back from China he planned to call in at 'Kuala Lumpur and other places' in connection with a project studying 'Imported Inflation'. The same leave of absence form lists seven other items of work that Seers was involved in and indicates which colleagues at IDS would be looking after such work while he was away. One such colleague, Sir Hans Singer, captured the spirit of vitality and intellectual turbulence that Seers habitually brought to life at the institute:

> Somehow, one always knew when he was around; the pulse of the place seemed to beat faster. When he was away, one held one's breath in anticipation of the new ideas, new plans, new projects with which he would come back . . . Wherever he went, with whatever he wrote, in whatever setting he argued, he created an aura of excitement, of stirring things up. (IDS, 1983)

The IDS was soon to attract a glittering fellowship, some of whom had made their name already, while others were to earn their reputations while working in the stimulating intellectual environment that Seers's leadership inspired. Research at home and abroad, overseas assignments and consultancies, post-graduate teaching and short-course training were the staples of the IDS programme. Seers was closely involved in the design and direction of IDS's two-year MPhil and in doctoral supervisions, the two main components of the institute's teaching programme.

Dudley Seers was born on 11 April 1920 into the family of an executive of General Motors, educated at a preparatory school and at Rugby, and then went up to Pembroke College, Cambridge, where Joan Robinson was one of his supervisors. Following the outbreak of war he joined the Royal Navy, was commissioned, saw action and was mentioned in dispatches. After demobilisation he spent two years in New Zealand, worked in the office of the prime minister, and wrote a pamphlet *The Challenge to New Zealand Labour* (1946).

In 1947 he returned to the UK and took up a sequence of appointments in the Oxford University Institute of Statistics, later to become the Institute of Economics and Statistics. His early publications were mainly on national income, production and consumption, on the construction of price indices, and on some of the practical problems involved in compiling estimates of the various components of national accounts. He was also very interested in income distribution, and in how that was changing. While still at Oxford he undertook assignments in Burma, on the Gold Coast (Ghana) with Dick Ross, and in Malta with Tommy Balogh.

In 1953 he became a research economist at UN headquarters before spending two years as statistical adviser, under UN technical assistance, to the islands of the Eastern Caribbean. In 1957 he moved to Chile to become Chief of the Survey Section of the Economic Commission for Latin America (ECLA), where he worked with Raul Prebisch and Osvaldo Sunkel and became familiar with the school of Latin American economists working on structural analysis and with dependency theory. The four years that he spent at ECLA were permanently to influence his perception of development issues. He tried to bring to the attention of 'Anglo Saxon economists' the problems faced by countries in Latin America with inflation, public finance and import substitution and to explain the debate between monetarists and structuralists. He was convinced that theories based upon Western industrialised models failed either to explain or to assist economies such as those he had been working on in Latin America and the Caribbean.

In 1961 Seers moved to Yale as a visiting professor and it was during his two years there that he wrote a number of his most pungent and influential articles, notably 'A theory of inflation and growth in under-developed economies' (1962c); 'A model of comparative rates of growth in the world economy' (1962b); 'Why visiting economists fail' (1962a); 'The limitations of the special case' (1963a); and 'Big companies and small countries' (1963c).

In 1963 Seers returned to the UN as Director of the Economic Development Division of the Economic Commission for Africa (ECA). While there he led a UN/FAO mission to Northern Rhodesia (shortly to become Zambia), which produced both an influential report in which distribution issues were explicitly addressed and a novel, modified input–output system for economic programming.

The victory of the Labour Party in the autumn elections of 1964 led to the creation of a new Ministry of Overseas Development (with Barbara Castle as minister). Seers was recruited as first director general of its Economic Planning Staff with direct access to the minister and a position just below that of the permanent under-secretary. From that vantage point he helped to organise and direct the work of the new ministry and also played a major role in the design and founding of the Institute of Development Studies at the University of Sussex before becoming, in 1967, its first substantive director. In 1972, the IDS directorship passed to Richard Jolly (later, Sir Richard), but Seers remained an exceptionally active, inspirational and influential Fellow until his death in March 1983.

In 1969, Seers became President of the Society for International Development (SID), having earlier been president of its UK chapter, and in 1975 he was elected the founding President of the European Association of Development Research Institutes (EADI). He was made a Companion of St Michael and St George (CMG) by the British government in 1975, having previously in 1970 been awarded the Order of Boyaca of Colombia.

Seers's familiarity with how statistics were actually compiled led him to question the relevance or appropriateness of standard accounting conventions as indicators of 'development' in African and Latin American conditions. If GDP grows but income distribution becomes more unequal, the number living in abject poverty increases, and the country becomes less self-reliant, would we want to call that development? Seers argued that sta-tistical offices in developing countries should switch away from feeding dubious numbers into a Eurocentric system of national accounts and towards identifying, measuring and tracking the key indicators of each nation's specific development goals. He advocated a similar switch in planning offices: from the construction of complex publishable models (largely useless for planning purposes) towards confidential staff work that would advise heads of government on the likely outcomes of alternative development strategies, includ-ing a review of their political, military, cultural and educational implications.

In the same vein, one strand of his work involved formulating new indicators of devel-opment and devising methods to measure these. In his later years he focused upon life pro-files for different social groups and different countries as a method of social accounting, providing a consistent framework for data collection and comparisons. Research on the construction of these 'active life profiles' was carried out with the help of statistical offices in Brazil, Hong Kong, Malaysia and Kenya.

Dudley Seers's written output was prolific. An attempt by the IDS Library to gather together his work produced over 300 items. But it was not until after his death that his only full-length book appeared. Nearly everything else that he wrote after the early years was either country or problem specific, and was usually aimed at getting something done. His favoured outlets were journal articles, discussion papers and country reports. He led a major post-revolutionary study of Cuba (1962), and after the Zambia report (1964), led or participated in other consultancy reports on Colombia (1970), Sri Lanka (1971), Uganda (1978) and Nigeria (1979). He was recognised as being masterly in moulding together contributions by a variety of team members into a single report with a strong central theme – often the need to increase employment and to attack poverty alleviation directly, while at the same time maintaining financial discipline.

He wrote three short booklets, presented numerous conference papers, gave visiting lec-tures, and contributed chapters to books being edited by others. There were also news-paper articles (mainly for *The Guardian*), letters to the editor, book and film reviews, background and briefing papers, interviews and broadcasts, a submission to a parlia-mentary select committee, and the fullest and most frequent 'journey reports' of any Fellow at the Institute. These last, since they were for internal circulation only, were frank, funny, ruminative, frequently rude but also packed with information, anecdotes, *obiter dicta* and appreciation of the work of others.

Seers's approach to work for the international agencies was distinctive. He was at his best working with an international team, sharing jokes and comradeship, setting impos-sible timetables for drafts – but then by example, organisation and support ensuring that they were met. His ideal team combined young and old, new and experienced, some from within the UN, some from outside, including if possible some with sharply contrasting viewpoints. For the ILO employment missions, Seers introduced the rule that he would take on the leadership only if he alone was to be responsible for the content of their final report – thereby bypassing the bureaucratic caution and excessive sensitivities that he felt too often blurred the message of most international documents. But he was a realist, as well as a romantic, and exercised these responsibilities to produce reports which were innovative but professional, provocative but not embarrassing. And as a point of profes-sional integrity, the contribution of every team member was fully acknowledged.

Of his own attitudes and published work, Seers observed:

I suppose I owe most, however, not to desk work in Britain, or the books I have read, but to the jobs I have done overseas. The world is a great laboratory of social experiments, but to take advantage of this wealth of experience one has to work in a variety of countries: the information available in print is very partial and biased. If I had stayed in an academic post at home, I would now view the world very differently: I would analyse it with much less attention to the social aspects and the practical issues of policy and administration in different environments. (Seers, 1983, p. ix)

The nature of those overseas assignments had made Seers particularly aware of the special problems of small countries *vis-à-vis* the Great Powers and less conscious than he later became of regional differences and the costs imposed by centralised bureaucracies. He listed 'teasing bureaucrats' among his recreations in *Who's Who* but – as Singer has pointed out – he teased not only bureaucrats, but also academics, Marxists, friends and foes, and also himself.

Challenging orthodoxies was another favoured occupation, and several of Seers's most memorable forays did precisely that. An early example was 'The limitations of the special case' (1963a), probably his most frequently reprinted publication. In this article, as Richard Jolly has written:

Seers warned against the dangers of naively transferring theories and analytical models from the 'special case' of developed countries to the rest of the world. Analysis of developing economies, he argued, must focus on the structural characteristics of these countries, for instance their heavy dependence on imports, fluctuating earnings from primary products, high proportions of population in agriculture and the rural areas, weak infrastructure and fragmented labour markets – and how these affected the dynamics of the countries, whether of the pattern of growth or of inflation. (Personal communication with author, 2003)

Seers particularly warned against the application of Keynesian prescriptions in open economies where the critical problem was much less likely to be deficiency of demand than bottlenecks in supply. In 'The birth, life and death of development economics' (1979a) Seers argues that 'from a professional point of view, the time has come . . . to dispose of development economics'. The reasons which he gives are similar to those which led to the institute which he helped to found being called the 'Institute of Development Studies', not of development economics. Implied in the choice of name was the need to take account of political, social and cultural factors – and of history – in explaining development and underdevelopment. The choice also reflected Seers's disapproval of the application of standard national income accounting conventions to less-developed economies. In a characteristic footnote, he observes 'in any economy which is predominantly rural (i.e typical) a competent statistician can produce almost any growth rate, even keeping strictly to the conventions of the UN System of National Accounts' (Seers, 1983).

Later on Seers was to align himself with Joan Robinson and Thomas Balogh in arguing that conventional textbook analysis was becoming decreasingly relevant even in Western economies. This in turn opened the way for his application to the industrialised economies of some of the concepts and techniques which had evolved in the analysis of developing countries.

Towards the end of his career, Seers became increasingly preoccupied with the problems of Europe, using the core–periphery model to analyse the situation and prospects of areas such as Greece, Southern Italy, Portugal, Eire and Scotland:

> We should abandon the convention that development is a problem only of the countries of Africa, Asia and Latin America which are eligible for aid. This approach which has been rooted in political expediency and paternalism now hinders the professionalisation of the subject . . . The significance of the European periphery is that it provides a bridge across which the subject can escape from its conventional, essentially tropical, boundaries . . . North Sea oil is a proper subject for development studies. (Ibid.)

His book *The Political Economy of Nationalism* (1983) takes these arguments further. In it he argues that the division of the globe into 'three worlds' had become obsolete by the 1970s while plans for a New International Economic Order are dismissed as no more than an attempt to reform (and thus prolong the life of) an existing neocolonial system. In their place, Seers foresees the emergence of several large regional groupings which will become increasingly self-reliant, and which can be expected to provide a more stable basis for an enlarged Europe and a better prospect for world peace.

To the surprise of some of his colleagues, and to the dismay of others, some delinking between the industrialised West and the less-developed world is recommended with a view to increasing this regional self-reliance. Seers also called for a reduction in the EEC foreign aid target to just 0.1 per cent of GDP since much of it, he argued, merely had the effect of keeping corrupt and inefficient governments in power. Twenty-one years before it happened, the book foresees the possibility of the countries in Soviet-dominated Eastern Europe becoming part of the European 'region', and predicts that attention and aid would be concentrated on integrating these countries and diverted away from former European colonies in what he thought was now inappropriately described as 'the Third World'.

In keeping with its un-academic style, the book contains amusing anecdotes of Seers's meetings with Kwame Nkrumah (who had not previously realised that his government could 'borrow' the surpluses of the Cocoa Marketing Board); with Fidel Castro (who is quoted as saying that the reason for a sharp rise in the birthrate soon after the revolution was that a big order for 'Dutch caps' had been read as an order for automotive gaskets); and with Dom Mintoff, whom Seers much admired for making the most of Malta's limited 'room for manoeuvre'.

His early death left innovative and exciting work undone. None the less his contribution to his chosen field was seminal and his influence massive. It has been said that he practically invented 'development studies' combining aspects of economics, political science, sociology, statistics, demography, geography and history in a sequence of country- or problem-specific studies. He also wrote with penetration on issues of measurement and methodology. If all these contributions together never quite added up to a single 'theory of development' that may have been because the breadth of his experience had convinced him that no single explanation as to why countries do or do not 'develop' could be either useful or true.

MIKE FABER

References and further reading

IDS (1983), 'IDS Annual Report, 1982', *IDS Handbook 1983*, Brighton: Institute of Development Studies, University of Sussex, pp. 2–5.

Seers, D. (1946), *The Challenges to New Zealand Labour*, Christchurch: Christchurch Cooperative Bank Society.

Seers, D. (1949), *Changes in the Cost of Living and the Distribution of Income since 1938*, Oxford: Basil Blackwell.

Seers, D. (1959), 'An approach to the short-period analysis of primary-producing economies', *Oxford Economic Papers*, **11** (1), 1–36.

Seers, D. (1962a), 'Why visiting economists fail', *Journal of Political Economy*, **70** (4), 325–38.

Seers, D. (1962b), 'A model of comparative rates of growth in the world economy', *Economic Journal*, **74** (285), 45–78.

Seers, D. (1962c), 'A theory of inflation and growth in under-developed economies based on the experience of Latin America', *Oxford Economic Papers*, **14** (2), 173–95.

Seers, D. (1963a), 'The limitations of the special case', Oxford University Institute of Economics and Statistics, *Bulletin*, **25** (2), 77–98.

Seers, D. (1963b), 'The role of industry in development: some fallacies', *Journal of Modern African Studies*, **1** (4), 461–5.

Seers, D. (1963c), 'Big companies and small countries: a practical proposal', *International Review for Social Sciences*, **16** (4), 509–608.

Seers, D. (1964a), *Report of the UN/ECA/FAO Economic Survey Mission on the Economic Development of Zambia*, Entebbe.

Seers, D. (1964b), 'The economic and social background', in Seers (ed.), *Cuba: The Economic and Social Revolution*, Chapel Hill, NC: University of North Carolina Press, pp. 3–61.

Seers, D. (1971), *Matching Employment Opportunities and Expectations: A Programme of Action for Ceylon*, Report of an Inter-Agency Team, Geneva: International Labour Organization.

Seers, D. (1972), 'What are we trying to measure?', *Journal of Development Studies*, **8** (2), 21–36.

Seers, D. (1976), 'A new look at the three world classification', *IDS Bulletin*, **7** (4), 8–13.

Seers, D. (1977), 'Life expectancy as an integrating concept in social and demographic analysis and planning', *Review of Income and Wealth*, **23** (3), 195–203.

Seers, D. (1979a), 'The birth, life and death of development economics', *Development and Change*, **10** (4), 707–19.

Seers, D. (1979b), *The Rehabilitation of the Economy of Uganda*, Report by a Commonwealth Team of Experts, Commonwealth Secretariat, London.

Seers, D. (1980), 'Muddling morality and mutuality: a review of the Brandt Report', *Third World Quarterly*, **2** (4), 681–93.

Seers, D. (1981), 'The life cycle of a petroleum economy and its implication for development', *Research for Development*, **1** (1) (Journal of the Nigerian Institute of Social and Economic Research).

Seers, D. (1982), 'Active life profiles for different social groups: a contribution to demographic accounting, a frame for social indicators and a tool of social and economic analysis', Discussion Paper 178, Institute of Development Studies, University of Sussex, Brighton.

Seers, D. (1983), *The Political Economy of Nationalism*, Oxford: Oxford University Press.

Toye, J. (ed.) (1989), Special Issue on 'Dudley Seers: His Work and Influence', *IDS Bulletin*, **20** (3), 1–70.

Sen, Amartya Kumar (b. 1933)

In the first post-war decades when development economics blossomed, the field was strongly influenced by the Harrod–Domar reformulation of John Maynard Keynes's short-run anti-cyclical ideas to address the problem of long-run growth. Savings, investment and sacrifices in current consumption to achieve greater capital accumulation were seen as the key elements in economic development. That view was shaken a bit by the mid-1950s growth models of Abramovitz (1956) and Solow (1957), which revealed how much of the growth experience is *not* explained by capital accumulation alone. Nevertheless, despite the important work of Kenneth Arrow, P.T. Bauer, Albert O. Hirschman, Gunnar Myrdal and others, attention was concentrated on savings behaviour, capital accumulation and transfer of technology, often to the relative neglect of human resources, culture and welfare outcomes. The shift in this paradigm that has occurred since the early days of development economics owes much to the influence of Amartya Sen, whose impact on the field began around 1960, when his *Choice of Techniques* was first published. In the years since, the field has evolved away from what Sen has called a 'blood, sweat and tears' approach of viewing the repression of current well-being as the price of greater invest-ment and growth. In its place, more complex and flexible paradigms have emerged that bring out not only the important roles of human capital formation, technological change and culture in development, but also take a more benign view of the development process, emphasising both the desirability and possibility of achieving substantial progress in 'human development' even at low levels of per capita income. Sen has been a major influ-ence in this evolution.

Sen's first book, *Choice of Techniques* (1960) was an essay in development economics. Although not the field for which he received the Nobel Prize in 1998, it has always been linked in his work to underlying welfare principles, and couched explicitly in a philo-sophical and welfare economics framework. Atkinson (1999, p. 187) notes:

> [T]he integrated view of the subject . . . runs through [Sen's] work in different fields and links the research at different stages of his career. This is apparent from the way in which the essays on development economics interlock with those on social justice. Concern with famine is linked to that with poverty, and writing on the measurement of poverty draws in turn on his more philo-sophical investigations.

Indeed, a truly comprehensive assessment of Amartya Sen's contributions to develop-ment economics would require consideration of his entire *oeuvre*, an impractical task in view of the fact that the list of his published work only through 1998 given by the *Scandinavian Journal of Economics* (1999) occupies some 13 pages of small, single-spaced text. Limiting discussion to Sen's contributions to development studies requires some arbitrary demarcations.

Choice of Techniques explored the connection between technical choice decisions and the resulting distribution of income between profits and wages and, therefore, the rate of saving. As Sen explained in the 'Introduction' to *Choice of Techniques* (3rd edn, reprinted as ch. 9 in Sen 1984), 'The determination of the optimum *size* of total savings and that of the optimum *capital-intensity* of investment are interdependent problems. This inter-dependence provides the starting point of this book' (p. 207, original emphasis). Because in an economy with surplus labour the social opportunity cost of labour was assumed to be zero in the sense of zero marginal labour productivity, many authors concluded that the optimum technology would be the most labour-intensive one. Sen argued that labour should not be regarded as costless under these circumstances *if* the savings volume is sub-optimal and more weight should be attached to extra investment *vis-à-vis* extra con-sumption. Thus there might be reason to favour a more capital-intensive technology in a capital-scarce country than would be chosen in a free market with factor prices deter-mined by factor endowments. While sacrificing some output in the near term, such a choice would lead to a higher growth rate and to higher output in the longer run.

Others, notably Galenson and Leibenstein (1955) and Maurice Dobb (1960), advocated adopting capital-intensive techniques precisely in order to maximise savings and growth. Sen's formulation, however, enabled the choice to depend on the suboptimality of savings and the resulting premium to be placed on extra saving and investment. That decision would depend on the planners' time horizon or social discount rate, but also presupposes the possibility of suboptimal saving under either market or planning conditions. This link embedded the choice of techniques discussion in a large literature on the optimal savings rate, to which Sen made important contributions (for instance, 1961, 1967, 1984).

The argument also led directly to reconsideration of the labour surplus model of Nurkse (1953), Lewis (1954), Ranis and Fei (1961) and others, in a classic paper (1966) showing that 'the assumption of zero marginal productivity of labour is neither a necessary nor a sufficient condition for the existence of surplus' (p. 46 of version in Sen 1984). This paper disarmed the protagonists on both sides of the ongoing debate over the existence of surplus labour: it showed, on the one hand, that existence did not necessarily imply such unlikely behaviour as working without producing anything, and on the other, that some results attributed to surplus labour did not in fact require it, while its limits needed also to be considered.

Sen later came to re-evaluate somewhat these early contributions in the context of the evolution of development economics away from preoccupation with physical capital accumulation and towards greater recognition both of the role of human capital and the importance of improving human well-being and the quality of life sooner rather than later in the process of development (1997a, fn. 5). Both trends in fact owe much to Sen's own contributions, which have also strongly influenced the formulation of the 'human development' concept now used extensively by the United Nations Development Programme (UNDP).

Rejection of the 'blood, sweat and tears' view was also an implicit theme of Sen's empirical work on hunger and famines (1981; Drèze and Sen, 1989). Starting from the 1981 book analysing four historical famines and culminating in the three-volume edited work (with Jean Drèze and Athar Hussain), *The Political Economy of Hunger* (1990), which brought together contributions by experts on much of the developing world, this corpus of work proposed and explored an 'entitlements' framework of understanding famine as a collapse in the ability of groups of individuals to acquire food, and it went on to analyse the conditions in which such entitlement losses could occur and the kinds of policies needed to prevent this. An important conclusion to emerge was that famines are neither impossible nor even very difficult to prevent even in very poor countries, given the necessary political conditions. From establishing that poor countries have had very different records with respect to famine prevention, it was not a large step to investigating the international comparative record of indicators of human well-being, such as longevity, morbidity and literacy. As it became clear that economic growth in low-income countries had been accompanied by a wide range of achievements in human development, the notion of an 'iron law' suppressing improvements in well-being through the 'dark Satanic mills' stages faded away, creating room for discussions of the public policy agenda needed to make economic growth friendlier to human development. Thus, recognition of the historical *feasibility* of a more humane approach to development, even at very low levels of income per capita, was an important root of the shift in view.

Another such root concerned the *urgency* of improving well-being now rather than waiting until some future time of greater affluence – the ethical dimension around which Sen's influence has been particularly felt. He framed this as the imperative, in an

intertemporal decision context, to place 'appropriate valuation on the terrible deprivations that exist right now' and to pay 'special attention to the priority of preventing deprivations that are known to be both *definitely disastrous* and *definitely preventable*' (1997a,
p. 9, original emphasis). Third, Sen along with others has underlined the *synergies* that
exist between improving health, nutrition and education, on the one hand, and promoting rapid economic growth, on the other – so that investing in human beings also stimulates development (see 1997a; also Strauss and Thomas, 1998). This recognition of the
importance of human resources in the development process relieves the starkness of the
classic perceived conflict between present and future welfare; now, future welfare is dependent on improvements in human resources, which in turn lift present welfare. Finally,
some aspects of development now recognised as important to both its conceptualisation
and accomplishment, such as improving the status of women and overcoming discrimination against them, are directly affected by present improvements in provision of health
and education. Here, too, Sen has been a contributor, both with respect to exploring such
individual issues as gender discrimination (for instance, chs 15 and 16 of 1984, as well as
1989, 1990a, b, and 1992b), and more generally in influencing the very way we conceptualise development.

While Sen's work on famine, which re-casts our understanding of its causes and means
of prevention, had a great impact, probably the most important influence of Sen's work
on development economics derives from his foundational re-definition of development
itself. He has made the case for regarding development not in terms of increasing commodity production, or income, or utility, or bringing about structural change or meeting
basic needs, but rather as an expansion of people's 'capabilities' (1984), which represent
'the various combinations of functionings (beings and doings) that the person can
achieve' (1992a, p. 40). Capabilities reflect the freedom that people have to do and be what
they wish to. Such a freedom-centred view of development is certainly not new; indeed,
Sen (1984) points to its roots at least as far back as Adam Smith and Karl Marx. However,
Sen's rigorous statement of this view and his convincing comparisons of it with rival concepts have given it a strong claim to be the best way to conceptualise development. The
argument, which is elucidated most fully in *Development as Freedom* (1999) focuses attention on development's basic human objectives (Sen's 'evaluative reason' for putting
freedom at the core of the development concept), as well as underlining the role of individual and collective human agency in accomplishing these objectives. If development is
the widening of freedom, then the empowerment of people to achieve it themselves is consistent with the goal. Sen's 'effectiveness reason' for regarding development as the expansion of freedom is that 'achievement of development is thoroughly dependent on the free
agency of people' (1999, p. 4).

Defining development in this way has many ramifications. To take but one example, it
suggests a basis other than the strictly instrumental or strictly ideological for evaluating
the respective roles of market and state in the pursuit of development. In his extensive
work on Indian development, as well as in commenting on the paths pursued by formerly
socialist countries, Sen has criticised both state interventions in areas more properly left
to the market, and also the *absence* of sufficient government role where it is warranted and
indispensable: 'There is . . . quite a deep complementarity between reducing, on the one
hand, the overactivity of the state in running a "license Raj," and, on the other, removing

the underactivity of the state in the continuing neglect of elementary education and other social opportunities' (1999, p. 127). This position, while perhaps out of synch with 'market fundamentalist' fashions, is both consistent with orthodox theories of market failure, especially as these have been supplemented in recent decades by considerations of information, incomplete markets and so on, and also sensitive to the issue of 'government failure'. The difference is that Sen's argument is based on the freedom criterion: deprivation of opportunities for market exchange is a limitation of freedom, but so is government default on its responsibility to supply public goods such as education and health, whose absence also constrains freedom by limiting the expansion of desired capabilities.

Although some major development issues (for example, the natural environment and its link to the issue of sustainable development) have escaped his attention, Sen has taken on many issues squarely in development studies as well as on its periphery. In addition to the contributions discussed already, he has written on the question of the conceptualisation and measurement of poverty (1976, 1983) and of inequality (1992a, 1997b; Sen and Foster, 1997). His work on investment appraisal and project evaluation (Sen et al., 1972), along with that of Little and Mirrlees (1974), provided pioneering guides to how project planning can accommodate differences between market and social valuations of investment alternatives. He has dealt with employment (1975), intra-household distribution (1988, originally published as 1984, ch. 15), population (1993, 1994a, b), and the usefulness of measures such as mortality or life expectancy at birth to investigate discrimination according to gender, race, caste or ethnicity (1989, 1990a, b, 1992b), and much more, as they say. What unifies these disparate contributions is their common grounding in a clear philosophical and analytical framework, their common concern for people suffering from poverty, discrimination or exploitation, and their Enlightenment optimism that humane values and the exercise of clear-headed thought can measurably improve the human condition.

CARL RISKIN

References

Abramovitz, Moses (1956), 'Resource and output trends in the United States since 1870', *American Economic Review*, **46** (2), 5–23.
Atkinson, Anthony B. (1999), 'The contributions of Amartya Sen to welfare economics', *Scandinavian Journal of Economics*, **101** (2), 173–90.
Dobb, Maurice (1960), *An Essay on Economic Growth and Planning*, London: Routledge.
Drèze, Jean and Amartya Sen (1989), *Hunger and Public Action*, Oxford: Clarendon.
Drèze, Jean, Amartya Sen and Athar Hussain (eds) (1990), *The Political Economy of Hunger*, Oxford: Clarendon.
Galenson, Walter and Harvey Leibenstein (1955), 'Investment criteria, productivity and economic development', *Quarterly Journal of Economics*, **69**, 343–70.
Lewis, W. Arthur (1954), 'Economic development with unlimited supplies of labour', *Manchester School*, **22**, 139–91.
Little, I.M.D. and James A. Mirrlees (1974), *Project Appraisal and Planning for Developing Countries*, London: Heinemann and New York: Basic Books.
Nurkse, Ragnar (1953), *Problems of Capital-Formation in Underdeveloped Countries*, Oxford: Oxford University Press.
Ranis, G. and J.C.H. Fei (1961), 'A theory of economic development', *American Economic Review*, **51**, 533–58.
Sen, Amartya (1960), *Choice of Techniques: An Aspect of the Theory of Planned Economic Development*, Oxford: Blackwell (3rd edn, 1968).
Sen, Amartya (1961), 'On optimising the rate of saving', *Economic Journal*, **71**, 479–96.
Sen, Amartya (1966), 'Peasants and dualism with or without surplus labour', *Journal of Political Economy*, **74**, 425–50.

Sen, Amartya (1967), 'Terminal capital and optimum savings', in C.H. Feinstein (ed.), *Socialism, Capitalism, and Economic Growth, Essays Presented to Maurice Dobb*, Cambridge: Cambridge University Press, pp. 40–53.

Sen, Amartya (1975), *Employment, Technology and Development: A Study Prepared for the International Office within the Framework of the World Employment Programme*, Oxford: Clarendon.

Sen, Amartya (1976), 'Poverty: an ordinal approach to measurement', *Econometrica*, **44** (2), 219–31.

Sen, Amartya (1981), *Poverty and Famines: An Essay on Entitlement and Deprivation*, Oxford and New York: Oxford University Press.

Sen, Amartya (1983), 'Poor, relatively speaking', *Oxford Economic Papers*, **35**, 153–69 (reprinted in Sen, 1984, Essay 14).

Sen, Amartya (1984), *Resources, Values, and Development*, Cambridge, MA: Harvard University Press.

Sen, Amartya (1988), 'Family and food: sex bias in poverty', in P. Bardhan and T.N. Srinivasan (eds), *Rural Poverty in South Asia*, New York: Columbia University Press, pp. 453–72.

Sen, Amartya (1989), 'Women's survival as a development problem', *Bulletin of the American Academy of Arts and Sciences*, **43**, 14–29.

Sen, Amartya (1990a), 'Gender and cooperative conflict', in Irene Tinker (ed.), *Persistent Inequalities*, Oxford and New York: Oxford University Press, pp. 123–49.

Sen, Amartya (1990b), 'More than one hundred million women are missing', *New York Review of Books*, **37** (20), 61–7.

Sen, Amartya (1992a), *Inequality Reexamined*, Oxford: Clarendon.

Sen, Amartya (1992b), 'Missing women', *British Medical Journal*, **304**, 586–7.

Sen, Amartya (1993), 'On the Darwinian view of progress', *Population and Development Review*, **19** (1), 130–37.

Sen, Amartya (1994a), 'Population and reasoned agency: food, fertility, and economic development', in Kerstin Lindahl-Kiessling and Hans Landberg (eds), *Population, Economic Development, and the Environment*, Oxford: Oxford University Press, pp. 51–78.

Sen, Amartya (1994b), 'Population: delusion and reality', *New York Review of Books*, **41** (15), 66–71.

Sen, Amartya (1997a), 'Development thinking at the beginning of the 21st century', Suntory and Toyota International Centres for Economics and Related Disciplines Discussion Paper no. DEDPS/2, London, www.sticerd.lse.ac.uk/dps/de/dedps 2.pdf.

Sen, Amartya (1997b), 'From income inequality to economic inequality', *Southern Economic Journal*, **64** (2), 384–401.

Sen, Amartya (1999), *Development As Freedom*, New York: Alfred A. Knopf and Oxford: Oxford University Press.

Sen, Amartya and James E. Foster (1997), *On Economic Inequality*, Oxford: Clarendon.

Sen, Amartya, Stephen Marglin and Partha Dasgupta (1972), *Guidelines for Project Evaluation*, New York: UNIDO.

Solow, Robert (1957), 'Technical change and the aggregate production function', *Review of Economics and Statistics*, **39** (4), 312–20.

Strauss, John and Duncan Thomas (1998), 'Health, nutrition and economic development', *Journal of Economic Literature*, **36** (2), 766–817.

Sharecropping

Historically, with settled agriculture, direct producers have worked the land under a variety of production relations. They have done so as peasant proprietors, who deploy predominantly family labour, with, perhaps, some wage labour at peak seasons; as tenants, who may be serfs or free, or in a range of unfree relationships with landlords; as slaves, who own nothing and are themselves the property of slave-owners; or as wage labourers, who own only their labour power and are most likely to work for rich peasants or capitalist farmers. In a particular social formation, these may coexist, although one may be the dominant form.

Where, from time immemorial, a landlord class, and, with it, tenancy, have existed, so, too has sharecropping. Sharecropping is the division of the crop in predetermined, proportionate terms, or in fixed shares, between landlord and tenant. The archetypal share of the gross produce in the historical record is 50:50, with, traditionally, the landlord supplying the land and the tenant everything else: this reflected in the notion of half being built into the word for sharecropping in various languages (for example, French, Italian, German, Dutch, and some of the regional languages of India). It has been suggested that there is a perceived justice in this. If so, it is a 'justice' that sharecroppers have not always acknowledged. In practice, however, there has been considerable variety around these apparent norms, with sharecroppers often parting with more than 50 per cent and sometimes with less; and sometimes with landlords supplying some of the inputs other than land, in cost–share leasing arrangements, and then taking a higher share of the crop.

Records are sparse, but sharecropping, rather than, or as well as, other rental forms (or forms of surplus appropriation) – such as labour rent, fixed produce rent, or fixed money rent – existed in several ancient societies. This has been so, for example, in ancient Greece, in sixth century BC Attica; in ancient China, in the Spring and Autumn Period, 722–481 BC; and in ancient India – it is mentioned in the Arthasastra of Kautilya, a celebrated manual of statecraft of the fourth century BC (on these instances, see Byres 1983, pp. 7–11).

Since ancient times, there are very few countries in which it has not existed, often persisting for several centuries. In Europe, England (in medieval England it was known as *champart* rent) and Scotland (where those who paid it were termed 'steel bow tenants') were unusual in the relative unimportance of share rent. The reasons for its relative absence in England are discussed in Hilton (1990). But in, for example, France (*métayage*), Italy (*mezzadria*) and Spain (*aparcería*) it was important and persisted from before the medieval era until 1945 and after. Elsewhere in Europe, it was common in, for example, parts of western Germany (*halbpacht* and *halfmann* or *halfen* and *halfwinner*), the eastern Netherlands (*helftwinning* and *deelpacht*), Belgium (*tierce part*, where the landlord's share was supposedly one-third), and Russia (*polovnichestvo*). On these European instances, see Byres (1983, pp. 11–25). In the American South, where it replaced slavery as the dominant mode of surplus appropriation after 1865, it did not disappear until the late 1950s (for its existence and the reasons for its ultimate demise there, see Byres, 1996, ch. 7, pp. 282–341). In all these cases, it was eliminated by capitalism, except in Russia, where it was socialist intervention that rooted it out. Once a productive technology emerged with significant economies of scale, and massively reduced labour input per acre, operating with wage labour became by far the most profitable option.

Outside of Europe it continued to exist, on a large scale, in both China and India, economically backward countries that contained the world's largest concentrations of population, right through to the post-1945 era. In, for example, Persia, there are records of the crop-sharing contract, the *muzare'h*, being dominant in the countryside from at least the third century AD through to the 1950s and beyond. On these cases, see Byres (1983, pp. 25–31). In China, it was eradicated in the 1950s, with land reform and then by collectivisation. It has not returned, to any extent. In India, its eradication has been the object of land reform programmes, in the various states, in the 1950s and 1960s; and a concerted attempt was made in West Bengal, from 1978 onwards, to secure the rights and improve the conditions of sharecroppers, in Operation *Barga* (*barga* is Bengali for sharecropping), with some success. Sharecropping is still in evidence in West Bengal and elsewhere in India, although it is now on the decline. In poor countries, generally, although sharecropping has been diminishing, with the progress of capitalism and the advance of technology, it retains some considerable presence: in Asia, outside of the countries noted, and with the exceptions of Japan, South Korea and Taiwan, where capitalism has done its work; in Latin America; and in Africa.

The virtual ubiquity and clear tenacity of sharecropping cry out for explanation. Yet, historians, with some honourable exceptions (for example, Hilton 1990), while noting its existence, have avoided such explanation. Sharecropping has not figured prominently in the historical literature. Economists, by contrast, have been much preoccupied by it and until recently have tended to condemn it roundly as inefficient. This raises a conundrum as to why it can have existed so widely and for so long.

If sharecropping has been so pervasive and, often, so difficult to dislodge, there has been considerable variety in the conditions attached to it. Apart from the variety in the share accruing to each party and in whether the landlord supplies any of the inputs other than land, already noted, this has been so with respect to whether the landlord was resident or absentee; whether the landlord invested in land improvements and farm buildings; and whether tenure was secure. Which of these prevailed, it has been argued, would influence how productively the land was worked, although there might be dispute over how and to what extent the influence operated: over, for example, whether the share itself, and its accompanying conditions, generated incentives or disincentives to produce, or compulsions to survive (and, therefore, to produce).

As already noted, its prevalence, in the past, in Europe (other than England and Scotland), and elsewhere, attracted the attention of economists. For example, among classical economists, Adam Smith (1976, pp. 390–91), was very influential; while, among neoclassicals, and even more influential, was Alfred Marshall (1979, pp. 534–7). Other classical economists who wrote on sharecropping included Arthur Young, Sismondi, Richard Jones, John Ramsay McCulloch and John Stuart Mill. A succinct treatment of their views, with the relevant references, may be seen in Johnson (1950, pp. 111–14) and Cheung (1969, pp. 30–42).

Usually, although not always, sharecropping attracted their censure, as inefficient. That inefficiency was held to derive from the disincentive to tenants associated with the share that automatically accrued to the landlord (which, in practice, might be more than the archetypal 50 per cent). Marshall was especially influential in formulating such a case: the Marshallian formulation remaining the essential neoclassical case against sharecropping from the 1890s until the late 1960s. It was an argument centring on the incentive to apply labour and to invest. The Marshallian prediction, rigorously formulated, and on the given assumptions, was that a sharecropper would apply less labour input and invest less per acre, and, therefore, produce less output per acre, than a peasant proprietor, a tenant paying fixed money rent, or a capitalist farmer (whether tenant or proprietor) using wage labour.

Marx, too, discussed it (1962, p. 783), but not in the aforementioned terms. Rather, he considered it in the context of the 'genesis of capitalist ground rent', as a 'transient form' between the 'original form of rent' and 'capitalist rent'. His expectation was that capitalist agriculture would be far more productive than farming pursued through sharecropping and would, ultimately, sweep it away. In the Marxist tradition, sharecropping's defining characteristic, which made it a preferred rental form for landlords, has been seen to be its capacity to maximise surplus appropriation. There was, then, in this tradition, no mystery as to why sharecropping has been so common historically and so stubbornly unyielding, in pre-capitalist conditions.

There was, however, as already indicated, a puzzle, for neoclassicals. Why, if it was so inefficient, had it been so widespread and so tenacious? Both landlord and sharecropper would, in principle, benefit from a shift to a more efficient way of working the land. Marshall suggested that the inefficiency might be overcome by 'constant interference' by the landlord to secure the maximum intensity of cultivation. That, of course, implied persistent monitoring of labour input. It might also be argued that the postulated inefficiency might, in part, be reduced, if not eliminated, where particular conditions accompanying sharecropping prevailed: where, for example, the landlord's share was less than 50 per cent, tenure was secure (Smith had stressed the disincentive associated with insecure tenure), or the landlord was resident and invested in improvements and buildings. Both Sismondi and Mill had argued, before Marshall, in favour of sharecropping, on such grounds, as it existed in nineteenth-century Italy (in Tuscany, at least), where there was secure tenure and landlords invested in farm buildings; although in France, where tenure was insecure, such a case could not be made. But for neoclassicals, the puzzle, apparently inherent in sharecropping, remained.

For Marxists, the puzzle did not exist. Nor did it exist for a latter-day neoclassical, D. Gale Johnson (1950), who, in an important article, wished to explain its existence in the American South – ironically, writing just as it was disappearing there. Johnson provided a powerful explanation for its persistence in terms of conditions imposed by landlords, in an unequal bargaining situation: cost–share leasing, with landlords supplying inputs, and so ensuring appropriate investment, and taking an appropriately larger share of the crop; insecure tenancies, which sharecroppers, fearful of losing the tenancy, would strive to have renewed through considerable effort (here insecurity acting as a spur to effort rather than as a disincentive); holdings that were deliberately small, which drew effort from sharecroppers to reach tolerable levels of subsistence. Given the absence of alternative employment opportunities (an opportunity cost of labour close to zero), something approaching output maximisation might emerge. So here was effective compulsion, which had the effect of maximising the rental return.

For the most part, until the late 1960s, the European tradition of condemnation prevailed, and its targeted eradication in poor countries was a common feature of land reform programmes. Marxists continued to see it as a feature of pre-capitalist relationships in the countryside of poor countries and do so down to the present (for example, Bhaduri, 1983 and Patnaik, 1983).

From the late 1960s, a new generation of neoclassical economists discovered its apparently positive properties. It was argued that in circumstances of endemic risk, such as characterised agriculture in poor countries, sharecropping's unique capacity to *disperse risk*, for both landlord and tenant, made it the optimal solution for each party. Assume, for example, a very bad harvest. If the landlord worked the land with wage labour, the whole risk would fall upon him, since he would have to pay the relevant wages. On the other hand, if there were tenancy, with a fixed money rent, the risk would fall upon the tenants. With sharecropping, however, risk is distributed equally between the two parties. The first rigorous case in these terms was made by Cheung (1969), who argued that sharecropping was the preferred option where the advantages deriving from risk dispersal exceeded the transaction costs (both negotiation costs and enforcement costs) associated with the sharecropping relationship. Such an argument has been developed, most notably by Joseph Stiglitz (1974, 1987, 1989), who posited that sharecropping, far from dampening incentives, raised them by dispersing risk and minimising the costs of monitoring labour inputs. Here, then, is an apparently convincing explanation of the puzzle of sharecropping's prevalence and longevity. This has been part of the so-called 'new development economics', whose dominant intellectual force has been Stiglitz (1986), who concisely states its major postulates. There has been a veritable explosion of writing on sharecropping and other 'agrarian institutions', in this tradition.

It is by no means the case, however, that the previous 'condemnation' or explanations for sharecropping's existence have disappeared. There are, indeed, those who argue that the new development economics casts little light upon the condition of sharecroppers in poor countries either now or at any point in their history, or upon sharecropping's remarkable incidence and persistence (for example, Bhaduri, 1986). Sharecroppers have never had any real bargaining power *vis-à-vis* landlords. Rather, the asymmetry of economic power has been marked. Any improvement in their lot, or, indeed, the elimination of sharecropping, has required either the active intervention of the state, whether socialist or capitalist, or a transformation wrought via the development of capitalism.

TERENCE J. BYRES

References

Bhaduri, Amit (1983), 'Cropsharing as a labour process: size of farm and supervision cost', *Journal of Peasant Studies*, **10** (2–3), 88–93. Special issue on Sharecropping and Sharecroppers.

Bhaduri, Amit (1986), 'Forced commerce and agrarian growth', *World Development*, **14** (2), 267–72.

Byres, Terence J. (1983), 'Historical perspectives on sharecropping', *Journal of Peasant Studies*, **10** (2–3), 7–40.

Byres, Terence J. (1996), *Capitalism from Above and Capitalism from Below: An Essay in Comparative Political Economy*, Basingstoke and London: Macmillan.

Cheung, Stephen N.S. (1969), *The Theory of Share Tenancy*, Chicago and London: University of Chicago Press.

Hilton, Rodney (1990), 'Why was there so little champart rent in medieval England?', *Journal of Peasant Studies*, **17** (4), 509–19.

Johnson, D. Gale (1950), 'Resource allocation under share contracts', *Journal of Political Economy*, **58**, 111–23.

Marshall, Alfred (1920 [1979]), *Principles of Economics*, 8th edn, London and Basingstoke: Macmillan (1st edn published in 1890).

Marx, Karl (1962), *Capital*, Vol. 3, Moscow: Foreign Languages Publishing House (1st edn published in German in 1894).

Patnaik, Utsa (1983), 'Classical theory of rent and its application to India: some preliminary thoughts on sharecropping', *Journal of Peasant Studies*, **10** (2–3), 71–93.

Smith, Adam (1776), *An Inquiry into the Nature and Causes of the Wealth of Nations*, reprinted in W.B. Todd (ed.) (1976), *Glasgow Edition of the Works and Correspondence of Adam Smith*, vol. I, Oxford: Oxford University Press.

Stiglitz, Joseph (1974), 'Incentives and risk-sharing in sharecropping', *Review of Economic Studies*, **41**, 219–55.

Stiglitz, Joseph (1986), 'The new development economics', *World Development*, **14** (2), 257–65.

Stiglitz, Joseph (1987), 'Sharecropping', in John Eatwell, Murray Milgate and Peter Newman (eds), *The New Palgrave: A Dictionary of Economics*, London: Macmillan.

Stiglitz, Joseph (1989), 'Rational peasants, efficient institutions, and a theory of rural organisation: methodological remarks for development economics', in Pranab Bardhan (ed.), *The Economic Theory of Agrarian Institutions*, Oxford: Clarendon pp. 18–29.

Singer, Hans (1910–2006)

Hans (later Sir Hans) Singer was one of the best-known and most respected development economists. His work was recognised in awards, honorary doctorates, and a knighthood in 1994 'for services to economic issues'. He received a Lifetime Achievement Award for his work in development economics at the UK Development Studies Association Conference in London on 6 November 2004. There can be few authorities with six *Festschrifts* in their honour (Cairncross and Puri, 1976; Clay and Shaw, 1987; Chen and Sapsford, 1997; Sapsford and Chen, 1998, 1999; Hatti and Tandon, 2006). They show the depth and breadth of Singer's influence in development economics – and the esteem and affection in which he was held.

Singer produced 450 publications since his first article appeared in 1935. (A complete list of his publications appears in Shaw, 2002 and 2004). They included over 100 books and pamphlets that he authored, co-authored or edited, or to which he contributed; over 80 reports for 13 UN organisations as well as for governments and bilateral and non-governmental bodies; 260 articles; in addition he wrote over 100 book reviews; and many letters to the editors of newspapers. The downside is that he dispersed his efforts so widely that he did not produced the one definitive work that he carries in him.

Twists of fate

The extraordinary story of Hans Singer's long and productive life shows the twists of fate that guided his development as development economist. The twists of fate started in 1929 when Singer entered Bonn University in Germany with the intention, encouraged by his father who was a doctor, of studying medicine. He switched to economics after attending a lecture by Joseph Schumpeter and came under his spell, and that of his economic masterpiece, *The Theory of Economic Development*. When he was forced to leave Nazi Germany in 1933, on the recommendation of Schumpeter, he received a two-year scholarship (1934–36) at King's College, Cambridge University in England to complete the PhD work that he had started in Bonn. At Cambridge, Singer came under another spell, that of John Maynard Keynes, precisely at the time when Keynes was producing his economic masterpiece, *The General Theory of Employment, Interest and Money*, and the supervision of Colin Clark. Singer's PhD dissertation was entitled 'Materials for the study of urban ground rent', which covered the period from 1845 to 1913 and showed his aptitude for analysing long-term data series. He was among the first group of students to receive a doctorate in economics from Cambridge University.

The hand of fate continued with Singer's first employment after university on a major two-year (1936–38) study of long-term unemployment in the depressed areas of the United Kingdom organised by the Pilgrim Trust under the chairmanship of Archbishop William Temple, with Sir William (later Lord) Beveridge as its main adviser (Pilgrim Trust, 1938). This made a strong impression on a young economist starting out on his professional career. The twists of fate continued when David Owen, who had worked with Singer on the unemployment study, was appointed as the first head of the department of economic and social affairs at the newly created United Nations. Owen sought the services of either Alec Cairncross or Hans Singer to strengthen his new department. As Cairncross was not available, Singer accepted a two-year secondment at the UN, which was to last 22 years.

The final twist came when on arriving at the UN in 1947, and in the absence of David Owen who was away on duty travel, Singer was assigned to work in a small section that dealt with the problems of developing countries. Simultaneously, he was appointed a professor in the graduate faculty of the New School for Social Research in New York. He welcomed the chance of maintaining his links with the academic world. Furthermore, it gave him the space and opportunity to think about the theoretical framework of economic development within which his work at the UN could be placed. And it gave him the opportunity to publish papers in his own name, a practice not allowed at the UN. Singer took full advantage of the opportunities these twists of fate provided to make pioneering contributions to the rapidly growing field of development economics, which were widely acknowledged and quoted.

Special attributes

What are some of the special attributes that set Singer apart from his contemporary development economists?

The combined influence of Schumpeter and Keynes

Singer came under the direct influence of *both* Schumpeter and Keynes, the two great beacons in his intellectual development as a development economist. The combination of these two forces gave a decisive form to Singer's ideas and writings. Schumpeter's views on the importance of technology and innovation and the role of the entrepreneur, and Keynes's thesis that economics is not a universal truth applicable to all countries and conditions but a framework to mould to different circumstances, provided Singer with an enabling framework for much of his work.

Terms of trade: the fulcrum

Singer's best-known contribution to development economics was his analysis of the terms of trade between industrialised and developing countries (Singer, 1949, 1950; UN, 1949). Recent research has shown conclusively that Singer's original work was subsequently used by Raul Prebisch in what became known as the Prebisch–Singer thesis, leading to a call to at least rename the concept the 'Singer–Prebisch thesis' (Toye and Toye, 2003). That thesis is generally taken to be the proposition that the net barter terms of trade between primary products and manufactures have been subject to a long-term downward trend. It contradicted the belief widely held among economists at the time that the long-term trend was in favour of primary products. Singer argued that economic history had been unkind to developing countries. Most of the secondary and cumulative effects of investment had been removed from the (developing) country in which the investment took place to the investing (industrial) country. And developing countries were diverted into types of activities offering less scope for technical progress, withholding a central factor of 'dynamic radiation' that revolutionised society in the industrialised countries. He emphasised the structural differences between countries where increased efficiency of production led to higher incomes and those where it led to falling product prices. His thesis also carried the message of historical injustice – that developing countries had helped to maintain a rising standard of living in the industrialised countries without receiving a corresponding equivalent contribution towards their own advancement.

Singer emphasised that his work was meant to be more a *policy guide* than a long-term projection. Developing countries were advised to diversify out of primary exports wherever possible by developing domestic markets and through industrialisation. Singer 'revisited' his original work on several occasions, when he put more emphasis on relations between types of countries, rather than types of commodities, and on the distribution of 'technological power' in more contemporary terms in answer to some of the criticisms of his original work. Singer also emphasised the important message the thesis contains of 'distributive justice', pointing to in-built, long-term inequalities between industrialised and developing countries. He constantly argued that unless there were fundamental changes in the world economic order, divergence rather than convergence will continue between them, threatening global economic and social advancement, stability and peace. The Prebisch–Singer thesis created a growth industry in the development economics literature. Increasingly sophisticated statistical and econometric analyses have vindicated the thesis, making it one of the very few hypotheses in economics that have stood the test of time (Sapsford and Chen, 1998).

Singer's work on the terms of trade was the fulcrum for many of the other issues he took up in order to achieve 'distributive justice' for the developing countries, including: industrialisation; science and technology; human investment; planning; trade and aid; technical assistance and pre-investment activities; regional cooperation; and international economic order with multilateral global governance.

Long service in the United Nations (1947–69)

Singer's long service in the United Nations during its formative years was also to benefit his development as a development economist. He carried out a wide range of assignments at UN headquarters in New York, in UN agencies and regional institutions, and in developing countries in Africa, Asia and Latin America. This enabled him to see at first hand conditions in the developing world, discuss with leaders and planners their developmental problems and aspirations, and set his own theoretical and conceptual framework against the background of concrete reality.

Theorist and pragmatist

Out of this milieu emerged Singer's perspectives on development including: the 'mechanics of development'; the role of the public sector in economic growth; 'a balanced view of balanced growth'; the concept of pre-investment financing; a programme, not project, approach to development; the 'myth' of counterpart funds; the notion of human investment; the interaction of population growth and education with economic growth; and, above all, his view that development is 'growth *plus* change', cultural, social and economic. Even his concept of 'redistribution from growth' to tackle poverty, which he formulated when co-leader of the ILO employment mission to Kenya in 1972, was firmly embedded in his UN experience (ILO, 1972). Singer was also one of the founding fathers of the structural analysis of development, which explains disequilibrium in the balance of trade and payments, unemployment and worsening income distribution by particular properties of demand and supply functions, and the role of institutions. In particular, he analysed the failure of the price mechanism to produce a satisfactory distribution of income.

Singer maintained that there can be no 'blueprint' for development (Schiavo-Campo and Singer, 1970). However, a number of themes permeated throughout Singer's 'perspectives' on development. The starting-point should be people, not money and wealth, which gave a whole new perspective on the development process. Sustained and equitable development depended not on the creation of wealth but on the capacity of people to create wealth. Hence, Singer's insistence on the importance of the human factor in economic development, and, following from that, on health, education and training, the well-being of children (the future generation), and food security; on science and appropriate technology; on employment and income distribution and the conquest of poverty; and on planning and sound institutions; all viewed in an international context in which trade and aid are conducted with distributive justice and efficiency so that all countries, developing and developed, might flourish and converge, not diverge.

But Singer was never content only to formulate the theoretical underpinnings of the problems of developing countries. He became involved in many pioneering ventures to overcome them. A number of the organisations he helped to set up or strengthen to tackle Third World problems are still operating today including: the United Nations Development Programme, the UN World Food Programme, the UN Research Institute for Social Development, the UNIDO, and the African Development Bank. He supported the changing focus of UNICEF from an emergency body to an organisation concerned with the long-term interests of children. He was also indirectly involved in the creation of the International Development Association (IDA), the soft-loan arm of the World Bank, which was established in part as a foil to prevent attempts to set up a UN Special Fund for Economic Development (SUNFED), with which Singer was intimately involved. But not all that he set out to accomplish was achieved, and there were disappointments along the way.

Work at IDS

From 1969, Singer was a professorial fellow of the Institute of Development Studies (IDS) at the University of Sussex in England, and professor (later emeritus) at the university. During this period, his activities and output were even more prolific than previously. He made a significant contribution to the activities of IDS, which is now recognised as one of the world's leading institutes of development studies. He is remembered with respect and affection by the cohorts of students who have passed through the institute as a source of almost unlimited help and inspiration. And he was in constant demand by governments, multilateral and bilateral aid agencies and non-governmental organisations for his creative intelligence, profound knowledge and wise advice. His commitment to the cause of a more just and equitable world economic order remains unquenched. His life and work serves as an inspiration for the next generation of development economists.

D. JOHN SHAW

References

Cairncross, A. and M. Puri (eds) (1976), *Employment, Income Distribution and Development Strategy. Problems of the Developing Countries. Essays in Honour of H.W. Singer*, Basingstoke and London: Macmillan.

Chen, J. and D. Sapsford (eds) (1997), 'Economic development and policy. Professor Sir Hans Singer's contribution to development economics', *World Development*, **25** (11), 1853–956.

Clay, E. and D.J. Shaw (eds) (1987), *Poverty, Development and Food. Essays in Honour of H.W. Singer on his 75th Birthday*, Basingstoke and London: Macmillan.

Hatti, N. and R. Tandon (eds) (2006), *Trade and Technology in a Globalizing World, Essays in Honour of H.W. Singer*, New Delhi: BPRC (India).

ILO (1972), *Employment, Incomes and Equality. A Strategy for Increasing Productive Employment in Kenya*, Technical Paper No. 6, Geneva: International Labour Office.

Pilgrim Trust (1938), *Men Without Work*, Cambridge: Cambridge University Press.

Sapsford, D. and J. Chen (eds) (1998), *Development Economics and Policy: The Conference Volume to Celebrate the 85th Birthday of Professor Sir Hans Singer*, Basingstoke and London: Macmillan.

Sapsford, D. and J. Chen (eds) (1999), 'The Prebisch–Singer thesis: a thesis for the new millennium', *Journal of International Development*, **11** (6), 863–916.

Schiavo-Campo, S. and H.W. Singer (1970), *Perspectives in Economic Development*, Boston, MA: Houghton-Mifflin.

Shaw, D. John (2002 and 2004), *Sir Hans Singer. The Life and Work of a Development Economist*, Basingstoke and New York: Palgrave Macmillan (hardback), New Delhi: BRPC (India) (paperback).

Singer, H.W. (1949), 'Economic progress in under-developed countries', *Social Research*, **16** (1), 236–66.

Singer, H.W. (1950), 'The distribution of gains between investing and borrowing countries', *American Economic Review*, **40** (2), 473–85.

Toye, J. and R. Toye (2003), 'The origins and interpretation of the Prebisch–Singer thesis', *History of Political Economy*, **35** (3), 437–67.

UN (1949), *Relative Prices of Exports and Imports for Under-Developed Countries. A Study of Post-War Terms of Trade between Under-Developed and Industrialized Countries*, 1949/II.B.3, New York: United Nations.

Smith, Adam (1723–1790)

Adam Smith provides the principal source of inspiration for free market economists. His two key works, the *Theory of Moral Sentiments* (1761) and the *Wealth of Nations* (1776), together constitute a comprehensive analysis of the fundamental issues in the political economy of development. His analysis of the market mechanism attempted to identify the fundamental laws governing economic development. While he believed that the free market was the fundamental driver of development, he also exposed its deep internal ethical contradictions, though he was unable to answer satisfactorily how its shortcomings might be resolved.

Smith identified two powerful drivers of economic progress, the division of labour and the accumulation of capital. The foundation of Smith's 'growth model' was the division of labour: 'The greatest improvement in the productive powers of labour, and the greater part of the skill, dexterity and judgement with which it is any where directed, or applied, seem to have been the effects of the division of labour' (Smith, 1776, vol. 1, p. 7). The fundamental driver of the accumulation process is the pursuit of profit: 'it is only for the sake of profit that any man employs a capital in the support of industry' (ibid., p. 477). The possessors of capital direct their stock of capital towards those industries that yield the greatest profit and are, therefore 'likely to be of the greatest value': '[B]y directing that industry in such a manner as its produce may be of the greatest value, he intends only his own gain, and he is in this, as in many other cases, led by the invisible hand to promote an end which was no part of his intention' (ibid.).

These principles are the key to 'economic development', or the 'wealth of nations': 'Little else is required to carry a state to the highest level of opulence from the lowest level of barbarism, but peace, easy taxes, and a tolerable administration of justice' (Smith quoted in Cannan, 1976, p. xl).

> The natural effort of every individual to better his own condition, when suffered to exert itself with freedom and security, is so powerful a principle, that it is alone, and without any assistance,

not only capable of carrying on the society to wealth and prosperity, but of surmounting a hundred impertinent obstructions with which the folly of human laws too often incumbers its operations . . . (Smith, 1776, vol. 2, pp. 49–50)

The system appears to be an elegant, harmonious integration of individual self-interest and social interests. However, alongside Smith's rigorous analysis of the growth process, was a deep awareness of the internal contradictions of that same process. He believed that people are born with relatively equal capacities for self-realisation. He considered that people's capability for self-realisation were largely dependent on their social environment, especially their work environment, not on inherited differences:

> The difference of natural talents in different men is, in reality, much less than we are aware of; and the very different genius which appears to distinguish men of different professions, when grown up to maturity, is not upon many occasions so much the cause as the effect of the division of labour. The differences between the most dissimilar characters, between a philosopher and a common street porter, for example, seems to arise not so much from nature, as from habit, custom and education. (Smith, 1776, vol. 1, pp. 19–20)

In the course of industrial advance, opportunities arise for greatly enhanced division of labour, which were not present in agriculture: 'The nature of agriculture, indeed, does not permit of so many subdivisions of labour, nor of so complete a separation of one business from another, as manufactures' (ibid., p. 9). The enhanced division of labour permits increased work intensity and increased worker dexterity, reducing the time lost in passing from one task to another; it allows intensified application of mechanisation to specialist tasks, providing opportunities for technical progress in the production of new types of machines by specialist machine-makers (ibid., pp. 9–14).

However, the division of labour stimulates productivity at a high price:

> In the progress of the division of labour, the employment of the far greater part of those who live by labour, that is the great body of the people, comes to be confined to a few very simple operations; frequently to one or two. But the understandings of the greater part of men are necessarily formed by their ordinary employments. The man whose whole life is spent in performing a few simple operations, of which the effects too are, perhaps, always the same, or very nearly the same, has no occasion to exert his understanding, or to exercise his invention in finding out expedients for removing difficulties which never occur. He naturally loses, therefore, the habit of such exertion, and generally becomes as stupid and ignorant as it is possible for a human creature to become. (Smith, 1776, vol. 2, pp. 302–3)

Smith warned: '[I]n every improved and civilized society this is the state into which the labouring poor, that is, the great body of the people, must necessarily fall, unless government takes some pains to prevent it' (ibid., p. 303). The only 'solution' that he was able to offer to this contradiction was the establishment of 'little school[s]' in each parish or district, 'where children may be taught for a reward so moderate, that even a common labourer may afford it' (ibid., p. 306).

Smith thought that great inequality and class conflicts were unavoidable in a society based on private property: 'Wherever there is great property, there is great inequality. For one very rich man, there must be at least five hundred poor, and the affluence of the few supposes the indigence of the many' (ibid., p. 232). He warned that without substantial 'trickle down' of the fruits of economic progress to the mass of the population, a society would be morally unsatisfactory and at risk due to social instability:

> Servants, labourers, and workmen of different kinds, make up the far greater part of every great political society. But what improves the circumstances of the greater part can never be regarded as an inconveniency to the whole. No society can surely be flourishing and happy, of which the far greater part of the members are poor and miserable. It is but equity, besides, that they who feed, cloath, and lodge the whole body of the people, should have such a share of the produce of their own labour as to be themselves tolerably well fed, cloathed and lodged. (Smith, 1776, vol. 1, p. 88)

In an economy like that of Britain in the late eighteenth century, it was difficult to achieve cooperative solutions to the great differences of socio-economic interests: 'The affluence of the rich excites the indignation of the poor, who are often driven by want, and prompted by envy, to invade his possessions' (Smith, 1776, vol. 2, p. 232). Smith concluded that it was a critical duty of the state to protect property-owners, the key instruments for economic progress: 'The acquisition of valuable and extensive property, therefore, necessarily requires the establishment of civil government . . . Civil government supposes a certain subordination . . . [which] give[s] some men some superiority over the greater part of their brethren' (ibid., p. 232).

Labour markets in late eighteenth-century England were basically antagonistic: 'The workmen desire to get as much, the masters to give as little as possible. The former are disposed to combine in order to raise, the latter in order to lower the wages of labour' (Smith, 1776, vol. 1, p. 74). The balance of power was tipped decisively towards the masters:

> The masters, being fewer in number, can combine much more easily; and law, besides, authorises or at least does not prohibit their combinations, while it prohibits those of the workmen. We have no acts of parliament against combining to lower the price of work; but many against combining to raise it. In all such disputes, the masters can hold out much longer . . . Many workmen could not subsist a week, few could subsist a month, and scarce any a year without employment. (ibid., pp. 74–5)

Smith believed that class stratification was a necessary condition of economic progress, facilitating the accumulation of capital and the division of labour. However, he acknowledged that this contained the high possibility not only of class conflict, but also of 'the corruption of our moral sentiments':

> [T]he disposition to admire, and almost to worship, the rich and powerful, and to despise, or, at least, to neglect persons of poor and mean condition, though necessary both to establish and to maintain the distinction of ranks and the order of society, is, at the same time, the great and most universal cause of the corruption of our moral sentiments. (Smith, 1761, p. 61)

Profit is the central motive for the accumulation of capital, and behind this lies an even deeper psychological drive, namely the desire to acquire 'wealth and greatness'. This fundamental driving force of economic progress contains its own 'deception', or inbuilt contradiction:

> The pleasures of wealth and greatness . . . strike the imagination as something grand and beautiful and noble, of which the attainment is well worth all the toil and anxiety which we are

apt to bestow upon it. And it is well that nature imposes upon us in this manner. It is this deception which rouses and keeps in continual motion the industry of mankind. (Ibid., p. 183)

Smith enumerates the dramatic effects of the application of this 'industry', impelled by the 'deception' of the pursuit of 'wealth and greatness':

> It is this which first prompted them to cultivate the ground, to build houses, to found cities and commonwealths and to invent and improve all the sciences and arts, which ennoble and embellish human life; which have entirely changed the whole face of the globe, have turned the rude forests of nature into agreeable and fertile plains, and made the trackless and barren ocean a new fund of subsistence, and the great high road of communication to the different nations of the earth. The earth by these labours of mankind has been obliged to redouble her natural fertility, and to maintain a greater multitude of inhabitants. (Ibid., pp. 183–4)

It is deeply paradoxical that the driving force for economic progress should be considered to be a 'deception'.

The pursuit of 'wealth and greatness' is a 'deception' because, beyond a certain modest level of consumption, additional consumption brings no increase in happiness, and often brings unhappiness. Smith compared 'power and riches', to 'immense fabrics' which 'requires the labour of life to raise':

> [They] threaten every moment to overwhelm the person that dwells in them, and which while they stand, though they may save him from some smaller inconveniences, can protect him from none of the severer inclemencies of the season. They keep off the summer shower, not the winter storm, but leave him always as much, and sometimes more exposed than before, to anxiety, to fear, and to sorrow; to diseases, to danger, and to death. (Ibid., p. 184)

For Smith 'frivolous consumption' brings no increase in happiness: 'How many people ruin themselves by laying out money on trinkets of frivolous utility . . . [W]ealth and greatness are mere trinkets of frivolous utility, no more adapted for procuring ease of body or tranquillity [sic] of mind than the tweezer-cases of the lovers of toys' (ibid., pp. 180–81).

Smith thought that the only worthwhile social goal was the pursuit of happiness. This is to be attained through 'tranquillity', not the pursuit of 'power and riches': 'Happiness consists in tranquillity and enjoyment. Without tranquillity there can be no enjoyment; and where there is perfect tranquillity there is scarce anything which is not capable of amusing' (ibid., p. 150). Smith believed that a good society was one in which people attained happiness through fulfilling basic human needs, not in the vain pursuit of unlimited wants:

> Two different roads are presented to us . . . the one, by the study of wisdom and the practice of virtue; the other, by the acquisition of wealth and greatness . . . the one, of proud ambition and ostentatious avidity, the other, of humble modesty and equitable justice . . . the one more gaudy and glittering in its colouring, the other more correct and more exquisitely beautiful in its outline . . . (Ibid., p. 62)

Smith considered that human psychology required social cohesion as the foundation of a good society in which all citizens could achieve happiness:

> All the members of human society stand in need of each others assistance . . . Where the neces-sary assistance is reciprocally afforded from love, from gratitude, from friendship, and esteem, the society flourishes and is happy. All the different members of it are bound together by the agreeable bands of love and affection, and are, as it were, drawn to one common centre of mutual good offices. (Ibid., p. 85)

The foundation of such cohesion was 'benevolence':

> And hence it is, that to feel much for others and little for ourselves, that to restrain our selfish, and to indulge our benevolent affections, constitutes the perfection of human nature; and can alone produce among mankind that harmony of sentiments and passions in which consists their whole grace and propriety. (Ibid., p. 25)

Benevolence, not the pursuit of 'wealth and greatness' allows the construction of a sense of duty which, in its turn, enables the realisation of social cohesion:

> The regard to those general rules of conduct, is what is properly called a sense of duty, a princi-ple of great consequence in human life, and the only principle by which the bulk of mankind are capable of directing their actions . . . Without this sacred regard to general rules, there is no man whose conduct can be much depended upon . . . [B]y acting according to the dictates of our moral faculties, we necessarily pursue the most effectual means for promoting the happiness of mankind . . . (Ibid., pp. 161–3, 166)

Smith believed that unless a society was 'just', there was a grave danger that it would dis-integrate into chaos:

> Justice, on the contrary, is the main pillar that upholds the whole edifice. If it is removed, the great, the immense fabric of human society, that fabric which to raise and support seems in this world, if I may say so, to have been the peculiar and darling care of Nature, must in a moment crumble into atoms. (Ibid., p. 86)

Smith's analysis of the contradictions of the market economy is highly relevant to fun-damental issues facing the world today. These include the nature of work for almost one billion people in developing countries employed as 'lumpen labour' in the non-farm sector for US$1–2 per day; class conflict between capital and labour in developing countries that are still in the early phase of capitalist industrialisation; the 'degradation of work' for a large fraction of service sector workers in rich countries, who work under intense pressure from 'remorseless monitoring' made possible by modern information technology, in order to increase 'labour intensity'; the erosion of a sense of social cohesion as 'state desertion', in order to provide a 'good investment environment' for global capital, becomes wide-spread across countries at all levels of development; widespread consumer fetishism pro-moted by the immense marketing expenditure of global giant firms, and commercialised global mass media; and even the very sustainability of life on the planet as fast-growing parts of developing countries move towards the immense per capita consumption levels of the advanced capitalist countries.

Peter Nolan

References
Cannan, Edwin T. (1976), 'Editor's Introduction', in Edwin T. Cannan (ed.), *The Wealth of Nations*, Chicago: University of Chicago Press, pp. xix–liv.
Smith, Adam (1761 [1982]), *The Theory of Moral Sentiments*, revised edn, edited by D.D. Raphael and A.L. Macfie, Liberty Classics, Indianapolis (first published 1759).
Smith, Adam (1776), *An Inquiry into the Nature and Causes of The Wealth of Nations*, Chicago, reprinted in Edwin T. Cannan (ed.) (1976), *The Wealth of Nations*, Chicago: University of Chicago Press.

Social Capital

Social capital shot to prominence across the social sciences in the 1990s. Not surprisingly, it has gained a strong presence in development studies (for example, Woolcock, 1998), not least because the World Bank has heavily promoted it through a dedicated website, a large research and policy programme, and numerous publications (see, for example, Dasgupta and Serageldin, 1999; Grootaert and van Bastelaer, 2002; and Fine, 2003 for a critique of the latter). So wide-ranging has social capital been in theoretical, empirical and policy work that it has become something of a cliché, deployed by all and sundry in whatever way that suits. Equally, it has attracted a significant undercurrent of criticism, especially from those with radical leanings and/or commitment to rigour and clarity in scholarship, terminology and meaning (for example, Fine, 2001; Smith and Kulynych, 2002).

The last point derives from the universally recognised chaos that surrounds the *definition* of social capital. In popular parlance, it draws its meaning from the quip that it is not what you know but whom you know that is important. More specifically, interpersonal relations can be helpful in getting things done. But, from this simple nostrum, any number of directions can be taken. First, what do we mean by who you know? Interpersonal relations from the family outwards represents a start but 'knowing me, knowing you', can be formal and informal, thereby incorporating the impersonal as well as the personal. Specifically, culture, social norms, associations, networks, trust, institutions and so on all become part of social capital. Further, as collective attributes, gender, ethnicity and other elements in social stratification are also seen as sources and/or embodiment of social capital.

Second, quite apart from ranging across the social sciences in method and technique, social capital has been equally gregarious in its subject matter. Whatever the topic, social capital is ready to be applied – to the sick, the poor, the criminal, the corrupt, the (dys)functional family, schooling, community life, work and organisation, democracy and governance, collective action, transitional societies, intangible assets or, indeed, to any aspect of social, cultural and economic performance, and equally across time and place, raising doubts over its relevance to the specificities of Africa, India and Latin America (see Harriss, 2001; Fine, 2002; and Molyneux, 2002 who adds a gender dimension). Not surprisingly, its attention has also been turned on development. Usually, the starting-point is that outcomes are enhanced by the presence of social capital, although critics are mindful of dark, perverse or negative social capital that gets things undone or the wrong things done through the Mafia, corruption or whatever. Indeed, one way of looking at social capital is as the more fully developed and expanded mirror image of the rent-seeking literature – the analytical structure is identical, the difference is that the non-market and 'connections' are perceived to be functional rather than dysfunctional.

In respect of its ambiguity and universal applicability, social capital is, once again, similar to many other concepts that have, seemingly, increasingly shot to prominence as academic fashions across the social sciences – good governance, civil society and, most dramatically of late, globalisation. As already indicated, social capital is marked like the latter by its astonishing range of application and approach. Its capacity for this is a consequence of its 'fit' with the evolving intellectual milieu across the social sciences. Specifically, this is marked by a dual retreat from the extreme excesses of both neoliberalism and postmodernism. On the one hand, the message that everything can be left to the market is wearing thin as more careful consideration is being given to the role of the non-market, if not necessarily the state, in reaction against the demonstrable failure of privatisation and austerity programmes (and of the neoliberal project itself as the state has remained of paramount importance). On the other hand, postmodernist preoccupation with identity, meaning and subjectivity has lost ground to a genuine concern for understanding material realities – not least what is the nature of contemporary capitalism and how might it be made to be different.

Of course, the rise of 'globalisation' is the most powerful reflection of these intellectual trends, not least because, on balance, it has been won away from its origins in neoliberalism and culturalism towards a focus on power, conflict, the role of the state, and their salience within the world system of contemporary capitalism. While social capital also reflects a turn away from neoliberalism and postmodernism, it does so in a way that is as wide-ranging if not as radical as globalisation. Thus, as already indicated, while social capital could in principle be almost anything – in approach and application – it has, in practice, incorporated a particular content and dynamic.

Most revealing in this respect is the way in which the perceived analytical origins of social capital have been shifted. Undoubtedly, the term essentially initiated with Pierre Bourdieu (1980 and 1983). His focus is upon how different social classes form and reproduce themselves in relation to one another, and with corresponding implications for the incidence of different types of privilege, oppression and resistance. Bourdieu also carefully distinguishes different types of non-economic capital – the cultural and the symbolic as well as the social – and how they mutually condition one another. While committed to avoiding (Marxist) determinism, Bourdieu has been particularly scathing against mainstream economics. His methodology also emphasises the context, meaning and specificity of the practices engaged in by social classes.

Increasingly, these critical elements in Bourdieu's approach have been written out of social capital, not least in deference to his displacement as founder by James Coleman (1988 and 1990), a rational choice sociologist committed to basing social theory on micro foundations. Social capital becomes functional. It seeks positive-sum outcomes out of cooperation rather than recognising endemic conflict of interest governed by the exercise of power. The different types of capital, other than the economic, are subsumed under social capital. This is part of a process of filling out explanatory factors – from a starting-point in physical, human, environmental capital or whatever. But it is also part of the process of stripping out the contextual content contained within Bourdieu's approach, substituting for preoccupation with meaning grounded in specific practices by universally applicable concepts such as trust, association, network, custom and so on. Especially through the work of social capital's most ardent proponent, Robert Putnam (1993 and

2000), reputedly the single most-cited author across the social sciences in the 1990s, social capital emphasises the role of civil society at the expense of the state, trade unions and political parties (except where social capital is deemed to make these more effective and participatory in some sense).

This is despite these social organisations and corresponding activities often being the most important sources of the collective participation from which social capital putatively derives. Not surprisingly in the light of its chameleon-like character, a critical if supportive literature is to be found among those who wish to bring back in the state, trade unions, politics, conflict, meaning and context, and so on, to a concept that has so readily and rapidly excluded them. Such attempts, with the equally critical recognition of the presence of negative social capital, merely add to the weight of ambiguity that burdens the definitions of social capital. It has been variously disaggregated or reaggregated into the bonding, bridging, linking, vertical, horizontal and so on, in acknowledgement of the diverse forms and content of social relations and the vain attempt to find some (social capital) homogeneity across them (for example, Woolcock and Narayan, 2000). But the more general the category in scope of application, the weaker is the extrapolation from one context to another whether for analytical, empirical or policy purposes. It remains remarkable the extent to which those who deploy the notion of social capital consider themselves to be discussing something in common.

No doubt this is encouraged by the terminology itself. The term refers to *social* capital or anything that is not directly economic but is collective in some sense beyond the private, the individual or the alienable – you might possess social capital but you cannot own and sell it. And it refers to social *capital* in the sense of any resource that is able to support the serving of some function or other more readily. In the first respect, there is an inclination, often implicit, to treat all other forms of capital as non-social, whether these be physical, natural, financial, human or whatever. In the second respect, there is the presumption that social capital complements and exhausts other forms of capital, providing a residual explanation for all outcomes once correcting for differential access to other resources.

These predispositions, however well recognised among those using social capital, play an influential role in the relationship between the discipline of economics and social capital, and between it and economic analysis. On the first count, social capital has a small but significant following within mainstream economics. It serves precisely as a residual explanatory factor after taking account of other types of capital – whether explaining difference in growth performance in Barro-type regressions or the incidence of inequality and poverty. The poor are deemed to live in societies that lack social capital although they may compensate for their poverty through more social support among themselves. More generally, with whatever measures are taken for social capital, these can be regressed on as independent variables to explain economic or, indeed, social outcomes at whatever level of analysis from the individual to the country.

Underlying such procedures are the ideas that the economy and markets do not work perfectly *and* that non-market factors can influence economic outcomes. In short, social capital serves as the proxy for the relationship between the non-economic and the economic in a vision of the world beset by market, especially informational, imperfections. In this respect, social capital represents an ideal illustration of what has been termed 'economic(s) imperialism' – the process by which economics extends its methods to the traditional terrain of the other social sciences. Both mainstream economics and (Colemanesque) social capital base their understanding on rational choice. Social capital neatly complements other forms of capital as a residual explanatory factor, not least in explaining differences in economic performance, narrowly conceived as total factor productivity as far as technological change is concerned. And there is no need, especially for a mainstream economics that remained untouched by postmodernism, to question the context, meaning or specificity of its concepts other than as game-theoretic, path-dependent equilibria.

Social capital, then, provides a natural conduit through which economics can stomp across the social sciences. And, in its market imperfection version, economics encounters very little resistance. In this case, despite its name, the social capital literature has generally been extremely weak in examining the economy. Essentially, it is taken for granted with the one proviso that it could be enhanced from a necessarily imperfect dependence upon the market (and state) if only the positive-sum gains from the cooperation can be realised. Far, then, from representing a critique of economics, as many of its practitioners believe through emphasis of the social on the economic, social capital is entirely consistent with the most recent fashions within mainstream economics (as opposed to neoliberal dogma). For these positively draw upon market imperfections both to explain inefficient market outcomes as well as the potential for non-market phenomena to correct or consolidate them.

So far the discussion has been almost entirely confined to the impact of social capital across the social sciences in general. Not surprisingly, given its characteristics, it has blossomed in development economics and studies, in part because of its putative universal applicability across time, place and context and, in great part, because of its heavy promotion by the World Bank in particular and other development agencies alongside (Bebbington et al., 2004). These two factors underpinning the rise of social capital across development studies correspond to the more general shifts, respectively, towards the new development economics and from the Washington to the post-Washington Consensus. Not surprisingly, Joseph Stiglitz has played a key role in each, if more muted in case of social capital for which serious mainstream economics retains a certain scepticism over its affinity to its core physicalist notion of capital. As the post-Washington Consensus, at least in scholarship and rhetoric if not policy, has accepted the heavy incidence of market and institutional failure, and has sought to divine a rationale for the gamut of economic and social interventions that accompany loans, so social capital serves the function of distracting attention from huge differences in economic and political power and privilege, and the inevitability of conflict over these. Instead, social capital delivers a dose of hope in the form of self-help raised from the individual to some level of community or collectivity.

To this end, detailed household surveys have been put in place in country after country in order to demonstrate that if only the poor would help, trust and support one another and their politicians, so improved outcomes are just around the corner. Significantly, a vision of development itself is restored in which developing countries need to emulate the developed – based on sound markets, sound institutions and sound social capital. This is a mere shadow of the previously discarded modernisation for that, at least, understood development as a process of transformation, heavily (if not too heavily) incorporating the role of the state in economic and social provision. With social capital, as with the post-Washington Consensus more generally, development has become means without ends! Its proponents view its analytical deficiencies as paltry beside its virtues in combating neoliberalism, bringing the social to the economic and, thereby, civilising economists. But its critics suggest that the issues are with what neoliberalism is to be replaced, the need to reconstruct the economic not append the social, and that economists are beyond being civilised in view of their rational choice and deterministic methodology.

BEN FINE

References

Bebbington, A., S. Guggenheim, E. Olson and M. Woolcock (2004), 'Exploring social capital debates at the World Bank', *Journal of Development Studies*, **40** (5), 33–64.

Bourdieu, P. (1980), 'Le Capital social: notes provisoires', *Actes de la Recherche en Sciences Sociales*, no. 31, 2–3.

Bourdieu, P. (1983), 'The forms of capital', in Richardson (ed.) (1986), pp. 241–58 (first published in German in 1983).

Coleman, J. (1988), 'Social capital in the creation of human capital', *American Journal of Sociology*, **94**, Supplement, 95–120, reproduced in R. Swedberg (ed.) (1996), *Economic Sociology*, Cheltenham, UK and Northampton, MA, USA: Edward Elgar, pp. 319–44.

Coleman, J. (1990), *Foundations of Social Theory*, Cambridge, MA: Harvard University Press.

Dasgupta, P. and I. Serageldin (eds) (1999), *Social Capital: A Multifaceted Perspective*, Washington, DC: World Bank.

Fine, B. (2001), *Social Capital versus Social Theory: Political Economy and Social Science at the Turn of the Millennium*, London: Routledge.

Fine, B. (2002), 'It ain't social, it ain't capital and it ain't Africa', *Studia Africana*, no. 13, 18–33.

Fine, B. (2003), 'Social capital: the World Bank's fungible friend', *Journal of Agrarian Change*, **3** (4), 586–603.

Grootaert, C. and T. van Bastelaer (eds) (2002), *The Role of Social Capital in Development: An Empirical Assessment*, Cambridge, MA: Harvard University Press.

Harriss, J. (2001), *Depoliticizing Development: The World Bank and Social Capital*, New Delhi: Leftword Books (revised edn, London: Anthem Press, 2002).

Molyneux, M. (2002), 'Gender and the silences of social capital: lessons from Latin America', *Development and Change*, **33** (2), 167–88.

Putnam, R. (1993), *Making Democracy Work: Civic Traditions in Modern Italy*, Princeton, NJ: Princeton University Press.

Putnam, R. (2000), *Bowling Alone: The Collapse and Revival of American Community*, New York: Simon & Schuster.

Richardson, J. (ed.) (1986), *Handbook of Theory and Research for the Sociology of Education*, New York: Greenwood.

Smith, S. and J. Kulynych (2002), 'It may be social, but why is it capital? The social construction of social capital and the politics of language', *Politics and Society*, **30** (1), 149–86.

Woolcock, M. (1998), 'Social capital and economic development: toward a theoretical synthesis and policy framework', *Theory and Society*, **27** (2), 151–208.

Woolcock, M. and D. Narayan (2000), 'Social capital: implications for development theory, research and policy', *World Bank Research Observer*, **15** (2), 225–49.

Social Exclusion

The concept of social exclusion has gained wide circulation in development studies in recent years. It started in Western Europe around the mid-1970s to refer to various categories of poor people who were unprotected by social insurance (Silver, 1994, p. 532). Later on, social exclusion has been used as a broader concept than poverty, encompassing the inability of the poor to participate effectively in economic, political and cultural life. Social exclusion involves distance and alienation from mainstream society (Green, 1997, p. 515).

Taken as a concept only, social exclusion is of limited utility in the social sciences, unless it is placed in a theoretical framework. As normative theory, favouring 'inclusion' policies, social exclusion has been widely discussed in the European and American social policy context (Silver, 1994; Green, 1997; Loury, 1999; Atkinson and Davoudi, 2000). As a positive theory, social exclusion theorists in the First World have developed the multifaceted nature of deprivation and the mechanisms and institutions of exclusion (Loury, 1999).

Social exclusion in development economics

In 1994, the ILO and the UNDP launched a joint research project that sought to 'deconstruct' the original concept of social exclusion with a view to examining its utility in the Third World. The first set of papers showing the theoretical and empirical results of this project appeared in Rodgers et al. (1995). This project may be considered the foundational event of social exclusion as positive theory of the Third World. In his review of the social exclusion concept, Sen (2000) points out its merits of focusing particularly on relational features of poverty. Thus, social exclusion would be more appropriate to deal with problems of relative poverty (inequality) rather than absolute poverty. In fact, in this entry, social exclusion is presented as a distribution theory of the Third World, which is largely based on Figueroa et al. (1996) and Figueroa (2001).

A stylised fact of the world capitalist economy is that the degree of income inequality is higher in the Third World than in the First World (Deininger and Squire, 1996). Standard economics cannot explain this difference. In fact, the ultra-familiar neoclassical Heckscher–Ohlin–Samuelson model of international trade predicts the opposite relation. Labour-abundant countries produce with more labour-intensive methods and thus will show a higher share of labour income in national income. Assume that the Third World is relatively labour abundant and you get the neoclassical result.

However, not all markets in the capitalist system are Walrasian. The potato market is an example of a Walrasian market because it does not exclude people willing to buy or sell potatoes at the market price. But the logic of profit maximisation of firms can create non-Walrasian markets, where, at the market price, individuals cannot exchange in the market all the quantities of the good they are willing to buy or sell. For instance, in the labour market, not all workers are able to sell their labour at the market wage rate. In the credit market, not all individuals willing to obtain a loan and able to repay it at the market interest rate can get it. The same thing can be said about the insurance markets. Non-Walrasian markets, therefore, exclude some people.

People are poor and remain poor because they have no access to jobs in the labour market or because they have no access to credit and insurance markets, which could allow them to set up their own firms and thus escape poverty. Labour, credit and insurance play a significant role in the reproduction of poverty and inequality; hence, they may be labelled 'basic markets'. Not all markets have the same hierarchy in the process of distribution. If initial individual endowments of capital are concentrated in society, the mechanism of market exclusion will reproduce that inequality.

Exclusion from basic markets occurs in all market economies. Is the degree of market exclusion higher in the Third World than in the First World? There is no empirical evidence on this difference, but it seems plausible. Even if this were the case, however, market exclusion would explain only part of the observed differences in inequality.

In a developed capitalist society, all individuals share the same rights. All are equal before the law. People cannot be excluded from access to public goods, especially from those that are important for human capital development, such as education, health and social protection. Call them 'basic public goods'. The society may even be multiethnic and multicultural, but that does not matter because all people have the same rights. Actually, standard economics implicitly assumes this type of abstract society, that is, a socially homogeneous society. The society may be multiethnic, but this difference is not an essential factor in the generation and reproduction of inequality. It is as if ethnicity did not exist or did not matter. For easy reference, this abstract society will be called the 'epsilon society'.

Social exclusion as distribution theory in the Third World

Consider now another abstract society, where rights are unequal among social groups. How would this situation come about in the first place? Consider a slavery society. This is a socially heterogeneous and hierarchical society. There are two ethnic groups (whites and blacks) and there is a social hierarchy among them. Consider a colonial system. The group that dominates and the dominated constitute two ethnic groups (whites and aboriginals) and there is a social hierarchy among them. More specifically, consider a society that was born to capitalism with a strong slavery and colonial heritage. Call it the 'sigma society'.

In a sigma society, political and cultural assets count, and they are unequally distributed among social groups. The political system operates with first- and second-class citizens. Not all people are equal before the law. Cultural assets refer to ethnic markers of individuals (language, race, religion and so on) and are also unequally distributed. These markers are called 'cultural assets' because their hierarchy is learned and transmitted from generation to generation. Cultural assets provide social groups with either social prestige or social stigma, which leads to segregation. Call the descendants of the slavery or dominated groups the 'z-workers', who by definition are endowed with low quantities of economic assets (land, human capital and physical capital) and with low quantities of political and cultural assets. Would this initial inequality get reproduced or vanish endogenously?

In a sigma society, z-workers are excluded from the basic markets. Because they are excluded from the credit and insurance markets, they cannot accumulate physical capital. Could they accumulate human capital? Human capital has two components: formal education and the corporate culture of the firm. Education can be obtained only in public schools, as a public good. The access to quantity and quality of education depends now not so much on real income, savings and financing, but on the degree of citizenship of the social group. But governments have no incentives to grant them the right to high-quality education. Governments seek to maximise votes subject to their budget constraint. This motivation leads to the use of budgets in discretionary expenses, not on rights. As a result of governments' rationality, second-rate citizens will get a second-rate education. Hence, human capital accumulation in the form of education is blocked. Human capital in the form of corporation culture cannot be accumulated because inequality in political and/or cultural assets leads to the segregation of z-workers.

The consequence is that z-workers are excluded from the high-skilled labour market. Their poverty does not come from a problem of wage discrimination in the labour market;

it is due to a problem of exclusion, the absence of z-workers in the high-skilled labour market.

Z-workers are also excluded from access to basic public goods. It was shown above that governments' motivations lead to exclusion from education. The same logic applies to health and social protection. They are also excluded from justice because not all people are equal before the law. If they could have access to these basic public goods, they could escape poverty. They may have access to other public goods of less significance, but that does not alter the result because not all public goods play the same role in the reproduction of poverty. There is also a hierarchy of public goods.

Analytically, the differences between sigma and epsilon societies are clear. They differ in their initial conditions. In the sigma society, individuals participate in the economic process endowed with unequal quantities of economic, political and cultural assets; in the epsilon society, by contrast, individuals participate in the economic process endowed with unequal quantities of economic assets only, for they are equally endowed with political and cultural assets. In addition, factor endowments in each society are such that sigma is a relatively labour-abundant economy. In the sigma society, given the initial inequality in the individual endowment of assets, together with the initial institutions (rules of the market system and of the political system), the general equilibrium solution of the economic process will determine both the level of output and its distribution between social groups. Z-workers constitute the poorest group in society.

Social relations in the sigma society include class relations and ethnic relations. There are two tiers in the degree of inequality that comes out of the economic process: the inequality within the capitalist sector and the inequality between ethnic groups. The first inequality is the result of exploitation and the second is the result of exclusion. The overall inequality is the aggregation of both tiers. As in the famous dialogue between F. Scott Fitzgerald and Ernest Hemingway, one may say that in the epsilon society the only difference between the rich and the poor is money. This is not the case in the sigma society. Sigma is a much more complex society.

In the long run, as physical capital and human capital are accumulated, the sigma economy reaches higher levels of output, higher levels of profits and real wages, but z-workers are left behind. The degrees of income inequality between classes and between ethnic groups do not fall; hence, the overall degree of inequality does not change much. Thus, the sigma theory predicts that the initial inequality between ethnic groups will be reproduced. The mechanisms of exclusion from the basic markets and from the basic public goods play a significant role in this outcome. These mechanisms set limits to economic and social mobility. In particular, there are blockages to the mobility of z-workers. In the sigma society, the poorest groups are the excluded, and vice versa. A sigma society will remain qualitatively a sigma society, always with z-workers, as a socially heterogeneous and hierarchical society. A sigma society will not become epsilon society endogenously.

Another prediction is that the degree of income inequality in a sigma society will tend to be higher than the corresponding degree of inequality in epsilon societies. The effect of having relatively more z-workers in the population is to increase the relative degree of inequality of the sigma society. The existence of social exclusion makes a society more unequal than if all workers were subject to capitalist exploitation. Workers would be better off if they were exploited rather than excluded; society would show a lower degree of inequality.

Empirical consistency and policy implications

The predictions of sigma theory seem to be consistent with the basic facts of most Third World countries. The fact that Latin America and Africa are the regions with the highest degree of colonial legacy and are, at the same time, the most unequal countries in income distribution (Deininger and Squire, 1996) is consistent with one of the predictions of sigma theory. Within Latin America, the same consistency is found. Countries that were born free to capitalism, such as Argentina, Uruguay and Costa Rica show the lowest degree of inequality among the countries of the region (Figueroa, 2001). The prediction that poverty is ethnically biased, that poverty has ethnic markers, such as skin colour, language, gender and geographical origin, is also consistent with the fact that poverty incidence is higher among the aboriginal populations, as is the case in Latin American countries (Psacharopoulos and Patrinos, 1994). The persistence of the peasant economy (largely aboriginal populations) in most Third World countries – in spite of the persistent disparity between urban and rural average incomes – is also consistent with sigma theory, which predicts blockages in the economic mobility of z-workers. In sum, most Third World countries seem to resemble the sigma society.

The observed degree of inequality of nations is thus explained by sigma theory. In the inequality of nations, their initial conditions matter. Those initial conditions generate path dependence, that is, history counts. But to conclude that history matters should not be taken as historical determinism. What this conclusion implies is that the policy implications of sigma theory are different from the policies applied so far in the Third World, which mostly come from standard economics. If the foundational event of a sigma society is very important in determining its high degree of inequality, its legacy must be eliminated. To eliminate the colonial heritage and to construct a socially homogeneous society implies the equalisation of economic, political and cultural rights, the removal of social exclusion. It implies the introduction of institutional innovations in society, that is, new rules and new organisations. Certainly, this transformation entails breaking with history – a kind of refoundational shock.

The big question is, which agent would have the incentive and the power to carry out such a transformation? Sigma theory does not have an answer because this transformation is exogenously determined.

Other contributions to social exclusion literature

Social exclusion is not part of standard economics. However, some recent developments in neoclassical economic theory have implications for the problem of social exclusion. What if people could make free choices as regards social group formation? Becker and Murphy (2000) show that free choice would lead to segregation by income and neighbourhood. Their theory also predicts segregation in a multiethnic society.

Akerlof and Kranton (2000) incorporate identity – a person's sense of self – into the theory of economic choice. With this theory, they discuss the case of a social environment characterised by poverty and social exclusion. They show that social exclusion would lead to problems of identity and to self-destructive behaviour among the excluded group.

Their theory predicts that exclusion causes self-defeating behaviour. There is nothing irrational about this behaviour; on the contrary, it is the result of a free choice of identity, an adjustment that people make not to suffer the guilt of failure derived from a high degree of social exclusion.

In the framework of sigma theory, these works show that the role of individual preferences is to reinforce the social structure of classes and ethnic relations; that is, to reinforce inequality. They strengthen the prediction that sigma society cannot endogenously become an epsilon society.

ADOLFO FIGUEROA

References

Akerlof, George and Rachel Kranton (2000), 'Economics and identity', *Quarterly Journal of Economics*, **155** (3), 715–53.

Atkinson, Rob and Simin Davoudi (2000), 'The concept of social exclusion in the European Union: context, development and possibilities', *Journal of Common Market Studies*, **38** (3), 427–48.

Becker, Gary and Kevin Murphy (2000), *Social Economics: Market Behavior in a Social Environment*, Cambridge, MA: The Belknap Press of Harvard University Press.

Deininger, Klaus and Lyn Squire (1996), 'A new data set measuring inequality', *World Bank Economic Review*, **10** (3), 569–91.

Figueroa, Adolfo (2001), 'Social exclusion as a distribution theory', in Estanislao Gacitúa, Carlos Sojo and Shelton Davis (eds), *Social Exclusion and Poverty Reduction in Latin America and the Caribbean*, Washington, DC: World Bank, pp. 23–48.

Figueroa, Adolfo, Teófilo Altamirano and Denis Sulmont (1996), *Social Exclusion and Inequality in Peru*, Geneva: International Institute for Labour Studies, ILO.

Green, A.E. (1997), 'Exclusion, unemployment and non-employment', *Regional Studies*, **31** (5), 505–20.

Loury, Glenn C. (1999), 'Social exclusion and ethnic groups: the challenge to economics', in Boris Pleskovic and Joseph Stiglitz (eds), *Annual World Bank Conference on Economic Development*, Washington, DC: World Bank, pp. 225–52.

Psacharopoulos, George and Harry Patrinos (1994), *Indigenous People and Poverty in Latin America. An Empirical Analysis*, Aldershot: Avebury.

Rodgers, Gerry, Charles Gore and Jose Figueredo (eds) (1995), *Social Exclusion: Rhetoric, Reality, Responses*, Geneva: International Institute for Labour Studies, ILO.

Sen, Amartya (2000), *Social Exclusion: Concept, Application and Scrutiny*, Manila: Asian Development Bank.

Silver, Hilary (1994), 'Social exclusion and social solidarity: three paradigms', *International Labour Review*, **133** (5–6), 531–78.

Social Justice

Theories of social justice address the way the benefits and burdens of social cooperation are distributed among the various groups or individuals within a society. A number of issues arise almost immediately from such a characterisation. First, does the concept presuppose some kind of agency with the capacity and task of realising some approved distributive pattern? Second, how are we to go about measuring and conceptualising the relevant benefits and burdens: what currency should we use to measure how well groups or individuals are doing? Third, what is the scope of the 'society' presupposed by social justice? Is social justice a problem for the domestic arrangements of nation states, or does it apply more broadly, perhaps extending so far as to encompass the distribution of benefits and burdens within global 'society'? To some extent these issues are interlinked, since, for example, a complaint that a distribution within some domain is unjust naturally raises the further question of whether some agency has responsibility to act so as to rectify that injustice.

Questions of social justice arise quite naturally from the policy dilemmas involved in economic development. Faced with a choice between a policy that would lead to a higher rate of growth and one which results in a more equal distribution of well-being among a population, theories of social justice can provide ways of thinking through the question. For example, how far is it legitimate to sacrifice the well-being of the very poorest in a society today in pursuit of economic growth that may well lead to a higher standard of living for the poorest in the future? How focused should we be on the maximisation of wealth and income as opposed to the concrete ability people have to enjoy various forms of life or such goods as equality of status?

Historically, many philosophers and other writers have discussed questions related to social justice. Examples are John Locke's theory of property acquisition and David Hume's contention that justice consists in respect for rules governing the distribution of property, rules that facilitate cooperation and are conducive to mutual advantage. But it is to John Stuart Mill in his *Utilitarianism* that we probably owe the entry of the term into the modern literature, though earlier uses can be traced in the writings of socially conscious Roman Catholic priests. Mill characterises as 'the highest abstract standard of social and distributive justice; to which all institutions, and the efforts of virtuous citizens should be made to converge' that 'society should treat all equally well who have deserved equally well' (Mill, 1861, ch. 5). The distributive currency that Mill employs here is a utilitarian one, although indirectly, since he writes not of making the equally deserving equally happy, but rather of furnishing them equally with the 'means of happiness'. The scope of Mill's concern, at least tacitly, is that of a nation, and the agency with the duty to realise standards of social justice is the state.

Hayek's critique of social justice

Mill's conception, and others of similar nature, was witheringly criticised by Friedrich Hayek in the second volume of his *Law, Legislation and Liberty* (1976). For Hayek, justice is first and foremost an attribute of individual conduct and the suggestion that it be treated instead as a property of something as abstract as an income distribution represents a fundamental misapplication of the idea. Moreover, it is, in Hayek's view a misapplication with extremely pernicious consequences, since it suggests that some agency has a responsibility for realising a just outcome. For Hayek, the distributive outcomes of a market order are not suitable objects of evaluation using concepts of justice. Since those outcomes are not the result of conscious human intentions but are rather the unintended result of individuals cooperating together, the issue of justice does not arise so long as everyone has acted in accordance with market norms and laws governing the ownership and transmission of property.

The great danger, in Hayek's view, of the misapprehensions involved in the concept of social justice, is that the state will be called upon to intervene more and more in search of 'just' social outcomes and will thus thwart the anonymous information-gathering process that enables the spontaneous market order to be such a successful engine of growth. As a consequence, the search for 'social justice' will leave everyone worse off. Hayek further argued that attempts to realise social justice would require continuous *ex post* interference in the transactions entered into by individuals, and would thus undermine both the freedom of the individual and the predictability characteristic of a society governed by the rule of law. Interestingly, though, Hayek explicitly exempted from his criticisms the theory of social justice advanced by John Rawls.

Rawls's theory of social justice

Hayek's critique did not apply to Rawls's (1971) theory because Rawls took as the direct object of evaluation for a theory of social justice not the outcomes generated by a social order, but rather the institutions, norms and procedures that give rise to such outcomes. Rejecting classical utilitarianism as a standard for social evaluation, Rawls considers what principles of justice should govern what he calls the 'basic structure' of a discrete society. To answer this question he uses a thought experiment, based in the social contract tradition in political philosophy, which examines which principles would be chosen by persons placed in a specially designed circumstance of choice called the 'original position'. In this original position, individuals concerned only for their own prospects, must, in ignorance of their own strengths and abilities, tastes, preferences and commitments, choose principles to govern the basic structure of a society in which they will be placed. Rawls argues that they would choose two principles. The first of these is that individuals would be a guaranteed package of 'basic liberties'. The second, subordinate to the first, assures individuals both of fair equality of opportunity in the competition for jobs and offices and then introduces a principle of defeasible equality to govern the way in which the basic structure generates distributions of wealth and income: the 'difference principle'.

Although it is only a subordinate part of Rawls's complete theory of social justice, debates about the ambiguities of the difference principle have been crucial to subsequent writing on social justice. The principle states: 'Social and economic inequalities are to be arranged so that they are . . . to the greatest benefit of the least advantaged' (Rawls, 1971, p. 302). Among the difficulties this raises are the identification of the least advantaged, the measurement of 'benefit', and the resolution of whether the principle should be interpreted as constraining relative inequalities or simply as promoting the best outcome for the least advantaged. Rawls himself favoured a 'resourcist' metric defined in terms of what he called 'primary goods'.

Contemporary debates

One important critic of the primary-goods metric has been the economist Amartya Sen. In his essay 'Equality of what?', Sen (1980) argued that we should be concerned neither with the resources available to a person, nor with the welfare that a person is able to derive from those resources, but rather with securing for individuals a set of 'capabilities'. These capabilities are objective states of a person that permit them to achieve a variety of functionings in the world. So, for example, we should be concerned with neither the amount of food available to a person (resource), nor the enjoyment that food affords them (welfare), but, rather, their securing of a state of adequate nutrition. Sen's approach has been highly influential in the world of development, informing as it does such projects as the United Nations Human Development Index, but there remain difficulties in deciding exactly which capabilities are morally significant and how the comparative well-being of individuals should be assessed using the approach. This problem, known as the 'indexing problem' has received extensive attention from the philosopher Martha Nussbaum (see, especially Nussbaum, 2000).

Also highly influential within the philosophical literature has been the approach of Ronald Dworkin. In a series of essays, and later, in his book *Sovereign Virtue* (2000), Dworkin has argued for a resource-based metric for social justice. Welfare-based metrics, he has claimed, are vulnerable to the problem of expensive tastes. Those who have chosen a lifestyle such that they can only enjoy average levels of welfare upon the provision of expensive goods, have no claim on society to afford them such additional resources. Via a series of thought experiments, Dworkin has extended the resource-based approach beyond Rawls's narrow focus on external goods and resources to encompass the personal attributes of individuals (such as their talents, abilities, good looks and intelligence). The master idea behind Dworkin's conception is that social justice requires that we compensate individuals for unchosen disadvantage. Thus, an individual's access to a bundle of resources less valuable than average is prima facie grounds for a corrective transfer where that disadvantage is the result of brute luck (the accident of birth, or other factors beyond an individual's control), but not where it results from the free choice of a person to pursue one occupation rather than another or to squander his/her resources in an unprofitable venture.

Following Dworkin's lead, a whole school of thinking on social distributive justice, known as 'luck egalitarianism' has emerged. Some of these theorists differ from Dworkin in the 'currency' they favour, but all support his basic insight that the aim of justice is to compensate individuals for unchosen disadvantage. Recently, this approach has attracted sharp criticism from philosophers such as Elizabeth Anderson (1999), who has argued that this focus on compensation for ill-luck neglects and even undermines important aspects of the egalitarian ideal. Drawing on Rawls's theory and on Sen's writings on capability, she has suggested that egalitarian theories of justice should be as much concerned about the quality of the relationships they foster among citizens, as they are about the quantities of resource those citizens get.

Anderson's writing also marks one division between theorists concerning the shape of the distribution of wealth and income that just social institutions should ideally realise or promote. Anderson rejects the notion that we should, in some sense, favour equality in the dimension of wealth and income. Rather, following earlier writers like Harry Frankfurt (1987), she argues that just so long as people have sufficient resources to achieve the politically and morally salient capabilities, there is no further issue of distributive justice to resolve. Among theorists who believe that some focus on distributive pattern – however indirectly realised – is appropriate, three broad schools of thought have emerged. Each of these views on the appropriate shape of distribution is, in principle, compatible with a range of different commitments on the 'currency' question.

Historically, the idea that justice should promote equality has been most prominent. It accords with the formal requirement of justice to treat like cases alike, and gains support from Kantian ideas about the equal moral worth of persons. But this egalitarian ideal has been challenged by philosophers such as Derek Parfit. Parfit (1997) has argued that we do not value equality as such, but rather that we have reason to give priority to the least advantaged. In the so-called 'levelling-down objection', Parfit claims that where we have a choice between a distribution of wealth and income that is more equal, and one that is less equal but where the least advantaged do better than they do in the equal distribution, we always have reason to prefer inequality. He concludes that equality has no independent weight as a distributive principle. These three theories: sufficiency, luck-egalitarianism and the prioritarian approach, currently command the territory of views that are, in a broader sense, egalitarian conceptions of social justice.

Hayek's objection to 'social justice' on the grounds that the concept presupposes some distributive agency gains some renewed force once some of the simplifying assumptions behind Rawls's theory are relaxed. Rawls originally restricted his theory of justice to a self-contained society and sought to implement the difference principle through the design of the basic social institutions and procedures. On this model, a just distribution of benefits and burdens would emerge from individuals freely pursuing their own good while observing justice-apt rules and procedures. But the question naturally arises of what social justice requires once its scope is extended beyond particular societies to the world as a whole.

Given the vast disparities of wealth and income in the world, the luck-egalitarian view looks especially demanding when extended to the global stage, since there are few more dramatic examples of brute bad luck than having the ill-fortune to be born in Burundi rather than, say, Boston, Massachusetts. But if social justice, most fundamentally, is about the compensation of unchosen disadvantage then what agency, if any, is to have the task of realising justice? Hayekian complaints about the way in which demands for social justice increase the power of governments may be sidestepped by a focus on rules and principles at the national level, but securing any particular pattern of global distribution would require extensive international government on a far more developed scale than anything that presently exists. Rawls himself favoured more relaxed criteria for distribution between states than exists where citizens share a framework of coercive law (Rawls, 1999).

Legal frameworks do, however, extend beyond national boundaries. Even on a narrow construal of what justice requires, one that focuses on conduct and process, it is possible to raise serious questions about the distribution of burdens and benefits among the world's population. In the first place, this is because many of the terms under which trade takes place between wealthy and poorer countries are not merely given but are the object of negotiation and agreement. We can intelligibly ask whether the rules, as agreed upon, are fair, and whether poor producers have a reasonable opportunity to sell their products in First World markets. Second, as the political philosopher Thomas Pogge (2002) has recently argued, there is an important difference between the domestic and the global legal frameworks that impacts negatively upon the very poorest, especially in natural resource-rich countries. Whereas people who seize assets by force within a domestic framework are seen as thieves and denied legal title to those assets, people who seize power within a country are able to sell its resources (such as oil or diamonds) on international markets. Such recognition provides incentives for *coups d'état* within countries and leads to corruption, as even democratic governments must buy off those with the capacity to seize power. De facto rulers of states also have the capacity to secure loans from international agencies and other governments, debts which continue to be enforced against future governments, however democratic.

Social justice and development

Recent theoretical work on social justice continues to be important for development in a variety of ways. The 'currency' issue is clearly crucial for our assessment of the economic and social well-being of nations and peoples. For example, choosing per capita income to assess nations' level of development will often lead to a very different view of their relative progress than will a judgement based on a measure like Sen's capabilities (see, for example, Sen, 1999). Which of these measures is, on balance, best is, however, open to debate. While the 'capability' measures may capture what is morally important, they can have significant policy drawbacks. For example, the use of such measures may give countries incentives to concentrate on getting some proportion of their population above a capability threshold (say for literacy) and the easiest way of doing this can be to concentrate on those who can most cheaply be helped, to the detriment of the most severely disadvantaged.

More fundamental, though, are the difficult choices posed by the egalitarian, prioritarian and sufficiency approaches, which can lead to significantly different policy choices. Prioritarian and sufficiency views can, for example, favour faster growth where egalitarian ones would not, because they do not see the pattern of wealth distribution above a certain threshold as being the morally significant issue.

But perhaps the most important work for the future is the extension of thought on social justice to the global sphere by Rawls himself, by Charles Beitz (1979), Thomas Pogge (2002) and others. The central question here is whether the same principles – egalitarian, prioritarian or sufficiency based – translate from the national context in which they were first conceived, to the cosmopolitan context to which philosophers are now turning. The argument between 'nationalists' and 'cosmopolitans' is set to continue for many years.

CHRISTOPHER BERTRAM

References

Anderson, Elizabeth S. (1999), 'What is the point of equality?', *Ethics*, **109** (2), 287–337.
Beitz, Charles (1979), *Political Theory and International Relations*, Princeton, NJ: Princeton University Press (2nd edn, 1999).
Dworkin, Ronald (2000), *Sovereign Virtue: The Theory and Practice of Equality*, Cambridge, MA: Harvard University Press.
Frankfurt, Harry (1987), 'Equality as a moral ideal', *Ethics*, **98**, 21–43.
Hayek, Friedrich (1976), *Law, Legislation and Liberty*, Vol. 2, London: Routledge & Kegan Paul.
Mill, John Stuart (1861), *Utilitarianism*, London.
Nussbaum, Martha (2000), *Women and Human Development*, Cambridge: Cambridge University Press.
Parfit, Derek (1997), 'Equality or priority?', *Ratio*, **10**, 202–21.
Pogge, Thomas (2002), *World Poverty and Human Rights*, Cambridge: Polity.
Rawls, John (1971), *A Theory of Justice*, Oxford: Clarendon (2nd edn published by Belknap, Harvard, 1999).
Rawls, John (1999), *The Law of Peoples*, Cambridge, MA: Harvard University Press.
Sen, Amartya (1980), 'Equality of what?', in S.M. McMurrin (ed.),*The Tanner Lectures on Human Values*, Vol. 1, Cambridge: Cambridge University Press, pp. 195–220.
Sen, Amartya (1999), *Development as Freedom*, Oxford: Oxford University Press.

The Solow–Swan Model

Often referred to as 'the neoclassical model of growth', the Solow–Swan model can be traced to two papers published in the same year – one by Robert Solow (1956) of MIT and the other by Trevor Swan (1956) from the Australian National University. Good introductory expositions may be found in Jones (2002) and in Solow (2000a and 2000b).

Originally seen as a theory of the rate of economic growth, the Solow–Swan model has more recently come to be seen as providing the foundation for a theory of the level of output per worker or of income per capita (see Mankiw et al., 1992 for an example). Both matters were present explicitly in the papers by Solow (especially) and Swan but they, like most writers in the two or three decades following the publication of their papers, stressed that part of the theory which dealt with the determination of the equilibrium rate of growth of aggregate output.

Based on an aggregate production function which is 'well-behaved', has constant returns to scale and allows substitution between inputs (or, more generally, with a variable input ratio), the key propositions of the Solow–Swan model are: (1) in conditions of steady growth, the output–capital ratio will be constant; (2) the capital–labour ratio and the output–labour ratio will be variable, even in conditions of steady growth; (3) given the levels and the (assumed constant) growth rates of population and technology, the capital–labour ratio (and thus the output–capital and the output–labour ratios) vary monotonically with the savings rate. As a result, as the savings rate increases or decreases, so too does the equilibrium capital–labour ratio but, given the savings rate, any attempt to maintain a capital–labour ratio higher or lower than this equilibrium level would be futile and unsustainable; (4) with population growth and technological progress going on at an exogenously given rate, the equilibrium growth rate depends upon the rate of growth in labour supply (population) and the rate of technological progress, but not upon the savings rate. Essentially, this is because a low savings rate can sustain a low capital–labour ratio while a high savings rate can sustain a high capital–labour ratio. For the growth rate to (say) be above that determined by technological progress and population growth rates, the capital–labour ratio would have to be rising. An increase in the savings rate can temporarily bring this about (provided the savings are matched by desired investment) but because of diminishing returns the higher growth rate cannot be sustained. Sooner or later the capital–labour ratio will rise to a level beyond which it cannot be sustained by the savings rate at which point the capital–labour ratio will stop rising and the rate of growth will return to that dictated by technical progress and population growth rates; (5) although a change in the savings rate does not permanently alter the equilibrium rate of growth, it will permanently alter the equilibrium level of capital per unit of labour. As a result, there will be a different equilibrium level of output per worker and thus per capita income (and per capita consumption) corresponding to each savings rate; (6) this creates the possibility that, on welfare grounds, one particular savings rate is to be preferred to all others; and finally (7) technological progress has to be of a particular 'labour-augmenting' type in order to be compatible with sustained equilibrium growth.

These propositions can be demonstrated as follows (for ease of exposition we assume an economy with no trade, no government, homogeneous labour and capital goods, that the consumption good and the capital good are one and the same and that there is no depreciation).

Assume that output (Y) over any period depends upon the level of technology (A), labour (L) and physical capital (K) inputs as characterised by a Cobb–Douglas production function such that:

$$Y_t = K_t^\alpha (A_t L_t)^{1-\alpha}. \tag{1}$$

Given our production function, it must be the case that the actual rate of growth of output in any period will equal:

$$\frac{dY}{Y} = \alpha\left(\frac{dK}{K}\right) + (1-\alpha)\left(\frac{dL}{L} + \frac{dA}{A}\right). \tag{2}$$

Equilibrium or steady-state growth is usually defined as an evolution along which aggregate output grows at the same, constant, rate. In the steady state the rate of profit (rate of interest) will be constant, as will the savings rate (actually, it is common to assume that the savings rate is also constant out of equilibrium), and the ratio of asset stocks to aggregate output or income. In particular, the output–capital ratio will be constant in growth equilibrium. One way to explain why this must be so is to recognise that constancy of the output–capital ratio is a logical corollary of the constancy of the savings propensity. If saving (S) is proportional to national income (Y) and the propensity to save (s) is constant (either by assumption or as a corollary of the model being in equilibrium), then the savings rate (S/Y) is constant. If investment (I) is equal to saving then it follows that the ratio of investment to output (I/Y) is also constant and this means that investment must be growing at the same rate as output. Now, 'investment' is the making of additions to the capital stock (that is, it is the amount by which the (net) capital stock changes between any two periods so, assuming no depreciation, $I = dK$) and if investment is growing at a constant rate equal to the rate of growth in output then the amount by which the capital stock changes in any period (dK) must be growing at a constant rate equal to the rate of growth in output. If we have steady growth the capital stock is growing at a constant rate (whatever rate it is) and the ratio (dK/K) must be constant. If any ratio is to be constant over time, its numerator and denominator must both grow at the same rate and this rule must be true of growth rates as well as any other ratio. So, if the rate of growth of the capital stock (dK/K) is constant, then the capital stock – the denominator (K) – must be rising at the same rate as the numerator (dK) – and so the capital stock must be growing at the same rate as investment. Since investment is growing at the same rate as output, it follows that the capital stock must also be growing at the same rate as output and so the output–capital ratio must be constant over time.

So, under conditions of growth equilibrium we must have:

$$\frac{dK}{K} = \frac{dY}{Y}. \tag{3}$$

Combining the equilibrium condition (3) with (2) we find that the equilibrium growth rate is the sum of the population (labour supply) growth rate (n) and the rate of technological progress (dA/A):

$$\frac{dY}{Y} = n + \frac{dA}{A}, \tag{4}$$

where, by assumption, dL/L, the rate of growth of labour input, is equal to n, the rate of population growth. Note that the propensity to save does not appear in this expression.

Combining (4) and (3), and remembering that $dK = I = sY$, we have as an equilibrium condition:

$$s\frac{Y_t}{K_t} = n + \frac{dA}{A}.$$ (5)

Logically, for this equality to be maintained with given rates of population growth and technological change, while the propensity to save changes, the output–capital ratio must change by an offsetting amount in the opposite direction. At the end of the day, it is for this reason that the equilibrium rate of growth (but not, as we shall see, the equilibrium *levels* of the capital–labour, output–capital and output–labour ratios) is independent of the savings rate in the Solow–Swan model and it is here that one of the main differences between it and its predecessor, the Harrod–Domar model of growth, is to be found.

We can rearrange (5) to give an expression for the equilibrium output–capital ratio (that is, capital productivity) of:

$$\frac{Y_t}{K_t} = \frac{n + (dA/A)}{s},$$ (6)

showing that there is a unique relationship between the output–capital ratio and the propensity to save (given the rate of population growth (n) and the rate of technological change (dA/A)).

What can we say about the other key ratios, the capital–labour ratio and the output–labour ratio? We will deal with each in turn.

From (1), we see that:

$$\frac{Y_t}{K_t} = A_t^{1-\alpha}\left(\frac{K_t}{L_t}\right)^{\alpha-1}.$$ (7)

Substitution of (7) into (6) and rearranging gives an expression for the value of capital per unit of labour in equilibrium of:

$$\left(\frac{K_t}{L_t}\right) = A_t\left(\frac{s}{n + (dA/A)}\right)^{\frac{1}{1-\alpha}},$$ (8)

showing that there is a unique and positive relationship between the capital–labour ratio and the propensity to save (given the rate of population growth (n), level of technology (A), the rate of technological change (dA/A) and the elasticity of output with respect to the capital stock (α)).

Also, it follows from (1) that the level of output per unit of labour (that is, labour productivity) in any period may be expressed as:

$$\frac{Y_t}{L_t} = A_t^{1-\alpha}\left(\frac{K_t}{L_t}\right)^{\alpha}.$$ (9)

Substitution of (8) into (9) gives an expression for equilibrium output per unit of labour as:

$$\frac{Y_t}{L_t} = A_t \left[\frac{s}{n + (dA/A)} \right]^{\frac{\alpha}{1-\alpha}}. \tag{10}$$

Equation (10) shows that there is a unique relationship between the level of output per unit of labour and the propensity to save (given the rate of population growth (n) and level of technology (A), the rate of technological change (dA/A) and the elasticity of output with respect to capital stock (α)).

Now, suppose technological progress (dA/A) is occurring at the steady rate a per period. Then (8) and (10) imply that in conditions of equilibrium growth, capital per unit of labour and output per unit of labour rise over time (and at the same rate, a per period) while equation (6) shows that the output–capital ratio does not change. This finding, that in equilibrium growth rising labour productivity is accompanied by constant capital productivity, leads naturally to a discussion of the following question: is any 'type' of technological progress consistent with equilibrium growth or is it the case that for equilibrium growth to be sustained, technological progress must be of a certain type?

We have seen that equilibrium growth necessarily entails constancy of the output–capital ratio over time. For the output–capital ratio (Y/K) to be constant in the presence of technological change, it must be the case that the (direct) effect of technological change on the output–capital ratio is completely offset by an (indirect) effect on the output–capital ratio of a change in the capital–labour ratio. Only if technological progress is 'labour augmenting' or 'Harrod neutral' (Harrod, 1948, ch. 1) will this happen. The mechanics of the process may be explained as follows. At a given capital–labour ratio, technological progress raises both the average and marginal product of capital. With a given interest rate this induces a higher rate of capital accumulation and so the capital–labour ratio starts to rise. It will only stop rising when the marginal product of capital is back to its original level (and is again equal to the (unchanged) interest rate) and the output–capital ratio has also returned to its original level. Thus technological progress is accompanied by rising capital–labour ratio (equation (8) above shows this) and output–labour ratio (equation (10) above shows this) while the output–capital ratio returns to its original level so that if we simply compare equilibria the output–capital ratio appears to be (and is) constant (equation (6) above shows this). Technological progress of this type (where the output–capital ratio remains constant between equilibria while the capital–labour ratio rises) is known as Harrod-neutral or labour-augmenting technological progress. An intuitive explanation goes like this: when we say technological progress is labour augmenting, we mean that a rise in the level of technology (a rise in A) is equivalent to an increase in labour input. Assuming diminishing returns, an increase in labour input (or the level of technology) with a given capital stock raises both the marginal and average product of capital. To restore the original marginal and average products, the capital stock has to increase, and the increase has to be in exactly the same proportion as the labour input (or the level of technology) has increased. Only then will the average (and marginal) product of capital be the same before and after the increase in labour input (or the level of technology). All of which is to say that only if technological progress is of this labour-augmenting Harrod-neutral type, will sustained equilibrium growth be possible. Given this, it should not be surprising to see as an essential adjunct of the Solow–Swan model, work on whether this is a 'natural outcome' of the workings of an economic system or model. Kennedy (1964) is a seminal paper in this area.

We have seen that in this model a rise in the savings rate, even if it were reflected in faster capital accumulation, would result in a higher capital–labour ratio but not a permanently higher rate of economic growth. But we should note two things. First, this does not say that the savings rate is completely irrelevant because different levels of capital–labour ratio would be associated with different levels of output per capita and (especially) with different levels of consumption per capita. So the possibility arises that by choosing one savings rate rather than another, an economy might grow at the same rate as would otherwise be the case, but with a higher sustainable level of consumption per head than otherwise. Hence there has been a stream of literature on optimal growth and the savings rate, of which Phelps (1961) is a seminal paper. Second, it is an implication of the model that an exogenous change to the savings rate could alter the equilibrium growth rate if the change in the savings rate led to a change in the rate of labour supply (population) growth or to a change in the rate of technological progress. The possibility that higher output per worker might induce a higher rate of population growth (and thus be associated with a low-level equilibrium trap) was raised in Solow's (1956) paper, while the possibility that savings (or the rate of time preference more generally) might influence technological change and/or human capital accumulation is an important feature of much of endogenous growth theory.

As is the case with any economic model, certain things are deemed to be important (are included in the model) but are taken as given, as exogenous. In early versions of the model both technological progress and population (labour force) growth was treated this way, but much work has been undertaken endogenising these variables. Other criticisms relate to the ability of the model and the equilibrium methodology to survive outside the one good world and especially in a world in which there are many capital goods. Cohen and Harcourt (2003) set out the issues involved.

The Solow–Swan model has proved to be a resilient foundation for a rich range of ideas and also lends itself to a large range of empirical analysis including studies of the contribution of various factors of production and other items (loosely named 'technological progress' or the 'residual') to economic growth. Indeed, few areas of macroeconomics, public finance, business-cycle analysis and development economics have not incorporated the model into their toolkit. In addition, the work of Solow and Swan gave considerable impetus to the important notion that macroeconomic policy, whether it be concerned with stabilisation or development, must be understood and evaluated in a context of growth and not statics.

ROBERT DIXON

References

Cohen, A.J. and G.C. Harcourt (2003), 'Whatever happened to the Cambridge capital theory controversies', *Journal of Economic Perspectives*, **17** (Winter), 199–214.
Harrod, R.F. (1948), *Towards a Dynamic Economics*, London: Macmillan.
Jones, C. (2002), *Introduction to Economic Growth*, 2nd edn, New York: Norton.

Kennedy, C. (1964), 'Induced bias in innovation and the theory of distribution', *Economic Journal*, **74** (September), 541–7.

Mankiw, N.G., D. Romer and D. Weil (1992), 'A contribution to the empirics of economic growth', *Quarterly Journal of Economics*, **107** (May), 407–37.

Phelps, E.S. (1961), 'The golden rule of accumulation', *American Economic Review*, **51** (September), 638–43.

Solow, R. (1956), 'A contribution to the theory of economic growth', *Quarterly Journal of Economics*, **70** (February), 65–94.

Solow, R. (2000a), *Growth Theory: An Exposition*, 2nd edn, Oxford and New York: Oxford University Press.

Solow, R. (2000b), 'The neoclassical theory of growth and distribution', *Banca Nazionale del Lavoro Quarterly Review*, **53** (December), 349–81.

Swan, T. (1956), 'Economic growth and capital accumulation', *Economic Record*, **32** (November), 334–61.

State and Development

That effective states are essential for promoting economic and social development is a proposition that is widely accepted. However, what constitutes an effective state, and the appropriate role of such a state in markets, are issues that evoke deep disagreements. On the one hand are scholars and practitioners of development who prefer limited government, both as an end in itself, and as a means to more prosperous economies. Conversely, a variety of critics hold that strong, interventionist states are needed instead to facilitate political order, economic growth, and greater equality in the developing world. Since these debates often combine scholarship and ideology, they are not easily settled. Related issues can nevertheless be explored by focusing on the state's role in development in a number of important areas.

State and orderly government

When discussing the modern state we generally refer to the political and the bureaucratic apparatus that helps maintain centralised control over the use of coercion in a given territory (Weber, 1994). Whereas excessive and arbitrary use of coercive power by rulers readily creates tyrannies, failure to centralise the legitimate use of coercion also creates deeply troubled polities. These are old and perennial concerns. At the dawn of the modern era, Thomas Hobbes (1968) worried about the insecurity of life and property without the power of a 'Leviathan'. In more recent times, Samuel Huntington (1968) strongly underlined the importance of political order for the process of development. He argued that numerous demanding groups are likely to overwhelm developing-country rulers because the power of these rulers often rests on fragile political institutions, such as political parties. While this analysis has subsequently been challenged effectively, arguing instead that ruling elites are as responsible for regime breakdowns as the demanding masses (Bermeo, 2003), no one would want to deny that a measure of political order remains a prerequisite for social and economic development.

Scarcity of political order is readily noticeable in parts of the developing world, especially in Sub-Saharan Africa, but also elsewhere. Symptoms include ineffective and short-lived governments, ethnic and class violence, and in a few cases, even civil wars. More extreme examples include the limited reach of the central government in such countries as the Congo/Zaire or Afghanistan, ethnic violence in Sri Lanka, pogroms in Rwanda, and civil wars in El Salvador and the Sudan. Less dramatic but more common examples of ineffective states are what scholars often refer to as neopatrimonial or predatory states, that is, states that are governed by personalistic and corrupt rulers who readily channel public resources for personal use (Callaghy and Ravenhill, 1994; Evans, 1995).

Ineffective states hurt development. It is well understood by scholars of development that political instability discourages private investment and that personalistic rulers divert public investment away from productive uses. Beyond issues of capital accumulation and growth, ineffective states also hurt the societies they govern because they are often manned by less-than-professional armed forces, civil bureaucracies, and police. Instead of pursuing the public good, state agents in these settings use the power at their disposal to repress and exploit common citizens. These problems take on an especially ominous dimension when the rulers and the ruled are distinct in terms of ethnic or class divisions. Victims of state repression may, in turn, organise and arm themselves as a form of self-protection, opening up the prospect for long-term violence. Ineffective states thus generally encourage social trends that development seeks to reverse, namely, economic stagnation, social insecurity and lack of individual opportunities.

While it is clear that ineffective states hurt development, the question of why some parts of the developing world have ended up with more ineffective states than others is considerably more difficult to answer. Whereas a South Korea or even an India is moderately well governed, a Nigeria or a Tanzania is not. Why? The reasons are complex and many (Kohli, 2004). First, modern states emerged in Europe and spread from there to the non-West, often via colonial imposition. The fit between the state as a political form and indigenous political units was especially poor in some parts of the developing world, such as in Sub-Saharan Africa, which lacked a tradition of large-scale, centralised political units. Second, and most important, the political impact of colonialism varied from place to place; for example, considerably more architectonic in a Korea or an India, where colonisers left behind well-functioning states, than in a Nigeria or a Tanzania. Third, revolutionary and nationalist movements proved to be important agents of state formation in the developing world; however, such movements emerged and succeeded only in some countries. And finally, well-organised militaries in power have at times succeeded in reforming developing-country states; the problem, however, is not only that such militaries can readily become tyrannical, but also that well-organised militaries remain scarce, especially in ineffective states.

State and economic growth

Developing-country states have helped both to promote and to hinder economic growth. Many East Asian countries, such as South Korea or Taiwan, exemplify how states have collaborated with private investors to facilitate rapid industrialisation. By contrast, the ruling elites in many African countries used state policies and resources, less to promote economic growth, but more to enrich themselves and their political supporters. In much of the developing world, exemplified, say, by an India or a Brazil, which fall somewhere between these extremes, states have been more supportive of growth promotion in some periods and in some areas than in others. Interpretation of this varied record has generated significant scholarly controversies.

To simplify these controversies, two major schools of thought developed over the last two to three decades: neoliberal and statist. Neoliberal scholars and policy makers believe that states that follow the logic of markets help efficient allocation of resources; these limited states are thus best suited to facilitate rapid economic growth (World Bank, 1987, 1991). States in rapidly growing East Asia are thus thought to have been minimal states that helped create open economies, including minimal protection and equilibrium exchange rates, which in turn set the framework for rapid exports of labour-intensive products (Balassa, 1988). Following a similar logic, states in Sub-Saharan Africa are viewed as serving mainly urban interests that distorted prices in the core agricultural sector, and thus contributed in the recent past to stagnant economies (Bates, 1981). Numerous other developing countries are also criticised for their early embrace of state intervention, economic planning and import-substitution policy regimes. These ideas contributed to the emergence of what came to be known during the 1980s and the 1990s as the 'Washington Consensus' on development; a set of ideas that emphasised macro-economic stability, minimal state intervention, open economies and the privatisation of public enterprises as the appropriate strategy for economic growth in debt-ridden developing countries (Williamson, 1990).

Neoliberal ideas proved to be very influential during the 1980s and beyond, especially in moulding the economic policies of Latin American and Sub-Saharan African countries, many of whom had acquired serious foreign debts in an earlier period, and who had little choice but to accept external pressure. Their political potency aside, the truth value of neoliberal ideas did not go unchallenged. Many scholars argued that rapid economic growth in East Asia was a product, not of minimal market-following states, but of highly interventionist market-leading states that picked economic winners, subsidised their export success, collaborated closely with business, and repressed labour so as to keep wages well behind productivity gains (Amsden, 1989; Wade, 1990). For Sub-Saharan Africa, dissenting scholars argued that the problem ran deeper than that of urban-biased states distorting agrarian markets; the roots of economic stagnation lay instead with the poorly formed, neopatrimonial states that were incapable of pursuing any type of coherent development (Sandbrook, 1985). In more mixed cases too, for example, scholars suggested that slow economic growth in a case like India may be a function less of an import-substitution policy regime but more a result of excessive distributive pressures on the state (Bardhan, 1989), or that the economic problems of Brazil may result from the state's inability to facilitate domestic savings, excessive dependence on external resources, and vulnerabilities to global economic shocks (Fishlow, 1980). Some scholars have pulled together a variety of such evidence to provide a coherent statist alternative to the neoliberal views (Evans, 1995; Kohli, 2004), stressing the central role of state and business collaboration in the promotion of rapid economic growth.

Adjudicating such debates as between neoliberal and statist scholars is not easy, especially because available evidence can be organised and reorganised in a manner so that it suits a scholar's prior normative commitments. The recent experience of many developing countries with neoliberal policies, however, is quite disturbing. After nearly two decades of an embrace of 'structural adjustment', including minimising the role of the state, economic growth in large parts of Sub-Saharan Africa (with some important exceptions like Botswana and Mauritius) remains anaemic (Van de Walle, 2001). The performance of Latin American countries is also highly uneven (Stallings and Peres, 2000). By contrast, such highly interventionist economies as China, India and Vietnam have emerged as some of the world's most rapid economic growers. Such experience has led to growing doubts about the validity of the Washington Consensus on development (Stiglitz, 2002). While nothing coherent has really replaced the Washington Consensus, there is a burgeoning realisation that no one solution may fit all developing countries, and that the role of an effective state and of other institutions in managing a developing-country economy remains very important.

State, poverty and inequality
Very few developing-country states have succeeded in directly attacking the roots of inequalities in their societies, and thus in rapidly reducing poverty. This is mainly because most developing-country states represent the interests of narrow economic and political elites. Even when state power in one country or another comes to rest on a broader social coalition, the political and bureaucratic capacity to push through such difficult reforms as land redistribution is often missing. Leaving aside a few occupied countries like South Korea in the 1950s, it is not surprising that radical redistribution of wealth and property succeeded in only a handful of revolutionary communist states; these states combined the power of centralised coercion with that of mobilised masses, mainly via well-organised communist parties. Such a strategy was pursued in countries like China and Cuba during certain periods, and indeed led to reduction in inequalities and to rapid alleviation of poverty. However, communist states also generated other well-known problems, including tyrannical concentration of power and a failure to encourage economic growth.

Growing economies of course help the poor in developing countries; the evidence in support of the proposition that economic growth helps alleviate poverty is fairly strong (Fields, 2001). Two important qualifications are nevertheless important, both of which suggest that states also need to play an important and direct role in poverty alleviation. First, the 'trickle-down' process is often very slow. Take, for example, the case of India. The percentage of population living in poverty in India has declined steadily but slowly. Nevertheless, the absolute number of poor people has for some decades remained at a stubborn 300 million, a number that ought to be morally and politically unacceptable. Second, as the United Nation's Human Development Report(s) regularly stress, a number of countries have defied the association between income and poverty, reducing more poverty than income levels alone would suggest (see especially UNDP, 1996, ch. 3). The lessons include that states have and can help the lot of the poor via a number of strategies: modifying the growth strategy to be more employment generating; effective taxation and public expenditures in such areas as health, education, and the promotion of employment via public works; and, of course, the more radical option of land redistribution.

Patterns of income inequality within developing countries do not seem to vary regularly with levels of income (Fields, 2001). Thus, for example, a middle-income country like Brazil is a lot more unequal than another middle-income country like South Korea. Similarly, income inequality in a poor country like India is a lot less skewed than in many Sub-Saharan African countries. While historical and demographic factors contribute to such variations, it is also the case that patterns of inequality reflect accumulation of past state actions. A South Korea is thus a relatively egalitarian society because of land reforms implemented during the 1950s and the subsequent pursuit of a more labour-intensive strategy of industrialisation. The state in Brazil, by contrast, has been considerably more elitist (at least until very recently), regularly channelling economic benefits to the few at the top of the social pyramid. Sustained democracy in India has put pressure on governments to limit wealth accumulation at the top and to channel some public resources to those at the bottom. In much of Sub-Saharan Africa, by contrast, the absence of sustained democracy has meant that the interests of peasant farmers have been regularly neglected, creating a serious city versus the countryside divide.

In sum, it ought to be clear that states have a very important role to play in moderating inequalities and in helping alleviate poverty in the developing world. What remains a troubling issue, however, is that the states that may be best suited to promote economic growth may not be the best suited for moderating inequalities and alleviating poverty. Whereas states that have proved to be the most effective agents of growth have been closely allied with business groups, well-organised social democratic governments in power are likely to be better at tackling poverty and inequality. With the introduction of democracy in much of the developing world, it is no surprise that governments that have proved effective at growth promotion find themselves challenged electorally because of their supposed neglect of the poor (for example, the 2004 elections in India). Conversely, when a left-leaning government comes into power (for example, Lula in Brazil), it is also no surprise that business groups act nervous, threaten to pull out capital, and need to be reassured so as to resume the growth of the economy. How to create effective democratic states and, within them, how to reconcile growth and redistribution will remain the primary challenge of development in the twenty-first century.

ATUL KOHLI

References

Amsden, Alice (1989), *Asia's Next Giant: South Korea and Late Industrialization*, Oxford and New York: Oxford University Press.
Balassa, Bela (1988), 'Lessons of East Asian development', *Economic Development and Cultural Change*, **36** (3), 273–90.
Bardhan, Pranab (1989), *The Political Economy of Development in India*, Oxford: Blackwell.
Bates, Robert H. (1981), *Markets and States in Tropical Africa: The Political Basis of Agricultural Policies*, Berkeley, CA: University of California Press.
Bermeo, Nancy G. (2003), *Ordinary People in Extraordinary Times: The Citizenry and the Breakdown of Democracy*, Princeton, NJ: Princeton University Press.
Callaghy, Thomas and John Ravenhill (eds) (1994), *Hemmed In: Responses to Africa's Economic Decline*, New York: Columbia University Press.
Evans, Peter (1995), *Embedded Autonomy: States and Industrial Transformation*, Princeton, NJ: Princeton University Press.
Fields, Gary (2001), *Distribution and Development: A New Look at the Developing World*, Cambridge, MA: MIT Press.
Fishlow, Albert (1980), 'Brazilian development in long-term perspective', *American Economic Review*, **70**, 102–8.
Hobbes, Thomas (1968), *Leviathan*, London and Baltimore, MD: Penguin Books.
Huntington, Samuel (1968), *Political Order in Changing Societies*, New Haven, CT: Yale University Press.
Kohli, Atul (2004), *State-Directed Development: Political Power and Industrialization in the Global Periphery*, Cambridge and New York: Cambridge University Press.
Sandbrook, Richard (1985), *Politics of Africa's Economic Stagnation*, Cambridge: Cambridge University Press.
Stallings, Barbara and Wilson Peres (2000), *Growth, Employment and Equity: The Impact of the Economic Reforms in Latin America and the Caribbean*, Washington, DC: Brookings Institution Press.
Stiglitz, Joseph (2002), *Globalization and its Discontents*, London: Allen Lane.
United Nations Development Programme (1996), *Human Development Report*, Oxford and New York: Oxford University Press.

Van de Walle, Nicholas (2001), *African Economies and the Politics of Permanent Crisis, 1979–1991*, Cambridge and New York: Cambridge University Press.

Wade, Robert (1990), *Governing the Market: Economic Theory and the Role of Government in East Asian Industrialization*, Princeton, NJ: Princeton University Press.

Weber, Max (1994), 'The profession and vocation of politics', in Weber, *Political Writings*, edited by P. Lassman and R. Speirs, Cambridge: Cambridge University Press, pp. 309–18.

Williamson, John (1990), 'What Washington means by policy reform', in Williamson (ed.), *The Progress of Policy Reform in Latin America*, Washington, DC: Institute of International Economics, pp. 32–5.

World Bank (1987), *World Development Report*, Oxford and New York: Oxford University Press.

World Bank (1991), *World Development Report*, Oxford and New York: Oxford University Press.

Stock Market and Economic Development

The stock market is widely regarded as a central institution of capitalism. It provides a mechanism, based on the buying and selling of shares, through which economic agents (households, corporations and financial intermediaries) allocate their savings to corporations and others who need capital. Behind this apparently simple apparatus lie a number of complex issues. The significance of the stock market for capitalist development and specifically for achieving, in the narrow sense of the term, faster economic growth in developing countries raises further questions.

The controversial role of stock markets

Long ago, John Maynard Keynes (1936) in the famous Chapter 12 of *The General Theory* stated the case against the stock market in the following terms:

> As the organization of investment markets improves, the risk of the predominance of speculation does, however, increase. In one of the greatest investment markets in the world, namely, New York, the influence of speculation in the above sense [i.e., the activity of forecasting the psychology of the market] is enormous . . . Speculators may do no harm as bubbles on a steady stream of enterprise. But the position is serious when enterprise becomes a bubble on a whirlpool of speculation. When the capital development of a country becomes a by-product of the activities of a casino, the job is likely ill-done.

Notwithstanding Keynes, the stock market has never lacked defenders: today they are to be found not just in orthodox economic circles but also among those whom one would normally expect to find its most vehement critics. To begin with the orthodox perspective, at a practical policy level, the case for establishing and expanding stock markets in developing countries is put forward by the Bretton Woods Institutions (BWIs) (see for example, World Bank, 1989, 2002). It is argued that state-directed financial institutions, which many developing countries (DCs) established in the post-Second World War period in order to provide long-term finance for industrialisation, often at subsidised interest rates for targeted firms or sectors, were unsuccessful. In many countries, such economic arrangements allegedly resulted in huge non-performing loans, crony capitalism and ultimately in inefficient inflationary finance. Even if in some cases these measures were successful, it would, in the BWIs' view, still be useful to have an alternative, competitive source of finance for industrial firms. The BWIs also suggest importantly that the establishment and growth of stock markets represents a natural progression in the course of economic development, that is, in the process of industrialisation, firms require recourse to stock market financing in order to supplement their normal sources of funds via banks and retained profits.

Those with a leftist outlook but who support the establishment of stock markets in developing countries includes the United Nation's World Institute for Development Economics Research, which, in the 1980s, appointed a high-level study group under the chairmanship of Kenneth Berrill. Its report called on DC governments to establish stock markets in order to attract portfolio capital from advanced countries (WIDER, 1990). The essential argument was that, because of the debt crisis, Western banks would be unwilling to lend to DCs. There were, however, huge accumulations of savings in advanced country (AC) pension funds and other savings vehicles which DCs could and should tap. This point was reinforced later by the OECD economist, Helmut Reisen (1994), who argued that this was a *Pareto optimal* solution to both the ageing problem in the West and DCs' needs for external finance. The former would gain from portfolio diversification and higher rates of return in young and more vigorous developing economies; the latter would benefit from the ever-expanding savings of wealthier populations.

In a similar vein, Zhao Zhi Yang, the then Secretary-General of the Chinese Communist Party, provided a memorable defence of the role of the stock market in a communist country like China at the Thirteenth Congress of the Chinese Communist Party in 1988. Zhao suggested that in a country at a low level of economic development such as China, the laws of 'commodity production' must prevail, that is, the market economy must predominate. Zhao raised the question if capitalist countries can benefit from stock markets, why should socialist countries also not do so? He went on to suggest that this question was particularly pertinent in view of the fact that a socialist country is better able to regulate the negative effects of stock markets than a capitalist economy (Singh, 1993).

Similarly, cutting across the normal 'party lines', there have also been critical voices in the very citadels of stock market capitalism, namely the United States and the UK. Thus, Michael Porter (1992) reported the findings of a large research project, sponsored by the Harvard Business School and the Council on Competitiveness on the US financial sector. The project included contributions by leading US economists and policy makers including Larry Summers a distinguished academic economist and later, US Treasury Secretary. The report broadly echoed Keynesian-type reservations regarding the role of the stock market. It suggested that the stock market-based US financial system was inefficient in allocating capital and was thereby undermining the economy's global competitiveness.

The controversy continues, particularly in relation to developing countries and especially in the light of the frequent acute financial crises – virtual meltdowns of the stock markets in some countries – in South East Asia, Latin America and Russia.

Stock markets and development: critical issues
The above controversy raises the following analytical, empirical and policy issues:

1. How does the stock market help or hinder economic development, at least in the narrow sense of achieving faster economic growth?
2. What are the channels through which these effects operate?

3. If the stock market system is not working well, can the government of whatever political complexion, communist or otherwise regulate the stock market so as to eliminate or minimise its negative features?

These questions are examined in turn below.

How stock markets affect economic development

In textbook economic analysis, stock markets can affect economic development in a number of different ways. First, through the pooling of small individual savings into large capital investments by corporations, it allows economic agents to hold titles to a small part of a steel mill or a shipyard. Without such a risk-sharing institution, there may not have been the large capital accumulations needed to finance lumpy investment projects. J.R. Hicks assigned particular importance to this function of the stock market in relation to the eighteenth-century English industrial revolution (Levine, 1997).

Second, the textbooks suggest that the stock market helps economic development through efficient allocation of capital, that is, to those firms that utilise it most profitably. This is achieved by the actions of a multitude of buyers and sellers of shares, with diverse views of future profits of companies. Efficient allocation is defined to occur when the market accords higher share prices for those companies with higher expected profitability and relatively lower prices for those which may be less profitable in the future. Broadly speaking this results in a lower cost of capital (that is, in market parlance, a higher *P/E* ratio) for efficient firms and a higher cost (that is, a lower *P/E* ratio) for the relatively inefficient firms. (In this analysis, in accordance with the normal calculus of a capitalist economy, efficiency and profitability are deemed to be synonymous, but such a calculus does not take into account externalities and other factors, by virtue of which the two may differ.)

Third, and importantly, the stock market is thought to provide a vehicle by means of which faster technical progress is achieved by virtue of selecting new projects on the basis of the pooling of wisdom of large numbers of buyers and sellers or, alternatively, by the activities of institutions such as venture capital funds. This point is particularly emphasised by the modern theory of endogenous growth and finance (King and Levine, 1993; Levine, 1997).

Fourth, stock markets are also thought to promote good corporate governance through takeovers and the market for corporate control. In textbook theory, if managers are pursuing goals other than that of maximising shareholder wealth, or are otherwise being slothful or inefficient, the firm's share price will fall, making it subject to a 'disciplinary takeover'.

Through the above processes, which include the stock market's risk-sharing, informational, monitoring and disciplinary functions, the market is thought to promote higher levels of investment and higher productivity growth.

Channels of transmission

The validity of the textbook theory and its ability to perform the tasks outlined above depends crucially on the efficiency of two market processes and their respective outcomes: (a) the determination of share prices and (b) the workings of the takeover mechanism.

A central empirical question is how efficient are the prices generated by stock markets in the real world. Similarly, a related question is the efficiency of actual takeovers.

Determination of share prices　In the orthodox paradigm of share-price determination, these prices are expected to be efficient since they emanate from perfect markets with large numbers of well-informed buyers and sellers in which no one buyer or seller can influence the price and where there is a homogeneous product, namely shares. There is, however, an alternative paradigm indicated by the above quotation from Keynes that regards stock markets essentially as gambling casinos dominated by speculators. Recent literature provides formalisation of the various elements of this paradigm (see Stiglitz, 1994; Allen and Gale, 2000; Shiller, 2000; Shleifer, 2000). In brief, this literature suggests that in the face of the highly uncertain future, share prices are likely to be influenced by the so-called 'noise traders', and by whims, fads and contagion. For similar psychological reasons, investors may also give much greater weight in price formation to near rather than long-term performance.

Until recently, the empirical literature has been dominated by the so-called 'efficient markets hypothesis' (EMH), which argues that real-world share prices are efficient in the sense that they incorporate all available information (Fama, 1970). In the 1970s, evidence in favour of this hypothesis was thought to be overwhelming, with enthusiasts regarding it as the best-documented hypothesis throughout the social sciences (Jensen, 1978). In the 1980s and 1990s, with (a) the 1987 US stock market crash, (b) the meltdown in the Asian stock markets in the 1990s and (c) the recent bursting of the technology stocks bubble, the EMH has suffered fundamental setbacks. In this context, a useful distinction can be made between two kinds of efficiency of stock markets: (a) the information arbitrage efficiency which ensures that all information concerning a firm's shares immediately percolates to all stock market participants, ensuring that no participant can make a profit on such public information; and (b) fundamental valuation efficiency, that is, share prices accurately reflect a firm's fundamentals, that is, its long-term expected profitability (Tobin, 1984). The growing consensus view is that, in these terms, stock markets may at best be regarded as being efficient in the sense of (a) but far from being efficient in the economically more important sense (b). (See the references in the previous paragraph.)

The takeover mechanism　Just as there are good theoretical reasons why share prices in the real world may not be efficient in the fundamental valuation sense, economists have identified a number of reasons why the takeover mechanism may not actually work in the way envisaged in the orthodox analysis. The reasons include: (a) imperfections in the market for corporate control, the most important of which is that, whereas large firms can take over small ones, the reverse is rarely the case (see further, below); (b) the huge transactions costs of takeovers, particularly when large firms are involved and bids are contested; and (c) the free-rider problem identified by Grossman and Hart (1980). An obvious additional reason is that acquirers themselves may be empire builders rather than shareholder welfare maximisers (Singh, 1992).

The empirical evidence on these issues indicates that, although there is a very active market for corporate control in the major Anglo-Saxon countries, it is seriously inefficient. Two kinds of evidence lead to this conclusion. First, studies of the takeover selection process indicate that selection in the market for corporate control takes place only to a limited extent on the basis of the targeted firm's performance but much more so on the basis of its size. A large relatively unprofitable firm has a much smaller chance of being acquired than a small profitable firm. Second, controlling for other relevant variables, studies of post-merger profitability of amalgamating firms indicate that there is at best no improvement on average in post-merger profits but most likely a decline (Ravenscraft and Scherer, 1987; Singh, 1992; Tichy, 2002). To the extent that any market power is associated with a merger, even a neutral effect suggests a micro-economy inefficiency in resource utilisation, certainly not an improvement.

A related set of financial studies – the so-called 'events studies' – suggest, however, that in US takeovers, the acquiring firms suffer a sizeable decline in share prices in the period of six months to three years following the merger. The gainers are mainly the acquired firms whose share prices may rise by up to 20 per cent on average (Jensen, 1988). This poses serious incentive problems as potential acquiring firms stand to lose rather than to gain. Equally importantly, in order to classify these gains to the shareholders of acquired firms as being social gains, the analysis has to assume that share prices are always efficient in the fundamental valuation sense, which, as indicated above, is far from being the case. The rise in the share price of the acquired firm may reflect simply the price for control which empire builders are willing to pay even to the detriment of their own shareholders.

Further, a priori analysis as well as evidence indicates that in practice the imperfections of the pricing and the takeover processes together may lead to 'short-termism' on the part of corporate managements. This is reflected in the fact that the latter are obliged to fulfil the market analysts' short-term (quarterly or six-monthly) expectations of the firms' earnings per share. Evidence suggests that if such short-term targets are not met, there is a fall in share prices, making the firm *ceteris paribus* vulnerable to takeover. In a closely related but more general sense, the dominance of stock markets can also result in the unhealthy ascendancy of finance over production, and that of financial engineering (through the takeover process) over the normal long-term entrepreneurial tasks of introducing technical change, reducing costs and improving products. Thus, the benefits of having large corporations dependent on a highly liquid equity market are far from being unambiguous (Singh, 1999).

Stock markets, savings, investment and economic growth   Apart from the evidence on share prices and takeovers, there is also direct information available on the relationship between economic growth and related variables and stock market development.

First, there is broad-brush evidence indicating comparative long-term records of stock market-dominated economies, for example, the USA and the UK, are not superior, but, if anything, inferior relative to those of countries where stock markets do not play a significant role (Germany, Japan, Italy and other continental European countries) (Pagano, 1993; Singh and Glen, forthcoming). Similarly, the post-Second World War economic miracle of former West Germany occurred without any help from the stock markets. With respect to Japan, there is evidence that after the war, the Japanese government deliberately discouraged the growth of stock markets in favour of banks in the organisation of its financial system (Hoshi and Kashyap, 2001). Equally importantly, the much bigger miracles of late industrialising countries like Taiwan and Korea over the last three decades have also been accomplished independently of the stock markets. In all the countries, the banks (in the case of Taiwan and South Korea, state-owned ones) have played the central role in promoting long-term industrialisation (World Bank, 1993).

The more detailed recent firm-level econometric studies suggest that there is a positive relationship between both stock market and banking development and corporate growth (Levine and Zervos, 1998). However, this research has significant limitations as it is based on reduced-form cross-sectional analysis where it is particularly difficult to assess causality (Singh, 1997; Arestis et al., 2001). Moreover, this research ignores altogether the evidence on the inefficiencies of the critical channels of transmission, that is those of the share prices and the takeover mechanism discussed here.

Stock market regulation and developing countries
Compared with the highly organised and extensively regulated stock market activity in the USA and the UK, most DCs do not have such well-functioning markets. Not only is there inadequate government regulation, but private information gathering and disseminating firms are also often absent in DCs. Notwithstanding these regulatory and informational deficits, there was an enormous expansion of DC stock markets in the 1980s and 1990s in the wake of financial liberalisation in many of these countries. Despite their breathtaking expansion, most DC markets remain 'immature' (that is, riddled with insider trading and lack of transparency) and relatively illiquid. Most trading takes place in a few blue-chip shares (Singh, 1995, 1997).

There are good theoretical reasons for expecting DC share prices to be volatile, an expectation which is confirmed by the data. Evidence suggests that DC share prices are far more unstable than those of ACs. Share-price volatility is a negative feature of stock markets, as, *inter alia*, it detracts from the efficiency of the price signals in allocating investment. The volatility is further accentuated if DCs allow external portfolio capital inflows. This greatly increases the vulnerability of the economy not only to international shocks, but also to domestic shocks, substantially magnifying their effects. The main reason for this is that capital inflows lead to an interaction between two inherently unstable markets – the stock market and the currency market. In the event of a large shock (domestic or external) these interactions generate a negative feedback that may lead to, or greatly worsen, a financial crisis.

DCs have found it difficult to regulate stock markets, as is indicated by frequent scams on DC stock markets. This should not be surprising as even highly regulated and well-functioning markets, such as those in the United States, from time to time experience episodes such as those of Enron and WorldCom. Nevertheless, Singh (1998) has argued that one regulatory reform that would be particularly useful for DCs, is to stop the creation of a market for corporate control. Such a market, as indicated above, exacerbates the negative effects of stock markets (for example, short-termism) from the perspective of economic development. This reform may, however, involve major changes in company law, reducing the role of shareholders and enhancing that of stakeholders or the government in takeover situations. DC governments need to find cheaper and more efficient ways of changing corporate managements than the lottery and the huge expense of the market for corporate control. They should also encourage product market competition to discipline corporations rather than rely on the stock market for this purpose.

Conclusion

To sum up, this entry suggests that stock markets may be potent symbols of capitalism, but paradoxically capitalism works as well, if not better, when stock markets do not have a major role in the economy. This is particularly so from the perspective of economic development in emerging countries.

AJIT SINGH

References

Allen, F. and D. Gale (2000), *Comparing Financial Systems*, Cambridge, MA: MIT Press.
Arestis, P., P. Demetriades and K. Luintel (2001), 'Financial development and economic growth: the role of stock markets', *Journal of Money, Credit and Banking*, **33** (1), 16–41.
Fama, E. (1970), 'Efficient capital markets: a review of theory and empirical work', *Journal of Finance*, **25**, 383–417.
Grossman, S. and O. Hart (1980), 'Takeover bids, the free-rider problem and the theory of the corporation', *Bell Journal of Economics*, **11**, 42–64.
Hoshi, T. and A. Kashyap (2001), *Corporate Financing and Governance in Japan: The Road to the Future*, Cambridge, MA: MIT Press.
Jensen, M. (1978), 'Some anomalies evidence regarding market efficiency', *Journal of Financial Economics*, **6**, 95–101.
Jensen, M. (1988), 'Take-overs: their causes and consequences', *Journal of Economic Perspectives*, **2** (1), 21–48.
Keynes, J.M. (1936), *The General Theory of Money, Interest and Employment*, London: Macmillan.
King, R.G. and R. Levine (1993), 'Financial intermediation and economic development', in Colin Mayer and Xavier Vives (eds), *Capital Markets and Financial Intermediation*, Cambridge: Cambridge University Press, pp. 156–93.
Levine, R. (1997), 'Financial development and economic growth: views and agenda', *Journal of Economic Literature*, **35** (2), June, 688–726.
Levine, R. and S. Zervos (1998), 'Stock markets, banks, and economic growth', *American Economic Review*, **88** (3), 537–58.
Pagano, M. (1993), 'Financial markets and growth: an overview', *American Economic Review*, **37**, 613–22.
Porter, M.E. (1992), 'Capital disadvantage: America's failing capital investment system', *Harvard Business Review*, **70** (5), 65–83.
Ravenscraft, D.J. and F.M. Scherer (1987), *Mergers, Sell Offs and Economic Effiiency*, Washington, DC: Brookings Institution.
Reisen, Helmut (1994), 'On the wealth of nations and retirees', in R. O'Brien (ed.), *Finance and the International Economy, 8: Prize Essays in Memory of Robert Marjolin*, Oxford and New York: Oxford University Press for American Express Bank Ltd, pp. 87–107.
Shiller, R.J. (2000), *Irrational Exuberance*, Princeton, NJ: Princeton University Press.
Shleifer, A. (2000), *Inefficient Markets: An Introduction to Behavioural Finance*, Oxford: Oxford University Press.
Singh, A. (1992), 'Corporate take-overs', in J. Eatwell, M. Milgate and P. Newman (eds), *The New Palgrave Dictionary of Money and Finance*, London: Macmillan, pp. 480–86.
Singh, A. (1993), 'The stock market and economic development: should developing countries encourage stock markets?', *UNCTAD Review*, **4**, 1–28.
Singh, A. (1995), 'Corporate financial patterns in industrialising economies: a comparative international study', IFC Technical Paper no. 2, Washington, DC: World Bank.
Singh, A. (1997), 'Financial liberalisation, stock markets and economic development', *Economic Journal*, **107**, 771–82.
Singh, A. (1998), 'Liberalisation, the stock market and the market for corporate control: a bridge too far for the Indian economy?', in Ishar Judge Ahluwalia and I.M.D. Little (eds), *India's Economic Reforms and Development: Essays for Manmohan Singh*, Oxford: Oxford University Press, pp. 169–96.
Singh, A. (1999), 'Should Africa promote stock market capitalism?', *Journal of International Development*, **11** (3), 343–65.
Singh, A. and J. Glen (forthcoming), 'Corporate governance, competition and finance: re-thinking lessons from the Asian Crisis', *Eastern Economic Journal*.
Stiglitz, J. (1994), 'The role of the state in financial markets', in M. Bruno and B. Pleskovic (eds), *Proceedings of the World Bank Annual Conference on Development Economics 1993*, Washington, DC: World Bank, pp. 19–52.

Tichy, G. (2002), 'What do we know about the success and failure of mergers?', *Journal of Industry Competition and Trade*, **1** (4), 347–94.

Tobin, J. (1984), 'On the efficiency of the financial system', *Lloyds Bank Review*, July, 1–15.

WIDER (1990), *Foreign Portfolio Investment in Emerging Equity Markets*, Study Group Series no. 5, Helsinki: World Institute for Development Economics Research of the United Nations University.

World Bank (1989), *World Development Report*, Oxford and New York: Oxford University Press.

World Bank (1993), *The East Asian Miracle*, Oxford and New York: Oxford University Press.

World Bank (2002), *World Development Report*, Oxford and New York: Oxford University Press.

Streeten, Paul Patrick (b. 1917)

A development economist and philosopher, whose most original and powerful work is on means of reducing world poverty, on ways of understanding the complexity and self-changing nature of social life, and on the indispensable role of values in social science.

Paul Hornig, who changed his name to Streeten as a British soldier, was born in Vienna in 1917. His family life and education introduced him to some of the city's notable philosophers, psychoanalysts, economists and writers. He was active in an unlawful youth movement that opposed tobacco and alcohol as passionately as it opposed the prevailing bourgeois culture and government. He has recorded three turning-points in that young life. The first, at fifteen, was from hiking and camping and group life towards intellectual and private interests in psychology and sociology. The second, at eighteen, was away from revolutionary action towards democratic reform, away from collectivism towards individualism and away from party doctrine towards individual conscience. The third, as a dissident Jewish law student, was his lucky escape from Austria after the *Anschluss* in 1938.

A Christian group called Blue Pilgrims arranged his passage to England. Two Streeten sisters offered him a home. Other members found him a place at the University of Aberdeen. He began work in political economy, but early in the war with Germany he was interned as an enemy alien. The prisoners, some of whom later won the Nobel Prize, ran camp universities. In 1941 those with anti-Nazi credentials were accepted for war service. After two laborious years in the British army's pioneer corps, Paul was recruited into a commando troop. To pretend British nationality if captured, its foreign members adopted English names and family histories. Thus Paul Hornig became Paul Streeten. He was severely wounded in the allied occupation of Sicily. His young experience of exile, prison, hard labour and warfare may have contributed to his lifelong regard for 'civil courage'.

When he recovered he was offered further education. He joined Balliol College, took a degree in philosophy, politics and economics, and was elected a Fellow in1948. He taught with Thomas Balogh, an adviser to British governments and designer of the British National Oil Corporation. Fifty years later he recalled that 'the genuine Athenian democracy of an Oxford College, the collegiate spirit, and the daily contact with brilliant colleagues from many areas and with excellent undergraduates provided a heady mixture. These were the happiest years of my life'. The same source – pp. 151–2 of his *Thinking About Development*, 1995, ironically a Cambridge University Press book – argues that 'Oxford-trained economists, though they have spent less time on economics than their Cambridge equivalents, are better economic theorists for having had to study philosophy . . . and better applied economists for having had to study politics'.

From 1964 to 1966 he helped to design Britain's overseas aid policies. As a professor at the University of Sussex, he founded its Institute of Development Studies. Returning to Oxford in 1968 as Warden of Queen Elizabeth House he turned that centre of Commonwealth studies into a centre of development studies. He moved to the US in 1976, worked for the World Bank's Basic Needs programme, and then joined Boston University in 1980. He directed its Center for Asian Development Studies until 1984, then its World Development Institute until 1989. He was a member until 2003 of the team writing the United Nations Development Programme's annual Human Development Reports. He has had an extraordinary number of consultant, advisory and visiting appointments, local and national and international. A list of them occupies two crowded pages (ix–x) of Sanjaya Lall and Frances Stewart (eds) *Theory and Reality in Development: Essays in Honour of Paul Streeten* (1986) which also records that his developing-country experience includes India, Pakistan, Bangladesh, China, the Philippines, Malaysia, Sri Lanka, Israel, Mauritius, Malta, Egypt, Nigeria, Ivory Coast, Kenya, Kuwait, Tanzania, Panama, Trinidad, Barbados, Argentina, Brazil, Chile, Venezuela and Mexico. Besides UNESCO, UNDP and the World Bank he has worked for UNCTAD, UNIDO, FAO, WHO, ILO, WFC, WFP, IFAD, UNICEF, the IMF, the Asian Development Bank, the African Development Bank, the African Research Consortium, ODA, CIDA, SIDA, the EU, the OECD, DAC, UNU (Tokyo) and for WIDER (Helsinki) whose founding paper he wrote.

Of the many honours conferred on Streeten in Europe, the United Kingdom and North America, one that most exactly celebrates his dual service to both the theory and the practice of humane development is perhaps the Wassily Leontief Prize awarded in 2001 by the Global Development and Environment Institute at Tufts University, Massachusetts, 'to recognize outstanding contributions to economic theory that address contemporary realities and support just and sustainable societies'.

That dual originality is rare and valuable. Theorists whose science is their main concern do look for elements of real life that accord with or discredit particular types or directions of theory. Others reverse that intent, to condemn as inefficient any practices that do not accord with prevailing theory. The best pragmatic economists bring open minds and institutional ingenuity to bear on the life which is itself their main concern. Streeten's main concern is with the quality and justice of life, especially the life of poor people in poor countries, and the harm they can suffer from bad theory. Too much of the prevailing neoclassical orthodoxy is both untrue and unadaptable to changing life. It conceals the values that necessarily shape its selections from life's complexity. It neglects its own self-verifying and self-falsifying effects on that life. Trying for a unanimous, value-free science of an isolable, internally determined economic system driven and kept efficient chiefly by individual selfishness is a threefold mistake: a moral, political and scientific mistake.

A colleague has observed that Streeten as theorist processes passages of reasoning, his own and others, impartially. He tries the effect of reversing each positive and each negative, running every model backwards as well as forwards and running it while varying each of its premises in turn, scanning every matrix for neglected boxes, and testing every proposition for truth, tautology, political realism, moral turpitude and undistributed middles. But those apparently pedantic skills serve strong moral and social concerns. When Streeten exposes an unstated premise it is always one that matters to real people.

Precision must not be sterile, imagination must not be impractical: they should join, he believes, to generate 'imaginative visions of alternative possibilities with close and precise attention to detail'.

He has worked at a wide range of development problems. His summaries of the history of development ideas through the last half-century have emphasised nine directions of change, to most of which he has been a leading contributor:

- From thinking measured economic growth would suffice, people learned that it often would not. Many elements of economic and social and cultural development had to be independently contrived. Growth is as much an effect as a cause of development.
- From relying on capital accumulation as the main engine of growth, people learned that many other economic and social and cultural conditions needed to be contrived.
- From 'growth will trickle down', or 'grow first, redistribute later', people learned that countries which grow first do not easily trickle or redistribute, and that redistributing first often helps growth.
- From expecting poor countries to follow the rich along a regular path of growth, people came to see more complex and variable relations between the developed and the underdeveloped. Those relations can both hinder and help late developers. Each successful modernisation alters conditions for the next, and continuing changes in the developed countries continue to change the forces they exert on the less developed.
- From seeing fast industrialisation as a main agent of development, people have learned what problems it can create, and how important it is in most circumstances to improve agriculture, including small-scale and subsistence agriculture, and the local material and social conditions that rural people need.
- From 'best' technology people have learned to look as well or instead, in many circumstances, for 'appropriate' technology that can improve output and distribution with least call on scarce capital or skills.
- From arguing *between* correct pricing, radical redistribution and technical innovation as strategies to end poverty and reduce inequality, many now accept that the three need to be applied together, in a right order and relation to one another.
- From thinking of population control as a simple effect of income growth, then as a condition as well as an effect of income growth, people have learned that it is a more complex, changing and partly independent problem. For example, if food, safe water and contraception are available, primary education for girls may do more to cut both death and birth rates than a lot of growth in other forms may do.
- Finally, as Streeten wrote in *Development Perspectives* (1981):

> it became clear that measured income and its growth is only a part of basic needs. Adequate nutrition and safe water at hand, continuing employment, secure and adequate livelihoods for the self-employed, more and better schooling for their children, better preventive medical services, adequate shelter, cheap transport, and (but not only) a higher and growing level of measured income: some or all of these would figure on the list of urgently felt needs of poor people. (p. 110)

Those concerns, together with a cool head, a clear eye, and patience with complexities, prompt his analysis of 'the judo trick'. Left and Right offer different simplifications of the relations between big business and the poor world's underdevelopment and underemployment. The Left see global firms exploiting or disemploying poor countries' labour, pre-empting their natural resources and obstructing their development. The Right see the developed economies as models for the rest of the world to follow, and unhindered global trade and investment as the means of doing it. Streeten shares both parties' anxieties, but reasons patiently, both practically and theoretically, against their simplicities.

Big traders and investors can indeed help poor countries to develop. But they may often do it better by dealing with the developing countries' small business and contract labour, rather than by themselves owning the resources and employing wage labour. The big firm provides the materials, the designs, the credit and the marketing, while the informal sector produces the clothes, the sport equipment, the electronic components, the cloth and woodwork for handicrafts, or the crops. The big firms, as importers to their rich countries, use their political influence to discourage protectionist policies. Their interest in low-cost, labour-intensive imports coincides with the poor producers' interests. As long as there are institutional safeguards against exploitation and sweated labour, 'firms such as Marks and Spencer can do more for the poor of the world than Marx and Engels'.

The institutional safeguards are vital. Characteristically, *Thinking about Development* lists some necessary conditions for the 'judo trick' to advance all the interests concerned. Exchange rates, interest rates and any export and import restraints must be helpfully designed. Poor people must have access to the necessary assets, including land and credit. Their returns must rise with their productivity, which must not all be captured by price-cutting wholesalers. Demand from their own countries must also be expanded by increasing poor incomes. They must have health services, education, and training in simple managerial, accounting, bookkeeping and marketing techniques. They must have necessary infrastructure and information services.

By those means, big and small business can be made complementary to one another in access to markets, inputs, information and technology. Small-scale firms get access to large-scale firms, domestic to foreign firms, public to private firms, and non-governmental organisations to governments. The process is hazardous. There are all-too-easy ways of exploiting and degrading poor adult and child labour, and forcing small enterprises to resort to those horrors by misusing political and market strength against them. In *Globalisation: Threat or Opportunity?* (2001) Streeten concludes that competent government and the long-term interests of international business can and should prevent those horrors:

> Policies must be designed to mobilize the energies of the small-scale firms, and to make use of their lower costs, more labour-intensive techniques, greater employment creation and wider dispersion of technology, without, on the one hand, sacrificing efficiency and innovation, and, on the other, depriving the informal sector, by under-pricing outputs or over-pricing inputs, of adequate rewards and humane working conditions. (p. 99)

Matching changes are in process in the developed world, in the move from standardised, large-scale production to small-scale flexible firms. The mass consumer has been replaced by a more sophisticated type with higher purchasing power and more-differentiated tastes. Energy and information technology allow some decentralised production by smaller firms. Within many of them 'the old confrontation between labour and capital is replaced by one between the managers, owners and workers in the small sub-contracting firms on the one hand, and the large buyers of their output on the other . . . All this holds out great productive and social promise for the informal sector, especially if supported by the right social policies' (p. 100).

Streeten's contributions to economic education have been as radical as his work on development. Neoclassical orthodoxies are perhaps less rigid and more responsive to their critics and to practical experience than they used to be. But many texts still distinguish 'positive' from 'normative' economics as different in kind, the one scientific and the other not. Myrdal and Streeten emphasise all three of (1) the genuine, testable truth of the many factual elements in economists' work; (2) the irreducible role of values in selecting the questions to ask, the identities and categories to impose on the subject matter, the strands of causation to trace, and thus the purposes that the work is capable of serving; and (3) the diverse and changing nature, complexity and interdependence of economic, social and political life. Those perceptions, and the inescapable moral and social responsibilities that they impose on teachers, deserve to be at the heart of economic education.

If they are not, it is not for want of persuasive publication. In his first three teaching years Streeten had papers published in English, German, Italian, French and American journals. His bibliography includes more than 400 articles, many of them reprinted in more than one journal or language. He has been editor then chairman of the journal *World Development* for more than 30 years. He translated Gunnar Myrdal's *The Political Element in the Development of Economic Theory* (1953) and contributed to Myrdal's *Asian Drama* (1968). He edited and contributed to *Value in Social Theory* (1958), *The Crisis of Indian Planning* (with Michael Lipton, 1968), *Unfashionable Economics* (1970), *Commonwealth Policy in a Global Context* (with Hugh Corbet, 1971), *Recent Issues in World Development* (with Richard Jolly, 1981), volume two of *Human Resources, Employment and Development* (with Harry Maier, 1983), *Beyond Adjustment* (1988) and *The United Nations and the Bretton Woods Institutions* (with Mahbub ul Haq et al., 1995). He wrote or co-authored *Economic Integration* (1961), *Diversification and Development* (with Diane Elson, 1971), *Aid to Africa* (1972a), *The Frontiers of Development Studies* (1972b), *Trade Strategies for Development* (1973), *The Limits of Development Research* (1975), *Foreign Investment, Transnationals and Developing Countries* (with Sanjaya Lall, 1977), *Development Perspectives* (1981), *First Things First* (with Shaid Burki et al., 1981), *What Price Food?* (1987), *Mobilizing Human Potential* (1989), *Paul Streeten in South Africa* (1992), *Strategies for Human Development* (1994), *Thinking About Development* (1995) and *Globalisation: Threat or Opportunity?* (2001). Chapter 25 of that latest book condenses into four pages Streeten's distinctive concerns with poverty, with theory and practice, with facts and values, and with utopian possibilities. It serves equally well as an introduction to his life's work, and to the threats and opportunities facing rich and poor humanity now.

HUGH STRETTON

References

Haq, Mahbub ul, Richard Jolly, Paul Streeten and Khadija Haq (1995), *The United Nations and the Bretton Woods Institutions: New Challenges for the Twenty-First Century*, Basingstoke: Macmillan.

Lall, Sanjaya and Frances Stewart (eds) (1986), *Theory and Reality in Development: Essays in Honour of Paul Streeten*, Basingstoke: Macmillan.

Lall, Sanjaya and Paul Streeten (1977), *Foreign Investment, Transnationals and Developing Countries*, London: Macmillan.

Myrdal, Gunnar (1953), *The Political Element in the Development of Economic Theory*, London: Routledge & Kegan Paul (translated from Swedish by Paul Streeten).

Myrdal, Gunnar (1958), *Value in Social Theory: A Selection of Essays on Methodology* (edited by Paul Streeten), London: Routledge & Kegan Paul.

Myrdal, Gunnar (1968), *Asian Drama: An Inquiry into the Poverty of Nations*, London: Penguin.

Streeten, Paul (1961), *Economic Integration: Aspects and Problems*, Leyden: A.W. Sijthoff.

Streeten, Paul (ed.) (1970), *Unfashionable Economics: Essays in Honour of Lord Balogh*, London: Weidenfeld & Nicolson.

Streeten, Paul (1972a), *Aid to Africa: A Policy Outline for the 1970s*, London: Praeger.

Streeten, Paul (1972b), *The Frontiers of Development Studies*, London: Macmillan.

Streeten, Paul (ed.) (1973), *Trade Strategies for Development*, London: Macmillan.

Streeten, Paul (1975), *The Limits of Development Research*, Oxford: Pergamon (reprinted from *World Development*, **2** (10–12), 1974).

Streeten, Paul (1981), *Development Perspectives*, London: Macmillan.

Streeten, Paul (1987), *What Price Food? Agricultural Price Policies in Developing Countries*, Basingstoke: Macmillan.

Streeten, Paul (ed.) (1988), *Beyond Adjustment: the Asian Experience*, Washington, DC: International Monetary Fund.

Streeten, Paul (1989), *Mobilizing Human Potential: The Challenge of Unemployment*, New York: United Nations Development Programme.

Streeten, Paul (1992), *Paul Streeten in South Africa: Reflections on a Journey*, Pretoria: Development Society of Southern Africa.

Streeten, Paul (1994), *Strategies for Human Development: Global Poverty and Unemployment*, Copenhagen: Handelshøjskolens Forlag.

Streeten, Paul (1995), *Thinking About Development*, Cambridge: Cambridge University Press.

Streeten, Paul (2001), *Globalisation: Threat or Opportunity?* Copenhagen: Copenhagen Business School Press.

Streeten, Paul, Shaid Burki, Mahbub ul Haq and Frances Stewart (1981), *First Things First: Meeting Basic Human Needs in the Developing Countries*, Oxford and New York: Oxford University Press for the World Bank.

Streeten, Paul and Hugh Corbet (eds) (1971), *Commonwealth Policy in a Global Context*, London: Cass.

Streeten, Paul and Diane Elson (1971), *Diversification and Development: The Case of Coffee*, New York: Praeger.

Streeten, Paul and Richard Jolly (eds) (1981), *Recent Issues in World Development*, Oxford: Pergamon.

Streeten, Paul and Michael Lipton (eds) (1968), *The Crisis of Indian Planning: Economic Planning in the 1960s*, London: Oxford University Press.

Streeten, Paul and Harry Maier (eds) (1983), *Human Resources, Employment and Development*, Vol. 2, London: Macmillan.

Structural Adjustment

Since 1980, the most ubiquitous and consequential set of policies affecting developing and transitional countries has been a series of economic reforms sponsored by the World Bank, the IMF and other multilateral and bilateral donors. From its inception, these policy measures or structural adjustment packages tied loans to a series of macroeconomic and sector targets. This strategy, sometimes referred to as 'neoliberalism', assumed that growth and development would arise from the stabilisation, liberalisation and privatisation of economies. Stabilisation, which focused on reducing trade deficits, constraining monetary growth and cutting government spending, was aimed at reducing inflation and imbalances in the current account and government budgets. Liberalisation retracted state intervention in markets in order to reverse the distortions to the price signals consumers and private producers need to make optimal choices. In addition to reducing government regulations, liberalisation often meant 'freeing up' prices by removing government controls or subsidies on output prices like food for consumers and input prices like fertiliser to farmers. User fees or charges to individuals for utilising public goods like education and healthcare were introduced to promote 'efficiency' in their allocation. Privatisation focused on selling state assets to the private sector in the belief that private property ownership would lead to higher levels of efficiency, investment and growth.

In its initial formulation the IMF was to focus on short-term demand management aimed at stabilising economies and the World Bank was to concentrate on medium-term programmes incorporating supply-side inducements that were to arise through economic reforms associated with liberalisation and privatisation. As we will see, over time the distinction between the content of programmes and terms of loans began to blur. Moreover, in many of the poorer regions, the model has seldom induced growth or development and often collapsed into a perpetual short-term focus on the ever-elusive goal of macroeconomic stabilisation. By 1995, in Sub-Saharan Africa, 37 countries had received structural adjustment loans (Kapur et al., 1997, p. 798). However, by 2001 according to the World Bank's own calculations the GNP per capita of the region had fallen by 43 per cent since 1980 when the first programmes were put in place (World Bank, 2003).

Despite more than two decades of disappointing results, the adjustment trinity (three closely related constructs denoting the same fealty to neoliberals as the Christian concept) of stabilisation, liberalisation and privatisation is still at the core of the policy conditionality of international aid, including the 'new' poverty-reduction strategies of the World Bank and the IMF. What are the changes if any to these policies, for example, has adjustment been adjusted? Why has there been such a strong adherence to structural adjustment? Why have the results been so disappointing? These and other questions will be explored in this entry, beginning with an examination of the origin and evolution of structural adjustment including the broadening of the policy agenda. This will be followed by an explanation of the poor track record of adjustment which focuses on its weak theoretical roots, and some reasons for the continuing adherence to these policies.

To understand the origins of adjustment one must begin with the development of the policy conditionality (loans contingent on policy changes) of the IMF. To John Maynard Keynes, who represented the British delegation in the 1944 negotiations, the Fund was to be largely a facilitator that would maximise policy sovereignty. However, the US delegation, led by Harry Dexter White, wanted the IMF to be conservative with the right to challenge any drawing from the Fund. In the end the Articles of Agreement permitted the Fund to intervene to declare member loan ineligibility (Article 5, Section 5). In September 1947, conditionality was formally introduced when Chile was told that approval of its drawings was contingent on changes to their fiscal and monetary policy. The executive board considered their right to impose conditions and decided that this was permitted since it was far less punitive than declaring complete ineligibility (under Article 5, section 5) (Horsefield, 1969, Vol. I, pp. 187–92).

With the introduction of standby agreements in 1952, which tied credit allocation to specific policy targets, conditionality became the IMF operational norm. The focus was on readily quantifiable targets like domestic credit expansion with a strong anti-inflationary bias. The aim was to maintain fixed exchange systems by adjusting the domestic absorption capacity in response to balance-of-payments problems. This monetarist approach was formalised by Polak (1957) and has become known as the 'financial programming model'. Even after the demise of the Bretton Woods fixed exchange rate system in 1973, the IMF continued to use the same model of stabilisation to generate the terms of its loan conditionality. In a world of greater exchange rate flexibility the IMF began to incorporate an expenditure-switching model (Salter–Swan) to justify devaluations to help reverse balance-of-payments deficits. In this two-good world, currency depreciations shift production to tradables exchanged on global markets (away from non-tradables) since it increases the return in domestic currency terms (Stein and Nissanke, 1999).

The major reason why stabilisation became a core policy in all bilateral and multilateral official lending had less to do with the IMF and more to do with changes in the World Bank. During the 1950s and 1960s, the Bank primarily lent funds in support of infrastructural expansion and upgrading. During the decade of the 1970s under the presidency of Robert McNamara, the World Bank became more concerned with income distribution, basic needs and poverty reduction. They expanded their project support into areas like agriculture, education and rural water access. There was some concern among the economists in the Bank that too much economic growth would be sacrificed to achieve these social goals. Moreover, the economics profession was becoming increasingly neoclassical and critical of most forms of state intervention in the economy, including the kind being supported by the World Bank (see, for example, Bauer, 1972).

A key change was the appointment of the economist Ernie Stern as the vice president in charge of operations. When McNamara set out to criticise the developed countries for their trade barriers, Stern convinced him not to provide unsolicited advice but to make a statement of broad principle by offering 'additional assistance to developing countries that undertake the needed structural adjustment for export promotion in line with their long-term comparative advantage' (Kapur et al., 1997, pp. 506–7). A series of events rapidly put structural adjustment policies at the centre of the new World Bank agenda including: the oil shock of 1979 and the need to find a new mechanism to disburse funds in support of balance of payments; the elections of the conservatives Margaret Thatcher (May 1979) and Ronald Reagan (November 1980); the replacement of McNamara by A.W. Clausen, a staunch conservative (July 1981); the departure in the early 1980s of proponents of anti-poverty strategies like Mahbub ul Haq and the appointment of the ultra-conservative and dogmatic neoliberal Anne Krueger (in 1982) as chief economist who systematically replaced most of the development research department with economists holding views similar to her own (Stein, forthcoming).

When structural adjustment was first suggested to the executive board there were some concerns over infringing on the IMF's sphere of responsibility and problems with the Bank's Articles which prohibited programme loans to 'exceptional' examples. The senior staff dealt with the dual problem by promising to coordinate their efforts with the macrostabilisation policies of the Fund and convincing the board that 'exceptional' would be defined as countries with Fund programmes. Thus the IMF, with its stabilisation policies was incorporated centrally into structural adjustment packages. IMF standby agreements rapidly became the prerequisite not only for World Bank loans but also for bilateral assistance as the World Bank increased its coordination functions by among other things organising and chairing annual donor meetings.

The remaining two parts of the trinity were introduced as part of World Bank structural adjustment packages. Liberalisation and privatisation arose from an array of neoclassical microeconomic models which assumed that consumers and producers would make optimal choices if prices properly reflected scarcity and choice. In this view, countries had difficulties because states distorted market signals through various forms of policy intervention, including direct ownership of productive assets. Deregulation and privatisation became part of both general macroeconomic policy conditionality (structural adjustment loans or SALs) and sector specific loans (sectoral adjustment loans or SECALs) in areas such as finance and agriculture. By 1988, adjustment lending by the International Bank for Reconstruction and Development (IBRD) and the International Development Association (IDA) (arm of the Bank lending to the poorest countries on concessional terms) reached nearly $5 billion or roughly 26 per cent of total lending (World Bank, 1988, pp. 65, 132).

While SALs and SECALs often involved multiyear programmes, the IMF primarily focused on short-term standby accords. In 1986, the IMF introduced structural adjustment facilities (SAFs), which allowed them to provide lower interest loans (subsidised by trust funds raised from selling gold holdings) for up to three years to poorer developing countries. By 1988, with the introduction of extended SAFs (ESAFs), which included World Bank-type conditionality like trade liberalisation and privatisation, there was little difference between the policy packages of the two Bretton Woods institutions.

The rather poor performance of economies under adjustment throughout the 1980s increasingly pushed the World Bank and the IMF to consider new policy conditionality without abandoning the core strategy. To the Bank and the Fund there was never a question of anything fundamentally wrong with the strategy, instead the focus was on the impediments on the recipient side. At the forefront was the issue of governance which in its initial formulation focused on an efficient and accountable public administration, freedom of the press, commitment to human rights, a reliable judiciary and pluralism in politics. In the early 1990s, in the World Bank, effort was aimed at reclassifying existing projects as having governance components. However, over time governance projects and spending became more consequential. The IMF also joined the governance issue by looking at the transparency of government accounts, public sector management effectiveness and the regulatory stability of the private sector. Both the Bank and the Fund increasingly began to bring a broader lexicon to the development discussion including poverty reduction, institutions, sustainable development and aid ownership. Nevertheless, in many countries the term 'adjustment' became highly pejorative. Poor people, failed businessmen and retrenched government workers accused the Fund and Bank of 'sapping' them of their livelihood and sustenance.

After the September 1999 joint annual meeting, the World Bank and the IMF began to formally abandon the term 'structural adjustment'. The IMF, almost immediately after, replaced their ESAFs with poverty reduction growth facilities (PRGFs). In May 2001, the World Bank introduced poverty reduction support credits (PRSCs). In August 2004, the Bank formally abandoned SALs and replaced them with development policy loans (DPLs). The last clear reference to adjustment was in the 1999 Annual Report of the World Bank and showed that through 1999, adjustment lending was still overwhelmingly dominant in many regions. In Africa, for example, adjustment lending accounted for

40 per cent of the total in 1997, 28.5 per cent in 1998 and 37.1 per cent in 1999. In all regions, World Bank adjustment lending spiked upward after the 1998 Asian crisis (World Bank, 1999). More recently, the World Bank estimates that one-third of their total loans in the fiscal year ending 30 June 2003 was in structural adjustment lending, including PRSCs.

As part of the change, countries were to take greater ownership of their policies by developing 'home-grown' poverty reduction strategy papers (PRSPs). In reality, PRSPs still contained the macro-stabilisation and other adjustment-type targets found in the PRGFs and were designed with the heavy input of the World Bank and the IMF. The PRSPs also did not remove the onerous new layers of governance-related conditionality. In the 1970s the Fund imposed an average of six conditions, rising to ten in the 1980s and a whopping 26 by the 1990s (Stein, forthcoming).

A final discussion needs to focus on the reasons for the poor performance of adjustment and the continued adherence to these policies despite the poor track record. A detailed exposition of the weaknesses of adjustment is beyond the scope of this brief entry. It has been explored elsewhere (Stein and Nissanke, 1999). The main point is that the problem with adjustment is fundamentally a theoretical one.

Development is a dynamic process that requires the transformation of lumpy institutions and structures that cannot be conceptualised by the neoclassical economic theories underlying adjustment. In contrast, these theories focus on marginal changes to financial variables, static equilibrium and rational deductive presumptions about how agents will react to new price relationships. They frequently assume full employment in their models even though most developing countries have at least double-digit unemployment levels. They also assume the existence of perfect competition and well-developed markets when the norm is one of oligopoly and poorly formed markets. In its pure form, neoclassical economics has no theory of institutions, yet institutional development is at the very heart of the transformation of economies. The models focus on atomistic economic individuals with a single optimal mode of behaviour. In contrast, when people are seen as social beings, development becomes synonymous with new forms of behaviour arising from new rules, roles and relations. Entrepreneurship and investment thrives best in a fostering climate with research and development, access to finance, expanding human capital, improving infrastructure and so on, not just having the correct price signals.

For most developing countries, development will not arise from the models underlying structural adjustment. A new vision based on a much broader array of social and economic theories is required. However, this is blocked not only by the dominance of neoclassical theory in the economics departments of most major universities but also by those that gain by the perpetuation of the existing policy paradigm. Liberalisation has meant the retraction of barriers to the movement of capital and goods to maximise the profitability of corporations based in developed countries without the comparable mobility of labour to seek the highest wage. There is little doubt that US corporations have gained enormously under this system and considerable evidence that US hegemony inside the World Bank and the IMF has been central in perpetuating the neoliberal agenda (Wade, 2002). Where states are still able to dictate the terms of investment and organise strategic intervention in markets (as in China) significant gains are still possible from foreign trade and investment. However, for most developing countries, this will not be an option as long as neoliberal policies continue to be at the core of the conditionality of the international financial institutions.

HOWARD STEIN

References

Bauer, Peter (1972), *Dissent on Development: Studies and Debates in Development Economics*, Cambridge, MA: Harvard University Press.
Horsefield, J. Keith (1969), *The International Monetary Fund, 1945–1965: Twenty Years of International Monetary Cooperation*, 3 vols, Washington, DC: IMF.
Kapur, Devesh, J.P Lewis and R. Webb (1997), *The World Bank: Its First Half Century*, Washington, DC: Brookings Institution.
Polak, J.J. (1957), 'Monetary analysis of income formation and payments problems', *IMF Staff Papers*, **6** (1), 1–50.
Stein, Howard (forthcoming), *Beyond the World Bank Agenda: An Institutional Approach to Development* (book manuscript).
Stein, Howard and Machiko Nissanke (1999), 'Structural adjustment and the African crisis: a theoretical appraisal', *Eastern Economic Journal*, **25** (4), 399–420.
Wade, Robert (2002), 'US hegemony and the World Bank: the fight over people and ideas', *Review of International Political Economy*, **9** (2), 201–29.
World Bank (1988), *Annual Report, 1988*, Washington, DC: World Bank.
World Bank (1999), *Annual Report, 1999*, Washington, DC: World Bank.
World Bank (2003), *African Development Indicators, 2003*, Washington, DC: World Bank.

Structural Transformation

Modern economic growth and the structural transformation

'Modern economic growth' (MEG) is the term applied by Simon Kuznets (1966) to describe the economic epoch of the last 250 years distinguished by the pervasive application of science-based technology to production. Its principal characteristics are 'a sustained increase in per capita or per worker product . . . and usually sweeping structural changes' (Kuznets, 1966, p. 1).

The process of modern economic growth has wide ramification besides the rise in productivity and accompanying structural transformation. They include the concentration of economic activity in urban centres with the consequent displacement of population, a switch to large-scale enterprises with a corresponding change from self-employment to employee status, and a move towards universal education. These and related trends lead to changes in the structure of families and in their roles as providers of safety nets, and to changes in social positions, expectations, and aspirations of various groups in the population.

The spread of MEG during the nineteenth century was part of the first major wave of integration of the world economy, which we label today 'globalisation', and of a related development, the domestic integration of the economies of most of today's nation states. The same forces that ignited and propelled the growth of productivity and structural change that defines MEG were also responsible for the unification of national economies and for the first wave of global market integration. Those were rapid technological changes in production and transportation, and other processes that combined to expand the size of markets and to reduce the cost of transacting in them.

One implication of the close relation between MEG and globalisation relates to the sectoral (industrial) structure of production and trade. We cannot conceive of globalisation, not even the earlier wave during the nineteenth century, without industrialisation and urbanisation, the hallmarks of MEG. Around 1750, the number of cities with a population larger than 100 000 was only 15. These cities accounted for about 3 per cent of the total population. By 1950 the number of such cities had grown to 384, accounting for about 24 per cent of the population (Tilly, 1975, p. 399).

The interrelated processes of structural change that accompany economic development are jointly referred to as 'structural transformation'. The central element of structural transformation is the process of industrialisation measured by changes in the sectoral shares in production and factor use. Structure also refers to some ratios derived from technological or behavioural relations. Input–output coefficients are an example of the former, and the aggregate saving ratio of the latter. The principal changes in structure emphasised in the development literature (see Syrquin, 1988 for references) are increases in the rates of accumulation (Walt Rostow, Arthur Lewis); shifts in the sectoral composition of economic activity (industrialisation) focusing initially on the allocation of employment (Allan G.B. Fisher, Colin Clark) and later on production and factor use in general (Simon Kuznets, Hollis Chenery); and changes in the location of economic activity (urbanisation) and other concomitant aspects of industrialisation (demographic transition, income distribution).

A major implication of comparative studies of structural transformation is that identifying the sources of long-term productivity growth requires a disaggregated, multi-sectoral approach but in an economy-wide framework.

Structure and growth
Structural change is at the centre of modern economic growth. It is therefore an essential ingredient for describing the process and for the construction of any comprehensive theory of development. More important is the hypothesis that growth and structural change are strongly interrelated. Most writers recognise their interdependence, and some emphasise the necessity of structural changes for growth. For Kuznets, 'structural changes, not only in economic but also in social institutions and beliefs, are required, without which modern economic growth would be impossible' (Kuznets, 1971, p. 348). The interdependence also appears as a cumulative process as when the structural transformations are seen as 'necessary conditions for aggregate growth, and once in train will serve to shape, constrain, or support subsequent growth' (Abramovitz, 1986, p. 245); or, more guardedly: 'Neither structural change nor growth in GDP is an exogenous variable; both result from a complex of interacting causes on the supply side and the demand side' (Matthews et al., 1982, p. 250).

Once we abandon the fictional world of homothetic preferences, neutral total factor productivity growth with no systematic sectoral effects, perfect mobility and markets that adjust instantaneously, structural change emerges as a central feature of the process of development and an essential element in accounting for the rate and pattern of growth. It can retard growth if its pace is too slow or its direction inefficient, but it can contribute to growth if it improves the allocation of resources by, for example, reducing the disparity in factor returns across sectors, or facilitating the exploitation of economies of scale. The gains can be far from negligible, accounting for as much as a third of the measured growth in total factor productivity (Syrquin, 1988). Structural change entails and is fuelled by innovation and adaptation which in a Schumpeterian process of creative destruction lead to the replacement of old by new products founded on novel technologies. This process underlies the explanation of Kuznets (1930) and Burns (1934) of their finding that growth rates of output of particular commodities tended invariably to slow down, while at the same time there was no evidence of retardation at the aggregate level.

The required adaptations are intrinsically conflictive, hence the necessity of mechanisms for conflict resolution and the emergence of the state as arbiter among group interests, and as mitigator of the adverse effects of economic change.

Some stylised facts
The long-term comparisons for industrial countries of Kuznets and others, and econometric estimates for large number of countries since 1950 within a common accounting framework, have yielded various robust features of the transformation which can be succinctly summarised in a set of stylised facts. I will focus primarily on sector proportions in a simple aggregate accounting framework.

The elements of sectoral transformation are linked by the following accounting identities. First, total gross domestic product (GDP) by use:

$$Y = (C + I + G) + (E - M) = D + T, \tag{1}$$

where Y is GDP, C is private consumption, G is government consumption, I is gross investment, E is exports, M is imports, D is domestic final demand and T is net trade. At the sectoral level from the material balance equation of the input–output accounts we find value added in sector j to equal:

$$V_j = v_j X_j = v_i (W_i + D_i + T_i), \tag{2}$$

where X_i is gross output of sector i, W_i is intermediate demand for the output of sector i, (D and T are defined above) and v_j is the value-added ratio in sector j. Adding up GDP by source yields:

$$V = \Sigma V_j = Y. \tag{3}$$

Structural transformation
Industrialisation has to be analysed in conjunction with changes in the structures of demand (final and intermediate) and trade. Results from an econometric study of the various elements of structural transformation are summarised in Table 14. The patterns of change in the table summarise the relationship that exists along growth paths where per capita income is the measure of development.

Demand
The best-established trends in the composition of final uses of output are the rise in the share of resources allocated to investment and the decline of the share of food in consumption. The latter (Engel's Law), is among the most robust empirical relationships in economics, but its implication of non-homothetic preference is rarely acknowledged in

Table 14   Shares of economic structure associated with levels of per capita income (%)

Component of economic structure	Income per capita (1980 US dollars)				
	Actual average ≤300	Predicted 300	Predicted 4000	Actual average ≥4000	Total change
Final demand					
Private consumption	79	73	60	60	−19
Investment	14	18	26	26	12
Exports	16	19	26	23	07
Food consumption	39	38	19	15	−24
Trade					
Merchandise exports	14	15	21	18	04
Primary	13	14	12	07	−06
Manufacturing	01	01	09	11	10
Production (value added)					
Agriculture	48	40	10	07	−41
Manufacturing	10	12	24	28	18
Utilities and construction	10	11	15	17	07
Services	31	32	45	47	16
Labour force					
Agriculture	81	75	24	13	−68
Industry	07	09	33	40	33
Services	12	16	43	47	35

Source: Syrquin and Chenery (1989).

theories of growth and international trade. During the process of development, the use of intermediates relative to total gross output tends to rise. A measure of this change is an increase in the density of the input–output matrix which reflects the evolution to a more complex system with a higher degree of fabrication, and the shift from handicrafts to factory production (Deutsch and Syrquin, 1989).

Trade
The rise in the ratio of capital (human and physical) to labour, and the observed higher rate of productivity growth in the modern sectors of the economy tend to shift the comparative advantage from primary activities to industrial ones. Accordingly, we find the composition of exports shifting systematically from primary products to manufactures mostly in the upper levels of the transition (Balassa, 1979).

Productivity growth
In most countries with available long-term sectoral information, total factor productivity (TFP) tends to be higher in manufacturing than in agriculture for extended periods

(Martin and Mitra, 2001, report faster TFP in agriculture than in manufacturing for a panel of around 50 countries during 1967–92). Unbalanced productivity growth is one of the reasons on the supply side behind the shift in comparative advantage and the transformation of the structure of production during the transition. The imbalance of TFP notwithstanding, successful industrialisation has always been preceded or accompanied by a significant rise in productivity in agriculture. While there are significant differences among the sectoral rates of TFP, these rates tend to be uniformly higher across sectors in countries with good average performance as well as within countries in periods of rapid growth of aggregate productivity. This finding suggests that the overall economic environment, which includes macroeconomic and trade policies, is an important factor in explaining differences in productivity growth.

Changes in the structures of production and employment
Changes in demand and trade reinforce each other. They combine with productivity growth to produce a more pronounced shift in the structures of production and labour use. The share of value added in agriculture declines sharply over the transition, whereas manufacturing, construction and utilities double their share and the services sector share rises by about 50 per cent. The decline in the share of agriculture in employment is more pronounced than in production, but since employment starts from a much higher level and its decline takes place at a relatively higher income level, it leads to a decline in the relative productivity of labour in agriculture. Only by the end of the transition does the trend reverse itself and the gap in average productivity begins to narrow.

Proximate sources of structural transformation
What accounts for the observed changes in industrial structure? The principal proximate factors accounting for this central feature of structural transformation are changes in domestic final demand (Engel effects), the growing intermediate use of industrial products, unbalanced productivity growth, and the evolution of comparative advantage as factor proportions change (on all this, see Syrquin, 1988, and references therein). The fall in the primary share is mostly due to Engel effects at low income levels, and to trade effects afterwards. Increased use of fabricated inputs (captured by changes in input–output coefficients) contributes to the decline in the primary share at all income levels.

The rise in the manufacturing share is due less to high income elasticities and more to trade and technology. Import substitution is quite significant at all income levels. The little noted increase in the overall density of the input–output matrix that accompanies development is especially important in heavy industry (Deutsch and Syrquin, 1989).

In a relatively closed economy the structure of production has to conform closely to the structure of demand, as stressed in the balanced-growth approach of the 1950s. The extent of a country's participation in the international economy is only weakly related to the level of development across countries. The variable most correlated to the share of trade in income across countries is the size of the economy. This relation, among the more robust of the empirical regularities has, until recently, been all but ignored by trade models. In small countries the shares of trade in GDP is relatively high, domestic markets relatively small, and the production structure, therefore, tends to be more specialised than in larger countries. An additional initial condition related to the commodity composition of trade and the type of specialisation is the availability of natural resources. Together with traditional factor proportions and commercial policy, they help to determine the extent and nature of a country's participation in international trade.

In practice, the evolution of comparative advantage and the bias in commercial policies have combined to create an export pattern that reinforces the shift from primary goods into industry, implicit in the pattern of domestic demand. The strength and timing of the reorientation of exports have not been the same across countries; small countries lacking a broad base of natural resources, had to develop manufactured exports at an earlier stage than resource-rich countries, where specialisation in primary exports persists to a much later stage of development. Large countries have shifted away from the specialisation in primary products through import substitution.

Reallocation of resources

The shift of resources among sectors is perhaps the most important element of structural transformation. In the absence of full equilibrium they are significant in accounting for aggregate productivity growth and its acceleration at middle-income levels. Paradoxically, the slack in the economy when resources are not allocated efficiently becomes a potential source of growth, and the disappearance of the slack can contribute to a one-time productivity slowdown.

Differences in returns to labour and capital across sectors may reflect quality differences as well as disequilibrium. Even if returns for homogeneous factors were always equal across sectors, accommodating the changes in sector proportions inherent in the process of growth would still remain a major undertaking and a potential brake on growth.

Resource shifts were central to the analyses of Kuznets and Edward Denison but not for most of the old and new growth approaches. Recently, aided perhaps by the growing availability of enterprise data sets, resource shifts have come to play a central role. Some representative examples are Timmer and Szirmai (2000) on growth in Asian manufacturing, Feinstein (1999) on structural change in the developed countries in the twentieth century, and Temple (2001) on structural change during Europe's golden age. These studies clearly illustrate the importance of resource reallocation for growth and the large degree of underestimation of those effects when we deal with relatively aggregate data. The broad definition of sectors, even in fairly disaggregated studies, hides all factor reallocations in those broadly defined sectors. In Taiwan, for example, Kuznets (1979) argues that the high rate of growth of product per worker, required 'a much greater rate of shift [than the] one now suggested in the three-sector classification and that the shifts from old to new subbranches within these sectors are particularly neglected' (p. 73).

An important data limitation is the treatment of quality changes and of new products in particular. The problem is not just one of aggregation. In addressing the issue, Kuznets found it 'frustrating that the available sectoral classifications fail to separate new industries from old, and distinguish those affected by technological innovations' (Kuznets, 1971, p. 315). An implication is that 'both the true rate of shift in production structure and its connection with the high rate of aggregate growth are grossly underestimated' (ibid.). New products do not just substitute for old ones, but they also tend to increase the variety of similar goods commonly grouped under the same classification. Increased product variety has been shown to be a significantly large source of consumer surplus gains (Brynjolfsson et al., 2003).

MOSHE SYRQUIN

References

Abramovitz, M. (1986), 'Simon Kuznets: 1901–1985', *Journal of Economic History*, **46**, 241–6.

Balassa, B. (1979), 'A "stages approach" to comparative advantage', in I. Adelman (ed.), *Economic Growth and Resources, Vol. 4: National and International Policies*, London: Macmillan, pp. 121–56.

Brynjolfsson, Erik, Yu (Jeffrey) Hu and Michael D. Smith (2003), 'Consumer surplus in the digital economy: estimating the value of increased product variety at online booksellers', *Management Science*, **49**, 1580–96.

Burns, A.F. (1934), *Production Trends in the United States since 1870*, New York: National Bureau of Economic Research.

Denison, Edward (1967), *Why Growth Rates Differ*, Washington, DC: Brookings Institution.

Deutsch, J. and M. Syrquin (1989), 'Economic development and the structure of production', *Economic Systems Research*, **1**, 447–64.

Feinstein, Charles (1999), 'Structural change in the developed countries in the twentieth century', *Oxford Review of Economic Policy*, **15**, 35–55.

Kuznets, S. (1930), *Secular Movements in Production and Prices*, Boston, MA and New York: Houghton Mifflin.

Kuznets, S. (1966), *Modern Economic Growth*, New Haven, CT: Yale University Press.

Kuznets, S. (1971), *Economic Growth of Nations: Total Output and Production Structure*, Cambridge, MA: Harvard University Press.

Kuznets, S. (1979), 'Growth and structural shifts', in W. Galenson (ed.), *Economic Growth and Structural Change in Taiwan: The Postwar Experience of the Republic of China*, Ithaca, NY: Cornell University Press, pp. 15–131.

Martin, Will and Devashish Mitra (2001), 'Productivity growth and convergence in agriculture versus manufacturing', *Economic Development & Cultural Change*, **49**, 403–22.

Matthews, R.C.O., C. Feinstein and C. Odling-Smee (1982), *British Economic Growth*, Oxford: Oxford University Press.

Syrquin, M. (1988), 'Patterns of structural change', in H.B. Chenery and T.N. Srinivasan (eds), *Handbook of Development Economics*, vol. 1, Amsterdam: North-Holland, pp. 203–73.

Syrquin, Moshe and Hollis B. Chenery (1989), 'Three decades of industrialization', *World Bank Economic Review*, **3**, 145–81.

Temple Jonathan (2001), 'Structural change and Europe's golden age', University of Bristol Discussion Paper no. 01/519.

Tilly, Charles (1975), 'Reflections on the history of European state-making', in Charles Tilly (ed.), *The Formation of National States in Western Europe*, Princeton, NJ: Princeton University Press, pp. 3–83.

Timmer, Marcel P. and Adam Szirmai (2000), 'Productivity growth in Asian manufacturing: the structural bonus hypothesis examined', *Structural Change and Economic Dynamics*, **11**, 371–92.

Structure and Agency

Since their origins, the social sciences have been characterised by a vivid and slowly evolving debate on structure: what is it, how does it relate to social action and, more generally, to development? Related to this is the question of how structure relates to agency, that is, the capability of actors to deviate from, or to change the normal course of events. How can actor–structure relations be conceptualised? This seemingly perennial debate, often typified by sharp contradictions, is, however, far from being an expression of an irresolvable impasse. Rather, it reflects, in the first place, that what de facto emerges as structural pattern, is highly dependent on time. Second, the issue of spatial heterogeneity has increasingly entered debates, research programmes and theories. This has led to a range of contrasting trajectories being identified that exist alongside the dominant development tendencies and processes. Similarly, the once overarching concept of structure has increasingly been decomposed in the notion of multiple structures – structures that at least partially overlap and compete with each other and allow contrasting development processes to emerge. And finally, actor–structure relations themselves have been rethought, particularly over the last two decades. As a consequence, structure is increasingly conceptualised as the set of parameters that actors use to order their practices.

Structural patterns can be highly variable through time and space. Structures evolve and change over time – sometimes abruptly, sometimes barely perceptible to those who are familiar with them. Equally, on a spatial level a considerable heterogeneity in structural patterns can be encountered in terms of their composition, dynamics and, especially, their effects (that is, what is explained). The structure of the Roman Empire, as described by Max Weber, is very different from that of Oriental despotism as analysed by Karl Marx. And the two contrast starkly with the main structural patterns in, for example, Norway at the beginning of the twentieth century – a point in time when Norway was a very poor and underdeveloped country, but one which was later to develop into one of the most prosperous societies of the world. It might be argued that this occurred because of rich oil reserves and fishing grounds. Yet, there are many Third World countries with a similar set of resources, which have not been able to 'translate' potential richness into such material growth and increased welfare. This points to *differences* in, and therefore to the *specificity* of, structures – both aspects are crucial to development studies. And even when 'structural patterns' are seemingly identical, their effects can be highly differentiated. Take, for example, the typical *latifundio–minifundio* complex of large landholdings surrounded by a multitude of small peasant farms which characterises large parts of rural areas in Africa, Latin America and, to a lesser degree, Asia and parts of Europe. The effects of these structurally identical complexes on the scale and intensity of farming, on the social position of peasants and on the nature and shape of social movements, have been quite different. In short: there are no unilinear cause–effect relations. 'Causes' are changing, effects are strongly differentiated and the relations interlinking the two are equally variable.

The next question regards how structure is identified, specified and disclosed. This increasingly differs as a result of the specialisation and division of labour within social sciences. Every discipline has its own favourite domain in which it locates structure. This can be illustrated with reference to the different structures that are assumed to govern agrarian and rural development processes. Following Hayami and Ruttan (1985), development economics tends to situate the main structural relations at the level of relative factor prices (and the associated institutional patterns that might reflect or distort these). Others locate 'structure' within the main commodity markets, while the neoinstitutional approach focuses on institutional patterns that govern different types of transaction. Sociologically inspired approaches, on the other hand, centre upon normative frameworks and the associated social patterns that order local regularities as well as micro–macro relations. The 'moral economy' and 'the weapons of the weak' (Scott, 1976, 1985) provide excellent illustrations of this. However, the same empirical phenomena might be 'explained' by referring to competing notions of 'structure' as, for example, rational choice models. Equally demographic relations (be they at the micro or the macro level), class and power relations (as in the *dependencia* tradition), social hierarchies and the countervailing impact of social movements have all been viewed as constituent parts, if not the backbone of structure (an overview which remains convincing to this day can be found in Harriss, 1992).

The reification of structure

In itself this state of affairs does not necessarily represent a problem. It shows that the notion of structure basically requires a research programme, which needs to empirically assess what actually functions as structure. The main problem with this position is that social sciences – and development studies are, in this respect, no exception – strongly reify their favourite delineation (and representation) of structure. That is, the chosen set of parameters tends to be represented as a set of laws that actually 'govern' social action and development and that can, therefore, be used to explain it. In consequence, the theoretical space for agency is eliminated. The identified structure emerges as the instrument that neatly delineates the possible from the impossible, opportunities from limitations, the rational and the promising from the irrational and the counterproductive and the domain of discourse from that of the indisputable (Bourdieu, 1977). In this way science and the associated expert systems become important modes of ordering; particularly when there is a close synergy between these expert systems on the one hand, and state apparatuses and vested power groups on the other (van der Ploeg, 2003). Technological and economic determinism are clear expressions of such tendencies. The same applies to structural determinism, which takes as inevitable the existing power hierarchies in today's societies. In all these forms of determinism, 'structure' is associated with causal complexes (be they technological, economic and/or related with unequal power balances) that 'inevitably' produce specific effects. In brief, structure is assumed to be *prior* to social action and development: it conditions, if not determines, social action.

These representations of structure give rise to three, interrelated problems in theory and research, as well as in policy making. First, structure is understood in an essentialist way. It is seen as a stable pattern, underlying and ordering developmental processes. In line with this is the assumption that scientists have a particular gift in being able to unravel this somewhat hidden structure and translate it into desirable ('rational') actions. Second, these structures are interpreted and represented through a wide range of scientific specialisations that often contradict one another. Third, the disclosed 'structures' are increasingly reified: that is, they are identified, not only as more or less given and hardly changeable, but also as active drivers, as ultimate causes of social action and development processes. As a result, science, and more specifically development studies, is in danger of becoming part of the problem, instead of being a building block for devising new solutions.

The 'turn' in development studies

Over the last decade, however, a clear 'turn' in focus (Booth, 1994; Schuurman, 1996) has begun to emerge. The concept of structure and the associated notions on actor and agency are being rethought and reconstituted. Actor network theory (Law, 1994), social construction of technology (Bijker et al., 1997), neoinstitutional economics (Saccomandi, 1998; North, 1990) and the actor orientated approach (Long, 2001) have turned out to be powerful drivers of this 'turn'. This has coincided with a fundamental shift in the *loci* of empirical research. Inquiry into heterogeneity, in different socio-material domains, is displacing the earlier focus on main trends (and their subsequent reification as 'dominant' trends). Analysis of (differential) processes is replacing the research on the existing state of affairs. Through these shifts, differences become as important as similarities. In interface analysis, structural discontinuities become central, displacing the attention previously paid to structural continuities. A special and highly innovative example is the study of interrelations between 'strategic niches' (that is, the places where novelties – potentially promising changes – are germinated and nurtured) and 'socio-technical regimes'. These regimes are understood as 'a grammar or rule set comprised in the coherent complex of scientific knowledge, engineering practices, production process technologies, product characteristics, skills and procedures, ways of handling relevant artefacts and persons, ways of defining problems – all of them embedded in institutions and infrastructures' (Rip and Kemp, 1998, p. 338). The multidimensional, multi-actor and multi-level interactions between regimes and niches reveal a world and describe development processes that are far more emergent and offer far more levers for practice than possible under previous, more 'structuralist' accounts. In short, it is a world loaded with agency – although the multiple forms of agency evidently face limitations, the reigning regimes being one of these.

These shifts in *focus* and *locus* are reflected in a progressive reconstitution of the notion of structure. Structure is now increasingly understood as being part of social action (instead of being prior to, and somehow located outside of it). Structure is what is being constructed and, as such, becomes an ordering principle for further constructions. In the aftermath of the 'turn', structure is now defined 'as an extremely fluid set of emergent properties, which, on the one hand, results from the interlocking and/or distantiation of [that is, disconnected from] various actors' projects, while on the other, functions as an important point of reference for the further elaboration, negotiation and confrontation of actors' projects' (Long and van der Ploeg, 1994, p. 75). Through their projects (Latour, 1991) and the implied interaction with the projects of others, actors are as much involved in the construction of structures, that is, the shared and simultaneously contested sets of expectations, infrastructures, artefacts and relations, as their practices are ordered (that is: structured) by these sets.

After the 'turn'
This redefinition, which increasingly underpins development studies, implies, in the first place, that structure is, at least partly, an actor-dependent concept. The elements and relations perceived, accepted, experienced and/or represented by groups of actors as guiding elements, and consequently translated into corresponding actions, emerge as crucial nodes of structure. From this it follows that *folk notions* of structure, and the associated classification schemes are central elements for both research and theory. Second, the emphasis, both in theory and research, has now definitely shifted towards relations rather than to 'things', such as state, markets and technology. Markets, for instance, are neither understood as determining economic behaviour nor seen as irrelevant. What is of primary importance is the way actors relate themselves, their practices and their projects to these markets. In this respect agency is decisive. Relative factor prices, derived from the (inter-relations among) the capital market, the labour market and the land market, do not order agricultural practices and/or rural development patterns in a universal and unilinear way. It is only when farming practices are strongly integrated in these markets (only when they have been made dependent upon them), that such structuring effects are exerted. At the same time it follows that where practices (be they in agriculture, trading, forestry, the construction of irrigation works, or whatever) have been distantiated from these markets, that

contrasting developmental trajectories and associated effects are produced (van der Ploeg, 1990). The same applies to specific state interventions (and especially its mega projects, see Scott, 1998) that aim at, and result in, changes in relative factor prices (for example, by making capital cheaper compared to labour). Market agencies, state apparatuses, technology, classes and so on, are part and parcel of these relational patterns. These entities, as well as their effects, are shaped, reshaped, negotiated and/or contested through *relational patterns* as much as these patterns are moulded and remoulded by each of these entities and by the resultant (and mostly unintended) effects. Hence, some of the most interesting research centres around micro–macro linkages (Knorr-Cetina, 1981).

Comparative approaches
The reconstituted concept of structure allows for a far more attuned analysis of *how* development processes are constructed and differentiated. An important difference here is that between exogenous and endogenous development. The latter refers to developmental processes that are mainly, though not exclusively, built on locally available and controlled resources and which imply a reallocation of produced wealth within the localities themselves (Lowe et al., 1995). Thus, self-generating forms of growth are triggered. On the other hand, exogenous forms of development are mainly based on the introduction of external resources (capital, technologies, organisational models, knowledge) and imply a redefinition of the value of local resources. A rich gamut of comparative studies (embracing both developed and underdeveloped countries) show that exogenous and endogenous development result not only in highly contrasting effects (for example, in terms of employment and income levels, the efficiency in the use of scarce resources, environmental pressures) but also in highly distinctive *relational* patterns, that is, in specific structures (Marsden, 2003). It is also to be noted that, after the 'turn', structures, and consequently actor–structure relations are no longer enclosed in the exclusive frameworks of highly segmented scientific disciplines, but are increasingly formulated and developed in a multidisciplinary way.

Thus, it is increasingly shown that the reconceptualisation of actor–structure relations allows for a comparative analysis and, consequently, an integrated reinterpretation of empirical entities that were once considered as separate 'structural constellations' as, for example, the *latifundio–minifundio* complex, modernised farming in Europe and the new peasant sector that is emerging out of land invasions and settlements in current Brazil. Or, to go beyond the rural, the Norwegian development model and that of, say, Venezuela or Peru. All these 'cases' entail specific actor–structure relations and specific expressions of agency. Therefore, they are all evolving in specific ways, which result in differentiated development trajectories. In this way, the comparative study of development not only contributes to a better understanding of specific time- and space-bounded constellations, but also renders new, fresh and often far-reaching insights into alternatives and new ways forward.

JAN DOUWE VAN DER PLOEG

References
Bijker, Wiebe E., Thomas P. Hughes and Trevor J. Pinch (1997), *The Social Construction of Technological Systems: New Directions in the Sociology and History of Technology*, Cambridge, MA and London: MIT Press.

Booth, David (ed.) (1994), *Rethinking Social Development: Theory, Research and Practice*, Harlow: Longman Scientific.

Bourdieu, Pierre (1977), *Outline of a Theory of Practice*, Cambridge: Cambridge University Press.

Harriss, John (1992), *Rural Development: Theories of Peasant Economy and Agrarian Change*, London: Hutchinson University Library.

Hayami, Yuri and Vernon W. Ruttan (1985), *Agricultural Development: An International Perspective*, revised and expanded edn, Baltimore, MD and London: Johns Hopkins University Press.

Knorr-Cetina, Karin D. (1981), 'The micro-sociological challenge of the macro-sociological: towards a reconstruction of social theory and methodology', in Karin D. Knorr-Cetina and A.V. Cicourel (eds), *Advances in Social Theory and Methodology: Towards an Integration of Micro- and Macro-sociologies*, Boston, MA: Routledge & Kegan Paul, pp. 1–47.

Latour, Bruno (1991), 'Transférer les projets dans la realité' (Transfer projects to reality), in D. Chevalier (ed.), *Savoir faire et pouvoir transmettre* (Know how and being able to transmit), Paris: Éditions de la Maison des sciences de l'homme, pp. 151–65.

Law, John (1994), *Organizing Modernity*, Oxford and Cambridge, MA: Blackwell.

Long, Norman (2001), *Development Sociology: Actor Perspectives*, London and New York: Routledge.

Long, Norman and Jan Douwe van der Ploeg (1994), 'Heterogeneity, actor and structure: towards a reconstitution of the concepts of structure', in Booth (ed.), pp. 62–89.

Lowe, Philip, Jonathan Murdoch and Neil Ward (1995), 'Networks in rural development: beyond exogenous and endogenous models', in Jan D. van der Ploeg and Gert van Dijk (eds), *Beyond Modernization: The Impact of Endogenous Rural Development*, Assen: Royal Van Gorcum, pp. 87–105.

Marsden, Terry (2003), *The Condition of Rural Sustainability*, Assen: Royal van Gorcum.

North, Douglass C. (1990), *Institutions, Institutional Change and Economic Performance*, Cambridge and New York: Cambridge University Press.

Rip, Arie and Richard Kemp (1998), 'Technological change', in S. Rayner and E.L. Malone (eds), *Human Choice and Climate Change*, Columbus, OH: Battelle Press, Vol. 2, ch. 6, pp. 327–99.

Saccomandi, Vito (1998), *Agricultural Market Economics: A Neo-Institutional Analysis of the Exchange, Circulation and Distribution of Agricultural Products*, Assen: Royal Van Gorcum.

Schuurman, Frans J. (1996), *Beyond the Impasse: New Directions in Development Theory*, London: Zed Books.

Scott, James C. (1976), *The Moral Economy of the Peasant*, New Haven, CT: Yale University Press.

Scott, James C. (1985), *Weapons of the Weak: Everyday Forms of Peasant Resistance*, New Haven, CT and London: Yale University Press.

Scott, James C. (1998), *Seeing Like a State: How Certain Schemes to Improve the Human Condition Have Failed*, New Haven, CT and London: Yale University Press.

van der Ploeg, Jan Douwe (1990), *Labor, Markets, and Agricultural Production*, Boulder, CO, San Francisco and London: Westview.

van der Ploeg, Jan Douwe (2003), *The Virtual Farmer: Past, Present and Future of the Dutch Peasantry*, Assen: Royal Van Gorcum.

Sustainable Consumption

Agenda 21, the major statement of global policy prepared at the Rio de Janeiro 'Earth Summit' in 1992 (UN, 1992) has widely been used to support arguments for major changes in the way the global economy is managed. *Agenda 21* introduced the notion of 'sustainable consumption', arguing that the world – and rich countries in particular – had to change their consumption 'patterns' if the world was to move on to sustainable paths. Unfortunately, *Agenda 21* shares much of the ambiguity surrounding discussions of sustainable development, speaking interchangeably of 'sustainable consumption patterns', 'lifestyle changes', 'sustainable consumption', 'optimisation of resource use' and the 'minimisation of waste', without offering definitions. For the most part, the thrust of *Agenda 21* is that the world needs to raise consumption while reducing resource use, that is, decoupling resource use from economic activity. This is equivalent to raising the productivity of natural resources, securing more 'development' for a given input of resources.

The potential for achieving major increases in resource productivity is discussed in the widely publicised work *Factor Four* (von Weizsäcker et al., 1997). But some people have read *Agenda 21* as calling for reductions in consumption levels in rich countries, a view consistent with opposition to the pursuit of economic growth as a goal of policy. 'Sustainable consumption' has thus come to mean very different things. While the focus on resource productivity is widely accepted, encouraging lifestyle change to reduce consumption itself is far more controversial.

The development of the economic theory of sustainable development does, however, permit a rigorous definition of sustainable consumption (see Sustainable Development and National Accounting, this volume). Sustainable development is about ensuring that there are rising per capita stocks of overall wealth. In turn, total wealth increases if and only if savings (capital formation) exceed depreciation on all forms of capital assets – man-made, human, environmental. Deducting this depreciation from the conventional notion of savings produces the notion of genuine savings. The maximum sustainable level of consumption is then that level which is consistent with genuine savings being zero. The formula for genuine savings is:

$$S_g = (GNP - C - \delta K_M - \delta K_N + \alpha K_H) \geq 0,$$

where:

S_g = genuine savings;
GNP = gross national product;
C = consumption;
δK_M = depreciation of man-made capital;
δK_N = depreciation of natural capital; and
αK_H = appreciation of human capital.

Setting $S_g = 0$, we have:

$$C_{max} = GNP - \delta K_M - \delta K_N + \alpha K_H.$$

C_{max} is now the maximum sustainable level of consumption.

The formula for maximum sustainable consumption defines a context in which *net* investment is actually zero. The amount of investment taking place is just sufficient to offset depreciation. This will not guarantee non-declining per capita well-being if population is growing, nor would it achieve some target rate of growth of well-being, for example, that people should be 'better off' as each year goes by. More generally, C_{max} is the maximum sustainable level of consumption, but it is not necessarily the optimal level of consumption. Thus, C_{max} is best thought of as some upper limit on optimal consumption.

The definition advanced above is consistent with that in Costanza et al. (1991, p. 8) of sustainable consumption as: 'that amount of consumption that can be continued indefinitely without degrading capital stocks, including natural stocks'. It is more likely that

Costanza et al. intended a different definition since the one they provide is consistent with weak sustainability, whereas their own views advocate strong sustainability (see below).

What policies would follow from a focus on the genuine savings/maximum sustainable consumption notion? The genuine savings approach shows that there are a number of policies which could ensure sustainable consumption – investment in education, investment in technology, investment in social capital, reduction of environmental damage through decoupling and, more generally, encouragement of savings via tax breaks and interest rate changes. The lessons are not new, but they now fit together in a coherent story of sustainable consumption.

The preceding definition is consistent with weak sustainability – that is, with the view that the total capital stock must rise through time, with substitution between different types of capital being permitted. Those who advocate strong sustainability argue that environmental assets are so 'special' that their stock must also not decline. The goal of maximum sustainable consumption needs to be redefined if the goal is strong sustainability. The basic difference is that there is an added constraint. In addition to requiring that $S_g \geq 0$, we require that $\delta K_n \leq 0$. The maximum sustainable consumption level is now:

$$C_{max,SS} = C_{max,WS} - OC_{CONS}$$

The expression OC_{CONS} is the sacrifice of consumption that has to be made in order to conserve natural capital at its existing level. It can be thought of as a *cost of conservation* or, analogously, an *abatement* cost such that the expenditure involved conserves the stock of natural capital. The maximum sustainable level of consumption is lower under strong sustainability by the cost of avoiding natural capital depreciation. This is because some consumption has to be diverted to replacing natural resources in order to honour the commitment to keep natural capital at least constant.

In economics, it tends to be assumed that consumption alone produces 'utility' or 'well-being'. In a world without population growth, then, the optimal level of consumption appears to be the highest level of consumption consistent with sustainability. That has already been defined as C_{max}. The reality is more complex for various reasons. First, population growth rates are usually positive, so that the pursuit of C_{max} above would not guarantee non-declining per capita consumption, which is the requirement for sustainability. Second, technological change needs to be considered as this will augment the efficiency of resources, that is, will raise the ability to generate consumption from given inputs. Third, optimality is usually derived from setting up the problem as one of maximising the discounted future flows of consumption, whereas sustainability might not be consistent with this formulation of the problem (Page, 1977; Pezzey, 1992). Fourth, for complex reasons, the two maximal sustainable consumption paths, C_{max} under weak and strong sustainability are not themselves optimal. It is possible that an optimal path with rising per capita consumption exists but it will involve significant technological change.

Figure 9 illustrates some stylised consumption paths. The traditional optimal consumption path is given by the inverted 'U' curve and results from maximising the present value of future consumption. While optimal, the path is not sustainable: consumption eventually goes to zero, a result that is mainly driven by the existence of positive discount rates (for utility). The two straight lines show the *maximal constant consumption levels* that

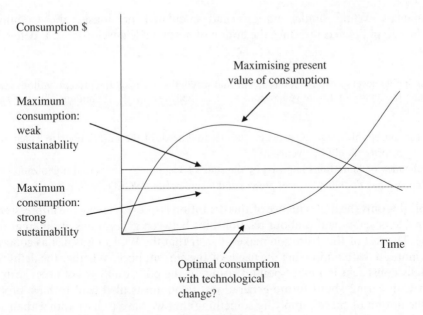

Figure 9   Sustainable and optimal consumption paths

are also sustainable. The upper line shows sustainable consumption under a weak sustainability approach and the lower shows maximal consumption under strong sustainability. Neither path is optimal, for complex reasons. The final upward-sloping curve combines sustainability and optimality. To achieve such a path requires technological change to accommodate population change and increasing depreciation on capital stocks.

DAVID PEARCE

References

Costanza, Robert, Herman Daly and Joy Bartholomew (1991), 'Goals, agenda and policy recommendations for ecological economics', in R. Costanza (ed.), *Ecological Economics: The Science and Management of Sustainability*, New York: Columbia University Press, pp. 1–21.

Page, Talbot (1977), *Conservation and Economic Efficiency: An Approach to Materials Policy*, Baltimore, MD: Johns Hopkins University Press for Resources for the Future.

Pezzey, Jack (1992), 'Sustainability: an interdisciplinary guide', *Environmental Values*, **1**, 321–62.

United Nations (1992), *Agenda 21*, reprinted in full in Stanley Johnson (1993), *The Earth Summit: The United Nations Conference on Environment and Development*, London: Graham & Trotman, pp. 125–508.

von Weizsäcker, Ernst, Amory Lovins and L. Hunter Lovins (1997), *Factor Four: Doubling Wealth, Halving Resource Use*, London: Earthscan.

Sustainable Development

The United Nations World Commission on Environment and Development's report in 1987 on North–South relations and the global environmental problem – the 'Brundtland Report' (WCED, 1987) – marked a watershed in integrative thinking about economic development. While similar notions had circulated previously, the Commission brought into political centrestage the notion of sustainable development. It defined it as follows:

> Sustainable development is development that meets the needs of the present without compromising the ability of future generations to meet their own needs. It contains within it two key concepts:
>
> - the concept of 'need', in particular the essential needs of the world's poor, to which overriding priority should be given, and
> - the idea of limitations imposed by the state of technology and social organization on the environment's ability to meet present and future needs. (WCED, 1987, p. 43)

Typically, only the first sentence of this definition is quoted, giving the impression that sustainable development is about relationships between generations at different points in time. The rest of the definition makes it clear that the WCED was just as concerned, if not more so, with addressing the needs of the current poor. Whether the definition is internally consistent is a moot point. Caring for the poor today is not necessarily consistent with caring about future generations. Economists also tend to have problems with the notion of 'need', implying something that we have to have rather than something it would be nice to choose. But the WCED chose 'needs' because they were concerned to stress the fact that what many take for granted – supplies of energy, clean water, clean air, political freedoms, protection from crime and war – are denied to many others.

The Brundtland Commission's goals were overtly political but the report stimulated extensive activity by economists into ways in which sustainable development could be made operational. Sustainable development is readily defined as a path of rising per capita well-being. Alternative definitions of well-being occupy a significant part of the literature, but one reason for being fairly relaxed about meaning is that defining development is not the same thing as searching for the necessary and sufficient conditions for achieving it. The conditions are likely to be very similar, if not the same, regardless of how development is defined.

Since wealth and technology define the capacity to generate well-being, it is natural to focus on these underlying constituents of wealth. Total wealth is defined as the sum of man-made capital (machinery, infrastructure and so on) – K_M; human capital (the stock of knowledge and skills) – K_H; environmental or natural capital (the stock of natural resources, environmental quality and environmental services) – K_N; and social capital (the 'glue' that binds societies together) – K_S. The largest strides have been made in addressing the first three capital stocks, but the ever-present nature of social discord and war is a reminder that social capital deserves a very high status in discussions about sustainability and development (Isham et al., 2002). Technological change raises capital productivity, that is, well-being per unit of capital. On the other hand, population change is most likely to dissipate capital stocks, lowering the prospects for sustainability, as indicated clearly by most of the optimal growth models of the 1970s. Thus, one underlying side rule for sustainability is to ensure not only that total wealth rises through time but also that technological change outpaces population growth.

Focusing on capital stocks, the basic rule for sustainability is that total wealth per capita should increase through time. This requirement can be written as:

$$\frac{d}{dt}\left(\frac{K}{N}\right) = \dot{k} \geq 0,$$

where K is total wealth, N is population, and t is time. This is the 'constant capital rule', that is, a rule that says per capita wealth must be at least constant through time. Differentiation yields:

$$\dot{k} = \frac{d}{dt}\left(\frac{K}{N}\right) = \frac{K}{N}\left(\frac{\dot{K}}{K} - \frac{\dot{N}}{N}\right) = \frac{K}{N}\left(\frac{\dot{K}}{K} - n\right),$$

where n is now the rate of change of population (expressed as a percentage). The expression $\dot{K}$ is genuine savings, or the net addition to wealth. Genuine savings is the excess of savings over depreciation, and is hence formally equivalent to net investment. However, investment now refers to a positive change in the total capital stocks. The constant capital rule assumes that all forms of capital are substitutable at the margin. This implies weak sustainability. Confusion reigns over the meaning of substitutability. Self-evidently *total* stocks of individual forms of capital cannot be substituted – the disappearance of, say, all the world's forests would be catastrophic. But it is hard to avoid the fact that capital stocks are substitutes at the margin, although little is known about the relevant elasticities of substitution. Finally, the constant capital rule above underlines the destructive role played by rapid population increase: if n exceeds the percentage rate of net investment, the bracketed expression is negative and non-sustainability ensues.

Those who argue that some forms of capital are not substitutable even at the margin, look for strong sustainability. This requires weak sustainability plus an added constraint that stocks of K_N should not decline. This constraint requires that resources be diverted to maintaining natural assets even though the apparent social rate of return to doing so is less than the opportunity cost of that conservation. Effectively, strong sustainability trades a lower growth path of well-being against an insurance policy to cover the risks of major losses from natural resource depletion. Global threats such as global warming would be a case in point. In this respect, strong sustainability offers a reasonably rigorous meaning to the *precautionary principle*. The difference in well-being growth paths between strong and weak sustainability contexts is shown in the entry on Sustainable Consumption, this volume.

Major developments have taken place in the measurement of total wealth and hence in indicators of sustainability. The World Bank now publishes total wealth estimates. The data problems are formidable, but information continues to improve with time. Some estimates are shown in Table 15.

Unsurprisingly, advanced nations such as the USA have per capita wealth stocks 10–20 times as large as those for poor countries. Perhaps more interesting is the suggested composition of wealth. Conventional, man-made capital accounts for around 20 per cent of total wealth in most countries, with human capital dominating the wealth estimates. Low levels of natural wealth are partly explained by the data limitations which generally omit major elements of the value of ecosystem services.

Table 15   Some estimates of total per capita wealth, 1990 (1990$)

Country	K_M/N	K_H/N	K_N/N	K/N	K_M as % of K
USA	76 000	308 000	17 000	401 000	19
UK	51 000	209 000	5000	266 000	19
Germany	66 000	211 000	4000	281 000	23
Saudi Arabia	30 000	69 000	72 000	171 000	18
Uganda	6000	8000	2000	15 000	37
India	4000	12 000	4000	20 000	22
China	6000	28 000	3000	37 000	16
Brazil	16 000	66 000	7000	89 000	18
Chile	17 000	116 000	14 000	148 000	12

Source: Kunte et al. (1998).

Table 16   Genuine savings as a percentage of GNP

Country	1970s	1980s	1990	1997
Mexico	9.1	−3.0	0.9	19.3
Peru	5.8	−0.8	4.1	21.7
China	14.1	6.6	10.5	38.0
Thailand	16.4	17.7	27.0	30.7
Saudi Arabia	−27.6	−25.5	−27.3	−10.7
India	8.4	7.1	8.8	12.7
Ghana	4.1	−6.0	1.4	6.7
Zambia	−5.7	−27.3	−32.0	6.2
UK	11.0	8.4	11.4	11.6
USA	11.0	9.0	8.2	13.2

Sources: 1970s to 1990 from Hamilton and Clemens (1999) and 1997 from Hamilton (2000).

The wealth estimates provide the data for K/N in the constant capital equation. The World Bank has separately estimated genuine savings and some estimates are shown in Table 16. A negative genuine savings figure is prima facie evidence of non-sustainability. It seems clear that Saudi Arabia and Zambia fall into this category. In Saudi Arabia's case what is happening is that the rate of depletion of oil is not being compensated for by the equivalent build-up of other capital assets: that is, some of the oil revenues are being consumed. Developed economies seem to have fairly stable genuine savings rates of 8–13 per cent, but it is notable that the genuine savings rates for China and Thailand are very much higher, revealing the rapid rates of net investment in those countries.

Given estimates of population and population change, genuine savings and total wealth, there is now sufficient evidence to compute the constant capital equation.

Hamilton (2000) illustrates the approach for the USA for the year 1997. This entry adopts revised estimates of total wealth:

$$K/N = \text{wealth per capita} = \$535\,000$$

$$S_g/N = K/N = \text{genuine savings per capita} = \$3\,900$$

$$n = \text{population growth rate} = 0.008.$$

Entering these values into the wealth equation yields the change in wealth per capita as – \$380, a *negative* change in wealth, an initially surprising result. This reveals the importance of not relying on genuine savings data alone, even though they provide a first indication of sustainability. One major reason for the result is the USA's low savings ratio, or to put it another way, its high consumption level out of current income. However, changing the assumptions has a marked effect on this result. If genuine savings per capita is measured to be \$4100 instead of \$3900, and the period over which consumption is discounted is 25 years instead of 30, the effect is to secure a *positive* change in wealth per capita of + \$612.

Changes in wealth per capita also turn out to be very sensitive to the population growth rate. Hamilton (2000) suggests that genuine savings rates below 10 per cent of GNP are consistent with negative changes in wealth per capita. Perhaps more significant is the relationship between wealth per capita and population: if population growth rates exceed 1.2 per cent per annum, then there is a real risk that the change in wealth per capita will be negative. Finally, countries with positive GNP growth rates can also have declining wealth per capita, a finding that underlines the limitations of GNP as an indicator of 'true' economic progress.

DAVID PEARCE

References

Hamilton, Kirk (2000), *Sustaining Economic Welfare: Estimating Changes in Wealth per Capita*, Washington, DC: World Bank, Environment Department.

Hamilton, Kirk and Michael Clemens (1999), 'Genuine saving in developing countries', *World Bank Economic Review*, **13** (2), 33–56.

Isham, Jonathan, Thomas Kelly and Sunder Ramaswamy (2002), *Social Capital and Economic Development: Well-being in Developing Countries*, Cheltenham, UK and Northampton, MA, USA: Edward Elgar.

Kunte, Arundate, Kirk Hamilton, John Dixon and Michael Clemens (1998), 'Estimating national wealth: Methodology and Results', Paper no. 57, Environmental Economics Series, World Bank, Washington, DC.

World Commission on Environment and Development (WCED) (1987), *Our Common Future*, Oxford: Oxford University Press.

Technology and Development

Poor countries need new technologies to develop. If they could effectively tap even a fraction of the technologies presently available, they would enjoy far higher levels of social and economic well-being. This is almost a truism, and few would seriously question it today. What *is* debated is how to best manage the transfer and use of technology. This entry deals with issues in manufacturing industry.

The debate on industrial technology and development has changed. Some two decades ago, it ranged around the 'appropriateness' of the technologies from developed countries for developing ones and whether FDI was the best way to transfer technologies. Today, there is little concern about appropriate technologies – all developing countries want new technologies to compete in world markets – and widespread desire to attract FDI. International competitiveness has become the *sine qua non* of industrial development, with falling transport and communication costs, trade liberalisation and rapid technical change (which often renders older vintages of technology uneconomical in developing countries, even at their low wages). Globalised production systems are spreading, with the manufacture of a product or component spread over several countries to take advantage of labour cost and other differences, and tightly linked by companies that organise the value chain in sophisticated ways.

There are two views on how this affects technology and development. The optimistic one is as follows. Technology is mobile internationally; the cost of transmitting information has fallen to very low levels; and transnational corporations (TNCs), the main innovators, are constantly searching for new sites in which to deploy new technology. As countries liberalise, technologies will flow to them if they manage their macro economies well, create market friendly environments and improve infrastructure and education. They will use these new technologies efficiently if they are in line with their factor endowments. No other policies are called for to develop healthy, growing industrial sectors – globalisation is assumed uniformly beneficial for development.

There is a less sanguine view: only a few countries are succeeding under globalisation because they have adopted targeted strategies to access and efficiently use new technologies. The vast majority of other poor countries are not succeeding industrially, and cannot unless they can reintroduce more proactive government strategies.

This view is based on four features of technology, ignored by free market proponents:

- New technologies are not easily transferred to and used efficiently by poor countries in free market conditions. Technologies need considerable effort to access, master, adapt and use efficiently – they need new capabilities. Building new capabilities is a costly and difficult process which faces widespread and diffuse market failures (Stiglitz, 1996; Lall, 2001). Thus, while *greater* openness to technologies and trade is desirable, *full and rapid* exposure to world markets may be harmful.

- New technologies have higher skill, technical and organisational demands, making the development of capabilities more difficult for new entrants. Moreover, capabilities develop cumulatively, so that countries with a head start can pull further ahead. This explains the growing divergence within the developing world between countries that have effective capability-building processes and those that have not (UNIDO, 2002).
- The growth of globalised production systems may reduce the need in developing countries to build local capabilities (in that multinationals transfer some of the factors the countries lack). However, given economies of scale and agglomeration and cumulative learning, these systems concentrate in a few sites.
- Economies of agglomeration exacerbate the inequitable spread of global production. Again, first movers can stay ahead for long periods by creating cumulative spillovers for their enterprises. Thus, while the mobility of knowledge and production makes it theoretically easier for all countries to access technologies and markets, the nature of capability development creates inexorable forces for divergence.

For sustained industrial development, it is necessary to take into account changing patterns of competitiveness. Technology intensive activities, with high rates of R&D spending, are growing much faster in trade and production than others (Lall, 2001). High-technology exports are the most dynamic set, driven by product innovation and the relocation of production (of labour-intensive processes) from rich to poor countries. While such relocation has also raised exports of low-technology products like apparel, this process is maturing. This is particularly worrying for developing countries, whose natural entry point into manufactured exports is low-technology activities. It is even more worrying that the largest export product in this category, apparel, which spread across poor countries because of quotas under the Multi-Fibre Arrangement (MFA), may shift significantly to China and India when the quota system ends in 2005. This will deprive many other low-wage countries of their main opportunity to develop a competitive industrial base: more sophisticated activities will be out of their reach.

East Asia dominates all manufactured exports and all categories apart from resource-based products. Its share is growing in all categories except for low-technology products; in high technology, it commands over 85 per cent of developing-world exports. The other outstanding performer is Mexico, with the North American Free Trade Agreement (NAFTA) driving rapid export growth in all categories; the rest of South America does rather poorly despite massive liberalisation (Lall et al., 2004). Sub-Saharan Africa is practically absent from the global industrial scene, with the minor exception of resource-based products. Even here, its presence is tiny despite its resource base. In Latin America and Africa, liberalisation has done nothing to promote export dynamism.

The lead taken by East Asia cannot, as the proponents of liberalisation argue, be explained by differences in trade or investment policies. It is due to structural forces based on industrial capabilities, and it cannot be reversed by persisting with liberalisation. Liberalisation does not have any in-built forces to reverse cumulative causation.

The ability of a country to build technological capabilities depends on its policies, natural and human resources, support institutions, infrastructure, business practices and social capital. Policies on trade, competition and labour affect learning via the signals firms receive from the market. The natural resource base affects the cost and benefit of different learning strategies, while the skill base determines how much and how quickly firms learn. Support institutions affect how inputs like information, technical assistance, skills or risk finance are provided to firms. Infrastructure determines the cost of operation and interacting with the outside world. Social capital and the business setting affect how well firms interact with each other and how they respond to government policies.

Conventional wisdom eschews trade interventions for industrialisation. It is based on neoclassical trade theory: free trade promotes the optimal allocation of resources (except when a country has monopoly power in trade). This is based upon stringent assumptions, including no scale economies or externalities, 'well-behaved' production functions, full information, identical technologies across countries, no learning costs, no risk or uncertainty and so on. All these assumptions are unrealistic and theorists have relaxed several of them over time. However, perhaps the most unrealistic assumption – and the one most ignored in subsequent refinements – is that there are no capabilities involved in using technologies in developing countries. It is on this basis that institutions like the World Bank (1993) recommend non-selective 'market-friendly' policies (passive liberalisation and free markets guiding resource allocation).

The capability approach suggests that free markets *cannot* ensure efficient resource allocation in the presence of market failures. Free trade leads to underinvestment in 'difficult' technologies in latecomers, because firms cannot recoup their costs fully when faced with competitors that have already undergone learning. The failures arise in encouraging entry into difficult technologies or those with widespread externalities, and in coordinating decisions by agents where there is collective learning. All the major industrialised countries used trade policy to develop their industrial sectors, though they are now intent on denying this option to developing ones (Chang, 2002).

However, protection by itself is not adequate industrial policy: it cannot lead to competitive capabilities if factor markets are deficient. If the labour market cannot provide the new skills needed, the financial market the capital to finance learning, or the technology market the information needed to master new technologies, protection will result in inefficiency. It is vital to combine protection with improvements in the relevant factor markets – trade policy must be part of a larger strategy.

Interventions to restore efficient allocation *must* vary by activity according to learning needs and linkages. Uniform support across activities makes as little sense as non-intervention. However, industrial policy only works if enterprises take advantage of protection to invest in building capabilities. If they collect rents in protected markets they end up with inadequate capabilities. The secret of effective trade policy lies in combining sheltered learning with a stimulus to build capabilities. The best stimulus comes from international competition. Combining protection with international competition is perfectly possible by giving limited protection or offsetting protection by strong export incentives. This is what the most successful Asian Tigers did.

Trade interventions must be geared to remedying market failures and be removed once the failures have been overcome. They should not be the haphazard, open-ended and non-selective protection used by import-substituting regimes. These regimes did not offset the cushion offered by protection with the sharp edge of competition.

Similar arguments apply to the *liberalisation* of protected regimes. Industries set up behind protective barriers are often technically inefficient. The remedy is not to expose them rapidly to international competition. Activities are not 'efficient' or 'inefficient' in some absolute sense; many can be made efficient if supported in 'relearning' capabilities. This needs time and support. Liberalisation has to be gradual and coordinated with factor market interventions.

Let us briefly consider the industrial strategies used in East Asia (Lall, 2001). Korea is the technological leader in the developing world and recently joined the OECD. In the 1960s, Korean income levels were lower than much of Africa and just ahead of South Asia. It started with light industry, but protected, subsidised and intervened in various ways to deepen its industrial structure. It directed (and subsidised) credit to complex technologies, forced firms to raise local content, restricted FDI and intervened in the technology transfer process to raise local innovative capabilities. It created giant conglomerates to lead its export and technological push, while guiding and promoting R&D and skill formation. It set up a massive technology infrastructure geared to the needs of selected industries, often ignoring intellectual property rights to promote reverse engineering. The government's efforts were greatly assisted by the external environment: the United States was prepared to support Korean efforts and import its products, MNCs were more willing than they are today to license new technologies and enter into arm's-length subcontracting ('original equipment manufacture') arrangements, and Japanese industry was seeking lower-cost locations to facilitate its upgrading. All these provided invaluable inputs into Korean technological development and export competitiveness.

However, many other countries could equally have benefited from these external conditions: what distinguishes Korea is its ability to mount comprehensive policies to build domestic capabilities to compete in global markets. These policies formed a coherent whole, targeted at entering progressively more difficult technologies and activities with significant local value added, under national ownership, and with a steady move into more innovative functions. The same strategic approach guided its trade liberalisation. Korea opened its economy gradually and in a controlled manner, behind a sustained export push that enabled firms to restructure and expand while building the ability to compete in world markets. The opening-up during the 1980s did not result in dislocation or unemployment. It was only later, when Korea attempted premature and rapid financial liberalisation, that the crash came.

The only other country to succeed in export competitiveness with a similar autonomous strategy was Taiwan. It also engaged in trade interventions, along with selective interventions in factor markets and institutions. It enjoyed a rapid development and deepening of indigenous skills and technological capabilities, with the ability to keep abreast of new technologies. Its myriad small and medium-sized enterprises are now dynamic exporters of high-technology products, aided by a comprehensive and proactive extension and research support and financing system.

Other Asian countries succeeded by relying on FDI and insertion into global production networks. There were substrategies, targeted and passive. Targeted FDI strategies – as in Singapore – also entailed considerable industrial policy, but the intensity of intervention was lower than with autonomous strategies (Lall, 1996). The source of technical change remained largely outside, in the hands of TNCs; this meant that there was less need to promote learning in national infant industries. However, industrial policy was needed to ensure the development of the relevant skills, capabilities and institutions required to ensure that TNCs keep transferring new technologies and functions.

Passive FDI strategies – as in Malaysia or Mexico – involved less industrial policy. TNCs were attracted mainly by low wages for unskilled or semi-skilled labour and good infrastructure, given a conducive macro environment and welcoming policies to FDI. Subsequent dynamism and upgrading did need more intervention, since with rising wages continued growth depends on whether TNCs can be induced to upgrade from simple assembly into more-advanced activities with greater local content. This upgrading has not gone far enough. Without more capability development, the initial spurt of growth may peter out.

Simply opening up to trade and investment flows is not an adequate strategy for countries at the low end of the technology ladder, as in Africa. Stabilisation and liberalisation can remove the constraints to growth caused by poor macro management, inefficient public enterprises, high entry costs for private enterprises and restrictions on FDI. However, it cannot allow the economy to build more-advanced capabilities. Evidence on Africa shows that after an initial spurt of growth, liberalising economies with static capabilities slow down as their initial advantages are exhausted (Lall, 1999). As import competition in product markets increase, enterprises find it difficult to cope and close down or withdraw into non-traded activities. Without strategic support from the government, they find it difficult to bridge the gap between their capabilities and those needed for international competitiveness. New enterprises find it more difficult to enter complex activities with stringent skill and technology requirements.

There is a danger, therefore, that industrial structures in low-income countries with passive industrial policy regress into simple activities that cannot sustain rapid growth. This is one reason why liberalisation has had poor results in Sub-Saharan Africa. Liberalisation has also led to technological regression in much of Latin America, with relatively weak growth and competitive performance. These countries have a large base of capabilities in such industries as food processing and automobile manufacture, but find it difficult to move into dynamic high-tech activities.

The rule-setting part of the international system (the Bretton Woods institutions and WTO) has been concerned with facilitating globalisation rather than helping countries cope with its demands. This approach has been based on the implicit premise that markets and rules to promote market forces will accomplish both objectives. As a result of external pressures as well as domestic changes, there has been considerable liberalisation in the developing and transition worlds. Governments are withdrawing from direct ownership of productive resources and also from the provision of a number of infrastructure services. They play a steadily diminishing role in the allocation of productive resources. The ultimate objective of the current phase of reforms is a liberal production, trading and investment framework where the driving force is private enterprises responding to market signals.

There is much to welcome in these trends. Many government interventions to promote development have a poor record and have constrained rather than helped growth and welfare. Giving greater play to market forces will contain many of the inefficiencies and rent seeking inherent in government intervention. However, as noted, simply opening up to market forces cannot deal with structural problems of development. The most successful developing countries intervened intensively in markets, with many different strategies to build up their competitive capabilities. Their experience suggests that there is a significant role for government in providing the 'collective goods' needed for sustained development. The issue is not *whether* governments should intervene, but *how*.

In the absence of renewed international support for (new forms of) industrial policy, current global forces will lead to further divergence in industrial and income growth. This will cause intolerable pressures in a world thrust closer together. Many policy makers and analysts see that inequities are rising, but so widespread and ingrained are the neoliberal arguments that they are unable to understand the structural forces at work. The first step must be to understand and explain these; the next must be to devise an appropriate policy response.

However, we must also be aware of structural limitations to industrialisation in a globalising world. International production systems may not be able to spread across the whole developing world, whatever governments do. Electronics was the main industry whose relocation drove East Asian success, and it is now 'settled' in that region. Cumulative first-mover advantages may prevent it from moving to other regions. No other high-technology industry has the same requirements of labour-intensive assembly combined with highly transportable products.

Low-technology industries may continue to spread to poorer developing countries, but, as noted, the abolition of the MFA raises the risk that the lead industry, apparel, will shift back to Asia. Other industries have demanding skill needs that the least developed countries may not be able to meet. One indicator is that the US African Growth and Opportunities Act (AGOA), which offers tariff- and quota-free entry to most African countries in most manufactured products, has not attracted any footwear, sports goods or other producers to Africa. Only apparel has responded, and that is mainly because of the quota system. Resource-based activities also do not offer much hope of industrial development: processing resources is demanding in scale, skills, technology and infrastructure. The least developed countries are likely to be competitive only in primary exports rather than in processed products.

Thus, it may turn out that the East Asian 'miracle' was unique not in the ability of governments to mount effective industrial policy but in the technological characteristics of the industries that drove its export success.

SANJAYA LALL

References

Chang, H.-J. (2002), *Kicking Away the Ladder: Development Strategy in Historical Perspective*, London: Anthem Press.

Lall, S. (1996), *Learning from the Asian Tigers: Studies in Technology and Industrial Policy*, London: Macmillan.

Lall, S. (ed.) (1999), *The Technological Response to Import Liberalization in Sub-Saharan Africa*, London: Macmillan.

Lall, S. (2001), *Competitiveness, Technology and Skills*, Cheltenham, UK and Northampton, MA, USA: Edward Elgar.

Lall, S., M. Albaladejo and M.M. Moreira (2004), *Latin American Industrial Competitiveness and the Challenge of Globalisation*, Washington, DC: Inter-American Development Bank.

Stiglitz, J.E. (1996), 'Some lessons from the East Asian miracle', *World Bank Research Observer*, **11** (2), 151–77.

UNIDO (2002), *Industrial Development Report 2002/2003*, Vienna: UN Industrial Development Organization.

World Bank (1993), *The East Asian Miracle*, Oxford: Oxford University Press.

Tinbergen, Jan (1903–1994)

Jan Tinbergen was born in The Hague into a teacher's family that brought five children into this world. Both his brother Nikolaas, a zoologist, and Jan, the physicist turned economist, received a Nobel Prize for work in their respective fields.

Tinbergen spans the entire twentieth century. He studied theoretical physics under Paul Ehrenfest at the University of Leiden, but turned to economics early on in his studies. This is reflected in the title of his doctoral dissertation, 'Minimum problemen in de Natuurkunde en de Ekonomie' (Minimum problems in physics and economics). This turning-point reflected his growing interest in solving the economic and social problems he saw around him during the crisis-ridden decades of the inter-bellum period.

Tinbergen's career can be divided into four periods:

1. The 1930s, when he pioneered quantitative methods in economics, thus initiating mathematical economics and econometrics. This resulted in his work on business-cycle theory and practice undertaken in the framework of the League of Nations before the Second World War. During this period he tried to understand the causes of the Great Depression and possible solutions.
2. His work on macroeconomic models as founder and first director of the Central Planning Bureau of the Netherlands between 1945 and 1955. This was not only a creative theoretical period but above all an eminently practical experience in the post-war reconstruction of the Dutch economy and its road to sustained economic and social development. This was his attempt at the national level to show in practical terms the way out of chaos and into prosperity.
3. His switch to development economics, advisor to many governments of developing countries, director of the Netherlands Economics Institute, chairman of the UN committee of development policy and planning and as such the main inspirer of the first two development decades of the United Nations. This period embraces the years from 1955 to 1975, during which he showed at the international level possible solutions to global inequalities by setting ambitious economic growth targets for developing countries and equally ambitious development assistance targets for the industrial countries.
4. His very active retirement period, during which he continued his interest in development, employment and income distribution problems, but during which he concentrated also on a lifelong interest in peace and security by launching himself into the economics of peace.

When Tinbergen was awarded the first Nobel Prize in economics in 1969 (shared with Ragnar Frisch), it was for 'introducing true dynamics into economics and for macro-econometric modeling in which this dynamics was applied'. In other words, it was for the work he had done during the first phase of his career. When he got the prize, Tinbergen was deeply engaged in the third phase, and many of his collaborators at the time were surprised that the Nobel committee did not mention that work, namely development economics. It is therefore important to review briefly Tinbergen's main contributions in each of the four phases of his career.

The first phase was his pioneering econometric period during which he concentrated on macro-econometric models of the Dutch, the US and the UK economies. One important aspect of Tinbergen's model of the Dutch economy, prepared in 1936, is that it provided means to tackle the problems of unemployment and financial deficits within a deteriorating economy. In 1939, Tinbergen and his research assistants produced for the League of Nations in Geneva the landmark study on business cycles in the United States. This was a much bigger system than the Dutch 1936 model, it paid more attention to economic explanations of the individual relationships that depicted aggregative economic behaviour, and it includes far superior dynamics. This was necessary because the US model had to be capable of generating economic movements like those that we have come to know as the business cycle.

The second phase of Tinbergen's career had its origin in the 1936 model of the Dutch economy. But it also reflected his interest in tackling the political consequences of his thinking and ideas. He became a lifelong member of the social-democratic party that came to power in the Netherlands after the Second World War. For these two reasons he was asked to set up and to direct the Central Planning Bureau that still exists. Thus, Tinbergen became one of the architects of the reconstruction of the Dutch economy after the war. During this period, which lasted from 1945 until 1955, he produced a theory of economic policy that combined qualitative as well as quantitative dimensions of economic policy which he elaborated in his book *Economic Policy: Principles and Design* (1956). Tinbergen has been criticised for the use of 'oversimplified models'. His reply was that the advantage of using quantitative models is that it is easy to check for completeness and that better approximations to reality can be introduced step by step. It is important to underline that these simplified models resulted in now familiar insights: that in order to reach a number of fixed targets an equal number of independent instruments is necessary. Not only did Tinbergen argue in favour of stepwise solutions, but he also pleaded for decentralised decision-making structures. Policy instruments that affect the entire country remain at the central level, but those that affect part of the country must be farmed out to lower levels of authority.

In 1955 – allegedly after a visit to Calcutta where he saw close up the misery and poverty of a developing country – Tinbergen left the Central Planning Bureau. After a year at Harvard, in 1957 he accepted a full professorship in mathematical economics and development planning at the Netherlands School of Economics at Rotterdam, later to become the economics department of Erasmus University. Thus starts the third phase of his career, when he published works on the optimum regime, planning in stages, the semi-input–output method, the international division of labour, educational planning, income distribution, the convergence theory of economic systems and many more topics.

This work is characterised by 'responsible simplification', also taking into account the availability of data in the developing countries. This is illustrated, for example, in his semi-input–output approach in which he adapts Wassily Leontief's input–output method to the situation in developing countries.

Tinbergen gave a good deal of attention to social sectors in general and to education in particular, thus continuing his interest in qualitative and cultural factors. He constructed an econometric model that quantifies the relation between education and economic growth, thereby combining quantitative and qualitative analysis. Obviously, he was attacked again – by Thomas Balogh in particular – and Tinbergen replied characteristic-ally: 'We have preferred to start with highly simplified models in the scientific tradition which is also well known in economics. The Keynesian multiplier model is an outstand-ing example of this tradition' (Tinbergen, 1965, p. 10).

Very quickly Tinbergen – together with P.C. Mahanalobis, the father of the early Indian five year plans – became the guru of the prevailing consensus during the 1950s and 1960s on planned government direction of the economy. His econometric techniques and the framework of his models were applied to many underdeveloped countries and the UN was swamped with requests to send him as advisor and consultant. The model-builder had himself become a model. Just as in the 1930s in his work for the League of Nations, when Tinbergen was ahead of his time by two decades, so it may prove again with his empha-sis on precise definition of objectives and means in macroeconomic planning, combined with normative values for income distribution and microeconomic equity.

From 1965 to 1975, Tinbergen was chairman of the UN Committee for Development Planning. He became the leader of a brilliant group of people including Gamani Corea, Saburo Okita, Josef Pajestka, K.N. Raj and M.L. Quereshi (among others). During Tinbergen's chairmanship, this group came closer than we have ever been before or since to fulfilling the function foreseen for the UN at the Bretton Woods and San Francisco conferences to be the focus of what we now call 'global macroeconomic governance'. His name is closely associated with the second UN development decade (1970–80) and the 0.7 per cent development aid target.

During the fourth phase of his career he continued to be interested in development studies, occupational and educational structures of the labour force, and the race between technological progress and income distribution. But he also became more and more focused on peace economics which he defined as 'economic science used for [the] purpose' of prohibiting the employment of war 'as an instrument of settling conflicts between nations' (Tinbergen, 1994, p. 3). Tinbergen's emphasis was on costs and gains. In what must have been one of his last articles – published in the summer of 1994 – he reviews many of the things to which he attached importance: war and peace, the establishment of a world government, and the reform of the United Nations. '[We] must calculate the costs of the wealth destroyed . . . and the money value of being killed or of a friend or one's partner or relative killed . . .' (ibid., p. 3).

Many view Tinbergen as a naïve idealist whose ideas are now totally out of date given the change in economic policies since 1980, the Washington Consensus, and the decline in the welfare state. However, when future governments return to the idea of welfare eco-nomics, his ideas may very well come up again as they are fundamental to the entire edifice.

A common error consists of judging a person's accomplishments by the techniques and state of the art of today. Obviously, a lot of his work during the first two phases of his career no longer conforms to the technical requirements which modern economists have embraced. His use of estimation techniques never was state of the art. Most of it was done by hand, or by Friden calculator, or by some form of primitive computer. Nevertheless, he showed how it was possible to find meaningful and even exciting results without using the technology that modern economists frequently use to hide their poverty of ideas, to quote Dutch economist Bernard van Praag.

As we have seen, Tinbergen became more of an idealist as time marched on. He had always put his quantitative techniques in the service of shaping a better world with less unemployment, a better income distribution within and between countries, and substantive financial transfers from the rich to the poor nations. During the fourth and final phase of his life and career, however, he tended to emphasise world government and peace economics. The change in economic policies since 1980 and this growing idealism meant that more and more observers considered Tinbergen naïve, *weltfremd*, and not in touch with reality. Only his former disciples would insist that Tinbergen was not only a great scientist but also a saint, so modest, so polite and so generous.

Both the critics and the disciples are wrong. Many of Tinbergen's contributions to economics remain valid and will become relevant again once the economic wisdom of the day changes in the direction of greater rationality. His modesty was only apparent and could border on arrogance. But he was sincere when he remarked in 1969, upon being awarded the Nobel Prize: 'I would have preferred the Nobel Prize for Peace'.

LOUIS EMMERIJ

Selected works

(1939), *Business Cycles in the United States of America, 1919–1932*, Geneva: League of Nations.
(1952), *On the Theory of Economic Policy*, Amsterdam: North-Holland.
(1956), *Economic Policy: Principles and Design*, Amsterdam: North-Holland.
(1958), *The Design of Development*, Baltimore, MD: Johns Hopkins University Press.
(1962a), *Mathematical Models of Economic Growth*, New York: McGraw-Hill.
(1962b), *Shaping the World Economy, Suggestions for an International Economic Policy*, New York: Twentieth Century Fund.
(1965), *Econometric Models of Education*, Paris: OECD.
(1975), *Income Distribution, Analysis and Policies*, Amsterdam: North-Holland.
(1976), *Reshaping the International Order*, A Report to the Club of Rome, New York: Dutton.
(1985), *Production, Income and Welfare: The Search for an Optimum Social Order*, Brighton: Wheatsheaf.
(1987), *Revitalizing the United Nations System*, Santa Barbara, CA: Nuclear Age Peace Foundation.
(1990), *World Security and Equity*, Aldershot, UK and Brookfield, US: Edward Elgar.
(1994), 'What is peace economics?', *Peace Economics, Peace Science and Public Policy*, **1** (4), 3–4.

Tourism and Development

International tourist arrivals increased from 25 million in 1950 to almost 715 million in 2002. Although tourism has experienced a downturn since 9/11, the share going to the South over the long term has increased from about 3 per cent in 1950 to almost 30 per cent in 2002 (WTO, 1991, 2003). Moreover, intra-regional tourism in the South has also grown rapidly and now accounts for more visitors than from the developed world. Tourism is now a major industry in many developing countries. It is of growing importance in terms of employment and foreign exchange and it accounts for a significant share of GDP. Indirectly tourism has an impact on the construction and related industries, agriculture, manufacturing, financial services, in addition to transport, trade and communications.

Orthodox economics stresses the gains from trade for all countries, and for developing countries international interaction is also assumed to play an important role in the diffusion of modern values, structures and institutions. Trade barriers and domestic resource constraints, however, limit the export potential of many developing countries. In contrast, international tourism is often regarded as an easy, low-cost – high-benefit option which promotes modernisation and offers 'limitless growth potential' (OECD, 1967, pp. 11–15). Tourism opens up new markets which are not subject to the tariffs, quotas and other barriers to trade that continue to limit the growth of Third World commodity exports.

The role of tourism in the process of modernisation and the consequences for development have been debated extensively within and across the social sciences. From an orthodox or mainstream perspective economic progress resulting from tourism cannot ensure increased economic independence, but it is assumed that tourism can enhance economic growth and this has the potential to underpin social development and poverty reduction, facilitate increased equality and help meet basic needs. In contrast, from a radical perspective, international tourism, which is increasingly dominated by global capital, is seen as providing new opportunities for exploiting developing countries. There is a considerable body of literature from within economics, sociology, anthropology, geography and political science which has addressed this topic (see Harrison, 2004).

The impact of tourism on host communities has been a major issue. Much of the literature to date has emphasised that tourism is a major force generating change (Hall, 1991; Nelson et al., 1993; Poon, 1993) but the relationship between tourism and development is a complex one. There are opportunity costs of tourism and it creates new problems and uncertainties. The 'advocacy' platform has given way to the 'cautionary' and later the 'adaptancy' and 'knowledge-based' platforms (Jafari, 1990; Harrison, 1992; Gayle, 1993; Patullo, 1996). While recognising the benefits that tourism can bring, many developing countries are also concerned about the growing dependency on tourism and the threat of neocolonialism.

As international tourism has expanded and travel has become a fashion good, competition between destinations has intensified. Sun, sea and sand is still a major determinant of tourism flows, but many developing countries have also turned to promoting their comparative advantage for alternative tourism based on culture, heritage or history. This development has not gone unchallenged. The notion that cultural (alternative) tourism is clean and green while mass tourism is 'bad' is inevitably a simplification. Moreover, as Butler (1992) has argued, alternative tourism may be the thin edge of the wedge. There is concern over the viability and sustainability of alternative tourism, growing opposition to the commoditisation of culture and fears for the social fabric and cohesion of traditional societies.

The impact of tourism depends on a range of factors including the number of visitors, the nature of the tourist encounter and how it is controlled. It cannot be assumed that tourism is a panacea for development. There is no guarantee that the benefits of tourism will trickle down to the poorest groups and those on the margins of society. Equally there is little evidence that tourist development reduces inequalities either within or between nation states (Harrison, 1992, p. 25). Part of the debate is located around issues of control. International tourism is now a global industry, dominated by multinational corporations that control almost all aspects of the industry. Sometimes other issues cloud the debate over control. In the Caribbean there is great sensitivity over who controls the tourism industry because of the history of slavery and colonialism. Rajotte (1987) captures the concerns of many when he expresses the fear that tourism might become 'a new form of sugar', with external capital creaming off monopoly profits while the host nation is left to bear the brunt of the costs. A more extreme, neocolonialist, version of this view argues that the economic and political sovereignty of small states may be under threat. Yet the presumption that inside control through local capital is good and outside control by international capital is bad simply cannot be asserted. Nevertheless, it is abundantly clear that the free market solution will not necessarily lead to sustainable tourist development. The major problem for many developing countries is how to manage and control tourism so as to achieve sustainability without being too prescriptive and thereby putting a brake on development.

International travel leads to contact between people from different societies. More often than not they speak a different language, but also differ with respect to values, beliefs and behaviour. For both, the experience is in some respects illusory. The guest is not only outside the indigenous culture but has also moved outside the bounds of his/her own culture. Visitors invariably have preconceptions about indigenous people and cultures – the 'savages' (Douglas, 1994) or the 'friendly natives' – which are often based on the (mis)information and images of illusory destinations. It is equally valid to suggest that hosts find it difficult to understand the everyday culture of the visitor, not least because tourists themselves have stepped outside their own culture. This mutual lack of understanding can give rise to resentment or offence and occasionally lead to conflict between hosts and guests.

There is a considerable body of literature on how host communities respond to the stranger in their midst (Price, 1996). Some residents may change their schedule to avoid tourists (Brown and Giles, 1994) while others change the timing of their festivals either to accommodate tourists (Brandes, 1988; Greenwood, 1989; Picard, 1990) or to prevent them attending (Boissevain, 1996). Boissevain suggests that communities adapt 'surprisingly quickly' and soon 'adopt business attitudes' towards profits (ibid., p. 15). They are also 'creative in investing and staging events' while managing to 'deflect the tourist gaze from private space and activities' (ibid., p. 22).

Tourism is an important agent of change but this cannot be understood purely in terms of the impact of individual or group interaction. More fundamentally, the growth of tourism represents a change in the value and use of resources which has important consequences for the organisation of labour and the form of social institutions and structures (Butler and Hinch, 1996). Tourism often leads to a growth in the demand for traditional products. In many instances this leads to the commercialisation of the production of handicrafts, and this in turn creates new demands for resources and sets up both backward and forward linkage effects. In the case of small islands there are numerous examples of natural resources having to be imported to meet the surge in demand for traditional goods, and this often has wide-ranging economic and social consequences (Milne, 1990).

Much of the literature relating to the socio-cultural impacts of tourism has been critical, but as Crick (1989, p. 335) points out it is often ethnocentric and sometimes shallow. Turner and Ash (1978, p. 197) refer to tourism as the 'enemy of authenticity and cultural identity' while Sofield (1996), argues that it is important to minimise the cultural impacts of tourism in order to preserve cultural diversity and maintain authenticity. Such assertions need to be contextualised but it is also important to consider the meaning and nature of authenticity. The importance of cultural diversity cannot simply be asserted, nor can it be presumed that some undefined notion of authenticity is something that needs to be preserved. There is a danger that traditional life is romanticised and bestowed with idyllic qualities. Modern societies may not have eradicated poverty or inequality and may have created new social ills, but traditional life 'with its customary exchange and obligation system' also has its problems (Forster, 1964, p. 222).

For some critics, globalisation is the problem. There is a fear that tourism contributes to the 'cola-isation' or standardisation of culture. Many are critical of the way culture is exploited and manipulated by transnational corporations for a growing global market. They often use emotive language to criticise the packaging and commoditisation of culture which is 'priced like . . . fast food' and 'is a violation of peoples' cultural rights' (Greenwood, 1989, pp. 176–7). Underlying these concerns are fears that the marketing and selling of culture for tourists represents a new form of colonialism and that in the process unique cultural identities will be lost.

Such views, however, have not gone unchallenged. Tourism can contribute to bringing traditional rituals or cultural forms in music, painting or handicrafts to the attention of the world. This aspect of tourism may be regarded as progressive, enlightening and educational. There are numerous instances where the introduction of tourism has helped small island communities to reverse a period of decline and outward migration. Although the commercial selling and production of traditional goods is often condemned, it may help to promote handicraft production, reinvigorate artistic skill and raise awareness of the artistic merit of traditional artefacts. As a consequence, tourism may help to revitalise and sustain indigenous cultures.

There is, however, the danger of idealising traditional cultural norms, values and institutions. Cultural practices and traditions may be a source of communal strength but they may also limit access to other cultures, discourage dissent and reinforce social divisions. These postmodern tensions are also present in the developed world. Without some idea of what development means it is impossible to assess social change or to determine what is to count as development. Moreover, as Nussbaum and Sen (1989) make clear, understanding a culture and its central values and traditions raises problems of observation, evidence, interpretation and assessment, and these difficulties are compounded where there is diversity within a community. The cultural changes that occur with tourism, or any other form of development, cannot be reduced to a list of positive or negative effects such that, for example, 'preserving tradition' is good and 'modernisation' is bad (ibid., p. 316).

There are no simple generalisations about the economic, social and environmental impacts of tourism. Much of the debate within developing countries indicates ambivalence towards tourist development and recognition that it must be sustainable. This implies that tourism must grow in harmony with the economy and be managed to prevent economic, social and environmental degradation. There are also other potential uses for the human and other resources absorbed by tourism, and it may be important to assess the benefits of alternative development strategies.

RON AYRES

References

Boissevain, J. (1996), 'Introduction', in Boissevain (ed.), *Coping with Tourists: European Reactions to Mass Tourism*, London: Berghahn, pp. 1–26.

Brandes, S. (1988), *Power and Persuasion: Fiestas and Social Control in Rural Mexico*, Philadelphia, PA: University of Pennsylvania Press.

Brown, G. and R. Giles (1994), 'Coping with tourism: an examination of resident responses to the social impact of tourism', in A. Seaton (ed.), *Tourism: The State of the Art*, Chichester: John Wiley & Sons, pp. 755–64.

Butler, R. (1992), 'Alternative tourism: the thin edge of the wedge', in V.L. Smith and W.R. Eadington (eds), *Tourism Alternatives: Potentials and Problems in the Development of Tourism*, Philadelphia, PA: University of Pennsylvania Press, pp. 31–46.

Butler, R. and T. Hinch (eds) (1996), *Tourism and Indigenous Peoples*, London: International Thomson Business Press.

Crick, M. (1989), 'Representations of international tourism in the social sciences: sun, sex, sights, savings and servility', *Annual Review of Anthropology*, **18**, 307–44.

Douglas, N. (1994), 'They came for savages', PhD thesis, University of Queensland, Brisbane.

Forster, J. (1964), 'The sociological consequences of tourism', *International Journal of Comparative Sociology*, **5**, 217–27.

Gayle, D.G. (1993), *Tourism, Marketing and Management in the Caribbean*, London: Routledge.

Greenwood, D. (1989), 'Culture by the pound: an anthropological perspective on tourism as cultural commoditisation', in V. Smith (ed.), *Hosts and Guests: The Anthropology of Tourism*, 2nd edn, Philadelphia, PA: University of Pennsylvania Press, pp. 171–85.

Hall, D. (1991), *Tourism and Economic Development in Eastern Europe and the Soviet Union*, London: Belhaven.

Harrison, D. (ed.) (1992), *Tourism and the Less Developed Countries*, London: Belhaven.

Harrison, D. (2004), *Tourism and the Less Developed World: Issues and Case Studies*, Oxford: Oxford University Press.

Jafari, J. (1990), 'Socio-cultural dimensions of tourism', paper presented at the Conference on Tourism and socio-cultural change in the Caribbean, Trinidad and Tobago, 25–28 June.

Milne, S. (1990), 'The impact of tourism development in small Pacific Island states: an overview', *New Zealand Journal of Geography*, **89**, 16–21.

Nelson, J.G., R. Butler and G. Wall (eds) (1993), *Tourism and Sustainable Development: Monitoring, Planning and Managing*, Waterloo, Ontario: Department of Geography, University of Waterloo.

Nussbaum, M.C. and A. Sen (1989), 'Internal criticism and Indian rationalist traditions', in M. Krausz (ed.), *Relativism, Interpretation and Confrontation*, Notre Dame, IN: Notre Dame, University Press, pp. 299–325.

OECD (1967), *Tourism Development and Economic Growth*, Paris: Organisation for Economic Cooperation and Development.

Patullo, P. (1996), *Last Resorts*, London: Cassell.

Picard, M. (1990), 'Cultural tourism in Bali: cultural performances as tourist attraction', *Indonesia*, **49**, 37–74.

Poon, A. (1993), *Tourism, Technology and Competitive Strategies*, Harmondsworth: CAB International.

Price, M.F. (1996), *People and Tourism in Fragile Environments*, Chichester: Wiley.

Rajotte, F. (ed.) (1987), 'Tourism: a new kind of sugar', occasional paper, University of Hawaii, Honolulu.

Sofield, T.H.B. (1996), 'Anuha Island resort: a case study of failure', in R. Butler and T. Hinch (eds), *Tourism and Indigenous Peoples*, London: International Thomson Business Press, pp. 176–202.

Turner, L. and J. Ash (1978), *The Golden Hordes*, New York: St. Martin's Press.

World Tourism Organization (1991), *Tourism to the Year 2000*, Madrid: WTO.

World Tourism Organization (2003), 'Tourism highlights', Facts and Figures section, www.world-tourism.org.

Trade and Industrial Policy

Trade and industrial policies are intertwined in all countries for the obvious reason that many industrial goods are traded in the international market. However, their interrelationship is even closer in developing countries, as industrial development in a developing country without some kind of control over trade flows is very difficult, if not totally impossible, due to the existence of superior producers abroad. This is the essence of the infant industry argument, which forms the central element in the trade and industrial policies of any developing country.

In the days of imperialism, weak countries were denied the right to use independent trade and industrial policies. In the main, this was achieved through the deprivation of tariff autonomy. That colonies do not have the ability to set their own tariffs may be obvious. However, even countries that were not technically colonies – post-independence Latin American countries, China, Thailand (formerly Siam), Turkey (formerly the Ottoman Empire) and Iran (formerly Persia) – were also deprived of tariff autonomy through 'unequal treaties'. This meant that none of the countries could use independent trade, and thus industrial, policies.

From the late nineteenth century, at least some of the nominally independent countries started regaining tariff autonomy. The larger Latin American countries were able to regain tariff autonomy from the 1880s, Japan only in 1911, and Turkey and China had to wait until 1929.

From the 1930s the regained tariff autonomy started to be translated into concrete trade and industrial policy actions at least in some of the countries concerned. The Great Depression and the subsequent collapse of the world trading system created the necessity. And the rise of planning following the emergence of the Soviet Union, together with the collapse of capitalism during the Great Depression, turned the political and intellectual tides towards active trade and industrial policies. Kemal Attaturk in Turkey, Juan Péron in Argentina, and Getúlio Vargas in Brazil are only some of the more famous political leaders who adopted a set of policies, commonly (if somewhat misleadingly) known as the import-substituting industrialisation (ISI) strategy during this period. When the developing countries in Asia and Africa gained independence between 1945, with the end of the Second World War, and the 1960s, most of them did the same.

According to the supporters of ISI, the conventional mode of economic activity in the developing countries, that is, relying on primary commodity exports to finance the import of manufactured products, was dangerous for a number of reasons. First, the collapse of international trade following the Great Depression demonstrated the fragility of the international trading system and the consequent danger of relying too heavily on it. Second, the volatility of their prices made primary commodities an unreliable source of foreign exchange. Third, it was suggested that there was a long-term tendency for the terms of trade for primary commodity exports to fall. Last but not least, given their low income elasticities of demand, the scope for increase in the exports of primary commodities over time was regarded as small. In contrast, manufacturing was seen as offering the opportunities for faster productivity growth and greater stability in income.

So, during the first quarter-century of the post-war period, in their desire to move their economies away from primary commodities towards manufacturing, most developing countries used tariff barriers, quantitative restrictions (quotas), industrial licensing, subsidies and other trade and industrial policy measures. Some countries, notably those in East Asia, also used export subsidies, governmental export marketing support, and other means to promote manufacturing exports.

From the 1970s, however, dissenting voices were beginning to be raised against the then orthodoxy of ISI (Little et al., 1970, is the classic example). It was pointed out that protectionist trade policy and interventionist industrial policy 'distort' market signals, thereby channelling resources into 'inefficient' industries that reduce economic welfare. On the basis of this diagnosis, it was recommended that trade should be liberalised while market-distorting domestic industrial policies such as subsidies and government creation of monopoly should be abolished.

From the early 1980s, when many developing countries got into economic trouble following the debt crisis, the 'recommendation' for free trade turned into a requirement. Following the debt crisis, the IMF and the World Bank jointly launched the so-called 'structural adjustment programmes' (SAPs), which involved 'conditionalities' that went beyond their traditional domains of foreign exchange reserves and infrastructural investment, respectively. Now their loans came with conditions that relate to policies in all sorts of areas. And given the belief in the virtues of free trade and free markets that prevailed in these organisations, it was natural that trade liberalisation and industrial deregulation became compulsory for countries that needed their finance.

However, the early 1980s was also the time when it began to be more widely known that the successful East Asian countries had not practised free trade, as the free trade economists had claimed for a long time. Many commentators pointed out that these countries actually had used a lot of policy measures similar to those used by the ISI countries. So, not being able to use the standard free trade–protectionism dichotomy in justifying their policies, the World Bank and their associates had to come up with a new discourse.

In this new discourse, it was claimed that, while they did not practise straightforward free trade, the East Asian countries practised a 'virtual free trade' by using subsidies and other measures for export promotion, which cancelled out the 'distortions' created by import tariffs and quotas. Calling this an 'outward-orientated' trade strategy, ISI was rechristened an 'inward-orientated' strategy, which was then 'shown' to be inferior to the former through numerous econometric exercises.

However, there are numerous criticisms to the discourse of inward- versus outward-orientated trade strategy (see the theoretical review by Helleiner, 1990; and the critical review of econometric studies by Rodriguez and Rodrik, 2001). The details of their criticisms need not detain us here, but basically the discourse has been convincingly shown to lack theoretical foundation (even in neoclassical terms) and is based on 'evidence' built with dubious methodologies and unreliable data.

Actually, trade liberalisation – and other 'market-orientated' reform measures – during the last two decades at the behest of the IMF and the World Bank, have produced very disappointing results. The 1980s and the 1990s have seen the average growth rate of per capita income in the developing countries being halved to 1.5 per cent from the 3 per cent recorded in the 'bad old days' of ISI in the 1960s and the 1970s. Even the disappointing 1.5 per cent rate would not have been possible without India and China, which *did* liberalise their trade and industrial policies in the last two decades, but still practise a wide range of strategic trade and industrial policies, not dissimilar to the ones practised by the East Asian countries until the 1980s. Therefore, one may ask, if ISI was such a failure and if an outward-orientated trade strategy is so good, why have the developing countries been growing at half the rate in the last two decades that they were under ISI?

Of course, this is not to say that everything was rosy under ISI. That the protected industries were uncompetitive by international standards *in the beginning* was natural – after all, they would not have needed protection in the first place if they were already competitive. However, in many countries too many infant industries had failed to 'grow up' even after decades of protection. With widespread state intervention, corruption and rent seeking abounded, which not only created inefficiencies and waste but also brought crises of political legitimacy to the whole exercise of ISI. Very often, there were balance-of-payment problems that were the results of the inability of many countries pursuing ISI to develop viable export industries, which crippled their macro economy.

However, these problems were the results of bad design and poor implementation rather than of inherent flaws in the logic supporting interventionist trade and industrial policies. Infant industries failing to grow up were either those that were overly ambitious, given the country's technological and managerial capabilities, or those that were not adequately supervised and disciplined by the government administering protection and subsidies. That this is the case is proved by the successes of many infant industries around the world, ranging from the Japanese automobile industry, to the Korean steel industry, to the Brazilian regional jet industry. It is also possible to contain the problems of corruption and rent seeking associated with interventionist trade and industrial policies, as can be seen in the cases of the East Asian countries and some European countries (for example, France, Austria, Finland). Export promotion programmes should be, and could have been, incorporated into the overall industrial strategy, as can be seen in the case of the East Asian countries.

Despite these limitations, the financial muscles of the IMF and the World Bank, as well as the donor governments, ensured that trade liberalisation programmes remained the order of the day. The push towards free trade and industrial deregulation has intensified over the last decade thanks to the establishment of the new world trading order through the WTO in 1995.

What is notable is that, contrary to what is usually believed, the WTO is not really a free trade organisation. For one thing, it still allows considerable degrees of protection in agriculture, especially by the developed countries, and certain designated manufacturing sectors in the developing countries. For another, in the form of the TRIPS (Trade Related Intellectual Property Rights) agreement, which concerns patents, copyrights and trademarks, the WTO explicitly prevents free trade in ideas.

Having said that, it is true that the WTO has pushed the developing countries significantly towards free trade because it has forced them to eliminate quotas, considerably reduce their tariffs, and limit their abilities to regulate foreign investments, through the TRIMS (Trade Related Investment Measures) agreement that prevents the application of important regulatory measures like local contents requirement and foreign exchange balancing requirement.

However, this does not allow us to conclude that there is no longer room for interventionist trade and industrial policies under the WTO regime. For example, the poorest countries (roughly those with less than $1000 per capita income) are allowed to use export subsidies, which are not allowed for other countries. There are other subsidies that all countries can still legitimately use, such as those for R&D, agriculture, reduction of regional disparity, and the development of environmentally friendly technology. Indeed, the developed countries have actively used these subsidies to promote their industries. As significant as the tariff reductions may have been, it is not as if countries had to adopt a zero tariff. In some industries, tariff ceilings are still quite high (30 per cent plus). TRIMS still allow the use of performance requirements such as those related to technology transfer or export ratio. And so on.

Unfortunately, the developed countries are working hard to reduce the remaining policy space for the developing countries even further. For example, the United States is pushing for its proposal that all manufacturing tariffs should be virtually eliminated in the next decade or so. Moreover, through the push for a multilateral investment agreement (MIA), the developed countries have tried to illegalise many more regulations regarding foreign investment than the ones prohibited by TRIMS. And in the face of the resistance that their proposal for an MIA have met, many developed countries, especially the United States, have resorted to bilateral investment treaties (BITs), which often carry even more restrictions on foreign investment regulation by the host country than there would be if the proposed MIA were adopted.

Thus, if all these further moves are realised, the policy space for the developing countries could indeed become insignificant. However, they are still to happen, and it will be unfortunate if developing countries jump to the mistaken conclusion that the space is already non-existent and give up the policy measures that are allowed under the current regime. Developing countries should use the existing policy space to the maximum possible degree.

Important as it may be to exploit the room for manoeuvre under the current regime, in the end it is necessary to change the WTO system in a way that is more development friendly. The developing countries should be allowed to use more tariffs and subsidies than they are now. They should be able to protect intellectual property rights less rigorously than is demanded under the present regime. After all, these are the policies that have been used by virtually all successful developers from eighteenth-century Britain, through nineteenth-century USA, Germany and Sweden, to late twentieth-century Japan, Korea and Taiwan in the earlier phase of their development (for details, see Chang, 2002).

HA-JOON CHANG

References

Chang, H.-J. (2002), *Kicking Away the Ladder: Development Strategy in Historical Perspective*, London: Anthem Press.
Helleiner, G. (1990), 'Trade strategy in medium-term adjustment', *World Development*, **18** (6), 879–97.
Little, I., T. Scitovsky and M. Scott (1970), *Industry in Trade in Some Developing Countries: A Comparative Study*, London: Oxford University Press.
Rodriguez, F. and D. Rodrik (2001), 'Trade policy and economic growth: a skeptic's guide to the cross-national evidence', *NBER Macroeconomics Annual 2000*, Cambridge, MA: MIT.

Trade Negotiations and Protectionism

Introduction

Negotiations are currently under way in the WTO to create new global obligations and rules that will subject all member countries to provide greater market access to each other's exports of goods and services. At the same time, these new obligations will institutionalise indefinitely the trade policies and profiles of its members. There are therefore grave concerns that the current trade talks will unnecessarily and inappropriately curtail and deprive developing countries of their trade policy measures used in pursuing their development objectives.

Subscribers to the notion of free trade, including the developed-country members of the WTO, disparage these reservations, since they believe that trade liberalisation in any case will benefit development as it enhances economic growth. From their point of view, the real problem has been governments' protectionist interference with trade that has prevented trade from being a real engine of development.

However, the case for free trade is far from clear. As a matter of fact, developing countries that have liberalised too rapidly have suffered debilitating consequences. Furthermore, the vilification of government trade measures as protectionism fails to realise the important nurturing role trade measures have played in the developmental experience of the industrialised countries and economically successful developing countries today.

The negotiations should not result in rules that will compel the developing-country members of the WTO to liberalise trade at a rate and manner which is inconsistent with their development priorities. More importantly, the new rules should not deprive developing countries of using trade measures as part of their policy options in their industrial and economic development strategies. The negotiations should instead take into fullest consideration the articulated development needs and interests of the developing countries, and consequently culminate in rules that respect and recognise their need for policy space.

Free trade theory: some criticisms
Free trade theorists contend that the liberalisation of trade will lead to greater economic growth and thereby reduce poverty. This is achieved through a more efficient allocation of resources according to the theory of comparative advantage (see International Trade, this volume), as countries trade. More significantly, according to free trade enthusiasts the increase in income level and other positive spillovers that accompany trade liberalisation can cause the growth rate of the country to be placed on a higher path. Hence trade liberalisation which induces one-time static gains in economic efficiency could lead to a dynamic increase in the rate of economic growth (see USITC, 1997; Bhala, 2001). Consequently government interventions that do not pursue free trade end up preventing this 'naturally' beneficial economic phenomenon from taking place.

Unfortunately the reality is not so simple. Resources are not perfectly mobile as assumed in the standard theory of comparative advantage. The transfer of resources from one sector to another in reality is not so straightforward. The time and costs of reallocating resources are tremendous.

> Factors of production . . . are often sector specific or product specific. A car mechanic cannot instantly become a textile machine operator, or a lathe used in machine tools industries cannot be transformed into a sewing machine to be used in the clothing sector. Expansion into new products and sectors requires investment in skills and equipment, rather than reshuffling and redeploying existing labor and equipment. (Akyüz, 2005, p. 7)

Unless this is forthcoming, the overall impact of trade liberalisation could be a 'decline in industrial employment and value added as firms go out of business, as a result of import liberalization, and cannot be fully replaced by new firms in sectors enjoying greater competitiveness' (ibid.).

There are several examples of closure of firms and factories and loss of industrial jobs following trade liberalisation, which are detailed below.

More importantly, when the initial damage inflicted on industry is deep, the process of industrial restructuring in response to new incentives may be delayed and the economy could remain depressed for prolonged periods. Avoiding such an outcome would require a gradual and phased approach to import liberalization, properly sequenced with the build up of a strong and flexible industrial and export capacity through a judicious combination of market discipline and policy intervention. (ibid., p. 8)

In relation to its free traders' assertion that liberalisation will lead to growth, there is no clear theoretical prediction that trade liberalisation either increases or decreases the rate of economic growth. The proposed linkage between trade liberalisation and the sources of growth such as labour, capital and technology vary from model to model (see USITC, 1997; Bhala, 2001). As such there is 'much ambiguity over how this is achieved and little consensus about the impact of trade openness on economic growth' (Akyüz, 2005, p. 8).

Advocates of free trade have therefore resorted to empirical studies to demonstrate the positive impact of trade liberalisation on economic growth.

As in theory, there is also much debate over the empirical evidence regarding the benefits of trade liberalisation in developing countries. Studies trying to show that there is a causal link between liberalisation and growth have been unable to do so convincingly because of their methodological and conceptual weakness (Rodriguez and Rodrik, 1999).

One major problem in these studies has been the failure to define with consistency and precision the notion of trade openness. Another serious shortcoming is the lapse in logic where correlation is inadequately explained and confused for causation. Coterminous periods of openness and growth, might not be because the latter flowed from the former. It could easily be the other way round.

These studies are unable to demonstrate persuasively a positive linkage between trade openness and growth, and do not support the claim that more open developing countries do better in terms of growth than those which are not.

Doha Round of trade negotiations
Despite the critique and criticisms levelled, the idea of trade liberalisation has none the less shaped and structured the current round of trade negotiations taking place in the WTO. The Doha Ministerial Declaration adopted at the fourth ministerial meeting of the WTO declares 'international trade can play a major role in the promotion of economic development and the alleviation of poverty' (WTO, 2001, para. 2). Member countries reiterated their commitment to the process of trade reform and liberalisation and 'pledge[d] to reject the use of protectionism' (ibid., para. 1).

The 'free trade' theory is further concretised through the appended Doha work programme (WTO, 2004), committing the member countries of the WTO to augment the opening up of their economies and provide greater market access to each other's exports of goods and services (WTO, 2001, paras 13 and 16). This is to be done through a set of rules or modalities to be negotiated to reduce or remove member countries' protectionist trade policies such as tariffs and subsidies (ibid.).

This is the 'logic' of the system that has informed the negotiating context and content for the bargaining on market opening that is taking place among the member countries. This in turn has been seized upon selectively by the developed-country members in the negotiations to push for the assumption of new obligations that will harmonise developing-country members' trade measures and subject them to reduction and eventual removal.

More specifically in the context of the Doha Round of negotiations on industrial goods, developed-country members have proposed that all tariff lines of a member are to be brought within the WTO system through a process of binding; the tariff structure is then to be made uniform or harmonised so that the standard deviation from the average tariff rate of that country is diminished. The tariff rates are to be subjected to dramatic reduction and eventual removal (Khor and Goh, 2004).

These potential obligations and constraints on countries' tariff profiles weigh in favour of the developed-country members. With respect to industrial or non-agricultural products, developed-country members generally have a low average tariff of around 3–4 per cent. They have bound virtually all their tariffs (99 per cent) (Hoda, 2002). There is little disparity between their bound and applied rates. More importantly, developed countries are more competitive in producing industrial products and are their main exporters. However, it should be noted that the developed countries took several rounds of tariff renegotiations to achieve their current tariff structures, while at the same time deepening and developing their economies.

Developing-country members on the other hand have higher average bound tariffs at about 30 per cent. The level of bindings is also lower at about 71 per cent, and many African countries have very low binding levels (Hoda, 2002). The disparity between the bound and the applied is also more pronounced when compared to developed countries. It needs to be highlighted, however, that this does not reflect the fact that many developing countries have undertaken significant trade liberalisation and their effective applied rates are actually low.

Hence these proposals which are dominating the negotiations will entail more significant and far-reaching changes and implications for the trade regimes of developing rather than developed countries. More importantly, these proposals do not pay adequate consideration to and are inconsistent with the developmental needs and interests of developing countries.

Protecting development

These proposals run counter to the development experiences and practices of the industrialised countries and the more recently successful East Asian economies, where protective trade barriers had been critical to their industrial development.

As documented and observed by Shaffaedin (1998), Chang (2002) and others, 'with the exception of Hong Kong, no country has developed its industrial base without prior infant industry protection . . . In the process of industrialization and export expansion, functional and selective intervention in trade has been an important factor' (Shafaedin, 1998, p. 2).

Industrial development is critical to economic development:

> The basic policy challenge facing most developing countries is how to establish a broad and robust industrial base as the key to successful development, and how best to channel investment and trade to this end. Shifting away from dependence on the production and export of primary commodities towards industrial products has often been viewed as a means of more effective

participation in the international division of labour. Manufactures are expected to offer better prospects for export earnings not only because they allow for a more rapid productivity growth and expansion of production, but also because they hold out the promise of greater price stability even as volume expands, thereby avoiding the declining terms of trade that has frustrated the development efforts of many commodity dependent economies. (Akyüz, 2004, pp. 16–17)

According to the founder of infant industry protection theory, Frederick List (1856), there are four phases in the development of international trade and industrialisation: (1) the expansion of imports of manufactured goods; (2) the starting up of domestic production with the help of protection; (3) satisfaction of the domestic market; and finally (4) the massive expansion of their exports (see Shafaeddin, 2000a and b).

Commensurately, the tariff profiles should reflect this process of industrial development, higher tariffs for the product that is being produced domestically and lower tariffs for the imports of capital goods required to manufacture those products. After successful industrialisation, tariffs for the product being produced could then be reduced to enhance efficiency and productivity. As the industrialisation process matures, and the country begins to produce the capital goods that were originally imported, then tariff measures could be used to promote the development of the capacity to produce those capital goods.

The uniformity to the tariff structure that would be imposed by the international trade rules under negotiations and the unidirectional treatment of tariffs, in having them reduced, will curtail the developing-country members' policy space and options to pursue an efficacious industrialisation and development strategy.

Negative impact of liberalisation: deindustrialisation and unemployment

In addition, rapid and across-the-board liberalisation as advocated by the developed-country members in this round of negotiations would damage and undermine the nascent, weak and vulnerable industrial base of many developing countries, as well as exacerbate the unemployment situation.

Many local firms and industries are still too weak to withstand competition from a large inflow of cheaper imports resulting from the lowering of import barriers. In many developing countries that have a weak and vulnerable industrial base, rapid import liberalisation has led to reduced production or even outright closure of local firms and labour retrenchment, while there has been no evidence of shifting of the displaced capital or labour to more efficient industries. In many developing countries, there has been a weakening of the industrial sector, and even a process of 'deindustrialisation'.

Following trade liberalisation in 1990,

> [F]ormal sector job growth slowed to a trickle in Zimbabwe and unemployment rate jumped from 10 to 20 percent. Adjustment in the nineties has also been difficult for much of the manufacturing sector in Mozambique, Cameroon, Tanzania, Malawi, and Zambia. Import competition precipitated sharp contractions in output and employment in the short run, with many firms closing down operations entirely. (African Development Bank, 1998, pp. 45, 51, cited in Buffie, 2001, p. 190)

In Sierra Leone, Zambia, Zaire, Uganda, Tanzania and the Sudan, liberalisation in the 1980s brought a tremendous surge in consumer imports and sharp cutbacks in foreign exchange available for purchases of intermediate inputs and capital goods. The effects on industrial output and employment were devastating. In Uganda, for example, the capacity utilisation rate in the industrial sector languished at 22 per cent while consumer imports claimed 40–60 per cent of total foreign exchange (Loxley, 1989, cited in Buffie, 2001, p. 191).

Nor is the evidence from other parts of Latin America particularly encouraging: 'Liberalisation in the early nineties seems to have resulted in large job losses in the formal sector and a substantial worsening in underemployment in Peru, Nicaragua, Ecuador and Brazil' (Buffie, 2001, pp. 190–91).

Developing-country members are also urged to provide deeper market access in the agriculture sector under this round of WTO negotiations.

Some developing countries have experienced adverse consequences as a result of trade liberalisation in this sector. Studies by the UN FAO found that in the 14 developing countries it examined there was a 'general trend towards the consolidation of farms as competitive pressures began to build up following trade liberalisation' and this has led to 'the displacement and marginalization of farm labourers, creating hardship that involved typically small farmers and food insecure population groups' (FAO, 2000, p. 25).

The effects of import liberalisation can be negative and sometimes devastating, reducing their prospects for industrialisation and indeed in some cases destroying the domestic industrial base. It contradicts the orthodox approach that import liberalisation necessarily leads to growth.

Furthermore, given the tight financial constraints faced by many developing countries, deep cuts to their tariff rates as envisaged in the negotiations by the developed-country members would diminish the customs revenue which developing-country governments are dependent on.

The Doha development agenda and the objectives of trade negotiations

These fundamental developmental and fiscal concerns of developing countries are formally recognised in the current round of negotiations under the Doha mandate and the GATT/WTO agreement, through the principles of special and differential treatment and less than full reciprocity, where developing countries' need for more flexibility in the treatment of their tariffs is recognised (WTO, 2001, para. 50). More generally, the imperative to place the needs and interests of developing countries at the heart of this round of negotiations is explicitly articulated in the Doha Ministerial Declaration (ibid., para. 2).

However, as pointed out by many developing-country members, the ongoing negotiations have failed to take on board and effectively incorporate these principles and precepts.

There is clear remit under the Doha mandate to recognise developing countries' need to have the flexibility and ability to vary their tariff levels and trade measures in line with their development, financial and trade needs. This has to be incorporated and fully taken account of in the modalities and the results of the negotiations.

In ensuring the development of developing countries, which is after all the *raison d'être* of this round of negotiations, and cautioned by the experiences of deindustrialisation resulting from inappropriate liberalisation, it is important to state that the aim of negotiations is not to achieve trade liberalisation in itself. It should be recognised that trade is only a means, to be used when appropriate and to be used carefully while development is the goal.

CHIEN YEN GOH

References

Akyüz, Yilmaz (2005), 'Trade, growth and industrilization in developing countries: issues, experience and policy challenges', *TWN Trade and Development Series No. 28*, Penang, Malaysia: Third World Network.

Bhala, Raj (2001), *International Trade Law: Theory and Practice*, 2nd edn, New York: Lexis.

Buffie, Edward (2001), *Trade Policy in Developing Countries*, Cambridge and New York: Cambridge University Press.

Chang, Ha-Joon (2002), *Kicking Away the Ladder: Development Strategy in Historical Perspective*, London: Anthem.

FAO (2000), *Agriculture, Trade and Food Security: Issues and Options in the WTO Negotiations from the Perspective of Developing Countries, Vol. II: Country Case Studies*, Rome: Food and Agriculture Organization.

Hoda, Anwarul (2002), *Tariff Negotiations and Re-Negotiations Under the GATT and the WTO: Procedures and Practices*, Cambridge: Cambridge University Press.

Khor, Martin and Goh Chien Yen (2004), 'The WTO negotiations on non agricultural market access: a development perspective', mimeo, Third World Network.

List, Frederick (1856), *National System of Political Economy*, Philadelphia, PA: Lippincott.

Rodriguez, Francisco and Dani Rodrik (1999), 'Trade policy and economic growth: a skeptic's guide to cross national evidence', NBER Working Paper no. 7081, National Bureau of Economic Research, Cambridge, MA.

Shafaeddin, Mehdi (1998), 'How did developed countries industrialise? The history of trade and industrial policy: the cases of Great Britain and the USA', UNCTAD Discussion Paper no. 139, UNCTAD, Geneva, www.unctad.org/en/docs/dp_139.en.pdf.

Shafaeddin, Mehdi (2000a), 'What did Frederick List actually say? Some clarifications on the infant industry argument', UNCTAD Discussion Paper no. 149, UNCTAD, Geneva, www.unctad.org/en/docs/dp_149.en.pdf.

Shafaeddin, Medhi (2000b), 'Free trade or fair trade? An enquiry into the causes of failure in recent trade negotiations', UNCTAD Discussion Paper no. 153, UNCTAD, Geneva, www.unctad.org/en/docs/dp_153.en.pdf.

USITC (1997), 'The dynamic effects of trade liberalization: an empirical analysis', Investigation No. 332-375, Publication 3069, United States International Trade Commission, Washington, DC, http://hotdocs.usitc.gov/docs/pubs/332/PUB3069.PDF.

WTO (2001), Doha Ministerial Declaration, WT/MIN(01)/DEC/1, Adopted on 14 November 2001, World Trade Organization, Geneva, www.wto.org/english/thewto_e/minist_e/min01_e/mindecl_e.pdf.

WTO (2004), 'Doha work program', General Council Decision of 1 August 2004, WT/L/579, World Trade Organization, Geneva, www.wto.org/english/tratop_e/dda_e/draft_text_gc_dg_31july04_e.htm.

Transition

'Transition' is a term which is widely used to describe the transformation of state socialist countries, which were characterised by state-controlled economies and political dictatorship, into democratic market economies. Transition in this sense is a phenomenon which began in 1989 when a number of countries (Poland, Hungary, Czechoslovakia and East Germany) freed themselves from Soviet control or domestic tyranny (Romania and Albania in 1991–92). It was extended to the former Soviet Union in 1992 after the dismantling of the USSR in December 1991.

The question arises whether China and Vietnam, which have also been transforming their economies in a market direction, should also be considered transition economies. This is controversial. Some international financial institutions such as the World Bank treat China and Vietnam as transition economies. On the other hand, the European Bank for Reconstruction and Development, which was set up to help finance transition, confines itself to the former USSR and the former Eastern Europe.

There are two (non-geographical) reasons for excluding China and Vietnam from the category of transition economies. First, the political processes in those countries are different from those in the countries of the former Soviet Union (FSU) and the former Eastern Europe. The countries in the last two categories (with some exceptions such as Belarus, Turkmenistan and Uzbekistan where political power has been captured by undemocratic elites) have undergone a dramatic democratisation process. In some of them (such as the Central European and Baltic countries) it is reasonable to assert that they have completed this process. In others (for example, Russia) great progress has been made, even if the current system does not entirely meet democratic criteria. On the other hand, in China and Vietnam power remains in the hands of the leaders of the Communist Party, legal opposition is not possible, and the population does not have any chance to choose the national leadership.

Second, the main aim of China's leaders has not been system change but economic growth. The system has been changed in a way intended to facilitate growth, and growth has resulted. However, system change as such has not been a goal.

As understood by mainstream economic opinion at the outset of the process, economic transition consisted mainly of stabilisation, liberalisation and privatisation. Stabilisation referred to the need to reduce inflation, both open and suppressed, and establish balance-of-payments equilibrium. For this a standard package of fiscal, monetary (and sometimes exchange rate and incomes policy) measures was recommended, together with price liberalisation so as to eliminate suppressed inflation (shortages and queues). Experience has shown that such packages if persisted in are successful in reducing disequilibrium, but that:

1. the political costs may be such as to make it impossible to persist in their implementation (as in Yugoslavia in 1990 where the adoption of such a package was one of the factors leading to the break-up of the country);
2. the time taken for the package to work may be far longer than anticipated (in Poland a stabilisation package was adopted at the beginning of 1990, but it was only nine years later, in 1999, that inflation finally fell below 10 per cent per annum);
3. it may contribute to a sharp decline in output and welfare (as in Russia after the unsuccessful attempt at shock therapy by Finance Minister, and subsequently acting Prime Minister, Yegor Gaidar at the beginning of 1992); and
4. one of the main aims, reducing inflation to a single-figure annual rate, is not actually a necessary condition for economic growth in post-socialist countries (as the experience first of Poland and then of Russia showed).

Liberalisation means the liberalising of prices, by removing or reducing subsidies and price controls (so that prices can reflect supply and demand and not cause shortages and queues), of internal trade (so that traders can meet market demand) and of external trade (to enable the country to take full advantage of the international division of labour). Liberalising prices was essential to the emergence of a market economy. However, sudden liberalisation under disequilibrium conditions gave rise to 'corrective inflation' (that is, the immediate price rises necessary to bring supply and demand into equilibrium) and, where fiscal policy remained destabilising, it gave rise to continued inflation (as in the CIS

(Commonwealth of Independent States) countries). Liberalising internal trade made more goods available and generated extra income, but was also a bonanza for protection racketeers, sellers of fake goods and tax evaders. Liberalising international trade was a major factor in overcoming the former shortages and queues, but frequently caused serious production declines by introducing international competition in previously protected markets and also facilitated capital flight (via various tricks such as double invoicing).

Privatisation was thought to be crucial for both political and economic reasons. Politically it created powerful interest groups with a stake in transition and strongly opposed to a restoration of the old system (which would have led to the loss of their newly acquired property). In addition it secured support and money from the West. Economically it was thought that only privately owned enterprises could operate successfully in a market economy. Experience has shown that:

1. at any rate in Central Europe, economic growth has come mainly not from newly privatised formerly state-owned enterprises, but from *de novo* enterprises, that is, newly created enterprises (which often use assets acquired from (formerly) state-owned enterprises);
2. the quick privatisation of the entire national economy often degenerates into large-scale looting. Although this is quick, and Coase-efficient, it undermines political support for the resulting social system by redistributing wealth to a small elite;
3. complete privatisation is not a necessary condition for economic growth. For example, in Poland a large part of the economy remained state owned years after economic growth resumed; and
4. the design of privatisation programmes has been more important for enterprise performance than initially expected. Some ownership reforms, such as voucher privatisation in the Czech Republic, introduced principal–agent problems by diluting ownership or by failing to result in control over management and incentives to raise efficiency and profitability.

In addition to these *intended* processes, the transition countries have also been marked by some *unintended* processes. Of these, the most important have been economic contraction, impoverishment, informalisation, increased corruption, demographic changes, criminalisation, capital flight and polarisation.

Although many economists expected immediate economic growth as a result of efficiency gains, the transition countries of the former Eastern Europe and the FSU (but not China and Vietnam which experienced prolonged high growth) experienced a huge economic contraction of between 18 and 75 per cent in the first few reform years. This led to a sharp decline in formal sector employment throughout the region. Although all have registered positive (but not always continuous) growth after this initial collapse, even in 2002 most of them had real GDP figures below the pre-transition level. The reasons for this depression are still a subject of debate, and may include disorganisation; state desertion; the absence (at any rate in some countries) of functioning markets for factors of production; an inheritance of military, value-subtracting and uneconomically located production for which there was little or no demand under the new circumstances; time lags which prevented the expansion of increased profit sectors being able to compensate immediately for the decline of reduced profit sectors; a fall in demand; and international competition.

A dramatic result of transition has been a huge increase in the absolute numbers of the poor and of their share in the total population. According to World Bank data, between 1987–88 (just before the beginning of transition) and 1993–95 (soon after its beginning), the share of the poor in the total population of (the former) Eastern Europe and the FSU rose from about 3 to about 25 per cent and in absolute numbers from 7 million to 89 million (Milanovic, 1998, pp. 67–77). This means that one of the first results of transition was to push more than a fifth of the population concerned below the poverty line. Children were particularly badly affected by increased poverty. With the resumption of economic growth, first in Central Europe and the Baltic countries, and subsequently in Russia and the other CIS countries, it is to be hoped that the share of the population in poverty will gradually decline.

A major result of the transition has been the emergence of a large informal sector of the economy. Partly this concerns new, often micro, enterprises which wish to escape the attention of bureaucrats, criminals and the tax authorities. Partly it concerns enterprises which already existed under the old system. These undertake substantial volumes of activity 'off the books' and make extensive use of barter. In addition there has been a widespread informalisation of the labour market. This takes the form of extensive unilateral management determination of wages and conditions, regardless of laws about these matters, disregard by employers of workers' rights to be paid on time, to receive paid maternity leave, to be protected from dangerous working conditions or to be represented by trade unions.

Transition has led to an increase in corruption (this has also happened in China and Vietnam). Indeed, in some countries kleptocracy has become an important part of the political system. This growth of corruption resulted from the new opportunities for enrichment and the widespread failure to introduce and enforce appropriate legal and cultural norms.

A striking feature of the transition was the demographic changes. There has been a significant increase in mortality, concentrated among adult men in Russia and Ukraine. This substantially increased the gender gap in life expectancy in Russia and Ukraine (women in Russia in 2000 had a life expectancy 13 years greater than that for men). It has also led to a huge gap between male life expectancy in Russia and Ukraine and that in the rest of Europe (in 2001 male life expectancy in Russia was only 59, which was 17 years less than the EU average). The explanation of these mass deaths among adult male Russians and Ukrainians is controversial. To what extent they are linked to the transition, and if they are linked to the nature of the transmission mechanism(s), are unclear. There was also a dramatic decline in fertility. Whether this should be considered a healthy process of Europeanisation, or a symptom of social stress, is controversial. The combined result of current trends in fertility, mortality and migration is that the population of many of the countries of the former Eastern Europe and the European FSU is expected to decline markedly in the coming decades.

A significant feature of transition has been the growth of crime and the widespread criminalisation of society. This has been particularly marked in the CIS countries. An important feature of these countries in the 1990s was the development of close links between the criminal, political and business worlds. Many economists have connected criminalisation with the inability of the state to perform even its night watchman functions. Hence the supply of property protection and rule enforcement was privatised, that is, taken over by criminal organisations.

Capital flight was a major factor in a number of countries, in particular in Russia in the 1990s, which resulted from the perceived insecurity of property in that country. This was caused by the absence of the rule of law, the political uncertainty during the Yeltsin period, criminalisation, and the legal right of the tax authorities and certain other bodies to help themselves to the contents of bank accounts without the prior agreement of the account-holder.

Transition has seen a sharp polarisation within and between countries. Within countries, inequality has increased significantly. This increase seems to be least in Central Europe and greatest in the CIS countries. Between countries, inequality has also increased. At the beginning of the twenty-first century there are a number of fairly successful countries (such as the eight new EU members – Slovenia, Czech Republic, Slovakia, Hungary, Poland, Lithuania, Latvia and Estonia) and many unsuccessful countries (such as Albania, Romania, Moldova, Ukraine, Belarus, Kyrgyzstan, Tadjikstan and Turkmenistan).

The main intellectual issue raised by the experience of transition has been the limitations of orthodox economics and its policy recommendations. Were the unexpected and disagreeable phenomena outlined above an inevitable result of the collapse of the old system (and in some cases of the very states themselves) or was it (partly) a result of bad policy and of the theory which underlay it? An important result of this debate, which has been long and sometimes acrimonious, has been the general recognition of the importance of the institutional environment within which economic activity takes place, of the need for an effective public administration, of the benefits of strategic integration into the world economy, and of the need to consider the social aspects of economic policy.

Initially, 'transition' was seen as a victory for Adam Smith and the doctrine of the 'invisible hand'. After some years of experience, however, it was increasingly realised that free prices and markets alone are insufficient to ensure economic growth in a healthy socioeconomic context. Hence, currently transition is widely seen as a *partial* vindication of Adam Smith, but also as a vindication of Karl Polanyi and his stress on the role of the state in creating markets, of Douglass North and the new institutional economics, of Thomas Hobbes and the need for a strong – but limited – state to protect property and enforce the economic rules of the game, of Deng Xiaoping and the benefits of strategic integration with the world economy, and of the Bismarck–Roosevelt–Beveridge stress on the need for welfare programmes to provide social support for the market economy.

MICHAEL ELLMAN

References and further reading

Beyer, J., J. Wielgohs and H. Wiesenthal (eds) (2001), *Successful Transitions*, Baden-Baden: Nomos.
Blanchard, O. and M. Kremer (1997), 'Disorganization', *Quarterly Journal of Economics*, **112** (4), 1091–126.
Buiter, W. (2000), 'From predation to accumulation?', *Economics of Transition*, **8** (3), 603–22.
Campos, N.F. and F. Coricelli (2002), 'Growth in transition: what we know, what we don't, and what we should', *Journal of Economic Literature*, **40** (3), 793–836.
Coase, R.H. (1992), 'The institutional structure of production', *American Economic Review*, **82** (4), 713–19.

Cornia, G.A. and R. Paniccià (eds) (2000), *The Mortality Crisis in Transitional Economies*, Oxford: Oxford University Press.

Dudwick, N., E. Gomarth, M. Alexandre and K. Keuhast (eds) (2003), *When Things Fall Apart: Qualitative Studies of Poverty in the Former Soviet Union*, Washington, DC: World Bank.

Economic Survey of Europe (biannual), New York and Geneva: United Nations.

Estrin, S. (2002), 'Competition and corporate governance in transition', *Journal of Economic Perspectives*, **16** (1), 101–24.

Granville, B. and P. Oppenheimer (eds) (2001), *Russia's Post-Communist Economy*, Oxford: Oxford University Press.

Kolodko, W. (2000), *From Shock to Therapy: The Political Economy of Postsocialist Transformation*, Oxford: Oxford University Press.

Kontorovich, V. (1996), 'Imperial legacy and the transformation of the Russian economy', *Transition* (Prague), **2** (17), 22–5.

Lokshin, M. and M. Ravallion (2000), 'Welfare impacts of the 1998 financial crisis in Russia and the response of the public safety net', *Economics of Transition*, **8** (2), 269–95.

Megginson, W.L. and J.M. Netter, (2001), 'From state to market: a survey of empirical studies on privatization', *Journal of Economic Literature*, **39** (2), 321–89.

Milanovic, B. (1998), *Income, Inequality and Poverty during the Transition from Planned to Market Economy*, Washington, DC: World Bank.

Naughton, B. (1993). 'Deng Xiaoping: the economist', *China Quarterly*, **135**, 491–514.

North, D. (1994), 'Economic performance through time', *American Economic Review*, **84** (3), 359–68.

Polishchuk, L. (1997), 'Missed markets: implications for economic behaviour and institutional changes', in J.M. Nelson, C. Tilley and L. Walker (eds), *Transforming Post-Communist Political Economies*, Washington, DC: National Academy Press, pp. 80–101.

Pomfret, R. (1997) 'Growth and transition: why has China's performance been so different?', *Journal of Comparative Economics*, **25** (4), 422–40.

Popov, V. (2000), 'Shock therapy versus gradualism: the end of the debate', *Comparative Economic Studies*, **42** (1), 1–57.

Rawski, T. (2001), 'What is happening to China's GDP statistics?', *China Economic Review*, **12** (4), 347–54.

Roland, G. (2000), *Transition and Economics*, Cambridge, MA: MIT Press.

Singh, A. (1995), 'The causes of fast economic growth in East Asia', in *UNCTAD Review 1995*, New York and Geneva: United Nations, pp. 91–128.

Transition (newsletter), World Bank, Washington, DC.

Transition Report (annual), European Bank for Reconstruction and Development, London.

Walder, A.G. (1995), 'China's transitional economy: interpreting its significance', *China Quarterly*, **144**, 963–79.

World Bank (2000), *Making Transition Work for Everyone: Poverty and Inequality in Europe and Central Asia*, Washington, DC: World Bank.

World Bank (2002a), *Building Institutions for Markets*, Oxford and New York: Oxford University Press.

World Bank (2002b), *Transition – The First Ten Years: Analysis and Lessons for Eastern Europe and the Former Soviet Union*, Washington, DC: World Bank.

Transnational Corporations

The operations of transnational corporations (TNCs) in less-developed countries (LDCs) have become an increasingly important and controversial aspect of the global economy. Collectively, TNCs – defined as companies with operations and employees in more than one country – command vast financial resources, global brands, marketing expertise, advanced technologies, and integrated production networks encompassing subsidiaries and extensive corporate alliances, which place them at the very centre of the process of economic globalisation. Since the mid-1980s and the broad shift in LDC economic policy towards less state intervention and fewer restrictions on foreign investment, the strategic decisions of TNCs have become even more important in the determination of the location of productive activity. The first section of this entry will describe some of the key theories that attempt to explain the phenomenon of the TNC and 'international production'. The second section will discuss some of the main policy issues regarding TNCs that confront developing countries.

Theories of the TNC

The TNC has always occupied an anomalous position in economic theory. It straddles the divide between international capital movements (a province of macroeconomics), on the one hand, and industrial economics and the theory of the firm (both areas of microeconomic analysis), on the other. Since the 1960s, studies have largely focused upon firm-level analyses that have progressively developed our knowledge of the TNC as a distinct economic actor endowed with a complex package of motivations and resources. The following section will provide a brief overview of some of the major theoretical perspectives on the TNC (for a survey of the literature, see Caves, 1996).

Until the 1960s, despite the long-standing interest of institutional economists in the study of the firm as an economic organisation and the development of theories of imperfect competition, mainstream economic thinking, in the words of Edith Penrose, 'continued to treat direct private foreign investment within the traditional framework of the pricing system and thus simply as capital flows determined by international differences in the rate of return on capital'. In terms of economic thinking, therefore, TNCs in the developing world were seen simply as an instrument through which capital was transferred from wealthy countries with abundant capital earning low returns to poor, capital-scarce countries where it earned high returns. Moreover, conceived in these terms, TNC operations were unequivocally benign and supportive of economic development.

This traditional conception of TNC operations was decisively challenged by Steven Hymer (1976) in his 1960 doctoral dissertation at the Massachusetts Institute of Technology, a contribution that marked the beginning of the modern analysis of international production. Hymer found that neither the geographical distribution of FDI nor the motivations of TNCs could be adequately explained by differences in interest rates, even when adjusted for risk. Instead, Hymer located the mainspring of international production in competitive conditions in particular markets, thus moving the locus of analysis to the industry or firm level. At the firm level, he identified three influences that could potentially propel a company to become a TNC: (1) the possession of ownership or monopolistic advantages which could be effectively transferred to foreign markets; (2) the removal of conflict through mergers of large firms in different countries; and (3) the internalisation of structural market imperfections. By opening these new vistas to economic analysis, he also encouraged economists to develop a more holistic conception of the TNC as a bundle of attributes and resources rather than as a simple agent of capital transfer. The various supply-side theories that are now dominant in the study of TNCs can trace their lineage, in varying degrees, to different aspects of Hymer's framework.

Richard Caves (1971) and Charles Kindleberger (1984) developed Hymer's hypothesis that the possession of ownership or monopolistic advantages by a company was a key factor motivating its decision to become a TNC. Since TNCs operating in foreign markets have certain intrinsic disadvantages relative to local firms (such as cultural and language barriers, knowledge of local market conditions, and a relative lack of business and governmental connections), they must possess exploitable advantages to offset them. For almost all TNCs, monopolistic advantages in the form of proprietary control over advanced technology and production processes, global brands, and institutional expertise in marketing, finance and management confer competitive advantages that overcome their disadvantages in foreign production. In contrast to the traditional 'benign' conception of TNC operations, this analysis suggests that the very existence of TNCs is based upon monopolistic advantages over domestic firms that, at least potentially, could impose welfare costs on the host country. While Kindleberger believed that the welfare benefits of TNC operations outweighed their costs, other analysts, such as Jenkins (1987), have emphasised the potential inefficiencies arising from the market power of TNCs and the possibility of collusive conduct between them.

While Hymer noted that the internalisation of market imperfections was a motivating factor in expanding the boundaries of the firm to encompass foreign operations, it was left to other economists, among them Williamson (1975) and Buckley and Casson (1976), to further develop the concept. The essential insight was provided by Ronald Coase's (1937) seminal article in which he argued that administered exchanges within the firm were efficient responses to transaction costs associated with the price mechanism. When the costs of market-based, arm's-length exchanges (arising from, among other factors, opportunism, asset specificity, bounded rationality and uncertainty) exceed those of administered exchanges, the boundary of the firm expands in order to reduce transaction costs. In the context of the TNC, this analysis suggests that coordinating the actions of agents in different countries through market-based transactions is less efficient than administrated exchanges within the TNC. Thus, depending on the type of foreign operations, by becoming a TNC a firm is internalising key markets, such as technology, managerial know-how, reputation, distribution or raw materials (Hennart, 2000).

John Dunning (1981, 2000), in both his 'eclectic' and 'ownership, location, internalisation' (OLI) paradigms, has, in addition to bringing the 'monopolistic advantages' and 'internalisation' theories together, brought in location-specific factors influencing foreign investment. As such, these paradigms do not purport to explain the TNC as a firm, but rather to explain the pattern of foreign investments they undertake. Although they are not discrete theories, they provide an analytical framework within which the complex phenomena of TNCs and international production can be empirically investigated and the connections between the various theories studied.

Within the heterodox tradition in economics, there is an extensive literature devoted to foreign investment and the TNC. Marxist writers, such as Rosa Luxemburg, and Baran and Sweezy (1966), argued that because of deficient effective demand (underconsumption) and falling profit rates, capitalist economies were intrinsically unstable. These periodic crises would effectively drive capitalist firms to foreign countries in search of new markets and higher profits. In order to facilitate this process, the capitalist state pursues imperialistic policies to open new frontiers for exploitation by transnational capital. In essence, if not in its particulars, the Marxist perspective also influenced many 'dependency' theorists, particularly in Latin America, who viewed TNCs as a central part of the mechanism that relegated developing countries on the periphery of the world system to permanent economic and technological backwardness. The clear policy implication was that TNCs were inimical to economic development and should therefore be excluded from the national economy altogether or heavily regulated to ensure that their operations conformed to the national interest.

A more modern example of the heterodox perspective is provided by Peoples and Sugden (2000), who view TNC operations through the prism of its distributional effects on capital and labour. They argue that TNCs leverage their control over highly mobile global capital to extract concessions from an immobile pool of labour isolated in national economies. Consequently, TNCs are able to pursue a policy of 'divide and rule' which weakens labour unions and shifts the distribution of profits decisively in capital's favour. In their view, international production is in part an attempt to control labour markets, and the objective of pursuing a divide-and-rule policy provides an explanation for the very existence of TNCs.

Policy issues

While TNC activity is still largely concentrated in the Triad (United States, Europe and Japan), an analysis of FDI inflows reveals that in the 1990s an increasing share was being directed towards LDCs. While LDCs accounted for a quarter of global FDI inflows in the 1970s and 1980s, in the 1990s their share rose to an average of 32 per cent (UNCTAD, 2002). TNC activities, however, extend beyond FDI to encompass non-equity alliances, research consortia, joint ventures, turnkey plants, licensing agreements and tight relationships with key suppliers. While the evidence indicates that TNC activities are heavily concentrated in the Triad and in a select group of developing countries, it also suggests that they are becoming increasingly important, in both a quantitative and qualitative sense, in an expanding number of LDCs.

Consequently, the policy issues surrounding TNC operations in LDCs, ranging from labour standards and intellectual property rights to corporate taxation and competition policy, have been given renewed prominence. Over the coming decade, LDCs will have to confront them domestically, bilaterally, and in the multilateral negotiations of the World Trade Organization (WTO) (for an overview, see Brewer and Young, 1998). The remainder of this entry will briefly outline the issues of competition policy and labour standards as they relate to TNCs, as well as comment on the broader question of TNC-led development.

As the 'monopolistic advantages' theory argued, TNCs possess, as a condition for their existence, strong competitive advantages over domestic rivals. In view of these advantages, coupled with their greater size, reputation and command over resources, TNC operations can have potentially adverse effects on the competitive environment in LDCs. By driving domestic firms out of the market (or indeed, by acquiring them) and inhibiting market entry, TNCs may diminish economic welfare by reducing output and raising prices. The continued expansion of TNC operations, therefore, means that it is imperative for LDCs to develop appropriate and effective competition policies (an aspect of economic policy that has been historically neglected in LDCs) and the institutional capacities to enforce them. In this connection, it is important to note that an effective competition policy and the drive to attract TNC investment can easily come into conflict. By granting subsidies to TNCs (either directly or through tax concessions) or by providing them with trade protection, LDCs can promote these anti-competitive and welfare-reducing effects.

Thus, a judicious balance must be struck between encouraging TNC investment and promoting competition by denying it a privileged position. In the multilateral context, the trend towards mergers and acquisitions among large TNCs that have potentially anti-competitive implications for LDC markets requires that developing countries become more closely involved in the formulation of an effective global competition strategy.

Access to cheap labour, while not the only motivating factor driving TNC investment in LDCs, is none the less a central consideration. With the expansion of export-orientated TNC operations (including both direct investment and subcontractor plants) in LDCs that supply highly competitive developed-country markets, the incentive to find low-wage sites that minimise costs has only increased over time. While working conditions and the treatment of workers vary considerably among plants, there are many instances in which these low wages are associated with sweatshop conditions, particularly in labour-intensive consumer goods such as garments, toys and sports equipment. While this issue clearly requires addressing from an ethical standpoint, it is also essential from a practical, policy perspective. A country that fails to raise the skills, wages and working conditions of its workforce consistently over time will risk limiting its competitive advantage to low labour costs and will be vulnerable to competition from still lower-wage countries. There are three areas in which LDCs must work to address this problem: (1) multilateral fora such as the WTO and the ILO; (2) voluntary measures for TNCs encompassing codes of conduct, certification mechanisms and compliance labelling; and (3) more effective national regulation and enforcement in LDCs. Beyond legal measures, a sustained policy of upgrading skills and technological capacities is required so that the country can move beyond those industry sectors where these conditions are the most prevalent (for a full discussion of this issue, see Moran, 2002).

While there are challenges that LDCs must confront in dealing with the power of TNCs, such as promoting competition and improving labour standards, it is important to note the more positive side of the ledger. In conjunction with effective government policies, TNCs can provide a powerful lever for economic development. The TNC comprises a powerful 'package' of both physical (technology, capital) and intangible assets (business techniques, management skills, marketing capabilities and so on), which can be harnessed by LDCs to penetrate international markets, upgrade skills, and transform domestic technological capabilities. However, contrary to some of the more euphoric assessments of TNCs, they are not a *deus ex machina* that, left to themselves, ensure economic development. Singapore, perhaps the country that has relied the most on TNC-led development, has also aggressively and successfully pursued policies to develop its competitive advantages that, over time, enable the country to move up the knowledge-value hierarchies within the TNC production networks. These policies have included, among others, a focus on education, improvements in infrastructure and public administration, and the promotion of strong linkages between TNCs and domestic firms. This reflected the understanding of Singaporean policy makers that instead of a passive 'trickle-down' strategy, domestic capabilities had to be 'built up' to take full advantage of TNC investment (ibid.). Thus, far from receding into the background within the context of TNC-led development, judicious, effective and proactive government policy remains a central determinant of economic success.

BRUCE WEISSE

References

Baran, P. and P. Sweezy (1966), *Monopoly Capital*, Harmondsworth: Penguin.
Brewer, T. and S. Young (1998), *The Multilateral Investment System and Multinational Enterprises*, Oxford: Oxford University Press.
Buckley, P. and M. Casson (1976), *The Future of Multinational Enterprise*, London: Macmillan.
Caves, Richard (1971), 'International corporations: the industrial economics of foreign investment', *Economica*, **38**, 1–27.
Caves, Richard (1996), *Multinational Enterprise and Economic Analysis*, 2nd edn, Cambridge: Cambridge University Press.
Coase, R. (1937), 'The nature of the firm', *Economica*, **4**, 386–405.
Dunning, John (1981), *International Production and Multinational Enterprise*, London: Allen & Unwin.
Dunning, John (2000), 'The eclectic paradigm of international production: a personal perspective', in C. Pitelis and R. Sugden (eds), *The Nature of the Transnational Firm*, 2nd edn, London: Routledge, pp. 119–39.
Hennart, J.-F. (2000), 'Transaction costs theory and the multinational enterprise', in C. Pitelis and R. Sugden (eds), *The Nature of the Transnational Firm*, 2nd edn, London: Routledge, pp. 72–118.
Hymer, Steven (1976), *The International Operations of National Firms: A Study of Foreign Direct Investment*, Cambridge, MA: MIT Press.
Jenkins, R. (1987), *Transnational Corporations and Uneven Development*, London: Methuen.
Kindleberger, Charles (1984), *Multinational Excursions*, Cambridge, MA: MIT Press.
Moran, Theodore (2002), *Beyond Sweatshops*, Washington, DC: Brookings Institution.
Peoples, J. and R. Sugden (2000), 'Divide and rule by transnational corporations', in C. Pitelis and R. Sugden (eds), *The Nature of the Transnational Firm*, 2nd edn, London: Routledge, pp. 174–92.
UNCTAD (2002), *World Investment Report*, New York and Geneva: United Nations.
Williamson, Oliver (1975), *Markets and Hierarchies*, New York: Free Press.

Uneconomic Growth

Uneconomic growth in theory
We are discovering that the limit to economic growth is the beginning of a phase of uneconomic growth. But can growth in GNP in fact be uneconomic? Before answering this macroeconomic question let us consider the analogous question in microeconomics – can growth in a microeconomic activity (firm production or household consumption) be uneconomic? Of course it can. Indeed, all of microeconomics is simply a variation on the theme of seeking the optimal scale or extent of each micro activity – the point where increasing marginal cost equals declining marginal benefit, and beyond which further growth in the activity would be uneconomic because it would increase costs more than benefits. Quite aptly, the $MB = MC$ condition is sometimes called the 'when to stop rule'.

But when we move to macroeconomics we no longer hear anything about optimal scale, or about marginal costs and benefits; nor is there anything like a 'when to stop rule'. Instead of separate accounts of costs and benefits compared at the margin we have just one account, GNP, which conflates cost and benefits into the single category of 'economic activity'. The faith is that activity overwhelmingly reflects benefits. There is no macroeconomic analogue of costs of activity to balance against and hold in check the growth of 'activity', identified with benefit, and measured by GNP. Unique among economic magnitudes, GNP is supposed to grow forever.

But of course there really are costs incurred by GNP growth, even if not usually measured. There are costs of depletion, pollution, disruption of ecological life-support services, sacrifice of leisure time, disutility of some kinds of labour, destruction of community in the interests of capital and labour mobility, takeover of habitat of other species, and running down a critical part of the inheritance of future generations. We not only fail to measure these costs, but frequently we implicitly count them as benefits, as when we include the costs of cleaning up pollution as a part of GNP, and when we fail to deduct for depreciation of renewable natural capital (productive capacity), and liquidation of non-renewable natural capital (inventories).

There is no a priori reason why at the margin the costs of growth in GNP could not be greater than the benefits. In fact, economic theory would lead us to expect that eventually to happen. The law of diminishing marginal utility of income tells us that we satisfy our most pressing wants first, and that each additional unit of income is dedicated to the satisfaction of a less pressing want. So the marginal benefit of growth declines. Similarly, the law of increasing marginal costs tells us that we first make use of the most productive and accessible factors of production – the most fertile land, the most concentrated and available mineral deposits, the best workers – and only use the less-productive factors as growth makes it necessary. Consequently, marginal costs increase with growth. When rising marginal costs equal falling marginal benefits then we are at the optimal level of

GNP (a measure of activity, remember, not welfare!), and further growth would be uneconomic – would increase costs more than it increased benefits.

Why is this simple extension of the basic logic of microeconomics treated as inconceivable in the domain of macroeconomics? Mainly because microeconomics deals with the part, and expansion of a part is limited by the opportunity cost inflicted on the rest of the whole. In a finite whole, growth of one part encroaches on other parts, imposing an opportunity cost. Macroeconomics deals with the whole, and the growth of the whole does not inflict an opportunity cost, because it does not encroach on anything – there is no 'rest of the whole' to suffer the cost. Ecological economists have pointed out that the macro economy is not the relevant whole, but is itself a part, a subsystem of the ecosystem, the larger economy of nature. Consequently, the expansion of the macro economy does encroach on a larger limited whole, it does not just expand into the infinite void, and therefore macroeconomic growth really does incur an opportunity cost.

The end of physical growth, or even growth of a value-weighted index of physical growth like GNP, is not the end of progress. Uneconomic growth is not the only thing that lies beyond growth. There is also the possibility of a biophysically steady-state economy in which the technical arts, as well as the art of living, go on improving even after population and capital stock have stopped growing. Many years ago John Stuart Mill envisaged just such an economy of biophysical equilibrium and moral growth. To avoid uneconomic growth we must learn to seek qualitative improvement, development, within the context of a biophysical steady state. However, we do not at present seek the alternative of a steady state because we do not recognise either the concept or the reality of 'uneconomic growth'.

No one is arguing that poverty is better than wealth – we all prefer wealth. The question is, does growth, as we measure it, really make us wealthier at the margin? Or might it not in reality be making us poorer? Has economic growth become uneconomic growth – or in John Ruskin's prescient words, could it not be that 'That which seems to be wealth may in verity be only the gilded index of far-reaching ruin' (Ruskin, 1860, p. 23).

Uneconomic growth in fact
One might accept the theoretical possibility of uneconomic growth, but argue that it is irrelevant for practical purposes since, it could be alleged, we are nowhere near the optimal scale. Economists all agree that GNP was not designed to be a measure of welfare, but only of activity. Nevertheless they assume that welfare is positively correlated with activity, so that increasing GNP will increase welfare, even if not on a one-for-one basis. This is equivalent to believing that the marginal benefit of GNP growth is greater than the marginal cost. This belief can be put to an empirical test. The results, for the United States and some other countries, turn out not to support the belief.

Evidence for doubting the positive correlation between GNP and welfare in the United States is taken from two sources.

First Nordhaus and Tobin (1973) asked, 'Is growth obsolete?' as a measure of welfare, and hence as a proper guide to policy. To answer their question they developed a direct index of welfare, called Measured Economic Welfare (MEW) and tested its correlation with GNP over the 1929–65 period. They found that, for the period as a whole, GNP and MEW were indeed positively correlated – for every six units of increase in GNP there was, on average, a four-unit increase in MEW. Economists breathed a sigh of relief, forgot about MEW, and concentrated again on GNP. Although GNP was not designed as a measure of welfare, it was and still is thought to be sufficiently well correlated with welfare to serve as a practical guide for policy.

Some 20 years later John Cobb, Clifford Cobb and I revisited the issue and began development of our Index of Sustainable Economic Welfare (ISEW) with a review of the Nordhaus and Tobin MEW. We discovered that if one takes only the latter half of their time series (that is, the 18 years from 1947 to 1965) the positive correlation between GNP and MEW *falls* dramatically. In this most recent period – surely the more relevant for projections into the future – a six-unit increase in GNP yielded on average only a one-unit increase in MEW. This suggests that GNP growth at this stage of the United States' history may be a quite inefficient way of improving economic welfare – certainly less efficient than in the past.

The ISEW was developed to replace MEW, since the latter omitted any correction for environmental costs, did not correct for distributional changes, and included leisure, which both dominated the MEW and introduced many arbitrary valuation decisions. The ISEW, like the MEW, though less so, was positively correlated with GNP up to a point (around 1980) beyond which the correlation turned slightly negative. Neither the MEW nor the ISEW considered the effect of individual country GNP growth on the *global* environment, and consequently on welfare of citizens of other countries. Nor was there any deduction for legal harmful products, such as tobacco or alcohol, or for illegal harmful products such as drugs. No deduction was made for diminishing marginal utility of income resulting from growth over time (although there was a distributional correction for the higher marginal utility of income to the poor). Such considerations would further push the correlation between GNP and welfare towards the negative. Also, GNP, MEW and ISEW all begin with personal consumption. Since all three measures have in common their largest single category, there is a significant auto-correlation bias, which makes the poor correlations between GNP and the two welfare measures all the more striking.

Measures of welfare are difficult and subject to many arbitrary judgements, so sweeping conclusions should be resisted. However, it seems fair to say that for the United States since 1947, the empirical evidence that GNP growth has increased welfare is weak, and since 1980 probably non-existent. Consequently, any impact on welfare via policies that increase GNP growth would also be weak or non-existent. In other words, the 'great benefit', for which US citizens are urged to sacrifice the environment, community standards, and industrial peace, appears, on closer inspection, likely not even to exist.

That GNP growth is becoming uneconomic at the present margin in rich countries does not mean that it was uneconomic in the past, or that it is currently uneconomic in poor countries. To avoid starvation it is worth consuming some capital, including natural capital. But only in exchange for food, clothing, and shelter for the very poor – not to swell aggregate GNP. The idea that increasing inequality does not matter as long as growth reduces absolute poverty seems to be premised on the faith that aggregate growth remains economic. If GNP growth is uneconomic, and it could be so even in a country with considerable poverty, then increasing the absolute income of the poor must come at the expense of the rich. Uneconomic growth cannot keep the problem of redistribution at bay the way economic growth has done, at least temporarily.

From permitting growth, to mandating growth, to limiting growth

The current macroeconomic paradigm permits growth forever but does not really mandate it. What pushed the growth-forever ideology was not neoclassical logic – indeed, the logic of optimisation clearly tells us that growth must stop at the optimum, lest it become uneconomic. Historically, the growth push came from the practical answers given by modern economists to three major problems, each associated with the name of a great economist: Thomas Malthus on overpopulation; Karl Marx on unjust distribution; and John Maynard Keynes on involuntary unemployment. Growth is the common answer to all three problems given by modern economists.

Overpopulation is thought to be cured by the demographic transition. When GNP per capita reaches a certain level, children become too expensive in terms of other goods forgone and the birth rate automatically falls. Economic growth is the best contraceptive, as the slogan goes. Whether the product of increased per capita consumption times the decreased birth rate of 'capitas' results in increasing total consumption beyond the optimal scale remains an unasked question. More concretely, is it necessary for Indian per capita consumption to rise to the Swedish level for Indian fertility to fall to the Swedish level, and if so what happens to the Indian ecosystem as a result of that level of total consumption?

Unjust distribution of wealth between classes, we are told, is rendered tolerable by growth, the rising tide that lifts all boats, to recall another slogan. Yet growth has in fact increased inequality both within and among nations. To make matters worse, even the metaphor is wrong, since a rising tide in one part of the world implies an ebbing tide somewhere else.

Unemployment is to be cured by increasing aggregate demand which requires that investment be stimulated, which of course implies growth. But how long can we continue to avoid unemployment by growth? Must we grow beyond optimal scale in pursuit of full employment? This is another unasked question.

Continuing this time-honoured tradition, the World Bank's 1992 *World Development Report* argued that more growth was also the automatic solution to the environmental problem. A so-called 'environmental Kuznets curve' was discovered, which was taken to reveal an inverted U-shaped relation between GNP and the emissions of a number of environmental pollutants. Consequently, one must persevere in growth because even though it initially is bad for the environment, it will later be good for the environment once we pass the hump of the inverted U.

Of course the assumption in all cases is that growth is 'economic', that it is making us richer rather than poorer. But now growth is becoming uneconomic. Uneconomic growth will not sustain the demographic transition and cure overpopulation. Nor will it help redress unjust distribution, or cure unemployment. Nor will it provide extra wealth to be devoted to environmental repair and clean up. Indirect, automatic, growth-based solutions to the big problems no longer work if growth is uneconomic.

We now need more direct and radical solutions to the problems of Malthus, Marx and Keynes: population control to deal with overpopulation; redistribution to deal with excessive inequality; and for unemployment, a public sector employer of last resort, and ecological tax reform to raise resource prices relative to labour.

These must be national policies. It is utopian (or dystopian) to think of them being carried out by a world authority. Many nations have made progress in controlling their population growth, in limiting domestic income inequality and in reducing unemployment. Some nations have improved resource productivity by internalising environmental and social costs into prices. But nations' efforts in this regard are undercut by the ideology of globalisation – a last gasp attempt to re-establish the conditions of the empty-world economy. Apparently, as countries feel the increasing weight of poverty resulting from uneconomic growth, they make a renewed effort to fight the increasing burden of poverty in the only way they know how, namely by more growth, presumed to still be economic. This 'full-world' growth pushes each country to further exploit the remaining global commons, and to try to grow into the ecological space and markets of other countries. This collective folly we call 'globalisation'. It is another subject, but the point is that its roots lie in a desire to escape limits to growth at a national level.

The focus of this entry has been on the 'economic limit' to growth (where marginal costs equal marginal benefits), because that should be the effective limit. If we fail to stop at the economic limit, however, there are two further limits. The 'catastrophe limit' occurs if the marginal costs suddenly become discontinuously large – for example, a new chemical previously thought to be benign suddenly and massively disrupts photosynthesis. Alternatively the 'futility limit' could be next in sequence – the marginal utility of further GNP could reach zero. This is more realistic than one might think. Recent research by experimental economists and psychologists reveals that, beyond some sufficiency threshold, self-reported happiness is a function of relative, not absolute income. Growth cannot increase everyone's relative income, and is thus powerless to increase aggregate benefit beyond that threshold, even if it imposed no ecological costs. The latter arguments have been developed by J.K. Galbraith, Fred Hirsch and Richard Easterlin, who argue for limits to growth quite independently of biophysical constraints. For policy purposes, of course, we should be governed by the economic limit.

HERMAN E. DALY

References and further reading

Cobb, Clifford and John Cobb (1994), *The Green National Product: A Proposed Index of Sustainable Economic Welfare*, Lanham, MD: University Press of America.

Daly, Herman and Joshua Farley (2004), *Ecological Economics: Principles and Applications*, Washington, DC: Island Press.

Easterlin, Richard (1995), 'Will raising the incomes of all increase the happiness of all?', *Journal of Economic Behavior and Organization*, **27**, 35–47.

Galbraith, John Kenneth (1958), *The Affluent Society*, Boston, MA: Houghton Mifflin.

Hirsch, Fred (1976), *The Social Limits to Growth*, Cambridge, MA: Harvard University Press.

Meadows, Donella (1972), *The Limits to Growth*, New York: Universe Books.

Mill, John Stuart (1857), *Principles of Political Economy*, London: John W. Parker.

Nordhaus, William and James Tobin (1973), 'Is growth obsolete?', in Milton Moss (ed.), *The Measurement of Economic and Social Performance*, Studies in Income and Wealth, vol. 38, Cambridge, MA: National Bureau of Economic Research, pp. 509–32.

Ruskin, John (1860 [1960]), *Unto This Last*, Lincoln, NB: University of Nebraska Press, edited by Lloyd J. Hubenka.

Schumacher, Ernst (1973), *Small Is Beautiful: Economics as if People Mattered*, New York: Harper & Row.

World Bank (1992), *World Development Report 1992: Development and the Environment*, Oxford: Oxford University Press.

Urban Livelihoods

The livelihoods open to both rural and urban people are determined by their assets; the economic, social and political context in which they live; and their capacity to deal with risks, shocks and stresses (Ellis, 1998; Rakodi, 1999, 2002). Understanding their capacity to assemble secure livelihoods 'thus requires focussing simultaneously on the characteristics of households, their endowment of resources and their structure of opportunities, particularly in their relationships to the market and the state' (González de la Rocha and Grinspun, 2001, pp. 56–7).

The economic context for urban livelihoods

In the past it was anticipated that urban economies would, with economic growth and 'modernisation', generate sufficient employment to absorb the growing labour force. For most in high- and many in middle-income countries, wage employment is available for a majority and wages make the largest contribution to household income. In such urban centres, poverty is associated with unemployment or unskilled low-paid jobs such as domestic service. However, the availability of full-time secure employment with wages sufficient to support a family has declined in the face of global economic trends, local economic restructuring and growth of the labour force. In many urban centres, economic crisis, liberalisation and adjustment policies have led to growing unemployment, increased job insecurity, job losses in both the public and private sectors, and declining real wages. Households in many countries in transition to a market economy have been particularly hard hit (González de la Rocha and Grinspun, 2001).

Reduced global demand, especially where urban centres are dependent on single industries, for example in the Zambian Copperbelt, may lead to long-term economic decline. Trade liberalisation benefits cities in some regions, at least temporarily (for example, in Mexico near the US border), while damaging the industrial base of others (for example, textiles and clothing in some African cities). Downsizing and privatisation of public sector employers has led to a loss of jobs. Maintenance of wage employment in East Asian cities as manufacturing relocates to lower-cost locations in China or Vietnam depends on their ability to diversify into hi-tech industry and services. Following the Asian financial crisis in 1997/8, urban households were badly affected by the loss of wage employment. Except where new factories provide jobs for women, formal employment continues to be predominantly secured by men.

As the availability of secure wage employment declines in absolute or relative terms, workers, especially women, become increasingly reliant on casual work or informal sector activities (Chant, 1999). Open unemployment has often increased, mainly among the professionally qualified and young people. Most of the poor cannot afford the luxury of unemployment and are forced to take low-wage and insecure work, or to seek openings in the informal sector. In Indonesia, for example, competition between informal sector enterprises, already fierce, was worsened by the economic crisis. Some retrenched workers returned to their rural homes. The purchasing power of remaining urban customers declined at the same time as the number of vendors competing for their custom increased (Mukherjee et al., 2002). However, occupations in the informal sector are neither temporary nor confined to the poor. They are a permanent part of urban economies worldwide, not only important to household survival strategies but also closely linked to the large-scale 'formal' sector.

Resources for household livelihoods

In difficult economic circumstances, households have to adjust their livelihoods to escape chronic poverty, avoid temporary impoverishment or, if possible, improve their well-being. Their capacity to do so varies not just with the context in which they live but also with the assets they command (Rakodi, 1999). Assets are often (and controversially) conceptualised as capital – stuff that can be accumulated, exchanged or depleted and put to work to generate a flow of income or other benefits without being totally consumed in use. As important as the stocks themselves are, the social relationships that permit households and individuals to access resources influence the way in which they are mobilised and used, and determine the way in which the proceeds are controlled and shared within households.

Human capital
Households are commonly defined as socio-economic units consisting of one or more individuals who live together and share a dwelling and food. In practice, it is hard to fit complex and dynamic social relationships and living arrangements into this definition. They are also the main units in which labour resources for productive and reproductive tasks are organised (Beall, 2002). The size of a household, the availability of adults able to earn incomes, and the education, skills and health of its members are the most crucial elements of human capital. Generally, households with few adults able to work in relation to the numbers of children, disabled, sick or elderly members are poor. Poverty is, therefore, associated with both household types (for example, single adult households with children, elderly people without family support) and stages in the household life cycle (for example, families with young children). It is also associated with low levels of educational attainment and lack of vocational skills. Ill health is closely linked to poverty – impoverishment often follows the illness or death of an income earner, and households may become trapped in a cycle of indebtedness and poverty, especially if the illness is long term (Harpham and Grant, 2002).

Faced with economic difficulties, households may be able to mobilise additional labour by sending additional members to work or working longer hours, or may attempt to diversify their economic activities. Such tactics can tide households over a crisis, enable them to cope and occasionally permit them to improve their economic position. However, they may also result in reduced time devoted to childcare, withdrawal of children from school, a heavier work burden for women, and increased ill health. Short-term survival or security is bought at the cost of longer-term investment in human capital (Wood, 2003).

Natural capital
Rural households draw heavily on natural capital for their livelihoods. The amount and quality of land is the most significant asset for many, but even those without land of their own can often gain access to other natural resources, such as water, forest products or building materials. Rural and urban livelihoods should not be regarded as separate or distinct (Jerve, 2001; Satterthwaite and Tacoli, 2002). In practice, many households straddle

rural and urban areas through migration and investment strategies, kinship ties, cultivation and livestock ownership. Many urban people regard themselves as temporary residents, working to sustain families and livelihoods based in rural areas; others attempt to access land for cultivation to supplement their urban incomes or improve their security. The land they cultivate may be in their home areas, on the urban periphery, on unused land close to their area of residence, or on residential plots (Binns and Lynch, 1998; Ellis and Sumberg, 1998). The opportunities to cultivate and keep livestock vary between countries, urban centres and households depending on the pattern of land ownership, system of land administration, population pressure, city size, the nature of kinship networks and entitlements, and the financial resources available to households for acquiring land. Where water and energy supply systems are inadequate, urban households may depend on groundwater and woodfuel. However, most of the land needed by urban households for residential and business purposes needs considerable investment before it is usable and generally access to basic utilities requires organised systems of piped water, energy supply and so on. Land may, therefore, be better conceptualised as physical than natural capital in urban areas. The infrastructure and services on which urban residents depend for their livelihoods and well-being should be given separate and specific emphasis.

Physical capital
Investment in physical assets enables households to improve their livelihoods and provides them with a hedge against insecurity. The purchase of equipment or a vehicle enables a business to start and grow. Consumer goods may relieve the pressure on household labour, especially that of women, improve access to knowledge and information, and be sold or pawned to provide emergency cash. Even more important is investment in housing (Moser, 1998). Evidence shows that most urban households aspire to house ownership, because it can provide secure accommodation, a place to do business, a source of income from renting and a (generally) appreciating asset that can be shared with and handed on to the next generation. Often, of course, increased commercialisation of land and housing markets and deficient land administration has placed secure land and house ownership beyond the reach of poor households. Instead, they have to rent their accommodation or live in areas that are inadequately serviced, unsuitable for residential use and vulnerable to eviction (UN-HABITAT, 2003a). The importance of house ownership to household livelihoods is demonstrated by the prevalence of home-based enterprises (33 per cent of households in Madina, Accra and 40 per cent in Mamelodi, Pretoria) (Gough et al., 2003), the frequency with which owners rent out rooms (UN-HABITAT, 2003b) and their reluctance to sell (Gilbert, 1999).

Financial capital
To invest and provide a buffer against misfortune, households need access to stocks of financial capital. The ability to save and/or borrow depends on their past and current capacity to generate income, the demands on that income, the financial services available to them and the social networks to which they have access. Generally the range of services offered by formal financial institutions is limited and unsuited to the needs of poor households, and they rarely have branches in the areas where the poor live. Although there have been efforts to develop alternative savings and credit facilities, generally through

micro-finance NGOs, their scale is generally limited and they are inaccessible to the poorest (Rutherford et al., 2002).

In the absence of formal services, households depend on informal alternatives, including their social and kinship networks, ROSCAs (rotating credit associations) and moneylenders, the range of which varies from place to place (Ruthven, 2002).

Social capital
Access to a job, a market stall, a vocational skill, land, a room to rent, childcare, a neighbour's tap or latrine, or a loan, in short most components of a livelihood, depends on social relationships (Phillips, 2002; Beall, 2004). The close-knit, stable (and often hierarchical, patriarchal and oppressive) social relationships said to typify village life may be absent in many urban settlements. True, mobility, unemployment, crime and HIV/AIDS pose threats to social resources. None the less, urban residents are able to draw to a greater or lesser extent on kin networks; develop mutually supportive relationships with neighbours, workmates and friends; and participate in informal and formal social groups that can provide a sense of identity, social support and welfare assistance. Such 'bonding' social capital may be essential to survival, but does not necessarily provide access to higher levels of resources. Poor residents are, therefore, likely to try and develop relationships with those better endowed with education, contacts or financial resources, including relatives, bureaucrats and NGOs – bridging social capital (Mitlin, 2001; Beall, 2004). Social organisation may enable residents to secure environmental improvements and make claims on the political system.

Political capital
Even with widespread democratisation and decentralisation, few political systems in developing countries provide access to basic services as of right. For residents coping with inadequate infrastructure, insecure tenure, and inappropriate regulatory systems, relationships with politicians are crucial (Benjamin, 2000). In most places, these relationships with community leaders, party officials and elected councillors are essentially clientelist. However, in particular political circumstances, voice can be exercised and accountability secured by poor residents (for example, in Brazil, South Africa or the Philippines) (Souza, 2001; Rakodi, 2004).

Livelihood strategies
Households and the individuals within them seek to manage complex and changing portfolios of assets to improve their well-being and safeguard their livelihoods (Moser, 1998). Security is at least as important as increased incomes and strategies such as diversification of income-generating activities or investment in housing and social relationships are designed to achieve these aims.

However, the economic and physical environments in which poor people live are risky and their limited resources render them vulnerable to impoverishment. Much of the time, therefore, responses have to focus on coping with shocks and stresses. As noted above, households do this partly by intensifying the use of household labour. But consumption-reducing strategies are also important, including consuming less and/or poorer-quality food; reducing expenditure on education, healthcare, transport, clothing, housing or remittances; drawing down savings; borrowing; pawning or selling assets; growing food; foraging or scavenging; and engaging in illegal or semi-legal activities ranging from drug dealing to prostitution, robbery or begging. Sometimes such strategies may enable households to cope in the short term and recover their position, as evidenced by the large proportion that experience transient poverty (Baulch and Hoddinott, 2000). However, successive crises or the exhaustion of one of more type of capital may trap households in poverty, at the worst perpetuated by indebtedness or the inability to invest in education and training from one generation to the next (Hulme and Shepherd, 2003).

The livelihoods approach lays emphasis on the assets available to households, their resourcefulness in managing these assets and their resilience in a risky environment. This should not, however, blind us to the limits imposed by structural constraints arising from economic restructuring, undemocratic politics, limited government capacity and the unequal distribution of wealth (Devas et al., 2004).

CAROLE RAKODI

References

Baulch, B. and J. Hoddinott (eds) (2000), *Economic Mobility and Poverty Dynamics in Developing Countries*, London: Frank Cass.

Beall, J. (2002), 'Living in the present, investing in the future – household security among the poor', in C. Rakodi with T. Lloyd-Jones (eds), *Urban Livelihoods: A People-Centred Approach to Reducing Poverty*, London: Earthscan, pp. 71–87.

Beall, J. (2004), 'Surviving in the city: livelihoods and linkages of the urban poor', in N. Devas (ed.), pp. 53–67.

Benjamin, S. (2000), 'Governance, economic settings and poverty in Bangalore', *Environment and Urbanization*, **12** (1), 35–56.

Binns, T. and K. Lynch (1998), 'Feeding Africa's growing cities into the 21st century: the potential of urban agriculture', *Journal of International Development*, **10**, 777–93.

Chant, S. (1999), 'Informal sector activity in the Third World city', in M. Pacione (ed.), *Applied Geography*, London: Routledge, 509–27.

Devas, N. (ed.), with P. Amis, J. Beall, U. Grant, D. Mitlin, F. Nunan and C. Rakodi (2004), *Urban Governance, Voice and Poverty in the Developing World*, London: Earthscan.

Ellis, F. (1998), 'Household strategies and rural livelihood diversification', *Journal of Development Studies*, **35** (1), 1–38.

Ellis, F. and J. Sumberg (1998), 'Food production, urban areas and policy responses', *World Development*, **26**, 213–25.

Gilbert, A. (1999), 'A home is for ever? Residential mobility and home ownership in self-help settlements', *Environment and Planning A*, **31** (6), 1073–92.

González de la Rocha, M. and A. Grinspun (2001), 'Private adjustments: household, crisis and work', in A. Grinspun (ed.), *Choices for the Poor: Lessons from National Poverty Strategies*, New York: UNDP, pp. 55–88.

Gough, K.V., A.G. Tipple and M. Napier (2003), 'Making a living in African cities: the role of home-based enterprises in Accra and Pretoria', *International Planning Studies*, **8** (4), 253–78.

Harpham, T. and E. Grant (2002), 'Health, health services and urban livelihoods', in C. Rakodi with T. Lloyd-Jones (eds), *Urban Livelihoods: A People-Centred Approach to Reducing Poverty*, London: Earthscan, pp. 165–79.

Hulme, D. and A. Shepherd (2003), 'Conceptualizing chronic poverty', *World Development*, **31** (3), 403–23.

Jerve, A.M. (2001), 'Rural-urban linkages and poverty analysis', in A. Grinspun (ed.), *Choices for the Poor: Lessons from National Poverty Strategies*, New York: UNDP, pp. 89–120.

Mitlin, D. (2001), 'The formal and informal worlds of state and civil society: what do they offer to the urban poor?', *International Planning Studies*, **6** (4), 377–92.

Moser, C. (1998), 'The asset vulnerability framework: reassessing urban poverty reduction strategies', *World Development*, **26** (1), 1–19.

Mukherjee, N., J. Hardjono and E. Carriere (2002), *People, Poverty and Livelihoods: Indonesia*, Jakarta: DFID.

Phillips, S. (2002), 'Social capital, local networks and community development', in C. Rakodi with T. Lloyd-Jones (eds), *Urban Livelihoods: A People-Centred Approach to Reducing Poverty*, London: Earthscan, pp. 133–50.

Rakodi, C. (1999), 'A capital assets framework for analysing household livelihood strategies', *Development Policy Review*, **17** (3), 315–42.

Rakodi, C. (2002), 'A livelihoods approach – conceptual issues and definitions', in C. Rakodi with T. Lloyd-Jones (eds), *Urban Livelihoods: A People-Centred Approach to Reducing Poverty*, London: Earthscan, pp. 3–22.

Rakodi, C. (2004), 'Urban politics: exclusion or empowerment?', in N. Devas (ed.), pp. 68–94.

Rutherford, S., M. Harper and J. Grierson (2002), 'Support for livelihood strategies', in C. Rakodi with T. Lloyd-Jones (eds), *Urban Livelihoods: A People-Centred Approach to Reducing Poverty*, London: Earthscan, pp. 112–32.

Ruthven, O. (2002), 'Money mosaics: financial choice and strategy in a West Delhi squatter settlement', *Journal of International Development*, **14** (2), 249–71.

Satterthwaite, D. and C. Tacoli (2002), 'Seeking an understanding of poverty that recognises rural–urban differences and rural–urban linkages', in C. Rakodi with T. Lloyd-Jones (eds), *Urban Livelihoods: A People-Centred Approach to Reducing Poverty*, London: Earthscan, pp. 52–70.

Souza, C. (2001), 'Participatory budgeting in Brazilian cities: limits and possibilities in building democratic institutions', *Environment and Urbanization*, **13** (1), 159–84.

UN-HABITAT (2003a), *The Challenge of Slums: Global Report on Human Settlements 2003*, London: Earthscan.

UN-HABITAT (2003b), *Rental Housing: An Essential Option for the Urban Poor in Developing Countries*, Nairobi: United Nations Human Settlements Programme.

Wood, G. (2003), 'Staying secure, staying poor: the "Faustian bargain"', *World Development*, **31** (3), 455–71.

Urbanisation and Third World Cities

Urbanisation is the process by which an increasing proportion of the population in any nation or region comes to live and work in urban centres. Its immediate cause is net rural to urban migration (natural increase may be the dominant cause of urban population growth in most nations but it contributes little or nothing to increasing the proportion of people living in urban areas). The term 'urbanisation' may also be used to refer to the change in land use from non-urban (usually agricultural) to urban.

Although urbanisation is widely acknowledged as one of the most significant changes taking place in low- and middle-income countries, there is little detailed study of its scale and nature in most such nations. In part, this is because urbanisation is often seen as a 'global trend' rather than as changes whose scale and nature are particular to each nation. In part, it is because of a lack of attention to the economic, social, political and demographic drivers of urbanisation whose form and relative importance are also particular to each nation.

The broad global trends are clear. During the twentieth century, the world's urban population increased more than tenfold. In 1900, urban centres had less than 15 per cent of the world's population; now they have close to half. UN projections suggest that urban centres may have 60 per cent of the world's population by 2020 and that most of the growth in the world's population between 2000 and 2020 will be in urban areas in low- and middle-income nations. These nations already have more than two-thirds of the world's urban population and the proportion is growing (see Tables 17 and 18).

Many aspects of urban change in these nations over the last 50 years have been unprecedented, including their level of urbanisation and the size and number of very large cities. Many cities had populations that grew ten- or even 20-fold in this period and some sprawl for thousands of square kilometres and concentrate more than 10 million people. But the scale of these changes is often overstated. Most low- and middle-income nations may be urbanising but a large proportion of their urban centres are not growing rapidly.

Table 17 Distribution of the world's urban population by region, 1950–2010

Region	1950	1970	1990	2000	Projection for 2010
Urban population (millions of inhabitants)					
World	733	1330	2273	2857	3505
Africa	33	83	199	295	417
Asia	232	486	1012	1367	1770
Europe	280	413	516	529	534
Latin America and the Caribbean	70	163	314	393	472
Northern America	110	171	214	250	286
Oceania	8	14	19	23	26
Percentage of population living in urban areas					
World	29.1	36.0	43.2	47.1	51.3
Africa	14.9	23.2	31.9	37.1	42.4
Asia	16.6	22.7	31.9	37.1	42.7
Europe	51.2	62.9	71.5	72.7	74.2
Latin America and the Caribbean	41.9	57.4	71.1	75.5	79.4
Northern America	63.9	73.8	75.4	79.1	82.3
Oceania	60.6	70.6	70.1	72.7	73.7
Percentage of the world's urban population living in:					
World	100	100	100	100	100
Africa	4.5	6.2	8.7	10.3	11.9
Asia	31.7	36.5	44.5	47.8	50.5
Europe	38.3	31.0	22.7	18.5	15.2
Latin America and the Caribbean	9.5	12.3	13.8	13.8	13.5
Northern America	15.0	12.9	9.4	8.8	8.2
Oceania	1.1	1.0	0.8	0.8	0.7

Source: United Nations (2004).

Many urban centres have more people moving out than in – including many of the world's largest cities such as Mexico City, São Paulo, Buenos Aires, Calcutta and Seoul. These are also among the many large cities that had several million fewer inhabitants in 2000 than had been predicted 25 years ago. The increasing number of 'mega cities' with more than ten million inhabitants may appear a cause for concern but by 2000, there were only 18 such cities and they concentrated less than 4 per cent of the world's population.

One reason for the concern with rapid urbanisation has been the very poor conditions in which large proportions of the urban population live, including high levels of over-crowding and much of the low-income population living in illegal or informal settlements with very inadequate provision for water, sanitation, drainage, healthcare and schools. However, this is not so much linked to rapid urbanisation as to the lack of attention to building local governance structures. Many of the worst urban conditions are found in

Table 18   Distribution of the world's largest cities by region, over time

Region	1800	1900	1950	2000
Number of 'million cities' (cities with more than a million inhabitants)				
World	2	17	86	387
Africa	0	0	2	35
Asia	1	4	31	194
Europe	1	9	30	62
Latin America and the Caribbean	0	0	7	49
Northern America	0	4	14	41
Oceania	0	0	2	6
Regional distribution of the world's largest 100 cities				
World	100	100	100	100
Africa	4	2	3	8
Asia	65	22	37	44
Europe	28	53	34	15
Latin America and the Caribbean	3	5	8	16
Northern America	0	16	16	15
Oceania	0	2	2	2
Average size of the world's 100 largest cities	187 000	725 000	2.2 m	6.3 m

Sources: Satterthwaite (2005); data for 1950 and 2000 drawn from United Nations (2004).

urban centres that have not grown rapidly, while some of the best are in cities with rapid growth or nations with rapid urbanisation.

The regional distribution of urban population
Urbanisation levels increased dramatically in Africa, Asia and Latin America between 1950 and 2000 (Table 17). The scale of this change and the number of nations experiencing rapid growth in urbanisation levels was unprecedented – although the rates of increase in levels of urbanisation were not; Japan, the USA and many countries in West Europe had periods when their level of urbanisation increased as rapidly (Preston, 1979).

Some qualifications are needed in regard to the accuracy of the statistics in Table 17. The statistics for 2000 draw wherever possible on national censuses held between 1999 and 2002, but for 45 per cent of nations with more than a million inhabitants in 2000 no census data after 1993 were available when the UN statistical compendium from which this table draws was compiled. For some nations in Sub-Saharan Africa, no census data were available since the 1970s or early 1980s so figures for their levels of urbanisation for 1990 and 2000 are based on estimates and projections. Other sources suggest that most of Sub-Saharan Africa urbanised much less than that suggested by the UN statistics (Potts, 1995; Bocquier, 2004).

Any nation's level of urbanisation is strongly influenced by how its government defines an urban centre, especially the proportion of 'small urban centres and large villages' classified as urban or rural. In virtually all nations, a significant proportion of the population lives in settlements with between 1000 and 20 000 inhabitants, most of which have both urban and rural characteristics. A nation's level of urbanisation is much influenced by what proportion of these are classified as urban. India would be predominantly urban if all settlements with more than 1000 inhabitants were classified as urban. Thus, the level of urbanisation in the world, in each region and each nation is best understood not as a precise figure. The world was not 48.3 per cent urban in 2003 but somewhere between 40 and 55 per cent, depending on which criteria are used to define urban centres (UN, 2004).

The largest cities
Just two centuries ago, there were only two cities with more than a million inhabitants – London and Beijing; by 2000 there were 387. A large (and increasing) proportion of these 'million cities' are in Africa, Asia and Latin America. This is often highlighted as a particular concern, but this is not so much a dramatic shift as a return to what was apparent prior to the industrial revolution (Bairoch, 1988). Throughout most of recorded history, Asia has had a high proportion of the world's largest cities. South and Central America and North Africa have long had large cities too. Most of the largest cities in these regions have also been important cities for centuries (see Table 18).

Economic drivers of urbanisation
Virtually all nations that have urbanised rapidly during the last 50 years have had long periods of rapid economic expansion and large shifts in employment patterns from agricultural and pastoral activities (dispersed among rural areas) to industrial, service and information activities (highly concentrated in urban areas). Much urban change is driven by where profit-seeking enterprises choose to concentrate (or to bypass or leave). In general, the higher the per capita income of a nation (or region within a nation), the higher the level of urbanisation. Although agriculture is often considered as separate from urban development, prosperous high-value agriculture has underpinned rapid development in many cities. So too has tourism – but in different locations the stimulus may come from local, national or international tourists and with large differences in the extent to which tourism spending benefits the local economy.

There is an economic logic underlying the distribution of the world's largest cities. In 2000, the world's five largest economies (USA, China, Japan, India and Germany) had half of the world's 18 mega cities and nearly half of its million cities. Similarly, within each of the world's regions, most of the largest cities are concentrated in the largest economies – for instance, Brazil, Mexico and Argentina in Latin America and China, Japan, India, Indonesia and the Republic of Korea in Asia.

The internationalisation of world production and trade has influenced urbanisation in most nations. Many cities owe their prosperity (or part of their employment base) to their roles within this increasingly internationalised production and distribution system. Growing cross-border flows of raw materials, goods, information, income and capital, much of it managed by transnational corporations, underpin a network of what can be termed 'global cities' that are the key sites for the management and servicing of the global economy (Sassen, 2002). Most international investment is concentrated in a relatively small proportion of cities. Many of the fastest-growing large cities are those that have most success in attracting international investment – for instance, Dhaka in Bangladesh and Bangalore in India. China has many examples of cities with rapid population growth rates, which is hardly surprising given the very rapid growth of its economy sustained over the last two decades. For instance, the city of Shenzhen close to Hong Kong has grown from a small border town to a major metropolis in the last 20 years.

However, the association between globalisation and large cities is moderated by two factors. The first is that advanced telecommunications systems allow a separation of the production from those who manage and finance it and benefit from its profits. The second is the more decentralised urban patterns that are possible within regions with well-developed transport and communications infrastructure – as in, for instance, south-east Brazil where smaller cities have attracted much new investment away from São Paulo. In the nations that have had effective decentralisations, urban authorities in smaller cities have more capacity to compete for new investment. Trade liberalisation and a greater emphasis on exports have also increased the comparative advantage of many smaller cities.

The many influences on urbanisation
Analyses of urban change within any nation over time provides a reminder of its diversity including the rising and falling importance of different urban centres; the largest cities are simply those that managed to retain their economic and/or political importance. These also point to the spatial influence of changes in government policies (for instance, from supporting import substitution to supporting export promotion, the extent and nature of decentralisation).

It is tempting to compare urbanisation trends between nations because data sets are available with each nation's level of urbanisation and each major city's population from 1950 to 2000 (with projections to 2030). But doing so is fraught with danger. First, there are the limitations in the data noted above. Second, the factors underlying urban change often differ greatly between nations. To illustrate the complexity, consider the example of Pakistan. An analysis of its 1998 census (Hasan, 2004) highlighted the impossibility of understanding urban change without understanding the influence of Pakistan's Partition from India in the late 1940s (which caused large migration flows to particular locations, especially to Karachi), of Pakistan's division (as Bangladesh became independent), of the civil war in Afghanistan (bringing many refugees to Pakistan and many Western agencies supporting the Afghans fighting the Soviet-backed government based in Pakistan), of the green revolution, of Pakistan's political structure and of a host of other factors. Inevitably, the very large population movements brought by these also brought many political conflicts – including those between long-term city dwellers and immigrants from India, between Pakistanis and Afghans, and between urban interests and rural interests. Now the whole nation's urban system is being influenced by the erosion of light industry due to cheap imports.

Perhaps the most important political influence on urban change in most nations in Africa and Asia over the last 50 years was the dissolving of the European powers' colonial empires. One reason why urbanisation has been so rapid in many nations is because it began from such a small base, as the colonial powers kept down urban populations by imposing restrictions on the rights of their national populations to live and work in urban centres (Potts, 1995). Another factor underpinning urbanisation was the need for newly independent governments to build the institutions of governance that nation states require and expand the education and healthcare system that had been so undeveloped under colonial rule. Urban change in many African nations has also been influenced by wars and civil conflicts – for instance, millions of people fled to urban areas in Angola, Mozambique and the Sudan during civil wars there in the 1980s and 1990s, just as they had done in Zimbabwe in the liberation struggle of the 1970s (ibid.).

So, while reviews of tables with urban population statistics for different nations may show some broad trends towards increasingly urbanised societies, the scale and nature of such trends and their underlying causes differ greatly from country to country. Even if globalisation is an increasing influence in most urban centres, it is important not to forget the unique mix of social, economic, political and demographic factors within each location that are influencing urban change there.

Conclusions

The world is likely to continue urbanising and to have more large cities – but perhaps less so than current projections suggest. There are good grounds for questioning whether most of the urban population will live in very large cities because more dispersed patterns of urban development are increasingly evident. There are also grounds for questioning whether urbanisation levels will continue to rise in virtually all low- and middle-income nations. For instance, Africa will only become increasingly urban if most of its more populous nations have greater economic success than they had during the 1990s.

The problems associated with urbanisation are not inherent to cities or to urban expansion. The knowledge of how to install and maintain the infrastructure and services that underpin good-quality city environments has developed over the last 150 years and cities have many economies of scale and proximity to support this. During the last 30 years has been added the knowledge of how to integrate this provision with a broader regional concern for sustainable resource use, good land-use management and minimising waste and pollution (Hardoy et al., 2001). It is not rapid urbanisation but the lack of attention to developing urban governance structures and economic stagnation that underpins most urban problems. Many factors constrain the development of appropriate governance structures, especially where these raise costs and limit choices for politically powerful enterprises and populations. Good governance recognises the rights of all citizens, not just the wealthy. It has to include actions to ensure that infrastructure and services are available to all and that revenues are raised from those who benefit from this. It will ensure 'the rule of law' through which the rights and entitlements of everyone and 'the public good' are protected and effective democratic processes are in place, including the values this implies such as accountability to citizens and transparency in the generation and use of public resources. This is a very different 'urban agenda' from the one that sees 'urbanisation' as the problem.

DAVID SATTERTHWAITE

References

Bairoch, P. (1988), *Cities and Economic Development: From the Dawn of History to the Present*, London: Mansell.

Bocquier, P. (2004), 'Analyzing urbanization in Sub-Saharan Africa', in Tony Champion and Graeme Hugo (eds), *New Forms of Urbanization; Beyond the Urban–Rural Dichotomy*, Aldershot: Ashgate, pp. 133–50.

Hardoy, J.E., D. Mitlin and D. Satterthwaite (2001), *Environmental Problems in an Urbanizing World: Finding Solutions for Cities in Africa, Asia and Latin America*, London: Earthscan.

Hasan, A. (2004), 'The process of socio-economic change in Pakistan', paper presented at a seminar on 'The Future of Pakistan: The Politics and Economics of Development in Pakistan', School of Advanced Studies, Johns Hopkins University, Baltimore, MD, 8 November.

Potts, D. (1995), 'Shall we go home? Increasing urban poverty in African cities and migration processes', *The Geographic Journal*, **161** (3), 245–64.

Preston, S.H. (1979), 'Urban growth in developing countries: a demographic reappraisal', *Population and Development Review*, **5** (2), 195–215.

Sassen, S. (2002), 'Locating cities on global circuits', *Environment and Urbanization*, **14** (1), 13–30.

Satterthwaite, D. (2005), *The Scale of Urban Change Worldwide 1950–2000 and its Underpinnings*, IIED Working Paper, International Institute for Environment and Development, London, www.iied.org/urban/index.html.

United Nations (2004), *World Urbanization Prospects: The 2003 Revision*, United Nations Population Division, Department of Economic and Social Affairs, ST/ESA/SER.A/237, New York.

Vulnerability and Coping

The concept of vulnerability has been around in the poverty and famine literature for a long time, yet ambiguities in its interpretation persist in food security and related literatures. This entry draws on an unpublished piece of work (Ellis, 2003) in order to clarify the concept. A succinct definition is provided by Devereux (2002, p. 1) to the effect that 'vulnerability denotes both exposure and sensitivity to livelihood shocks'. At the same time, the phrase 'living on the edge' provokes a graphic image of the livelihood circumstances that vulnerability tries to convey (Pearce et al., 1996). Living on the edge evokes the sense of a small push sending a person or people over the edge, and it is just this knife-edge between ability to survive and thrive, and sudden loss of ability to do so, that vulnerability seeks to describe. Rising vulnerability over time is then a matter of how close to the edge people are being pushed by factors that are outside their control.

A paper by Alwang et al. (2001) seeks to synthesise differing understandings of vulnerability into a single framework that can be widely shared, and the ideas that they put forward, drawing on the work of many others, are helpful for clarifying the vulnerability concept. In the first instance, it is important to be clear about the thing or status that a person or population is vulnerable to. Typically, the interest is in vulnerability to an acute decline in access to food. However, people can be vulnerable to many other things: income falling below a certain level; a wide variety of illnesses and infectious diseases; accidents at work; atmospheric pollution and so on.

Although it has been stated often enough, there is no harm in reaffirming that vulnerability is not the same as poverty. Poverty, certainly as defined by economists, describes a state with respect to an absolute or relative norm (for example, a poverty line). Vulnerability, by contrast, refers to proneness to a sudden, catastrophic, fall in the level of a variable, in this instance access to enough food (that is, once again it is about susceptibility to falling over the edge). Of course, rising poverty is a factor contributing to rising vulnerability (being pushed closer to the edge), but this does not make it the same thing. Poor people may not be vulnerable if they live in relatively stable contexts with good infrastructure, communications and social support systems. Conversely, non-poor people can be vulnerable if they live in unstable contexts characterised by widespread uncertainty.

Vulnerability is a 'forward-looking' concept (Alwang et al., 2001, p. 1): it seeks to describe people's proneness to a future acute loss in their capability to acquire food. It is for this reason that vulnerability ideas can play an important role in predicting the onset of food crises, a consideration that this entry returns to in due course. One useful way of capturing this forward-looking feature is to view vulnerability as a sequence, described by Alwang et al. as a 'risk chain':

- people confront a variety of risks in the routine pursuit of their livelihoods; some of these risks pertain to potentially catastrophic events or 'shocks' (for example, floods, droughts), while others represent pervasive uncertainty in the livelihood environment stemming from numerous short-, medium- and long-run causes;

- people actively manage risk in a variety of ways; some of them to do with anticipating the eventuality of shocks in advance (*ex ante* risk management) and some to do with actions after a shock has occurred (*ex post* coping) (Webb et al., 1992; Carter, 1997);
- examples of *ex ante* risk management include building up stores, making savings, nurturing social networks, growing drought-resistant crops, building up livestock herds, diversifying crops and income sources, and so on (Walker and Jodha, 1986; Swift, 1989); successful management reduces risk overall by spreading it across assets and activities that have different types of risk associated with them (so-called 'risk spreading');
- examples of *ex post* coping include seeking off-farm employment, migrating, removing children from school, having fewer meals, selling livestock and so on (more on coping strategies below); and
- coping behaviours result in outcomes: success or failure to avert acute food failure.

This simplified vulnerability sequence is illustrated in Figure 10. Critical to the degree of vulnerability represented by risk management and coping within the chain is the asset status of households and how this is changing over different time periods. This is where vulnerability links closely to the sustainable livelihoods (SL) framework with its emphasis on assets, activities and outcomes within vulnerability and institutional contexts (Carney, 1998; Scoones, 1998). The SL framework itself represents an extended version, particularly on the policy and institutions side, of a preceding approach referred to as the 'asset vulnerability framework' (Swift, 1989; Moser, 1998).

Referring to Figure 10, *ex ante* risk management strategies are largely to do with building up assets in order to provide the household with buffers against uncertain events (Swift, 1989). They are also about diversifying both on- and off-farm activities (Ellis, 1998, 2000). In order to have the greatest possible risk ameliorating effect, this diversity needs to comprise activities that have differing risk profiles from each other (for example, a brother with a bicycle taxi in town, rather than a job on the next farm). Successful asset building can result in virtuous spirals of accumulation, in which assets are traded up in sequence, for example, chickens to goats, to cattle, to land; or, cash from non-farm income

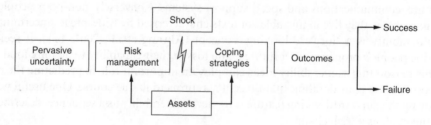

Source: Author's interpretation of Alwang et al. (2001).

Figure 10   Vulnerability as a risk sequence

to farm inputs to higher farm income to land or to livestock. The scope to do this is curtailed in national economies undergoing generalised economic stagnation or crisis, and this is often relevant to interpreting some of the mosaic of factors that precipitate food crises in low-income countries.

Ex post coping behaviours include non-erosive responses (reducing consumption of non-food items, sending a family member to town to look for work, gathering wild food, doing with less food); and erosive responses (selling assets), causing a downward spiral in the asset status of the social unit. Much has been written on the sequences of asset disposal that distinguish the downside response to a gathering crisis (Watts, 1983; Corbett, 1988; Davies, 1993, 1996; Devereux, 1993, 2001). In general, families will seek to protect their ability to recover from the shock, and therefore will dispose of movable assets first: savings, stocks, livestock. Later on, they may dispose of implements, buildings, even land, thus placing themselves in the position of inability to recover from the shock in the future.

Vulnerability assessments undertaken during the course of a food security crisis that occurred in southern Africa in 2001–03 found the full range of coping behaviours that have been observed in other places and other times. These included:

- reducing expenditure on non-food items;
- substitution between foods (cassava for maize);
- smaller meals;
- fewer meals per day;
- payment in food for casual labour;
- bartering for food;
- collection and consumption of wild food;
- drawing down on social networks;
- livestock sales;
- withdrawing children from school;
- increased prostitution; and
- borrowing from moneylenders.

Coping behaviours have proved insightful for devising indicators of rising vulnerability, and these form part of the basis of vulnerability assessment methods that seek to identify a population in difficulty in time to avert a full-blown crisis. Certain interlinked processes that occur within coping are worth noting. Since ability to acquire food is the critical issue, it is price ratios between what people do to raise cash, and the price of food that is important, not the price of food on its own. The advent of sharply adverse trends in the ratio of wage rates or livestock sales prices compared to the maize price is one indicator that a local economy may be entering coping mode. The relative exhaustion of food reserves, food rationing within the household, withdrawing children from school, sending children to live with relatives elsewhere, and sending away family members that would normally be in residence to search for work, are complementary pieces of evidence.

Further ideas that have been used to deepen the concept of vulnerability are those of resilience and sensitivity, which originate in ecological (Holling, 1973) and natural resource management literatures (Blaikie and Brookfield, 1987; Bayliss-Smith, 1991). Resilience refers to the ability of an ecological or livelihood system to 'bounce back' from

		Resilience	
		High	**Low**
Sensitivity	**High**	Vulnerable	Highly vulnerable
	Low	Robust	Vulnerable

Source: Adapted from Davies (1996).

Figure 11   Resilience and sensitivity as vulnerability dimensions

stress or shocks. Diversity is an important factor contributing to resilience in both natural and human systems (Altieri, 1995). For example, a farming system can be said to be resilient when a mid-season rain failure adversely affects only a proportion of the multiple crops cultivated. Sensitivity refers to the magnitude of a system's response to an external event, for example, if a small change in the price of rice rapidly causes widespread undernutrition in a human population, then the livelihood system is acutely sensitive to even this minor shock. When applied to natural resource systems, sensitivity refers to the magnitude of the change in ecological systems set in motion by a particular process of human interference.

Resilience and sensitivity permit livelihoods to be described as a gradation from being highly robust to highly vulnerable, with respect to food security outcomes. The most robust livelihood system is one that displays high resilience and low sensitivity, while the most vulnerable displays low resilience and high sensitivity (see Figure 11). Low resilience can result either from failure to recover fully from an earlier shock or from adverse trends that erode household assets and opportunities over time. The latter would correspond to Davies's (1996) notion of gradual livelihood adaptation towards less resilience than prevailed before.

In summary, vulnerability is defined here following Devereux (2002) as degree of exposure and sensitivity to livelihood shocks; or, in short, living on the edge. It is apparent that vulnerability has both narrow and wide interpretations. Its narrow interpretation refers to the micro level of the household or similar social unit (compound and so on) and seeks to describe the risks that people confront, the anticipatory management of those risks and what happens when one or other (or a combination) of those uncertain events come to pass, in the form of mitigation, coping and outcomes. This micro-level approach can be, and is, scaled up horizontally when vulnerability assessment mapping is undertaken as part of food crisis information gathering at subnational, national or regional levels. However, vulnerability potentially has a broader application. People's livelihood chances are not just determined by local level events, but by political, social and economic trends that are national, regional and sometimes even global in character.

FRANK ELLIS

References

Altieri, M.A. (1995), *Agroecology: The Science of Sustainable Agriculture*, 2nd edn, London: IT Publications.

Alwang, J., P. Siegel and S. Jorgensen (2001), 'Vulnerability: a view from different disciplines', Social Protection Discussion Paper Series no. 115, Washington, DC: World Bank, Social Protection Unit.

Bayliss-Smith, T. (1991), 'Food security and agricultural sustainability in the New Guinea Highlands: vulnerable people, vulnerable places', *IDS Bulletin*, **22** (3), 5–11.

Blaikie, P. and H. Brookfield (eds) (1987), *Land Degradation and Society*, London: Methuen.

Carney, D. (1998), 'Implementing the sustainable rural livelihoods approach', Ch. 1 in Carney (ed.), *Sustainable Rural Livelihoods: What Contribution Can We Make?*, London: Department for International Development.

Carter, M.R. (1997), 'Environment, technology, and the social articulation of risk in West African agriculture', *Economic Development and Cultural Change*, **45** (3), 557–91.

Corbett, J. (1988), 'Famine and household coping strategies', *World Development*, **16** (9), 1099–112.

Davies, S. (1993), 'Are coping strategies a cop out?', *IDS Bulletin*, **24** (4), 60–72.

Davies, S. (1996), *Adaptable Livelihoods: Coping with Food Insecurity in the Malian Sahel*, London: Macmillan.

Devereux, S. (1993), 'Goats before ploughs: dilemmas of household response sequencing during food shortages', *IDS Bulletin*, **24** (4), 52–9.

Devereux, S. (2001), 'Famine in Africa', Ch. 5 in S. Devereux and S. Maxwell (eds), *Food Security in Sub-Saharan Africa*, London: Intermediate Technology Development Group, pp. 117–48.

Devereux, S. (2002), 'Poverty, livelihoods and famine', paper prepared for the Ending Famine in the 21st Century Conference, 27 February–1 March, Institute of Development Studies, University of Sussex, Brighton.

Ellis, F. (1998), 'Survey article: household strategies and rural livelihood diversification', *Journal of Development Studies*, **35** (1), 1–38.

Ellis, F. (2000), *Rural Livelihoods and Diversity in Developing Countries*, Oxford: Oxford University Press.

Ellis, F. (2003), 'Human vulnerability and food insecurity: policy implications', Forum for Food Security in Southern Africa, Theme Paper No. 3, London: Overseas Development Institute, July, processed.

Holling, C.S. (1973), 'Resilience and stability of ecological systems', *Annual Review of Ecology and Systematics*, **4**, 1–23.

Moser, C.O.N. (1998), 'The asset vulnerability framework: reassessing urban poverty reduction strategies', *World Development*, **26** (1), pp. 1–19.

Pearce, J., A. Ngwira and G. Chimseu (1996), *Living on the Edge: A Study of the Rural Food Economy in the Mchinji and Salima Districts of Malawi*, London: Save the Children Fund (UK).

Scoones, I. (1998), 'Sustainable rural livelihoods: a framework for analysis', IDS Working Paper No. 72, Institute of Development Studies, University of Sussex, Brighton.

Swift, J. (1989), 'Why are rural people vulnerable to famine?', *IDS Bulletin*, **20** (2), 8–15.

Walker, T.S. and N.S. Jodha (1986), 'How small farm households adapt to risk', in P. Hazell, C. Pomareda and A. Valdes (eds), *Crop Insurance for Agricultural Development*, Baltimore, MD: Johns Hopkins University Press, pp. 17–34.

Watts, M. (1983), *Silent Violence: Food, Famine and Peasantry in Northern Nigeria*, Berkeley, CA: University of California Press.

Webb, P., J. von Braun and Y. Yohannes (1992), 'Famine in Ethiopia: policy implications of coping failure at national and household levels', Research Report No. 92, Washington, DC: International Food Policy Research Institute.

Washington Consensus

In 1982, the government of Mexico announced that it would suspend servicing its external debt, which provoked a fear among major international financial institutions that other debtor countries might follow. This carried the threat of bankruptcy of major international banks. The debt accumulation which provoked this threat of crisis occurred during the 1970s, when favourable terms of trade and low real interest rates made the debt burdens appear sustainable. However, at the beginning of the 1980s restrictive monetary policy in several developed countries brought real interest rates to nigh unprecedented levels in world money markets, and the terms of trade for primary products declined drastically. Facing threat of widespread default or partial payment of debts, international financial interests sought a strategy by which their assets would be preserved. This strategy came to be called the 'Washington Consensus'. Most of the heavily indebted countries to which the strategy was applied were in Latin America, with the largest debts being those of Brazil and Mexico.

The Washington Consensus was a work-in-progress, evolving through a series of conferences and meetings during the mid-1980s, with the major role played by the creditor banks, the governments of the countries in which those banks were based, and the major multilateral financial institutions (the IMF and later, in a supporting role, the World Bank), with analytical justification provided by sympathetic academic economists. John Williamson is commonly said to be the term's originator (Williamson, 1990), though by one account its first use was by Hans Singer (of Singer–Prebisch fame), who said that its policy package represented a consensus 'only in Washington'. The Consensus reigned hegemonic in international development policy from the early 1980s to the mid-1990s, when it came under sustained attack.

Its elements derived from an economic ideology that came to be encapsulated in the term 'neoliberalism'. The essential parts included: (1) restrictive monetary and fiscal policy ('fiscal discipline' and 'interest rate liberalisation'); (2) elimination of controls on the capital movements, implying severe curtailment of government management of national currencies ('a competitive exchange rate'); (3) elimination of export taxes and import quotas, and dramatic reduction of tariffs ('trade liberalisation'); (4) removing government interventions in domestic markets, including financial and labour markets ('deregulation'); (5) rapid sale of public assets ('privatisation'); and (6) redirection of public expenditure consistent with a narrow definition of public goods. This package of measures implied a radical shift in the policy regime in almost all developing countries, and became a focal point for debate over appropriate economic policies for development, and, as time passed, was viewed by many critics as the quintessence of a 'globalisation' process that gave little priority to human welfare.

The impact of the Consensus had a dynamic which transcended Latin America and the debt question. Policy conditionality began with IMF lending immediately after the

Second World War, and the stabilisation component of the Consensus became orthodoxy in the 1950s. Convergence from the World Bank side began in May 1979, when Robert McNamara proposed the idea of structural adjustment in an UNCTAD speech in Manila. This became the basis of a new policy instrument of programme loans to governments of developing countries. The Bank, concerned about restrictions in its 'Articles' on programme lending, and on infringing on IMF territory, proposed that IMF standby agreements become a prerequisite for Bank programme loans. The election of Ronald Reagan as US president and his appointment of A.W. ('Tom') Clausen as head of the World Bank set the stage for the coordination that would be the basis of the consensus. Clausen appointed the dogmatic neoliberal Anne Krueger as chief economist in 1982, and she established many of the details of the Consensus in the 1980s.

In 2002, Williamson himself referred to 'the Washington Consensus' as 'a damaged brand name', protesting that he never intended it to refer to a neoliberal agenda for transforming policy in developing countries. In summarising his view of the Consensus, he referred to the basic elements being as generally embraced as 'motherhood and apple pie'. He wrote, 'the three big ideas [in the Consensus] are macroeconomic discipline, a market economy, and openness to the world . . . in respect of trade and [foreign direct investment]' (Williamson, 2002, p. 1). By most definitions the 'three big ideas' would seem necessary if not sufficient to qualify the Consensus for neoliberal status. The neoliberal credentials of the Consensus were enhanced by the addition of other elements, in what Dani Rodrik (2001) called the 'Augmented Washington Consensus': corporate governance, good governance in the public sector (that is, anti-corruption), flexible labour markets, conformity with WTO rules, independent central banks, and 'targeted' poverty reduction instruments. The inclusion of these 'add-ons' in IMF and World Bank conditionality in the 1980s and 1990s prompted Ravi Kanbur (formerly chief economist for the African region of the World Bank) to conclude, 'in the 1980s, and to a certain extent well into the 1990s, many [Washington institutions] saw the main task as . . . storming the citadel of statist development strategies', so that 'the negotiators from Washington always took a more purist stance, a more extreme stance than even their own intellectual framework permitted' (Kanbur, 1999, p. 2).

One should not exaggerate the extent to which the Washington Consensus policy package was 'forced' upon 'unwilling' governments. Had the governments of heavily indebted countries been strongly opposed, it is likely that they had the bargaining power to form a 'debtors' cartel' to alter substantially the policies they subsequently adopted. Moreover, the package required institutional and policy changes that significantly threatened major interests within the countries. It remains to be explained why debtor governments did not mount an organised challenge.

Closely associated with the Washington Consensus policy package was the 'Programme for Sustained Growth' proposed by the US Secretary of the Treasury, James Baker (the 'Baker Plan'), presented to the joint annual meeting of the IMF and the World Bank in Seoul in October 1985. The plan offered funding of US$29 billion to 15 'major' debtors, which would be explicitly linked to Consensus-specified 'comprehensive macroeconomic and market-oriented structural adjustment policies' (Hang-Sheng, 1985, p 2; see also, Structural Adjustment in this volume). About US$9 billion would come from the World Bank and the Inter-American Development Bank (IDB), and US$20 billion from private banks. The IMF was assigned the key role of specifying and monitoring the policy changes, in what came to be called its 'gate-keeper' role.

Some supporters of the Consensus stressed its alleged positive impact on the economic health of the countries whose governments embraced its policies. However, it would be difficult to deny that the basic function of the Washington Consensus was to facilitate the servicing of external debt. To achieve this outcome, macro policies were the keystone. First, a restrictive fiscal policy was necessary to generate a budget surplus for the payment of debt service, both in accounting terms and for macro management. Much of the debt was to governments, and over time governments were forced to assume responsibility for private external debts as domestic borrowers defaulted (even the government of Chile nationalised the country's foreign debt under pressure from creditors). Therefore, governments faced the choice of generating net revenue to cover debt service, or suffering from inflation-generating deficits. In practice, it proved difficult to achieve increased revenue as economies contracted. Second, servicing debts would imply a surplus on the external current account, which in practice required import compression via output contraction (since foreign trade controls would be eliminated as part of the policy package). In practice, output contraction proved far greater than was necessary for debt servicing (de Pinies, 1989).

Largely on the basis of the Baker Plan, debtor governments and their commercial bank creditors engaged in repeated rounds of ad hoc rescheduling and restructuring sovereign and private sector debt. At a formal level the rescheduling and restructuring reflected the optimism that the debt crisis was a temporary phenomenon that would end as the debtor economies rebounded. A key characteristic of the Baker Plan was the prevention, in as far as possible, of a secondary market in sovereign debt; that is, governments were prohibited from selling their debt below its nominal value. This prohibition eliminated one of the most obvious and effective market-based vehicles for exiting the debt crisis. By the end of the 1980s, it became clear that many loans would never be entirely repaid, and that some form of substantial debt relief was necessary for these nations and their fragile economies to resume growth and to regain access to the global capital markets.

This recognition prompted the Brady Plan (named after Nicholas F. Brady, who followed Baker as the US Secretary of the Treasury). As with the Baker Plan, Brady linked debt relief to policy conditionalities. Its new features were two: (i) bank creditors would grant debt relief in exchange for guarantees that what remained would be paid without fail; and (ii) the new debt paper would be sold on international financial markets. The latter allowed for the discounting of debt, which the Baker Plan had prohibited. This shift, from non-market-administered debt management, to market-based debt reduction, could be implemented because the major creditor banks had achieved considerable replenishment of their reserves during the 1980s.

The failure of the Washington Consensus to achieve orderly debt management, macro stability, or recovery of debt-affected countries was generally recognised by the 1990s (Stiglitz, 1998). World Bank sources showed that by 1997, just prior to the Asian financial crisis, the percentage of private non-guaranteed debt reached 23 per cent of total debt to Latin America and the Caribbean, which was well above the level of the 1980s. In as far as developing-country debts were managed at all, it was on an ad hoc, case-by-case basis which dragged on through the 1980s. Far from stabilising economies, the Washington

Consensus policy package was coincident with hyperinflation in several of the highly indebted Latin American countries (Argentina and Brazil, for example). Per capita income of these countries declined during the 1980s. When recovery came in the 1990s, it proved to be patchy, with countries enjoying a few years of rapid expansion on the basis of excess capacity, followed by instability, in some cases resulting from the transmission of international financial crises, which the elimination of capital account controls facilitated. By the middle of the first decade of the twenty-first century, very few of the highly indebted countries had sustained growth rates equal to those recorded in the 1960s and 1970s.

A collateral effect of the adoption of the Washington Consensus package by governments of the highly indebted middle-income countries was its progressive extension to countries of the sub-Saharan region. While the very low growth rates of the majority of these countries suggested a need for a change in the basic policy framework, few of the countries conformed to the characteristics of countries to which the Consensus initially applied, neither high debts to private banks (their debts were primarily to bilateral multilateral development institutions), nor severe inflationary pressures.

From the standpoint of the twenty-first century, perhaps the most striking aspect of the Washington Consensus was the process itself. In the wake of the Copenhagen Social Summit in 1995, bilateral and multilateral agencies providing development assistance committed themselves to a new approach to 'partnerships' between the governments of developed and developing countries, based on a process of policy formulation that would be 'country led' and 'nationally owned', including 'broad participation by civil society' (Malloch Brown, 2002). By these criteria, the Washington Consensus process seemed from another era, with the formulation of a radical change in policy direction carried out behind closed doors, primarily among private and public sector representatives from creditor countries, with the role of the International Monetary Fund and the World Bank involving heavy and detailed policy conditionalities. The Washington Consensus process was very much a product of the 1980s.

JOHN WEEKS
HOWARD STEIN

References and further reading

de Pinies, Jaime (1989), 'Debt sustainability and overadjustment', *World Development*, **17** (1), 29–43.

Fine, Ben, Costas Lapavitsas and Jonathan Pincus (2003), *Development Policy in the Twenty-first Century: Beyond the Post-Washington Consensus*, London: Routledge.

Hang-Sheng, Cheng (1985), 'The Baker Plan: a new initiative', *Federal Reserve Bank of San Francisco Newsletter*, 22 November.

Kanbur, Ravi (1999), 'The strange case of the Washington Consensus; a brief note on John Williamson's "What should the World Bank think about the Washington Consensus?"', unpublished, Ithaca NY: Cornell University, www.people.cornell.edu/pages/sk145/papers.htm.

Kuczynski, Pedro-Pablo and John Williamson (2003), *After the Washington Consensus: Restarting Growth and Reform in Latin America*, Washington, DC: Institute for International Economics.

Malloch Brown, Mark (2002), 'Address by UNDP Administrator Mark Malloch Brown', International Conference on Financing for Development, Monterrey, Mexico, 18 March.

Rodrik, Dani (2001), *The Global Governance of Trade As If Development Really Mattered*, New York: UNDP.

Stiglitz, Joseph (1998), 'More instruments and broader goals: moving toward the post-Washington Consensus', UNU/ WIDER Annual Lectures 2, (Helsinki: UNU/WIDER.

Weeks, John (1989), 'Losers pay reparations, or how the Third World lost the lending war,' in J. Weeks (ed.), *Debt Disaster? Banks, Governments and Multilaterals Confront the Crisis*, New York: New York University Press, pp. 41–63.

Williamson, John (1990), 'What Washington means by policy reform', in J. Williamson (ed.), *Latin American Adjustment: How Much Has Happened?*, Washington, DC: Institute for International Economics, pp. 5–20.
Williamson, John (2002), 'Did the Washington Consensus fail?', Outline of Remarks at Center for Strategic and International Studies, Washington, DC: Institute for International Economics, 6 November.

Water and Development

The evolution of water policy

Both human communities and living organisms adapt to and depend on natural hydrological cycles. One of the key factors that influence the way in which cities throughout the world expand is the supply of water. Rivers, desertification and floods have shaped civilisations. Man's obsession with controlling the natural hydrological cycle can be traced back to 560 BC when the first enclosed and covered spring was recorded in Athens (Morton, 1966). Storing and moving water is a major engineering feat, providing the foundation on which human civilisation has been able to develop. Over the centuries, problems of water scarcity were solved by developing infrastructure and relying on hydraulic assignments, such as the aqueduct in AD 226, a proof of human ingenuity and the triumph of Roman engineering.

The twentieth century was the era of dam building. Today around 3800 km³ of fresh water is withdrawn annually from the world's lakes, rivers and aquifers, twice the volume extracted just 50 years ago (WCD, 2000, p. 3). Driven by modern science whose philosophy was to control, rather than to understand, nature (Turton, 2001), the consequences of large dams have been mostly disastrous. The Turkwel Gorge Dam in Northern Kenya threatens the thin strip of remaining forest as the water table is crucial to the survival of the trees and very large floods are essential for their regeneration. The Masinga Dam in the Tana River Basin (Kenya) has reduced the size of the largest floods and in the long run the forest will cease to replace itself (Adams, 1992). The World Commission on Dams (2000) has shown that, globally, the largest numbers of dams were constructed in the 1970s. The stories of vanishing waters, man's arrogance and domination over nature and the disastrous consequences of this, have been well captured in Reisner's (1986) classic on the mismanagement of water, *Cadillac Desert*.

Over the past 30 years there have been four important paradigm shifts affecting the water sector: (1) the recognition of water as a human right; (2) the focus on the software and not just the hardware aspect of water delivery; (3) the acknowledgement of water as an economic good; and (4) the shift from supply – with its socially and politically oppressive consequences – to demand. In an attempt to secure sustainable development and conserve water, a new water management paradigm emerged during the 1990s. The emphasis was on integrated water resource management (IWRM) and the decentralised management of water resources with an insistence on local user-group participation and action rooted in designated watershed areas (Ostrom, 1996; Farrington et al., 1999). IWRM is a process which promotes the coordinated development and management of water, land and related resources without compromising the sustainability of vital ecosystems.

Water is a multi-stakeholder issue and interested and affected parties are viable mechanisms to address human and ecological needs and to translate IWRM into practice.

Despite the change in focus, the domain of water remains dominated by technological and economistic discourse where in-stream flows, pumps, pipes and the 'scientific' discourse of water delivery reverberate forcefully. The participatory approach involving water users at all levels and specifically focusing on ordinary water users is not easy to practice, and it has been more or less successfully implemented in developing and developed contexts (Ostrom, 1996; Farrington et al., 1999).

Of critical importance in terms of the conceptual split introduced by IWRM, is how people adapt to changes in the supply of water rather than the availability of this resource itself (Ohlsson, 1999). The capabilities for organisation at the level of dwelling, village or town are as critical as the power structures and political agendas that drive water allocation and determine where and how much will be directed to satisfy the consumption needs of industry, agriculture, households and tourism. Rising incomes, rapid industrialisation and agricultural production do not always match water availability. Water stress, defined by Turton et al. (2003) as an annual availability of less than 1600 m^3 per person, influences water allocation. Poor management of water has consequences in terms of cost and time and the capacity to manage water on all fronts is not just 'nice to have' but is fundamental for sustainable development.

Water and poverty

According to the *World Development Report*, more than a billion people in low-and middle-income countries, and 50 million people in high-income countries, lacked access to safe water for drinking, personal hygiene and domestic use in 1995 (World Bank, 2003, p. 2). Water supply services contribute directly and indirectly to income generation, health and education. Actual or even potential water shortages lead to significant social stress as well as physiological stress in individuals and communities (MacKay, 2004). Scarcity of water curtails economic production, food security and health. A Water Poverty Index (WPI) is currently being refined in an attempt to establish an international measure comparing performance in the water sector across countries in a holistic way (see Lawrence et al., 2002). The index is intended to capture the diverse aspects of everyday living that are affected by water deprivation. Similar criticisms to those made against the United Nation's Human Development Index can be made of this index, but the WPI is a significant interdisciplinary management tool. It makes the links between poverty, social deprivation, health, environmental integrity and water availability explicit, enabling policy makers to identify appropriate mechanisms to deal with the causes of poverty and water stress.

The International Conference on Water and the Environment, held in Dublin in 1992, set out the four 'Dublin principles' that are still relevant:

- *Principle one* holds that fresh water is a finite and vulnerable resource, essential to sustain life, development and the environment, and
- *Principle two* that water development and management should be based on a participatory approach involving users, planners and policy makers at all levels.
- *Principle three* addresses gender issues: because women play a central role in the provision, management and safeguarding of household water, gender equality is crucial in determining a just allocation of water at the community and household levels.

- *Principle four* concerns the pricing and costing of water and declares that water has an economic value in all its competing uses and should be recognised as an economic good.

At the operational level these agreed principles are not always easy to translate into concrete action.

Besides the UN Conference on the Environment and Development in 1992 that produced *Agenda 21*, other significant international events that debated and confirmed the Dublin principles were the Millennium Summit in New York (2000), the Second World Water Forum in The Hague (2000), the World Summit on Sustainable Development in Rio (2002), the Monterrey Conference (2002), the World Summit on Sustainable Development (WSSD) in Johannesburg (2003), and the Third World Water Forum in Kyoto (2003). These events all highlighted the importance of water for development and set goals and targets for action. One of the outcomes of the Johannesburg WSSD was that the United States declared $970 million available over the next three years for water and sanitation projects and the United Nations an extra $20 million in resources for water and sanitation, particularly aimed at improving living conditions for the rural poor of developing nations. The task of providing water and sanitation is a huge one and the World Commission on Water predicts that water users will increase by 50 per cent over the coming 30 years and that four billion people will live under conditions of severe water stress by 2025 (World Bank, 2003). Given the scale of the task, the Third World Water Forum recognised that $18 billion will be required annually to produce water security over the next 25 years.

Water and livelihoods
Agriculture is the world's biggest consumer of water and although 80–90 per cent of all consumed water goes onto fields, only half of that touches crops. Unwise planning in irrigation has resulted in unworkable canals and heavy debt. Water and livelihoods are intimately connected because water is a constraint on food production. Enhancing the productivity of land, water and human resources is a key feature of global poverty reduction strategies. Unsurprisingly, some of the most progressive work in this domain is closely linked with managing the commons, small-scale agriculture and land-use practices of the poor. In this field of research, the focus on conservation and sustainable use of scarce resources is paramount. A balance is required between the use of water for human needs and the use of water for the survival of ecosystems on which people depend. Poor people depend more on commons than rich people do, as they do not have the resources to buy land, and the way that food is produced depends on the availability of water. Unless communities are able to increasingly understand the water cycle and its effect on the environment in the catchment or watershed region in which they are living, and to influence decision-making processes that concern them, their long-term social and economic well-being will remain threatened. The politics of power continues to define how much water is distributed, at what cost and to whom, giving rise to a new academic discipline called 'hydropolitics' (Turton, 2002, p. 16).

The price of water
There are presently 261 international river basins, and 145 nations have territory in shared

basins (Turton et al., 2003). Political and watershed boundaries do not coincide neatly and progress in managing transboundary aquifers is slow. Despite alarmist claims concerning the acceleration of 'water wars' (Starr, 1991), Wolf (2002) considers that the record of cooperation is vastly superior to that of conflict, and posits that water is much more a vector of cooperation than a source of conflict.

Water projects have provided examples for a number of pilot cases in developing country contexts that span an array of innovations in development planning. A recent study in Bolivia, for instance, has shown that the form, quality and conditions of access to water and sanitation are indicators of social segregation (Laurie and Crespo, 2003). The debates about water as a public good or water as an economic good continue, but global trends favour privatisation and full recovery of costs to the consumer. Although these trends are fairly recent in developing contexts, there is some evidence that health problems are exacerbated when poor people are expected to pay. Several studies show that the urban poor pay high prices for water supply and spend a high proportion of their income on water. On the other hand, data on water vending suggests that households can afford to spend about 2–3 per cent of their income on water (Conradie et al., 2001). Jakarta et al. (in ibid.) found that households pay up to 50 times what they would pay for piped water when purchasing water from vendors. In Ukunda, Kenya, water vending is a competitive industry and households spend up to 9 per cent of their average annual income on water. According to the same source, in Onitsha, Nigeria, only 1 per cent of households have access to piped water and poor households spend 18 per cent of their income on water in the dry season (Conradie et al., 2001).

The shift to cost recovery has increased prices for those connected to the piped networks, however, many of the poorest and those living in low-income settlements have not been connected. Low-income households that have to buy from private water vendors spend a considerable proportion of their income on water and because these households struggle to pay connection costs and regular charges, increasing recognition is being given to the potential role of water subsidies.

Water and health

According to the *Global Water Supply and Sanitation Assessment Report* (WHO, 2000), Africa is lagging behind in water supply coverage both in urban (85 per cent) and rural (47 per cent) areas. In Latin America and the Caribbean, 85 per cent of the population in 2000, or 77 million people, lacked access to safe water – 51 million are rural and 26 million urban water users. In Asia, 65 per cent of the population are unserved – 60 per cent of the world's population but only 36 per cent of the world's water supply – and water deprivation is a grave concern. Five million South Africans still need access to a basic supply of water. These are people who take water directly from dams, pools, streams, rivers and springs, or purchase water from water vendors. At the household level, being forced to live in areas that have poor water services not only entrenches poverty in social well-being, health and hygiene but also creates economic inertia.

Although water is the most widely occurring substance on the earth, only 2.53 per cent is fresh water while the remainder is salt water (World Bank, 2003). According to Professor Eugene Cloete (Vice President of the International Water Association), the problems experienced around water can be summed up as follows: there is either 'too much or too little or it is too dirty' (interview Cloete, 2003). Uncontrolled urban discharges, climate changes, intensified agricultural practices and dense human settlements are some of the problems that provoke the widespread degradation of the environment and jeopardise the well-being of communities. Contrary to popular belief, problems of water pollution are not only due to overcrowding in dense population settlements. Mining activities in South Africa, for example, have resulted in radioactivity entering the sediment of streams and rivers in certain catchment areas (Wade et al., 2002) with unknown consequences for human health once this enters the food chain. In sparsely populated rural areas, where animal and human excrement mix with drinking water, water becomes microbiologically unsafe. Since 1991, between 200,000 and 600,000 cases of cholera have been reported worldwide on a yearly basis. In 1999 Africa accounted for 81 per cent of the cases reported worldwide (WHO, 2000). Sudden large outbreaks are usually caused by contaminated drinking water. Mobile populations are particularly at risk as the movement of people between countries (as in Southern Africa) encourages the spread of cholera.

Water-related diseases are among the most common causes of illness and death, affecting mainly the poor in developing countries. More than three million people each year, mostly the more vulnerable segments of the population (for instance, children under the age of five) die from waterborne diseases such as gastro-enteritis and diarrhoea, which are caused by contaminated drinking water. According to the World Water Development Report (2003), in 2000 the estimated mortality rate due to water-sanitation-hygiene-associated diarrhoeas was 2,213,000. Six hundred children in the world die daily from diseases caused by contaminated water, the equivalent of a jumbo jet crashing every day.

The World Health Organization specifies reasonable access to water of *at least* 25 litres per person per day from an approved source within 1 km of the user's dwelling. Recent research has shown that in those dwellings where there is no piped water, the child mortality rate is twice as high, and for those households that do not have flush sanitation the child morality rate is four times as high. Evidently both water and sanitation have an acute effect on child mortality rates – a tragedy, as such deaths are usually preventable.

The health gains from the provision of improved water supply and sanitation are obvious, and in the light of these appalling statistics, positive health externalities confirm the rationale for government subsidisation of basic water services. Generally, poor hygiene practices go hand in hand with poor health. Good hand-washing practices depend on higher levels of consumption of water, and rural and poor populations are lacking in this respect, thus health-related diseases such as diarrhoea, opportunistic diseases that stem from HIV/AIDS and cholera take their toll (Ashton and Ramasar, 2002). Poverty reduction and better water management are inextricably linked. It is recognised that ill health is a very significant cause of households moving from having low incomes, but managing, to being chronically poor. Thus the international agreed target is to halve the proportion of people without access to drinking water and improved sanitation by 2015.

But poor people are not only vulnerable to diseases related to water contamination. Between 1991 and 2000, more than 665,000 people died in natural disasters, of which 90 per cent were water related. Floods caused 15 per cent of deaths, droughts 42 per cent of deaths, and some 97 per cent of all natural disaster deaths occurred in developing countries (World Bank, 2003). Alarmingly, according to the World Water Development Report (2003), the number of hydro-meteorological disasters (floods and droughts) has more than doubled since 1996. The poorest of the poor, the elderly, women and children, are the most affected. In 1988, floods devastated large parts of Dhaka in Bangladesh and donor countries evolved a strategy plan costing between 1 and 6 billion dollars to build huge dikes to 'control' the floods. A counter plan suggested that the construction would cost $6 million to maintain every year and that the solution was to build on the ingenuity of the people and their ability to adapt to floods.

The problems of water delivery are no longer to do with engineering and controlling nature. Key concerns in the water sector include understanding ways in which communities respond and adapt to water scarcity since the availability of social resources is as critical as the availability of water. Ignorance and lack of governance and ingenuity in managing water take their toll. Resolving the tension between water as an economic good and water as a public good includes taking into account the concerns around equity and efficiency and addressing the issue of politics and power and how unequal power relations in the domain of water impact on people.

JAQUI GOLDIN

References

Adams, W. (1992), *Wasting the Rain: Rivers, People and Planning in Africa*, London: Earthscan.
Ashton, P. and V. Ramasar (2002), 'Water and HIV/AIDS: some strategic considerations in Southern Africa', in A.R. Turton and R. Henwood (eds), *Hydropolitics in the Developing World: A Southern African Perspective*, Pretoria: African Water Issues Research Unit (AWIRU), pp. 217–235.
Conradie, B., J. Goldin, A. Leiman. B. Standish and M. Visser (2001), 'Competition policy and privatization in the South African water industry', DPRU Working Paper 01/45, Development Policy Research Unit, University of Cape Town, South Africa.
Farrington, J., C. Turton and A. James (eds), (1999), *Participatory Watershed Development Challenges for the Twenty First Century*, Oxford and New Delhi: Oxford University Press.
Laurie, N. and C. Crespo (2003), ' "Pro-poor" water privatisation: ideology confounded in Bolivia?' *id21 Research Highlights*, 26 November, Brighton: Institute for Development Studies.
Lawrence, P., J. Meigh C. Sullivan (2002), 'The Water Poverty Index: an international comparison', *Keele Economics Research Papers*, KERP 2002/19, Department of Economics, Keele University, UK.
MacKay, H.M. (2004), 'Water policies and practices', in D. Reed and M. de Wit *Towards a Just South Africa: The Political Economy of Natural Resourced Wealth*, Pretoria: World Wildlife Fund and CSIR Environmentek, pp. 49–84.
Morton, H.V. (1966), *The Waters of Rome*, London: Michael Joseph.
Ohlsson, L. (1999), *Water and Security in Southern Africa*, Publications on Water Resources 1, Department for Natural Resources and the Environment, Swedish International Development Cooperation Agency, Stockholm.
Ostrom, E. (1996), *Incentives, Rules of the Game and Development*, Annual World Bank Conference on Development Economics, Washington, DC: World Bank.
Reisner, M. (1986), *Cadillac Desert*, London: Secker & Warburg.
Starr, J.R. (1991), 'Water wars', *Foreign Policy*, **82**, 17–36.
Turton, A. (2001), 'The problematic of WDM as a concept and a policy: towards the development of a set of guidelines for Southern Africa', unpublished paper, African Water Issues Research Unit (AWIRU), University of Pretoria.
Turton, A. (2002), 'Water and state sovereignty: the hydropolitical challenge for states in arid regions', in Wolf (ed.), pp. 516–33.
Turton, A., P. Ashton and E. Cloete (eds) (2003), *Transboundary Rivers, Sovereignty and Development: Hydropolitical Drivers in the Okavango River Basin*, Geneva: African Water Issues Research Unit and Green Cross International.
Wade, P.W., S. Woodbourne, W.M. Morris, P. Vos and N.W. Jarvis (2002), *Tier 1 Risk Assessment of Selected Radionuclides in Sediments of the Mooi River Catchment*, Pretoria: Water Research Commission.

WHO (2000), *Global Water Supply and Sanitation Assessment Report*, Geneva: World Health Organization/United Nations Children's Fund.

Wolf, A. (2002), *Conflict Prevention and Resolution in Water Systems*, Cheltenham, UK and Northampton, MA, USA: Edward Elgar.

World Bank (2003), *World Development Report*, Oxford: Oxford University Press.

World Commission on Dams (WCD) (2000), *Dams and Development: A New Framework for Decision Making: The Report of the World Commission on Dams*, London: Earthscan, www.dams.org/report/.

World Water Development Report (2003), *Water for People, Water for Life. World Water Assessment Programme*, New York: United Nations.

Index